Dimensions and Use of the Scholarly Information Environment:

Introduction to a Data Set Assembled by the Digital Library Federation and Outsell, Inc.

by Amy Friedlander

November 2002

Digital Library Federation
Council on Library and Information Resources
Washington, D.C.

About the Author

Amy Friedlander is special projects associate at the Council on Library and Information Resources. She is primarily responsible for CLIR's work with the Library of Congress on its National Digital Information Infrastructure Preservation Program (NDIIPP). Before joining CLIR, she was the founding editor of *D-Lib Magazine* and *iMP: The Magazine on Information Impacts*. She has published on the implications of higher education for the historical role of women and on the history of large-scale technology-based infrastructures.

ISBN 1-887334-94-7

Published by:

Digital Library Federation
Council on Library and Information Resources
1755 Massachusetts Avenue, NW, Suite 500
Washington, DC 20036
Web site at http://www.clir.org

Additional copies are available for $40 per copy. Orders must be placed through CLIR's Web site.

The paper in this publication meets the minimum requirements of the American National Standard for Information Sciences—Permanence of Paper for Printed Library Materials ANSI Z39.48-1984.

Contents

Preface

We know from anecdotal evidence that users' expectations of libraries are changing as they find more information directly from the Web. Anecdotal evidence, though, is hardly enough for developing persuasive plans for new library services. The Digital Library Federation (DLF) and Council on Library and Information Resources (CLIR) commissioned Outsell, Inc., to conduct a large-scale study of undergraduates, graduate students, and faculty members from academic institutions ranging from the small liberal arts college to the largest research university. Our hope was that a picture of user behavior would emerge.

This report presents a summary of the findings and 158 selected data tables; it should be viewed as an entry to a much larger data set. The full set of 659 data tables provided by Outsell will be mounted on the Web later this year. We encourage readers to make use of these tables and ask that you share with us your analyses of the data. In addition, CLIR will deposit the raw data with the Inter-University Consortium for Political and Social Research.

CLIR and DLF expect to commission additional work based on the data. We welcome proposals from readers with an interest in performing more detailed studies.

Deanna B. Marcum
President, CLIR

NARRATIVE

INTRODUCTION

Academic and research libraries face numerous challenges in managing their information resources in the digital age. Like many other organizations, the Digital Library Federation (DLF) has become concerned about changing patterns of information use for teaching, learning, and research and about the implications of these patterns for libraries and library directors, who require reliable information for strategic planning. In collaboration with the Council on Library and Information Resources (CLIR) and Outsell, Inc., the DLF has initiated a planning and research process to understand how library use is changing and to support future investigation and analysis. The survey conducted by Outsell and described herein is only one of several activities under way or recently completed. Related projects include

- A survey by DLF Distinguished Fellow Denise Troll Covey of methods applied by leading research libraries to assess the use and usability of online collections and services (Troll Covey 2002)
- A survey by former DLF Director Daniel Greenstein and Indiana University Dean of Libraries Suzanne Thorin of the policy, organizational, and financial environments in which leading research libraries are developing their digital libraries (Greenstein and Thorin 2002)
- A study by Charles McClure and colleagues into methods of assessing quality in digital reference services (McClure et al. 2002)

Outsell developed the survey questionnaire with guidance from the DLF advisory group on user studies. Interviews began in fall 2001 and continued over two and one-half months. The primary goal of the survey questionnaire was to collect data on the relevance of existing and possible future services as well as on student and faculty perceptions of the library's value in the context of the scholarly information environment. Other objectives included determining (1) what information resources are used to support research, teaching, and learning, and (2) how those sources and services are located, evaluated, and used by faculty and students at different kinds of institutions of higher education and in different disciplines. It is expected that the data will support evaluations of the library's current and potential future roles as well as more detailed studies on the development and use of collections.

This report includes 158 of the 659 data tables provided by Outsell, a few summary observations, and a brief discussion of some possible implications of the findings. In addition to publishing this report, CLIR will post to the Web all 659 of the data tables, and will deposit the raw data tapes with the Inter-University Consortium for Political and Social Research (ICPSR).[1]

In this document, the tables have been grouped in three categories: (1) Faculty and Students; (2) Infrastructure, Facilities, and Services; and (3) Formats. The information presented in the tables overlaps to some extent; however, the tables included in Faculty and Students primarily contain data about who participated and what they do. Tables included in Infrastructure, Facilities, and Services contain data related to where faculty and students access information. Finally, tables grouped within Formats contain comparative data on the formats and media that faculty and students use for research, teaching, and coursework.

Data Collection

Data were collected at three types of institutions of higher education: public (state-funded) universities, private doctoral research institutions, and liberal arts colleges. These categories correspond as follows to the Carnegie Classification of Institutions of Higher Education[2]:

Study Classification	Carnegie Classification
Leading public (state-funded) research university	Doctoral Research Universities– Extensive – Public Institutions
Leading private research university	Doctoral Research Universities– Extensive – Private, Not-for-Profit Institutions
Leading liberal arts colleges	Baccalaureate Colleges– Liberal Arts – Private, Not-for-Profit Institutions

These institutions of higher education have well-defined missions with respect to research and teaching. The design of the survey has enabled investigators to recover data reflecting potential differences among these institutional types as well as across academic disciplines, as discussed in the following paragraphs. Most or all of these institutions house libraries that are also documented in other data collection efforts, such as those developed by the Association of Research Libraries, the Oberlin group of liberal arts colleges, and the

[1] As of this writing, Outsell is developing a codebook to accompany the data. When the codebook is complete, the data will be deposited and available from ICPSR at www.icpsr.umich.edu.

[2] The Carnegie Classification was originally published in 1973 and has been updated in 1976, 1987, and 1994. The Carnegie Foundation expects to undertake a revision of the classification system to be concluded in 2005. The classification is available at http://www.carnegiefoundation.org/.

Association of College and Research Libraries. The information provided by these other data collection efforts could be used in conjunction with the results of this survey to enable further studies.

Outsell interviewed a total of 3,234 faculty members, graduate students, and undergraduate students from the three types of educational institutions (there were no graduate students in the liberal arts college sample) in the Carnegie Classification (see Appendix 1). The distribution of respondents is illustrated in the table that follows. Within each institution type, an equal number of members of the faculty were selected across the seven disciplines studied (arts and humanities, biological sciences, business, engineering, law, physical sciences/mathematics, and social sciences). Students were selected by institution type and level (graduate or undergraduate). Quotas for each subset of the sample were established by respondent type, institution type, and discipline to ensure representation from all combinations. The sample is considered representative of the underlying population at this set of institutions.

Distribution of Respondents

Institution Type	Faculty	Graduate Students	Undergraduate Students	Total
Leading doctoral research university, public	272	657	407	1,336
Leading doctoral research university, private	337	399	135	872
Baccalaureate colleges–liberal arts, private	321	0	705	1,026
Total	930	1,056	1,248	3,234

Trained interviewers worked randomly through the sample, using phone numbers of faculty members and departments. For students, a telephone sample for each institution was obtained, allowing investigators to dial into a student's apartment or dormitory room. After screening the students for type (graduate or undergraduate) and discipline, the interviewers administered the questionnaire to those who agreed to participate.

The intent had been to conduct a 30-minute interview. However, tests showed that more than an hour was generally required to complete the interviews. To limit the length of the interview without eliminating any of the questions, a rotation scheme was developed. Some questions were asked of all respondents, and subsets of questions were asked of different segments of the respondent population. In all, six versions of the questionnaire were used. Frequency distributions were constructed for responses to the full questionnaire. Data were aggregated by status (faculty, graduate student, and undergraduate student); type of institution (public Ph.D.-granting institution, private Ph.D.-granting institution, and liberal arts college), and discipline. The full set of 659 tables contains data on all subsets of respondents. Summary tables of a subset of these tables, including weighted averages, are included in this report.

Weighting factors were used to enable generalizations to the population represented by this sample (that is, faculty and students at Ph.D.-granting public and private universities and liberal arts colleges). The initial sample reflected the underlying distribution according to status (faculty, graduate student, and undergraduate student).

Weighting factors were constructed by reviewing the percentage of degrees conferred by public research, private research, and liberal arts colleges in each of the seven disciplines in the last year available (1997-1998) to balance the results of the study with the population by discipline. Investigators achieved a 95 percent confidence level with a precision of 3 to 5 percent for all targeted segments. Tests of reliability are indicated in each table. When testing proportions for significant differences, investigators used a *z*-test. When testing means, investigators used a *t*-test.

PART 1: FACULTY AND STUDENTS

Part I: Faculty and Students contains 28 tables that summarize information describing basic demographic characteristics, major and minor responsibilities, use of different media, satisfactions, and frustrations. About 40 percent (41.3%) of those interviewed were associated with public research universities, 27 percent with private research universities, and just under 32 percent (31.7%) with liberal arts colleges (Table 1[3]). The distributions across disciplines were roughly proportional by type of institution, with somewhat higher representation of arts and humanities at the liberal arts colleges (39.9%) and greater representation in the biological sciences and engineering (43.0% and 54.4%, respectively) at the public research universities. Just under 29 percent (28.8%) of the sample were faculty members, 32.7 percent were graduate students, and 38.6 percent were undergraduates (Table 2). There was a slight concentration (47.4%) of undergraduates in arts and humanities; graduate students were somewhat concentrated in the biological sciences, engineering, and law. Faculty members were fairly evenly distributed across disciplines, although there was a disproportionate representation (40.3%) within the physical sciences/mathematics.

Somewhat more than half of the study population was male (56.4%); 43.6 percent was female (Table 3). Faculty members were predominantly men (77.5%), but the gender distribution was more equitable among graduate and undergraduate students. Indeed, more than half of the respondents in the undergraduate sample studied were women (54.2%). Men clearly concentrate in physical sciences/mathematics, engineering, business and law, and women are more evenly distributed among all seven disciplines studied. Rough-

[3] Tables have been renumbered for publication in this document; original table numbers are also provided in a chart at the end of this narrative to enable readers to link the subset of tables herein presented to the full set made available on the Web.

ly half of the respondents in the biological sciences, social sciences, and arts and humanities were women.

The median age of the study group was the early 20s; mean age, which is more sensitive to extreme values, was the early 30s (Table 4). Members of the faculty have been teaching on average 15.4 years (Table 6). Students reported working toward their current degrees for an average of 2.4 years (Table 8). Almost half of the respondents (48.6%) worked part-time, and 5.9 percent worked full-time (Table 7). More than half of the undergraduate population (52.2%) worked part-time, and 54.5 percent of the undergraduates at liberal arts colleges worked part-time. More than 40 percent (44.4%) of graduate students worked part-time; almost a third (30.1%) worked full-time. Eighty-three percent of the undergraduates have yet to decide on a major (Table 9) and 51.7 percent of the study respondents, including 24.8 percent of the undergraduates, lived off-campus (Table 10).

Respondents among the faculty and graduate students divide their time among teaching, research, and service (Table 13). Among the faculty at public and private Ph.D.-granting institutions, research was the dominant activity; 75.3 percent and 80.5 percent of the faculty at these institutions, respectively, reported research as a responsibility; only 55.8 percent and 62.7 percent of the faculty at these respective types of institutions think teaching is a responsibility. In contrast, at the liberal arts colleges, 99.4 percent of the faculty and graduate students consider teaching a responsibility and 84.3 percent consider research a responsibility. Research is an important activity across all seven disciplines; however, respondents from the arts and humanities tended to emphasize teaching over research. The balance between teaching and research seems most even among respondents from business (59.3% considered research a responsibility and 60.8% thought teaching was a responsibility).

Faculty and graduate students spend most of their time engaged in research, although full faculty members spend, on average, more of their time on teaching than on research (Table 14). Faculty reported spending an average of 15.79 hours weekly obtaining, reviewing, and analyzing information from all sources to support both teaching and research (Table 15). Respondents from public and private universities reported spending on average about one to two hours more per week on these activities than the average time reported by all faculty members in the sample. Respondents at the liberal arts colleges, in contrast, report significantly less time invested in these information-related activities—an average of 12.24 hours. Although these results for public and private doctoral universities reflect aggregated responses from faculty and students, the findings nonetheless indicate that faculty and graduate students at Ph.D. granting universities invest more of their time in information-seeking and analytical activities than their colleagues at liberal arts colleges do. This finding is consistent with the research focus of these institutions.

Tables 16 through 24 summarize information on the use of print and electronic media for research, teaching, and coursework. Overall, faculty members and students use a combination of media. At the extremes, 67.8 percent of the faculty members and 61 percent of the graduate students reported using print sources exclusively for their research (Table 16). Just under 35 percent (34.7%) of the faculty members and just under half (49.2%) of the graduate students said they rely exclusively or almost exclusively on electronic sources for their research (Table 17). This trend was fairly consistent across disciplines, with the possible exception of the arts and humanities, where there seemed to be a greater need for print materials. More than three-quarters (78.4%) of the respondents in arts and humanities said that they rely all or most of the time on print materials for their research (Table 16).

Across the board, print figures importantly in teaching. More than 70 percent of the faculty members and graduate students reported using print all or most of the time in teaching, and well over 70 percent of the respondents in physical sciences/mathematics, social sciences, and arts and humanities said they rely most or almost most of the time on print for the classroom (Table 19). Less than 25 percent of respondents across all institution types and all disciplines—except for business (41.9%) and law (29.8%)—rely all or most of the time on electronic sources for teaching (Table 20).

Graduate students rely strongly on print resources (Table 22) while undergraduates seem more willing to rely on electronic sources. Just over half of undergraduates (51.6%) responded that they relied all or most of the time on print sources, in contrast to the more than 70 percent among graduate students and faculty. About half (49.2%) of undergraduates reported that they used electronic materials exclusively or almost exclusively (Table 23). Reliance on electronic sources is strongest among business students, 62.9 percent of whom reported using electronic sources all or most of the time. Less than half of the students in the biological, physical sciences/mathematics, social sciences, engineering, and arts and humanities reported this preference (Table 23).

Tables 25-27 summarize information documenting unmet needs and challenges. About one-quarter of the faculty members (25.6%) and well over one-third (38.3%) of graduate students expressed a need for more online journals (Table 25). A greater frustration is lack of time. Nearly 40 percent (38.8%) of the total sample of respondents and 60 percent (60.2%) of the faculty reported "having enough time" as their major problem (Table 26). Respondents expressed minor frustrations with finding information, determining its credibility, and getting access to and analyzing it (Table 27). Indeed, 38.4 percent of respondents saw having insufficient training on how to search for information as an impediment. This finding was roughly consistent across institutions and disciplines.

Finally, the library has a commanding authority. Slightly more than 98 percent (98.2%) of those surveyed agreed with the statement, "My institution's library contains information from credible and known sources" (Table 28). There were less than three percentage points of variability across types of institutions and disciplines (Table 28). By way of contrast, 75.4 percent of respondents agreed with the statement, "The Internet provides high-quality information." Only 45.9 percent of respondents reported using information from the Internet without additional verification.

Parts 2 and 3 of this document examine findings relating to infrastructure and facilities and use of formats. The major themes in this section suggest that the library is perceived to have a central role in higher education, particularly with respect to maintaining the quality of information available to faculty and students. However, libraries appear to be serving multiple constituencies with variable needs. Higher education comprises a spectrum of subgroups, ranging from faculty with long tenure and well-articulated research interests and teaching needs to undergraduate students who have been on campus for only a short time and perhaps have yet to declare a major. More than half of the students are working at least part-time, and about half of the total study population do not live on campus. Faculty and graduate students seem to expect a hybrid environment of print and electronic resources, while undergraduates seem more willing to live in a wholly online world.

PART 2: INFRASTRUCTURE, FACILITIES, AND SERVICES

Faculty and students use a range of equipment in their offices, at the library, and at home or in dorm rooms (Tables 29-31). Respondents seem most reliant on desktop computers, but for those who also use a computer from their off-campus residences, a laptop is important. Faculty members seem to prefer to access information from their offices; they reported spending 73.95 percent[4] of their time accessing information for teaching and research from their offices (Table 32). Only 9.68 percent of their time devoted to accessing information is spent at a physical library. Undergraduates, in contrast, reported that about one-third of the time (33.58%) they devote to accessing information is spent at a physical library. About 40 percent of their information access/acquisition time (38.22%) occurs from their residences, and the remainder is spent in labs, classrooms, and other unspecified locations. Graduate students display an even greater mix of behaviors in their use of facilities.

On the other hand, when asked about the role of the physical *and virtual* library in providing access to information for purposes of research, faculty and graduate students reported that they made substantial use of these facilities. On average,[5] faculty respondents said that almost 60 percent (59.34%) of the information they use for research comes from the library, and the percentages are even higher

[4] Some of the percentages are given to one decimal; others are provided at two decimals. The results cited in this introduction to the summary tables are reported as given in the tables.

[5] In the tables, both mean and median are given. In this introduction, the mean, which is the more commonly cited statistic, is given unless otherwise indicated.

among graduate students and graduate students who are also members of the faculty[6] (Table 33). Faculty and graduate students meet their information needs through a mix of print and online sources (Tables 34-42), but even then, the library's Web site is an important conduit to relevant material. When asked what percentage of their online information needs relative to research were met by the library's Web site, faculty members responded on average 61.65 percent. Graduate students reported roughly the same (65.81%) (Table 36).

At the same time, on average, 58.08 percent of faculty members' and graduate students' information needs relating to research are reportedly met by the Internet[7] (Table 37). When asked about the role of the library relative to teaching, faculty (including graduate students who were members of the faculty) placed less reliance on the physical and virtual library than graduate students did. But all three subgroups (faculty, graduate students, and graduate students who were members of the faculty) responded that on average, about half (53.65%) of their information needs were met by the physical and virtual library (Table 38). All three subgroups found information related to teaching online and on the Internet (Tables 40 and 42), but the library's Web site also plays an important role. On average and across all three subgroups, 59.10 percent of the online information needs related to teaching are met through the library's site (Table 41).

Collectively, these findings suggest that advanced researchers—faculty and graduate students—use multiple on- and offline sources to support research and teaching. They do not perceive a competition between library-based information and information they find on the Internet through search engines, the library's Web site, and other tools (Table 43). At the same time, faculty and graduate students are skeptical of the authenticity and credibility of Internet-based information and employ various strategies to vet the information (Tables 44 and 45).

Undergraduates' reliance on electronic sources suggests that their perceptions and behaviors might differ from those of faculty and graduate students. All students rely heavily on the physical and virtual library for their coursework; on average, between 65 and 70 percent of their information needs are satisfied through these facilities (Table 46). All students also rely heavily on the library's Web site for access to the online resources they use; on average, well over 60 percent of the online sources they use are accessed through the li-

---

[6] In questions related to teaching, the study differentiated between graduate students and graduate students who are also members of the faculty.

[7] Investigators asked two questions (1) how information needs were met by the campus library's Web site (and other campus-based Web-enabled resources, such as department Web sites) and (2) how information needs were met by going out to the Internet. Respondents may have been confused by this survey question. A local Web site can serve as a portal to local resources as well as to hyperlinked, non-local Internet resources. A user might also find the latter by going out onto the Internet independently. Thus, responses that reflect use of a locally constructed Web portal might be masking non-local Internet resources served up on a local Web page through a set of hyperlinks. How users differentiate between Internet resources and those organized and made accessible through local, Web-enabled resources remains an interesting question.

brary's site (Table 49). On average, undergraduates use Internet sources for their coursework more than graduate students do; 66.53 percent of the former, versus 58.84 percent of the latter, claimed that their information needs were met on the Net (Table 50). Like faculty and graduate students, undergraduates seem to need the library's Web site to find relevant material.

The Web has also emerged as an important mode of communication among faculty members and students; however, it appears to have augmented, not replaced, more traditional modes. Tables 51–55 summarize data on where faculty members make information available about courses (e.g., syllabi) and course readings for graduate and undergraduate students. Handouts are still popular, but 67.9 percent faculty also maintain Web pages with this information for their undergraduate students (Table 51). The information is available on reserve at the library, the campus bookstore, and the copy center as well. Faculty members still favor the local bookstore for making course readings available to undergraduates, but readings are also made available for undergraduates in handouts, on reserve in the library, in the library's general holdings, and through course Web sites (Table 52). Similar patterns characterize information about courses and course readings for graduate students (Tables 53 and 54).

Students' perceptions relative to their coursework differ somewhat in emphasis. They rely heavily on handouts for information about course requirements and use the course Web page as a backup (Table 55). The most frequently cited source for obtaining course readings is the bookstore, followed by holdings in the general collections at the library, reserve readings at the library, handouts, and the course Web page (Table 56). Faculty members expect both undergraduate and graduate students to find at least some of the course readings independently (Tables 57 and 58). Students, faced with juggling multiple courses, not surprisingly seem to perceive finding resources independently a slightly greater burden than do their teachers, but the trajectory of the responses is roughly aligned (Table 59).

For example, most of the faculty believe that their graduate students need to find all or some of the supplementary course readings (that is, course readings necessary for the class but not specified in the syllabus) independently. Slightly under half (49.4%) thought that "some of the readings" had to be secured independently, and 29.1 percent of the faculty respondents thought "it is all there for them" (Table 58). About one-fourth of the graduate students (25.4%) agreed that "it is all there," and 54.7 percent believed that they had to find at least some of the readings for themselves (Table 59).

When asked to evaluate the extent to which they relied on different institutions and services for keeping current with developments in their field, 33.3 percent of the entire study sample identified the library as one of the sources they consulted, and 32.8 percent rated it as the "most important" source (Table 60). This finding was consistent across faculty, graduate students, and undergraduates as well as across disciplines. Respondents in the arts and humanities are most reliant on the library; 37.5 percent consider it their most important resource for staying current. Respondents in business are least reliant on the library, but 22.5 percent still consider it their most important source.

Other sources for keeping current include the "open" Internet, personal libraries and subscriptions, professional meetings, interaction with colleagues, department and library Web pages, the bookstore, and online alerting services. The extent of reliance on these sources varied. Faculty place high value on their personal libraries and subscriptions to journals (55.9 percent think that these resources are the most important way to stay current). Thirty-eight percent of undergraduates, compared with only 21.4 percent of faculty, consider the open Internet to be their most important source for keeping abreast of developments. Again, notions of what constitutes "keeping current" are presumably different among demographic groups at different stages of their academic and professional development, and these differences in perceptions of relative value of the Internet versus the library or specific formats (such as journals) merit further scrutiny.

Respondents were asked a series of questions designed to determine the adequacy of existing sources in all media and of modes of delivery (Table 61). About half (54.7%) considered the medium important. Respondents had high standards, placing value on such variables as speed of delivery, ease of access, quality, currency, ability to search, coverage, and printing. However, less than half (43.8%) feel that their needs are being met. This finding appears to hold across all media and subgroups and disciplines. An interesting study might be conceived that systematically examined the differences between value placed on various attributes and system features (for example, speed of delivery, ease of access, search, printing, coverage) and the extent to which different user groups and disciplines believe that a given system or medium performs satisfactorily.

Respondents are basically satisfied with the content and services that the library provides (Tables 62–65). Slightly over 14 percent (14.3%) requested more print journals, and 10.7 percent would like more electronic journals (Table 62). These needs seem concentrated among faculty members and graduate students, and among respondents in the biological sciences, physical sciences/mathematics, and engineering. However, when asked what types of content were no longer necessary, 61.3 percent of the total sample responded "Can't think of anything/everything is useful" (Table 64). This finding was fairly consistent across faculty members and students as well as across disciplines. When asked about library services, the level of satisfaction was even higher: 75.1 percent of the sample responded, "Can't think of anything/nothing" (Table 65). Allegiance is particularly strong among liberal arts colleges and law, where almost 90 percent (86.5% and 88.9%, respectively) of respondents voiced this sentiment.

Loyalty to the library and its content and services notwithstanding, respondents believe that they are changing how they go about their work (Table 66). About 40 percent of the total (41.5%) reported that they work and study away from campus more than they used to. This finding was more pronounced among graduate students and those who are affiliated with public research universities than among other survey respondents. About one-third of the sample (34.5%) reported that they use the library less frequently than they used to, with a preponderance among the faculty and, again, graduate students. Less than a fourth (23.9%) of the respondents participate in distance learning, but those who do tend to be disproportionately represented among undergraduates and respondents in the social sciences, engineering, and business. Relatively few—a little more than 15 percent (15.7%)—agreed with the statement, "The Internet has not changed the way I use the library."

Overall, higher education places great value on the library and its services. The library is, however, only one of many elements in a complex information infrastructure. Clearly, teaching faculty and graduate students rely on the library and its collections, as well as the bookstore, copy center, and other modalities to provide coursework for their students. Moreover, traditional library-based functions of information selection, organization, and aggregation appear to be migrating to the Web as libraries build Web sites that users employ to access a broad range of online sources. Many respondents appear to welcome the proliferation of different media. This would suggest that the net effect of electronic sources is additive, and only occasionally does one medium appear to substitute for another. This "substitution effect," while weak, is evident primarily among undergraduates. Whether this observation portends a wholesale change, or whether undergraduates' attitudes toward the relative value of all elements in information infrastructure will evolve, is an open question.

PART 3: FORMATS

Faculty and students seek and use information from multiple sources, in different formats, and at many venues on- and off-campus. Outsell has collected consistent information on 17 formats: print/Hard-copy books; print/Hard-copy journals; electronic books; electronic journals; magazines; papers delivered at professional meetings; print abstracts and indices; online abstracts and indices; online databases, data sets, or data sources; manuscripts; proprietary software; data; photographs, prints, and other visual resources; technical reports; preprints; dissertations; and news. How electronic information is used has engaged the attention of a wide variety of researchers. One of the great strengths of the Outsell data is that they are based on a survey of multiple user groups, because this will make it possible for future scholars of communication to examine one format or set of formats from multiple perspectives on a large scale. A few observations on some of the basic trends and themes follow.

When asked which categories of information they used for their "job/coursework,"[8] the most frequently cited answer was reference. Just under half of all respondents (47.3%) placed it among the sources they use regularly (Table 67). The second most frequently cited category of information is scientific and technical information (39.9%). Social science information ranks third (29.4%) and humanities fourth (22.2%). When asked which category of information was most important, the top choice was scientific and technical information (28.6%), followed by reference (19.5%), social science information (16.8%), and humanities (12.4%). However, the most frequently cited second most important type of information was reference (27.8%). These priorities, particularly the pattern in first choice, more or less track the priorities of the faculty. However, undergraduates placed a greater value on reference information than faculty members did: 14.0 percent of faculty members, in contrast to 25.6 percent of undergraduates, considered reference information most important.

The distribution across disciplines tended to track the patterns evidenced across the sample with a few notable exceptions. Respondents in the biological sciences, physical sciences, and engineering placed a strong emphasis on scientific information, while respondents in the social sciences and arts and humanities placed less emphasis on material in their respective disciplines. For example, 85.5 percent of the respondents in engineering say they regularly use scientific and technical information, and 72.7 percent considered this their most important category of information (Table 67). By contrast, only 60.5 percent of the social science respondents regularly used social science information, and of them, only 41.9 percent considered this category of information the most important.

These patterns suggest several possibilities. The questionnaire was constructed to differentiate among information used in research, teaching, and coursework. Respondents, particularly faculty, may have interpreted the question to mean information they used daily, perhaps related to teaching rather than research. It is also possible that they construe their original research as separate from the literature they may consult as part of that process. In view of the effort faculty and graduate students invest in staying abreast of developments (see Part 2), the literature, particularly the journal literature, is clearly vital to the research process.

When asked which information types were used for research, 97.2 percent of all respondents cited print/Hard-copy journals, followed by print/Hard-copy books (96.6 %), online abstracts and indexes (88.2%), papers given at conferences (84.5%), data (82.1%), online databases, etc. (81.8%), and manuscripts and other primary source documents (81.1%) (Table 68). All the other formats investigated are used, but not as broadly. On the other hand, scholars and students in different disciplines rely on different information formats. More than 80 percent of respondents in the biological sciences

[8] The term "job/coursework" is employed in the more detailed tables summarized in Table 67. For use of the term, see Table 57 in the full compilation.

and physical sciences/mathematics use electronic journals; the sample-wide response to this question was 74.9 percent. Only 59.2 percent of the respondents in arts and humanities reported needing "data" for their research activities. Technical reports are disproportionately used by respondents in the biological sciences, physical sciences/mathematics, and engineering, reflecting a long-standing tradition for early distribution of research results in this format. Preprints figure prominently among respondents in the physical sciences/mathematics, as well as to a somewhat lesser extent in the biological sciences and in engineering, where this format has also historically been important.

When it comes to teaching, priorities are somewhat different. Slightly more than 95 percent (95.8%) of the respondents, who include faculty members and graduate students only, cite print/Hard-copy books rather than journals (Table 69). Print/Hard-copy books are followed in frequency of use by print/Hard-copy journals (81.1%), news (66.3%), and photographs, etc. (62.9%). These priorities are fairly consistent across disciplines, all of which reported using print/Hard-copy books most frequently. Respondents in business and law stand out in their use of news (89.6% and 89.4%, respectively) while those in the biological sciences and arts and humanities are particularly active in their use of photographs and visual resources for teaching (83.3% and 78.3%, respectively).

Students' use of information types represents a mix of their professors' and instructors' preferences and the materials they might need for research projects. Print/Hard-copy books are the most frequently used format (93.3%) (Table 70). The next four most frequently used types among all students are print/Hard-copy journals (80.6%), online data databases, etc. (80.2%), data (75.2%), and online abstracts and indexes (73.1%). Compared with the researchers' use, students' use of information for coursework thus appears to be more concentrated in books than in journals and other formats. This suggests that although the interests of faculty and graduate students are well defined and focused, their information requirements are fairly broad in terms of formats. Undergraduate students seem to be quite the opposite: their intellectual and professional interests are not as well formed, yet they rely fairly heavily on one format, books.

A selection of the findings follows. It is focused on findings relative to print/Hard-copy books, print/Hard-copy journals, and electronic journals (Tables 71–88). Print/Hard-copy books and journals figure importantly in research and teaching; electronic journals have been the subject of intense discussion among librarians, publishers, and researchers about patterns in scholarly communication. This interest justifies a preliminary look at the e-journal format as well as the formats that appear to be more frequently used on campus. Still, analysis of the other, somewhat less frequently used formats (for example, dissertations, manuscripts, technical reports, and data) awaits more sophisticated investigation. Remaining summary data are contained in Tables 89–162.

Print/Hard-copy Books

The investigators asked two related questions about each format: Where do you go to find information *about* material? and Where do you go to find the *material itself*? In response to the first question, with respect to print/Hard-copy books used for research, the overwhelming response within the study sample is "Go online" (82.7%) (Table 71). Less than half of respondents (47.7%) go to print sources, such as finding aids, to find information about material, and less than one-fourth (23.2%) ask for assistance. The finding was consistent across faculty members and graduate students (undergraduates were not asked this question) and across all disciplines. When asked where they went to find the material itself, 90.3 percent of respondents went to the campus library (Table 72). The second most frequent way to find the books is to go online, but only 16.8 percent of respondents find print/Hard-copy books in this way.

To find information about books for teaching, faculty and instructors cast their nets somewhat more broadly (Table 73). Slightly more than 65 percent (65.2%) of the entire study sample go online, including online library catalogs and finding aids, and 54.6 percent use print aids at the campus library. About 30 percent (30.3%) seek some form of personal assistance, either from a colleague or, rarely, from a librarian (9.2%). Otherwise, professors and instructors use a wide range of tools and strategies: personal libraries, Web directories/subject-related Web pages, search engines, their institution's Web sites, and online reference services. To find the information itself, 64.7 percent of the respondents go to the campus library (Table 74). Less frequently used places to find the material include the bookstore (15.2%), online access (13.1%), and the publisher (11.3%).

When students look for information about print/Hard-copy books needed for a course, they also go online (70.7%) (Table 75). To a substantially lesser extent, they ask for help (33.6%), typically from a member of the faculty or a librarian. Less than one-third of students (31.5%) also consult print aids, primarily at their libraries. Still, when they go online, they are accessing services offered by the library; in descending order, online finding aids they consulted included the online catalog (21.4%), the institution's Web site (16.7%), and Internet search engines (16.3%). To find or use the material itself, 84.6 percent of the undergraduate and graduate students go to the library, which is by far the most frequently used location (Table 76). The next most frequently cited place for finding print/Hard-copy books is the physical bookstore, where 18.8 percent of respondents reported that they purchase the books they need for coursework.

Print/Hard-copy Journals

When asked where users go to find information about print or Hard-copy journals for use in research, the most frequent response was "online" among all groups studied (87.2%) (Table 77). Within the general category of "online," however, respondents in all disciplines use an array of sources: databases, the library catalog and finding aids, the university or college Web site, Web directories/subject-related Web pages, Internet searches, and online abstracting and indexing services. Respondents in the arts and humanities rely disproportionately on the library's online services; 41.0 percent reported library catalogs and finding aids as their *preferred* source. Nearly one-fourth (23.1%) of respondents reported using the library's online aids, but only 14.6 percent consider it their preferred source. Just under half (48.7%) of the whole group also use print sources as discovery tools; these are generally located at the campus library, although only 14.7 percent of respondents consider using print sources at the library the preferred method. Just under one-fourth (24.4%) asked for personal assistance. Only 13.9 percent ask a librarian, and a bare 3.2 percent consider consulting a librarian a preferred way of identifying information related to journals.

On the other hand, the campus library figures prominently in use of print/Hard-copy journals. Almost 90 percent (87.1%) of all respondents cited the library as the place where they find such journals for research, and 61.5 percent consider the library the preferred source (Table 78). This finding was fairly consistent across disciplines, although the percentage was slightly lower among respondents in the biological sciences (78.7%). Moreover, only about half of the respondents in the biological sciences (49.3%) consider the library their preferred location for finding print/Hard-copy journals related to their research. The highest usage is among respondents in the arts and humanities, where 95.1 percent of the respondents reported finding print/Hard-copy journals for research at their campus libraries and 83.6 percent consider the library the *preferred* location. In declining frequency of use, respondents named online access, interlibrary loan, borrowing from other libraries, personal holdings, and consulting colleagues as sources for locating print/Hard-copy journals.

Online resources are the principal means by which faculty members and teaching graduate students obtain information about print/Hard-copy journals they use for teaching (Table 79). About three-fourths (74.6%) find this information through one of several online tools (for example, databases, search engines, Web directories/subject-related Web sites, their institution's Web site, and online library catalogs and finding aids). About 60 percent (61.1%) reported using print sources as well, and about half (49.3%) find these sources in the campus library. Just over 20 percent (20.5%) of the respondents consider finding information about print/Hard-copy journals for teaching in the library to be their preferred strategy. As is the case in use of online resources for identifying relevant teaching material in print/hard-copy books, respondents use a range of strategies when they look for information about print/Hard-copy journals among offline resources. Sources include their own collections, personal subscriptions, references or citations in books and journals, abstracting and indexing tools, and so on. About one-fifth (20.9%) asks for help in several ways: from colleagues on campus (14.0%), librarians (9.6%), colleagues at other institutions (4.0%), and elsewhere.

The trajectories of use reflected in Table 79 seem to be similar across disciplines and types of institutions, although the liberal arts colleges tend to show higher uses of both print and online resources to support the use of journals in teaching and more frequent use of the library. For example, 74.0 percent of the respondents at these institutions reported using print resources (as opposed to the sample-wide response of 61.1 percent). Almost one-fourth (24.4%) of liberal arts college respondents said they consulted with others (as opposed to 20.9% across the entire sample), and 15.2 percent asked a librarian for assistance (as opposed to the sample-wide response, 9.6%).

Just under 80 percent (79.5%) of all respondents in the subgroup of faculty members and graduate students who teach reported that when they use print/hard journals, they use them at or borrow them from the library (Table 80). For 57.6 percent, the library is the preferred venue. This finding appears consistent across all institution types and disciplines, although the liberal arts colleges and arts and humanities are somewhat more prominently represented (62.3% and 62.5%, respectively). Somewhat over one-fourth of all respondents in this subgroup (26.9%) said that they found these journals online. Otherwise, respondents find print/Hard-copy journals in a variety of ways: through personal collections, personal subscriptions, interlibrary loan, course Web sites, and the campus bookstore, and from colleagues and collections within their departments, on-demand document delivery services, and publishers.

Nearly three-fourths (73.4%) of graduate and undergraduate students go online to find information about print/Hard-copy journals they need or use for coursework (Table 81). About one-third (32.4%) asks for help, most frequently from a librarian (22.6%) or from faculty (16.7%). Finally, 29.1 percent of the students look for this information in the library. These patterns appear to hold across all institution types and disciplines. Undergraduates and respondents from liberal arts colleges and from arts and humanities, engineering, and business seemed somewhat more willing to seek personal assistance, generally from a librarian. Respondents from private research universities as well as those in the arts and humanities and law seem to take greater advantage of library facilities than respondents in the other types of institutions and disciplines surveyed.

Use of print/Hard-copy journals for coursework is centered in the library; 87.1 percent of respondents said they either borrow journals or use them within the library (Table 82). More than one-fourth (27.9%) of the respondents have access to the material online. Additional access strategies include borrowing from other libraries, interlibrary loan, purchase at the bookstore, loans from faculty, personal holdings, on-demand document-delivery services, and so on.

As had been suggested by the patterns exhibited in association with print/Hard-copy books, the information summarized in this section further confirms the importance of the library in supporting identification and use of print/Hard-copy journals for research, teaching, and coursework. The relevance of the library's resources to teaching and coursework appears particularly important. Undergraduates seem more willing than graduate students and faculty members to ask for help, but even intellectually sophisticated scholars appear to need the library's organizational and selection functions—even though that functionality may be available online rather than in the library building itself. It is also important to note that faculty and instructors display a range of information-seeking and use behaviors. It is unclear whether this creativity has always been a hallmark of scholarship and teaching or whether it represents a response to perceived (or real) limitations in existing tools and services or to changes in the way that scholars now work.

Electronic Journals (E-journals)

Nearly all respondents who use e-journals for research (92.7%) find out about them online (Table 83). Finding aids include online databases (21.8%), search engines (18.2%), Web/subject-related directories (15.1%), and Internet searches (10.8%), as well as a host of other services, including online abstracting/indexing services, online reference services, department Web pages, and so on. Only 21.7 percent of the respondents who use e-journals for research identify them through print sources, frequently at the campus library. Among e-journal users, a disproportionate number of respondents in the biological sciences (24.1%) reported using print sources to identify e-journals, although only 3.4 percent considered this their preferred mode. Consistent with earlier observations, 16.5 percent of all respondents ask for personal assistance and only 2.5 percent prefer to ask a librarian.

Just over 80 percent (81.2%) of those who use e-journals for research access them online, and about three-fourths (74.1%) of the respondents consider online access the preferred modality (Table 84). Nearly one-fourth (23.0%) reported using electronic journals in the library or borrowing them from the library, but only 13.9 percent consider this a preferred strategy. Otherwise, respondents again displayed a wide range of access strategies (for example, office use, interlibrary loan, and personal holdings). Respondents at liberal arts colleges are disproportionately represented among online users of e-journals (96.8%), while respondents at public research universities are represented in a relatively low proportion (76.0%).

Across the disciplines, the most frequent users of e-journals are in law (94.7%); individuals in this discipline use e-journals more frequently than persons in the biological sciences, physical sciences/mathematics, and engineering. However, the sample sizes in these subjects (specifically law) are low, which means that results should be approached with some caution. Physical sciences/mathematics and engineering have a tradition of using preprints and technical reports for early release of results, which may affect the scholars' use of the formal literature for research. How the availability of multiple communication modalities within given disciplines or sets of disciplines affects relative use of the available formats is an important question for future research.

Just over 86 percent (86.7%) of those who use e-journals for teaching obtain information about them online (Table 85). These respondents use an array of discovery tools with little obvious preference: search engines (18.6%), online databases (18.4%), online library catalogs and finding aids (17.3%), institutions' Web sites (16.0%), Web directories/subject-related sites (14.8%), and Internet searches (12.8%), together with a variety of other strategies and services. None of these strategies fares particularly well among the respondents as a preferred approach. For example, only 9.5 percent of the respondents consider search engines, the most frequently cited tool, a "preferred source of information" about e-journals for teaching. These findings seem to hold across institutions and disciplines, although private universities and liberal arts colleges are relatively frequent users of online library catalogs and finding aids (24.6% and 20.2%, respectively), as are respondents in the biological sciences (23.8%) and arts and humanities (30.4%).

Other means of identifying relevant e-journals for teaching include print materials (22.8%), which are most frequently accessed at the library, and personal assistance (22.3%). Requests for personal assistance conform to the patterns observed with respect to formats. Somewhat more than 10 percent (11.3%) consult a librarian, and only 4.4 percent consider asking a librarian a preferred strategy. Faculty and graduate students are most likely to ask a colleague (13.4%).

Among those faculty members and graduate students who use electronic journals for teaching, 80.5 percent reported finding the materials online, and this is the preferred source for 75.3 percent of the respondents (Table 86). Another 22.7 percent borrow or use e-journals at the library, but only 14.7 percent consider this a preferred strategy. In addition, respondents in this subgroup employ a broad range of strategies and tools: access in their offices, on-demand document delivery, interlibrary loan, and purchase. Less than 1 percent (0.6%) own e-journals in their personal collections, and less than 1 percent (0.6%) acquire them from the publishers directly. The low level of ownership suggests that, at least for teaching purposes, faculty and graduate students rely on third-party access, presumably the library, which may make the material available online through its Web site. This suggestion, which is consistent with earlier observations about reliance on the library's Web site, points to the importance of the Web site as an element in the infrastructure of higher education. This topic might be profitably explored in future studies.

Nearly 90 percent (88.1%) of students who use e-journals for coursework find out about them online (Table 87). Discovery tools include online library catalogs/finding aids (22.7%), institutional Web sites (22.5%), search engines (21.0%), online databases (19.2%), and Internet searches (11.3%), among others. About 20 percent (20.1%) ask for help in some form: from librarians (12.8%), faculty (10.5%), and other students (4.1%). Undergraduates are clearly the most willing to ask for help (23.5%), particularly those who have yet to declare a major (41.7%).

Seventy-five percent of students who use e-journals for their coursework access the journals themselves online, and for 68.5% percent, this is the preferred strategy (Table 88). Nearly 40 percent (39.5%) use or borrow the material from the campus library, and 25.5 percent consider this the preferred method. Other strategies are also employed at very low levels, including interlibrary loan (2.8%), borrowing from other libraries (2.2%), and on-demand document-delivery systems (0.5%). These observations seem to hold across institution types and disciplines, although arts and humanities are underrepresented within the group who access e-journals online; 68.5 percent of the arts and humanities respondents reported such use. However, a disproportionately high percentage of respondents in the arts and humanities (48.1%), social sciences (43.7%), and biological sciences (43.3%) borrow e-journals from the library or use the material there.

OBSERVATIONS AND IMPLICATIONS

These data characterize key segments of the higher education population—faculty, graduate students, and undergraduates—from several perspectives, enabling us to view behaviors and preferences in terms of different roles and functions. The information needs of the faculty are represented in terms of the functional roles of researcher and teacher, and both roles are then considered independently relative to the library. Similarly, the students' views, whether graduate or undergraduate, are treated independently, making it possible to see how information needs may evolve as intellectual interests become more focused and more sophisticated. In this regard, graduate students occupy a telling middle ground: at some times their information preferences and behaviors are generally aligned with those of undergraduates; at other times, for example, in their roles as instructors, the graduate students' interests and preferences converge with those of the faculty. It is a point that might yield interesting results from further study.

At least two categories of future studies can be envisaged. The first category would delve more deeply into subsets of the data. The second would contextualize the data in comparative studies with other information-intensive user populations (e.g., full-time researchers in industry, research institutes, and government) or other segments of the higher education community (e.g., part-time/adjunct faculty or students in remote or continuing education settings who may pursue additional training not related to an academic degree). Studies that plumb the data more deeply might examine differences across and within disciplines and across status.

Preliminary observations have brought to light several examples in which respondents in the liberal arts colleges and in the biological sciences and arts and humanities seem to rely on the library and its functions and services more than their peers in the other disciplines do. Respondents in law also seem to show greater use of the library and its functions. This suggests, for example, that law may require and reward skills that rely on a tightly integrated use of library facilities to support notions of acceptable evidence and the style of argument that is part of the legal culture, which borrows heavily from precedent and may resemble, for example, historical and literary research. This understanding of the nature of evidence and argument may differ substantially from that that prevails in laboratory or experimental sciences, which have their own canons of evidence and interpretation. Thus, the legal profession may selectively draw on graduates from liberal arts colleges and on the cognitive frameworks that students in the arts and humanities and biological sciences develop. How the intellectual content of these and other disciplines interact may be a fruitful topic for further study, as is the question of how institutions of higher education incubate learning styles and scholarship, and of how the library and its functions support that process. Other topics are sure to be imagined as researchers become familiar with this data set.

Library directors and college and university administrators face an increasingly complex institutional and informational environment. The population they serve is far from homogeneous in its level of sophistication, information needs and infrastructure requirements. Faculty and graduate students, in particular, seem to be omnivorous in their appetite for information, creative in their strategies for seeking and acquiring information in all forms, and very independent. They appear to seek tools, services, and facilities that they can use where and when they need them. So far, most faculty, graduate students and undergraduates seem to prefer a hybrid information environment in which information in electronic form does not supplant information in print but adds to the range of equipment, resources, and services available to teachers and students.

Like the bookstore and copy center, the library is a facility that serves campus information needs and is vital to teaching, learning, and research. For example, faculty members place course readings on reserve and require use of items in the general collection as part of their curricula, continuing to take advantage of the physical facility and the analog collections. In addition, many of the librarian's functions—as selector, organizer, guarantor of quality, and perhaps as teacher—seem to be finding expression in the electronic medium, where the library's Web site, for example, is seen as an important element in the local information infrastructure. Liberal arts colleges, where the teaching mission is particularly important, also seem to be institutions in which there is consistently greater reliance on the library and where the library has a greater presence in supporting the curriculum. Undergraduates, far more than graduate students and faculty, ask librarians for help in their coursework, adding to the function of the librarian as teacher as well as editor, selector, and guide. Thus, integrating librarians' functions and services into the undergraduate learning experience may prove a fertile area for future growth.

REFERENCES

Greenstein, Daniel, and Suzanne E. Thorin. 2002. *The Digital Library: A Biography*. Washington, D.C.: Digital Library Federation and Council on Library and Information Resources. Available from: http://www.clir.org/pubs/abstract/pub109abst.html.

McClure, Charles, et al. 2002. *Statistics, Measures and Quality Standards for Assessing Digital Reference Library Services: Guidelines and Procedures*. Syracuse, N.Y., and Tallahassee, Fla.: Syracuse University and Florida State University. Available from: http://quartz.syr.edu/quality/.

Troll Covey, Denise. 2002. *Usage and Usability Assessment: Library Practices and Concerns*. Washington, D.C.: Digital Library Federation and Council on Library and Information Resources. Available from: http://www.clir.org/pubs/abstract/pub105abst.html.

SELECTED DATA TABLES

Key to Tables

The following tables contain summaries of the survey data. Each table contains the responses to one survey question, with the possible responses down the left-hand side, and frequencies and percentages of those responses in the body of the table. The first column represents the results from the total number of respondents to the question. The remaining column headings represent subsets of respondents to that question by respondent type, institution type, discipline, and gender. The base samples for the total responding to that question and for the other subsets is listed just below the column heading.

Letters appear next to some of the values. These letters correspond to the letters beneath the column headings, and they indicate significant differences identified by statistical testing. It means that the value is statistically different from the values given for other respondent groups represented by the letters. The results are tested at the 95 percent level of confidence (that is, there is a 5 percent or less chance that the differences between the data are due to chance). The number with the greater magnitude has the significance letter attached to it, indicating that it is "significantly greater" than at least one other comparative number.

Questions that were open-ended (e.g., "How many hours do you spend on research?") show actual responses followed by the mean and/or median and standard deviation.

This document includes 158 of the 659 data tables provided by Outsell. Each of these 158 tables has been numbered according to its order of appearance in the narrative. The numbers assigned for this publication, therefore, differ from those that were originally given by Outsell. The List of Tables that follows matches each table used in this document with its original table number.

Most, but not all, of the tables presented in the following pages are specifically referenced in the narrative.

List of Tables

Part 1: The Sample: Faculty and Students

27	630	Minor problem summary table
28	601	Top two box summary table [values perceived in different forms of information access]

Part 2: Infrastructure, Facilities, and Services

29	54	Summary table: What equipment do you use for accessing information from your off-campus residence?
30	55	Summary table: What equipment is available at the library?
31	56	Summary table: What equipment do you have in your office?
32	45	Thinking about the past year, what percent of the time that you are accessing information for your (teaching or research/studies) is spent at each location?
33	181	What percent of the information that you use for your research comes from your institution's physical or virtual library?
34	182	What percent of the information that you use for your research comes from another source?
35	186	What percent of your current information needs for your research are available online?
36	187	What percent of your current information needs for your research that are available online are available through your institution's library Web site?
37	188	And, what percent of your current information needs for your research that are available online are available through the Internet?
38	309	What percent of the information that you use for teaching comes from your institution's physical or virtual library?
39	310	What percent of the information that you use for your teaching comes from another source?
40	314	What percent of your current information needs for your teaching are available online?
41	315	And, what percent of your current information needs for your teaching that are available online are available through your institution's library Web site?
42	316	And, what percent of your current information needs for your teaching that are available online are available through the Internet?
43	602	Once you've gained access to the Internet, how do you usually get pointed to the right information sources?
44	603	How do you verify the information you receive from the Internet? That is, how do you establish the accuracy of the information you receive from the open Internet?
45	604	How do you determine the authoritativeness of the information you receive from the Internet? That is, how do you decide how much it should influence your current thinking?
46	437	What percent of the information that you use for your coursework comes from your institution's physical or virtual library?
47	438	What percent of the information that you use for your coursework comes from another source?
48	442	What percent of your current information needs for your classes are available online?
49	443	And, what percent of your current information needs for your classes that are available online are available through your institution's library Web site?
50	444	And, what percent of your current information needs for your classes that are available online are available through the Internet?
51	482	All/most summary table [availability of course information to undergraduates]
52	494	All/most summary table [availability of course readings to undergraduates]

53	507	All/most summary table [availability of course information for graduate students]
54	519	All/most summary table [availability of course readings for graduate students]
55	532	All/most summary table [availability of course information by instructors]
56	544	All/most summary table [availability of course readings]
57	495	How many additional course readings, beyond what you make available, do your undergraduate students need to access to meet the requirements of their class? Would you say they have to independently find [all, most, some, none, don't know/refused]?
58	520	How many additional course readings, beyond what you make available, do your graduate students need to access to meet the requirements of their class? Would you say they have to independently find [all, most, some, none, don't know/refused]?
59	545	How many additional course readings, beyond what your instructors make available, do you need to access to meet the requirements of your class? Would you say you have to independently find [all, most, some, none, don't know/refused]?
60	548	Summary table [resources to stay abreast of developments]
61	579	Summary table [adequacy of current systems]
62	589	What additional information content does your library need to provide to meet your needs? What else?
63	590	What services would you like your institution's library to offer?
64	591	What types of information content does your academic library offer that you find no longer necessary? Why isn't this information content necessary?
65	592	What types of information services does your academic library offer that are no longer necessary? Why aren't these information services necessary?
66	650	Top two box summary table [current and anticipated use of systems and facilities]

Part 3: Formats

67	60	Summary table: Of those information categories you just mentioned as using, which is the most important? And which is the second most important?
68	61	Which of the following information types do you use for your research?
69	189	Which of the following information types do you use for your teaching?
70	317	Which of the following information types do you use for your coursework?
71	62	When you are doing research, how do you find information about print or hardcopy books? [about research]
72	68	Print or hardcopy books summary table [research]
73	193	Print or hardcopy books summary table [about teaching materials]
74	196	Print or hardcopy books summary table [teaching materials]
75	321	Print or hardcopy books summary table [coursework]
76	324	Print or hardcopy books summary table [coursework]
77	72	When you are doing research, how do you find information about print or hardcopy journals? [research]
78	75	Print or hardcopy journals summary table [research]
79	200	Print or hardcopy journals summary table [teaching materials]
80	203	Print or hardcopy journals summary table [teaching materials]
81	328	Print or hardcopy journals summary table [coursework]

82	331	Print or hardcopy journals summary table [coursework]
83	86	When you are doing research, how do you find information about e-journals? [research]
84	89	E-journals summary table [research]
85	214	E-journals summary table [teaching materials]
86	217	E-journals summary table [teaching materials]
87	342	E-journals summary table [coursework]
88	345	E-journals summary table [coursework]
89	82	E-books summary table [research]
90	96	Magazines summary table [research]
91	103	Papers delivered at professional meetings summary table [research]
92	110	Print abstracts and indexes summary table [research]
93	117	Online abstracts and indexes summary table [research]
94	124	Online databases, data sets or data sources summary table [research]
95	131	Manuscripts and other primary source documents summary table [research
96	138	Proprietary software or application summary table [research]
97	145	Data summary table [research]
98	152	Photographs, prints and other visual resources summary table [research]
99	159	Technical reports summary table [research]
100	166	Pre-prints summary table [research]
101	173	Dissertations summary table [research]
102	180	News summary table [research]
103	207	E-books summary table [teaching materials]
104	210	E-books summary table [teaching materials]
105	221	Magazines summary table [teaching materials]
106	224	Magazines summary table [teaching materials]
107	228	Papers delivered at professional meetings summary table [teaching materials]
108	231	Papers delivered at professional meetings summary table [teaching materials]
109	235	Print abstracts and indexes summary table [teaching materials]
110	238	Print abstracts and indexes summary table [teaching materials]
111	242	Online abstracts and indexes summary table [teaching materials]
112	245	Online abstracts and indexes summary table [teaching materials]
113	249	Online databases, data sets or data sources summary table [teaching materials]
114	252	Online databases, data sets or data sources summary table [teaching materials]
115	256	Manuscripts and other primary source documents summary table [teaching materials]
116	259	Manuscripts and other primary source documents summary table [teaching materials]
117	263	Proprietary software or application summary table [teaching materials]
118	266	Proprietary software or application summary table [teaching materials]
119	270	Data summary table [teaching materials]
120	273	Data summary table [teaching materials]
121	277	Photographs, prints and other visual resources summary table [teaching materials]
122	280	Photographs, prints and other visual resources summary table [teaching materials]
123	284	Technical reports summary table [teaching materials]

TABLE 1
INSTITUTION TYPE:

	TOTAL SAMPLE	RESPONDENT TYPE: FACULTY MEMBER (A)	GRAD. STUDENT (B)	FACULTY /GRAD (C)	UNDER GRAD. STUDENT (D)	INSTITUTION TYPE: PUBLIC (E)	PRIVATE (F)	LIBERAL ARTS (G)	DISCIPLINE: BIOLOGIAL SCIENCES (H)	PHYSICAL SCIENCES /MATH (I)	SOCIAL SCIENCES (J)	ARTS AND HUMAN. (K)	ENGI-NEERING (L)	BUSINESS (M)	LAW (N)	UNDEC. MAJOR	GENDER: MALE (P)	FEMALE (Q)
Base - Total Respondents	3234	930	1056	1986	1248	1336	872	1026	465	511	993	600	125	406	32	102	1823	1411
Public (state funded) research university	1336 41.3%	272 29.2%	657 62.2%AD	929 46.8%D	407 32.6%	1336 100.0%FG	0 0	0 0	200 43.0%IK	183 35.8%	474 47.7%IK	214 35.6%	68 54.4%HIJ KMN	168 41.4%	14 41.9%	16 15.7%	702 38.5%	634 44.9%P
Private research university	872 27.0%	337 36.3%D	399 37.8%D	736 37.1%D	135 10.9%	0 0	872 100.0%EG	0 0	159 34.3%IJK	115 22.5%	259 26.1%	147 24.4%	48 38.8%IJK M	120 29.5%I	16 48.7%HIJ KLM	7 6.9%	551 30.2%Q	321 22.7%
Liberal arts college	1026 31.7%	321 34.5%B	0 0	321 16.2%	705 56.5%ABC	0 0	0 0	1026 100.0%EF	106 22.7%LN	213 41.7%HJL MN	259 26.1%LN	240 39.9%HJL MN	8 6.7%	118 29.1%HLN	3 9.4%	79 77.5%	570 31.3%	456 32.3%

Proportions/Means: Columns Tested (5% risk level) - A/B/D - C/D - E/F/G - H/I/J/K/L/M/N - P/Q

Table 1
Page 1

Outsell/Digital Library Federation Study (2002)
Weighted Tables

TABLE 2

QA1. RESPONDENT TYPE:

		RESPONDENT TYPE				INSTITUTION TYPE			DISCIPLINE									GENDER	
	TOTAL SAMPLE	FACULTY MEMBER	GRAD. STUDENT	FACULTY /GRAD	UNDER GRAD. STUDENT	PUBLIC	PRIVATE	LIBERAL ARTS	BIOLOGIAL SCIENCES	PHYSICAL SCIENCES /MATH	SOCIAL SCIENCES	ARTS AND HUMAN.	ENGI-NEERING	BUSINESS	LAW	UNDEC. MAJOR	MALE	FEMALE
		(A)	(B)	(C)	(D)	(E)	(F)	(G)	(H)	(I)	(J)	(K)	(L)	(M)	(N)		(P)	(Q)
Base - Total Respondents	3234	930	1056	1986	1248	1336	872	1026	465	511	993	600	125	406	32	102	1823	1411
FACULTY MEMBER	930 28.8%	930 100.0%BD	0 0	930 46.8%D	0 0	272 20.3%	337 38.7%EG	321 31.3%E	157 33.7%JKL N	206 40.3%HJK LN	222 22.3%	164 27.2%	34 27.4%	140 34.6%JK LN	7 23.0%	0 0	721 39.5%Q	209 14.8%
GRADUATE STUDENT	1056 32.7%	0 0	1056 100.0%AD	1056 53.2%D	0 0	657 49.2%G	399 45.8%G	0 0	183 39.4%IKM	163 31.9%K	368 37.1%KM	152 25.4%	59 47.0%HIJ KM	109 26.8%	22 67.5%HIJKL M	0 0	530 29.1%	526 37.3%P
UNDERGRADUATE STUDENT	1248 38.6%	0 0	0 0	0 0	1248 100.0%A BC	407 30.5%F	135 15.5%	705 68.7%EF	125 26.9%N	142 27.8%N	402 40.5%HI LN	284 47.4%HI JLMN	32 25.6%N	157 38.7%HIL N	3 9.4%	102 100.0%	572 31.4%	676 47.9%P

Proportions/Means: Columns Tested (5% risk level) - A/B/D - C/D - E/F/G - H/I/J/K/L/M/N - P/Q

Table 2
Page 2

Outsell/Digital Library Federation Study (2002)
Weighted Tables

TABLE 3

Q35. Gender:

		RESPONDENT TYPE				INSTITUTION TYPE			DISCIPLINE								GENDER	
	TOTAL SAMPLE	FACULTY MEMBER	GRAD. STUDENT	FACULTY /GRAD	UNDER GRAD. STUDENT	PUBLIC	PRIVATE	LIBERAL ARTS	BIOLOGIAL SCIENCES	PHYSICAL SCIENCES /MATH	SOCIAL SCIENCES	ARTS AND HUMAN.	ENGI-NEERING	BUSINESS	LAW	UNDEC. MAJOR	MALE	FEMALE
		(A)	(B)	(C)	(D)	(E)	(F)	(G)	(H)	(I)	(J)	(K)	(L)	(M)	(N)		(P)	(Q)
Base - Total Respondents	3234	930	1056	1986	1248	1336	872	1026	465	511	993	600	125	406	32	102	1823	1411
Male	1823	721	530	1251	572	702	551	570	232	379	487	297	99	261	19	48	1823	0
	56.4%	77.5%BD	50.2%	63.0%D	45.8%	52.6%	63.2%EG	55.5%	50.0%	74.2%HJK MN	49.1%	49.4%	79.5%HJK MN	64.3%HJ K	59.7%HJ K	47.1%	100.0%Q	0
Female	1411	209	526	735	676	634	321	456	232	132	506	304	26	145	13	54	0	1411
	43.6%	22.5%	49.8%A	37.0%	54.2%A C	47.4%F	36.8%	44.5%F	50.0%ILM N	25.8%	50.9%IL MN	50.6%IL MN	20.5%	35.7%IL	40.3%IL	52.9%	0	100.0%P

Proportions/Means: Columns Tested (5% risk level) - A/B/D - C/D - E/F/G - H/I/J/K/L/M/N - P/Q

TABLE 4

Q34. Which of the following categories includes your age?

	TOTAL SAMPLE	RESPONDENT TYPE: FACULTY MEMBER	RESPONDENT TYPE: GRAD. STUDENT	RESPONDENT TYPE: FACULTY /GRAD	RESPONDENT TYPE: UNDER GRAD. STUDENT	INSTITUTION TYPE: PUBLIC	INSTITUTION TYPE: PRIVATE	INSTITUTION TYPE: LIBERAL ARTS	DISCIPLINE: BIOLOGIAL SCIENCES	DISCIPLINE: PHYSICAL SCIENCES /MATH	DISCIPLINE: SOCIAL SCIENCES	DISCIPLINE: ARTS AND HUMAN.	DISCIPLINE: ENGI-NEERING	DISCIPLINE: BUSINESS	DISCIPLINE: LAW	DISCIPLINE: UNDEC. MAJOR	GENDER: MALE	GENDER: FEMALE
		(A)	(B)	(C)	(D)	(E)	(F)	(G)	(H)	(I)	(J)	(K)	(L)	(M)	(N)		(P)	(Q)
Base - Total Respondents	3234	930	1056	1986	1248	1336	872	1026	465	511	993	600	125	406	32	102	1823	1411
Less than 18 (17)	6 0.2%	0 0	* *	* *	6 0.5%C	4 0.3%	1 0.1%	2 0.2%	1 0.2%	2 0.4%	0 0	2 0.4%	* 0.2%J	0 0	0 0	1 1.0%	2 0.1%	5 0.3%
18-24 (21)	1455 45.0%	0 0	268 25.4%A	268 13.5%	1187 95.1%A BC	518 38.7%F	241 27.7%	696 67.8%EF	162 34.8%	194 38.0%	474 47.7%HI LM	301 50.2%HI LMN	48 38.4%	163 40.0%	14 41.9%	100 98.0%	663 36.4%	792 56.1%P
25-34 (29.5)	824 25.5%	138 14.9%D	646 61.2%AD	785 39.5%D	39 3.1%	462 34.6%G	299 34.3%G	63 6.1%	144 31.1%IK	126 24.7%	265 26.7%K	124 20.7%	44 35.1%IJK M	109 26.8%K	11 35.1%IJKM	0 0	452 24.8%	372 26.4%
35-44 (39.5)	346 10.7%	241 25.9%BD	97 9.2%D	338 17.0%D	8 0.7%	139 10.4%	113 12.9%G	94 9.2%	67 14.4%JKN	70 13.7%JN	85 8.5%	63 10.4%	14 10.9%N	47 11.4%N	2 5.8%	0 0	229 12.5%Q	118 8.3%
45-54 (49.5	339 10.5%	308 33.1%BD	29 2.8%D	337 17.0%D	2 0.2%	132 9.9%	108 12.4%	100 9.7%	55 11.9%L	66 12.9%L	92 9.3%	63 10.4%	10 7.7%	50 12.4%L	3 9.9%	0 0	252 13.8%Q	88 6.2%
55-64 (59.5)	213 6.6%	200 21.5%BD	12 1.1%D	212 10.7%D	1 0.1%	69 5.2%	83 9.6%EG	61 5.9%	30 6.4%	48 9.4%JL	56 5.7%	39 6.5%	7 5.6%	31 7.6%	2 6.8%	0 0	186 10.2%Q	28 2.0%
65 or over (67)	40 1.2%	40 4.3%BD	0 0	40 2.0%D	0 0	9 0.7%	21 2.4%EG	10 1.0%	4 0.8%	5 1.0%	15 1.5%	8 1.3%	3 2.1%H	6 1.4%	0 0	0 0	35 1.9%Q	5 0.4%
Refused	10 0.3%	4 0.4%	3 0.3%	7 0.3%	4 0.3%	4 0.3%	6 0.6%	1 0.1%	2 0.4%	0 0	6 0.6%	0 0	0 0	2 0.5%	* 0.5%IK	1 1.0%	6 0.3%	5 0.3%
Median	22.55	42.24	24.40	28.82	19.08	23.67	26.42	19.93	25.04	25.01	21.63	20.96	23.76	24.09	22.90	18.98	25.58	20.53
Mean	31.26	46.83BD	29.15D	37.43D	21.46	30.99G	34.70EG	28.71	32.57JKN	33.36JKL N	30.43	30.77	31.30	32.51JK	30.55	20.96	34.19Q	27.48

Proportions/Means: Columns Tested (5% risk level) - A/B/D - C/D - E/F/G - H/I/J/K/L/M/N - P/Q

Table 658
Page 2181

Outsell/Digital Library Federation Study (2002)
Weighted Tables

TABLE 4, continued

Q34. Which of the following categories includes your age?

		RESPONDENT TYPE				INSTITUTION TYPE			DISCIPLINE								GENDER	
	TOTAL SAMPLE	FACULTY MEMBER	GRAD. STUDENT	FACULTY /GRAD	UNDER GRAD. STUDENT	PUBLIC	PRIVATE	LIBERAL ARTS	BIOLOGIAL SCIENCES	PHYSICAL SCIENCES /MATH	SOCIAL SCIENCES	ARTS AND HUMAN.	ENGI-NEERING	BUSINESS	LAW	UNDEC. MAJOR	MALE	FEMALE
		(A)	(B)	(C)	(D)	(E)	(F)	(G)	(H)	(I)	(J)	(K)	(L)	(M)	(N)		(P)	(Q)
Base - Total Respondents	3234	930	1056	1986	1248	1336	872	1026	465	511	993	600	125	406	32	102	1823	1411
Standard Deviation	12.63	10.65	7.00	12.52	2.69	11.51	13.30	12.80	12.15	13.31	12.36	12.84	12.14	13.01	11.88	0.40	13.83	9.65
Standard Error	0.22	0.34	0.21	0.27	0.08	0.31	0.43	0.42	0.53	0.59	0.54	0.55	0.59	0.62	0.86	0.04	0.31	0.27

Proportions/Means: Columns Tested (5% risk level) - A/B/D - C/D - E/F/G - H/I/J/K/L/M/N - P/Q

TABLE 5

Q27. What is your position title?

	TOTAL SAMPLE	RESPONDENT TYPE: FACULTY MEMBER	GRAD. STUDENT	FACULTY /GRAD	UNDER GRAD. STUDENT	INSTITUTION TYPE: PUBLIC	PRIVATE	LIBERAL ARTS	DISCIPLINE: BIOLOGIAL SCIENCES	PHYSICAL SCIENCES /MATH	SOCIAL SCIENCES	ARTS AND HUMAN.	ENGI-NEERING	BUSINESS	LAW	UNDEC. MAJOR	GENDER: MALE	FEMALE
		(A)	(B)	(C)	(D)	(E)	(F)	(G)	(H)	(I)	(J)	(K)	(L)	(M)	(N)		(P)	(Q)
Base - Faculty	930	930	0**	930	0**	272	337	321	157	206	222	164	34	140	7*	0*	721	209
Professor/Associate Professor	547 58.8%	547 58.8%	0 0	547 58.8%	0 0	162 59.5%	209 62.0%	176 54.8%	99 62.9%M	130 63.1%M	137 61.9%M	91 55.5%	19 56.8%	67 47.7%	4 54.5%	0 0	457 63.4%Q	90 43.0%
Assistant Professor	250 26.9%	250 26.9%	0 0	250 26.9%	0 0	63 23.3%	76 22.5%	111 34.5%EF	41 26.4%	57 27.7%	60 27.1%	39 24.0%	8 24.6%	43 30.5%	1 15.9%	0 0	164 22.8%	86 41.0%P
Instructor/Lecturer	57 6.2%	57 6.2%	0 0	57 6.2%	0 0	20 7.3%	20 6.0%	17 5.4%	6 3.9%	9 4.4%	4 1.7%	20 12.3%HIJ	2 5.1%	16 11.3%HIJ	1 9.1%J	0 0	38 5.3%	19 9.2%
Dean/Ass't Dean or Department Head/ Chair	44 4.8%	44 4.8%	0 0	44 4.8%	0 0	12 4.5%	21 6.2%	11 3.5%	4 2.8%	7 3.4%	15 6.8%	6 3.4%	4 11.0%HIK	7 5.3%	1 15.9%HIJKM	0 0	39 5.4%	6 2.7%
Research Professor	4 0.4%	4 0.4%	0 0	4 0.4%	0 0	1 0.3%	3 0.9%	0 0	1 0.6%	2 1.0%	0 0	0 0	0 0	1 0.7%	0 0	0 0	4 0.5%	0 0
Post Doc/Research Associate	1 0.1%	1 0.1%	0 0	1 0.1%	0 0	* 0.1%	* 0.1%	1 0.3%	1 0.6%	0 0	0 0	0 0	* 0.8%I	0 0	* 2.3%IJKM	0 0	1 0.2%	0 0
Other	25 2.7%	25 2.7%	0 0	25 2.7%	0 0	13 4.9%G	8 2.4%	4 1.2%	4 2.8%	1 0.5%	6 2.5%	8 4.8%I	1 1.7%	6 4.0%I	* 2.3%	0 0	16 2.3%	9 4.2%
Don't Know/Refused	1 0.1%	1 0.1%	0 0	1 0.1%	0 0	0 0	0 0	1 0.3%	0 0	0 0	0 0	0 0	0 0	1 0.7%	0 0	0 0	1 0.1%	0 0

Proportions/Means: Columns Tested (5% risk level) - A/B/D - C/D - E/F/G - H/I/J/K/L/M/N - P/Q
* small base; ** very small base (under 30) ineligible for sig testing

Table 651
Page 2172

Outsell/Digital Library Federation Study (2002)
Weighted Tables

TABLE 6

Q28. How many years have you been teaching?

		RESPONDENT TYPE				INSTITUTION TYPE			DISCIPLINE								GENDER	
	TOTAL SAMPLE	FACULTY MEMBER	GRAD. STUDENT	FACULTY /GRAD	UNDER GRAD. STUDENT	PUBLIC	PRIVATE	LIBERAL ARTS	BIOLOGIAL SCIENCES	PHYSICAL SCIENCES /MATH	SOCIAL SCIENCES	ARTS AND HUMAN.	ENGI-NEERING	BUSINESS	LAW	UNDEC. MAJOR	MALE	FEMALE
		(A)	(B)	(C)	(D)	(E)	(F)	(G)	(H)	(I)	(J)	(K)	(L)	(M)	(N)		(P)	(Q)
Base - Faculty	930	930	0**	930	0**	272	337	321	157	206	222	164	34	140	7*	0*	721	209
Less than 1 year (1)	5	5	0	5	0	*	4	1	0	0	2	2	*	1	0	0	1	4
	0.6%	0.6%	0	0.6%	0	0.1%	1.2%	0.3%	0	0	0.8%	1.4%	0.8%I	0.7%	0	0	0.2%	2.0%P
1-5 years (3)	181	181	0	181	0	43	61	77	39	34	43	27	7	30	1	0	118	63
	19.4%	19.4%	0	19.4%	0	15.9%	18.1%	23.8%E	24.7%IN	16.5%	19.5%	16.4%	21.2%	21.2%	9.1%	0	16.4%	29.9%P
6-10 years (8)	155	155	0	155	0	53	45	57	24	38	34	22	7	29	2	0	103	52
	16.7%	16.7%	0	16.7%	0	19.6%	13.3%	17.8%	15.2%	18.4%	15.3%	13.7%	19.5%	20.5%	22.7%	0	14.3%	24.8%P
11-15 years (13)	116	116	0	116	0	37	41	38	22	27	30	16	6	14	1	0	88	27
	12.4%	12.4%	0	12.4%	0	13.5%	12.0%	11.9%	14.0%	13.1%	13.6%	9.6%	16.9%	9.9%	15.9%	0	12.2%	13.1%
16-20 years (18)	108	108	0	108	0	36	37	36	19	28	21	18	5	17	1	0	86	22
	11.6%	11.6%	0	11.6%	0	13.2%	10.8%	11.1%	12.4%	13.6%	9.3%	11.0%	13.6%	11.9%	9.1%	0	11.9%	10.6%
Over 20 years (25)	362	362	0	362	0	102	149	111	51	79	92	77	10	50	3	0	321	41
	38.9%	38.9%	0	38.9%	0	37.5%	44.1%G	34.7%	32.6%	38.3%	41.5%L	47.3%HL M	28.0%	35.8%	38.6%	0	44.6%Q	19.5%
Don't Know	2	2	0	2	0	*	1	1	1	0	0	1	0	0	*	0	2	0
	0.2%	0.2%	0	0.2%	0	0.1%	0.3%	0.3%	0.6%	0	0	0.7%	0	0	2.3%IJLM	0	0.3%	0
Refused	1	1	0	1	0	*	1	0	1	0	0	0	0	0	*	0	1	*
	0.1%	0.1%	0	0.1%	0	0.1%	0.3%	0	0.6%	0	0	0	0	0	2.3%IJKLM	0	0.1%	0.1%
Median	13.31	13.31	0	13.31	0	13.32	15.41	11.28	11.40	13.71	13.45	16.91	10.50	11.83	13.00	0	15.81	6.64
Mean	15.42	15.42	0	15.42	0	15.59	16.25G	14.40	14.31	15.71	15.64	16.75HL M	13.84	14.66	16.19	0	16.59Q	11.40
Standard Deviation	8.83	8.83	0	8.83	0	8.48	8.91	8.95	8.84	8.53	8.95	8.93	8.51	8.92	8.76	0	8.66	8.22

Proportions/Means: Columns Tested (5% risk level) - A/B/D - C/D - E/F/G - H/I/J/K/L/M/N - P/Q
* small base; ** very small base (under 30) ineligible for sig testing

Table 652
Page 2173

Outsell/Digital Library Federation Study (2002)
Weighted Tables

TABLE 6, continued

Q28. How many years have you been teaching?

	TOTAL SAMPLE	RESPONDENT TYPE				INSTITUTION TYPE			DISCIPLINE								GENDER	
		FACULTY MEMBER	GRAD. STUDENT	FACULTY /GRAD	UNDER GRAD. STUDENT	PUBLIC	PRIVATE	LIBERAL ARTS	BIOLOGIAL SCIENCES	PHYSICAL SCIENCES /MATH	SOCIAL SCIENCES	ARTS AND HUMAN.	ENGI-NEERING	BUSINESS	LAW	UNDEC. MAJOR	MALE	FEMALE
		(A)	(B)	(C)	(D)	(E)	(F)	(G)	(H)	(I)	(J)	(K)	(L)	(M)	(N)		(P)	(Q)
Base - Faculty	930	930	0**	930	0**	272	337	321	157	206	222	164	34	140	7*	0*	721	209
Standard Error	0.29	0.29	0	0.29	0	0.47	0.50	0.51	0.67	0.59	0.82	0.74	0.78	0.73	1.35	0	0.32	0.57

Proportions/Means: Columns Tested (5% risk level) - A/B/D - C/D - E/F/G - H/I/J/K/L/M/N - P/Q
* small base; ** very small base (under 30) ineligible for sig testing

Table 652
Page 2174

Outsell/Digital Library Federation Study (2002)
Weighted Tables

TABLE 7

Q29. Are you employed full-time, part-time or are you not employed?

		RESPONDENT TYPE				INSTITUTION TYPE			DISCIPLINE								GENDER	
	TOTAL SAMPLE	FACULTY MEMBER	GRAD. STUDENT	FACULTY /GRAD	UNDER GRAD. STUDENT	PUBLIC	PRIVATE	LIBERAL ARTS	BIOLOGIAL SCIENCES	PHYSICAL SCIENCES /MATH	SOCIAL SCIENCES	ARTS AND HUMAN.	ENGI-NEERING	BUSINESS	LAW	UNDEC. MAJOR	MALE	FEMALE
		(A)	(B)	(C)	(D)	(E)	(F)	(G)	(H)	(I)	(J)	(K)	(L)	(M)	(N)		(P)	(Q)
Base - Students	2304	0**	1056	1056	1248	1065	534	705	308	305	771	437	90	266	25	102	1102	1202
Employed full-time	367 15.9%	0 0	318 30.1%D	318 30.1%D	49 3.9%	230 21.6%G	118 22.1%G	19 2.7%	67 21.7%JKM N	86 28.2%JKM N	113 14.6%MN	52 11.8%N	26 28.2%HJKM N	21 8.0%N	1 2.7%	2 2.0%	196 17.8%Q	170 14.2%
Employed part-time	1120 48.6%	0 0	467 44.2%	467 44.2%	653 52.3%B C	525 49.3%F	211 39.4%	384 54.5%F	111 36.0%	133 43.6%HN	419 54.4%HI LN	242 55.4%HI LMN	36 40.1%N	126 47.6%HN	7 29.3%	45 44.1%	484 43.9%	636 52.9%P
Not employed	811 35.2%	0 0	267 25.3%	267 25.3%	544 43.6%B C	308 29.0%	201 37.6%E	302 42.8%E	129 42.0%IJK L	84 27.5%	237 30.7%	143 32.8%	28 30.8%	118 44.4%IJ KL	17 67.3%HI JKLM	55 53.9%	416 37.7%Q	395 32.9%
Don't Know/Refused	6 0.3%	0 0	4 0.4%	4 0.4%	2 0.2%	1 0.1%	4 0.8%G	0 0	1 0.3%	2 0.7%	2 0.2%	0 0	1 1.0%KM	0 0	* 0.7%KM	0 0	6 0.5%Q	* *

Proportions/Means: Columns Tested (5% risk level) - A/B/D - C/D - E/F/G - H/I/J/K/L/M/N - P/Q
** very small base (under 30) ineligible for sig testing

Table 653
Page 2175

Outsell/Digital Library Federation Study (2002)
Weighted Tables

TABLE 8

Q30. How many years have you been working towards your current degree?

		RESPONDENT TYPE				INSTITUTION TYPE			DISCIPLINE								GENDER	
	TOTAL SAMPLE	FACULTY MEMBER	GRAD. STUDENT	FACULTY /GRAD	UNDER GRAD. STUDENT	PUBLIC	PRIVATE	LIBERAL ARTS	BIOLOGIAL SCIENCES	PHYSICAL SCIENCES /MATH	SOCIAL SCIENCES	ARTS AND HUMAN.	ENGI-NEERING	BUSINESS	LAW	UNDEC. MAJOR	MALE	FEMALE
		(A)	(B)	(C)	(D)	(E)	(F)	(G)	(H)	(I)	(J)	(K)	(L)	(M)	(N)		(P)	(Q)
Base - Students	2304	0**	1056	1056	1248	1065	534	705	308	305	771	437	90	266	25	102	1102	1202
Less than 1 year (.5)	436	0	149	149	287	158	122	155	41	50	128	74	14	61	4	63	213	223
	18.9%	0	14.1%	14.1%	23.0%BC	14.9%	22.8%E	22.0%E	13.4%	16.4%	16.6%	16.9%	15.7%	23.1%HIJKL	15.6%	61.8%	19.3%	18.5%
1-2 years (1.5)	879	0	449	449	430	380	229	270	106	112	288	166	44	117	12	35	429	450
	38.2%	0	42.5%D	42.5%D	34.5%	35.7%	42.9%E	38.3%	34.6%	36.7%	37.3%	37.9%	48.1%HIJK	44.1%H	46.9%HIJ	34.3%	39.0%	37.4%
3-4 years (3.5)	791	0	318	318	473	382	135	273	122	115	282	167	25	69	8	3	367	424
	34.3%	0	30.1%	30.1%	37.9%BC	35.9%F	25.3%	38.8%F	39.7%LM	37.7%LM	36.6%LM	38.2%LM	27.2%	25.9%	32.7%	2.9%	33.3%	35.3%
5-6 years (5.5)	138	0	93	93	45	101	32	4	27	21	47	19	7	16	*	0	63	75
	6.0%	0	8.8%D	8.8%D	3.6%	9.5%FG	6.1%G	0.6%	8.9%KN	6.9%N	6.1%N	4.4%	8.0%KN	5.9%N	1.4%	0	5.7%	6.2%
7-8 years (7.5)	28	0	25	25	3	19	9	*	8	7	8	3	*	2	*	0	15	13
	1.2%	0	2.4%D	2.4%D	0.3%	1.8%G	1.6%G	*	2.6%KL	2.3%	1.0%	0.8%	0.3%	0.7%	1.4%	0	1.3%	1.1%
9-10 years (9.5)	12	0	10	10	2	10	2	0	1	0	6	4	1	0	*	0	5	6
	0.5%	0	0.9%D	0.9%D	0.2%	0.9%G	0.4%	0	0.3%	0	0.7%	1.0%	0.6%I	0	1.4%IM	0	0.5%	0.5%
Over 10 years (12)	14	0	10	10	5	10	2	2	1	0	11	1	0	0	*	1	6	9
	0.6%	0	0.9%	0.9%	0.4%	1.0%	0.4%	0.3%	0.3%	0	1.5%	0.3%	0	0	0.7%IM	1.0%	0.5%	0.7%
Don't Know	3	0	2	2	1	2	1	0	1	0	0	1	0	1	0	0	2	1
	0.1%	0	0.2%	0.2%	0.1%	0.2%	0.2%	0	0.3%	0	0	0.3%	0	0.3%	0	0	0.2%	0.1%
Refused	3	0	1	1	2	1	2	0	0	0	2	1	0	0	0	0	2	1
	0.1%	0	0.1%	0.1%	0.2%	0.1%	0.4%	0	0	0	0.2%	0.3%	0	0	0	0	0.2%	0.1%
Median	1.31	0	1.34	1.34	1.28	1.48	1.13	1.23	1.59	1.42	1.39	1.36	1.21	1.11	1.23	0.40	1.28	1.34

Proportions/Means: Columns Tested (5% risk level) - A/B/D - C/D - E/F/G - H/I/J/K/L/M/N - P/Q
** very small base (under 30) ineligible for sig testing

Table 654
Page 2176

Outsell/Digital Library Federation Study (2002)
Weighted Tables

TABLE 8, continued

Q30. How many years have you been working towards your current degree?

		RESPONDENT TYPE				INSTITUTION TYPE			DISCIPLINE									GENDER	
	TOTAL SAMPLE	FACULTY MEMBER	GRAD. STUDENT	FACULTY /GRAD	UNDER GRAD. STUDENT	PUBLIC	PRIVATE	LIBERAL ARTS	BIOLOGIAL SCIENCES	PHYSICAL SCIENCES /MATH	SOCIAL SCIENCES	ARTS AND HUMAN.	ENGI- NEERING	BUSINESS	LAW	UNDEC. MAJOR	MALE	FEMALE
		(A)	(B)	(C)	(D)	(E)	(F)	(G)	(H)	(I)	(J)	(K)	(L)	(M)	(N)		(P)	(Q)
Base - Students	2304	0**	1056	1056	1248	1065	534	705	308	305	771	437	90	266	25	102	1102	1202
Mean	2.42	0	2.63D	2.63D	2.24	2.74FG	2.19	2.11	2.72KLMN	2.50M	2.58LM	2.43M	2.28	2.07	2.31	1.04	2.38	2.46
Standard Deviation	1.77	0	1.99	1.99	1.55	1.98	1.73	1.35	1.76	1.61	1.97	1.67	1.57	1.47	1.81	1.27	1.75	1.80
Standard Error	0.04	0	0.06	0.06	0.05	0.06	0.07	0.05	0.09	0.09	0.10	0.08	0.09	0.09	0.15	0.13	0.05	0.05

Proportions/Means: Columns Tested (5% risk level) - A/B/D - C/D - E/F/G - H/I/J/K/L/M/N - P/Q
** very small base (under 30) ineligible for sig testing

Table 654
Page 2177

Outsell/Digital Library Federation Study (2002)
Weighted Tables

TABLE 9

Q31. What degree are you working towards?

		RESPONDENT TYPE				INSTITUTION TYPE			DISCIPLINE								GENDER	
	TOTAL SAMPLE	FACULTY MEMBER	GRAD. STUDENT	FACULTY /GRAD	UNDER GRAD. STUDENT	PUBLIC	PRIVATE	LIBERAL ARTS	BIOLOGIAL SCIENCES	PHYSICAL SCIENCES /MATH	SOCIAL SCIENCES	ARTS AND HUMAN.	ENGI-NEERING	BUSINESS	LAW	UNDEC. MAJOR	MALE	FEMALE
		(A)	(B)	(C)	(D)	(E)	(F)	(G)	(H)	(I)	(J)	(K)	(L)	(M)	(N)		(P)	(Q)
Base - Students	2304	0**	1056	1056	1248	1065	534	705	308	305	771	437	90	266	25	102	1102	1202
Bachelors	1159	0	7	7	1152	380	130	649	114	126	382	271	30	148	3	85	528	631
	50.3%	0	0.7%	0.7%	92.3%B C	35.7%F	24.2%	92.1%EF	36.9%N	41.3%N	49.5%HI LN	62.1%HI JLN	33.7%N	55.6%HI LN	12.9%	83.3%	47.9%	52.5%
Masters	444	0	419	419	25	271	163	10	40	42	162	83	25	92	1	0	209	235
	19.3%	0	39.7%D	39.7%D	2.0%	25.5%G	30.5%G	1.5%	12.9%N	13.8%N	21.0%HI N	19.0%HN	27.6%HIJ KN	34.6%HIJ KN	3.4%	0	18.9%	19.6%
Doctorate (Ph.D, Ed.D.).	564	0	551	551	13	359	202	4	109	129	205	72	34	11	4	0	303	262
	24.5%	0	52.2%D	52.2%D	1.1%	33.7%G	37.8%G	0.5%	35.4%JKM N	42.3%JKM N	26.6%KM N	16.4%M	37.8%JKMN	4.2%	17.0%M	0	27.5%Q	21.8%
Professional Degree (MD, DMD, JD)	73	0	73	73	0	37	36	0	37	4	8	2	*	6	16	0	32	40
	3.1%	0	6.9%D	6.9%D	0	3.5%G	6.7%EG	0	12.0%IJKL M	1.3%	1.0%	0.5%	0.3%	2.1%	63.9%HIJKL M	0	2.9%	3.4%
Certificate	6	0	2	2	4	1	1	4	1	1	2	1	0	0	0	1	1	5
	0.3%	0	0.2%	0.2%	0.3%	0.1%	0.2%	0.6%	0.3%	0.3%	0.2%	0.3%	0	0	0	1.0%	0.1%	0.4%
Undeclared	12	0	0	0	12	3	0	9	0	0	0	1	0	0	0	11	8	4
	0.5%	0	0	0	1.0%BC	0.3%	0	1.3%EF	0	0	0	0.3%	0	0	0	10.8%	0.7%	0.3%
Other	42	0	4	4	38	14	3	26	8	3	13	6	1	8	1	3	21	22
	1.8%	0	0.4%	0.4%	3.0%BC	1.3%	0.5%	3.7%EF	2.6%	1.0%	1.7%	1.3%	0.6%	3.1%	2.7%L	2.9%	1.9%	1.8%
DK/Refused	4	0	0	0	4	0	1	3	0	0	0	1	0	1	0	2	1	3
	0.2%	0	0	0	0.3%	0	0.2%	0.4%	0	0	0	0.3%	0	0.3%	0	2.0%	0.1%	0.2%

Proportions/Means: Columns Tested (5% risk level) - A/B/D - C/D - E/F/G - H/I/J/K/L/M/N - P/Q
** very small base (under 30) ineligible for sig testing

Table 655
Page 2178

Outsell/Digital Library Federation Study (2002)
Weighted Tables

TABLE 10

Q32. Do you live in on-campus housing or off-campus?

		RESPONDENT TYPE				INSTITUTION TYPE			DISCIPLINE									GENDER	
	TOTAL SAMPLE	FACULTY MEMBER	GRAD. STUDENT	FACULTY /GRAD	UNDER GRAD. STUDENT	PUBLIC	PRIVATE	LIBERAL ARTS	BIOLOGIAL SCIENCES	PHYSICAL SCIENCES /MATH	SOCIAL SCIENCES	ARTS AND HUMAN.	ENGI-NEERING	BUSINESS	LAW	UNDEC. MAJOR	MALE	FEMALE
		(A)	(B)	(C)	(D)	(E)	(F)	(G)	(H)	(I)	(J)	(K)	(L)	(M)	(N)		(P)	(Q)
Base - Students	2304	0**	1056	1056	1248	1065	534	705	308	305	771	437	90	266	25	102	1102	1202
On campus	1108 48.1%	0 0	173 16.3%	173 16.3%	936 75.0%B C	308 28.9%	157 29.4%	644 91.3%EF	113 36.6%N	151 49.5%HN	333 43.2%N	245 56.2%HJ LMN	41 45.8%HN	122 45.8%HN	6 25.9%	97 95.1%	538 48.8%	571 47.5%
Off campus	1191 51.7%	0 0	882 83.5%D	882 83.5%D	309 24.8%	756 71.0%G	375 70.1%G	60 8.6%	194 62.9%IKL M	154 50.5%	436 56.6%K	192 43.8%	49 54.2%K	143 53.8%K	19 74.1%HIJ KLM	5 4.9%	561 50.9%	630 52.4%
Don't Know/Refused	5 0.2%	0 0	2 0.2%	2 0.2%	3 0.2%	1 0.1%	3 0.5%	1 0.1%	2 0.6%	0 0	2 0.2%	0 0	0 0	1 0.3%	0 0	0 0	3 0.3%	2 0.2%

Proportions/Means: Columns Tested (5% risk level) - A/B/D - C/D - E/F/G - H/I/J/K/L/M/N - P/Q
** very small base (under 30) ineligible for sig testing

Table 656
Page 2179

Outsell/Digital Library Federation Study (2002)
Weighted Tables

TABLE 11

Q33. What year of college are you in?

		RESPONDENT TYPE				INSTITUTION TYPE			DISCIPLINE								GENDER	
	TOTAL SAMPLE	FACULTY MEMBER	GRAD. STUDENT	FACULTY /GRAD	UNDER GRAD. STUDENT	PUBLIC	PRIVATE	LIBERAL ARTS	BIOLOGIAL SCIENCES	PHYSICAL SCIENCES /MATH	SOCIAL SCIENCES	ARTS AND HUMAN.	ENGI-NEERING	BUSINESS	LAW	UNDEC. MAJOR	MALE	FEMALE
		(A)	(B)	(C)	(D)	(E)	(F)	(G)	(H)	(I)	(J)	(K)	(L)	(M)	(N)		(P)	(Q)
Base - Undergraduate Students	1248	0**	0**	0**	1248	407	135	705	125	142	402	284	32	157	3**	102	572	676
Freshman	374	0	0	0	374	111	42	221	34	39	98	76	8	38	*	80	172	202
	30.0%	0	0	0	30.0%	27.2%	31.3%	31.3%	27.5%	27.5%	24.3%	26.8%	26.4%	24.3%	11.1%	78.4%	30.1%	29.8%
Sophomore	272	0	0	0	272	54	36	182	25	31	85	72	8	33	1	18	134	138
	21.8%	0	0	0	21.8%	13.3%	26.6%E	25.8%E	19.7%	21.8%	21.0%	25.2%	26.4%	20.7%	27.8%	17.6%	23.5%	20.3%
Junior	244	0	0	0	244	89	26	128	30	23	94	56	7	30	1	3	114	130
	19.5%	0	0	0	19.5%	21.9%	19.4%	18.2%	23.9%	16.2%	23.4%	19.7%	21.8%	18.9%	33.3%	2.9%	20.0%	19.2%
Senior (including 5th year seniors)	345	0	0	0	345	143	28	174	33	48	124	76	8	54	1	1	142	203
	27.7%	0	0	0	27.7%	35.1%FG	20.7%	24.7%	26.8%	33.8%	30.8%	26.8%	24.5%	34.3%	27.8%	1.0%	24.9%	30.0%
Other	9	0	0	0	9	8	1	0	3	1	0	3	*	2	0	0	6	3
	0.7%	0	0	0	0.7%	2.0%G	0.6%	0	2.1%J	0.7%	0	1.2%	0.9%J	1.2%J	0	0	1.0%	0.5%
Don't Know/Refused	4	0	0	0	4	2	2	0	0	0	2	1	0	1	0	0	3	1
	0.3%	0	0	0	0.3%	0.5%	1.4%G	0	0	0	0.5%	0.4%	0	0.6%	0	0	0.5%	0.1%

Proportions/Means: Columns Tested (5% risk level) - A/B/D - C/D - E/F/G - H/I/J/K/L/M/N - P/Q
** very small base (under 30) ineligible for sig testing

Table 657
Page 2180

Outsell/Digital Library Federation Study (2002)
Weighted Tables

TABLE 12

QB. What is your primary area of work or research/study within your college/university?

		RESPONDENT TYPE				INSTITUTION TYPE			DISCIPLINE								GENDER	
	TOTAL SAMPLE	FACULTY MEMBER	GRAD. STUDENT	FACULTY /GRAD	UNDER GRAD. STUDENT	PUBLIC	PRIVATE	LIBERAL ARTS	BIOLOGIAL SCIENCES	PHYSICAL SCIENCES /MATH	SOCIAL SCIENCES	ARTS AND HUMAN.	ENGI-NEERING	BUSINESS	LAW	UNDEC. MAJOR	MALE	FEMALE
		(A)	(B)	(C)	(D)	(E)	(F)	(G)	(H)	(I)	(J)	(K)	(L)	(M)	(N)		(P)	(Q)
Base - Total Weighted Respondents	3132	930	1056	1986	1146	1320	865	947	465	511	993	600	125	406	32	0*	1775	1357
Social sciences	993 31.7%	222 23.9%	368 34.9%A	590 29.7%	402 35.1%A C	474 35.9%FG	259 30.0%	259 27.4%	0 0	0 0	993 100.0%HIKLM N	0 0	0 0	0 0	0 0	0 0	487 27.4%	506 37.3%P
Arts and humanities	600 19.2%	164 17.6%	152 14.4%	316 15.9%	284 24.8%A BC	214 16.2%	147 17.0%	240 25.3%EF	0 0	0 0	0 0	600 100.0%HIJLM N	0 0	0 0	0 0	0 0	297 16.7%	304 22.4%P
Physical sciences/ Math	511 16.3%	206 22.1%BD	163 15.4%	369 18.6%D	142 12.4%	183 13.9%	115 13.3%	213 22.5%EF	0 0	511 100.0%HJKLMN	0 0	0 0	0 0	0 0	0 0	0 0	379 21.4%Q	132 9.7%
Biological sciences	465 14.8%	157 16.8%D	183 17.3%D	340 17.1%D	125 10.9%	200 15.1%G	159 18.4%G	106 11.1%	465 100.0%IJKLMN	0 0	0 0	0 0	0 0	0 0	0 0	0 0	232 13.1%	232 17.1%P
Business	406 13.0%	140 15.1%B	109 10.3%	249 12.5%	157 13.7%B	168 12.7%	120 13.9%	118 12.5%	0 0	0 0	0 0	0 0	0 0	406 100.0%HIJKL N	0 0	0 0	261 14.7%Q	145 10.7%
Engineering	125 4.0%	34 3.7%	59 5.5%D	93 4.7%D	32 2.8%	68 5.1%G	48 5.6%G	8 0.9%	0 0	0 0	0 0	0 0	125 100.0%HIJKMN	0 0	0 0	0 0	99 5.6%Q	26 1.9%
Law	32 1.0%	7 0.8%	22 2.1%AD	29 1.5%D	3 0.3%	14 1.0%	16 1.8%G	3 0.3%	0 0	0 0	0 0	0 0	0 0	0 0	32 100.0%HIJKL M	0 0	19 1.1%	13 1.0%

Proportions/Means: Columns Tested (5% risk level) - A/B/D - C/D - E/F/G - H/I/J/K/L/M/N - P/Q
* small base

Table 4
Page 4

Outsell/Digital Library Federation Study (2002)
Weighted Tables

TABLE 13

Q1a. For each of the following, please tell me if this is one of your responsibilities.

	TOTAL SAMPLE	RESPONDENT TYPE: FACULTY MEMBER	RESPONDENT TYPE: GRAD. STUDENT	RESPONDENT TYPE: FACULTY /GRAD	RESPONDENT TYPE: UNDER GRAD. STUDENT	INSTITUTION TYPE: PUBLIC	INSTITUTION TYPE: PRIVATE	INSTITUTION TYPE: LIBERAL ARTS	DISCIPLINE: BIOLOGIAL SCIENCES	DISCIPLINE: PHYSICAL SCIENCES /MATH	DISCIPLINE: SOCIAL SCIENCES	DISCIPLINE: ARTS AND HUMAN.	DISCIPLINE: ENGI-NEERING	DISCIPLINE: BUSINESS	DISCIPLINE: LAW	DISCIPLINE: UNDEC. MAJOR	GENDER: MALE	GENDER: FEMALE
		(A)	(B)	(C)	(D)	(E)	(F)	(G)	(H)	(I)	(J)	(K)	(L)	(M)	(N)		(P)	(Q)
Base - Faculty or Graduate student	1986	930	1056	1986	0**	929	736	321	340	369	590	316	93	249	29	0*	1251	735
Research	1563 78.7%	811 87.2%B	752 71.2%	1563 78.7%	0 0	699 75.3%	593 80.5%E	271 84.3%E	269 79.3%MN	320 86.7%HKM N	491 83.1%KM N	239 75.5%MN	79 85.0%KMN	148 59.3%	18 59.5%	0 0	1023 81.8%Q	540 73.4%
Teaching	1299 65.4%	920 99.0%B	379 35.9%	1299 65.4%	0 0	518 55.8%	461 62.7%E	319 99.4%EF	206 60.6%N	282 76.4%HJL MN	344 58.3%N	258 81.6%HJ LMN	50 53.7%N	152 60.8%N	8 27.2%	0 0	912 72.9%Q	387 52.6%
Service	1181 59.5%	867 93.2%B	314 29.7%	1181 59.5%	0 0	435 46.9%	439 59.7%E	306 95.4%EF	196 57.8%LN	231 62.6%LN	329 55.7%LN	214 67.7%HJ LN	43 46.6%	156 62.7%LN	11 38.7%	0 0	827 66.1%Q	354 48.1%
Attending classes	873 44.0%	0 0	873 82.7%A	873 44.0%	0 0	540 58.2%FG	333 45.2%G	0 0	152 44.8%I	119 32.2%	308 52.2%IK M	121 38.3%	46 49.4%IK	105 42.2%I	22 73.4%HIJKL M	0 0	431 34.4%	442 60.2%P
Other	12 0.6%	4 0.4%	8 0.8%	12 0.6%	0 0	7 0.7%	5 0.7%	1 0.3%	2 0.5%	0 0	4 0.6%	4 1.4%I	1 0.6%I	2 0.7%	0 0	0 0	4 0.3%	8 1.1%

Proportions/Means: Columns Tested (5% risk level) - A/B/D - C/D - E/F/G - H/I/J/K/L/M/N - P/Q
* small base; ** very small base (under 30) ineligible for sig testing

Table 5
Page 5

Outsell/Digital Library Federation Study (2002)
Weighted Tables

TABLE 14

Q14c. MEAN SUMMARY TABLE

		RESPONDENT TYPE				INSTITUTION TYPE			DISCIPLINE									GENDER	
	TOTAL SAMPLE	FACULTY MEMBER	GRAD. STUDENT	FACULTY /GRAD	UNDER GRAD. STUDENT	PUBLIC	PRIVATE	LIBERAL ARTS	BIOLOGIAL SCIENCES	PHYSICAL SCIENCES /MATH	SOCIAL SCIENCES	ARTS AND HUMAN.	ENGI-NEERING	BUSINESS	LAW	UNDEC. MAJOR	MALE	FEMALE
		(A)	(B)	(C)	(D)	(E)	(F)	(G)	(H)	(I)	(J)	(K)	(L)	(M)	(N)		(P)	(Q)
Base - Faculty and graduate students	1986	930	1056	1986	0**	929	736	321	340	369	590	316	93	249	29	0*	1251	735
Research	47.30	45.36	49.00A	47.30	0	49.04G	48.95G	38.44	52.20KMN	50.75KMN	49.15KM N	43.21MN	56.76IJK MN	34.05	34.76	0	47.59	46.80
Teaching	26.63	47.69B	8.11	26.63	0	19.42	23.16E	55.60EF	24.00LN	32.28HJL N	21.44N	32.21HJ LN	19.36N	31.67HJ LN	12.33	0	30.57Q	19.83
Service	5.76	6.96B	4.71	5.76	0	5.79	5.65	5.96	5.47	4.50	6.62ILN	6.93ILN	3.91	5.45	3.86	0	5.73	5.81
Coursework	38.43	0	38.43	38.43	0	36.62	41.45E	0	34.73	28.86	36.35I	37.12I	31.86	65.93HI JKL	65.79HIJKL	0	37.94	38.92

Proportions/Means: Columns Tested (5% risk level) - A/B/D - C/D - E/F/G - H/I/J/K/L/M/N - P/Q
* small base; ** very small base (under 30) ineligible for sig testing

Table 587
Page 2078

Outsell/Digital Library Federation Study (2002)
Weighted Tables

TABLE 15

Q14a. On average, about how many hours did you yourself spend each week obtaining, reviewing, and analyzing information from all sources to assist you in your (teaching or research/studies)?

		RESPONDENT TYPE				INSTITUTION TYPE			DISCIPLINE								GENDER	
	TOTAL SAMPLE	FACULTY MEMBER	GRAD. STUDENT	FACULTY /GRAD	UNDER GRAD. STUDENT	PUBLIC	PRIVATE	LIBERAL ARTS	BIOLOGIAL SCIENCES	PHYSICAL SCIENCES /MATH	SOCIAL SCIENCES	ARTS AND HUMAN.	ENGI-NEERING	BUSINESS	LAW	UNDEC. MAJOR	MALE	FEMALE
		(A)	(B)	(C)	(D)	(E)	(F)	(G)	(H)	(I)	(J)	(K)	(L)	(M)	(N)		(P)	(Q)
Base - Total Respondents	3234	930	1056	1986	1248	1336	872	1026	465	511	993	600	125	406	32	102	1823	1411
5 hours or less	783 24.2%	176 18.9%	203 19.2%	378 19.1%	405 32.4%A BC	301 22.5%	174 20.0%	308 30.0%EF	122 26.3%JN	127 24.9%N	211 21.2%	150 25.0%N	33 26.7%JN	99 24.3%N	5 16.2%	36 35.3%	431 23.6%	352 24.9%
6 - 10 hours	871 26.9%	259 27.9%B	249 23.6%	508 25.6%	363 29.1%B C	341 25.5%	225 25.8%	306 29.8%E	116 25.0%	162 31.7%HJN	241 24.2%	159 26.5%N	34 27.0%N	121 29.7%N	6 18.8%	33 32.4%	494 27.1%	377 26.7%
11 - 20 hours	891 27.6%	289 31.0%D	292 27.6%	580 29.2%D	311 24.9%	377 28.2%	245 28.1%	269 26.2%	136 29.4%	133 26.0%	297 29.9%	159 26.5%	33 26.3%	105 25.9%	10 30.4%	18 17.6%	512 28.1%	379 26.9%
Over 20 hours	658 20.3%	195 21.0%D	309 29.2%AD	504 25.4%D	154 12.3%	303 22.7%G	223 25.6%G	132 12.9%	89 19.1%	87 17.0%	235 23.7%I	124 20.7%	24 19.1%	78 19.2%	11 34.0%HIJ KLM	10 9.8%	373 20.5%	285 20.2%
DK/REF	30 0.9%	11 1.2%	4 0.4%	15 0.8%	15 1.2%	14 1.1%	5 0.5%	11 1.1%	1 0.2%	2 0.4%	9 0.9%	8 1.3%H	1 0.9%	4 0.9%	* 0.5%	5 4.9%	12 0.7%	18 1.3%
Median	9.90	11.78	14.35	14.13	9.23	11.41	14.00	9.42	9.91	9.29	13.58	9.88	9.49HIJK M	9.78	17.10HIJ KLM	7.28	9.94	9.86
Mean	15.48	15.79D	19.22AD	17.62D	12.04	16.57G	17.59G	12.24	15.07	14.25	16.78HI LM	15.82	14.68	14.89	20.97HI JKLM	10.04	15.51	15.42
Standard Deviation	13.68	11.93	16.67	14.75	10.95	14.79	15.02	9.91	15.00	12.56	13.63	14.40	13.26	12.92	16.26	8.36	13.46	13.98
Standard Error	0.24	0.39	0.49	0.32	0.32	0.40	0.49	0.33	0.65	0.56	0.60	0.63	0.64	0.62	1.18	0.85	0.31	0.39

Proportions/Means: Columns Tested (5% risk level) - A/B/D - C/D - E/F/G - H/I/J/K/L/M/N - P/Q

Table 580
Page 2071

Outsell/Digital Library Federation Study (2002)
Weighted Tables

TABLE 16

R8b_1. Do you use hard copy print all of the time, most of the time, some of the time, or none of the time?

	TOTAL SAMPLE	FACULTY MEMBER	GRAD. STUDENT	FACULTY /GRAD	UNDER GRAD. STUDENT	PUBLIC	PRIVATE	LIBERAL ARTS	BIOLOGIAL SCIENCES	PHYSICAL SCIENCES /MATH	SOCIAL SCIENCES	ARTS AND HUMAN.	ENGI-NEERING	BUSINESS	LAW	UNDEC. MAJOR	MALE	FEMALE
		RESPONDENT TYPE				INSTITUTION TYPE			DISCIPLINE								GENDER	
		(A)	(B)	(C)	(D)	(E)	(F)	(G)	(H)	(I)	(J)	(K)	(L)	(M)	(N)		(P)	(Q)
Base - Responsibility is Research	1563	811	752	1563	0**	699	593	271	269	320	491	239	79	148	18	0*	1023	540
All of the time/ Most of the time (NET)	1008 64.5%	549 67.8%B	459 61.0%	1008 64.5%	0 0	463 66.2%F	355 60.0%	190 70.1%F	158 58.8%N	199 62.2%N	331 67.4%HL MN	187 78.4%HI JLMN	46 58.5%N	80 54.1%N	7 38.8%	0 0	657 64.2%	351 65.0%
All of the time	187 12.0%	108 13.3%	80 10.6%	187 12.0%	0 0	90 12.9%	74 12.5%	23 8.7%	24 8.8%	33 10.3%	75 15.3%HL N	34 14.1%LN	6 7.7%	15 10.1%	1 4.9%	0 0	128 12.5%	59 10.9%
Most of the time	821 52.5%	442 54.5%	379 50.4%	821 52.5%	0 0	373 53.3%	281 47.5%	166 61.4%EF	135 50.0%N	166 51.9%N	256 52.1%N	153 64.3%HI JLMN	40 50.7%N	65 44.0%	6 34.0%	0 0	529 51.7%	292 54.1%
Some of the time	548 35.1%	260 32.1%	288 38.3%A	548 35.1%	0 0	231 33.1%	236 39.8%EG	81 29.9%	109 40.5%JK	119 37.2%K	160 32.6%K	52 21.6%	32 40.8%JK	66 44.7%JK	11 60.2%HIJKL M	0 0	360 35.2%	188 34.8%
None of the time	6 0.4%	1 0.1%	5 0.7%	6 0.4%	0 0	5 0.7%	1 0.2%	0 0	2 0.7%	2 0.6%	0 0	0 0	* 0.4%	2 1.3%J	* 1.0%JK	0 0	5 0.5%	1 0.2%
DK/Refused	* *	* *	0 0	* *	0 0	* *	0 0	0 0	0 0	0 0	0 0	0 0	* 0.4%	0 0	0 0	0 0	* *	0 0

Proportions/Means: Columns Tested (5% risk level) - A/B/D - C/D - E/F/G - H/I/J/K/L/M/N - P/Q
* small base; ** very small base (under 30) ineligible for sig testing

Table 183
Page 685

Outsell/Digital Library Federation Study (2002)
Weighted Tables

TABLE 17

R8b_2. Do you use electronic sources all of the time, most of the time, some of the time, or none of the time?

		RESPONDENT TYPE				INSTITUTION TYPE			DISCIPLINE									GENDER	
	TOTAL SAMPLE	FACULTY MEMBER	GRAD. STUDENT	FACULTY /GRAD	UNDER GRAD. STUDENT	PUBLIC	PRIVATE	LIBERAL ARTS	BIOLOGIAL SCIENCES	PHYSICAL SCIENCES /MATH	SOCIAL SCIENCES	ARTS AND HUMAN.	ENGI-NEERING	BUSINESS	LAW	UNDEC. MAJOR	MALE	FEMALE
		(A)	(B)	(C)	(D)	(E)	(F)	(G)	(H)	(I)	(J)	(K)	(L)	(M)	(N)		(P)	(Q)
Base - Responsibility is Research	1563	811	752	1563	0**	699	593	271	269	320	491	239	79	148	18	0*	1023	540
All of the time/ Most of the time (NET)	651 41.7%	281 34.7%	370 49.2%A	651 41.7%	0 0	309 44.2%G	267 45.1%G	75 27.6%	130 48.4%JK	149 46.6%JK	180 36.8%K	59 24.9%	38 48.2%JK	83 56.0%JK	11 65.0%HIJKL	0 0	405 39.6%	246 45.5%P
All of the time	125 8.0%	38 4.7%	87 11.5%A	125 8.0%	0 0	68 9.7%G	53 8.9%G	5 1.7%	27 10.1%K	23 7.2%	36 7.3%	9 3.8%	8 10.3%K	20 13.2%IJ K	2 12.6%K	0 0	81 7.9%	44 8.1%
Most of the time	526 33.7%	243 30.0%	283 37.7%A	526 33.7%	0 0	242 34.6%G	214 36.2%G	70 25.9%	103 38.2%JK	126 39.4%JK	145 29.5%K	50 21.1%	30 37.9%JK	63 42.8%JK	9 52.4%HIJKL	0 0	324 31.7%	202 37.4%P
Some of the time	867 55.5%	500 61.6%B	368 48.9%	867 55.5%	0 0	371 53.1%	307 51.8%	189 69.8%EF	134 49.7%N	165 51.6%MN	291 59.4%HL MN	170 71.4%HI JLMN	40 50.4%N	61 41.5%	6 32.0%	0 0	584 57.1%	283 52.5%
None of the time	40 2.5%	25 3.1%	15 1.9%	40 2.5%	0 0	16 2.4%	16 2.7%	7 2.6%	4 1.6%	5 1.6%	17 3.4%	9 3.8%	1 1.5%	3 1.9%	* 1.9%	0 0	30 2.9%	10 1.8%
DK/Refused	5 0.3%	5 0.6%	0 0	5 0.3%	0 0	2 0.3%	3 0.5%	0 0	1 0.3%	1 0.3%	2 0.4%	0 0	0 0	1 0.6%	* 1.0%KL	0 0	4 0.4%	1 0.2%

Proportions/Means: Columns Tested (5% risk level) - A/B/D - C/D - E/F/G - H/I/J/K/L/M/N - P/Q
* small base; ** very small base (under 30) ineligible for sig testing

Table 184
Page 686

Outsell/Digital Library Federation Study (2002)
Weighted Tables

TABLE 18

R8b_3. Do you use some other medium all of the time, most of the time, some of the time, or none of the time?

	RESPONDENT TYPE					INSTITUTION TYPE			DISCIPLINE									GENDER	
	TOTAL SAMPLE	FACULTY MEMBER	GRAD. STUDENT	FACULTY /GRAD	UNDER GRAD. STUDENT	PUBLIC	PRIVATE	LIBERAL ARTS	BIOLOGIAL SCIENCES	PHYSICAL SCIENCES /MATH	SOCIAL SCIENCES	ARTS AND HUMAN.	ENGI-NEERING	BUSINESS	LAW	UNDEC. MAJOR	MALE	FEMALE
		(A)	(B)	(C)	(D)	(E)	(F)	(G)	(H)	(I)	(J)	(K)	(L)	(M)	(N)		(P)	(Q)
Base - Responsibility is Research	1563	811	752	1563	0**	699	593	271	269	320	491	239	79	148	18	0*	1023	540
All of the time/ Most of the time (NET)	51 3.2%	37 4.6%B	14 1.8%	51 3.2%	0 0	23 3.3%	17 2.9%	10 3.8%	8 2.9%	7 2.2%	15 3.1%	18 7.5%HIJ LM	1 1.8%	1 0.6%	* 1.9%	0 0	31 3.0%	20 3.6%
All of the time	13 0.8%	10 1.2%	3 0.4%	13 0.8%	0 0	6 0.9%	5 0.9%	2 0.7%	3 1.0%	2 0.6%	4 0.8%	3 1.4%	* 0.4%	1 0.6%	* 1.0%	0 0	9 0.9%	4 0.7%
Most of the time	37 2.4%	27 3.4%B	10 1.4%	37 2.4%	0 0	17 2.5%	12 2.0%	8 3.1%	5 2.0%	5 1.6%	11 2.3%	15 6.1%HIJ LM	1 1.5%M	0 0	* 1.0%M	0 0	22 2.1%	16 2.9%
Some of the time	703 45.0%	308 38.0%	395 52.6%A	703 45.0%	0 0	334 47.8%G	266 44.9%	103 38.0%	114 42.2%	116 36.3%	241 49.0%I	125 52.6%HI N	36 45.6%I	65 44.0%	7 37.9%	0 0	448 43.8%	255 47.3%
None of the time	782 50.1%	448 55.3%B	334 44.5%	782 50.1%	0 0	333 47.5%	297 50.2%	152 56.3%E	143 52.9%K	191 59.7%JKL	227 46.4%	92 38.5%	40 50.7%K	79 53.5%K	11 60.2%JK	0 0	523 51.1%	259 48.0%
DK/Refused	26 1.7%	18 2.2%	9 1.2%	26 1.7%	0 0	9 1.4%	12 2.0%	5 1.8%	5 2.0%	6 1.9%	8 1.5%	3 1.4%	1 1.8%	3 1.9%	0 0	0 0	21 2.0%	5 1.0%

Proportions/Means: Columns Tested (5% risk level) - A/B/D - C/D - E/F/G - H/I/J/K/L/M/N - P/Q
* small base; ** very small base (under 30) ineligible for sig testing

TABLE 19

T8b_1. Do you use Hard copy print all of the time, most of the time, some of the time, or none of the time?

		RESPONDENT TYPE				INSTITUTION TYPE			DISCIPLINE								GENDER	
	TOTAL SAMPLE	FACULTY MEMBER	GRAD. STUDENT	FACULTY /GRAD	UNDER GRAD. STUDENT	PUBLIC	PRIVATE	LIBERAL ARTS	BIOLOGIAL SCIENCES	PHYSICAL SCIENCES /MATH	SOCIAL SCIENCES	ARTS AND HUMAN.	ENGI-NEERING	BUSINESS	LAW	UNDEC. MAJOR	MALE	FEMALE
		(A)	(B)	(C)	(D)	(E)	(F)	(G)	(H)	(I)	(J)	(K)	(L)	(M)	(N)		(P)	(Q)
Base - Responsibility is Teaching	1299	920	379	1299	0**	518	461	319	206	282	344	258	50	152	8*	0*	912	387
All of the time/ Most of the time (NET)	949 73.1%	676 73.5%	273 72.1%	949 73.1%	0 0	370 71.4%	338 73.3%	241 75.4%	131 63.7%	219 77.7%HM	256 74.3%HM	206 80.0%HM N	37 74.4%HM	95 62.6%	5 66.0%	0 0	654 71.7%	295 76.3%
All of the time	289 22.2%	188 20.4%	100 26.5%A	289 22.2%	0 0	131 25.2%G	101 22.0%	56 17.7%	29 14.1%	73 25.9%H	85 24.6%H	63 24.3%H	9 18.0%	28 18.4%	2 29.8%H	0 0	184 20.2%	105 27.1%P
Most of the time	660 50.8%	488 53.0%B	173 45.6%	660 50.8%	0 0	240 46.2%	237 51.3%	184 57.7%E	102 49.6%	146 51.8%N	171 49.7%	143 55.7%MN	28 56.4%MN	67 44.2%	3 36.2%	0 0	470 51.5%	190 49.2%
Some of the time	331 25.5%	234 25.5%	96 25.5%	331 25.5%	0 0	134 25.8%	119 25.7%	79 24.6%	70 33.8%IKL	58 20.6%	86 25.1%	49 19.1%	12 23.8%	53 35.0%IJ KL	3 34.0%IK	0 0	247 27.1%	84 21.7%
None of the time	17 1.3%	8 0.9%	9 2.4%	17 1.3%	0 0	12 2.3%G	5 1.0%	0 0	4 2.1%	4 1.4%	2 0.5%	2 0.9%	1 1.2%	4 2.5%	0 0	0 0	10 1.1%	7 1.8%
DK/Refused	2 0.2%	2 0.2%	* 0.1%	2 0.2%	0 0	2 0.4%	0 0	0 0	1 0.4%	1 0.4%	0 0	0 0	* 0.6%J	0 0	0 0	0 0	1 0.1%	1 0.2%

Proportions/Means: Columns Tested (5% risk level) - A/B/D - C/D - E/F/G - H/I/J/K/L/M/N - P/Q
* small base; ** very small base (under 30) ineligible for sig testing

Table 311
Page 1289

TABLE 20

T8b_2. Do you use Electronic sources all of the time, most of the time, some of the time, or none of the time?

	RESPONDENT TYPE					INSTITUTION TYPE			DISCIPLINE								GENDER	
	TOTAL SAMPLE	FACULTY MEMBER	GRAD. STUDENT	FACULTY /GRAD	UNDER GRAD. STUDENT	PUBLIC	PRIVATE	LIBERAL ARTS	BIOLOGIAL SCIENCES	PHYSICAL SCIENCES /MATH	SOCIAL SCIENCES	ARTS AND HUMAN.	ENGI-NEERING	BUSINESS	LAW	UNDEC. MAJOR	MALE	FEMALE
		(A)	(B)	(C)	(D)	(E)	(F)	(G)	(H)	(I)	(J)	(K)	(L)	(M)	(N)		(P)	(Q)
Base - Responsibility is Teaching	1299	920	379	1299	0**	518	461	319	206	282	344	258	50	152	8*	0*	912	387
All of the time/ Most of the time (NET)	284 21.9%	209 22.7%	75 19.7%	284 21.9%	0 0	119 23.0%	93 20.3%	72 22.4%	45 21.8%K	50 17.7%	79 23.0%K	35 13.5%	11 21.5%K	62 41.1%HI JKL	2 29.8%IK	0 0	188 20.6%	96 24.8%
All of the time	67 5.2%	42 4.6%	25 6.7%	67 5.2%	0 0	32 6.2%	23 4.9%	12 3.9%	9 4.3%	9 3.2%	28 8.2%IK	9 3.5%	2 4.7%	9 6.1%	1 8.5%	0 0	39 4.2%	29 7.4%P
Most of the time	217 16.7%	167 18.2%B	49 13.0%	217 16.7%	0 0	87 16.8%	71 15.4%	59 18.5%	36 17.5%K	41 14.5%	51 14.8%	26 10.0%	8 16.9%K	53 35.0%HI JKL	2 21.3%K	0 0	149 16.4%	67 17.4%
Some of the time	872 67.1%	635 69.0%B	237 62.6%	872 67.1%	0 0	322 62.1%	323 70.0%E	228 71.2%E	146 70.9%MN	181 64.2%M	235 68.3%M	189 73.5%IM N	34 67.4%M	83 54.6%	4 55.3%	0 0	623 68.4%	249 64.3%
None of the time	138 10.6%	71 7.7%	67 17.6%A	138 10.6%	0 0	74 14.3%FG	43 9.3%	20 6.4%	14 6.8%	50 17.7%HJLM	28 8.2%	32 12.6%HM	5 10.5%M	7 4.3%	1 14.9%M	0 0	98 10.7%	40 10.4%
DK/Refused	5 0.4%	5 0.5%	* 0.1%	5 0.4%	0 0	3 0.6%	2 0.4%	0 0	1 0.4%	1 0.4%	2 0.5%	1 0.4%	* 0.6%	0 0	0 0	0 0	3 0.3%	2 0.5%

Proportions/Means: Columns Tested (5% risk level) - A/B/D - C/D - E/F/G - H/I/J/K/L/M/N - P/Q
* small base; ** very small base (under 30) ineligible for sig testing

Table 312
Page 1290

Outsell/Digital Library Federation Study (2002)
Weighted Tables

TABLE 21

T8b_3. Do you use Some other medium all of the time, most of the time, some of the time, or none of the time?

	RESPONDENT TYPE				INSTITUTION TYPE			DISCIPLINE								GENDER	
	TOTAL SAMPLE	FACULTY MEMBER	GRAD. STUDENT	FACULTY /GRAD	UNDER GRAD. STUDENT	PUBLIC	PRIVATE	LIBERAL ARTS	BIOLOGIAL SCIENCES	PHYSICAL SCIENCES /MATH	SOCIAL SCIENCES	ARTS AND HUMAN.	ENGI-NEERING	BUSINESS	LAW	UNDEC. MAJOR	MALE	FEMALE
		(A)	(B)	(C)	(D)	(E)	(F)	(G)	(H)	(I)	(J)	(K)	(L)	(M)	(N)		(P)	(Q)
Base - Responsibility is Teaching	1299	920	379	1299	0**	518	461	319	206	282	344	258	50	152	8*	0*	912	387
All of the time/ Most of the time (NET)	85 6.6%	51 5.6%	34 9.0%A	85 6.6%	0 0	42 8.0%	25 5.4%	19 5.9%	11 5.6%L	14 5.0%	19 5.5%	29 11.3%HIJ L	1 1.2%	11 7.4%L	* 4.3%	0 0	63 6.9%	23 5.9%
All of the time	21 1.6%	12 1.3%	9 2.4%	21 1.6%	0 0	12 2.3%	5 1.1%	4 1.3%	0 0	1 0.4%	8 2.2%	10 3.9%HIL	0 0	3 1.8%H	0 0	0 0	13 1.5%	8 2.1%
Most of the time	64 4.9%	39 4.2%	25 6.6%	64 4.9%	0 0	30 5.7%	20 4.3%	15 4.6%	11 5.6%L	13 4.6%	11 3.3%	19 7.4%L	1 1.2%	8 5.5%	* 4.3%	0 0	49 5.4%	15 3.8%
Some of the time	587 45.2%	418 45.5%	169 44.6%	587 45.2%	0 0	214 41.3%	221 47.9%	152 47.7%	105 50.9%IM	106 37.6%	160 46.4%	134 52.2%IM	22 43.6%	57 37.4%	4 48.9%	0 0	394 43.2%	193 49.8%P
None of the time	611 47.1%	438 47.6%	173 45.8%	611 47.1%	0 0	257 49.6%	208 45.1%	146 45.8%	89 43.2%	159 56.4%HJK	160 46.4%K	93 36.1%	26 52.3%K	81 53.4%HK	4 46.8%	0 0	443 48.5%	169 43.6%
DK/Refused	15 1.1%	12 1.3%	2 0.6%	15 1.1%	0 0	6 1.1%	7 1.6%	2 0.6%	1 0.4%	3 1.1%	6 1.6%	1 0.4%	1 2.9%HK	3 1.8%	0 0	0 0	12 1.3%	3 0.7%

Proportions/Means: Columns Tested (5% risk level) - A/B/D - C/D - E/F/G - H/I/J/K/L/M/N - P/Q
* small base; ** very small base (under 30) ineligible for sig testing

Table 313
Page 1291

Outsell/Digital Library Federation Study (2002)
Weighted Tables

TABLE 22

R8b_1. Do you use Hard copy print all of the time, most of the time, some of the time, or none of the time?

		RESPONDENT TYPE				INSTITUTION TYPE			DISCIPLINE								GENDER	
	TOTAL SAMPLE	FACULTY MEMBER	GRAD. STUDENT	FACULTY /GRAD	UNDER GRAD. STUDENT	PUBLIC	PRIVATE	LIBERAL ARTS	BIOLOGIAL SCIENCES	PHYSICAL SCIENCES /MATH	SOCIAL SCIENCES	ARTS AND HUMAN.	ENGI-NEERING	BUSINESS	LAW	UNDEC. MAJOR	MALE	FEMALE
		(A)	(B)	(C)	(D)	(E)	(F)	(G)	(H)	(I)	(J)	(K)	(L)	(M)	(N)		(P)	(Q)
Base - Student	2304	0**	1056	1056	1248	1065	534	705	308	305	771	437	90	266	25	102	1102	1202
All of the time/ Most of the time (NET)	1400 60.8%	0 0	756 71.6%D	756 71.6%D	644 51.6%	664 62.4%G	341 63.9%G	395 56.0%	177 57.4%M	192 63.0%M	491 63.7%M	292 66.9%HM	61 67.0%HM	114 43.0%	16 65.3%M	57 55.9%	661 60.0%	739 61.5%
All of the time	280 12.1%	0 0	197 18.6%D	197 18.6%D	83 6.7%	153 14.4%G	70 13.1%G	57 8.1%	25 8.0%	52 17.0%HJM	92 12.0%	62 14.1%HM	13 14.4%HM	24 9.1%	6 24.5%HJK LM	6 5.9%	157 14.2%Q	123 10.2%
Most of the time	1120 48.6%	0 0	559 53.0%D	559 53.0%D	561 45.0%	511 48.0%	271 50.8%	338 47.9%	152 49.4%M	140 45.9%M	399 51.7%MN	231 52.8%MN	48 52.6%MN	90 33.9%	10 40.8%	51 50.0%	504 45.8%	616 51.3%P
Some of the time	846 36.7%	0 0	263 24.9%	263 24.9%	583 46.7%B C	364 34.2%	175 32.7%	307 43.5%EF	126 40.9%JKL	103 33.8%	259 33.7%	130 29.7%	28 31.1%	146 54.9%HI JKLN	9 34.0%	45 44.1%	413 37.5%	432 36.0%
None of the time	43 1.9%	0 0	23 2.2%	23 2.2%	20 1.6%	28 2.7%G	13 2.3%G	2 0.3%	5 1.7%	6 2.0%	15 2.0%	10 2.3%	1 1.0%	6 2.1%	* 0.7%	0 0	18 1.6%	25 2.1%
DK/Refused	15 0.7%	0 0	14 1.3%D	14 1.3%D	1 0.1%	8 0.8%	6 1.0%G	1 0.1%	0 0	4 1.3%H	6 0.7%	4 1.0%	1 1.0%HM	0 0	0 0	0 0	10 0.9%	5 0.4%

Proportions/Means: Columns Tested (5% risk level) - A/B/D - C/D - E/F/G - H/I/J/K/L/M/N - P/Q
** very small base (under 30) ineligible for sig testing

Table 439
Page 1886

Outsell/Digital Library Federation Study (2002)
Weighted Tables

TABLE 23

R8b_2. Do you use Electronic sources all of the time, most of the time, some of the time, or none of the time?

		RESPONDENT TYPE				INSTITUTION TYPE			DISCIPLINE									GENDER	
	TOTAL SAMPLE	FACULTY MEMBER	GRAD. STUDENT	FACULTY /GRAD	UNDER GRAD. STUDENT	PUBLIC	PRIVATE	LIBERAL ARTS	BIOLOGIAL SCIENCES	PHYSICAL SCIENCES /MATH	SOCIAL SCIENCES	ARTS AND HUMAN.	ENGI-NEERING	BUSINESS	LAW	UNDEC. MAJOR	MALE	FEMALE
		(A)	(B)	(C)	(D)	(E)	(F)	(G)	(H)	(I)	(J)	(K)	(L)	(M)	(N)		(P)	(Q)
Base - Student	2304	0**	1056	1056	1248	1065	534	705	308	305	771	437	90	266	25	102	1102	1202
All of the time/ Most of the time (NET)	986 42.8%	0 0	372 35.2%	372 35.2%	614 49.2%B C	451 42.3%	210 39.4%	325 46.1%F	141 45.7%IKL	115 37.7%K	353 45.9%IK L	121 27.7%	32 35.6%K	167 62.9%HI JKLN	10 40.1%K	46 45.1%	471 42.7%	515 42.9%
All of the time	221 9.6%	0 0	86 8.2%	86 8.2%	135 10.8%	110 10.3%	44 8.3%	67 9.5%	21 6.9%	31 10.2%	79 10.2%	32 7.4%	9 9.6%	41 15.4%HJK L	2 8.8%	6 5.9%	97 8.8%	124 10.4%
Most of the time	764 33.2%	0 0	285 27.0%	285 27.0%	479 38.4%B C	341 32.0%	166 31.1%	258 36.5%	120 38.9%IKL	84 27.5%K	274 35.6%IK L	88 20.3%	23 26.0%	126 47.6%HI JKLN	8 31.3%K	40 39.2%	374 33.9%	391 32.5%
Some of the time	1199 52.0%	0 0	590 55.9%D	590 55.9%D	609 48.8%	548 51.4%	283 52.9%	369 52.3%	158 51.1%M	161 52.8%M	384 49.8%M	287 65.6%HI JLMN	52 57.7%JM	91 34.3%	13 51.7%M	54 52.9%	566 51.4%	633 52.7%
None of the time	104 4.5%	0 0	80 7.6%D	80 7.6%D	24 1.9%	58 5.5%G	35 6.5%G	11 1.5%	8 2.6%	27 8.9%HJM	28 3.7%	25 5.6%HM	5 5.8%HM	7 2.4%	2 8.2%HJM	2 2.0%	57 5.2%	47 3.9%
DK/Refused	16 0.7%	0 0	15 1.4%D	15 1.4%D	1 0.1%	8 0.8%	6 1.2%G	1 0.1%	2 0.6%	2 0.7%	6 0.7%	4 1.0%	1 1.0%	1 0.3%	0 0	0 0	9 0.8%	7 0.6%

Proportions/Means: Columns Tested (5% risk level) - A/B/D - C/D - E/F/G - H/I/J/K/L/M/N - P/Q
** very small base (under 30) ineligible for sig testing

Table 440
Page 1887

TABLE 24

R8b_3. Do you use Some other medium all of the time, most of the time, some of the time, or none of the time?

		RESPONDENT TYPE				INSTITUTION TYPE			DISCIPLINE								GENDER	
	TOTAL SAMPLE	FACULTY MEMBER	GRAD. STUDENT	FACULTY /GRAD	UNDER GRAD. STUDENT	PUBLIC	PRIVATE	LIBERAL ARTS	BIOLOGIAL SCIENCES	PHYSICAL SCIENCES /MATH	SOCIAL SCIENCES	ARTS AND HUMAN.	ENGI- NEERING	BUSINESS	LAW	UNDEC. MAJOR	MALE	FEMALE
		(A)	(B)	(C)	(D)	(E)	(F)	(G)	(H)	(I)	(J)	(K)	(L)	(M)	(N)		(P)	(Q)
Base - Student	2304	0**	1056	1056	1248	1065	534	705	308	305	771	437	90	266	25	102	1102	1202
All of the time/ Most of the time (NET)	104 4.5%	0 0	37 3.5%	37 3.5%	67 5.4%	44 4.1%	21 3.9%	39 5.5%	11 3.4%	15 4.9%	30 3.9%	27 6.2%L	2 2.6%	12 4.5%	1 3.4%	6 5.9%	56 5.1%	48 4.0%
All of the time	16 0.7%	0 0	7 0.7%	7 0.7%	9 0.7%	6 0.6%	3 0.6%	7 1.0%	3 0.9%	0 0	4 0.5%	6 1.3%	1 1.3%I	3 1.0%	* 0.7%I	0 0	9 0.9%	7 0.6%
Most of the time	88 3.8%	0 0	29 2.8%	29 2.8%	58 4.7%BC	38 3.5%	18 3.3%	32 4.6%	8 2.6%	15 4.9%L	26 3.4%	21 4.9%L	1 1.3%	9 3.5%	1 2.7%	6 5.9%	47 4.2%	41 3.4%
Some of the time	1263 54.8%	0 0	511 48.4%	511 48.4%	752 60.3%B C	586 55.1%F	254 47.6%	423 60.0%F	173 56.3%ILN	143 46.9%N	417 54.1%N	260 59.5%IL N	43 47.4%N	164 61.5%IL N	8 32.0%	55 53.9%	591 53.6%	672 55.9%
None of the time	897 38.9%	0 0	478 45.2%D	478 45.2%D	420 33.6%	405 38.1%	250 46.7%EG	242 34.4%	121 39.1%	141 46.2%KM	305 39.5%	143 32.8%	43 47.8%HJK M	87 32.9%	16 64.6%HI JKLM	41 40.2%	434 39.4%	463 38.5%
DK/Refused	40 1.7%	0 0	31 2.9%D	31 2.9%D	9 0.7%	29 2.8%G	10 1.8%G	1 0.1%	4 1.1%	6 2.0%	19 2.4%	7 1.5%	2 2.2%	3 1.0%	0 0	0 0	21 1.9%	19 1.5%

Proportions/Means: Columns Tested (5% risk level) - A/B/D - C/D - E/F/G - H/I/J/K/L/M/N - P/Q
** very small base (under 30) ineligible for sig testing

Table 441
Page 1888

Outsell/Digital Library Federation Study (2002)
Weighted Tables

TABLE 25

Q15a. What unmet needs for information types and content do you have?

	TOTAL SAMPLE	RESPONDENT TYPE: FACULTY MEMBER	GRAD. STUDENT	FACULTY /GRAD	UNDER GRAD. STUDENT	INSTITUTION TYPE: PUBLIC	PRIVATE	LIBERAL ARTS	DISCIPLINE: BIOLOGICAL SCIENCES	PHYSICAL SCIENCES /MATH	SOCIAL SCIENCES	ARTS AND HUMAN.	ENGI-NEERING	BUSINESS	LAW	UNDEC. MAJOR	GENDER: MALE	FEMALE
		(A)	(B)	(C)	(D)	(E)	(F)	(G)	(H)	(I)	(J)	(K)	(L)	(M)	(N)		(P)	(Q)
Base - Total Respondents	1592	453	530	983	608	659	430	504	238	237	500	296	60	192	17	52*	897	695
More online journals	426 26.7%	116 25.6%D	203 38.3%AD	319 32.4%D	107 17.5%	219 33.2%G	133 30.9%G	74 14.8%	92 38.7%IJK MN	68 28.7%KN	147 29.3%KN	44 14.8%	23 37.7%IKM N	45 23.3%KN	2 10.0%	6 11.5%	228 25.5%	197 28.4%
More print journals	184 11.6%	45 9.8%	71 13.3%	115 11.7%	69 11.3%	92 14.0%	42 9.8%	50 9.9%	30 12.5%N	28 11.8%N	58 11.7%N	41 14.0%N	6 9.7%	16 8.3%	1 4.0%	4 7.7%	97 10.8%	87 12.5%
Online materials	72 4.5%	28 6.1%D	25 4.7%	53 5.4%	19 3.2%	24 3.7%	21 5.0%	27 5.3%	12 5.2%	12 5.1%	26 5.3%	9 3.0%	4 6.8%KN	8 4.4%	* 1.0%	0 0	50 5.5%	23 3.3%
Print materials	43 2.7%	9 1.9%	16 3.1%	25 2.5%	18 3.0%	18 2.8%	8 1.9%	17 3.3%	6 2.6%	2 0.8%	13 2.6%	15 4.9%IL	1 1.0%	6 2.9%	* 1.0%	1 1.9%	22 2.5%	21 3.0%
Other	189 11.9%	84 18.5%BD	55 10.3%	139 14.1%D	51 8.4%	78 11.8%	53 12.3%	59 11.7%	20 8.5%	30 12.7%	55 10.9%	48 16.3%H	7 11.1%	24 12.6%	2 10.0%	4 7.7%	105 11.7%	85 12.2%
None	801 50.3%	228 50.4%B	207 39.0%	435 44.3%	366 60.1%A BC	279 42.4%	210 49.0%	311 61.9%EF	100 42.1%	120 50.6%	243 48.5%	160 54.2%HL	25 41.5%	103 53.9%HL	13 76.0%HI JKLM	37 71.2%	464 51.7%	337 48.5%

Proportions/Means: Columns Tested (5% risk level) - A/B/D - C/D - E/F/G - H/I/J/K/L/M/N - P/Q
* small base

Table 588
Page 2079

Outsell/Digital Library Federation Study (2002)
Weighted Tables

TABLE 26

Q25. MAJOR PROBLEM SUMMARY TABLE

	RESPONDENT TYPE					INSTITUTION TYPE			DISCIPLINE									GENDER	
	TOTAL SAMPLE	FACULTY MEMBER	GRAD. STUDENT	FACULTY /GRAD	UNDER GRAD. STUDENT	PUBLIC	PRIVATE	LIBERAL ARTS	BIOLOGIAL SCIENCES	PHYSICAL SCIENCES /MATH	SOCIAL SCIENCES	ARTS AND HUMAN.	ENGI-NEERING	BUSINESS	LAW	UNDEC. MAJOR	MALE	FEMALE
		(A)	(B)	(C)	(D)	(E)	(F)	(G)	(H)	(I)	(J)	(K)	(L)	(M)	(N)		(P)	(Q)
Base - Total Respondents	1076	296	370	666	410	436	302	338	162	149	357	197	38	125	12*	36*	592	484
Having enough time	417 38.8%	178 60.2%BD	136 36.8%D	314 47.2%D	103 25.2%	174 40.1%	125 41.6%	117 34.6%	69 42.4%	64 43.2%	133 37.4%	75 38.1%	17 43.8%	47 38.1%	4 31.9%	8 22.2%	226 38.2%	191 39.5%
Knowing what's available	195 18.1%	67 22.8%D	64 17.3%	131 19.7%	63 15.4%	87 20.0%	56 18.6%	52 15.3%	28 17.4%	31 20.8%	58 16.3%	37 18.9%	8 20.6%	25 20.1%	1 9.7%	6 16.7%	112 19.0%	82 17.0%
Having access to all information from one place	118 11.0%	24 8.3%	59 15.9%AD	83 12.5%	35 8.5%	59 13.6%G	38 12.5%G	21 6.3%	19 12.0%	9 6.1%	47 13.2%I	21 10.8%	6 15.4%IN	12 9.7%	1 4.2%	3 8.3%	49 8.3%	69 14.3%P
Determining the quality/ credibility/ accuracy of information	115 10.7%	31 10.5%	38 10.3%	69 10.4%	46 11.3%	42 9.5%	39 13.0%	35 10.3%	15 9.3%	11 7.4%	32 8.9%	21 10.8%	4 10.7%	25 20.1%HIJ KLN	1 6.9%	6 16.7%	73 12.3%	43 8.8%
Having sufficient training on how to search for information	112 10.4%	32 11.0%	38 10.4%	71 10.6%	41 10.0%	54 12.4%	30 10.1%	27 8.1%	20 12.5%	12 8.1%	36 10.0%	22 11.4%	3 9.2%	13 10.4%	1 6.9%	4 11.1%	52 8.8%	59 12.3%
Accessing information once you find what you want	100 9.3%	28 9.4%	47 12.6%D	74 11.2%D	25 6.2%	48 11.1%G	32 10.6%G	19 5.7%	18 10.9%	10 6.7%	34 9.5%	16 8.0%	3 8.4%	16 12.7%	1 4.2%	3 8.3%	39 6.5%	61 12.6%P

Proportions/Means: Columns Tested (5% risk level) - A/B/D - C/D - E/F/G - H/I/J/K/L/M/N - P/Q
* small base

Table 629
Page 2141

Outsell/Digital Library Federation Study (2002)
Weighted Tables

TABLE 26, continued

Q25. MAJOR PROBLEM SUMMARY TABLE

		RESPONDENT TYPE				INSTITUTION TYPE			DISCIPLINE									GENDER	
	TOTAL SAMPLE	FACULTY MEMBER	GRAD. STUDENT	FACULTY /GRAD	UNDER GRAD. STUDENT	PUBLIC	PRIVATE	LIBERAL ARTS	BIOLOGIAL SCIENCES	PHYSICAL SCIENCES /MATH	SOCIAL SCIENCES	ARTS AND HUMAN.	ENGI- NEERING	BUSINESS	LAW	UNDEC. MAJOR	MALE	FEMALE
		(A)	(B)	(C)	(D)	(E)	(F)	(G)	(H)	(I)	(J)	(K)	(L)	(M)	(N)		(P)	(Q)
Being able to compare across information alternatives, e.g. library vs. web sites	87 8.2%	28 9.5%	32 8.7%	60 9.1%	27 6.7%	28 6.5%	26 8.6%	33 10.0%	14 8.7%	12 8.1%	26 7.5%	13 6.9%	3 8.7%	17 13.4%N	* 2.8%	1 2.8%	62 10.4%Q	25 5.4%
Finding information	81 7.6%	24 8.1%	32 8.8%	56 8.4%	25 6.2%	38 8.8%	22 7.4%	21 6.1%	11 6.5%	12 8.1%	28 7.9%	10 5.1%	6 15.3%HIJK MN	9 7.5%	1 4.2%	5 13.9%	40 6.8%	41 8.6%
Having training and advice about the effective use of online information sources	80 7.4%	23 7.7%	31 8.4%	54 8.1%	26 6.3%	40 9.2%	22 7.4%	17 5.2%	12 7.6%	7 4.7%	34 9.5%	17 8.6%	1 3.9%	6 4.5%	1 5.6%	2 5.6%	34 5.7%	46 9.5%P
Not enough access to networked computers	80 7.4%	13 4.3%	37 10.0%A	50 7.5%	30 7.3%	41 9.3%	21 7.0%	18 5.2%	11 7.1%	8 5.4%	24 6.8%	17 8.5%	4 10.7%	13 10.4%	1 6.9%	1 2.8%	42 7.1%	38 7.8%
Getting information in a timely manner	79 7.4%	20 6.7%	27 7.3%	47 7.1%	32 7.9%	32 7.3%	27 8.9%	21 6.1%	11 6.5%	12 8.1%	19 5.3%	18 9.1%	3 8.5%	13 10.4%	1 5.6%	3 8.3%	37 6.3%	42 8.7%
All information at my institution is not available from different locations within the institution	72 6.8%	25 8.6%D	35 9.4%D	59 9.0%D	13 3.2%	36 8.3%G	24 8.2%G	12 3.6%	12 7.7%IN	4 2.7%	28 7.9%N	15 7.5%N	5 13.0%IN	8 6.8%	0 0	0 0	31 5.3%	41 8.6%

Proportions/Means: Columns Tested (5% risk level) - A/B/D - C/D - E/F/G - H/I/J/K/L/M/N - P/Q
* small base

Table 629
Page 2142

Outsell/Digital Library Federation Study (2002)
Weighted Tables

TABLE 26, continued

Q25. MAJOR PROBLEM SUMMARY TABLE

		RESPONDENT TYPE				INSTITUTION TYPE			DISCIPLINE									GENDER	
	TOTAL SAMPLE	FACULTY MEMBER	GRAD. STUDENT	FACULTY /GRAD	UNDER GRAD. STUDENT	PUBLIC	PRIVATE	LIBERAL ARTS	BIOLOGIAL SCIENCES	PHYSICAL SCIENCES /MATH	SOCIAL SCIENCES	ARTS AND HUMAN.	ENGI-NEERING	BUSINESS	LAW	UNDEC. MAJOR	MALE	FEMALE
		(A)	(B)	(C)	(D)	(E)	(F)	(G)	(H)	(I)	(J)	(K)	(L)	(M)	(N)		(P)	(Q)
Not being able to log onto the library's website (lines busy, site down, etc.)	65 6.1%	10 3.4%	27 7.2%	36 5.5%	29 7.1%	34 7.7%	17 5.5%	15 4.5%	11 7.1%	6 4.0%	19 5.3%	11 5.7%	3 9.2%I	11 9.0%	* 2.8%	3 8.3%	34 5.7%	32 6.6%
Having to go to a library	61 5.7%	19 6.3%D	32 8.7%D	51 7.6%D	11 2.6%	37 8.5%G	19 6.4%G	5 1.5%	13 8.2%IN	3 2.0%	24 6.8%N	8 4.0%	3 6.9%IN	8 6.7%I	0 0	2 5.6%	22 3.6%	40 8.2%P
Having people who can help you find information or who search for information for you	60 5.6%	19 6.3%	26 7.0%	44 6.7%	15 3.8%	24 5.5%	21 6.8%	15 4.6%	9 5.4%	8 5.4%	19 5.3%	10 5.2%	2 6.2%	10 8.2%	1 4.2%	1 2.9%	30 5.1%	29 6.1%
Your own comfort level with electronic information	53 4.9%	20 6.6%B	11 3.0%	31 4.6%	22 5.4%	24 5.6%	12 4.0%	16 4.8%	9 5.5%	7 4.7%	13 3.7%	17 8.5%JLM	1 2.3%	4 3.0%	* 1.4%	2 5.6%	28 4.7%	24 5.1%

Proportions/Means: Columns Tested (5% risk level) - A/B/D - C/D - E/F/G - H/I/J/K/L/M/N - P/Q
* small base

Table 629
Page 2143

Outsell/Digital Library Federation Study (2002)
Weighted Tables

TABLE 27

Q25. MINOR PROBLEM SUMMARY TABLE

		RESPONDENT TYPE				INSTITUTION TYPE			DISCIPLINE								GENDER	
	TOTAL SAMPLE	FACULTY MEMBER	GRAD. STUDENT	FACULTY /GRAD	UNDER GRAD. STUDENT	PUBLIC	PRIVATE	LIBERAL ARTS	BIOLOGIAL SCIENCES	PHYSICAL SCIENCES /MATH	SOCIAL SCIENCES	ARTS AND HUMAN.	ENGI- NEERING	BUSINESS	LAW	UNDEC. MAJOR	MALE	FEMALE
		(A)	(B)	(C)	(D)	(E)	(F)	(G)	(H)	(I)	(J)	(K)	(L)	(M)	(N)		(P)	(Q)
Base - Total Respondents	1076	296	370	666	410	436	302	338	162	149	357	197	38	125	12*	36*	592	484
Knowing what's available	531 49.4%	153 51.9%	180 48.8%	333 50.1%	198 48.2%	198 45.5%	154 51.1%	179 52.9%	74 45.7%	76 51.0%	180 50.5%	91 46.3%	19 49.6%	65 52.2%	6 48.6%	20 55.6%	296 50.0%	235 48.7%
Finding information	488 45.4%	149 50.3%	165 45.0%	314 47.4%	174 42.3%	187 43.0%	146 48.5%	155 45.9%	84 52.2%N	64 43.0%	154 43.2%	90 45.7%	17 43.5%	62 50.4%N	4 32.4%	13 36.1%	260 44.0%	228 47.2%
Determining the quality/ credibility/ accuracy of information	474 44.1%	130 44.3%	146 39.6%	277 41.7%	197 48.1%B	188 43.1%	123 40.9%	163 48.3%	70 43.7%N	70 47.3%N	167 46.8%N	77 39.2%	17 44.3%N	56 44.8%N	3 27.8%	13 36.1%	261 44.2%	213 44.0%
Accessing information once you find what you want	458 42.7%	142 48.2%D	154 41.7%	296 44.5%	163 39.6%	181 41.6%	133 44.1%	144 42.7%	76 47.0%N	63 42.3%N	154 43.2%N	86 44.0%N	16 42.7%N	46 36.6%N	2 19.4%	15 41.7%	250 42.2%	209 43.2%
Being able to compare across information alternatives, e.g. library vs. web sites	420 39.4%	109 37.6%	139 37.9%	248 37.8%	171 42.1%	169 39.3%	114 38.0%	137 40.8%	70 43.2%N	55 36.9%	130 36.9%	75 38.7%	15 41.3%	56 44.8%N	4 29.2%	16 44.4%	226 38.3%	194 40.9%
Having sufficient training on how to search for information	413 38.4%	130 43.8%	132 35.9%	262 39.4%	151 36.7%	155 35.7%	123 40.7%	135 39.8%	62 38.0%	61 41.2%	126 35.3%	86 43.8%	16 42.0%	45 35.8%	4 34.7%	13 36.1%	241 40.6%	172 35.6%

Proportions/Means: Columns Tested (5% risk level) - A/B/D - C/D - E/F/G - H/I/J/K/L/M/N - P/Q
* small base

Table 630
Page 2144

Outsell/Digital Library Federation Study (2002)
Weighted Tables

TABLE 27, continued

Q25. MINOR PROBLEM SUMMARY TABLE

	TOTAL SAMPLE	RESPONDENT TYPE: FACULTY MEMBER (A)	RESPONDENT TYPE: GRAD. STUDENT (B)	RESPONDENT TYPE: FACULTY /GRAD (C)	RESPONDENT TYPE: UNDER GRAD. STUDENT (D)	INSTITUTION TYPE: PUBLIC (E)	INSTITUTION TYPE: PRIVATE (F)	INSTITUTION TYPE: LIBERAL ARTS (G)	DISCIPLINE: BIOLOGIAL SCIENCES (H)	DISCIPLINE: PHYSICAL SCIENCES /MATH (I)	DISCIPLINE: SOCIAL SCIENCES (J)	DISCIPLINE: ARTS AND HUMAN. (K)	DISCIPLINE: ENGI-NEERING (L)	DISCIPLINE: BUSINESS (M)	DISCIPLINE: LAW (N)	DISCIPLINE: UNDEC. MAJOR	GENDER: MALE (P)	GENDER: FEMALE (Q)
Getting information in a timely manner	412 38.4%	121 40.9%	133 36.1%	253 38.3%	158 38.5%	163 37.6%	108 36.0%	140 41.4%	60 37.0%N	59 39.9%N	154 43.4%MN	71 35.8%N	14 38.8%N	40 32.1%	3 20.8%	11 30.6%	227 38.3%	185 38.4%
Having enough time	404 37.6%	77 25.9%	151 40.9%A	227 34.2%	176 43.0%A C	160 36.7%	100 33.1%	144 42.7%F	54 33.2%	55 37.2%	139 38.9%	77 39.2%	11 29.2%	46 36.6%	5 41.7%	17 47.2%	216 36.5%	188 38.9%
All information at my institution is not available from different locations within the institution	391 36.7%	83 28.9%	139 37.6%A	222 33.8%	169 41.5%A C	167 39.0%	99 33.1%	124 37.1%	67 42.0%KN	58 39.2%N	128 36.0%	59 30.6%	15 39.7%N	47 38.3%	3 24.6%	14 38.9%	211 36.0%	180 37.6%
Having access to all information from one place	365 34.0%	90 30.6%	134 36.3%	224 33.8%	141 34.5%	152 34.8%	96 31.9%	118 34.9%	56 35.0%	61 41.2%KN	130 36.3%K	50 25.6%	13 33.8%	39 31.3%	3 26.4%	13 36.1%	199 33.6%	167 34.5%
Having training and advice about the effective use of online information sources	362 33.7%	124 42.2%BD	108 29.3%	232 35.0%	130 31.7%	134 31.0%	108 35.8%	120 35.4%	50 31.0%	55 36.9%	115 32.1%	69 35.6%	16 42.6%HN	44 35.1%	3 25.0%	10 27.8%	212 35.8%	150 31.1%
Having to go to a library	333 30.9%	102 34.3%D	123 33.2%	224 33.7%D	108 26.4%	141 32.3%	101 33.4%	91 26.9%	54 33.2%	48 32.2%	113 31.6%	55 27.8%	14 36.6%	36 29.1%	3 25.0%	10 27.8%	189 31.9%	144 29.7%
Having people who can help you find information or who search for information for you	284 26.5%	90 30.6%D	102 27.8%	192 29.0%D	91 22.3%	112 26.0%	92 30.6%	79 23.4%	45 27.7%	37 24.8%	100 27.9%	50 26.0%	12 30.8%	30 23.9%	3 26.4%	7 20.0%	145 24.6%	139 28.8%

Proportions/Means: Columns Tested (5% risk level) - A/B/D - C/D - E/F/G - H/I/J/K/L/M/N - P/Q
* small base

Table 630
Page 2145

Outsell/Digital Library Federation Study (2002)
Weighted Tables

TABLE 27, continued

Q25. MINOR PROBLEM SUMMARY TABLE

		RESPONDENT TYPE				INSTITUTION TYPE			DISCIPLINE									GENDER	
	TOTAL SAMPLE	FACULTY MEMBER	GRAD. STUDENT	FACULTY /GRAD	UNDER GRAD. STUDENT	PUBLIC	PRIVATE	LIBERAL ARTS	BIOLOGIAL SCIENCES	PHYSICAL SCIENCES /MATH	SOCIAL SCIENCES	ARTS AND HUMAN.	ENGI-NEERING	BUSINESS	LAW	UNDEC. MAJOR	MALE	FEMALE
		(A)	(B)	(C)	(D)	(E)	(F)	(G)	(H)	(I)	(J)	(K)	(L)	(M)	(N)		(P)	(Q)
Your own comfort level with electronic information	240 22.3%	62 20.9%	71 19.2%	133 20.0%	107 26.0%B C	98 22.5%	59 19.5%	83 24.5%	33 20.8%	32 21.5%	75 21.1%	57 29.0%LN	6 16.0%	26 20.9%	2 13.9%	8 22.2%	111 18.7%	129 26.7%P
Not being able to log onto the library's website (lines busy, site down, etc.)	192 17.9%	33 11.3%	79 21.4%A	112 16.9%	80 19.4%A	83 19.1%	54 18.1%	55 16.2%	31 19.1%	23 15.4%	58 16.3%	46 23.3%L	5 13.1%	22 18.0%	3 23.6%	4 11.1%	88 14.8%	104 21.7%P
Not enough access to networked computers	186 17.3%	36 12.3%	79 21.3%A	115 17.3%	71 17.4%	86 19.6%G	58 19.2%G	43 12.7%	28 17.4%	20 13.4%	62 17.4%	45 22.7%I	6 16.8%	20 16.4%	2 12.5%	3 8.3%	88 14.9%	98 20.3%P

Proportions/Means: Columns Tested (5% risk level) - A/B/D - C/D - E/F/G - H/I/J/K/L/M/N - P/Q
* small base

Table 630
Page 2146

Outsell/Digital Library Federation Study (2002)
Weighted Tables

TABLE 28

Q19. TOP TWO BOX SUMMARY TABLE

		RESPONDENT TYPE				INSTITUTION TYPE			DISCIPLINE								GENDER	
	TOTAL SAMPLE	FACULTY MEMBER	GRAD. STUDENT	FACULTY /GRAD	UNDER GRAD. STUDENT	PUBLIC	PRIVATE	LIBERAL ARTS	BIOLOGIAL SCIENCES	PHYSICAL SCIENCES /MATH	SOCIAL SCIENCES	ARTS AND HUMAN.	ENGI-NEERING	BUSINESS	LAW	UNDEC. MAJOR	MALE	FEMALE
		(A)	(B)	(C)	(D)	(E)	(F)	(G)	(H)	(I)	(J)	(K)	(L)	(M)	(N)		(P)	(Q)
Base - Total Respondents	1054	309	335	644	410	436	280	338	152	176	301	207	44	131	10*	33*	603	451
My institution's library contains information from credible and known sources	1033 98.2%	300 97.7%	335 99.9%AD	635 98.8%	398 97.3%	429 98.5%	279 99.5%G	325 96.8%	150 98.8%	173 98.3%	295 98.1%	202 98.4%	43 98.0%	129 98.6%	10 98.3%	31 93.9%	590 98.3%	443 98.2%
My institution's library provides high quality information	1031 97.9%	294 95.5%	333 99.3%A	626 97.5%	404 98.5%A	427 98.0%	272 97.2%	331 98.2%	150 98.3%	170 96.6%	299 99.4%IM	202 97.8%	43 98.0%	126 96.5%	10 100.0%	31 93.9%	589 97.9%	441 97.9%
My institution's library provides information that I use and cite in my research papers	991 94.8%	272 90.4%	320 95.9%A	592 93.3%	398 97.0%A C	413 95.2%	270 97.0%G	308 92.2%	142 94.2%	162 92.0%	295 98.1%HI M	193 95.0%M	42 97.3%M	115 89.2%	10 98.3%	32 97.0%	561 94.0%	430 95.8%
My institution's library provides information that I use and trust without additional verification	938 89.0%	266 86.3%	298 89.0%	564 87.7%	374 91.1%	384 88.3%	246 88.0%	307 90.8%	136 89.0%	163 92.6%J	256 85.0%	183 88.1%	40 91.4%	121 92.9%J	9 90.0%	31 93.9%	535 88.8%	403 89.4%
The Internet provides information that I use and cite in my research papers	814 77.9%	211 69.9%	252 75.7%	463 72.9%	351 85.5%A BC	329 76.3%	211 76.0%	274 81.5%	104 69.0%	142 80.7%HK	231 77.4%	144 70.9%	35 81.1%HK	115 89.2%HI JKL	9 88.3%H K	33 100.0%	458 76.4%	356 79.9%

Proportions/Means: Columns Tested (5% risk level) - A/B/D - C/D - E/F/G - H/I/J/K/L/M/N - P/Q
* small base

Table 601
Page 2100

Outsell/Digital Library Federation Study (2002)
Weighted Tables

TABLE 28, continued

Q19. TOP TWO BOX SUMMARY TABLE

		RESPONDENT TYPE				INSTITUTION TYPE			DISCIPLINE									GENDER	
	TOTAL SAMPLE	FACULTY MEMBER	GRAD. STUDENT	FACULTY /GRAD	UNDER GRAD. STUDENT	PUBLIC	PRIVATE	LIBERAL ARTS	BIOLOGIAL SCIENCES	PHYSICAL SCIENCES /MATH	SOCIAL SCIENCES	ARTS AND HUMAN.	ENGI- NEERING	BUSINESS	LAW	UNDEC. MAJOR	MALE	FEMALE
		(A)	(B)	(C)	(D)	(E)	(F)	(G)	(H)	(I)	(J)	(K)	(L)	(M)	(N)		(P)	(Q)
The Internet provides high quality information	793 75.4%	209 68.2%	244 72.8%	453 70.6%	341 83.0%A BC	330 75.6%	197 70.4%	267 79.3%F	112 73.8%	136 77.3%K	237 79.2%K	134 64.9%	33 76.2%K	100 75.9%K	9 91.7%HI JKLM	32 97.0%	453 75.2%	340 75.7%
The Internet contains information from credible and known sources	779 74.3%	223 73.2%	241 72.1%	464 72.6%	315 76.9%	328 75.5%	203 72.7%	248 74.1%	106 70.3%	130 73.9%	227 76.1%	143 69.9%	33 75.5%	105 80.7%HK	8 83.1%	25 75.8%	449 74.7%	330 73.8%
The Internet provides information that I use and trust without additional verification	481 45.9%	103 33.5%	158 47.6%A	261 40.8%	220 53.7%A C	221 51.0%F	104 37.2%	156 46.4%F	61 39.9%	89 51.1%HK	135 45.3%	77 37.3%	21 47.0%	74 57.1%HJ K	6 59.3%HK	18 54.5%	264 43.9%	217 48.6%

Proportions/Means: Columns Tested (5% risk level) - A/B/D - C/D - E/F/G - H/I/J/K/L/M/N - P/Q
* small base

Table 601
Page 2101

TABLE 29

Q4EH. SUMMARY TABLE: What equipment do you use for accessing information from your off-campus residence?

	TOTAL SAMPLE	RESPONDENT TYPE: FACULTY MEMBER (A)	GRAD. STUDENT (B)	FACULTY /GRAD (C)	UNDER GRAD. STUDENT (D)	INSTITUTION TYPE: PUBLIC (E)	PRIVATE (F)	LIBERAL ARTS (G)	DISCIPLINE: BIOLOGIAL SCIENCES (H)	PHYSICAL SCIENCES /MATH (I)	SOCIAL SCIENCES (J)	ARTS AND HUMAN. (K)	ENGI-NEERING (L)	BUSINESS (M)	LAW (N)	UNDEC. MAJOR	GENDER: MALE (P)	FEMALE (Q)
Base - Base - Access off campus	440	164	197	361	79*	211	154	74*	66*	61*	158*	78*	15*	53*	7*	1*	258	182
Desktop computer (NET)	376 85.4%	145 88.7%B	157 79.9%	303 83.9%	73 92.5%B	186 88.0%	127 82.4%	62 84.1%	55 84.0%N	56 91.8%MN	139 88.1%N	67 85.7%N	13 84.6%N	42 78.9%N	2 30.2%	1 100.0%	227 88.1%	148 81.7%
Unaided	325 73.8%	121 73.9%	136 69.3%	258 71.4%	67 85.0%B C	162 76.8%	107 69.6%	55 74.0%	50 76.0%N	51 83.6%LN	109 69.0%N	64 81.4%N	10 67.3%N	38 71.9%N	1 18.6%	1 100.0%	195 75.5%	130 71.5%
Aided	51 11.6%	24 14.8%	21 10.5%	45 12.5%	6 7.5%	24 11.2%	20 12.8%	8 10.1%	5 8.0%	5 8.2%	30 19.0%K	3 4.3%	3 17.3%K	4 7.0%	1 11.6%	0 0	32 12.5%	19 10.2%
Laptop computer (NET)	272 62.0%	115 70.2%D	119 60.6%	234 65.0%D	38 48.2%	117 55.3%	105 68.3%E	50 67.7%	44 66.7%K	35 57.4%	105 66.7%K	36 45.7%	10 67.3%K	35 66.7%K	7 93.0%HIJKL M	0 0	164 63.5%	108 59.7%
Unaided	170 38.8%	66 40.4%	82 41.5%	148 41.0%	23 28.6%	67 31.7%	65 42.0%	39 52.1%E	26 40.0%K	21 34.4%	68 42.9%K	19 24.3%	7 46.2%K	23 43.9%K	6 83.7%HIJKL M	0 0	99 38.3%	72 39.5%
Aided	102 23.2%	49 29.7%B	38 19.2%	86 24.0%	15 19.6%	50 23.6%	40 26.3%	12 15.6%	18 26.7%N	14 23.0%	38 23.8%	17 21.4%	3 21.2%	12 22.8%	1 9.3%	0 0	65 25.3%	37 20.2%
Scanner (NET)	197 44.8%	72 44.0%	90 45.7%	162 44.9%	35 44.4%	100 47.4%	62 40.0%	35 47.7%	30 45.3%	28 45.9%	71 45.2%	36 45.7%	8 51.9%	21 40.4%	3 37.2%	0 0	127 49.3%Q	70 38.5%
Unaided	18 4.2%	6 3.7%	10 5.1%	16 4.5%	2 2.8%	12 5.9%	4 2.4%	2 3.1%	3 4.0%	1 1.6%	9 6.0%	4 5.7%	1 5.8%M	0 0	0 0	0 0	10 3.9%	8 4.6%
Aided	179 40.7%	66 40.3%	80 40.6%	146 40.5%	33 41.6%	88 41.5%	58 37.6%	33 44.6%	27 41.3%	27 44.3%	62 39.3%	31 40.0%	7 46.2%	21 40.4%	3 37.2%	0 0	117 45.4%Q	62 33.9%

Proportions/Means: Columns Tested (5% risk level) - A/B/D - C/D - E/F/G - H/I/J/K/L/M/N - P/Q
* small base

Table 54
Page 60

TABLE 29, continued

Q4EH. SUMMARY TABLE: What equipment do you use for accessing information from your off-campus residence?

		RESPONDENT TYPE				INSTITUTION TYPE			DISCIPLINE									GENDER	
	TOTAL SAMPLE	FACULTY MEMBER	GRAD. STUDENT	FACULTY /GRAD	UNDER GRAD. STUDENT	PUBLIC	PRIVATE	LIBERAL ARTS	BIOLOGIAL SCIENCES	PHYSICAL SCIENCES /MATH	SOCIAL SCIENCES	ARTS AND HUMAN.	ENGI-NEERING	BUSINESS	LAW	UNDEC. MAJOR	MALE	FEMALE
		(A)	(B)	(C)	(D)	(E)	(F)	(G)	(H)	(I)	(J)	(K)	(L)	(M)	(N)		(P)	(Q)
Base - Base - Access off campus	440	164	197	361	79*	211	154	74*	66*	61*	158*	78*	15*	53*	7*	1*	258	182
Laser printer (NET)	194 44.2%	76 46.4%	85 43.3%	161 44.7%	33 41.7%	98 46.5%	64 41.3%	32 43.6%	27 41.3%	20 32.8%	83 52.4%I	29 37.1%	6 42.3%	25 47.4%	3 34.9%	1 100.0%	107 41.5%	87 47.9%
Unaided	28 6.3%	9 5.6%	13 6.4%	22 6.1%	6 7.5%	15 7.1%	12 7.5%	1 1.7%	4 6.7%	3 4.9%	11 7.1%	4 5.7%	1 3.8%	4 7.0%	* 4.7%	0 0	15 5.9%	12 6.9%
Aided	166 37.8%	67 40.8%	72 36.8%	139 38.6%	27 34.2%	83 39.4%	52 33.8%	31 41.8%	23 34.7%	17 27.9%	71 45.2%I	25 31.4%	6 38.5%	21 40.4%	2 30.2%	1 100.0%	92 35.6%	75 41.1%
Fax machine (NET)	138 31.3%	64 39.2%B	49 24.8%	113 31.4%	25 31.2%	66 31.1%	40 26.1%	32 43.0%F	15 22.7%	24 39.3%HN	49 31.0%	25 31.4%	3 23.1%	20 38.6%N	1 18.6%	0 0	94 36.6%Q	43 23.9%
Unaided	7 1.6%	4 2.5%	3 1.6%	7 2.0%	0 0	3 1.6%	2 1.2%	2 2.5%	2 2.7%	1 1.6%	4 2.4%	0 0	1 3.8%KM	0 0	0 0	0 0	3 1.2%	4 2.2%
Aided	131 29.7%	60 36.7%B	46 23.3%	106 29.4%	25 31.2%	62 29.5%	38 24.9%	30 40.5%F	13 20.0%	23 37.7%HLN	45 28.6%	25 31.4%	3 19.2%	20 38.6%HL N	1 18.6%	0 0	91 35.4%Q	39 21.6%
Palmtop or PDA (NET)	108 24.6%	39 23.6%	49 24.7%	87 24.2%	21 26.5%	54 25.3%	41 26.6%	14 18.3%	19 29.3%IK	8 13.1%	41 26.2%	11 14.3%	6 36.5%IK	21 40.4%IK N	1 18.6%	0 0	71 27.5%	37 20.5%
Unaided	8 1.7%	3 1.8%	3 1.4%	6 1.6%	2 2.4%	4 1.9%	4 2.4%	0 0	1 1.3%	0 0	4 2.4%	1 1.4%	0 0	2 3.5%	0 0	0 0	6 2.2%	2 1.0%
Aided	101 22.9%	36 21.8%	46 23.2%	82 22.6%	19 24.1%	50 23.5%	37 24.2%	14 18.3%	18 28.0%IK	8 13.1%	38 23.8%	10 12.9%	6 36.5%IK	20 36.8%IK	1 18.6%	0 0	65 25.3%	35 19.5%

Proportions/Means: Columns Tested (5% risk level) - A/B/D - C/D - E/F/G - H/I/J/K/L/M/N - P/Q
* small base

Table 54
Page 61

TABLE 29, continued

Q4EH. SUMMARY TABLE: What equipment do you use for accessing information from your off-campus residence?

		RESPONDENT TYPE				INSTITUTION TYPE			DISCIPLINE									GENDER	
	TOTAL SAMPLE	FACULTY MEMBER	GRAD. STUDENT	FACULTY /GRAD	UNDER GRAD. STUDENT	PUBLIC	PRIVATE	LIBERAL ARTS	BIOLOGIAL SCIENCES	PHYSICAL SCIENCES /MATH	SOCIAL SCIENCES	ARTS AND HUMAN.	ENGI- NEERING	BUSINESS	LAW	UNDEC. MAJOR	MALE	FEMALE
		(A)	(B)	(C)	(D)	(E)	(F)	(G)	(H)	(I)	(J)	(K)	(L)	(M)	(N)		(P)	(Q)
Base - Base - Access off campus	440	164	197	361	79*	211	154	74*	66*	61*	158*	78*	15*	53*	7*	1*	258	182
Other (NET)	54 12.2%	27 16.3%	20 10.3%	47 13.0%	7 8.3%	25 11.6%	18 11.8%	11 14.7%	4 5.3%	9 14.8%	19 11.9%	10 12.9%	2 13.5%	9 17.5%H	1 11.6%	0 0	37 14.5%	16 8.9%
Unaided	30 6.8%	24 14.9%BD	6 2.8%	30 8.3%D	0 0	10 4.8%	11 7.1%	9 12.0%	2 2.7%	5 8.2%	11 7.1%	7 8.6%	2 11.5%H	3 5.3%	1 9.3%	0 0	26 9.9%Q	4 2.4%
Aided	25 5.6%	3 2.0%	15 7.4%A	18 5.0%	7 8.3%A	15 7.2%	7 4.7%	2 2.7%	2 2.7%	4 6.6%	8 4.8%	3 4.3%	* 1.9%	7 14.0%HJK	* 2.3%	0 0	12 4.6%	13 7.0%

Proportions/Means: Columns Tested (5% risk level) - A/B/D - C/D - E/F/G - H/I/J/K/L/M/N - P/Q
* small base

TABLE 30

Q4FI. SUMMARY TABLE: What equipment is available at the library?

		RESPONDENT TYPE				INSTITUTION TYPE			DISCIPLINE								GENDER	
	TOTAL SAMPLE	FACULTY MEMBER	GRAD. STUDENT	FACULTY /GRAD	UNDER GRAD. STUDENT	PUBLIC	PRIVATE	LIBERAL ARTS	BIOLOGIAL SCIENCES	PHYSICAL SCIENCES /MATH	SOCIAL SCIENCES	ARTS AND HUMAN.	ENGI-NEERING	BUSINESS	LAW	UNDEC. MAJOR	MALE	FEMALE
		(A)	(B)	(C)	(D)	(E)	(F)	(G)	(H)	(I)	(J)	(K)	(L)	(M)	(N)		(P)	(Q)
Base - Access information from physical library	907	193	314	507	399	322	254	330	115	128	301	194	28*	94	11*	35*	518	388
Desktop computer (NET)	800 88.3%	173 89.4%	280 89.3%	453 89.3%	347 86.9%	287 89.0%	224 88.3%	289 87.5%	106 91.6%K	115 89.8%	261 86.9%	161 83.2%	25 86.7%	92 98.0%HI JKLN	10 89.6%	30 85.7%	451 87.1%	349 89.8%
Unaided	700 77.3%	143 74.2%	250 79.4%	393 77.5%	308 77.0%	253 78.5%	195 76.7%	252 76.4%	97 84.0%KL	101 78.9%	231 76.9%	136 69.9%	20 70.4%	80 85.1%KL	9 77.6%	27 77.1%	394 76.0%	307 79.0%
Aided	100 11.0%	29 15.2%	31 9.8%	60 11.9%	40 9.9%	34 10.5%	29 11.6%	36 11.1%	9 7.6%	14 10.9%	30 10.0%	26 13.3%	5 16.3%H	12 12.9%	1 11.9%	3 8.6%	58 11.1%	42 10.9%
Laser printer (NET)	767 84.6%	137 70.9%	273 86.9%A	410 80.8%	358 89.5%A C	282 87.3%	205 80.7%	281 85.0%	103 89.3%JL	108 84.4%	241 80.0%	160 82.7%	23 80.6%	88 94.1%IJ KL	10 91.0%	34 97.1%	427 82.4%	340 87.6%
Unaided	136 15.0%	17 9.0%	60 19.2%A	78 15.3%	58 14.6%	68 20.9%G	39 15.2%G	30 9.1%	30 26.0%IJK LM	13 10.2%	41 13.7%	29 15.0%	4 14.3%	10 10.9%	2 20.9%I	6 17.1%	75 14.6%	61 15.6%
Aided	631 69.6%	119 61.9%	213 67.7%	332 65.5%	299 74.9%A C	214 66.4%	167 65.6%	251 75.9%EF	73 63.4%	95 74.2%	199 66.2%	131 67.6%	19 66.3%	78 83.2%HJ KLN	8 70.1%	28 80.0%	352 67.9%	279 72.0%
Scanner (NET)	551 60.7%	108 55.7%	177 56.3%	285 56.1%	266 66.6%A BC	187 58.0%	149 58.5%	215 65.1%	81 70.2%JKN	81 63.3%	167 55.6%	113 58.4%	17 60.2%	62 66.3%N	6 50.7%	23 65.7%	321 61.9%	230 59.2%
Unaided	78 8.6%	10 4.9%	34 10.7%A	43 8.5%	35 8.7%	29 9.0%	24 9.4%	25 7.5%	16 13.7%IN	6 4.7%	24 8.1%	15 7.5%	3 9.2%	8 8.9%	* 1.5%	6 17.1%	40 7.7%	38 9.8%

Proportions/Means: Columns Tested (5% risk level) - A/B/D - C/D - E/F/G - H/I/J/K/L/M/N - P/Q
* small base

Table 55
Page 63

Outsell/Digital Library Federation Study (2002)
Weighted Tables

TABLE 30, continued

Q4FI. SUMMARY TABLE: What equipment is available at the library?

	TOTAL SAMPLE	RESPONDENT TYPE: FACULTY MEMBER (A)	GRAD. STUDENT (B)	FACULTY /GRAD (C)	UNDER GRAD. STUDENT (D)	INSTITUTION TYPE: PUBLIC (E)	PRIVATE (F)	LIBERAL ARTS (G)	DISCIPLINE: BIOLOGIAL SCIENCES (H)	PHYSICAL SCIENCES /MATH (I)	SOCIAL SCIENCES (J)	ARTS AND HUMAN. (K)	ENGI-NEERING (L)	BUSINESS (M)	LAW (N)	UNDEC. MAJOR	GENDER: MALE (P)	FEMALE (Q)
Base - Access information from physical library	907	193	314	507	399	322	254	330	115	128	301	194	28*	94	11*	35*	518	388
Aided	473 52.1%	98 50.8%	143 45.7%	241 47.6%	231 57.9%B C	158 49.0%	125 49.1%	190 57.5%	65 56.5%	75 58.6%	143 47.5%	99 50.9%	14 51.0%	54 57.4%	6 49.3%	17 48.6%	281 54.2%	192 49.4%
Fax machine (NET)	384 42.3%	86 44.8%	113 35.9%	199 39.3%	184 46.2%B	119 36.9%	112 44.1%	153 46.2%E	51 44.3%	60 46.9%	107 35.6%	85 43.9%	10 36.7%	47 50.5%J	7 65.7%HI JKL	15 42.9%	233 45.0%	150 38.7%
Unaided	35 3.8%	8 3.9%	13 4.1%	21 4.0%	14 3.5%	18 5.6%G	11 4.5%	5 1.5%	5 4.6%	5 3.9%	11 3.7%	9 4.6%	1 3.1%	2 2.0%	* 3.0%	1 2.9%	23 4.4%	12 3.0%
Aided	349 38.5%	79 40.9%	100 31.8%	179 35.2%	170 42.7%B C	101 31.3%	101 39.6%	148 44.7%E	46 39.7%	55 43.0%	96 31.9%	76 39.3%	10 33.7%	46 48.5%JL	7 62.7%HI JKL	14 40.0%	211 40.6%	139 35.7%
Laptop computer (NET)	317 35.0%	63 32.5%	97 30.8%	159 31.4%	158 39.6%B C	106 32.8%	75 29.5%	137 41.4%EF	43 37.4%	44 34.4%	94 31.2%	69 35.8%	8 26.5%	41 43.6%JL	5 47.8%JL	13 37.1%	184 35.6%	133 34.3%
Unaided	98 10.9%	15 7.7%	33 10.4%	48 9.4%	51 12.7%	40 12.5%	21 8.2%	38 11.4%	23 19.8%IJK	7 5.5%	26 8.7%	19 9.8%	3 11.2%	13 13.9%I	2 17.9%IJ	5 14.3%	54 10.4%	44 11.4%
Aided	219 24.2%	48 24.7%	64 20.4%	112 22.1%	107 26.8%	66 20.3%	54 21.3%	99 30.1%EF	20 17.6%	37 28.9%HL	68 22.5%	50 26.0%	4 15.3%	28 29.7%HL	3 29.9%HL	8 22.9%	130 25.1%	89 22.9%
Palmtop or PDA (NET)	59 6.5%	14 7.3%	21 6.5%	35 6.9%	24 6.1%	15 4.7%	20 7.7%	24 7.4%	9 7.6%	5 3.9%	24 8.1%K	6 2.9%	2 6.1%	9 9.9%K	1 10.4%IK	3 8.6%	35 6.8%	24 6.2%

Proportions/Means: Columns Tested (5% risk level) - A/B/D - C/D - E/F/G - H/I/J/K/L/M/N - P/Q
* small base

Table 55
Page 64

Outsell/Digital Library Federation Study (2002)
Weighted Tables

TABLE 30, continued

Q4FI. SUMMARY TABLE: What equipment is available at the library?

		RESPONDENT TYPE				INSTITUTION TYPE			DISCIPLINE									GENDER	
	TOTAL SAMPLE	FACULTY MEMBER	GRAD. STUDENT	FACULTY /GRAD	UNDER GRAD. STUDENT	PUBLIC	PRIVATE	LIBERAL ARTS	BIOLOGIAL SCIENCES	PHYSICAL SCIENCES /MATH	SOCIAL SCIENCES	ARTS AND HUMAN.	ENGI- NEERING	BUSINESS	LAW	UNDEC. MAJOR	MALE	FEMALE
		(A)	(B)	(C)	(D)	(E)	(F)	(G)	(H)	(I)	(J)	(K)	(L)	(M)	(N)		(P)	(Q)
Base - Access information from physical library	907	193	314	507	399	322	254	330	115	128	301	194	28*	94	11*	35*	518	388
Unaided	6 0.6%	0 0	3 0.9%	3 0.5%	3 0.7%	4 1.2%	2 0.7%	0 0	1 0.8%	1 0.8%	4 1.2%	0 0	0 0	0 0	0 0	0 0	2 0.4%	4 1.0%
Aided	53 5.9%	14 7.3%	18 5.7%	32 6.3%	21 5.4%	11 3.5%	18 7.0%	24 7.4%	8 6.9%	4 3.1%	21 6.9%	6 2.9%	2 6.1%	9 9.9%IK	1 10.4%IK	3 8.6%	33 6.4%	20 5.2%
Other (NET)	288 31.8%	73 38.0%	91 29.1%	165 32.5%	123 30.9%	99 30.7%	81 32.0%	108 32.7%	29 25.2%	47 36.7%H	88 29.4%	72 37.0%H	11 37.8%H	26 27.7%	3 28.4%	12 34.3%	183 35.2%Q	105 27.2%
Unaided	263 29.0%	67 34.8%	81 25.9%	149 29.3%	114 28.5%	93 28.8%	70 27.7%	99 30.1%	25 21.4%	42 32.8%H	79 26.2%	68 35.3%H	10 34.7%H	25 26.7%	3 23.9%	11 31.4%	165 31.8%	98 25.1%
Aided	45 5.0%	16 8.4%D	15 4.9%	32 6.2%	14 3.5%	15 4.7%	15 5.8%	16 4.7%	5 4.6%	10 7.8%	19 6.2%	6 2.9%	2 7.1%M	2 2.0%	1 7.5%M	1 2.9%	36 7.0%Q	9 2.3%

Proportions/Means: Columns Tested (5% risk level) - A/B/D - C/D - E/F/G - H/I/J/K/L/M/N - P/Q
* small base

TABLE 31

Q4GJ. SUMMARY TABLE: What equipment do you have in your office?

		RESPONDENT TYPE				INSTITUTION TYPE			DISCIPLINE								GENDER	
	TOTAL SAMPLE	FACULTY MEMBER	GRAD. STUDENT	FACULTY /GRAD	UNDER GRAD. STUDENT	PUBLIC	PRIVATE	LIBERAL ARTS	BIOLOGIAL SCIENCES	PHYSICAL SCIENCES /MATH	SOCIAL SCIENCES	ARTS AND HUMAN.	ENGI-NEERING	BUSINESS	LAW	UNDEC. MAJOR	MALE	FEMALE
		(A)	(B)	(C)	(D)	(E)	(F)	(G)	(H)	(I)	(J)	(K)	(L)	(M)	(N)		(P)	(Q)
Base - Total Respondents	627	453	167	620	7**	236	226	165	89	147	179*	95*	33	80*	5**	0*	456	171
Desktop computer (NET)	598 95.4%	437 96.3%	157 94.0%	593 95.7%	5 68.1%	225 95.3%	217 96.1%	156 94.6%	85 96.0%	140 95.2%	171 95.8%	91 95.3%	32 97.3%	74 93.0%	5 100.0%	0 0	432 94.7%	166 97.2%
Unaided	557 88.8%	410 90.5%	142 85.0%	552 89.0%	5 68.1%	211 89.3%	204 90.1%	142 86.2%	79 89.1%	131 89.1%L	162 90.5%L	86 90.6%L	26 80.5%	68 84.9%	4 92.6%	0 0	401 88.1%	155 90.7%
Aided	41 6.6%	27 5.8%	15 8.9%	41 6.7%	0 0	14 5.9%	14 6.0%	14 8.4%	6 6.9%	9 6.1%	9 5.3%	4 4.7%	6 16.8%HIJK	7 8.1%	* 7.4%	0 0	30 6.6%	11 6.5%
Laser printer (NET)	559 89.2%	405 89.4%	148 89.0%	554 89.3%	5 77.3%	208 88.3%	202 89.4%	149 90.1%	77 87.1%	128 87.1%	164 91.6%	81 84.7%	30 91.2%	75 94.2%K	4 92.6%	0 0	406 89.0%	153 89.5%
Unaided	123 19.6%	86 18.9%	37 22.1%	123 19.8%	* 4.2%	47 19.9%	56 24.6%G	20 12.2%	18 19.8%	25 17.0%	41 23.2%	16 16.5%	7 20.4%	16 19.8%	1 14.8%	0 0	81 17.7%	42 24.6%
Aided	436 69.6%	320 70.5%	112 66.9%	431 69.5%	5 73.2%	161 68.4%	146 64.8%	128 77.9%F	60 67.3%	103 70.1%	122 68.4%	65 68.2%	23 70.8%	60 74.4%	4 77.8%	0 0	325 71.3%	111 64.9%
Fax machine (NET)	488 77.8%	368 81.2%B	117 70.0%	485 78.2%	3 45.5%	177 75.1%	178 78.7%	133 80.3%	65 73.3%	111 75.5%	143 80.0%	71 74.1%	24 74.3%	70 87.2%HI KL	4 88.9%	0 0	359 78.8%	129 75.1%
Unaided	37 5.9%	18 4.1%	18 10.6%A	36 5.8%	1 16.1%	15 6.6%	17 7.4%	5 3.0%	9 9.9%	8 5.4%	9 5.3%	6 5.9%	1 4.4%	4 4.7%	* 3.7%	0 0	27 5.9%	10 5.9%
Aided	451 71.9%	350 77.1%B	99 59.4%	449 72.3%	2 29.4%	162 68.5%	161 71.4%	128 77.3%	56 63.4%	103 70.1%	133 74.7%	65 68.2%	23 69.9%	66 82.6%HI KL	4 85.2%	0 0	332 72.9%	118 69.2%

Proportions/Means: Columns Tested (5% risk level) - A/B/D - C/D - E/F/G - H/I/J/K/L/M/N - P/Q
* small base; ** very small base (under 30) ineligible for sig testing

Table 56
Page 66

Outsell/Digital Library Federation Study (2002)
Weighted Tables

TABLE 31, continued

Q4GJ. SUMMARY TABLE: What equipment do you have in your office?

		RESPONDENT TYPE				INSTITUTION TYPE			DISCIPLINE									GENDER	
	TOTAL SAMPLE	FACULTY MEMBER	GRAD. STUDENT	FACULTY /GRAD	UNDER GRAD. STUDENT	PUBLIC	PRIVATE	LIBERAL ARTS	BIOLOGIAL SCIENCES	PHYSICAL SCIENCES /MATH	SOCIAL SCIENCES	ARTS AND HUMAN.	ENGI- NEERING	BUSINESS	LAW	UNDEC. MAJOR	MALE	FEMALE
		(A)	(B)	(C)	(D)	(E)	(F)	(G)	(H)	(I)	(J)	(K)	(L)	(M)	(N)		(P)	(Q)
Base - Total Respondents	627	453	167	620	7**	236	226	165	89	147	179*	95*	33	80*	5**	0*	456	171
Scanner (NET)	447 71.3%	338 74.7%B	104 62.5%	443 71.4%	4 61.3%	161 68.2%	158 69.8%	128 77.8%	66 74.3%	106 72.1%	126 70.5%	60 63.5%	23 71.7%	62 77.9%K	3 59.3%	0 0	326 71.4%	121 70.9%
Unaided	56 9.0%	42 9.2%	15 8.7%	56 9.1%	* 4.2%	13 5.7%	29 13.0%E	14 8.3%	14 15.8%I	10 6.8%	15 8.4%	8 8.2%	4 11.5%	6 7.0%	* 3.7%	0 0	36 8.0%	20 11.8%
Aided	390 62.3%	297 65.5%B	90 53.8%	386 62.3%	4 57.1%	147 62.4%	129 56.9%	115 69.5%F	52 58.4%	96 65.3%	111 62.1%	53 55.3%	20 60.2%	57 70.9%K	3 55.6%	0 0	289 63.4%	101 59.2%
Laptop computer (NET)	353 56.3%	263 58.0%	84 50.5%	347 56.0%	6 81.5%	131 55.3%	130 57.5%	92 56.0%	62 70.3%IJK	82 55.8%K	100 55.8%K	37 38.8%	21 65.5%K	47 59.3%K	3 63.0%	0 0	272 59.6%Q	81 47.5%
Unaided	138 22.0%	97 21.4%	38 22.7%	135 21.7%	3 47.9%	52 22.2%	50 22.0%	36 21.8%	25 27.7%K	27 18.4%	41 23.2%K	10 10.6%	9 26.5%K	26 32.6%IK	* 7.4%	0 0	108 23.7%	30 17.7%
Aided	215 34.2%	166 36.6%	46 27.8%	212 34.2%	2 33.6%	78 33.1%	80 35.5%	56 34.2%	38 42.6%KM	55 37.4%	58 32.6%	27 28.2%	13 38.9%	21 26.7%	3 55.6%	0 0	164 35.9%	51 29.8%
Palmtop or PDA (NET)	109 17.4%	80 17.7%	26 15.4%	106 17.1%	3 45.5%	34 14.6%	51 22.7%E	23 14.2%	18 19.8%	18 12.2%	30 16.8%	15 15.3%	8 24.8%I	20 24.4%I	1 25.9%	0 0	88 19.2%	22 12.6%
Unaided	10 1.5%	6 1.3%	3 1.7%	9 1.4%	1 13.3%	4 1.5%	3 1.3%	3 1.8%	1 1.0%	2 1.4%	0 0	2 2.4%	1 2.7%J	4 4.7%J	0 0	0 0	7 1.6%	2 1.4%
Aided	99 15.8%	74 16.4%	23 13.8%	97 15.7%	2 32.1%	31 13.0%	48 21.3%EG	20 12.4%	17 18.8%	16 10.9%	30 16.8%	12 12.9%	7 22.1%I	16 19.8%	1 25.9%	0 0	80 17.6%	19 11.2%
Other (NET)	156 24.9%	114 25.1%	39 23.6%	153 24.7%	3 42.0%	60 25.6%	57 25.4%	38 23.1%	22 24.8%	33 22.4%	47 26.3%	25 25.9%	9 26.5%	20 24.4%	1 25.9%	0 0	119 26.1%	37 21.6%

Proportions/Means: Columns Tested (5% risk level) - A/B/D - C/D - E/F/G - H/I/J/K/L/M/N - P/Q
* small base; ** very small base (under 30) ineligible for sig testing

Table 56
Page 67

Outsell/Digital Library Federation Study (2002)
Weighted Tables

TABLE 31, continued

Q4GJ. SUMMARY TABLE: What equipment do you have in your office?

		RESPONDENT TYPE				INSTITUTION TYPE			DISCIPLINE									GENDER	
	TOTAL SAMPLE	FACULTY MEMBER	GRAD. STUDENT	FACULTY /GRAD	UNDER GRAD. STUDENT	PUBLIC	PRIVATE	LIBERAL ARTS	BIOLOGIAL SCIENCES	PHYSICAL SCIENCES /MATH	SOCIAL SCIENCES	ARTS AND HUMAN.	ENGI-NEERING	BUSINESS	LAW	UNDEC. MAJOR	MALE	FEMALE
		(A)	(B)	(C)	(D)	(E)	(F)	(G)	(H)	(I)	(J)	(K)	(L)	(M)	(N)		(P)	(Q)
Base - Total Respondents	627	453	167	620	7**	236	226	165	89	147	179*	95*	33	80*	5**	0*	456	171
Unaided	98 15.6%	74 16.2%	22 13.5%	96 15.5%	2 27.7%	35 14.7%	34 15.0%	29 17.9%	11 12.9%	17 11.6%	32 17.9%	21 22.4%I	5 15.0%	10 12.8%	1 25.9%	0 0	72 15.9%	26 15.0%
Aided	62 9.9%	44 9.7%	17 10.1%	61 9.8%	1 14.3%	27 11.3%	25 11.0%	10 6.3%	12 13.9%K	17 11.6%K	15 8.4%	3 3.5%	5 15.0%K	9 11.6%K	0 0	0 0	49 10.7%	13 7.7%

Proportions/Means: Columns Tested (5% risk level) - A/B/D - C/D - E/F/G - H/I/J/K/L/M/N - P/Q
* small base; ** very small base (under 30) ineligible for sig testing

TABLE 32

Q4bSUM. Thinking about the past year, what percent of the time that you are accessing information for your [teaching or research/studies] is spent at each location?

MEAN SUMMARY TABLE

		RESPONDENT TYPE				INSTITUTION TYPE			DISCIPLINE								GENDER	
	TOTAL SAMPLE	FACULTY MEMBER	GRAD. STUDENT	FACULTY /GRAD	UNDER GRAD. STUDENT	PUBLIC	PRIVATE	LIBERAL ARTS	BIOLOGIAL SCIENCES	PHYSICAL SCIENCES /MATH	SOCIAL SCIENCES	ARTS AND HUMAN.	ENGI- NEERING	BUSINESS	LAW	UNDEC. MAJOR	MALE	FEMALE
		(A)	(B)	(C)	(D)	(E)	(F)	(G)	(H)	(I)	(J)	(K)	(L)	(M)	(N)		(P)	(Q)
Base - Total Respondents	1656	475	539	1014	642	687	442	527	229	264	528	300	62	206	16*	51*	941	715
Office	28.04	73.95BD	19.94D	45.23D	0.89	25.14	36.83EG	24.45	31.64JKN	43.46HJK MN	22.66	21.31	39.99HJK MN	31.81JK N	20.27	0.00	36.44Q	16.97
Physical library	25.57	9.68	30.01A	20.50	33.58A C	23.89	24.20	28.92E	22.38	17.58	28.42HI LM	34.33HI LM	17.64	20.01	35.11HI LM	29.29	23.60	28.17P
On-campus residence	16.60	0.48	5.03A	2.90	38.22A BC	12.12F	7.65	29.92EF	12.89	13.14	16.31N	18.48N	12.68	16.24N	8.24	51.78	13.67	20.44P
Off-campus residence	13.08	10.79	20.64AD	16.03D	8.43	18.41G	14.55G	4.91	12.68IL	8.42	16.71IL	13.39IL	8.02	13.22IL	24.20HIJ KLM	1.76	11.74	14.85P
Scientific laboratory	1.95	0.85D	5.18AD	3.16D	0.05	2.55G	2.93G	0.35	5.74JKMN	6.17JKMN	0.12	0.00	3.57JKMN	0.00	0.00	0.00	2.21	1.62
Computer lab	5.32	0.14	8.38A	4.52	6.59AC	6.67G	4.98	3.86	5.14	5.25	4.34	5.33	9.63HIJK	6.68	7.18	5.39	4.78	6.04
Classroom	1.90	0.47	2.44A	1.52	2.51A	2.85G	1.35	1.13	2.43	1.48	1.85	1.29	2.10	2.74	1.86	2.25	1.23	2.78P
Other	7.41	3.39	8.18A	5.94	9.73AC	8.22	7.53	6.25	7.09	4.11	9.59IKN	5.50	6.37	9.31IN	3.14	9.51	6.22	8.97P

Proportions/Means: Columns Tested (5% risk level) - A/B/D - C/D - E/F/G - H/I/J/K/L/M/N - P/Q
* small base; ** very small base (under 30) ineligible for sig testing

Table 45
Page 50

Outsell/Digital Library Federation Study (2002)
Weighted Tables

TABLE 33

R8a1. What percent of the information that you use for your research comes from your institution's physical or virtual library?

		RESPONDENT TYPE				INSTITUTION TYPE			DISCIPLINE								GENDER	
	TOTAL SAMPLE	FACULTY MEMBER	GRAD. STUDENT	FACULTY /GRAD	UNDER GRAD. STUDENT	PUBLIC	PRIVATE	LIBERAL ARTS	BIOLOGICAL SCIENCES	PHYSICAL SCIENCES /MATH	SOCIAL SCIENCES	ARTS AND HUMAN.	ENGI-NEERING	BUSINESS	LAW	UNDEC. MAJOR	MALE	FEMALE
		(A)	(B)	(C)	(D)	(E)	(F)	(G)	(H)	(I)	(J)	(K)	(L)	(M)	(N)		(P)	(Q)
Base - Responsibility is research	1563	811	752	1563	0**	699	593	271	269	320	491	239	79	148	18	0*	1023	540
25% or less	229 14.7%	154 19.0%B	75 10.0%	229 14.7%	0 0	73 10.5%	92 15.5%E	64 23.7%EF	27 10.1%	72 22.5%HJK L	55 11.1%	34 14.1%	11 13.6%	27 18.2%HJ	4 24.3%HJKL	0 0	164 16.0%	65 12.1%
26% - 50%	319 20.4%	191 23.5%B	128 17.1%	319 20.4%	0 0	141 20.1%	104 17.5%	75 27.7%EF	46 17.0%	69 21.6%	100 20.3%	54 22.5%	17 22.1%	30 20.1%	4 22.3%	0 0	215 21.0%	104 19.3%
51% - 75%	314 20.1%	175 21.6%	139 18.4%	314 20.1%	0 0	136 19.5%	129 21.8%	48 17.8%	58 21.6%N	54 16.9%	115 23.4%N	44 18.3%	14 18.0%	27 18.2%	2 11.7%	0 0	215 21.1%	98 18.2%
76% - 100%	695 44.5%	287 35.4%	408 54.3%A	695 44.5%	0 0	348 49.8%G	267 45.1%G	79 29.3%	138 51.3%I	123 38.4%	222 45.2%	105 44.1%	36 45.6%	63 42.8%	7 41.7%	0 0	425 41.5%	270 50.0%P
Don't Know	6 0.4%	4 0.5%	1 0.2%	6 0.4%	0 0	1 0.2%	1 0.1%	4 1.5%EF	0 0	2 0.6%	0 0	2 0.9%	1 0.7%HJ	1 0.6%	0 0	0 0	4 0.4%	2 0.3%
Median	73.07	59.96	76.92	73.07	0	74.91	73.51	49.16EF	75.56IJ	67.64J	72.60	71.62IJ	70.77HIJ KM	69.50HI JK	59.17HIJKM	0	72.06	75.10P
Mean	64.99	59.34	71.06A	64.99	0	68.83FG	65.48G	53.85	70.19IKL MN	59.31	67.05IN	64.48I	64.73I	62.53	58.98	0	63.07	68.62P
Standard Deviation	28.33	28.93	26.38	28.33	0	26.71	28.28	29.77	26.62	30.65	27.18	27.66	27.35	28.91	33.56	0	28.43	27.81
Standard Error	0.70	1.01	0.93	0.70	0	1.00	1.10	1.86	1.52	1.72	1.68	1.90	1.66	2.30	3.31	0	0.85	1.24

Proportions/Means: Columns Tested (5% risk level) - A/B/D - C/D - E/F/G - H/I/J/K/L/M/N - P/Q
* small base; ** very small base (under 30) ineligible for sig testing

Table 181
Page 683

Outsell/Digital Library Federation Study (2002)
Weighted Tables

TABLE 34

R8a2. What percent of the information that you use for your research comes from another source?

	TOTAL SAMPLE	RESPONDENT TYPE: FACULTY MEMBER (A)	GRAD. STUDENT (B)	FACULTY /GRAD (C)	UNDER GRAD. STUDENT (D)	INSTITUTION TYPE: PUBLIC (E)	PRIVATE (F)	LIBERAL ARTS (G)	DISCIPLINE: BIOLOGIAL SCIENCES (H)	PHYSICAL SCIENCES /MATH (I)	SOCIAL SCIENCES (J)	ARTS AND HUMAN. (K)	ENGI-NEERING (L)	BUSINESS (M)	LAW (N)	UNDEC. MAJOR	GENDER: MALE (P)	FEMALE (Q)
Base - Responsibility is Research	1563	811	752	1563	0**	699	593	271	269	320	491	239	79	148	18	0*	1023	540
25% or less	823 52.7%	357 44.1%	466 62.0%A	823 52.7%	0 0	398 56.9%G	325 54.8%G	101 37.2%	163 60.5%ILM N	147 45.9%	271 55.2%IN	124 52.1%	39 49.6%	72 48.4%	8 43.7%	0 0	509 49.8%	314 58.1%P
26% - 50%	332 21.3%	197 24.3%B	135 18.0%	332 21.3%	0 0	153 21.9%	118 19.9%	61 22.7%	59 21.9%	61 19.1%	103 21.1%	53 22.1%	20 25.0%	33 22.6%	3 18.4%	0 0	228 22.3%	104 19.3%
51% - 75%	222 14.2%	131 16.2%B	91 12.1%	222 14.2%	0 0	86 12.3%	84 14.2%	52 19.1%E	27 10.1%	56 17.5%H	73 14.9%	36 15.0%	10 12.5%	17 11.3%	3 16.5%	0 0	153 14.9%	69 12.8%
76% - 100%	178 11.4%	122 15.0%B	57 7.5%	178 11.4%	0 0	60 8.6%	65 10.9%	54 19.9%EF	20 7.5%	54 16.9%HJK	43 8.8%	24 9.9%	9 11.0%	25 17.0%HJ K	4 20.4%HJKL	0 0	128 12.5%	51 9.4%
Don't Know	7 0.4%	4 0.4%	3 0.4%	7 0.4%	0 0	3 0.4%	1 0.2%	3 1.1%	0 0	2 0.6%	0 0	2 0.9%	1 1.8%HJ	1 0.6%	* 1.0%HJ	0 0	5 0.5%	2 0.3%
Median	23.26	35.12	18.11	23.26	0	20.11	22.51	41.83EF	19.44	29.29J	22.40	23.38J	24.38HIJ KM	25.83HI JK	36.67HIJKLM	0	24.97	19.90
Mean	35.06	40.70B	28.98	35.06	0	31.21	34.54	46.24EF	29.81	40.88HJK L	32.95	35.52H	35.43H	37.47H	41.32HJ	0	37.01Q	31.38
Standard Deviation	28.35	28.94	26.40	28.35	0	26.73	28.28	29.75	26.62	30.64	27.18	27.66	27.45	28.91	33.58	0	28.45	27.81
Standard Error	0.70	1.01	0.93	0.70	0	1.00	1.11	1.86	1.52	1.72	1.68	1.90	1.68	2.30	3.32	0	0.85	1.24

Proportions/Means: Columns Tested (5% risk level) - A/B/D - C/D - E/F/G - H/I/J/K/L/M/N - P/Q
* small base; ** very small base (under 30) ineligible for sig testing

Table 182
Page 684

Outsell/Digital Library Federation Study (2002)
Weighted Tables

TABLE 35

R8C. What percent of your current information needs for your research are available online?

	RESPONDENT TYPE				INSTITUTION TYPE			DISCIPLINE								GENDER	
	TOTAL SAMPLE	FACULTY MEMBER	GRAD. STUDENT	FACULTY /GRAD	UNDER GRAD. STUDENT	PUBLIC	PRIVATE	LIBERAL ARTS	BIOLOGIAL SCIENCES	PHYSICAL SCIENCES /MATH	SOCIAL SCIENCES	ARTS AND HUMAN.	ENGI-NEERING	BUSINESS	LAW	UNDEC. MAJOR	MALE	FEMALE
		(A)	(B)	(C)	(D)	(E)	(F)	(G)	(H)	(I)	(J)	(K)	(L)	(M)	(N)		(P)	(Q)
Base - Responsibility is Research	1563	811	752	1563	0**	699	593	271	269	320	491	239	79	148	18	0*	1023	540
25% or less	352	206	146	352	0	145	138	69	37	49	115	115	15	20	1	0	234	118
	22.5%	25.4%B	19.4%	22.5%	0	20.7%	23.4%	25.6%	13.7%N	15.3%N	23.4%HI MN	48.4%HI JLMN	19.1%N	13.8%N	4.9%	0	22.9%	21.9%
26% - 50%	464	248	215	464	0	211	166	87	77	88	169	66	23	38	2	0	300	164
	29.7%	30.6%	28.7%	29.7%	0	30.1%	28.0%	32.0%	28.4%N	27.5%N	34.5%N	27.7%N	29.8%N	25.8%N	12.6%	0	29.3%	30.3%
51% - 75%	346	163	182	346	0	149	147	50	66	86	107	29	21	33	3	0	232	113
	22.1%	20.1%	24.3%	22.1%	0	21.3%	24.8%	18.4%	24.5%K	26.9%KN	21.8%K	12.2%	26.5%KN	22.6%K	16.5%	0	22.7%	21.0%
76% - 100%	363	162	200	363	0	181	129	53	85	90	83	22	18	53	11	0	227	136
	23.2%	20.0%	26.6%A	23.2%	0	25.8%	21.7%	19.5%	31.7%JKL	28.1%JK	16.9%K	9.4%	22.4%K	35.8%JK L	65.0%HIJKL M	0	22.1%	25.2%
Don't Know	39	31	8	39	0	14	12	12	4	7	17	6	2	3	*	0	30	8
	2.5%	3.8%B	1.0%	2.5%	0	2.0%	2.1%	4.5%	1.6%	2.2%	3.4%	2.3%	2.2%	1.9%	1.0%	0	3.0%	1.6%
Median	48.84	47.39	55.70	48.84	0	49.37	49.16	44.00EF	65.08JK	58.65JK	46.71	25.25	50.00HIJ KM	60.00HI JK	82.14HIJKM	0	48.78	48.95P
Mean	52.71	49.98	55.57A	52.71	0	54.28G	52.18	49.72	60.54JKL	58.44JK	48.85K	35.75	54.72JK	61.76JK L	77.93HIJKLM	0	52.26	53.55
Standard Deviation	27.56	27.14	27.72	27.56	0	27.78	27.56	26.79	25.92	26.13	26.16	26.45	26.29	25.77	23.04	0	27.68	27.33
Standard Error	0.69	0.96	0.98	0.69	0	1.05	1.08	1.70	1.49	1.48	1.65	1.83	1.61	2.06	2.28	0	0.83	1.23

Proportions/Means: Columns Tested (5% risk level) - A/B/D - C/D - E/F/G - H/I/J/K/L/M/N - P/Q
* small base; ** very small base (under 30) ineligible for sig testing

Table 186
Page 688

TABLE 36

R8D1. What percent of your current information needs for your research that are available online are available Through your institution's library web site?

	TOTAL SAMPLE	FACULTY MEMBER (A)	GRAD. STUDENT (B)	FACULTY /GRAD (C)	UNDER GRAD. STUDENT (D)	PUBLIC (E)	PRIVATE (F)	LIBERAL ARTS (G)	BIOLOGIAL SCIENCES (H)	PHYSICAL SCIENCES /MATH (I)	SOCIAL SCIENCES (J)	ARTS AND HUMAN. (K)	ENGI- NEERING (L)	BUSINESS (M)	LAW (N)	UNDEC. MAJOR	MALE (P)	FEMALE (Q)
		RESPONDENT TYPE				INSTITUTION TYPE			DISCIPLINE								GENDER	
Base - At least one percent of current information needs for research are available online	1519	778	742	1519	0**	684	577	259	265	312	474	230	77	145	17	0*	990	529
25% or less	266 17.5%	148 19.0%	118 15.8%	266 17.5%	0 0	128 18.7%	90 15.6%	48 18.4%	38 14.3%	63 20.2%	73 15.5%	53 22.9%HJ M	13 16.6%	20 14.1%	6 32.7%HIJLM	0 0	186 18.8%	80 15.1%
26% - 50%	307 20.2%	176 22.6%B	131 17.6%	307 20.2%	0 0	114 16.7%	129 22.4%E	63 24.3%E	49 18.6%	67 21.5%	105 22.2%	36 15.6%	18 23.0%K	29 19.9%	3 16.8%	0 0	200 20.2%	107 20.2%
51% - 75%	248 16.4%	100 12.9%	148 20.0%A	248 16.4%	0 0	118 17.3%	95 16.5%	35 13.7%	40 15.0%N	42 13.5%N	88 18.7%N	32 14.1%N	10 13.2%N	35 24.4%HIK LN	1 3.0%	0 0	154 15.5%	95 17.9%
76% - 100%	657 43.2%	318 40.9%	339 45.7%	657 43.2%	0 0	312 45.6%	245 42.5%	100 38.6%	134 50.5%JKM	133 42.6%	196 41.3%	95 41.5%	33 43.4%	59 40.4%	7 43.6%	0 0	426 43.0%	231 43.7%
Don't Know	42 2.7%	36 4.6%B	6 0.8%	42 2.7%	0 0	12 1.7%	17 3.0%	13 5.0%E	4 1.7%	7 2.2%	11 2.4%	13 5.9%HIJ M	3 3.8%	2 1.3%	1 4.0%	0 0	25 2.5%	17 3.2%
Median	70.96	68.57	72.59	70.96	0	72.89	69.01	67.60EF	75.56J	69.32J	70.68	66.88J	68.13HIJ KM	68.75HI JK	48.50HIJKM	0	70.64	71.53P
Mean	63.72	61.65	65.81A	63.72	0	64.51	64.02	60.87	68.39IKL N	61.38	64.38N	60.72	61.99N	64.62N	54.29	0	62.89	65.29
Standard Deviation	31.94	32.76	30.97	31.94	0	32.26	31.03	33.06	30.11	33.26	31.24	34.38	31.50	29.32	39.66	0	32.55	30.72

Proportions/Means: Columns Tested (5% risk level) - A/B/D - C/D - E/F/G - H/I/J/K/L/M/N - P/Q
* small base; ** very small base (under 30) ineligible for sig testing

Table 187
Page 689

Outsell/Digital Library Federation Study (2002)
Weighted Tables

TABLE 36, continued

R8D1. What percent of your current information needs for your research that are available online are available Through your institution's library web site?

		RESPONDENT TYPE				INSTITUTION TYPE			DISCIPLINE								GENDER	
	TOTAL SAMPLE	FACULTY MEMBER	GRAD. STUDENT	FACULTY /GRAD	UNDER GRAD. STUDENT	PUBLIC	PRIVATE	LIBERAL ARTS	BIOLOGIAL SCIENCES	PHYSICAL SCIENCES /MATH	SOCIAL SCIENCES	ARTS AND HUMAN.	ENGI-NEERING	BUSINESS	LAW	UNDEC. MAJOR	MALE	FEMALE
		(A)	(B)	(C)	(D)	(E)	(F)	(G)	(H)	(I)	(J)	(K)	(L)	(M)	(N)		(P)	(Q)
Base - At least one percent of current information needs for research are available online	1519	778	742	1519	0**	684	577	259	265	312	474	230	77	145	17	0*	990	529
Standard Error	0.81	1.18	1.11	0.81	0	1.23	1.24	2.14	1.75	1.90	1.99	2.47	1.97	2.36	4.03	0	1.00	1.41

Proportions/Means: Columns Tested (5% risk level) - A/B/D - C/D - E/F/G - H/I/J/K/L/M/N - P/Q
* small base; ** very small base (under 30) ineligible for sig testing

Table 187
Page 690

TABLE 37

R8D2. And, what percent of your current information needs for your research that are available online are available Through the Internet?

		RESPONDENT TYPE				INSTITUTION TYPE			DISCIPLINE								GENDER	
	TOTAL SAMPLE	FACULTY MEMBER	GRAD. STUDENT	FACULTY /GRAD	UNDER GRAD. STUDENT	PUBLIC	PRIVATE	LIBERAL ARTS	BIOLOGIAL SCIENCES	PHYSICAL SCIENCES /MATH	SOCIAL SCIENCES	ARTS AND HUMAN.	ENGI-NEERING	BUSINESS	LAW	UNDEC. MAJOR	MALE	FEMALE
		(A)	(B)	(C)	(D)	(E)	(F)	(G)	(H)	(I)	(J)	(K)	(L)	(M)	(N)		(P)	(Q)
Base - At least one percent of current information needs for research are available online	1519	778	742	1519	0**	684	577	259	265	312	474	230	77	145	17	0*	990	529
25% or less	368 24.2%	183 23.5%	186 25.0%	368 24.2%	0 0	169 24.8%	144 24.9%	56 21.5%	79 29.9%IMN	57 18.3%	109 23.0%N	72 31.2%IJ MN	20 25.7%IN	30 20.5%	2 10.9%	0 0	234 23.6%	135 25.5%
26% - 50%	350 23.1%	173 22.3%	177 23.9%	350 23.1%	0 0	176 25.7%F	117 20.3%	58 22.3%	56 21.3%N	63 20.2%N	128 27.0%N	54 23.4%N	15 19.6%	33 22.4%N	2 10.9%	0 0	217 21.9%	134 25.3%
51% - 75%	173 11.4%	76 9.7%	97 13.1%	173 11.4%	0 0	65 9.5%	75 12.9%	34 13.1%	26 10.0%	39 12.5%K	55 11.5%	15 6.3%	11 14.7%K	25 17.3%HK	2 12.9%K	0 0	117 11.8%	56 10.6%
76% - 100%	572 37.6%	300 38.6%	271 36.6%	572 37.6%	0 0	259 37.9%	223 38.6%	90 34.8%	96 36.2%	139 44.6%HJK L	164 34.5%	80 34.6%	28 35.8%	56 38.5%	11 61.4%HIJKL M	0 0	392 39.6%	180 34.0%
Don't Know	56 3.7%	46 5.9%B	10 1.3%	56 3.7%	0 0	15 2.2%	19 3.3%	21 8.3%EF	7 2.7%	14 4.5%	19 4.0%	10 4.4%	3 4.2%	2 1.3%	1 4.0%	0 0	31 3.1%	25 4.7%
Median	56.09	56.65	55.52	56.09	0	49.44	58.50	54.37EF	48.26J	72.22J	49.17	46.82J	57.73HIJ KM	63.33HI JK	84.17HIJKM	0	59.58	47.31
Mean	58.08	58.92	57.25	58.08	0	57.18	58.30	60.11	55.62	64.30HJK L	56.81	52.83	57.39	60.06K	75.28HIJKLM	0	59.74Q	54.93
Standard Deviation	33.82	33.96	33.68	33.82	0	33.88	34.31	32.49	34.76	32.60	33.39	35.06	34.07	32.44	28.66	0	33.67	33.91
Standard Error	0.86	1.24	1.21	0.86	0	1.30	1.37	2.15	2.03	1.89	2.15	2.50	2.14	2.61	2.91	0	1.03	1.57

Proportions/Means: Columns Tested (5% risk level) - A/B/D - C/D - E/F/G - H/I/J/K/L/M/N - P/Q
* small base; ** very small base (under 30) ineligible for sig testing

Table 188
Page 691

Outsell/Digital Library Federation Study (2002)
Weighted Tables

TABLE 38

T8A1. What percent of the information that you use for your teaching comes from your institution's physical or virtual library?

		RESPONDENT TYPE				INSTITUTION TYPE			DISCIPLINE								GENDER	
	TOTAL SAMPLE	FACULTY MEMBER	GRAD. STUDENT	FACULTY /GRAD	UNDER GRAD. STUDENT	PUBLIC	PRIVATE	LIBERAL ARTS	BIOLOGIAL SCIENCES	PHYSICAL SCIENCES /MATH	SOCIAL SCIENCES	ARTS AND HUMAN.	ENGI-NEERING	BUSINESS	LAW	UNDEC. MAJOR	MALE	FEMALE
		(A)	(B)	(C)	(D)	(E)	(F)	(G)	(H)	(I)	(J)	(K)	(L)	(M)	(N)		(P)	(Q)
Base - Responsibility is teaching	1299	920	379	1299	0**	518	461	319	206	282	344	258	50	152	8*	0*	912	387
25% or less	371 28.6%	292 31.8%B	79 20.8%	371 28.6%	0 0	162 31.2%F	109 23.7%	100 31.4%F	45 21.8%	103 36.5%HJK	81 23.5%	56 21.7%	17 33.1%HJK	67 44.2%HJ KL	3 38.3%HJK	0 0	270 29.6%	101 26.1%
26% - 50%	308 23.7%	242 26.3%B	67 17.6%	308 23.7%	0 0	116 22.4%	106 23.0%	86 27.0%	49 23.9%	53 18.8%	103 30.1%IL	56 21.7%	10 19.2%	35 23.3%	2 21.3%	0 0	215 23.5%	94 24.2%
51% - 75%	183 14.1%	132 14.3%	51 13.5%	183 14.1%	0 0	65 12.6%	66 14.4%	51 16.1%	30 14.5%	35 12.4%	43 12.6%	53 20.4%IJ LM	6 12.2%	15 9.8%	1 12.8%	0 0	133 14.6%	50 12.8%
76% - 100%	427 32.9%	247 26.8%	180 47.5%A	427 32.9%	0 0	171 33.1%G	177 38.3%G	79 24.6%	81 39.3%M	90 31.9%M	113 32.8%M	91 35.2%M	17 33.7%M	33 22.1%	2 25.5%	0 0	288 31.6%	139 35.8%
Don't Know/Refused	10 0.8%	7 0.8%	3 0.7%	10 0.8%	0 0	4 0.8%	3 0.6%	3 0.9%	1 0.4%	1 0.4%	4 1.1%	2 0.9%	1 1.7%	1 0.6%	* 2.1%	0 0	6 0.6%	4 1.0%
Median	47.87	43.96	72.50A	47.87	0	46.62	55.65	43.09	55.94IJ	43.54	47.41	58.75IJ	47.25HIJ KM	35.00IJ	33.33HIJKM	0	47.16	49.39P
Mean	53.65	49.69	63.26A	53.65	0	53.00	57.85EG	48.61	58.28IMN	50.41M	54.81M	58.81IL MN	52.29M	42.85	46.26	0	52.94	55.33
Standard Deviation	32.15	30.80	33.35	32.15	0	33.10	32.07	29.92	31.07	34.32	31.13	29.97	33.33	31.86	37.13	0	32.12	32.20
Standard Error	0.89	1.00	1.76	0.89	.0	1.43	1.51	1.71	2.04	2.05	2.31	1.98	2.56	2.50	5.47	0	1.04	1.71

Proportions/Means: Columns Tested (5% risk level) - A/B/D - C/D - E/F/G - H/I/J/K/L/M/N - P/Q
* small base; ** very small base (under 30) ineligible for sig testing

Table 309
Page 1287

Outsell/Digital Library Federation Study (2002)
Weighted Tables

TABLE 39

Q8A2. What percent of the information that you use for your teaching comes from another source?

		RESPONDENT TYPE				INSTITUTION TYPE			DISCIPLINE									GENDER	
	TOTAL SAMPLE	FACULTY MEMBER	GRAD. STUDENT	FACULTY /GRAD	UNDER GRAD. STUDENT	PUBLIC	PRIVATE	LIBERAL ARTS	BIOLOGIAL SCIENCES	PHYSICAL SCIENCES /MATH	SOCIAL SCIENCES	ARTS AND HUMAN.	ENGI-NEERING	BUSINESS	LAW	UNDEC. MAJOR	MALE	FEMALE
		(A)	(B)	(C)	(D)	(E)	(F)	(G)	(H)	(I)	(J)	(K)	(L)	(M)	(N)		(P)	(Q)
Base - Responsibility is teaching	1299	920	379	1299	0**	518	461	319	206	282	344	258	50	152	8*	0*	912	387
25% or less	485 37.3%	288 31.3%	196 51.9%A	485 37.3%	0 0	193 37.2%	195 42.3%G	97 30.3%	89 43.2%M	102 36.2%M	128 37.2%M	108 41.7%M	19 37.2%M	37 24.5%	3 34.0%	0 0	331 36.3%	153 39.6%
26% - 50%	288 22.2%	218 23.7%	70 18.5%	288 22.2%	0 0	105 20.3%	110 23.9%	73 22.9%	50 24.4%I	46 16.3%	83 24.0%I	69 27.0%IN	10 20.3%	29 19.0%	1 12.8%	0 0	202 22.2%	86 22.3%
51% - 75%	203 15.6%	160 17.4%B	42 11.2%	203 15.6%	0 0	79 15.2%	62 13.4%	62 19.4%F	32 15.4%	41 14.5%	60 17.5%	30 11.7%	7 14.5%	31 20.2%K	2 19.1%	0 0	148 16.2%	55 14.1%
76% - 100%	312 24.0%	245 26.6%B	68 17.8%	312 24.0%	0 0	137 26.5%F	91 19.8%	84 26.1%	33 16.2%	91 32.3%HJK	70 20.2%	48 18.7%	13 26.7%HK	54 35.6%HJ K	3 34.0%HJK	0 0	224 24.6%	88 22.7%
Don't Know/Refused	11 0.9%	9 1.0%	2 0.6%	11 0.9%	0 0	4 0.8%	3 0.6%	4 1.3%	2 0.9%	2 0.7%	4 1.1%	2 0.9%	1 1.2%	1 0.6%	0 0	0 0	6 0.7%	5 1.3%
Median	42.14	46.04	22.55	42.14	0	43.31	37.18	47.03EF	35.62	46.67	42.59	38.25	43.00HIJ KM	60.00HI JK	55.00HIJKM	0	42.80	40.71P
Mean	46.32	50.26B	36.79	46.32	0	46.92F	42.15	51.43F	41.47	49.62HK	45.19	41.19	48.02HK	57.15HI JKL	52.60HK	0	47.01	44.69
Standard Deviation	32.15	30.80	33.39	32.15	0	33.07	32.07	29.96	30.90	34.38	31.13	29.97	33.48	31.86	37.60	0	32.10	32.25
Standard Error	0.89	1.00	1.76	0.89	0	1.42	1.51	1.71	2.03	2.05	2.31	1.98	2.57	2.50	5.48	0	1.04	1.71

Proportions/Means: Columns Tested (5% risk level) - A/B/D - C/D - E/F/G - H/I/J/K/L/M/N - P/Q
* small base; ** very small base (under 30) ineligible for sig testing

Table 310
Page 1288

Outsell/Digital Library Federation Study (2002)
Weighted Tables

TABLE 40

T8C. What percent of your current information needs for your teaching are available online?

	TOTAL SAMPLE	RESPONDENT TYPE: FACULTY MEMBER	GRAD. STUDENT	FACULTY /GRAD	UNDER GRAD. STUDENT	INSTITUTION TYPE: PUBLIC	PRIVATE	LIBERAL ARTS	DISCIPLINE: BIOLOGIAL SCIENCES	PHYSICAL SCIENCES /MATH	SOCIAL SCIENCES	ARTS AND HUMAN.	ENGI- NEERING	BUSINESS	LAW	UNDEC. MAJOR	GENDER: MALE	FEMALE
		(A)	(B)	(C)	(D)	(E)	(F)	(G)	(H)	(I)	(J)	(K)	(L)	(M)	(N)		(P)	(Q)
Base - Responsibility is teaching	1299	920	379	1299	0**	518	461	319	206	282	344	258	50	152	8*	0*	912	387
25% or less	439 33.8%	299 32.5%	140 36.9%	439 33.8%	0 0	176 34.0%	156 33.8%	106 33.3%	55 26.9%	111 39.4%HJN	96 27.9%	111 43.0%HJ MN	17 34.9%N	47 30.7%	2 19.1%	0 0	312 34.2%	127 32.8%
26% - 50%	393 30.2%	313 34.0%B	79 21.0%	393 30.2%	0 0	146 28.2%	132 28.6%	115 35.9%EF	62 30.3%	76 27.0%	117 33.9%	76 29.6%	18 35.5%	41 27.0%	3 34.0%	0 0	290 31.8%	103 26.6%
51% - 75%	184 14.1%	121 13.1%	63 16.6%	184 14.1%	0 0	77 14.9%	74 15.9%G	33 10.4%	40 19.7%IKL	32 11.3%	58 16.9%K	24 9.1%	5 9.3%	23 15.3%	2 19.1%K	0 0	119 13.1%	65 16.7%
76% - 100%	208 16.0%	124 13.4%	85 22.4%A	208 16.0%	0 0	90 17.4%	75 16.3%	43 13.5%	36 17.5%	44 15.6%	53 15.3%	29 11.3%	8 16.9%	36 23.9%IJ K	2 23.4%K	0 0	137 15.1%	71 18.4%
Don't Know/Refused	76 5.8%	64 7.0%B	12 3.1%	76 5.8%	0 0	29 5.5%	25 5.4%	22 6.9%	11 5.6%	19 6.7%	21 6.0%	18 7.0%	2 3.5%	5 3.1%	* 4.3%	0 0	54 5.9%	22 5.6%
Median	38.69	38.10	41.35A	38.69	0	39.80	37.59	37.61	44.27IJK	31.32	37.35	28.78	36.82HIJ KM	44.44IJ K	46.43HIJKM	0	38.44	38.85P
Mean	43.58	42.48	46.15	43.58	0	44.72	43.50	41.83	49.38IKL	40.65	44.79K	36.60	42.36K	49.78IK L	53.22IKL	0	42.83	45.35
Standard Deviation	28.60	26.90	32.12	28.60	0	29.96	28.58	26.25	27.20	30.30	26.83	27.26	30.04	29.88	30.94	0	28.58	28.61
Standard Error	0.81	0.90	1.71	0.81	0	1.32	1.37	1.55	1.83	1.87	2.05	1.86	2.33	2.38	4.61	0	0.95	1.55

Proportions/Means: Columns Tested (5% risk level) - A/B/D - C/D - E/F/G - H/I/J/K/L/M/N - P/Q
* small base; ** very small base (under 30) ineligible for sig testing

Table 314
Page 1292

Outsell/Digital Library Federation Study (2002)
Weighted Tables

TABLE 41

T8D1. And, what percent of your current information needs for your teaching that are available online are available Through your institution's library web site?

	RESPONDENT TYPE				INSTITUTION TYPE			DISCIPLINE								GENDER	
	TOTAL SAMPLE	FACULTY MEMBER	GRAD. STUDENT	FACULTY /GRAD	UNDER GRAD. STUDENT	PUBLIC	PRIVATE	LIBERAL ARTS	BIOLOGIAL SCIENCES	PHYSICAL SCIENCES /MATH	SOCIAL SCIENCES	ARTS AND HUMAN.	ENGI-NEERING	BUSINESS	LAW	UNDEC. MAJOR	MALE	FEMALE
		(A)	(B)	(C)	(D)	(E)	(F)	(G)	(H)	(I)	(J)	(K)	(L)	(M)	(N)		(P)	(Q)
Base - At least one percent of current information needs for teaching are available online	1166	833	333	1166	0**	455	422	289	191	238	314	228	44	143	7*	0*	819	347
25% or less	299 25.7%	229 27.5%B	70 21.1%	299 25.7%	0 0	110 24.2%	102 24.2%	87 30.1%	48 25.3%	70 29.4%J	64 20.4%	62 27.0%	17 37.9%HJK M	36 25.3%	2 32.6%	0 0	221 27.0%	78 22.6%
26% - 50%	228 19.6%	173 20.8%	55 16.5%	228 19.6%	0 0	91 20.0%	87 20.7%	50 17.2%	32 16.6%	43 18.1%	73 23.4%	39 17.2%	9 19.6%	31 21.4%	2 20.9%	0 0	162 19.7%	67 19.2%
51% - 75%	127 10.9%	76 9.1%	51 15.3%A	127 10.9%	0 0	51 11.3%	46 11.0%	29 10.1%	25 12.9%	20 8.4%	41 13.2%	22 9.8%	3 7.2%	15 10.4%	1 9.3%	0 0	82 10.0%	45 13.0%
76% - 100%	470 40.3%	323 38.7%	147 44.2%	470 40.3%	0 0	186 40.8%	171 40.6%	113 39.1%	84 43.8%L	95 39.9%	130 41.3%	92 40.2%	15 33.3%	53 37.0%	2 27.9%	0 0	330 40.3%	140 40.3%
Don't Know/Refused	42 3.6%	32 3.9%	10 2.9%	42 3.6%	0 0	17 3.7%	14 3.4%	10 3.6%	3 1.4%	10 4.2%	6 1.8%	13 5.9%HJ	1 2.0%	8 5.8%HJ	1 9.3%HJL	0 0	25 3.0%	17 4.8%
Median	59.83	49.86	70.39A	59.83	0	65.64	59.62	54.16	70.00IJK	51.43	65.00	57.86	42.35HIJ KM	51.25IJ K	40.00HIJKM	0	56.83	62.66P
Mean	59.10	57.20	63.80A	59.10	0	60.10	60.12	56.04	61.17L	56.86	61.45LN	59.33L	49.67	57.81L	49.03	0	58.59	60.32
Standard Deviation	35.66	35.81	34.90	35.66	0	35.47	35.54	36.09	35.55	37.39	33.49	36.90	37.23	34.87	39.65	0	36.24	34.25
Standard Error	1.06	1.25	1.99	1.06	0	1.65	1.77	2.20	2.43	2.48	2.61	2.66	3.04	2.90	6.35	0	1.26	1.96

Proportions/Means: Columns Tested (5% risk level) - A/B/D - C/D - E/F/G - H/I/J/K/L/M/N - P/Q
* small base; ** very small base (under 30) ineligible for sig testing

Table 315
Page 1293

Outsell/Digital Library Federation Study (2002)
Weighted Tables

TABLE 42

T8D2. And, what percent of your current information needs for your teaching that are available online are available Through the Internet?

		RESPONDENT TYPE				INSTITUTION TYPE			DISCIPLINE								GENDER	
	TOTAL SAMPLE	FACULTY MEMBER	GRAD. STUDENT	FACULTY /GRAD	UNDER GRAD. STUDENT	PUBLIC	PRIVATE	LIBERAL ARTS	BIOLOGIAL SCIENCES	PHYSICAL SCIENCES /MATH	SOCIAL SCIENCES	ARTS AND HUMAN.	ENGI-NEERING	BUSINESS	LAW	UNDEC. MAJOR	MALE	FEMALE
		(A)	(B)	(C)	(D)	(E)	(F)	(G)	(H)	(I)	(J)	(K)	(L)	(M)	(N)		(P)	(Q)
Base - At least one percent of current information needs for teaching are available online	1166	833	333	1166	0**	455	422	289	191	238	314	228	44	143	7*	0*	819	347
25% or less	260 22.3%	180 21.6%	79 23.8%	260 22.3%	0 0	101 22.2%	93 22.1%	65 22.6%	50 26.3%M	52 21.8%	62 19.8%	55 24.0%	14 31.4%IJM	25 17.5%	2 20.9%	0 0	185 22.5%	75 21.6%
26% - 50%	249 21.3%	182 21.8%	67 20.1%	249 21.3%	0 0	94 20.6%	94 22.3%	61 21.1%	33 17.5%	46 19.3%	77 24.6%	53 23.0%	9 20.3%	29 20.1%	2 23.3%	0 0	177 21.6%	72 20.7%
51% - 75%	119 10.2%	76 9.2%	42 12.7%	119 10.2%	0 0	48 10.6%	41 9.7%	29 10.1%	19 10.1%	21 8.8%	26 8.4%	32 14.2%L	3 6.5%	16 11.0%	1 11.6%	0 0	77 9.4%	42 12.1%
76% - 100%	497 42.6%	363 43.6%	134 40.1%	497 42.6%	0 0	196 43.0%	177 41.8%	125 43.3%	86 45.2%K	112 47.1%K	139 44.3%K	74 32.4%	17 38.6%	66 46.1%K	3 37.2%	0 0	355 43.4%	142 40.9%
Don't Know/Refused	42 3.6%	31 3.8%	11 3.2%	42 3.6%	0 0	16 3.6%	17 4.0%	9 3.0%	2 0.9%	7 2.9%	9 3.0%	15 6.4%H	1 3.3%	7 5.2%H	1 7.0%H	0 0	26 3.2%	16 4.7%
Median	66.53	67.56	65.05A	66.53	0	66.80	64.34	65.96EF	63.75JK	72.81JK	64.00	49.92	47.22HIJ KM	73.33HI JK	56.67HIJKM	0	67.11	65.73P
Mean	62.08	62.53	60.94	62.08	0	62.66	61.15	62.50	61.18	64.91KL	62.31	58.11	56.01	66.26KL	59.65	0	62.11	61.99
Standard Deviation	33.94	33.73	34.47	33.94	0	33.73	34.81	33.07	34.77	33.81	34.07	33.23	36.39	32.57	37.08	0	34.16	33.46

Proportions/Means: Columns Tested (5% risk level) - A/B/D - C/D - E/F/G - H/I/J/K/L/M/N - P/Q
* small base; ** very small base (under 30) ineligible for sig testing

Table 316
Page 1294

Outsell/Digital Library Federation Study (2002)
Weighted Tables

TABLE 43

Q20. Once you've gained access to the Internet, how do you usually get pointed to the right information sources?

		RESPONDENT TYPE				INSTITUTION TYPE			DISCIPLINE								GENDER	
	TOTAL SAMPLE	FACULTY MEMBER	GRAD. STUDENT	FACULTY /GRAD	UNDER GRAD. STUDENT	PUBLIC	PRIVATE	LIBERAL ARTS	BIOLOGIAL SCIENCES	PHYSICAL SCIENCES /MATH	SOCIAL SCIENCES	ARTS AND HUMAN.	ENGI-NEERING	BUSINESS	LAW	UNDEC. MAJOR	MALE	FEMALE
		(A)	(B)	(C)	(D)	(E)	(F)	(G)	(H)	(I)	(J)	(K)	(L)	(M)	(N)		(P)	(Q)
Base - Total Respondents	1054	309	335	644	410	436	280	338	152	176	301	207	44	131	10*	33*	603	451
Through search engines	502 47.6%	146 47.4%	134 39.9%	280 43.5%	222 54.1%B C	217 49.6%	118 42.2%	167 49.5%	61 39.9%	96 54.5%HJN	120 40.0%	104 50.3%H	23 52.3%HJN	75 57.4%HJ N	4 36.7%	19 57.6%	308 51.1%Q	194 43.0%
Through the library's website	349 33.1%	98 31.6%	138 41.1%AD	235 36.5%D	114 27.7%	145 33.3%	101 36.2%	103 30.4%	63 41.6%ILM N	48 27.3%	111 36.9%	66 31.9%	13 29.1%	35 27.0%	3 26.7%	10 30.3%	187 31.1%	162 35.9%
Through websites recommended by collegues/ instructors	105 9.9%	28 9.1%	33 9.8%	61 9.4%	44 10.7%	36 8.3%	28 10.1%	40 11.9%	16 10.4%	14 8.0%	34 11.2%	20 9.7%	5 11.9%	10 7.8%	2 15.0%	4 12.1%	53 8.8%	52 11.5%
Through web-directories	40 3.8%	11 3.5%	9 2.8%	20 3.1%	20 4.8%	11 2.6%	13 4.6%	15 4.5%	5 3.5%	6 3.4%	15 5.0%	8 3.8%	1 2.0%	4 2.8%	1 10.0%HIKLM	0 0	21 3.4%	19 4.3%
Through websites recommended by friends	9 0.8%	* 0.1%	6 1.9%A	7 1.0%	2 0.5%	6 1.4%	3 1.0%	0 0	2 1.2%	2 1.1%	2 0.6%	1 0.5%	1 2.6%K	1 0.7%	0 0	0 0	5 0.8%	4 0.9%
Other	29 2.7%	11 3.5%	11 3.3%	22 3.4%	7 1.7%	14 3.2%	10 3.5%	5 1.5%	3 1.7%	5 2.8%	13 4.4%	2 1.1%	1 2.0%	4 2.8%	1 11.7%HIJKL M	0 0	17 2.8%	12 2.7%
Do not use the Internet	8 0.8%	7 2.1%D	2 0.6%	8 1.3%D	0 0	3 0.7%	4 1.3%	2 0.6%	2 1.2%	1 0.6%	6 1.9%	0 0	0 0	0 0	0 0	0 0	5 0.8%	4 0.8%

Proportions/Means: Columns Tested (5% risk level) - A/B/D - C/D - E/F/G - H/I/J/K/L/M/N - P/Q
* small base

Table 602
Page 2102

Outsell/Digital Library Federation Study (2002)
Weighted Tables

TABLE 43, continued

Q20. Once you've gained access to the Internet, how do you usually get pointed to the right information sources?

		RESPONDENT TYPE				INSTITUTION TYPE			DISCIPLINE									GENDER	
	TOTAL SAMPLE	FACULTY MEMBER	GRAD. STUDENT	FACULTY /GRAD	UNDER GRAD. STUDENT	PUBLIC	PRIVATE	LIBERAL ARTS	BIOLOGIAL SCIENCES	PHYSICAL SCIENCES /MATH	SOCIAL SCIENCES	ARTS AND HUMAN.	ENGI-NEERING	BUSINESS	LAW	UNDEC. MAJOR	MALE	FEMALE
		(A)	(B)	(C)	(D)	(E)	(F)	(G)	(H)	(I)	(J)	(K)	(L)	(M)	(N)		(P)	(Q)
Base - Total Respondents	1054	309	335	644	410	436	280	338	152	176	301	207	44	131	10*	33*	603	451
DK/Refused	12 1.2%	8 2.7%D	2 0.6%	10 1.6%	2 0.5%	4 0.9%	3 1.1%	5 1.5%	1 0.6%	4 2.3%J	0 0	6 2.7%J	0 0	2 1.4%	0 0	0 0	8 1.3%	4 0.9%

Proportions/Means: Columns Tested (5% risk level) - A/B/D - C/D - E/F/G - H/I/J/K/L/M/N - P/Q
* small base

Table 602
Page 2103

TABLE 44

Q21. How do you verify the information you receive from the Internet? That is, how do you establish the accuracy of the information you receive from the open Internet?

		RESPONDENT TYPE				INSTITUTION TYPE			DISCIPLINE									GENDER	
	TOTAL SAMPLE	FACULTY MEMBER	GRAD. STUDENT	FACULTY /GRAD	UNDER GRAD. STUDENT	PUBLIC	PRIVATE	LIBERAL ARTS	BIOLOGIAL SCIENCES	PHYSICAL SCIENCES /MATH	SOCIAL SCIENCES	ARTS AND HUMAN.	ENGI- NEERING	BUSINESS	LAW	UNDEC. MAJOR	MALE	FEMALE
		(A)	(B)	(C)	(D)	(E)	(F)	(G)	(H)	(I)	(J)	(K)	(L)	(M)	(N)		(P)	(Q)
Base - Total Respondents	1046	302	333	635	410	433	276	336	150	175	295	207	44	131	10*	33*	599	447
Don't Know/Refused	29 2.8%	8 2.6%	12 3.5%	20 3.1%	10 2.4%	17 4.0%F	3 1.1%	9 2.7%	2 1.2%	6 3.4%	8 2.5%	6 2.7%	1 3.3%	4 2.8%	* 3.3%	3 9.1%	17 2.8%	12 2.8%
Base - Total Responding	1017	294	322	616	401	416	273	327	149	169	288	202	42	127	10*	30*	582	435
Check it against another source	399 39.3%	129 44.0%B	109 34.0%	239 38.7%	161 40.1%	159 38.3%	98 35.9%	142 43.3%	49 33.1%	62 36.7%	107 37.3%	99 48.9%HI J	19 44.5%H	51 40.1%	4 43.1%	8 26.7%	232 39.8%	168 38.5%
Only reference known sources	210 20.7%	64 21.9%	72 22.4%	136 22.1%	74 18.4%	73 17.4%	66 24.2%E	72 21.9%	26 17.2%	41 24.3%L	66 22.9%	34 16.7%	6 14.4%	30 23.4%	2 15.5%	7 23.3%	128 22.0%	82 19.0%
Trust the sponsoring organization/ publisher	86 8.4%	29 9.8%	29 9.2%	58 9.5%	28 6.9%	33 8.0%	25 9.2%	27 8.3%	18 11.8%	15 8.9%	19 6.5%	16 7.8%	4 10.3%	9 7.3%	1 10.3%	4 13.3%	51 8.7%	35 8.0%
Only reference academic sources provided by an accredited institution	82 8.1%	19 6.5%	24 7.5%	43 7.0%	39 9.7%	28 6.8%	25 9.3%	28 8.7%	13 8.9%KL	17 10.1%KL	32 11.1%KL	6 2.8%	1 2.1%	10 8.0%KL	1 12.1%KL	2 6.7%	47 8.0%	35 8.1%
Trust the web site	73 7.2%	19 6.4%	30 9.2%	49 7.9%	25 6.2%	30 7.3%	26 9.6%	17 5.1%	10 6.5%	16 9.5%	19 6.5%	10 5.0%	6 14.4%HJK	11 8.8%	1 5.2%	1 3.3%	46 7.8%	28 6.4%

Proportions/Means: Columns Tested (5% risk level) - A/B/D - C/D - E/F/G - H/I/J/K/L/M/N - P/Q
* small base

Table 603
Page 2104

Outsell/Digital Library Federation Study (2002)
Weighted Tables

TABLE 44, continued

Q21. How do you verify the information you receive from the Internet? That is, how do you establish the accuracy of the information you receive from the open Internet?

		RESPONDENT TYPE				INSTITUTION TYPE			DISCIPLINE								GENDER	
	TOTAL SAMPLE	FACULTY MEMBER	GRAD. STUDENT	FACULTY /GRAD	UNDER GRAD. STUDENT	PUBLIC	PRIVATE	LIBERAL ARTS	BIOLOGIAL SCIENCES	PHYSICAL SCIENCES /MATH	SOCIAL SCIENCES	ARTS AND HUMAN.	ENGI-NEERING	BUSINESS	LAW	UNDEC. MAJOR	MALE	FEMALE
		(A)	(B)	(C)	(D)	(E)	(F)	(G)	(H)	(I)	(J)	(K)	(L)	(M)	(N)		(P)	(Q)
Base - Total Responding	1017	294	322	616	401	416	273	327	149	169	288	202	42	127	10*	30*	582	435
Trust the author	70 6.9%	26 8.8%	21 6.6%	47 7.6%	23 5.7%	27 6.6%	26 9.3%	17 5.2%	7 4.7%	18 10.7%HJM	13 4.6%	20 10.0%	5 11.0%HJM	6 4.4%	* 3.4%	1 3.3%	47 8.1%	23 5.2%
Discuss with professor	67 6.6%	0 0	19 6.1%A	19 3.2%	48 11.9%AB C	21 5.1%	9 3.2%	37 11.4%EF	4 2.4%	13 7.7%HM	26 9.2%HM	17 8.3%HM	2 5.5%M	2 1.5%	1 5.2%	3 10.0%	32 5.6%	35 8.0%
Peer reviewed	43 4.2%	23 7.8%BD	12 3.7%	35 5.7%D	8 1.9%	20 4.9%	12 4.2%	11 3.3%	10 6.5%K	9 5.3%	11 3.9%	4 2.2%	2 5.5%	5 3.6%	* 1.7%	1 3.3%	25 4.3%	17 4.0%
Trust the library/ collection	42 4.2%	9 3.1%	21 6.5%	30 4.8%	13 3.1%	26 6.2%G	9 3.5%	7 2.1%	6 4.1%	6 3.6%	11 3.9%	11 5.6%	3 6.8%	4 2.9%	* 1.7%	1 3.3%	19 3.3%	23 5.3%
Only reference sites recommended by colleague or peer	34 3.4%	6 2.2%	9 2.9%	16 2.6%	19 4.7%	11 2.6%	11 4.1%	13 3.9%	2 1.2%	4 2.4%	9 3.3%	16 7.8%HIL M	1 1.4%	2 1.5%	* 1.7%	1 3.3%	17 2.9%	18 4.1%
Do a search on the author	30 2.9%	3 1.0%	7 2.2%	10 1.6%	20 4.9%AC	11 2.7%	5 2.0%	13 3.9%	2 1.2%	6 3.6%M	15 5.2%LM	7 3.3%M	0 0	0 0	0 0	0 0	15 2.5%	15 3.4%
Self investigation	26 2.5%	11 3.9%B	3 0.9%	14 2.3%	11 2.8%	5 1.3%	7 2.6%	13 4.1%E	4 3.0%	5 3.0%	8 2.6%	3 1.7%	1 3.4%	2 1.5%	* 1.7%	2 6.7%	12 2.1%	14 3.1%
Trust if it is fee based site	0 0	0 0	0 0	0 0	0 0	0 0	0 0	0 0	0 0	0 0	0 0	0 0	0 0	0 0	0 0	0 0	0 0	0 0

Proportions/Means: Columns Tested (5% risk level) - A/B/D - C/D - E/F/G - H/I/J/K/L/M/N - P/Q
* small base

Table 603
Page 2105

Outsell/Digital Library Federation Study (2002)
Weighted Tables

TABLE 44, continued

Q21. How do you verify the information you receive from the Internet? That is, how do you establish the accuracy of the information you receive from the open Internet?

		RESPONDENT TYPE				INSTITUTION TYPE			DISCIPLINE								GENDER	
	TOTAL SAMPLE	FACULTY MEMBER	GRAD. STUDENT	FACULTY /GRAD	UNDER GRAD. STUDENT	PUBLIC	PRIVATE	LIBERAL ARTS	BIOLOGIAL SCIENCES	PHYSICAL SCIENCES /MATH	SOCIAL SCIENCES	ARTS AND HUMAN.	ENGI-NEERING	BUSINESS	LAW	UNDEC. MAJOR	MALE	FEMALE
		(A)	(B)	(C)	(D)	(E)	(F)	(G)	(H)	(I)	(J)	(K)	(L)	(M)	(N)		(P)	(Q)
Base - Total Responding	1017	294	322	616	401	416	273	327	149	169	288	202	42	127	10*	30*	582	435
Other	117 11.5%	53 18.1%BD	28 8.8%	82 13.2%	35 8.8%	40 9.7%	40 14.8%	36 11.1%	26 17.2%JM	24 14.2%M	23 7.8%	25 12.2%	4 10.3%	8 6.6%	2 15.5%M	6 20.0%	74 12.6%	43 10.0%
Do not verify information	39 3.9%	6 2.0%	15 4.7%	21 3.4%	18 4.5%	18 4.4%	10 3.8%	11 3.2%	4 3.0%	4 2.4%	9 3.3%	4 2.2%	1 3.4%	12 9.5%HIJ K	* 3.4%	3 10.0%	25 4.4%	14 3.2%

Proportions/Means: Columns Tested (5% risk level) - A/B/D - C/D - E/F/G - H/I/J/K/L/M/N - P/Q
* small base

Table 603
Page 2106

TABLE 45

Q22. How do you determine the authoritativeness of the information you receive from the Internet? That is, how do you decide how much it should influence your current thinking?

		RESPONDENT TYPE				INSTITUTION TYPE			DISCIPLINE								GENDER	
	TOTAL SAMPLE	FACULTY MEMBER	GRAD. STUDENT	FACULTY /GRAD	UNDER GRAD. STUDENT	PUBLIC	PRIVATE	LIBERAL ARTS	BIOLOGIAL SCIENCES	PHYSICAL SCIENCES /MATH	SOCIAL SCIENCES	ARTS AND HUMAN.	ENGI-NEERING	BUSINESS	LAW	UNDEC. MAJOR	MALE	FEMALE
		(A)	(B)	(C)	(D)	(E)	(F)	(G)	(H)	(I)	(J)	(K)	(L)	(M)	(N)		(P)	(Q)
Base - Total Respondents	1046	302	333	635	410	433	276	336	150	175	295	207	44	131	10*	33*	599	447
Don't Know/Refused	94 9.0%	14 4.6%	34 10.3%A	48 7.6%	46 11.2%A	46 10.5%	18 6.4%	31 9.2%	11 7.0%	10 5.7%	32 10.8%	18 8.6%	5 11.9%I	11 8.5%	1 11.7%	6 18.2%	47 7.8%	47 10.6%
Base - Total Responding	952	288	299	587	365	388	259	305	140	165	263	189	39	120	9*	27*	552	400
Only reference known sources	181 19.1%	63 22.0%D	64 21.3%	127 21.6%D	55 15.0%	76 19.5%	51 19.7%	55 17.9%	30 21.4%	32 19.4%	51 19.3%	29 15.4%	6 14.3%	29 24.0%	1 15.1%	4 14.8%	109 19.7%	73 18.2%
Check with alternative sources	133 14.0%	43 14.8%	37 12.4%	80 13.6%	53 14.6%	43 11.0%	35 13.4%	56 18.3%E	16 11.3%	26 15.8%	38 14.3%	29 15.4%	5 12.8%	14 11.6%	1 7.5%	5 18.5%	66 12.0%	67 16.8%
Trust the author	124 13.0%	46 15.9%B	29 9.5%	74 12.7%	50 13.7%	41 10.5%	38 14.5%	46 15.0%	18 12.6%	25 15.2%	26 10.0%	28 14.8%	7 18.8%J	16 13.2%	2 24.5%HJM	2 7.4%	80 14.5%	44 11.0%
Trust the sponsoring organization/ publisher	85 8.9%	42 14.4%D	29 9.5%D	70 11.9%D	15 4.1%	38 9.8%	22 8.6%	25 8.2%	17 11.9%	13 7.9%	17 6.4%	19 10.1%	4 11.3%	12 10.1%	2 22.6%HIJ KLM	1 3.7%	53 9.6%	32 8.1%
Trust the web site	79 8.3%	24 8.4%	24 8.0%	48 8.2%	31 8.5%	27 7.0%	27 10.5%	25 8.1%	11 7.5%	14 8.5%	19 7.1%	15 7.7%	6 14.3%HJK	12 10.1%	2 17.0%HJK	2 7.4%	44 7.9%	35 8.8%
Only reference academic sources provided by an accredited institution	67 7.1%	16 5.4%	25 8.4%	41 6.9%	26 7.2%	25 6.4%	22 8.5%	20 6.7%	11 8.2%L	17 10.3%L	19 7.1%	9 4.7%	1 1.5%	8 7.0%	1 11.3%L	1 3.7%	42 7.6%	25 6.2%

Proportions/Means: Columns Tested (5% risk level) - A/B/D - C/D - E/F/G - H/I/J/K/L/M/N - P/Q
* small base

Table 604
Page 2107

Outsell/Digital Library Federation Study (2002)
Weighted Tables

TABLE 45, continued

Q22. How do you determine the authoritativeness of the information you receive from the Internet? That is, how do you decide how much it should influence your current thinking?

		RESPONDENT TYPE				INSTITUTION TYPE			DISCIPLINE									GENDER	
	TOTAL SAMPLE	FACULTY MEMBER	GRAD. STUDENT	FACULTY /GRAD	UNDER GRAD. STUDENT	PUBLIC	PRIVATE	LIBERAL ARTS	BIOLOGIAL SCIENCES	PHYSICAL SCIENCES /MATH	SOCIAL SCIENCES	ARTS AND HUMAN.	ENGI-NEERING	BUSINESS	LAW	UNDEC. MAJOR	MALE	FEMALE
		(A)	(B)	(C)	(D)	(E)	(F)	(G)	(H)	(I)	(J)	(K)	(L)	(M)	(N)		(P)	(Q)
Base - Total Responding	952	288	299	587	365	388	259	305	140	165	263	189	39	120	9*	27*	552	400
Peer reviewed	61 6.4%	21 7.3%	23 7.7%	44 7.5%	17 4.7%	28 7.3%	14 5.5%	19 6.1%	15 10.7%M	13 7.9%	13 5.0%	11 5.9%	4 10.5%M	5 3.9%	* 1.9%	0 0	36 6.6%	25 6.2%
Only reference sites recommended by colleague or peer	44 4.7%	8 2.9%	21 6.9%A	29 4.9%	15 4.2%	16 4.0%	14 5.5%	14 4.7%	5 3.8%	4 2.4%	13 5.0%	15 7.7%I	1 3.8%	5 3.9%	* 1.9%	1 3.7%	26 4.7%	19 4.6%
Base it on my own opinions	38 4.0%	23 8.0%BD	7 2.3%	30 5.1%	9 2.3%	16 4.0%	10 3.8%	13 4.2%	6 4.4%	6 3.6%	6 2.1%	12 6.5%	1 1.5%	7 5.4%	0 0	1 3.7%	27 5.0%	11 2.7%
Depends on source/ information	34 3.6%	14 5.0%D	13 4.4%	28 4.7%D	7 1.9%	19 4.8%	9 3.5%	7 2.3%	6 4.4%	8 4.8%	9 3.6%	7 3.6%	1 1.5%	3 2.3%	1 7.5%L	0 0	21 3.7%	14 3.4%
Trust the library/ collection	28 3.0%	6 2.0%	14 4.7%	20 3.4%	9 2.3%	21 5.4%FG	3 1.3%	4 1.3%	8 5.7%	5 3.0%	6 2.1%	4 2.4%	1 3.0%	3 2.3%	* 3.8%	1 3.7%	10 1.8%	18 4.6%P
Ask around	25 2.6%	2 0.7%	10 3.4%A	12 2.1%	13 3.4%A	13 3.4%	4 1.4%	8 2.5%	4 2.5%	7 4.2%	6 2.1%	3 1.8%	2 6.0%JKM	1 0.8%	0 0	2 7.4%	12 2.2%	13 3.1%
Trust if it is fee based site	1 0.1%	0 0	0 0	0 0	1 0.3%	0 0	0 0	1 0.3%	0 0	0 0	0 0	0 0	0 0	0 0	0 0	1 3.7%	1 0.2%	0 0
Other	169 17.7%	50 17.3%	42 14.2%	92 15.7%	77 21.0%B	64 16.4%	47 18.3%	58 18.9%	26 18.2%	23 13.9%	47 17.9%	44 23.1%IM	7 18.0%	16 13.2%	2 20.8%	5 18.5%	93 16.8%	76 19.0%
Not concerned with authoritativeness	62 6.5%	8 2.8%	15 5.1%	23 4.0%	39 10.6%AB C	24 6.2%	13 5.0%	25 8.2%	5 3.8%	8 4.8%	19 7.1%	13 7.1%	1 2.3%	12 10.1%HL	1 5.7%	3 11.1%	44 8.0%	18 4.5%

Proportions/Means: Columns Tested (5% risk level) - A/B/D - C/D - E/F/G - H/I/J/K/L/M/N - P/Q
* small base

Table 604
Page 2108

Outsell/Digital Library Federation Study (2002)
Weighted Tables

TABLE 46

S8A1. What percent of the information that you use for your coursework comes from your institution's physical or virtual library?

		RESPONDENT TYPE				INSTITUTION TYPE			DISCIPLINE								GENDER	
	TOTAL SAMPLE	FACULTY MEMBER	GRAD. STUDENT	FACULTY /GRAD	UNDER GRAD. STUDENT	PUBLIC	PRIVATE	LIBERAL ARTS	BIOLOGIAL SCIENCES	PHYSICAL SCIENCES /MATH	SOCIAL SCIENCES	ARTS AND HUMAN.	ENGI-NEERING	BUSINESS	LAW	UNDEC. MAJOR	MALE	FEMALE
		(A)	(B)	(C)	(D)	(E)	(F)	(G)	(H)	(I)	(J)	(K)	(L)	(M)	(N)		(P)	(Q)
Base - Student	2304	0**	1056	1056	1248	1065	534	705	308	305	771	437	90	266	25	102	1102	1202
25% or less	298 13.0%	0 0	132 12.5%	132 12.5%	166 13.3%	142 13.3%	84 15.8%G	72 10.3%	40 12.9%	41 13.4%	70 9.0%	52 11.8%	19 21.2%HIJK	59 22.0%HIJK	7 27.9%HIJK	12 11.8%	159 14.4%	140 11.6%
26% - 50%	430 18.7%	0 0	202 19.2%	202 19.2%	227 18.2%	204 19.2%	95 17.7%	131 18.6%	44 14.3%	55 18.0%K	160 20.7%HK	55 12.6%	20 21.8%HK	67 25.2%HIK	6 25.9%HIK	23 22.5%	197 17.9%	232 19.3%
51% - 75%	471 20.5%	0 0	165 15.6%	165 15.6%	306 24.5%BC	209 19.7%	88 16.4%	174 24.7%EF	61 19.7%N	46 15.1%	179 23.2%ILN	93 21.3%IN	15 16.7%N	54 20.3%N	2 8.2%	22 21.6%	227 20.6%	245 20.3%
76% - 100%	1075 46.7%	0 0	531 50.3%D	531 50.3%D	544 43.6%	496 46.6%	254 47.6%	325 46.1%	162 52.6%LMN	157 51.5%LMN	353 45.9%M	230 52.6%LMN	35 38.8%	85 31.8%	10 38.1%	44 43.1%	502 45.6%	573 47.7%
Don't Know/Refused	29 1.3%	0 0	26 2.4%D	26 2.4%D	4 0.3%	14 1.3%	13 2.5%G	2 0.3%	2 0.6%	6 2.0%	9 1.2%	8 1.8%	1 1.6%	2 0.7%	0 0	1 1.0%	17 1.6%	12 1.0%
Median	73.01	0	75.59	75.59	71.67	72.85	73.66E	72.96E	76.28JK	76.04JK	72.50	76.27J	66.38HIJKM	56.92J	48.69HIJKLM	70.36	72.33	73.65
Mean	67.13	0	68.00	68.00	66.40	66.71	66.05	68.55	69.79LMN	68.70LMN	68.39LMN	70.78LMN	60.24	56.35	55.02	66.62	66.06	68.10
Standard Deviation	27.98	0	28.59	28.59	27.45	28.12	29.95	26.17	27.97	29.09	26.00	26.85	31.19	29.52	34.53	27.19	28.53	27.44
Standard Error	0.59	0	0.85	0.85	0.81	0.88	1.20	1.05	1.50	1.68	1.29	1.37	1.78	1.75	2.85	2.71	0.83	0.83

Proportions/Means: Columns Tested (5% risk level) - A/B/D - C/D - E/F/G - H/I/J/K/L/M/N - P/Q
** very small base (under 30) ineligible for sig testing

Table 437
Page 1884

TABLE 47

Q8A2. What percent of the information that you use for your coursework comes from another source?

		RESPONDENT TYPE				INSTITUTION TYPE			DISCIPLINE								GENDER	
	TOTAL SAMPLE	FACULTY MEMBER	GRAD. STUDENT	FACULTY /GRAD	UNDER GRAD. STUDENT	PUBLIC	PRIVATE	LIBERAL ARTS	BIOLOGICAL SCIENCES	PHYSICAL SCIENCES /MATH	SOCIAL SCIENCES	ARTS AND HUMAN.	ENGI-NEERING	BUSINESS	LAW	UNDEC. MAJOR	MALE	FEMALE
		(A)	(B)	(C)	(D)	(E)	(F)	(G)	(H)	(I)	(J)	(K)	(L)	(M)	(N)		(P)	(Q)
Base - Student	2304	0**	1056	1056	1248	1065	534	705	308	305	771	437	90	266	25	102	1102	1202
25% or less	1230 53.4%	0 0	569 53.9%	569 53.9%	661 53.0%	562 52.8%	279 52.1%	389 55.2%	185 60.0%LMN	166 54.4%LMN	408 52.9%LM N	270 61.8%JL MN	41 44.9%	100 37.4%	11 42.2%	51 50.0%	578 52.4%	652 54.3%
26% - 50%	552 24.0%	0 0	236 22.4%	236 22.4%	316 25.3%	260 24.4%	114 21.3%	179 25.4%	60 19.4%	71 23.3%	212 27.6%HK N	76 17.4%	23 25.3%K	74 28.0%HK N	5 18.4%	31 30.4%	262 23.7%	291 24.2%
51% - 75%	244 10.6%	0 0	113 10.7%	113 10.7%	131 10.5%	106 10.0%	62 11.6%	76 10.8%	26 8.3%	29 9.5%	85 11.0%	43 9.7%	10 10.9%	38 14.3%H	4 15.0%H	11 10.8%	115 10.4%	129 10.8%
76% - 100%	244 10.6%	0 0	109 10.4%	109 10.4%	135 10.8%	121 11.4%G	67 12.6%G	56 7.9%	33 10.9%	31 10.2%	56 7.3%	40 9.2%	16 17.6%HIJ K	52 19.6%HI JK	6 24.5%HIJ K	9 8.8%	130 11.8%	115 9.5%
Don't Know/Refused	33 1.4%	0 0	28 2.7%D	28 2.7%D	5 0.4%	15 1.4%	13 2.4%G	5 0.6%	4 1.4%	8 2.6%	9 1.2%	8 1.8%	1 1.3%	2 0.7%	0 0	0 0	18 1.6%	15 1.2%
Median	21.99	0	19.46	19.46	23.30	22.28	21.27E	21.96	18.91J	18.96J	22.50	18.63	28.50HIJ KM	38.08HI JK	42.62HI JKLM	27.50	22.63	21.41
Mean	32.85	0	32.01	32.01	33.54	33.39	33.84	31.30	30.31	31.16	31.61	29.02	39.64HIJ K	43.66HI JK	44.98HI JK	33.78	33.86	31.93
Standard Deviation	27.95	0	28.58	28.58	27.41	28.14	29.93	26.06	27.89	28.98	26.00	26.79	31.20	29.52	34.53	27.37	28.51	27.41
Standard Error	0.59	0	0.85	0.85	0.81	0.88	1.20	1.04	1.50	1.68	1.29	1.37	1.78	1.75	2.85	2.71	0.83	0.83

Proportions/Means: Columns Tested (5% risk level) - A/B/D - C/D - E/F/G - H/I/J/K/L/M/N - P/Q
** very small base (under 30) ineligible for sig testing

Table 438
Page 1885

Outsell/Digital Library Federation Study (2002)
Weighted Tables

TABLE 48

S8C. What percent of your current information needs for your classes are available online?

		RESPONDENT TYPE				INSTITUTION TYPE		
	TOTAL SAMPLE	FACULTY MEMBER	GRAD. STUDENT	FACULTY /GRAD	UNDER GRAD. STUDENT	PUBLIC	PRIVATE	LIBERAL ARTS
		(A)	(B)	(C)	(D)	(E)	(F)	(G)
Base - Total Respondents	2304	0**	1056	1056	1248	1065	534	705
25% or less	490 21.3%	0 0	306 28.9%D	306 28.9%D	184 14.8%	236 22.2%	126 23.5%G	128 18.1%
26% - 50%	631 27.4%	0 0	300 28.4%	300 28.4%	331 26.5%	279 26.2%	147 27.5%	204 29.0%
51% - 75%	441 19.1%	0 0	179 16.9%	179 16.9%	262 21.0%B C	204 19.1%	94 17.6%	143 20.3%
76% - 100%	698 30.3%	0 0	243 23.0%	243 23.0%	455 36.4%B C	322 30.2%	156 29.3%	220 31.2%
Don't Know/Refused	45 2.0%	0 0	29 2.8%D	29 2.8%D	16 1.3%	24 2.2%	11 2.1%	10 1.4%
Median	55.29	0	46.84	46.84	66.17	55.31	49.34E	53.47
Mean	56.18	0	49.18	49.18	62.02B C	55.52	54.39	58.53F
Standard Deviation	29.32	0	29.86	29.86	27.55	29.93	29.60	28.07

	DISCIPLINE								GENDER	
	BIOLOGIAL SCIENCES	PHYSICAL SCIENCES /MATH	SOCIAL SCIENCES	ARTS AND HUMAN.	ENGI-NEERING	BUSINESS	LAW	UNDEC. MAJOR	MALE	FEMALE
	(H)	(I)	(J)	(K)	(L)	(M)	(N)		(P)	(Q)
Base - Total Respondents	308	305	771	437	90	266	25	102	1102	1202
25% or less	59 19.1%M	82 26.9%HM	162 21.0%M	123 28.2%HJ M	21 23.7%M	24 9.1%	8 33.3%HJL M	10 9.8%	246 22.3%	244 20.3%
26% - 50%	76 24.6%	78 25.6%	231 30.0%N	127 29.0%N	23 26.0%	62 23.4%	4 17.7%	29 28.4%	306 27.8%	324 27.0%
51% - 75%	70 22.9%KN	56 18.4%N	143 18.5%N	72 16.4%	17 18.9%N	61 23.1%KN	2 9.5%	19 18.6%	218 19.8%	223 18.5%
76% - 100%	99 32.0%IK	76 24.9%	227 29.5%	104 23.8%	26 29.2%	116 43.7%HI JKL	10 39.5%IJ KL	39 38.2%	305 27.7%	393 32.7%P
Don't Know/Refused	4 1.4%	13 4.3%HJMN	8 1.0%	11 2.6%	2 2.2%	2 0.7%	0 0	5 4.9%	27 2.4%	18 1.5%
Median	58.56JK	48.21J	49.53	47.57J	49.73HIJ KM	71.96HI JK	49.25HI JKLM	70.25	49.56	56.61
Mean	58.26IK	51.83	55.48K	50.50	54.86K	67.32HI JKLN	55.33	64.41	55.11	57.16
Standard Deviation	28.34	30.51	29.80	28.57	29.43	25.54	35.04	26.47	29.45	29.19

Proportions/Means: Columns Tested (5% risk level) - A/B/D - C/D - E/F/G - H/I/J/K/L/M/N - P/Q
** very small base (under 30) ineligible for sig testing

Table 442
Page 1889

TABLE 49

S8D1. And, what percent of your current information needs for your classes that are available online are available Through your institution's library web site?

		RESPONDENT TYPE				INSTITUTION TYPE			DISCIPLINE								GENDER	
	TOTAL SAMPLE	FACULTY MEMBER	GRAD. STUDENT	FACULTY /GRAD	UNDER GRAD. STUDENT	PUBLIC	PRIVATE	LIBERAL ARTS	BIOLOGIAL SCIENCES	PHYSICAL SCIENCES /MATH	SOCIAL SCIENCES	ARTS AND HUMAN.	ENGI- NEERING	BUSINESS	LAW	UNDEC. MAJOR	MALE	FEMALE
		(A)	(B)	(C)	(D)	(E)	(F)	(G)	(H)	(I)	(J)	(K)	(L)	(M)	(N)		(P)	(Q)
Base - At least one percent of current information needs for coursework are available online	2214	0**	991	991	1223	1018	509	687	303	278	748	417	87	261	24	96*	1053	1160
25% or less	320	0	177	177	143	164	74	82	39	44	115	54	16	41	9	3	156	164
	14.4%	0	17.8%D	17.8%D	11.7%	16.1%G	14.6%	11.9%	12.8%	15.8%	15.3%	12.9%	18.7%HK	15.7%	35.2%HIJ KLM	3.1%	14.8%	14.2%
26% - 50%	454	0	211	211	243	204	122	128	65	58	167	77	19	48	3	16	227	227
	20.5%	0	21.3%	21.3%	19.9%	20.0%	24.0%G	18.6%	21.5%N	20.9%N	22.4%N	18.5%	21.7%N	18.5%	12.7%	16.7%	21.5%	19.6%
51% - 75%	338	0	130	130	208	169	70	100	39	40	117	59	12	53	2	17	154	184
	15.3%	0	13.1%	13.1%	17.0%B C	16.6%	13.7%	14.5%	12.8%	14.4%N	15.6%N	14.2%N	13.7%N	20.3%HKL N	7.0%	17.7%	14.6%	15.9%
76% - 100%	1037	0	459	459	578	453	230	354	156	123	333	215	36	108	10	56	485	552
	46.8%	0	46.3%	46.3%	47.3%	44.5%	45.2%	51.5%EF	51.5%LM	44.2%	44.5%	51.6%JL M	41.8%	41.3%	43.0%	58.3%	46.0%	47.6%
Don't Know/Refused	65	0	14	14	50	28	13	23	4	13	17	11	3	11	1	4	32	33
	2.9%	0	1.4%	1.4%	4.1%BC	2.8%	2.5%	3.4%	1.5%	4.7%H	2.3%	2.7%	4.0%H	4.3%H	2.1%	4.2%	3.0%	2.8%
Median	74.40	0	71.61	71.61	74.80	73.58	71.44E	76.68E	76.04JK	72.21JK	70.83	76.41J	69.64HIJ KM	68.37JK	58.17HI JKM	79.55	74.16	74.08
Mean	66.95	0	64.79	64.79	68.74B C	65.18	66.02	70.28EF	69.17LMN	65.49N	65.62N	69.68LM N	62.15	63.75N	56.07	78.25	66.29	67.54
Standard Deviation	30.98	0	32.63	32.63	29.44	31.67	31.05	29.65	30.37	32.06	31.08	30.39	32.86	30.93	40.29	23.00	31.63	30.39

Proportions/Means: Columns Tested (5% risk level) - A/B/D - C/D - E/F/G - H/I/J/K/L/M/N - P/Q
* small base; ** very small base (under 30) ineligible for sig testing

Table 443
Page 1890

Outsell/Digital Library Federation Study (2002)
Weighted Tables

TABLE 50

S8D2. And, what percent of your current information needs for your classes that are available online are available Through the Internet?

		RESPONDENT TYPE				INSTITUTION TYPE			DISCIPLINE								GENDER	
	TOTAL SAMPLE	FACULTY MEMBER	GRAD. STUDENT	FACULTY /GRAD	UNDER GRAD. STUDENT	PUBLIC	PRIVATE	LIBERAL ARTS	BIOLOGIAL SCIENCES	PHYSICAL SCIENCES /MATH	SOCIAL SCIENCES	ARTS AND HUMAN.	ENGI-NEERING	BUSINESS	LAW	UNDEC. MAJOR	MALE	FEMALE
		(A)	(B)	(C)	(D)	(E)	(F)	(G)	(H)	(I)	(J)	(K)	(L)	(M)	(N)		(P)	(Q)
Base - At least one percent of current information needs for coursework are available online	2214	0**	991	991	1223	1018	509	687	303	278	748	417	87	261	24	96*	1053	1160
25% or less	411 18.6%	0 0	232 23.4%D	232 23.4%D	180 14.7%	202 19.9%G	109 21.3%G	101 14.7%	60 19.8%M	55 19.8%M	160 21.4%LM	82 19.6%M	13 15.1%	33 12.5%	3 14.1%	6 6.3%	183 17.4%	228 19.7%
26% - 50%	514 23.2%	0 0	247 25.0%	247 25.0%	267 21.8%	257 25.2%	114 22.3%	144 20.9%	77 25.6%	57 20.5%	180 24.1%	97 23.4%	22 25.8%	57 21.7%	5 19.7%	18 18.8%	261 24.7%	253 21.8%
51% - 75%	295 13.3%	0 0	107 10.8%	107 10.8%	188 15.4%B C	131 12.8%	58 11.3%	107 15.6%	34 11.3%N	41 14.7%N	94 12.6%N	62 14.8%N	13 15.1%N	42 16.0%N	1 4.9%	8 8.3%	147 14.0%	148 12.7%
76% - 100%	942 42.5%	0 0	386 38.9%	386 38.9%	556 45.5%B C	408 40.1%	217 42.6%	317 46.1%E	124 41.0%	119 42.8%	301 40.2%	158 37.9%	36 41.8%	128 49.1%HJ K	14 59.2%HI JKL	61 63.5%	443 42.0%	499 43.0%
Don't Know/Refused	52 2.3%	0 0	19 1.9%	19 1.9%	33 2.7%	20 2.0%	12 2.4%	19 2.7%	7 2.3%	6 2.2%	13 1.8%	18 4.3%JM	2 2.3%	2 0.7%	1 2.1%	3 3.1%	20 1.9%	32 2.7%
Median	69.66	0	55.71	55.71	74.45	62.82	67.60E	72.81E	65.00JK	70.95JK	64.17	65.00J	67.31HIJ KM	74.25HJ K	85.54HI JKM	87.05	69.62	68.46
Mean	63.07	0	58.84	58.84	66.53B C	60.92	61.97	67.11EF	60.94	64.54	60.18	61.10	63.94	68.63HJ K	72.19HI JKL	78.32	63.46	62.73
Standard Deviation	32.46	0	34.35	34.35	30.41	33.00	33.31	30.64	33.20	32.90	33.55	31.51	31.04	29.83	32.72	25.85	32.03	32.87

Proportions/Means: Columns Tested (5% risk level) - A/B/D - C/D - E/F/G - H/I/J/K/L/M/N - P/Q
* small base; ** very small base (under 30) ineligible for sig testing

Table 444
Page 1891

Outsell/Digital Library Federation Study (2002)
Weighted Tables

TABLE 51

Q9B. ALL/MOST SUMMARY TABLE

		RESPONDENT TYPE				INSTITUTION TYPE			DISCIPLINE									GENDER	
	TOTAL SAMPLE	FACULTY MEMBER	GRAD. STUDENT	FACULTY /GRAD	UNDER GRAD. STUDENT	PUBLIC	PRIVATE	LIBERAL ARTS	BIOLOGIAL SCIENCES	PHYSICAL SCIENCES /MATH	SOCIAL SCIENCES	ARTS AND HUMAN.	ENGI- NEERING	BUSINESS	LAW	UNDEC. MAJOR	MALE	FEMALE
		(A)	(B)	(C)	(D)	(E)	(F)	(G)	(H)	(I)	(J)	(K)	(L)	(M)	(N)		(P)	(Q)
Base - Faculty and graduate students who teach undergraduates	628	448	180	628	0**	252	216	161	99	145	160*	119	22*	81*	3**	0*	446	182
In handouts	375	265	111	375	0	133	126	116	60	82	96	85	10	41	1	0	260	115
	77.0%	74.9%	82.5%	77.0%	0	72.8%	75.9%	83.7%E	73.9%	74.5%	81.0%L	82.6%L	63.6%	72.1%	57.1%	0	75.0%	82.0%
On course web page	232	171	61	232	0	87	88	57	35	72	45	30	11	38	1	0	169	64
	67.2%	67.9%	65.4%	67.2%	0	64.2%	70.9%	66.7%	65.6%	71.3%	60.0%	64.3%	67.9%	74.5%	42.9%	0	66.8%	68.2%
In campus library on reserve	17	11	6	17	0	7	3	7	2	5	8	2	1	0	0	0	5	13
	64.8%	57.2%	85.8%	64.8%	0	87.4%	42.1%	64.7%	33.3%	71.4%	66.7%	100.0%	100.0%	0	0	0	33.0%	100.0%
In campus library in general holdings	6	3	3	6	0	3	3	0	2	1	2	0	0	1	0	0	3	3
	66.9%	49.4%	100.0%	66.9%	0	100.0%	59.5%	0	66.7%	100.0%	50.0%	0	0	100.0%	0	0	49.4%	100.0%
At a local bookstore	5	3	1	5	0	3	1	0	0	1	2	0	1	1	0	0	4	*
	70.1%	77.2%	56.3%	70.1%	0	63.4%	100.0%	0	0	33.3%	100.0%	0	100.0%	100.0%	0	0	68.7%	100.0%
On library e-reserve	4	4	0	4	0	2	1	1	1	0	0	1	0	2	0	0	2	2
	20.7%	25.9%	0	20.7%	0	30.0%	11.4%	33.1%	25.0%	0	0	100.0%	0	100.0%	0	0	13.7%	49.1%
At a copy center	4	2	2	4	0	2	2	0	0	0	4	0	0	0	0	0	2	2
	62.1%	62.7%	61.6%	62.1%	0	45.1%	100.0%	0	0	0	100.0%	0	0	0	0	0	45.1%	100.0%
On personalized information service	4	4	0	4	0	0	0	4	2	1	0	0	0	1	0	0	3	1
	80.7%	100.0%	0	80.7%	0	0	0	100.0%	66.7%	100.0%	0	0	0	100.0%	0	0	100.0%	53.2%
Through personal holdings	3	3	0	3	0	2	0	1	1	0	0	0	0	2	0	0	3	0
	36.1%	59.6%	0	36.1%	0	32.1%	0	100.0%	50.0%	0	0	0	0	50.0%	0	0	50.0%	0

Proportions/Means: Columns Tested (5% risk level) - A/B/D - C/D - E/F/G - H/I/J/K/L/M/N - P/Q
* small base; ** very small base (under 30) ineligible for sig testing

Table 482
Page 1950

Outsell/Digital Library Federation Study (2002)
Weighted Tables

TABLE 51, continued

Q9B. ALL/MOST SUMMARY TABLE

		RESPONDENT TYPE				INSTITUTION TYPE			DISCIPLINE									GENDER	
	TOTAL SAMPLE	FACULTY MEMBER	GRAD. STUDENT	FACULTY /GRAD	UNDER GRAD. STUDENT	PUBLIC	PRIVATE	LIBERAL ARTS	BIOLOGIAL SCIENCES	PHYSICAL SCIENCES /MATH	SOCIAL SCIENCES	ARTS AND HUMAN.	ENGI-NEERING	BUSINESS	LAW	UNDEC. MAJOR	MALE	FEMALE
		(A)	(B)	(C)	(D)	(E)	(F)	(G)	(H)	(I)	(J)	(K)	(L)	(M)	(N)		(P)	(Q)
Other	26 58.1%	21 64.9%	5 40.4%	26 58.1%	0 0	6 48.1%	8 51.0%	12 73.6%	4 62.5%	5 55.6%	8 80.0%	6 41.7%	1 66.7%	3 60.0%	0 0	0 0	18 63.0%	8 49.1%

Proportions/Means: Columns Tested (5% risk level) - A/B/D - C/D - E/F/G - H/I/J/K/L/M/N - P/Q
* small base; ** very small base (under 30) ineligible for sig testing

TABLE 52

Q9D. ALL/MOST SUMMARY TABLE

		RESPONDENT TYPE				INSTITUTION TYPE			DISCIPLINE									GENDER	
	TOTAL SAMPLE	FACULTY MEMBER	GRAD. STUDENT	FACULTY /GRAD	UNDER GRAD. STUDENT	PUBLIC	PRIVATE	LIBERAL ARTS	BIOLOGIAL SCIENCES	PHYSICAL SCIENCES /MATH	SOCIAL SCIENCES	ARTS AND HUMAN.	ENGI-NEERING	BUSINESS	LAW	UNDEC. MAJOR	MALE	FEMALE
		(A)	(B)	(C)	(D)	(E)	(F)	(G)	(H)	(I)	(J)	(K)	(L)	(M)	(N)		(P)	(Q)
Base - Faculty and graduate students who teach undergraduates	657	477	180	657	0**	265	230	162	107	151	167*	120	23*	85*	4**	0*	467	190
At a local bookstore	139 80.1%	108 81.3%	31 76.2%	139 80.1%	0 0	51 77.8%	49 84.6%	39 77.8%	13 78.9%	38 82.6%	39 75.0%	30 84.4%	5 88.9%	13 77.8%	1 100.0%	0 0	103 84.3%	36 70.1%
In Handouts	116 50.8%	84 49.7%	32 53.8%	116 50.8%	0 0	44 50.6%	42 56.7%	30 44.5%	31 60.3%I	17 37.0%	21 55.0%	24 44.7%	4 59.1%	20 58.3%	1 57.1%	0 0	87 49.5%	29 55.2%
In campus library on reserve	98 46.4%	67 41.2%	31 63.9%A	98 46.4%	0 0	35 56.2%G	34 48.4%	30 37.2%	13 40.5%	19 41.3%	32 51.5%	22 54.1%	4 54.2%	7 34.8%	* 33.3%	0 0	65 42.9%	33 55.3%
On course web page	86 58.0%	58 53.9%	28 69.2%	86 58.0%	0 0	37 60.4%	32 60.4%	17 50.0%	18 58.3%	22 62.9%	21 57.9%	7 35.3%	3 64.7%	15 69.6%	0 0	0 0	63 56.5%	23 62.7%
In campus library in general holdings	31 54.0%	20 44.7%	10 92.1%	31 54.0%	0 0	10 65.1%	15 51.6%	6 46.6%	3 33.3%	4 33.3%	11 75.0%	6 55.6%	1 71.4%	6 60.0%	0 0	0 0	23 50.0%	8 71.1%
Through personal holdings	12 65.0%	12 69.2%	0 0	12 65.0%	0 0	4 42.0%	5 82.0%	3 100.0%	1 100.0%	3 100.0%	2 50.0%	2 40.0%	* 50.0%	4 80.0%	0 0	0 0	7 61.6%	5 70.6%
On library e-reserve	8 33.8%	7 35.9%	1 22.7%	8 33.8%	0 0	4 59.0%	2 25.9%	2 20.0%	4 57.1%	2 50.0%	0 0	1 25.0%	* 33.3%	1 33.3%	* 100.0%	0 0	6 34.8%	2 31.3%
At a copy center	6 40.4%	2 26.1%	4 57.7%	6 40.4%	0 0	5 49.4%	1 23.0%	0 0	0 0	0 0	4 40.0%	1 50.0%	0 0	1 50.0%	0 0	0 0	3 31.0%	3 59.9%
On personalized information service	1 48.2%	1 48.2%	0 0	1 48.2%	0 0	1 100.0%	0 0	0 0	0 0	0 0	0 0	0 0	0 0	1 100.0%	0 0	0 0	1 48.2%	0 0

Proportions/Means: Columns Tested (5% risk level) - A/B/D - C/D - E/F/G - H/I/J/K/L/M/N - P/Q
* small base; ** very small base (under 30) ineligible for sig testing

Table 494
Page 1964

Outsell/Digital Library Federation Study (2002)
Weighted Tables

TABLE 52, continued

Q9D. ALL/MOST SUMMARY TABLE

		RESPONDENT TYPE				INSTITUTION TYPE			DISCIPLINE									GENDER	
	TOTAL SAMPLE	FACULTY MEMBER	GRAD. STUDENT	FACULTY /GRAD	UNDER GRAD. STUDENT	PUBLIC	PRIVATE	LIBERAL ARTS	BIOLOGIAL SCIENCES	PHYSICAL SCIENCES /MATH	SOCIAL SCIENCES	ARTS AND HUMAN.	ENGI-NEERING	BUSINESS	LAW	UNDEC. MAJOR	MALE	FEMALE
		(A)	(B)	(C)	(D)	(E)	(F)	(G)	(H)	(I)	(J)	(K)	(L)	(M)	(N)		(P)	(Q)
Other	26	16	10	26	0	11	12	4	3	10	4	6	*	4	*	0	15	11
	50.0%	45.2%	59.7%	50.0%	0	40.3%	74.5%	38.0%	37.5%	76.9%	25.0%	71.4%	33.3%	44.4%	100.0%	0	48.3%	52.8%

Proportions/Means: Columns Tested (5% risk level) - A/B/D - C/D - E/F/G - H/I/J/K/L/M/N - P/Q
* small base; ** very small base (under 30) ineligible for sig testing

TABLE 53

Q10B. ALL/MOST SUMMARY TABLE

		RESPONDENT TYPE				INSTITUTION TYPE			DISCIPLINE								GENDER	
	TOTAL SAMPLE	FACULTY MEMBER	GRAD. STUDENT	FACULTY /GRAD	UNDER GRAD. STUDENT	PUBLIC	PRIVATE	LIBERAL ARTS	BIOLOGIAL SCIENCES	PHYSICAL SCIENCES /MATH	SOCIAL SCIENCES	ARTS AND HUMAN.	ENGI-NEERING	BUSINESS	LAW	UNDEC. MAJOR	MALE	FEMALE
		(A)	(B)	(C)	(D)	(E)	(F)	(G)	(H)	(I)	(J)	(K)	(L)	(M)	(N)		(P)	(Q)
Base - Faculty who teach graduate students	235	235	0**	235	0**	116	108*	11**	42*	38*	68*	35*	13*	37*	2**	0*	197	38*
In Handouts	118	118	0	118	0	60	53	5	17	16	43	17	4	20	1	0	103	15
	73.8%	73.8%	0	73.8%	0	72.8%	74.1%	84.7%	57.6%	61.5%	88.5%	68.2%	57.7%	87.5%	100.0%	0	74.1%	72.2%
On course web page	77	77	0	77	0	37	36	4	14	13	24	2	5	18	1	0	63	14
	72.7%	72.7%	0	72.7%	0	71.2%	73.6%	78.7%	80.0%	81.3%	76.5%	33.3%	66.7%	70.4%	57.1%	0	73.2%	70.7%
In campus library on reserve	14	14	0	14	0	10	3	1	2	3	4	3	1	1	*	0	12	2
	53.0%	53.0%	0	53.0%	0	82.5%	22.9%	56.0%	40.0%	50.0%	66.7%	42.9%	75.0%	100.0%	100.0%	0	53.4%	50.6%
In campus library in general holdings	5	5	0	5	0	2	3	0	3	0	0	1	*	1	0	0	5	0
	44.2%	44.2%	0	44.2%	0	89.0%	30.6%	0	75.0%	0	0	33.3%	50.0%	100.0%	0	0	44.2%	0
At a local bookstore	5	5	0	5	0	2	0	3	0	1	2	0	1	1	*	0	5	0
	55.2%	55.2%	0	55.2%	0	40.1%	0	76.2%	0	100.0%	50.0%	0	75.0%	100.0%	100.0%	0	63.7%	0
On library e-reserve	4	4	0	4	0	2	1	1	3	0	0	0	0	1	0	0	2	2
	92.5%	92.5%	0	92.5%	0	100.0%	75.2%	100.0%	100.0%	0	0	0	0	100.0%	0	0	86.2%	100.0%
Through personal holdings	2	2	0	2	0	2	0	0	0	1	0	0	*	1	0	0	2	0
	70.5%	70.5%	0	70.5%	0	70.5%	0	0	0	100.0%	0	0	100.0%	50.0%	0	0	70.5%	0
On personalized information service	0	0	0	0	0	0	0	0	0	0	0	0	0	0	0	0	0	0
	0	0	0	0	0	0	0	0	0	0	0	0	0	0	0	0	0	0
At a copy center	0	0	0	0	0	0	0	0	0	0	0	0	0	0	0	0	0	0
	0	0	0	0	0	0	0	0	0	0	0	0	0	0	0	0	0	0
Other	4	4	0	4	0	*	3	1	2	0	0	1	*	1	*	0	3	2
	35.3%	35.3%	0	35.3%	0	8.3%	51.7%	100.0%	50.0%	0	0	100.0%	20.0%	33.3%	50.0%	0	30.9%	44.2%

Proportions/Means: Columns Tested (5% risk level) - A/B/D - C/D - E/F/G - H/I/J/K/L/M/N - P/Q
* small base; ** very small base (under 30) ineligible for sig testing

Table 507
Page 1979

Outsell/Digital Library Federation Study (2002)
Weighted Tables

TABLE 54
Q10D. ALL/MOST SUMMARY TABLE

		RESPONDENT TYPE				INSTITUTION TYPE			DISCIPLINE								GENDER	
	TOTAL SAMPLE	FACULTY MEMBER	GRAD. STUDENT	FACULTY /GRAD	UNDER GRAD. STUDENT	PUBLIC	PRIVATE	LIBERAL ARTS	BIOLOGIAL SCIENCES	PHYSICAL SCIENCES /MATH	SOCIAL SCIENCES	ARTS AND HUMAN.	ENGI-NEERING	BUSINESS	LAW	UNDEC. MAJOR	MALE	FEMALE
		(A)	(B)	(C)	(D)	(E)	(F)	(G)	(H)	(I)	(J)	(K)	(L)	(M)	(N)		(P)	(Q)
Base - Faculty who teach graduate students	235	235	0**	235	0**	116	108*	11**	42*	38*	68*	35*	13*	37*	2**	0*	197	38*
In Handouts	63 62.8%	63 62.8%	0 0	63 62.8%	0 0	26 53.8%	31 70.0%	6 76.2%	11 61.9%	9 60.0%	24 86.7%	4 30.8%	1 33.3%	12 59.1%	* 66.7%	0 0	53 61.4%	10 71.3%
At a local bookstore	34 76.7%	34 76.7%	0 0	34 76.7%	0 0	22 80.4%	10 72.7%	2 61.8%	2 100.0%	4 80.0%	13 70.0%	4 80.0%	3 84.6%	7 77.8%	1 100.0%	0 0	25 73.8%	8 87.1%
In campus library on reserve	33 52.1%	33 52.1%	0 0	33 52.1%	0 0	15 48.3%	17 58.1%	1 35.9%	8 75.0%	5 41.7%	9 50.0%	8 70.0%	2 42.9%	1 14.3%	* 100.0%	0 0	28 51.0%	5 59.1%
On course web page	27 49.3%	27 49.3%	0 0	27 49.3%	0 0	12 43.0%	14 58.3%	1 33.1%	8 64.3%	3 60.0%	8 36.4%	0 0	1 41.7%	7 58.3%	* 100.0%	0 0	25 53.7%	1 17.6%
In campus library in general holdings	19 54.3%	19 54.3%	0 0	19 54.3%	0 0	9 58.4%	10 51.4%	0 0	5 75.0%	0 0	8 80.0%	3 42.9%	1 30.0%	2 33.3%	* 50.0%	0 0	16 54.1%	3 55.4%
Through personal holdings	5 40.8%	5 40.8%	0 0	5 40.8%	0 0	4 80.6%	1 12.3%	0 0	1 100.0%	2 66.7%	0 0	0 0	* 50.0%	2 100.0%	0 0	0 0	3 30.3%	2 100.0%
On library e-reserve	2 15.0%	2 15.0%	0 0	2 15.0%	0 0	1 33.6%	1 11.5%	0 0	0 0	1 50.0%	0 0	0 0	0 0	1 100.0%	* 50.0%	0 0	2 20.6%	0 0
On personalized information service	0 0	0 0	0 0	0 0	0 0	0 0	0 0	0 0	0 0	0 0	0 0	0 0	0 0	0 0	0 0	0 0	0 0	0 0
At a copy center	0 0	0 0	0 0	0 0	0 0	0 0	0 0	0 0	0 0	0 0	0 0	0 0	0 0	0 0	0 0	0 0	0 0	0 0
Other	5 37.3%	5 37.3%	0 0	5 37.3%	0 0	3 35.8%	2 39.1%	0 0	0 0	1 25.0%	0 0	2 100.0%	1 100.0%	1 50.0%	* 100.0%	0 0	4 33.2%	1 58.1%

Proportions/Means: Columns Tested (5% risk level) - A/B/D - C/D - E/F/G - H/I/J/K/L/M/N - P/Q
* small base; ** very small base (under 30) ineligible for sig testing

Table 519
Page 1992

Outsell/Digital Library Federation Study (2002)
Weighted Tables

TABLE 55

Q11B. ALL/MOST SUMMARY TABLE

		RESPONDENT TYPE				INSTITUTION TYPE			DISCIPLINE									GENDER	
	TOTAL SAMPLE	FACULTY MEMBER	GRAD. STUDENT	FACULTY /GRAD	UNDER GRAD. STUDENT	PUBLIC	PRIVATE	LIBERAL ARTS	BIOLOGIAL SCIENCES	PHYSICAL SCIENCES /MATH	SOCIAL SCIENCES	ARTS AND HUMAN.	ENGI-NEERING	BUSINESS	LAW	UNDEC. MAJOR	MALE	FEMALE
		(A)	(B)	(C)	(D)	(E)	(F)	(G)	(H)	(I)	(J)	(K)	(L)	(M)	(N)		(P)	(Q)
Base - Students	1165	0**	526	526	639	532	273	360	143	160	389	226	48	138	12*	50*	552	614
In Handouts	686 83.1%	0 0	304 79.3%	304 79.3%	382 86.3%B C	270 80.0%	167 82.5%	250 87.1%E	90 82.3%	101 82.8%	235 87.4%K	137 77.7%	21 83.7%	66 79.8%	6 76.6%	31 88.6%	318 81.0%	369 84.9%
On course web page	517 68.3%	0 0	189 64.5%	189 64.5%	327 70.7%	211 69.7%	123 67.2%	183 67.5%	66 71.4%N	77 64.2%	147 67.8%	78 59.3%	27 72.1%KN	92 82.5%HI JKLN	4 54.2%	25 65.8%	250 71.2%	266 65.8%
In campus library on reserve	41 48.3%	0 0	22 48.8%	22 48.8%	19 47.7%	20 54.8%	11 40.7%	11 46.5%	4 45.5%	5 50.0%	19 47.6%	11 52.6%	1 37.5%	0 0	* 100.0%	1 50.0%	26 60.4%	16 36.1%
In campus library in general holdings	26 70.1%	0 0	18 75.1%	18 75.1%	8 60.4%	14 67.4%	9 79.4%	3 61.5%	1 100.0%	6 66.7%	9 62.5%	7 85.7%	1 80.0%	1 50.0%	1 100.0%	0 0	15 65.4%	10 78.6%
At a local bookstore	14 49.4%	0 0	9 44.5%	9 44.5%	5 61.4%	7 48.0%	4 50.6%	2 52.2%	0 0	1 100.0%	8 57.1%	3 50.0%	1 66.7%	1 20.0%	* 100.0%	0 0	8 78.3%	6 33.1%
Through personal holdings	8 74.3%	0 0	2 47.0%	2 47.0%	6 91.1%	3 51.4%	4 100.0%	1 100.0%	1 100.0%	2 66.7%	0 0	1 50.0%	0 0	3 100.0%	0 0	1 100.0%	4 92.9%	4 62.3%
On library e-reserve	6 18.7%	0 0	1 6.3%	1 6.3%	5 34.8%	3 17.9%	1 11.1%	2 30.3%	1 20.0%	1 33.3%	2 14.3%	1 10.0%	* 100.0%	0 0	0 0	1 100.0%	4 19.2%	2 17.5%
At a copy center	6 40.0%	0 0	4 32.7%	4 32.7%	2 67.2%	5 39.6%	0 0	1 100.0%	0 0	0 0	4 66.7%	1 33.3%	0 0	1 33.3%	0 0	0 0	2 26.9%	4 54.4%
On personalized information service	5 46.7%	0 0	2 42.6%	2 42.6%	3 50.0%	3 41.2%	1 100.0%	1 45.4%	2 66.7%	1 50.0%	0 0	1 50.0%	* 100.0%	1 50.0%	0 0	0 0	1 20.0%	4 77.8%
Other	21 49.5%	0 0	11 50.0%	11 50.0%	10 49.1%	14 56.4%	4 41.0%	3 37.7%	4 50.0%	4 80.0%	6 37.5%	3 37.5%	2 70.0%	1 100.0%	1 61.5%	0 0	8 49.2%	12 49.7%

Proportions/Means: Columns Tested (5% risk level) - A/B/D - C/D - E/F/G - H/I/J/K/L/M/N - P/Q
* small base; ** very small base (under 30) ineligible for sig testing

Table 532
Page 2006

Outsell/Digital Library Federation Study (2002)
Weighted Tables

TABLE 56

Q11D. ALL/MOST SUMMARY TABLE

		RESPONDENT TYPE				INSTITUTION TYPE			DISCIPLINE									GENDER	
	TOTAL SAMPLE	FACULTY MEMBER	GRAD. STUDENT	FACULTY /GRAD	UNDER GRAD. STUDENT	PUBLIC	PRIVATE	LIBERAL ARTS	BIOLOGIAL SCIENCES	PHYSICAL SCIENCES /MATH	SOCIAL SCIENCES	ARTS AND HUMAN.	ENGI-NEERING	BUSINESS	LAW	UNDEC. MAJOR	MALE	FEMALE
		(A)	(B)	(C)	(D)	(E)	(F)	(G)	(H)	(I)	(J)	(K)	(L)	(M)	(N)		(P)	(Q)
Base - Students	1165	0**	526	526	639	532	273	360	143	160	389	226	48	138	12*	50*	552	614
At a local bookstore	258 82.0%	0 0	76 68.6%	76 68.6%	182 89.3%B C	87 73.8%	47 78.4%	124 90.6%EF	24 77.1%	27 71.1%	85 84.9%	64 85.1%	10 78.6%	30 78.0%	4 92.9%	15 93.8%	112 81.5%	146 82.4%
In campus library on reserve	241 59.5%	0 0	115 61.1%	115 61.1%	126 58.2%	96 65.7%	58 58.1%	87 54.7%	30 60.7%	39 68.4%	86 59.7%	50 54.9%	9 68.2%	16 56.7%	1 50.0%	9 50.0%	112 59.4%	128 59.6%
In Handouts	221 59.7%	0 0	103 56.9%	103 56.9%	117 62.4%	83 55.8%	61 58.8%	77 65.5%	38 65.2%	30 66.7%	64 53.1%	45 58.8%	8 59.6%	28 71.4%	1 46.2%	7 46.7%	96 59.2%	124 60.1%
On course web page	157 46.5%	0 0	74 51.5%	74 51.5%	83 42.8%	76 48.1%	40 51.4%	41 40.1%	23 48.1%	23 51.1%	45 43.6%	20 42.9%	7 47.2%	29 50.0%	2 47.8%	8 44.4%	76 47.9%	81 45.3%
In campus library in general holdings	120 63.2%	0 0	61 65.2%	61 65.2%	59 61.3%	59 66.3%	28 63.5%	33 58.1%	16 60.0%	20 66.7%	34 60.0%	27 64.9%	8 61.9%	9 71.4%	1 66.7%	5 62.5%	63 62.7%	57 63.8%
On library e-reserve	22 31.6%	0 0	6 23.1%	6 23.1%	15 37.4%	11 36.7%	2 12.9%	9 36.0%	4 45.5%	0 0	11 40.0%	3 18.8%	0 0	3 37.5%	0 0	0 0	9 26.7%	13 36.1%
At a copy center	15 45.4%	0 0	14 53.5%	14 53.5%	1 14.5%	8 43.9%	7 53.8%	0 0	1 50.0%	1 33.3%	9 55.6%	2 50.0%	1 66.7%	1 16.7%	0 0	0 0	6 50.1%	9 42.4%
Through personal holdings	6 50.8%	0 0	4 50.8%	4 50.8%	2 50.9%	3 47.5%	2 57.1%	1 50.0%	3 75.0%	1 50.0%	2 100.0%	0 0	0 0	0 0	0 0	0 0	4 74.5%	2 30.3%
On personalized information service	3 53.2%	0 0	1 30.6%	1 30.6%	3 71.7%	3 55.8%	1 100.0%	0 0	1 100.0%	0 0	0 0	2 100.0%	* 100.0%	0 0	0 0	0 0	3 55.8%	1 46.8%
Other	88 68.5%	0 0	33 65.4%	33 65.4%	55 70.5%	38 72.0%	20 69.7%	31 63.8%	6 53.8%	17 70.8%	32 85.0%	16 48.3%	2 70.0%	11 80.0%	1 80.0%	3 60.0%	34 69.0%	55 68.1%

Proportions/Means: Columns Tested (5% risk level) - A/B/D - C/D - E/F/G - H/I/J/K/L/M/N - P/Q
* small base; ** very small base (under 30) ineligible for sig testing

Table 544
Page 2019

Outsell/Digital Library Federation Study (2002)
Weighted Tables

TABLE 57

Q9E. How many additional course readings, beyond what you make available, do your undergraduate students need to access to meet the requirements of their class? Would you say they have to independently find:

	TOTAL SAMPLE	RESPONDENT TYPE: FACULTY MEMBER	GRAD. STUDENT	FACULTY /GRAD	UNDER GRAD. STUDENT	INSTITUTION TYPE: PUBLIC	PRIVATE	LIBERAL ARTS	DISCIPLINE: BIOLOGIAL SCIENCES	PHYSICAL SCIENCES /MATH	SOCIAL SCIENCES	ARTS AND HUMAN.	ENGI-NEERING	BUSINESS	LAW	UNDEC. MAJOR	GENDER: MALE	FEMALE
		(A)	(B)	(C)	(D)	(E)	(F)	(G)	(H)	(I)	(J)	(K)	(L)	(M)	(N)		(P)	(Q)
Base - Faculty and graduate students who teach undergraduates	628	448	180	628	0**	252	216	161	99	145	160*	119	22*	81*	3**	0*	446	182
NET ALL/MOST	65 10.3%	49 10.8%	16 9.0%	65 10.3%	0 0	20 8.0%	29 13.6%	15 9.5%	10 9.7%	13 9.0%	21 12.9%	10 8.5%	2 8.0%	9 11.5%	* 12.5%	0 0	49 10.9%	16 8.8%
All of the course readings	12 2.0%	9 2.1%	3 1.6%	12 2.0%	0 0	5 2.1%	2 1.0%	5 3.0%	0 0	2 1.4%	4 2.4%	3 2.8%	* 1.3%	3 3.4%	* 6.3%	0 0	12 2.8%Q	0 0
Most of the course readings	52 8.3%	39 8.7%	13 7.4%	52 8.3%	0 0	15 5.9%	27 12.6%E	10 6.5%	10 9.7%	11 7.6%	17 10.6%	7 5.7%	1 6.7%	7 8.0%	* 6.3%	0 0	36 8.1%	16 8.8%
Some of the course readings	268 42.6%	201 44.8%	67 37.1%	268 42.6%	0 0	102 40.3%	80 37.1%	86 53.5%EF	54 54.0%KL	61 42.1%L	66 41.2%	45 37.7%	6 28.0%	34 42.5%	2 68.7%	0 0	192 43.1%	75 41.3%
None of the course readings, it is all there for them	280 44.6%	190 42.3%	91 50.3%	280 44.6%	0 0	125 49.6%G	101 46.8%G	54 33.7%	36 36.3%	68 46.9%	70 43.5%	57 48.1%	14 62.7%HIJ M	35 43.7%	1 18.7%	0 0	195 43.7%	85 46.8%
DK/Refused	16 2.5%	9 2.0%	7 3.7%	16 2.5%	0 0	5 2.0%	5 2.5%	5 3.2%	0 0	3 2.1%	4 2.4%	7 5.7%H	* 1.3%	2 2.3%	0 0	0 0	10 2.3%	5 3.0%

Proportions/Means: Columns Tested (5% risk level) - A/B/D - C/D - E/F/G - H/I/J/K/L/M/N - P/Q
* small base; ** very small base (under 30) ineligible for sig testing

Table 495
Page 1966

Outsell/Digital Library Federation Study (2002)
Weighted Tables

TABLE 58

Q10E. How many additional course readings, beyond what you make available, do your graduate students need to access to meet the requirements of their class? Would you say they have to independently find:

		RESPONDENT TYPE				INSTITUTION TYPE			DISCIPLINE									GENDER	
	TOTAL SAMPLE	FACULTY MEMBER	GRAD. STUDENT	FACULTY /GRAD	UNDER GRAD. STUDENT	PUBLIC	PRIVATE	LIBERAL ARTS	BIOLOGIAL SCIENCES	PHYSICAL SCIENCES /MATH	SOCIAL SCIENCES	ARTS AND HUMAN.	ENGI-NEERING	BUSINESS	LAW	UNDEC. MAJOR	MALE	FEMALE
		(A)	(B)	(C)	(D)	(E)	(F)	(G)	(H)	(I)	(J)	(K)	(L)	(M)	(N)		(P)	(Q)
Base - Faculty who teach graduate students	235	235	0**	235	0**	116	108*	11**	42*	38*	68*	35*	13*	37*	2**	0*	197	38*
NET ALL/MOST	46 19.4%	46 19.4%	0 0	46 19.4%	0 0	17 14.5%	28 25.7%	1 8.8%	8 18.8%I	1 2.6%	21 30.6%I	9 25.8%I	2 15.6%I	5 12.5%	* 18.2%	0 0	36 18.2%	10 25.8%
All of the course readings	14 5.8%	14 5.8%	0 0	14 5.8%	0 0	3 2.5%	10 9.0%	1 8.8%	0 0	0 0	8 11.1%	3 9.7%H	1 6.7%HI	2 5.0%	0 0	0 0	12 5.9%	2 5.0%
Most of the course readings	32 13.6%	32 13.6%	0 0	32 13.6%	0 0	14 12.0%	18 16.7%	0 0	8 18.8%I	1 2.6%	13 19.4%I	6 16.1%	1 8.9%	3 7.5%	* 18.2%	0 0	24 12.3%	8 20.8%
Some of the course readings	116 49.4%	116 49.4%	0 0	116 49.4%	0 0	60 51.5%	50 45.9%	7 62.8%	22 52.1%	24 63.2%K	28 41.7%	13 38.7%	8 57.8%	20 52.5%	1 72.7%	0 0	97 49.3%	19 50.3%
None of the course readings, it is all there for them	68 29.1%	68 29.1%	0 0	68 29.1%	0 0	38 32.3%	28 25.6%	3 28.4%	11 27.1%	12 31.6%	17 25.0%	11 32.3%	3 26.7%	13 35.0%	* 9.1%	0 0	59 30.1%	9 23.9%
DK/Refused	5 2.1%	5 2.1%	0 0	5 2.1%	0 0	2 1.6%	3 2.8%	0 0	1 2.1%	1 2.6%	2 2.8%	1 3.2%	0 0	0 0	0 0	0 0	5 2.5%	0 0

Proportions/Means: Columns Tested (5% risk level) - A/B/D - C/D - E/F/G - H/I/J/K/L/M/N - P/Q
* small base; ** very small base (under 30) ineligible for sig testing

Table 520
Page 1993

TABLE 59

Q11E. How many additional course readings, beyond what your instructors make available, do you need to access to meet the requirements of your classes? Would you say you have to independently find:

		RESPONDENT TYPE				INSTITUTION TYPE			DISCIPLINE								GENDER	
	TOTAL SAMPLE	FACULTY MEMBER	GRAD. STUDENT	FACULTY /GRAD	UNDER GRAD. STUDENT	PUBLIC	PRIVATE	LIBERAL ARTS	BIOLOGIAL SCIENCES	PHYSICAL SCIENCES /MATH	SOCIAL SCIENCES	ARTS AND HUMAN.	ENGI-NEERING	BUSINESS	LAW	UNDEC. MAJOR	MALE	FEMALE
		(A)	(B)	(C)	(D)	(E)	(F)	(G)	(H)	(I)	(J)	(K)	(L)	(M)	(N)		(P)	(Q)
Base - Students	1165	0**	526	526	639	532	273	360	143	160	389	226	48	138	12*	50*	552	614
NET ALL/MOST	158 13.6%	0 0	92 17.6%D	92 17.6%D	66 10.3%	93 17.6%G	44 16.3%G	21 5.7%	26 17.9%I	16 10.0%	58 15.0%	28 12.4%	8 16.4%	15 10.8%	2 15.7%	6 12.0%	72 13.1%	86 14.0%
All of the course readings	34 2.9%	0 0	15 2.8%	15 2.8%	20 3.1%	19 3.6%	5 1.8%	10 2.8%	9 6.2%JM	5 3.1%	9 2.4%	7 3.0%	2 4.2%	2 1.4%	1 4.3%	0 0	14 2.6%	20 3.3%
Most of the course readings	124 10.6%	0 0	78 14.8%D	78 14.8%D	46 7.3%	74 13.9%G	40 14.5%G	11 2.9%	17 11.7%	11 6.9%	49 12.6%	21 9.4%	6 12.1%	13 9.5%	1 11.4%	6 12.0%	58 10.6%	66 10.7%
Some of the course readings	644 55.3%	0 0	288 54.7%	288 54.7%	356 55.7%	281 52.8%	162 59.2%	202 56.0%	74 51.9%	85 53.1%	227 58.5%	123 54.5%	25 52.1%	76 55.4%	5 45.7%	28 56.0%	316 57.3%	328 53.5%
None of the course readings, it is all there for them	351 30.1%	0 0	134 25.4%	134 25.4%	217 33.9%B C	149 28.0%	64 23.4%	138 38.3%EF	42 29.6%	56 35.0%J	100 25.6%	71 31.2%	15 31.5%	47 33.8%	5 38.6%J	16 32.0%	156 28.3%	195 31.7%
DK/Refused	12 1.0%	0 0	12 2.3%D	12 2.3%D	0 0	9 1.7%G	3 1.2%	0 0	1 0.6%	3 1.9%	4 1.0%	4 2.0%	0 0	0 0	0 0	0 0	7 1.3%	5 0.8%

Proportions/Means: Columns Tested (5% risk level) - A/B/D - C/D - E/F/G - H/I/J/K/L/M/N - P/Q
* small base; ** very small base (under 30) ineligible for sig testing

Table 545
Page 2020

TABLE 60

Q12A/B. SUMMARY TABLE

	RESPONDENT TYPE				INSTITUTION TYPE			DISCIPLINE									GENDER	
	TOTAL SAMPLE	FACULTY MEMBER	GRAD. STUDENT	FACULTY /GRAD	UNDER GRAD. STUDENT	PUBLIC	PRIVATE	LIBERAL ARTS	BIOLOGIAL SCIENCES	PHYSICAL SCIENCES /MATH	SOCIAL SCIENCES	ARTS AND HUMAN.	ENGI-NEERING	BUSINESS	LAW	UNDEC. MAJOR	MALE	FEMALE
		(A)	(B)	(C)	(D)	(E)	(F)	(G)	(H)	(I)	(J)	(K)	(L)	(M)	(N)		(P)	(Q)
Base - Total Responding	1642	477	526	1003	639	678	442	523	226	274	493	305	65	215	15*	50*	926	716
Your own institution's physical academic library and all its resources	547 33.3%	155 32.4%	167 31.7%	321 32.0%	225 35.2%	218 32.1%	138 31.3%	191 36.5%	71 31.5%M	95 34.7%M	180 36.6%M	115 37.9%M	19 29.6%	50 23.4%	4 26.4%	11 22.0%	327 35.3%	219 30.6%
Rely on	547 33.3%	155 32.4%	167 31.7%	321 32.0%	225 35.2%	218 32.1%	138 31.3%	191 36.5%	71 31.5%M	95 34.7%M	180 36.6%M	115 37.9%M	19 29.6%	50 23.4%	4 26.4%	11 22.0%	327 35.3%	219 30.6%
Most important	539 32.8%	147 30.9%	167 31.7%	314 31.3%	225 35.2%	217 32.0%	138 31.2%	185 35.3%	70 31.1%M	92 33.6%M	180 36.6%M	114 37.5%M	19 29.1%	48 22.5%	4 26.4%	11 22.0%	320 34.6%	219 30.6%
Open Internet	493 30.0%	120 25.1%	129 24.5%	249 24.8%	244 38.2%A BC	181 26.8%	127 28.6%	185 35.3%EF	62 27.2%	79 28.8%	135 27.5%	94 30.9%	16 24.2%	83 38.5%HI JL	5 33.0%	19 38.0%	262 28.3%	231 32.2%
Rely on	493 30.0%	120 25.1%	129 24.5%	249 24.8%	244 38.2%A BC	181 26.8%	127 28.6%	185 35.3%EF	62 27.2%	79 28.8%	135 27.5%	94 30.9%	16 24.2%	83 38.5%HI JL	5 33.0%	19 38.0%	262 28.3%	231 32.2%
Most important	471 28.7%	102 21.4%	126 23.9%	228 22.7%	243 38.0%A BC	177 26.2%	118 26.7%	176 33.6%EF	57 25.3%	74 27.0%	132 26.7%	88 29.0%	15 22.9%	81 37.7%HI JKL	5 33.0%	19 38.0%	245 26.5%	226 31.5%P
Personal library/ files, including personal journal subscriptions	480 29.2%	269 56.4%BD	134 25.5%D	403 40.2%D	77 12.0%	174 25.6%	163 37.0%EG	143 27.3%	66 29.2%	82 29.9%	149 30.2%	94 30.9%	18 27.4%	60 27.7%	5 30.8%	7 14.0%	320 34.5%Q	160 22.3%

Proportions/Means: Columns Tested (5% risk level) - A/B/D - C/D - E/F/G - H/I/J/K/L/M/N - P/Q

* small base

Table 548
Page 2027

Outsell/Digital Library Federation Study (2002)
Weighted Tables

TABLE 60, continued

Q12A/B. SUMMARY TABLE

	TOTAL SAMPLE	RESPONDENT TYPE: FACULTY MEMBER (A)	GRAD. STUDENT (B)	FACULTY /GRAD (C)	UNDER GRAD. STUDENT (D)	INSTITUTION TYPE: PUBLIC (E)	PRIVATE (F)	LIBERAL ARTS (G)	DISCIPLINE: BIOLOGIAL SCIENCES (H)	PHYSICAL SCIENCES /MATH (I)	SOCIAL SCIENCES (J)	ARTS AND HUMAN. (K)	ENGI-NEERING (L)	BUSINESS (M)	LAW (N)	UNDEC. MAJOR	GENDER: MALE (P)	FEMALE (Q)
Base - Total Responding	1642	477	526	1003	639	678	442	523	226	274	493	305	65	215	15*	50*	926	716
Rely on	480 29.2%	269 56.4%BD	134 25.5%D	403 40.2%D	77 12.0%	174 25.6%	163 37.0%EG	143 27.3%	66 29.2%	82 29.9%	149 30.2%	94 30.9%	18 27.4%	60 27.7%	5 30.8%	7 14.0%	320 34.5%Q	160 22.3%
Most important	469 28.5%	267 55.9%BD	130 24.7%D	397 39.6%D	72 11.2%	171 25.3%	159 35.9%EG	139 26.5%	66 29.2%	82 29.9%	145 29.4%	91 29.8%	17 26.0%	57 26.4%	5 29.7%	7 14.0%	312 33.7%Q	157 21.9%
Professional meetings	164 10.0%	118 24.7%BD	38 7.2%D	156 15.5%D	8 1.3%	54 8.0%	66 14.8%EG	44 8.5%	22 9.7%	35 12.8%	41 8.4%	32 10.7%	11 16.6%HJK MN	21 10.0%	1 5.5%	0 0	115 12.4%Q	49 6.9%
Rely on	164 10.0%	118 24.7%BD	38 7.2%D	156 15.5%D	8 1.3%	54 8.0%	66 14.8%EG	44 8.5%	22 9.7%	35 12.8%	41 8.4%	32 10.7%	11 16.6%HJK MN	21 10.0%	1 5.5%	0 0	115 12.4%Q	49 6.9%
Most important	148 9.0%	105 22.1%BD	36 6.9%D	142 14.1%D	6 0.9%	50 7.4%	59 13.2%EG	39 7.5%	22 9.7%	31 11.3%	39 8.0%	27 8.8%	10 15.2%JKMN	18 8.2%	1 4.4%	0 0	102 11.1%Q	45 6.3%
Online databases	146 8.9%	42 8.9%D	69 13.1%D	111 11.1%D	35 5.5%	57 8.4%	56 12.7%EG	33 6.4%	34 15.2%IJKM	25 9.1%M	47 9.5%M	19 6.3%	6 9.0%M	8 3.9%	4 24.2%HIJ KLM	3 6.0%	75 8.1%	72 10.0%
Rely on	146 8.9%	42 8.9%D	69 13.1%D	111 11.1%D	35 5.5%	57 8.4%	56 12.7%EG	33 6.4%	34 15.2%IJKM	25 9.1%M	47 9.5%M	19 6.3%	6 9.0%M	8 3.9%	4 24.2%HIJ KLM	3 6.0%	75 8.1%	72 10.0%
Most important	141 8.6%	40 8.4%D	68 13.0%AD	109 10.8%D	32 5.1%	55 8.2%	53 12.0%G	32 6.2%	33 14.8%IKLM	25 9.1%M	47 9.5%M	17 5.5%	6 8.5%M	7 3.5%	4 24.2%HIJ KLM	2 4.0%	72 7.8%	69 9.6%

Proportions/Means: Columns Tested (5% risk level) - A/B/D - C/D - E/F/G - H/I/J/K/L/M/N - P/Q
* small base

Table 548
Page 2028

Outsell/Digital Library Federation Study (2002)
Weighted Tables

TABLE 60, continued

Q12A/B. SUMMARY TABLE

		RESPONDENT TYPE				INSTITUTION TYPE			DISCIPLINE								GENDER	
	TOTAL SAMPLE	FACULTY MEMBER	GRAD. STUDENT	FACULTY /GRAD	UNDER GRAD. STUDENT	PUBLIC	PRIVATE	LIBERAL ARTS	BIOLOGIAL SCIENCES	PHYSICAL SCIENCES /MATH	SOCIAL SCIENCES	ARTS AND HUMAN.	ENGI- NEERING	BUSINESS	LAW	UNDEC. MAJOR	MALE	FEMALE
		(A)	(B)	(C)	(D)	(E)	(F)	(G)	(H)	(I)	(J)	(K)	(L)	(M)	(N)		(P)	(Q)
Base - Total Responding	1642	477	526	1003	639	678	442	523	226	274	493	305	65	215	15*	50*	926	716
Colleagues/peers inside your institution	136 8.3%	49 10.2%D	59 11.2%D	107 10.7%D	29 4.5%	53 7.8%	44 10.0%	39 7.5%	16 7.0%	26 9.5%J	23 4.6%	45 14.7%HJ M	8 11.7%J	18 8.2%	2 12.1%J	0 0	79 8.5%	58 8.1%
Rely on	136 8.3%	49 10.2%D	59 11.2%D	107 10.7%D	29 4.5%	53 7.8%	44 10.0%	39 7.5%	16 7.0%	26 9.5%J	23 4.6%	45 14.7%HJ M	8 11.7%J	18 8.2%	2 12.1%J	0 0	79 8.5%	58 8.1%
Most important	125 7.6%	39 8.3%D	58 11.0%D	97 9.7%D	28 4.3%	51 7.5%	39 8.8%	35 6.7%	15 6.6%	23 8.4%	23 4.6%	41 13.6%HJ M	7 11.2%J	14 6.5%	2 11.0%J	0 0	70 7.6%	55 7.7%
Your own institution's academic library resources on the library web page	132 8.1%	36 7.4%	51 9.7%	87 8.6%	46 7.1%	65 9.6%	32 7.4%	35 6.7%	19 8.6%	27 9.9%	32 6.5%	22 7.4%	6 8.5%	20 9.1%	2 9.9%	5 10.0%	82 8.8%	51 7.1%
Rely on	132 8.1%	36 7.4%	51 9.7%	87 8.6%	46 7.1%	65 9.6%	32 7.4%	35 6.7%	19 8.6%	27 9.9%	32 6.5%	22 7.4%	6 8.5%	20 9.1%	2 9.9%	5 10.0%	82 8.8%	51 7.1%
Most important	121 7.4%	27 5.6%	51 9.7%A	78 7.8%	43 6.7%	64 9.4%G	28 6.3%	29 5.5%	18 7.8%	24 8.8%	28 5.7%	22 7.4%	6 8.5%	18 8.2%	1 8.8%	4 8.0%	74 8.0%	47 6.6%
Department web page	79 4.8%	10 2.0%	30 5.6%A	39 3.9%	40 6.2%A	39 5.8%	22 5.0%	18 3.5%	11 5.1%	11 4.0%	24 5.0%	15 4.8%	4 6.3%	9 4.3%	1 3.3%	4 8.0%	48 5.2%	32 4.4%
Rely on	79 4.8%	10 2.0%	30 5.6%A	39 3.9%	40 6.2%A	39 5.8%	22 5.0%	18 3.5%	11 5.1%	11 4.0%	24 5.0%	15 4.8%	4 6.3%	9 4.3%	1 3.3%	4 8.0%	48 5.2%	32 4.4%

Proportions/Means: Columns Tested (5% risk level) - A/B/D - C/D - E/F/G - H/I/J/K/L/M/N - P/Q
* small base

Table 548
Page 2029

TABLE 60, continued

Q12A/B. SUMMARY TABLE

		RESPONDENT TYPE				INSTITUTION TYPE			DISCIPLINE									GENDER	
	TOTAL SAMPLE	FACULTY MEMBER	GRAD. STUDENT	FACULTY /GRAD	UNDER GRAD. STUDENT	PUBLIC	PRIVATE	LIBERAL ARTS	BIOLOGIAL SCIENCES	PHYSICAL SCIENCES /MATH	SOCIAL SCIENCES	ARTS AND HUMAN.	ENGI-NEERING	BUSINESS	LAW	UNDEC. MAJOR	MALE	FEMALE
		(A)	(B)	(C)	(D)	(E)	(F)	(G)	(H)	(I)	(J)	(K)	(L)	(M)	(N)		(P)	(Q)
Base - Total Responding	1642	477	526	1003	639	678	442	523	226	274	493	305	65	215	15*	50*	926	716
Most important	78 4.8%	9 2.0%	30 5.6%A	39 3.9%	39 6.1%A	39 5.8%	21 4.7%	18 3.5%	11 4.7%	11 4.0%	24 5.0%	15 4.8%	4 5.8%	9 4.3%	1 3.3%	4 8.0%	47 5.1%	31 4.3%
Colleagues/peers outside your institution	73 4.5%	52 10.9%BD	13 2.6%	65 6.5%D	8 1.3%	17 2.5%	28 6.3%E	28 5.4%E	10 4.3%	19 6.9%J	11 2.3%	19 6.3%J	4 5.8%J	10 4.8%	* 2.2%	0 0	50 5.4%Q	23 3.2%
Rely on	73 4.5%	52 10.9%BD	13 2.6%	65 6.5%D	8 1.3%	17 2.5%	28 6.3%E	28 5.4%E	10 4.3%	19 6.9%J	11 2.3%	19 6.3%J	4 5.8%J	10 4.8%	* 2.2%	0 0	50 5.4%Q	23 3.2%
Most important	55 3.4%	39 8.3%BD	10 1.9%	49 4.9%D	6 0.9%	14 2.0%	21 4.7%E	21 4.0%	8 3.5%	15 5.5%JN	9 1.9%	12 4.0%	3 4.9%JN	7 3.5%	0 0	0 0	37 4.0%	19 2.6%
Instructors/faculty	62 3.8%	0 0	0 0	0 0	62 9.7%AB C	11 1.6%	3 0.7%	48 9.2%EF	8 3.5%	5 1.8%	19 3.8%	17 5.5%IN	2 3.1%	6 2.6%	0 0	6 12.0%	17 1.9%	45 6.3%P
Rely on	62 3.8%	0 0	0 0	0 0	62 9.7%AB C	11 1.6%	3 0.7%	48 9.2%EF	8 3.5%	5 1.8%	19 3.8%	17 5.5%IN	2 3.1%	6 2.6%	0 0	6 12.0%	17 1.9%	45 6.3%P
Most important	61 3.7%	0 0	0 0	0 0	61 9.5%AB C	11 1.6%	3 0.7%	47 9.0%EF	8 3.5%	5 1.8%	19 3.8%	16 5.1%I	2 3.1%	6 2.6%	0 0	6 12.0%	17 1.9%	44 6.1%P
Another library	29 1.8%	13 2.8%D	10 1.9%	23 2.3%	6 0.9%	7 1.0%	16 3.7%EG	6 1.1%	4 1.6%	4 1.5%	11 2.3%	9 2.9%M	* 0.4%	1 0.4%	* 1.1%	0 0	16 1.8%	13 1.8%

Proportions/Means: Columns Tested (5% risk level) - A/B/D - C/D - E/F/G - H/I/J/K/L/M/N - P/Q
* small base

Table 548
Page 2030

Outsell/Digital Library Federation Study (2002)
Weighted Tables

TABLE 60, continued

Q12A/B. SUMMARY TABLE

		RESPONDENT TYPE				INSTITUTION TYPE			DISCIPLINE									GENDER	
	TOTAL SAMPLE	FACULTY MEMBER	GRAD. STUDENT	FACULTY /GRAD	UNDER GRAD. STUDENT	PUBLIC	PRIVATE	LIBERAL ARTS	BIOLOGIAL SCIENCES	PHYSICAL SCIENCES /MATH	SOCIAL SCIENCES	ARTS AND HUMAN.	ENGI-NEERING	BUSINESS	LAW	UNDEC. MAJOR	MALE	FEMALE
		(A)	(B)	(C)	(D)	(E)	(F)	(G)	(H)	(I)	(J)	(K)	(L)	(M)	(N)		(P)	(Q)
Base - Total Responding	1642	477	526	1003	639	678	442	523	226	274	493	305	65	215	15*	50*	926	716
Rely on	29 1.8%	13 2.8%D	10 1.9%	23 2.3%	6 0.9%	7 1.0%	16 3.7%EG	6 1.1%	4 1.6%	4 1.5%	11 2.3%	9 2.9%M	* 0.4%	1 0.4%	* 1.1%	0 0	16 1.8%	13 1.8%
Most important	27 1.6%	11 2.3%	10 1.9%	21 2.1%	6 0.9%	7 1.0%	15 3.5%EG	5 0.9%	4 1.6%	3 1.1%	11 2.3%	8 2.6%	* 0.4%	1 0.4%	* 1.1%	0 0	14 1.5%	13 1.8%
Your own institution's web portal	28 1.7%	5 1.1%	15 2.9%	21 2.1%	8 1.2%	20 3.0%G	7 1.6%G	1 0.2%	5 2.3%K	7 2.6%K	8 1.5%	1 0.4%	2 2.7%K	6 2.6%K	* 1.1%	0 0	18 2.0%	10 1.4%
Rely on	28 1.7%	5 1.1%	15 2.9%	21 2.1%	8 1.2%	20 3.0%G	7 1.6%G	1 0.2%	5 2.3%K	7 2.6%K	8 1.5%	1 0.4%	2 2.7%K	6 2.6%K	* 1.1%	0 0	18 2.0%	10 1.4%
Most important	27 1.6%	3 0.7%	15 2.9%A	19 1.9%	8 1.2%	20 3.0%G	6 1.4%G	0 0	4 1.9%	7 2.6%K	8 1.5%	1 0.4%	2 2.7%K	5 2.2%	* 1.1%	0 0	16 1.8%	10 1.4%
Bookstore	27 1.7%	4 0.9%	5 1.0%	10 1.0%	18 2.8%AC	6 0.8%	7 1.6%	14 2.7%E	2 0.8%	4 1.5%	8 1.5%	4 1.5%	1 1.8%	4 1.7%	1 3.3%H	4 8.0%	13 1.4%	14 2.0%
Rely on	27 1.7%	4 0.9%	5 1.0%	10 1.0%	18 2.8%AC	6 0.8%	7 1.6%	14 2.7%E	2 0.8%	4 1.5%	8 1.5%	4 1.5%	1 1.8%	4 1.7%	1 3.3%H	4 8.0%	13 1.4%	14 2.0%
Most important	25 1.5%	3 0.6%	5 1.0%	8 0.8%	17 2.6%AC	5 0.8%	7 1.6%	12 2.3%	2 0.8%	4 1.5%	8 1.5%	3 1.1%	1 1.8%	4 1.7%	* 2.2%	3 6.0%	12 1.2%	13 1.9%
Online alerting service	24 1.5%	7 1.4%	11 2.2%	18 1.8%	6 1.0%	12 1.8%	10 2.2%G	3 0.5%	6 2.7%	2 0.7%	6 1.1%	2 0.7%	2 3.1%IK	6 2.6%	1 4.4%IJK	0 0	13 1.4%	11 1.6%

Proportions/Means: Columns Tested (5% risk level) - A/B/D - C/D - E/F/G - H/I/J/K/L/M/N - P/Q
* small base

Table 548
Page 2031

Outsell/Digital Library Federation Study (2002)
Weighted Tables

TABLE 60, continued

Q12A/B. SUMMARY TABLE

	TOTAL SAMPLE	RESPONDENT TYPE: FACULTY MEMBER (A)	GRAD. STUDENT (B)	FACULTY /GRAD (C)	UNDER GRAD. STUDENT (D)	INSTITUTION TYPE: PUBLIC (E)	PRIVATE (F)	LIBERAL ARTS (G)	DISCIPLINE: BIOLOGIAL SCIENCES (H)	PHYSICAL SCIENCES /MATH (I)	SOCIAL SCIENCES (J)	ARTS AND HUMAN. (K)	ENGI-NEERING (L)	BUSINESS (M)	LAW (N)	UNDEC. MAJOR	GENDER: MALE (P)	FEMALE (Q)
Base - Total Responding	1642	477	526	1003	639	678	442	523	226	274	493	305	65	215	15*	50*	926	716
Rely on	24 1.5%	7 1.4%	11 2.2%	18 1.8%	6 1.0%	12 1.8%	10 2.2%G	3 0.5%	6 2.7%	2 0.7%	6 1.1%	2 0.7%	2 3.1%IK	6 2.6%	1 4.4%IJK	0 0	13 1.4%	11 1.6%
Most important	21 1.3%	5 0.9%	11 2.1%	16 1.6%	5 0.8%	12 1.7%G	7 1.6%	2 0.3%	5 2.3%IK	1 0.4%	6 1.1%	1 0.4%	2 2.7%IK	6 2.6%IK	1 3.3%IK	0 0	11 1.2%	10 1.4%
E-mail listservs	24 1.4%	15 3.1%D	7 1.4%	22 2.2%D	2 0.3%	12 1.7%	7 1.6%	5 0.9%	5 2.3%	4 1.5%	4 0.8%	4 1.5%	* 0.4%	6 2.6%	* 1.1%	0 0	14 1.5%	10 1.4%
Rely on	24 1.4%	15 3.1%D	7 1.4%	22 2.2%D	2 0.3%	12 1.7%	7 1.6%	5 0.9%	5 2.3%	4 1.5%	4 0.8%	4 1.5%	* 0.4%	6 2.6%	* 1.1%	0 0	14 1.5%	10 1.4%
Most important	22 1.3%	15 3.1%D	6 1.1%D	21 2.1%D	1 0.1%	12 1.7%	5 1.2%	5 0.9%	4 1.9%	4 1.5%	4 0.8%	3 1.1%	* 0.4%	6 2.6%	* 1.1%	0 0	12 1.3%	9 1.3%
Class	10 0.6%	0 0	3 0.6%	3 0.3%	7 1.1%A	3 0.5%	2 0.5%	5 0.9%	3 1.2%	1 0.4%	2 0.4%	3 1.1%	1 0.9%M	0 0	* 2.2%IJM	0 0	3 0.4%	6 0.9%
Rely on	10 0.6%	0 0	3 0.6%	3 0.3%	7 1.1%A	3 0.5%	2 0.5%	5 0.9%	3 1.2%	1 0.4%	2 0.4%	3 1.1%	1 0.9%M	0 0	* 2.2%IJM	0 0	3 0.4%	6 0.9%
Most important	9 0.5%	0 0	3 0.6%	3 0.3%	6 0.9%	2 0.3%	2 0.5%	5 0.9%	2 0.8%	1 0.4%	2 0.4%	3 1.1%	1 0.9%M	0 0	* 2.2%IJM	0 0	3 0.4%	5 0.8%
Information Types - Unspecified	186 11.3%	55 11.6%	45 8.6%	101 10.0%	85 13.3%B	61 9.0%	51 11.6%	74 14.1%E	18 7.8%	29 10.6%	47 9.5%	40 13.2%H	5 8.1%	40 18.6%HIJ L	2 9.9%	5 10.0%	112 12.1%	73 10.2%

Proportions/Means: Columns Tested (5% risk level) - A/B/D - C/D - E/F/G - H/I/J/K/L/M/N - P/Q
* small base

Table 548
Page 2032

Outsell/Digital Library Federation Study (2002)
Weighted Tables

TABLE 60, continued

Q12A/B. SUMMARY TABLE

		RESPONDENT TYPE				INSTITUTION TYPE			DISCIPLINE									GENDER	
	TOTAL SAMPLE	FACULTY MEMBER	GRAD. STUDENT	FACULTY /GRAD	UNDER GRAD. STUDENT	PUBLIC	PRIVATE	LIBERAL ARTS	BIOLOGIAL SCIENCES	PHYSICAL SCIENCES /MATH	SOCIAL SCIENCES	ARTS AND HUMAN.	ENGI-NEERING	BUSINESS	LAW	UNDEC. MAJOR	MALE	FEMALE
		(A)	(B)	(C)	(D)	(E)	(F)	(G)	(H)	(I)	(J)	(K)	(L)	(M)	(N)		(P)	(Q)
Base - Total Responding	1642	477	526	1003	639	678	442	523	226	274	493	305	65	215	15*	50*	926	716
Rely on	186 11.3%	55 11.6%	45 8.6%	101 10.0%	85 13.3%B	61 9.0%	51 11.6%	74 14.1%E	18 7.8%	29 10.6%	47 9.5%	40 13.2%H	5 8.1%	40 18.6%HIJ L	2 9.9%	5 10.0%	112 12.1%	73 10.2%
Most important	172 10.5%	50 10.5%	41 7.8%	91 9.1%	80 12.6%BC	58 8.5%	48 10.9%	66 12.6%E	17 7.4%	26 9.5%	41 8.4%	38 12.5%	5 8.1%	38 17.7%HIJ LN	1 7.7%	5 10.0%	104 11.2%	68 9.5%
Other	156 9.5%	72 15.1%BD	35 6.6%	107 10.7%	49 7.7%	47 7.0%	49 11.2%E	60 11.4%E	20 8.9%	26 9.5%	38 7.6%	35 11.4%	5 7.2%	30 13.9%JL	2 15.4%JL	1 2.0%	89 9.6%	67 9.4%
Most important	149 9.1%	69 14.5%BD	35 6.6%	104 10.4%D	45 7.0%	43 6.4%	49 11.0%E	57 10.9%E	19 8.6%	25 9.1%	34 6.9%	34 11.0%	5 7.2%	29 13.4%JL	2 15.4%JL	1 2.0%	85 9.2%	63 8.9%
Rely on	135 8.2%	61 12.8%BD	32 6.0%	93 9.2%	43 6.6%	43 6.3%	42 9.4%	51 9.7%	18 8.2%	24 8.8%	32 6.5%	28 9.2%	5 7.2%	26 12.1%J	2 13.2%J	0 0	77 8.3%	58 8.2%
DK/Refused	27 1.7%	2 0.4%	5 1.0%	7 0.7%	20 3.2%AB C	11 1.6%	4 1.0%	12 2.3%	1 0.4%	6 2.2%M	6 1.1%	6 1.8%M	1 1.8%M	0 0	* 1.1%M	8 16.0%	16 1.7%	12 1.7%

Proportions/Means: Columns Tested (5% risk level) - A/B/D - C/D - E/F/G - H/I/J/K/L/M/N - P/Q
* small base

TABLE 61
Q13A/B SUMMARY TABLE

	RESPONDENT TYPE					INSTITUTION TYPE			DISCIPLINE								GENDER	
	TOTAL SAMPLE	FACULTY MEMBER	GRAD. STUDENT	FACULTY /GRAD	UNDER GRAD. STUDENT	PUBLIC	PRIVATE	LIBERAL ARTS	BIOLOGIAL SCIENCES	PHYSICAL SCIENCES /MATH	SOCIAL SCIENCES	ARTS AND HUMAN.	ENGI-NEERING	BUSINESS	LAW	UNDEC. MAJOR	MALE	FEMALE
		(A)	(B)	(C)	(D)	(E)	(F)	(G)	(H)	(I)	(J)	(K)	(L)	(M)	(N)		(P)	(Q)
Base - Total Respondents	1391	426	427	853	537	546	375	469	190	242	404	251	55	191	15*	43*	791	600
Medium																		
Important (4,5)	761 54.7%	227 53.2%	252 58.9%	479 56.1%	283 52.6%	321 58.9%G	211 56.4%G	228 48.6%	115 60.6%IL	116 47.9%	229 56.7%	138 54.9%	28 50.3%	109 57.1%	9 56.8%	18 41.9%	422 53.3%	339 56.6%
Meeting Needs (4,5)	609 43.8%	184 43.1%	193 45.1%	376 44.1%	233 43.3%	242 44.4%	167 44.6%	199 42.5%	89 46.8%	95 39.3%	177 43.7%	114 45.5%	23 42.9%	84 43.9%	8 54.5%I	19 44.2%	354 44.8%	255 42.5%
Speed of delivery																		
Important (4,5)	1026 73.8%	313 73.5%	327 76.4%	640 75.0%	386 71.8%	407 74.5%	290 77.4%G	329 70.0%	147 77.3%K	170 70.2%	297 73.5%	171 68.3%	41 74.1%	154 81.0%IK	11 75.0%	34 79.1%	567 71.7%	458 76.4%
Meeting Needs (4,5)	574 41.2%	186 43.6%	182 42.6%	368 43.1%	205 38.3%	222 40.7%	165 44.1%	186 39.6%	85 44.9%K	100 41.3%	158 39.1%	85 33.9%	24 43.9%K	99 51.7%IJ K	7 50.0%K	15 34.9%	329 41.6%	244 40.7%
Ease of access																		
Important (4,5)	1235 88.8%	384 90.1%	385 90.2%	769 90.1%	465 86.7%	488 89.4%	334 89.1%	413 87.9%	172 90.7%	210 86.8%	359 88.8%	220 87.5%	51 92.6%	170 89.3%	14 92.0%	39 90.7%	682 86.2%	553 92.2%P
Meeting Needs (4,5)	655 47.1%	188 44.2%	209 48.9%	397 46.5%	258 48.0%	274 50.2%G	180 48.1%	200 42.7%	99 51.9%	106 43.8%	190 47.0%	112 44.6%	26 46.6%	96 50.2%	8 55.7%	19 44.2%	376 47.6%	279 46.4%
Quality																		
Important (4,5)	1268 91.2%	384 90.1%	397 92.9%	781 91.5%	487 90.6%	501 91.8%	341 91.0%	425 90.5%	175 92.1%	213 88.0%	376 93.0%	232 92.4%	49 88.9%	172 90.2%	13 88.6%	38 88.4%	723 91.4%	545 90.9%
Meeting Needs (4,5)	713 51.3%	199 46.8%	241 56.4%A	440 51.6%	273 50.8%	282 51.6%	200 53.2%	232 49.4%	93 49.1%	114 47.1%	229 56.7%I	124 49.6%	26 48.1%	95 49.8%	10 65.9%HI KLM	21 48.8%	398 50.3%	315 52.6%

Proportions/Means: Columns Tested (5% risk level) - A/B/D - C/D - E/F/G - H/I/J/K/L/M/N - P/Q
* small base

Table 579
Page 2067

Outsell/Digital Library Federation Study (2002)
Weighted Tables

TABLE 61, continued

Q13A/B SUMMARY TABLE

		RESPONDENT TYPE				INSTITUTION TYPE			DISCIPLINE								GENDER	
	TOTAL SAMPLE	FACULTY MEMBER	GRAD. STUDENT	FACULTY /GRAD	UNDER GRAD. STUDENT	PUBLIC	PRIVATE	LIBERAL ARTS	BIOLOGIAL SCIENCES	PHYSICAL SCIENCES /MATH	SOCIAL SCIENCES	ARTS AND HUMAN.	ENGI-NEERING	BUSINESS	LAW	UNDEC. MAJOR	MALE	FEMALE
		(A)	(B)	(C)	(D)	(E)	(F)	(G)	(H)	(I)	(J)	(K)	(L)	(M)	(N)		(P)	(Q)
Base - Total Respondents	1391	426	427	853	537	546	375	469	190	242	404	251	55	191	15*	43*	791	600
Update frequency																		
Important (4,5)	898 64.6%	260 61.1%	317 74.2%AD	577 67.6%D	321 59.7%	390 71.5%G	244 65.0%G	264 56.1%	129 68.1%IK	140 57.9%	269 66.5%	148 58.9%	36 65.1%	139 73.2%IK	13 84.1%HI JKL	24 55.8%	502 63.5%	396 65.9%
Meeting Needs (4,5)	580 41.7%	164 38.4%	199 46.5%A	362 42.4%	217 40.5%	232 42.6%	167 44.4%	181 38.4%	91 47.7%K	97 40.1%	160 39.5%	94 37.5%	21 38.1%	88 46.3%	10 65.9%HI JKLM	19 44.2%	338 42.7%	242 40.3%
Delivery frequency																		
Important (4,5)	589 42.3%	163 38.2%	187 43.7%	349 40.9%	239 44.5%	233 42.7%	164 43.7%	191 40.7%	85 44.9%I	84 34.7%	190 47.0%IL	97 38.8%	20 36.0%	88 46.3%IL	7 45.5%	17 39.5%	311 39.3%	278 46.3%P
Meeting Needs (4,5)	475 34.1%	152 35.7%	137 32.1%	289 33.9%	186 34.5%	177 32.5%	144 38.5%	153 32.6%	68 35.6%	79 32.6%	133 33.0%	84 33.5%	18 33.3%	73 38.0%	6 38.6%	14 32.6%	285 36.0%	190 31.7%
Search functions																		
Important (4,5)	1095 78.7%	323 75.8%	368 86.2%AD	691 81.0%D	404 75.1%	444 81.4%G	306 81.6%G	345 73.4%	147 77.3%	184 76.0%	335 82.8%	196 78.1%	42 76.2%	147 77.1%	12 78.4%	33 76.7%	611 77.3%	484 80.7%
Meeting Needs (4,5)	587 42.2%	161 37.8%	196 45.9%A	357 41.8%	230 42.8%	234 42.8%	170 45.4%	183 39.0%	84 44.4%	91 37.6%	179 44.2%	102 40.6%	22 40.2%	81 42.4%	8 54.5%IK L	20 46.5%	335 42.4%	252 42.0%
Coverage period																		
Important (4,5)	742 53.4%	255 59.8%D	236 55.3%D	491 57.5%D	251 46.7%	309 56.5%G	210 56.1%G	223 47.5%	108 56.9%IK	115 47.5%	241 59.5%IK	114 45.5%	28 51.9%	111 58.0%IK	10 65.9%IK L	15 34.9%	428 54.1%	314 52.3%

Proportions/Means: Columns Tested (5% risk level) - A/B/D - C/D - E/F/G - H/I/J/K/L/M/N - P/Q
* small base

Table 579
Page 2068

Outsell/Digital Library Federation Study (2002)
Weighted Tables

TABLE 61, continued

Q13A/B SUMMARY TABLE

		RESPONDENT TYPE				INSTITUTION TYPE			DISCIPLINE									GENDER	
	TOTAL SAMPLE	FACULTY MEMBER	GRAD. STUDENT	FACULTY /GRAD	UNDER GRAD. STUDENT	PUBLIC	PRIVATE	LIBERAL ARTS	BIOLOGIAL SCIENCES	PHYSICAL SCIENCES /MATH	SOCIAL SCIENCES	ARTS AND HUMAN.	ENGI-NEERING	BUSINESS	LAW	UNDEC. MAJOR	MALE	FEMALE
		(A)	(B)	(C)	(D)	(E)	(F)	(G)	(H)	(I)	(J)	(K)	(L)	(M)	(N)		(P)	(Q)
Base - Total Respondents	1391	426	427	853	537	546	375	469	190	242	404	251	55	191	15*	43*	791	600
Meeting Needs (4,5)	421 30.2%	124 29.0%	131 30.6%	254 29.8%	166 30.9%	170 31.2%	118 31.6%	132 28.1%	68 35.6%K	75 31.0%	113 27.9%	66 26.3%	15 27.0%	66 34.6%	7 47.7%HI JKLM	11 25.6%	242 30.6%	179 29.8%
Geographic coverage Important (4,5)	430 31.0%	137 32.2%	132 30.9%	269 31.6%	161 30.0%	169 31.0%	122 32.4%	140 29.8%	50 26.4%L	61 25.2%L	150 37.2%HI L	86 34.4%IL	9 16.4%	57 29.8%L	5 33.0%L	12 27.9%	250 31.6%	180 30.1%
Meeting Needs (4,5)	421 30.3%	131 30.7%	129 30.2%	260 30.5%	161 29.9%	167 30.7%	124 33.1%	129 27.6%	60 31.5%	76 31.4%	120 29.8%	71 28.1%	13 24.3%	62 32.7%	7 44.3%HI JKL	12 27.9%	242 30.6%	179 29.8%
Subject coverage Important (4,5)	1160 83.4%	368 86.4%D	373 87.4%D	742 86.9%D	419 77.9%	468 85.8%G	319 85.0%	373 79.5%	163 85.6%	198 81.8%	338 83.7%	207 82.6%	45 82.0%	160 83.9%	13 86.4%	36 83.7%	639 80.8%	521 86.9%P
Meeting Needs (4,5)	666 47.9%	194 45.6%	209 48.9%	403 47.3%	262 48.9%	254 46.5%	178 47.4%	234 49.9%	102 53.7%JKL	136 56.2%JKL	167 41.4%	108 42.9%	23 41.3%	97 50.7%	10 63.6%JK LM	24 55.8%	373 47.2%	293 48.8%
Search options Important (4,5)	1042 74.9%	308 72.4%	334 78.1%	642 75.2%	400 74.4%	424 77.7%G	292 77.7%G	326 69.4%	143 75.5%	184 76.0%	305 75.3%	177 70.5%	42 76.2%	149 78.0%	12 81.8%K	30 69.8%	576 72.9%	466 77.6%
Meeting Needs (4,5)	596 42.8%	169 39.6%	190 44.6%	359 42.1%	236 44.0%	240 44.0%	169 45.2%	186 39.6%	89 46.8%	95 39.3%	160 39.5%	109 43.3%	23 42.9%	89 46.8%	8 51.1%	23 53.5%	328 41.5%	267 44.6%

Proportions/Means: Columns Tested (5% risk level) - A/B/D - C/D - E/F/G - H/I/J/K/L/M/N - P/Q
* small base

Table 579
Page 2069

Outsell/Digital Library Federation Study (2002)
Weighted Tables

TABLE 61, continued

Q13A/B SUMMARY TABLE

	TOTAL SAMPLE	RESPONDENT TYPE: FACULTY MEMBER	GRAD. STUDENT	FACULTY /GRAD	UNDER GRAD. STUDENT	INSTITUTION TYPE: PUBLIC	PRIVATE	LIBERAL ARTS	DISCIPLINE: BIOLOGIAL SCIENCES	PHYSICAL SCIENCES /MATH	SOCIAL SCIENCES	ARTS AND HUMAN.	ENGI- NEERING	BUSINESS	LAW	UNDEC. MAJOR	GENDER: MALE	FEMALE
		(A)	(B)	(C)	(D)	(E)	(F)	(G)	(H)	(I)	(J)	(K)	(L)	(M)	(N)		(P)	(Q)
Base - Total Respondents	1391	426	427	853	537	546	375	469	190	242	404	251	55	191	15*	43*	791	600
Display options																		
Important (4,5)	446	128	155	284	162	193	130	123	65	64	128	85	19	68	4	12	251	194
	32.0%	30.1%	36.3%	33.2%	30.2%	35.3%G	34.7%G	26.2%	34.3%	26.4%	31.6%	33.9%	35.4%I	35.6%I	28.4%	27.9%	31.8%	32.4%
Meeting Needs (4,5)	443	136	140	276	167	178	127	138	63	75	115	87	18	62	5	17	257	186
	31.8%	32.0%	32.7%	32.3%	31.1%	32.6%	33.9%	29.4%	33.3%	31.0%	28.4%	34.8%	32.3%	32.7%	36.4%	39.5%	32.5%	31.0%
Support																		
Important (4,5)	723	232	191	423	299	268	173	282	99	111	205	151	25	97	7	28	392	331
	52.0%	54.5%B	44.7%	49.6%	55.7%B C	49.0%	46.0%	60.1%EF	51.9%	45.9%	50.7%	60.3%IJ LMN	46.0%	50.7%	46.6%	65.1%	49.5%	55.2%
Meeting Needs (4,5)	499	140	142	282	217	189	132	178	71	75	150	95	19	67	6	15	280	219
	35.8%	32.9%	33.2%	33.0%	40.4%A BC	34.6%	35.2%	37.9%	37.5%	31.0%	37.2%	37.9%	33.9%	35.1%	40.9%	34.9%	35.4%	36.5%
Use privileges																		
Important (4,5)	802	255	250	505	297	319	227	257	121	130	237	137	27	116	10	24	444	358
	57.7%	59.7%	58.6%	59.2%	55.3%	58.3%	60.5%	54.6%	63.9%IKL	53.7%	58.6%	54.5%	49.7%	61.0%L	63.6%L	55.8%	56.2%	59.7%
Meeting Needs (4,5)	501	141	156	297	205	206	126	170	75	84	130	100	15	72	6	20	288	214
	36.1%	33.0%	36.5%	34.8%	38.1%	37.7%	33.6%	36.1%	39.4%L	34.7%	32.1%	39.7%L	28.0%	37.6%L	42.0%L	46.5%	36.4%	35.7%
Printing and downloading																		
Important (4,5)	1144	352	364	716	428	461	313	371	162	199	331	193	48	169	12	31	634	511
	82.3%	82.5%	85.3%D	83.9%	79.8%	84.5%G	83.3%	78.9%	85.2%K	82.2%	81.9%	76.8%	86.8%K	88.8%K	81.8%	72.1%	80.2%	85.1%P
Meeting Needs (4,5)	711	209	204	413	298	280	179	253	97	131	190	128	28	103	8	26	422	289
	51.1%	49.1%	47.7%	48.4%	55.5%B C	51.2%	47.6%	53.8%	50.9%	54.1%	47.0%	50.9%	51.9%	54.1%	54.5%	60.5%	53.4%	48.2%

Proportions/Means: Columns Tested (5% risk level) - A/B/D - C/D - E/F/G - H/I/J/K/L/M/N - P/Q
* small base

Table 579
Page 2070

Outsell/Digital Library Federation Study (2002)
Weighted Tables

TABLE 62

Q15b. What additional information content does your library need to provide to meet your needs? What else?

		RESPONDENT TYPE				INSTITUTION TYPE			DISCIPLINE									GENDER	
	TOTAL SAMPLE	FACULTY MEMBER	GRAD. STUDENT	FACULTY /GRAD	UNDER GRAD. STUDENT	PUBLIC	PRIVATE	LIBERAL ARTS	BIOLOGIAL SCIENCES	PHYSICAL SCIENCES /MATH	SOCIAL SCIENCES	ARTS AND HUMAN.	ENGI- NEERING	BUSINESS	LAW	UNDEC. MAJOR	MALE	FEMALE
		(A)	(B)	(C)	(D)	(E)	(F)	(G)	(H)	(I)	(J)	(K)	(L)	(M)	(N)		(P)	(Q)
Base - Unmet needs	791	225	323	548	243	379	219	192	138	117	258	136	35	88*	4**	15*	433	358
Print Journal	113 14.3%	39 17.4%D	54 16.6%D	93 16.9%D	20 8.3%	56 14.8%	28 12.7%	29 15.2%	24 17.2%	27 23.1%JKL M	32 12.4%	16 11.6%	4 11.6%	9 10.5%	* 8.3%	1 6.7%	56 12.9%	57 16.0%
E-Journal	85 10.7%	23 10.0%	50 15.6%D	73 13.3%D	12 4.9%	38 10.1%	34 15.5%G	12 6.5%	26 19.1%JKM	14 12.0%	24 9.5%	8 5.8%	6 18.2%JKM	5 5.3%	0 0	1 6.7%	43 9.9%	42 11.7%
More books	60 7.6%	16 7.2%	27 8.4%	43 7.9%	17 6.8%	27 7.1%	22 9.9%	11 5.9%	5 3.8%	12 10.3%H	19 7.3%	15 10.7%H	3 7.4%	4 4.2%	0 0	3 20.0%	32 7.4%	28 7.8%
Online information	46 5.9%	6 2.7%	30 9.3%AD	36 6.6%	10 4.2%	28 7.5%	10 4.6%	8 4.1%	7 5.1%	2 1.7%	24 9.5%I	6 4.1%	3 7.4%I	4 4.2%	0 0	1 6.7%	28 6.3%	19 5.3%
More computers	26 3.2%	10 4.3%	7 2.3%	17 3.1%	9 3.5%	11 2.8%	9 3.9%	7 3.4%	4 2.5%	4 3.4%	11 4.4%	2 1.7%	0 0	5 5.3%L	0 0	0 0	16 3.7%	9 2.6%
Better organized reference center	10 1.2%	0 0	2 0.7%	2 0.4%	8 3.1%AB C	3 0.9%	7 3.0%G	0 0	1 0.6%	0 0	8 2.9%	1 0.8%	* 0.8%	0 0	0 0	0 0	7 1.6%	3 0.8%
Nothing/Can't think of anything	324 41.0%	74 32.8%	134 41.4%	207 37.9%	117 48.2%A C	173 45.5%F	76 34.8%	75 39.2%	56 40.8%	47 40.2%	107 41.6%	49 36.4%	14 40.5%	41 46.3%	3 62.5%	7 46.7%	169 38.9%	156 43.6%
All others	165 20.9%	65 29.0%BD	53 16.3%	118 21.5%	48 19.6%	59 15.4%	60 27.2%E	47 24.6%E	21 15.3%	19 16.2%	47 18.2%	45 33.1%HI JL	7 20.7%	23 26.3%H	1 25.0%	2 13.3%	97 22.4%	68 19.1%

Proportions/Means: Columns Tested (5% risk level) - A/B/D - C/D - E/F/G - H/I/J/K/L/M/N - P/Q
* small base; ** very small base (under 30) ineligible for sig testing

Table 589
Page 2080

Outsell/Digital Library Federation Study (2002)
Weighted Tables

TABLE 62, continued

Q15b. What additional information content does your library need to provide to meet your needs? What else?

		RESPONDENT TYPE				INSTITUTION TYPE			DISCIPLINE									GENDER	
	TOTAL SAMPLE	FACULTY MEMBER	GRAD. STUDENT	FACULTY /GRAD	UNDER GRAD. STUDENT	PUBLIC	PRIVATE	LIBERAL ARTS	BIOLOGIAL SCIENCES	PHYSICAL SCIENCES /MATH	SOCIAL SCIENCES	ARTS AND HUMAN.	ENGI- NEERING	BUSINESS	LAW	UNDEC. MAJOR	MALE	FEMALE
		(A)	(B)	(C)	(D)	(E)	(F)	(G)	(H)	(I)	(J)	(K)	(L)	(M)	(N)		(P)	(Q)
Base - Unmet needs	791	225	323	548	243	379	219	192	138	117	258	136	35	88*	4**	15*	433	358
Don't Know/Refused	25 3.2%	7 3.0%	6 1.7%	12 2.2%	13 5.4%BC	13 3.5%	5 2.1%	8 4.0%	5 3.8%	5 4.3%	4 1.5%	6 4.1%	1 2.5%	4 4.2%	* 4.2%	1 6.7%	14 3.1%	12 3.3%

Proportions/Means: Columns Tested (5% risk level) - A/B/D - C/D - E/F/G - H/I/J/K/L/M/N - P/Q
* small base; ** very small base (under 30) ineligible for sig testing

Table 589
Page 2081

TABLE 63

Q16a. What services would you like your institution's library to offer?

		RESPONDENT TYPE				INSTITUTION TYPE			DISCIPLINE								GENDER	
	TOTAL SAMPLE	FACULTY MEMBER	GRAD. STUDENT	FACULTY /GRAD	UNDER GRAD. STUDENT	PUBLIC	PRIVATE	LIBERAL ARTS	BIOLOGIAL SCIENCES	PHYSICAL SCIENCES /MATH	SOCIAL SCIENCES	ARTS AND HUMAN.	ENGI-NEERING	BUSINESS	LAW	UNDEC. MAJOR	MALE	FEMALE
		(A)	(B)	(C)	(D)	(E)	(F)	(G)	(H)	(I)	(J)	(K)	(L)	(M)	(N)		(P)	(Q)
Base - Total Respondents	1592	453	530	983	608	659	430	504	238	237	500	296	60	192	17	52*	897	695
Can't think of anything	182 11.5%	41 9.0%	64 12.0%	104 10.6%	78 12.8%	74 11.3%	51 12.0%	57 11.3%	26 11.1%	38 16.0%J	36 7.1%	40 13.6%J	6 10.6%	19 9.7%	2 12.0%	15 28.8%	95 10.6%	87 12.5%
More electronic materials	53 3.3%	9 2.0%	26 4.9%A	35 3.6%	18 2.9%	23 3.5%	14 3.2%	16 3.3%	18 7.4%IJK	6 2.5%	11 2.3%	4 1.5%	3 5.8%JK	7 3.9%	1 3.0%	2 3.8%	32 3.5%	21 3.0%
Making information available from different locations	48 3.0%	3 0.7%	29 5.4%AD	32 3.3%	16 2.7%A	39 5.9%FG	8 1.9%G	1 0.2%	8 3.3%	2 0.8%	21 4.1%I	10 3.4%	2 2.9%	5 2.4%	* 1.0%	1 1.9%	18 2.0%	30 4.3%P
Coffee shop	42 2.7%	6 1.3%	13 2.4%	19 1.9%	24 3.9%AC	12 1.8%	13 3.1%	17 3.4%	4 1.5%	5 2.1%	13 2.6%	12 4.2%	1 2.4%	5 2.4%	* 2.0%	2 3.8%	29 3.3%	13 1.9%
More electronic hardware (computer, copier)	41 2.6%	6 1.4%	17 3.3%	24 2.4%	17 2.8%	19 2.8%	9 2.1%	13 2.6%	8 3.3%	5 2.1%	11 2.3%	8 2.7%	1 1.9%	5 2.4%	1 6.0%IJL	2 3.8%	18 2.0%	23 3.3%
Selecting high quality online information	39 2.4%	4 0.9%	21 3.9%A	25 2.5%	14 2.3%	29 4.4%FG	7 1.7%	3 0.6%	5 2.2%	5 2.1%	15 3.0%	7 2.3%	2 3.4%	5 2.4%	0 0	0 0	20 2.3%	18 2.7%
Consultation on organizing online information	32 2.0%	3 0.6%	16 3.1%A	19 1.9%	13 2.2%	25 3.8%FG	6 1.5%	1 0.2%	5 2.2%	2 0.8%	13 2.6%	6 1.9%	1 2.4%	5 2.4%	* 2.0%	0 0	15 1.6%	18 2.5%
Lounge area to eat or study	32 2.0%	7 1.6%	15 2.9%	23 2.3%	10 1.6%	10 1.6%	11 2.6%	11 2.2%	2 0.7%	4 1.7%	13 2.6%	7 2.3%	0 0	6 2.9%L	0 0	1 1.9%	23 2.6%	9 1.3%

Proportions/Means: Columns Tested (5% risk level) - A/B/D - C/D - E/F/G - H/I/J/K/L/M/N - P/Q
* small base

Table 590
Page 2082

TABLE 63, continued

Q16a. What services would you like your institution's library to offer?

		RESPONDENT TYPE				INSTITUTION TYPE			DISCIPLINE								GENDER	
	TOTAL SAMPLE	FACULTY MEMBER	GRAD. STUDENT	FACULTY /GRAD	UNDER GRAD. STUDENT	PUBLIC	PRIVATE	LIBERAL ARTS	BIOLOGIAL SCIENCES	PHYSICAL SCIENCES /MATH	SOCIAL SCIENCES	ARTS AND HUMAN.	ENGI-NEERING	BUSINESS	LAW	UNDEC. MAJOR	MALE	FEMALE
		(A)	(B)	(C)	(D)	(E)	(F)	(G)	(H)	(I)	(J)	(K)	(L)	(M)	(N)		(P)	(Q)
Base - Total Respondents	1592	453	530	983	608	659	430	504	238	237	500	296	60	192	17	52*	897	695
Assistance in library	27 1.7%	7 1.5%	6 1.2%	13 1.3%	13 2.2%	2 0.3%	7 1.6%E	17 3.4%E	5 2.2%	2 0.8%	9 1.9%	2 0.8%	1 1.4%	4 1.9%	0 0	3 5.8%	11 1.3%	15 2.2%
Book and photocopying delivery service	25 1.6%	10 2.2%D	13 2.5%D	23 2.4%D	2 0.3%	16 2.4%	6 1.3%	4 0.7%	6 2.6%	2 0.8%	6 1.1%	8 2.7%	1 1.9%	2 1.0%	* 2.0%	0 0	11 1.2%	14 2.0%
More print material	25 1.5%	7 1.6%	10 2.0%	18 1.8%	7 1.1%	15 2.3%G	7 1.5%	3 0.6%	7 3.0%	5 2.1%	6 1.1%	2 0.8%	2 2.9%K	3 1.5%	* 1.0%	0 0	14 1.6%	10 1.5%
Managing traditional library and archival collections	23 1.4%	7 1.6%	9 1.8%	17 1.7%	6 1.0%	15 2.3%G	7 1.5%G	1 0.2%	2 0.7%	0 0	13 2.6%I	7 2.3%I	* 0.5%	1 0.5%	0 0	0 0	13 1.4%	10 1.5%
Laptop computer loan program	23 1.4%	8 1.7%	5 1.0%	13 1.3%	10 1.6%	12 1.8%	7 1.6%	4 0.8%	2 0.7%	1 0.4%	13 2.6%	4 1.5%	0 0	2 1.0%	* 2.0%L	0 0	8 0.9%	15 2.1%
Recommending high quality information	20 1.3%	2 0.5%	7 1.3%	9 1.0%	11 1.8%	13 1.9%	4 0.9%	4 0.7%	4 1.5%	0 0	11 2.3%I	3 1.1%	1 1.4%I	1 0.5%	* 2.0%I	0 0	10 1.1%	10 1.5%
Expanded hours	19 1.2%	2 0.5%	10 1.9%	12 1.2%	7 1.1%	10 1.5%	7 1.7%	2 0.4%	7 3.0%IJ	0 0	4 0.8%	4 1.5%	1 1.0%I	3 1.5%	* 1.0%I	0 0	9 1.0%	10 1.5%
Group study space	15 0.9%	2 0.3%	7 1.3%	9 0.9%	6 1.0%	8 1.2%	3 0.7%	4 0.8%	1 0.4%	3 1.3%	2 0.4%	3 1.1%	1 1.4%	3 1.5%	1 5.0%HIJ KLM	1 1.9%	7 0.8%	7 1.1%
24/7 real-time digital reference service	9 0.6%	2 0.5%	3 0.6%	5 0.5%	4 0.7%	6 1.0%	2 0.5%	1 0.2%	1 0.4%	0 0	6 1.1%	2 0.8%	1 1.0%IM	0 0	0 0	0 0	2 0.2%	8 1.1%P

Proportions/Means: Columns Tested (5% risk level) - A/B/D - C/D - E/F/G - H/I/J/K/L/M/N - P/Q
* small base

Table 590
Page 2083

Outsell/Digital Library Federation Study (2002)
Weighted Tables

TABLE 63, continued

Q16a. What services would you like your institution's library to offer?

	TOTAL SAMPLE	RESPONDENT TYPE: FACULTY MEMBER (A)	GRAD. STUDENT (B)	FACULTY /GRAD (C)	UNDER GRAD. STUDENT (D)	INSTITUTION TYPE: PUBLIC (E)	PRIVATE (F)	LIBERAL ARTS (G)	DISCIPLINE: BIOLOGIAL SCIENCES (H)	PHYSICAL SCIENCES /MATH (I)	SOCIAL SCIENCES (J)	ARTS AND HUMAN. (K)	ENGI-NEERING (L)	BUSINESS (M)	LAW (N)	UNDEC. MAJOR	GENDER: MALE (P)	FEMALE (Q)
Base - Total Respondents	1592	453	530	983	608	659	430	504	238	237	500	296	60	192	17	52*	897	695
Personalized library web page	9 0.6%	1 0.3%	5 0.9%	6 0.6%	3 0.5%	7 1.0%	* 0.1%	2 0.4%	2 0.7%	1 0.4%	6 1.1%	0 0	1 1.0%KM	0 0	0 0	0 0	2 0.2%	7 1.0%
Alerting service	9 0.5%	1 0.3%	6 1.2%	8 0.8%	1 0.2%	7 1.0%G	2 0.5%	0 0	1 0.4%	1 0.4%	2 0.4%	2 0.8%	1 1.4%	2 1.0%	0 0	0 0	5 0.5%	4 0.6%
Other	204 12.8%	60 13.1%	73 13.7%	132 13.5%	71 11.7%	83 12.6%	61 14.1%	60 12.0%	26 11.1%	19 8.0%	77 15.4%IM	47 15.9%IM	9 15.5%IM	16 8.3%	4 25.0%HIJ KLM	5 9.6%	116 12.9%	88 12.7%
DK/Refused	821 51.6%	280 61.7%BD	231 43.6%	511 51.9%	310 51.0%B	301 45.7%	224 52.2%	295 58.7%E	109 45.8%	140 59.1%HKL N	261 52.3%	144 48.9%	29 47.8%	110 57.3%H	8 46.0%	20 38.5%	486 54.2%Q	335 48.2%

Proportions/Means: Columns Tested (5% risk level) - A/B/D - C/D - E/F/G - H/I/J/K/L/M/N - P/Q
* small base

Table 590
Page 2084

Outsell/Digital Library Federation Study (2002)
Weighted Tables

TABLE 64

Q17. What types of information content does your academic library offer that you find no longer necessary? Why isn't this information content necessary?

		RESPONDENT TYPE				INSTITUTION TYPE			DISCIPLINE								GENDER	
	TOTAL SAMPLE	FACULTY MEMBER	GRAD. STUDENT	FACULTY /GRAD	UNDER GRAD. STUDENT	PUBLIC	PRIVATE	LIBERAL ARTS	BIOLOGIAL SCIENCES	PHYSICAL SCIENCES /MATH	SOCIAL SCIENCES	ARTS AND HUMAN.	ENGI-NEERING	BUSINESS	LAW	UNDEC. MAJOR	MALE	FEMALE
		(A)	(B)	(C)	(D)	(E)	(F)	(G)	(H)	(I)	(J)	(K)	(L)	(M)	(N)		(P)	(Q)
Base - Faculty and graduate students	983	453	530	983	0**	460	364	159	175	171	299	161	45	117	15*	0*	610	373
Can't think of anything / Everything is useful	603 61.3%	246 54.2%	357 67.4%A	603 61.3%	0 0	280 60.9%G	243 66.6%G	80 50.5%	118 67.3%M	105 61.4%M	180 60.4%M	109 67.4%M	27 60.4%M	54 46.0%	10 65.6%M	0 0	361 59.2%	242 64.8%
Print materials (magazines, journals etc.)	93 9.5%	70 15.5%B	23 4.3%	93 9.5%	0 0	37 8.0%	22 6.0%	35 21.9%EF	13 7.5%	23 13.5%	23 7.5%	12 7.6%	3 7.8%	17 14.3%	2 13.3%	0 0	73 12.0%Q	20 5.4%
Out of date materials	41 4.2%	13 2.8%	29 5.4%	41 4.2%	0 0	25 5.5%	13 3.7%	3 1.8%	6 3.5%	6 3.5%	19 6.3%	4 2.8%	1 2.6%	5 4.0%	* 1.1%	0 0	18 3.0%	23 6.2%P
Microfiche	25 2.5%	12 2.6%	13 2.5%	25 2.5%	0 0	10 2.2%	8 2.3%	6 3.9%	4 2.0%	1 0.6%	13 4.4%I	4 2.8%	1 3.2%I	1 0.8%	* 2.2%	0 0	13 2.1%	12 3.2%
Card catalogues	19 1.9%	5 1.0%	14 2.6%	19 1.9%	0 0	10 2.3%	6 1.7%	2 1.2%	4 2.5%	1 0.6%	8 2.5%	4 2.8%	* 0.6%	1 0.8%	0 0	0 0	14 2.2%	5 1.4%
All Others	64 6.5%	37 8.2%	27 5.0%	64 6.5%	0 0	28 6.0%	24 6.5%	13 7.9%	9 5.0%	14 8.2%	17 5.7%	6 3.5%	4 9.1%K	13 11.1%HK	2 10.0%K	0 0	45 7.3%	19 5.1%
Don't Know/Refused	144 14.7%	73 16.1%	71 13.5%	144 14.7%	0 0	72 15.6%	52 14.3%	20 12.8%	21 12.1%	21 12.3%	45 15.1%	21 13.2%	8 16.9%	27 23.0%HIK N	1 7.8%	0 0	87 14.2%	57 15.4%

Proportions/Means: Columns Tested (5% risk level) - A/B/D - C/D - E/F/G - H/I/J/K/L/M/N - P/Q
* small base; ** very small base (under 30) ineligible for sig testing

Table 591
Page 2085

TABLE 65

Q18. What types of information services does your academic library offer that are no longer necessary? Why aren't these information services necessary?

		RESPONDENT TYPE				INSTITUTION TYPE			DISCIPLINE								GENDER	
	TOTAL SAMPLE	FACULTY MEMBER	GRAD. STUDENT	FACULTY /GRAD	UNDER GRAD. STUDENT	PUBLIC	PRIVATE	LIBERAL ARTS	BIOLOGIAL SCIENCES	PHYSICAL SCIENCES /MATH	SOCIAL SCIENCES	ARTS AND HUMAN.	ENGI-NEERING	BUSINESS	LAW	UNDEC. MAJOR	MALE	FEMALE
		(A)	(B)	(C)	(D)	(E)	(F)	(G)	(H)	(I)	(J)	(K)	(L)	(M)	(N)		(P)	(Q)
Base - Faculty and graduate students	983	453	530	983	0**	460	364	159	175	171	299	161	45	117	15*	0*	610	373
Can't think of anything/Nothing	738 75.1%	351 77.5%	387 73.0%	738 75.1%	0 0	329 71.6%	271 74.5%	137 86.5%EF	135 76.9%M	132 77.2%M	233 78.0%M	119 73.6%	32 70.8%	74 63.5%	14 88.9%HIJKL M	0 0	464 76.0%	274 73.5%
Don't Know/Refused	174 17.7%	67 14.7%	107 20.2%A	174 17.7%	0 0	92 19.9%G	64 17.7%	18 11.2%	27 15.6%	29 17.0%	45 15.1%	31 19.4%N	9 20.8%N	31 26.2%HJN	1 7.8%	0 0	99 16.2%	75 20.1%
All others	71 7.3%	35 7.8%	36 6.8%	71 7.3%	0 0	39 8.5%G	29 7.8%G	4 2.4%	13 7.5%	10 5.8%	21 6.9%	11 6.9%	4 8.4%	12 10.3%	1 3.3%	0 0	48 7.8%	24 6.4%

Proportions/Means: Columns Tested (5% risk level) - A/B/D - C/D - E/F/G - H/I/J/K/L/M/N - P/Q
* small base; ** very small base (under 30) ineligible for sig testing

Table 592
Page 2086

Outsell/Digital Library Federation Study (2002)
Weighted Tables

TABLE 66

Q26. TOP TWO BOX SUMMARY TABLE

	TOTAL SAMPLE	RESPONDENT TYPE: FACULTY MEMBER	GRAD. STUDENT	FACULTY /GRAD	UNDER GRAD. STUDENT	INSTITUTION TYPE: PUBLIC	PRIVATE	LIBERAL ARTS	DISCIPLINE: BIOLOGICAL SCIENCES	PHYSICAL SCIENCES /MATH	SOCIAL SCIENCES	ARTS AND HUMAN.	ENGI-NEERING	BUSINESS	LAW	UNDEC. MAJOR	GENDER: MALE	FEMALE
		(A)	(B)	(C)	(D)	(E)	(F)	(G)	(H)	(I)	(J)	(K)	(L)	(M)	(N)		(P)	(Q)
Base - Total Responding	1076	296	370	666	410	436	302	338	162	149	357	197	38	125	12*	36*	592	484
I am comfortable locating and using print information	1021 94.8%	285 96.4%	349 94.3%	634 95.2%	387 94.2%	414 95.0%	288 95.4%	319 94.2%	152 94.0%	141 94.6%	344 96.3%M	187 94.9%	36 93.9%	113 91.0%	11 91.7%	36 100.0%	560 94.6%	461 95.2%
I am comfortable using my institution's web site	1017 94.7%	270 91.7%	358 97.2%A	629 94.7%	388 94.5%	415 95.5%	283 94.2%	318 94.1%	155 96.2%N	141 94.6%	340 95.3%N	180 92.0%	36 95.4%	118 94.8%	11 88.7%	35 97.2%	555 94.0%	462 95.4%
I am comfortable retrieving and using information electronically	1009 93.9%	271 91.6%	350 94.8%	621 93.4%	388 94.6%	409 93.8%	280 93.2%	319 94.5%	153 95.1%K	144 96.6%K	337 94.2%K	175 88.6%	35 93.1%	120 96.3%K	11 93.0%	34 94.4%	551 93.1%	458 94.8%
Printed books and journals will continue to be important sources for me for the next five years	973 90.5%	283 95.6%BD	325 87.9%	608 91.3%	364 89.2%	387 88.7%	271 89.7%	315 93.6%E	143 88.0%	135 90.6%MN	329 92.6%MN	186 94.3%HM N	35 91.6%MN	101 81.3%	10 80.6%	34 94.4%	544 91.8%	429 89.0%
I am finding more relevant information on the Internet than I did two years ago	935 87.2%	264 89.6%	312 84.4%	576 86.7%	359 87.9%	374 85.8%	259 86.1%	302 89.8%	143 88.5%	127 85.2%	305 85.7%	170 86.4%	35 91.5%	115 92.5%	11 90.1%	30 83.3%	513 87.1%	422 87.2%
My campus library meets most of my information needs	922 85.9%	226 76.8%	316 85.3%A	541 81.6%	381 92.8%A BC	380 87.4%	251 83.2%	291 86.3%	143 88.0%	121 81.8%	301 84.2%	175 88.6%	32 85.5%	105 85.0%	11 95.7%IJ LM	34 94.4%	500 84.6%	422 87.4%

Proportions/Means: Columns Tested (5% risk level) - A/B/D - C/D - E/F/G - H/I/J/K/L/M/N - P/Q
* small base

Table 650
Page 2169

Outsell/Digital Library Federation Study (2002)
Weighted Tables

TABLE 66, continued

Q26. TOP TWO BOX SUMMARY TABLE

		RESPONDENT TYPE				INSTITUTION TYPE			DISCIPLINE								GENDER	
	TOTAL SAMPLE	FACULTY MEMBER	GRAD. STUDENT	FACULTY /GRAD	UNDER GRAD. STUDENT	PUBLIC	PRIVATE	LIBERAL ARTS	BIOLOGIAL SCIENCES	PHYSICAL SCIENCES /MATH	SOCIAL SCIENCES	ARTS AND HUMAN.	ENGI-NEERING	BUSINESS	LAW	UNDEC. MAJOR	MALE	FEMALE
		(A)	(B)	(C)	(D)	(E)	(F)	(G)	(H)	(I)	(J)	(K)	(L)	(M)	(N)		(P)	(Q)
When I find information online, I print it out to read it	829 77.2%	232 78.7%	301 81.7%D	534 80.4%D	295 71.9%	342 78.7%	230 76.5%	256 75.7%	126 78.1%	111 75.0%	293 82.1%M	148 75.0%	28 74.6%	89 71.6%	10 84.7%M	23 63.9%	434 73.6%	395 81.6%P
I often find I have an urgent need for information	646 60.0%	185 62.4%	229 62.0%	414 62.2%	232 56.5%	265 60.9%	187 62.2%	193 57.0%	101 62.5%	81 54.4%	222 62.1%	120 60.8%	28 73.1%IJK M	72 57.5%	9 70.4%I	14 38.9%	348 58.8%	297 61.5%
I need access to information 24 hours a day, 7 days a week (24/7)	601 55.9%	110 37.3%	238 64.3%A	348 52.3%	253 61.7%A C	260 59.8%	157 52.0%	184 54.3%	94 58.2%I	65 43.6%	211 58.9%I	103 52.6%	27 70.2%HIJ K	74 59.7%I	8 65.3%I	19 52.8%	315 53.2%	286 59.1%
Browsing the stacks or journal shelves in a library is an important way for me to get information	595 55.4%	163 55.4%	187 50.5%	350 52.6%	245 59.7%B C	229 52.5%	156 51.7%	210 62.3%EF	77 47.8%	76 51.0%	196 54.7%M	141 71.6%HI JLMN	22 57.3%M	53 42.9%	6 51.4%	24 66.7%	344 58.1%	251 52.0%
I can find everything I need on my institution's web site	589 55.1%	135 46.5%	187 50.5%	322 48.8%	267 65.1%A BC	235 54.0%	157 52.7%	197 58.6%	93 57.6%I	65 44.2%	211 59.3%I	101 51.4%	20 52.3%	72 57.9%I	6 49.3%	22 61.1%	301 51.2%	288 59.8%P
Having a personal library is more important to me now than it was two years ago	566 52.7%	89 30.0%	214 57.9%A	303 45.5%	264 64.3%A C	227 52.2%	155 51.2%	184 54.5%	75 46.2%	67 45.0%	194 54.2%	114 58.0%HI	21 54.6%	66 53.4%	6 49.3%	24 66.7%	287 48.5%	279 57.8%P

Proportions/Means: Columns Tested (5% risk level) - A/B/D - C/D - E/F/G - H/I/J/K/L/M/N - P/Q
* small base

Table 650
Page 2170

Outsell/Digital Library Federation Study (2002)
Weighted Tables

TABLE 66, continued

Q26. TOP TWO BOX SUMMARY TABLE

		RESPONDENT TYPE				INSTITUTION TYPE			DISCIPLINE								GENDER	
	TOTAL SAMPLE	FACULTY MEMBER	GRAD. STUDENT	FACULTY /GRAD	UNDER GRAD. STUDENT	PUBLIC	PRIVATE	LIBERAL ARTS	BIOLOGIAL SCIENCES	PHYSICAL SCIENCES /MATH	SOCIAL SCIENCES	ARTS AND HUMAN.	ENGI- NEERING	BUSINESS	LAW	UNDEC. MAJOR	MALE	FEMALE
		(A)	(B)	(C)	(D)	(E)	(F)	(G)	(H)	(I)	(J)	(K)	(L)	(M)	(N)		(P)	(Q)
I work/study off campus more than I used to	445 41.5%	107 36.6%	212 57.2%AD	319 48.1%D	126 31.0%	237 54.3%FG	125 41.6%G	83 24.9%	66 40.8%	48 32.2%	179 50.3%IK	71 35.8%	17 43.5%I	53 42.9%	6 47.2%I	7 20.0%	234 39.8%	211 43.7%
I use the library significantly less than I did two years ago	370 34.5%	126 42.7%D	139 37.8%D	266 40.0%D	104 25.5%	164 37.7%G	115 38.2%G	91 27.0%	59 36.6%	51 34.2%	117 32.6%	55 27.8%	17 44.6%JK	60 48.5%HI JKN	4 33.3%	7 20.6%	207 35.1%	162 33.7%
I find reading information on screen satisfactory and rarely print out information	296 27.6%	57 19.3%	89 24.0%	146 21.9%	151 36.8%A BC	127 29.1%	74 24.8%	95 28.1%	41 25.7%	45 30.2%N	94 26.3%	54 27.3%	11 29.8%N	37 29.9%N	2 15.5%	12 33.3%	182 30.8%Q	114 23.6%
I often can't get information when I need it	256 23.8%	77 26.2%	95 25.6%	172 25.9%	84 20.5%	108 24.8%	72 24.0%	76 22.5%	47 28.8%N	34 22.8%N	85 23.7%N	43 21.6%N	10 25.2%N	30 24.1%N	1 8.3%	8 22.2%	143 24.1%	114 23.5%
I participate in distance learning opportunities at my institution	250 23.9%	60 21.5%	75 20.8%	136 21.1%	114 28.5%B C	104 24.4%	72 24.4%	74 22.9%	33 20.8%	32 21.9%	88 26.1%	40 20.8%	13 34.6%HIK N	34 27.8%	2 18.3%	7 20.0%	135 23.6%	115 24.4%
The Internet has not changed the way I use the library	169 15.7%	36 12.2%	52 14.0%	88 13.2%	81 19.9%A C	71 16.3%	43 14.4%	55 16.2%	24 14.8%	26 17.4%	49 13.7%	37 18.8%	6 16.0%	20 15.7%	2 12.5%	6 17.6%	99 16.7%	70 14.5%
I need help finding information 24 hours a day, 7 days a week (24/7)	149 13.8%	16 5.5%	69 18.8%A	86 12.9%	63 15.4%A	80 18.2%FG	35 11.8%	34 10.0%	20 12.5%	12 8.1%	58 16.3%I	28 14.2%	6 16.8%I	18 14.2%	2 18.1%I	4 11.1%	79 13.3%	70 14.5%

Proportions/Means: Columns Tested (5% risk level) - A/B/D - C/D - E/F/G - H/I/J/K/L/M/N - P/Q
* small base

Table 650
Page 2171

Outsell/Digital Library Federation Study (2002)
Weighted Tables

TABLE 67

Q5b. SUMMARY TABLE: Of those information categories you just mentioned as using, which is the most important? And which is the second most important?

		RESPONDENT TYPE				INSTITUTION TYPE			DISCIPLINE								GENDER	
	TOTAL SAMPLE	FACULTY MEMBER	GRAD. STUDENT	FACULTY /GRAD	UNDER GRAD. STUDENT	PUBLIC	PRIVATE	LIBERAL ARTS	BIOLOGIAL SCIENCES	PHYSICAL SCIENCES /MATH	SOCIAL SCIENCES	ARTS AND HUMAN.	ENGI-NEERING	BUSINESS	LAW	UNDEC. MAJOR	MALE	FEMALE
		(A)	(B)	(C)	(D)	(E)	(F)	(G)	(H)	(I)	(J)	(K)	(L)	(M)	(N)		(P)	(Q)
Base - Regularly use at least one category of information	3221	928	1049	1977	1244	1330	866	1025	463	505	991	598	124	406	32	101	1819	1402
Reference Information	1524 47.3%	459 49.4%	506 48.2%	964 48.8%	560 45.0%	664 49.9%	403 46.6%	457 44.6%	236 51.0%JMN	351 69.5%HJK LMN	368 37.2%M	323 53.9%JM N	78 62.7%HJK MN	106 26.1%	13 38.7%	50 49.5%	889 48.9%	636 45.3%
Most Important	629 19.5%	130 14.0%	180 17.2%	311 15.7%	318 25.6%A BC	294 22.1%F	135 15.6%	199 19.4%	77 16.7%MN	80 15.8%MN	207 20.9%IM N	166 27.7%HI JLMN	23 18.2%MN	45 11.0%	2 5.8%	30 29.7%	323 17.8%	306 21.8%P
2nd Most Important	895 27.8%	328 35.4%D	325 31.0%D	654 33.1%D	242 19.4%	370 27.8%	268 30.9%G	258 25.2%	158 34.2%JKM	271 53.7%HJK LMN	162 16.3%	157 26.2%JM	55 44.5%HJK MN	61 15.1%	11 33.0%JM	20 19.8%	566 31.1%Q	329 23.5%
Scientific and technical information	1285 39.9%	499 53.8%BD	474 45.2%D	974 49.2%D	311 25.0%	569 42.7%G	368 42.5%G	349 34.0%	346 74.7%JKM N	426 84.4%HJK MN	222 22.4%KN	69 11.6%N	106 85.5%HJK MN	92 22.7%KN	2 4.7%	22 21.8%	843 46.4%Q	442 31.5%
Most Important	921 28.6%	377 40.6%BD	343 32.7%D	720 36.4%D	202 16.2%	396 29.8%	262 30.3%G	263 25.7%	258 55.7%JKM N	363 71.9%HJK MN	128 12.9%KN	29 4.9%N	90 72.7%HJK MN	43 10.5%KN	* 1.0%	10 9.9%	625 34.4%Q	296 21.1%
2nd Most Important	364 11.3%	122 13.2%D	132 12.6%D	254 12.8%D	110 8.8%	173 13.0%G	106 12.2%G	85 8.3%	88 19.0%IJK LMN	63 12.5%KN	94 9.5%N	40 6.7%	16 12.8%KN	49 12.1%KN	1 3.7%	12 11.9%	218 12.0%	146 10.4%
Business Information	410 12.7%	130 14.0%	126 12.0%	256 13.0%	154 12.4%	160 12.1%	131 15.1%G	119 11.6%	4 1.0%	16 3.2%H	58 5.9%HIK	17 2.8%H	7 5.8%HIK	300 73.9%HIJ KLN	3 9.4%HIK	4 4.0%	273 15.0%Q	138 9.8%

Proportions/Means: Columns Tested (5% risk level) - A/B/D - C/D - E/F/G - H/I/J/K/L/M/N - P/Q
* small base

Table 60
Page 75

Outsell/Digital Library Federation Study (2002)
Weighted Tables

TABLE 67, continued

Q5b. SUMMARY TABLE: Of those information categories you just mentioned as using, which is the most important? And which is the second most important?

		RESPONDENT TYPE				INSTITUTION TYPE			DISCIPLINE								GENDER	
	TOTAL SAMPLE	FACULTY MEMBER	GRAD. STUDENT	FACULTY /GRAD	UNDER GRAD. STUDENT	PUBLIC	PRIVATE	LIBERAL ARTS	BIOLOGIAL SCIENCES	PHYSICAL SCIENCES /MATH	SOCIAL SCIENCES	ARTS AND HUMAN.	ENGI-NEERING	BUSINESS	LAW	UNDEC. MAJOR	MALE	FEMALE
		(A)	(B)	(C)	(D)	(E)	(F)	(G)	(H)	(I)	(J)	(K)	(L)	(M)	(N)		(P)	(Q)
Most Important	263 8.2%	85 9.1%	85 8.1%	169 8.6%	94 7.6%	104 7.8%	78 9.1%	81 7.9%	3 0.6%	6 1.2%	19 1.9%	7 1.1%	2 1.6%	225 55.4%HIJKL N	0 0	2 2.0%	174 9.5%Q	90 6.4%
2nd Most Important	147 4.6%	46 4.9%	41 3.9%	87 4.4%	60 4.8%	56 4.2%	52 6.0%G	38 3.7%	2 0.4%	10 2.0%H	39 4.0%HK	10 1.7%H	5 4.2%HIK	75 18.5%HIJ KLN	3 9.4%HIJ KL	2 2.0%	99 5.5%Q	48 3.4%
Humanities Information	714 22.2%	167 18.0%	186 17.8%	353 17.9%	361 29.1%A BC	239 18.0%	167 19.3%	309 30.1%EF	11 2.5%	30 5.9%HM	239 24.1%HI LMN	377 63.1%HIJ LMN	4 3.5%	11 2.7%	2 6.8%HM	39 38.6%	340 18.7%	374 26.7%P
Most Important	401 12.4%	106 11.4%	102 9.7%	208 10.5%	193 15.5%AB C	126 9.4%	111 12.8%E	164 16.0%E	2 0.4%	11 2.2%H	90 9.1%HI LMN	270 45.1%HIJ LMN	2 1.4%H	5 1.1%	1 1.6%H	21 20.8%	212 11.7%	189 13.5%
2nd Most Important	314 9.7%	61 6.5%	84 8.0%	145 7.3%	169 13.6%AB C	113 8.5%	56 6.5%	144 14.1%EF	10 2.1%	19 3.8%M	149 15.0%HI LMN	108 18.0%HIL MN	3 2.1%	7 1.6%	2 5.2%HL M	18 17.8%	128 7.1%	185 13.2%P
Social science information	945 29.4%	275 29.6%	309 29.5%	584 29.5%	361 29.0%	384 28.9%	245 28.3%	316 30.9%	32 6.8%	36 7.1%	600 60.5%HI KLMN	174 29.0%HIL M	7 5.4%	68 16.7%HI L	8 24.1%HI LM	22 21.8%	461 25.3%	485 34.6%P
Most Important	541 16.8%	158 17.0%	191 18.2%	349 17.7%	191 15.4%	230 17.3%	134 15.5%	177 17.2%	11 2.3%	11 2.2%	415 41.9%HI KLMN	62 10.3%HIL	2 1.6%	28 6.9%HIL	2 6.8%HIL	10 9.9%	239 13.1%	302 21.5%P
2nd Most Important	405 12.6%	117 12.6%	118 11.2%	235 11.9%	170 13.7%	154 11.6%	111 12.8%	140 13.6%	21 4.6%	25 5.0%	184 18.6%HI LM	112 18.7%HIL M	5 3.7%	40 9.8%HI L	6 17.3%HI LM	12 11.9%	222 12.2%	183 13.0%
Legal Data	175 5.4%	58 6.3%	63 6.0%	121 6.1%D	54 4.3%	79 6.0%	55 6.4%G	41 4.0%	6 1.3%	5 1.0%	81 8.2%HIK L	15 2.4%	3 2.3%	33 8.2%HI KL	29 90.6%HIJ KLM	3 3.0%	102 5.6%	74 5.3%

Proportions/Means: Columns Tested (5% risk level) - A/B/D - C/D - E/F/G - H/I/J/K/L/M/N - P/Q
* small base

Table 60
Page 76

Outsell/Digital Library Federation Study (2002)
Weighted Tables

TABLE 67, continued

Q5b. SUMMARY TABLE: Of those information categories you just mentioned as using, which is the most important? And which is the second most important?

		RESPONDENT TYPE				INSTITUTION TYPE			DISCIPLINE								GENDER	
	TOTAL SAMPLE	FACULTY MEMBER	GRAD. STUDENT	FACULTY /GRAD	UNDER GRAD. STUDENT	PUBLIC	PRIVATE	LIBERAL ARTS	BIOLOGIAL SCIENCES	PHYSICAL SCIENCES /MATH	SOCIAL SCIENCES	ARTS AND HUMAN.	ENGI-NEERING	BUSINESS	LAW	UNDEC. MAJOR	MALE	FEMALE
		(A)	(B)	(C)	(D)	(E)	(F)	(G)	(H)	(I)	(J)	(K)	(L)	(M)	(N)		(P)	(Q)
Most Important	67 2.1%	23 2.5%D	29 2.7%D	52 2.6%D	15 1.2%	25 1.9%	29 3.3%G	13 1.3%	0 0	2 0.4%	21 2.1%HIL	8 1.3%H	* 0.2%	8 2.1%HI L	27 82.2%HIJ KLM	1 1.0%	40 2.2%	26 1.9%
2nd Most Important	108 3.4%	35 3.8%	34 3.3%	69 3.5%	39 3.1%	54 4.1%	26 3.1%	28 2.7%	6 1.3%	3 0.6%	60 6.1%HIK L	7 1.1%	3 2.1%I	25 6.2%HIK L	3 8.4%HIK L	2 2.0%	61 3.4%	47 3.4%
Medical Information	346 10.7%	88 9.5%	144 13.8%AD	232 11.7%D	113 9.1%	141 10.6%	118 13.6%EG	87 8.5%	202 43.7%IJKL M	46 9.1%KMN	70 7.0%KMN	10 1.7%M	10 7.7%KMN	1 0.2%	0 0	7 6.9%	158 8.7%	188 13.4%P
Most Important	145 4.5%	20 2.2%	74 7.1%AD	95 4.8%	50 4.0%A	71 5.4%G	54 6.3%G	19 1.8%	101 21.9%IJKL MN	15 3.0%KMN	21 2.1%KM	3 0.6%	1 1.2%M	1 0.2%	0 0	2 2.0%	59 3.3%	85 6.1%P
2nd Most Important	201 6.2%	68 7.3%	70 6.7%	138 7.0%	63 5.1%	69 5.2%	63 7.3%	68 6.7%	101 21.9%IJKL MN	31 6.1%KMN	49 4.9%KMN	7 1.1%M	8 6.5%KMN	0 0	0 0	5 5.0%	98 5.4%	103 7.3%P
News	569 17.7%	112 12.0%	118 11.3%	230 11.6%	339 27.2%A BC	181 13.6%	136 15.7%	252 24.6%EF	34 7.4%	48 9.5%	197 19.9%HI L	113 18.9%HIL	12 9.3%	120 29.5%HI JKLN	6 19.9%HI L	38 37.6%	325 17.9%	244 17.4%
Most Important	175 5.4%	23 2.5%	21 2.0%	44 2.2%	131 10.6%AB C	56 4.2%	41 4.7%	79 7.7%EF	8 1.7%	11 2.2%	66 6.6%HIL N	37 6.2%HIL N	1 1.2%	33 8.0%HIL N	1 2.1%	19 18.8%	103 5.7%	72 5.1%
2nd Most Important	394 12.2%	89 9.6%	97 9.3%	186 9.4%	208 16.7%A BC	125 9.4%	95 11.0%	173 16.9%EF	26 5.7%	37 7.3%	132 13.3%HI L	76 12.7%HIL	10 8.2%	87 21.5%HI JKL	6 17.8%HI L	19 18.8%	222 12.2%	172 12.2%
General interest and consumer information	191 5.9%	39 4.2%	37 3.5%	76 3.8%	115 9.2%AB C	62 4.6%	47 5.5%	81 7.9%E	9 1.9%	19 3.8%	51 5.1%HN	41 6.9%HIN	6 4.9%HN	51 12.6%HIJ KLN	* 1.0%	13 12.9%	108 5.9%	83 5.9%

Proportions/Means: Columns Tested (5% risk level) - A/B/D - C/D - E/F/G - H/I/J/K/L/M/N - P/Q
* small base

Table 60
Page 77

Outsell/Digital Library Federation Study (2002)
Weighted Tables

TABLE 67, continued

Q5b. SUMMARY TABLE: Of those information categories you just mentioned as using, which is the most important? And which is the second most important?

		RESPONDENT TYPE				INSTITUTION TYPE			DISCIPLINE								GENDER	
	TOTAL SAMPLE	FACULTY MEMBER	GRAD. STUDENT	FACULTY /GRAD	UNDER GRAD. STUDENT	PUBLIC	PRIVATE	LIBERAL ARTS	BIOLOGIAL SCIENCES	PHYSICAL SCIENCES /MATH	SOCIAL SCIENCES	ARTS AND HUMAN.	ENGI- NEERING	BUSINESS	LAW	UNDEC. MAJOR	MALE	FEMALE
		(A)	(B)	(C)	(D)	(E)	(F)	(G)	(H)	(I)	(J)	(K)	(L)	(M)	(N)		(P)	(Q)
Most Important	56 1.7%	2 0.2%	10 1.0%A	12 0.6%	44 3.5%AB C	19 1.4%	12 1.4%	25 2.4%	1 0.2%	5 1.0%	15 1.5%H	12 2.1%H	2 1.6%H	15 3.7%HIJN	0 0	6 5.9%	34 1.8%	23 1.6%
2nd Most Important	134 4.2%	37 4.0%	27 2.5%	64 3.2%	71 5.7%BC	43 3.2%	35 4.1%	56 5.5%E	8 1.7%	14 2.8%	36 3.6%	29 4.9%HN	4 3.3%	36 8.9%HIJ KLN	* 1.0%	7 6.9%	74 4.1%	60 4.3%

Proportions/Means: Columns Tested (5% risk level) - A/B/D - C/D - E/F/G - H/I/J/K/L/M/N - P/Q
* small base

Table 60
Page 78

TABLE 68

R6SUM. %YES: Which of the following information types do you use for your research?

	TOTAL SAMPLE	RESPONDENT TYPE: FACULTY MEMBER (A)	GRAD. STUDENT (B)	FACULTY /GRAD (C)	UNDER GRAD. STUDENT (D)	INSTITUTION TYPE: PUBLIC (E)	PRIVATE (F)	LIBERAL ARTS (G)	DISCIPLINE: BIOLOGIAL SCIENCES (H)	PHYSICAL SCIENCES /MATH (I)	SOCIAL SCIENCES (J)	ARTS AND HUMAN. (K)	ENGI-NEERING (L)	BUSINESS (M)	LAW (N)	UNDEC. MAJOR	GENDER: MALE (P)	FEMALE (Q)
Base - Responsibility is Research	1563	811	752	1563	0**	699	593	271	269	320	491	239	79	148	18	0*	1023	540
Print or hardcopy journals	1520 97.2%	790 97.5%	729 97.0%	1520 97.2%	0 0	681 97.4%	572 96.6%	266 98.4%	262 97.4%	312 97.5%	487 99.2%KL MN	227 95.3%	75 95.2%	139 94.3%	17 95.1%	0 0	992 97.0%	527 97.7%
Print or hardcopy books	1510 96.6%	786 97.0%	723 96.2%	1510 96.6%	0 0	675 96.6%	571 96.4%	263 97.2%	256 95.1%M	308 96.3%M	483 98.5%HM	237 99.5%HI LMN	76 96.7%M	132 89.3%	17 96.1%	0 0	985 96.3%	525 97.2%
Online abstracts and indexes	1378 88.2%	695 85.7%	683 90.9%A	1378 88.2%	0 0	612 87.5%	529 89.2%	237 87.6%	249 92.5%KN	288 90.0%KN	434 88.5%KN	187 78.4%	71 89.7%KN	135 91.2%KN	14 80.6%	0 0	903 88.3%	475 87.9%
Papers delivered at professional meetings	1320 84.5%	737 90.8%B	584 77.6%	1320 84.5%	0 0	575 82.2%	504 85.1%	242 89.3%E	235 87.3%N	273 85.3%N	412 83.9%N	194 81.2%N	70 89.0%KN	127 86.2%N	9 53.4%	0 0	870 85.0%	451 83.5%
Data	1284 82.1%	649 80.0%	635 84.4%A	1284 82.1%	0 0	589 84.2%G	486 82.1%	208 77.0%	235 87.3%KN	262 81.9%K	431 87.7%IK N	141 59.2%	67 85.3%KN	135 91.2%IK N	13 73.8%K	0 0	829 81.0%	455 84.3%
Online databases, data sets or data sources	1279 81.8%	645 79.6%	633 84.3%A	1279 81.8%	0 0	563 80.5%	504 85.0%G	212 78.2%	230 85.3%IL	251 78.4%	402 82.0%	192 80.3%	62 78.7%	126 85.5%	16 90.3%IKL	0 0	832 81.3%	447 82.8%
Manuscripts and other primary source documents	1267 81.1%	672 82.8%	595 79.2%	1267 81.1%	0 0	567 81.0%	493 83.1%G	208 76.7%	230 85.3%ILM N	245 76.6%M	419 85.4%IL MN	203 85.0%IL MN	57 72.4%	100 67.9%	13 72.8%	0 0	819 80.1%	447 82.9%

Proportions/Means: Columns Tested (5% risk level) - A/B/D - C/D - E/F/G - H/I/J/K/L/M/N - P/Q
* small base; ** very small base (under 30) ineligible for sig testing

Table 61
Page 79

Outsell/Digital Library Federation Study (2002)
Weighted Tables

TABLE 68, continued

R6SUM. %YES: Which of the following information types do you use for your research?

		RESPONDENT TYPE				INSTITUTION TYPE			DISCIPLINE								GENDER	
	TOTAL SAMPLE	FACULTY MEMBER	GRAD. STUDENT	FACULTY /GRAD	UNDER GRAD. STUDENT	PUBLIC	PRIVATE	LIBERAL ARTS	BIOLOGIAL SCIENCES	PHYSICAL SCIENCES /MATH	SOCIAL SCIENCES	ARTS AND HUMAN.	ENGI- NEERING	BUSINESS	LAW	UNDEC. MAJOR	MALE	FEMALE
		(A)	(B)	(C)	(D)	(E)	(F)	(G)	(H)	(I)	(J)	(K)	(L)	(M)	(N)		(P)	(Q)
Base - Responsibility is Research	1563	811	752	1563	0**	699	593	271	269	320	491	239	79	148	18	0*	1023	540
Print abstracts and indexes	1223 78.3%	613 75.6%	610 81.2%A	1223 78.3%	0 0	545 78.0%	475 80.2%	203 74.9%	223 82.7%KN	250 78.1%KN	399 81.2%KN	165 69.0%	61 77.6%K	114 77.4%	12 68.0%	0 0	788 77.1%	435 80.6%
e-journals	1171 74.9%	567 70.0%	603 80.2%A	1171 74.9%	0 0	548 78.4%G	436 73.6%	187 69.0%	224 83.3%JKL MN	259 80.9%JKL N	357 72.8%KN	150 62.9%	59 74.3%KN	111 74.8%KN	11 62.1%	0 0	737 72.0%	434 80.4%P
Dissertations	1102 70.5%	540 66.6%	563 74.8%A	1102 70.5%	0 0	512 73.2%G	432 72.8%G	159 58.7%	175 65.0%N	238 74.4%HMN	350 71.3%MN	183 76.5%HM N	66 84.2%HIJ KMN	86 57.9%N	5 29.1%	0 0	707 69.1%	395 73.2%
Technical reports	903 57.8%	478 58.9%	425 56.6%	903 57.8%	0 0	403 57.6%	351 59.2%	149 55.1%	191 70.9%JKM N	227 70.9%JKM N	259 52.9%KN	64 26.8%	71 89.7%HIJ KMN	86 57.9%KN	5 31.1%	0 0	612 59.8%Q	291 54.0%
Proprietary software or application	860 55.0%	458 56.4%	402 53.5%	860 55.0%	0 0	380 54.4%	327 55.2%	153 56.3%	167 62.1%JKN	211 65.9%JKN	244 49.8%K	93 39.0%	51 65.1%JKN	85 57.2%K	8 47.6%	0 0	589 57.6%Q	270 50.1%
News	838 53.6%	475 58.6%B	363 48.3%	838 53.6%	0 0	355 50.7%	317 53.5%	166 61.3%EF	106 39.2%	114 35.6%	299 60.9%HI L	156 65.3%HI L	34 43.4%	116 78.6%HI JKL	13 75.7%HIJL	0 0	551 53.9%	287 53.1%
Magazines	768 49.2%	413 51.0%	355 47.2%	768 49.2%	0 0	326 46.6%	289 48.7%	153 56.6%EF	90 33.3%	143 44.7%H	233 47.5%H	155 64.8%HI JLN	42 52.9%HI	98 66.0%HI JLN	8 47.6%H	0 0	526 51.4%Q	242 44.8%

Proportions/Means: Columns Tested (5% risk level) - A/B/D - C/D - E/F/G - H/I/J/K/L/M/N - P/Q
* small base; ** very small base (under 30) ineligible for sig testing

Table 61
Page 80

TABLE 68, continued

R6SUM. %YES: Which of the following information types do you use for your research?

	TOTAL SAMPLE	RESPONDENT TYPE: FACULTY MEMBER	GRAD. STUDENT	FACULTY /GRAD	UNDER GRAD. STUDENT	INSTITUTION TYPE: PUBLIC	PRIVATE	LIBERAL ARTS	DISCIPLINE: BIOLOGIAL SCIENCES	PHYSICAL SCIENCES /MATH	SOCIAL SCIENCES	ARTS AND HUMAN.	ENGI-NEERING	BUSINESS	LAW	UNDEC. MAJOR	GENDER: MALE	FEMALE
		(A)	(B)	(C)	(D)	(E)	(F)	(G)	(H)	(I)	(J)	(K)	(L)	(M)	(N)		(P)	(Q)
Base - Responsibility is Research	1563	811	752	1563	0**	699	593	271	269	320	491	239	79	148	18	0*	1023	540
Photographs, prints and other visual resources	761 48.7%	380 46.8%	381 50.7%	761 48.7%	0 0	337 48.2%	299 50.5%	125 46.1%	177 65.7%IJL MN	142 44.4%MN	192 39.1%MN	167 70.0%IJ LMN	42 53.7%IJM N	38 25.8%	3 16.5%	0 0	500 48.9%	261 48.3%
Pre-prints	614 39.3%	357 44.0%B	257 34.1%	614 39.3%	0 0	262 37.5%	235 39.7%	116 42.9%	128 47.7%JKM N	215 67.2%HJK LMN	124 25.3%	50 21.1%	42 53.7%JKM N	48 32.7%K	5 28.2%	0 0	445 43.5%Q	168 31.2%
e-books	288 18.4%	122 15.0%	166 22.1%A	288 18.4%	0 0	140 20.0%G	117 19.7%G	31 11.5%	48 18.0%	45 14.1%	102 20.7%I	44 18.3%	20 25.7%HIK M	25 17.0%	4 20.4%	0 0	182 17.8%	105 19.5%

Proportions/Means: Columns Tested (5% risk level) - A/B/D - C/D - E/F/G - H/I/J/K/L/M/N - P/Q
* small base; ** very small base (under 30) ineligible for sig testing

Table 61
Page 81

TABLE 69

T6SUM. %YES: Which of the following information types do you use for your teaching?

		RESPONDENT TYPE				INSTITUTION TYPE			DISCIPLINE								GENDER	
	TOTAL SAMPLE	FACULTY MEMBER	GRAD. STUDENT	FACULTY /GRAD	UNDER GRAD. STUDENT	PUBLIC	PRIVATE	LIBERAL ARTS	BIOLOGIAL SCIENCES	PHYSICAL SCIENCES /MATH	SOCIAL SCIENCES	ARTS AND HUMAN.	ENGI-NEERING	BUSINESS	LAW	UNDEC. MAJOR	MALE	FEMALE
		(A)	(B)	(C)	(D)	(E)	(F)	(G)	(H)	(I)	(J)	(K)	(L)	(M)	(N)		(P)	(Q)
Base - Responsibility is Teaching	1299	920	379	1299	0**	518	461	319	206	282	344	258	50	152	8*	0*	912	387
Print or hardcopy books	1245 95.8%	894 97.2%B	350 92.5%	1245 95.8%	0 0	496 95.6%	439 95.1%	311 97.2%	193 93.6%	270 95.7%	337 97.8%HL M	249 96.5%	47 93.6%	142 93.9%	8 97.9%	0 0	878 96.3%	367 94.7%
Print or hardcopy journals	1054 81.1%	797 86.6%B	257 67.9%	1054 81.1%	0 0	399 77.0%	379 82.1%	276 86.5%E	181 88.0%ILM	199 70.6%	297 86.3%IL	213 82.6%IL	36 71.5%	121 79.8%I	7 89.4%IL	0 0	754 82.7%Q	300 77.5%
News	861 66.3%	666 72.4%B	194 51.3%	861 66.3%	0 0	317 61.1%	295 63.9%	249 77.9%EF	125 60.7%L	150 53.2%L	258 74.9%HI KL	166 64.3%IL	19 39.0%	136 89.6%HI JKL	7 89.4%HIJKL	0 0	598 65.6%	262 67.8%
Photographs, prints and other visual resources	817 62.9%	572 62.2%	244 64.6%	817 62.9%	0 0	308 59.5%	303 65.8%	205 64.1%	172 83.3%IJL MN	156 55.3%MN	186 54.1%N	202 78.3%IJ LMN	32 65.1%IJM N	66 43.6%	3 34.0%	0 0	571 62.6%	246 63.5%
Data	814 62.7%	597 64.9%B	217 57.3%	814 62.7%	0 0	311 60.0%	289 62.7%	214 67.1%	149 72.2%IKL N	177 62.8%KL	239 69.4%KL N	120 46.5%	27 53.5%	100 65.6%KL N	4 48.9%	0 0	590 64.7%Q	224 57.9%
Online databases, data sets or data sources	773 59.5%	572 62.1%B	202 53.3%	773 59.5%	0 0	291 56.2%	278 60.3%	204 63.7%E	125 60.7%L	164 58.2%	218 63.4%L	146 56.5%	24 48.8%	91 60.1%L	5 66.0%L	0 0	562 61.6%Q	211 54.6%
Manuscripts and other primary source documents	743 57.2%	531 57.6%	213 56.2%	743 57.2%	0 0	301 58.2%	266 57.7%	176 55.0%	145 70.5%IJL MN	133 47.2%	209 60.7%IL M	167 64.8%IL MN	23 47.1%	62 41.1%	4 48.9%	0 0	535 58.7%	208 53.8%

Proportions/Means: Columns Tested (5% risk level) - A/B/D - C/D - E/F/G - H/I/J/K/L/M/N - P/Q
* small base; ** very small base (under 30) ineligible for sig testing

Table 189
Page 692

Outsell/Digital Library Federation Study (2002)
Weighted Tables

TABLE 69, continued

T6SUM. %YES: Which of the following information types do you use for your teaching?

		RESPONDENT TYPE				INSTITUTION TYPE			DISCIPLINE									GENDER	
	TOTAL SAMPLE	FACULTY MEMBER	GRAD. STUDENT	FACULTY /GRAD	UNDER GRAD. STUDENT	PUBLIC	PRIVATE	LIBERAL ARTS	BIOLOGIAL SCIENCES	PHYSICAL SCIENCES /MATH	SOCIAL SCIENCES	ARTS AND HUMAN.	ENGI- NEERING	BUSINESS	LAW	UNDEC. MAJOR	MALE	FEMALE
		(A)	(B)	(C)	(D)	(E)	(F)	(G)	(H)	(I)	(J)	(K)	(L)	(M)	(N)		(P)	(Q)
Base - Responsibility is Teaching	1299	920	379	1299	0**	518	461	319	206	282	344	258	50	152	8*	0*	912	387
Magazines	709 54.6%	559 60.7%B	150 39.7%	709 54.6%	0 0	249 48.0%	241 52.3%	219 68.7%EF	90 43.6%	132 46.8%	173 50.3%	171 66.5%HI JL	20 40.7%	118 77.9%HI JKLN	4 55.3%	0 0	503 55.2%	206 53.2%
Papers delivered at professional meetings	625 48.1%	497 54.0%B	128 33.8%	625 48.1%	0 0	228 44.1%	239 51.7%E	158 49.5%	105 50.9%I	112 39.7%	179 51.9%I	120 46.5%	30 61.0%HIK N	76 50.3%I	3 42.6%	0 0	451 49.4%	174 45.0%
Proprietary software or application	587 45.2%	441 47.9%B	146 38.5%	587 45.2%	0 0	217 41.8%	185 40.2%	185 57.9%EF	99 47.9%K	153 54.3%JKN	137 39.9%	88 34.3%	32 63.4%HJK MN	75 49.7%K	3 36.2%	0 0	431 47.2%Q	156 40.4%
Online abstracts and indexes	564 43.4%	420 45.6%B	144 38.1%	564 43.4%	0 0	214 41.3%	188 40.8%	161 50.5%EF	125 60.7%IJK LMN	103 36.5%	154 44.8%	101 39.1%	19 39.0%	59 38.7%	3 38.3%	0 0	385 42.2%	179 46.4%
Print abstracts and indexes	490 37.7%	355 38.6%	135 35.6%	490 37.7%	0 0	189 36.6%	172 37.2%	128 40.2%	103 50.0%IJK LM	88 31.2%	130 37.7%	99 38.3%	20 40.1%	47 31.3%	3 36.2%	0 0	347 38.0%	143 36.9%
e-journals	476 36.6%	348 37.8%	128 33.7%	476 36.6%	0 0	186 35.8%	162 35.1%	128 40.1%	114 55.1%IJK LMN	93 33.0%	120 35.0%	81 31.3%	17 33.1%	49 32.5%	2 27.7%	0 0	329 36.0%	147 37.9%
Technical reports	429 33.1%	337 36.6%B	93 24.4%	429 33.1%	0 0	167 32.2%	156 33.9%	106 33.2%	90 43.6%IKN	96 34.0%K	124 36.1%K	35 13.5%	25 50.0%IJK MN	58 38.0%K	2 27.7%K	0 0	327 35.8%Q	103 26.5%

Proportions/Means: Columns Tested (5% risk level) - A/B/D - C/D - E/F/G - H/I/J/K/L/M/N - P/Q
* small base; ** very small base (under 30) ineligible for sig testing

Table 189
Page 693

Outsell/Digital Library Federation Study (2002)
Weighted Tables

TABLE 69, continued

T6SUM. %YES: Which of the following information types do you use for your teaching?

		RESPONDENT TYPE				INSTITUTION TYPE			DISCIPLINE								GENDER	
	TOTAL SAMPLE	FACULTY MEMBER	GRAD. STUDENT	FACULTY /GRAD	UNDER GRAD. STUDENT	PUBLIC	PRIVATE	LIBERAL ARTS	BIOLOGIAL SCIENCES	PHYSICAL SCIENCES /MATH	SOCIAL SCIENCES	ARTS AND HUMAN.	ENGI-NEERING	BUSINESS	LAW	UNDEC. MAJOR	MALE	FEMALE
		(A)	(B)	(C)	(D)	(E)	(F)	(G)	(H)	(I)	(J)	(K)	(L)	(M)	(N)		(P)	(Q)
Base - Responsibility is Teaching	1299	920	379	1299	0**	518	461	319	206	282	344	258	50	152	8*	0*	912	387
Pre-prints	282 21.7%	228 24.8%B	54 14.3%	282 21.7%	0 0	112 21.6%	110 23.9%	61 19.0%	55 26.9%K	64 22.7%K	75 21.9%	37 14.3%	17 34.9%IJK M	32 20.9%	2 21.3%	0 0	211 23.1%	72 18.5%
Dissertations	277 21.3%	198 21.6%	78 20.7%	277 21.3%	0 0	119 23.0%G	107 23.1%G	51 15.9%	45 21.8%M	46 16.3%	79 23.0%M	72 27.8%IM N	15 29.7%IMN	20 12.9%	1 12.8%	0 0	203 22.2%	74 19.1%
e-books	134 10.3%	92 10.0%	42 11.1%	134 10.3%	0 0	49 9.5%	53 11.4%	32 10.2%	21 10.3%	18 6.4%	51 14.8%IM	27 10.4%	6 12.8%IM	10 6.7%	1 8.5%	0 0	93 10.2%	41 10.5%

Proportions/Means: Columns Tested (5% risk level) - A/B/D - C/D - E/F/G - H/I/J/K/L/M/N - P/Q
* small base; ** very small base (under 30) ineligible for sig testing

Table 189
Page 694

TABLE 70

S6SUM. %YES: Which of the following information types do you use for your coursework?

		RESPONDENT TYPE				INSTITUTION TYPE			DISCIPLINE									GENDER	
	TOTAL SAMPLE	FACULTY MEMBER	GRAD. STUDENT	FACULTY /GRAD	UNDER GRAD. STUDENT	PUBLIC	PRIVATE	LIBERAL ARTS	BIOLOGIAL SCIENCES	PHYSICAL SCIENCES /MATH	SOCIAL SCIENCES	ARTS AND HUMAN.	ENGI-NEERING	BUSINESS	LAW	UNDEC. MAJOR	MALE	FEMALE
		(A)	(B)	(C)	(D)	(E)	(F)	(G)	(H)	(I)	(J)	(K)	(L)	(M)	(N)		(P)	(Q)
Base - Student	2304	0**	1056	1056	1248	1065	534	705	308	305	771	437	90	266	25	102	1102	1202
Print or hardcopy books	2150 93.3%	0 0	973 92.2%	973 92.2%	1177 94.3%	984 92.4%	497 93.1%	669 94.9%	279 90.6%	284 93.1%	724 93.9%	413 94.6%H	83 91.3%	245 92.0%	24 95.9%	99 97.1%	1023 92.8%	1127 93.8%
Print or hardcopy journals	1858 80.6%	0 0	904 85.6%D	904 85.6%D	954 76.4%	865 81.2%	440 82.4%	552 78.4%	258 83.7%ILM	219 71.8%	679 88.0%IK LMN	352 80.5%I	68 74.7%	199 74.8%	20 78.9%	64 62.7%	861 78.1%	997 82.9%P
Online databases, data sets or data sources	1849 80.2%	0 0	774 73.2%	774 73.2%	1075 86.2%B C	818 76.8%	424 79.4%	607 86.0%EF	249 80.9%IL	209 68.5%	649 84.1%IK L	344 78.7%IL	64 70.2%	229 86.0%IK L	21 83.7%IL	85 83.3%	864 78.4%	984 81.9%
Data	1734 75.2%	0 0	727 68.8%	727 68.8%	1007 80.7%B C	786 73.8%	370 69.2%	578 82.0%EF	234 76.0%KN	223 73.1%KN	617 80.0%IK LN	276 63.1%N	65 72.1%KN	227 85.3%HI KLN	13 53.1%	79 77.5%	848 77.0%	885 73.7%
Online abstracts and indexes	1685 73.1%	0 0	756 71.6%	756 71.6%	929 74.4%	779 73.2%	378 70.8%	528 74.9%	233 75.7%IKL N	193 63.3%	613 79.5%IK LN	300 68.7%	58 64.4%	204 76.6%IK LN	15 59.9%	69 67.6%	764 69.3%	921 76.7%P
News	1484 64.4%	0 0	496 46.9%	496 46.9%	988 79.2%B C	600 56.4%	308 57.7%	575 81.6%EF	153 49.7%IL	120 39.3%	532 69.0%HI L	310 71.0%HI L	38 42.0%	227 85.3%HI JKLN	16 62.6%HI L	88 86.3%	695 63.0%	789 65.7%
Manuscripts and other primary source documents	1474 64.0%	0 0	641 60.7%	641 60.7%	833 66.8%B C	635 59.6%	324 60.7%	515 73.0%EF	194 63.1%ILM	156 51.1%	549 71.2%HI LMN	319 73.1%HI LMN	41 45.8%	131 49.3%	15 58.5%L	68 66.7%	658 59.7%	816 67.9%P
Photographs, prints and other visual resources	1371 59.5%	0 0	502 47.5%	502 47.5%	869 69,6%B C	593 55.7%	294 55.0%	484 68.7%EF	195 63.4%ILN	154 50.5%N	440 57.1%N	307 70.3%HI JLMN	48 52.9%N	153 57.7%N	5 21.1%	68 66.7%	651 59.0%	720 59.9%

Proportions/Means: Columns Tested (5% risk level) - A/B/D - C/D - E/F/G - H/I/J/K/L/M/N - P/Q
** very small base (under 30) ineligible for sig testing

Table 317
Page 1295

Outsell/Digital Library Federation Study (2002)
Weighted Tables

TABLE 70, continued

S6SUM. %YES: Which of the following information types do you use for your coursework?

		RESPONDENT TYPE				INSTITUTION TYPE			DISCIPLINE								GENDER	
	TOTAL SAMPLE	FACULTY MEMBER (A)	GRAD. STUDENT (B)	FACULTY /GRAD (C)	UNDER GRAD. STUDENT (D)	PUBLIC (E)	PRIVATE (F)	LIBERAL ARTS (G)	BIOLOGICAL SCIENCES (H)	PHYSICAL SCIENCES /MATH (I)	SOCIAL SCIENCES (J)	ARTS AND HUMAN. (K)	ENGI-NEERING (L)	BUSINESS (M)	LAW (N)	UNDEC. MAJOR	MALE (P)	FEMALE (Q)
Base - Student	2304	0**	1056	1056	1248	1065	534	705	308	305	771	437	90	266	25	102	1102	1202
Print abstracts and indexes	1361 59.1%	0 0	656 62.1%D	656 62.1%D	706 56.5%	655 61.5%G	311 58.2%	395 56.1%	190 61.7%IL	151 49.5%	521 67.6%IK LMN	256 58.7%IL	45 49.4%	144 54.2%	13 53.1%	41 40.2%	595 54.0%	766 63.7%P
Magazines	1310 56.9%	0 0	452 42.8%	452 42.8%	858 68.8%B C	553 52.0%	277 51.8%	480 68.1%EF	142 46.0%N	120 39.3%N	440 57.1%HI LN	300 68.7%HI JLN	41 45.5%N	189 71.0%HI JLN	7 29.3%	71 69.6%	630 57.1%	680 56.6%
e-journals	1227 53.3%	0 0	592 56.0%D	592 56.0%D	635 50.9%	562 52.8%	305 57.2%	360 51.1%	190 61.7%IKL N	150 49.2%N	449 58.3%IK LN	202 46.2%N	39 43.6%	144 54.2%KL N	9 34.7%	44 43.1%	562 51.0%	666 55.4%
Proprietary software or application	958 41.6%	0 0	451 42.7%	451 42.7%	507 40.6%	454 42.7%G	245 45.9%G	258 36.6%	128 41.7%KN	140 45.9%KN	299 38.8%	142 32.6%	56 61.5%HIJ KN	150 56.3%HI JKN	7 29.9%	35 34.3%	510 46.2%Q	448 37.3%
Papers delivered at professional meetings	947 41.1%	0 0	590 55.9%D	590 55.9%D	356 28.5%	501 47.1%G	240 45.0%G	205 29.1%	130 42.3%KMN	115 37.7%	400 52.0%HI KLMN	148 33.8%	39 43.3%KMN	87 32.9%	7 29.9%	19 18.6%	433 39.3%	514 42.8%
Technical reports	883 38.3%	0 0	448 42.4%D	448 42.4%D	436 34.9%	445 41.8%G	199 37.3%	239 33.9%	139 45.1%KN	150 49.2%JKN	303 39.3%KN	78 17.9%	59 65.7%HIJ KMN	127 47.9%JK N	4 17.7%	22 21.6%	472 42.9%Q	411 34.2%
Dissertations	866 37.6%	0 0	465 44.0%D	465 44.0%D	400 32.1%	412 38.7%	197 36.9%	257 36.5%	94 30.6%MN	91 29.8%MN	376 48.8%HI LMN	187 42.8%HI LMN	31 34.3%MN	60 22.4%	5 19.7%	22 21.6%	405 36.8%	461 38.3%

Proportions/Means: Columns Tested (5% risk level) - A/B/D - C/D - E/F/G - H/I/J/K/L/M/N - P/Q
** very small base (under 30) ineligible for sig testing

Table 317
Page 1296

Outsell/Digital Library Federation Study (2002)
Weighted Tables

TABLE 70, continued

S6SUM. %YES: Which of the following information types do you use for your coursework?

	TOTAL SAMPLE	RESPONDENT TYPE: FACULTY MEMBER	RESPONDENT TYPE: GRAD. STUDENT	RESPONDENT TYPE: FACULTY /GRAD	RESPONDENT TYPE: UNDER GRAD. STUDENT	INSTITUTION TYPE: PUBLIC	INSTITUTION TYPE: PRIVATE	INSTITUTION TYPE: LIBERAL ARTS	DISCIPLINE: BIOLOGIAL SCIENCES	DISCIPLINE: PHYSICAL SCIENCES /MATH	DISCIPLINE: SOCIAL SCIENCES	DISCIPLINE: ARTS AND HUMAN.	DISCIPLINE: ENGI-NEERING	DISCIPLINE: BUSINESS	DISCIPLINE: LAW	DISCIPLINE: UNDEC. MAJOR	GENDER: MALE	GENDER: FEMALE
		(A)	(B)	(C)	(D)	(E)	(F)	(G)	(H)	(I)	(J)	(K)	(L)	(M)	(N)		(P)	(Q)
Base - Student	2304	0**	1056	1056	1248	1065	534	705	308	305	771	437	90	266	25	102	1102	1202
Pre-prints	487	0	293	293	194	254	124	110	68	80	180	59	22	57	5	16	260	227
	21.1%	0	27.8%D	27.8%D	15.5%	23.8%G	23.2%G	15.6%	22.0%K	26.2%K	23.4%K	13.6%	24.4%K	21.3%K	19.7%	15.7%	23.6%Q	18.9%
e-books	456	0	170	170	286	196	95	164	55	42	171	85	20	57	3	23	207	249
	19.8%	0	16.1%	16.1%	22.9%B C	18.4%	17.9%	23.3%EF	18.0%	13.8%	22.2%IN	19.5%IN	21.8%IN	21.3%IN	10.9%	22.5%	18.8%	20.7%

Proportions/Means: Columns Tested (5% risk level) - A/B/D - C/D - E/F/G - H/I/J/K/L/M/N - P/Q
** very small base (under 30) ineligible for sig testing

Table 317
Page 1297

Outsell/Digital Library Federation Study (2002)
Weighted Tables

TABLE 71

R7a_1. When you are doing research, how do you find information about Print or hardcopy books? That is, as you gather references and citations for your research, but before you actually try to get the specific information?

		RESPONDENT TYPE				INSTITUTION TYPE			DISCIPLINE								GENDER	
	TOTAL SAMPLE	FACULTY MEMBER	GRAD. STUDENT	FACULTY /GRAD	UNDER GRAD. STUDENT	PUBLIC	PRIVATE	LIBERAL ARTS	BIOLOGIAL SCIENCES	PHYSICAL SCIENCES /MATH	SOCIAL SCIENCES	ARTS AND HUMAN.	ENGI- NEERING	BUSINESS	LAW	UNDEC. MAJOR	MALE	FEMALE
		(A)	(B)	(C)	(D)	(E)	(F)	(G)	(H)	(I)	(J)	(K)	(L)	(M)	(N)		(P)	(Q)
Base - Responsibility is Research	404	190	214	404	0**	189	148	67*	62*	78*	139*	65*	17*	36*	7*	0*	272	132*
Ask someone to assist you	94 23.2%	56 29.7%B	37 17.4%	94 23.2%	0 0	35 18.7%	44 29.9%E	14 20.9%	13 21.4%	20 25.6%	26 18.9%	15 22.4%	6 35.1%J	12 33.3%	2 23.8%	0 0	71 26.1%	23 17.2%
Go to print sources	191 47.4%	122 64.3%B	69 32.4%	191 47.4%	0 0	69 36.8%	76 51.6%E	46 68.1%EF	24 38.6%	38 48.7%	58 41.9%	40 62.1%HJ	8 45.6%	20 53.8%	4 54.8%	0 0	149 54.7%Q	43 32.4%
Go online	334 82.7%	162 85.0%	172 80.7%	334 82.7%	0 0	151 79.9%	123 83.3%	60 89.6%	54 87.1%	67 85.9%	111 79.7%	52 79.3%	14 87.7%	31 84.6%	6 78.6%	0 0	223 82.1%	111 84.1%

Proportions/Means: Columns Tested (5% risk level) - A/B/D - C/D - E/F/G - H/I/J/K/L/M/N - P/Q
* small base; ** very small base (under 30) ineligible for sig testing

Table 62
Page 82

Outsell/Digital Library Federation Study (2002)
Weighted Tables

TABLE 72

R7D/E_1. Print or hardcopy books SUMMARY TABLE

	TOTAL SAMPLE	RESPONDENT TYPE: FACULTY MEMBER (A)	GRAD. STUDENT (B)	FACULTY /GRAD (C)	UNDER GRAD. STUDENT (D)	INSTITUTION TYPE: PUBLIC (E)	PRIVATE (F)	LIBERAL ARTS (G)
Base - Use Print or hardcopy books for research	404	190	214	404	0**	189	148	67*
Borrow from or use in campus library (NET)	365	166	198	365	0	179	128	57
	90.3%	87.5%	92.9%	90.3%	0	95.0%FG	86.7%	85.2%
All sources of info	365	166	198	365	0	179	128	57
	90.3%	87.5%	92.9%	90.3%	0	95.0%FG	86.7%	85.2%
preferred source of info	316	134	183	316	0	160	109	47
	78.4%	70.2%	85.7%A	78.4%	0	84.7%FG	73.9%	70.6%
Access online (NET)	68	37	31	68	0	26	27	15
	16.8%	19.6%	14.4%	16.8%	0	14.0%	18.1%	21.9%
All sources of info	68	37	31	68	0	26	27	15
	16.8%	19.6%	14.4%	16.8%	0	14.0%	18.1%	21.9%
preferred source of info	39	21	18	39	0	14	20	5
	9.6%	10.9%	8.4%	9.6%	0	7.4%	13.3%	7.5%
Interlibrary loan (NET)	57	44	13	57	0	10	23	23
	14.1%	23.2%B	5.9%	14.1%	0	5.6%	15.6%E	34.7%EF
All sources of info	57	44	13	57	0	10	23	23
	14.1%	23.2%B	5.9%	14.1%	0	5.6%	15.6%E	34.7%EF
preferred source of info	10	10	*	10	0	1	*	9
	2.5%	5.2%B	0.1%	2.5%	0	0.6%	0.1%	13.2%EF

	DISCIPLINE: BIOLOGICAL SCIENCES (H)	PHYSICAL SCIENCES /MATH (I)	SOCIAL SCIENCES (J)	ARTS AND HUMAN. (K)	ENGI-NEERING (L)	BUSINESS (M)	LAW (N)	UNDEC. MAJOR	GENDER: MALE (P)	FEMALE (Q)
Base - Use Print or hardcopy books for research	62*	78*	139*	65*	17*	36*	7*	0*	272	132*
Borrow from or use in campus library (NET)	58	69	128	58	13	32	7	0	243	122
	94.3%L	88.5%	91.9%L	89.7%	78.9%	87.2%	95.2%L	0	89.3%	92.6%
All sources of info	58	69	128	58	13	32	7	0	243	122
	94.3%L	88.5%	91.9%L	89.7%	78.9%	87.2%	95.2%L	0	89.3%	92.6%
preferred source of info	48	60	117	54	11	20	6	0	205	111
	78.6%M	76.9%M	83.8%LM	82.8%LM	66.7%	56.4%	88.1%LM	0	75.5%	84.5%
Access online (NET)	11	12	23	8	3	10	1	0	46	22
	18.6%	15.4%	16.2%	12.1%	19.3%	28.2%K	9.5%	0	17.0%	16.5%
All sources of info	11	12	23	8	3	10	1	0	46	22
	18.6%	15.4%	16.2%	12.1%	19.3%	28.2%K	9.5%	0	17.0%	16.5%
preferred source of info	8	7	11	3	1	7	*	0	26	12
	12.9%	9.0%	8.1%	5.2%	8.8%	20.5%JKN	2.4%	0	9.7%	9.3%
Interlibrary loan (NET)	11	14	19	6	1	6	1	0	47	10
	17.1%	17.9%	13.5%	8.6%	7.0%	15.4%	14.3%	0	17.2%Q	7.5%
All sources of info	11	14	19	6	1	6	1	0	47	10
	17.1%	17.9%	13.5%	8.6%	7.0%	15.4%	14.3%	0	17.2%Q	7.5%
preferred source of info	1	4	2	1	*	2	*	0	8	2
	1.4%	5.1%	1.4%	1.7%	1.8%	5.1%	2.4%	0	3.1%	1.4%

Proportions/Means: Columns Tested (5% risk level) - A/B/D - C/D - E/F/G - H/I/J/K/L/M/N - P/Q
* small base; ** very small base (under 30) ineligible for sig testing

Table 68
Page 110

Outsell/Digital Library Federation Study (2002)
Weighted Tables

TABLE 72, continued

R7D/E_1. Print or hardcopy books SUMMARY TABLE

		RESPONDENT TYPE				INSTITUTION TYPE			DISCIPLINE									GENDER	
	TOTAL SAMPLE	FACULTY MEMBER	GRAD. STUDENT	FACULTY /GRAD	UNDER GRAD. STUDENT	PUBLIC	PRIVATE	LIBERAL ARTS	BIOLOGIAL SCIENCES	PHYSICAL SCIENCES /MATH	SOCIAL SCIENCES	ARTS AND HUMAN.	ENGI-NEERING	BUSINESS	LAW	UNDEC. MAJOR	MALE	FEMALE
		(A)	(B)	(C)	(D)	(E)	(F)	(G)	(H)	(I)	(J)	(K)	(L)	(M)	(N)		(P)	(Q)
Base - Use Print or hardcopy books for research	404	190	214	404	0**	189	148	67*	62*	78*	139*	65*	17*	36*	7*	0*	272	132*
Borrow from or use in other libraries (NET)	35 8.6%	21 11.3%	13 6.1%	35 8.6%	0 0	11 5.8%	14 9.5%	9 14.1%	1 1.4%	9 11.5%H	9 6.8%	10 15.5%H	1 3.5%	4 10.3%H	1 11.9%H	0 0	26 9.6%	8 6.3%
All sources of info	35 8.6%	21 11.3%	13 6.1%	35 8.6%	0 0	11 5.8%	14 9.5%	9 14.1%	1 1.4%	9 11.5%H	9 6.8%	10 15.5%H	1 3.5%	4 10.3%H	1 11.9%H	0 0	26 9.6%	8 6.3%
preferred source of info	8 1.9%	4 2.2%	4 1.6%	8 1.9%	0 0	2 1.0%	6 3.8%	0 0	0 0	1 1.3%	2 1.4%	3 5.2%	* 1.8%	1 2.6%	* 2.4%H	0 0	7 2.4%	1 0.9%
Purchase from online bookstore (NET)	32 7.9%	25 13.4%B	6 3.0%	32 7.9%	0 0	6 3.3%	17 11.3%E	9 13.2%E	7 11.4%K	9 11.5%K	9 6.8%	1 1.7%	1 8.8%K	4 10.3%	0 0	0 0	28 10.2%Q	4 3.0%
All sources of info	32 7.9%	25 13.4%B	6 3.0%	32 7.9%	0 0	6 3.3%	17 11.3%E	9 13.2%E	7 11.4%K	9 11.5%K	9 6.8%	1 1.7%	1 8.8%K	4 10.3%	0 0	0 0	28 10.2%Q	4 3.0%
preferred source of info	5 1.2%	5 2.5%B	0 0	5 1.2%	0 0	1 0.6%	2 1.0%	2 2.9%	0 0	1 1.3%	0 0	0 0	1 5.3%HJK	3 7.7%HJK	0 0	0 0	5 1.7%	0 0
Purchase from physical book store (NET)	28 7.0%	16 8.6%	12 5.5%	28 7.0%	0 0	15 7.8%	9 6.3%	4 6.1%	4 5.7%	7 9.0%J	2 1.4%	8 12.1%J	4 22.8%HIJ N	4 10.3%J	* 4.8%	0 0	25 9.0%Q	4 2.7%
All sources of info	28 7.0%	16 8.6%	12 5.5%	28 7.0%	0 0	15 7.8%	9 6.3%	4 6.1%	4 5.7%	7 9.0%J	2 1.4%	8 12.1%J	4 22.8%HIJ N	4 10.3%J	* 4.8%	0 0	25 9.0%Q	4 2.7%

Proportions/Means: Columns Tested (5% risk level) - A/B/D - C/D - E/F/G - H/I/J/K/L/M/N - P/Q
* small base; ** very small base (under 30) ineligible for sig testing

Table 68
Page 111

Outsell/Digital Library Federation Study (2002)
Weighted Tables

TABLE 72, continued

R7D/E_1. Print or hardcopy books SUMMARY TABLE

		RESPONDENT TYPE				INSTITUTION TYPE			DISCIPLINE									GENDER	
	TOTAL SAMPLE	FACULTY MEMBER	GRAD. STUDENT	FACULTY /GRAD	UNDER GRAD. STUDENT	PUBLIC	PRIVATE	LIBERAL ARTS	BIOLOGIAL SCIENCES	PHYSICAL SCIENCES /MATH	SOCIAL SCIENCES	ARTS AND HUMAN.	ENGI-NEERING	BUSINESS	LAW	UNDEC. MAJOR	MALE	FEMALE
		(A)	(B)	(C)	(D)	(E)	(F)	(G)	(H)	(I)	(J)	(K)	(L)	(M)	(N)		(P)	(Q)
Base - Use Print or hardcopy books for research	404	190	214	404	0**	189	148	67*	62*	78*	139*	65*	17*	36*	7*	0*	272	132*
preferred source of info	8 1.9%	2 1.1%	5 2.5%	8 1.9%	0 0	5 2.5%	3 1.9%	0 0	2 2.9%	2 2.6%	2 1.4%	0 0	2 10.5%HIJKM	0 0	* 2.4%K	0 0	6 2.3%	1 1.0%
Colleague (NET)	8 1.9%	3 1.7%	5 2.1%	8 1.9%	0 0	2 1.2%	4 2.4%	2 3.0%	4 7.1%JK	3 3.8%J	0 0	0 0	* 1.8%J	0 0	0 0	0 0	7 2.5%	1 0.7%
All sources of info	8 1.9%	3 1.7%	5 2.1%	8 1.9%	0 0	2 1.2%	4 2.4%	2 3.0%	4 7.1%JK	3 3.8%J	0 0	0 0	* 1.8%J	0 0	0 0	0 0	7 2.5%	1 0.7%
preferred source of info	1 0.2%	0 0	1 0.5%	1 0.2%	0 0	1 0.5%	0 0	0 0	0 0	1 1.3%	0 0	0 0	0 0	0 0	0 0	0 0	1 0.4%	0 0
Personal holdings (NET)	8 1.9%	7 3.8%B	* 0.1%	8 1.9%	0 0	4 2.2%	2 1.5%	1 1.7%	0 0	0 0	4 2.7%	2 3.4%	1 3.5%HI	1 2.6%	0 0	0 0	5 2.0%	2 1.6%
All sources of info	8 1.9%	7 3.8%B	* 0.1%	8 1.9%	0 0	4 2.2%	2 1.5%	1 1.7%	0 0	0 0	4 2.7%	2 3.4%	1 3.5%HI	1 2.6%	0 0	0 0	5 2.0%	2 1.6%
preferred source of info	5 1.2%	5 2.5%B	0 0	5 1.2%	0 0	3 1.5%	2 1.3%	0 0	0 0	0 0	4 2.7%	0 0	0 0	1 2.6%	0 0	0 0	4 1.4%	1 0.7%
Sources (NET)	5 1.2%	4 2.0%	1 0.4%	5 1.2%	0 0	* 0.2%	4 2.4%	1 1.3%	3 4.3%J	0 0	0 0	0 0	* 1.8%J	2 5.1%IJ	0 0	0 0	4 1.4%	1 0.7%
All sources of info	5 1.2%	4 2.0%	1 0.4%	5 1.2%	0 0	* 0.2%	4 2.4%	1 1.3%	3 4.3%J	0 0	0 0	0 0	* 1.8%J	2 5.1%IJ	0 0	0 0	4 1.4%	1 0.7%

Proportions/Means: Columns Tested (5% risk level) - A/B/D - C/D - E/F/G - H/I/J/K/L/M/N - P/Q
* small base; ** very small base (under 30) ineligible for sig testing

Table 68
Page 112

Outsell/Digital Library Federation Study (2002)
Weighted Tables

TABLE 72, continued

R7D/E_1. Print or hardcopy books SUMMARY TABLE

		RESPONDENT TYPE				INSTITUTION TYPE			DISCIPLINE									GENDER	
	TOTAL SAMPLE	FACULTY MEMBER	GRAD. STUDENT	FACULTY /GRAD	UNDER GRAD. STUDENT	PUBLIC	PRIVATE	LIBERAL ARTS	BIOLOGIAL SCIENCES	PHYSICAL SCIENCES /MATH	SOCIAL SCIENCES	ARTS AND HUMAN.	ENGI- NEERING	BUSINESS	LAW	UNDEC. MAJOR	MALE	FEMALE
		(A)	(B)	(C)	(D)	(E)	(F)	(G)	(H)	(I)	(J)	(K)	(L)	(M)	(N)		(P)	(Q)
Base - Use Print or hardcopy books for research	404	190	214	404	0**	189	148	67*	62*	78*	139*	65*	17*	36*	7*	0*	272	132*
preferred source of info	3 0.7%	2 1.1%	1 0.4%	3 0.7%	0 0	* 0.2%	2 1.2%	1 1.3%	2 2.9%	0 0	0 0	0 0	* 1.8%J	1 2.6%	0 0	0 0	2 0.8%	1 0.7%
Order from on demand document delivery service (NET)	4 1.0%	2 1.1%	2 0.9%	4 1.0%	0 0	2 1.0%	1 0.8%	1 1.4%	0 0	0 0	2 1.4%	0 0	* 1.8%	2 5.1%I	0 0	0 0	2 0.8%	2 1.4%
All sources of info	4 1.0%	2 1.1%	2 0.9%	4 1.0%	0 0	2 1.0%	1 0.8%	1 1.4%	0 0	0 0	2 1.4%	0 0	* 1.8%	2 5.1%I	0 0	0 0	2 0.8%	2 1.4%
preferred source of info	1 0.2%	1 0.5%	0 0	1 0.2%	0 0	0 0	0 0	1 1.4%	0 0	0 0	0 0	0 0	0 0	1 2.6%	0 0	0 0	1 0.3%	0 0
Ask library to purchase source (NET)	2 0.5%	2 1.0%	0 0	2 0.5%	0 0	0 0	2 1.3%	0 0	0 0	0 0	2 1.4%	0 0	0 0	0 0	0 0	0 0	2 0.7%	0 0
All sources of info	2 0.5%	2 1.0%	0 0	2 0.5%	0 0	0 0	2 1.3%	0 0	0 0	0 0	2 1.4%	0 0	0 0	0 0	0 0	0 0	2 0.7%	0 0
preferred source of info	2 0.5%	2 1.0%	0 0	2 0.5%	0 0	0 0	2 1.3%	0 0	0 0	0 0	2 1.4%	0 0	0 0	0 0	0 0	0 0	2 0.7%	0 0
Faculty (NET)	1 0.3%	0 0	1 0.6%	1 0.3%	0 0	0 0	1 0.9%	0 0	0 0	1 1.3%	0 0	0 0	* 1.8%J	0 0	0 0	0 0	0 0	1 1.0%

Proportions/Means: Columns Tested (5% risk level) - A/B/D - C/D - E/F/G - H/I/J/K/L/M/N - P/Q
* small base; ** very small base (under 30) ineligible for sig testing

TABLE 72, continued

R7D/E_1. Print or hardcopy books SUMMARY TABLE

		RESPONDENT TYPE				INSTITUTION TYPE			DISCIPLINE								GENDER	
	TOTAL SAMPLE	FACULTY MEMBER	GRAD. STUDENT	FACULTY /GRAD	UNDER GRAD. STUDENT	PUBLIC	PRIVATE	LIBERAL ARTS	BIOLOGIAL SCIENCES	PHYSICAL SCIENCES /MATH	SOCIAL SCIENCES	ARTS AND HUMAN.	ENGI- NEERING	BUSINESS	LAW	UNDEC. MAJOR	MALE	FEMALE
		(A)	(B)	(C)	(D)	(E)	(F)	(G)	(H)	(I)	(J)	(K)	(L)	(M)	(N)		(P)	(Q)
Base - Use Print or hardcopy books for research	404	190	214	404	0**	189	148	67*	62*	78*	139*	65*	17*	36*	7*	0*	272	132*
All sources of info	1 0.3%	0 0	1 0.6%	1 0.3%	0 0	0 0	1 0.9%	0 0	0 0	1 1.3%	0 0	0 0	* 1.8%J	0 0	0 0	0 0	0 0	1 1.0%
preferred source of info	1 0.2%	0 0	1 0.5%	1 0.2%	0 0	0 0	1 0.7%	0 0	0 0	1 1.3%	0 0	0 0	0 0	0 0	0 0	0 0	0 0	1 0.8%
Printed material (NET)	1 0.2%	1 0.5%	0 0	1 0.2%	0 0	1 0.5%	0 0	0 0	0 0	0 0	0 0	0 0	0 0	1 2.6%	0 0	0 0	1 0.3%	0 0
All sources of info	1 0.2%	1 0.5%	0 0	1 0.2%	0 0	1 0.5%	0 0	0 0	0 0	0 0	0 0	0 0	0 0	1 2.6%	0 0	0 0	1 0.3%	0 0
preferred source of info	0 0	0 0	0 0	0 0	0 0	0 0	0 0	0 0	0 0	0 0	0 0	0 0	0 0	0 0	0 0	0 0	0 0	0 0
Office (NET)	* *	* 0.1%	0 0	* *	0 0	* 0.1%	0 0	0 0	0 0	0 0	0 0	0 0	0 0	0 0	* 2.4%HIJK	0 0	* 0.1%	0 0
All sources of info	* *	* 0.1%	0 0	* *	0 0	* 0.1%	0 0	0 0	0 0	0 0	0 0	0 0	0 0	0 0	* 2.4%HIJK	0 0	* 0.1%	0 0
preferred source of info	0 0	0 0	0 0	0 0	0 0	0 0	0 0	0 0	0 0	0 0	0 0	0 0	0 0	0 0	0 0	0 0	0 0	0 0
E-journals (NET)	0 0	0 0	0 0	0 0	0 0	0 0	0 0	0 0	0 0	0 0	0 0	0 0	0 0	0 0	0 0	0 0	0 0	0 0

Proportions/Means: Columns Tested (5% risk level) - A/B/D - C/D - E/F/G - H/I/J/K/L/M/N - P/Q
* small base; ** very small base (under 30) ineligible for sig testing

Table 68
Page 114

Outsell/Digital Library Federation Study (2002)
Weighted Tables

TABLE 72, continued

R7D/E_1. Print or hardcopy books SUMMARY TABLE

		RESPONDENT TYPE				INSTITUTION TYPE			DISCIPLINE									GENDER	
	TOTAL SAMPLE	FACULTY MEMBER	GRAD. STUDENT	FACULTY /GRAD	UNDER GRAD. STUDENT	PUBLIC	PRIVATE	LIBERAL ARTS	BIOLOGIAL SCIENCES	PHYSICAL SCIENCES /MATH	SOCIAL SCIENCES	ARTS AND HUMAN.	ENGI-NEERING	BUSINESS	LAW	UNDEC. MAJOR	MALE	FEMALE
		(A)	(B)	(C)	(D)	(E)	(F)	(G)	(H)	(I)	(J)	(K)	(L)	(M)	(N)		(P)	(Q)
Base - Use Print or hardcopy books for research	404	190	214	404	0**	189	148	67*	62*	78*	139*	65*	17*	36*	7*	0*	272	132*
All sources of info	0 0	0 0	0 0	0 0	0 0	0 0	0 0	0 0	0 0	0 0	0 0	0 0	0 0	0 0	0 0	0 0	0 0	0 0
preferred source of info	0 0	0 0	0 0	0 0	0 0	0 0	0 0	0 0	0 0	0 0	0 0	0 0	0 0	0 0	0 0	0 0	0 0	0 0
Access book/journal/ journal article elsewhere online (NET)	0 0	0 0	0 0	0 0	0 0	0 0	0 0	0 0	0 0	0 0	0 0	0 0	0 0	0 0	0 0	0 0	0 0	0 0
All sources of info	0 0	0 0	0 0	0 0	0 0	0 0	0 0	0 0	0 0	0 0	0 0	0 0	0 0	0 0	0 0	0 0	0 0	0 0
preferred source of info	0 0	0 0	0 0	0 0	0 0	0 0	0 0	0 0	0 0	0 0	0 0	0 0	0 0	0 0	0 0	0 0	0 0	0 0
Meetings/conferences (NET)	0 0	0 0	0 0	0 0	0 0	0 0	0 0	0 0	0 0	0 0	0 0	0 0	0 0	0 0	0 0	0 0	0 0	0 0
All sources of info	0 0	0 0	0 0	0 0	0 0	0 0	0 0	0 0	0 0	0 0	0 0	0 0	0 0	0 0	0 0	0 0	0 0	0 0
preferred source of info	0 0	0 0	0 0	0 0	0 0	0 0	0 0	0 0	0 0	0 0	0 0	0 0	0 0	0 0	0 0	0 0	0 0	0 0
Access from course website (NET)	0 0	0 0	0 0	0 0	0 0	0 0	0 0	0 0	0 0	0 0	0 0	0 0	0 0	0 0	0 0	0 0	0 0	0 0

Proportions/Means: Columns Tested (5% risk level) - A/B/D - C/D - E/F/G - H/I/J/K/L/M/N - P/Q
* small base; ** very small base (under 30) ineligible for sig testing

Table 68
Page 115

Outsell/Digital Library Federation Study (2002)
Weighted Tables

TABLE 72, continued

R7D/E_1. Print or hardcopy books SUMMARY TABLE

		RESPONDENT TYPE				INSTITUTION TYPE			DISCIPLINE									GENDER	
	TOTAL SAMPLE	FACULTY MEMBER	GRAD. STUDENT	FACULTY /GRAD	UNDER GRAD. STUDENT	PUBLIC	PRIVATE	LIBERAL ARTS	BIOLOGIAL SCIENCES	PHYSICAL SCIENCES /MATH	SOCIAL SCIENCES	ARTS AND HUMAN.	ENGI- NEERING	BUSINESS	LAW	UNDEC. MAJOR	MALE	FEMALE
		(A)	(B)	(C)	(D)	(E)	(F)	(G)	(H)	(I)	(J)	(K)	(L)	(M)	(N)		(P)	(Q)
Base - Use Print or hardcopy books for research	404	190	214	404	0**	189	148	67*	62*	78*	139*	65*	17*	36*	7*	0*	272	132*
All sources of info	0 0	0 0	0 0	0 0	0 0	0 0	0 0	0 0	0 0	0 0	0 0	0 0	0 0	0 0	0 0	0 0	0 0	0 0
preferred source of info	0 0	0 0	0 0	0 0	0 0	0 0	0 0	0 0	0 0	0 0	0 0	0 0	0 0	0 0	0 0	0 0	0 0	0 0
Other (NET)	10 2.6%	4 2.1%	6 3.0%	10 2.6%	0 0	6 3.4%	4 2.7%	0 0	2 2.9%	2 2.6%	2 1.4%	3 5.2%	* 1.8%	1 2.6%	* 2.4%	0 0	6 2.4%	4 3.0%
All sources of info	9 2.3%	3 1.6%	6 3.0%	9 2.3%	0 0	6 3.3%	3 2.1%	0 0	1 1.4%	2 2.6%	2 1.4%	3 5.2%	* 1.8%	1 2.6%	0 0	0 0	5 2.0%	4 3.0%
preferred source of info	2 0.6%	2 1.1%	* 0.1%	2 0.6%	0 0	* 0.2%	2 1.4%	0 0	1 1.4%	0 0	0 0	1 1.7%	* 1.8%J	0 0	* 2.4%IJ	0 0	2 0.9%	0 0
DK/Refused	4 0.9%	3 1.7%	* 0.1%	4 0.9%	0 0	1 0.6%	* 0.2%	2 3.2%	0 0	1 1.3%	0 0	2 3.4%	* 1.8%J	0 0	0 0	0 0	2 0.9%	1 0.9%

Proportions/Means: Columns Tested (5% risk level) - A/B/D - C/D - E/F/G - H/I/J/K/L/M/N - P/Q
* small base; ** very small base (under 30) ineligible for sig testing

Table 68
Page 116

Outsell/Digital Library Federation Study (2002)
Weighted Tables

TABLE 73

T7sum_1. Print or hardcopy books SUMMARY TABLE

		RESPONDENT TYPE				INSTITUTION TYPE			DISCIPLINE								GENDER	
	TOTAL SAMPLE	FACULTY MEMBER	GRAD. STUDENT	FACULTY /GRAD	UNDER GRAD. STUDENT	PUBLIC	PRIVATE	LIBERAL ARTS	BIOLOGIAL SCIENCES	PHYSICAL SCIENCES /MATH	SOCIAL SCIENCES	ARTS AND HUMAN.	ENGI-NEERING	BUSINESS	LAW	UNDEC. MAJOR	MALE	FEMALE
		(A)	(B)	(C)	(D)	(E)	(F)	(G)	(H)	(I)	(J)	(K)	(L)	(M)	(N)		(P)	(Q)
Base - USe Print or hardcopy books for teaching	529	360	169	529	0**	222	184	123	73*	135	130*	110*	21*	57*	4**	0*	373	156
ONLINE	345	262	83	345	0	135	113	97	55	81	79	72	14	42	3	0	247	98
	65.2%	72.7%B	49.3%	65.2%	0	60.6%	61.4%	79.4%EF	74.7%I	60.0%	60.9%	65.3%	65.8%	73.8%	86.4%	0	66.1%	63.1%
Online library catalogues and finding aids	72	50	22	72	0	28	29	15	11	12	26	16	2	6	*	0	50	22
	13.6%	14.0%	12.7%	13.6%	0	12.4%	15.8%	12.6%	14.5%	8.9%	20.3%I	14.3%	8.2%	9.8%	4.5%	0	13.4%	14.1%
All sources of info	72	50	22	72	0	28	29	15	11	12	26	16	2	6	*	0	50	22
	13.6%	14.0%	12.7%	13.6%	0	12.4%	15.8%	12.6%	14.5%	8.9%	20.3%I	14.3%	8.2%	9.8%	4.5%	0	13.4%	14.1%
preferred source of info	53	35	18	53	0	20	21	13	8	9	23	8	1	5	*	0	36	18
	10.1%	9.8%	10.6%	10.1%	0	8.9%	11.3%	10.3%	10.8%	6.7%	17.4%I	7.1%	5.5%	8.2%	4.5%	0	9.6%	11.2%
Web directory/ subject related web site	64	57	7	64	0	15	18	31	9	21	11	9	3	9	1	0	42	22
	12.0%	15.9%B	3.8%	12.0%	0	6.7%	9.8%	25.1%EF	12.0%	15.6%	8.7%	8.2%	16.4%	16.4%	22.7%	0	11.2%	14.1%
All sources of info	64	57	7	64	0	15	18	31	9	21	11	9	3	9	1	0	42	22
	12.0%	15.9%B	3.8%	12.0%	0	6.7%	9.8%	25.1%EF	12.0%	15.6%	8.7%	8.2%	16.4%	16.4%	22.7%	0	11.2%	14.1%
preferred source of info	27	24	3	27	0	5	9	13	4	8	6	2	1	5	*	0	17	9
	5.0%	6.6%B	1.8%	5.0%	0	2.1%	5.1%	10.3%E	6.0%	5.9%	4.3%	2.0%	6.8%	8.2%	9.1%	0	4.7%	6.0%
Search engine	62	45	17	62	0	24	25	13	7	17	9	17	3	8	1	0	47	15
	11.7%	12.5%	10.0%	11.7%	0	10.7%	13.7%	10.5%	9.6%	12.6%	7.2%	15.3%	12.3%	14.8%	18.2%	0	12.7%	9.3%
All sources of info	62	45	17	62	0	24	25	13	7	17	9	17	3	8	1	0	47	15
	11.7%	12.5%	10.0%	11.7%	0	10.7%	13.7%	10.5%	9.6%	12.6%	7.2%	15.3%	12.3%	14.8%	18.2%	0	12.7%	9.3%

Proportions/Means: Columns Tested (5% risk level) - A/B/D - C/D - E/F/G - H/I/J/K/L/M/N - P/Q
* small base; ** very small base (under 30) ineligible for sig testing

Table 193
Page 706

Outsell/Digital Library Federation Study (2002)
Weighted Tables

TABLE 73, continued

T7sum_1. Print or hardcopy books SUMMARY TABLE

		RESPONDENT TYPE				INSTITUTION TYPE			DISCIPLINE								GENDER	
	TOTAL SAMPLE	FACULTY MEMBER	GRAD. STUDENT	FACULTY /GRAD	UNDER GRAD. STUDENT	PUBLIC	PRIVATE	LIBERAL ARTS	BIOLOGIAL SCIENCES	PHYSICAL SCIENCES /MATH	SOCIAL SCIENCES	ARTS AND HUMAN.	ENGI- NEERING	BUSINESS	LAW	UNDEC. MAJOR	MALE	FEMALE
		(A)	(B)	(C)	(D)	(E)	(F)	(G)	(H)	(I)	(J)	(K)	(L)	(M)	(N)		(P)	(Q)
Base - USe Print or hardcopy books for teaching	529	360	169	529	0**	222	184	123	73*	135	130*	110*	21*	57*	4**	0*	373	156
preferred source of info	24 4.4%	16 4.5%	7 4.3%	24 4.4%	0 0	7 3.3%	8 4.6%	8 6.3%	5 7.2%J	9 6.7%J	0 0	4 4.1%	1 4.1%J	4 6.6%J	* 4.5%	0 0	17 4.6%	6 4.1%
Your own institution's web site	57 10.8%	36 10.0%	21 12.4%	57 10.8%	0 0	27 12.1%	19 10.5%	11 8.7%	10 13.3%IL	6 4.4%	21 15.9%IL	11 10.2%L	* 1.4%	8 14.8%IL	1 18.2%	0 0	32 8.6%	25 16.0%P
All sources of info	57 10.8%	36 10.0%	21 12.4%	57 10.8%	0 0	27 12.1%	19 10.5%	11 8.7%	10 13.3%IL	6 4.4%	21 15.9%IL	11 10.2%L	* 1.4%	8 14.8%IL	1 18.2%	0 0	32 8.6%	25 16.0%P
preferred source of info	35 6.5%	23 6.5%	11 6.6%	35 6.5%	0 0	18 8.3%	8 4.6%	8 6.4%	5 7.2%	5 3.7%	9 7.2%	7 6.1%	* 1.4%	7 13.1%IL	1 13.6%	0 0	19 5.0%	16 10.3%P
Online reference service	49 9.3%	45 12.5%B	4 2.4%	49 9.3%	0 0	21 9.6%	15 8.4%	12 10.0%	4 6.0%	10 7.4%	9 7.2%	7 6.1%	6 26.0%HIJ K	12 21.3%HI JK	1 22.7%	0 0	37 10.0%	12 7.4%
All sources of info	49 9.3%	45 12.5%B	4 2.4%	49 9.3%	0 0	21 9.6%	15 8.4%	12 10.0%	4 6.0%	10 7.4%	9 7.2%	7 6.1%	6 26.0%HIJ K	12 21.3%HI JK	1 22.7%	0 0	37 10.0%	12 7.4%
preferred source of info	25 4.6%	22 6.1%B	3 1.5%	25 4.6%	0 0	11 5.0%	8 4.6%	5 4.1%	3 3.6%	9 6.7%	4 2.9%	2 2.0%	3 13.7%HJK	4 6.6%	* 9.1%	0 0	16 4.4%	8 5.3%
Internet searches	45 8.5%	35 9.8%	10 5.8%	45 8.5%	0 0	17 7.5%	15 8.2%	13 10.6%	6 8.4%	10 7.4%	8 5.8%	12 11.2%	2 9.6%	7 11.5%	* 9.1%	0 0	38 10.1%	7 4.6%
All sources of info	45 8.5%	35 9.8%	10 5.8%	45 8.5%	0 0	17 7.5%	15 8.2%	13 10.6%	6 8.4%	10 7.4%	8 5.8%	12 11.2%	2 9.6%	7 11.5%	* 9.1%	0 0	38 10.1%	7 4.6%

Proportions/Means: Columns Tested (5% risk level) - A/B/D - C/D - E/F/G - H/I/J/K/L/M/N - P/Q
* small base; ** very small base (under 30) ineligible for sig testing

Table 193
Page 707

Outsell/Digital Library Federation Study (2002)
Weighted Tables

TABLE 73, continued

T7sum_1. Print or hardcopy books SUMMARY TABLE

	TOTAL SAMPLE	RESPONDENT TYPE: FACULTY MEMBER	GRAD. STUDENT	FACULTY /GRAD	UNDER GRAD. STUDENT	INSTITUTION TYPE: PUBLIC	PRIVATE	LIBERAL ARTS	DISCIPLINE: BIOLOGIAL SCIENCES	PHYSICAL SCIENCES /MATH	SOCIAL SCIENCES	ARTS AND HUMAN.	ENGI-NEERING	BUSINESS	LAW	UNDEC. MAJOR	GENDER: MALE	FEMALE
		(A)	(B)	(C)	(D)	(E)	(F)	(G)	(H)	(I)	(J)	(K)	(L)	(M)	(N)		(P)	(Q)
Base - USe Print or hardcopy books for teaching	529	360	169	529	0**	222	184	123	73*	135	130*	110*	21*	57*	4**	0*	373	156
preferred source of info	14 2.7%	9 2.4%	6 3.4%	14 2.7%	0 0	9 3.9%	2 1.2%	3 2.6%	3 3.6%	3 2.2%	0 0	6 5.1%J	1 5.5%J	2 3.3%	0 0	0 0	12 3.3%	2 1.3%
Online databases	43 8.2%	34 9.3%	10 5.7%	43 8.2%	0 0	20 9.2%	9 4.8%	14 11.5%F	7 9.6%	11 8.1%	8 5.8%	12 11.2%	2 8.2%	3 4.9%	1 22.7%	0 0	33 8.9%	10 6.4%
All sources of info	43 8.2%	34 9.3%	10 5.7%	43 8.2%	0 0	20 9.2%	9 4.8%	14 11.5%F	7 9.6%	11 8.1%	8 5.8%	12 11.2%	2 8.2%	3 4.9%	1 22.7%	0 0	33 8.9%	10 6.4%
preferred source of info	29 5.4%	24 6.7%	4 2.6%	29 5.4%	0 0	13 5.8%	8 4.3%	8 6.5%	4 6.0%	6 4.4%	6 4.3%	9 8.2%	1 6.8%	2 3.3%	* 9.1%	0 0	24 6.5%	5 2.9%
Online bookstore	32 6.0%	30 8.5%B	1 0.8%	32 6.0%	0 0	8 3.7%	11 6.0%	13 10.2%E	6 8.4%	6 4.4%	8 5.8%	4 4.1%	1 4.1%	7 11.5%	* 4.5%	0 0	29 7.9%Q	2 1.5%
All sources of info	32 6.0%	30 8.5%B	1 0.8%	32 6.0%	0 0	8 3.7%	11 6.0%	13 10.2%E	6 8.4%	6 4.4%	8 5.8%	4 4.1%	1 4.1%	7 11.5%	* 4.5%	0 0	29 7.9%Q	2 1.5%
preferred source of info	8 1.5%	8 2.2%	0 0	8 1.5%	0 0	1 0.5%	4 2.1%	3 2.3%	3 3.6%	2 1.5%	0 0	1 1.0%	* 1.4%	2 3.3%	0 0	0 0	7 1.7%	1 0.9%
Online abstracting and indexing services	9 1.7%	8 2.1%	1 0.8%	9 1.7%	0 0	1 0.4%	4 2.3%	4 3.2%E	1 1.2%	3 2.2%	2 1.4%	1 1.0%	* 1.4%	2 3.3%	0 0	0 0	7 1.9%	2 1.4%
All sources of info	9 1.7%	8 2.1%	1 0.8%	9 1.7%	0 0	1 0.4%	4 2.3%	4 3.2%E	1 1.2%	3 2.2%	2 1.4%	1 1.0%	* 1.4%	2 3.3%	0 0	0 0	7 1.9%	2 1.4%

Proportions/Means: Columns Tested (5% risk level) - A/B/D - C/D - E/F/G - H/I/J/K/L/M/N - P/Q
* small base; ** very small base (under 30) ineligible for sig testing

Table 193
Page 708

Outsell/Digital Library Federation Study (2002)
Weighted Tables

TABLE 73, continued

T7sum_1. Print or hardcopy books SUMMARY TABLE

		RESPONDENT TYPE				INSTITUTION TYPE			DISCIPLINE									GENDER	
	TOTAL SAMPLE	FACULTY MEMBER	GRAD. STUDENT	FACULTY /GRAD	UNDER GRAD. STUDENT	PUBLIC	PRIVATE	LIBERAL ARTS	BIOLOGIAL SCIENCES	PHYSICAL SCIENCES /MATH	SOCIAL SCIENCES	ARTS AND HUMAN.	ENGI- NEERING	BUSINESS	LAW	UNDEC. MAJOR	MALE	FEMALE
		(A)	(B)	(C)	(D)	(E)	(F)	(G)	(H)	(I)	(J)	(K)	(L)	(M)	(N)		(P)	(Q)
Base - USe Print or hardcopy books for teaching	529	360	169	529	0**	222	184	123	73*	135	130*	110*	21*	57*	4**	0*	373	156
preferred source of info	3 0.6%	3 0.8%	* 0.2%	3 0.6%	0 0	0 0	1 0.6%	2 1.6%	1 1.2%	2 1.5%	0 0	0 0	* 1.4%	0 0	0 0	0 0	3 0.8%	0 0
Department web page	6 1.2%	1 0.4%	5 2.9%A	6 1.2%	0 0	4 1.7%	1 0.7%	1 0.8%	2 2.4%	3 2.2%	0 0	1 1.0%	* 1.4%	0 0	0 0	0 0	4 1.1%	2 1.2%
All sources of info	6 1.2%	1 0.4%	5 2.9%A	6 1.2%	0 0	4 1.7%	1 0.7%	1 0.8%	2 2.4%	3 2.2%	0 0	1 1.0%	* 1.4%	0 0	0 0	0 0	4 1.1%	2 1.2%
preferred source of info	3 0.5%	1 0.3%	2 1.1%	3 0.5%	0 0	2 0.8%	0 0	1 0.8%	1 1.2%	2 1.5%	0 0	0 0	0 0	0 0	0 0	0 0	1 0.3%	2 1.2%
Your own personal electronic library/files	3 0.6%	3 0.9%	0 0	3 0.6%	0 0	3 1.3%	* 0.2%	0 0	0 0	0 0	2 1.4%	0 0	* 1.4%I	1 1.6%	0 0	0 0	3 0.8%	0 0
All sources of info	3 0.6%	3 0.9%	0 0	3 0.6%	0 0	3 1.3%	* 0.2%	0 0	0 0	0 0	2 1.4%	0 0	* 1.4%I	1 1.6%	0 0	0 0	3 0.8%	0 0
preferred source of info	1 0.2%	1 0.3%	0 0	1 0.2%	0 0	1 0.4%	0 0	0 0	0 0	0 0	0 0	0 0	0 0	1 1.6%	0 0	0 0	1 0.2%	0 0
E-mail listservs	1 0.2%	1 0.3%	0 0	1 0.2%	0 0	0 0	* 0.1%	1 0.7%	1 1.2%	0 0	0 0	0 0	0 0	0 0	* 4.5%	0 0	1 0.2%	* 0.1%
All sources of info	1 0.2%	1 0.3%	0 0	1 0.2%	0 0	0 0	* 0.1%	1 0.7%	1 1.2%	0 0	0 0	0 0	0 0	0 0	* 4.5%	0 0	1 0.2%	* 0.1%

Proportions/Means: Columns Tested (5% risk level) - A/B/D - C/D - E/F/G - H/I/J/K/L/M/N - P/Q
* small base; ** very small base (under 30) ineligible for sig testing

Table 193
Page 709

Outsell/Digital Library Federation Study (2002)
Weighted Tables

TABLE 73, continued

T7sum_1. Print or hardcopy books SUMMARY TABLE

		RESPONDENT TYPE				INSTITUTION TYPE			DISCIPLINE								GENDER	
	TOTAL SAMPLE	FACULTY MEMBER	GRAD. STUDENT	FACULTY /GRAD	UNDER GRAD. STUDENT	PUBLIC	PRIVATE	LIBERAL ARTS	BIOLOGIAL SCIENCES	PHYSICAL SCIENCES /MATH	SOCIAL SCIENCES	ARTS AND HUMAN.	ENGI- NEERING	BUSINESS	LAW	UNDEC. MAJOR	MALE	FEMALE
		(A)	(B)	(C)	(D)	(E)	(F)	(G)	(H)	(I)	(J)	(K)	(L)	(M)	(N)		(P)	(Q)
Base - USe Print or hardcopy books for teaching	529	360	169	529	0**	222	184	123	73*	135	130*	110*	21*	57*	4**	0*	373	156
preferred source of info	0 0	0 0	0 0	0 0	0 0	0 0	0 0	0 0	0 0	0 0	0 0	0 0	0 0	0 0	0 0	0 0	0 0	0 0
LIBRARY/PRINT	289 54.6%	224 62.1%B	66 38.7%	289 54.6%	0 0	99 44.5%	107 57.9%E	84 68.2%E	49 67.5%JLM	73 54.1%L	66 50.7%L	65 59.2%L	7 32.9%	27 47.5%	2 59.1%	0 0	220 58.9%Q	69 44.4%
Campus library	207 39.1%	158 43.9%B	49 28.9%	207 39.1%	0 0	67 30.0%	82 44.5%E	58 47.6%E	36 49.4%LM	50 37.0%L	51 39.1%	48 43.9%LM	5 23.3%	16 27.9%	1 36.4%	0 0	154 41.4%	53 33.8%
All sources of info	207 39.1%	158 43.9%B	49 28.9%	207 39.1%	0 0	67 30.0%	82 44.5%E	58 47.6%E	36 49.4%LM	50 37.0%L	51 39.1%	48 43.9%LM	5 23.3%	16 27.9%	1 36.4%	0 0	154 41.4%	53 33.8%
preferred source of info	97 18.2%	62 17.2%	34 20.3%	97 18.2%	0 0	38 17.1%	41 22.0%	18 14.6%	16 21.7%M	22 16.3%	32 24.6%M	20 18.4%M	2 11.0%	4 6.6%	1 13.6%	0 0	63 16.9%	33 21.3%
Your own personal physical library/ files/bookshelves	76 14.4%	65 18.1%B	11 6.5%	76 14.4%	0 0	26 11.7%	27 14.7%	23 18.8%	11 15.7%	20 14.8%	19 14.5%	15 13.3%	2 8.2%	9 16.4%	* 9.1%	0 0	62 16.5%	15 9.4%
All sources of info	76 14.4%	65 18.1%B	11 6.5%	76 14.4%	0 0	26 11.7%	27 14.7%	23 18.8%	11 15.7%	20 14.8%	19 14.5%	15 13.3%	2 8.2%	9 16.4%	* 9.1%	0 0	62 16.5%	15 9.4%
preferred source of info	52 9.8%	43 11.9%B	9 5.2%	52 9.8%	0 0	18 8.3%	17 9.2%	16 13.2%	5 7.2%	17 12.6%L	13 10.1%	9 8.2%	1 2.7%	7 11.5%	* 4.5%	0 0	43 11.6%Q	8 5.3%

Proportions/Means: Columns Tested (5% risk level) - A/B/D - C/D - E/F/G - H/I/J/K/L/M/N - P/Q
* small base; ** very small base (under 30) ineligible for sig testing

Table 193
Page 710

Outsell/Digital Library Federation Study (2002)
Weighted Tables

TABLE 73, continued

T7sum_1. Print or hardcopy books SUMMARY TABLE

	RESPONDENT TYPE				INSTITUTION TYPE			DISCIPLINE									GENDER	
	TOTAL SAMPLE	FACULTY MEMBER	GRAD. STUDENT	FACULTY /GRAD	UNDER GRAD. STUDENT	PUBLIC	PRIVATE	LIBERAL ARTS	BIOLOGIAL SCIENCES	PHYSICAL SCIENCES /MATH	SOCIAL SCIENCES	ARTS AND HUMAN.	ENGI-NEERING	BUSINESS	LAW	UNDEC. MAJOR	MALE	FEMALE
		(A)	(B)	(C)	(D)	(E)	(F)	(G)	(H)	(I)	(J)	(K)	(L)	(M)	(N)		(P)	(Q)
Base - USe Print or hardcopy books for teaching	529	360	169	529	0**	222	184	123	73*	135	130*	110*	21*	57*	4**	0*	373	156
Personal subscriptions to newspapers, magazines and journals	25 4.8%	24 6.7%B	1 0.5%	25 4.8%	0 0	6 2.7%	12 6.3%	8 6.2%	4 4.8%	4 3.0%	9 7.2%	2 2.0%	1 5.5%	5 8.2%	* 4.5%	0 0	23 6.1%Q	2 1.5%
All sources of info	25 4.8%	24 6.7%B	1 0.5%	25 4.8%	0 0	6 2.7%	12 6.3%	8 6.2%	4 4.8%	4 3.0%	9 7.2%	2 2.0%	1 5.5%	5 8.2%	* 4.5%	0 0	23 6.1%Q	2 1.5%
preferred source of info	7 1.4%	7 2.1%	0 0	7 1.4%	0 0	3 1.6%	1 0.6%	3 2.3%	1 1.2%	2 1.5%	0 0	2 2.0%	* 1.4%	2 3.3%	* 4.5%	0 0	7 1.9%	* 0.1%
References cited in books or journal articles	24 4.5%	20 5.5%	4 2.4%	24 4.5%	0 0	8 3.4%	9 5.0%	7 5.7%	5 7.2%	8 5.9%	4 2.9%	3 3.1%	1 2.7%	3 4.9%	* 4.5%	0 0	19 5.1%	5 3.2%
All sources of info	24 4.5%	20 5.5%	4 2.4%	24 4.5%	0 0	8 3.4%	9 5.0%	7 5.7%	5 7.2%	8 5.9%	4 2.9%	3 3.1%	1 2.7%	3 4.9%	* 4.5%	0 0	19 5.1%	5 3.2%
preferred source of info	11 2.1%	9 2.5%	2 1.3%	11 2.1%	0 0	3 1.2%	4 2.2%	4 3.4%	1 1.2%	3 2.2%	4 2.9%	2 2.0%	0 0	1 1.6%	* 4.5%	0 0	10 2.6%	1 0.7%
Another library	19 3.5%	15 4.1%	4 2.3%	19 3.5%	0 0	3 1.4%	11 5.8%E	5 4.1%	4 4.8%	5 3.7%	6 4.3%	2 2.0%	0 0	2 3.3%	1 13.6%	0 0	14 3.9%	4 2.8%
All sources of info	19 3.5%	15 4.1%	4 2.3%	19 3.5%	0 0	3 1.4%	11 5.8%E	5 4.1%	4 4.8%	5 3.7%	6 4.3%	2 2.0%	0 0	2 3.3%	1 13.6%	0 0	14 3.9%	4 2.8%

Proportions/Means: Columns Tested (5% risk level) - A/B/D - C/D - E/F/G - H/I/J/K/L/M/N - P/Q
* small base; ** very small base (under 30) ineligible for sig testing

Table 193
Page 711

Outsell/Digital Library Federation Study (2002)
Weighted Tables

TABLE 73, continued

T7sum_1. Print or hardcopy books SUMMARY TABLE

	RESPONDENT TYPE					INSTITUTION TYPE			DISCIPLINE								GENDER	
	TOTAL SAMPLE	FACULTY MEMBER	GRAD. STUDENT	FACULTY /GRAD	UNDER GRAD. STUDENT	PUBLIC	PRIVATE	LIBERAL ARTS	BIOLOGIAL SCIENCES	PHYSICAL SCIENCES /MATH	SOCIAL SCIENCES	ARTS AND HUMAN.	ENGI-NEERING	BUSINESS	LAW	UNDEC. MAJOR	MALE	FEMALE
		(A)	(B)	(C)	(D)	(E)	(F)	(G)	(H)	(I)	(J)	(K)	(L)	(M)	(N)		(P)	(Q)
Base - USe Print or hardcopy books for teaching	529	360	169	529	0**	222	184	123	73*	135	130*	110*	21*	57*	4**	0*	373	156
preferred source of info	2 0.4%	* *	2 1.1%	2 0.4%	0 0	* 0.1%	2 1.0%	0 0	0 0	0 0	2 1.4%	0 0	0 0	0 0	* 4.5%	0 0	2 0.5%	* 0.1%
Physical bookstore	14 2.7%	11 3.1%	3 1.7%	14 2.7%	0 0	9 4.1%	3 1.6%	2 1.6%	4 4.8%	2 1.5%	2 1.4%	4 4.1%	* 1.4%	2 3.3%	* 4.5%	0 0	9 2.4%	5 3.3%
All sources of info	14 2.7%	11 3.1%	3 1.7%	14 2.7%	0 0	9 4.1%	3 1.6%	2 1.6%	4 4.8%	2 1.5%	2 1.4%	4 4.1%	* 1.4%	2 3.3%	* 4.5%	0 0	9 2.4%	5 3.3%
preferred source of info	5 0.9%	2 0.5%	3 1.7%	5 0.9%	0 0	5 2.1%	0 0	0 0	2 2.4%	2 1.5%	0 0	0 0	0 0	1 1.6%	0 0	0 0	4 1.0%	1 0.6%
Printed library catalogues and finding aids	7 1.4%	6 1.8%	1 0.6%	7 1.4%	0 0	2 1.0%	3 1.8%	2 1.6%	1 1.2%	1 0.7%	0 0	6 5.1%IJ	0 0	0 0	0 0	0 0	6 1.7%	1 0.7%
All sources of info	7 1.4%	6 1.8%	1 0.6%	7 1.4%	0 0	2 1.0%	3 1.8%	2 1.6%	1 1.2%	1 0.7%	0 0	6 5.1%IJ	0 0	0 0	0 0	0 0	6 1.7%	1 0.7%
preferred source of info	4 0.8%	4 1.2%	0 0	4 0.8%	0 0	1 0.5%	2 1.2%	1 0.9%	0 0	0 0	0 0	4 4.1%I	0 0	0 0	0 0	0 0	3 0.9%	1 0.7%
Printed abstracting and indexing services	4 0.7%	3 0.8%	1 0.7%	4 0.7%	0 0	0 0	3 1.6%	1 0.8%	2 2.4%	1 0.7%	0 0	1 1.0%	0 0	0 0	0 0	0 0	3 0.7%	1 0.7%
All sources of info	4 0.7%	3 0.8%	1 0.7%	4 0.7%	0 0	0 0	3 1.6%	1 0.8%	2 2.4%	1 0.7%	0 0	1 1.0%	0 0	0 0	0 0	0 0	3 0.7%	1 0.7%

Proportions/Means: Columns Tested (5% risk level) - A/B/D - C/D - E/F/G - H/I/J/K/L/M/N - P/Q
* small base; ** very small base (under 30) ineligible for sig testing

Table 193
Page 712

Outsell/Digital Library Federation Study (2002)
Weighted Tables

TABLE 73, continued

T7sum_1. Print or hardcopy books SUMMARY TABLE

		RESPONDENT TYPE				INSTITUTION TYPE			DISCIPLINE								GENDER	
	TOTAL SAMPLE	FACULTY MEMBER	GRAD. STUDENT	FACULTY /GRAD	UNDER GRAD. STUDENT	PUBLIC	PRIVATE	LIBERAL ARTS	BIOLOGIAL SCIENCES	PHYSICAL SCIENCES /MATH	SOCIAL SCIENCES	ARTS AND HUMAN.	ENGI- NEERING	BUSINESS	LAW	UNDEC. MAJOR	MALE	FEMALE
		(A)	(B)	(C)	(D)	(E)	(F)	(G)	(H)	(I)	(J)	(K)	(L)	(M)	(N)		(P)	(Q)
Base - USe Print or hardcopy books for teaching	529	360	169	529	0**	222	184	123	73*	135	130*	110*	21*	57*	4**	0*	373	156
preferred source of info	0 0	0 0	0 0	0 0	0 0	0 0	0 0	0 0	0 0	0 0	0 0	0 0	0 0	0 0	0 0	0 0	0 0	0 0
PERSONAL ASSISTANCE	160 30.3%	92 25.6%	68 40.2%A	160 30.3%	0 0	73 32.9%	56 30.4%	31 25.4%	18 25.3%	45 33.3%J	24 18.8%	43 38.8%J	9 43.8%HJ	20 34.4%J	1 27.3%	0 0	110 29.3%	51 32.6%
Colleagues inside your institution	122 23.0%	62 17.1%	60 35.5%A	122 23.0%	0 0	59 26.4%G	43 23.3%	20 16.4%	12 16.9%	37 27.4%	21 15.9%	30 27.6%	8 37.0%HJ	13 23.0%	1 18.2%	0 0	83 22.1%	39 25.1%
All sources of info	122 23.0%	62 17.1%	60 35.5%A	122 23.0%	0 0	59 26.4%G	43 23.3%	20 16.4%	12 16.9%	37 27.4%	21 15.9%	30 27.6%	8 37.0%HJ	13 23.0%	1 18.2%	0 0	83 22.1%	39 25.1%
preferred source of info	64 12.2%	22 6.1%	42 25.1%A	64 12.2%	0 0	35 15.7%G	23 12.6%G	6 5.2%	4 6.0%	26 19.3%HJ	9 7.2%	15 13.3%	5 24.7%HJKM	5 8.2%	* 4.5%	0 0	41 11.0%	23 14.9%
A librarian in your institution	49 9.2%	39 10.8%	10 5.8%	49 9.2%	0 0	15 6.7%	20 10.9%	14 11.2%	8 10.8%	9 6.7%	8 5.8%	15 13.3%	2 8.2%	7 13.1%	1 18.2%	0 0	36 9.6%	13 8.3%
All sources of info	49 9.2%	39 10.8%	10 5.8%	49 9.2%	0 0	15 6.7%	20 10.9%	14 11.2%	8 10.8%	9 6.7%	8 5.8%	15 13.3%	2 8.2%	7 13.1%	1 18.2%	0 0	36 9.6%	13 8.3%
preferred source of info	13 2.4%	9 2.5%	4 2.2%	13 2.4%	0 0	6 2.9%	5 2.9%	1 0.8%	1 1.2%	1 0.7%	4 2.9%	2 2.0%	1 5.5%I	4 6.6%I	0 0	0 0	9 2.4%	4 2.4%
Colleagues outside your institution	28 5.3%	27 7.5%B	1 0.7%	28 5.3%	0 0	8 3.5%	7 3.9%	13 10.6%EF	4 6.0%	8 5.9%	2 1.4%	10 9.2%J	1 4.1%	3 4.9%	0 0	0 0	22 5.8%	6 4.0%

Proportions/Means: Columns Tested (5% risk level) - A/B/D - C/D - E/F/G - H/I/J/K/L/M/N - P/Q
* small base; ** very small base (under 30) ineligible for sig testing

Table 193
Page 713

Outsell/Digital Library Federation Study (2002)
Weighted Tables

TABLE 73, continued

T7sum_1. Print or hardcopy books SUMMARY TABLE

		RESPONDENT TYPE				INSTITUTION TYPE			DISCIPLINE								GENDER	
	TOTAL SAMPLE	FACULTY MEMBER	GRAD. STUDENT	FACULTY /GRAD	UNDER GRAD. STUDENT	PUBLIC	PRIVATE	LIBERAL ARTS	BIOLOGICAL SCIENCES	PHYSICAL SCIENCES /MATH	SOCIAL SCIENCES	ARTS AND HUMAN.	ENGI- NEERING	BUSINESS	LAW	UNDEC. MAJOR	MALE	FEMALE
		(A)	(B)	(C)	(D)	(E)	(F)	(G)	(H)	(I)	(J)	(K)	(L)	(M)	(N)		(P)	(Q)
Base - USe Print or hardcopy books for teaching	529	360	169	529	0**	222	184	123	73*	135	130*	110*	21*	57*	4**	0*	373	156
All sources of info	28 5.3%	27 7.5%B	1 0.7%	28 5.3%	0 0	8 3.5%	7 3.9%	13 10.6%EF	4 6.0%	8 5.9%	2 1.4%	10 9.2%J	1 4.1%	3 4.9%	0 0	0 0	22 5.8%	6 4.0%
preferred source of info	5 1.0%	5 1.4%	0 0	5 1.0%	0 0	1 0.4%	3 1.6%	1 0.9%	0 0	0 0	2 1.4%	2 2.0%	0 0	1 1.6%	0 0	0 0	5 1.4%	0 0
Professional meetings	7 1.4%	7 1.9%	* 0.2%	7 1.4%	0 0	6 2.7%	1 0.6%	0 0	1 1.2%	2 1.5%	4 2.9%	0 0	1 2.7%K	0 0	0 0	0 0	5 1.4%	2 1.2%
All sources of info	7 1.4%	7 1.9%	* 0.2%	7 1.4%	0 0	6 2.7%	1 0.6%	0 0	1 1.2%	2 1.5%	4 2.9%	0 0	1 2.7%K	0 0	0 0	0 0	5 1.4%	2 1.2%
preferred source of info	3 0.6%	3 0.8%	* 0.2%	3 0.6%	0 0	3 1.3%	* 0.2%	0 0	0 0	1 0.7%	2 1.4%	0 0	* 1.4%	0 0	0 0	0 0	1 0.3%	2 1.2%
Another institution's librarian	2 0.4%	2 0.6%	0 0	2 0.4%	0 0	0 0	2 1.1%	0 0	0 0	0 0	0 0	1 1.0%	0 0	1 1.6%	0 0	0 0	2 0.5%	0 0
All sources of info	2 0.4%	2 0.6%	0 0	2 0.4%	0 0	0 0	2 1.1%	0 0	0 0	0 0	0 0	1 1.0%	0 0	1 1.6%	0 0	0 0	2 0.5%	0 0
preferred source of info	0 0	0 0	0 0	0 0	0 0	0 0	0 0	0 0	0 0	0 0	0 0	0 0	0 0	0 0	0 0	0 0	0 0	0 0
Students	4 0.8%	4 1.1%	* 0.2%	4 0.8%	0 0	2 0.8%	1 0.7%	1 0.9%	0 0	1 0.7%	2 1.4%	1 1.0%	* 1.4%	0 0	0 0	0 0	4 1.1%	0 0

Proportions/Means: Columns Tested (5% risk level) - A/B/D - C/D - E/F/G - H/I/J/K/L/M/N - P/Q
* small base; ** very small base (under 30) ineligible for sig testing

Table 193
Page 714

Outsell/Digital Library Federation Study (2002)
Weighted Tables

TABLE 73, continued

T7sum_1. Print or hardcopy books SUMMARY TABLE

		RESPONDENT TYPE				INSTITUTION TYPE			DISCIPLINE									GENDER	
	TOTAL SAMPLE	FACULTY MEMBER	GRAD. STUDENT	FACULTY /GRAD	UNDER GRAD. STUDENT	PUBLIC	PRIVATE	LIBERAL ARTS	BIOLOGIAL SCIENCES	PHYSICAL SCIENCES /MATH	SOCIAL SCIENCES	ARTS AND HUMAN.	ENGI-NEERING	BUSINESS	LAW	UNDEC. MAJOR	MALE	FEMALE
		(A)	(B)	(C)	(D)	(E)	(F)	(G)	(H)	(I)	(J)	(K)	(L)	(M)	(N)		(P)	(Q)
Base - USe Print or hardcopy books for teaching	529	360	169	529	0**	222	184	123	73*	135	130*	110*	21*	57*	4**	0*	373	156
All sources of info	4 0.8%	4 1.1%	* 0.2%	4 0.8%	0 0	2 0.8%	1 0.7%	1 0.9%	0 0	1 0.7%	2 1.4%	1 1.0%	* 1.4%	0 0	0 0	0 0	4 1.1%	0 0
preferred source of info	* 0.1%	0 0	* 0.2%	* 0.1%	0 0	0 0	* 0.2%	0 0	0 0	0 0	0 0	0 0	* 1.4%I	0 0	0 0	0 0	* 0.1%	0 0
Personal office/lab	1 0.2%	0 0	1 0.5%	1 0.2%	0 0	0 0	1 0.5%	0 0	1 1.2%	0 0	0 0	0 0	0 0	0 0	0 0	0 0	0 0	1 0.6%
All sources of info	1 0.2%	0 0	1 0.5%	1 0.2%	0 0	0 0	1 0.5%	0 0	1 1.2%	0 0	0 0	0 0	0 0	0 0	0 0	0 0	0 0	1 0.6%
preferred source of info	0 0	0 0	0 0	0 0	0 0	0 0	0 0	0 0	0 0	0 0	0 0	0 0	0 0	0 0	0 0	0 0	0 0	0 0
Online (unspecified)	* 0.1%	0 0	* 0.2%	* 0.1%	0 0	0 0	* 0.2%	0 0	0 0	0 0	0 0	0 0	* 1.4%I	0 0	0 0	0 0	* 0.1%	0 0
All sources of info	* 0.1%	0 0	* 0.2%	* 0.1%	0 0	0 0	* 0.2%	0 0	0 0	0 0	0 0	0 0	* 1.4%I	0 0	0 0	0 0	* 0.1%	0 0
preferred source of info	0 0	0 0	0 0	0 0	0 0	0 0	0 0	0 0	0 0	0 0	0 0	0 0	0 0	0 0	0 0	0 0	0 0	0 0
Author	0 0	0 0	0 0	0 0	0 0	0 0	0 0	0 0	0 0	0 0	0 0	0 0	0 0	0 0	0 0	0 0	0 0	0 0
All sources of info	0 0	0 0	0 0	0 0	0 0	0 0	0 0	0 0	0 0	0 0	0 0	0 0	0 0	0 0	0 0	0 0	0 0	0 0

Proportions/Means: Columns Tested (5% risk level) - A/B/D - C/D - E/F/G - H/I/J/K/L/M/N - P/Q
* small base; ** very small base (under 30) ineligible for sig testing

Table 193
Page 715

Outsell/Digital Library Federation Study (2002)
Weighted Tables

TABLE 73, continued

T7sum_1. Print or hardcopy books SUMMARY TABLE

	RESPONDENT TYPE				INSTITUTION TYPE			DISCIPLINE									GENDER	
	TOTAL SAMPLE	FACULTY MEMBER	GRAD. STUDENT	FACULTY /GRAD	UNDER GRAD. STUDENT	PUBLIC	PRIVATE	LIBERAL ARTS	BIOLOGIAL SCIENCES	PHYSICAL SCIENCES /MATH	SOCIAL SCIENCES	ARTS AND HUMAN.	ENGI-NEERING	BUSINESS	LAW	UNDEC. MAJOR	MALE	FEMALE
		(A)	(B)	(C)	(D)	(E)	(F)	(G)	(H)	(I)	(J)	(K)	(L)	(M)	(N)		(P)	(Q)
Base - USe Print or hardcopy books for teaching	529	360	169	529	0**	222	184	123	73*	135	130*	110*	21*	57*	4**	0*	373	156
preferred source of info	0 0	0 0	0 0	0 0	0 0	0 0	0 0	0 0	0 0	0 0	0 0	0 0	0 0	0 0	0 0	0 0	0 0	0 0
Other	53 10.1%	36 10.1%	17 10.0%	53 10.1%	0 0	30 13.3%	13 6.8%	11 9.1%	7 9.6%	10 7.4%	17 13.0%	11 10.2%	3 13.7%	5 8.2%	1 13.6%	0 0	35 9.3%	19 11.9%
All sources of info	49 9.3%	34 9.4%	15 8.9%	49 9.3%	0 0	27 12.3%	12 6.7%	9 7.4%	6 8.4%	10 7.4%	15 11.6%	10 9.2%	3 13.7%	5 8.2%	* 4.5%	0 0	33 8.7%	16 10.6%
preferred source of info	24 4.6%	13 3.7%	11 6.5%	24 4.6%	0 0	15 6.7%F	3 1.8%	6 4.9%	4 4.8%	5 3.7%	9 7.2%	4 4.1%	1 2.7%	1 1.6%	* 9.1%	0 0	18 4.9%	6 3.7%
DK/Refused	25 4.7%	15 4.2%	10 6.0%	25 4.7%	0 0	11 4.8%	11 6.1%	3 2.5%	4 4.8%	2 1.5%	8 5.8%	9 8.2%I	1 4.1%	2 3.3%	* 9.1%	0 0	14 3.7%	11 7.1%

Proportions/Means: Columns Tested (5% risk level) - A/B/D - C/D - E/F/G - H/I/J/K/L/M/N - P/Q
* small base; ** very small base (under 30) ineligible for sig testing

TABLE 74

T7D/E_1. Print or hardcopy books SUMMARY TABLE

		RESPONDENT TYPE				INSTITUTION TYPE			DISCIPLINE								GENDER	
	TOTAL SAMPLE	FACULTY MEMBER	GRAD. STUDENT	FACULTY /GRAD	UNDER GRAD. STUDENT	PUBLIC	PRIVATE	LIBERAL ARTS	BIOLOGIAL SCIENCES	PHYSICAL SCIENCES /MATH	SOCIAL SCIENCES	ARTS AND HUMAN.	ENGI-NEERING	BUSINESS	LAW	UNDEC. MAJOR	MALE	FEMALE
		(A)	(B)	(C)	(D)	(E)	(F)	(G)	(H)	(I)	(J)	(K)	(L)	(M)	(N)		(P)	(Q)
Base - Use Print or hardcopy books for teaching	529	360	169	529	0**	222	184	123	73*	135	130*	110*	21*	57*	4**	0*	373	156
Borrow from or use in campus library (NET)	342 64.7%	228 63.3%	114 67.5%	342 64.7%	0 0	140 62.8%	125 67.8%	78 63.3%	55 74.7%ILM	78 57.8%	81 62.3%M	90 81.6%IJ LM	12 56.2%	25 44.3%	2 59.1%	0 0	242 64.9%	100 64.2%
All sources of info	342 64.7%	228 63.3%	114 67.5%	342 64.7%	0 0	140 62.8%	125 67.8%	78 63.3%	55 74.7%ILM	78 57.8%	81 62.3%M	90 81.6%IJ LM	12 56.2%	25 44.3%	2 59.1%	0 0	242 64.9%	100 64.2%
preferred source of info	273 51.6%	173 48.1%	100 59.0%A	273 51.6%	0 0	114 51.1%	103 56.0%	56 45.9%	40 55.4%LM	63 46.7%M	71 55.1%LM	72 65.3%IL M	8 37.0%	17 29.5%	2 45.5%	0 0	192 51.5%	80 51.6%
Purchase from physical book store (NET)	81 15.2%	65 18.0%B	16 9.4%	81 15.2%	0 0	28 12.7%	32 17.5%	20 16.4%	11 14.5%	14 10.4%	19 14.5%	24 21.4%I	5 21.9%I	8 14.8%	1 18.2%	0 0	57 15.2%	24 15.3%
All sources of info	81 15.2%	65 18.0%B	16 9.4%	81 15.2%	0 0	28 12.7%	32 17.5%	20 16.4%	11 14.5%	14 10.4%	19 14.5%	24 21.4%I	5 21.9%I	8 14.8%	1 18.2%	0 0	57 15.2%	24 15.3%
preferred source of info	38 7.2%	28 7.8%	10 5.9%	38 7.2%	0 0	15 6.8%	15 8.2%	8 6.4%	6 8.4%	7 5.2%	9 7.2%	10 9.2%	2 11.0%	3 4.9%	* 9.1%	0 0	29 7.7%	9 6.0%
Access online (NET)	69 13.1%	52 14.3%	18 10.4%	69 13.1%	0 0	31 13.9%	19 10.2%	19 15.8%	10 13.3%	13 9.6%	13 10.1%	16 14.3%	3 15.1%	14 24.6%IJ	1 13.6%	0 0	52 13.9%	17 11.1%
All sources of info	69 13.1%	52 14.3%	18 10.4%	69 13.1%	0 0	31 13.9%	19 10.2%	19 15.8%	10 13.3%	13 9.6%	13 10.1%	16 14.3%	3 15.1%	14 24.6%IJ	1 13.6%	0 0	52 13.9%	17 11.1%

Proportions/Means: Columns Tested (5% risk level) - A/B/D - C/D - E/F/G - H/I/J/K/L/M/N - P/Q
* small base; ** very small base (under 30) ineligible for sig testing

Table 196
Page 723

Outsell/Digital Library Federation Study (2002)
Weighted Tables

TABLE 74, continued

T7D/E_1. Print or hardcopy books SUMMARY TABLE

		RESPONDENT TYPE				INSTITUTION TYPE			DISCIPLINE								GENDER	
	TOTAL SAMPLE	FACULTY MEMBER	GRAD. STUDENT	FACULTY /GRAD	UNDER GRAD. STUDENT	PUBLIC	PRIVATE	LIBERAL ARTS	BIOLOGIAL SCIENCES	PHYSICAL SCIENCES /MATH	SOCIAL SCIENCES	ARTS AND HUMAN.	ENGI-NEERING	BUSINESS	LAW	UNDEC. MAJOR	MALE	FEMALE
		(A)	(B)	(C)	(D)	(E)	(F)	(G)	(H)	(I)	(J)	(K)	(L)	(M)	(N)		(P)	(Q)
Base - Use Print or hardcopy books for teaching	529	360	169	529	0**	222	184	123	73*	135	130*	110*	21*	57*	4**	0*	373	156
preferred source of info	42 7.8%	29 8.0%	13 7.5%	42 7.8%	0 0	20 8.8%	9 4.9%	13 10.5%	10 13.3%J	9 6.7%	4 2.9%	6 5.1%	3 13.7%JK	10 18.0%IJK	* 9.1%	0 0	29 7.8%	13 8.1%
Publisher (NET)	60 11.3%	56 15.5%B	4 2.5%	60 11.3%	0 0	25 11.1%	18 10.0%	17 13.8%	5 7.2%	18 13.3%	15 11.6%	7 6.1%	5 23.3%HJK	9 16.4%K	1 18.2%	0 0	45 12.1%	15 9.6%
All sources of info	60 11.3%	56 15.5%B	4 2.5%	60 11.3%	0 0	25 11.1%	18 10.0%	17 13.8%	5 7.2%	18 13.3%	15 11.6%	7 6.1%	5 23.3%HJK	9 16.4%K	1 18.2%	0 0	45 12.1%	15 9.6%
preferred source of info	44 8.4%	41 11.5%B	3 1.8%	44 8.4%	0 0	15 6.9%	15 8.1%	14 11.4%	4 6.0%	15 11.1%K	9 7.2%	3 3.1%	3 15.1%HK	8 14.8%K	1 18.2%	0 0	31 8.2%	14 8.8%
Personal Collection/ Holdings (NET)	46 8.8%	39 10.9%B	7 4.1%	46 8.8%	0 0	21 9.5%	12 6.3%	14 11.1%	4 4.8%	16 11.9%	9 7.2%	7 6.1%	1 6.8%	9 16.4%HK	0 0	0 0	41 11.1%Q	5 3.3%
All sources of info	46 8.8%	39 10.9%B	7 4.1%	46 8.8%	0 0	21 9.5%	12 6.3%	14 11.1%	4 4.8%	16 11.9%	9 7.2%	7 6.1%	1 6.8%	9 16.4%HK	0 0	0 0	41 11.1%Q	5 3.3%
preferred source of info	33 6.3%	27 7.5%	6 3.5%	33 6.3%	0 0	18 8.2%F	4 2.3%	11 8.8%F	2 2.4%	12 8.9%	8 5.8%	4 4.1%	1 4.1%	7 11.5%H	0 0	0 0	28 7.5%	5 3.3%
Purchase from online bookstore (NET)	38 7.1%	32 9.0%B	5 3.1%	38 7.1%	0 0	11 4.9%	12 6.6%	15 12.0%E	3 3.6%	9 6.7%	9 7.2%	8 7.1%	2 9.6%	7 11.5%	* 4.5%	0 0	27 7.3%	10 6.6%
All sources of info	38 7.1%	32 9.0%B	5 3.1%	38 7.1%	0 0	11 4.9%	12 6.6%	15 12.0%E	3 3.6%	9 6.7%	9 7.2%	8 7.1%	2 9.6%	7 11.5%	* 4.5%	0 0	27 7.3%	10 6.6%

Proportions/Means: Columns Tested (5% risk level) - A/B/D - C/D - E/F/G - H/I/J/K/L/M/N - P/Q
* small base; ** very small base (under 30) ineligible for sig testing

Table 196
Page 724

Outsell/Digital Library Federation Study (2002)
Weighted Tables

TABLE 74, continued

T7D/E_1. Print or hardcopy books SUMMARY TABLE

		RESPONDENT TYPE				INSTITUTION TYPE			DISCIPLINE								GENDER	
	TOTAL SAMPLE	FACULTY MEMBER	GRAD. STUDENT	FACULTY /GRAD	UNDER GRAD. STUDENT	PUBLIC	PRIVATE	LIBERAL ARTS	BIOLOGIAL SCIENCES	PHYSICAL SCIENCES /MATH	SOCIAL SCIENCES	ARTS AND HUMAN.	ENGI- NEERING	BUSINESS	LAW	UNDEC. MAJOR	MALE	FEMALE
		(A)	(B)	(C)	(D)	(E)	(F)	(G)	(H)	(I)	(J)	(K)	(L)	(M)	(N)		(P)	(Q)
Base - Use Print or hardcopy books for teaching	529	360	169	529	0**	222	184	123	73*	135	130*	110*	21*	57*	4**	0*	373	156
preferred source of info	15 2.9%	11 3.0%	4 2.6%	15 2.9%	0 0	8 3.4%	4 2.2%	4 3.1%	1 1.2%	3 2.2%	6 4.3%	2 2.0%	1 2.7%	3 4.9%	* 4.5%	0 0	10 2.7%	5 3.3%
Interlibrary loan (NET)	35 6.6%	32 8.8%B	3 1.9%	35 6.6%	0 0	4 1.7%	20 10.6%E	12 9.5%E	6 8.4%	5 3.7%	13 10.1%	7 6.1%	1 4.1%	3 4.9%	* 9.1%	0 0	27 7.2%	8 5.2%
All sources of info	35 6.6%	32 8.8%B	3 1.9%	35 6.6%	0 0	4 1.7%	20 10.6%E	12 9.5%E	6 8.4%	5 3.7%	13 10.1%	7 6.1%	1 4.1%	3 4.9%	* 9.1%	0 0	27 7.2%	8 5.2%
preferred source of info	12 2.2%	11 3.1%B	* 0.2%	12 2.2%	0 0	* 0.1%	8 4.6%E	3 2.3%	3 3.6%I	0 0	6 4.3%I	1 1.0%	* 1.4%I	2 3.3%I	0 0	0 0	9 2.3%	3 1.8%
Borrow from or use in other libraries (NET)	24 4.5%	19 5.2%	5 2.9%	24 4.5%	0 0	7 3.0%	8 4.4%	9 7.2%	5 7.2%	6 4.4%	4 2.9%	6 5.1%	* 1.4%	2 3.3%	1 22.7%	0 0	18 4.9%	5 3.3%
All sources of info	24 4.5%	19 5.2%	5 2.9%	24 4.5%	0 0	7 3.0%	8 4.4%	9 7.2%	5 7.2%	6 4.4%	4 2.9%	6 5.1%	* 1.4%	2 3.3%	1 22.7%	0 0	18 4.9%	5 3.3%
preferred source of info	6 1.2%	4 1.2%	2 1.1%	6 1.2%	0 0	2 1.1%	3 1.6%	1 0.8%	0 0	1 0.7%	4 2.9%	0 0	* 1.4%	1 1.6%	* 9.1%	0 0	5 1.4%	1 0.8%
Department (NET)	10 1.9%	2 0.5%	8 4.9%A	10 1.9%	0 0	8 3.7%G	2 1.1%	0 0	0 0	9 6.7%HJK	0 0	0 0	* 1.4%	1 1.6%	0 0	0 0	6 1.7%	4 2.6%
All sources of info	10 1.9%	2 0.5%	8 4.9%A	10 1.9%	0 0	8 3.7%G	2 1.1%	0 0	0 0	9 6.7%HJK	0 0	0 0	* 1.4%	1 1.6%	0 0	0 0	6 1.7%	4 2.6%

Proportions/Means: Columns Tested (5% risk level) - A/B/D - C/D - E/F/G - H/I/J/K/L/M/N - P/Q
* small base; ** very small base (under 30) ineligible for sig testing

Table 196
Page 725

TABLE 74, continued

T7D/E_1. Print or hardcopy books SUMMARY TABLE

		RESPONDENT TYPE				INSTITUTION TYPE			DISCIPLINE								GENDER	
	TOTAL SAMPLE	FACULTY MEMBER	GRAD. STUDENT	FACULTY /GRAD	UNDER GRAD. STUDENT	PUBLIC	PRIVATE	LIBERAL ARTS	BIOLOGIAL SCIENCES	PHYSICAL SCIENCES /MATH	SOCIAL SCIENCES	ARTS AND HUMAN.	ENGI- NEERING	BUSINESS	LAW	UNDEC. MAJOR	MALE	FEMALE
		(A)	(B)	(C)	(D)	(E)	(F)	(G)	(H)	(I)	(J)	(K)	(L)	(M)	(N)		(P)	(Q)
Base - Use Print or hardcopy books for teaching	529	360	169	529	0**	222	184	123	73*	135	130*	110*	21*	57*	4**	0*	373	156
preferred source of info	9 1.7%	1 0.3%	8 4.9%A	9 1.7%	0 0	7 3.2%	2 1.1%	0 0	0 0	8 5.9%HJK	0 0	0 0	* 1.4%	1 1.6%	0 0	0 0	5 1.4%	4 2.6%
Order from on demand document delivery service (NET)	9 1.8%	9 2.6%	0 0	9 1.8%	0 0	2 1.0%	0 0	7 5.8%EF	1 1.2%	5 3.7%	0 0	2 2.0%	* 1.4%	1 1.6%	0 0	0 0	6 1.6%	3 2.2%
All sources of info	9 1.8%	9 2.6%	0 0	9 1.8%	0 0	2 1.0%	0 0	7 5.8%EF	1 1.2%	5 3.7%	0 0	2 2.0%	* 1.4%	1 1.6%	0 0	0 0	6 1.6%	3 2.2%
preferred source of info	8 1.6%	8 2.3%	0 0	8 1.6%	0 0	2 1.0%	0 0	6 4.9%EF	1 1.2%	5 3.7%	0 0	1 1.0%	* 1.4%	1 1.6%	0 0	0 0	6 1.6%	2 1.5%
Office (NET)	9 1.7%	6 1.7%	3 1.7%	9 1.7%	0 0	2 0.9%	4 2.1%	3 2.6%	2 2.4%	2 1.5%	0 0	3 3.1%	0 0	2 3.3%	* 4.5%	0 0	5 1.4%	4 2.4%
All sources of info	9 1.7%	6 1.7%	3 1.7%	9 1.7%	0 0	2 0.9%	4 2.1%	3 2.6%	2 2.4%	2 1.5%	0 0	3 3.1%	0 0	2 3.3%	* 4.5%	0 0	5 1.4%	4 2.4%
preferred source of info	7 1.3%	4 1.1%	3 1.7%	7 1.3%	0 0	1 0.4%	4 2.1%	2 1.7%	2 2.4%	2 1.5%	0 0	2 2.0%	0 0	1 1.6%	0 0	0 0	3 0.8%	4 2.4%
Colleagues (NET)	6 1.2%	4 1.2%	2 1.3%	6 1.2%	0 0	4 1.6%	1 0.5%	2 1.7%	1 1.2%	1 0.7%	0 0	3 3.1%	* 1.4%	1 1.6%	0 0	0 0	1 0.2%	6 3.5%P
All sources of info	6 1.2%	4 1.2%	2 1.3%	6 1.2%	0 0	4 1.6%	1 0.5%	2 1.7%	1 1.2%	1 0.7%	0 0	3 3.1%	* 1.4%	1 1.6%	0 0	0 0	1 0.2%	6 3.5%P

Proportions/Means: Columns Tested (5% risk level) - A/B/D - C/D - E/F/G - H/I/J/K/L/M/N - P/Q
* small base; ** very small base (under 30) ineligible for sig testing

Table 196
Page 726

Outsell/Digital Library Federation Study (2002)
Weighted Tables

TABLE 74, continued

T7D/E_1. Print or hardcopy books SUMMARY TABLE

	RESPONDENT TYPE					INSTITUTION TYPE			DISCIPLINE									GENDER	
	TOTAL SAMPLE	FACULTY MEMBER	GRAD. STUDENT	FACULTY /GRAD	UNDER GRAD. STUDENT	PUBLIC	PRIVATE	LIBERAL ARTS	BIOLOGIAL SCIENCES	PHYSICAL SCIENCES /MATH	SOCIAL SCIENCES	ARTS AND HUMAN.	ENGI-NEERING	BUSINESS	LAW	UNDEC. MAJOR	MALE	FEMALE
		(A)	(B)	(C)	(D)	(E)	(F)	(G)	(H)	(I)	(J)	(K)	(L)	(M)	(N)		(P)	(Q)
Base - Use Print or hardcopy books for teaching	529	360	169	529	0**	222	184	123	73*	135	130*	110*	21*	57*	4**	0*	373	156
preferred source of info	4 0.8%	2 0.6%	2 1.3%	4 0.8%	0 0	3 1.5%	1 0.5%	0 0	1 1.2%	1 0.7%	0 0	2 2.0%	0 0	0 0	0 0	0 0	0 0	4 2.6%P
Access from course website (NET)	6 1.1%	5 1.3%	1 0.7%	6 1.1%	0 0	2 0.8%	2 1.2%	2 1.5%	1 1.2%	0 0	2 1.4%	2 2.0%	0 0	1 1.6%	0 0	0 0	5 1.3%	1 0.7%
All sources of info	6 1.1%	5 1.3%	1 0.7%	6 1.1%	0 0	2 0.8%	2 1.2%	2 1.5%	1 1.2%	0 0	2 1.4%	2 2.0%	0 0	1 1.6%	0 0	0 0	5 1.3%	1 0.7%
preferred source of info	1 0.2%	1 0.3%	0 0	1 0.2%	0 0	0 0	1 0.6%	0 0	0 0	0 0	0 0	1 1.0%	0 0	0 0	0 0	0 0	1 0.3%	0 0
Faculty (NET)	5 0.9%	0 0	5 2.7%A	5 0.9%	0 0	2 1.0%	2 1.3%	0 0	0 0	2 1.5%	0 0	1 1.0%	1 2.7%HJ	1 1.6%	0 0	0 0	4 0.9%	1 0.7%
All sources of info	5 0.9%	0 0	5 2.7%A	5 0.9%	0 0	2 1.0%	2 1.3%	0 0	0 0	2 1.5%	0 0	1 1.0%	1 2.7%HJ	1 1.6%	0 0	0 0	4 0.9%	1 0.7%
preferred source of info	5 0.9%	0 0	5 2.7%A	5 0.9%	0 0	2 1.0%	2 1.3%	0 0	0 0	2 1.5%	0 0	1 1.0%	1 2.7%HJ	1 1.6%	0 0	0 0	4 0.9%	1 0.7%
Ask library to purchase source (NET)	4 0.7%	1 0.4%	2 1.5%	4 0.7%	0 0	1 0.4%	2 1.2%	1 0.7%	1 1.2%	0 0	2 1.4%	0 0	1 5.5%IKM	0 0	0 0	0 0	1 0.2%	3 2.0%
All sources of info	4 0.7%	1 0.4%	2 1.5%	4 0.7%	0 0	1 0.4%	2 1.2%	1 0.7%	1 1.2%	0 0	2 1.4%	0 0	1 5.5%IKM	0 0	0 0	0 0	1 0.2%	3 2.0%

Proportions/Means: Columns Tested (5% risk level) - A/B/D - C/D - E/F/G - H/I/J/K/L/M/N - P/Q
* small base; ** very small base (under 30) ineligible for sig testing

Table 196
Page 727

Outsell/Digital Library Federation Study (2002)
Weighted Tables

TABLE 74, continued

T7D/E_1. Print or hardcopy books SUMMARY TABLE

		RESPONDENT TYPE				INSTITUTION TYPE			DISCIPLINE									GENDER	
	TOTAL SAMPLE	FACULTY MEMBER	GRAD. STUDENT	FACULTY /GRAD	UNDER GRAD. STUDENT	PUBLIC	PRIVATE	LIBERAL ARTS	BIOLOGIAL SCIENCES	PHYSICAL SCIENCES /MATH	SOCIAL SCIENCES	ARTS AND HUMAN.	ENGI-NEERING	BUSINESS	LAW	UNDEC. MAJOR	MALE	FEMALE
		(A)	(B)	(C)	(D)	(E)	(F)	(G)	(H)	(I)	(J)	(K)	(L)	(M)	(N)		(P)	(Q)
Base - Use Print or hardcopy books for teaching	529	360	169	529	0**	222	184	123	73*	135	130*	110*	21*	57*	4**	0*	373	156
preferred source of info	4 0.7%	1 0.4%	2 1.5%	4 0.7%	0 0	1 0.4%	2 1.2%	1 0.7%	1 1.2%	0 0	2 1.4%	0 0	1 5.5%IKM	0 0	0 0	0 0	1 0.2%	3 2.0%
Author	1 0.2%	1 0.3%	0 0	1 0.2%	0 0	0 0	0 0	1 0.8%	0 0	1 0.7%	0 0	0 0	0 0	0 0	0 0	0 0	1 0.3%	0 0
All sources of info	1 0.2%	1 0.3%	0 0	1 0.2%	0 0	0 0	0 0	1 0.8%	0 0	1 0.7%	0 0	0 0	0 0	0 0	0 0	0 0	1 0.3%	0 0
preferred source of info	0 0	0 0	0 0	0 0	0 0	0 0	0 0	0 0	0 0	0 0	0 0	0 0	0 0	0 0	0 0	0 0	0 0	0 0
Meeting/Conferences (NET)	0 0	0 0	0 0	0 0	0 0	0 0	0 0	0 0	0 0	0 0	0 0	0 0	0 0	0 0	0 0	0 0	0 0	0 0
All sources of info	0 0	0 0	0 0	0 0	0 0	0 0	0 0	0 0	0 0	0 0	0 0	0 0	0 0	0 0	0 0	0 0	0 0	0 0
preferred source of info	0 0	0 0	0 0	0 0	0 0	0 0	0 0	0 0	0 0	0 0	0 0	0 0	0 0	0 0	0 0	0 0	0 0	0 0
Home (NET)	0 0	0 0	0 0	0 0	0 0	0 0	0 0	0 0	0 0	0 0	0 0	0 0	0 0	0 0	0 0	0 0	0 0	0 0
All sources of info	0 0	0 0	0 0	0 0	0 0	0 0	0 0	0 0	0 0	0 0	0 0	0 0	0 0	0 0	0 0	0 0	0 0	0 0

Proportions/Means: Columns Tested (5% risk level) - A/B/D - C/D - E/F/G - H/I/J/K/L/M/N - P/Q
* small base; ** very small base (under 30) ineligible for sig testing

Table 196
Page 728

Outsell/Digital Library Federation Study (2002)
Weighted Tables

TABLE 74, continued

T7D/E_1. Print or hardcopy books SUMMARY TABLE

		RESPONDENT TYPE				INSTITUTION TYPE			DISCIPLINE									GENDER	
	TOTAL SAMPLE	FACULTY MEMBER	GRAD. STUDENT	FACULTY /GRAD	UNDER GRAD. STUDENT	PUBLIC	PRIVATE	LIBERAL ARTS	BIOLOGIAL SCIENCES	PHYSICAL SCIENCES /MATH	SOCIAL SCIENCES	ARTS AND HUMAN.	ENGI-NEERING	BUSINESS	LAW	UNDEC. MAJOR	MALE	FEMALE
		(A)	(B)	(C)	(D)	(E)	(F)	(G)	(H)	(I)	(J)	(K)	(L)	(M)	(N)		(P)	(Q)
Base - Use Print or hardcopy books for teaching	529	360	169	529	0**	222	184	123	73*	135	130*	110*	21*	57*	4**	0*	373	156
preferred source of info	0 0	0 0	0 0	0 0	0 0	0 0	0 0	0 0	0 0	0 0	0 0	0 0	0 0	0 0	0 0	0 0	0 0	0 0
Access book/journal/ journal article elsewhere online (NET)	0 0	0 0	0 0	0 0	0 0	0 0	0 0	0 0	0 0	0 0	0 0	0 0	0 0	0 0	0 0	0 0	0 0	0 0
All sources of info	0 0	0 0	0 0	0 0	0 0	0 0	0 0	0 0	0 0	0 0	0 0	0 0	0 0	0 0	0 0	0 0	0 0	0 0
preferred source of info	0 0	0 0	0 0	0 0	0 0	0 0	0 0	0 0	0 0	0 0	0 0	0 0	0 0	0 0	0 0	0 0	0 0	0 0
Other (NET)	30 5.6%	18 5.0%	12 6.9%	30 5.6%	0 0	14 6.3%	11 5.8%	5 4.1%	4 4.8%	8 5.9%	9 7.2%	2 2.0%	1 4.1%	6 9.8%K	* 4.5%	0 0	21 5.6%	9 5.6%
All sources of info	25 4.8%	14 3.8%	12 6.9%	25 4.8%	0 0	12 5.3%	11 5.8%	3 2.4%	4 4.8%K	7 5.2%K	9 7.2%K	0 0	1 4.1%K	5 8.2%K	0 0	0 0	18 4.8%	8 4.9%
preferred source of info	20 3.8%	11 3.0%	10 5.6%	20 3.8%	0 0	10 4.4%	8 4.1%	3 2.5%	3 3.6%	5 3.7%	8 5.8%	2 2.0%	0 0	3 4.9%	* 4.5%	0 0	13 3.6%	7 4.4%
DK/Refused	7 1.4%	6 1.7%	1 0.8%	7 1.4%	0 0	4 1.9%	2 1.2%	1 0.9%	0 0	2 1.5%	4 2.9%	1 1.0%	1 2.7%H	0 0	0 0	0 0	7 1.9%	* 0.2%

Proportions/Means: Columns Tested (5% risk level) - A/B/D - C/D - E/F/G - H/I/J/K/L/M/N - P/Q
* small base; ** very small base (under 30) ineligible for sig testing

Table 196
Page 729

Outsell/Digital Library Federation Study (2002)
Weighted Tables

TABLE 75

S7sum_1. Print or hardcopy books SUMMARY TABLE

		RESPONDENT TYPE				INSTITUTION TYPE			DISCIPLINE									GENDER	
	TOTAL SAMPLE	FACULTY MEMBER	GRAD. STUDENT	FACULTY /GRAD	UNDER GRAD. STUDENT	PUBLIC	PRIVATE	LIBERAL ARTS	BIOLOGIAL SCIENCES	PHYSICAL SCIENCES /MATH	SOCIAL SCIENCES	ARTS AND HUMAN.	ENGI- NEERING	BUSINESS	LAW	UNDEC. MAJOR	MALE	FEMALE
		(A)	(B)	(C)	(D)	(E)	(F)	(G)	(H)	(I)	(J)	(K)	(L)	(M)	(N)		(P)	(Q)
Base - Use Print or hardcopy books for coursework	780	0**	376	376	404	369	192	219	95	134	237	140	34	89*	12*	39*	382	398
ONLINE	551 70.7%	0 0	260 69.2%	260 69.2%	291 72.1%	256 69.5%	133 69.3%	162 73.9%	71 75.0%LN	92 68.7%N	177 74.6%LN	92 65.6%	19 56.9%	64 71.9%LN	6 52.1%	30 76.9%	245 64.2%	306 76.9%P
Online library catalogues and finding aids (NET)	167 21.4%	0 0	83 22.1%	83 22.1%	84 20.7%	75 20.3%	44 22.8%	48 21.9%	18 18.5%	20 14.9%	62 26.2%IL N	36 25.6%IL N	5 14.7%	16 17.7%	2 12.7%	9 23.1%	72 18.7%	95 23.9%
All sources of info	167 21.4%	0 0	83 22.1%	83 22.1%	84 20.7%	75 20.3%	44 22.8%	48 21.9%	18 18.5%	20 14.9%	62 26.2%IL N	36 25.6%IL N	5 14.7%	16 17.7%	2 12.7%	9 23.1%	72 18.7%	95 23.9%
preferred source of info	129 16.5%	0 0	65 17.3%	65 17.3%	64 15.8%	65 17.6%	31 16.3%	33 14.9%	13 13.9%	15 11.2%	51 21.4%I	26 18.4%	5 13.8%	11 12.5%	1 11.3%	7 17.9%	59 15.3%	70 17.7%
Your own institution's web site (NET)	130 16.7%	0 0	53 14.2%	53 14.2%	77 19.0%	61 16.6%	23 12.2%	45 20.7%F	15 15.7%	25 18.7%	36 15.1%	27 19.2%L	3 9.5%	13 14.6%	1 9.9%	10 25.6%	57 14.9%	73 18.4%
All sources of info	130 16.7%	0 0	53 14.2%	53 14.2%	77 19.0%	61 16.6%	23 12.2%	45 20.7%F	15 15.7%	25 18.7%	36 15.1%	27 19.2%L	3 9.5%	13 14.6%	1 9.9%	10 25.6%	57 14.9%	73 18.4%
preferred source of info	100 12.8%	0 0	44 11.6%	44 11.6%	56 13.9%	47 12.7%	17 8.7%	36 16.6%F	10 10.2%	21 15.7%L	26 11.1%	20 14.4%	2 6.9%	12 13.5%	1 9.9%	7 17.9%	47 12.2%	53 13.3%
Search engine (NET)	127 16.3%	0 0	36 9.5%	36 9.5%	91 22.6%B C	38 10.3%	33 17.0%E	56 25.8%E	17 17.6%	27 20.1%	28 11.9%	25 17.6%	4 11.2%	19 20.8%	1 9.9%	7 17.9%	57 15.0%	70 17.5%

Proportions/Means: Columns Tested (5% risk level) - A/B/D - C/D - E/F/G - H/I/J/K/L/M/N - P/Q
* small base; ** very small base (under 30) ineligible for sig testing

Table 321
Page 1309

Outsell/Digital Library Federation Study (2002)
Weighted Tables

TABLE 75, continued

S7sum_1. Print or hardcopy books SUMMARY TABLE

		RESPONDENT TYPE				INSTITUTION TYPE			DISCIPLINE								GENDER	
	TOTAL SAMPLE	FACULTY MEMBER	GRAD. STUDENT	FACULTY /GRAD	UNDER GRAD. STUDENT	PUBLIC	PRIVATE	LIBERAL ARTS	BIOLOGIAL SCIENCES	PHYSICAL SCIENCES /MATH	SOCIAL SCIENCES	ARTS AND HUMAN.	ENGI- NEERING	BUSINESS	LAW	UNDEC. MAJOR	MALE	FEMALE
		(A)	(B)	(C)	(D)	(E)	(F)	(G)	(H)	(I)	(J)	(K)	(L)	(M)	(N)		(P)	(Q)
Base - Use Print or hardcopy books for coursework	780	0**	376	376	404	369	192	219	95	134	237	140	34	89*	12*	39*	382	398
All sources of info	127 16.3%	0 0	36 9.5%	36 9.5%	91 22.6%B C	38 10.3%	33 17.0%E	56 25.8%E	17 17.6%	27 20.1%	28 11.9%	25 17.6%	4 11.2%	19 20.8%	1 9.9%	7 17.9%	57 15.0%	70 17.5%
preferred source of info	55 7.1%	0 0	22 5.9%	22 5.9%	33 8.2%	18 5.0%	19 9.8%E	18 8.3%	10 10.2%	8 6.0%	15 6.3%	7 4.8%	2 6.0%	9 10.4%	1 4.2%	4 10.3%	26 6.7%	30 7.4%
Online databases (NET)	86 11.1%	0 0	46 12.4%	46 12.4%	40 9.9%	29 7.9%	32 16.7%E	25 11.5%	12 13.0%L	15 11.2%	34 14.3%L	12 8.8%	1 4.3%	7 7.3%	2 15.5%L	3 7.7%	43 11.2%	44 11.0%
All sources of info	86 11.1%	0 0	46 12.4%	46 12.4%	40 9.9%	29 7.9%	32 16.7%E	25 11.5%	12 13.0%L	15 11.2%	34 14.3%L	12 8.8%	1 4.3%	7 7.3%	2 15.5%L	3 7.7%	43 11.2%	44 11.0%
preferred source of info	48 6.2%	0 0	30 7.9%	30 7.9%	19 4.6%	15 4.2%	20 10.2%E	13 6.1%	7 7.4%	10 7.5%	21 8.7%K	3 2.4%	1 3.4%	5 5.2%	2 12.7%KLM	0 0	21 5.5%	27 6.9%
Internet searches (NET)	52 6.6%	0 0	25 6.6%	25 6.6%	27 6.6%	35 9.4%F	5 2.8%	12 5.2%	12 13.0%JKN	10 7.5%N	13 5.6%	7 4.8%	4 11.2%KN	5 5.2%	0 0	1 2.6%	24 6.4%	27 6.9%
All sources of info	52 6.6%	0 0	25 6.6%	25 6.6%	27 6.6%	35 9.4%F	5 2.8%	12 5.2%	12 13.0%JKN	10 7.5%N	13 5.6%	7 4.8%	4 11.2%KN	5 5.2%	0 0	1 2.6%	24 6.4%	27 6.9%
preferred source of info	26 3.3%	0 0	13 3.5%	13 3.5%	13 3.2%	19 5.2%F	2 1.2%	5 2.1%	4 4.6%	5 3.7%	9 4.0%	1 0.8%	2 6.9%KN	4 4.2%	0 0	0 0	16 4.2%	10 2.5%
Web directory/ subject related web site (NET)	39 5.0%	0 0	21 5.7%	21 5.7%	18 4.4%	20 5.3%	8 4.2%	12 5.2%	4 3.7%	7 5.2%	13 5.6%	3 2.4%	2 5.2%	7 7.3%	1 7.0%	3 7.7%	19 5.0%	20 5.0%

Proportions/Means: Columns Tested (5% risk level) - A/B/D - C/D - E/F/G - H/I/J/K/L/M/N - P/Q
* small base; ** very small base (under 30) ineligible for sig testing

Table 321
Page 1310

Outsell/Digital Library Federation Study (2002)
Weighted Tables

TABLE 75, continued

S7sum_1. Print or hardcopy books SUMMARY TABLE

		RESPONDENT TYPE				INSTITUTION TYPE			DISCIPLINE									GENDER	
	TOTAL SAMPLE	FACULTY MEMBER	GRAD. STUDENT	FACULTY /GRAD	UNDER GRAD. STUDENT	PUBLIC	PRIVATE	LIBERAL ARTS	BIOLOGIAL SCIENCES	PHYSICAL SCIENCES /MATH	SOCIAL SCIENCES	ARTS AND HUMAN.	ENGI- NEERING	BUSINESS	LAW	UNDEC. MAJOR	MALE	FEMALE
		(A)	(B)	(C)	(D)	(E)	(F)	(G)	(H)	(I)	(J)	(K)	(L)	(M)	(N)		(P)	(Q)
Base - Use Print or hardcopy books for coursework	780	0**	376	376	404	369	192	219	95	134	237	140	34	89*	12*	39*	382	398
All sources of info	39 5.0%	0 0	21 5.7%	21 5.7%	18 4.4%	20 5.3%	8 4.2%	12 5.2%	4 3.7%	7 5.2%	13 5.6%	3 2.4%	2 5.2%	7 7.3%	1 7.0%	3 7.7%	19 5.0%	20 5.0%
preferred source of info	27 3.5%	0 0	14 3.7%	14 3.7%	14 3.4%	16 4.4%	4 1.9%	8 3.5%	3 2.8%	4 3.0%	9 4.0%	2 1.6%	1 2.6%	6 6.2%	1 5.6%K	2 5.1%	16 4.1%	12 3.0%
Department web page (NET)	24 3.1%	0 0	13 3.5%	13 3.5%	11 2.7%	13 3.6%	7 3.6%	4 1.9%	4 4.6%	5 3.7%	8 3.2%	1 0.8%	2 5.2%K	5 5.2%K	0 0	0 0	10 2.6%	14 3.6%
All sources of info	24 3.1%	0 0	13 3.5%	13 3.5%	11 2.7%	13 3.6%	7 3.6%	4 1.9%	4 4.6%	5 3.7%	8 3.2%	1 0.8%	2 5.2%K	5 5.2%K	0 0	0 0	10 2.6%	14 3.6%
preferred source of info	19 2.4%	0 0	9 2.4%	9 2.4%	10 2.4%	8 2.1%	7 3.6%	4 1.9%	3 2.8%	3 2.2%	8 3.2%	1 0.8%	1 2.6%	4 4.2%	0 0	0 0	7 2.0%	11 2.9%
Online bookstore (NET)	22 2.9%	0 0	17 4.6%D	17 4.6%D	5 1.2%	11 3.1%	8 4.0%	3 1.4%	5 5.6%K	4 3.0%	6 2.4%	1 0.8%	* 0.9%	6 6.2%K	* 2.8%	0 0	7 1.8%	15 3.9%
All sources of info	22 2.9%	0 0	17 4.6%D	17 4.6%D	5 1.2%	11 3.1%	8 4.0%	3 1.4%	5 5.6%K	4 3.0%	6 2.4%	1 0.8%	* 0.9%	6 6.2%K	* 2.8%	0 0	7 1.8%	15 3.9%
preferred source of info	9 1.2%	0 0	8 2.2%D	8 2.2%D	1 0.2%	6 1.5%	3 1.4%	1 0.4%	4 3.7%K	1 0.7%	2 0.8%	0 0	0 0	3 3.1%K	0 0	0 0	4 1.0%	5 1.4%
Online reference service (NET)	17 2.2%	0 0	10 2.6%	10 2.6%	7 1.8%	11 2.9%	4 2.0%	2 1.1%	2 1.9%	3 2.2%	4 1.6%	2 1.6%	1 3.4%	5 5.2%	1 4.2%	0 0	2 0.6%	15 3.7%P

Proportions/Means: Columns Tested (5% risk level) - A/B/D - C/D - E/F/G - H/I/J/K/L/M/N - P/Q
* small base; ** very small base (under 30) ineligible for sig testing

Table 321
Page 1311

Outsell/Digital Library Federation Study (2002)
Weighted Tables

TABLE 75, continued

S7sum_1. Print or hardcopy books SUMMARY TABLE

	TOTAL SAMPLE	RESPONDENT TYPE: FACULTY MEMBER (A)	GRAD. STUDENT (B)	FACULTY /GRAD (C)	UNDER GRAD. STUDENT (D)	INSTITUTION TYPE: PUBLIC (E)	PRIVATE (F)	LIBERAL ARTS (G)	DISCIPLINE: BIOLOGIAL SCIENCES (H)	PHYSICAL SCIENCES /MATH (I)	SOCIAL SCIENCES (J)	ARTS AND HUMAN. (K)	ENGI-NEERING (L)	BUSINESS (M)	LAW (N)	UNDEC. MAJOR	GENDER: MALE (P)	FEMALE (Q)
Base - Use Print or hardcopy books for coursework	780	0**	376	376	404	369	192	219	95	134	237	140	34	89*	12*	39*	382	398
All sources of info	17 2.2%	0 0	10 2.6%	10 2.6%	7 1.8%	11 2.9%	4 2.0%	2 1.1%	2 1.9%	3 2.2%	4 1.6%	2 1.6%	1 3.4%	5 5.2%	1 4.2%	0 0	2 0.6%	15 3.7%P
preferred source of info	8 1.0%	0 0	4 1.0%	4 1.0%	4 1.0%	6 1.7%	1 0.3%	1 0.5%	0 0	1 0.7%	2 0.8%	1 0.8%	1 1.7%	3 3.1%	1 4.2%HIJK	0 0	1 0.3%	7 1.7%
Online abstracting and indexing services (NET)	16 2.1%	0 0	9 2.4%	9 2.4%	7 1.7%	5 1.3%	9 4.9%EG	2 0.9%	2 1.9%	5 3.7%	6 2.4%	3 2.4%	* 0.9%	0 0	0 0	0 0	9 2.4%	7 1.8%
All sources of info	16 2.1%	0 0	9 2.4%	9 2.4%	7 1.7%	5 1.3%	9 4.9%EG	2 0.9%	2 1.9%	5 3.7%	6 2.4%	3 2.4%	* 0.9%	0 0	0 0	0 0	9 2.4%	7 1.8%
preferred source of info	9 1.2%	0 0	5 1.4%	5 1.4%	4 1.0%	2 0.5%	5 2.8%E	2 0.9%	0 0	4 3.0%	4 1.6%	1 0.8%	* 0.9%	0 0	0 0	0 0	4 1.0%	5 1.3%
Your own personal electronic library/files (NET)	4 0.5%	0 0	2 0.5%	2 0.5%	2 0.5%	* 0.1%	2 1.0%	2 0.9%	1 0.9%	0 0	2 0.8%	0 0	* 0.9%	0 0	0 0	1 2.6%	* 0.1%	4 0.9%
All sources of info	4 0.5%	0 0	2 0.5%	2 0.5%	2 0.5%	* 0.1%	2 1.0%	2 0.9%	1 0.9%	0 0	2 0.8%	0 0	* 0.9%	0 0	0 0	1 2.6%	* 0.1%	4 0.9%
preferred source of info	1 0.2%	0 0	0 0	0 0	1 0.3%	* 0.1%	0 0	1 0.5%	0 0	0 0	0 0	0 0	* 0.9%J	0 0	0 0	1 2.6%	* 0.1%	1 0.3%
E-mail listservs (NET)	1 0.1%	0 0	0 0	0 0	1 0.2%	1 0.3%	0 0	0 0	0 0	0 0	0 0	0 0	0 0	0 0	0 0	1 2.6%	1 0.3%	0 0

Proportions/Means: Columns Tested (5% risk level) - A/B/D - C/D - E/F/G - H/I/J/K/L/M/N - P/Q
* small base; ** very small base (under 30) ineligible for sig testing

Table 321
Page 1312

Outsell/Digital Library Federation Study (2002)
Weighted Tables

TABLE 75, continued

S7sum_1. Print or hardcopy books SUMMARY TABLE

	TOTAL SAMPLE	RESPONDENT TYPE: FACULTY MEMBER (A)	GRAD. STUDENT (B)	FACULTY /GRAD (C)	UNDER GRAD. STUDENT (D)	INSTITUTION TYPE: PUBLIC (E)	PRIVATE (F)	LIBERAL ARTS (G)	DISCIPLINE: BIOLOGIAL SCIENCES (H)	PHYSICAL SCIENCES /MATH (I)	SOCIAL SCIENCES (J)	ARTS AND HUMAN. (K)	ENGI-NEERING (L)	BUSINESS (M)	LAW (N)	UNDEC. MAJOR	GENDER: MALE (P)	FEMALE (Q)
Base - Use Print or hardcopy books for coursework	780	0**	376	376	404	369	192	219	95	134	237	140	34	89*	12*	39*	382	398
All sources of info	1 0.1%	0 0	0 0	0 0	1 0.2%	1 0.3%	0 0	0 0	0 0	0 0	0 0	0 0	0 0	0 0	0 0	1 2.6%	1 0.3%	0 0
preferred source of info	1 0.1%	0 0	0 0	0 0	1 0.2%	1 0.3%	0 0	0 0	0 0	0 0	0 0	0 0	0 0	0 0	0 0	1 2.6%	1 0.3%	0 0
PERSONAL ASSISTANCE	262 33.6%	0 0	119 31.7%	119 31.7%	143 35.4%	116 31.6%	61 32.0%	84 38.5%	34 36.1%J	52 38.8%J	56 23.8%	55 39.2%J	13 38.8%J	33 36.5%J	5 42.3%J	14 35.9%	137 35.9%	125 31.4%
Faculty members inside your institution (NET)	154 19.8%	0 0	80 21.2%	80 21.2%	75 18.5%	76 20.6%	39 20.3%	40 18.0%	18 19.4%	40 29.9%JK	30 12.7%	27 19.2%	9 27.6%J	21 24.0%J	2 18.3%	6 15.4%	84 22.0%	70 17.7%
All sources of info	154 19.8%	0 0	80 21.2%	80 21.2%	75 18.5%	76 20.6%	39 20.3%	40 18.0%	18 19.4%	40 29.9%JK	30 12.7%	27 19.2%	9 27.6%J	21 24.0%J	2 18.3%	6 15.4%	84 22.0%	70 17.7%
preferred source of info	86 11.0%	0 0	43 11.5%	43 11.5%	42 10.4%	40 10.8%	24 12.2%	22 10.1%	10 10.2%	20 14.9%K	23 9.5%	10 7.2%	7 19.8%HJK	13 14.6%	2 12.7%	2 5.1%	54 14.1%Q	32 8.0%
A librarian in your institution (NET)	145 18.6%	0 0	46 12.2%	46 12.2%	99 24.5%B C	48 13.1%	29 15.2%	67 30.6%EF	20 21.3%	19 14.2%	34 14.3%	37 26.4%IJ L	4 12.1%	15 16.7%	4 31.0%IJ LM	12 30.8%	66 17.3%	79 19.7%
All sources of info	145 18.6%	0 0	46 12.2%	46 12.2%	99 24.5%B C	48 13.1%	29 15.2%	67 30.6%EF	20 21.3%	19 14.2%	34 14.3%	37 26.4%IJ L	4 12.1%	15 16.7%	4 31.0%IJ LM	12 30.8%	66 17.3%	79 19.7%

Proportions/Means: Columns Tested (5% risk level) - A/B/D - C/D - E/F/G - H/I/J/K/L/M/N - P/Q
* small base; ** very small base (under 30) ineligible for sig testing

Table 321
Page 1313

Outsell/Digital Library Federation Study (2002)
Weighted Tables

TABLE 75, continued

S7sum_1. Print or hardcopy books SUMMARY TABLE

	TOTAL SAMPLE	RESPONDENT TYPE: FACULTY MEMBER	GRAD. STUDENT	FACULTY /GRAD	UNDER GRAD. STUDENT	INSTITUTION TYPE: PUBLIC	PRIVATE	LIBERAL ARTS	DISCIPLINE: BIOLOGIAL SCIENCES	PHYSICAL SCIENCES /MATH	SOCIAL SCIENCES	ARTS AND HUMAN.	ENGI-NEERING	BUSINESS	LAW	UNDEC. MAJOR	GENDER: MALE	FEMALE
		(A)	(B)	(C)	(D)	(E)	(F)	(G)	(H)	(I)	(J)	(K)	(L)	(M)	(N)		(P)	(Q)
Base - Use Print or hardcopy books for coursework	780	0**	376	376	404	369	192	219	95	134	237	140	34	89*	12*	39*	382	398
preferred source of info	60 7.6%	0 0	20 5.2%	20 5.2%	40 9.9%BC	22 6.0%	13 6.7%	25 11.3%E	11 11.1%I	4 3.0%	11 4.8%	17 12.0%IJ	2 6.9%	9 10.4%I	1 11.3%IJ	4 10.3%	29 7.6%	30 7.6%
Other students inside your institution (NET)	35 4.5%	0 0	18 4.7%	18 4.7%	17 4.2%	15 4.0%	11 5.7%	9 4.2%	4 3.7%	9 6.7%	9 4.0%	6 4.0%	1 4.3%	5 5.2%	* 1.4%	1 2.6%	23 6.1%Q	11 2.9%
All sources of info	35 4.5%	0 0	18 4.7%	18 4.7%	17 4.2%	15 4.0%	11 5.7%	9 4.2%	4 3.7%	9 6.7%	9 4.0%	6 4.0%	1 4.3%	5 5.2%	* 1.4%	1 2.6%	23 6.1%Q	11 2.9%
preferred source of info	6 0.8%	0 0	5 1.5%	5 1.5%	1 0.2%	2 0.6%	4 2.1%G	0 0	2 1.9%	4 3.0%JK	0 0	0 0	1 1.7%JK	0 0	0 0	0 0	4 1.0%	2 0.6%
Faculty members outside your institution (NET)	11 1.4%	0 0	4 1.1%	4 1.1%	7 1.7%	4 1.1%	4 2.1%	3 1.4%	1 0.9%	5 3.7%	2 0.8%	3 2.4%	0 0	0 0	0 0	0 0	7 1.8%	4 1.0%
All sources of info	11 1.4%	0 0	4 1.1%	4 1.1%	7 1.7%	4 1.1%	4 2.1%	3 1.4%	1 0.9%	5 3.7%	2 0.8%	3 2.4%	0 0	0 0	0 0	0 0	7 1.8%	4 1.0%
preferred source of info	1 0.1%	0 0	0 0	0 0	1 0.2%	0 0	0 0	1 0.5%	0 0	1 0.7%	0 0	0 0	0 0	0 0	0 0	0 0	0 0	1 0.3%
Another institution's librarian (NET)	6 0.8%	0 0	1 0.3%	1 0.3%	5 1.2%	4 1.1%	1 0.7%	1 0.5%	0 0	3 2.2%	2 0.8%	1 0.8%	* 0.9%	0 0	0 0	0 0	2 0.6%	4 1.0%
All sources of info	6 0.8%	0 0	1 0.3%	1 0.3%	5 1.2%	4 1.1%	1 0.7%	1 0.5%	0 0	3 2.2%	2 0.8%	1 0.8%	* 0.9%	0 0	0 0	0 0	2 0.6%	4 1.0%

Proportions/Means: Columns Tested (5% risk level) - A/B/D - C/D - E/F/G - H/I/J/K/L/M/N - P/Q
* small base; ** very small base (under 30) ineligible for sig testing

Table 321
Page 1314

Outsell/Digital Library Federation Study (2002)
Weighted Tables

TABLE 75, continued

S7sum_1. Print or hardcopy books SUMMARY TABLE

	TOTAL SAMPLE	RESPONDENT TYPE: FACULTY MEMBER (A)	GRAD. STUDENT (B)	FACULTY /GRAD (C)	UNDER GRAD. STUDENT (D)	INSTITUTION TYPE: PUBLIC (E)	PRIVATE (F)	LIBERAL ARTS (G)	DISCIPLINE: BIOLOGIAL SCIENCES (H)	PHYSICAL SCIENCES /MATH (I)	SOCIAL SCIENCES (J)	ARTS AND HUMAN. (K)	ENGI-NEERING (L)	BUSINESS (M)	LAW (N)	UNDEC. MAJOR	GENDER: MALE (P)	FEMALE (Q)
Base - Use Print or hardcopy books for coursework	780	0**	376	376	404	369	192	219	95	134	237	140	34	89*	12*	39*	382	398
preferred source of info	0 0	0 0	0 0	0 0	0 0	0 0	0 0	0 0	0 0	0 0	0 0	0 0	0 0	0 0	0 0	0 0	0 0	0 0
Other students outside your institution (NET)	2 0.3%	0 0	1 0.2%	1 0.2%	1 0.3%	0 0	1 0.5%	1 0.5%	1 0.9%	0 0	0 0	1 0.8%	0 0	0 0	0 0	0 0	0 0	2 0.5%
All sources of info	2 0.3%	0 0	1 0.2%	1 0.2%	1 0.3%	0 0	1 0.5%	1 0.5%	1 0.9%	0 0	0 0	1 0.8%	0 0	0 0	0 0	0 0	0 0	2 0.5%
preferred source of info	0 0	0 0	0 0	0 0	0 0	0 0	0 0	0 0	0 0	0 0	0 0	0 0	0 0	0 0	0 0	0 0	0 0	0 0
Professional meetings (NET)	1 0.2%	0 0	1 0.3%	1 0.3%	* 0.1%	1 0.4%	0 0	0 0	0 0	0 0	0 0	1 0.8%	* 0.9%J	0 0	0 0	0 0	1 0.4%	0 0
All sources of info	1 0.2%	0 0	1 0.3%	1 0.3%	* 0.1%	1 0.4%	0 0	0 0	0 0	0 0	0 0	1 0.8%	* 0.9%J	0 0	0 0	0 0	1 0.4%	0 0
preferred source of info	1 0.1%	0 0	1 0.3%	1 0.3%	0 0	1 0.3%	0 0	0 0	0 0	0 0	0 0	1 0.8%	0 0	0 0	0 0	0 0	1 0.3%	0 0
LIBRARY FACILITIES/ PRINT	246 31.5%	0 0	117 31.0%	117 31.0%	129 32.0%	113 30.5%	58 30.1%	75 34.3%	27 28.7%	50 37.3%M	70 29.4%	58 41.6%HJ M	10 29.3%	17 18.7%	5 40.8%M	9 23.1%	119 31.1%	127 31.9%
Campus library (NET)	213 27.3%	0 0	100 26.6%	100 26.6%	113 27.9%	92 25.0%	50 26.1%	70 32.1%	21 22.2%	45 33.6%LM	62 26.2%M	54 38.4%HJ LM	7 21.6%	12 13.5%	3 28.2%M	8 20.5%	102 26.6%	111 27.9%

Proportions/Means: Columns Tested (5% risk level) - A/B/D - C/D - E/F/G - H/I/J/K/L/M/N - P/Q
* small base; ** very small base (under 30) ineligible for sig testing

Table 321
Page 1315

Outsell/Digital Library Federation Study (2002)
Weighted Tables

TABLE 75, continued

S7sum_1. Print or hardcopy books SUMMARY TABLE

	TOTAL SAMPLE	RESPONDENT TYPE: FACULTY MEMBER	GRAD. STUDENT	FACULTY /GRAD	UNDER GRAD. STUDENT	INSTITUTION TYPE: PUBLIC	PRIVATE	LIBERAL ARTS	DISCIPLINE: BIOLOGIAL SCIENCES	PHYSICAL SCIENCES /MATH	SOCIAL SCIENCES	ARTS AND HUMAN.	ENGI-NEERING	BUSINESS	LAW	UNDEC. MAJOR	GENDER: MALE	FEMALE
		(A)	(B)	(C)	(D)	(E)	(F)	(G)	(H)	(I)	(J)	(K)	(L)	(M)	(N)		(P)	(Q)
Base - Use Print or hardcopy books for coursework	780	0**	376	376	404	369	192	219	95	134	237	140	34	89*	12*	39*	382	398
All sources of info	213 27.3%	0 0	100 26.6%	100 26.6%	113 27.9%	92 25.0%	50 26.1%	70 32.1%	21 22.2%	45 33.6%LM	62 26.2%M	54 38.4%HJ LM	7 21.6%	12 13.5%	3 28.2%M	8 20.5%	102 26.6%	111 27.9%
preferred source of info	137 17.5%	0 0	66 17.6%	66 17.6%	71 17.5%	66 17.9%	33 17.0%	38 17.3%	9 9.3%	26 19.4%HM	43 18.3%M	41 29.6%HJ LMN	5 15.5%M	5 5.2%	1 11.3%	6 15.4%	65 17.1%	71 17.9%
Physical bookstore (NET)	29 3.8%	0 0	18 4.7%	18 4.7%	12 2.9%	10 2.8%	11 5.8%	8 3.6%	5 5.6%	4 3.0%	8 3.2%	4 3.2%	3 7.8%	4 4.2%	1 7.0%	1 2.6%	16 4.2%	13 3.4%
All sources of info	29 3.8%	0 0	18 4.7%	18 4.7%	12 2.9%	10 2.8%	11 5.8%	8 3.6%	5 5.6%	4 3.0%	8 3.2%	4 3.2%	3 7.8%	4 4.2%	1 7.0%	1 2.6%	16 4.2%	13 3.4%
preferred source of info	11 1.4%	0 0	5 1.4%	5 1.4%	6 1.4%	4 1.0%	4 2.1%	3 1.4%	1 0.9%	2 1.5%	2 0.8%	1 0.8%	1 4.3%JK	2 2.1%	1 5.6%HIJ K	1 2.6%	8 2.1%	3 0.7%
Another library (NET)	10 1.3%	0 0	1 0.4%	1 0.4%	9 2.2%BC	6 1.6%	* 0.1%	4 1.9%	1 0.9%	2 1.5%	4 1.6%	3 2.4%	0 0	0 0	* 2.8%LM	0 0	4 1.0%	6 1.6%
All sources of info	10 1.3%	0 0	1 0.4%	1 0.4%	9 2.2%BC	6 1.6%	* 0.1%	4 1.9%	1 0.9%	2 1.5%	4 1.6%	3 2.4%	0 0	0 0	* 2.8%LM	0 0	4 1.0%	6 1.6%
preferred source of info	2 0.3%	0 0	* *	* *	2 0.5%	2 0.5%	* 0.1%	0 0	0 0	0 0	2 0.8%	0 0	0 0	0 0	* 1.4%HIKM	0 0	* *	2 0.5%

Proportions/Means: Columns Tested (5% risk level) - A/B/D - C/D - E/F/G - H/I/J/K/L/M/N - P/Q
* small base; ** very small base (under 30) ineligible for sig testing

Table 321
Page 1316

Outsell/Digital Library Federation Study (2002)
Weighted Tables

TABLE 75, continued

S7sum_1. Print or hardcopy books SUMMARY TABLE

		RESPONDENT TYPE				INSTITUTION TYPE			DISCIPLINE									GENDER	
	TOTAL SAMPLE	FACULTY MEMBER	GRAD. STUDENT	FACULTY /GRAD	UNDER GRAD. STUDENT	PUBLIC	PRIVATE	LIBERAL ARTS	BIOLOGIAL SCIENCES	PHYSICAL SCIENCES /MATH	SOCIAL SCIENCES	ARTS AND HUMAN.	ENGI-NEERING	BUSINESS	LAW	UNDEC. MAJOR	MALE	FEMALE
		(A)	(B)	(C)	(D)	(E)	(F)	(G)	(H)	(I)	(J)	(K)	(L)	(M)	(N)		(P)	(Q)
Base - Use Print or hardcopy books for coursework	780	0**	376	376	404	369	192	219	95	134	237	140	34	89*	12*	39*	382	398
References cited in books or journal articles (NET)	10 1.3%	0 0	4 0.9%	4 0.9%	7 1.6%	7 1.8%	* 0.1%	3 1.5%	2 1.9%	1 0.7%	2 0.8%	3 2.4%	1 1.7%	0 0	1 4.2%IJM	1 2.6%	8 2.1%	2 0.5%
All sources of info	10 1.3%	0 0	4 0.9%	4 0.9%	7 1.6%	7 1.8%	* 0.1%	3 1.5%	2 1.9%	1 0.7%	2 0.8%	3 2.4%	1 1.7%	0 0	1 4.2%IJM	1 2.6%	8 2.1%	2 0.5%
preferred source of info	2 0.3%	0 0	1 0.3%	1 0.3%	1 0.3%	1 0.3%	0 0	1 0.5%	0 0	0 0	0 0	2 1.6%	0 0	0 0	* 1.4%HIJM	0 0	2 0.6%	0 0
Printed library catalogues and finding aids (NET)	9 1.1%	0 0	2 0.5%	2 0.5%	7 1.7%	5 1.3%	1 0.6%	3 1.4%	2 1.9%	1 0.7%	2 0.8%	1 0.8%	1 1.7%	2 2.1%	1 5.6%IJK	0 0	3 0.8%	6 1.5%
All sources of info	9 1.1%	0 0	2 0.5%	2 0.5%	7 1.7%	5 1.3%	1 0.6%	3 1.4%	2 1.9%	1 0.7%	2 0.8%	1 0.8%	1 1.7%	2 2.1%	1 5.6%IJK	0 0	3 0.8%	6 1.5%
preferred source of info	5 0.7%	0 0	1 0.2%	1 0.2%	5 1.2%	1 0.4%	1 0.6%	3 1.3%	1 0.9%	1 0.7%	2 0.8%	0 0	1 1.7%K	1 1.0%	* 1.4%K	0 0	2 0.4%	4 1.0%
Your own personal physical library/ files/bookshelves (NET)	7 0.9%	0 0	5 1.3%	5 1.3%	2 0.5%	4 1.1%	2 1.0%	1 0.5%	3 2.8%J	3 2.2%J	0 0	1 0.8%	* 0.9%J	0 0	0 0	0 0	2 0.6%	5 1.2%
All sources of info	7 0.9%	0 0	5 1.3%	5 1.3%	2 0.5%	4 1.1%	2 1.0%	1 0.5%	3 2.8%J	3 2.2%J	0 0	1 0.8%	* 0.9%J	0 0	0 0	0 0	2 0.6%	5 1.2%

Proportions/Means: Columns Tested (5% risk level) - A/B/D - C/D - E/F/G - H/I/J/K/L/M/N - P/Q
* small base; ** very small base (under 30) ineligible for sig testing

Table 321
Page 1317

Outsell/Digital Library Federation Study (2002)
Weighted Tables

TABLE 75, continued

S7sum_1. Print or hardcopy books SUMMARY TABLE

		RESPONDENT TYPE				INSTITUTION TYPE			DISCIPLINE								GENDER	
	TOTAL SAMPLE	FACULTY MEMBER	GRAD. STUDENT	FACULTY /GRAD	UNDER GRAD. STUDENT	PUBLIC	PRIVATE	LIBERAL ARTS	BIOLOGIAL SCIENCES	PHYSICAL SCIENCES /MATH	SOCIAL SCIENCES	ARTS AND HUMAN.	ENGI-NEERING	BUSINESS	LAW	UNDEC. MAJOR	MALE	FEMALE
		(A)	(B)	(C)	(D)	(E)	(F)	(G)	(H)	(I)	(J)	(K)	(L)	(M)	(N)		(P)	(Q)
Base - Use Print or hardcopy books for coursework	780	0**	376	376	404	369	192	219	95	134	237	140	34	89*	12*	39*	382	398
preferred source of info	1 0.2%	0 0	1 0.2%	1 0.2%	* 0.1%	1 0.3%	0 0	0 0	1 0.9%	0 0	0 0	0 0	* 0.9%J	0 0	0 0	0 0	* 0.1%	1 0.2%
Printed abstracting and indexing services (NET)	2 0.3%	0 0	1 0.3%	1 0.3%	1 0.2%	1 0.2%	* 0.1%	1 0.5%	1 0.9%	1 0.7%	0 0	0 0	0 0	0 0	* 1.4%JKM	0 0	2 0.5%	0 0
All sources of info	2 0.3%	0 0	1 0.3%	1 0.3%	1 0.2%	1 0.2%	* 0.1%	1 0.5%	1 0.9%	1 0.7%	0 0	0 0	0 0	0 0	* 1.4%JKM	0 0	2 0.5%	0 0
preferred source of info	1 0.1%	0 0	1 0.3%	1 0.3%	0 0	1 0.2%	* 0.1%	0 0	1 0.9%	0 0	0 0	0 0	0 0	0 0	* 1.4%IJKM	0 0	1 0.3%	0 0
Personal subscriptions to newspapers, magazines and journals (NET)	0 0	0 0	0 0	0 0	0 0	0 0	0 0	0 0	0 0	0 0	0 0	0 0	0 0	0 0	0 0	0 0	0 0	0 0
All sources of info	0 0	0 0	0 0	0 0	0 0	0 0	0 0	0 0	0 0	0 0	0 0	0 0	0 0	0 0	0 0	0 0	0 0	0 0
preferred source of info	0 0	0 0	0 0	0 0	0 0	0 0	0 0	0 0	0 0	0 0	0 0	0 0	0 0	0 0	0 0	0 0	0 0	0 0
Other (NET)	33 4.2%	0 0	20 5.3%	20 5.3%	13 3.1%	21 5.8%G	7 3.5%	4 2.0%	4 4.6%	3 2.2%	9 4.0%	6 4.0%	1 4.3%	5 5.2%	1 8.5%I	3 7.7%	11 2.8%	22 5.5%

Proportions/Means: Columns Tested (5% risk level) - A/B/D - C/D - E/F/G - H/I/J/K/L/M/N - P/Q
* small base; ** very small base (under 30) ineligible for sig testing

Table 321
Page 1318

Outsell/Digital Library Federation Study (2002)
Weighted Tables

TABLE 75, continued

S7sum_1. Print or hardcopy books SUMMARY TABLE

		RESPONDENT TYPE				INSTITUTION TYPE			DISCIPLINE								GENDER	
	TOTAL SAMPLE	FACULTY MEMBER	GRAD. STUDENT	FACULTY /GRAD	UNDER GRAD. STUDENT	PUBLIC	PRIVATE	LIBERAL ARTS	BIOLOGIAL SCIENCES	PHYSICAL SCIENCES /MATH	SOCIAL SCIENCES	ARTS AND HUMAN.	ENGI- NEERING	BUSINESS	LAW	UNDEC. MAJOR	MALE	FEMALE
		(A)	(B)	(C)	(D)	(E)	(F)	(G)	(H)	(I)	(J)	(K)	(L)	(M)	(N)		(P)	(Q)
Base - Use Print or hardcopy books for coursework	780	0**	376	376	404	369	192	219	95	134	237	140	34	89*	12*	39*	382	398
All sources of info	27 3.4%	0 0	16 4.3%	16 4.3%	11 2.6%	17 4.5%	6 3.0%	4 2.0%	4 3.7%	3 2.2%	8 3.2%	6 4.0%	1 4.3%	3 3.1%	1 8.5%I	2 5.1%	10 2.5%	17 4.3%
preferred source of info	15 2.0%	0 0	8 2.2%	8 2.2%	7 1.8%	11 3.0%	2 1.2%	2 0.9%	4 3.7%	1 0.7%	2 0.8%	2 1.6%	* 0.9%	3 3.1%	1 5.6%IJK L	3 7.7%	6 1.5%	10 2.4%
Online (unspecified)	7 0.9%	0 0	3 0.7%	3 0.7%	4 1.0%	5 1.4%	1 0.8%	0 0	1 0.9%	0 0	4 1.6%	0 0	1 3.4%IK	1 1.0%	0 0	0 0	4 1.0%	3 0.8%
All sources of info	7 0.9%	0 0	3 0.7%	3 0.7%	4 1.0%	5 1.4%	1 0.8%	0 0	1 0.9%	0 0	4 1.6%	0 0	1 3.4%IK	1 1.0%	0 0	0 0	4 1.0%	3 0.8%
preferred source of info	3 0.4%	0 0	2 0.7%	2 0.7%	* 0.1%	2 0.7%	* 0.2%	0 0	0 0	0 0	2 0.8%	0 0	1 2.6%HIKM	0 0	0 0	0 0	1 0.2%	2 0.5%
E-journals	1 0.1%	0 0	0 0	0 0	1 0.3%	0 0	0 0	1 0.5%	0 0	0 0	0 0	1 0.8%	0 0	0 0	0 0	0 0	1 0.3%	0 0
All sources of info	1 0.1%	0 0	0 0	0 0	1 0.3%	0 0	0 0	1 0.5%	0 0	0 0	0 0	1 0.8%	0 0	0 0	0 0	0 0	1 0.3%	0 0
preferred source of info	0 0	0 0	0 0	0 0	0 0	0 0	0 0	0 0	0 0	0 0	0 0	0 0	0 0	0 0	0 0	0 0	0 0	0 0
DK/Refused	20 2.6%	0 0	9 2.4%	9 2.4%	11 2.7%	11 2.9%	5 2.7%	4 1.8%	4 3.7%	4 3.0%	4 1.6%	3 2.4%	1 1.7%	4 4.2%	0 0	1 2.6%	9 2.4%	11 2.7%

Proportions/Means: Columns Tested (5% risk level) - A/B/D - C/D - E/F/G - H/I/J/K/L/M/N - P/Q
* small base; ** very small base (under 30) ineligible for sig testing

Table 321
Page 1319

Outsell/Digital Library Federation Study (2002)
Weighted Tables

TABLE 76

S7D/E_1. Print or hardcopy books SUMMARY TABLE

		RESPONDENT TYPE				INSTITUTION TYPE			DISCIPLINE									GENDER	
	TOTAL SAMPLE	FACULTY MEMBER	GRAD. STUDENT	FACULTY /GRAD	UNDER GRAD. STUDENT	PUBLIC	PRIVATE	LIBERAL ARTS	BIOLOGIAL SCIENCES	PHYSICAL SCIENCES /MATH	SOCIAL SCIENCES	ARTS AND HUMAN.	ENGI-NEERING	BUSINESS	LAW	UNDEC. MAJOR	MALE	FEMALE
		(A)	(B)	(C)	(D)	(E)	(F)	(G)	(H)	(I)	(J)	(K)	(L)	(M)	(N)		(P)	(Q)
Base - Use Print or hardcopy books for coursework	780	0**	376	376	404	369	192	219	95	134	237	140	34	89*	12*	39*	382	398
Borrow from or use in campus library (NET)	660 84.6%	0 0	297 78.9%	297 78.9%	363 90.0%B C	295 80.1%	164 85.6%	200 91.4%E	78 82.4%M	114 85.1%MN	209 88.1%LM N	129 92.0%HL MN	26 77.6%	61 68.8%	9 73.2%	34 87.2%	313 81.9%	347 87.3%
All sources of info	660 84.6%	0 0	297 78.9%	297 78.9%	363 90.0%B C	295 80.1%	164 85.6%	200 91.4%E	78 82.4%M	114 85.1%MN	209 88.1%LM N	129 92.0%HL MN	26 77.6%	61 68.8%	9 73.2%	34 87.2%	313 81.9%	347 87.3%
preferred source of info	575 73.7%	0 0	252 67.0%	252 67.0%	323 80.0%B C	253 68.7%	138 72.1%	183 83.6%EF	66 69.4%	96 71.6%M	186 78.6%LM N	115 82.4%HI LMN	21 62.9%	50 56.3%	7 59.2%	33 84.6%	279 73.1%	296 74.4%
Purchase from physical book store (NET)	147 18.8%	0 0	84 22.4%D	84 22.4%D	62 15.4%	66 17.8%	38 20.0%	43 19.4%	15 15.7%	32 23.9%K	39 16.7%	13 9.6%	10 29.3%HJK	27 30.2%HJ K	3 25.4%K	7 17.9%	82 21.5%	65 16.3%
All sources of info	147 18.8%	0 0	84 22.4%D	84 22.4%D	62 15.4%	66 17.8%	38 20.0%	43 19.4%	15 15.7%	32 23.9%K	39 16.7%	13 9.6%	10 29.3%HJK	27 30.2%HJ K	3 25.4%K	7 17.9%	82 21.5%	65 16.3%
preferred source of info	83 10.6%	0 0	51 13.5%D	51 13.5%D	32 8.0%	45 12.1%	22 11.7%	16 7.3%	11 11.1%K	18 13.4%K	19 7.9%	4 3.2%	6 17.2%JK	19 20.8%JK	3 22.5%HJ K	4 10.3%	47 12.4%	36 9.0%
Access online (NET)	118 15.1%	0 0	67 17.8%	67 17.8%	51 12.5%	65 17.7%G	31 16.1%	21 9.8%	18 19.4%K	22 16.4%	38 15.9%	13 9.6%	6 16.4%	14 15.6%	2 14.1%	5 12.8%	53 14.0%	64 16.2%

Proportions/Means: Columns Tested (5% risk level) - A/B/D - C/D - E/F/G - H/I/J/K/L/M/N - P/Q
* small base; ** very small base (under 30) ineligible for sig testing

Table 324
Page 1326

Outsell/Digital Library Federation Study (2002)
Weighted Tables

TABLE 76, continued

S7D/E_1. Print or hardcopy books SUMMARY TABLE

		RESPONDENT TYPE				INSTITUTION TYPE			DISCIPLINE									GENDER	
	TOTAL SAMPLE	FACULTY MEMBER	GRAD. STUDENT	FACULTY /GRAD	UNDER GRAD. STUDENT	PUBLIC	PRIVATE	LIBERAL ARTS	BIOLOGIAL SCIENCES	PHYSICAL SCIENCES /MATH	SOCIAL SCIENCES	ARTS AND HUMAN.	ENGI-NEERING	BUSINESS	LAW	UNDEC. MAJOR	MALE	FEMALE
		(A)	(B)	(C)	(D)	(E)	(F)	(G)	(H)	(I)	(J)	(K)	(L)	(M)	(N)		(P)	(Q)
Base - Use Print or hardcopy books for coursework	780	0**	376	376	404	369	192	219	95	134	237	140	34	89*	12*	39*	382	398
All sources of info	118 15.1%	0 0	67 17.8%	67 17.8%	51 12.5%	65 17.7%G	31 16.1%	21 9.8%	18 19.4%K	22 16.4%	38 15.9%	13 9.6%	6 16.4%	14 15.6%	2 14.1%	5 12.8%	53 14.0%	64 16.2%
preferred source of info	85 10.9%	0 0	50 13.4%D	50 13.4%D	34 8.5%	51 14.0%G	21 10.9%	12 5.7%	14 14.8%K	14 10.4%	30 12.7%	8 5.6%	3 10.3%	12 13.5%K	1 9.9%	2 5.1%	37 9.6%	48 12.1%
Borrow from or use in other libraries (NET)	39 5.0%	0 0	13 3.6%	13 3.6%	26 6.4%	13 3.7%	8 4.4%	18 8.0%E	2 1.9%	10 7.5%	8 3.2%	16 11.2%HJL M	1 2.6%	2 2.1%	1 5.6%	1 2.6%	16 4.3%	23 5.8%
All sources of info	39 5.0%	0 0	13 3.6%	13 3.6%	26 6.4%	13 3.7%	8 4.4%	18 8.0%E	2 1.9%	10 7.5%	8 3.2%	16 11.2%HJL M	1 2.6%	2 2.1%	1 5.6%	1 2.6%	16 4.3%	23 5.8%
preferred source of info	8 1.1%	0 0	3 0.8%	3 0.8%	5 1.3%	3 0.9%	2 1.0%	3 1.4%	0 0	1 0.7%	0 0	6 4.0%HJ	1 1.7%J	1 1.0%	* 2.8%HJ	0 0	4 1.0%	4 1.1%
Purchase from online bookstore (NET)	34 4.3%	0 0	23 6.1%D	23 6.1%D	11 2.6%	11 3.1%	13 6.6%	10 4.4%	4 4.6%	7 5.2%	4 1.6%	7 4.8%	3 7.8%J	7 8.3%J	1 5.6%J	1 2.6%	20 5.1%	14 3.5%
All sources of info	34 4.3%	0 0	23 6.1%D	23 6.1%D	11 2.6%	11 3.1%	13 6.6%	10 4.4%	4 4.6%	7 5.2%	4 1.6%	7 4.8%	3 7.8%J	7 8.3%J	1 5.6%J	1 2.6%	20 5.1%	14 3.5%
preferred source of info	9 1.1%	0 0	8 2.0%D	8 2.0%D	1 0.3%	4 1.2%	3 1.7%	1 0.5%	1 0.9%	1 0.7%	0 0	1 0.8%	1 2.6%J	5 5.2%IJK	* 1.4%J	0 0	4 1.1%	4 1.1%
Interlibrary loan (NET)	19 2.4%	0 0	6 1.6%	6 1.6%	12 3:1%	5 1.5%	3 1.3%	11 4.8%E	4 4.6%	2 1.5%	6 2.4%	3 2.4%	* 0.9%	2 2.1%	0 0	1 2.6%	9 2.4%	10 2.4%

Proportions/Means: Columns Tested (5% risk level) - A/B/D - C/D - E/F/G - H/I/J/K/L/M/N - P/Q
* small base; ** very small base (under 30) ineligible for sig testing

Table 324
Page 1327

Outsell/Digital Library Federation Study (2002)
Weighted Tables

TABLE 76, continued

S7D/E_1. Print or hardcopy books SUMMARY TABLE

		RESPONDENT TYPE				INSTITUTION TYPE			DISCIPLINE									GENDER	
	TOTAL SAMPLE	FACULTY MEMBER	GRAD. STUDENT	FACULTY /GRAD	UNDER GRAD. STUDENT	PUBLIC	PRIVATE	LIBERAL ARTS	BIOLOGICAL SCIENCES	PHYSICAL SCIENCES /MATH	SOCIAL SCIENCES	ARTS AND HUMAN.	ENGI- NEERING	BUSINESS	LAW	UNDEC. MAJOR	MALE	FEMALE
		(A)	(B)	(C)	(D)	(E)	(F)	(G)	(H)	(I)	(J)	(K)	(L)	(M)	(N)		(P)	(Q)
Base - Use Print or hardcopy books for coursework	780	0**	376	376	404	369	192	219	95	134	237	140	34	89*	12*	39*	382	398
All sources of info	19 2.4%	0 0	6 1.6%	6 1.6%	12 3.1%	5 1.5%	3 1.3%	11 4.8%E	4 4.6%	2 1.5%	6 2.4%	3 2.4%	* 0.9%	2 2.1%	0 0	1 2.6%	9 2.4%	10 2.4%
preferred source of info	2 0.2%	0 0	1 0.2%	1 0.2%	1 0.2%	2 0.5%	0 0	0 0	2 1.9%	0 0	0 0	0 0	0 0	0 0	0 0	0 0	0 0	2 0.4%
Faculty (NET)	12 1.6%	0 0	7 1.9%	7 1.9%	5 1.3%	2 0.6%	5 2.5%	5 2.4%	2 1.9%	2 1.5%	2 0.8%	7 4.8%JM	0 0	0 0	0 0	0 0	5 1.3%	7 1.8%
All sources of info	12 1.6%	0 0	7 1.9%	7 1.9%	5 1.3%	2 0.6%	5 2.5%	5 2.4%	2 1.9%	2 1.5%	2 0.8%	7 4.8%JM	0 0	0 0	0 0	0 0	5 1.3%	7 1.8%
preferred source of info	4 0.5%	0 0	2 0.5%	2 0.5%	2 0.6%	1 0.3%	1 0.5%	2 1.0%	1 0.9%	0 0	0 0	3 2.4%J	0 0	0 0	0 0	0 0	1 0.3%	3 0.8%
Colleagues (NET)	5 0.7%	0 0	3 0.9%	3 0.9%	2 0.5%	2 0.5%	2 0.8%	2 0.9%	0 0	1 0.7%	2 0.8%	0 0	1 1.7%K	0 0	0 0	2 5.1%	2 0.6%	3 0.8%
All sources of info	5 0.7%	0 0	3 0.9%	3 0.9%	2 0.5%	2 0.5%	2 0.8%	2 0.9%	0 0	1 0.7%	2 0.8%	0 0	1 1.7%K	0 0	0 0	2 5.1%	2 0.6%	3 0.8%
preferred source of info	1 0.2%	0 0	1 0.3%	1 0.3%	0 0	0 0	1 0.7%	0 0	0 0	1 0.7%	0 0	0 0	* 0.9%J	0 0	0 0	0 0	1 0.3%	0 0
Ask library to purchase source (NET)	3 0.4%	0 0	2 0.5%	2 0.5%	1 0.2%	3 0.8%	0 0	0 0	0 0	0 0	2 0.8%	0 0	0 0	0 0	0 0	1 2.6%	3 0.8%	0 0

Proportions/Means: Columns Tested (5% risk level) - A/B/D - C/D - E/F/G - H/I/J/K/L/M/N - P/Q
* small base; ** very small base (under 30) ineligible for sig testing

Table 324
Page 1328

Outsell/Digital Library Federation Study (2002)
Weighted Tables

TABLE 76, continued

S7D/E_1. Print or hardcopy books SUMMARY TABLE

	TOTAL SAMPLE	RESPONDENT TYPE: FACULTY MEMBER (A)	GRAD. STUDENT (B)	FACULTY /GRAD (C)	UNDER GRAD. STUDENT (D)	INSTITUTION TYPE: PUBLIC (E)	PRIVATE (F)	LIBERAL ARTS (G)	DISCIPLINE: BIOLOGIAL SCIENCES (H)	PHYSICAL SCIENCES /MATH (I)	SOCIAL SCIENCES (J)	ARTS AND HUMAN. (K)	ENGI-NEERING (L)	BUSINESS (M)	LAW (N)	UNDEC. MAJOR	GENDER: MALE (P)	FEMALE (Q)
Base - Use Print or hardcopy books for coursework	780	0**	376	376	404	369	192	219	95	134	237	140	34	89*	12*	39*	382	398
All sources of info	3 0.4%	0 0	2 0.5%	2 0.5%	1 0.2%	3 0.8%	0 0	0 0	0 0	0 0	2 0.8%	0 0	0 0	0 0	0 0	1 2.6%	3 0.8%	0 0
preferred source of info	2 0.2%	0 0	2 0.5%	2 0.5%	0 0	2 0.5%	0 0	0 0	0 0	0 0	2 0.8%	0 0	0 0	0 0	0 0	0 0	2 0.5%	0 0
Order from on demand document delivery service (NET)	2 0.2%	0 0	2 0.5%	2 0.5%	0 0	1 0.3%	1 0.5%	0 0	0 0	1 0.7%	0 0	0 0	0 0	1 1.0%	0 0	0 0	1 0.3%	1 0.2%
All sources of info	2 0.2%	0 0	2 0.5%	2 0.5%	0 0	1 0.3%	1 0.5%	0 0	0 0	1 0.7%	0 0	0 0	0 0	1 1.0%	0 0	0 0	1 0.3%	1 0.2%
preferred source of info	0 0	0 0	0 0	0 0	0 0	0 0	0 0	0 0	0 0	0 0	0 0	0 0	0 0	0 0	0 0	0 0	0 0	0 0
Home (NET)	2 0.2%	0 0	2 0.5%	2 0.5%	0 0	0 0	2 1.0%	0 0	0 0	0 0	2 0.8%	0 0	0 0	0 0	0 0	0 0	0 0	2 0.5%
All sources of info	2 0.2%	0 0	2 0.5%	2 0.5%	0 0	0 0	2 1.0%	0 0	0 0	0 0	2 0.8%	0 0	0 0	0 0	0 0	0 0	0 0	2 0.5%
preferred source of info	0 0	0 0	0 0	0 0	0 0	0 0	0 0	0 0	0 0	0 0	0 0	0 0	0 0	0 0	0 0	0 0	0 0	0 0
Personal Holdings (NET)	1 0.2%	0 0	1 0.4%	1 0.4%	0 0	1 0.3%	* 0.2%	0 0	0 0	0 0	0 0	1 0.8%	* 0.9%J	0 0	0 0	0 0	* 0.1%	1 0.3%

Proportions/Means: Columns Tested (5% risk level) - A/B/D - C/D - E/F/G - H/I/J/K/L/M/N - P/Q
* small base; ** very small base (under 30) ineligible for sig testing

Table 324
Page 1329

Outsell/Digital Library Federation Study (2002)
Weighted Tables

TABLE 76, continued

S7D/E_1. Print or hardcopy books SUMMARY TABLE

	TOTAL SAMPLE	RESPONDENT TYPE: FACULTY MEMBER	RESPONDENT TYPE: GRAD. STUDENT	RESPONDENT TYPE: FACULTY /GRAD	UNDER GRAD. STUDENT	INSTITUTION TYPE: PUBLIC	INSTITUTION TYPE: PRIVATE	INSTITUTION TYPE: LIBERAL ARTS	DISCIPLINE: BIOLOGIAL SCIENCES	DISCIPLINE: PHYSICAL SCIENCES /MATH	DISCIPLINE: SOCIAL SCIENCES	DISCIPLINE: ARTS AND HUMAN.	DISCIPLINE: ENGI-NEERING	DISCIPLINE: BUSINESS	DISCIPLINE: LAW	DISCIPLINE: UNDEC. MAJOR	GENDER: MALE	GENDER: FEMALE
		(A)	(B)	(C)	(D)	(E)	(F)	(G)	(H)	(I)	(J)	(K)	(L)	(M)	(N)		(P)	(Q)
Base - Use Print or hardcopy books for coursework	780	0**	376	376	404	369	192	219	95	134	237	140	34	89*	12*	39*	382	398
All sources of info	1 0.2%	0 0	1 0.4%	1 0.4%	0 0	1 0.3%	* 0.2%	0 0	0 0	0 0	0 0	1 0.8%	* 0.9%J	0 0	0 0	0 0	* 0.1%	1 0.3%
preferred source of info	* *	0 0	* 0.1%	* 0.1%	0 0	0 0	* 0.2%	0 0	0 0	0 0	0 0	0 0	* 0.9%J	0 0	0 0	0 0	* 0.1%	0 0
Access book/journal/ journal article elsewhere online (NET)	0 0	0 0	0 0	0 0	0 0	0 0	0 0	0 0	0 0	0 0	0 0	0 0	0 0	0 0	0 0	0 0	0 0	0 0
All sources of info	0 0	0 0	0 0	0 0	0 0	0 0	0 0	0 0	0 0	0 0	0 0	0 0	0 0	0 0	0 0	0 0	0 0	0 0
preferred source of info	0 0	0 0	0 0	0 0	0 0	0 0	0 0	0 0	0 0	0 0	0 0	0 0	0 0	0 0	0 0	0 0	0 0	0 0
In class (NET)	0 0	0 0	0 0	0 0	0 0	0 0	0 0	0 0	0 0	0 0	0 0	0 0	0 0	0 0	0 0	0 0	0 0	0 0
All sources of info	0 0	0 0	0 0	0 0	0 0	0 0	0 0	0 0	0 0	0 0	0 0	0 0	0 0	0 0	0 0	0 0	0 0	0 0
preferred source of info	0 0	0 0	0 0	0 0	0 0	0 0	0 0	0 0	0 0	0 0	0 0	0 0	0 0	0 0	0 0	0 0	0 0	0 0
Dorm room (NET)	0 0	0 0	0 0	0 0	0 0	0 0	0 0	0 0	0 0	0 0	0 0	0 0	0 0	0 0	0 0	0 0	0 0	0 0

Proportions/Means: Columns Tested (5% risk level) - A/B/D - C/D - E/F/G - H/I/J/K/L/M/N - P/Q
* small base; ** very small base (under 30) ineligible for sig testing

Table 324
Page 1330

Outsell/Digital Library Federation Study (2002)
Weighted Tables

TABLE 76, continued

S7D/E_1. Print or hardcopy books SUMMARY TABLE

		RESPONDENT TYPE				INSTITUTION TYPE			DISCIPLINE								GENDER	
	TOTAL SAMPLE	FACULTY MEMBER	GRAD. STUDENT	FACULTY /GRAD	UNDER GRAD. STUDENT	PUBLIC	PRIVATE	LIBERAL ARTS	BIOLOGIAL SCIENCES	PHYSICAL SCIENCES /MATH	SOCIAL SCIENCES	ARTS AND HUMAN.	ENGI- NEERING	BUSINESS	LAW	UNDEC. MAJOR	MALE	FEMALE
		(A)	(B)	(C)	(D)	(E)	(F)	(G)	(H)	(I)	(J)	(K)	(L)	(M)	(N)		(P)	(Q)
Base - Use Print or hardcopy books for coursework	780	0**	376	376	404	369	192	219	95	134	237	140	34	89*	12*	39*	382	398
All sources of info	0 0	0 0	0 0	0 0	0 0	0 0	0 0	0 0	0 0	0 0	0 0	0 0	0 0	0 0	0 0	0 0	0 0	0 0
preferred source of info	0 0	0 0	0 0	0 0	0 0	0 0	0 0	0 0	0 0	0 0	0 0	0 0	0 0	0 0	0 0	0 0	0 0	0 0
Access from course website (NET)	0 0	0 0	0 0	0 0	0 0	0 0	0 0	0 0	0 0	0 0	0 0	0 0	0 0	0 0	0 0	0 0	0 0	0 0
All sources of info	0 0	0 0	0 0	0 0	0 0	0 0	0 0	0 0	0 0	0 0	0 0	0 0	0 0	0 0	0 0	0 0	0 0	0 0
preferred source of info	0 0	0 0	0 0	0 0	0 0	0 0	0 0	0 0	0 0	0 0	0 0	0 0	0 0	0 0	0 0	0 0	0 0	0 0
Other (NET)	10 1.3%	0 0	6 1.7%	6 1.7%	4 1.0%	5 1.4%	4 2.1%	1 0.5%	1 0.9%	3 2.2%J	0 0	1 0.8%	0 0	5 5.2%JKL	1 5.6%HJKL	0 0	7 1.8%	3 0.8%
All sources of info	10 1.3%	0 0	6 1.7%	6 1.7%	4 1.0%	5 1.4%	4 2.1%	1 0.5%	1 0.9%	3 2.2%J	0 0	1 0.8%	0 0	5 5.2%JKL	1 5.6%HJKL	0 0	7 1.8%	3 0.8%
preferred source of info	4 0.5%	0 0	1 0.4%	1 0.4%	2 0.5%	2 0.6%	* 0.1%	1 0.5%	0 0	1 0.7%	0 0	1 0.8%	0 0	1 1.0%	1 4.2%HIJKL	0 0	2 0.5%	1 0.4%
DK/Refused	6 0.8%	0 0	5 1.2%	5 1.2%	1 0.3%	4 1.0%	2 1.1%	0 0	0 0	2 1.5%	0 0	1 0.8%	1 2.6%HJ	2 2.1%J	0 0	0 0	4 1.0%	2 0.5%

Proportions/Means: Columns Tested (5% risk level) - A/B/D - C/D - E/F/G - H/I/J/K/L/M/N - P/Q
* small base; ** very small base (under 30) ineligible for sig testing

TABLE 77

R7sum_2. When you are doing research, how do you find information about Print or hardcopy journals ? Do you ...

	TOTAL SAMPLE	RESPONDENT TYPE: FACULTY MEMBER	GRAD. STUDENT	FACULTY /GRAD	UNDER GRAD. STUDENT	INSTITUTION TYPE: PUBLIC	PRIVATE	LIBERAL ARTS	DISCIPLINE: BIOLOGIAL SCIENCES	PHYSICAL SCIENCES /MATH	SOCIAL SCIENCES	ARTS AND HUMAN.	ENGI-NEERING	BUSINESS	LAW	UNDEC. MAJOR	GENDER: MALE	FEMALE
		(A)	(B)	(C)	(D)	(E)	(F)	(G)	(H)	(I)	(J)	(K)	(L)	(M)	(N)		(P)	(Q)
Base - Use Print or hardcopy journals for research	434	220	214	434	0**	188	158	88*	66*	94*	141*	68*	23*	36*	5*	0*	292	143
ONLINE	379 87.2%	190 86.1%	189 88.3%	379 87.2%	0 0	168 89.4%	133 84.4%	77 87.5%	62 93.3%L	82 87.2%	122 86.7%	57 83.6%	19 81.5%	32 87.2%	5 96.8%	0 0	250 85.7%	129 90.3%
Online databases	119 27.4%	64 29.1%	55 25.7%	119 27.4%	0 0	47 24.8%	42 26.8%	30 34.1%	18 26.7%	26 27.7%	36 25.3%	21 31.1%	5 19.8%	10 28.2%	4 67.7%HIJKL M	0 0	78 26.6%	41 29.0%
All sources of info	119 27.4%	64 29.1%	55 25.7%	119 27.4%	0 0	47 24.8%	42 26.8%	30 34.1%	18 26.7%	26 27.7%	36 25.3%	21 31.1%	5 19.8%	10 28.2%	4 67.7%HIJKL M	0 0	78 26.6%	41 29.0%
preferred source of info	82 18.9%	42 19.0%	40 18.8%	82 18.9%	0 0	34 17.8%	29 18.5%	20 22.2%	11 17.3%	18 19.1%L	30 21.3%L	13 19.7%	2 7.4%	5 12.8%	3 54.8%HIJKL M	0 0	49 16.8%	33 23.3%
Online library catalogues and finding aids	100 23.1%	48 21.7%	52 24.5%	100 23.1%	0 0	47 24.7%	34 21.6%	20 22.4%	14 21.3%	11 11.7%	38 26.7%I	28 41.0%HI LMN	3 14.8%	6 15.4%	1 9.7%	0 0	56 19.2%	44 30.9%P
All sources of info	100 23.1%	48 21.7%	52 24.5%	100 23.1%	0 0	47 24.7%	34 21.6%	20 22.4%	14 21.3%	11 11.7%	38 26.7%I	28 41.0%HI LMN	3 14.8%	6 15.4%	1 9.7%	0 0	56 19.2%	44 30.9%P
preferred source of info	63 14.6%	23 10.6%	40 18.7%A	63 14.6%	0 0	37 19.8%G	20 12.6%	6 6.9%	10 14.7%	7 7.4%	26 18.7%I	13 19.7%I	3 12.3%	4 10.3%	* 3.2%	0 0	33 11.4%	30 21.0%P

Proportions/Means: Columns Tested (5% risk level) - A/B/D - C/D - E/F/G - H/I/J/K/L/M/N - P/Q
* small base; ** very small base (under 30) ineligible for sig testing

Table 72
Page 128

Outsell/Digital Library Federation Study (2002)
Weighted Tables

TABLE 77, continued

R7sum_2. When you are doing research, how do you find information about Print or hardcopy journals ? Do you ...

		RESPONDENT TYPE				INSTITUTION TYPE			DISCIPLINE								GENDER	
	TOTAL SAMPLE	FACULTY MEMBER	GRAD. STUDENT	FACULTY /GRAD	UNDER GRAD. STUDENT	PUBLIC	PRIVATE	LIBERAL ARTS	BIOLOGIAL SCIENCES	PHYSICAL SCIENCES /MATH	SOCIAL SCIENCES	ARTS AND HUMAN.	ENGI-NEERING	BUSINESS	LAW	UNDEC. MAJOR	MALE	FEMALE
		(A)	(B)	(C)	(D)	(E)	(F)	(G)	(H)	(I)	(J)	(K)	(L)	(M)	(N)		(P)	(Q)
Base - Use Print or hardcopy journals for research	434	220	214	434	0**	188	158	88*	66*	94*	141*	68*	23*	36*	5*	0*	292	143
Search engine	67 15.4%	43 19.4%B	24 11.2%	67 15.4%	0 0	22 11.9%	26 16.8%	18 20.3%	17 25.3%J	16 17.0%J	9 6.7%	9 13.1%	5 21.0%J	10 28.2%J	1 9.7%	0 0	53 18.3%Q	13 9.5%
All sources of info	67 15.4%	43 19.4%B	24 11.2%	67 15.4%	0 0	22 11.9%	26 16.8%	18 20.3%	17 25.3%J	16 17.0%J	9 6.7%	9 13.1%	5 21.0%J	10 28.2%J	1 9.7%	0 0	53 18.3%Q	13 9.5%
preferred source of info	30 6.9%	17 7.8%	13 6.0%	30 6.9%	0 0	12 6.3%	11 7.3%	7 7.7%	10 14.7%JK	10 10.6%JK	4 2.7%	1 1.6%	3 11.1%JK	3 7.7%	* 3.2%	0 0	22 7.6%	8 5.7%
Your own institution's web site	65 15.0%	29 13.0%	36 17.0%	65 15.0%	0 0	31 16.7%	27 16.9%	7 7.9%	8 12.0%	7 7.4%	30 21.3%IKN	6 8.2%	5 22.2%IKN	9 25.6%IKN	0 0	0 0	46 15.7%	19 13.4%
All sources of info	65 15.0%	29 13.0%	36 17.0%	65 15.0%	0 0	31 16.7%	27 16.9%	7 7.9%	8 12.0%	7 7.4%	30 21.3%IKN	6 8.2%	5 22.2%IKN	9 25.6%IKN	0 0	0 0	46 15.7%	19 13.4%
preferred source of info	38 8.8%	17 7.7%	21 9.9%	38 8.8%	0 0	18 9.5%	16 10.2%	4 4.7%	3 4.0%	5 5.3%	19 13.3%	4 6.6%	3 11.1%	5 12.8%	0 0	0 0	26 9.0%	12 8.3%
Web directory/ subject related web site	60 13.7%	34 15.3%	26 12.1%	60 13.7%	0 0	19 10.0%	23 14.7%	17 19.8%E	11 16.0%	23 24.5%JKL	9 6.7%	8 11.5%	2 9.9%	6 15.4%	1 16.1%	0 0	38 13.0%	22 15.2%
All sources of info	60 13.7%	34 15.3%	26 12.1%	60 13.7%	0 0	19 10.0%	23 14.7%	17 19.8%E	11 16.0%	23 24.5%JKL	9 6.7%	8 11.5%	2 9.9%	6 15.4%	1 16.1%	0 0	38 13.0%	22 15.2%

Proportions/Means: Columns Tested (5% risk level) - A/B/D - C/D - E/F/G - H/I/J/K/L/M/N - P/Q
* small base; ** very small base (under 30) ineligible for sig testing

Table 72
Page 129

TABLE 77, continued

R7sum_2. When you are doing research, how do you find information about Print or hardcopy journals ? Do you ...

		RESPONDENT TYPE				INSTITUTION TYPE			DISCIPLINE								GENDER	
	TOTAL SAMPLE	FACULTY MEMBER	GRAD. STUDENT	FACULTY /GRAD	UNDER GRAD. STUDENT	PUBLIC	PRIVATE	LIBERAL ARTS	BIOLOGIAL SCIENCES	PHYSICAL SCIENCES /MATH	SOCIAL SCIENCES	ARTS AND HUMAN.	ENGI- NEERING	BUSINESS	LAW	UNDEC. MAJOR	MALE	FEMALE
		(A)	(B)	(C)	(D)	(E)	(F)	(G)	(H)	(I)	(J)	(K)	(L)	(M)	(N)		(P)	(Q)
Base - Use Print or hardcopy journals for research	434	220	214	434	0**	188	158	88*	66*	94*	141*	68*	23*	36*	5*	0*	292	143
preferred source of info	37	17	21	37	0	15	14	8	9	13	9	1	1	4	1	0	22	15
	8.6%	7.6%	9.6%	8.6%	0	8.2%	8.8%	9.2%	13.3%K	13.8%KL	6.7%	1.6%	3.7%	10.3%K	9.7%K	0	7.5%	10.8%
Internet searches	47	23	24	47	0	24	16	8	11	8	13	3	4	7	*	0	32	15
	10.9%	10.6%	11.2%	10.9%	0	12.6%	10.1%	8.7%	17.3%K	8.5%	9.3%	4.9%	16.0%K	20.5%K	3.2%	0	11.0%	10.6%
All sources of info	47	23	24	47	0	24	16	8	11	8	13	3	4	7	*	0	32	15
	10.9%	10.6%	11.2%	10.9%	0	12.6%	10.1%	8.7%	17.3%K	8.5%	9.3%	4.9%	16.0%K	20.5%K	3.2%	0	11.0%	10.6%
preferred source of info	20	5	15	20	0	15	4	2	5	4	6	2	1	2	0	0	11	9
	4.7%	2.3%	7.2%A	4.7%	0	7.7%	2.5%	2.3%	8.0%	4.3%	4.0%	3.3%	6.2%	5.1%	0	0	3.9%	6.5%
Online abstracting and indexing services	33	16	17	33	0	12	12	8	3	11	13	2	1	2	*	0	24	8
	7.5%	7.2%	7.9%	7.5%	0	6.6%	7.9%	8.9%	4.0%	11.7%	9.3%	3.3%	6.2%	5.1%	6.5%	0	8.4%	5.8%
All sources of info	33	16	17	33	0	12	12	8	3	11	13	2	1	2	*	0	24	8
	7.5%	7.2%	7.9%	7.5%	0	6.6%	7.9%	8.9%	4.0%	11.7%	9.3%	3.3%	6.2%	5.1%	6.5%	0	8.4%	5.8%
preferred source of info	18	10	8	18	0	4	9	5	3	7	6	1	1	1	*	0	14	5
	4.2%	4.6%	3.7%	4.2%	0	2.2%	5.8%	5.5%	4.0%	7.4%	4.0%	1.6%	2.5%	2.6%	3.2%	0	4.6%	3.2%
Online reference service	9	6	3	9	0	5	3	1	2	2	2	0	1	2	1	0	8	1
	2.0%	2.9%	1.2%	2.0%	0	2.6%	2.0%	1.1%	2.7%	2.1%	1.3%	0	3.7%K	5.1%	9.7%IJK	0	2.8%	0.4%
All sources of info	9	6	3	9	0	5	3	1	2	2	2	0	1	2	1	0	8	1
	2.0%	2.9%	1.2%	2.0%	0	2.6%	2.0%	1.1%	2.7%	2.1%	1.3%	0	3.7%K	5.1%	9.7%IJK	0	2.8%	0.4%

Proportions/Means: Columns Tested (5% risk level) - A/B/D - C/D - E/F/G - H/I/J/K/L/M/N - P/Q
* small base; ** very small base (under 30) ineligible for sig testing

Table 72
Page 130

Outsell/Digital Library Federation Study (2002)
Weighted Tables

TABLE 77, continued

R7sum_2. When you are doing research, how do you find information about Print or hardcopy journals ? Do you ...

		RESPONDENT TYPE				INSTITUTION TYPE			DISCIPLINE								GENDER	
	TOTAL SAMPLE	FACULTY MEMBER	GRAD. STUDENT	FACULTY /GRAD	UNDER GRAD. STUDENT	PUBLIC	PRIVATE	LIBERAL ARTS	BIOLOGIAL SCIENCES	PHYSICAL SCIENCES /MATH	SOCIAL SCIENCES	ARTS AND HUMAN.	ENGI-NEERING	BUSINESS	LAW	UNDEC. MAJOR	MALE	FEMALE
		(A)	(B)	(C)	(D)	(E)	(F)	(G)	(H)	(I)	(J)	(K)	(L)	(M)	(N)		(P)	(Q)
Base - Use Print or hardcopy journals for research	434	220	214	434	0**	188	158	88*	66*	94*	141*	68*	23*	36*	5*	0*	292	143
preferred source of info	6 1.3%	4 2.0%	1 0.6%	6 1.3%	0 0	4 2.1%	1 0.6%	1 1.1%	1 1.3%	1 1.1%	2 1.3%	0 0	1 2.5%	1 2.6%	1 9.7%HIJK	0 0	5 1.8%	1 0.4%
Department web page	6 1.5%	2 0.8%	5 2.2%	6 1.5%	0 0	3 1.5%	3 1.8%	1 1.0%	2 2.7%	1 1.1%	2 1.3%	0 0	1 3.7%K	1 2.6%	0 0	0 0	6 1.9%	1 0.6%
All sources of info	6 1.5%	2 0.8%	5 2.2%	6 1.5%	0 0	3 1.5%	3 1.8%	1 1.0%	2 2.7%	1 1.1%	2 1.3%	0 0	1 3.7%K	1 2.6%	0 0	0 0	6 1.9%	1 0.6%
preferred source of info	5 1.1%	2 0.8%	3 1.4%	5 1.1%	0 0	2 1.2%	2 1.1%	1 1.0%	2 2.7%	0 0	2 1.3%	0 0	* 1.2%	1 2.6%	0 0	0 0	4 1.4%	1 0.6%
E-mail listservs	4 0.9%	4 1.7%	0 0	4 0.9%	0 0	1 0.5%	2 1.2%	1 1.0%	1 1.3%	2 2.1%	0 0	0 0	0 0	1 2.6%	0 0	0 0	4 1.3%	0 0
All sources of info	4 0.9%	4 1.7%	0 0	4 0.9%	0 0	1 0.5%	2 1.2%	1 1.0%	1 1.3%	2 2.1%	0 0	0 0	0 0	1 2.6%	0 0	0 0	4 1.3%	0 0
preferred source of info	1 0.2%	1 0.5%	0 0	1 0.2%	0 0	1 0.5%	0 0	0 0	0 0	1 1.1%	0 0	0 0	0 0	0 0	0 0	0 0	1 0.3%	0 0
Your own personal electronic library/files	2 0.4%	0 0	2 0.9%	2 0.4%	0 0	0 0	2 1.2%	0 0	0 0	0 0	2 1.3%	0 0	0 0	0 0	0 0	0 0	0 0	2 1.3%
All sources of info	2 0.4%	0 0	2 0.9%	2 0.4%	0 0	0 0	2 1.2%	0 0	0 0	0 0	2 1.3%	0 0	0 0	0 0	0 0	0 0	0 0	2 1.3%

Proportions/Means: Columns Tested (5% risk level) - A/B/D - C/D - E/F/G - H/I/J/K/L/M/N - P/Q
* small base; ** very small base (under 30) ineligible for sig testing

Table 72
Page 131

Outsell/Digital Library Federation Study (2002)
Weighted Tables

TABLE 77, continued

R7sum_2. When you are doing research, how do you find information about Print or hardcopy journals ? Do you ...

	RESPONDENT TYPE				INSTITUTION TYPE			DISCIPLINE								GENDER	
	TOTAL SAMPLE	FACULTY MEMBER	GRAD. STUDENT	FACULTY /GRAD	UNDER GRAD. STUDENT	PUBLIC	PRIVATE	LIBERAL ARTS	BIOLOGIAL SCIENCES	PHYSICAL SCIENCES /MATH	SOCIAL SCIENCES	ARTS AND HUMAN.	ENGI-NEERING	BUSINESS	LAW	UNDEC. MAJOR	MALE	FEMALE
		(A)	(B)	(C)	(D)	(E)	(F)	(G)	(H)	(I)	(J)	(K)	(L)	(M)	(N)		(P)	(Q)
Base - Use Print or hardcopy journals for research	434	220	214	434	0**	188	158	88*	66*	94*	141*	68*	23*	36*	5*	0*	292	143
preferred source of info	0 0	0 0	0 0	0 0	0 0	0 0	0 0	0 0	0 0	0 0	0 0	0 0	0 0	0 0	0 0	0 0	0 0	0 0
Online bookstore	1 0.2%	1 0.4%	0 0	1 0.2%	0 0	0 0	1 0.6%	0 0	1 1.3%	0 0	0 0	0 0	0 0	0 0	0 0	0 0	0 0	1 0.6%
All sources of info	1 0.2%	1 0.4%	0 0	1 0.2%	0 0	0 0	1 0.6%	0 0	1 1.3%	0 0	0 0	0 0	0 0	0 0	0 0	0 0	0 0	1 0.6%
preferred source of info	0 0	0 0	0 0	0 0	0 0	0 0	0 0	0 0	0 0	0 0	0 0	0 0	0 0	0 0	0 0	0 0	0 0	0 0
LIBRARY/PRINT	211 48.7%	138 62.7%B	73 34.2%	211 48.7%	0 0	70 37.2%	76 48.3%	65 73.9%EF	28 42.7%	56 59.6%HJ	55 38.7%	44 63.9%HJ M	12 49.4%	15 41.0%	3 48.4%	0 0	158 54.1%Q	54 37.7%
Campus library	175 40.3%	116 52.8%B	59 27.4%	175 40.3%	0 0	54 28.7%	66 41.9%E	55 62.1%EF	25 37.3%	46 48.9%JM	43 30.7%	40 59.0%HJ LM	9 39.5%	9 25.6%	2 41.9%	0 0	132 45.2%Q	43 30.3%
All sources of info	175 40.3%	116 52.8%B	59 27.4%	175 40.3%	0 0	54 28.7%	66 41.9%E	55 62.1%EF	25 37.3%	46 48.9%JM	43 30.7%	40 59.0%HJ LM	9 39.5%	9 25.6%	2 41.9%	0 0	132 45.2%Q	43 30.3%
preferred source of info	64 14.7%	39 17.8%	24 11.4%	64 14.7%	0 0	19 10.1%	28 17.5%	17 19.4%	10 14.7%	11 11.7%	15 10.7%	20 29.5%HI JM	4 18.5%	3 7.7%	1 12.9%	0 0	49 16.8%	15 10.4%

Proportions/Means: Columns Tested (5% risk level) - A/B/D - C/D - E/F/G - H/I/J/K/L/M/N - P/Q
* small base; ** very small base (under 30) ineligible for sig testing

Table 72
Page 132

Outsell/Digital Library Federation Study (2002)
Weighted Tables

TABLE 77, continued

R7sum_2. When you are doing research, how do you find information about Print or hardcopy journals ? Do you ...

	RESPONDENT TYPE				INSTITUTION TYPE			DISCIPLINE								GENDER	
	TOTAL SAMPLE	FACULTY MEMBER	GRAD. STUDENT	FACULTY /GRAD	UNDER GRAD. STUDENT	PUBLIC	PRIVATE	LIBERAL ARTS	BIOLOGIAL SCIENCES	PHYSICAL SCIENCES /MATH	SOCIAL SCIENCES	ARTS AND HUMAN.	ENGI-NEERING	BUSINESS	LAW	UNDEC. MAJOR	MALE	FEMALE
		(A)	(B)	(C)	(D)	(E)	(F)	(G)	(H)	(I)	(J)	(K)	(L)	(M)	(N)		(P)	(Q)
Base - Use Print or hardcopy journals for research	434	220	214	434	0**	188	158	88*	66*	94*	141*	68*	23*	36*	5*	0*	292	143
References cited in books or journal articles	33 7.7%	25 11.4%B	8 3.9%	33 7.7%	0 0	10 5.5%	10 6.1%	14 15.4%EF	3 4.0%	10 10.6%	8 5.3%	4 6.6%	2 9.9%	7 17.9%HJN	0 0	0 0	27 9.1%	7 4.8%
All sources of info	33 7.7%	25 11.4%B	8 3.9%	33 7.7%	0 0	10 5.5%	10 6.1%	14 15.4%EF	3 4.0%	10 10.6%	8 5.3%	4 6.6%	2 9.9%	7 17.9%HJN	0 0	0 0	27 9.1%	7 4.8%
preferred source of info	6 1.4%	3 1.5%	3 1.3%	6 1.4%	0 0	3 1.7%	1 0.6%	2 2.3%	0 0	4 4.3%J	0 0	1 1.6%	1 3.7%HJ	0 0	0 0	0 0	5 1.7%	1 0.7%
Another library	31 7.2%	24 10.8%B	8 3.5%	31 7.2%	0 0	8 4.2%	13 8.3%	10 11.7%E	3 4.0%	8 8.5%	9 6.7%	7 9.8%	1 6.2%	3 7.7%	* 6.5%	0 0	24 8.2%	7 5.1%
All sources of info	31 7.2%	24 10.8%B	8 3.5%	31 7.2%	0 0	8 4.2%	13 8.3%	10 11.7%E	3 4.0%	8 8.5%	9 6.7%	7 9.8%	1 6.2%	3 7.7%	* 6.5%	0 0	24 8.2%	7 5.1%
preferred source of info	2 0.4%	0 0	2 0.9%	2 0.4%	0 0	2 1.0%	0 0	0 0	0 0	0 0	2 1.3%	0 0	0 0	0 0	0 0	0 0	2 0.6%	0 0
Personal subscriptions to newspapers, magazines and journals	22 5.0%	18 8.0%B	4 1.9%	22 5.0%	0 0	9 4.7%	6 3.9%	7 7.6%	2 2.7%	5 5.3%	9 6.7%	0 0	1 3.7%K	5 12.8%HK	0 0	0 0	21 7.0%Q	1 0.8%
All sources of info	22 5.0%	18 8.0%B	4 1.9%	22 5.0%	0 0	9 4.7%	6 3.9%	7 7.6%	2 2.7%	5 5.3%	9 6.7%	0 0	1 3.7%K	5 12.8%HK	0 0	0 0	21 7.0%Q	1 0.8%

Proportions/Means: Columns Tested (5% risk level) - A/B/D - C/D - E/F/G - H/I/J/K/L/M/N - P/Q
* small base; ** very small base (under 30) ineligible for sig testing

Table 72
Page 133

Outsell/Digital Library Federation Study (2002)
Weighted Tables

TABLE 77, continued

R7sum_2. When you are doing research, how do you find information about Print or hardcopy journals ? Do you ...

	TOTAL SAMPLE	RESPONDENT TYPE: FACULTY MEMBER	RESPONDENT TYPE: GRAD. STUDENT	RESPONDENT TYPE: FACULTY /GRAD	RESPONDENT TYPE: UNDER GRAD. STUDENT	INSTITUTION TYPE: PUBLIC	INSTITUTION TYPE: PRIVATE	INSTITUTION TYPE: LIBERAL ARTS	DISCIPLINE: BIOLOGIAL SCIENCES	DISCIPLINE: PHYSICAL SCIENCES /MATH	DISCIPLINE: SOCIAL SCIENCES	DISCIPLINE: ARTS AND HUMAN.	DISCIPLINE: ENGI-NEERING	DISCIPLINE: BUSINESS	DISCIPLINE: LAW	DISCIPLINE: UNDEC. MAJOR	GENDER: MALE	GENDER: FEMALE
		(A)	(B)	(C)	(D)	(E)	(F)	(G)	(H)	(I)	(J)	(K)	(L)	(M)	(N)		(P)	(Q)
Base - Use Print or hardcopy journals for research	434	220	214	434	0**	188	158	88*	66*	94*	141*	68*	23*	36*	5*	0*	292	143
preferred source of info	9	9	0	9	0	3	4	3	1	2	6	0	0	1	0	0	9	0
	2.2%	4.3%B	0	2.2%	0	1.5%	2.3%	3.3%	1.3%	2.1%	4.0%	0	0	2.6%	0	0	3.2%	0
Your own personal physical library/ files/bookshelves	15	13	2	15	0	4	2	10	3	4	6	2	1	0	0	0	14	1
	3.5%	5.9%B	1.0%	3.5%	0	2.1%	1.0%	10.9%EF	4.0%	4.3%	4.0%	3.3%	2.5%	0	0	0	4.8%	0.8%
All sources of info	15	13	2	15	0	4	2	10	3	4	6	2	1	0	0	0	14	1
	3.5%	5.9%B	1.0%	3.5%	0	2.1%	1.0%	10.9%EF	4.0%	4.3%	4.0%	3.3%	2.5%	0	0	0	4.8%	0.8%
preferred source of info	2	2	0	2	0	0	1	1	0	2	0	0	0	0	0	0	2	0
	0.5%	0.9%	0	0.5%	0	0	0.6%	1.1%	0	2.1%	0	0	0	0	0	0	0.7%	0
Printed abstracting and indexing services	10	6	4	10	0	2	6	2	3	1	4	1	0	1	*	0	6	3
	2.2%	2.5%	1.9%	2.2%	0	1.0%	3.7%	2.1%	4.0%	1.1%	2.7%	1.6%	0	2.6%	3.2%L	0	2.2%	2.2%
All sources of info	10	6	4	10	0	2	6	2	3	1	4	1	0	1	*	0	6	3
	2.2%	2.5%	1.9%	2.2%	0	1.0%	3.7%	2.1%	4.0%	1.1%	2.7%	1.6%	0	2.6%	3.2%L	0	2.2%	2.2%
preferred source of info	0	0	0	0	0	0	0	0	0	0	0	0	0	0	0	0	0	0
	0	0	0	0	0	0	0	0	0	0	0	0	0	0	0	0	0	0
Printed library catalogues and finding aids	6	3	3	6	0	2	1	3	0	0	4	2	0	0	*	0	3	3
	1.4%	1.4%	1.5%	1.4%	0	1.0%	0.8%	3.4%	0	0	2.7%	3.3%	0	0	3.2%HILM	0	1.0%	2.2%

Proportions/Means: Columns Tested (5% risk level) - A/B/D - C/D - E/F/G - H/I/J/K/L/M/N - P/Q
* small base; ** very small base (under 30) ineligible for sig testing

Table 72
Page 134

Outsell/Digital Library Federation Study (2002)
Weighted Tables

TABLE 77, continued

R7sum_2. When you are doing research, how do you find information about Print or hardcopy journals ? Do you ...

	TOTAL SAMPLE	RESPONDENT TYPE: FACULTY MEMBER (A)	GRAD. STUDENT (B)	FACULTY /GRAD (C)	UNDER GRAD. STUDENT (D)	INSTITUTION TYPE: PUBLIC (E)	PRIVATE (F)	LIBERAL ARTS (G)	DISCIPLINE: BIOLOGIAL SCIENCES (H)	PHYSICAL SCIENCES /MATH (I)	SOCIAL SCIENCES (J)	ARTS AND HUMAN. (K)	ENGI-NEERING (L)	BUSINESS (M)	LAW (N)	UNDEC. MAJOR	GENDER: MALE (P)	FEMALE (Q)
Base - Use Print or hardcopy journals for research	434	220	214	434	0**	188	158	88*	66*	94*	141*	68*	23*	36*	5*	0*	292	143
All sources of info	6 1.4%	3 1.4%	3 1.5%	6 1.4%	0 0	2 1.0%	1 0.8%	3 3.4%	0 0	0 0	4 2.7%	2 3.3%	0 0	0 0	* 3.2%HILM	0 0	3 1.0%	3 2.2%
preferred source of info	0 0	0 0	0 0	0 0	0 0	0 0	0 0	0 0	0 0	0 0	0 0	0 0	0 0	0 0	0 0	0 0	0 0	0 0
Physical bookstore	4 1.0%	3 1.5%	1 0.4%	4 1.0%	0 0	3 1.6%	1 0.7%	0 0	1 1.3%	0 0	2 1.3%	0 0	1 2.5%I	1 2.6%	0 0	0 0	4 1.4%	* 0.2%
All sources of info	4 1.0%	3 1.5%	1 0.4%	4 1.0%	0 0	3 1.6%	1 0.7%	0 0	1 1.3%	0 0	2 1.3%	0 0	1 2.5%I	1 2.6%	0 0	0 0	4 1.4%	* 0.2%
preferred source of info	0 0	0 0	0 0	0 0	0 0	0 0	0 0	0 0	0 0	0 0	0 0	0 0	0 0	0 0	0 0	0 0	0 0	0 0
PERSONAL ASSISTANCE	106 24.4%	59 26.9%	47 21.9%	106 24.4%	0 0	40 21.1%	41 25.7%	26 29.2%	10 14.7%	29 30.9%HJ	21 14.7%	21 31.1%HJ	8 33.3%HJ	17 46.2%HJ N	1 16.1%	0 0	81 27.8%Q	25 17.4%
A librarian in your institution	60 13.9%	38 17.3%	22 10.4%	60 13.9%	0 0	21 11.2%	18 11.6%	21 23.7%EF	5 8.0%	14 14.9%	13 9.3%	15 21.3%HJ	3 13.6%	9 25.6%HJ	1 16.1%	0 0	48 16.6%Q	12 8.4%
All sources of info	60 13.9%	38 17.3%	22 10.4%	60 13.9%	0 0	21 11.2%	18 11.6%	21 23.7%EF	5 8.0%	14 14.9%	13 9.3%	15 21.3%HJ	3 13.6%	9 25.6%HJ	1 16.1%	0 0	48 16.6%Q	12 8.4%
preferred source of info	14 3.2%	6 2.8%	8 3.7%	14 3.2%	0 0	6 3.3%	4 2.6%	4 4.3%	1 1.3%	2 2.1%	6 4.0%	1 1.6%	1 2.5%	4 10.3%HIK	* 3.2%	0 0	11 3.8%	3 2.1%

Proportions/Means: Columns Tested (5% risk level) - A/B/D - C/D - E/F/G - H/I/J/K/L/M/N - P/Q
* small base; ** very small base (under 30) ineligible for sig testing

Table 72
Page 135

Outsell/Digital Library Federation Study (2002)
Weighted Tables

TABLE 77, continued

R7sum_2. When you are doing research, how do you find information about Print or hardcopy journals ? Do you ...

	RESPONDENT TYPE				INSTITUTION TYPE			DISCIPLINE								GENDER	
	TOTAL SAMPLE	FACULTY MEMBER	GRAD. STUDENT	FACULTY /GRAD	UNDER GRAD. STUDENT	PUBLIC	PRIVATE	LIBERAL ARTS	BIOLOGIAL SCIENCES	PHYSICAL SCIENCES /MATH	SOCIAL SCIENCES	ARTS AND HUMAN.	ENGI- NEERING	BUSINESS	LAW	UNDEC. MAJOR	MALE	FEMALE
		(A)	(B)	(C)	(D)	(E)	(F)	(G)	(H)	(I)	(J)	(K)	(L)	(M)	(N)		(P)	(Q)
Base - Use Print or hardcopy journals for research	434	220	214	434	0**	188	158	88*	66*	94*	141*	68*	23*	36*	5*	0*	292	143
Colleagues inside your institution	60 13.7%	29 13.0%	31 14.5%	60 13.7%	0 0	26 13.6%	22 14.2%	12 13.2%	4 5.3%	18 19.1%HJ	11 8.0%	10 14.8%	4 18.5%HJ	12 33.3%HJK N	* 6.5%	0 0	41 14.2%	18 12.8%
All sources of info	60 13.7%	29 13.0%	31 14.5%	60 13.7%	0 0	26 13.6%	22 14.2%	12 13.2%	4 5.3%	18 19.1%HJ	11 8.0%	10 14.8%	4 18.5%HJ	12 33.3%HJK N	* 6.5%	0 0	41 14.2%	18 12.8%
preferred source of info	11 2.5%	6 2.7%	5 2.3%	11 2.5%	0 0	3 1.7%	6 3.7%	2 2.2%	0 0	2 2.1%	4 2.7%	2 3.3%	1 4.9%H	2 5.1%	0 0	0 0	6 1.9%	5 3.7%
Colleagues outside your institution	21 4.9%	18 8.2%B	3 1.5%	21 4.9%	0 0	7 3.9%	6 3.9%	8 9.0%	2 2.7%	10 10.6%J	2 1.3%	3 4.9%	1 2.5%	4 10.3%J	0 0	0 0	18 6.3%	3 2.1%
All sources of info	21 4.9%	18 8.2%B	3 1.5%	21 4.9%	0 0	7 3.9%	6 3.9%	8 9.0%	2 2.7%	10 10.6%J	2 1.3%	3 4.9%	1 2.5%	4 10.3%J	0 0	0 0	18 6.3%	3 2.1%
preferred source of info	0 0	0 0	0 0	0 0	0 0	0 0	0 0	0 0	0 0	0 0	0 0	0 0	0 0	0 0	0 0	0 0	0 0	0 0
Another institution's librarian	7 1.6%	7 3.2%B	0 0	7 1.6%	0 0	1 0.6%	4 2.5%	2 2.4%	1 1.3%	1 1.1%	2 1.3%	3 4.9%	0 0	0 0	0 0	0 0	7 2.4%	0 0
All sources of info	7 1.6%	7 3.2%B	0 0	7 1.6%	0 0	1 0.6%	4 2.5%	2 2.4%	1 1.3%	1 1.1%	2 1.3%	3 4.9%	0 0	0 0	0 0	0 0	7 2.4%	0 0

Proportions/Means: Columns Tested (5% risk level) - A/B/D - C/D - E/F/G - H/I/J/K/L/M/N - P/Q
* small base; ** very small base (under 30) ineligible for sig testing

Table 72
Page 136

TABLE 77, continued

R7sum_2. When you are doing research, how do you find information about Print or hardcopy journals ? Do you ...

		RESPONDENT TYPE				INSTITUTION TYPE			DISCIPLINE								GENDER	
	TOTAL SAMPLE	FACULTY MEMBER	GRAD. STUDENT	FACULTY /GRAD	UNDER GRAD. STUDENT	PUBLIC	PRIVATE	LIBERAL ARTS	BIOLOGIAL SCIENCES	PHYSICAL SCIENCES /MATH	SOCIAL SCIENCES	ARTS AND HUMAN.	ENGI- NEERING	BUSINESS	LAW	UNDEC. MAJOR	MALE	FEMALE
		(A)	(B)	(C)	(D)	(E)	(F)	(G)	(H)	(I)	(J)	(K)	(L)	(M)	(N)		(P)	(Q)
Base - Use Print or hardcopy journals for research	434	220	214	434	0**	188	158	88*	66*	94*	141*	68*	23*	36*	5*	0*	292	143
preferred source of info	1 0.3%	1 0.5%	0 0	1 0.3%	0 0	0 0	1 0.7%	0 0	0 0	0 0	0 0	1 1.6%	0 0	0 0	0 0	0 0	1 0.4%	0 0
Professional meetings	3 0.7%	2 0.8%	1 0.6%	3 0.7%	0 0	2 1.2%	1 0.6%	0 0	0 0	1 1.1%	0 0	0 0	1 4.9%HJK	1 2.6%	0 0	0 0	2 0.7%	1 0.7%
All sources of info	3 0.7%	2 0.8%	1 0.6%	3 0.7%	0 0	2 1.2%	1 0.6%	0 0	0 0	1 1.1%	0 0	0 0	1 4.9%HJK	1 2.6%	0 0	0 0	2 0.7%	1 0.7%
preferred source of info	1 0.2%	1 0.3%	* 0.1%	1 0.2%	0 0	* 0.2%	1 0.4%	0 0	0 0	0 0	0 0	0 0	1 3.7%HIJK	0 0	0 0	0 0	1 0.3%	0 0
Online (unspecified)	2 0.5%	2 0.8%	* 0.1%	2 0.5%	0 0	1 0.3%	1 0.9%	0 0	0 0	0 0	0 0	1 1.6%	1 3.7%HIJ	0 0	0 0	0 0	2 0.6%	* 0.2%
All sources of info	2 0.5%	2 0.8%	* 0.1%	2 0.5%	0 0	1 0.3%	1 0.9%	0 0	0 0	0 0	0 0	1 1.6%	1 3.7%HIJ	0 0	0 0	0 0	2 0.6%	* 0.2%
preferred source of info	2 0.4%	2 0.8%	0 0	2 0.4%	0 0	* 0.2%	1 0.9%	0 0	0 0	0 0	0 0	1 1.6%	1 2.5%IJ	0 0	0 0	0 0	2 0.6%	0 0
E-Journals	1 0.3%	* 0.1%	1 0.5%	1 0.3%	0 0	1 0.7%	0 0	0 0	0 0	0 0	0 0	1 1.6%	* 1.2%	0 0	0 0	0 0	1 0.5%	0 0
All sources of info	1 0.3%	* 0.1%	1 0.5%	1 0.3%	0 0	1 0.7%	0 0	0 0	0 0	0 0	0 0	1 1.6%	* 1.2%	0 0	0 0	0 0	1 0.5%	0 0

Proportions/Means: Columns Tested (5% risk level) - A/B/D - C/D - E/F/G - H/I/J/K/L/M/N - P/Q
* small base; ** very small base (under 30) ineligible for sig testing

Table 72
Page 137

Outsell/Digital Library Federation Study (2002)
Weighted Tables

TABLE 77, continued

R7sum_2. When you are doing research, how do you find information about Print or hardcopy journals ? Do you ...

	TOTAL SAMPLE	RESPONDENT TYPE: FACULTY MEMBER	GRAD. STUDENT	FACULTY /GRAD	UNDER GRAD. STUDENT	INSTITUTION TYPE: PUBLIC	PRIVATE	LIBERAL ARTS	DISCIPLINE: BIOLOGIAL SCIENCES	PHYSICAL SCIENCES /MATH	SOCIAL SCIENCES	ARTS AND HUMAN.	ENGI-NEERING	BUSINESS	LAW	UNDEC. MAJOR	GENDER: MALE	FEMALE
		(A)	(B)	(C)	(D)	(E)	(F)	(G)	(H)	(I)	(J)	(K)	(L)	(M)	(N)		(P)	(Q)
Base - Use Print or hardcopy journals for research	434	220	214	434	0**	188	158	88*	66*	94*	141*	68*	23*	36*	5*	0*	292	143
preferred source of info	* 0.1%	* 0.1%	0 0	* 0.1%	0 0	* 0.2%	0 0	0 0	0 0	0 0	0 0	0 0	* 1.2%	0 0	0 0	0 0	* 0.1%	0 0
Author	* 0.1%	0 0	* 0.1%	* 0.1%	0 0	0 0	* 0.2%	0 0	0 0	0 0	0 0	0 0	* 1.2%	0 0	0 0	0 0	* 0.1%	0 0
All sources of info	* 0.1%	0 0	* 0.1%	* 0.1%	0 0	0 0	* 0.2%	0 0	0 0	0 0	0 0	0 0	* 1.2%	0 0	0 0	0 0	* 0.1%	0 0
preferred source of info	0 0	0 0	0 0	0 0	0 0	0 0	0 0	0 0	0 0	0 0	0 0	0 0	0 0	0 0	0 0	0 0	0 0	0 0
Personal office/lab	0 0	0 0	0 0	0 0	0 0	0 0	0 0	0 0	0 0	0 0	0 0	0 0	0 0	0 0	0 0	0 0	0 0	0 0
All sources of info	0 0	0 0	0 0	0 0	0 0	0 0	0 0	0 0	0 0	0 0	0 0	0 0	0 0	0 0	0 0	0 0	0 0	0 0
preferred source of info	0 0	0 0	0 0	0 0	0 0	0 0	0 0	0 0	0 0	0 0	0 0	0 0	0 0	0 0	0 0	0 0	0 0	0 0
Other	31 7.2%	19 8.7%	12 5.7%	31 7.2%	0 0	12 6.1%	16 10.0%	4 4.6%	4 5.3%	9 9.6%	8 5.3%	8 11.5%	1 6.2%	2 5.1%	* 3.2%	0 0	24 8.1%	8 5.4%
All sources of info	31 7.2%	19 8.7%	12 5.5%	31 7.2%	0 0	11 6.0%	16 10.0%	4 4.6%	4 5.3%	9 9.6%	8 5.3%	8 11.5%	1 4.9%	2 5.1%	* 3.2%	0 0	24 8.1%	7 5.2%

Proportions/Means: Columns Tested (5% risk level) - A/B/D - C/D - E/F/G - H/I/J/K/L/M/N - P/Q
* small base; ** very small base (under 30) ineligible for sig testing

Table 72
Page 138

Outsell/Digital Library Federation Study (2002)
Weighted Tables

TABLE 77, continued

R7sum_2. When you are doing research, how do you find information about Print or hardcopy journals ? Do you ...

		RESPONDENT TYPE				INSTITUTION TYPE			DISCIPLINE								GENDER	
	TOTAL SAMPLE	FACULTY MEMBER	GRAD. STUDENT	FACULTY /GRAD	UNDER GRAD. STUDENT	PUBLIC	PRIVATE	LIBERAL ARTS	BIOLOGIAL SCIENCES	PHYSICAL SCIENCES /MATH	SOCIAL SCIENCES	ARTS AND HUMAN.	ENGI-NEERING	BUSINESS	LAW	UNDEC. MAJOR	MALE	FEMALE
		(A)	(B)	(C)	(D)	(E)	(F)	(G)	(H)	(I)	(J)	(K)	(L)	(M)	(N)		(P)	(Q)
Base - Use Print or hardcopy journals for research	434	220	214	434	0**	188	158	88*	66*	94*	141*	68*	23*	36*	5*	0*	292	143
preferred source of info	7 1.6%	2 1.0%	5 2.3%	7 1.6%	0 0	4 2.2%	3 1.9%	0 0	1 1.3%	2 2.1%	2 1.3%	1 1.6%	* 1.2%	1 2.6%	0 0	0 0	5 1.7%	2 1.5%
DK/Refused	14 3.1%	8 3.8%	5 2.4%	14 3.1%	0 0	5 2.9%	2 1.5%	6 6.7%F	1 1.3%	4 4.3%	4 2.7%	2 3.3%	1 3.7%	2 5.1%	0 0	0 0	11 3.9%	2 1.6%

Proportions/Means: Columns Tested (5% risk level) - A/B/D - C/D - E/F/G - H/I/J/K/L/M/N - P/Q
* small base; ** very small base (under 30) ineligible for sig testing

Table 72
Page 139

TABLE 78

R7D/E_2. Print or hardcopy journals SUMMARY TABLE

	TOTAL SAMPLE	RESPONDENT TYPE FACULTY MEMBER	GRAD. STUDENT	FACULTY /GRAD	UNDER GRAD. STUDENT	INSTITUTION TYPE PUBLIC	PRIVATE	LIBERAL ARTS	DISCIPLINE BIOLOGIAL SCIENCES	PHYSICAL SCIENCES /MATH	SOCIAL SCIENCES	ARTS AND HUMAN.	ENGI-NEERING	BUSINESS	LAW	UNDEC. MAJOR	GENDER MALE	FEMALE
		(A)	(B)	(C)	(D)	(E)	(F)	(G)	(H)	(I)	(J)	(K)	(L)	(M)	(N)		(P)	(Q)
Base - Use Print or hardcopy journals for research	434	220	214	434	0**	188	158	88*	66*	94*	141*	68*	23*	36*	5*	0*	292	143
Borrow from or use in campus library (NET)	378 87.1%	198 89.7%	181 84.4%	378 87.1%	0 0	158 83.9%	143 90.4%	77 87.8%	52 78.7%	80 85.1%	126 89.3%	65 95.1%HL	20 85.2%	31 84.6%	5 87.1%	0 0	252 86.3%	126 88.6%
All sources of info	378 87.1%	198 89.7%	181 84.4%	378 87.1%	0 0	158 83.9%	143 90.4%	77 87.8%	52 78.7%	80 85.1%	126 89.3%	65 95.1%HL	20 85.2%	31 84.6%	5 87.1%	0 0	252 86.3%	126 88.6%
preferred source of info	267 61.5%	125 56.9%	142 66.3%	267 61.5%	0 0	126 66.7%G	96 60.5%	46 52.2%	33 49.3%	57 60.6%	86 61.3%	57 83.6%HI JLMN	14 59.3%	17 46.2%	3 64.5%	0 0	170 58.2%	97 68.3%
Access online (NET)	155 35.6%	83 37.5%	72 33.7%	155 35.6%	0 0	56 29.6%	68 42.8%E	31 35.7%	34 52.0%IJK	33 35.1%K	47 33.3%	12 18.0%	9 37.0%K	17 46.2%K	3 51.6%K	0 0	110 37.6%	45 31.7%
All sources of info	155 35.6%	83 37.5%	72 33.7%	155 35.6%	0 0	56 29.6%	68 42.8%E	31 35.7%	34 52.0%IJK	33 35.1%K	47 33.3%	12 18.0%	9 37.0%K	17 46.2%K	3 51.6%K	0 0	110 37.6%	45 31.7%
preferred source of info	118 27.1%	59 26.8%	59 27.4%	118 27.1%	0 0	48 25.2%	46 29.4%	24 26.8%	26 40.0%IK	22 23.4%K	41 29.3%K	4 6.6%	8 33.3%K	14 38.5%K	2 29.0%K	0 0	83 28.5%	34 24.2%
Interlibrary loan (NET)	65 14.8%	53 24.1%B	11 5.3%	65 14.8%	0 0	12 6.4%	25 15.6%E	28 31.7%EF	12 18.7%J	17 18.1%J	11 8.0%	15 21.3%J	2 9.9%	7 17.9%	1 9.7%	0 0	48 16.6%	16 11.3%
All sources of info	65 14.8%	53 24.1%B	11 5.3%	65 14.8%	0 0	12 6.4%	25 15.6%E	28 31.7%EF	12 18.7%J	17 18.1%J	11 8.0%	15 21.3%J	2 9.9%	7 17.9%	1 9.7%	0 0	48 16.6%	16 11.3%

Proportions/Means: Columns Tested (5% risk level) - A/B/D - C/D - E/F/G - H/I/J/K/L/M/N - P/Q
* small base; ** very small base (under 30) ineligible for sig testing

Table 75
Page 146

Outsell/Digital Library Federation Study (2002)
Weighted Tables

TABLE 78, continued

R7D/E_2. Print or hardcopy journals SUMMARY TABLE

		RESPONDENT TYPE				INSTITUTION TYPE			DISCIPLINE									GENDER	
	TOTAL SAMPLE	FACULTY MEMBER	GRAD. STUDENT	FACULTY /GRAD	UNDER GRAD. STUDENT	PUBLIC	PRIVATE	LIBERAL ARTS	BIOLOGIAL SCIENCES	PHYSICAL SCIENCES /MATH	SOCIAL SCIENCES	ARTS AND HUMAN.	ENGI- NEERING	BUSINESS	LAW	UNDEC. MAJOR	MALE	FEMALE
		(A)	(B)	(C)	(D)	(E)	(F)	(G)	(H)	(I)	(J)	(K)	(L)	(M)	(N)		(P)	(Q)
Base - Use Print or hardcopy journals for research	434	220	214	434	0**	188	158	88*	66*	94*	141*	68*	23*	36*	5*	0*	292	143
preferred source of info	9 2.0%	5 2.2%	4 1.9%	9 2.0%	0 0	3 1.5%	2 1.4%	4 4.4%	2 2.7%	3 3.2%	0 0	2 3.3%	0 0	2 5.1%J	0 0	0 0	4 1.3%	5 3.5%
Borrow from or use in other libraries (NET)	53 12.2%	31 14.3%	22 10.1%	53 12.2%	0 0	10 5.5%	28 17.7%E	15 16.9%E	7 10.7%	14 14.9%L	15 10.7%	12 18.0%L	1 3.7%	4 10.3%	* 3.2%	0 0	32 11.1%	21 14.5%
All sources of info	53 12.2%	31 14.3%	22 10.1%	53 12.2%	0 0	10 5.5%	28 17.7%E	15 16.9%E	7 10.7%	14 14.9%L	15 10.7%	12 18.0%L	1 3.7%	4 10.3%	* 3.2%	0 0	32 11.1%	21 14.5%
preferred source of info	10 2.3%	4 1.9%	6 2.7%	10 2.3%	0 0	4 2.0%	5 3.2%	1 1.3%	0 0	4 4.3%	4 2.7%	2 3.3%	0 0	0 0	0 0	0 0	6 2.1%	4 2.7%
Personal holdings (NET)	20 4.6%	19 8.6%B	1 0.6%	20 4.6%	0 0	8 4.3%	4 2.7%	8 9.0%F	3 4.0%	6 6.4%	6 4.0%	2 3.3%	1 3.7%	3 7.7%	0 0	0 0	18 6.3%Q	2 1.3%
All sources of info	20 4.6%	19 8.6%B	1 0.6%	20 4.6%	0 0	8 4.3%	4 2.7%	8 9.0%F	3 4.0%	6 6.4%	6 4.0%	2 3.3%	1 3.7%	3 7.7%	0 0	0 0	18 6.3%Q	2 1.3%
preferred source of info	13 3.0%	13 5.7%B	* 0.1%	13 3.0%	0 0	5 2.6%	4 2.7%	4 4.3%	2 2.7%	1 1.1%	6 4.0%	1 1.6%	1 2.5%	3 7.7%I	0 0	0 0	13 4.4%Q	0 0
Colleague (NET)	5 1.1%	4 1.8%	1 0.3%	5 1.1%	0 0	0 0	1 0.4%	4 4.6%EF	0 0	2 2.1%	0 0	1 1.6%	1 2.5%J	1 2.6%	0 0	0 0	4 1.2%	1 0.7%
All sources of info	5 1.1%	4 1.8%	1 0.3%	5 1.1%	0 0	0 0	1 0.4%	4 4.6%EF	0 0	2 2.1%	0 0	1 1.6%	1 2.5%J	1 2.6%	0 0	0 0	4 1.2%	1 0.7%

Proportions/Means: Columns Tested (5% risk level) - A/B/D - C/D - E/F/G - H/I/J/K/L/M/N - P/Q
* small base; ** very small base (under 30) ineligible for sig testing

Table 75
Page 147

Outsell/Digital Library Federation Study (2002)
Weighted Tables

TABLE 78, continued

R7D/E_2. Print or hardcopy journals SUMMARY TABLE

		RESPONDENT TYPE				INSTITUTION TYPE			DISCIPLINE									GENDER	
	TOTAL SAMPLE	FACULTY MEMBER	GRAD. STUDENT	FACULTY /GRAD	UNDER GRAD. STUDENT	PUBLIC	PRIVATE	LIBERAL ARTS	BIOLOGIAL SCIENCES	PHYSICAL SCIENCES /MATH	SOCIAL SCIENCES	ARTS AND HUMAN.	ENGI-NEERING	BUSINESS	LAW	UNDEC. MAJOR	MALE	FEMALE
		(A)	(B)	(C)	(D)	(E)	(F)	(G)	(H)	(I)	(J)	(K)	(L)	(M)	(N)		(P)	(Q)
Base - Use Print or hardcopy journals for research	434	220	214	434	0**	188	158	88*	66*	94*	141*	68*	23*	36*	5*	0*	292	143
preferred source of info	1 0.2%	1 0.5%	0 0	1 0.2%	0 0	0 0	0 0	1 1.1%	0 0	1 1.1%	0 0	0 0	0 0	0 0	0 0	0 0	1 0.3%	0 0
Sources (NET)	5 1.1%	5 2.1%	0 0	5 1.1%	0 0	3 1.7%	* 0.2%	1 1.1%	0 0	4 4.3%J	0 0	0 0	1 2.5%J	0 0	0 0	0 0	5 1.6%	0 0
All sources of info	5 1.1%	5 2.1%	0 0	5 1.1%	0 0	3 1.7%	* 0.2%	1 1.1%	0 0	4 4.3%J	0 0	0 0	1 2.5%J	0 0	0 0	0 0	5 1.6%	0 0
preferred source of info	1 0.2%	1 0.5%	0 0	1 0.2%	0 0	1 0.5%	0 0	0 0	0 0	1 1.1%	0 0	0 0	0 0	0 0	0 0	0 0	1 0.3%	0 0
Order from on demand document delivery service (NET)	4 0.9%	4 1.8%	0 0	4 0.9%	0 0	0 0	0 0	4 4.4%EF	0 0	2 2.1%	2 1.3%	0 0	0 0	0 0	0 0	0 0	4 1.3%	0 0
All sources of info	4 0.9%	4 1.8%	0 0	4 0.9%	0 0	0 0	0 0	4 4.4%EF	0 0	2 2.1%	2 1.3%	0 0	0 0	0 0	0 0	0 0	4 1.3%	0 0
preferred source of info	3 0.7%	3 1.3%	0 0	3 0.7%	0 0	0 0	0 0	3 3.3%EF	0 0	1 1.1%	2 1.3%	0 0	0 0	0 0	0 0	0 0	3 1.0%	0 0
Purchase from online bookstore (NET)	3 0.8%	3 1.5%	0 0	3 0.8%	0 0	* 0.1%	0 0	3 3.7%EF	0 0	1 1.1%	0 0	2 3.3%	0 0	0 0	* 3.2%HJLM	0 0	3 1.2%	0 0
All sources of info	3 0.8%	3 1.5%	0 0	3 0.8%	0 0	* 0.1%	0 0	3 3.7%EF	0 0	1 1.1%	0 0	2 3.3%	0 0	0 0	* 3.2%HJLM	0 0	3 1.2%	0 0

Proportions/Means: Columns Tested (5% risk level) - A/B/D - C/D - E/F/G - H/I/J/K/L/M/N - P/Q
* small base; ** very small base (under 30) ineligible for sig testing

Table 75
Page 148

Outsell/Digital Library Federation Study (2002)
Weighted Tables

TABLE 78, continued

R7D/E_2. Print or hardcopy journals SUMMARY TABLE

	TOTAL SAMPLE	RESPONDENT TYPE: FACULTY MEMBER (A)	GRAD. STUDENT (B)	FACULTY /GRAD (C)	UNDER GRAD. STUDENT (D)	INSTITUTION TYPE: PUBLIC (E)	PRIVATE (F)	LIBERAL ARTS (G)	DISCIPLINE: BIOLOGIAL SCIENCES (H)	PHYSICAL SCIENCES /MATH (I)	SOCIAL SCIENCES (J)	ARTS AND HUMAN. (K)	ENGI-NEERING (L)	BUSINESS (M)	LAW (N)	UNDEC. MAJOR	GENDER: MALE (P)	FEMALE (Q)
Base - Use Print or hardcopy journals for research	434	220	214	434	0**	188	158	88*	66*	94*	141*	68*	23*	36*	5*	0*	292	143
preferred source of info	2 0.5%	2 1.0%	0 0	2 0.5%	0 0	0 0	0 0	2 2.4%	0 0	1 1.1%	0 0	1 1.6%	0 0	0 0	0 0	0 0	2 0.7%	0 0
Faculty (NET)	2 0.6%	0 0	2 1.1%	2 0.6%	0 0	2 1.2%	* 0.2%	0 0	0 0	0 0	2 1.3%	0 0	1 2.5%I	0 0	0 0	0 0	2 0.8%	0 0
All sources of info	2 0.6%	0 0	2 1.1%	2 0.6%	0 0	2 1.2%	* 0.2%	0 0	0 0	0 0	2 1.3%	0 0	1 2.5%I	0 0	0 0	0 0	2 0.8%	0 0
preferred source of info	* 0.1%	0 0	* 0.1%	* 0.1%	0 0	0 0	* 0.2%	0 0	0 0	0 0	0 0	0 0	* 1.2%	0 0	0 0	0 0	* 0.1%	0 0
Office (NET)	2 0.5%	1 0.5%	1 0.5%	2 0.5%	0 0	1 0.6%	1 0.6%	0 0	0 0	1 1.1%	0 0	1 1.6%	0 0	0 0	0 0	0 0	1 0.3%	1 0.8%
All sources of info	2 0.5%	1 0.5%	1 0.5%	2 0.5%	0 0	1 0.6%	1 0.6%	0 0	0 0	1 1.1%	0 0	1 1.6%	0 0	0 0	0 0	0 0	1 0.3%	1 0.8%
preferred source of info	1 0.2%	1 0.5%	0 0	1 0.2%	0 0	0 0	1 0.6%	0 0	0 0	1 1.1%	0 0	0 0	0 0	0 0	0 0	0 0	1 0.3%	0 0
Ask library to purchase source (NET)	2 0.5%	1 0.4%	1 0.5%	2 0.5%	0 0	1 0.5%	1 0.8%	0 0	1 1.3%	0 0	0 0	0 0	* 1.2%	1 2.6%	0 0	0 0	2 0.7%	0 0
All sources of info	2 0.5%	1 0.4%	1 0.5%	2 0.5%	0 0	1 0.5%	1 0.8%	0 0	1 1.3%	0 0	0 0	0 0	* 1.2%	1 2.6%	0 0	0 0	2 0.7%	0 0

Proportions/Means: Columns Tested (5% risk level) - A/B/D - C/D - E/F/G - H/I/J/K/L/M/N - P/Q
* small base; ** very small base (under 30) ineligible for sig testing

Table 75
Page 149

Outsell/Digital Library Federation Study (2002)
Weighted Tables

TABLE 78, continued

R7D/E_2. Print or hardcopy journals SUMMARY TABLE

	RESPONDENT TYPE					INSTITUTION TYPE			DISCIPLINE									GENDER	
	TOTAL SAMPLE	FACULTY MEMBER	GRAD. STUDENT	FACULTY /GRAD	UNDER GRAD. STUDENT	PUBLIC	PRIVATE	LIBERAL ARTS	BIOLOGIAL SCIENCES	PHYSICAL SCIENCES /MATH	SOCIAL SCIENCES	ARTS AND HUMAN.	ENGI- NEERING	BUSINESS	LAW	UNDEC. MAJOR	MALE	FEMALE
		(A)	(B)	(C)	(D)	(E)	(F)	(G)	(H)	(I)	(J)	(K)	(L)	(M)	(N)		(P)	(Q)
Base - Use Print or hardcopy journals for research	434	220	214	434	0**	188	158	88*	66*	94*	141*	68*	23*	36*	5*	0*	292	143
preferred source of info	0 0	0 0	0 0	0 0	0 0	0 0	0 0	0 0	0 0	0 0	0 0	0 0	0 0	0 0	0 0	0 0	0 0	0 0
Purchase from physical book store (NET)	2 0.4%	1 0.6%	* 0.1%	2 0.4%	0 0	* 0.1%	* 0.2%	1 1.3%	0 0	0 0	0 0	1 1.6%	* 1.2%	0 0	* 3.2%HIJM	0 0	2 0.5%	0 0
All sources of info	2 0.4%	1 0.6%	* 0.1%	2 0.4%	0 0	* 0.1%	* 0.2%	1 1.3%	0 0	0 0	0 0	1 1.6%	* 1.2%	0 0	* 3.2%HIJM	0 0	2 0.5%	0 0
preferred source of info	0 0	0 0	0 0	0 0	0 0	0 0	0 0	0 0	0 0	0 0	0 0	0 0	0 0	0 0	0 0	0 0	0 0	0 0
Printed material (NET)	1 0.1%	0 0	1 0.3%	1 0.1%	0 0	* 0.2%	* 0.2%	0 0	0 0	0 0	0 0	0 0	1 2.5%IJ	0 0	0 0	0 0	1 0.2%	0 0
All sources of info	1 0.1%	0 0	1 0.3%	1 0.1%	0 0	* 0.2%	* 0.2%	0 0	0 0	0 0	0 0	0 0	1 2.5%IJ	0 0	0 0	0 0	1 0.2%	0 0
preferred source of info	* 0.1%	0 0	* 0.1%	* 0.1%	0 0	* 0.2%	0 0	0 0	0 0	0 0	0 0	0 0	* 1.2%	0 0	0 0	0 0	* 0.1%	0 0
Meetings/conferences (NET)	* 0.1%	* 0.1%	0 0	* 0.1%	0 0	0 0	* 0.2%	0 0	0 0	0 0	0 0	0 0	* 1.2%	0 0	0 0	0 0	* 0.1%	0 0
All sources of info	* 0.1%	* 0.1%	0 0	* 0.1%	0 0	0 0	* 0.2%	0 0	0 0	0 0	0 0	0 0	* 1.2%	0 0	0 0	0 0	* 0.1%	0 0

Proportions/Means: Columns Tested (5% risk level) - A/B/D - C/D - E/F/G - H/I/J/K/L/M/N - P/Q
* small base; ** very small base (under 30) ineligible for sig testing

Table 75
Page 150

Outsell/Digital Library Federation Study (2002)
Weighted Tables

TABLE 78, continued

R7D/E_2. Print or hardcopy journals SUMMARY TABLE

		RESPONDENT TYPE				INSTITUTION TYPE			DISCIPLINE								GENDER	
	TOTAL SAMPLE	FACULTY MEMBER	GRAD. STUDENT	FACULTY /GRAD	UNDER GRAD. STUDENT	PUBLIC	PRIVATE	LIBERAL ARTS	BIOLOGIAL SCIENCES	PHYSICAL SCIENCES /MATH	SOCIAL SCIENCES	ARTS AND HUMAN.	ENGI-NEERING	BUSINESS	LAW	UNDEC. MAJOR	MALE	FEMALE
		(A)	(B)	(C)	(D)	(E)	(F)	(G)	(H)	(I)	(J)	(K)	(L)	(M)	(N)		(P)	(Q)
Base - Use Print or hardcopy journals for research	434	220	214	434	0**	188	158	88*	66*	94*	141*	68*	23*	36*	5*	0*	292	143
preferred source of info	* 0.1%	* 0.1%	0 0	* 0.1%	0 0	0 0	* 0.2%	0 0	0 0	0 0	0 0	0 0	* 1.2%	0 0	0 0	0 0	* 0.1%	0 0
Access from course website (NET)	0 0	0 0	0 0	0 0	0 0	0 0	0 0	0 0	0 0	0 0	0 0	0 0	0 0	0 0	0 0	0 0	0 0	0 0
All sources of info	0 0	0 0	0 0	0 0	0 0	0 0	0 0	0 0	0 0	0 0	0 0	0 0	0 0	0 0	0 0	0 0	0 0	0 0
preferred source of info	0 0	0 0	0 0	0 0	0 0	0 0	0 0	0 0	0 0	0 0	0 0	0 0	0 0	0 0	0 0	0 0	0 0	0 0
Access book/journal/ journal article elsewhere online (NET)	0 0	0 0	0 0	0 0	0 0	0 0	0 0	0 0	0 0	0 0	0 0	0 0	0 0	0 0	0 0	0 0	0 0	0 0
All sources of info	0 0	0 0	0 0	0 0	0 0	0 0	0 0	0 0	0 0	0 0	0 0	0 0	0 0	0 0	0 0	0 0	0 0	0 0
preferred source of info	0 0	0 0	0 0	0 0	0 0	0 0	0 0	0 0	0 0	0 0	0 0	0 0	0 0	0 0	0 0	0 0	0 0	0 0
E-journals (NET)	0 0	0 0	0 0	0 0	0 0	0 0	0 0	0 0	0 0	0 0	0 0	0 0	0 0	0 0	0 0	0 0	0 0	0 0
All sources of info	0 0	0 0	0 0	0 0	0 0	0 0	0 0	0 0	0 0	0 0	0 0	0 0	0 0	0 0	0 0	0 0	0 0	0 0

Proportions/Means: Columns Tested (5% risk level) - A/B/D - C/D - E/F/G - H/I/J/K/L/M/N - P/Q
* small base; ** very small base (under 30) ineligible for sig testing

Table 75
Page 151

Outsell/Digital Library Federation Study (2002)
Weighted Tables

TABLE 78, continued

R7D/E_2. Print or hardcopy journals SUMMARY TABLE

		RESPONDENT TYPE				INSTITUTION TYPE			DISCIPLINE								GENDER	
	TOTAL SAMPLE	FACULTY MEMBER	GRAD. STUDENT	FACULTY /GRAD	UNDER GRAD. STUDENT	PUBLIC	PRIVATE	LIBERAL ARTS	BIOLOGIAL SCIENCES	PHYSICAL SCIENCES /MATH	SOCIAL SCIENCES	ARTS AND HUMAN.	ENGI-NEERING	BUSINESS	LAW	UNDEC. MAJOR	MALE	FEMALE
		(A)	(B)	(C)	(D)	(E)	(F)	(G)	(H)	(I)	(J)	(K)	(L)	(M)	(N)		(P)	(Q)
Base - Use Print or hardcopy journals for research	434	220	214	434	0**	188	158	88*	66*	94*	141*	68*	23*	36*	5*	0*	292	143
preferred source of info	0	0	0	0	0	0	0	0	0	0	0	0	0	0	0	0	0	0
	0	0	0	0	0	0	0	0	0	0	0	0	0	0	0	0	0	0
Other (NET)	17	11	6	17	0	9	5	3	4	1	8	2	1	1	*	0	14	4
	4.0%	5.2%	2.8%	4.0%	0	4.8%	3.4%	3.5%	6.7%I	1.1%	5.3%	3.3%	4.9%	2.6%	3.2%	0	4.7%	2.6%
All sources of info	15	9	6	15	0	9	5	1	4	0	8	2	1	0	0	0	13	3
	3.5%	4.2%	2.8%	3.5%	0	4.7%	3.4%	1.3%	6.7%I	0	5.3%	3.3%	4.9%I	0	0	0	4.3%	1.9%
preferred source of info	6	3	3	6	0	2	2	2	4	1	0	0	*	1	*	0	4	2
	1.4%	1.4%	1.4%	1.4%	0	1.2%	1.1%	2.2%	5.3%J	1.1%	0	0	1.2%	2.6%	3.2%JK	0	1.4%	1.3%
DK/Refused	3	3	0	3	0	*	1	2	0	1	2	0	0	0	*	0	3	0
	0.7%	1.4%	0	0.7%	0	0.1%	0.6%	2.1%	0	1.1%	1.3%	0	0	0	3.2%HKLM	0	1.0%	0

Proportions/Means: Columns Tested (5% risk level) - A/B/D - C/D - E/F/G - H/I/J/K/L/M/N - P/Q
* small base; ** very small base (under 30) ineligible for sig testing

Table 75
Page 152

Outsell/Digital Library Federation Study (2002)
Weighted Tables

TABLE 79

T7sum_2. Print or hardcopy journals SUMMARY TABLE

		RESPONDENT TYPE				INSTITUTION TYPE			DISCIPLINE								GENDER	
	TOTAL SAMPLE	FACULTY MEMBER	GRAD. STUDENT	FACULTY /GRAD	UNDER GRAD. STUDENT	PUBLIC	PRIVATE	LIBERAL ARTS	BIOLOGIAL SCIENCES	PHYSICAL SCIENCES /MATH	SOCIAL SCIENCES	ARTS AND HUMAN.	ENGI-NEERING	BUSINESS	LAW	UNDEC. MAJOR	MALE	FEMALE
		(A)	(B)	(C)	(D)	(E)	(F)	(G)	(H)	(I)	(J)	(K)	(L)	(M)	(N)		(P)	(Q)
Base - USe Print or hardcopy journals for teaching	425	321	105*	425	0**	148	162	115	65*	85*	133*	81*	12*	47*	3**	0*	288	137*
ONLINE	317 74.6%	245 76.5%	72 68.7%	317 74.6%	0 0	99 67.0%	119 73.3%	99 86.1%EF	55 83.8%	63 74.1%	94 70.4%	60 75.0%	9 75.6%	34 74.0%	2 62.5%	0 0	214 74.1%	104 75.6%
Online databases	83 19.5%	59 18.4%	24 22.6%	83 19.5%	0 0	26 17.4%	35 21.7%	22 19.0%	17 25.7%LM	12 14.1%	32 23.9%L	17 20.8%L	* 2.4%	5 10.0%	* 12.5%	0 0	44 15.4%	38 28.0%P
All sources of info	83 19.5%	59 18.4%	24 22.6%	83 19.5%	0 0	26 17.4%	35 21.7%	22 19.0%	17 25.7%LM	12 14.1%	32 23.9%L	17 20.8%L	* 2.4%	5 10.0%	* 12.5%	0 0	44 15.4%	38 28.0%P
preferred source of info	50 11.7%	35 11.0%	14 13.8%	50 11.7%	0 0	16 11.0%	22 13.4%	12 10.1%	10 14.9%	8 9.4%	21 15.5%	8 9.7%	* 2.4%	3 6.0%	* 12.5%	0 0	22 7.6%	28 20.3%P
Search engine	62 14.6%	57 17.9%B	5 4.4%	62 14.6%	0 0	20 13.2%	15 9.2%	28 23.8%EF	11 16.2%J	18 21.2%J	8 5.6%	12 15.3%J	3 22.0%J	10 22.0%J	1 25.0%	0 0	47 16.3%	15 10.9%
All sources of info	62 14.6%	57 17.9%B	5 4.4%	62 14.6%	0 0	20 13.2%	15 9.2%	28 23.8%EF	11 16.2%J	18 21.2%J	8 5.6%	12 15.3%J	3 22.0%J	10 22.0%J	1 25.0%	0 0	47 16.3%	15 10.9%
preferred source of info	25 5.9%	24 7.6%B	1 1.0%	25 5.9%	0 0	7 4.8%	7 4.1%	12 10.0%	7 10.8%J	7 8.2%J	2 1.4%	4 5.6%	1 9.8%J	4 8.0%J	0 0	0 0	20 7.1%	5 3.6%
Web directory/ subject related web site	62 14.5%	55 17.1%B	7 6.5%	62 14.5%	0 0	10 7.1%	23 14.1%	28 24.6%EF	11 17.6%	16 18.8%	13 9.9%	12 15.3%	1 9.8%	7 16.0%	* 6.3%	0 0	46 16.1%	15 11.1%
All sources of info	62 14.5%	55 17.1%B	7 6.5%	62 14.5%	0 0	10 7.1%	23 14.1%	28 24.6%EF	11 17.6%	16 18.8%	13 9.9%	12 15.3%	1 9.8%	7 16.0%	* 6.3%	0 0	46 16.1%	15 11.1%

Proportions/Means: Columns Tested (5% risk level) - A/B/D - C/D - E/F/G - H/I/J/K/L/M/N - P/Q
* small base; ** very small base (under 30) ineligible for sig testing

Table 200
Page 741

Outsell/Digital Library Federation Study (2002)
Weighted Tables

TABLE 79, continued

T7sum_2. Print or hardcopy journals SUMMARY TABLE

	TOTAL SAMPLE	RESPONDENT TYPE: FACULTY MEMBER (A)	GRAD. STUDENT (B)	FACULTY /GRAD (C)	UNDER GRAD. STUDENT (D)	INSTITUTION TYPE: PUBLIC (E)	PRIVATE (F)	LIBERAL ARTS (G)	DISCIPLINE: BIOLOGIAL SCIENCES (H)	PHYSICAL SCIENCES /MATH (I)	SOCIAL SCIENCES (J)	ARTS AND HUMAN. (K)	ENGI-NEERING (L)	BUSINESS (M)	LAW (N)	UNDEC. MAJOR	GENDER: MALE (P)	FEMALE (Q)
Base - USe Print or hardcopy journals for teaching	425	321	105*	425	0**	148	162	115	65*	85*	133*	81*	12*	47*	3**	0*	288	137*
preferred source of info	27 6.4%	23 7.1%	4 4.1%	27 6.4%	0 0	3 2.0%	13 8.3%E	11 9.2%E	6 9.5%	7 8.2%	6 4.2%	2 2.8%	* 2.4%	6 12.0%K	* 6.3%	0 0	21 7.1%	7 4.8%
Your own institution's web site	59 13.9%	46 14.2%	14 12.9%	59 13.9%	0 0	19 13.0%	26 16.4%	13 11.6%	10 14.9%	8 9.4%	23 16.9%	7 8.3%	3 22.0%IK	9 20.0%	* 6.3%	0 0	39 13.6%	20 14.4%
All sources of info	59 13.9%	46 14.2%	14 12.9%	59 13.9%	0 0	19 13.0%	26 16.4%	13 11.6%	10 14.9%	8 9.4%	23 16.9%	7 8.3%	3 22.0%IK	9 20.0%	* 6.3%	0 0	39 13.6%	20 14.4%
preferred source of info	31 7.3%	24 7.6%	7 6.6%	31 7.3%	0 0	15 10.4%	8 5.2%	8 6.5%	5 8.1%	4 4.7%	9 7.0%	2 2.8%	2 14.6%IK	8 18.0%IJK	* 6.3%	0 0	20 7.0%	11 8.1%
Online library catalogues and finding aids	57 13.3%	36 11.4%	20 19.3%	57 13.3%	0 0	16 10.8%	24 14.7%	17 14.5%	10 14.9%	6 7.1%	19 14.1%	17 20.8%I	1 12.2%	4 8.0%	* 6.3%	0 0	44 15.2%	13 9.3%
All sources of info	57 13.3%	36 11.4%	20 19.3%	57 13.3%	0 0	16 10.8%	24 14.7%	17 14.5%	10 14.9%	6 7.1%	19 14.1%	17 20.8%I	1 12.2%	4 8.0%	* 6.3%	0 0	44 15.2%	13 9.3%
preferred source of info	34 8.0%	18 5.7%	16 15.2%A	34 8.0%	0 0	12 7.9%	13 8.1%	10 8.2%	6 9.5%	3 3.5%	13 9.9%	9 11.1%	1 7.3%	2 4.0%	* 6.3%	0 0	23 8.1%	11 8.0%
Internet searches	36 8.6%	30 9.3%	7 6.4%	36 8.6%	0 0	15 9.8%	10 6.4%	12 10.0%	7 10.8%	8 9.4%	8 5.6%	7 8.3%	1 4.9%	7 14.0%	0 0	0 0	29 10.2%	7 5.0%
All sources of info	36 8.6%	30 9.3%	7 6.4%	36 8.6%	0 0	15 9.8%	10 6.4%	12 10.0%	7 10.8%	8 9.4%	8 5.6%	7 8.3%	1 4.9%	7 14.0%	0 0	0 0	29 10.2%	7 5.0%

Proportions/Means: Columns Tested (5% risk level) - A/B/D - C/D - E/F/G - H/I/J/K/L/M/N - P/Q
* small base; ** very small base (under 30) ineligible for sig testing

Table 200
Page 742

Outsell/Digital Library Federation Study (2002)
Weighted Tables

TABLE 79, continued

T7sum_2. Print or hardcopy journals SUMMARY TABLE

	TOTAL SAMPLE	FACULTY MEMBER	GRAD. STUDENT	FACULTY /GRAD	UNDER GRAD. STUDENT	PUBLIC	PRIVATE	LIBERAL ARTS	BIOLOGIAL SCIENCES	PHYSICAL SCIENCES /MATH	SOCIAL SCIENCES	ARTS AND HUMAN.	ENGI-NEERING	BUSINESS	LAW	UNDEC. MAJOR	MALE	FEMALE
		RESPONDENT TYPE				INSTITUTION TYPE			DISCIPLINE								GENDER	
		(A)	(B)	(C)	(D)	(E)	(F)	(G)	(H)	(I)	(J)	(K)	(L)	(M)	(N)		(P)	(Q)
Base - USe Print or hardcopy journals for teaching	425	321	105*	425	0**	148	162	115	65*	85*	133*	81*	12*	47*	3**	0*	288	137*
preferred source of info	16 3.7%	12 3.8%	4 3.5%	16 3.7%	0 0	6 4.0%	5 3.2%	5 4.2%	3 4.1%	2 2.4%	6 4.2%	2 2.8%	1 4.9%	3 6.0%	0 0	0 0	12 4.1%	4 2.9%
Online abstracting and indexing services	27 6.4%	18 5.6%	9 8.8%	27 6.4%	0 0	7 4.6%	10 5.9%	11 9.3%	3 4.1%	10 11.8%	8 5.6%	4 5.6%	1 4.9%	2 4.0%	0 0	0 0	16 5.7%	11 7.9%
All sources of info	27 6.4%	18 5.6%	9 8.8%	27 6.4%	0 0	7 4.6%	10 5.9%	11 9.3%	3 4.1%	10 11.8%	8 5.6%	4 5.6%	1 4.9%	2 4.0%	0 0	0 0	16 5.7%	11 7.9%
preferred source of info	13 2.9%	7 2.1%	6 5.5%	13 2.9%	0 0	5 3.1%	4 2.5%	4 3.4%	2 2.7%	4 4.7%	6 4.2%	1 1.4%	0 0	0 0	0 0	0 0	5 1.7%	8 5.6%
Online reference service	17 4.0%	14 4.4%	3 2.9%	17 4.0%	0 0	7 4.4%	6 3.9%	4 3.7%	4 5.4%	2 2.4%	4 2.8%	4 5.6%	1 9.8%I	2 4.0%	* 12.5%	0 0	12 4.2%	5 3.6%
All sources of info	17 4.0%	14 4.4%	3 2.9%	17 4.0%	0 0	7 4.4%	6 3.9%	4 3.7%	4 5.4%	2 2.4%	4 2.8%	4 5.6%	1 9.8%I	2 4.0%	* 12.5%	0 0	12 4.2%	5 3.6%
preferred source of info	5 1.1%	4 1.1%	1 1.0%	5 1.1%	0 0	1 0.7%	3 1.7%	1 0.8%	2 2.7%	1 1.2%	2 1.4%	0 0	0 0	0 0	0 0	0 0	3 1.0%	2 1.4%
Online bookstore	4 1.0%	4 1.3%	0 0	4 1.0%	0 0	1 0.7%	1 0.8%	2 1.7%	1 1.4%	2 2.4%	0 0	1 1.4%	* 2.4%J	0 0	0 0	0 0	4 1.5%	0 0
All sources of info	4 1.0%	4 1.3%	0 0	4 1.0%	0 0	1 0.7%	1 0.8%	2 1.7%	1 1.4%	2 2.4%	0 0	1 1.4%	* 2.4%J	0 0	0 0	0 0	4 1.5%	0 0

Proportions/Means: Columns Tested (5% risk level) - A/B/D - C/D - E/F/G - H/I/J/K/L/M/N - P/Q
* small base; ** very small base (under 30) ineligible for sig testing

Table 200
Page 743

Outsell/Digital Library Federation Study (2002)
Weighted Tables

TABLE 79, continued

T7sum_2. Print or hardcopy journals SUMMARY TABLE

		RESPONDENT TYPE				INSTITUTION TYPE			DISCIPLINE								GENDER	
	TOTAL SAMPLE	FACULTY MEMBER	GRAD. STUDENT	FACULTY /GRAD	UNDER GRAD. STUDENT	PUBLIC	PRIVATE	LIBERAL ARTS	BIOLOGIAL SCIENCES	PHYSICAL SCIENCES /MATH	SOCIAL SCIENCES	ARTS AND HUMAN.	ENGI- NEERING	BUSINESS	LAW	UNDEC. MAJOR	MALE	FEMALE
		(A)	(B)	(C)	(D)	(E)	(F)	(G)	(H)	(I)	(J)	(K)	(L)	(M)	(N)		(P)	(Q)
Base - USe Print or hardcopy journals for teaching	425	321	105*	425	0**	148	162	115	65*	85*	133*	81*	12*	47*	3**	0*	288	137*
preferred source of info	0 0	0 0	0 0	0 0	0 0	0 0	0 0	0 0	0 0	0 0	0 0	0 0	0 0	0 0	0 0	0 0	0 0	0 0
Your own personal electronic library/files	3 0.7%	3 1.0%	0 0	3 0.7%	0 0	3 2.1%	0 0	0 0	0 0	1 1.2%	0 0	1 1.4%	0 0	1 2.0%	0 0	0 0	2 0.7%	1 0.7%
All sources of info	3 0.7%	3 1.0%	0 0	3 0.7%	0 0	3 2.1%	0 0	0 0	0 0	1 1.2%	0 0	1 1.4%	0 0	1 2.0%	0 0	0 0	2 0.7%	1 0.7%
preferred source of info	0 0	0 0	0 0	0 0	0 0	0 0	0 0	0 0	0 0	0 0	0 0	0 0	0 0	0 0	0 0	0 0	0 0	0 0
Department web page	3 0.6%	2 0.6%	1 0.8%	3 0.6%	0 0	1 0.6%	0 0	2 1.6%	2 2.7%	1 1.2%	0 0	0 0	0 0	0 0	0 0	0 0	2 0.7%	1 0.6%
All sources of info	3 0.6%	2 0.6%	1 0.8%	3 0.6%	0 0	1 0.6%	0 0	2 1.6%	2 2.7%	1 1.2%	0 0	0 0	0 0	0 0	0 0	0 0	2 0.7%	1 0.6%
preferred source of info	2 0.4%	1 0.3%	1 0.8%	2 0.4%	0 0	1 0.6%	0 0	1 0.8%	2 2.7%	0 0	0 0	0 0	0 0	0 0	0 0	0 0	1 0.3%	1 0.6%
E-mail listservs	2 0.5%	2 0.6%	0 0	2 0.5%	0 0	* 0.1%	0 0	2 1.6%	1 1.4%	1 1.2%	0 0	0 0	0 0	0 0	* 6.3%	0 0	2 0.7%	* 0.1%
All sources of info	2 0.5%	2 0.6%	0 0	2 0.5%	0 0	* 0.1%	0 0	2 1.6%	1 1.4%	1 1.2%	0 0	0 0	0 0	0 0	* 6.3%	0 0	2 0.7%	* 0.1%

Proportions/Means: Columns Tested (5% risk level) - A/B/D - C/D - E/F/G - H/I/J/K/L/M/N - P/Q
* small base; ** very small base (under 30) ineligible for sig testing

Table 200
Page 744

Outsell/Digital Library Federation Study (2002)
Weighted Tables

TABLE 79, continued

T7sum_2. Print or hardcopy journals SUMMARY TABLE

		RESPONDENT TYPE				INSTITUTION TYPE			DISCIPLINE								GENDER	
	TOTAL SAMPLE	FACULTY MEMBER	GRAD. STUDENT	FACULTY /GRAD	UNDER GRAD. STUDENT	PUBLIC	PRIVATE	LIBERAL ARTS	BIOLOGIAL SCIENCES	PHYSICAL SCIENCES /MATH	SOCIAL SCIENCES	ARTS AND HUMAN.	ENGI-NEERING	BUSINESS	LAW	UNDEC. MAJOR	MALE	FEMALE
		(A)	(B)	(C)	(D)	(E)	(F)	(G)	(H)	(I)	(J)	(K)	(L)	(M)	(N)		(P)	(Q)
Base - USe Print or hardcopy journals for teaching	425	321	105*	425	0**	148	162	115	65*	85*	133*	81*	12*	47*	3**	0*	288	137*
preferred source of info	0 0	0 0	0 0	0 0	0 0	0 0	0 0	0 0	0 0	0 0	0 0	0 0	0 0	0 0	0 0	0 0	0 0	0 0
LIBRARY/PRINT	260 61.1%	220 68.5%B	40 38.4%	260 61.1%	0 0	83 56.3%	91 56.3%	85 74.0%EF	38 58.1%	62 72.9%J	70 52.1%	52 63.9%	7 56.1%	31 66.0%	2 62.5%	0 0	184 64.0%	76 55.2%
Campus library	210 49.3%	176 55.0%B	33 31.7%	210 49.3%	0 0	71 48.1%	73 45.3%	65 56.3%	32 48.6%	53 62.4%J	55 40.8%	43 52.8%	5 43.9%	21 46.0%	1 43.7%	0 0	144 50.1%	65 47.5%
All sources of info	210 49.3%	176 55.0%B	33 31.7%	210 49.3%	0 0	71 48.1%	73 45.3%	65 56.3%	32 48.6%	53 62.4%J	55 40.8%	43 52.8%	5 43.9%	21 46.0%	1 43.7%	0 0	144 50.1%	65 47.5%
preferred source of info	87 20.5%	69 21.4%	19 18.0%	87 20.5%	0 0	37 24.8%	29 18.0%	21 18.6%	6 9.5%	19 22.4%H	30 22.5%H	24 29.2%HM	2 19.5%	6 12.0%	1 25.0%	0 0	60 20.7%	28 20.3%
Your own personal physical library/ files/bookshelves	57 13.5%	54 16.9%B	3 3.1%	57 13.5%	0 0	18 12.1%	20 12.3%	20 17.0%	11 16.2%	14 16.5%	11 8.5%	10 12.5%	1 9.8%	10 22.0%J	* 6.3%	0 0	47 16.3%Q	11 7.7%
All sources of info	57 13.5%	54 16.9%B	3 3.1%	57 13.5%	0 0	18 12.1%	20 12.3%	20 17.0%	11 16.2%	14 16.5%	11 8.5%	10 12.5%	1 9.8%	10 22.0%J	* 6.3%	0 0	47 16.3%Q	11 7.7%
preferred source of info	32 7.5%	31 9.7%B	1 1.0%	32 7.5%	0 0	6 4.1%	15 9.3%	11 9.5%	4 6.8%	7 8.2%	9 7.0%	6 6.9%	1 7.3%	5 10.0%	* 6.3%	0 0	27 9.5%	5 3.5%

Proportions/Means: Columns Tested (5% risk level) - A/B/D - C/D - E/F/G - H/I/J/K/L/M/N - P/Q
* small base; ** very small base (under 30) ineligible for sig testing

Table 200
Page 745

Outsell/Digital Library Federation Study (2002)
Weighted Tables

TABLE 79, continued

T7sum_2. Print or hardcopy journals SUMMARY TABLE

	TOTAL SAMPLE	RESPONDENT TYPE: FACULTY MEMBER	GRAD. STUDENT	FACULTY /GRAD	UNDER GRAD. STUDENT	INSTITUTION TYPE: PUBLIC	PRIVATE	LIBERAL ARTS	DISCIPLINE: BIOLOGIAL SCIENCES	PHYSICAL SCIENCES /MATH	SOCIAL SCIENCES	ARTS AND HUMAN.	ENGI-NEERING	BUSINESS	LAW	UNDEC. MAJOR	GENDER: MALE	FEMALE
		(A)	(B)	(C)	(D)	(E)	(F)	(G)	(H)	(I)	(J)	(K)	(L)	(M)	(N)		(P)	(Q)
Base - USe Print or hardcopy journals for teaching	425	321	105*	425	0**	148	162	115	65*	85*	133*	81*	12*	47*	3**	0*	288	137*
Personal subscriptions to newspapers, magazines and journals	47 11.1%	41 12.8%	6 5.7%	47 11.1%	0 0	12 8.2%	13 7.9%	22 19.2%EF	6 9.5%	13 15.3%	15 11.3%	6 6.9%	1 4.9%	7 14.0%	* 6.3%	0 0	37 13.0%	10 7.0%
All sources of info	47 11.1%	41 12.8%	6 5.7%	47 11.1%	0 0	12 8.2%	13 7.9%	22 19.2%EF	6 9.5%	13 15.3%	15 11.3%	6 6.9%	1 4.9%	7 14.0%	* 6.3%	0 0	37 13.0%	10 7.0%
preferred source of info	18 4.1%	16 4.9%	2 1.8%	18 4.1%	0 0	3 2.3%	7 4.1%	8 6.6%	1 1.4%	5 5.9%K	9 7.0%K	0 0	* 2.4%K	2 4.0%	* 6.3%	0 0	15 5.1%	3 2.1%
References cited in books or journal articles	27 6.3%	23 7.1%	4 3.9%	27 6.3%	0 0	10 6.8%	11 6.5%	6 5.5%	1 1.4%	4 4.7%	8 5.6%	10 12.5%H	1 4.9%	4 8.0%	* 6.3%	0 0	19 6.7%	8 5.6%
All sources of info	27 6.3%	23 7.1%	4 3.9%	27 6.3%	0 0	10 6.8%	11 6.5%	6 5.5%	1 1.4%	4 4.7%	8 5.6%	10 12.5%H	1 4.9%	4 8.0%	* 6.3%	0 0	19 6.7%	8 5.6%
preferred source of info	10 2.3%	7 2.3%	2 2.1%	10 2.3%	0 0	4 2.7%	5 2.9%	1 0.9%	1 1.4%	1 1.2%	4 2.8%	2 2.8%	0 0	2 4.0%	0 0	0 0	5 1.8%	5 3.4%
Another library	13 3.0%	11 3.5%	2 1.7%	13 3.0%	0 0	2 1.4%	2 1.3%	9 7.6%EF	4 5.4%J	7 8.2%J	0 0	1 1.4%	* 2.4%J	1 2.0%	0 0	0 0	8 2.8%	5 3.4%
All sources of info	13 3.0%	11 3.5%	2 1.7%	13 3.0%	0 0	2 1.4%	2 1.3%	9 7.6%EF	4 5.4%J	7 8.2%J	0 0	1 1.4%	* 2.4%J	1 2.0%	0 0	0 0	8 2.8%	5 3.4%

Proportions/Means: Columns Tested (5% risk level) - A/B/D - C/D - E/F/G - H/I/J/K/L/M/N - P/Q
* small base; ** very small base (under 30) ineligible for sig testing

Table 200
Page 746

Outsell/Digital Library Federation Study (2002)
Weighted Tables

TABLE 79, continued

T7sum_2. Print or hardcopy journals SUMMARY TABLE

	TOTAL SAMPLE	RESPONDENT TYPE: FACULTY MEMBER (A)	GRAD. STUDENT (B)	FACULTY /GRAD (C)	UNDER GRAD. STUDENT (D)	INSTITUTION TYPE: PUBLIC (E)	PRIVATE (F)	LIBERAL ARTS (G)	DISCIPLINE: BIOLOGIAL SCIENCES (H)	PHYSICAL SCIENCES /MATH (I)	SOCIAL SCIENCES (J)	ARTS AND HUMAN. (K)	ENGI-NEERING (L)	BUSINESS (M)	LAW (N)	UNDEC. MAJOR	GENDER: MALE (P)	FEMALE (Q)
Base - USe Print or hardcopy journals for teaching	425	321	105*	425	0**	148	162	115	65*	85*	133*	81*	12*	47*	3**	0*	288	137*
preferred source of info	0 0	0 0	0 0	0 0	0 0	0 0	0 0	0 0	0 0	0 0	0 0	0 0	0 0	0 0	0 0	0 0	0 0	0 0
Printed abstracting and indexing services	11 2.7%	10 3.0%	2 1.8%	11 2.7%	0 0	3 2.0%	5 2.9%	4 3.2%	2 2.7%	1 1.2%	8 5.6%	0 0	0 0	1 2.0%	* 6.3%	0 0	10 3.3%	2 1.4%
All sources of info	11 2.7%	10 3.0%	2 1.8%	11 2.7%	0 0	3 2.0%	5 2.9%	4 3.2%	2 2.7%	1 1.2%	8 5.6%	0 0	0 0	1 2.0%	* 6.3%	0 0	10 3.3%	2 1.4%
preferred source of info	4 0.9%	4 1.2%	0 0	4 0.9%	0 0	0 0	2 1.2%	2 1.6%	1 1.4%	0 0	2 1.4%	0 0	0 0	1 2.0%	0 0	0 0	4 1.3%	0 0
Physical bookstore	5 1.2%	3 1.0%	2 1.9%	5 1.2%	0 0	2 1.5%	2 1.2%	1 1.0%	2 2.7%	0 0	0 0	3 4.2%J	0 0	0 0	* 6.3%	0 0	4 1.4%	1 0.9%
All sources of info	5 1.2%	3 1.0%	2 1.9%	5 1.2%	0 0	2 1.5%	2 1.2%	1 1.0%	2 2.7%	0 0	0 0	3 4.2%J	0 0	0 0	* 6.3%	0 0	4 1.4%	1 0.9%
preferred source of info	0 0	0 0	0 0	0 0	0 0	0 0	0 0	0 0	0 0	0 0	0 0	0 0	0 0	0 0	0 0	0 0	0 0	0 0
Printed library catalogues and finding aids	4 0.9%	4 1.2%	0 0	4 0.9%	0 0	0 0	1 0.6%	3 2.6%	0 0	0 0	2 1.4%	1 1.4%	0 0	1 2.0%	0 0	0 0	3 1.0%	1 0.7%
All sources of info	4 0.9%	4 1.2%	0 0	4 0.9%	0 0	0 0	1 0.6%	3 2.6%	0 0	0 0	2 1.4%	1 1.4%	0 0	1 2.0%	0 0	0 0	3 1.0%	1 0.7%

Proportions/Means: Columns Tested (5% risk level) - A/B/D - C/D - E/F/G - H/I/J/K/L/M/N - P/Q
* small base; ** very small base (under 30) ineligible for sig testing

Table 200
Page 747

Outsell/Digital Library Federation Study (2002)
Weighted Tables

TABLE 79, continued

T7sum_2. Print or hardcopy journals SUMMARY TABLE

		RESPONDENT TYPE				INSTITUTION TYPE			DISCIPLINE									GENDER	
	TOTAL SAMPLE	FACULTY MEMBER	GRAD. STUDENT	FACULTY /GRAD	UNDER GRAD. STUDENT	PUBLIC	PRIVATE	LIBERAL ARTS	BIOLOGIAL SCIENCES	PHYSICAL SCIENCES /MATH	SOCIAL SCIENCES	ARTS AND HUMAN.	ENGI-NEERING	BUSINESS	LAW	UNDEC. MAJOR	MALE	FEMALE
		(A)	(B)	(C)	(D)	(E)	(F)	(G)	(H)	(I)	(J)	(K)	(L)	(M)	(N)		(P)	(Q)
Base - USe Print or hardcopy journals for teaching	425	321	105*	425	0**	148	162	115	65*	85*	133*	81*	12*	47*	3**	0*	288	137*
preferred source of info	3 0.7%	3 0.9%	0 0	3 0.7%	0 0	0 0	0 0	3 2.6%	0 0	0 0	2 1.4%	1 1.4%	0 0	0 0	0 0	0 0	3 1.0%	0 0
PERSONAL ASSISTANCE	89 20.9%	63 19.6%	26 24.9%	89 20.9%	0 0	30 20.2%	31 19.1%	28 24.4%	10 14.9%	27 31.8%HJ	15 11.3%	20 25.0%J	3 22.0%	14 30.0%HJ	1 18.7%	0 0	64 22.1%	25 18.5%
Colleagues inside your institution	60 14.0%	39 12.1%	21 20.1%	60 14.0%	0 0	21 14.3%	25 15.3%	14 11.9%	7 10.8%	20 23.5%HJ	8 5.6%	12 15.3%J	1 12.2%	11 24.0%J	* 6.3%	0 0	45 15.7%	14 10.4%
All sources of info	60 14.0%	39 12.1%	21 20.1%	60 14.0%	0 0	21 14.3%	25 15.3%	14 11.9%	7 10.8%	20 23.5%HJ	8 5.6%	12 15.3%J	1 12.2%	11 24.0%J	* 6.3%	0 0	45 15.7%	14 10.4%
preferred source of info	22 5.3%	5 1.5%	18 16.8%A	22 5.3%	0 0	7 4.7%	13 7.7%	3 2.5%	5 8.1%	9 10.6%J	4 2.8%	2 2.8%	* 2.4%	2 4.0%	0 0	0 0	18 6.4%	4 3.0%
A librarian in your institution	41 9.6%	35 10.8%	6 5.9%	41 9.6%	0 0	15 10.1%	8 5.2%	18 15.2%F	4 6.8%	10 11.8%	8 5.6%	15 18.1%HJ	1 9.8%	3 6.0%	* 12.5%	0 0	29 10.0%	12 8.6%
All sources of info	41 9.6%	35 10.8%	6 5.9%	41 9.6%	0 0	15 10.1%	8 5.2%	18 15.2%F	4 6.8%	10 11.8%	8 5.6%	15 18.1%HJ	1 9.8%	3 6.0%	* 12.5%	0 0	29 10.0%	12 8.6%
preferred source of info	13 3.0%	10 3.0%	3 3.1%	13 3.0%	0 0	7 4.6%	5 3.2%	1 0.9%	0 0	2 2.4%	4 2.8%	4 5.6%	1 7.3%H	2 4.0%	0 0	0 0	9 3.1%	4 2.9%
Colleagues outside your institution	17 4.0%	17 5.3%B	0 0	17 4.0%	0 0	3 2.0%	8 5.0%	6 5.1%	1 1.4%	5 5.9%	2 1.4%	6 6.9%	0 0	4 8.0%J	0 0	0 0	11 3.9%	6 4.2%

Proportions/Means: Columns Tested (5% risk level) - A/B/D - C/D - E/F/G - H/I/J/K/L/M/N - P/Q
* small base; ** very small base (under 30) ineligible for sig testing

Table 200
Page 748

Outsell/Digital Library Federation Study (2002)
Weighted Tables

TABLE 79, continued

T7sum_2. Print or hardcopy journals SUMMARY TABLE

		RESPONDENT TYPE				INSTITUTION TYPE			DISCIPLINE									GENDER	
	TOTAL SAMPLE	FACULTY MEMBER	GRAD. STUDENT	FACULTY /GRAD	UNDER GRAD. STUDENT	PUBLIC	PRIVATE	LIBERAL ARTS	BIOLOGIAL SCIENCES	PHYSICAL SCIENCES /MATH	SOCIAL SCIENCES	ARTS AND HUMAN.	ENGI- NEERING	BUSINESS	LAW	UNDEC. MAJOR	MALE	FEMALE
		(A)	(B)	(C)	(D)	(E)	(F)	(G)	(H)	(I)	(J)	(K)	(L)	(M)	(N)		(P)	(Q)
Base - USe Print or hardcopy journals for teaching	425	321	105*	425	0**	148	162	115	65*	85*	133*	81*	12*	47*	3**	0*	288	137*
All sources of info	17 4.0%	17 5.3%B	0 0	17 4.0%	0 0	3 2.0%	8 5.0%	6 5.1%	1 1.4%	5 5.9%	2 1.4%	6 6.9%	0 0	4 8.0%J	0 0	0 0	11 3.9%	6 4.2%
preferred source of info	2 0.5%	2 0.6%	0 0	2 0.5%	0 0	0 0	2 1.3%	0 0	0 0	0 0	0 0	1 1.4%	0 0	1 2.0%	0 0	0 0	1 0.4%	1 0.7%
Another institution's librarian	4 1.0%	2 0.7%	2 1.9%	4 1.0%	0 0	2 1.4%	1 0.7%	1 0.9%	1 1.4%	1 1.2%	0 0	2 2.8%	0 0	0 0	0 0	0 0	2 0.7%	2 1.5%
All sources of info	4 1.0%	2 0.7%	2 1.9%	4 1.0%	0 0	2 1.4%	1 0.7%	1 0.9%	1 1.4%	1 1.2%	0 0	2 2.8%	0 0	0 0	0 0	0 0	2 0.7%	2 1.5%
preferred source of info	1 0.2%	0 0	1 0.8%	1 0.2%	0 0	1 0.6%	0 0	0 0	1 1.4%	0 0	0 0	0 0	0 0	0 0	0 0	0 0	0 0	1 0.6%
Professional meetings	3 0.7%	2 0.6%	1 1.1%	3 0.7%	0 0	1 0.9%	0 0	2 1.6%	0 0	0 0	2 1.4%	1 1.4%	0 0	0 0	* 6.3%	0 0	3 1.0%	* 0.1%
All sources of info	3 0.7%	2 0.6%	1 1.1%	3 0.7%	0 0	1 0.9%	0 0	2 1.6%	0 0	0 0	2 1.4%	1 1.4%	0 0	0 0	* 6.3%	0 0	3 1.0%	* 0.1%
preferred source of info	* *	* 0.1%	0 0	* *	0 0	* 0.1%	0 0	0 0	0 0	0 0	0 0	0 0	0 0	0 0	* 6.3%	0 0	0 0	* 0.1%
Online (unspecified)	6 1.4%	6 1.9%	0 0	6 1.4%	0 0	1 0.7%	5 3.1%	0 0	2 2.7%	1 1.2%	2 1.4%	1 1.4%	* 2.4%	0 0	0 0	0 0	4 1.4%	2 1.4%

Proportions/Means: Columns Tested (5% risk level) - A/B/D - C/D - E/F/G - H/I/J/K/L/M/N - P/Q
* small base; ** very small base (under 30) ineligible for sig testing

Table 200
Page 749

Outsell/Digital Library Federation Study (2002)
Weighted Tables

TABLE 79, continued

T7sum_2. Print or hardcopy journals SUMMARY TABLE

		RESPONDENT TYPE				INSTITUTION TYPE			DISCIPLINE								GENDER	
	TOTAL SAMPLE	FACULTY MEMBER	GRAD. STUDENT	FACULTY /GRAD	UNDER GRAD. STUDENT	PUBLIC	PRIVATE	LIBERAL ARTS	BIOLOGIAL SCIENCES	PHYSICAL SCIENCES /MATH	SOCIAL SCIENCES	ARTS AND HUMAN.	ENGI- NEERING	BUSINESS	LAW	UNDEC. MAJOR	MALE	FEMALE
		(A)	(B)	(C)	(D)	(E)	(F)	(G)	(H)	(I)	(J)	(K)	(L)	(M)	(N)		(P)	(Q)
Base - USe Print or hardcopy journals for teaching	425	321	105*	425	0**	148	162	115	65*	85*	133*	81*	12*	47*	3**	0*	288	137*
All sources of info	6 1.4%	6 1.9%	0 0	6 1.4%	0 0	1 0.7%	5 3.1%	0 0	2 2.7%	1 1.2%	2 1.4%	1 1.4%	* 2.4%	0 0	0 0	0 0	4 1.4%	2 1.4%
preferred source of info	4 1.0%	4 1.3%	0 0	4 1.0%	0 0	1 0.7%	3 1.9%	0 0	1 1.4%	1 1.2%	2 1.4%	0 0	* 2.4%K	0 0	0 0	0 0	2 0.8%	2 1.4%
Students	4 0.9%	4 1.2%	0 0	4 0.9%	0 0	1 0.6%	0 0	3 2.5%	1 1.4%	1 1.2%	2 1.4%	0 0	0 0	0 0	0 0	0 0	3 1.0%	1 0.7%
All sources of info	4 0.9%	4 1.2%	0 0	4 0.9%	0 0	1 0.6%	0 0	3 2.5%	1 1.4%	1 1.2%	2 1.4%	0 0	0 0	0 0	0 0	0 0	3 1.0%	1 0.7%
preferred source of info	0 0	0 0	0 0	0 0	0 0	0 0	0 0	0 0	0 0	0 0	0 0	0 0	0 0	0 0	0 0	0 0	0 0	0 0
Personal office/lab	1 0.3%	1 0.3%	* 0.3%	1 0.3%	0 0	1 0.7%	* 0.2%	0 0	0 0	0 0	0 0	0 0	* 2.4%HIJK	1 2.0%	* 6.3%	0 0	1 0.4%	* 0.2%
All sources of info	1 0.3%	1 0.3%	* 0.3%	1 0.3%	0 0	1 0.7%	* 0.2%	0 0	0 0	0 0	0 0	0 0	* 2.4%HIJK	1 2.0%	* 6.3%	0 0	1 0.4%	* 0.2%
preferred source of info	1 0.2%	1 0.3%	0 0	1 0.2%	0 0	1 0.6%	0 0	0 0	0 0	0 0	0 0	0 0	0 0	1 2.0%	0 0	0 0	1 0.3%	0 0
Author	0 0	0 0	0 0	0 0	0 0	0 0	0 0	0 0	0 0	0 0	0 0	0 0	0 0	0 0	0 0	0 0	0 0	0 0
All sources of info	0 0	0 0	0 0	0 0	.0 0	0 0	0 0	0 0	0 0	0 0	0 0	0 0	0 0	0 0	0 0	0 0	0 0	0 0

Proportions/Means: Columns Tested (5% risk level) - A/B/D - C/D - E/F/G - H/I/J/K/L/M/N - P/Q
* small base; ** very small base (under 30) ineligible for sig testing

Table 200
Page 750

Outsell/Digital Library Federation Study (2002)
Weighted Tables

TABLE 79, continued

T7sum_2. Print or hardcopy journals SUMMARY TABLE

		RESPONDENT TYPE				INSTITUTION TYPE			DISCIPLINE								GENDER	
	TOTAL SAMPLE	FACULTY MEMBER	GRAD. STUDENT	FACULTY /GRAD	UNDER GRAD. STUDENT	PUBLIC	PRIVATE	LIBERAL ARTS	BIOLOGIAL SCIENCES	PHYSICAL SCIENCES /MATH	SOCIAL SCIENCES	ARTS AND HUMAN.	ENGI-NEERING	BUSINESS	LAW	UNDEC. MAJOR	MALE	FEMALE
		(A)	(B)	(C)	(D)	(E)	(F)	(G)	(H)	(I)	(J)	(K)	(L)	(M)	(N)		(P)	(Q)
Base - USe Print or hardcopy journals for teaching	425	321	105*	425	0**	148	162	115	65*	85*	133*	81*	12*	47*	3**	0*	288	137*
preferred source of info	0 0	0 0	0 0	0 0	0 0	0 0	0 0	0 0	0 0	0 0	0 0	0 0	0 0	0 0	0 0	0 0	0 0	0 0
Other	28 6.6%	24 7.6%	3 3.3%	28 6.6%	0 0	11 7.6%	9 5.8%	7 6.3%	5 8.1%	5 5.9%	4 2.8%	8 9.7%	1 7.3%	5 10.0%	1 18.7%	0 0	22 7.6%	6 4.4%
All sources of info	26 6.1%	24 7.4%	2 2.2%	26 6.1%	0 0	9 6.3%	9 5.8%	7 6.3%	4 6.8%	5 5.9%	4 2.8%	7 8.3%	1 7.3%	5 10.0%	1 18.7%	0 0	21 7.2%	5 3.8%
preferred source of info	13 2.9%	9 2.8%	3 3.3%	13 2.9%	0 0	6 3.7%	5 3.0%	2 1.9%	3 4.1%	1 1.2%	2 1.4%	6 6.9%	1 7.3%IJM	0 0	1 18.7%	0 0	7 2.6%	5 3.7%
DK/Refused	14 3.2%	12 3.7%	2 1.6%	14 3.2%	0 0	8 5.5%	3 1.9%	2 2.0%	0 0	4 4.7%J	0 0	7 8.3%HJ	2 14.6%HIJM	1 2.0%	* 6.3%	0 0	11 3.9%	2 1.8%

Proportions/Means: Columns Tested (5% risk level) - A/B/D - C/D - E/F/G - H/I/J/K/L/M/N - P/Q
* small base; ** very small base (under 30) ineligible for sig testing

Table 200
Page 751

Outsell/Digital Library Federation Study (2002)
Weighted Tables

TABLE 80

T7D/E_2. Print or hardcopy journals SUMMARY TABLE

		RESPONDENT TYPE				INSTITUTION TYPE			DISCIPLINE								GENDER	
	TOTAL SAMPLE	FACULTY MEMBER	GRAD. STUDENT	FACULTY /GRAD	UNDER GRAD. STUDENT	PUBLIC	PRIVATE	LIBERAL ARTS	BIOLOGIAL SCIENCES	PHYSICAL SCIENCES /MATH	SOCIAL SCIENCES	ARTS AND HUMAN.	ENGI-NEERING	BUSINESS	LAW	UNDEC. MAJOR	MALE	FEMALE
		(A)	(B)	(C)	(D)	(E)	(F)	(G)	(H)	(I)	(J)	(K)	(L)	(M)	(N)		(P)	(Q)
Base - Use Print or hardcopy journals for teaching	425	321	105*	425	0**	148	162	115	65*	85*	133*	81*	12*	47*	3**	0*	288	137*
Borrow from or use in campus library (NET)	338 79.5%	259 80.7%	80 76.0%	338 79.5%	0 0	113 76.5%	129 80.0%	96 82.7%	56 86.5%M	68 80.0%	103 77.5%	66 81.9%	10 82.9%	33 70.0%	2 75.0%	0 0	237 82.2%	101 73.9%
All sources of info	338 79.5%	259 80.7%	80 76.0%	338 79.5%	0 0	113 76.5%	129 80.0%	96 82.7%	56 86.5%M	68 80.0%	103 77.5%	66 81.9%	10 82.9%	33 70.0%	2 75.0%	0 0	237 82.2%	101 73.9%
preferred source of info	245 57.6%	184 57.5%	61 58.0%	245 57.6%	0 0	76 51.3%	97 60.1%	72 62.3%	39 59.5%M	50 58.8%M	81 60.6%M	50 62.5%M	6 51.2%	18 38.0%	1 50.0%	0 0	174 60.4%	71 51.8%
Access online (NET)	114 26.9%	85 26.5%	29 27.9%	114 26.9%	0 0	42 28.4%	48 29.5%	24 21.2%	18 28.4%	21 24.7%	34 25.4%	15 18.1%	5 43.9%IJK	20 44.0%IJK	1 25.0%	0 0	74 25.7%	40 29.3%
All sources of info	114 26.9%	85 26.5%	29 27.9%	114 26.9%	0 0	42 28.4%	48 29.5%	24 21.2%	18 28.4%	21 24.7%	34 25.4%	15 18.1%	5 43.9%IJK	20 44.0%IJK	1 25.0%	0 0	74 25.7%	40 29.3%
preferred source of info	74 17.3%	54 16.8%	20 18.8%	74 17.3%	0 0	28 19.2%	29 18.1%	16 13.7%	15 23.0%K	15 17.6%	19 14.1%	7 8.3%	4 31.7%JK	14 30.0%JK	1 18.7%	0 0	46 15.9%	28 20.3%
Personal Collection/ Holdings (NET)	37 8.6%	36 11.1%B	1 1.0%	37 8.6%	0 0	15 9.9%	8 5.0%	14 12.0%	4 6.8%	12 14.1%	8 5.6%	6 6.9%	1 12.2%	6 12.0%	* 6.3%	0 0	28 9.7%	9 6.5%
All sources of info	37 8.6%	36 11.1%B	1 1.0%	37 8.6%	0 0	15 9.9%	8 5.0%	14 12.0%	4 6.8%	12 14.1%	8 5.6%	6 6.9%	1 12.2%	6 12.0%	* 6.3%	0 0	28 9.7%	9 6.5%

Proportions/Means: Columns Tested (5% risk level) - A/B/D - C/D - E/F/G - H/I/J/K/L/M/N - P/Q
* small base; ** very small base (under 30) ineligible for sig testing

Table 203
Page 758

Outsell/Digital Library Federation Study (2002)
Weighted Tables

TABLE 80, continued

T7D/E_2. Print or hardcopy journals SUMMARY TABLE

		RESPONDENT TYPE				INSTITUTION TYPE			DISCIPLINE								GENDER	
	TOTAL SAMPLE	FACULTY MEMBER	GRAD. STUDENT	FACULTY /GRAD	UNDER GRAD. STUDENT	PUBLIC	PRIVATE	LIBERAL ARTS	BIOLOGIAL SCIENCES	PHYSICAL SCIENCES /MATH	SOCIAL SCIENCES	ARTS AND HUMAN.	ENGI-NEERING	BUSINESS	LAW	UNDEC. MAJOR	MALE	FEMALE
		(A)	(B)	(C)	(D)	(E)	(F)	(G)	(H)	(I)	(J)	(K)	(L)	(M)	(N)		(P)	(Q)
Base - Use Print or hardcopy journals for teaching	425	321	105*	425	0**	148	162	115	65*	85*	133*	81*	12*	47*	3**	0*	288	137*
preferred source of info	23 5.4%	22 6.8%B	1 1.0%	23 5.4%	0 0	12 7.8%F	3 1.9%	8 7.0%	3 4.1%	7 8.2%	6 4.2%	3 4.2%	1 9.8%	3 6.0%	* 6.3%	0 0	17 5.9%	6 4.3%
Interlibrary loan (NET)	35 8.3%	33 10.4%B	2 1.8%	35 8.3%	0 0	6 4.3%	11 6.7%	18 15.7%EF	5 8.1%	9 10.6%	6 4.2%	9 11.1%	1 12.2%	5 10.0%	* 12.5%	0 0	26 9.2%	9 6.5%
All sources of info	35 8.3%	33 10.4%B	2 1.8%	35 8.3%	0 0	6 4.3%	11 6.7%	18 15.7%EF	5 8.1%	9 10.6%	6 4.2%	9 11.1%	1 12.2%	5 10.0%	* 12.5%	0 0	26 9.2%	9 6.5%
preferred source of info	10 2.4%	10 3.2%	0 0	10 2.4%	0 0	2 1.3%	5 3.2%	3 2.8%	0 0	1 1.2%	4 2.8%	6 6.9%H	0 0	0 0	0 0	0 0	9 3.2%	1 0.8%
Access from course website (NET)	25 5.9%	23 7.3%	2 1.8%	25 5.9%	0 0	5 3.2%	4 2.4%	17 14.3%EF	4 5.4%	8 9.4%	8 5.6%	2 2.8%	0 0	4 8.0%	* 6.3%	0 0	18 6.1%	8 5.5%
All sources of info	25 5.9%	23 7.3%	2 1.8%	25 5.9%	0 0	5 3.2%	4 2.4%	17 14.3%EF	4 5.4%	8 9.4%	8 5.6%	2 2.8%	0 0	4 8.0%	* 6.3%	0 0	18 6.1%	8 5.5%
preferred source of info	14 3.4%	13 3.9%	2 1.8%	14 3.4%	0 0	4 2.5%	1 0.6%	10 8.4%F	2 2.7%	5 5.9%	4 2.8%	1 1.4%	0 0	3 6.0%	0 0	0 0	9 3.0%	6 4.2%
Borrow from or use in other libraries (NET)	19 4.5%	15 4.8%	4 3.5%	19 4.5%	0 0	5 3.2%	6 3.9%	8 6.9%	4 5.4%	8 9.4%J	2 1.4%	3 4.2%	* 2.4%	2 4.0%	* 6.3%	0 0	11 4.0%	8 5.6%
All sources of info	19 4.5%	15 4.8%	4 3.5%	19 4.5%	0 0	5 3.2%	6 3.9%	8 6.9%	4 5.4%	8 9.4%J	2 1.4%	3 4.2%	* 2.4%	2 4.0%	* 6.3%	0 0	11 4.0%	8 5.6%

Proportions/Means: Columns Tested (5% risk level) - A/B/D - C/D - E/F/G - H/I/J/K/L/M/N - P/Q
* small base; ** very small base (under 30) ineligible for sig testing

Table 203
Page 759

TABLE 80, continued

T7D/E_2. Print or hardcopy journals SUMMARY TABLE

	RESPONDENT TYPE				INSTITUTION TYPE			DISCIPLINE								GENDER	
	TOTAL SAMPLE	FACULTY MEMBER	GRAD. STUDENT	FACULTY /GRAD	UNDER GRAD. STUDENT	PUBLIC	PRIVATE	LIBERAL ARTS	BIOLOGIAL SCIENCES	PHYSICAL SCIENCES /MATH	SOCIAL SCIENCES	ARTS AND HUMAN.	ENGI-NEERING	BUSINESS	LAW	UNDEC. MAJOR	MALE	FEMALE
		(A)	(B)	(C)	(D)	(E)	(F)	(G)	(H)	(I)	(J)	(K)	(L)	(M)	(N)		(P)	(Q)
Base - Use Print or hardcopy journals for teaching	425	321	105*	425	0**	148	162	115	65*	85*	133*	81*	12*	47*	3**	0*	288	137*
preferred source of info	7 1.7%	4 1.3%	3 2.6%	7 1.7%	0 0	2 1.3%	5 3.2%	0 0	1 1.4%	1 1.2%	2 1.4%	1 1.4%	* 2.4%	2 4.0%	0 0	0 0	3 1.1%	4 2.9%
Purchase from physical book store (NET)	13 3.1%	11 3.4%	2 2.2%	13 3.1%	0 0	5 3.1%	6 3.7%	3 2.4%	2 2.7%	2 2.4%	2 1.4%	6 6.9%	* 2.4%	2 4.0%	0 0	0 0	8 2.9%	5 3.6%
All sources of info	13 3.1%	11 3.4%	2 2.2%	13 3.1%	0 0	5 3.1%	6 3.7%	3 2.4%	2 2.7%	2 2.4%	2 1.4%	6 6.9%	* 2.4%	2 4.0%	0 0	0 0	8 2.9%	5 3.6%
preferred source of info	7 1.6%	7 2.1%	0 0	7 1.6%	0 0	1 0.8%	4 2.4%	2 1.6%	2 2.7%	0 0	2 1.4%	2 2.8%	0 0	1 2.0%	0 0	0 0	3 1.0%	4 2.8%
Colleagues (NET)	9 2.1%	4 1.2%	5 4.9%A	9 2.1%	0 0	3 1.8%	5 3.2%	1 1.0%	1 1.4%	2 2.4%	0 0	4 5.6%J	1 4.9%J	1 2.0%	0 0	0 0	5 1.6%	4 3.0%
All sources of info	9 2.1%	4 1.2%	5 4.9%A	9 2.1%	0 0	3 1.8%	5 3.2%	1 1.0%	1 1.4%	2 2.4%	0 0	4 5.6%J	1 4.9%J	1 2.0%	0 0	0 0	5 1.6%	4 3.0%
preferred source of info	4 0.9%	0 0	4 3.8%A	4 0.9%	0 0	1 0.8%	3 1.8%	0 0	1 1.4%	2 2.4%	0 0	1 1.4%	0 0	0 0	0 0	0 0	2 0.7%	2 1.5%
Order from on demand document delivery service (NET)	9 2.1%	7 2.2%	2 1.8%	9 2.1%	0 0	2 1.3%	5 3.1%	2 1.7%	0 0	1 1.2%	6 4.2%	0 0	* 2.4%HK	2 4.0%	0 0	0 0	8 2.7%	1 0.7%

Proportions/Means: Columns Tested (5% risk level) - A/B/D - C/D - E/F/G - H/I/J/K/L/M/N - P/Q
* small base; ** very small base (under 30) ineligible for sig testing

Table 203
Page 760

TABLE 80, continued

T7D/E_2. Print or hardcopy journals SUMMARY TABLE

		RESPONDENT TYPE				INSTITUTION TYPE			DISCIPLINE									GENDER	
	TOTAL SAMPLE	FACULTY MEMBER	GRAD. STUDENT	FACULTY /GRAD	UNDER GRAD. STUDENT	PUBLIC	PRIVATE	LIBERAL ARTS	BIOLOGIAL SCIENCES	PHYSICAL SCIENCES /MATH	SOCIAL SCIENCES	ARTS AND HUMAN.	ENGI-NEERING	BUSINESS	LAW	UNDEC. MAJOR	MALE	FEMALE
		(A)	(B)	(C)	(D)	(E)	(F)	(G)	(H)	(I)	(J)	(K)	(L)	(M)	(N)		(P)	(Q)
Base - Use Print or hardcopy journals for teaching	425	321	105*	425	0**	148	162	115	65*	85*	133*	81*	12*	47*	3**	0*	288	137*
All sources of info	9 2.1%	7 2.2%	2 1.8%	9 2.1%	0 0	2 1.3%	5 3.1%	2 1.7%	0 0	1 1.2%	6 4.2%	0 0	* 2.4%HK	2 4.0%	0 0	0 0	8 2.7%	1 0.7%
preferred source of info	8 1.8%	6 1.8%	2 1.8%	8 1.8%	0 0	2 1.3%	5 2.9%	1 0.8%	0 0	0 0	6 4.2%	0 0	0 0	2 4.0%	0 0	0 0	7 2.3%	1 0.7%
Publisher (NET)	8 1.9%	7 2.2%	1 1.1%	8 1.9%	0 0	3 2.0%	1 0.7%	4 3.6%	1 1.4%	1 1.2%	2 1.4%	3 4.2%	0 0	1 2.0%	* 6.3%	0 0	5 1.8%	3 2.2%
All sources of info	8 1.9%	7 2.2%	1 1.1%	8 1.9%	0 0	3 2.0%	1 0.7%	4 3.6%	1 1.4%	1 1.2%	2 1.4%	3 4.2%	0 0	1 2.0%	* 6.3%	0 0	5 1.8%	3 2.2%
preferred source of info	3 0.7%	3 1.0%	0 0	3 0.7%	0 0	3 2.0%	0 0	* 0.1%	1 1.4%	0 0	0 0	1 1.4%	0 0	1 2.0%	* 6.3%	0 0	1 0.4%	2 1.5%
Office (NET)	8 1.8%	8 2.4%	0 0	8 1.8%	0 0	1 0.7%	5 2.9%	2 1.6%	0 0	0 0	6 4.2%	0 0	0 0	2 4.0%	* 6.3%	0 0	6 2.0%	2 1.4%
All sources of info	8 1.8%	8 2.4%	0 0	8 1.8%	0 0	1 0.7%	5 2.9%	2 1.6%	0 0	0 0	6 4.2%	0 0	0 0	2 4.0%	* 6.3%	0 0	6 2.0%	2 1.4%
preferred source of info	6 1.4%	6 1.8%	0 0	6 1.4%	0 0	1 0.7%	3 1.7%	2 1.6%	0 0	0 0	4 2.8%	0 0	0 0	2 4.0%	* 6.3%	0 0	4 1.4%	2 1.4%
Ask library to purchase source (NET)	6 1.5%	6 1.9%	0 0	6 1.5%	0 0	* 0.1%	4 2.5%	2 1.6%	1 1.4%	1 1.2%	2 1.4%	2 2.8%	0 0	0 0	* 6.3%	0 0	4 1.4%	2 1.5%

Proportions/Means: Columns Tested (5% risk level) - A/B/D - C/D - E/F/G - H/I/J/K/L/M/N - P/Q
* small base; ** very small base (under 30) ineligible for sig testing

Table 203
Page 761

Outsell/Digital Library Federation Study (2002)
Weighted Tables

TABLE 80, continued

T7D/E_2. Print or hardcopy journals SUMMARY TABLE

	TOTAL SAMPLE	RESPONDENT TYPE: FACULTY MEMBER (A)	RESPONDENT TYPE: GRAD. STUDENT (B)	RESPONDENT TYPE: FACULTY /GRAD (C)	RESPONDENT TYPE: UNDER GRAD. STUDENT (D)	INSTITUTION TYPE: PUBLIC (E)	INSTITUTION TYPE: PRIVATE (F)	INSTITUTION TYPE: LIBERAL ARTS (G)	DISCIPLINE: BIOLOGIAL SCIENCES (H)	DISCIPLINE: PHYSICAL SCIENCES /MATH (I)	DISCIPLINE: SOCIAL SCIENCES (J)	DISCIPLINE: ARTS AND HUMAN. (K)	DISCIPLINE: ENGI- NEERING (L)	DISCIPLINE: BUSINESS (M)	DISCIPLINE: LAW (N)	DISCIPLINE: UNDEC. MAJOR	GENDER: MALE (P)	GENDER: FEMALE (Q)
Base - Use Print or hardcopy journals for teaching	425	321	105*	425	0**	148	162	115	65*	85*	133*	81*	12*	47*	3**	0*	288	137*
All sources of info	6 1.5%	6 1.9%	0 0	6 1.5%	0 0	* 0.1%	4 2.5%	2 1.6%	1 1.4%	1 1.2%	2 1.4%	2 2.8%	0 0	0 0	* 6.3%	0 0	4 1.4%	2 1.5%
preferred source of info	* *	* 0.1%	0 0	* *	0 0	* 0.1%	0 0	0 0	0 0	0 0	0 0	0 0	0 0	0 0	* 6.3%	0 0	0 0	* 0.1%
Home (NET)	6 1.4%	4 1.3%	2 1.8%	6 1.4%	0 0	2 1.3%	2 1.4%	2 1.6%	0 0	0 0	4 2.8%	2 2.8%	0 0	0 0	0 0	0 0	4 1.4%	2 1.4%
All sources of info	6 1.4%	4 1.3%	2 1.8%	6 1.4%	0 0	2 1.3%	2 1.4%	2 1.6%	0 0	0 0	4 2.8%	2 2.8%	0 0	0 0	0 0	0 0	4 1.4%	2 1.4%
preferred source of info	6 1.4%	4 1.3%	2 1.8%	6 1.4%	0 0	2 1.3%	2 1.4%	2 1.6%	0 0	0 0	4 2.8%	2 2.8%	0 0	0 0	0 0	0 0	4 1.4%	2 1.4%
Faculty (NET)	5 1.1%	0 0	5 4.3%A	5 1.1%	0 0	1 1.0%	3 1.9%	0 0	0 0	2 2.4%	0 0	2 2.8%	* 2.4%HJ	0 0	0 0	0 0	2 0.8%	2 1.5%
All sources of info	5 1.1%	0 0	5 4.3%A	5 1.1%	0 0	1 1.0%	3 1.9%	0 0	0 0	2 2.4%	0 0	2 2.8%	* 2.4%HJ	0 0	0 0	0 0	2 0.8%	2 1.5%
preferred source of info	5 1.1%	0 0	5 4.3%A	5 1.1%	0 0	1 1.0%	3 1.9%	0 0	0 0	2 2.4%	0 0	2 2.8%	* 2.4%HJ	0 0	0 0	0 0	2 0.8%	2 1.5%
Department (NET)	4 0.9%	3 0.9%	1 1.0%	4 0.9%	0 0	2 1.2%	1 0.6%	1 0.9%	1 1.4%	2 2.4%	0 0	0 0	0 0	1 2.0%	0 0	0 0	2 0.7%	2 1.4%

Proportions/Means: Columns Tested (5% risk level) - A/B/D - C/D - E/F/G - H/I/J/K/L/M/N - P/Q
* small base; ** very small base (under 30) ineligible for sig testing

Table 203
Page 762

Outsell/Digital Library Federation Study (2002)
Weighted Tables

TABLE 80, continued

T7D/E_2. Print or hardcopy journals SUMMARY TABLE

	RESPONDENT TYPE					INSTITUTION TYPE			DISCIPLINE									GENDER	
	TOTAL SAMPLE	FACULTY MEMBER	GRAD. STUDENT	FACULTY /GRAD	UNDER GRAD. STUDENT	PUBLIC	PRIVATE	LIBERAL ARTS	BIOLOGIAL SCIENCES	PHYSICAL SCIENCES /MATH	SOCIAL SCIENCES	ARTS AND HUMAN.	ENGI-NEERING	BUSINESS	LAW	UNDEC. MAJOR	MALE	FEMALE
		(A)	(B)	(C)	(D)	(E)	(F)	(G)	(H)	(I)	(J)	(K)	(L)	(M)	(N)		(P)	(Q)
Base - Use Print or hardcopy journals for teaching	425	321	105*	425	0**	148	162	115	65*	85*	133*	81*	12*	47*	3**	0*	288	137*
All sources of info	4 0.9%	3 0.9%	1 1.0%	4 0.9%	0 0	2 1.2%	1 0.6%	1 0.9%	1 1.4%	2 2.4%	0 0	0 0	0 0	1 2.0%	0 0	0 0	2 0.7%	2 1.4%
preferred source of info	0 0	0 0	0 0	0 0	0 0	0 0	0 0	0 0	0 0	0 0	0 0	0 0	0 0	0 0	0 0	0 0	0 0	0 0
Purchase from online bookstore (NET)	3 0.7%	3 0.9%	* 0.2%	3 0.7%	0 0	2 1.4%	* 0.1%	1 0.8%	2 2.7%	0 0	0 0	1 1.4%	0 0	0 0	* 6.3%	0 0	3 1.0%	* 0.1%
All sources of info	3 0.7%	3 0.9%	* 0.2%	3 0.7%	0 0	2 1.4%	* 0.1%	1 0.8%	2 2.7%	0 0	0 0	1 1.4%	0 0	0 0	* 6.3%	0 0	3 1.0%	* 0.1%
preferred source of info	1 0.2%	1 0.3%	* 0.2%	1 0.2%	0 0	1 0.6%	* 0.1%	0 0	1 1.4%	0 0	0 0	0 0	0 0	0 0	* 6.3%	0 0	1 0.3%	* 0.1%
Author	2 0.5%	2 0.6%	0 0	2 0.5%	0 0	1 0.6%	1 0.6%	0 0	0 0	1 1.2%	0 0	0 0	0 0	1 2.0%	0 0	0 0	2 0.7%	0 0
All sources of info	2 0.5%	2 0.6%	0 0	2 0.5%	0 0	1 0.6%	1 0.6%	0 0	0 0	1 1.2%	0 0	0 0	0 0	1 2.0%	0 0	0 0	2 0.7%	0 0
preferred source of info	1 0.2%	1 0.3%	0 0	1 0.2%	0 0	1 0.6%	0 0	0 0	0 0	0 0	0 0	0 0	0 0	1 2.0%	0 0	0 0	1 0.3%	0 0
Meeting/Conferences (NET)	1 0.2%	1 0.3%	0 0	1 0.2%	0 0	1 0.6%	0 0	0 0	0 0	0 0	0 0	0 0	0 0	1 2.0%	0 0	0 0	0 0	1 0.7%

Proportions/Means: Columns Tested (5% risk level) - A/B/D - C/D - E/F/G - H/I/J/K/L/M/N - P/Q
* small base; ** very small base (under 30) ineligible for sig testing

Table 203
Page 763

Outsell/Digital Library Federation Study (2002)
Weighted Tables

TABLE 80, continued

T7D/E_2. Print or hardcopy journals SUMMARY TABLE

		RESPONDENT TYPE				INSTITUTION TYPE			DISCIPLINE									GENDER	
	TOTAL SAMPLE	FACULTY MEMBER	GRAD. STUDENT	FACULTY /GRAD	UNDER GRAD. STUDENT	PUBLIC	PRIVATE	LIBERAL ARTS	BIOLOGIAL SCIENCES	PHYSICAL SCIENCES /MATH	SOCIAL SCIENCES	ARTS AND HUMAN.	ENGI-NEERING	BUSINESS	LAW	UNDEC. MAJOR	MALE	FEMALE
		(A)	(B)	(C)	(D)	(E)	(F)	(G)	(H)	(I)	(J)	(K)	(L)	(M)	(N)		(P)	(Q)
Base - Use Print or hardcopy journals for teaching	425	321	105*	425	0**	148	162	115	65*	85*	133*	81*	12*	47*	3**	0*	288	137*
All sources of info	1 0.2%	1 0.3%	0 0	1 0.2%	0 0	1 0.6%	0 0	0 0	0 0	0 0	0 0	0 0	0 0	1 2.0%	0 0	0 0	0 0	1 0.7%
preferred source of info	0 0	0 0	0 0	0 0	0 0	0 0	0 0	0 0	0 0	0 0	0 0	0 0	0 0	0 0	0 0	0 0	0 0	0 0
Access book/journal/ journal article elsewhere online (NET)	0 0	0 0	0 0	0 0	0 0	0 0	0 0	0 0	0 0	0 0	0 0	0 0	0 0	0 0	0 0	0 0	0 0	0 0
All sources of info	0 0	0 0	0 0	0 0	0 0	0 0	0 0	0 0	0 0	0 0	0 0	0 0	0 0	0 0	0 0	0 0	0 0	0 0
preferred source of info	0 0	0 0	0 0	0 0	0 0	0 0	0 0	0 0	0 0	0 0	0 0	0 0	0 0	0 0	0 0	0 0	0 0	0 0
Other (NET)	8 1.9%	5 1.5%	3 3.0%	8 1.9%	0 0	4 2.8%	3 1.8%	1 0.8%	1 1.4%	1 1.2%	4 2.8%	0 0	* 2.4%K	2 4.0%	* 6.3%	0 0	2 0.8%	6 4.1%P
All sources of info	7 1.7%	4 1.2%	3 3.0%	7 1.7%	0 0	3 2.2%	3 1.8%	1 0.8%	0 0	1 1.2%	4 2.8%	0 0	* 2.4%HK	2 4.0%	* 6.3%	0 0	2 0.8%	5 3.4%
preferred source of info	5 1.2%	2 0.6%	3 3.0%	5 1.2%	0 0	4 2.7%	1 0.6%	0 0	1 1.4%	1 1.2%	2 1.4%	0 0	* 2.4%K	1 2.0%	0 0	0 0	1 0.4%	4 2.7%

Proportions/Means: Columns Tested (5% risk level) - A/B/D - C/D - E/F/G - H/I/J/K/L/M/N - P/Q
* small base; ** very small base (under 30) ineligible for sig testing

Table 203
Page 764

Outsell/Digital Library Federation Study (2002)
Weighted Tables

TABLE 80, continued

T7D/E_2. Print or hardcopy journals SUMMARY TABLE

		RESPONDENT TYPE				INSTITUTION TYPE			DISCIPLINE								GENDER	
	TOTAL SAMPLE	FACULTY MEMBER	GRAD. STUDENT	FACULTY /GRAD	UNDER GRAD. STUDENT	PUBLIC	PRIVATE	LIBERAL ARTS	BIOLOGIAL SCIENCES	PHYSICAL SCIENCES /MATH	SOCIAL SCIENCES	ARTS AND HUMAN.	ENGI-NEERING	BUSINESS	LAW	UNDEC. MAJOR	MALE	FEMALE
		(A)	(B)	(C)	(D)	(E)	(F)	(G)	(H)	(I)	(J)	(K)	(L)	(M)	(N)		(P)	(Q)
Base - Use Print or hardcopy journals for teaching	425	321	105*	425	0**	148	162	115	65*	85*	133*	81*	12*	47*	3**	0*	288	137*
DK/Refused	7	4	3	7	0	7	0	0	1	1	2	3	0	0	0	0	4	3
	1.7%	1.3%	2.9%	1.7%	0	4.8%FG	0	0	1.4%	1.2%	1.4%	4.2%	0	0	0	0	1.5%	2.0%

Proportions/Means: Columns Tested (5% risk level) - A/B/D - C/D - E/F/G - H/I/J/K/L/M/N - P/Q
* small base; ** very small base (under 30) ineligible for sig testing

TABLE 81

S7sum_2. Print or hardcopy journals SUMMARY TABLE

		RESPONDENT TYPE				INSTITUTION TYPE			DISCIPLINE									GENDER	
	TOTAL SAMPLE	FACULTY MEMBER	GRAD. STUDENT	FACULTY /GRAD	UNDER GRAD. STUDENT	PUBLIC	PRIVATE	LIBERAL ARTS	BIOLOGIAL SCIENCES	PHYSICAL SCIENCES /MATH	SOCIAL SCIENCES	ARTS AND HUMAN.	ENGI-NEERING	BUSINESS	LAW	UNDEC. MAJOR	MALE	FEMALE
		(A)	(B)	(C)	(D)	(E)	(F)	(G)	(H)	(I)	(J)	(K)	(L)	(M)	(N)		(P)	(Q)
Base - Use Print or hardcopy journals for coursework	596	0**	318	318	279	294	132	170	86*	79*	209	110*	22*	60*	9*	21*	279	317
ONLINE	438	0	239	239	199	203	106	129	64	59	154	77	15	47	6	15	195	243
	73.4%	0	75.3%	75.3%	71.3%	69.0%	80.3%E	75.8%	74.5%	74.7%	73.9%	70.4%	66.2%	78.5%	68.6%	71.4%	69.8%	76.7%
Online library catalogues and finding aids (NET)	124	0	64	64	59	57	25	42	19	8	55	22	3	11	1	4	54	69
	20.8%	0	20.3%	20.3%	21.3%	19.3%	19.0%	24.5%	22.4%I	10.1%	26.1%IL	20.4%	13.0%	18.5%	15.7%	19.0%	19.4%	21.9%
All sources of info	124	0	64	64	59	57	25	42	19	8	55	22	3	11	1	4	54	69
	20.8%	0	20.3%	20.3%	21.3%	19.3%	19.0%	24.5%	22.4%I	10.1%	26.1%IL	20.4%	13.0%	18.5%	15.7%	19.0%	19.4%	21.9%
preferred source of info	101	0	55	55	46	52	16	33	15	5	51	16	2	7	1	4	41	60
	16.9%	0	17.2%	17.2%	16.6%	17.6%	11.9%	19.7%	17.3%I	6.3%	24.3%IL	14.3%	9.1%	12.3%	11.8%	19.0%	14.6%	19.0%
Your own institution's web site (NET)	109	0	51	51	58	42	26	42	16	16	28	29	2	9	1	7	44	65
	18.3%	0	16.0%	16.0%	20.9%	14.1%	19.4%	24.6%E	18.4%	20.3%	13.5%	26.5%JL	10.4%	15.4%	13.7%	33.3%	15.7%	20.5%
All sources of info	109	0	51	51	58	42	26	42	16	16	28	29	2	9	1	7	44	65
	18.3%	0	16.0%	16.0%	20.9%	14.1%	19.4%	24.6%E	18.4%	20.3%	13.5%	26.5%JL	10.4%	15.4%	13.7%	33.3%	15.7%	20.5%
preferred source of info	85	0	45	45	40	35	21	29	13	15	19	24	1	8	1	4	34	51
	14.3%	0	14.2%	14.2%	14.4%	12.1%	15.8%	17.1%	15.3%	19.0%JL	9.0%	21.4%JL	6.5%	13.8%	11.8%	19.0%	12.3%	16.1%
Online databases (NET)	94	0	58	58	36	32	36	25	16	12	32	19	2	9	3	1	38	55
	15.7%	0	18.2%	18.2%	12.9%	11.0%	27.4%EG	15.0%	18.4%	15.2%	15.3%	17.3%	9.1%	15.4%	31.4%IJK LM	4.8%	13.8%	17.5%

Proportions/Means: Columns Tested (5% risk level) - A/B/D - C/D - E/F/G - H/I/J/K/L/M/N - P/Q
* small base; ** very small base (under 30) ineligible for sig testing

Table 328
Page 1343

Outsell/Digital Library Federation Study (2002)
Weighted Tables

TABLE 81, continued

S7sum_2. Print or hardcopy journals SUMMARY TABLE

	TOTAL SAMPLE	RESPONDENT TYPE: FACULTY MEMBER (A)	GRAD. STUDENT (B)	FACULTY /GRAD (C)	UNDER GRAD. STUDENT (D)	INSTITUTION TYPE: PUBLIC (E)	PRIVATE (F)	LIBERAL ARTS (G)	DISCIPLINE: BIOLOGIAL SCIENCES (H)	PHYSICAL SCIENCES /MATH (I)	SOCIAL SCIENCES (J)	ARTS AND HUMAN. (K)	ENGI-NEERING (L)	BUSINESS (M)	LAW (N)	UNDEC. MAJOR	GENDER: MALE (P)	FEMALE (Q)
Base - Use Print or hardcopy journals for coursework	596	0**	318	318	279	294	132	170	86*	79*	209	110*	22*	60*	9*	21*	279	317
All sources of info	94 15.7%	0 0	58 18.2%	58 18.2%	36 12.9%	32 11.0%	36 27.4%EG	25 15.0%	16 18.4%	12 15.2%	32 15.3%	19 17.3%	2 9.1%	9 15.4%	3 31.4%IJK LM	1 4.8%	38 13.8%	55 17.5%
preferred source of info	56 9.3%	0 0	38 11.8%D	38 11.8%D	18 6.5%	21 7.0%	23 17.4%EG	12 7.1%	6 7.1%	11 13.9%	23 10.8%	7 6.1%	1 6.5%	6 9.2%	2 23.5%HJKLM	0 0	19 6.8%	36 11.5%
Search engine (NET)	78 13.0%	0 0	37 11.7%	37 11.7%	41 14.5%	25 8.4%	20 15.4%E	33 19.3%E	10 11.2%	11 13.9%	21 9.9%	17 15.3%	4 16.9%	12 20.0%	1 7.8%	3 14.3%	46 16.5%Q	32 9.9%
All sources of info	78 13.0%	0 0	37 11.7%	37 11.7%	41 14.5%	25 8.4%	20 15.4%E	33 19.3%E	10 11.2%	11 13.9%	21 9.9%	17 15.3%	4 16.9%	12 20.0%	1 7.8%	3 14.3%	46 16.5%Q	32 9.9%
preferred source of info	35 5.9%	0 0	20 6.4%	20 6.4%	15 5.3%	17 5.8%	7 5.5%	11 6.5%	4 4.1%	8 10.1%K	11 5.4%	1 1.0%	3 11.7%HK	7 12.3%K	* 2.0%	1 4.8%	22 7.9%	13 4.1%
Internet searches (NET)	54 9.0%	0 0	24 7.6%	24 7.6%	30 10.6%	35 12.0%	8 6.1%	10 6.1%	8 9.2%	9 11.4%	17 8.1%	9 8.2%	2 9.1%	7 12.3%	1 5.9%	1 4.8%	26 9.5%	27 8.6%
All sources of info	54 9.0%	0 0	24 7.6%	24 7.6%	30 10.6%	35 12.0%	8 6.1%	10 6.1%	8 9.2%	9 11.4%	17 8.1%	9 8.2%	2 9.1%	7 12.3%	1 5.9%	1 4.8%	26 9.5%	27 8.6%
preferred source of info	29 4.9%	0 0	13 4.1%	13 4.1%	16 5.9%	24 8.2%FG	3 2.4%	2 1.2%	4 4.1%	4 5.1%	9 4.5%	4 4.1%	2 7.8%	5 7.7%	1 5.9%	1 4.8%	14 5.2%	15 4.7%
Web directory/ subject related web site (NET)	45 7.5%	0 0	24 7.5%	24 7.5%	21 7.6%	18 6.0%	15 11.2%	12 7.3%	9 10.2%	5 6.3%	15 7.2%	6 5.1%	2 9.1%	7 10.8%	1 11.8%	1 4.8%	21 7.5%	24 7.6%

Proportions/Means: Columns Tested (5% risk level) - A/B/D - C/D - E/F/G - H/I/J/K/L/M/N - P/Q
* small base; ** very small base (under 30) ineligible for sig testing

Table 328
Page 1344

Outsell/Digital Library Federation Study (2002)
Weighted Tables

TABLE 81, continued

S7sum_2. Print or hardcopy journals SUMMARY TABLE

		RESPONDENT TYPE				INSTITUTION TYPE			DISCIPLINE								GENDER	
	TOTAL SAMPLE	FACULTY MEMBER	GRAD. STUDENT	FACULTY /GRAD	UNDER GRAD. STUDENT	PUBLIC	PRIVATE	LIBERAL ARTS	BIOLOGIAL SCIENCES	PHYSICAL SCIENCES /MATH	SOCIAL SCIENCES	ARTS AND HUMAN.	ENGI-NEERING	BUSINESS	LAW	UNDEC. MAJOR	MALE	FEMALE
		(A)	(B)	(C)	(D)	(E)	(F)	(G)	(H)	(I)	(J)	(K)	(L)	(M)	(N)		(P)	(Q)
Base - Use Print or hardcopy journals for coursework	596	0**	318	318	279	294	132	170	86*	79*	209	110*	22*	60*	9*	21*	279	317
All sources of info	45	0	24	24	21	18	15	12	9	5	15	6	2	7	1	1	21	24
	7.5%	0	7.5%	7.5%	7.6%	6.0%	11.2%	7.3%	10.2%	6.3%	7.2%	5.1%	9.1%	10.8%	11.8%	4.8%	7.5%	7.6%
preferred source of info	30	0	16	16	14	13	9	9	6	1	15	2	2	4	1	0	14	17
	5.1%	0	5.1%	5.1%	5.1%	4.3%	6.5%	5.4%	7.1%	1.3%	7.2%	2.0%	7.8%IK	6.2%	5.9%	0	4.9%	5.3%
Department web page (NET)	20	0	10	10	10	11	2	7	5	3	6	2	2	1	0	1	10	10
	3.4%	0	3.2%	3.2%	3.6%	3.9%	1.4%	4.0%	6.1%	3.8%	2.7%	2.0%	9.1%JKMN	1.5%	0	4.8%	3.8%	3.0%
All sources of info	20	0	10	10	10	11	2	7	5	3	6	2	2	1	0	1	10	10
	3.4%	0	3.2%	3.2%	3.6%	3.9%	1.4%	4.0%	6.1%	3.8%	2.7%	2.0%	9.1%JKMN	1.5%	0	4.8%	3.8%	3.0%
preferred source of info	13	0	8	8	5	8	2	3	4	2	2	2	2	1	0	0	7	6
	2.2%	0	2.5%	2.5%	1.9%	2.9%	1.4%	1.7%	5.1%J	2.5%	0.9%	2.0%	7.8%JKM	1.5%	0	0	2.7%	1.8%
Online abstracting and indexing services (NET)	17	0	10	10	7	6	9	2	3	3	6	4	*	1	*	0	7	10
	2.9%	0	3.2%	3.2%	2.5%	2.0%	7.0%EG	1.2%	3.1%	3.8%	2.7%	4.1%	1.3%	1.5%	3.9%	0	2.6%	3.1%
All sources of info	17	0	10	10	7	6	9	2	3	3	6	4	*	1	*	0	7	10
	2.9%	0	3.2%	3.2%	2.5%	2.0%	7.0%EG	1.2%	3.1%	3.8%	2.7%	4.1%	1.3%	1.5%	3.9%	0	2.6%	3.1%
preferred source of info	8	0	6	6	2	4	4	0	3	2	2	0	0	1	*	0	4	4
	1.3%	0	1.8%	1.8%	0.7%	1.3%	2.9%G	0	3.1%	2.5%	0.9%	0	0	1.5%	2.0%K	0	1.4%	1.2%
Online reference service (NET)	11	0	6	6	5	7	2	2	2	1	4	0	0	2	*	2	7	4
	1.8%	0	1.8%	1.8%	1.7%	2.2%	1.5%	1.2%	2.0%	1.3%	1.8%	0	0	3.1%	2.0%K	9.5%	2.4%	1.2%

Proportions/Means: Columns Tested (5% risk level) - A/B/D - C/D - E/F/G - H/I/J/K/L/M/N - P/Q
* small base; ** very small base (under 30) ineligible for sig testing

Table 328
Page 1345

Outsell/Digital Library Federation Study (2002)
Weighted Tables

TABLE 81, continued

S7sum_2. Print or hardcopy journals SUMMARY TABLE

		RESPONDENT TYPE				INSTITUTION TYPE			DISCIPLINE									GENDER	
	TOTAL SAMPLE	FACULTY MEMBER	GRAD. STUDENT	FACULTY /GRAD	UNDER GRAD. STUDENT	PUBLIC	PRIVATE	LIBERAL ARTS	BIOLOGIAL SCIENCES	PHYSICAL SCIENCES /MATH	SOCIAL SCIENCES	ARTS AND HUMAN.	ENGI-NEERING	BUSINESS	LAW	UNDEC. MAJOR	MALE	FEMALE
		(A)	(B)	(C)	(D)	(E)	(F)	(G)	(H)	(I)	(J)	(K)	(L)	(M)	(N)		(P)	(Q)
Base - Use Print or hardcopy journals for coursework	596	0**	318	318	279	294	132	170	86*	79*	209	110*	22*	60*	9*	21*	279	317
All sources of info	11 1.8%	0 0	6 1.8%	6 1.8%	5 1.7%	7 2.2%	2 1.5%	2 1.2%	2 2.0%	1 1.3%	4 1.8%	0 0	0 0	2 3.1%	* 2.0%K	2 9.5%	7 2.4%	4 1.2%
preferred source of info	5 0.8%	0 0	2 0.6%	2 0.6%	3 1.0%	4 1.3%	1 0.7%	0 0	1 1.0%	0 0	2 0.9%	0 0	0 0	2 3.1%	* 2.0%IK	0 0	4 1.4%	1 0.3%
Your own personal electronic library/files (NET)	6 1.1%	0 0	4 1.4%	4 1.4%	2 0.7%	5 1.8%	0 0	1 0.6%	0 0	2 2.5%	2 0.9%	0 0	1 2.6%HK	1 1.5%	0 0	1 4.8%	5 1.9%	1 0.3%
All sources of info	6 1.1%	0 0	4 1.4%	4 1.4%	2 0.7%	5 1.8%	0 0	1 0.6%	0 0	2 2.5%	2 0.9%	0 0	1 2.6%HK	1 1.5%	0 0	1 4.8%	5 1.9%	1 0.3%
preferred source of info	3 0.6%	0 0	2 0.7%	2 0.7%	1 0.4%	2 0.8%	0 0	1 0.6%	0 0	2 2.5%J	0 0	0 0	* 1.3%J	0 0	0 0	1 4.8%	2 0.8%	1 0.3%
Online bookstore (NET)	5 0.8%	0 0	5 1.6%	5 1.6%	0 0	3 1.0%	2 1.6%	0 0	0 0	0 0	2 0.9%	2 2.0%	0 0	1 1.5%	0 0	0 0	3 1.1%	2 0.6%
All sources of info	5 0.8%	0 0	5 1.6%	5 1.6%	0 0	3 1.0%	2 1.6%	0 0	0 0	0 0	2 0.9%	2 2.0%	0 0	1 1.5%	0 0	0 0	3 1.1%	2 0.6%
preferred source of info	0 0	0 0	0 0	0 0	0 0	0 0	0 0	0 0	0 0	0 0	0 0	0 0	0 0	0 0	0 0	0 0	0 0	0 0
E-mail listservs (NET)	0 0	0 0	0 0	0 0	0 0	0 0	0 0	0 0	0 0	0 0	0 0	0 0	0 0	0 0	0 0	0 0	0 0	0 0

Proportions/Means: Columns Tested (5% risk level) - A/B/D - C/D - E/F/G - H/I/J/K/L/M/N - P/Q
* small base; ** very small base (under 30) ineligible for sig testing

Table 328
Page 1346

Outsell/Digital Library Federation Study (2002)
Weighted Tables

TABLE 81, continued

S7sum_2. Print or hardcopy journals SUMMARY TABLE

		RESPONDENT TYPE				INSTITUTION TYPE			DISCIPLINE									GENDER	
	TOTAL SAMPLE	FACULTY MEMBER	GRAD. STUDENT	FACULTY /GRAD	UNDER GRAD. STUDENT	PUBLIC	PRIVATE	LIBERAL ARTS	BIOLOGIAL SCIENCES	PHYSICAL SCIENCES /MATH	SOCIAL SCIENCES	ARTS AND HUMAN.	ENGI-NEERING	BUSINESS	LAW	UNDEC. MAJOR	MALE	FEMALE
		(A)	(B)	(C)	(D)	(E)	(F)	(G)	(H)	(I)	(J)	(K)	(L)	(M)	(N)		(P)	(Q)
Base - Use Print or hardcopy journals for coursework	596	0**	318	318	279	294	132	170	86*	79*	209	110*	22*	60*	9*	21*	279	317
All sources of info	0 0	0 0	0 0	0 0	0 0	0 0	0 0	0 0	0 0	0 0	0 0	0 0	0 0	0 0	0 0	0 0	0 0	0 0
preferred source of info	0 0	0 0	0 0	0 0	0 0	0 0	0 0	0 0	0 0	0 0	0 0	0 0	0 0	0 0	0 0	0 0	0 0	0 0
PERSONAL ASSISTANCE	193 32.4%	0 0	81 25.4%	81 25.4%	112 40.3%B C	84 28.5%	41 31.3%	68 39.8%E	23 26.5%	22 27.8%	58 27.9%	43 38.8%	9 39.0%	23 38.5%	2 25.5%	13 61.9%	95 33.9%	98 31.0%
A librarian in your institution (NET)	135 22.6%	0 0	37 11.5%	37 11.5%	98 35.2%B C	54 18.5%	22 16.8%	58 34.2%EF	18 20.4%	10 12.7%	45 21.6%L	30 27.6%ILN	2 9.1%	20 32.3%IL N	1 11.8%	9 42.9%	61 21.7%	74 23.4%
All sources of info	135 22.6%	0 0	37 11.5%	37 11.5%	98 35.2%B C	54 18.5%	22 16.8%	58 34.2%EF	18 20.4%	10 12.7%	45 21.6%L	30 27.6%ILN	2 9.1%	20 32.3%IL N	1 11.8%	9 42.9%	61 21.7%	74 23.4%
preferred source of info	64 10.8%	0 0	9 3.0%	9 3.0%	55 19.6%B C	30 10.1%F	5 3.6%	30 17.4%EF	8 9.2%	3 3.8%	24 11.7%	13 12.2%IL	1 2.6%	8 13.8%IL	* 3.9%	6 28.6%	31 11.2%	33 10.4%
Faculty members inside your institution (NET)	99 16.7%	0 0	52 16.5%	52 16.5%	47 16.9%	40 13.8%	27 20.3%	32 19.0%	12 14.3%	14 17.7%	23 10.8%	25 22.4%J	7 32.5%HIJ M	11 18.5%	2 17.6%	6 28.6%	45 16.2%	54 17.1%
All sources of info	99 16.7%	0 0	52 16.5%	52 16.5%	47 16:9%	40 13.8%	27 20.3%	32 19.0%	12 14.3%	14 17.7%	23 10.8%	25 22.4%J	7 32.5%HIJ M	11 18.5%	2 17.6%	6 28.6%	45 16.2%	54 17.1%

Proportions/Means: Columns Tested (5% risk level) - A/B/D - C/D - E/F/G - H/I/J/K/L/M/N - P/Q
* small base; ** very small base (under 30) ineligible for sig testing

Table 328
Page 1347

Outsell/Digital Library Federation Study (2002)
Weighted Tables

TABLE 81, continued

S7sum_2. Print or hardcopy journals SUMMARY TABLE

	TOTAL SAMPLE	RESPONDENT TYPE: FACULTY MEMBER	GRAD. STUDENT	FACULTY /GRAD	UNDER GRAD. STUDENT	INSTITUTION TYPE: PUBLIC	PRIVATE	LIBERAL ARTS	DISCIPLINE: BIOLOGIAL SCIENCES	PHYSICAL SCIENCES /MATH	SOCIAL SCIENCES	ARTS AND HUMAN.	ENGI-NEERING	BUSINESS	LAW	UNDEC. MAJOR	GENDER: MALE	FEMALE
		(A)	(B)	(C)	(D)	(E)	(F)	(G)	(H)	(I)	(J)	(K)	(L)	(M)	(N)		(P)	(Q)
Base - Use Print or hardcopy journals for coursework	596	0**	318	318	279	294	132	170	86*	79*	209	110*	22*	60*	9*	21*	279	317
preferred source of info	41 6.8%	0 0	27 8.4%	27 8.4%	14 5.0%	19 6.6%	13 9.7%	8 4.9%	4 4.1%	8 10.1%J	6 2.7%	12 11.2%J	5 20.8%HIJM	4 6.2%	1 7.8%	2 9.5%	22 7.8%	19 5.9%
Other students inside your institution (NET)	28 4.7%	0 0	21 6.5%	21 6.5%	7 2.7%	10 3.4%	11 8.3%E	7 4.2%	2 2.0%	6 7.6%	8 3.6%	4 4.1%	1 6.5%	5 7.7%	* 2.0%	2 9.5%	13 4.7%	15 4.7%
All sources of info	28 4.7%	0 0	21 6.5%	21 6.5%	7 2.7%	10 3.4%	11 8.3%E	7 4.2%	2 2.0%	6 7.6%	8 3.6%	4 4.1%	1 6.5%	5 7.7%	* 2.0%	2 9.5%	13 4.7%	15 4.7%
preferred source of info	5 0.8%	0 0	4 1.3%	4 1.3%	1 0.4%	1 0.3%	3 2.3%	1 0.6%	1 1.0%	4 5.1%JK	0 0	0 0	0 0	0 0	* 2.0%JKM	0 0	5 1.7%Q	* 0.1%
Faculty members outside your institution (NET)	4 0.7%	0 0	4 1.3%	4 1.3%	0 0	3 1.0%	1 0.8%	0 0	0 0	0 0	2 0.9%	2 2.0%	0 0	0 0	0 0	0 0	1 0.4%	3 0.9%
All sources of info	4 0.7%	0 0	4 1.3%	4 1.3%	0 0	3 1.0%	1 0.8%	0 0	0 0	0 0	2 0.9%	2 2.0%	0 0	0 0	0 0	0 0	1 0.4%	3 0.9%
preferred source of info	0 0	0 0	0 0	0 0	0 0	0 0	0 0	0 0	0 0	0 0	0 0	0 0	0 0	0 0	0 0	0 0	0 0	0 0
Other students outside your institution (NET)	2 0.3%	0 0	2 0.6%	2 0.6%	0 0	2 0.6%	0 0	0 0	0 0	0 0	2 0.9%	0 0	0 0	0 0	0 0	0 0	0 0	2 0.6%
All sources of info	2 0.3%	0 0	2 0.6%	2 0.6%	0 0	2 0.6%	0 0	0 0	0 0	0 0	2 0.9%	0 0	0 0	0 0	0 0	0 0	0 0	2 0.6%

Proportions/Means: Columns Tested (5% risk level) - A/B/D - C/D - E/F/G - H/I/J/K/L/M/N - P/Q
* small base; ** very small base (under 30) ineligible for sig testing

Table 328
Page 1348

Outsell/Digital Library Federation Study (2002)
Weighted Tables

TABLE 81, continued

S7sum_2. Print or hardcopy journals SUMMARY TABLE

		RESPONDENT TYPE				INSTITUTION TYPE			DISCIPLINE									GENDER	
	TOTAL SAMPLE	FACULTY MEMBER	GRAD. STUDENT	FACULTY /GRAD	UNDER GRAD. STUDENT	PUBLIC	PRIVATE	LIBERAL ARTS	BIOLOGIAL SCIENCES	PHYSICAL SCIENCES /MATH	SOCIAL SCIENCES	ARTS AND HUMAN.	ENGI-NEERING	BUSINESS	LAW	UNDEC. MAJOR	MALE	FEMALE
		(A)	(B)	(C)	(D)	(E)	(F)	(G)	(H)	(I)	(J)	(K)	(L)	(M)	(N)		(P)	(Q)
Base - Use Print or hardcopy journals for coursework	596	0**	318	318	279	294	132	170	86*	79*	209	110*	22*	60*	9*	21*	279	317
preferred source of info	0 0	0 0	0 0	0 0	0 0	0 0	0 0	0 0	0 0	0 0	0 0	0 0	0 0	0 0	0 0	0 0	0 0	0 0
Another institution's librarian (NET)	1 0.2%	0 0	0 0	0 0	1 0.4%	0 0	0 0	1 0.6%	0 0	1 1.3%	0 0	0 0	0 0	0 0	0 0	0 0	1 0.4%	0 0
All sources of info	1 0.2%	0 0	0 0	0 0	1 0.4%	0 0	0 0	1 0.6%	0 0	1 1.3%	0 0	0 0	0 0	0 0	0 0	0 0	1 0.4%	0 0
preferred source of info	0 0	0 0	0 0	0 0	0 0	0 0	0 0	0 0	0 0	0 0	0 0	0 0	0 0	0 0	0 0	0 0	0 0	0 0
Professional meetings (NET)	0 0	0 0	0 0	0 0	0 0	0 0	0 0	0 0	0 0	0 0	0 0	0 0	0 0	0 0	0 0	0 0	0 0	0 0
All sources of info	0 0	0 0	0 0	0 0	0 0	0 0	0 0	0 0	0 0	0 0	0 0	0 0	0 0	0 0	0 0	0 0	0 0	0 0
preferred source of info	0 0	0 0	0 0	0 0	0 0	0 0	0 0	0 0	0 0	0 0	0 0	0 0	0 0	0 0	0 0	0 0	0 0	0 0
LIBRARY FACILITIES/ PRINT	174 29.1%	0 0	98 30.8%	98 30.8%	76 27.1%	70 23.8%	50 38.1%E	53 31.4%	20 23.5%	23 29.1%	60 28.8%	41 37.8%H	8 33.8%	14 23.1%	3 37.3%	4 19.0%	95 33.9%Q	79 24.9%
Campus library (NET)	152 25.5%	0 0	85 26.8%	85 26.8%	67 24.1%	63 21.3%	41 31.1%E	49 28.6%	18 20.4%	22 27.8%	51 24.3%	38 34.7%HM	7 32.5%M	10 16.9%	2 27.5%	4 19.0%	84 30.1%Q	68 21.5%

Proportions/Means: Columns Tested (5% risk level) - A/B/D - C/D - E/F/G - H/I/J/K/L/M/N - P/Q
* small base; ** very small base (under 30) ineligible for sig testing

Table 328
Page 1349

Outsell/Digital Library Federation Study (2002)
Weighted Tables

TABLE 81, continued

S7sum_2. Print or hardcopy journals SUMMARY TABLE

	TOTAL SAMPLE	FACULTY MEMBER (A)	GRAD. STUDENT (B)	FACULTY /GRAD (C)	UNDER GRAD. STUDENT (D)	PUBLIC (E)	PRIVATE (F)	LIBERAL ARTS (G)	BIOLOGIAL SCIENCES (H)	PHYSICAL SCIENCES /MATH (I)	SOCIAL SCIENCES (J)	ARTS AND HUMAN. (K)	ENGI-NEERING (L)	BUSINESS (M)	LAW (N)	UNDEC. MAJOR	MALE (P)	FEMALE (Q)
		RESPONDENT TYPE				INSTITUTION TYPE			DISCIPLINE								GENDER	
Base - Use Print or hardcopy journals for coursework	596	0**	318	318	279	294	132	170	86*	79*	209	110*	22*	60*	9*	21*	279	317
All sources of info	152 25.5%	0 0	85 26.8%	85 26.8%	67 24.1%	63 21.3%	41 31.1%E	49 28.6%	18 20.4%	22 27.8%	51 24.3%	38 34.7%HM	7 32.5%M	10 16.9%	2 27.5%	4 19.0%	84 30.1%Q	68 21.5%
preferred source of info	82 13.8%	0 0	45 14.3%	45 14.3%	37 13.2%	41 13.9%	13 9.8%	28 16.6%	10 11.2%	12 15.2%	32 15.3%	19 17.3%M	3 15.6%M	4 6.2%	1 13.7%	1 4.8%	43 15.3%	39 12.4%
References cited in books or journal articles (NET)	12 2.0%	0 0	10 3.1%	10 3.1%	2 0.7%	5 1.7%	7 5.1%G	0 0	1 1.0%	1 1.3%	8 3.6%	2 2.0%	0 0	0 0	0 0	0 0	2 0.8%	10 3.0%
All sources of info	12 2.0%	0 0	10 3.1%	10 3.1%	2 0.7%	5 1.7%	7 5.1%G	0 0	1 1.0%	1 1.3%	8 3.6%	2 2.0%	0 0	0 0	0 0	0 0	2 0.8%	10 3.0%
preferred source of info	4 0.7%	0 0	4 1.2%	4 1.2%	0 0	1 0.4%	3 2.1%	0 0	1 1.0%	0 0	2 0.9%	1 1.0%	0 0	0 0	0 0	0 0	1 0.4%	3 0.9%
Your own personal physical library/ files/bookshelves (NET)	8 1.3%	0 0	8 2.4%D	8 2.4%D	0 0	2 0.7%	5 4.1%EG	0 0	1 1.0%	1 1.3%	2 0.9%	3 3.1%	* 1.3%	0 0	* 2.0%M	0 0	8 2.7%Q	0 0
All sources of info	8 1.3%	0 0	8 2.4%D	8 2.4%D	0 0	2 0.7%	5 4.1%EG	0 0	1 1.0%	1 1.3%	2 0.9%	3 3.1%	* 1.3%	0 0	* 2.0%M	0 0	8 2.7%Q	0 0
preferred source of info	4 0.6%	0 0	4 1.1%	4 1.1%	0 0	0 0	4 2.7%EG	0 0	0 0	0 0	0 0	3 3.1%J	0 0	0 0	* 2.0%HIJM	0 0	4 1.3%	0 0

Proportions/Means: Columns Tested (5% risk level) - A/B/D - C/D - E/F/G - H/I/J/K/L/M/N - P/Q
* small base; ** very small base (under 30) ineligible for sig testing

Table 328
Page 1350

Outsell/Digital Library Federation Study (2002)
Weighted Tables

TABLE 81, continued

S7sum_2. Print or hardcopy journals SUMMARY TABLE

		RESPONDENT TYPE				INSTITUTION TYPE			DISCIPLINE								GENDER	
	TOTAL SAMPLE	FACULTY MEMBER	GRAD. STUDENT	FACULTY /GRAD	UNDER GRAD. STUDENT	PUBLIC	PRIVATE	LIBERAL ARTS	BIOLOGIAL SCIENCES	PHYSICAL SCIENCES /MATH	SOCIAL SCIENCES	ARTS AND HUMAN.	ENGI-NEERING	BUSINESS	LAW	UNDEC. MAJOR	MALE	FEMALE
		(A)	(B)	(C)	(D)	(E)	(F)	(G)	(H)	(I)	(J)	(K)	(L)	(M)	(N)		(P)	(Q)
Base - Use Print or hardcopy journals for coursework	596	0**	318	318	279	294	132	170	86*	79*	209	110*	22*	60*	9*	21*	279	317
Physical bookstore (NET)	6 1.1%	0 0	5 1.6%	5 1.6%	1 0.4%	5 1.8%	1 0.8%	0 0	1 1.0%	1 1.3%	2 0.9%	1 1.0%	* 1.3%	1 1.5%	* 2.0%	0 0	4 1.6%	2 0.6%
All sources of info	6 1.1%	0 0	5 1.6%	5 1.6%	1 0.4%	5 1.8%	1 0.8%	0 0	1 1.0%	1 1.3%	2 0.9%	1 1.0%	* 1.3%	1 1.5%	* 2.0%	0 0	4 1.6%	2 0.6%
preferred source of info	3 0.5%	0 0	2 0.6%	2 0.6%	1 0.4%	2 0.7%	1 0.8%	0 0	1 1.0%	0 0	0 0	1 1.0%	0 0	1 1.5%	* 2.0%IJ	0 0	2 0.8%	1 0.3%
Another library (NET)	5 0.9%	0 0	1 0.4%	1 0.4%	4 1.4%	1 0.5%	2 1.4%	2 1.2%	0 0	0 0	2 0.9%	2 2.0%	* 1.3%	0 0	0 0	1 4.8%	1 0.5%	4 1.3%
All sources of info	5 0.9%	0 0	1 0.4%	1 0.4%	4 1.4%	1 0.5%	2 1.4%	2 1.2%	0 0	0 0	2 0.9%	2 2.0%	* 1.3%	0 0	0 0	1 4.8%	1 0.5%	4 1.3%
preferred source of info	2 0.3%	0 0	0 0	0 0	2 0.7%	0 0	2 1.4%	0 0	0 0	0 0	2 0.9%	0 0	0 0	0 0	0 0	0 0	0 0	2 0.6%
Printed abstracting and indexing services (NET)	5 0.9%	0 0	1 0.4%	1 0.4%	4 1.3%	1 0.4%	* 0.1%	4 2.2%	1 1.0%	0 0	4 1.8%	0 0	0 0	0 0	1 5.9%HIKLM	0 0	3 1.1%	2 0.6%
All sources of info	5 0.9%	0 0	1 0.4%	1 0.4%	4 1.3%	1 0.4%	* 0.1%	4 2.2%	1 1.0%	0 0	4 1.8%	0 0	0 0	0 0	1 5.9%HIKLM	0 0	3 1.1%	2 0.6%
preferred source of info	0 0	0 0	0 0	0 0	0 0	0 0	0 0	0 0	0 0	0 0	0 0	0 0	0 0	0 0	0 0	0 0	0 0	0 0

Proportions/Means: Columns Tested (5% risk level) - A/B/D - C/D - E/F/G - H/I/J/K/L/M/N - P/Q
* small base; ** very small base (under 30) ineligible for sig testing

Table 328
Page 1351

Outsell/Digital Library Federation Study (2002)
Weighted Tables

TABLE 81, continued

S7sum_2. Print or hardcopy journals SUMMARY TABLE

		RESPONDENT TYPE				INSTITUTION TYPE			DISCIPLINE									GENDER	
	TOTAL SAMPLE	FACULTY MEMBER	GRAD. STUDENT	FACULTY /GRAD	UNDER GRAD. STUDENT	PUBLIC	PRIVATE	LIBERAL ARTS	BIOLOGIAL SCIENCES	PHYSICAL SCIENCES /MATH	SOCIAL SCIENCES	ARTS AND HUMAN.	ENGI-NEERING	BUSINESS	LAW	UNDEC. MAJOR	MALE	FEMALE
		(A)	(B)	(C)	(D)	(E)	(F)	(G)	(H)	(I)	(J)	(K)	(L)	(M)	(N)		(P)	(Q)
Base - Use Print or hardcopy journals for coursework	596	0**	318	318	279	294	132	170	86*	79*	209	110*	22*	60*	9*	21*	279	317
Printed library catalogues and finding aids (NET)	4 0.6%	0 0	2 0.6%	2 0.6%	2 0.6%	2 0.6%	1 0.8%	1 0.5%	2 2.0%	0 0	0 0	0 0	0 0	2 3.1%J	* 2.0%IJK	0 0	3 1.0%	1 0.3%
All sources of info	4 0.6%	0 0	2 0.6%	2 0.6%	2 0.6%	2 0.6%	1 0.8%	1 0.5%	2 2.0%	0 0	0 0	0 0	0 0	2 3.1%J	* 2.0%IJK	0 0	3 1.0%	1 0.3%
preferred source of info	2 0.3%	0 0	1 0.3%	1 0.3%	1 0.3%	2 0.6%	0 0	0 0	2 2.0%	0 0	0 0	0 0	0 0	0 0	0 0	0 0	1 0.3%	1 0.3%
Personal subscriptions to newspapers, magazines and journals (NET)	1 0.2%	0 0	1 0.3%	1 0.3%	0 0	0 0	1 0.8%	0 0	0 0	0 0	0 0	0 0	0 0	1 1.5%	* 2.0%HIJK	0 0	1 0.4%	0 0
All sources of info	1 0.2%	0 0	1 0.3%	1 0.3%	0 0	0 0	1 0.8%	0 0	0 0	0 0	0 0	0 0	0 0	1 1.5%	* 2.0%HIJK	0 0	1 0.4%	0 0
preferred source of info	0 0	0 0	0 0	0 0	0 0	0 0	0 0	0 0	0 0	0 0	0 0	0 0	0 0	0 0	0 0	0 0	0 0	0 0
Other (NET)	24 4.0%	0 0	16 4.9%	16 4.9%	8 2.9%	12 4.2%	6 4.5%	5 3.1%	4 4.1%	4 5.1%	8 3.6%	3 3.1%	* 1.3%	4 6.2%	* 2.0%	1 4.8%	11 3.9%	13 4.0%
All sources of info	24 4.0%	0 0	16 4.9%	16 4.9%	8 2.9%	12 4.2%	6 4.5%	5 3.1%	4 4.1%	4 5.1%	8 3.6%	3 3.1%	* 1.3%	4 6.2%	* 2.0%	1 4.8%	11 3.9%	13 4.0%

Proportions/Means: Columns Tested (5% risk level) - A/B/D - C/D - E/F/G - H/I/J/K/L/M/N - P/Q
* small base; ** very small base (under 30) ineligible for sig testing

Table 328
Page 1352

Outsell/Digital Library Federation Study (2002)
Weighted Tables

TABLE 81, continued

S7sum_2. Print or hardcopy journals SUMMARY TABLE

		RESPONDENT TYPE				INSTITUTION TYPE			DISCIPLINE									GENDER	
	TOTAL SAMPLE	FACULTY MEMBER	GRAD. STUDENT	FACULTY /GRAD	UNDER GRAD. STUDENT	PUBLIC	PRIVATE	LIBERAL ARTS	BIOLOGIAL SCIENCES	PHYSICAL SCIENCES /MATH	SOCIAL SCIENCES	ARTS AND HUMAN.	ENGI-NEERING	BUSINESS	LAW	UNDEC. MAJOR	MALE	FEMALE
		(A)	(B)	(C)	(D)	(E)	(F)	(G)	(H)	(I)	(J)	(K)	(L)	(M)	(N)		(P)	(Q)
Base - Use Print or hardcopy journals for coursework	596	0**	318	318	279	294	132	170	86*	79*	209	110*	22*	60*	9*	21*	279	317
preferred source of info	12	0	9	9	3	8	3	1	4	1	4	2	*	1	*	0	5	7
	2.0%	0	2.8%	2.8%	1.1%	2.6%	2.4%	0.7%	4.1%	1.3%	1.8%	2.0%	1.3%	1.5%	2.0%	0	1.8%	2.2%
E-journals	7	0	6	6	1	6	0	1	1	1	4	1	0	0	0	0	0	7
	1.1%	0	1.8%	1.8%	0.4%	1.9%	0	0.7%	1.0%	1.3%	1.8%	1.0%	0	0	0	0	0	2.1%P
All sources of info	7	0	6	6	1	6	0	1	1	1	4	1	0	0	0	0	0	7
	1.1%	0	1.8%	1.8%	0.4%	1.9%	0	0.7%	1.0%	1.3%	1.8%	1.0%	0	0	0	0	0	2.1%P
preferred source of info	2	0	2	2	0	2	0	0	0	0	2	0	0	0	0	0	0	2
	0.3%	0	0.6%	0.6%	0	0.6%	0	0	0	0	0.9%	0	0	0	0	0	0	0.6%
Online (unspecified)	4	0	3	3	1	2	1	1	0	0	2	1	0	1	*	0	1	3
	0.7%	0	0.9%	0.9%	0.5%	0.7%	0.8%	0.7%	0	0	0.9%	1.0%	0	1.5%	3.9%HIL	0	0.4%	1.0%
All sources of info	4	0	3	3	1	2	1	1	0	0	2	1	0	1	*	0	1	3
	0.7%	0	0.9%	0.9%	0.5%	0.7%	0.8%	0.7%	0	0	0.9%	1.0%	0	1.5%	3.9%HIL	0	0.4%	1.0%
preferred source of info	3	0	3	3	0	2	1	0	0	0	2	0	0	1	*	0	1	2
	0.5%	0	0.9%	0.9%	0	0.7%	0.7%	0	0	0	0.9%	0	0	1.5%	2.0%HIK	0	0.3%	0.6%
DK/Refused	7	0	3	3	4	6	0	1	3	2	0	1	*	0	0	1	3	4
	1.2%	0	1.0%	1.0%	1.3%	2.1%	0	0.6%	3.1%J	2.5%J	0	1.0%	1.3%J	0	0	4.8%	1.2%	1.1%

Proportions/Means: Columns Tested (5% risk level) - A/B/D - C/D - E/F/G - H/I/J/K/L/M/N - P/Q
* small base; ** very small base (under 30) ineligible for sig testing

Table 328
Page 1353

Outsell/Digital Library Federation Study (2002)
Weighted Tables

TABLE 82

S7D/E_2. Print or hardcopy journals SUMMARY TABLE

		RESPONDENT TYPE				INSTITUTION TYPE			DISCIPLINE								GENDER	
	TOTAL SAMPLE	FACULTY MEMBER	GRAD. STUDENT	FACULTY /GRAD	UNDER GRAD. STUDENT	PUBLIC	PRIVATE	LIBERAL ARTS	BIOLOGIAL SCIENCES	PHYSICAL SCIENCES /MATH	SOCIAL SCIENCES	ARTS AND HUMAN.	ENGI-NEERING	BUSINESS	LAW	UNDEC. MAJOR	MALE	FEMALE
		(A)	(B)	(C)	(D)	(E)	(F)	(G)	(H)	(I)	(J)	(K)	(L)	(M)	(N)		(P)	(Q)
Base - Use Print or hardcopy journals for coursework	596	0**	318	318	279	294	132	170	86*	79*	209	110*	22*	60*	9*	21*	279	317
Borrow from or use in campus library (NET)	519 87.1%	0 0	267 84.1%	267 84.1%	252 90.4%B C	245 83.2%	115 86.9%	160 93.9%E	73 84.7%	65 82.3%	188 90.1%N	99 89.8%N	19 84.4%	50 83.1%	6 72.5%	19 90.5%	238 85.4%	280 88.5%
All sources of info	519 87.1%	0 0	267 84.1%	267 84.1%	252 90.4%B C	245 83.2%	115 86.9%	160 93.9%E	73 84.7%	65 82.3%	188 90.1%N	99 89.8%N	19 84.4%	50 83.1%	6 72.5%	19 90.5%	238 85.4%	280 88.5%
preferred source of info	424 71.1%	0 0	205 64.6%	205 64.6%	218 78.4%B C	201 68.4%	87 66.0%	135 79.6%EF	56 65.3%	54 68.4%N	147 70.3%N	90 81.6%HI MN	16 70.1%N	39 64.6%	4 51.0%	18 85.7%	194 69.5%	230 72.5%
Access online (NET)	166 27.9%	0 0	100 31.6%	100 31.6%	66 23.5%	83 28.1%	42 32.1%	41 24.2%	29 33.7%K	30 38.0%K	55 26.1%	17 15.3%	7 32.5%K	21 35.4%K	3 35.3%K	4 19.0%	86 30.8%	80 25.3%
All sources of info	166 27.9%	0 0	100 31.6%	100 31.6%	66 23.5%	83 28.1%	42 32.1%	41 24.2%	29 33.7%K	30 38.0%K	55 26.1%	17 15.3%	7 32.5%K	21 35.4%K	3 35.3%K	4 19.0%	86 30.8%	80 25.3%
preferred source of info	126 21.2%	0 0	85 26.9%D	85 26.9%D	41 14.6%	67 22.7%G	36 27.4%G	23 13.6%	25 28.6%K	22 27.8%K	41 19.8%	11 10.2%	5 23.4%K	16 26.2%K	3 33.3%JK	3 14.3%	63 22.7%	63 19.8%
Borrow from or use in other libraries (NET)	24 4.0%	0 0	8 2.5%	8 2.5%	16 5.8%	6 2.2%	5 3.5%	13 7.7%E	4 5.1%	3 3.8%	4 1.8%	10 9.2%J	* 1.3%	1 1.5%	1 5.9%	1 4.8%	10 3.5%	14 4.5%
All sources of info	24 4.0%	0 0	8 2.5%	8 2.5%	16 5.8%	6 2.2%	5 3.5%	13 7.7%E	4 5.1%	3 3.8%	4 1.8%	10 9.2%J	* 1.3%	1 1.5%	1 5.9%	1 4.8%	10 3.5%	14 4.5%

Proportions/Means: Columns Tested (5% risk level) - A/B/D - C/D - E/F/G - H/I/J/K/L/M/N - P/Q
* small base; ** very small base (under 30) ineligible for sig testing

Table 331
Page 1360

Outsell/Digital Library Federation Study (2002)
Weighted Tables

TABLE 82, continued

S7D/E_2. Print or hardcopy journals SUMMARY TABLE

	TOTAL SAMPLE	RESPONDENT TYPE: FACULTY MEMBER	GRAD. STUDENT	FACULTY /GRAD	UNDER GRAD. STUDENT	INSTITUTION TYPE: PUBLIC	PRIVATE	LIBERAL ARTS	DISCIPLINE: BIOLOGIAL SCIENCES	PHYSICAL SCIENCES /MATH	SOCIAL SCIENCES	ARTS AND HUMAN.	ENGI-NEERING	BUSINESS	LAW	UNDEC. MAJOR	GENDER: MALE	FEMALE
		(A)	(B)	(C)	(D)	(E)	(F)	(G)	(H)	(I)	(J)	(K)	(L)	(M)	(N)		(P)	(Q)
Base - Use Print or hardcopy journals for coursework	596	0**	318	318	279	294	132	170	86*	79*	209	110*	22*	60*	9*	21*	279	317
preferred source of info	10 1.7%	0 0	3 1.0%	3 1.0%	7 2.5%	5 1.7%	1 0.9%	4 2.3%	3 3.1%	1 1.3%	2 0.9%	3 3.1%	0 0	1 1.5%	* 3.9%L	0 0	3 1.0%	7 2.3%
Interlibrary loan (NET)	24 3.9%	0 0	9 3.0%	9 3.0%	14 5.1%	6 2.1%	5 3.4%	13 7.6%E	5 6.1%	2 2.5%	6 2.7%	8 7.1%	1 2.6%	2 3.1%	* 3.9%	0 0	15 5.2%	9 2.8%
All sources of info	24 3.9%	0 0	9 3.0%	9 3.0%	14 5.1%	6 2.1%	5 3.4%	13 7.6%E	5 6.1%	2 2.5%	6 2.7%	8 7.1%	1 2.6%	2 3.1%	* 3.9%	0 0	15 5.2%	9 2.8%
preferred source of info	2 0.4%	0 0	1 0.4%	1 0.4%	1 0.3%	* 0.1%	1 0.7%	1 0.5%	1 1.0%	0 0	0 0	0 0	* 1.3%J	1 1.5%	0 0	0 0	2 0.8%	0 0
Purchase from physical book store (NET)	21 3.5%	0 0	11 3.5%	11 3.5%	10 3.5%	8 2.7%	5 3.8%	8 4.6%	2 2.0%	3 3.8%	8 3.6%	3 3.1%	1 2.6%	3 4.6%	1 7.8%H	1 4.8%	11 4.1%	9 2.9%
All sources of info	21 3.5%	0 0	11 3.5%	11 3.5%	10 3.5%	8 2.7%	5 3.8%	8 4.6%	2 2.0%	3 3.8%	8 3.6%	3 3.1%	1 2.6%	3 4.6%	1 7.8%H	1 4.8%	11 4.1%	9 2.9%
preferred source of info	7 1.2%	0 0	5 1.6%	5 1.6%	2 0.7%	3 1.0%	2 1.7%	2 1.1%	0 0	1 1.3%	4 1.8%	0 0	0 0	2 3.1%	* 3.9%HKL	0 0	3 1.1%	4 1.3%
Faculty (NET)	11 1.8%	0 0	7 2.1%	7 2.1%	4 1.5%	4 1.4%	4 2.8%	3 1.8%	2 2.0%	2 2.5%	2 0.9%	3 3.1%	1 2.6%	1 1.5%	* 2.0%	0 0	3 1.0%	8 2.5%
All sources of info	11 1.8%	0 0	7 2.1%	7 2.1%	4 1.5%	4 1.4%	4 2.8%	3 1.8%	2 2.0%	2 2.5%	2 0.9%	3 3.1%	1 2.6%	1 1.5%	* 2.0%	0 0	3 1.0%	8 2.5%

Proportions/Means: Columns Tested (5% risk level) - A/B/D - C/D - E/F/G - H/I/J/K/L/M/N - P/Q
* small base; ** very small base (under 30) ineligible for sig testing

Table 331
Page 1361

Outsell/Digital Library Federation Study (2002)
Weighted Tables

TABLE 82, continued

S7D/E_2. Print or hardcopy journals SUMMARY TABLE

		RESPONDENT TYPE				INSTITUTION TYPE			DISCIPLINE									GENDER	
	TOTAL SAMPLE	FACULTY MEMBER	GRAD. STUDENT	FACULTY /GRAD	UNDER GRAD. STUDENT	PUBLIC	PRIVATE	LIBERAL ARTS	BIOLOGIAL SCIENCES	PHYSICAL SCIENCES /MATH	SOCIAL SCIENCES	ARTS AND HUMAN.	ENGI-NEERING	BUSINESS	LAW	UNDEC. MAJOR	MALE	FEMALE
		(A)	(B)	(C)	(D)	(E)	(F)	(G)	(H)	(I)	(J)	(K)	(L)	(M)	(N)		(P)	(Q)
Base - Use Print or hardcopy journals for coursework	596	0**	318	318	279	294	132	170	86*	79*	209	110*	22*	60*	9*	21*	279	317
preferred source of info	6 1.0%	0 0	4 1.2%	4 1.2%	2 0.7%	1 0.4%	3 2.0%	2 1.2%	1 1.0%	0 0	2 0.9%	2 2.0%	1 2.6%I	0 0	* 2.0%IM	0 0	1 0.2%	5 1.6%
Purchase from online bookstore (NET)	5 0.8%	0 0	2 0.6%	2 0.6%	3 1.0%	1 0.4%	2 1.3%	2 1.1%	1 1.0%	0 0	2 0.9%	1 1.0%	1 2.6%I	0 0	* 3.9%IM	0 0	3 1.2%	1 0.4%
All sources of info	5 0.8%	0 0	2 0.6%	2 0.6%	3 1.0%	1 0.4%	2 1.3%	2 1.1%	1 1.0%	0 0	2 0.9%	1 1.0%	1 2.6%I	0 0	* 3.9%IM	0 0	3 1.2%	1 0.4%
preferred source of info	1 0.2%	0 0	1 0.4%	1 0.4%	0 0	0 0	1 1.0%	0 0	0 0	0 0	0 0	1 1.0%	0 0	0 0	* 2.0%HIJM	0 0	1 0.4%	* 0.1%
Personal Holdings (NET)	5 0.8%	0 0	3 0.9%	3 0.9%	2 0.7%	3 1.0%	0 0	2 1.1%	0 0	0 0	4 1.8%	0 0	0 0	1 1.5%	0 0	0 0	3 1.0%	2 0.6%
All sources of info	5 0.8%	0 0	3 0.9%	3 0.9%	2 0.7%	3 1.0%	0 0	2 1.1%	0 0	0 0	4 1.8%	0 0	0 0	1 1.5%	0 0	0 0	3 1.0%	2 0.6%
preferred source of info	1 0.2%	0 0	1 0.3%	1 0.3%	0 0	1 0.3%	0 0	0 0	0 0	0 0	0 0	0 0	0 0	1 1.5%	0 0	0 0	1 0.3%	0 0
Order from on demand document delivery service (NET)	3 0.5%	0 0	2 0.6%	2 0.6%	1 0.4%	2 0.6%	0 0	1 0.7%	0 0	0 0	2 0.9%	1 1.0%	0 0	0 0	0 0	0 0	3 1.1%	0 0
All sources of info	3 0.5%	0 0	2 0.6%	2 0.6%	1 0.4%	2 0.6%	0 0	1 0.7%	0 0	0 0	2 0.9%	1 1.0%	0 0	0 0	0 0	0 0	3 1.1%	0 0

Proportions/Means: Columns Tested (5% risk level) - A/B/D - C/D - E/F/G - H/I/J/K/L/M/N - P/Q
* small base; ** very small base (under 30) ineligible for sig testing

Table 331
Page 1362

Outsell/Digital Library Federation Study (2002)
Weighted Tables

TABLE 82, continued

S7D/E_2. Print or hardcopy journals SUMMARY TABLE

		RESPONDENT TYPE				INSTITUTION TYPE			DISCIPLINE									GENDER	
	TOTAL SAMPLE	FACULTY MEMBER	GRAD. STUDENT	FACULTY /GRAD	UNDER GRAD. STUDENT	PUBLIC	PRIVATE	LIBERAL ARTS	BIOLOGIAL SCIENCES	PHYSICAL SCIENCES /MATH	SOCIAL SCIENCES	ARTS AND HUMAN.	ENGI-NEERING	BUSINESS	LAW	UNDEC. MAJOR	MALE	FEMALE
		(A)	(B)	(C)	(D)	(E)	(F)	(G)	(H)	(I)	(J)	(K)	(L)	(M)	(N)		(P)	(Q)
Base - Use Print or hardcopy journals for coursework	596	0**	318	318	279	294	132	170	86*	79*	209	110*	22*	60*	9*	21*	279	317
preferred source of info	2 0.3%	0 0	2 0.6%	2 0.6%	0 0	2 0.6%	0 0	0 0	0 0	0 0	2 0.9%	0 0	0 0	0 0	0 0	0 0	2 0.7%	0 0
In class (NET)	2 0.3%	0 0	0 0	0 0	2 0.7%	2 0.6%	0 0	0 0	0 0	0 0	2 0.9%	0 0	0 0	0 0	0 0	0 0	2 0.7%	0 0
All sources of info	2 0.3%	0 0	0 0	0 0	2 0.7%	2 0.6%	0 0	0 0	0 0	0 0	2 0.9%	0 0	0 0	0 0	0 0	0 0	2 0.7%	0 0
preferred source of info	2 0.3%	0 0	0 0	0 0	2 0.7%	2 0.6%	0 0	0 0	0 0	0 0	2 0.9%	0 0	0 0	0 0	0 0	0 0	2 0.7%	0 0
Home (NET)	2 0.3%	0 0	2 0.6%	2 0.6%	0 0	2 0.6%	0 0	0 0	0 0	0 0	2 0.9%	0 0	0 0	0 0	0 0	0 0	0 0	2 0.6%
All sources of info	2 0.3%	0 0	2 0.6%	2 0.6%	0 0	2 0.6%	0 0	0 0	0 0	0 0	2 0.9%	0 0	0 0	0 0	0 0	0 0	0 0	2 0.6%
preferred source of info	2 0.3%	0 0	2 0.6%	2 0.6%	0 0	2 0.6%	0 0	0 0	0 0	0 0	2 0.9%	0 0	0 0	0 0	0 0	0 0	0 0	2 0.6%
Ask library to purchase source (NET)	2 0.3%	0 0	1 0.3%	1 0.3%	1 0.3%	1 0.3%	0 0	1 0.5%	2 2.0%	0 0	0 0	0 0	0 0	0 0	0 0	0 0	1 0.3%	1 0.3%
All sources of info	2 0.3%	0 0	1 0.3%	1 0.3%	1 0.3%	1 0.3%	0 0	1 0.5%	2 2.0%	0 0	0 0	0 0	0 0	0 0	0 0	0 0	1 0.3%	1 0.3%

Proportions/Means: Columns Tested (5% risk level) - A/B/D - C/D - E/F/G - H/I/J/K/L/M/N - P/Q
* small base; ** very small base (under 30) ineligible for sig testing

Table 331
Page 1363

Outsell/Digital Library Federation Study (2002)
Weighted Tables

TABLE 82, continued

S7D/E_2. Print or hardcopy journals SUMMARY TABLE

		RESPONDENT TYPE				INSTITUTION TYPE			DISCIPLINE									GENDER	
	TOTAL SAMPLE	FACULTY MEMBER	GRAD. STUDENT	FACULTY /GRAD	UNDER GRAD. STUDENT	PUBLIC	PRIVATE	LIBERAL ARTS	BIOLOGIAL SCIENCES	PHYSICAL SCIENCES /MATH	SOCIAL SCIENCES	ARTS AND HUMAN.	ENGI-NEERING	BUSINESS	LAW	UNDEC. MAJOR	MALE	FEMALE
		(A)	(B)	(C)	(D)	(E)	(F)	(G)	(H)	(I)	(J)	(K)	(L)	(M)	(N)		(P)	(Q)
Base - Use Print or hardcopy journals for coursework	596	0**	318	318	279	294	132	170	86*	79*	209	110*	22*	60*	9*	21*	279	317
preferred source of info	0 0	0 0	0 0	0 0	0 0	0 0	0 0	0 0	0 0	0 0	0 0	0 0	0 0	0 0	0 0	0 0	0 0	0 0
Colleagues (NET)	0 0	0 0	0 0	0 0	0 0	0 0	0 0	0 0	0 0	0 0	0 0	0 0	0 0	0 0	0 0	0 0	0 0	0 0
All sources of info	0 0	0 0	0 0	0 0	0 0	0 0	0 0	0 0	0 0	0 0	0 0	0 0	0 0	0 0	0 0	0 0	0 0	0 0
preferred source of info	0 0	0 0	0 0	0 0	0 0	0 0	0 0	0 0	0 0	0 0	0 0	0 0	0 0	0 0	0 0	0 0	0 0	0 0
Access book/journal/ journal article elsewhere online (NET)	0 0	0 0	0 0	0 0	0 0	0 0	0 0	0 0	0 0	0 0	0 0	0 0	0 0	0 0	0 0	0 0	0 0	0 0
All sources of info	0 0	0 0	0 0	0 0	0 0	0 0	0 0	0 0	0 0	0 0	0 0	0 0	0 0	0 0	0 0	0 0	0 0	0 0
preferred source of info	0 0	0 0	0 0	0 0	0 0	0 0	0 0	0 0	0 0	0 0	0 0	0 0	0 0	0 0	0 0	0 0	0 0	0 0
Dorm room (NET)	0 0	0 0	0 0	0 0	0 0	0 0	0 0	0 0	0 0	0 0	0 0	0 0	0 0	0 0	0 0	0 0	0 0	0 0
All sources of info	0 0	0 0	0 0	0 0	0 0	0 0	0 0	0 0	0 0	0 0	0 0	0 0	0 0	0 0	0 0	0 0	0 0	0 0

Proportions/Means: Columns Tested (5% risk level) - A/B/D - C/D - E/F/G - H/I/J/K/L/M/N - P/Q
* small base; ** very small base (under 30) ineligible for sig testing

Table 331
Page 1364

Outsell/Digital Library Federation Study (2002)
Weighted Tables

TABLE 82, continued

S7D/E_2. Print or hardcopy journals SUMMARY TABLE

		RESPONDENT TYPE				INSTITUTION TYPE			DISCIPLINE								GENDER	
	TOTAL SAMPLE	FACULTY MEMBER	GRAD. STUDENT	FACULTY /GRAD	UNDER GRAD. STUDENT	PUBLIC	PRIVATE	LIBERAL ARTS	BIOLOGIAL SCIENCES	PHYSICAL SCIENCES /MATH	SOCIAL SCIENCES	ARTS AND HUMAN.	ENGI- NEERING	BUSINESS	LAW	UNDEC. MAJOR	MALE	FEMALE
		(A)	(B)	(C)	(D)	(E)	(F)	(G)	(H)	(I)	(J)	(K)	(L)	(M)	(N)		(P)	(Q)
Base - Use Print or hardcopy journals for coursework	596	0**	318	318	279	294	132	170	86*	79*	209	110*	22*	60*	9*	21*	279	317
preferred source of info	0 0	0 0	0 0	0 0	0 0	0 0	0 0	0 0	0 0	0 0	0 0	0 0	0 0	0 0	0 0	0 0	0 0	0 0
Access from course website (NET)	0 0	0 0	0 0	0 0	0 0	0 0	0 0	0 0	0 0	0 0	0 0	0 0	0 0	0 0	0 0	0 0	0 0	0 0
All sources of info	0 0	0 0	0 0	0 0	0 0	0 0	0 0	0 0	0 0	0 0	0 0	0 0	0 0	0 0	0 0	0 0	0 0	0 0
preferred source of info	0 0	0 0	0 0	0 0	0 0	0 0	0 0	0 0	0 0	0 0	0 0	0 0	0 0	0 0	0 0	0 0	0 0	0 0
Other (NET)	18 2.9%	0 0	13 4.0%	13 4.0%	5 1.8%	14 4.6%G	3 2.2%	1 0.6%	2 2.0%	4 5.1%	8 3.6%	1 1.0%	1 2.6%	2 3.1%	1 7.8%HK	0 0	6 2.0%	12 3.8%
All sources of info	15 2.4%	0 0	11 3.4%	11 3.4%	4 1.4%	11 3.6%	3 2.2%	1 0.6%	2 2.0%	4 5.1%K	6 2.7%	0 0	1 2.6%K	2 3.1%	1 7.8%HK	0 0	4 1.6%	10 3.2%
preferred source of info	9 1.5%	0 0	6 2.0%	6 2.0%	3 1.1%	9 3.0%G	* 0.3%	0 0	1 1.0%	0 0	6 2.7%	1 1.0%	* 1.3%	1 1.5%	* 3.9%I	0 0	3 1.2%	6 1.9%
DK/Refused	4 0.7%	0 0	1 0.4%	1 0.4%	3 1.0%	1 0.4%	0 0	3 1.7%	0 0	1 1.3%	2 0.9%	1 1.0%	0 0	0 0	0 0	0 0	4 1.4%	0 0

Proportions/Means: Columns Tested (5% risk level) - A/B/D - C/D - E/F/G - H/I/J/K/L/M/N - P/Q
* small base; ** very small base (under 30) ineligible for sig testing

Table 331
Page 1365

TABLE 83

R7sum_4. When you are doing research, how do you find information about e-journals ? Do you ...

		RESPONDENT TYPE				INSTITUTION TYPE			DISCIPLINE								GENDER	
	TOTAL SAMPLE	FACULTY MEMBER	GRAD. STUDENT	FACULTY /GRAD	UNDER GRAD. STUDENT	PUBLIC	PRIVATE	LIBERAL ARTS	BIOLOGIAL SCIENCES	PHYSICAL SCIENCES /MATH	SOCIAL SCIENCES	ARTS AND HUMAN.	ENGI-NEERING	BUSINESS	LAW	UNDEC. MAJOR	MALE	FEMALE
		(A)	(B)	(C)	(D)	(E)	(F)	(G)	(H)	(I)	(J)	(K)	(L)	(M)	(N)		(P)	(Q)
Base - Use e-journals for research	266	122	144	266	0**	147	89*	29**	51*	60*	77*	35*	13*	27**	3**	0*	160	105*
ONLINE	246 92.7%	115 94.6%	131 91.1%	246 92.7%	0 0	136 92.0%	83 92.5%	28 97.0%	48 94.8%K	56 93.3%K	75 97.6%KL	27 77.4%	11 88.6%	26 96.6%	3 78.9%	0 0	147 92.0%	99 93.8%
Online databases	58 21.8%	23 19.3%	35 24.0%	58 21.8%	0 0	31 21.0%	22 24.6%	5 17.4%	9 17.2%	12 20.0%	19 24.4%	7 19.4%	2 18.2%	8 31.0%	1 31.6%	0 0	31 19.5%	27 25.4%
All sources of info	58 21.8%	23 19.3%	35 24.0%	58 21.8%	0 0	31 21.0%	22 24.6%	5 17.4%	9 17.2%	12 20.0%	19 24.4%	7 19.4%	2 18.2%	8 31.0%	1 31.6%	0 0	31 19.5%	27 25.4%
preferred source of info	48 18.1%	18 15.0%	30 20.8%	48 18.1%	0 0	24 16.4%	19 21.2%	5 17.4%	8 15.5%	9 15.0%	17 22.0%	4 12.9%	2 13.6%	7 27.6%	1 21.1%	0 0	26 16.0%	23 21.4%
Your own institution's web site	58 21.8%	29 23.7%	29 20.2%	58 21.8%	0 0	28 19.1%	23 26.0%	6 22.3%	11 20.7%	12 20.0%	17 22.0%	7 19.4%	3 25.0%	8 31.0%	* 5.3%	0 0	38 23.7%	20 18.9%
All sources of info	58 21.8%	29 23.7%	29 20.2%	58 21.8%	0 0	28 19.1%	23 26.0%	6 22.3%	11 20.7%	12 20.0%	17 22.0%	7 19.4%	3 25.0%	8 31.0%	* 5.3%	0 0	38 23.7%	20 18.9%
preferred source of info	45 16.9%	20 16.3%	25 17.4%	45 16.9%	0 0	24 16.5%	16 17.9%	5 16.1%	10 19.0%	11 18.3%	11 14.6%	4 12.9%	2 15.9%	7 24.1%	0 0	0 0	28 17.6%	17 15.9%
Search engine	48 18.2%	26 21.2%	23 15.7%	48 18.2%	0 0	28 18.8%	15 16.6%	6 20.4%	11 22.4%	9 15.0%	9 12.2%	10 29.0%	2 18.2%	5 17.2%	2 47.4%	0 0	28 17.2%	21 19.7%
All sources of info	48 18.2%	26 21.2%	23 15.7%	48 18.2%	0 0	28 18.8%	15 16.6%	6 20.4%	11 22.4%	9 15.0%	9 12.2%	10 29.0%	2 18.2%	5 17.2%	2 47.4%	0 0	28 17.2%	21 19.7%

Proportions/Means: Columns Tested (5% risk level) - A/B/D - C/D - E/F/G - H/I/J/K/L/M/N - P/Q
* small base; ** very small base (under 30) ineligible for sig testing

Table 86
Page 199

TABLE 83, continued

R7sum_4. When you are doing research, how do you find information about e-journals ? Do you ...

	RESPONDENT TYPE				INSTITUTION TYPE			DISCIPLINE								GENDER	
	TOTAL SAMPLE	FACULTY MEMBER	GRAD. STUDENT	FACULTY /GRAD	UNDER GRAD. STUDENT	PUBLIC	PRIVATE	LIBERAL ARTS	BIOLOGIAL SCIENCES	PHYSICAL SCIENCES /MATH	SOCIAL SCIENCES	ARTS AND HUMAN.	ENGI-NEERING	BUSINESS	LAW	UNDEC. MAJOR	MALE	FEMALE
		(A)	(B)	(C)	(D)	(E)	(F)	(G)	(H)	(I)	(J)	(K)	(L)	(M)	(N)		(P)	(Q)
Base - Use e-journals for research	266	122	144	266	0**	147	89*	29**	51*	60*	77*	35*	13*	27**	3**	0*	160	105*
preferred source of info	24 9.0%	12 10.1%	12 8.0%	24 9.0%	0 0	14 9.8%	7 8.1%	2 7.7%	4 8.6%	4 6.7%	6 7.3%	6 16.1%	1 6.8%	2 6.9%	2 47.4%	0 0	14 8.5%	10 9.7%
Online library catalogues and finding aids	47 17.6%	13 11.1%	33 23.1%A	47 17.6%	0 0	27 18.2%	18 20.3%	2 6.5%	9 17.2%	7 11.7%	21 26.8%	6 16.1%	3 22.7%	2 6.9%	0 0	0 0	22 13.7%	25 23.6%
All sources of info	47 17.6%	13 11.1%	33 23.1%A	47 17.6%	0 0	27 18.2%	18 20.3%	2 6.5%	9 17.2%	7 11.7%	21 26.8%	6 16.1%	3 22.7%	2 6.9%	0 0	0 0	22 13.7%	25 23.6%
preferred source of info	36 13.5%	12 9.6%	24 16.8%	36 13.5%	0 0	21 14.2%	13 14.6%	2 6.5%	6 12.1%	7 11.7%	15 19.5%	4 12.9%	2 18.2%	1 3.4%	0 0	0 0	18 10.9%	18 17.4%
Web directory/ subject related web site	40 15.1%	25 20.9%B	15 10.3%	40 15.1%	0 0	19 12.9%	14 16.0%	7 23.7%	10 19.0%	17 28.3%J	6 7.3%	4 12.9%	2 18.2%	1 3.4%	* 5.3%	0 0	25 15.8%	15 14.1%
All sources of info	40 15.1%	25 20.9%B	15 10.3%	40 15.1%	0 0	19 12.9%	14 16.0%	7 23.7%	10 19.0%	17 28.3%J	6 7.3%	4 12.9%	2 18.2%	1 3.4%	* 5.3%	0 0	25 15.8%	15 14.1%
preferred source of info	26 9.7%	18 14.7%B	8 5.4%	26 9.7%	0 0	11 7.4%	9 9.8%	6 20.3%	9 17.2%J	11 18.3%J	2 2.4%	2 6.5%	2 13.6%J	0 0	0 0	0 0	16 9.8%	10 9.5%
Internet searches	29 10.8%	8 6.7%	21 14.2%	29 10.8%	0 0	18 12.3%	7 7.8%	4 12.7%	5 10.3%	9 15.0%K	9 12.2%	0 0	1 9.1%K	4 13.8%	* 5.3%	0 0	18 11.1%	11 10.3%

Proportions/Means: Columns Tested (5% risk level) - A/B/D - C/D - E/F/G - H/I/J/K/L/M/N - P/Q
* small base; ** very small base (under 30) ineligible for sig testing

Table 86
Page 200

Outsell/Digital Library Federation Study (2002)
Weighted Tables

TABLE 83, continued

R7sum_4. When you are doing research, how do you find information about e-journals ? Do you ...

		RESPONDENT TYPE				INSTITUTION TYPE			DISCIPLINE								GENDER	
	TOTAL SAMPLE	FACULTY MEMBER	GRAD. STUDENT	FACULTY /GRAD	UNDER GRAD. STUDENT	PUBLIC	PRIVATE	LIBERAL ARTS	BIOLOGIAL SCIENCES	PHYSICAL SCIENCES /MATH	SOCIAL SCIENCES	ARTS AND HUMAN.	ENGI-NEERING	BUSINESS	LAW	UNDEC. MAJOR	MALE	FEMALE
		(A)	(B)	(C)	(D)	(E)	(F)	(G)	(H)	(I)	(J)	(K)	(L)	(M)	(N)		(P)	(Q)
Base - Use e-journals for research	266	122	144	266	0**	147	89*	29**	51*	60*	77*	35*	13*	27**	3**	0*	160	105*
All sources of info	29 10.8%	8 6.7%	21 14.2%	29 10.8%	0 0	18 12.3%	7 7.8%	4 12.7%	5 10.3%	9 15.0%K	9 12.2%	0 0	1 9.1%K	4 13.8%	* 5.3%	0 0	18 11.1%	11 10.3%
preferred source of info	19 7.0%	6 4.9%	13 8.7%	19 7.0%	0 0	10 7.1%	5 5.9%	3 9.7%	4 6.9%	6 10.0%	6 7.3%	0 0	1 4.5%	3 10.3%	0 0	0 0	15 9.2%	4 3.6%
Online abstracting and indexing services	14 5.2%	8 6.7%	6 4.0%	14 5.2%	0 0	6 3.9%	5 5.8%	3 9.9%	3 5.2%	3 5.0%	8 9.8%	0 0	1 4.5%	0 0	* 5.3%	0 0	11 7.1%	2 2.3%
All sources of info	14 5.2%	8 6.7%	6 4.0%	14 5.2%	0 0	6 3.9%	5 5.8%	3 9.9%	3 5.2%	3 5.0%	8 9.8%	0 0	1 4.5%	0 0	* 5.3%	0 0	11 7.1%	2 2.3%
preferred source of info	9 3.3%	4 3.3%	5 3.3%	9 3.3%	0 0	2 1.3%	4 4.5%	3 9.9%	1 1.7%	2 3.3%	6 7.3%	0 0	* 2.3%	0 0	0 0	0 0	8 4.7%	1 1.2%
Online reference service	12 4.6%	7 5.8%	5 3.7%	12 4.6%	0 0	7 4.7%	4 4.9%	1 3.4%	2 3.4%	3 5.0%	4 4.9%	2 6.5%	* 2.3%	1 3.4%	* 10.5%	0 0	8 4.7%	5 4.5%
All sources of info	12 4.6%	7 5.8%	5 3.7%	12 4.6%	0 0	7 4.7%	4 4.9%	1 3.4%	2 3.4%	3 5.0%	4 4.9%	2 6.5%	* 2.3%	1 3.4%	* 10.5%	0 0	8 4.7%	5 4.5%
preferred source of info	5 2.0%	5 4.0%B	* 0.2%	5 2.0%	0 0	5 3.4%	* 0.2%	0 0	1 1.7%	1 1.7%	2 2.4%	1 3.2%	0 0	0 0	* 10.5%	0 0	3 2.1%	2 1.8%
Department web page	7 2.7%	3 2.3%	4 3.0%	7 2.7%	0 0	4 2.9%	2 2.1%	1 3.2%	1 1.7%	2 3.3%	2 2.4%	1 3.2%	* 2.3%	1 3.4%	0 0	0 0	4 2.6%	3 2.7%

Proportions/Means: Columns Tested (5% risk level) - A/B/D - C/D - E/F/G - H/I/J/K/L/M/N - P/Q
* small base; ** very small base (under 30) ineligible for sig testing

Table 86
Page 201

Outsell/Digital Library Federation Study (2002)
Weighted Tables

TABLE 83, continued

R7sum_4. When you are doing research, how do you find information about e-journals ? Do you ...

	RESPONDENT TYPE					INSTITUTION TYPE			DISCIPLINE								GENDER	
	TOTAL SAMPLE	FACULTY MEMBER	GRAD. STUDENT	FACULTY /GRAD	UNDER GRAD. STUDENT	PUBLIC	PRIVATE	LIBERAL ARTS	BIOLOGIAL SCIENCES	PHYSICAL SCIENCES /MATH	SOCIAL SCIENCES	ARTS AND HUMAN.	ENGI-NEERING	BUSINESS	LAW	UNDEC. MAJOR	MALE	FEMALE
		(A)	(B)	(C)	(D)	(E)	(F)	(G)	(H)	(I)	(J)	(K)	(L)	(M)	(N)		(P)	(Q)
Base - Use e-journals for research	266	122	144	266	0**	147	89*	29**	51*	60*	77*	35*	13*	27**	3**	0*	160	105*
All sources of info	7 2.7%	3 2.3%	4 3.0%	7 2.7%	0 0	4 2.9%	2 2.1%	1 3.2%	1 1.7%	2 3.3%	2 2.4%	1 3.2%	* 2.3%	1 3.4%	0 0	0 0	4 2.6%	3 2.7%
preferred source of info	6 2.3%	3 2.3%	3 2.3%	6 2.3%	0 0	3 2.2%	2 2.1%	1 3.2%	1 1.7%	1 1.7%	2 2.4%	1 3.2%	* 2.3%	1 3.4%	0 0	0 0	4 2.6%	2 1.8%
E-mail listservs	3 1.3%	3 2.7%	0 0	3 1.3%	0 0	1 0.6%	1 1.6%	1 3.4%	0 0	1 1.7%	0 0	1 3.2%	* 2.3%	1 3.4%	0 0	0 0	1 0.9%	2 1.8%
All sources of info	3 1.3%	3 2.7%	0 0	3 1.3%	0 0	1 0.6%	1 1.6%	1 3.4%	0 0	1 1.7%	0 0	1 3.2%	* 2.3%	1 3.4%	0 0	0 0	1 0.9%	2 1.8%
preferred source of info	1 0.5%	1 1.0%	0 0	1 0.5%	0 0	1 0.6%	* 0.3%	0 0	0 0	0 0	0 0	0 0	* 2.3%	1 3.4%	0 0	0 0	* 0.2%	1 0.9%
Your own personal electronic library/files	1 0.5%	* 0.4%	1 0.6%	1 0.5%	0 0	1 0.9%	0 0	0 0	1 1.7%	0 0	0 0	0 0	* 2.3%	0 0	* 5.3%	0 0	1 0.8%	0 0
All sources of info	1 0.5%	* 0.4%	1 0.6%	1 0.5%	0 0	1 0.9%	0 0	0 0	1 1.7%	0 0	0 0	0 0	* 2.3%	0 0	* 5.3%	0 0	1 0.8%	0 0
preferred source of info	1 0.4%	* 0.2%	1 0.6%	1 0.4%	0 0	1 0.8%	0 0	0 0	1 1.7%	0 0	0 0	0 0	* 2.3%	0 0	0 0	0 0	1 0.7%	0 0
Online bookstore	0 0	0 0	0 0	0 0	0 0	0 0	0 0	0 0	0 0	0 0	0 0	0 0	0 0	0 0	0 0	0 0	0 0	0 0

Proportions/Means: Columns Tested (5% risk level) - A/B/D - C/D - E/F/G - H/I/J/K/L/M/N - P/Q
* small base; ** very small base (under 30) ineligible for sig testing

Table 86
Page 202

Outsell/Digital Library Federation Study (2002)
Weighted Tables

TABLE 83, continued

R7sum_4. When you are doing research, how do you find information about e-journals ? Do you ...

	TOTAL SAMPLE	RESPONDENT TYPE: FACULTY MEMBER	GRAD. STUDENT	FACULTY /GRAD	UNDER GRAD. STUDENT	INSTITUTION TYPE: PUBLIC	PRIVATE	LIBERAL ARTS	DISCIPLINE: BIOLOGIAL SCIENCES	PHYSICAL SCIENCES /MATH	SOCIAL SCIENCES	ARTS AND HUMAN.	ENGI-NEERING	BUSINESS	LAW	UNDEC. MAJOR	GENDER: MALE	FEMALE
		(A)	(B)	(C)	(D)	(E)	(F)	(G)	(H)	(I)	(J)	(K)	(L)	(M)	(N)		(P)	(Q)
Base - Use e-journals for research	266	122	144	266	0**	147	89*	29**	51*	60*	77*	35*	13*	27**	3**	0*	160	105*
All sources of info	0 0	0 0	0 0	0 0	0 0	0 0	0 0	0 0	0 0	0 0	0 0	0 0	0 0	0 0	0 0	0 0	0 0	0 0
preferred source of info	0 0	0 0	0 0	0 0	0 0	0 0	0 0	0 0	0 0	0 0	0 0	0 0	0 0	0 0	0 0	0 0	0 0	0 0
LIBRARY/PRINT	58 21.7%	30 24.3%	28 19.5%	58 21.7%	0 0	34 22.8%	15 17.1%	9 30.1%	12 24.1%	13 21.7%	15 19.5%	7 19.4%	3 20.5%	7 27.6%	1 15.8%	0 0	42 25.9%	16 15.2%
Campus library	45 16.9%	22 17.7%	23 16.2%	45 16.9%	0 0	26 18.0%	12 13.2%	7 22.8%	8 15.5%	9 15.0%	13 17.1%	6 16.1%	2 18.2%	7 24.1%	* 10.5%	0 0	31 19.1%	14 13.4%
All sources of info	45 16.9%	22 17.7%	23 16.2%	45 16.9%	0 0	26 18.0%	12 13.2%	7 22.8%	8 15.5%	9 15.0%	13 17.1%	6 16.1%	2 18.2%	7 24.1%	* 10.5%	0 0	31 19.1%	14 13.4%
preferred source of info	11 4.3%	3 2.6%	8 5.7%	11 4.3%	0 0	9 6.3%	2 2.4%	0 0	2 3.4%	2 3.3%	4 4.9%	1 3.2%	1 6.8%	2 6.9%	0 0	0 0	8 4.7%	4 3.6%
References cited in books or journal articles	15 5.6%	8 6.5%	7 4.9%	15 5.6%	0 0	7 4.9%	5 5.4%	3 10.3%	4 8.6%	4 6.7%	4 4.9%	1 3.2%	1 4.5%	1 3.4%	* 5.3%	0 0	10 6.4%	5 4.4%
All sources of info	15 5.6%	8 6.5%	7 4.9%	15 5.6%	0 0	7 4.9%	5 5.4%	3 10.3%	4 8.6%	4 6.7%	4 4.9%	1 3.2%	1 4.5%	1 3.4%	* 5.3%	0 0	10 6.4%	5 4.4%
preferred source of info	2 0.7%	1 0.7%	1 0.7%	2 0.7%	0 0	1 0.7%	0 0	1 3.0%	1 1.7%	1 1.7%	0 0	0 0	0 0	0 0	0 0	0 0	0 0	2 1.8%

Proportions/Means: Columns Tested (5% risk level) - A/B/D - C/D - E/F/G - H/I/J/K/L/M/N - P/Q
* small base; ** very small base (under 30) ineligible for sig testing

Table 86
Page 203

Outsell/Digital Library Federation Study (2002)
Weighted Tables

TABLE 83, continued

R7sum_4. When you are doing research, how do you find information about e-journals ? Do you ...

		RESPONDENT TYPE				INSTITUTION TYPE			DISCIPLINE									GENDER	
	TOTAL SAMPLE	FACULTY MEMBER	GRAD. STUDENT	FACULTY /GRAD	UNDER GRAD. STUDENT	PUBLIC	PRIVATE	LIBERAL ARTS	BIOLOGIAL SCIENCES	PHYSICAL SCIENCES /MATH	SOCIAL SCIENCES	ARTS AND HUMAN.	ENGI-NEERING	BUSINESS	LAW	UNDEC. MAJOR	MALE	FEMALE
		(A)	(B)	(C)	(D)	(E)	(F)	(G)	(H)	(I)	(J)	(K)	(L)	(M)	(N)		(P)	(Q)
Base - Use e-journals for research	266	122	144	266	0**	147	89*	29**	51*	60*	77*	35*	13*	27**	3**	0*	160	105*
Personal subscriptions to newspapers, magazines and journals	8 3.2%	7 5.5%	2 1.2%	8 3.2%	0 0	5 3.3%	3 3.0%	1 3.0%	5 10.3%I	1 1.7%	2 2.4%	0 0	* 2.3%	0 0	0 0	0 0	8 4.7%	1 0.8%
All sources of info	8 3.2%	7 5.5%	2 1.2%	8 3.2%	0 0	5 3.3%	3 3.0%	1 3.0%	5 10.3%I	1 1.7%	2 2.4%	0 0	* 2.3%	0 0	0 0	0 0	8 4.7%	1 0.8%
preferred source of info	0 0	0 0	0 0	0 0	0 0	0 0	0 0	0 0	0 0	0 0	0 0	0 0	0 0	0 0	0 0	0 0	0 0	0 0
Your own personal physical library/ files/bookshelves	6 2.1%	4 3.0%	2 1.3%	6 2.1%	0 0	3 1.8%	2 2.0%	1 3.4%	1 1.7%	2 3.3%	0 0	1 3.2%	1 4.5%J	1 3.4%	0 0	0 0	4 2.2%	2 1.9%
All sources of info	6 2.1%	4 3.0%	2 1.3%	6 2.1%	0 0	3 1.8%	2 2.0%	1 3.4%	1 1.7%	2 3.3%	0 0	1 3.2%	1 4.5%J	1 3.4%	0 0	0 0	4 2.2%	2 1.9%
preferred source of info	2 0.8%	1 1.1%	1 0.6%	2 0.8%	0 0	1 0.9%	1 1.0%	0 0	0 0	1 1.7%	0 0	0 0	* 2.3%	1 3.4%	0 0	0 0	2 1.4%	0 0
Another library	4 1.6%	2 1.9%	2 1.3%	4 1.6%	0 0	2 1.6%	2 2.1%	0 0	1 1.7%	1 1.7%	2 2.4%	0 0	* 2.3%	0 0	* 5.3%	0 0	3 2.1%	1 0.8%
All sources of info	4 1.6%	2 1.9%	2 1.3%	4 1.6%	0 0	2 1.6%	2 2.1%	0 0	1 1.7%	1 1.7%	2 2.4%	0 0	* 2.3%	0 0	* 5.3%	0 0	3 2.1%	1 0.8%

Proportions/Means: Columns Tested (5% risk level) - A/B/D - C/D - E/F/G - H/I/J/K/L/M/N - P/Q
* small base; ** very small base (under 30) ineligible for sig testing

Table 86
Page 204

Outsell/Digital Library Federation Study (2002)
Weighted Tables

TABLE 83, continued

R7sum_4. When you are doing research, how do you find information about e-journals ? Do you ...

		RESPONDENT TYPE				INSTITUTION TYPE			DISCIPLINE								GENDER	
	TOTAL SAMPLE	FACULTY MEMBER	GRAD. STUDENT	FACULTY /GRAD	UNDER GRAD. STUDENT	PUBLIC	PRIVATE	LIBERAL ARTS	BIOLOGIAL SCIENCES	PHYSICAL SCIENCES /MATH	SOCIAL SCIENCES	ARTS AND HUMAN.	ENGI-NEERING	BUSINESS	LAW	UNDEC. MAJOR	MALE	FEMALE
		(A)	(B)	(C)	(D)	(E)	(F)	(G)	(H)	(I)	(J)	(K)	(L)	(M)	(N)		(P)	(Q)
Base - Use e-journals for research	266	122	144	266	0**	147	89*	29**	51*	60*	77*	35*	13*	27**	3**	0*	160	105*
preferred source of info	0 0	0 0	0 0	0 0	0 0	0 0	0 0	0 0	0 0	0 0	0 0	0 0	0 0	0 0	0 0	0 0	0 0	0 0
Printed abstracting and indexing services	3 1.0%	2 1.4%	1 0.6%	3 1.0%	0 0	2 1.2%	1 1.0%	0 0	3 5.2%	0 0	0 0	0 0	0 0	0 0	0 0	0 0	2 1.1%	1 0.8%
All sources of info	3 1.0%	2 1.4%	1 0.6%	3 1.0%	0 0	2 1.2%	1 1.0%	0 0	3 5.2%	0 0	0 0	0 0	0 0	0 0	0 0	0 0	2 1.1%	1 0.8%
preferred source of info	1 0.3%	1 0.7%	0 0	1 0.3%	0 0	1 0.6%	0 0	0 0	1 1.7%	0 0	0 0	0 0	0 0	0 0	0 0	0 0	1 0.5%	0 0
Physical bookstore	2 0.7%	2 1.5%	0 0	2 0.7%	0 0	2 1.3%	0 0	0 0	0 0	0 0	2 2.4%	0 0	0 0	0 0	0 0	0 0	2 1.2%	0 0
All sources of info	2 0.7%	2 1.5%	0 0	2 0.7%	0 0	2 1.3%	0 0	0 0	0 0	0 0	2 2.4%	0 0	0 0	0 0	0 0	0 0	2 1.2%	0 0
preferred source of info	0 0	0 0	0 0	0 0	0 0	0 0	0 0	0 0	0 0	0 0	0 0	0 0	0 0	0 0	0 0	0 0	0 0	0 0
Printed library catalogues and finding aids	0 0	0 0	0 0	0 0	0 0	0 0	0 0	0 0	0 0	0 0	0 0	0 0	0 0	0 0	0 0	0 0	0 0	0 0
All sources of info	0 0	0 0	0 0	0 0	0 0	0 0	0 0	0 0	0 0	0 0	0 0	0 0	0 0	0 0	0 0	0 0	0 0	0 0

Proportions/Means: Columns Tested (5% risk level) - A/B/D - C/D - E/F/G - H/I/J/K/L/M/N - P/Q
* small base; ** very small base (under 30) ineligible for sig testing

Table 86
Page 205

Outsell/Digital Library Federation Study (2002)
Weighted Tables

TABLE 83, continued

R7sum_4. When you are doing research, how do you find information about e-journals ? Do you ...

	RESPONDENT TYPE				INSTITUTION TYPE			DISCIPLINE									GENDER	
	TOTAL SAMPLE	FACULTY MEMBER	GRAD. STUDENT	FACULTY /GRAD	UNDER GRAD. STUDENT	PUBLIC	PRIVATE	LIBERAL ARTS	BIOLOGIAL SCIENCES	PHYSICAL SCIENCES /MATH	SOCIAL SCIENCES	ARTS AND HUMAN.	ENGI-NEERING	BUSINESS	LAW	UNDEC. MAJOR	MALE	FEMALE
		(A)	(B)	(C)	(D)	(E)	(F)	(G)	(H)	(I)	(J)	(K)	(L)	(M)	(N)		(P)	(Q)
Base - Use e-journals for research	266	122	144	266	0**	147	89*	29**	51*	60*	77*	35*	13*	27**	3**	0*	160	105*
preferred source of info	0 0	0 0	0 0	0 0	0 0	0 0	0 0	0 0	0 0	0 0	0 0	0 0	0 0	0 0	0 0	0 0	0 0	0 0
PERSONAL ASSISTANCE	44 16.5%	24 19.6%	20 14.0%	44 16.5%	0 0	24 16.5%	13 14.2%	7 23.8%	7 13.8%	12 20.0%	9 12.2%	7 19.4%	1 11.4%	7 24.1%	1 26.3%	0 0	25 15.4%	19 18.2%
A librarian in your institution	28 10.4%	16 12.8%	12 8.5%	28 10.4%	0 0	15 10.4%	5 6.1%	7 23.8%	4 6.9%	7 11.7%	6 7.3%	4 12.9%	1 6.8%	6 20.7%	1 21.1%	0 0	19 12.0%	9 8.1%
All sources of info	28 10.4%	16 12.8%	12 8.5%	28 10.4%	0 0	15 10.4%	5 6.1%	7 23.8%	4 6.9%	7 11.7%	6 7.3%	4 12.9%	1 6.8%	6 20.7%	1 21.1%	0 0	19 12.0%	9 8.1%
preferred source of info	7 2.5%	3 2.7%	3 2.3%	7 2.5%	0 0	2 1.5%	3 2.9%	2 6.2%	1 1.7%	0 0	2 2.4%	2 6.5%	* 2.3%	1 3.4%	* 10.5%	0 0	5 2.8%	2 1.9%
Colleagues inside your institution	19 7.2%	11 9.1%	8 5.6%	19 7.2%	0 0	11 7.1%	8 8.5%	1 3.4%	2 3.4%	7 11.7%	4 4.9%	4 12.9%	1 6.8%	1 3.4%	* 10.5%	0 0	10 6.4%	9 8.4%
All sources of info	19 7.2%	11 9.1%	8 5.6%	19 7.2%	0 0	11 7.1%	8 8.5%	1 3.4%	2 3.4%	7 11.7%	4 4.9%	4 12.9%	1 6.8%	1 3.4%	* 10.5%	0 0	10 6.4%	9 8.4%
preferred source of info	1 0.3%	0 0	1 0.6%	1 0.3%	0 0	1 0.6%	0 0	0 0	1 1.7%	0 0	0 0	0 0	0 0	0 0	0 0	0 0	0 0	1 0.8%
Colleagues outside your institution	7 2.6%	5 4.2%	2 1.3%	7 2.6%	0 0	5 3.3%	1 1.1%	1 3.4%	2 3.4%	3 5.0%	2 2.4%	0 0	* 2.3%	0 0	0 0	0 0	5 3.2%	2 1.7%

Proportions/Means: Columns Tested (5% risk level) - A/B/D - C/D - E/F/G - H/I/J/K/L/M/N - P/Q
* small base; ** very small base (under 30) ineligible for sig testing

Table 86
Page 206

Outsell/Digital Library Federation Study (2002)
Weighted Tables

TABLE 83, continued

R7sum_4. When you are doing research, how do you find information about e-journals ? Do you ...

		RESPONDENT TYPE				INSTITUTION TYPE			DISCIPLINE									GENDER	
	TOTAL SAMPLE	FACULTY MEMBER	GRAD. STUDENT	FACULTY /GRAD	UNDER GRAD. STUDENT	PUBLIC	PRIVATE	LIBERAL ARTS	BIOLOGIAL SCIENCES	PHYSICAL SCIENCES /MATH	SOCIAL SCIENCES	ARTS AND HUMAN.	ENGI-NEERING	BUSINESS	LAW	UNDEC. MAJOR	MALE	FEMALE
		(A)	(B)	(C)	(D)	(E)	(F)	(G)	(H)	(I)	(J)	(K)	(L)	(M)	(N)		(P)	(Q)
Base - Use e-journals for research	266	122	144	266	0**	147	89*	29**	51*	60*	77*	35*	13*	27**	3**	0*	160	105*
All sources of info	7 2.6%	5 4.2%	2 1.3%	7 2.6%	0 0	5 3.3%	1 1.1%	1 3.4%	2 3.4%	3 5.0%	2 2.4%	0 0	* 2.3%	0 0	0 0	0 0	5 3.2%	2 1.7%
preferred source of info	0 0	0 0	0 0	0 0	0 0	0 0	0 0	0 0	0 0	0 0	0 0	0 0	0 0	0 0	0 0	0 0	0 0	0 0
Professional meetings	2 0.7%	1 0.7%	1 0.6%	2 0.7%	0 0	1 0.6%	1 1.0%	0 0	2 3.4%	0 0	0 0	0 0	0 0	0 0	0 0	0 0	0 0	2 1.7%
All sources of info	2 0.7%	1 0.7%	1 0.6%	2 0.7%	0 0	1 0.6%	1 1.0%	0 0	2 3.4%	0 0	0 0	0 0	0 0	0 0	0 0	0 0	0 0	2 1.7%
preferred source of info	0 0	0 0	0 0	0 0	0 0	0 0	0 0	0 0	0 0	0 0	0 0	0 0	0 0	0 0	0 0	0 0	0 0	0 0
Another institution's librarian	0 0	0 0	0 0	0 0	0 0	0 0	0 0	0 0	0 0	0 0	0 0	0 0	0 0	0 0	0 0	0 0	0 0	0 0
All sources of info	0 0	0 0	0 0	0 0	0 0	0 0	0 0	0 0	0 0	0 0	0 0	0 0	0 0	0 0	0 0	0 0	0 0	0 0
preferred source of info	0 0	0 0	0 0	0 0	0 0	0 0	0 0	0 0	0 0	0 0	0 0	0 0	0 0	0 0	0 0	0 0	0 0	0 0
Online (unspecified)	5 1.9%	1 0.9%	4 2.8%	5 1.9%	0 0	2 1.3%	3 3.6%	0 0	0 0	1 1.7%	2 2.4%	1 3.2%	0 0	1 3.4%	* 5.3%	0 0	2 1.3%	3 2.8%

Proportions/Means: Columns Tested (5% risk level) - A/B/D - C/D - E/F/G - H/I/J/K/L/M/N - P/Q
* small base; ** very small base (under 30) ineligible for sig testing

Table 86
Page 207

Outsell/Digital Library Federation Study (2002)
Weighted Tables

TABLE 83, continued

R7sum_4. When you are doing research, how do you find information about e-journals ? Do you ...

	RESPONDENT TYPE				INSTITUTION TYPE			DISCIPLINE								GENDER	
	TOTAL SAMPLE	FACULTY MEMBER	GRAD. STUDENT	FACULTY /GRAD	UNDER GRAD. STUDENT	PUBLIC	PRIVATE	LIBERAL ARTS	BIOLOGIAL SCIENCES	PHYSICAL SCIENCES /MATH	SOCIAL SCIENCES	ARTS AND HUMAN.	ENGI-NEERING	BUSINESS	LAW	UNDEC. MAJOR	MALE	FEMALE
		(A)	(B)	(C)	(D)	(E)	(F)	(G)	(H)	(I)	(J)	(K)	(L)	(M)	(N)		(P)	(Q)
Base - Use e-journals for research	266	122	144	266	0**	147	89*	29**	51*	60*	77*	35*	13*	27**	3**	0*	160	105*
All sources of info	5 1.9%	1 0.9%	4 2.8%	5 1.9%	0 0	2 1.3%	3 3.6%	0 0	0 0	1 1.7%	2 2.4%	1 3.2%	0 0	1 3.4%	* 5.3%	0 0	2 1.3%	3 2.8%
preferred source of info	1 0.4%	0 0	1 0.8%	1 0.4%	0 0	0 0	1 1.3%	0 0	0 0	1 1.7%	0 0	0 0	0 0	0 0	* 5.3%	0 0	1 0.7%	0 0
E-Journals	1 0.3%	0 0	1 0.6%	1 0.3%	0 0	1 0.6%	0 0	0 0	1 1.7%	0 0	0 0	0 0	0 0	0 0	0 0	0 0	1 0.5%	0 0
All sources of info	1 0.3%	0 0	1 0.6%	1 0.3%	0 0	1 0.6%	0 0	0 0	1 1.7%	0 0	0 0	0 0	0 0	0 0	0 0	0 0	1 0.5%	0 0
preferred source of info	0 0	0 0	0 0	0 0	0 0	0 0	0 0	0 0	0 0	0 0	0 0	0 0	0 0	0 0	0 0	0 0	0 0	0 0
Personal office/lab	0 0	0 0	0 0	0 0	0 0	0 0	0 0	0 0	0 0	0 0	0 0	0 0	0 0	0 0	0 0	0 0	0 0	0 0
All sources of info	0 0	0 0	0 0	0 0	0 0	0 0	0 0	0 0	0 0	0 0	0 0	0 0	0 0	0 0	0 0	0 0	0 0	0 0
preferred source of info	0 0	0 0	0 0	0 0	0 0	0 0	0 0	0 0	0 0	0 0	0 0	0 0	0 0	0 0	0 0	0 0	0 0	0 0
Author	0 0	0 0	0 0	0 0	0 0	0 0	0 0	0 0	0 0	0 0	0 0	0 0	0 0	0 0	0 0	0 0	0 0	0 0

Proportions/Means: Columns Tested (5% risk level) - A/B/D - C/D - E/F/G - H/I/J/K/L/M/N - P/Q
* small base; ** very small base (under 30) ineligible for sig testing

Table 86
Page 208

Outsell/Digital Library Federation Study (2002)
Weighted Tables

TABLE 83, continued

R7sum_4. When you are doing research, how do you find information about e-journals ? Do you ...

		RESPONDENT TYPE				INSTITUTION TYPE			DISCIPLINE									GENDER	
	TOTAL SAMPLE	FACULTY MEMBER	GRAD. STUDENT	FACULTY /GRAD	UNDER GRAD. STUDENT	PUBLIC	PRIVATE	LIBERAL ARTS	BIOLOGIAL SCIENCES	PHYSICAL SCIENCES /MATH	SOCIAL SCIENCES	ARTS AND HUMAN.	ENGI-NEERING	BUSINESS	LAW	UNDEC. MAJOR	MALE	FEMALE
		(A)	(B)	(C)	(D)	(E)	(F)	(G)	(H)	(I)	(J)	(K)	(L)	(M)	(N)		(P)	(Q)
Base - Use e-journals for research	266	122	144	266	0**	147	89*	29**	51*	60*	77*	35*	13*	27**	3**	0*	160	105*
All sources of info	0 0	0 0	0 0	0 0	0 0	0 0	0 0	0 0	0 0	0 0	0 0	0 0	0 0	0 0	0 0	0 0	0 0	0 0
preferred source of info	0 0	0 0	0 0	0 0	0 0	0 0	0 0	0 0	0 0	0 0	0 0	0 0	0 0	0 0	0 0	0 0	0 0	0 0
Other	15 5.7%	7 6.0%	8 5.5%	15 5.7%	0 0	10 6.6%	5 6.0%	0 0	1 1.7%	4 6.7%	2 2.4%	4 12.9%H	2 13.6%HJ	2 6.9%	* 10.5%	0 0	11 7.1%	4 3.6%
All sources of info	14 5.3%	6 5.2%	8 5.5%	14 5.3%	0 0	9 6.0%	5 6.0%	0 0	1 1.7%	3 5.0%	2 2.4%	4 12.9%H	2 13.6%HJ	2 6.9%	* 10.5%	0 0	10 6.5%	4 3.6%
preferred source of info	7 2.6%	3 2.2%	4 3.0%	7 2.6%	0 0	5 3.7%	2 1.8%	0 0	0 0	2 3.3%	0 0	3 9.7%HJ	1 4.5%HJ	1 3.4%	* 5.3%	0 0	5 2.9%	2 2.3%
DK/Refused	10 3.9%	8 6.2%	3 1.9%	10 3.9%	0 0	5 3.5%	5 5.9%	0 0	1 1.7%	0 0	4 4.9%	4 12.9%HI	* 2.3%	1 3.4%	0 0	0 0	4 2.7%	6 5.7%

Proportions/Means: Columns Tested (5% risk level) - A/B/D - C/D - E/F/G - H/I/J/K/L/M/N - P/Q
* small base; ** very small base (under 30) ineligible for sig testing

TABLE 84

R7D/E_4. e-journals SUMMARY TABLE

		RESPONDENT TYPE				INSTITUTION TYPE			DISCIPLINE								GENDER	
	TOTAL SAMPLE	FACULTY MEMBER	GRAD. STUDENT	FACULTY /GRAD	UNDER GRAD. STUDENT	PUBLIC	PRIVATE	LIBERAL ARTS	BIOLOGIAL SCIENCES	PHYSICAL SCIENCES /MATH	SOCIAL SCIENCES	ARTS AND HUMAN.	ENGI- NEERING	BUSINESS	LAW	UNDEC. MAJOR	MALE	FEMALE
		(A)	(B)	(C)	(D)	(E)	(F)	(G)	(H)	(I)	(J)	(K)	(L)	(M)	(N)		(P)	(Q)
Base - Use e-journals for research	266	122	144	266	0**	147	89*	29**	51*	60*	77*	35*	13*	27**	3**	0*	160	105*
Access online (NET)	216 81.2%	107 87.7%B	109 75.7%	216 81.2%	0 0	112 76.0%	76 84.8%	28 96.8%	40 79.3%	52 86.7%	60 78.0%	28 80.6%	11 84.1%	21 79.3%	3 94.7%	0 0	126 78.5%	90 85.3%
All sources of info	216 81.2%	107 87.7%B	109 75.7%	216 81.2%	0 0	112 76.0%	76 84.8%	28 96.8%	40 79.3%	52 86.7%	60 78.0%	28 80.6%	11 84.1%	21 79.3%	3 94.7%	0 0	126 78.5%	90 85.3%
preferred source of info	197 74.1%	95 78.3%	102 70.6%	197 74.1%	0 0	101 68.5%	68 75.9%	28 96.8%	39 75.9%	52 86.7%J	49 63.4%	25 71.0%	10 79.5%	20 72.4%	3 94.7%	0 0	115 71.8%	82 77.6%
Borrow from or use in campus library (NET)	61 23.0%	26 21.1%	35 24.6%	61 23.0%	0 0	36 24.6%	22 24.7%	3 9.9%	17 32.8%	13 21.7%	13 17.1%	8 22.6%	4 29.5%	7 24.1%	* 5.3%	0 0	40 24.7%	22 20.4%
All sources of info	61 23.0%	26 21.1%	35 24.6%	61 23.0%	0 0	36 24.6%	22 24.7%	3 9.9%	17 32.8%	13 21.7%	13 17.1%	8 22.6%	4 29.5%	7 24.1%	* 5.3%	0 0	40 24.7%	22 20.4%
preferred source of info	37 13.9%	11 9.3%	26 17.7%	37 13.9%	0 0	22 14.7%	15 17.0%	0 0	10 19.0%	6 10.0%	11 14.6%	4 12.9%	2 13.6%	4 13.8%	0 0	0 0	24 14.7%	13 12.6%
Office (NET)	9 3.4%	5 4.4%	4 2.6%	9 3.4%	0 0	5 3.4%	4 4.5%	0 0	2 3.4%	0 0	4 4.9%	2 6.5%	* 2.3%	1 3.4%	0 0	0 0	8 4.9%	1 1.1%
All sources of info	9 3.4%	5 4.4%	4 2.6%	9 3.4%	0 0	5 3.4%	4 4.5%	0 0	2 3.4%	0 0	4 4.9%	2 6.5%	* 2.3%	1 3.4%	0 0	0 0	8 4.9%	1 1.1%
preferred source of info	8 2.9%	5 4.1%	3 1.9%	8 2.9%	0 .0	5 3.2%	3 3.5%	0 0	1 1.7%	0 0	4 4.9%	2 6.5%	0 0	1 3.4%	0 0	0 0	7 4.2%	1 1.1%

Proportions/Means: Columns Tested (5% risk level) - A/B/D - C/D - E/F/G - H/I/J/K/L/M/N - P/Q
* small base; ** very small base (under 30) ineligible for sig testing

Table 89
Page 216

Outsell/Digital Library Federation Study (2002)
Weighted Tables

TABLE 84, continued

R7D/E_4. e-journals SUMMARY TABLE

		RESPONDENT TYPE				INSTITUTION TYPE			DISCIPLINE								GENDER	
	TOTAL SAMPLE	FACULTY MEMBER	GRAD. STUDENT	FACULTY /GRAD	UNDER GRAD. STUDENT	PUBLIC	PRIVATE	LIBERAL ARTS	BIOLOGIAL SCIENCES	PHYSICAL SCIENCES /MATH	SOCIAL SCIENCES	ARTS AND HUMAN.	ENGI-NEERING	BUSINESS	LAW	UNDEC. MAJOR	MALE	FEMALE
		(A)	(B)	(C)	(D)	(E)	(F)	(G)	(H)	(I)	(J)	(K)	(L)	(M)	(N)		(P)	(Q)
Base - Use e-journals for research	266	122	144	266	0**	147	89*	29**	51*	60*	77*	35*	13*	27**	3**	0*	160	105*
Interlibrary loan (NET)	8 3.2%	3 2.3%	6 3.9%	8 3.2%	0 0	6 4.3%	0 0	2 7.2%	1 1.7%	2 3.3%	4 4.9%	0 0	1 4.5%	1 3.4%	* 10.5%	0 0	3 1.7%	6 5.4%
All sources of info	8 3.2%	3 2.3%	6 3.9%	8 3.2%	0 0	6 4.3%	0 0	2 7.2%	1 1.7%	2 3.3%	4 4.9%	0 0	1 4.5%	1 3.4%	* 10.5%	0 0	3 1.7%	6 5.4%
preferred source of info	0 0	0 0	0 0	0 0	0 0	0 0	0 0	0 0	0 0	0 0	0 0	0 0	0 0	0 0	0 0	0 0	0 0	0 0
Borrow from or use in other libraries (NET)	6 2.3%	0 0	6 4.3%A	6 2.3%	0 0	4 2.7%	2 2.4%	0 0	0 0	0 0	6 7.3%	0 0	1 4.5%HI	0 0	0 0	0 0	2 1.5%	4 3.6%
All sources of info	6 2.3%	0 0	6 4.3%A	6 2.3%	0 0	4 2.7%	2 2.4%	0 0	0 0	0 0	6 7.3%	0 0	1 4.5%HI	0 0	0 0	0 0	2 1.5%	4 3.6%
preferred source of info	4 1.5%	0 0	4 2.8%	4 1.5%	0 0	2 1.5%	2 2.1%	0 0	0 0	0 0	4 4.9%	0 0	* 2.3%	0 0	0 0	0 0	2 1.4%	2 1.8%
Personal holdings (NET)	4 1.5%	1 0.9%	3 2.0%	4 1.5%	0 0	4 2.7%	0 0	0 0	0 0	1 1.7%	2 2.4%	1 3.2%	0 0	0 0	0 0	0 0	1 0.6%	3 2.8%
All sources of info	4 1.5%	1 0.9%	3 2.0%	4 1.5%	0 0	4 2.7%	0 0	0 0	0 0	1 1.7%	2 2.4%	1 3.2%	0 0	0 0	0 0	0 0	1 0.6%	3 2.8%
preferred source of info	4 1.5%	1 0.9%	3 2.0%	4 1.5%	0 0	4 2.7%	0 0	0 0	0 0	1 1.7%	2 2.4%	1 3.2%	0 0	0 0	0 0	0 0	1 0.6%	3 2.8%

Proportions/Means: Columns Tested (5% risk level) - A/B/D - C/D - E/F/G - H/I/J/K/L/M/N - P/Q
* small base; ** very small base (under 30) ineligible for sig testing

Table 89
Page 217

Outsell/Digital Library Federation Study (2002)
Weighted Tables

TABLE 84, continued

R7D/E_4. e-journals SUMMARY TABLE

	RESPONDENT TYPE				INSTITUTION TYPE			DISCIPLINE								GENDER	
	TOTAL SAMPLE	FACULTY MEMBER	GRAD. STUDENT	FACULTY /GRAD	UNDER GRAD. STUDENT	PUBLIC	PRIVATE	LIBERAL ARTS	BIOLOGIAL SCIENCES	PHYSICAL SCIENCES /MATH	SOCIAL SCIENCES	ARTS AND HUMAN.	ENGI- NEERING	BUSINESS	LAW	UNDEC. MAJOR	MALE	FEMALE
		(A)	(B)	(C)	(D)	(E)	(F)	(G)	(H)	(I)	(J)	(K)	(L)	(M)	(N)		(P)	(Q)
Base - Use e-journals for research	266	122	144	266	0**	147	89*	29**	51*	60*	77*	35*	13*	27**	3**	0*	160	105*
E-journals (NET)	4 1.4%	0 0	4 2.6%	4 1.4%	0 0	4 2.6%	0 0	0 0	1 1.7%	1 1.7%	2 2.4%	0 0	0 0	0 0	0 0	0 0	1 0.5%	3 2.7%
All sources of info	4 1.4%	0 0	4 2.6%	4 1.4%	0 0	4 2.6%	0 0	0 0	1 1.7%	1 1.7%	2 2.4%	0 0	0 0	0 0	0 0	0 0	1 0.5%	3 2.7%
preferred source of info	2 0.7%	0 0	2 1.3%	2 0.7%	0 0	2 1.3%	0 0	0 0	0 0	0 0	2 2.4%	0 0	0 0	0 0	0 0	0 0	0 0	2 1.8%
Printed material (NET)	4 1.4%	3 2.4%	1 0.6%	4 1.4%	0 0	4 2.6%	0 0	0 0	1 1.7%	1 1.7%	2 2.4%	0 0	0 0	0 0	0 0	0 0	3 1.8%	1 0.8%
All sources of info	4 1.4%	3 2.4%	1 0.6%	4 1.4%	0 0	4 2.6%	0 0	0 0	1 1.7%	1 1.7%	2 2.4%	0 0	0 0	0 0	0 0	0 0	3 1.8%	1 0.8%
preferred source of info	1 0.3%	0 0	1 0.6%	1 0.3%	0 0	1 0.6%	0 0	0 0	1 1.7%	0 0	0 0	0 0	0 0	0 0	0 0	0 0	0 0	1 0.8%
Sources (NET)	1 0.5%	1 1.0%	0 0	1 0.5%	0 0	* 0.2%	0 0	1 3.2%	0 0	0 0	0 0	0 0	* 2.3%	1 3.4%	0 0	0 0	1 0.8%	0 0
All sources of info	1 0.5%	1 1.0%	0 0	1 0.5%	0 0	* 0.2%	0 0	1 3.2%	0 0	0 0	0 0	0 0	* 2.3%	1 3.4%	0 0	0 0	1 0.8%	0 0
preferred source of info	1 0.3%	1 0.8%	0 0	1 0.3%	0 0	0 0	0 0	1 3.2%	0 0	0 0	0 0	0 0	0 0	1 3.4%	0 0	0 0	1 0.6%	0 0

Proportions/Means: Columns Tested (5% risk level) - A/B/D - C/D - E/F/G - H/I/J/K/L/M/N - P/Q
* small base; ** very small base (under 30) ineligible for sig testing

Table 89
Page 218

Outsell/Digital Library Federation Study (2002)
Weighted Tables

TABLE 84, continued

R7D/E_4. e-journals SUMMARY TABLE

		RESPONDENT TYPE				INSTITUTION TYPE			DISCIPLINE								GENDER	
	TOTAL SAMPLE	FACULTY MEMBER	GRAD. STUDENT	FACULTY /GRAD	UNDER GRAD. STUDENT	PUBLIC	PRIVATE	LIBERAL ARTS	BIOLOGIAL SCIENCES	PHYSICAL SCIENCES /MATH	SOCIAL SCIENCES	ARTS AND HUMAN.	ENGI- NEERING	BUSINESS	LAW	UNDEC. MAJOR	MALE	FEMALE
		(A)	(B)	(C)	(D)	(E)	(F)	(G)	(H)	(I)	(J)	(K)	(L)	(M)	(N)		(P)	(Q)
Base - Use e-journals for research	266	122	144	266	0**	147	89*	29**	51*	60*	77*	35*	13*	27**	3**	0*	160	105*
Order from on demand document delivery service (NET)	1 0.5%	1 1.0%	0 0	1 0.5%	0 0	1 0.8%	0 0	0 0	0 0	0 0	0 0	0 0	* 2.3%	1 3.4%	0 0	0 0	1 0.8%	0 0
All sources of info	1 0.5%	1 1.0%	0 0	1 0.5%	0 0	1 0.8%	0 0	0 0	0 0	0 0	0 0	0 0	* 2.3%	1 3.4%	0 0	0 0	1 0.8%	0 0
preferred source of info	1 0.3%	1 0.8%	0 0	1 0.3%	0 0	1 0.6%	0 0	0 0	0 0	0 0	0 0	0 0	0 0	1 3.4%	0 0	0 0	1 0.6%	0 0
Purchase from online bookstore (NET)	1 0.4%	1 0.9%	0 0	1 0.4%	0 0	1 0.8%	0 0	0 0	0 0	0 0	0 0	1 3.2%	0 0	0 0	0 0	0 0	1 0.7%	0 0
All sources of info	1 0.4%	1 0.9%	0 0	1 0.4%	0 0	1 0.8%	0 0	0 0	0 0	0 0	0 0	1 3.2%	0 0	0 0	0 0	0 0	1 0.7%	0 0
preferred source of info	0 0	0 0	0 0	0 0	0 0	0 0	0 0	0 0	0 0	0 0	0 0	0 0	0 0	0 0	0 0	0 0	0 0	0 0
Purchase from physical book store (NET)	0 0	0 0	0 0	0 0	0 0	0 0	0 0	0 0	0 0	0 0	0 0	0 0	0 0	0 0	0 0	0 0	0 0	0 0
All sources of info	0 0	0 0	0 0	0 0	0 0	0 0	0 0	0 0	0 0	0 0	0 0	0 0	0 0	0 0	0 0	0 0	0 0	0 0
preferred source of info	0 0	0 0	0 0	0 0	0 0	0 0	0 0	0 0	0 0	0 0	0 0	0 0	0 0	0 0	0 0	0 0	0 0	0 0

Proportions/Means: Columns Tested (5% risk level) - A/B/D - C/D - E/F/G - H/I/J/K/L/M/N - P/Q
* small base; ** very small base (under 30) ineligible for sig testing

Table 89
Page 219

Outsell/Digital Library Federation Study (2002)
Weighted Tables

TABLE 84, continued

R7D/E_4. e-journals SUMMARY TABLE

		RESPONDENT TYPE				INSTITUTION TYPE			DISCIPLINE								GENDER	
	TOTAL SAMPLE	FACULTY MEMBER	GRAD. STUDENT	FACULTY /GRAD	UNDER GRAD. STUDENT	PUBLIC	PRIVATE	LIBERAL ARTS	BIOLOGIAL SCIENCES	PHYSICAL SCIENCES /MATH	SOCIAL SCIENCES	ARTS AND HUMAN.	ENGI-NEERING	BUSINESS	LAW	UNDEC. MAJOR	MALE	FEMALE
		(A)	(B)	(C)	(D)	(E)	(F)	(G)	(H)	(I)	(J)	(K)	(L)	(M)	(N)		(P)	(Q)
Base - Use e-journals for research	266	122	144	266	0**	147	89*	29**	51*	60*	77*	35*	13*	27**	3**	0*	160	105*
Meetings/conferences (NET)	0	0	0	0	0	0	0	0	0	0	0	0	0	0	0	0	0	0
	0	0	0	0	0	0	0	0	0	0	0	0	0	0	0	0	0	0
All sources of info	0	0	0	0	0	0	0	0	0	0	0	0	0	0	0	0	0	0
	0	0	0	0	0	0	0	0	0	0	0	0	0	0	0	0	0	0
preferred source of info	0	0	0	0	0	0	0	0	0	0	0	0	0	0	0	0	0	0
	0	0	0	0	0	0	0	0	0	0	0	0	0	0	0	0	0	0
Access book/journal/ journal article elsewhere online (NET)	0	0	0	0	0	0	0	0	0	0	0	0	0	0	0	0	0	0
	0	0	0	0	0	0	0	0	0	0	0	0	0	0	0	0	0	0
All sources of info	0	0	0	0	0	0	0	0	0	0	0	0	0	0	0	0	0	0
	0	0	0	0	0	0	0	0	0	0	0	0	0	0	0	0	0	0
preferred source of info	0	0	0	0	0	0	0	0	0	0	0	0	0	0	0	0	0	0
	0	0	0	0	0	0	0	0	0	0	0	0	0	0	0	0	0	0
Access from course website (NET)	0	0	0	0	0	0	0	0	0	0	0	0	0	0	0	0	0	0
	0	0	0	0	0	0	0	0	0	0	0	0	0	0	0	0	0	0
All sources of info	0	0	0	0	0	0	0	0	0	0	0	0	0	0	0	0	0	0
	0	0	0	0	0	0	0	0	0	0	0	0	0	0	0	0	0	0
preferred source of info	0	0	0	0	0	0	0	0	0	0	0	0	0	0	0	0	0	0
	0	0	0	0	0	0	0	0	0	0	0	0	0	0	0	0	0	0

Proportions/Means: Columns Tested (5% risk level) - A/B/D - C/D - E/F/G - H/I/J/K/L/M/N - P/Q
* small base; ** very small base (under 30) ineligible for sig testing

Table 89
Page 220

Outsell/Digital Library Federation Study (2002)
Weighted Tables

TABLE 84, continued

R7D/E_4. e-journals SUMMARY TABLE

		RESPONDENT TYPE				INSTITUTION TYPE			DISCIPLINE								GENDER	
	TOTAL SAMPLE	FACULTY MEMBER	GRAD. STUDENT	FACULTY /GRAD	UNDER GRAD. STUDENT	PUBLIC	PRIVATE	LIBERAL ARTS	BIOLOGIAL SCIENCES	PHYSICAL SCIENCES /MATH	SOCIAL SCIENCES	ARTS AND HUMAN.	ENGI- NEERING	BUSINESS	LAW	UNDEC. MAJOR	MALE	FEMALE
		(A)	(B)	(C)	(D)	(E)	(F)	(G)	(H)	(I)	(J)	(K)	(L)	(M)	(N)		(P)	(Q)
Base - Use e-journals for research	266	122	144	266	0**	147	89*	29**	51*	60*	77*	35*	13*	27**	3**	0*	160	105*
Faculty (NET)	0	0	0	0	0	0	0	0	0	0	0	0	0	0	0	0	0	0
	0	0	0	0	0	0	0	0	0	0	0	0	0	0	0	0	0	0
All sources of info	0	0	0	0	0	0	0	0	0	0	0	0	0	0	0	0	0	0
	0	0	0	0	0	0	0	0	0	0	0	0	0	0	0	0	0	0
preferred source of info	0	0	0	0	0	0	0	0	0	0	0	0	0	0	0	0	0	0
	0	0	0	0	0	0	0	0	0	0	0	0	0	0	0	0	0	0
Ask library to purchase source (NET)	0	0	0	0	0	0	0	0	0	0	0	0	0	0	0	0	0	0
	0	0	0	0	0	0	0	0	0	0	0	0	0	0	0	0	0	0
All sources of info	0	0	0	0	0	0	0	0	0	0	0	0	0	0	0	0	0	0
	0	0	0	0	0	0	0	0	0	0	0	0	0	0	0	0	0	0
preferred source of info	0	0	0	0	0	0	0	0	0	0	0	0	0	0	0	0	0	0
	0	0	0	0	0	0	0	0	0	0	0	0	0	0	0	0	0	0
Colleague (NET)	0	0	0	0	0	0	0	0	0	0	0	0	0	0	0	0	0	0
	0	0	0	0	0	0	0	0	0	0	0	0	0	0	0	0	0	0
All sources of info	0	0	0	0	0	0	0	0	0	0	0	0	0	0	0	0	0	0
	0	0	0	0	0	0	0	0	0	0	0	0	0	0	0	0	0	0
preferred source of info	0	0	0	0	0	0	0	0	0	0	0	0	0	0	0	0	0	0
	0	0	0	0	0	0	0	0	0	0	0	0	0	0	0	0	0	0

Proportions/Means: Columns Tested (5% risk level) - A/B/D - C/D - E/F/G - H/I/J/K/L/M/N - P/Q
* small base; ** very small base (under 30) ineligible for sig testing

Table 89
Page 221

Outsell/Digital Library Federation Study (2002)
Weighted Tables

TABLE 84, continued

R7D/E_4. e-journals SUMMARY TABLE

	TOTAL SAMPLE	RESPONDENT TYPE: FACULTY MEMBER	GRAD. STUDENT	FACULTY /GRAD	UNDER GRAD. STUDENT	INSTITUTION TYPE: PUBLIC	PRIVATE	LIBERAL ARTS	DISCIPLINE: BIOLOGIAL SCIENCES	PHYSICAL SCIENCES /MATH	SOCIAL SCIENCES	ARTS AND HUMAN.	ENGI-NEERING	BUSINESS	LAW	UNDEC. MAJOR	GENDER: MALE	FEMALE
		(A)	(B)	(C)	(D)	(E)	(F)	(G)	(H)	(I)	(J)	(K)	(L)	(M)	(N)		(P)	(Q)
Base - Use e-journals for research	266	122	144	266	0**	147	89*	29**	51*	60*	77*	35*	13*	27**	3**	0*	160	105*
Other (NET)	15 5.6%	10 7.9%	5 3.7%	15 5.6%	0 0	13 8.5%F	1 1.6%	1 3.2%	2 3.4%	2 3.3%	8 9.8%	1 3.2%	* 2.3%	2 6.9%	* 10.5%	0 0	13 8.4%Q	1 1.4%
All sources of info	12 4.6%	8 6.3%	4 3.1%	12 4.6%	0 0	10 6.6%	1 1.6%	1 3.2%	1 1.7%	2 3.3%	6 7.3%	1 3.2%	* 2.3%	2 6.9%	* 10.5%	0 0	11 6.7%	1 1.4%
preferred source of info	7 2.6%	4 3.1%	3 2.3%	7 2.6%	0 0	7 4.7%	* 0.2%	0 0	1 1.7%	1 1.7%	4 4.9%	0 0	* 2.3%	1 3.4%	* 5.3%	0 0	7 4.1%	* 0.4%
DK/Refused	4 1.7%	3 2.7%	1 0.8%	4 1.7%	0 0	3 2.2%	1 1.3%	0 0	0 0	0 0	2 2.4%	2 6.5%	* 2.3%	0 0	0 0	0 0	3 2.1%	1 1.1%

Proportions/Means: Columns Tested (5% risk level) - A/B/D - C/D - E/F/G - H/I/J/K/L/M/N - P/Q
* small base; ** very small base (under 30) ineligible for sig testing

TABLE 85

T7sum_4. e-journals SUMMARY TABLE

		RESPONDENT TYPE				INSTITUTION TYPE			DISCIPLINE								GENDER	
	TOTAL SAMPLE	FACULTY MEMBER	GRAD. STUDENT	FACULTY /GRAD	UNDER GRAD. STUDENT	PUBLIC	PRIVATE	LIBERAL ARTS	BIOLOGIAL SCIENCES	PHYSICAL SCIENCES /MATH	SOCIAL SCIENCES	ARTS AND HUMAN.	ENGI-NEERING	BUSINESS	LAW	UNDEC. MAJOR	MALE	FEMALE
		(A)	(B)	(C)	(D)	(E)	(F)	(G)	(H)	(I)	(J)	(K)	(L)	(M)	(N)		(P)	(Q)
Base - USe e-journals for teaching	156	103*	53*	156	0**	75*	49*	33**	37*	31*	39**	26**	6**	16**	1**	0*	110*	46*
ONLINE	135 86.7%	95 92.5%B	40 75.5%	135 86.7%	0 0	65 86.8%	40 83.3%	30 91.6%	34 92.9%	26 83.9%	32 81.0%	22 87.0%	6 95.5%	14 88.2%	1 100.0%	0 0	96 87.6%	39 84.7%
Search engine	29 18.6%	23 22.0%	6 11.7%	29 18.6%	0 0	14 19.2%	8 15.7%	7 21.3%	7 19.0%	5 16.1%	9 23.8%	3 13.0%	1 18.2%	3 17.6%	* 33.3%	0 0	26 23.8%Q	3 5.9%
All sources of info	29 18.6%	23 22.0%	6 11.7%	29 18.6%	0 0	14 19.2%	8 15.7%	7 21.3%	7 19.0%	5 16.1%	9 23.8%	3 13.0%	1 18.2%	3 17.6%	* 33.3%	0 0	26 23.8%Q	3 5.9%
preferred source of info	15 9.5%	11 10.2%	4 8.1%	15 9.5%	0 0	6 8.4%	3 5.7%	6 17.7%	4 11.9%	4 12.9%	2 4.8%	3 13.0%	* 4.5%	1 5.9%	0 0	0 0	14 12.7%	1 1.9%
Online databases	29 18.4%	20 18.9%	9 17.3%	29 18.4%	0 0	14 18.2%	9 18.9%	6 18.0%	6 16.7%	9 29.0%	6 14.3%	4 17.4%	1 18.2%	2 11.8%	* 66.7%	0 0	23 20.7%	6 12.7%
All sources of info	29 18.4%	20 18.9%	9 17.3%	29 18.4%	0 0	14 18.2%	9 18.9%	6 18.0%	6 16.7%	9 29.0%	6 14.3%	4 17.4%	1 18.2%	2 11.8%	* 66.7%	0 0	23 20.7%	6 12.7%
preferred source of info	24 15.1%	16 15.1%	8 15.2%	24 15.1%	0 0	10 14.1%	8 16.6%	5 15.3%	4 11.9%	8 25.8%	6 14.3%	3 13.0%	1 13.6%	1 5.9%	* 66.7%	0 0	19 17.4%	4 9.6%
Online library catalogues and finding aids	27 17.3%	17 16.1%	10 19.7%	27 17.3%	0 0	8 11.3%	12 24.6%	7 20.2%	9 23.8%	2 6.5%	6 14.3%	8 30.4%	1 13.6%	2 11.8%	0 0	0 0	14 13.2%	13 27.4%
All sources of info	27 17.3%	17 16.1%	10 19.7%	27 17.3%	0 0	8 11.3%	12 24.6%	7 20.2%	9 23.8%	2 6.5%	6 14.3%	8 30.4%	1 13.6%	2 11.8%	0 0	0 0	14 13.2%	13 27.4%

Proportions/Means: Columns Tested (5% risk level) - A/B/D - C/D - E/F/G - H/I/J/K/L/M/N - P/Q
* small base; ** very small base (under 30) ineligible for sig testing

Table 214
Page 810

Outsell/Digital Library Federation Study (2002)
Weighted Tables

TABLE 85, continued

T7sum_4. e-journals SUMMARY TABLE

		RESPONDENT TYPE				INSTITUTION TYPE			DISCIPLINE								GENDER	
	TOTAL SAMPLE	FACULTY MEMBER	GRAD. STUDENT	FACULTY /GRAD	UNDER GRAD. STUDENT	PUBLIC	PRIVATE	LIBERAL ARTS	BIOLOGIAL SCIENCES	PHYSICAL SCIENCES /MATH	SOCIAL SCIENCES	ARTS AND HUMAN.	ENGI-NEERING	BUSINESS	LAW	UNDEC. MAJOR	MALE	FEMALE
		(A)	(B)	(C)	(D)	(E)	(F)	(G)	(H)	(I)	(J)	(K)	(L)	(M)	(N)		(P)	(Q)
Base - USe e-journals for teaching	156	103*	53*	156	0**	75*	49*	33**	37*	31*	39**	26**	6**	16**	1**	0*	110*	46*
preferred source of info	24 15.5%	15 14.4%	9 17.5%	24 15.5%	0 0	8 11.3%	9 18.6%	7 20.2%	7 19.0%	2 6.5%	6 14.3%	7 26.1%	1 13.6%	2 11.8%	0 0	0 0	13 11.6%	11 24.9%
Your own institution's web site	25 16.0%	17 16.0%	8 16.0%	25 16.0%	0 0	12 16.3%	10 20.4%	3 8.8%	6 16.7%	3 9.7%	6 14.3%	6 21.7%	2 27.3%	3 17.6%	0 0	0 0	13 11.6%	12 26.5%P
All sources of info	25 16.0%	17 16.0%	8 16.0%	25 16.0%	0 0	12 16.3%	10 20.4%	3 8.8%	6 16.7%	3 9.7%	6 14.3%	6 21.7%	2 27.3%	3 17.6%	0 0	0 0	13 11.6%	12 26.5%P
preferred source of info	20 12.5%	11 10.8%	8 16.0%	20 12.5%	0 0	12 15.9%	6 12.2%	2 5.4%	4 11.9%	2 6.5%	6 14.3%	4 17.4%	1 18.2%	2 11.8%	0 0	0 0	9 8.6%	10 22.0%P
Web directory/ subject related web site	23 14.8%	22 21.2%B	1 2.2%	23 14.8%	0 0	8 10.3%	4 9.0%	11 33.5%	4 11.9%	7 22.6%	4 9.5%	3 13.0%	2 27.3%	3 17.6%	0 0	0 0	16 14.5%	7 15.5%
All sources of info	23 14.8%	22 21.2%B	1 2.2%	23 14.8%	0 0	8 10.3%	4 9.0%	11 33.5%	4 11.9%	7 22.6%	4 9.5%	3 13.0%	2 27.3%	3 17.6%	0 0	0 0	16 14.5%	7 15.5%
preferred source of info	13 8.6%	12 12.1%	1 1.7%	13 8.6%	0 0	6 8.3%	1 2.5%	6 18.3%	2 4.8%	4 12.9%	4 9.5%	1 4.3%	1 13.6%	2 11.8%	0 0	0 0	10 9.5%	3 6.3%
Internet searches	20 12.8%	15 14.5%	5 9.5%	20 12.8%	0 0	9 11.9%	8 15.5%	4 11.1%	7 19.0%	3 9.7%	6 14.3%	2 8.7%	1 18.2%	1 5.9%	0 0	0 0	18 16.6%	2 3.8%
All sources of info	20 12.8%	15 14.5%	5 9.5%	20 12.8%	0 0	9 11.9%	8 15.5%	4 11.1%	7 19.0%	3 9.7%	6 14.3%	2 8.7%	1 18.2%	1 5.9%	0 0	0 0	18 16.6%	2 3.8%

Proportions/Means: Columns Tested (5% risk level) - A/B/D - C/D - E/F/G - H/I/J/K/L/M/N - P/Q
* small base; ** very small base (under 30) ineligible for sig testing

Table 214
Page 811

Outsell/Digital Library Federation Study (2002)
Weighted Tables

TABLE 85, continued

T7sum_4. e-journals SUMMARY TABLE

		RESPONDENT TYPE				INSTITUTION TYPE			DISCIPLINE									GENDER	
	TOTAL SAMPLE	FACULTY MEMBER	GRAD. STUDENT	FACULTY /GRAD	UNDER GRAD. STUDENT	PUBLIC	PRIVATE	LIBERAL ARTS	BIOLOGIAL SCIENCES	PHYSICAL SCIENCES /MATH	SOCIAL SCIENCES	ARTS AND HUMAN.	ENGI-NEERING	BUSINESS	LAW	UNDEC. MAJOR	MALE	FEMALE
		(A)	(B)	(C)	(D)	(E)	(F)	(G)	(H)	(I)	(J)	(K)	(L)	(M)	(N)		(P)	(Q)
Base - USe e-journals for teaching	156	103*	53*	156	0**	75*	49*	33**	37*	31*	39**	26**	6**	16**	1**	0*	110*	46*
preferred source of info	12 7.8%	9 8.8%	3 5.9%	12 7.8%	0 0	4 5.1%	7 13.7%	2 5.4%	6 16.7%	1 3.2%	2 4.8%	2 8.7%	0 0	1 5.9%	0 0	0 0	10 9.5%	2 3.8%
Online abstracting and indexing services	7 4.3%	2 1.8%	5 9.0%	7 4.3%	0 0	4 5.0%	1 2.1%	2 5.7%	1 2.4%	2 6.5%	4 9.5%	0 0	0 0	0 0	0 0	0 0	4 3.5%	3 6.0%
All sources of info	7 4.3%	2 1.8%	5 9.0%	7 4.3%	0 0	4 5.0%	1 2.1%	2 5.7%	1 2.4%	2 6.5%	4 9.5%	0 0	0 0	0 0	0 0	0 0	4 3.5%	3 6.0%
preferred source of info	4 2.4%	0 0	4 7.1%A	4 2.4%	0 0	4 5.0%	0 0	0 0	0 0	0 0	4 9.5%	0 0	0 0	0 0	0 0	0 0	2 1.7%	2 4.1%
E-mail listservs	4 2.4%	4 3.6%	0 0	4 2.4%	0 0	3 3.8%	1 1.8%	0 0	1 2.4%	1 3.2%	0 0	0 0	0 0	2 11.8%	0 0	0 0	3 2.6%	1 2.0%
All sources of info	4 2.4%	4 3.6%	0 0	4 2.4%	0 0	3 3.8%	1 1.8%	0 0	1 2.4%	1 3.2%	0 0	0 0	0 0	2 11.8%	0 0	0 0	3 2.6%	1 2.0%
preferred source of info	3 1.8%	3 2.8%	0 0	3 1.8%	0 0	3 3.8%	0 0	0 0	0 0	1 3.2%	0 0	0 0	0 0	2 11.8%	0 0	0 0	2 1.8%	1 2.0%
Department web page	3 2.0%	1 1.2%	2 3.3%	3 2.0%	0 0	2 2.4%	1 2.7%	0 0	2 4.8%	1 3.2%	0 0	0 0	* 4.5%	0 0	0 0	0 0	2 2.0%	1 1.9%
All sources of info	3 2.0%	1 1.2%	2 3.3%	3 2.0%	0 0	2 2.4%	1 2.7%	0 0	2 4.8%	1 3.2%	0 0	0 0	* 4.5%	0 0	0 0	0 0	2 2.0%	1 1.9%

Proportions/Means: Columns Tested (5% risk level) - A/B/D - C/D - E/F/G - H/I/J/K/L/M/N - P/Q
* small base; ** very small base (under 30) ineligible for sig testing

Table 214
Page 812

Outsell/Digital Library Federation Study (2002)
Weighted Tables

TABLE 85, continued

T7sum_4. e-journals SUMMARY TABLE

	TOTAL SAMPLE	RESPONDENT TYPE: FACULTY MEMBER	RESPONDENT TYPE: GRAD. STUDENT	RESPONDENT TYPE: FACULTY /GRAD	RESPONDENT TYPE: UNDER GRAD. STUDENT	INSTITUTION TYPE: PUBLIC	INSTITUTION TYPE: PRIVATE	INSTITUTION TYPE: LIBERAL ARTS	DISCIPLINE: BIOLOGIAL SCIENCES	DISCIPLINE: PHYSICAL SCIENCES /MATH	DISCIPLINE: SOCIAL SCIENCES	DISCIPLINE: ARTS AND HUMAN.	DISCIPLINE: ENGI- NEERING	DISCIPLINE: BUSINESS	DISCIPLINE: LAW	DISCIPLINE: UNDEC. MAJOR	GENDER: MALE	GENDER: FEMALE
		(A)	(B)	(C)	(D)	(E)	(F)	(G)	(H)	(I)	(J)	(K)	(L)	(M)	(N)		(P)	(Q)
Base - USe e-journals for teaching	156	103*	53*	156	0**	75*	49*	33**	37*	31*	39**	26**	6**	16**	1**	0*	110*	46*
preferred source of info	2 1.3%	* 0.3%	2 3.3%	2 1.3%	0 0	2 2.4%	* 0.6%	0 0	2 4.8%	0 0	0 0	0 0	* 4.5%	0 0	0 0	0 0	1 1.1%	1 1.9%
Online reference service	2 1.5%	2 2.3%	0 0	2 1.5%	0 0	* 0.4%	2 4.3%	0 0	1 2.4%	0 0	0 0	0 0	1 9.1%	1 5.9%	0 0	0 0	1 0.8%	1 3.2%
All sources of info	2 1.5%	2 2.3%	0 0	2 1.5%	0 0	* 0.4%	2 4.3%	0 0	1 2.4%	0 0	0 0	0 0	1 9.1%	1 5.9%	0 0	0 0	1 0.8%	1 3.2%
preferred source of info	1 0.8%	1 1.2%	0 0	1 0.8%	0 0	0 0	1 2.5%	0 0	0 0	0 0	0 0	0 0	* 4.5%	1 5.9%	0 0	0 0	1 0.8%	* 0.6%
Your own personal electronic library/files	1 0.6%	1 1.0%	0 0	1 0.6%	0 0	1 1.3%	0 0	0 0	0 0	1 3.2%	0 0	0 0	0 0	0 0	0 0	0 0	0 0	1 2.2%
All sources of info	1 0.6%	1 1.0%	0 0	1 0.6%	0 0	1 1.3%	0 0	0 0	0 0	1 3.2%	0 0	0 0	0 0	0 0	0 0	0 0	0 0	1 2.2%
preferred source of info	0 0	0 0	0 0	0 0	0 0	0 0	0 0	0 0	0 0	0 0	0 0	0 0	0 0	0 0	0 0	0 0	0 0	0 0
Online bookstore	0 0	0 0	0 0	0 0	0 0	0 0	0 0	0 0	0 0	0 0	0 0	0 0	0 0	0 0	0 0	0 0	0 0	0 0
All sources of info	0 0	0 0	0 0	0 0	0 0	0 0	0 0	0 0	0 0	0 0	0 0	0 0	0 0	0 0	0 0	0 0	0 0	0 0

Proportions/Means: Columns Tested (5% risk level) - A/B/D - C/D - E/F/G - H/I/J/K/L/M/N - P/Q
* small base; ** very small base (under 30) ineligible for sig testing

Table 214
Page 813

Outsell/Digital Library Federation Study (2002)
Weighted Tables

TABLE 85, continued

T7sum_4. e-journals SUMMARY TABLE

		RESPONDENT TYPE				INSTITUTION TYPE			DISCIPLINE									GENDER	
	TOTAL SAMPLE	FACULTY MEMBER	GRAD. STUDENT	FACULTY /GRAD	UNDER GRAD. STUDENT	PUBLIC	PRIVATE	LIBERAL ARTS	BIOLOGIAL SCIENCES	PHYSICAL SCIENCES /MATH	SOCIAL SCIENCES	ARTS AND HUMAN.	ENGI-NEERING	BUSINESS	LAW	UNDEC. MAJOR	MALE	FEMALE
		(A)	(B)	(C)	(D)	(E)	(F)	(G)	(H)	(I)	(J)	(K)	(L)	(M)	(N)		(P)	(Q)
Base - USe e-journals for teaching	156	103*	53*	156	0**	75*	49*	33**	37*	31*	39**	26**	6**	16**	1**	0*	110*	46*
preferred source of info	0 0	0 0	0 0	0 0	0 0	0 0	0 0	0 0	0 0	0 0	0 0	0 0	0 0	0 0	0 0	0 0	0 0	0 0
LIBRARY/PRINT	36 22.8%	26 25.1%	10 18.4%	36 22.8%	0 0	15 20.7%	12 24.0%	8 25.8%	6 16.7%	11 35.5%	8 19.0%	6 21.7%	2 36.4%	3 17.6%	* 33.3%	0 0	30 26.8%	6 13.2%
Campus library	27 17.5%	20 19.0%	8 14.4%	27 17.5%	0 0	10 13.7%	11 22.0%	6 19.2%	6 16.7%	8 25.8%	4 9.5%	4 17.4%	2 31.8%	3 17.6%	0 0	0 0	21 19.2%	6 13.2%
All sources of info	27 17.5%	20 19.0%	8 14.4%	27 17.5%	0 0	10 13.7%	11 22.0%	6 19.2%	6 16.7%	8 25.8%	4 9.5%	4 17.4%	2 31.8%	3 17.6%	0 0	0 0	21 19.2%	6 13.2%
preferred source of info	6 4.0%	5 4.7%	1 2.7%	6 4.0%	0 0	3 4.2%	2 4.7%	1 2.7%	3 7.1%	1 3.2%	0 0	1 4.3%	1 9.1%	1 5.9%	0 0	0 0	5 4.4%	1 3.1%
References cited in books or journal articles	9 5.9%	6 6.0%	3 5.7%	9 5.9%	0 0	5 6.5%	2 4.5%	2 6.6%	1 2.4%	3 9.7%	4 9.5%	1 4.3%	* 4.5%	0 0	* 33.3%	0 0	8 7.6%	1 1.9%
All sources of info	9 5.9%	6 6.0%	3 5.7%	9 5.9%	0 0	5 6.5%	2 4.5%	2 6.6%	1 2.4%	3 9.7%	4 9.5%	1 4.3%	* 4.5%	0 0	* 33.3%	0 0	8 7.6%	1 1.9%
preferred source of info	1 0.6%	1 1.0%	0 0	1 0.6%	0 0	0 0	0 0	1 3.1%	0 0	1 3.2%	0 0	0 0	0 0	0 0	0 0	0 0	1 0.9%	0 0

Proportions/Means: Columns Tested (5% risk level) - A/B/D - C/D - E/F/G - H/I/J/K/L/M/N - P/Q
* small base; ** very small base (under 30) ineligible for sig testing

TABLE 85, continued

T7sum_4. e-journals SUMMARY TABLE

	TOTAL SAMPLE	RESPONDENT TYPE: FACULTY MEMBER	GRAD. STUDENT	FACULTY /GRAD	UNDER GRAD. STUDENT	INSTITUTION TYPE: PUBLIC	PRIVATE	LIBERAL ARTS	DISCIPLINE: BIOLOGIAL SCIENCES	PHYSICAL SCIENCES /MATH	SOCIAL SCIENCES	ARTS AND HUMAN.	ENGI-NEERING	BUSINESS	LAW	UNDEC. MAJOR	GENDER: MALE	FEMALE
		(A)	(B)	(C)	(D)	(E)	(F)	(G)	(H)	(I)	(J)	(K)	(L)	(M)	(N)		(P)	(Q)
Base - USe e-journals for teaching	156	103*	53*	156	0**	75*	49*	33**	37*	31*	39**	26**	6**	16**	1**	0*	110*	46*
Personal subscriptions to newspapers, magazines and journals	5	5	0	5	0	2	2	1	1	1	2	1	*	0	0	0	4	1
	3.3%	5.0%	0	3.3%	0	2.5%	4.7%	3.1%	2.4%	3.2%	4.8%	4.3%	4.5%	0	0	0	3.9%	1.9%
All sources of info	5	5	0	5	0	2	2	1	1	1	2	1	*	0	0	0	4	1
	3.3%	5.0%	0	3.3%	0	2.5%	4.7%	3.1%	2.4%	3.2%	4.8%	4.3%	4.5%	0	0	0	3.9%	1.9%
preferred source of info	0	0	0	0	0	0	0	0	0	0	0	0	0	0	0	0	0	0
	0	0	0	0	0	0	0	0	0	0	0	0	0	0	0	0	0	0
Your own personal physical library/ files/bookshelves	2	2	0	2	0	*	0	1	0	1	0	0	1	0	0	0	2	0
	1.0%	1.5%	0	1.0%	0	0.4%	0	3.9%	0	3.2%	0	0	9.1%	0	0	0	1.4%	0
All sources of info	2	2	0	2	0	*	0	1	0	1	0	0	1	0	0	0	2	0
	1.0%	1.5%	0	1.0%	0	0.4%	0	3.9%	0	3.2%	0	0	9.1%	0	0	0	1.4%	0
preferred source of info	1	1	0	1	0	*	0	1	0	1	0	0	*	0	0	0	1	0
	0.8%	1.2%	0	0.8%	0	0.4%	0	3.1%	0	3.2%	0	0	4.5%	0	0	0	1.2%	0
Another library	1	1	0	1	0	0	0	1	0	0	0	1	*	0	0	0	1	0
	0.9%	1.4%	0	0.9%	0	0	0	4.3%	0	0	0	4.3%	4.5%	0	0	0	1.3%	0
All sources of info	1	1	0	1	0	0	0	1	0	0	0	1	*	0	0	0	1	0
	0.9%	1.4%	0	0.9%	0	0	0	4.3%	0	0	0	4.3%	4.5%	0	0	0	1.3%	0

Proportions/Means: Columns Tested (5% risk level) - A/B/D - C/D - E/F/G - H/I/J/K/L/M/N - P/Q
* small base; ** very small base (under 30) ineligible for sig testing

Table 214
Page 815

Outsell/Digital Library Federation Study (2002)
Weighted Tables

TABLE 85, continued

T7sum_4. e-journals SUMMARY TABLE

		RESPONDENT TYPE				INSTITUTION TYPE			DISCIPLINE								GENDER	
	TOTAL SAMPLE	FACULTY MEMBER	GRAD. STUDENT	FACULTY /GRAD	UNDER GRAD. STUDENT	PUBLIC	PRIVATE	LIBERAL ARTS	BIOLOGIAL SCIENCES	PHYSICAL SCIENCES /MATH	SOCIAL SCIENCES	ARTS AND HUMAN.	ENGI-NEERING	BUSINESS	LAW	UNDEC. MAJOR	MALE	FEMALE
		(A)	(B)	(C)	(D)	(E)	(F)	(G)	(H)	(I)	(J)	(K)	(L)	(M)	(N)		(P)	(Q)
Base - USe e-journals for teaching	156	103*	53*	156	0**	75*	49*	33**	37*	31*	39**	26**	6**	16**	1**	0*	110*	46*
preferred source of info	0 0	0 0	0 0	0 0	0 0	0 0	0 0	0 0	0 0	0 0	0 0	0 0	0 0	0 0	0 0	0 0	0 0	0 0
Printed abstracting and indexing services	1 0.6%	1 1.0%	0 0	1 0.6%	0 0	0 0	0 0	1 3.1%	0 0	1 3.2%	0 0	0 0	0 0	0 0	0 0	0 0	1 0.9%	0 0
All sources of info	1 0.6%	1 1.0%	0 0	1 0.6%	0 0	0 0	0 0	1 3.1%	0 0	1 3.2%	0 0	0 0	0 0	0 0	0 0	0 0	1 0.9%	0 0
preferred source of info	0 0	0 0	0 0	0 0	0 0	0 0	0 0	0 0	0 0	0 0	0 0	0 0	0 0	0 0	0 0	0 0	0 0	0 0
Physical bookstore	* 0.2%	* 0.3%	0 0	* 0.2%	0 0	* 0.4%	0 0	0 0	0 0	0 0	0 0	0 0	* 4.5%	0 0	0 0	0 0	* 0.3%	0 0
All sources of info	* 0.2%	* 0.3%	0 0	* 0.2%	0 0	* 0.4%	0 0	0 0	0 0	0 0	0 0	0 0	* 4.5%	0 0	0 0	0 0	* 0.3%	0 0
preferred source of info	0 0	0 0	0 0	0 0	0 0	0 0	0 0	0 0	0 0	0 0	0 0	0 0	0 0	0 0	0 0	0 0	0 0	0 0
Printed library catalogues and finding aids	0 0	0 0	0 0	0 0	0 0	0 0	0 0	0 0	0 0	0 0	0 0	0 0	0 0	0 0	0 0	0 0	0 0	0 0
All sources of info	0 0	0 0	0 0	0 0	0 0	0 0	0 0	0 0	0 0	0 0	0 0	0 0	0 0	0 0	0 0	0 0	0 0	0 0

Proportions/Means: Columns Tested (5% risk level) - A/B/D - C/D - E/F/G - H/I/J/K/L/M/N - P/Q
* small base; ** very small base (under 30) ineligible for sig testing

Table 214
Page 816

Outsell/Digital Library Federation Study (2002)
Weighted Tables

TABLE 85, continued

T7sum_4. e-journals SUMMARY TABLE

		RESPONDENT TYPE				INSTITUTION TYPE			DISCIPLINE									GENDER	
	TOTAL SAMPLE	FACULTY MEMBER	GRAD. STUDENT	FACULTY /GRAD	UNDER GRAD. STUDENT	PUBLIC	PRIVATE	LIBERAL ARTS	BIOLOGIAL SCIENCES	PHYSICAL SCIENCES /MATH	SOCIAL SCIENCES	ARTS AND HUMAN.	ENGI-NEERING	BUSINESS	LAW	UNDEC. MAJOR	MALE	FEMALE
		(A)	(B)	(C)	(D)	(E)	(F)	(G)	(H)	(I)	(J)	(K)	(L)	(M)	(N)		(P)	(Q)
Base - USe e-journals for teaching	156	103*	53*	156	0**	75*	49*	33**	37*	31*	39**	26**	6**	16**	1**	0*	110*	46*
preferred source of info	0 0	0 0	0 0	0 0	0 0	0 0	0 0	0 0	0 0	0 0	0 0	0 0	0 0	0 0	0 0	0 0	0 0	0 0
PERSONAL ASSISTANCE	35 22.3%	21 20.0%	14 27.0%	35 22.3%	0 0	14 18.2%	13 27.8%	8 23.9%	4 11.9%	10 32.3%H	8 19.0%	6 21.7%	2 27.3%	6 35.3%	0 0	0 0	26 23.9%	9 18.6%
Colleagues inside your institution	21 13.4%	10 9.2%	11 21.5%	21 13.4%	0 0	9 12.3%	12 24.2%	0 0	1 2.4%	5 16.1%H	6 14.3%	4 17.4%	1 18.2%	4 23.5%	0 0	0 0	14 12.9%	7 14.5%
All sources of info	21 13.4%	10 9.2%	11 21.5%	21 13.4%	0 0	9 12.3%	12 24.2%	0 0	1 2.4%	5 16.1%H	6 14.3%	4 17.4%	1 18.2%	4 23.5%	0 0	0 0	14 12.9%	7 14.5%
preferred source of info	11 7.0%	5 4.8%	6 11.3%	11 7.0%	0 0	4 5.2%	7 14.4%	0 0	1 2.4%	4 12.9%	2 4.8%	2 8.7%	0 0	2 11.8%	0 0	0 0	7 6.4%	4 8.3%
A librarian in your institution	18 11.3%	12 11.4%	6 11.2%	18 11.3%	0 0	7 9.2%	4 8.2%	7 20.8%	4 9.5%	4 12.9%	4 9.5%	3 13.0%	1 18.2%	2 11.8%	0 0	0 0	14 13.1%	3 7.2%
All sources of info	18 11.3%	12 11.4%	6 11.2%	18 11.3%	0 0	7 9.2%	4 8.2%	7 20.8%	4 9.5%	4 12.9%	4 9.5%	3 13.0%	1 18.2%	2 11.8%	0 0	0 0	14 13.1%	3 7.2%
preferred source of info	7 4.4%	2 2.0%	5 9.0%	7 4.4%	0 0	5 6.8%	2 3.6%	0 0	2 4.8%	1 3.2%	4 9.5%	0 0	* 4.5%	0 0	0 0	0 0	5 4.2%	2 4.7%
Colleagues outside your institution	3 1.9%	2 1.8%	1 2.1%	3 1.9%	0 0	2 2.4%	1 2.3%	0 0	1 2.4%	0 0	0 0	1 4.3%	0 0	1 5.9%	0 0	0 0	2 1.6%	1 2.4%
All sources of info	3 1.9%	2 1.8%	1 2.1%	3 1.9%	0 0	2 2.4%	1 2.3%	0 0	1 2.4%	0 0	0 0	1 4.3%	0 0	1 5.9%	0 0	0 0	2 1.6%	1 2.4%

Proportions/Means: Columns Tested (5% risk level) - A/B/D - C/D - E/F/G - H/I/J/K/L/M/N - P/Q
* small base; ** very small base (under 30) ineligible for sig testing

Table 214
Page 817

Outsell/Digital Library Federation Study (2002)
Weighted Tables

TABLE 85, continued

T7sum_4. e-journals SUMMARY TABLE

	TOTAL SAMPLE	RESPONDENT TYPE: FACULTY MEMBER	GRAD. STUDENT	FACULTY /GRAD	UNDER GRAD. STUDENT	INSTITUTION TYPE: PUBLIC	PRIVATE	LIBERAL ARTS	DISCIPLINE: BIOLOGIAL SCIENCES	PHYSICAL SCIENCES /MATH	SOCIAL SCIENCES	ARTS AND HUMAN.	ENGI-NEERING	BUSINESS	LAW	UNDEC. MAJOR	GENDER: MALE	FEMALE
		(A)	(B)	(C)	(D)	(E)	(F)	(G)	(H)	(I)	(J)	(K)	(L)	(M)	(N)		(P)	(Q)
Base - USe e-journals for teaching	156	103*	53*	156	0**	75*	49*	33**	37*	31*	39**	26**	6**	16**	1**	0*	110*	46*
preferred source of info	0 0	0 0	0 0	0 0	0 0	0 0	0 0	0 0	0 0	0 0	0 0	0 0	0 0	0 0	0 0	0 0	0 0	0 0
Professional meetings	2 1.4%	1 1.0%	1 2.1%	2 1.4%	0 0	0 0	1 2.3%	1 3.1%	0 0	1 3.2%	0 0	1 4.3%	0 0	0 0	0 0	0 0	1 0.9%	1 2.4%
All sources of info	2 1.4%	1 1.0%	1 2.1%	2 1.4%	0 0	0 0	1 2.3%	1 3.1%	0 0	1 3.2%	0 0	1 4.3%	0 0	0 0	0 0	0 0	1 0.9%	1 2.4%
preferred source of info	0 0	0 0	0 0	0 0	0 0	0 0	0 0	0 0	0 0	0 0	0 0	0 0	0 0	0 0	0 0	0 0	0 0	0 0
Another institution's librarian	1 0.9%	1 1.4%	0 0	1 0.9%	0 0	* 0.4%	0 0	1 3.4%	0 0	0 0	0 0	1 4.3%	* 4.5%	0 0	0 0	0 0	1 1.3%	0 0
All sources of info	1 0.9%	1 1.4%	0 0	1 0.9%	0 0	* 0.4%	0 0	1 3.4%	0 0	0 0	0 0	1 4.3%	* 4.5%	0 0	0 0	0 0	1 1.3%	0 0
preferred source of info	0 0	0 0	0 0	0 0	0 0	0 0	0 0	0 0	0 0	0 0	0 0	0 0	0 0	0 0	0 0	0 0	0 0	0 0
Personal office/lab	2 1.4%	2 1.8%	* 0.6%	2 1.4%	0 0	2 2.5%	* 0.6%	0 0	0 0	0 0	2 4.8%	0 0	* 4.5%	0 0	0 0	0 0	2 1.7%	* 0.6%
All sources of info	2 1.4%	2 1.8%	* 0.6%	2 1.4%	0 0	2 2.5%	* 0.6%	0 0	0 0	0 0	2 4.8%	0 0	* 4.5%	0 0	0 0	0 0	2 1.7%	* 0.6%

Proportions/Means: Columns Tested (5% risk level) - A/B/D - C/D - E/F/G - H/I/J/K/L/M/N - P/Q
* small base; ** very small base (under 30) ineligible for sig testing

Table 214
Page 818

Outsell/Digital Library Federation Study (2002)
Weighted Tables

TABLE 85, continued

T7sum_4. e-journals SUMMARY TABLE

	RESPONDENT TYPE					INSTITUTION TYPE			DISCIPLINE									GENDER	
	TOTAL SAMPLE	FACULTY MEMBER	GRAD. STUDENT	FACULTY /GRAD	UNDER GRAD. STUDENT	PUBLIC	PRIVATE	LIBERAL ARTS	BIOLOGIAL SCIENCES	PHYSICAL SCIENCES /MATH	SOCIAL SCIENCES	ARTS AND HUMAN.	ENGI-NEERING	BUSINESS	LAW	UNDEC. MAJOR	MALE	FEMALE
		(A)	(B)	(C)	(D)	(E)	(F)	(G)	(H)	(I)	(J)	(K)	(L)	(M)	(N)		(P)	(Q)
Base - USe e-journals for teaching	156	103*	53*	156	0**	75*	49*	33**	37*	31*	39**	26**	6**	16**	1**	0*	110*	46*
preferred source of info	2 1.2%	2 1.8%	0 0	2 1.2%	0 0	2 2.5%	0 0	0 0	0 0	0 0	2 4.8%	0 0	0 0	0 0	0 0	0 0	2 1.7%	0 0
Students	1 0.6%	1 0.9%	0 0	1 0.6%	0 0	1 1.2%	0 0	0 0	1 2.4%	0 0	0 0	0 0	0 0	0 0	0 0	0 0	1 0.8%	0 0
All sources of info	1 0.6%	1 0.9%	0 0	1 0.6%	0 0	1 1.2%	0 0	0 0	1 2.4%	0 0	0 0	0 0	0 0	0 0	0 0	0 0	1 0.8%	0 0
preferred source of info	0 0	0 0	0 0	0 0	0 0	0 0	0 0	0 0	0 0	0 0	0 0	0 0	0 0	0 0	0 0	0 0	0 0	0 0
Online (unspecified)	0 0	0 0	0 0	0 0	0 0	0 0	0 0	0 0	0 0	0 0	0 0	0 0	0 0	0 0	0 0	0 0	0 0	0 0
All sources of info	0 0	0 0	0 0	0 0	0 0	0 0	0 0	0 0	0 0	0 0	0 0	0 0	0 0	0 0	0 0	0 0	0 0	0 0
preferred source of info	0 0	0 0	0 0	0 0	0 0	0 0	0 0	0 0	0 0	0 0	0 0	0 0	0 0	0 0	0 0	0 0	0 0	0 0
Author	0 0	0 0	0 0	0 0	0 0	0 0	0 0	0 0	0 0	0 0	0 0	0 0	0 0	0 0	0 0	0 0	0 0	0 0
All sources of info	0 0	0 0	0 0	0 0	0 0	0 0	0 0	0 0	0 0	0 0	0 0	0 0	0 0	0 0	0 0	0 0	0 0	0 0
preferred source of info	0 0	0 0	0 0	0 0	0 0	0 0	0 0	0 0	0 0	0 0	0 0	0 0	0 0	0 0	0 0	0 0	0 0	0 0

Proportions/Means: Columns Tested (5% risk level) - A/B/D - C/D - E/F/G - H/I/J/K/L/M/N - P/Q
* small base; ** very small base (under 30) ineligible for sig testing

Table 214
Page 819

Outsell/Digital Library Federation Study (2002)
Weighted Tables

TABLE 85, continued

T7sum_4. e-journals SUMMARY TABLE

		RESPONDENT TYPE				INSTITUTION TYPE			DISCIPLINE									GENDER	
	TOTAL SAMPLE	FACULTY MEMBER	GRAD. STUDENT	FACULTY /GRAD	UNDER GRAD. STUDENT	PUBLIC	PRIVATE	LIBERAL ARTS	BIOLOGIAL SCIENCES	PHYSICAL SCIENCES /MATH	SOCIAL SCIENCES	ARTS AND HUMAN.	ENGI-NEERING	BUSINESS	LAW	UNDEC. MAJOR	MALE	FEMALE
		(A)	(B)	(C)	(D)	(E)	(F)	(G)	(H)	(I)	(J)	(K)	(L)	(M)	(N)		(P)	(Q)
Base - USe e-journals for teaching	156	103*	53*	156	0**	75*	49*	33**	37*	31*	39**	26**	6**	16**	1**	0*	110*	46*
Other	16 10.0%	9 8.5%	7 13.1%	16 10.0%	0 0	7 9.1%	5 10.2%	4 11.9%	3 7.1%	2 6.5%	8 19.0%	2 8.7%	* 4.5%	1 5.9%	0 0	0 0	12 10.7%	4 8.5%
All sources of info	15 9.5%	8 7.6%	7 13.1%	15 9.5%	0 0	7 9.1%	4 8.3%	4 11.9%	2 4.8%	2 6.5%	8 19.0%	2 8.7%	* 4.5%	1 5.9%	0 0	0 0	12 10.7%	3 6.5%
preferred source of info	6 3.8%	5 4.7%	1 2.1%	6 3.8%	0 0	2 2.7%	1 2.4%	3 8.4%	2 4.8%	0 0	2 4.8%	1 4.3%	* 4.5%	1 5.9%	0 0	0 0	4 3.6%	2 4.4%
DK/Refused	4 2.7%	4 4.1%	0 0	4 2.7%	0 0	3 3.9%	1 2.5%	* 0.5%	0 0	1 3.2%	2 4.8%	0 0	* 4.5%	1 5.9%	* 33.3%	0 0	3 3.0%	1 2.2%

Proportions/Means: Columns Tested (5% risk level) - A/B/D - C/D - E/F/G - H/I/J/K/L/M/N - P/Q
* small base; ** very small base (under 30) ineligible for sig testing

Table 214
Page 820

Outsell/Digital Library Federation Study (2002)
Weighted Tables

TABLE 86

T7D/E_4. e-journals SUMMARY TABLE

		RESPONDENT TYPE				INSTITUTION TYPE			DISCIPLINE								GENDER	
	TOTAL SAMPLE	FACULTY MEMBER	GRAD. STUDENT	FACULTY /GRAD	UNDER GRAD. STUDENT	PUBLIC	PRIVATE	LIBERAL ARTS	BIOLOGIAL SCIENCES	PHYSICAL SCIENCES /MATH	SOCIAL SCIENCES	ARTS AND HUMAN.	ENGI-NEERING	BUSINESS	LAW	UNDEC. MAJOR	MALE	FEMALE
		(A)	(B)	(C)	(D)	(E)	(F)	(G)	(H)	(I)	(J)	(K)	(L)	(M)	(N)		(P)	(Q)
Base - Use e-journals for teaching	156	103*	53*	156	0**	75*	49*	33**	37*	31*	39**	26**	6**	16**	1**	0*	110*	46*
Access online (NET)	125	88	37	125	0	58	39	28	27	28	30	20	6	14	1	0	90	36
	80.5%	85.4%	71.0%	80.5%	0	78.3%	80.2%	85.8%	73.8%	90.3%	76.2%	78.3%	86.4%	88.2%	100.0%	0	81.6%	78.0%
All sources of info	125	88	37	125	0	58	39	28	27	28	30	20	6	14	1	0	90	36
	80.5%	85.4%	71.0%	80.5%	0	78.3%	80.2%	85.8%	73.8%	90.3%	76.2%	78.3%	86.4%	88.2%	100.0%	0	81.6%	78.0%
preferred source of info	117	84	33	117	0	55	34	28	26	28	26	17	6	14	*	0	85	32
	75.3%	81.4%B	63.2%	75.3%	0	74.3%	69.9%	85.3%	71.4%	90.3%	66.7%	65.2%	86.4%	88.2%	66.7%	0	77.2%	70.6%
Borrow from or use in campus library (NET)	35	15	20	35	0	18	11	6	10	3	15	6	2	0	*	0	24	12
	22.7%	15.0%	37.8%A	22.7%	0	24.6%	23.2%	17.7%	26.2%	9.7%	38.1%	21.7%	27.3%	0	66.7%	0	21.4%	25.9%
All sources of info	35	15	20	35	0	18	11	6	10	3	15	6	2	0	*	0	24	12
	22.7%	15.0%	37.8%A	22.7%	0	24.6%	23.2%	17.7%	26.2%	9.7%	38.1%	21.7%	27.3%	0	66.7%	0	21.4%	25.9%
preferred source of info	23	10	13	23	0	12	8	3	7	1	9	4	1	0	*	0	15	8
	14.7%	9.5%	25.0%A	14.7%	0	16.4%	16.1%	8.9%	19.0%I	3.2%	23.8%	17.4%	13.6%	0	33.3%	0	13.3%	18.1%
Office (NET)	8	7	1	8	0	3	4	1	4	0	2	2	0	0	0	0	4	4
	4.9%	6.3%	2.1%	4.9%	0	4.0%	7.7%	2.7%	9.5%	0	4.8%	8.7%	0	0	0	0	3.3%	8.7%
All sources of info	8	7	1	8	0	3	4	1	4	0	2	2	0	0	0	0	4	4
	4.9%	6.3%	2.1%	4.9%	0	4.0%	7.7%	2.7%	9.5%	0	4.8%	8.7%	0	0	0	0	3.3%	8.7%
preferred source of info	7	6	1	7	0	3	4	0	3	0	2	2	0	0	0	0	4	3
	4.3%	5.5%	2.1%	4.3%	0	4.0%	7.7%	0	7.1%	0	4.8%	8.7%	0	0	0	0	3.3%	6.8%

Proportions/Means: Columns Tested (5% risk level) - A/B/D - C/D - E/F/G - H/I/J/K/L/M/N - P/Q
* small base; ** very small base (under 30) ineligible for sig testing

Table 217
Page 827

Outsell/Digital Library Federation Study (2002)
Weighted Tables

TABLE 86, continued

T7D/E_4. e-journals SUMMARY TABLE

		RESPONDENT TYPE				INSTITUTION TYPE			DISCIPLINE								GENDER	
	TOTAL SAMPLE	FACULTY MEMBER	GRAD. STUDENT	FACULTY /GRAD	UNDER GRAD. STUDENT	PUBLIC	PRIVATE	LIBERAL ARTS	BIOLOGIAL SCIENCES	PHYSICAL SCIENCES /MATH	SOCIAL SCIENCES	ARTS AND HUMAN.	ENGI-NEERING	BUSINESS	LAW	UNDEC. MAJOR	MALE	FEMALE
		(A)	(B)	(C)	(D)	(E)	(F)	(G)	(H)	(I)	(J)	(K)	(L)	(M)	(N)		(P)	(Q)
Base - Use e-journals for teaching	156	103*	53*	156	0**	75*	49*	33**	37*	31*	39**	26**	6**	16**	1**	0*	110*	46*
Order from on demand document delivery service (NET)	4 2.4%	2 1.8%	2 3.6%	4 2.4%	0 0	2 2.5%	2 3.9%	0 0	0 0	0 0	4 9.5%	0 0	0 0	0 0	0 0	0 0	4 3.4%	0 0
All sources of info	4 2.4%	2 1.8%	2 3.6%	4 2.4%	0 0	2 2.5%	2 3.9%	0 0	0 0	0 0	4 9.5%	0 0	0 0	0 0	0 0	0 0	4 3.4%	0 0
preferred source of info	2 1.2%	0 0	2 3.6%	2 1.2%	0 0	2 2.5%	0 0	0 0	0 0	0 0	2 4.8%	0 0	0 0	0 0	0 0	0 0	2 1.7%	0 0
Borrow from or use in other libraries (NET)	3 2.0%	2 1.9%	1 2.1%	3 2.0%	0 0	0 0	1 2.3%	2 6.1%	0 0	2 6.5%	0 0	1 4.3%	0 0	0 0	0 0	0 0	2 1.8%	1 2.4%
All sources of info	3 2.0%	2 1.9%	1 2.1%	3 2.0%	0 0	0 0	1 2.3%	2 6.1%	0 0	2 6.5%	0 0	1 4.3%	0 0	0 0	0 0	0 0	2 1.8%	1 2.4%
preferred source of info	1 0.7%	0 0	1 2.1%	1 0.7%	0 0	0 0	1 2.3%	0 0	0 0	0 0	0 0	1 4.3%	0 0	0 0	0 0	0 0	0 0	1 2.4%
Interlibrary loan (NET)	3 1.9%	2 1.8%	1 2.1%	3 1.9%	0 0	0 0	1 2.3%	2 5.7%	1 2.4%	1 3.2%	0 0	1 4.3%	0 0	0 0	0 0	0 0	1 0.9%	2 4.4%
All sources of info	3 1.9%	2 1.8%	1 2.1%	3 1.9%	0 0	0 0	1 2.3%	2 5.7%	1 2.4%	1 3.2%	0 0	1 4.3%	0 0	0 0	0 0	0 0	1 0.9%	2 4.4%
preferred source of info	0 0	0 0	0 0	0 0	0 0	0 0	0 0	0 0	0 0	0 0	0 0	0 0	0 0	0 0	0 0	0 0	0 0	0 0

Proportions/Means: Columns Tested (5% risk level) - A/B/D - C/D - E/F/G - H/I/J/K/L/M/N - P/Q
* small base; ** very small base (under 30) ineligible for sig testing

Table 217
Page 828

Outsell/Digital Library Federation Study (2002)
Weighted Tables

TABLE 86, continued

T7D/E_4. e-journals SUMMARY TABLE

	TOTAL SAMPLE	RESPONDENT TYPE: FACULTY MEMBER	GRAD. STUDENT	FACULTY /GRAD	UNDER GRAD. STUDENT	INSTITUTION TYPE: PUBLIC	PRIVATE	LIBERAL ARTS	DISCIPLINE: BIOLOGIAL SCIENCES	PHYSICAL SCIENCES /MATH	SOCIAL SCIENCES	ARTS AND HUMAN.	ENGI-NEERING	BUSINESS	LAW	UNDEC. MAJOR	GENDER: MALE	FEMALE
		(A)	(B)	(C)	(D)	(E)	(F)	(G)	(H)	(I)	(J)	(K)	(L)	(M)	(N)		(P)	(Q)
Base - Use e-journals for teaching	156	103*	53*	156	0**	75*	49*	33**	37*	31*	39**	26**	6**	16**	1**	0*	110*	46*
Ask library to purchase source (NET)	2 1.2%	2 1.8%	0 0	2 1.2%	0 0	0 0	2 3.9%	0 0	0 0	0 0	2 4.8%	0 0	0 0	0 0	0 0	0 0	2 1.7%	0 0
All sources of info	2 1.2%	2 1.8%	0 0	2 1.2%	0 0	0 0	2 3.9%	0 0	0 0	0 0	2 4.8%	0 0	0 0	0 0	0 0	0 0	2 1.7%	0 0
preferred source of info	0 0	0 0	0 0	0 0	0 0	0 0	0 0	0 0	0 0	0 0	0 0	0 0	0 0	0 0	0 0	0 0	0 0	0 0
Purchase from physical book store (NET)	1 0.7%	0 0	1 2.1%	1 0.7%	0 0	1 1.5%	0 0	0 0	0 0	0 0	0 0	1 4.3%	0 0	0 0	0 0	0 0	1 1.0%	0 0
All sources of info	1 0.7%	0 0	1 2.1%	1 0.7%	0 0	1 1.5%	0 0	0 0	0 0	0 0	0 0	1 4.3%	0 0	0 0	0 0	0 0	1 1.0%	0 0
preferred source of info	1 0.7%	0 0	1 2.1%	1 0.7%	0 0	1 1.5%	0 0	0 0	0 0	0 0	0 0	1 4.3%	0 0	0 0	0 0	0 0	1 1.0%	0 0
Faculty (NET)	1 0.6%	0 0	1 1.9%	1 0.6%	0 0	0 0	1 2.1%	0 0	0 0	1 3.2%	0 0	0 0	0 0	0 0	0 0	0 0	1 0.9%	0 0
All sources of info	1 0.6%	0 0	1 1.9%	1 0.6%	0 0	0 0	1 2.1%	0 0	0 0	1 3.2%	0 0	0 0	0 0	0 0	0 0	0 0	1 0.9%	0 0
preferred source of info	1 0.6%	0 0	1 1.9%	1 0.6%	0 0	0 0	1 2.1%	0 0	0 0	1 3.2%	0 0	0 0	0 0	0 0	0 0	0 0	1 0.9%	0 0

Proportions/Means: Columns Tested (5% risk level) - A/B/D - C/D - E/F/G - H/I/J/K/L/M/N - P/Q
* small base; ** very small base (under 30) ineligible for sig testing

Table 217
Page 829

Outsell/Digital Library Federation Study (2002)
Weighted Tables

TABLE 86, continued

T7D/E_4. e-journals SUMMARY TABLE

		RESPONDENT TYPE				INSTITUTION TYPE			DISCIPLINE									GENDER	
	TOTAL SAMPLE	FACULTY MEMBER	GRAD. STUDENT	FACULTY /GRAD	UNDER GRAD. STUDENT	PUBLIC	PRIVATE	LIBERAL ARTS	BIOLOGIAL SCIENCES	PHYSICAL SCIENCES /MATH	SOCIAL SCIENCES	ARTS AND HUMAN.	ENGI-NEERING	BUSINESS	LAW	UNDEC. MAJOR	MALE	FEMALE
		(A)	(B)	(C)	(D)	(E)	(F)	(G)	(H)	(I)	(J)	(K)	(L)	(M)	(N)		(P)	(Q)
Base - Use e-journals for teaching	156	103*	53*	156	0**	75*	49*	33**	37*	31*	39**	26**	6**	16**	1**	0*	110*	46*
Personal Collection/ Holdings (NET)	1 0.6%	1 1.0%	0 0	1 0.6%	0 0	0 0	0 0	1 3.1%	0 0	1 3.2%	0 0	0 0	0 0	0 0	0 0	0 0	1 0.9%	0 0
All sources of info	1 0.6%	1 1.0%	0 0	1 0.6%	0 0	0 0	0 0	1 3.1%	0 0	1 3.2%	0 0	0 0	0 0	0 0	0 0	0 0	1 0.9%	0 0
preferred source of info	0 0	0 0	0 0	0 0	0 0	0 0	0 0	0 0	0 0	0 0	0 0	0 0	0 0	0 0	0 0	0 0	0 0	0 0
Publisher (NET)	1 0.6%	1 0.9%	0 0	1 0.6%	0 0	1 1.2%	0 0	0 0	0 0	0 0	0 0	0 0	0 0	1 5.9%	0 0	0 0	1 0.8%	0 0
All sources of info	1 0.6%	1 0.9%	0 0	1 0.6%	0 0	1 1.2%	0 0	0 0	0 0	0 0	0 0	0 0	0 0	1 5.9%	0 0	0 0	1 0.8%	0 0
preferred source of info	1 0.6%	1 0.9%	0 0	1 0.6%	0 0	1 1.2%	0 0	0 0	0 0	0 0	0 0	0 0	0 0	1 5.9%	0 0	0 0	1 0.8%	0 0
Colleagues (NET)	1 0.6%	1 0.9%	0 0	1 0.6%	0 0	0 0	1 1.9%	0 0	0 0	0 0	0 0	0 0	0 0	1 5.9%	0 0	0 0	0 0	1 2.0%
All sources of info	1 0.6%	1 0.9%	0 0	1 0.6%	0 0	0 0	1 1.9%	0 0	0 0	0 0	0 0	0 0	0 0	1 5.9%	0 0	0 0	0 0	1 2.0%
preferred source of info	1 0.6%	1 0.9%	0 0	1 0.6%	0 0	0 0	1 1.9%	0 0	0 0	0 0	0 0	0 0	0 0	1 5.9%	0 0	0 0	0 0	1 2.0%

Proportions/Means: Columns Tested (5% risk level) - A/B/D - C/D - E/F/G - H/I/J/K/L/M/N - P/Q
* small base; ** very small base (under 30) ineligible for sig testing

Table 217
Page 830

Outsell/Digital Library Federation Study (2002)
Weighted Tables

TABLE 86, continued

T7D/E_4. e-journals SUMMARY TABLE

		RESPONDENT TYPE				INSTITUTION TYPE			DISCIPLINE								GENDER	
	TOTAL SAMPLE	FACULTY MEMBER	GRAD. STUDENT	FACULTY /GRAD	UNDER GRAD. STUDENT	PUBLIC	PRIVATE	LIBERAL ARTS	BIOLOGIAL SCIENCES	PHYSICAL SCIENCES /MATH	SOCIAL SCIENCES	ARTS AND HUMAN.	ENGI- NEERING	BUSINESS	LAW	UNDEC. MAJOR	MALE	FEMALE
		(A)	(B)	(C)	(D)	(E)	(F)	(G)	(H)	(I)	(J)	(K)	(L)	(M)	(N)		(P)	(Q)
Base - Use e-journals for teaching	156	103*	53*	156	0**	75*	49*	33**	37*	31*	39**	26**	6**	16**	1**	0*	110*	46*
Access from course website (NET)	* 0.2%	* 0.3%	0 0	* 0.2%	0 0	* 0.4%	0 0	0 0	0 0	0 0	0 0	0 0	* 4.5%	0 0	0 0	0 0	* 0.3%	0 0
All sources of info	* 0.2%	* 0.3%	0 0	* 0.2%	0 0	* 0.4%	0 0	0 0	0 0	0 0	0 0	0 0	* 4.5%	0 0	0 0	0 0	* 0.3%	0 0
preferred source of info	0 0	0 0	0 0	0 0	0 0	0 0	0 0	0 0	0 0	0 0	0 0	0 0	0 0	0 0	0 0	0 0	0 0	0 0
Meeting/Conferences (NET)	0 0	0 0	0 0	0 0	0 0	0 0	0 0	0 0	0 0	0 0	0 0	0 0	0 0	0 0	0 0	0 0	0 0	0 0
All sources of info	0 0	0 0	0 0	0 0	0 0	0 0	0 0	0 0	0 0	0 0	0 0	0 0	0 0	0 0	0 0	0 0	0 0	0 0
preferred source of info	0 0	0 0	0 0	0 0	0 0	0 0	0 0	0 0	0 0	0 0	0 0	0 0	0 0	0 0	0 0	0 0	0 0	0 0
Purchase from online bookstore (NET)	0 0	0 0	0 0	0 0	0 0	0 0	0 0	0 0	0 0	0 0	0 0	0 0	0 0	0 0	0 0	0 0	0 0	0 0
All sources of info	0 0	0 0	0 0	0 0	0 0	0 0	0 0	0 0	0 0	0 0	0 0	0 0	0 0	0 0	0 0	0 0	0 0	0 0
preferred source of info	0 0	0 0	0 0	0 0	0 0	0 0	0 0	0 0	0 0	0 0	0 0	0 0	0 0	0 0	0 0	0 0	0 0	0 0

Proportions/Means: Columns Tested (5% risk level) - A/B/D - C/D - E/F/G - H/I/J/K/L/M/N - P/Q
* small base; ** very small base (under 30) ineligible for sig testing

Table 217
Page 831

Outsell/Digital Library Federation Study (2002)
Weighted Tables

TABLE 86, continued

T7D/E_4. e-journals SUMMARY TABLE

		RESPONDENT TYPE				INSTITUTION TYPE			DISCIPLINE								GENDER	
	TOTAL SAMPLE	FACULTY MEMBER	GRAD. STUDENT	FACULTY /GRAD	UNDER GRAD. STUDENT	PUBLIC	PRIVATE	LIBERAL ARTS	BIOLOGIAL SCIENCES	PHYSICAL SCIENCES /MATH	SOCIAL SCIENCES	ARTS AND HUMAN.	ENGI- NEERING	BUSINESS	LAW	UNDEC. MAJOR	MALE	FEMALE
		(A)	(B)	(C)	(D)	(E)	(F)	(G)	(H)	(I)	(J)	(K)	(L)	(M)	(N)		(P)	(Q)
Base - Use e-journals for teaching	156	103*	53*	156	0**	75*	49*	33**	37*	31*	39**	26**	6**	16**	1**	0*	110*	46*
Department (NET)	0 0	0 0	0 0	0 0	0 0	0 0	0 0	0 0	0 0	0 0	0 0	0 0	0 0	0 0	0 0	0 0	0 0	0 0
All sources of info	0 0	0 0	0 0	0 0	0 0	0 0	0 0	0 0	0 0	0 0	0 0	0 0	0 0	0 0	0 0	0 0	0 0	0 0
preferred source of info	0 0	0 0	0 0	0 0	0 0	0 0	0 0	0 0	0 0	0 0	0 0	0 0	0 0	0 0	0 0	0 0	0 0	0 0
Author	0 0	0 0	0 0	0 0	0 0	0 0	0 0	0 0	0 0	0 0	0 0	0 0	0 0	0 0	0 0	0 0	0 0	0 0
All sources of info	0 0	0 0	0 0	0 0	0 0	0 0	0 0	0 0	0 0	0 0	0 0	0 0	0 0	0 0	0 0	0 0	0 0	0 0
preferred source of info	0 0	0 0	0 0	0 0	0 0	0 0	0 0	0 0	0 0	0 0	0 0	0 0	0 0	0 0	0 0	0 0	0 0	0 0
Home (NET)	0 0	0 0	0 0	0 0	0 0	0 0	0 0	0 0	0 0	0 0	0 0	0 0	0 0	0 0	0 0	0 0	0 0	0 0
All sources of info	0 0	0 0	0 0	0 0	0 0	0 0	0 0	0 0	0 0	0 0	0 0	0 0	0 0	0 0	0 0	0 0	0 0	0 0
preferred source of info	0 0	0 0	0 0	0 0	0 0	0 0	0 0	0 0	0 0	0 0	0 0	0 0	0 0	0 0	0 0	0 0	0 0	0 0

Proportions/Means: Columns Tested (5% risk level) - A/B/D - C/D - E/F/G - H/I/J/K/L/M/N - P/Q
* small base; ** very small base (under 30) ineligible for sig testing

Table 217
Page 832

TABLE 86, continued

T7D/E_4. e-journals SUMMARY TABLE

		RESPONDENT TYPE				INSTITUTION TYPE			DISCIPLINE									GENDER	
	TOTAL SAMPLE	FACULTY MEMBER	GRAD. STUDENT	FACULTY /GRAD	UNDER GRAD. STUDENT	PUBLIC	PRIVATE	LIBERAL ARTS	BIOLOGIAL SCIENCES	PHYSICAL SCIENCES /MATH	SOCIAL SCIENCES	ARTS AND HUMAN.	ENGI-NEERING	BUSINESS	LAW	UNDEC. MAJOR	MALE	FEMALE
		(A)	(B)	(C)	(D)	(E)	(F)	(G)	(H)	(I)	(J)	(K)	(L)	(M)	(N)		(P)	(Q)
Base - Use e-journals for teaching	156	103*	53*	156	0**	75*	49*	33**	37*	31*	39**	26**	6**	16**	1**	0*	110*	46*
Access book/journal/ journal article elsewhere online (NET)	0 0	0 0	0 0	0 0	0 0	0 0	0 0	0 0	0 0	0 0	0 0	0 0	0 0	0 0	0 0	0 0	0 0	0 0
All sources of info	0 0	0 0	0 0	0 0	0 0	0 0	0 0	0 0	0 0	0 0	0 0	0 0	0 0	0 0	0 0	0 0	0 0	0 0
preferred source of info	0 0	0 0	0 0	0 0	0 0	0 0	0 0	0 0	0 0	0 0	0 0	0 0	0 0	0 0	0 0	0 0	0 0	0 0
Other (NET)	2 1.2%	2 1.8%	0 0	2 1.2%	0 0	0 0	0 0	2 5.7%	1 2.4%	1 3.2%	0 0	0 0	0 0	0 0	0 0	0 0	2 1.7%	0 0
preferred source of info	2 1.2%	2 1.8%	0 0	2 1.2%	0 0	0 0	0 0	2 5.7%	1 2.4%	1 3.2%	0 0	0 0	0 0	0 0	0 0	0 0	2 1.7%	0 0
All sources of info	1 0.6%	1 0.9%	0 0	1 0.6%	0 0	0 0	0 0	1 2.7%	1 2.4%	0 0	0 0	0 0	0 0	0 0	0 0	0 0	1 0.8%	0 0
DK/Refused	0 0	0 0	0 0	0 0	0 0	0 0	0 0	0 0	0 0	0 0	0 0	0 0	0 0	0 0	0 0	0 0	0 0	0 0

Proportions/Means: Columns Tested (5% risk level) - A/B/D - C/D - E/F/G - H/I/J/K/L/M/N - P/Q
* small base; ** very small base (under 30) ineligible for sig testing

Table 217
Page 833

Outsell/Digital Library Federation Study (2002)
Weighted Tables

TABLE 87

S7sum_4. e-journals SUMMARY TABLE

		RESPONDENT TYPE				INSTITUTION TYPE			DISCIPLINE									GENDER	
	TOTAL SAMPLE	FACULTY MEMBER	GRAD. STUDENT	FACULTY /GRAD	UNDER GRAD. STUDENT	PUBLIC	PRIVATE	LIBERAL ARTS	BIOLOGIAL SCIENCES	PHYSICAL SCIENCES /MATH	SOCIAL SCIENCES	ARTS AND HUMAN.	ENGI-NEERING	BUSINESS	LAW	UNDEC. MAJOR	MALE	FEMALE
		(A)	(B)	(C)	(D)	(E)	(F)	(G)	(H)	(I)	(J)	(K)	(L)	(M)	(N)		(P)	(Q)
Base - Use e-journals for coursework	360	0**	165	165	195	166	86*	108*	53*	45*	133*	60*	12*	42*	2**	12*	153	207
ONLINE	317 88.1%	0 0	148 89.8%	148 89.8%	169 86.7%	144 87.0%	80 92.5%	93 86.3%	47 88.3%L	39 86.7%L	122 91.5%L	52 85.2%	9 69.8%	37 88.9%L	2 100.0%	10 83.3%	133 87.0%	184 88.9%
Online library catalogues and finding aids (NET)	82 22.7%	0 0	39 23.3%	39 23.3%	43 22.1%	37 22.3%	17 19.4%	28 25.8%	15 28.3%	8 17.8%	26 19.7%	18 29.6%	2 16.3%	9 22.2%	0 0	3 25.0%	35 22.7%	47 22.6%
All sources of info	82 22.7%	0 0	39 23.3%	39 23.3%	43 22.1%	37 22.3%	17 19.4%	28 25.8%	15 28.3%	8 17.8%	26 19.7%	18 29.6%	2 16.3%	9 22.2%	0 0	3 25.0%	35 22.7%	47 22.6%
preferred source of info	63 17.6%	0 0	37 22.5%	37 22.5%	26 13.5%	36 21.6%	14 16.7%	13 12.4%	14 26.7%J	8 17.8%	17 12.7%	15 24.1%	1 11.6%	7 17.8%	0 0	1 8.3%	29 19.2%	34 16.5%
Your own institution's web site (NET)	81 22.5%	0 0	39 23.6%	39 23.6%	42 21.6%	29 17.3%	21 24.4%	31 29.1%E	6 11.7%	12 26.7%M	38 28.2%HM	18 29.6%HM	2 18.6%	4 8.9%	* 20.0%	1 8.3%	26 16.8%	55 26.7%
All sources of info	81 22.5%	0 0	39 23.6%	39 23.6%	42 21.6%	29 17.3%	21 24.4%	31 29.1%E	6 11.7%	12 26.7%M	38 28.2%HM	18 29.6%HM	2 18.6%	4 8.9%	* 20.0%	1 8.3%	26 16.8%	55 26.7%
preferred source of info	71 19.6%	0 0	32 19.4%	32 19.4%	39 19.8%	24 14.7%	18 20.9%	28 26.1%E	6 11.7%	11 24.4%M	32 23.9%M	16 25.9%M	2 16.3%	3 6.7%	0 0	1 8.3%	19 12.3%	52 25.0%P
Search engine (NET)	76 21.0%	0 0	25 15.0%	25 15.0%	51 26.2%B C	25 14.9%	26 30.5%E	25 22.8%	10 18.3%	9 20.0%	15 11.3%	17 27.8%J	3 23.3%	17 40.0%HI J	1 30.0%	5 41.7%	34 22.5%	41 20.0%

Proportions/Means: Columns Tested (5% risk level) - A/B/D - C/D - E/F/G - H/I/J/K/L/M/N - P/Q
* small base; ** very small base (under 30) ineligible for sig testing

Table 342
Page 1409

Outsell/Digital Library Federation Study (2002)
Weighted Tables

TABLE 87, continued

S7sum_4. e-journals SUMMARY TABLE

	TOTAL SAMPLE	RESPONDENT TYPE: FACULTY MEMBER	GRAD. STUDENT	FACULTY /GRAD	UNDER GRAD. STUDENT	INSTITUTION TYPE: PUBLIC	PRIVATE	LIBERAL ARTS	DISCIPLINE: BIOLOGIAL SCIENCES	PHYSICAL SCIENCES /MATH	SOCIAL SCIENCES	ARTS AND HUMAN.	ENGI-NEERING	BUSINESS	LAW	UNDEC. MAJOR	GENDER: MALE	FEMALE
		(A)	(B)	(C)	(D)	(E)	(F)	(G)	(H)	(I)	(J)	(K)	(L)	(M)	(N)		(P)	(Q)
Base - Use e-journals for coursework	360	0**	165	165	195	166	86*	108*	53*	45*	133*	60*	12*	42*	2**	12*	153	207
All sources of info	76 21.0%	0 0	25 15.0%	25 15.0%	51 26.2%B C	25 14.9%	26 30.5%E	25 22.8%	10 18.3%	9 20.0%	15 11.3%	17 27.8%J	3 23.3%	17 40.0%HI J	1 30.0%	5 41.7%	34 22.5%	41 20.0%
preferred source of info	45 12.6%	0 0	15 8.9%	15 8.9%	31 15.7%	18 11.0%	15 17.2%	12 11.4%	7 13.3%	5 11.1%	9 7.0%	6 9.3%	2 14.0%	11 26.7%JK	* 20.0%	5 41.7%	23 15.0%	22 10.8%
Online databases (NET)	69 19.2%	0 0	35 21.1%	35 21.1%	34 17.5%	29 17.6%	17 19.7%	23 21.2%	6 11.7%	7 15.6%	43 32.4%HK LM	8 13.0%	1 4.7%	3 6.7%	* 20.0%	1 8.3%	35 23.2%	34 16.2%
All sources of info	69 19.2%	0 0	35 21.1%	35 21.1%	34 17.5%	29 17.6%	17 19.7%	23 21.2%	6 11.7%	7 15.6%	43 32.4%HK LM	8 13.0%	1 4.7%	3 6.7%	* 20.0%	1 8.3%	35 23.2%	34 16.2%
preferred source of info	51 14.1%	0 0	28 16.9%	28 16.9%	23 11.7%	20 11.8%	14 16.0%	17 15.9%	4 8.3%	6 13.3%	30 22.5%HL M	7 11.1%	* 2.3%	3 6.7%	* 20.0%	0 0	26 17.3%	24 11.7%
Internet searches (NET)	41 11.3%	0 0	16 9.6%	16 9.6%	25 12.7%	24 14.5%	10 11.2%	7 6.4%	4 8.3%	5 11.1%	19 14.1%	8 13.0%	1 7.0%	4 8.9%	0 0	0 0	14 8.9%	27 13.1%
All sources of info	41 11.3%	0 0	16 9.6%	16 9.6%	25 12.7%	24 14.5%	10 11.2%	7 6.4%	4 8.3%	5 11.1%	19 14.1%	8 13.0%	1 7.0%	4 8.9%	0 0	0 0	14 8.9%	27 13.1%
preferred source of info	24 6.6%	0 0	5 3.1%	5 3.1%	19 9.7%B C	17 10.3%	3 3.3%	4 3.6%	1 1.7%	3 6.7%	13 9.9%	2 3.7%	1 7.0%	4 8.9%	0 0	0 0	10 6.9%	13 6.5%

Proportions/Means: Columns Tested (5% risk level) - A/B/D - C/D - E/F/G - H/I/J/K/L/M/N - P/Q
* small base; ** very small base (under 30) ineligible for sig testing

Table 342
Page 1410

Outsell/Digital Library Federation Study (2002)
Weighted Tables

TABLE 87, continued

S7sum_4. e-journals SUMMARY TABLE

		RESPONDENT TYPE				INSTITUTION TYPE			DISCIPLINE								GENDER	
	TOTAL SAMPLE	FACULTY MEMBER	GRAD. STUDENT	FACULTY /GRAD	UNDER GRAD. STUDENT	PUBLIC	PRIVATE	LIBERAL ARTS	BIOLOGIAL SCIENCES	PHYSICAL SCIENCES /MATH	SOCIAL SCIENCES	ARTS AND HUMAN.	ENGI-NEERING	BUSINESS	LAW	UNDEC. MAJOR	MALE	FEMALE
		(A)	(B)	(C)	(D)	(E)	(F)	(G)	(H)	(I)	(J)	(K)	(L)	(M)	(N)		(P)	(Q)
Base - Use e-journals for coursework	360	0**	165	165	195	166	86*	108*	53*	45*	133*	60*	12*	42*	2**	12*	153	207
Web directory/ subject related web site (NET)	25 7.0%	0 0	13 7.6%	13 7.6%	13 6.5%	11 6.4%	8 8.9%	7 6.5%	5 10.0%	3 6.7%	4 2.8%	2 3.7%	1 9.3%	8 20.0%JK	1 30.0%	1 8.3%	12 7.6%	14 6.6%
All sources of info	25 7.0%	0 0	13 7.6%	13 7.6%	13 6.5%	11 6.4%	8 8.9%	7 6.5%	5 10.0%	3 6.7%	4 2.8%	2 3.7%	1 9.3%	8 20.0%JK	1 30.0%	1 8.3%	12 7.6%	14 6.6%
preferred source of info	19 5.4%	0 0	8 5.1%	8 5.1%	11 5.6%	8 4.7%	5 5.4%	7 6.5%	5 10.0%	2 4.4%	4 2.8%	2 3.7%	1 7.0%	4 8.9%	1 30.0%	1 8.3%	9 5.8%	11 5.1%
Online abstracting and indexing services (NET)	11 3.0%	0 0	7 4.3%	7 4.3%	4 2.0%	7 4.0%	3 3.9%	1 0.9%	1 1.7%	2 4.4%	6 4.2%	0 0	1 4.7%K	2 4.4%	0 0	0 0	7 4.7%	4 1.8%
All sources of info	11 3.0%	0 0	7 4.3%	7 4.3%	4 2.0%	7 4.0%	3 3.9%	1 0.9%	1 1.7%	2 4.4%	6 4.2%	0 0	1 4.7%K	2 4.4%	0 0	0 0	7 4.7%	4 1.8%
preferred source of info	7 1.9%	0 0	5 3.0%	5 3.0%	2 1.0%	3 1.7%	3 3.6%	1 0.9%	1 1.7%	2 4.4%	2 1.4%	0 0	* 2.3%	2 4.4%	0 0	0 0	5 3.3%	2 0.9%
Department web page (NET)	11 3.0%	0 0	6 3.4%	6 3.4%	5 2.6%	7 3.9%	1 1.2%	3 3.0%	4 8.3%M	1 2.2%	4 2.8%	1 1.9%	* 2.3%	0 0	* 10.0%	0 0	4 2.5%	7 3.3%
All sources of info	11 3.0%	0 0	6 3.4%	6 3.4%	5 2.6%	7 3.9%	1 1.2%	3 3.0%	4 8.3%M	1 2.2%	4 2.8%	1 1.9%	* 2.3%	0 0	* 10.0%	0 0	4 2.5%	7 3.3%
preferred source of info	7 1.9%	0 0	4 2.2%	4 2.2%	3 1.7%	5 2.7%	1 1.2%	1 1.2%	4 6.7%K	1 2.2%	2 1.4%	0 0	* 2.3%	0 0	* 10.0%	0 0	2 1.2%	5 2.4%

Proportions/Means: Columns Tested (5% risk level) - A/B/D - C/D - E/F/G - H/I/J/K/L/M/N - P/Q
* small base; ** very small base (under 30) ineligible for sig testing

Table 342
Page 1411

Outsell/Digital Library Federation Study (2002)
Weighted Tables

TABLE 87, continued

S7sum_4. e-journals SUMMARY TABLE

		RESPONDENT TYPE				INSTITUTION TYPE			DISCIPLINE									GENDER	
	TOTAL SAMPLE	FACULTY MEMBER	GRAD. STUDENT	FACULTY /GRAD	UNDER GRAD. STUDENT	PUBLIC	PRIVATE	LIBERAL ARTS	BIOLOGIAL SCIENCES	PHYSICAL SCIENCES /MATH	SOCIAL SCIENCES	ARTS AND HUMAN.	ENGI-NEERING	BUSINESS	LAW	UNDEC. MAJOR	MALE	FEMALE
		(A)	(B)	(C)	(D)	(E)	(F)	(G)	(H)	(I)	(J)	(K)	(L)	(M)	(N)		(P)	(Q)
Base - Use e-journals for coursework	360	0**	165	165	195	166	86*	108*	53*	45*	133*	60*	12*	42*	2**	12*	153	207
Online reference service (NET)	7 1.9%	0 0	4 2.5%	4 2.5%	3 1.5%	3 1.8%	3 3.3%	1 0.9%	1 1.7%	1 2.2%	2 1.4%	0 0	* 2.3%	2 4.4%	0 0	1 8.3%	3 2.1%	4 1.8%
All sources of info	7 1.9%	0 0	4 2.5%	4 2.5%	3 1.5%	3 1.8%	3 3.3%	1 0.9%	1 1.7%	1 2.2%	2 1.4%	0 0	* 2.3%	2 4.4%	0 0	1 8.3%	3 2.1%	4 1.8%
preferred source of info	4 1.1%	0 0	3 1.7%	3 1.7%	1 0.5%	0 0	3 3.3%E	1 0.9%	0 0	1 2.2%	2 1.4%	0 0	0 0	0 0	0 0	1 8.3%	2 1.3%	2 0.9%
Your own personal electronic library/files (NET)	4 1.2%	0 0	4 2.5%	4 2.5%	0 0	4 2.5%	0 0	0 0	1 1.7%	0 0	2 1.4%	1 1.9%	* 2.3%	0 0	0 0	0 0	4 2.5%	* 0.1%
All sources of info	4 1.2%	0 0	4 2.5%	4 2.5%	0 0	4 2.5%	0 0	0 0	1 1.7%	0 0	2 1.4%	1 1.9%	* 2.3%	0 0	0 0	0 0	4 2.5%	* 0.1%
preferred source of info	1 0.3%	0 0	1 0.7%	1 0.7%	0 0	1 0.7%	0 0	0 0	1 1.7%	0 0	0 0	0 0	* 2.3%J	0 0	0 0	0 0	1 0.6%	* 0.1%
E-mail listservs (NET)	4 1.0%	0 0	3 1.7%	3 1.7%	1 0.5%	4 2.2%	0 0	0 0	1 1.7%	0 0	2 1.4%	0 0	0 0	1 2.2%	0 0	0 0	0 0	4 1.8%
All sources of info	4 1.0%	0 0	3 1.7%	3 1.7%	1 0.5%	4 2.2%	0 0	0 0	1 1.7%	0 0	2 1.4%	0 0	0 0	1 2.2%	0 0	0 0	0 0	4 1.8%
preferred source of info	2 0.5%	0 0	2 1.1%	2 1.1%	0 0	2 1.1%	0 0	0 0	0 0	0 0	2 1.4%	0 0	0 0	0 0	0 0	0 0	0 0	2 0.9%

Proportions/Means: Columns Tested (5% risk level) - A/B/D - C/D - E/F/G - H/I/J/K/L/M/N - P/Q
* small base; ** very small base (under 30) ineligible for sig testing

Table 342
Page 1412

Outsell/Digital Library Federation Study (2002)
Weighted Tables

TABLE 87, continued

S7sum_4. e-journals SUMMARY TABLE

		RESPONDENT TYPE				INSTITUTION TYPE			DISCIPLINE									GENDER	
	TOTAL SAMPLE	FACULTY MEMBER	GRAD. STUDENT	FACULTY /GRAD	UNDER GRAD. STUDENT	PUBLIC	PRIVATE	LIBERAL ARTS	BIOLOGIAL SCIENCES	PHYSICAL SCIENCES /MATH	SOCIAL SCIENCES	ARTS AND HUMAN.	ENGI-NEERING	BUSINESS	LAW	UNDEC. MAJOR	MALE	FEMALE
		(A)	(B)	(C)	(D)	(E)	(F)	(G)	(H)	(I)	(J)	(K)	(L)	(M)	(N)		(P)	(Q)
Base - Use e-journals for coursework	360	0**	165	165	195	166	86*	108*	53*	45*	133*	60*	12*	42*	2**	12*	153	207
Online bookstore (NET)	2 0.5%	0 0	2 1.1%	2 1.1%	0 0	2 1.1%	0 0	0 0	0 0	0 0	2 1.4%	0 0	0 0	0 0	0 0	0 0	2 1.2%	0 0
All sources of info	2 0.5%	0 0	2 1.1%	2 1.1%	0 0	2 1.1%	0 0	0 0	0 0	0 0	2 1.4%	0 0	0 0	0 0	0 0	0 0	2 1.2%	0 0
preferred source of info	0 0	0 0	0 0	0 0	0 0	0 0	0 0	0 0	0 0	0 0	0 0	0 0	0 0	0 0	0 0	0 0	0 0	0 0
PERSONAL ASSISTANCE	72 20.1%	0 0	27 16.2%	27 16.2%	46 23.5%	25 15.0%	19 22.5%	28 26.1%	10 18.3%	9 20.0%	17 12.7%	17 27.8%J	4 34.9%HJ	10 24.4%	1 30.0%	5 41.7%	39 25.4%	34 16.3%
A librarian in your institution (NET)	46 12.8%	0 0	11 6.5%	11 6.5%	36 18.2%B C	17 10.0%	6 7.5%	23 21.4%EF	4 8.3%	4 8.9%	15 11.3%	11 18.5%	1 11.6%	6 13.3%	1 30.0%	4 33.3%	24 15.7%	22 10.8%
All sources of info	46 12.8%	0 0	11 6.5%	11 6.5%	36 18.2%B C	17 10.0%	6 7.5%	23 21.4%EF	4 8.3%	4 8.9%	15 11.3%	11 18.5%	1 11.6%	6 13.3%	1 30.0%	4 33.3%	24 15.7%	22 10.8%
preferred source of info	18 5.0%	0 0	5 3.2%	5 3.2%	13 6.6%	8 4.7%	2 2.9%	8 7.2%	1 1.7%	0 0	6 4.2%	4 7.4%	1 9.3%HI	4 8.9%I	* 10.0%	2 16.7%	8 5.0%	10 5.0%
Faculty members inside your institution (NET)	38 10.5%	0 0	17 10.4%	17 10.4%	21 10.7%	14 8.4%	12 13.8%	12 11.2%	7 13.3%J	4 8.9%	6 4.2%	10 16.7%J	3 20.9%J	6 13.3%	0 0	3 25.0%	22 14.2%	16 7.9%

Proportions/Means: Columns Tested (5% risk level) - A/B/D - C/D - E/F/G - H/I/J/K/L/M/N - P/Q
* small base; ** very small base (under 30) ineligible for sig testing

Table 342
Page 1413

TABLE 87, continued

S7sum_4. e-journals SUMMARY TABLE

	TOTAL SAMPLE	RESPONDENT TYPE: FACULTY MEMBER	GRAD. STUDENT	FACULTY /GRAD	UNDER GRAD. STUDENT	INSTITUTION TYPE: PUBLIC	PRIVATE	LIBERAL ARTS	DISCIPLINE: BIOLOGIAL SCIENCES	PHYSICAL SCIENCES /MATH	SOCIAL SCIENCES	ARTS AND HUMAN.	ENGI-NEERING	BUSINESS	LAW	UNDEC. MAJOR	GENDER: MALE	FEMALE
		(A)	(B)	(C)	(D)	(E)	(F)	(G)	(H)	(I)	(J)	(K)	(L)	(M)	(N)		(P)	(Q)
Base - Use e-journals for coursework	360	0**	165	165	195	166	86*	108*	53*	45*	133*	60*	12*	42*	2**	12*	153	207
All sources of info	38 10.5%	0 0	17 10.4%	17 10.4%	21 10.7%	14 8.4%	12 13.8%	12 11.2%	7 13.3%J	4 8.9%	6 4.2%	10 16.7%J	3 20.9%J	6 13.3%	0 0	3 25.0%	22 14.2%	16 7.9%
preferred source of info	16 4.5%	0 0	8 5.1%	8 5.1%	8 4.0%	9 5.3%	4 5.2%	3 2.8%	5 10.0%J	1 2.2%	2 1.4%	4 7.4%	2 14.0%IJ	2 4.4%	0 0	0 0	8 5.2%	8 4.0%
Other students inside your institution (NET)	15 4.1%	0 0	6 3.6%	6 3.6%	9 4.6%	5 3.1%	4 5.2%	5 4.8%	2 3.3%	2 4.4%	4 2.8%	3 5.6%	1 9.3%	3 6.7%	0 0	0 0	8 5.3%	7 3.2%
All sources of info	15 4.1%	0 0	6 3.6%	6 3.6%	9 4.6%	5 3.1%	4 5.2%	5 4.8%	2 3.3%	2 4.4%	4 2.8%	3 5.6%	1 9.3%	3 6.7%	0 0	0 0	8 5.3%	7 3.2%
preferred source of info	3 0.9%	0 0	1 0.6%	1 0.6%	2 1.1%	* 0.2%	1 1.1%	2 1.7%	0 0	0 0	2 1.4%	0 0	* 2.3%	1 2.2%	0 0	0 0	1 0.8%	2 0.9%
Faculty members outside your institution (NET)	1 0.3%	0 0	1 0.6%	1 0.6%	0 0	0 0	1 1.2%	0 0	0 0	1 2.2%	0 0	0 0	0 0	0 0	0 0	0 0	1 0.7%	0 0
All sources of info	1 0.3%	0 0	1 0.6%	1 0.6%	0 0	0 0	1 1.2%	0 0	0 0	1 2.2%	0 0	0 0	0 0	0 0	0 0	0 0	1 0.7%	0 0
preferred source of info	0 0	0 0	0 0	0 0	0 0	0 0	0 0	0 0	0 0	0 0	0 0	0 0	0 0	0 0	0 0	0 0	0 0	0 0
Other students outside your institution (NET)	1 0.3%	0 0	1 0.6%	1 0.6%	0 0	0 0	1 1.1%	0 0	0 0	0 0	0 0	0 0	0 0	1 2.2%	0 0	0 0	1 0.6%	0 0

Proportions/Means: Columns Tested (5% risk level) - A/B/D - C/D - E/F/G - H/I/J/K/L/M/N - P/Q
* small base; ** very small base (under 30) ineligible for sig testing

Table 342
Page 1414

Outsell/Digital Library Federation Study (2002)
Weighted Tables

TABLE 87, continued

S7sum_4. e-journals SUMMARY TABLE

		RESPONDENT TYPE				INSTITUTION TYPE			DISCIPLINE									GENDER	
	TOTAL SAMPLE	FACULTY MEMBER	GRAD. STUDENT	FACULTY /GRAD	UNDER GRAD. STUDENT	PUBLIC	PRIVATE	LIBERAL ARTS	BIOLOGIAL SCIENCES	PHYSICAL SCIENCES /MATH	SOCIAL SCIENCES	ARTS AND HUMAN.	ENGI-NEERING	BUSINESS	LAW	UNDEC. MAJOR	MALE	FEMALE
		(A)	(B)	(C)	(D)	(E)	(F)	(G)	(H)	(I)	(J)	(K)	(L)	(M)	(N)		(P)	(Q)
Base - Use e-journals for coursework	360	0**	165	165	195	166	86*	108*	53*	45*	133*	60*	12*	42*	2**	12*	153	207
All sources of info	1 0.3%	0 0	1 0.6%	1 0.6%	0 0	0 0	1 1.1%	0 0	0 0	0 0	0 0	0 0	0 0	1 2.2%	0 0	0 0	1 0.6%	0 0
preferred source of info	0 0	0 0	0 0	0 0	0 0	0 0	0 0	0 0	0 0	0 0	0 0	0 0	0 0	0 0	0 0	0 0	0 0	0 0
Another institution's librarian (NET)	0 0	0 0	0 0	0 0	0 0	0 0	0 0	0 0	0 0	0 0	0 0	0 0	0 0	0 0	0 0	0 0	0 0	0 0
All sources of info	0 0	0 0	0 0	0 0	0 0	0 0	0 0	0 0	0 0	0 0	0 0	0 0	0 0	0 0	0 0	0 0	0 0	0 0
preferred source of info	0 0	0 0	0 0	0 0	0 0	0 0	0 0	0 0	0 0	0 0	0 0	0 0	0 0	0 0	0 0	0 0	0 0	0 0
Professional meetings (NET)	0 0	0 0	0 0	0 0	0 0	0 0	0 0	0 0	0 0	0 0	0 0	0 0	0 0	0 0	0 0	0 0	0 0	0 0
All sources of info	0 0	0 0	0 0	0 0	0 0	0 0	0 0	0 0	0 0	0 0	0 0	0 0	0 0	0 0	0 0	0 0	0 0	0 0
preferred source of info	0 0	0 0	0 0	0 0	0 0	0 0	0 0	0 0	0 0	0 0	0 0	0 0	0 0	0 0	0 0	0 0	0 0	0 0
LIBRARY FACILITIES/ PRINT	49 13.6%	0 0	25 15.1%	25 15.1%	24 12.3%	21 12.9%	11 12.4%	17 15.6%	4 6.7%	3 6.7%	21 15.5%	13 22.2%HI	1 9.3%	5 11.1%	1 30.0%	2 16.7%	23 15.1%	26 12.5%

Proportions/Means: Columns Tested (5% risk level) - A/B/D - C/D - E/F/G - H/I/J/K/L/M/N - P/Q
* small base; ** very small base (under 30) ineligible for sig testing

Table 342
Page 1415

Outsell/Digital Library Federation Study (2002)
Weighted Tables

TABLE 87, continued

S7sum_4. e-journals SUMMARY TABLE

		RESPONDENT TYPE				INSTITUTION TYPE			DISCIPLINE									GENDER	
	TOTAL SAMPLE	FACULTY MEMBER	GRAD. STUDENT	FACULTY /GRAD	UNDER GRAD. STUDENT	PUBLIC	PRIVATE	LIBERAL ARTS	BIOLOGIAL SCIENCES	PHYSICAL SCIENCES /MATH	SOCIAL SCIENCES	ARTS AND HUMAN.	ENGI-NEERING	BUSINESS	LAW	UNDEC. MAJOR	MALE	FEMALE
		(A)	(B)	(C)	(D)	(E)	(F)	(G)	(H)	(I)	(J)	(K)	(L)	(M)	(N)		(P)	(Q)
Base - Use e-journals for coursework	360	0**	165	165	195	166	86*	108*	53*	45*	133*	60*	12*	42*	2**	12*	153	207
Campus library (NET)	39 10.8%	0 0	19 11.8%	19 11.8%	20 10.0%	16 9.6%	10 11.3%	13 12.3%	3 5.0%	3 6.7%	17 12.7%	10 16.7%	1 9.3%	3 6.7%	* 20.0%	2 16.7%	21 13.5%	18 8.8%
All sources of info	39 10.8%	0 0	19 11.8%	19 11.8%	20 10.0%	16 9.6%	10 11.3%	13 12.3%	3 5.0%	3 6.7%	17 12.7%	10 16.7%	1 9.3%	3 6.7%	* 20.0%	2 16.7%	21 13.5%	18 8.8%
preferred source of info	14 3.8%	0 0	5 3.2%	5 3.2%	8 4.3%	6 3.7%	1 1.6%	6 5.7%	1 1.7%	0 0	8 5.6%	4 7.4%	1 4.7%IM	0 0	* 10.0%	0 0	6 4.1%	7 3.6%
References cited in books or journal articles (NET)	4 1.1%	0 0	3 1.7%	3 1.7%	1 0.6%	2 1.1%	1 1.1%	1 1.0%	0 0	0 0	2 1.4%	1 1.9%	0 0	1 2.2%	0 0	0 0	2 1.3%	2 0.9%
All sources of info	4 1.1%	0 0	3 1.7%	3 1.7%	1 0.6%	2 1.1%	1 1.1%	1 1.0%	0 0	0 0	2 1.4%	1 1.9%	0 0	1 2.2%	0 0	0 0	2 1.3%	2 0.9%
preferred source of info	0 0	0 0	0 0	0 0	0 0	0 0	0 0	0 0	0 0	0 0	0 0	0 0	0 0	0 0	0 0	0 0	0 0	0 0
Another library (NET)	3 0.8%	0 0	0 0	0 0	3 1.5%	0 0	0 0	3 2.8%	0 0	0 0	2 1.4%	1 1.9%	0 0	0 0	0 0	0 0	3 2.0%	0 0
All sources of info	3 0.8%	0 0	0 0	0 0	3 1.5%	0 0	0 0	3 2.8%	0 0	0 0	2 1.4%	1 1.9%	0 0	0 0	0 0	0 0	3 2.0%	0 0
preferred source of info	0 0	0 0	0 0	0 0	0 0	0 0	0 0	0 0	0 0	0 0	0 0	0 0	0 0	0 0	0 0	0 0	0 0	0 0

Proportions/Means: Columns Tested (5% risk level) - A/B/D - C/D - E/F/G - H/I/J/K/L/M/N - P/Q
* small base; ** very small base (under 30) ineligible for sig testing

Table 342
Page 1416

Outsell/Digital Library Federation Study (2002)
Weighted Tables

TABLE 87, continued

S7sum_4. e-journals SUMMARY TABLE

		RESPONDENT TYPE				INSTITUTION TYPE			DISCIPLINE									GENDER	
	TOTAL SAMPLE	FACULTY MEMBER	GRAD. STUDENT	FACULTY /GRAD	UNDER GRAD. STUDENT	PUBLIC	PRIVATE	LIBERAL ARTS	BIOLOGIAL SCIENCES	PHYSICAL SCIENCES /MATH	SOCIAL SCIENCES	ARTS AND HUMAN.	ENGI-NEERING	BUSINESS	LAW	UNDEC. MAJOR	MALE	FEMALE
		(A)	(B)	(C)	(D)	(E)	(F)	(G)	(H)	(I)	(J)	(K)	(L)	(M)	(N)		(P)	(Q)
Base - Use e-journals for coursework	360	0**	165	165	195	166	86*	108*	53*	45*	133*	60*	12*	42*	2**	12*	153	207
Your own personal physical library/ files/bookshelves (NET)	3 0.8%	0 0	3 1.8%	3 1.8%	0 0	3 1.8%	0 0	0 0	0 0	0 0	2 1.4%	1 1.9%	0 0	0 0	0 0	0 0	1 0.7%	2 0.9%
All sources of info	3 0.8%	0 0	3 1.8%	3 1.8%	0 0	3 1.8%	0 0	0 0	0 0	0 0	2 1.4%	1 1.9%	0 0	0 0	0 0	0 0	1 0.7%	2 0.9%
preferred source of info	0 0	0 0	0 0	0 0	0 0	0 0	0 0	0 0	0 0	0 0	0 0	0 0	0 0	0 0	0 0	0 0	0 0	0 0
Personal subscriptions to newspapers, magazines and journals (NET)	3 0.8%	0 0	3 1.8%	3 1.8%	0 0	2 1.2%	1 1.1%	0 0	0 0	0 0	0 0	1 1.9%	0 0	2 4.4%J	0 0	0 0	2 1.3%	1 0.4%
All sources of info	3 0.8%	0 0	3 1.8%	3 1.8%	0 0	2 1.2%	1 1.1%	0 0	0 0	0 0	0 0	1 1.9%	0 0	2 4.4%J	0 0	0 0	2 1.3%	1 0.4%
preferred source of info	0 0	0 0	0 0	0 0	0 0	0 0	0 0	0 0	0 0	0 0	0 0	0 0	0 0	0 0	0 0	0 0	0 0	0 0
Printed library catalogues and finding aids (NET)	3 0.8%	0 0	1 0.6%	1 0.6%	2 1.1%	2 1.1%	0 0	1 1.0%	0 0	0 0	0 0	1 1.9%	0 0	2 4.4%J	0 0	0 0	1 0.6%	2 1.0%

Proportions/Means: Columns Tested (5% risk level) - A/B/D - C/D - E/F/G - H/I/J/K/L/M/N - P/Q
* small base; ** very small base (under 30) ineligible for sig testing

Table 342
Page 1417

TABLE 87, continued

S7sum_4. e-journals SUMMARY TABLE

		RESPONDENT TYPE				INSTITUTION TYPE			DISCIPLINE								GENDER	
	TOTAL SAMPLE	FACULTY MEMBER	GRAD. STUDENT	FACULTY /GRAD	UNDER GRAD. STUDENT	PUBLIC	PRIVATE	LIBERAL ARTS	BIOLOGIAL SCIENCES	PHYSICAL SCIENCES /MATH	SOCIAL SCIENCES	ARTS AND HUMAN.	ENGI-NEERING	BUSINESS	LAW	UNDEC. MAJOR	MALE	FEMALE
		(A)	(B)	(C)	(D)	(E)	(F)	(G)	(H)	(I)	(J)	(K)	(L)	(M)	(N)		(P)	(Q)
Base - Use e-journals for coursework	360	0**	165	165	195	166	86*	108*	53*	45*	133*	60*	12*	42*	2**	12*	153	207
All sources of info	3 0.8%	0 0	1 0.6%	1 0.6%	2 1.1%	2 1.1%	0 0	1 1.0%	0 0	0 0	0 0	1 1.9%	0 0	2 4.4%J	0 0	0 0	1 0.6%	2 1.0%
preferred source of info	0 0	0 0	0 0	0 0	0 0	0 0	0 0	0 0	0 0	0 0	0 0	0 0	0 0	0 0	0 0	0 0	0 0	0 0
Printed abstracting and indexing services (NET)	1 0.3%	0 0	1 0.5%	1 0.5%	* 0.1%	1 0.5%	0 0	* 0.2%	1 1.7%	0 0	0 0	0 0	0 0	0 0	* 10.0%	0 0	* 0.1%	1 0.4%
All sources of info	1 0.3%	0 0	1 0.5%	1 0.5%	* 0.1%	1 0.5%	0 0	* 0.2%	1 1.7%	0 0	0 0	0 0	0 0	0 0	* 10.0%	0 0	* 0.1%	1 0.4%
preferred source of info	0 0	0 0	0 0	0 0	0 0	0 0	0 0	0 0	0 0	0 0	0 0	0 0	0 0	0 0	0 0	0 0	0 0	0 0
Physical bookstore (NET)	0 0	0 0	0 0	0 0	0 0	0 0	0 0	0 0	0 0	0 0	0 0	0 0	0 0	0 0	0 0	0 0	0 0	0 0
All sources of info	0 0	0 0	0 0	0 0	0 0	0 0	0 0	0 0	0 0	0 0	0 0	0 0	0 0	0 0	0 0	0 0	0 0	0 0
preferred source of info	0 0	0 0	0 0	0 0	0 0	0 0	0 0	0 0	0 0	0 0	0 0	0 0	0 0	0 0	0 0	0 0	0 0	0 0
Other (NET)	13 3.6%	0 0	7 4.2%	7 4.2%	6 3.0%	7 4.2%	3 3.3%	3 2.8%	1 1.7%	3 6.7%	6 4.2%	1 1.9%	* 2.3%	2 4.4%	0 0	0 0	5 3.3%	8 3.7%

Proportions/Means: Columns Tested (5% risk level) - A/B/D - C/D - E/F/G - H/I/J/K/L/M/N - P/Q
* small base; ** very small base (under 30) ineligible for sig testing

Table 342
Page 1418

Outsell/Digital Library Federation Study (2002)
Weighted Tables

TABLE 87, continued

S7sum_4. e-journals SUMMARY TABLE

	TOTAL SAMPLE	RESPONDENT TYPE: FACULTY MEMBER (A)	RESPONDENT TYPE: GRAD. STUDENT (B)	RESPONDENT TYPE: FACULTY /GRAD (C)	RESPONDENT TYPE: UNDER GRAD. STUDENT (D)	INSTITUTION TYPE: PUBLIC (E)	INSTITUTION TYPE: PRIVATE (F)	INSTITUTION TYPE: LIBERAL ARTS (G)	DISCIPLINE: BIOLOGIAL SCIENCES (H)	DISCIPLINE: PHYSICAL SCIENCES /MATH (I)	DISCIPLINE: SOCIAL SCIENCES (J)	DISCIPLINE: ARTS AND HUMAN. (K)	DISCIPLINE: ENGI-NEERING (L)	DISCIPLINE: BUSINESS (M)	DISCIPLINE: LAW (N)	DISCIPLINE: UNDEC. MAJOR	GENDER: MALE (P)	GENDER: FEMALE (Q)
Base - Use e-journals for coursework	360	0**	165	165	195	166	86*	108*	53*	45*	133*	60*	12*	42*	2**	12*	153	207
All sources of info	12 3.3%	0 0	7 4.2%	7 4.2%	5 2.5%	6 3.6%	3 3.3%	3 2.8%	1 1.7%	3 6.7%	6 4.2%	1 1.9%	* 2.3%	1 2.2%	0 0	0 0	5 3.3%	7 3.3%
preferred source of info	3 0.8%	0 0	1 0.6%	1 0.6%	2 1.0%	3 1.7%	0 0	0 0	0 0	1 2.2%	0 0	0 0	0 0	2 4.4%J	0 0	0 0	1 0.6%	2 0.9%
E-journals	1 0.3%	0 0	1 0.6%	1 0.6%	0 0	1 0.6%	0 0	0 0	0 0	1 2.2%	0 0	0 0	0 0	0 0	0 0	0 0	0 0	1 0.5%
All sources of info	1 0.3%	0 0	1 0.6%	1 0.6%	0 0	1 0.6%	0 0	0 0	0 0	1 2.2%	0 0	0 0	0 0	0 0	0 0	0 0	0 0	1 0.5%
preferred source of info	0 0	0 0	0 0	0 0	0 0	0 0	0 0	0 0	0 0	0 0	0 0	0 0	0 0	0 0	0 0	0 0	0 0	0 0
Online (unspecified)	1 0.2%	0 0	1 0.5%	1 0.5%	0 0	1 0.5%	0 0	0 0	1 1.7%	0 0	0 0	0 0	0 0	0 0	0 0	0 0	0 0	1 0.4%
All sources of info	1 0.2%	0 0	1 0.5%	1 0.5%	0 0	1 0.5%	0 0	0 0	1 1.7%	0 0	0 0	0 0	0 0	0 0	0 0	0 0	0 0	1 0.4%
preferred source of info	1 0.2%	0 0	1 0.5%	1 0.5%	0 0	1 0.5%	0 0	0 0	1 1.7%	0 0	0 0	0 0	0 0	0 0	0 0	0 0	0 0	1 0.4%
DK/Refused	8 2.4%	0 0	3 2.1%	3 2.1%	5 2.6%	4 2.4%	1 0.7%	4 3.6%	1 1.7%	3 6.7%	2 1.4%	1 1.9%	1 4.7%M	0 0	0 0	1 8.3%	1 0.8%	7 3.5%

Proportions/Means: Columns Tested (5% risk level) - A/B/D - C/D - E/F/G - H/I/J/K/L/M/N - P/Q
* small base; ** very small base (under 30) ineligible for sig testing

Table 342
Page 1419

TABLE 88

S7D/E_4. e-journals SUMMARY TABLE

	TOTAL SAMPLE	RESPONDENT TYPE: FACULTY MEMBER	RESPONDENT TYPE: GRAD. STUDENT	RESPONDENT TYPE: FACULTY /GRAD	RESPONDENT TYPE: UNDER GRAD. STUDENT	INSTITUTION TYPE: PUBLIC	INSTITUTION TYPE: PRIVATE	INSTITUTION TYPE: LIBERAL ARTS	DISCIPLINE: BIOLOGIAL SCIENCES	DISCIPLINE: PHYSICAL SCIENCES /MATH	DISCIPLINE: SOCIAL SCIENCES	DISCIPLINE: ARTS AND HUMAN.	DISCIPLINE: ENGI-NEERING	DISCIPLINE: BUSINESS	DISCIPLINE: LAW	DISCIPLINE: UNDEC. MAJOR	GENDER: MALE	GENDER: FEMALE
		(A)	(B)	(C)	(D)	(E)	(F)	(G)	(H)	(I)	(J)	(K)	(L)	(M)	(N)		(P)	(Q)
Base - Use e-journals for coursework	360	0**	165	165	195	166	86*	108*	53*	45*	133*	60*	12*	42*	2**	12*	153	207
Access online (NET)	270 75.0%	0 0	131 79.3%	131 79.3%	139 71.4%	116 70.0%	70 81.8%	83 77.3%	40 75.0%	38 84.4%	98 73.2%	41 68.5%	9 74.4%	33 80.0%	1 70.0%	9 75.0%	120 78.6%	150 72.3%
All sources of info	270 75.0%	0 0	131 79.3%	131 79.3%	139 71.4%	116 70.0%	70 81.8%	83 77.3%	40 75.0%	38 84.4%	98 73.2%	41 68.5%	9 74.4%	33 80.0%	1 70.0%	9 75.0%	120 78.6%	150 72.3%
preferred source of info	246 68.5%	0 0	117 71.0%	117 71.0%	129 66.4%	102 61.4%	66 77.0%E	78 72.6%	35 66.7%	36 80.0%	86 64.8%	39 64.8%	9 69.8%	31 73.3%	1 70.0%	9 75.0%	111 72.7%	136 65.4%
Borrow from or use in campus library (NET)	142 39.5%	0 0	58 35.1%	58 35.1%	84 43.2%	71 43.1%	27 30.8%	44 40.9%	23 43.3%I	9 20.0%	58 43.7%I	29 48.1%I	3 27.9%	16 37.8%	1 30.0%	3 25.0%	51 33.3%	91 44.1%
All sources of info	142 39.5%	0 0	58 35.1%	58 35.1%	84 43.2%	71 43.1%	27 30.8%	44 40.9%	23 43.3%I	9 20.0%	58 43.7%I	29 48.1%I	3 27.9%	16 37.8%	1 30.0%	3 25.0%	51 33.3%	91 44.1%
preferred source of info	92 25.5%	0 0	34 20.7%	34 20.7%	58 29.5%	49 29.5%	15 17.9%	28 25.5%	16 30.0%I	6 13.3%	36 26.8%	18 29.6%	3 20.9%	11 26.7%	1 30.0%	2 16.7%	31 20.5%	60 29.2%
Interlibrary loan (NET)	10 2.8%	0 0	* 0.2%	* 0.2%	10 5.1%BC	5 3.2%	0 0	5 4.5%	2 3.3%	0 0	4 2.8%	3 5.6%	* 2.3%	0 0	0 0	1 8.3%	4 2.7%	6 2.9%
All sources of info	10 2.8%	0 0	* 0.2%	* 0.2%	10 5.1%BC	5 3.2%	0 0	5 4.5%	2 3.3%	0 0	4 2.8%	3 5.6%	* 2.3%	0 0	0 0	1 8.3%	4 2.7%	6 2.9%
preferred source of info	4 1.2%	0 0	* 0.2%	* 0.2%	4 2.0%	4 2.5%	0 0	0 0	1 1.7%	0 0	2 1.4%	1 1.9%	* 2.3%	0 0	0 0	0 0	4 2.7%Q	0 0

Proportions/Means: Columns Tested (5% risk level) - A/B/D - C/D - E/F/G - H/I/J/K/L/M/N - P/Q
* small base; ** very small base (under 30) ineligible for sig testing

Table 345
Page 1426

Outsell/Digital Library Federation Study (2002)
Weighted Tables

TABLE 88, continued

S7D/E_4. e-journals SUMMARY TABLE

		RESPONDENT TYPE				INSTITUTION TYPE			DISCIPLINE									GENDER	
	TOTAL SAMPLE	FACULTY MEMBER	GRAD. STUDENT	FACULTY /GRAD	UNDER GRAD. STUDENT	PUBLIC	PRIVATE	LIBERAL ARTS	BIOLOGIAL SCIENCES	PHYSICAL SCIENCES /MATH	SOCIAL SCIENCES	ARTS AND HUMAN.	ENGI-NEERING	BUSINESS	LAW	UNDEC. MAJOR	MALE	FEMALE
		(A)	(B)	(C)	(D)	(E)	(F)	(G)	(H)	(I)	(J)	(K)	(L)	(M)	(N)		(P)	(Q)
Base - Use e-journals for coursework	360	0**	165	165	195	166	86*	108*	53*	45*	133*	60*	12*	42*	2**	12*	153	207
Borrow from or use in other libraries (NET)	8 2.2%	0 0	3 1.7%	3 1.7%	5 2.5%	5 2.9%	0 0	3 2.8%	0 0	1 2.2%	6 4.2%	1 1.9%	0 0	0 0	0 0	0 0	1 0.7%	7 3.3%
All sources of info	8 2.2%	0 0	3 1.7%	3 1.7%	5 2.5%	5 2.9%	0 0	3 2.8%	0 0	1 2.2%	6 4.2%	1 1.9%	0 0	0 0	0 0	0 0	1 0.7%	7 3.3%
preferred source of info	3 0.8%	0 0	3 1.7%	3 1.7%	0 0	3 1.7%	0 0	0 0	0 0	1 2.2%	2 1.4%	0 0	0 0	0 0	0 0	0 0	1 0.7%	2 0.9%
Order from on demand document delivery service (NET)	2 0.5%	0 0	2 1.1%	2 1.1%	0 0	2 1.1%	0 0	0 0	0 0	0 0	2 1.4%	0 0	0 0	0 0	0 0	0 0	2 1.2%	0 0
All sources of info	2 0.5%	0 0	2 1.1%	2 1.1%	0 0	2 1.1%	0 0	0 0	0 0	0 0	2 1.4%	0 0	0 0	0 0	0 0	0 0	2 1.2%	0 0
preferred source of info	2 0.5%	0 0	2 1.1%	2 1.1%	0 0	2 1.1%	0 0	0 0	0 0	0 0	2 1.4%	0 0	0 0	0 0	0 0	0 0	2 1.2%	0 0
Ask library to purchase source (NET)	2 0.5%	0 0	2 1.1%	2 1.1%	0 0	2 1.1%	0 0	0 0	0 0	0 0	2 1.4%	0 0	0 0	0 0	0 0	0 0	2 1.2%	0 0
All sources of info	2 0.5%	0 0	2 1.1%	2 1.1%	0 0	2 1.1%	0 0	0 0	0 0	0 0	2 1.4%	0 0	0 0	0 0	0 0	0 0	2 1.2%	0 0
preferred source of info	2 0.5%	0 0	2 1.1%	2 1.1%	0 0	2 1.1%	0 0	0 0	0 0	0 0	2 1.4%	0 0	0 0	0 0	0 0	0 0	2 1.2%	0 0

Proportions/Means: Columns Tested (5% risk level) - A/B/D - C/D - E/F/G - H/I/J/K/L/M/N - P/Q
* small base; ** very small base (under 30) ineligible for sig testing

Table 345
Page 1427

Outsell/Digital Library Federation Study (2002)
Weighted Tables

TABLE 88, continued

S7D/E_4. e-journals SUMMARY TABLE

	TOTAL SAMPLE	RESPONDENT TYPE: FACULTY MEMBER	RESPONDENT TYPE: GRAD. STUDENT	RESPONDENT TYPE: FACULTY /GRAD	RESPONDENT TYPE: UNDER GRAD. STUDENT	INSTITUTION TYPE: PUBLIC	INSTITUTION TYPE: PRIVATE	INSTITUTION TYPE: LIBERAL ARTS	DISCIPLINE: BIOLOGIAL SCIENCES	DISCIPLINE: PHYSICAL SCIENCES /MATH	DISCIPLINE: SOCIAL SCIENCES	DISCIPLINE: ARTS AND HUMAN.	DISCIPLINE: ENGI-NEERING	DISCIPLINE: BUSINESS	DISCIPLINE: LAW	DISCIPLINE: UNDEC. MAJOR	GENDER: MALE	GENDER: FEMALE
		(A)	(B)	(C)	(D)	(E)	(F)	(G)	(H)	(I)	(J)	(K)	(L)	(M)	(N)		(P)	(Q)
Base - Use e-journals for coursework	360	0**	165	165	195	166	86*	108*	53*	45*	133*	60*	12*	42*	2**	12*	153	207
Dorm room (NET)	2	0	0	0	2	2	0	0	0	0	2	0	0	0	0	0	0	2
	0.5%	0	0	0	1.0%	1.1%	0	0	0	0	1.4%	0	0	0	0	0	0	0.9%
All sources of info	2	0	0	0	2	2	0	0	0	0	2	0	0	0	0	0	0	2
	0.5%	0	0	0	1.0%	1.1%	0	0	0	0	1.4%	0	0	0	0	0	0	0.9%
preferred source of info	2	0	0	0	2	2	0	0	0	0	2	0	0	0	0	0	0	2
	0.5%	0	0	0	1.0%	1.1%	0	0	0	0	1.4%	0	0	0	0	0	0	0.9%
Colleagues (NET)	1	0	1	1	0	0	1	0	0	0	0	0	*	1	0	0	1	0
	0.3%	0	0.7%	0.7%	0	0	1.4%	0	0	0	0	0	2.3%J	2.2%	0	0	0.8%	0
All sources of info	1	0	1	1	0	0	1	0	0	0	0	0	*	1	0	0	1	0
	0.3%	0	0.7%	0.7%	0	0	1.4%	0	0	0	0	0	2.3%J	2.2%	0	0	0.8%	0
preferred source of info	0	0	0	0	0	0	0	0	0	0	0	0	0	0	0	0	0	0
	0	0	0	0	0	0	0	0	0	0	0	0	0	0	0	0	0	0
Home (NET)	1	0	1	1	0	0	1	0	1	0	0	0	0	0	0	0	1	0
	0.2%	0	0.5%	0.5%	0	0	1.0%	0	1.7%	0	0	0	0	0	0	0	0.6%	0
All sources of info	1	0	1	1	0	0	1	0	1	0	0	0	0	0	0	0	1	0
	0.2%	0	0.5%	0.5%	0	0	1.0%	0	1.7%	0	0	0	0	0	0	0	0.6%	0
preferred source of info	1	0	1	1	0	0	1	0	1	0	0	0	0	0	0	0	1	0
	0.2%	0	0.5%	0.5%	0	0	1.0%	0	1.7%	0	0	0	0	0	0	0	0.6%	0
Purchase from online bookstore (NET)	0	0	0	0	0	0	0	0	0	0	0	0	0	0	0	0	0	0
	0	0	0	0	0	0	0	0	0	0	0	0	0	0	0	0	0	0

Proportions/Means: Columns Tested (5% risk level) - A/B/D - C/D - E/F/G - H/I/J/K/L/M/N - P/Q
* small base; ** very small base (under 30) ineligible for sig testing

Table 345
Page 1428

Outsell/Digital Library Federation Study (2002)
Weighted Tables

TABLE 88, continued

S7D/E_4. e-journals SUMMARY TABLE

		RESPONDENT TYPE				INSTITUTION TYPE			DISCIPLINE									GENDER	
	TOTAL SAMPLE	FACULTY MEMBER	GRAD. STUDENT	FACULTY /GRAD	UNDER GRAD. STUDENT	PUBLIC	PRIVATE	LIBERAL ARTS	BIOLOGIAL SCIENCES	PHYSICAL SCIENCES /MATH	SOCIAL SCIENCES	ARTS AND HUMAN.	ENGI-NEERING	BUSINESS	LAW	UNDEC. MAJOR	MALE	FEMALE
		(A)	(B)	(C)	(D)	(E)	(F)	(G)	(H)	(I)	(J)	(K)	(L)	(M)	(N)		(P)	(Q)
Base - Use e-journals for coursework	360	0**	165	165	195	166	86*	108*	53*	45*	133*	60*	12*	42*	2**	12*	153	207
All sources of info	0 0	0 0	0 0	0 0	0 0	0 0	0 0	0 0	0 0	0 0	0 0	0 0	0 0	0 0	0 0	0 0	0 0	0 0
preferred source of info	0 0	0 0	0 0	0 0	0 0	0 0	0 0	0 0	0 0	0 0	0 0	0 0	0 0	0 0	0 0	0 0	0 0	0 0
Purchase from physical book store (NET)	0 0	0 0	0 0	0 0	0 0	0 0	0 0	0 0	0 0	0 0	0 0	0 0	0 0	0 0	0 0	0 0	0 0	0 0
All sources of info	0 0	0 0	0 0	0 0	0 0	0 0	0 0	0 0	0 0	0 0	0 0	0 0	0 0	0 0	0 0	0 0	0 0	0 0
preferred source of info	0 0	0 0	0 0	0 0	0 0	0 0	0 0	0 0	0 0	0 0	0 0	0 0	0 0	0 0	0 0	0 0	0 0	0 0
Faculty (NET)	0 0	0 0	0 0	0 0	0 0	0 0	0 0	0 0	0 0	0 0	0 0	0 0	0 0	0 0	0 0	0 0	0 0	0 0
All sources of info	0 0	0 0	0 0	0 0	0 0	0 0	0 0	0 0	0 0	0 0	0 0	0 0	0 0	0 0	0 0	0 0	0 0	0 0
preferred source of info	0 0	0 0	0 0	0 0	0 0	0 0	0 0	0 0	0 0	0 0	0 0	0 0	0 0	0 0	0 0	0 0	0 0	0 0
Access from course website (NET)	0 0	0 0	0 0	0 0	0 0	0 0	0 0	0 0	0 0	0 0	0 0	0 0	0 0	0 0	0 0	0 0	0 0	0 0

Proportions/Means: Columns Tested (5% risk level) - A/B/D - C/D - E/F/G - H/I/J/K/L/M/N - P/Q
* small base; ** very small base (under 30) ineligible for sig testing

Table 345
Page 1429

Outsell/Digital Library Federation Study (2002)
Weighted Tables

TABLE 88, continued

S7D/E_4. e-journals SUMMARY TABLE

		RESPONDENT TYPE				INSTITUTION TYPE			DISCIPLINE								GENDER	
	TOTAL SAMPLE	FACULTY MEMBER	GRAD. STUDENT	FACULTY /GRAD	UNDER GRAD. STUDENT	PUBLIC	PRIVATE	LIBERAL ARTS	BIOLOGIAL SCIENCES	PHYSICAL SCIENCES /MATH	SOCIAL SCIENCES	ARTS AND HUMAN.	ENGI- NEERING	BUSINESS	LAW	UNDEC. MAJOR	MALE	FEMALE
		(A)	(B)	(C)	(D)	(E)	(F)	(G)	(H)	(I)	(J)	(K)	(L)	(M)	(N)		(P)	(Q)
Base - Use e-journals for coursework	360	0**	165	165	195	166	86*	108*	53*	45*	133*	60*	12*	42*	2**	12*	153	207
All sources of info	0 0	0 0	0 0	0 0	0 0	0 0	0 0	0 0	0 0	0 0	0 0	0 0	0 0	0 0	0 0	0 0	0 0	0 0
preferred source of info	0 0	0 0	0 0	0 0	0 0	0 0	0 0	0 0	0 0	0 0	0 0	0 0	0 0	0 0	0 0	0 0	0 0	0 0
In class (NET)	0 0	0 0	0 0	0 0	0 0	0 0	0 0	0 0	0 0	0 0	0 0	0 0	0 0	0 0	0 0	0 0	0 0	0 0
All sources of info	0 0	0 0	0 0	0 0	0 0	0 0	0 0	0 0	0 0	0 0	0 0	0 0	0 0	0 0	0 0	0 0	0 0	0 0
preferred source of info	0 0	0 0	0 0	0 0	0 0	0 0	0 0	0 0	0 0	0 0	0 0	0 0	0 0	0 0	0 0	0 0	0 0	0 0
Access book/journal/ journal article elsewhere online (NET)	0 0	0 0	0 0	0 0	0 0	0 0	0 0	0 0	0 0	0 0	0 0	0 0	0 0	0 0	0 0	0 0	0 0	0 0
All sources of info	0 0	0 0	0 0	0 0	0 0	0 0	0 0	0 0	0 0	0 0	0 0	0 0	0 0	0 0	0 0	0 0	0 0	0 0
preferred source of info	0 0	0 0	0 0	0 0	0 0	0 0	0 0	0 0	0 0	0 0	0 0	0 0	0 0	0 0	0 0	0 0	0 0	0 0
Personal Holdings (NET)	0 0	0 0	0 0	0 0	0 0	0 0	0 0	0 0	0 0	0 0	0 0	0 0	0 0	0 0	0 0	0 0	0 0	0 0

Proportions/Means: Columns Tested (5% risk level) - A/B/D - C/D - E/F/G - H/I/J/K/L/M/N - P/Q
* small base; ** very small base (under 30) ineligible for sig testing

Table 345
Page 1430

Outsell/Digital Library Federation Study (2002)
Weighted Tables

TABLE 88, continued

S7D/E_4. e-journals SUMMARY TABLE

		RESPONDENT TYPE				INSTITUTION TYPE			DISCIPLINE									GENDER	
	TOTAL SAMPLE	FACULTY MEMBER	GRAD. STUDENT	FACULTY /GRAD	UNDER GRAD. STUDENT	PUBLIC	PRIVATE	LIBERAL ARTS	BIOLOGIAL SCIENCES	PHYSICAL SCIENCES /MATH	SOCIAL SCIENCES	ARTS AND HUMAN.	ENGI-NEERING	BUSINESS	LAW	UNDEC. MAJOR	MALE	FEMALE
		(A)	(B)	(C)	(D)	(E)	(F)	(G)	(H)	(I)	(J)	(K)	(L)	(M)	(N)		(P)	(Q)
Base - Use e-journals for coursework	360	0**	165	165	195	166	86*	108*	53*	45*	133*	60*	12*	42*	2**	12*	153	207
All sources of info	0 0	0 0	0 0	0 0	0 0	0 0	0 0	0 0	0 0	0 0	0 0	0 0	0 0	0 0	0 0	0 0	0 0	0 0
preferred source of info	0 0	0 0	0 0	0 0	0 0	0 0	0 0	0 0	0 0	0 0	0 0	0 0	0 0	0 0	0 0	0 0	0 0	0 0
Other (NET)	6 1.6%	0 0	5 3.0%	5 3.0%	1 0.5%	3 1.7%	3 3.5%	0 0	1 1.7%	1 2.2%	2 1.4%	1 1.9%	0 0	1 2.2%	0 0	0 0	1 0.6%	5 2.4%
All sources of info	6 1.6%	0 0	5 3.0%	5 3.0%	1 0.5%	3 1.7%	3 3.5%	0 0	1 1.7%	1 2.2%	2 1.4%	1 1.9%	0 0	1 2.2%	0 0	0 0	1 0.6%	5 2.4%
preferred source of info	4 1.1%	0 0	4 2.4%	4 2.4%	0 0	1 0.6%	3 3.5%	0 0	0 0	1 2.2%	2 1.4%	1 1.9%	0 0	0 0	0 0	0 0	0 0	4 1.9%
DK/Refused	4 1.1%	0 0	2 1.1%	2 1.1%	2 1.1%	1 0.8%	1 0.7%	2 2.0%	0 0	1 2.2%	0 0	1 1.9%	1 7.0%HJM	0 0	0 0	1 8.3%	1 0.4%	3 1.6%

Proportions/Means: Columns Tested (5% risk level) - A/B/D - C/D - E/F/G - H/I/J/K/L/M/N - P/Q
* small base; ** very small base (under 30) ineligible for sig testing

Table 345
Page 1431

TABLE 89

R7D/E_3. e-books SUMMARY TABLE

	TOTAL SAMPLE	RESPONDENT TYPE: FACULTY MEMBER	GRAD. STUDENT	FACULTY /GRAD	UNDER GRAD. STUDENT	INSTITUTION TYPE: PUBLIC	PRIVATE	LIBERAL ARTS	DISCIPLINE: BIOLOGIAL SCIENCES	PHYSICAL SCIENCES /MATH	SOCIAL SCIENCES	ARTS AND HUMAN.	ENGI-NEERING	BUSINESS	LAW	UNDEC. MAJOR	GENDER: MALE	FEMALE
		(A)	(B)	(C)	(D)	(E)	(F)	(G)	(H)	(I)	(J)	(K)	(L)	(M)	(N)		(P)	(Q)
Base - Use e-books for research	58*	26**	31**	58*	0**	26**	26**	6**	13**	7**	15**	12**	4**	6**	1**	0*	44*	14**
Access online (NET)	47 82.0%	21 79.6%	26 84.1%	47 82.0%	0 0	22 84.4%	23 86.2%	3 52.3%	10 73.3%	7 100.0%	13 87.5%	10 81.8%	3 78.6%	4 66.7%	1 100.0%	0 0	38 85.6%	10 70.8%
All sources of info	47 82.0%	21 79.6%	26 84.1%	47 82.0%	0 0	22 84.4%	23 86.2%	3 52.3%	10 73.3%	7 100.0%	13 87.5%	10 81.8%	3 78.6%	4 66.7%	1 100.0%	0 0	38 85.6%	10 70.8%
preferred source of info	42 73.5%	17 64.6%	25 80.9%	42 73.5%	0 0	19 76.1%	20 75.6%	3 52.3%	10 73.3%	6 85.7%	11 75.0%	9 72.7%	3 78.6%	3 50.0%	1 100.0%	0 0	33 74.3%	10 70.8%
Borrow from or use in campus library (NET)	15 25.5%	9 32.7%	6 19.5%	15 25.5%	0 0	8 31.3%	4 15.1%	3 47.7%	4 26.7%	1 14.3%	2 12.5%	4 36.4%	1 21.4%	3 50.0%	* 33.3%	0 0	9 21.1%	5 39.3%
All sources of info	15 25.5%	9 32.7%	6 19.5%	15 25.5%	0 0	8 31.3%	4 15.1%	3 47.7%	4 26.7%	1 14.3%	2 12.5%	4 36.4%	1 21.4%	3 50.0%	* 33.3%	0 0	9 21.1%	5 39.3%
preferred source of info	12 20.7%	8 32.0%	4 11.2%	12 20.7%	0 0	6 21.7%	4 14.0%	3 47.7%	3 20.0%	1 14.3%	2 12.5%	3 27.3%	* 7.1%	3 50.0%	0 0	0 0	8 18.0%	4 29.2%
Interlibrary loan (NET)	2 3.1%	2 6.9%	0 0	2 3.1%	0 0	0 0	0 0	2 31.5%	1 6.7%	0 0	0 0	0 0	0 0	1 16.7%	0 0	0 0	2 4.1%	0 0
All sources of info	2 3.1%	2 6.9%	0 0	2 3.1%	0 0	0 0	0 0	2 31.5%	1 6.7%	0 0	0 0	0 0	0 0	1 16.7%	0 0	0 0	2 4.1%	0 0
preferred source of info	0 0	0 0	0 0	0 0	0 0	0 0	0 0	0 0	0 0	0 0	0 0	0 0	0 0	0 0	0 0	0 0	0 0	0 0

Proportions/Means: Columns Tested (5% risk level) - A/B/D - C/D - E/F/G - H/I/J/K/L/M/N - P/Q
* small base; ** very small base (under 30) ineligible for sig testing

Table 82
Page 181

Outsell/Digital Library Federation Study (2002)
Weighted Tables

TABLE 89, continued

R7D/E_3. e-books SUMMARY TABLE

		RESPONDENT TYPE				INSTITUTION TYPE			DISCIPLINE									GENDER	
	TOTAL SAMPLE	FACULTY MEMBER	GRAD. STUDENT	FACULTY /GRAD	UNDER GRAD. STUDENT	PUBLIC	PRIVATE	LIBERAL ARTS	BIOLOGIAL SCIENCES	PHYSICAL SCIENCES /MATH	SOCIAL SCIENCES	ARTS AND HUMAN.	ENGI-NEERING	BUSINESS	LAW	UNDEC. MAJOR	MALE	FEMALE
		(A)	(B)	(C)	(D)	(E)	(F)	(G)	(H)	(I)	(J)	(K)	(L)	(M)	(N)		(P)	(Q)
Base - Use e-books for research	58*	26**	31**	58*	0**	26**	26**	6**	13**	7**	15**	12**	4**	6**	1**	0*	44*	14**
Order from on demand document delivery service (NET)	1 1.9%	0 0	1 3.6%	1 1.9%	0 0	1 4.4%	0 0	0 0	0 0	0 0	0 0	1 9.1%	0 0	0 0	0 0	0 0	1 2.6%	0 0
All sources of info	1 1.9%	0 0	1 3.6%	1 1.9%	0 0	1 4.4%	0 0	0 0	0 0	0 0	0 0	1 9.1%	0 0	0 0	0 0	0 0	1 2.6%	0 0
preferred source of info	0 0	0 0	0 0	0 0	0 0	0 0	0 0	0 0	0 0	0 0	0 0	0 0	0 0	0 0	0 0	0 0	0 0	0 0
Borrow from or use in other libraries (NET)	* 0.5%	0 0	* 0.9%	* 0.5%	0 0	* 1.1%	0 0	0 0	0 0	0 0	0 0	0 0	* 7.1%	0 0	0 0	0 0	* 0.7%	0 0
All sources of info	* 0.5%	0 0	* 0.9%	* 0.5%	0 0	* 1.1%	0 0	0 0	0 0	0 0	0 0	0 0	* 7.1%	0 0	0 0	0 0	* 0.7%	0 0
preferred source of info	* 0.5%	0 0	* 0.9%	* 0.5%	0 0	* 1.1%	0 0	0 0	0 0	0 0	0 0	0 0	* 7.1%	0 0	0 0	0 0	* 0.7%	0 0
Purchase from online bookstore (NET)	0 0	0 0	0 0	0 0	0 0	0 0	0 0	0 0	0 0	0 0	0 0	0 0	0 0	0 0	0 0	0 0	0 0	0 0
All sources of info	0 0	0 0	0 0	0 0	0 0	0 0	0 0	0 0	0 0	0 0	0 0	0 0	0 0	0 0	0 0	0 0	0 0	0 0
preferred source of info	0 0	0 0	0 0	0 0	0 0	0 0	0 0	0 0	0 0	0 0	0 0	0 0	0 0	0 0	0 0	0 0	0 0	0 0

Proportions/Means: Columns Tested (5% risk level) - A/B/D - C/D - E/F/G - H/I/J/K/L/M/N - P/Q
* small base; ** very small base (under 30) ineligible for sig testing

Table 82
Page 182

Outsell/Digital Library Federation Study (2002)
Weighted Tables

TABLE 89, continued

R7D/E_3. e-books SUMMARY TABLE

		RESPONDENT TYPE				INSTITUTION TYPE			DISCIPLINE									GENDER	
	TOTAL SAMPLE	FACULTY MEMBER	GRAD. STUDENT	FACULTY /GRAD	UNDER GRAD. STUDENT	PUBLIC	PRIVATE	LIBERAL ARTS	BIOLOGIAL SCIENCES	PHYSICAL SCIENCES /MATH	SOCIAL SCIENCES	ARTS AND HUMAN.	ENGI-NEERING	BUSINESS	LAW	UNDEC. MAJOR	MALE	FEMALE
		(A)	(B)	(C)	(D)	(E)	(F)	(G)	(H)	(I)	(J)	(K)	(L)	(M)	(N)		(P)	(Q)
Base - Use e-books for research	58*	26**	31**	58*	0**	26**	26**	6**	13**	7**	15**	12**	4**	6**	1**	0*	44*	14**
Ask library to purchase source (NET)	0 0	0 0	0 0	0 0	0 0	0 0	0 0	0 0	0 0	0 0	0 0	0 0	0 0	0 0	0 0	0 0	0 0	0 0
All sources of info	0 0	0 0	0 0	0 0	0 0	0 0	0 0	0 0	0 0	0 0	0 0	0 0	0 0	0 0	0 0	0 0	0 0	0 0
preferred source of info	0 0	0 0	0 0	0 0	0 0	0 0	0 0	0 0	0 0	0 0	0 0	0 0	0 0	0 0	0 0	0 0	0 0	0 0
Access book/journal/ journal article elsewhere online (NET)	0 0	0 0	0 0	0 0	0 0	0 0	0 0	0 0	0 0	0 0	0 0	0 0	0 0	0 0	0 0	0 0	0 0	0 0
All sources of info	0 0	0 0	0 0	0 0	0 0	0 0	0 0	0 0	0 0	0 0	0 0	0 0	0 0	0 0	0 0	0 0	0 0	0 0
preferred source of info	0 0	0 0	0 0	0 0	0 0	0 0	0 0	0 0	0 0	0 0	0 0	0 0	0 0	0 0	0 0	0 0	0 0	0 0
Access from course website (NET)	0 0	0 0	0 0	0 0	0 0	0 0	0 0	0 0	0 0	0 0	0 0	0 0	0 0	0 0	0 0	0 0	0 0	0 0
All sources of info	0 0	0 0	0 0	0 0	0 0	0 0	0 0	0 0	0 0	0 0	0 0	0 0	0 0	0 0	0 0	0 0	0 0	0 0
preferred source of info	0 0	0 0	0 0	0 0	0 0	0 0	0 0	0 0	0 0	0 0	0 0	0 0	0 0	0 0	0 0	0 0	0 0	0 0

Proportions/Means: Columns Tested (5% risk level) - A/B/D - C/D - E/F/G - H/I/J/K/L/M/N - P/Q
* small base; ** very small base (under 30) ineligible for sig testing

Table 82
Page 183

Outsell/Digital Library Federation Study (2002)
Weighted Tables

TABLE 89, continued

R7D/E_3. e-books SUMMARY TABLE

		RESPONDENT TYPE				INSTITUTION TYPE			DISCIPLINE								GENDER	
	TOTAL SAMPLE	FACULTY MEMBER	GRAD. STUDENT	FACULTY /GRAD	UNDER GRAD. STUDENT	PUBLIC	PRIVATE	LIBERAL ARTS	BIOLOGIAL SCIENCES	PHYSICAL SCIENCES /MATH	SOCIAL SCIENCES	ARTS AND HUMAN.	ENGI-NEERING	BUSINESS	LAW	UNDEC. MAJOR	MALE	FEMALE
		(A)	(B)	(C)	(D)	(E)	(F)	(G)	(H)	(I)	(J)	(K)	(L)	(M)	(N)		(P)	(Q)
Base - Use e-books for research	58*	26**	31**	58*	0**	26**	26**	6**	13**	7**	15**	12**	4**	6**	1**	0*	44*	14**
Purchase from physical book store (NET)	0	0	0	0	0	0	0	0	0	0	0	0	0	0	0	0	0	0
	0	0	0	0	0	0	0	0	0	0	0	0	0	0	0	0	0	0
All sources of info	0	0	0	0	0	0	0	0	0	0	0	0	0	0	0	0	0	0
	0	0	0	0	0	0	0	0	0	0	0	0	0	0	0	0	0	0
preferred source of info	0	0	0	0	0	0	0	0	0	0	0	0	0	0	0	0	0	0
	0	0	0	0	0	0	0	0	0	0	0	0	0	0	0	0	0	0
Colleague (NET)	0	0	0	0	0	0	0	0	0	0	0	0	0	0	0	0	0	0
	0	0	0	0	0	0	0	0	0	0	0	0	0	0	0	0	0	0
All sources of info	0	0	0	0	0	0	0	0	0	0	0	0	0	0	0	0	0	0
	0	0	0	0	0	0	0	0	0	0	0	0	0	0	0	0	0	0
preferred source of info	0	0	0	0	0	0	0	0	0	0	0	0	0	0	0	0	0	0
	0	0	0	0	0	0	0	0	0	0	0	0	0	0	0	0	0	0
Office (NET)	0	0	0	0	0	0	0	0	0	0	0	0	0	0	0	0	0	0
	0	0	0	0	0	0	0	0	0	0	0	0	0	0	0	0	0	0
All sources of info	0	0	0	0	0	0	0	0	0	0	0	0	0	0	0	0	0	0
	0	0	0	0	0	0	0	0	0	0	0	0	0	0	0	0	0	0
preferred source of info	0	0	0	0	0	0	0	0	0	0	0	0	0	0	0	0	0	0
	0	0	0	0	0	0	0	0	0	0	0	0	0	0	0	0	0	0

Proportions/Means: Columns Tested (5% risk level) - A/B/D - C/D - E/F/G - H/I/J/K/L/M/N - P/Q
* small base; ** very small base (under 30) ineligible for sig testing

Table 82
Page 184

Outsell/Digital Library Federation Study (2002)
Weighted Tables

TABLE 89, continued
R7D/E_3. e-books SUMMARY TABLE

		RESPONDENT TYPE				INSTITUTION TYPE			DISCIPLINE								GENDER	
	TOTAL SAMPLE	FACULTY MEMBER	GRAD. STUDENT	FACULTY /GRAD	UNDER GRAD. STUDENT	PUBLIC	PRIVATE	LIBERAL ARTS	BIOLOGIAL SCIENCES	PHYSICAL SCIENCES /MATH	SOCIAL SCIENCES	ARTS AND HUMAN.	ENGI- NEERING	BUSINESS	LAW	UNDEC. MAJOR	MALE	FEMALE
		(A)	(B)	(C)	(D)	(E)	(F)	(G)	(H)	(I)	(J)	(K)	(L)	(M)	(N)		(P)	(Q)
Base - Use e-books for research	58*	26**	31**	58*	0**	26**	26**	6**	13**	7**	15**	12**	4**	6**	1**	0*	44*	14**
Meetings/conferences (NET)	0 0	0 0	0 0	0 0	0 0	0 0	0 0	0 0	0 0	0 0	0 0	0 0	0 0	0 0	0 0	0 0	0 0	0 0
All sources of info	0 0	0 0	0 0	0 0	0 0	0 0	0 0	0 0	0 0	0 0	0 0	0 0	0 0	0 0	0 0	0 0	0 0	0 0
preferred source of info	0 0	0 0	0 0	0 0	0 0	0 0	0 0	0 0	0 0	0 0	0 0	0 0	0 0	0 0	0 0	0 0	0 0	0 0
Sources (NET)	0 0	0 0	0 0	0 0	0 0	0 0	0 0	0 0	0 0	0 0	0 0	0 0	0 0	0 0	0 0	0 0	0 0	0 0
All sources of info	0 0	0 0	0 0	0 0	0 0	0 0	0 0	0 0	0 0	0 0	0 0	0 0	0 0	0 0	0 0	0 0	0 0	0 0
preferred source of info	0 0	0 0	0 0	0 0	0 0	0 0	0 0	0 0	0 0	0 0	0 0	0 0	0 0	0 0	0 0	0 0	0 0	0 0
E-journals (NET)	0 0	0 0	0 0	0 0	0 0	0 0	0 0	0 0	0 0	0 0	0 0	0 0	0 0	0 0	0 0	0 0	0 0	0 0
All sources of info	0 0	0 0	0 0	0 0	0 0	0 0	0 0	0 0	0 0	0 0	0 0	0 0	0 0	0 0	0 0	0 0	0 0	0 0
preferred source of info	0 0	0 0	0 0	0 0	0 0	0 0	0 0	0 0	0 0	0 0	0 0	0 0	0 0	0 0	0 0	0 0	0 0	0 0
Faculty (NET)	0 0	0 0	0 0	0 0	0 0	0 0	0 0	0 0	0 0	0 0	0 0	0 0	0 0	0 0	0 0	0 0	0 0	0 0

Proportions/Means: Columns Tested (5% risk level) - A/B/D - C/D - E/F/G - H/I/J/K/L/M/N - P/Q
* small base; ** very small base (under 30) ineligible for sig testing

Table 82
Page 185

Outsell/Digital Library Federation Study (2002)
Weighted Tables

TABLE 89, continued

R7D/E_3. e-books SUMMARY TABLE

		RESPONDENT TYPE				INSTITUTION TYPE			DISCIPLINE								GENDER	
	TOTAL SAMPLE	FACULTY MEMBER	GRAD. STUDENT	FACULTY /GRAD	UNDER GRAD. STUDENT	PUBLIC	PRIVATE	LIBERAL ARTS	BIOLOGIAL SCIENCES	PHYSICAL SCIENCES /MATH	SOCIAL SCIENCES	ARTS AND HUMAN.	ENGI- NEERING	BUSINESS	LAW	UNDEC. MAJOR	MALE	FEMALE
		(A)	(B)	(C)	(D)	(E)	(F)	(G)	(H)	(I)	(J)	(K)	(L)	(M)	(N)		(P)	(Q)
Base - Use e-books for research	58*	26**	31**	58*	0**	26**	26**	6**	13**	7**	15**	12**	4**	6**	1**	0*	44*	14**
All sources of info	0 0	0 0	0 0	0 0	0 0	0 0	0 0	0 0	0 0	0 0	0 0	0 0	0 0	0 0	0 0	0 0	0 0	0 0
preferred source of info	0 0	0 0	0 0	0 0	0 0	0 0	0 0	0 0	0 0	0 0	0 0	0 0	0 0	0 0	0 0	0 0	0 0	0 0
Personal holdings (NET)	0 0	0 0	0 0	0 0	0 0	0 0	0 0	0 0	0 0	0 0	0 0	0 0	0 0	0 0	0 0	0 0	0 0	0 0
All sources of info	0 0	0 0	0 0	0 0	0 0	0 0	0 0	0 0	0 0	0 0	0 0	0 0	0 0	0 0	0 0	0 0	0 0	0 0
preferred source of info	0 0	0 0	0 0	0 0	0 0	0 0	0 0	0 0	0 0	0 0	0 0	0 0	0 0	0 0	0 0	0 0	0 0	0 0
Printed material (NET)	0 0	0 0	0 0	0 0	0 0	0 0	0 0	0 0	0 0	0 0	0 0	0 0	0 0	0 0	0 0	0 0	0 0	0 0
All sources of info	0 0	0 0	0 0	0 0	0 0	0 0	0 0	0 0	0 0	0 0	0 0	0 0	0 0	0 0	0 0	0 0	0 0	0 0
preferred source of info	0 0	0 0	0 0	0 0	0 0	0 0	0 0	0 0	0 0	0 0	0 0	0 0	0 0	0 0	0 0	0 0	0 0	0 0
Other (NET)	1 2.5%	1 3.3%	1 1.8%	1 2.5%	0 0	1 2.3%	1 3.3%	0 0	1 6.7%	0 0	0 0	0 0	1 14.3%	0 0	0 0	0 0	1 3.3%	0 0
All sources of info	1 2.5%	1 3.3%	1 1.8%	1 2.5%	0 0	1 2.3%	1 3.3%	0 0	1 6.7%	0 0	0 0	0 0	1 14.3%	0 0	0 0	0 0	1 3.3%	0 0

Proportions/Means: Columns Tested (5% risk level) - A/B/D - C/D - E/F/G - H/I/J/K/L/M/N - P/Q
* small base; ** very small base (under 30) ineligible for sig testing

Table 82
Page 186

Outsell/Digital Library Federation Study (2002)
Weighted Tables

TABLE 89, continued

R7D/E_3. e-books SUMMARY TABLE

		RESPONDENT TYPE				INSTITUTION TYPE			DISCIPLINE									GENDER	
	TOTAL SAMPLE	FACULTY MEMBER	GRAD. STUDENT	FACULTY /GRAD	UNDER GRAD. STUDENT	PUBLIC	PRIVATE	LIBERAL ARTS	BIOLOGIAL SCIENCES	PHYSICAL SCIENCES /MATH	SOCIAL SCIENCES	ARTS AND HUMAN.	ENGI-NEERING	BUSINESS	LAW	UNDEC. MAJOR	MALE	FEMALE
		(A)	(B)	(C)	(D)	(E)	(F)	(G)	(H)	(I)	(J)	(K)	(L)	(M)	(N)		(P)	(Q)
Base - Use e-books for research	58*	26**	31**	58*	0**	26**	26**	6**	13**	7**	15**	12**	4**	6**	1**	0*	44*	14**
preferred source of info	1 2.0%	1 3.3%	* 0.9%	1 2.0%	0 0	* 1.1%	1 3.3%	0 0	1 6.7%	0 0	0 0	0 0	* 7.1%	0 0	0 0	0 0	1 2.7%	0 0
DK/Refused	2 3.3%	0 0	2 6.0%	2 3.3%	0 0	0 0	2 7.1%	0 0	0 0	0 0	2 12.5%	0 0	0 0	0 0	0 0	0 0	2 4.3%	0 0

Proportions/Means: Columns Tested (5% risk level) - A/B/D - C/D - E/F/G - H/I/J/K/L/M/N - P/Q
* small base; ** very small base (under 30) ineligible for sig testing

Table 82
Page 187

Outsell/Digital Library Federation Study (2002)
Weighted Tables

TABLE 90

R7D/E_5. Magazines SUMMARY TABLE

		RESPONDENT TYPE				INSTITUTION TYPE			DISCIPLINE									GENDER	
	TOTAL SAMPLE	FACULTY MEMBER	GRAD. STUDENT	FACULTY /GRAD	UNDER GRAD. STUDENT	PUBLIC	PRIVATE	LIBERAL ARTS	BIOLOGIAL SCIENCES	PHYSICAL SCIENCES /MATH	SOCIAL SCIENCES	ARTS AND HUMAN.	ENGI- NEERING	BUSINESS	LAW	UNDEC. MAJOR	MALE	FEMALE
		(A)	(B)	(C)	(D)	(E)	(F)	(G)	(H)	(I)	(J)	(K)	(L)	(M)	(N)		(P)	(Q)
Base - Use Magazines for research	196	120	77*	196	0**	83*	73*	40*	24**	28**	60*	45*	10*	27**	3**	0*	137	60*
Borrow from or use in campus library (NET)	147 75.0%	90 75.3%	57 74.6%	147 75.0%	0 0	61 72.9%	53 72.7%	33 83.7%	18 77.8%	24 85.7%	41 68.7%	38 85.0%	7 69.7%	16 58.6%	3 94.4%	0 0	105 77.0%	42 70.4%
All sources of info	147 75.0%	90 75.3%	57 74.6%	147 75.0%	0 0	61 72.9%	53 72.7%	33 83.7%	18 77.8%	24 85.7%	41 68.7%	38 85.0%	7 69.7%	16 58.6%	3 94.4%	0 0	105 77.0%	42 70.4%
preferred source of info	92 46.7%	48 40.1%	44 57.0%A	92 46.7%	0 0	39 46.4%	33 45.3%	20 49.9%	11 48.1%	11 39.3%	26 43.7%	27 60.0%L	3 36.4%	11 41.4%	1 44.4%	0 0	62 45.2%	30 50.0%
Access online (NET)	84 43.0%	58 48.3%	27 34.7%	84 43.0%	0 0	35 41.9%	35 48.0%	14 36.0%	11 48.1%	12 42.9%	26 43.7%	11 25.0%	6 63.6%K	16 58.6%	2 50.0%	0 0	60 43.7%	25 41.4%
All sources of info	84 43.0%	58 48.3%	27 34.7%	84 43.0%	0 0	35 41.9%	35 48.0%	14 36.0%	11 48.1%	12 42.9%	26 43.7%	11 25.0%	6 63.6%K	16 58.6%	2 50.0%	0 0	60 43.7%	25 41.4%
preferred source of info	73 37.1%	49 40.5%	24 31.7%	73 37.1%	0 0	31 37.1%	30 40.2%	12 31.2%	9 37.0%	10 35.7%	24 40.6%	10 22.5%	5 54.5%K	13 48.3%	1 38.9%	0 0	51 37.3%	22 36.6%
Interlibrary loan (NET)	20 10.0%	18 14.7%B	2 2.5%	20 10.0%	0 0	8 10.2%	3 4.2%	8 19.9%F	1 3.7%	4 14.3%	4 6.2%	7 15.0%	* 3.0%	4 13.8%	* 5.6%	0 0	13 9.2%	7 11.6%
All sources of info	20 10.0%	18 14.7%B	2 2.5%	20 10.0%	0 0	8 10.2%	3 4.2%	8 19.9%F	1 3.7%	4 14.3%	4 6.2%	7 15.0%	* 3.0%	4 13.8%	* 5.6%	0 0	13 9.2%	7 11.6%
preferred source of info	3 1.5%	3 2.5%	0 0	3 1.5%	0 0	0 0	1 1.5%	2 4.7%	0 0	0 0	2 3.1%	1 2.5%	0 0	0 0	0 0	0 0	0 0	3 5.0%P

Proportions/Means: Columns Tested (5% risk level) - A/B/D - C/D - E/F/G - H/I/J/K/L/M/N - P/Q
* small base; ** very small base (under 30) ineligible for sig testing

Table 96
Page 251

Outsell/Digital Library Federation Study (2002)
Weighted Tables

TABLE 90, continued

R7D/E_5. Magazines SUMMARY TABLE

	TOTAL SAMPLE	RESPONDENT TYPE: FACULTY MEMBER	GRAD. STUDENT	FACULTY /GRAD	UNDER GRAD. STUDENT	INSTITUTION TYPE: PUBLIC	PRIVATE	LIBERAL ARTS	DISCIPLINE: BIOLOGIAL SCIENCES	PHYSICAL SCIENCES /MATH	SOCIAL SCIENCES	ARTS AND HUMAN.	ENGI-NEERING	BUSINESS	LAW	UNDEC. MAJOR	GENDER: MALE	FEMALE
		(A)	(B)	(C)	(D)	(E)	(F)	(G)	(H)	(I)	(J)	(K)	(L)	(M)	(N)		(P)	(Q)
Base - Use Magazines for research	196	120	77*	196	0**	83*	73*	40*	24**	28**	60*	45*	10*	27**	3**	0*	137	60*
Borrow from or use in other libraries (NET)	15 7.8%	13 11.0%	2 2.9%	15 7.8%	0 0	3 3.1%	7 9.6%	6 14.5%E	1 3.7%	2 7.1%	6 9.4%	2 5.0%	1 6.1%	4 13.8%	* 11.1%	0 0	15 10.6%	1 1.5%
All sources of info	15 7.8%	13 11.0%	2 2.9%	15 7.8%	0 0	3 3.1%	7 9.6%	6 14.5%E	1 3.7%	2 7.1%	6 9.4%	2 5.0%	1 6.1%	4 13.8%	* 11.1%	0 0	15 10.6%	1 1.5%
preferred source of info	3 1.5%	2 1.6%	1 1.3%	3 1.5%	0 0	1 1.2%	2 2.6%	0 0	0 0	2 7.1%	0 0	0 0	0 0	1 3.4%	0 0	0 0	3 2.1%	0 0
Personal holdings (NET)	11 5.8%	10 8.0%	2 2.5%	11 5.8%	0 0	3 4.2%	1 1.5%	7 17.3%EF	1 3.7%	3 10.7%	4 6.2%	3 7.5%	* 3.0%	0 0	* 5.6%	0 0	8 5.5%	4 6.5%
All sources of info	11 5.8%	10 8.0%	2 2.5%	11 5.8%	0 0	3 4.2%	1 1.5%	7 17.3%EF	1 3.7%	3 10.7%	4 6.2%	3 7.5%	* 3.0%	0 0	* 5.6%	0 0	8 5.5%	4 6.5%
preferred source of info	5 2.7%	5 4.5%	0 0	5 2.7%	0 0	* 0.6%	1 1.5%	4 9.4%E	1 3.7%	1 3.6%	2 3.1%	1 2.5%	* 3.0%	0 0	* 5.6%	0 0	4 3.3%	1 1.5%
Purchase from physical book store (NET)	11 5.7%	6 5.3%	5 6.4%	11 5.7%	0 0	6 7.5%	3 4.1%	2 5.0%	2 7.4%	2 7.1%	2 3.1%	6 12.5%	0 0	0 0	0 0	0 0	7 5.3%	4 6.7%
All sources of info	11 5.7%	6 5.3%	5 6.4%	11 5.7%	0 0	6 7.5%	3 4.1%	2 5.0%	2 7.4%	2 7.1%	2 3.1%	6 12.5%	0 0	0 0	0 0	0 0	7 5.3%	4 6.7%
preferred source of info	6 3.1%	4 3.4%	2 2.6%	6 3.1%	0 0	5 6.3%	0 0	1 2.2%	2 7.4%	1 3.6%	0 0	3 7.5%	0 0	0 0	0 0	0 0	5 3.7%	1 1.9%

Proportions/Means: Columns Tested (5% risk level) - A/B/D - C/D - E/F/G - H/I/J/K/L/M/N - P/Q
* small base; ** very small base (under 30) ineligible for sig testing

Table 96
Page 252

Outsell/Digital Library Federation Study (2002)
Weighted Tables

TABLE 90, continued

R7D/E_5. Magazines SUMMARY TABLE

		RESPONDENT TYPE				INSTITUTION TYPE			DISCIPLINE									GENDER	
	TOTAL SAMPLE	FACULTY MEMBER	GRAD. STUDENT	FACULTY /GRAD	UNDER GRAD. STUDENT	PUBLIC	PRIVATE	LIBERAL ARTS	BIOLOGIAL SCIENCES	PHYSICAL SCIENCES /MATH	SOCIAL SCIENCES	ARTS AND HUMAN.	ENGI- NEERING	BUSINESS	LAW	UNDEC. MAJOR	MALE	FEMALE
		(A)	(B)	(C)	(D)	(E)	(F)	(G)	(H)	(I)	(J)	(K)	(L)	(M)	(N)		(P)	(Q)
Base - Use Magazines for research	196	120	77*	196	0**	83*	73*	40*	24**	28**	60*	45*	10*	27**	3**	0*	137	60*
Order from on demand document delivery service (NET)	6 2.9%	6 4.7%	0 0	6 2.9%	0 0	1 1.1%	3 3.9%	2 4.7%	1 3.7%	2 7.1%	2 3.1%	0 0	0 0	1 3.4%	0 0	0 0	5 3.5%	1 1.5%
All sources of info	6 2.9%	6 4.7%	0 0	6 2.9%	0 0	1 1.1%	3 3.9%	2 4.7%	1 3.7%	2 7.1%	2 3.1%	0 0	0 0	1 3.4%	0 0	0 0	5 3.5%	1 1.5%
preferred source of info	3 1.5%	3 2.4%	0 0	3 1.5%	0 0	0 0	3 3.9%	0 0	0 0	1 3.6%	2 3.1%	0 0	0 0	0 0	0 0	0 0	3 2.1%	0 0
Purchase from online bookstore (NET)	2 1.1%	1 0.9%	1 1.5%	2 1.1%	0 0	1 1.3%	0 0	1 2.8%	0 0	0 0	0 0	2 5.0%	0 0	0 0	0 0	0 0	1 0.8%	1 1.9%
All sources of info	2 1.1%	1 0.9%	1 1.5%	2 1.1%	0 0	1 1.3%	0 0	1 2.8%	0 0	0 0	0 0	2 5.0%	0 0	0 0	0 0	0 0	1 0.8%	1 1.9%
preferred source of info	0 0	0 0	0 0	0 0	0 0	0 0	0 0	0 0	0 0	0 0	0 0	0 0	0 0	0 0	0 0	0 0	0 0	0 0
Colleague (NET)	2 1.1%	2 1.5%	* 0.4%	2 1.1%	0 0	1 1.5%	1 1.2%	0 0	1 3.7%	0 0	0 0	0 0	* 3.0%	1 3.4%	0 0	0 0	1 0.9%	1 1.5%
All sources of info	2 1.1%	2 1.5%	* 0.4%	2 1.1%	0 0	1 1.5%	1 1.2%	0 0	1 3.7%	0 0	0 0	0 0	* 3.0%	1 3.4%	0 0	0 0	1 0.9%	1 1.5%
preferred source of info	0 0	0 0	0 0	0 0	0 0	0 0	0 0	0 0	0 0	0 0	0 0	0 0	0 0	0 0	0 0	0 0	0 0	0 0

Proportions/Means: Columns Tested (5% risk level) - A/B/D - C/D - E/F/G - H/I/J/K/L/M/N - P/Q
* small base; ** very small base (under 30) ineligible for sig testing

Table 96
Page 253

Outsell/Digital Library Federation Study (2002)
Weighted Tables

TABLE 90, continued

R7D/E_5. Magazines SUMMARY TABLE

		RESPONDENT TYPE				INSTITUTION TYPE			DISCIPLINE									GENDER	
	TOTAL SAMPLE	FACULTY MEMBER	GRAD. STUDENT	FACULTY /GRAD	UNDER GRAD. STUDENT	PUBLIC	PRIVATE	LIBERAL ARTS	BIOLOGIAL SCIENCES	PHYSICAL SCIENCES /MATH	SOCIAL SCIENCES	ARTS AND HUMAN.	ENGI- NEERING	BUSINESS	LAW	UNDEC. MAJOR	MALE	FEMALE
		(A)	(B)	(C)	(D)	(E)	(F)	(G)	(H)	(I)	(J)	(K)	(L)	(M)	(N)		(P)	(Q)
Base - Use Magazines for research	196	120	77*	196	0**	83*	73*	40*	24**	28**	60*	45*	10*	27**	3**	0*	137	60*
Ask library to purchase source (NET)	2 1.0%	0 0	2 2.5%	2 1.0%	0 0	2 2.3%	0 0	0 0	0 0	0 0	2 3.1%	0 0	0 0	0 0	0 0	0 0	2 1.4%	0 0
All sources of info	2 1.0%	0 0	2 2.5%	2 1.0%	0 0	2 2.3%	0 0	0 0	0 0	0 0	2 3.1%	0 0	0 0	0 0	0 0	0 0	2 1.4%	0 0
preferred source of info	2 1.0%	0 0	2 2.5%	2 1.0%	0 0	2 2.3%	0 0	0 0	0 0	0 0	2 3.1%	0 0	0 0	0 0	0 0	0 0	2 1.4%	0 0
Office (NET)	1 0.6%	1 0.9%	0 0	1 0.6%	0 0	1 1.3%	0 0	0 0	0 0	0 0	0 0	1 2.5%	0 0	0 0	0 0	0 0	0 0	1 1.9%
All sources of info	1 0.6%	1 0.9%	0 0	1 0.6%	0 0	1 1.3%	0 0	0 0	0 0	0 0	0 0	1 2.5%	0 0	0 0	0 0	0 0	0 0	1 1.9%
preferred source of info	1 0.6%	1 0.9%	0 0	1 0.6%	0 0	1 1.3%	0 0	0 0	0 0	0 0	0 0	1 2.5%	0 0	0 0	0 0	0 0	0 0	1 1.9%
E-journals (NET)	1 0.4%	0 0	1 1.2%	1 0.4%	0 0	1 1.1%	0 0	0 0	1 3.7%	0 0	0 0	0 0	0 0	0 0	0 0	0 0	0 0	1 1.5%
All sources of info	1 0.4%	0 0	1 1.2%	1 0.4%	0 0	1 1.1%	0 0	0 0	1 3.7%	0 0	0 0	0 0	0 0	0 0	0 0	0 0	0 0	1 1.5%
preferred source of info	0 0	0 0	0 0	0 0	0 0	0 0	0 0	0 0	0 0	0 0	0 0	0 0	0 0	0 0	0 0	0 0	0 0	0 0

Proportions/Means: Columns Tested (5% risk level) - A/B/D - C/D - E/F/G - H/I/J/K/L/M/N - P/Q
* small base; ** very small base (under 30) ineligible for sig testing

Table 96
Page 254

Outsell/Digital Library Federation Study (2002)
Weighted Tables

TABLE 90, continued

R7D/E_5. Magazines SUMMARY TABLE

		RESPONDENT TYPE				INSTITUTION TYPE			DISCIPLINE								GENDER	
	TOTAL SAMPLE	FACULTY MEMBER	GRAD. STUDENT	FACULTY /GRAD	UNDER GRAD. STUDENT	PUBLIC	PRIVATE	LIBERAL ARTS	BIOLOGIAL SCIENCES	PHYSICAL SCIENCES /MATH	SOCIAL SCIENCES	ARTS AND HUMAN.	ENGI-NEERING	BUSINESS	LAW	UNDEC. MAJOR	MALE	FEMALE
		(A)	(B)	(C)	(D)	(E)	(F)	(G)	(H)	(I)	(J)	(K)	(L)	(M)	(N)		(P)	(Q)
Base - Use Magazines for research	196	120	77*	196	0**	83*	73*	40*	24**	28**	60*	45*	10*	27**	3**	0*	137	60*
Sources (NET)	* 0.1%	* 0.1%	0 0	* 0.1%	0 0	* 0.2%	0 0	0 0	0 0	0 0	0 0	0 0	0 0	0 0	* 5.6%	0 0	* 0.1%	0 0
All sources of info	* 0.1%	* 0.1%	0 0	* 0.1%	0 0	* 0.2%	0 0	0 0	0 0	0 0	0 0	0 0	0 0	0 0	* 5.6%	0 0	* 0.1%	0 0
preferred source of info	* 0.1%	* 0.1%	0 0	* 0.1%	0 0	* 0.2%	0 0	0 0	0 0	0 0	0 0	0 0	0 0	0 0	* 5.6%	0 0	* 0.1%	0 0
Access from course website (NET)	0 0	0 0	0 0	0 0	0 0	0 0	0 0	0 0	0 0	0 0	0 0	0 0	0 0	0 0	0 0	0 0	0 0	0 0
All sources of info	0 0	0 0	0 0	0 0	0 0	0 0	0 0	0 0	0 0	0 0	0 0	0 0	0 0	0 0	0 0	0 0	0 0	0 0
preferred source of info	0 0	0 0	0 0	0 0	0 0	0 0	0 0	0 0	0 0	0 0	0 0	0 0	0 0	0 0	0 0	0 0	0 0	0 0
Access book/journal/ journal article elsewhere online (NET)	0 0	0 0	0 0	0 0	0 0	0 0	0 0	0 0	0 0	0 0	0 0	0 0	0 0	0 0	0 0	0 0	0 0	0 0
All sources of info	0 0	0 0	0 0	0 0	0 0	0 0	0 0	0 0	0 0	0 0	0 0	0 0	0 0	0 0	0 0	0 0	0 0	0 0
preferred source of info	0 0	0 0	0 0	0 0	0 0	0 0	0 0	0 0	0 0	0 0	0 0	0 0	0 0	0 0	0 0	0 0	0 0	0 0

Proportions/Means: Columns Tested (5% risk level) - A/B/D - C/D - E/F/G - H/I/J/K/L/M/N - P/Q
* small base; ** very small base (under 30) ineligible for sig testing

Table 96
Page 255

Outsell/Digital Library Federation Study (2002)
Weighted Tables

TABLE 90, continued

R7D/E_5. Magazines SUMMARY TABLE

		RESPONDENT TYPE				INSTITUTION TYPE			DISCIPLINE									GENDER	
	TOTAL SAMPLE	FACULTY MEMBER	GRAD. STUDENT	FACULTY /GRAD	UNDER GRAD. STUDENT	PUBLIC	PRIVATE	LIBERAL ARTS	BIOLOGIAL SCIENCES	PHYSICAL SCIENCES /MATH	SOCIAL SCIENCES	ARTS AND HUMAN.	ENGI-NEERING	BUSINESS	LAW	UNDEC. MAJOR	MALE	FEMALE
		(A)	(B)	(C)	(D)	(E)	(F)	(G)	(H)	(I)	(J)	(K)	(L)	(M)	(N)		(P)	(Q)
Base - Use Magazines for research	196	120	77*	196	0**	83*	73*	40*	24**	28**	60*	45*	10*	27**	3**	0*	137	60*
Faculty (NET)	0 0	0 0	0 0	0 0	0 0	0 0	0 0	0 0	0 0	0 0	0 0	0 0	0 0	0 0	0 0	0 0	0 0	0 0
All sources of info	0 0	0 0	0 0	0 0	0 0	0 0	0 0	0 0	0 0	0 0	0 0	0 0	0 0	0 0	0 0	0 0	0 0	0 0
preferred source of info	0 0	0 0	0 0	0 0	0 0	0 0	0 0	0 0	0 0	0 0	0 0	0 0	0 0	0 0	0 0	0 0	0 0	0 0
Meetings/conferences (NET)	0 0	0 0	0 0	0 0	0 0	0 0	0 0	0 0	0 0	0 0	0 0	0 0	0 0	0 0	0 0	0 0	0 0	0 0
All sources of info	0 0	0 0	0 0	0 0	0 0	0 0	0 0	0 0	0 0	0 0	0 0	0 0	0 0	0 0	0 0	0 0	0 0	0 0
preferred source of info	0 0	0 0	0 0	0 0	0 0	0 0	0 0	0 0	0 0	0 0	0 0	0 0	0 0	0 0	0 0	0 0	0 0	0 0
Printed material (NET)	0 0	0 0	0 0	0 0	0 0	0 0	0 0	0 0	0 0	0 0	0 0	0 0	0 0	0 0	0 0	0 0	0 0	0 0
All sources of info	0 0	0 0	0 0	0 0	0 0	0 0	0 0	0 0	0 0	0 0	0 0	0 0	0 0	0 0	0 0	0 0	0 0	0 0
preferred source of info	0 0	0 0	0 0	0 0	0 0	0 0	0 0	0 0	0 0	0 0	0 0	0 0	0 0	0 0	0 0	0 0	0 0	0 0
Other (NET)	14 7.1%	10 8.2%	4 5.4%	14 7.1%	0 0	8 10.1%	4 4.9%	2 5.0%	1 3.7%	3 10.7%	2 3.1%	2 5.0%	1 12.1%	5 17.2%	* 5.6%	0 0	12 8.9%	2 3.1%

Proportions/Means: Columns Tested (5% risk level) - A/B/D - C/D - E/F/G - H/I/J/K/L/M/N - P/Q
* small base; ** very small base (under 30) ineligible for sig testing

Table 96
Page 256

Outsell/Digital Library Federation Study (2002)
Weighted Tables

TABLE 90, continued

R7D/E_5. Magazines SUMMARY TABLE

		RESPONDENT TYPE				INSTITUTION TYPE			DISCIPLINE								GENDER	
	TOTAL SAMPLE	FACULTY MEMBER	GRAD. STUDENT	FACULTY /GRAD	UNDER GRAD. STUDENT	PUBLIC	PRIVATE	LIBERAL ARTS	BIOLOGIAL SCIENCES	PHYSICAL SCIENCES /MATH	SOCIAL SCIENCES	ARTS AND HUMAN.	ENGI-NEERING	BUSINESS	LAW	UNDEC. MAJOR	MALE	FEMALE
		(A)	(B)	(C)	(D)	(E)	(F)	(G)	(H)	(I)	(J)	(K)	(L)	(M)	(N)		(P)	(Q)
Base - Use Magazines for research	196	120	77*	196	0**	83*	73*	40*	24**	28**	60*	45*	10*	27**	3**	0*	137	60*
All sources of info	14 7.0%	10 8.1%	4 5.4%	14 7.0%	0 0	8 9.9%	4 4.9%	2 5.0%	1 3.7%	3 10.7%	2 3.1%	2 5.0%	1 12.1%	5 17.2%	0 0	0 0	12 8.7%	2 3.1%
preferred source of info	8 4.3%	5 3.9%	4 5.0%	8 4.3%	0 0	4 4.7%	4 4.9%	1 2.5%	1 3.7%	2 7.1%	2 3.1%	1 2.5%	1 6.1%	2 6.9%	* 5.6%	0 0	7 4.8%	2 3.1%
DK/Refused	0 0	0 0	0 0	0 0	0 0	0 0	0 0	0 0	0 0	0 0	0 0	0 0	0 0	0 0	0 0	0 0	0 0	0 0

Proportions/Means: Columns Tested (5% risk level) - A/B/D - C/D - E/F/G - H/I/J/K/L/M/N - P/Q
* small base; ** very small base (under 30) ineligible for sig testing

TABLE 91

R7D/E_6. Papers delivered at professional meetings SUMMARY TABLE

	TOTAL SAMPLE	RESPONDENT TYPE: FACULTY MEMBER (A)	GRAD. STUDENT (B)	FACULTY /GRAD (C)	UNDER GRAD. STUDENT (D)	INSTITUTION TYPE: PUBLIC (E)	PRIVATE (F)	LIBERAL ARTS (G)	DISCIPLINE: BIOLOGIAL SCIENCES (H)	PHYSICAL SCIENCES /MATH (I)	SOCIAL SCIENCES (J)	ARTS AND HUMAN. (K)	ENGI-NEERING (L)	BUSINESS (M)	LAW (N)	UNDEC. MAJOR	GENDER: MALE (P)	FEMALE (Q)
Base - Use Papers delivered at professional meetings for research	359	198	160	359	0**	164	126	69*	54*	78*	118*	59*	19*	29*	2**	0*	227	131*
Access online (NET)	178 49.7%	102 51.7%	76 47.1%	178 49.7%	0 0	77 47.3%	64 50.9%	36 53.0%	35 65.6%JK	45 57.7%K	49 41.3%	20 34.0%	12 61.5%JK	17 58.1%K	1 33.3%	0 0	120 52.8%	58 44.1%
All sources of info	178 49.7%	102 51.7%	76 47.1%	178 49.7%	0 0	77 47.3%	64 50.9%	36 53.0%	35 65.6%JK	45 57.7%K	49 41.3%	20 34.0%	12 61.5%JK	17 58.1%K	1 33.3%	0 0	120 52.8%	58 44.1%
preferred source of info	150 41.9%	85 42.7%	65 40.8%	150 41.9%	0 0	68 41.3%	52 41.4%	30 44.0%	33 60.7%JK	37 47.4%K	41 34.9%	15 24.5%	9 49.2%K	15 51.6%K	1 33.3%	0 0	102 45.1%	48 36.3%
Borrow from or use in campus library (NET)	136 37.8%	50 25.4%	85 53.1%A	136 37.8%	0 0	72 44.3%	42 32.9%	22 31.2%	25 45.9%JM	35 44.9%JM	30 25.4%	30 50.9%JM	10 55.4%JM	5 16.1%	1 33.3%	0 0	79 34.6%	57 43.3%
All sources of info	136 37.8%	50 25.4%	85 53.1%A	136 37.8%	0 0	72 44.3%	42 32.9%	22 31.2%	25 45.9%JM	35 44.9%JM	30 25.4%	30 50.9%JM	10 55.4%JM	5 16.1%	1 33.3%	0 0	79 34.6%	57 43.3%
preferred source of info	74 20.7%	19 9.5%	55 34.5%A	74 20.7%	0 0	46 28.2%G	22 17.2%	6 9.2%	9 16.4%	17 21.8%	15 12.7%	25 41.5%HI JM	6 29.2%JM	3 9.7%	* 22.2%	0 0	43 18.9%	31 23.8%
Meetings/conferences (NET)	54 15.1%	40 20.4%B	14 8.5%	54 15.1%	0 0	22 13.3%	17 13.5%	15 22.2%	7 13.1%	6 7.7%	26 22.2%IL	9 15.1%	1 7.7%	4 12.9%	1 33.3%	0 0	30 13.4%	24 18.0%
All sources of info	54 15.1%	40 20.4%B	14 8.5%	54 15.1%	0 0	22 13.3%	17 13.5%	15 22.2%	7 13.1%	6 7.7%	26 22.2%IL	9 15.1%	1 7.7%	4 12.9%	1 33.3%	0 0	30 13.4%	24 18.0%

Proportions/Means: Columns Tested (5% risk level) - A/B/D - C/D - E/F/G - H/I/J/K/L/M/N - P/Q
* small base; ** very small base (under 30) ineligible for sig testing

Table 103
Page 287

Outsell/Digital Library Federation Study (2002)
Weighted Tables

TABLE 91, continued

R7D/E_6. Papers delivered at professional meetings SUMMARY TABLE

	TOTAL SAMPLE	RESPONDENT TYPE: FACULTY MEMBER (A)	GRAD. STUDENT (B)	FACULTY /GRAD (C)	UNDER GRAD. STUDENT (D)	INSTITUTION TYPE: PUBLIC (E)	PRIVATE (F)	LIBERAL ARTS (G)	DISCIPLINE: BIOLOGIAL SCIENCES (H)	PHYSICAL SCIENCES /MATH (I)	SOCIAL SCIENCES (J)	ARTS AND HUMAN. (K)	ENGI- NEERING (L)	BUSINESS (M)	LAW (N)	UNDEC. MAJOR	GENDER: MALE (P)	FEMALE (Q)
Base - Use Papers delivered at professional meetings for research	359	198	160	359	0**	164	126	69*	54*	78*	118*	59*	19*	29*	2**	0*	227	131*
preferred source of info	45	36	8	45	0	17	16	12	7	3	23	8	1	3	1	0	26	19
	12.4%	18.3%B	5.2%	12.4%	0	10.1%	12.5%	17.9%	13.1%I	3.8%	19.0%IL	13.2%	4.6%	9.7%	33.3%	0	11.3%	14.4%
Sources (NET)	43	34	9	43	0	17	15	11	3	7	23	8	1	3	0	0	33	11
	12.1%	17.4%B	5.6%	12.1%	0	10.7%	11.6%	16.4%	4.9%	9.0%	19.0%HL	13.2%	3.1%	9.7%	0	0	14.4%	8.1%
All sources of info	43	34	9	43	0	17	15	11	3	7	23	8	1	3	0	0	33	11
	12.1%	17.4%B	5.6%	12.1%	0	10.7%	11.6%	16.4%	4.9%	9.0%	19.0%HL	13.2%	3.1%	9.7%	0	0	14.4%	8.1%
preferred source of info	28	22	6	28	0	12	8	7	1	6	13	4	*	3	0	0	18	9
	7.7%	11.1%B	3.5%	7.7%	0	7.5%	6.5%	10.4%	1.6%	7.7%	11.1%	7.5%	1.5%	9.7%	0	0	8.0%	7.2%
Interlibrary loan (NET)	28	21	7	28	0	10	9	9	6	10	4	6	2	0	*	0	21	7
	7.8%	10.4%	4.6%	7.8%	0	6.1%	7.2%	13.1%	11.5%	12.8%JM	3.2%	9.4%	12.3%JM	0	11.1%	0	9.4%	5.0%
All sources of info	28	21	7	28	0	10	9	9	6	10	4	6	2	0	*	0	21	7
	7.8%	10.4%	4.6%	7.8%	0	6.1%	7.2%	13.1%	11.5%	12.8%JM	3.2%	9.4%	12.3%JM	0	11.1%	0	9.4%	5.0%
preferred source of info	4	3	1	4	0	*	1	3	1	1	2	0	*	0	*	0	1	3
	1.2%	1.6%	0.7%	1.2%	0	0.1%	0.9%	4.2%E	1.6%	1.3%	1.6%	0	1.5%	0	11.1%	0	0.6%	2.1%
Colleague (NET)	13	5	7	13	0	4	8	1	3	4	2	3	1	0	0	0	8	4
	3.6%	2.7%	4.6%	3.6%	0	2.4%	6.0%	1.6%	4.9%	5.1%	1.6%	5.7%	4.6%	0	0	0	3.7%	3.3%
All sources of info	13	5	7	13	0	4	8	1	3	4	2	3	1	0	0	0	8	4
	3.6%	2.7%	4.6%	3.6%	0	2.4%	6.0%	1.6%	4.9%	5.1%	1.6%	5.7%	4.6%	0	0	0	3.7%	3.3%

Proportions/Means: Columns Tested (5% risk level) - A/B/D - C/D - E/F/G - H/I/J/K/L/M/N - P/Q
* small base; ** very small base (under 30) ineligible for sig testing

Table 103
Page 288

Outsell/Digital Library Federation Study (2002)
Weighted Tables

TABLE 91, continued

R7D/E_6. Papers delivered at professional meetings SUMMARY TABLE

		RESPONDENT TYPE				INSTITUTION TYPE			DISCIPLINE								GENDER	
	TOTAL SAMPLE	FACULTY MEMBER	GRAD. STUDENT	FACULTY /GRAD	UNDER GRAD. STUDENT	PUBLIC	PRIVATE	LIBERAL ARTS	BIOLOGIAL SCIENCES	PHYSICAL SCIENCES /MATH	SOCIAL SCIENCES	ARTS AND HUMAN.	ENGI- NEERING	BUSINESS	LAW	UNDEC. MAJOR	MALE	FEMALE
		(A)	(B)	(C)	(D)	(E)	(F)	(G)	(H)	(I)	(J)	(K)	(L)	(M)	(N)		(P)	(Q)
Base - Use Papers delivered at professional meetings for research	359	198	160	359	0**	164	126	69*	54*	78*	118*	59*	19*	29*	2**	0*	227	131*
preferred source of info	4 1.2%	* 0.1%	4 2.4%	4 1.2%	0 0	1 0.6%	3 2.5%	0 0	1 1.6%	3 3.8%	0 0	0 0	* 1.5%	0 0	0 0	0 0	3 1.4%	1 0.8%
Borrow from or use in other libraries (NET)	12 3.3%	6 3.0%	6 3.8%	12 3.3%	0 0	3 1.9%	6 4.7%	3 4.4%	2 3.3%	5 6.4%	2 1.6%	3 5.7%	0 0	0 0	0 0	0 0	6 2.6%	6 4.6%
All sources of info	12 3.3%	6 3.0%	6 3.8%	12 3.3%	0 0	3 1.9%	6 4.7%	3 4.4%	2 3.3%	5 6.4%	2 1.6%	3 5.7%	0 0	0 0	0 0	0 0	6 2.6%	6 4.6%
preferred source of info	2 0.6%	1 0.5%	1 0.6%	2 0.6%	0 0	1 0.6%	1 0.8%	0 0	0 0	2 2.6%	0 0	0 0	0 0	0 0	0 0	0 0	2 0.9%	0 0
Printed material (NET)	11 3.0%	5 2.5%	6 3.7%	11 3.0%	0 0	4 2.4%	6 4.6%	1 1.5%	0 0	4 5.1%	4 3.2%	1 1.9%	0 0	2 6.5%	0 0	0 0	7 3.1%	4 2.9%
All sources of info	11 3.0%	5 2.5%	6 3.7%	11 3.0%	0 0	4 2.4%	6 4.6%	1 1.5%	0 0	4 5.1%	4 3.2%	1 1.9%	0 0	2 6.5%	0 0	0 0	7 3.1%	4 2.9%
preferred source of info	8 2.2%	3 1.4%	5 3.0%	8 2.2%	0 0	3 1.8%	5 3.8%	0 0	0 0	1 1.3%	4 3.2%	1 1.9%	0 0	2 6.5%	0 0	0 0	4 1.7%	4 2.9%
Order from on demand document delivery service (NET)	11 3.0%	6 3.1%	4 2.8%	11 3.0%	0 0	4 2.2%	4 3.1%	3 4.5%	2 3.3%	2 2.6%	4 3.2%	2 3.8%	1 4.6%	0 0	0 0	0 0	7 3.0%	4 3.0%

Proportions/Means: Columns Tested (5% risk level) - A/B/D - C/D - E/F/G - H/I/J/K/L/M/N - P/Q
* small base; ** very small base (under 30) ineligible for sig testing

Table 103
Page 289

Outsell/Digital Library Federation Study (2002)
Weighted Tables

TABLE 91, continued

R7D/E_6. Papers delivered at professional meetings SUMMARY TABLE

		RESPONDENT TYPE				INSTITUTION TYPE			DISCIPLINE								GENDER	
	TOTAL SAMPLE	FACULTY MEMBER	GRAD. STUDENT	FACULTY /GRAD	UNDER GRAD. STUDENT	PUBLIC	PRIVATE	LIBERAL ARTS	BIOLOGIAL SCIENCES	PHYSICAL SCIENCES /MATH	SOCIAL SCIENCES	ARTS AND HUMAN.	ENGI-NEERING	BUSINESS	LAW	UNDEC. MAJOR	MALE	FEMALE
		(A)	(B)	(C)	(D)	(E)	(F)	(G)	(H)	(I)	(J)	(K)	(L)	(M)	(N)		(P)	(Q)
Base - Use Papers delivered at professional meetings for research	359	198	160	359	0**	164	126	69*	54*	78*	118*	59*	19*	29*	2**	0*	227	131*
All sources of info	11 3.0%	6 3.1%	4 2.8%	11 3.0%	0 0	4 2.2%	4 3.1%	3 4.5%	2 3.3%	2 2.6%	4 3.2%	2 3.8%	1 4.6%	0 0	0 0	0 0	7 3.0%	4 3.0%
preferred source of info	5 1.3%	2 0.9%	3 1.7%	5 1.3%	0 0	2 1.1%	3 2.2%	0 0	1 1.6%	0 0	4 3.2%	0 0	0 0	0 0	0 0	0 0	2 0.8%	3 2.1%
Personal holdings (NET)	9 2.5%	9 4.4%B	0 0	9 2.5%	0 0	0 0	2 1.5%	7 10.1%EF	1 1.6%	2 2.6%	6 4.8%	0 0	* 1.5%	0 0	0 0	0 0	8 3.4%	1 0.8%
All sources of info	9 2.5%	9 4.4%B	0 0	9 2.5%	0 0	0 0	2 1.5%	7 10.1%EF	1 1.6%	2 2.6%	6 4.8%	0 0	* 1.5%	0 0	0 0	0 0	8 3.4%	1 0.8%
preferred source of info	4 1.0%	4 1.9%	0 0	4 1.0%	0 0	0 0	2 1.5%	2 2.7%	0 0	0 0	4 3.2%	0 0	0 0	0 0	0 0	0 0	4 1.7%	0 0
Faculty (NET)	6 1.7%	1 0.5%	5 3.3%	6 1.7%	0 0	3 2.0%	2 1.6%	1 1.4%	1 1.6%	0 0	2 1.6%	2 3.8%	* 1.5%	1 3.2%	0 0	0 0	4 1.9%	2 1.5%
All sources of info	6 1.7%	1 0.5%	5 3.3%	6 1.7%	0 0	3 2.0%	2 1.6%	1 1.4%	1 1.6%	0 0	2 1.6%	2 3.8%	* 1.5%	1 3.2%	0 0	0 0	4 1.9%	2 1.5%
preferred source of info	3 0.8%	1 0.5%	2 1.2%	3 0.8%	0 0	2 1.1%	0 0	1 1.4%	0 0	0 0	2 1.6%	0 0	0 0	1 3.2%	0 0	0 0	3 1.2%	0 0

Proportions/Means: Columns Tested (5% risk level) - A/B/D - C/D - E/F/G - H/I/J/K/L/M/N - P/Q
* small base; ** very small base (under 30) ineligible for sig testing

Table 103
Page 290

Outsell/Digital Library Federation Study (2002)
Weighted Tables

TABLE 91, continued

R7D/E_6. Papers delivered at professional meetings SUMMARY TABLE

	RESPONDENT TYPE				INSTITUTION TYPE			DISCIPLINE									GENDER	
	TOTAL SAMPLE	FACULTY MEMBER	GRAD. STUDENT	FACULTY /GRAD	UNDER GRAD. STUDENT	PUBLIC	PRIVATE	LIBERAL ARTS	BIOLOGIAL SCIENCES	PHYSICAL SCIENCES /MATH	SOCIAL SCIENCES	ARTS AND HUMAN.	ENGI-NEERING	BUSINESS	LAW	UNDEC. MAJOR	MALE	FEMALE
		(A)	(B)	(C)	(D)	(E)	(F)	(G)	(H)	(I)	(J)	(K)	(L)	(M)	(N)		(P)	(Q)
Base - Use Papers delivered at professional meetings for research	359	198	160	359	0**	164	126	69*	54*	78*	118*	59*	19*	29*	2**	0*	227	131*
Ask library to purchase source (NET)	5 1.3%	3 1.4%	2 1.2%	5 1.3%	0 0	1 0.5%	4 3.0%	0 0	1 1.6%	0 0	4 3.2%	0 0	0 0	0 0	0 0	0 0	2 0.8%	3 2.1%
All sources of info	5 1.3%	3 1.4%	2 1.2%	5 1.3%	0 0	1 0.5%	4 3.0%	0 0	1 1.6%	0 0	4 3.2%	0 0	0 0	0 0	0 0	0 0	2 0.8%	3 2.1%
preferred source of info	5 1.3%	3 1.4%	2 1.2%	5 1.3%	0 0	1 0.5%	4 3.0%	0 0	1 1.6%	0 0	4 3.2%	0 0	0 0	0 0	0 0	0 0	2 0.8%	3 2.1%
Office (NET)	2 0.5%	2 1.0%	0 0	2 0.5%	0 0	0 0	1 0.7%	1 1.5%	0 0	1 1.3%	0 0	0 0	0 0	1 3.2%	0 0	0 0	2 0.8%	0 0
All sources of info	2 0.5%	2 1.0%	0 0	2 0.5%	0 0	0 0	1 0.7%	1 1.5%	0 0	1 1.3%	0 0	0 0	0 0	1 3.2%	0 0	0 0	2 0.8%	0 0
preferred source of info	1 0.3%	1 0.5%	0 0	1 0.3%	0 0	0 0	1 0.7%	0 0	0 0	0 0	0 0	0 0	0 0	1 3.2%	0 0	0 0	1 0.4%	0 0
Purchase from physical book store (NET)	2 0.5%	2 1.0%	0 0	2 0.5%	0 0	0 0	2 1.5%	0 0	0 0	1 1.3%	0 0	0 0	0 0	1 3.2%	0 0	0 0	2 0.8%	0 0
All sources of info	2 0.5%	2 1.0%	0 0	2 0.5%	0 0	0 0	2 1.5%	0 0	0 0	1 1.3%	0 0	0 0	0 0	1 3.2%	0 0	0 0	2 0.8%	0 0

Proportions/Means: Columns Tested (5% risk level) - A/B/D - C/D - E/F/G - H/I/J/K/L/M/N - P/Q
* small base; ** very small base (under 30) ineligible for sig testing

Table 103
Page 291

Outsell/Digital Library Federation Study (2002)
Weighted Tables

TABLE 91, continued

R7D/E_6. Papers delivered at professional meetings SUMMARY TABLE

		RESPONDENT TYPE				INSTITUTION TYPE			DISCIPLINE									GENDER	
	TOTAL SAMPLE	FACULTY MEMBER	GRAD. STUDENT	FACULTY /GRAD	UNDER GRAD. STUDENT	PUBLIC	PRIVATE	LIBERAL ARTS	BIOLOGIAL SCIENCES	PHYSICAL SCIENCES /MATH	SOCIAL SCIENCES	ARTS AND HUMAN.	ENGI- NEERING	BUSINESS	LAW	UNDEC. MAJOR	MALE	FEMALE
		(A)	(B)	(C)	(D)	(E)	(F)	(G)	(H)	(I)	(J)	(K)	(L)	(M)	(N)		(P)	(Q)
Base - Use Papers delivered at professional meetings for research	359	198	160	359	0**	164	126	69*	54*	78*	118*	59*	19*	29*	2**	0*	227	131*
preferred source of info	1 0.3%	1 0.5%	0 0	1 0.3%	0 0	0 0	1 0.7%	0 0	0 0	0 0	0 0	0 0	0 0	1 3.2%	0 0	0 0	1 0.4%	0 0
E-journals (NET)	1 0.2%	0 0	1 0.5%	1 0.2%	0 0	1 0.5%	0 0	0 0	1 1.6%	0 0	0 0	0 0	0 0	0 0	0 0	0 0	0 0	1 0.7%
All sources of info	1 0.2%	0 0	1 0.5%	1 0.2%	0 0	1 0.5%	0 0	0 0	1 1.6%	0 0	0 0	0 0	0 0	0 0	0 0	0 0	0 0	1 0.7%
preferred source of info	1 0.2%	0 0	1 0.5%	1 0.2%	0 0	1 0.5%	0 0	0 0	1 1.6%	0 0	0 0	0 0	0 0	0 0	0 0	0 0	0 0	1 0.7%
Purchase from online bookstore (NET)	* 0.1%	0 0	* 0.2%	* 0.1%	0 0	* 0.2%	0 0	0 0	0 0	0 0	0 0	0 0	* 1.5%	0 0	0 0	0 0	* 0.1%	0 0
All sources of info	* 0.1%	0 0	* 0.2%	* 0.1%	0 0	* 0.2%	0 0	0 0	0 0	0 0	0 0	0 0	* 1.5%	0 0	0 0	0 0	* 0.1%	0 0
preferred source of info	* 0.1%	0 0	* 0.2%	* 0.1%	0 0	* 0.2%	0 0	0 0	0 0	0 0	0 0	0 0	* 1.5%	0 0	0 0	0 0	* 0.1%	0 0
Access from course website (NET)	0 0	0 0	0 0	0 0	0 0	0 0	0 0	0 0	0 0	0 0	0 0	0 0	0 0	0 0	0 0	0 0	0 0	0 0
All sources of info	0 0	0 0	0 0	0 0	0 0	0 0	0 0	0 0	0 0	0 0	0 0	0 0	0 0	0 0	0 0	0 0	0 0	0 0

Proportions/Means: Columns Tested (5% risk level) - A/B/D - C/D - E/F/G - H/I/J/K/L/M/N - P/Q
* small base; ** very small base (under 30) ineligible for sig testing

Table 103
Page 292

Outsell/Digital Library Federation Study (2002)
Weighted Tables

TABLE 91, continued

R7D/E_6. Papers delivered at professional meetings SUMMARY TABLE

		RESPONDENT TYPE				INSTITUTION TYPE			DISCIPLINE									GENDER	
	TOTAL SAMPLE	FACULTY MEMBER	GRAD. STUDENT	FACULTY /GRAD	UNDER GRAD. STUDENT	PUBLIC	PRIVATE	LIBERAL ARTS	BIOLOGIAL SCIENCES	PHYSICAL SCIENCES /MATH	SOCIAL SCIENCES	ARTS AND HUMAN.	ENGI-NEERING	BUSINESS	LAW	UNDEC. MAJOR	MALE	FEMALE
		(A)	(B)	(C)	(D)	(E)	(F)	(G)	(H)	(I)	(J)	(K)	(L)	(M)	(N)		(P)	(Q)
Base - Use Papers delivered at professional meetings for research	359	198	160	359	0**	164	126	69*	54*	78*	118*	59*	19*	29*	2**	0*	227	131*
preferred source of info	0 0	0 0	0 0	0 0	0 0	0 0	0 0	0 0	0 0	0 0	0 0	0 0	0 0	0 0	0 0	0 0	0 0	0 0
Access book/journal/ journal article elsewhere online (NET)	0 0	0 0	0 0	0 0	0 0	0 0	0 0	0 0	0 0	0 0	0 0	0 0	0 0	0 0	0 0	0 0	0 0	0 0
All sources of info	0 0	0 0	0 0	0 0	0 0	0 0	0 0	0 0	0 0	0 0	0 0	0 0	0 0	0 0	0 0	0 0	0 0	0 0
preferred source of info	0 0	0 0	0 0	0 0	0 0	0 0	0 0	0 0	0 0	0 0	0 0	0 0	0 0	0 0	0 0	0 0	0 0	0 0
Other (NET)	46 12.9%	34 17.3%B	12 7.5%	46 12.9%	0 0	15 8.9%	21 16.4%	11 15.8%	3 4.9%	9 11.5%	13 11.1%	12 20.8%H	3 18.5%H	6 19.4%H	0 0	0 0	36 15.6%	11 8.1%
All sources of info	44 12.3%	32 16.3%B	12 7.5%	44 12.3%	0 0	15 8.9%	20 15.6%	10 14.3%	3 4.9%	7 9.0%	13 11.1%	12 20.8%H	3 18.5%H	6 19.4%H	0 0	0 0	34 14.7%	11 8.1%
preferred source of info	16 4.3%	12 6.1%	3 2.1%	16 4.3%	0 0	6 3.4%	4 3.2%	6 8.8%	0 0	4 5.1%	2 1.6%	7 11.3%HJ	2 10.8%HJ	1 3.2%	0 0	0 0	11 4.9%	4 3.3%
DK/Refused	10 2.7%	6 3.0%	4 2.3%	10 2.7%	0 0	5 2.9%	4 3.1%	1 1.5%	0 0	4 5.1%	6 4.8%	0 0	0 0	0 0	0 0	0 0	4 1.7%	6 4.4%

Proportions/Means: Columns Tested (5% risk level) - A/B/D - C/D - E/F/G - H/I/J/K/L/M/N - P/Q
* small base; ** very small base (under 30) ineligible for sig testing

Table 103
Page 293

TABLE 92

R7D/E_7. Print abstracts and indexes SUMMARY TABLE

		RESPONDENT TYPE				INSTITUTION TYPE			DISCIPLINE								GENDER	
	TOTAL SAMPLE	FACULTY MEMBER	GRAD. STUDENT	FACULTY /GRAD	UNDER GRAD. STUDENT	PUBLIC	PRIVATE	LIBERAL ARTS	BIOLOGIAL SCIENCES	PHYSICAL SCIENCES /MATH	SOCIAL SCIENCES	ARTS AND HUMAN.	ENGI- NEERING	BUSINESS	LAW	UNDEC. MAJOR	MALE	FEMALE
		(A)	(B)	(C)	(D)	(E)	(F)	(G)	(H)	(I)	(J)	(K)	(L)	(M)	(N)		(P)	(Q)
Base - Use Print abstracts and indexes for research	292	156	136	292	0**	129*	115*	49*	49*	60*	102*	30**	17*	32*	3**	0*	189	104*
Borrow from or use in campus library (NET)	222 75.9%	120 77.1%	101 74.5%	222 75.9%	0 0	100 78.0%	88 76.6%	34 68.9%	36 73.2%	42 70.0%	81 79.6%	25 81.5%	13 75.9%	23 73.5%	2 81.2%	0 0	147 77.9%	75 72.2%
All sources of info	222 75.9%	120 77.1%	101 74.5%	222 75.9%	0 0	100 78.0%	88 76.6%	34 68.9%	36 73.2%	42 70.0%	81 79.6%	25 81.5%	13 75.9%	23 73.5%	2 81.2%	0 0	147 77.9%	75 72.2%
preferred source of info	139 47.7%	71 45.7%	68 50.0%	139 47.7%	0 0	67 52.0%	51 44.3%	22 44.4%	19 39.3%	29 48.3%	51 50.0%	21 70.4%	6 37.9%	11 35.3%	2 56.2%	0 0	86 45.5%	54 51.8%
Access online (NET)	161 55.0%	81 52.2%	79 58.2%	161 55.0%	0 0	66 51.1%	70 60.9%	25 51.2%	33 66.1%	34 56.7%	55 53.7%	9 29.6%	10 58.6%	20 61.8%	1 43.7%	0 0	103 54.4%	58 56.1%
All sources of info	161 55.0%	81 52.2%	79 58.2%	161 55.0%	0 0	66 51.1%	70 60.9%	25 51.2%	33 66.1%	34 56.7%	55 53.7%	9 29.6%	10 58.6%	20 61.8%	1 43.7%	0 0	103 54.4%	58 56.1%
preferred source of info	133 45.6%	67 43.1%	66 48.5%	133 45.6%	0 0	53 41.2%	57 50.1%	23 46.7%	27 55.4%	29 48.3%	43 42.6%	6 18.5%	8 50.0%	19 58.8%	1 43.7%	0 0	84 44.8%	49 47.1%
Interlibrary loan (NET)	28 9.5%	20 12.6%	8 5.9%	28 9.5%	0 0	9 7.1%	8 6.7%	11 22.3%EF	4 7.1%	11 18.3%JM	6 5.6%	4 14.8%	2 10.3%	1 2.9%	* 12.5%	0 0	19 10.2%	8 8.2%
All sources of info	28 9.5%	20 12.6%	8 5.9%	28 9.5%	0 0	9 7.1%	8 6.7%	11 22.3%EF	4 7.1%	11 18.3%JM	6 5.6%	4 14.8%	2 10.3%	1 2.9%	* 12.5%	0 0	19 10.2%	8 8.2%
preferred source of info	2 0.8%	2 1.3%	* 0.2%	2 0.8%	0 0	* 0.2%	0 0	2 4.2%F	2 3.6%	0 0	0 0	0 0	1 3.4%IJ	0 0	0 0	0 0	2 1.2%	0 0

Proportions/Means: Columns Tested (5% risk level) - A/B/D - C/D - E/F/G - H/I/J/K/L/M/N - P/Q
* small base; ** very small base (under 30) ineligible for sig testing

Table 110
Page 322

Outsell/Digital Library Federation Study (2002)
Weighted Tables

TABLE 92, continued

R7D/E_7. Print abstracts and indexes SUMMARY TABLE

		RESPONDENT TYPE				INSTITUTION TYPE			DISCIPLINE								GENDER	
	TOTAL SAMPLE	FACULTY MEMBER	GRAD. STUDENT	FACULTY /GRAD	UNDER GRAD. STUDENT	PUBLIC	PRIVATE	LIBERAL ARTS	BIOLOGIAL SCIENCES	PHYSICAL SCIENCES /MATH	SOCIAL SCIENCES	ARTS AND HUMAN.	ENGI-NEERING	BUSINESS	LAW	UNDEC. MAJOR	MALE	FEMALE
		(A)	(B)	(C)	(D)	(E)	(F)	(G)	(H)	(I)	(J)	(K)	(L)	(M)	(N)		(P)	(Q)
Base - Use Print abstracts and indexes for research	292	156	136	292	0**	129*	115*	49*	49*	60*	102*	30**	17*	32*	3**	0*	189	104*
Borrow from or use in other libraries (NET)	27 9.2%	18 11.4%	9 6.7%	27 9.2%	0 0	7 5.1%	14 12.5%	6 12.4%	5 10.7%	6 10.0%	8 7.4%	6 18.5%	* 1.7%	2 5.9%	* 12.5%	0 0	17 9.1%	10 9.3%
All sources of info	27 9.2%	18 11.4%	9 6.7%	27 9.2%	0 0	7 5.1%	14 12.5%	6 12.4%	5 10.7%	6 10.0%	8 7.4%	6 18.5%	* 1.7%	2 5.9%	* 12.5%	0 0	17 9.1%	10 9.3%
preferred source of info	5 1.7%	4 2.5%	1 0.8%	5 1.7%	0 0	1 0.7%	3 2.7%	1 2.0%	1 1.8%	1 1.7%	0 0	2 7.4%	0 0	1 2.9%	0 0	0 0	4 2.1%	1 1.1%
Personal holdings (NET)	4 1.3%	4 2.5%	0 0	4 1.3%	0 0	3 2.1%	1 1.0%	0 0	1 1.8%	0 0	0 0	1 3.7%	0 0	2 5.9%J	0 0	0 0	4 2.0%	0 0
All sources of info	4 1.3%	4 2.5%	0 0	4 1.3%	0 0	3 2.1%	1 1.0%	0 0	1 1.8%	0 0	0 0	1 3.7%	0 0	2 5.9%J	0 0	0 0	4 2.0%	0 0
preferred source of info	1 0.3%	1 0.6%	0 0	1 0.3%	0 0	1 0.7%	0 0	0 0	0 0	0 0	0 0	0 0	0 0	1 2.9%	0 0	0 0	1 0.5%	0 0
Colleague (NET)	3 1.1%	3 1.9%	* 0.2%	3 1.1%	0 0	0 0	1 1.1%	2 4.1%E	0 0	3 5.0%	0 0	0 0	* 1.7%	0 0	0 0	0 0	3 1.6%	* 0.3%
All sources of info	3 1.1%	3 1.9%	* 0.2%	3 1.1%	0 0	0 0	1 1.1%	2 4.1%E	0 0	3 5.0%	0 0	0 0	* 1.7%	0 0	0 0	0 0	3 1.6%	* 0.3%
preferred source of info	1 0.3%	1 0.6%	0 0	1 0.3%	0 0	0 0	0 0	1 2.0%	0 0	1 1.7%	0 0	0 0	0 0	0 0	0 0	0 0	1 0.5%	0 0

Proportions/Means: Columns Tested (5% risk level) - A/B/D - C/D - E/F/G - H/I/J/K/L/M/N - P/Q
* small base; ** very small base (under 30) ineligible for sig testing

Table 110
Page 323

Outsell/Digital Library Federation Study (2002)
Weighted Tables

TABLE 92, continued

R7D/E_7. Print abstracts and indexes SUMMARY TABLE

		RESPONDENT TYPE				INSTITUTION TYPE			DISCIPLINE								GENDER	
	TOTAL SAMPLE	FACULTY MEMBER	GRAD. STUDENT	FACULTY /GRAD	UNDER GRAD. STUDENT	PUBLIC	PRIVATE	LIBERAL ARTS	BIOLOGIAL SCIENCES	PHYSICAL SCIENCES /MATH	SOCIAL SCIENCES	ARTS AND HUMAN.	ENGI-NEERING	BUSINESS	LAW	UNDEC. MAJOR	MALE	FEMALE
		(A)	(B)	(C)	(D)	(E)	(F)	(G)	(H)	(I)	(J)	(K)	(L)	(M)	(N)		(P)	(Q)
Base - Use Print abstracts and indexes for research	292	156	136	292	0**	129*	115*	49*	49*	60*	102*	30**	17*	32*	3**	0*	189	104*
Printed material (NET)	3 0.9%	3 1.8%	0 0	3 0.9%	0 0	2 1.5%	0 0	1 1.8%	1 1.8%	0 0	2 1.9%	0 0	0 0	0 0	0 0	0 0	3 1.5%	0 0
All sources of info	3 0.9%	3 1.8%	0 0	3 0.9%	0 0	2 1.5%	0 0	1 1.8%	1 1.8%	0 0	2 1.9%	0 0	0 0	0 0	0 0	0 0	3 1.5%	0 0
preferred source of info	2 0.6%	2 1.2%	0 0	2 0.6%	0 0	2 1.5%	0 0	0 0	0 0	0 0	2 1.9%	0 0	0 0	0 0	0 0	0 0	2 1.0%	0 0
Purchase from online bookstore (NET)	1 0.3%	1 0.6%	0 0	1 0.3%	0 0	0 0	1 0.8%	0 0	0 0	0 0	0 0	0 0	0 0	1 2.9%	0 0	0 0	0 0	1 0.9%
All sources of info	1 0.3%	1 0.6%	0 0	1 0.3%	0 0	0 0	1 0.8%	0 0	0 0	0 0	0 0	0 0	0 0	1 2.9%	0 0	0 0	0 0	1 0.9%
preferred source of info	0 0	0 0	0 0	0 0	0 0	0 0	0 0	0 0	0 0	0 0	0 0	0 0	0 0	0 0	0 0	0 0	0 0	0 0
Sources (NET)	1 0.2%	* 0.2%	* 0.2%	1 0.2%	0 0	* 0.2%	* 0.3%	0 0	0 0	0 0	0 0	0 0	1 3.4%IJ	0 0	0 0	0 0	1 0.3%	0 0
All sources of info	1 0.2%	* 0.2%	* 0.2%	1 0.2%	0 0	* 0.2%	* 0.3%	0 0	0 0	0 0	0 0	0 0	1 3.4%IJ	0 0	0 0	0 0	1 0.3%	0 0
preferred source of info	* 0.1%	* 0.2%	0 0	* 0.1%	0 0	* 0.2%	0 0	0 0	0 0	0 0	0 0	0 0	* 1.7%	0 0	0 0	0 0	* 0.2%	0 0

Proportions/Means: Columns Tested (5% risk level) - A/B/D - C/D - E/F/G - H/I/J/K/L/M/N - P/Q
* small base; ** very small base (under 30) ineligible for sig testing

Table 110
Page 324

Outsell/Digital Library Federation Study (2002)
Weighted Tables

TABLE 92, continued

R7D/E_7. Print abstracts and indexes SUMMARY TABLE

		RESPONDENT TYPE				INSTITUTION TYPE			DISCIPLINE								GENDER	
	TOTAL SAMPLE	FACULTY MEMBER	GRAD. STUDENT	FACULTY /GRAD	UNDER GRAD. STUDENT	PUBLIC	PRIVATE	LIBERAL ARTS	BIOLOGIAL SCIENCES	PHYSICAL SCIENCES /MATH	SOCIAL SCIENCES	ARTS AND HUMAN.	ENGI- NEERING	BUSINESS	LAW	UNDEC. MAJOR	MALE	FEMALE
		(A)	(B)	(C)	(D)	(E)	(F)	(G)	(H)	(I)	(J)	(K)	(L)	(M)	(N)		(P)	(Q)
Base - Use Print abstracts and indexes for research	292	156	136	292	0**	129*	115*	49*	49*	60*	102*	30**	17*	32*	3**	0*	189	104*
Ask library to purchase source (NET)	* 0.1%	* 0.2%	0 0	* 0.1%	0 0	* 0.2%	0 0	0 0	0 0	0 0	0 0	0 0	* 1.7%	0 0	0 0	0 0	* 0.2%	0 0
All sources of info	* 0.1%	* 0.2%	0 0	* 0.1%	0 0	* 0.2%	0 0	0 0	0 0	0 0	0 0	0 0	* 1.7%	0 0	0 0	0 0	* 0.2%	0 0
preferred source of info	0 0	0 0	0 0	0 0	0 0	0 0	0 0	0 0	0 0	0 0	0 0	0 0	0 0	0 0	0 0	0 0	0 0	0 0
Order from on demand document delivery service (NET)	* 0.1%	* 0.2%	0 0	* 0.1%	0 0	* 0.2%	0 0	0 0	0 0	0 0	0 0	0 0	* 1.7%	0 0	0 0	0 0	* 0.2%	0 0
All sources of info	* 0.1%	* 0.2%	0 0	* 0.1%	0 0	* 0.2%	0 0	0 0	0 0	0 0	0 0	0 0	* 1.7%	0 0	0 0	0 0	* 0.2%	0 0
preferred source of info	* 0.1%	* 0.2%	0 0	* 0.1%	0 0	* 0.2%	0 0	0 0	0 0	0 0	0 0	0 0	* 1.7%	0 0	0 0	0 0	* 0.2%	0 0
Meetings/conferences (NET)	* 0.1%	0 0	* 0.2%	* 0.1%	0 0	0 0	* 0.3%	0 0	0 0	0 0	0 0	0 0	* 1.7%	0 0	0 0	0 0	* 0.2%	0 0
All sources of info	* 0.1%	0 0	* 0.2%	* 0.1%	0 0	0 0	* 0.3%	0 0	0 0	0 0	0 0	0 0	* 1.7%	0 0	0 0	0 0	* 0.2%	0 0
preferred source of info	* 0.1%	0 0	* 0.2%	* 0.1%	0 0	0 0	* 0.3%	0 0	0 0	0 0	0 0	0 0	* 1.7%	0 0	0 0	0 0	* 0.2%	0 0

Proportions/Means: Columns Tested (5% risk level) - A/B/D - C/D - E/F/G - H/I/J/K/L/M/N - P/Q
* small base; ** very small base (under 30) ineligible for sig testing

Table 110
Page 325

Outsell/Digital Library Federation Study (2002)
Weighted Tables

TABLE 92, continued

R7D/E_7. Print abstracts and indexes SUMMARY TABLE

		RESPONDENT TYPE				INSTITUTION TYPE			DISCIPLINE								GENDER	
	TOTAL SAMPLE	FACULTY MEMBER	GRAD. STUDENT	FACULTY /GRAD	UNDER GRAD. STUDENT	PUBLIC	PRIVATE	LIBERAL ARTS	BIOLOGIAL SCIENCES	PHYSICAL SCIENCES /MATH	SOCIAL SCIENCES	ARTS AND HUMAN.	ENGI-NEERING	BUSINESS	LAW	UNDEC. MAJOR	MALE	FEMALE
		(A)	(B)	(C)	(D)	(E)	(F)	(G)	(H)	(I)	(J)	(K)	(L)	(M)	(N)		(P)	(Q)
Base - Use Print abstracts and indexes for research	292	156	136	292	0**	129*	115*	49*	49*	60*	102*	30**	17*	32*	3**	0*	189	104*
Access from course website (NET)	0 0	0 0	0 0	0 0	0 0	0 0	0 0	0 0	0 0	0 0	0 0	0 0	0 0	0 0	0 0	0 0	0 0	0 0
All sources of info	0 0	0 0	0 0	0 0	0 0	0 0	0 0	0 0	0 0	0 0	0 0	0 0	0 0	0 0	0 0	0 0	0 0	0 0
preferred source of info	0 0	0 0	0 0	0 0	0 0	0 0	0 0	0 0	0 0	0 0	0 0	0 0	0 0	0 0	0 0	0 0	0 0	0 0
Purchase from physical book store (NET)	0 0	0 0	0 0	0 0	0 0	0 0	0 0	0 0	0 0	0 0	0 0	0 0	0 0	0 0	0 0	0 0	0 0	0 0
All sources of info	0 0	0 0	0 0	0 0	0 0	0 0	0 0	0 0	0 0	0 0	0 0	0 0	0 0	0 0	0 0	0 0	0 0	0 0
preferred source of info	0 0	0 0	0 0	0 0	0 0	0 0	0 0	0 0	0 0	0 0	0 0	0 0	0 0	0 0	0 0	0 0	0 0	0 0
E-journals (NET)	0 0	0 0	0 0	0 0	0 0	0 0	0 0	0 0	0 0	0 0	0 0	0 0	0 0	0 0	0 0	0 0	0 0	0 0
All sources of info	0 0	0 0	0 0	0 0	0 0	0 0	0 0	0 0	0 0	0 0	0 0	0 0	0 0	0 0	0 0	0 0	0 0	0 0
preferred source of info	0 0	0 0	0 0	0 0	0 0	0 0	0 0	0 0	0 0	0 0	0 0	0 0	0 0	0 0	0 0	0 0	0 0	0 0

Proportions/Means: Columns Tested (5% risk level) - A/B/D - C/D - E/F/G - H/I/J/K/L/M/N - P/Q
* small base; ** very small base (under 30) ineligible for sig testing

Table 110
Page 326

TABLE 92, continued

R7D/E_7. Print abstracts and indexes SUMMARY TABLE

		RESPONDENT TYPE				INSTITUTION TYPE			DISCIPLINE								GENDER	
	TOTAL SAMPLE	FACULTY MEMBER	GRAD. STUDENT	FACULTY /GRAD	UNDER GRAD. STUDENT	PUBLIC	PRIVATE	LIBERAL ARTS	BIOLOGIAL SCIENCES	PHYSICAL SCIENCES /MATH	SOCIAL SCIENCES	ARTS AND HUMAN.	ENGI-NEERING	BUSINESS	LAW	UNDEC. MAJOR	MALE	FEMALE
		(A)	(B)	(C)	(D)	(E)	(F)	(G)	(H)	(I)	(J)	(K)	(L)	(M)	(N)		(P)	(Q)
Base - Use Print abstracts and indexes for research	292	156	136	292	0**	129*	115*	49*	49*	60*	102*	30**	17*	32*	3**	0*	189	104*
Faculty (NET)	0 0	0 0	0 0	0 0	0 0	0 0	0 0	0 0	0 0	0 0	0 0	0 0	0 0	0 0	0 0	0 0	0 0	0 0
All sources of info	0 0	0 0	0 0	0 0	0 0	0 0	0 0	0 0	0 0	0 0	0 0	0 0	0 0	0 0	0 0	0 0	0 0	0 0
preferred source of info	0 0	0 0	0 0	0 0	0 0	0 0	0 0	0 0	0 0	0 0	0 0	0 0	0 0	0 0	0 0	0 0	0 0	0 0
Access book/journal/ journal article elsewhere online (NET)	0 0	0 0	0 0	0 0	0 0	0 0	0 0	0 0	0 0	0 0	0 0	0 0	0 0	0 0	0 0	0 0	0 0	0 0
All sources of info	0 0	0 0	0 0	0 0	0 0	0 0	0 0	0 0	0 0	0 0	0 0	0 0	0 0	0 0	0 0	0 0	0 0	0 0
preferred source of info	0 0	0 0	0 0	0 0	0 0	0 0	0 0	0 0	0 0	0 0	0 0	0 0	0 0	0 0	0 0	0 0	0 0	0 0
Office (NET)	0 0	0 0	0 0	0 0	0 0	0 0	0 0	0 0	0 0	0 0	0 0	0 0	0 0	0 0	0 0	0 0	0 0	0 0
All sources of info	0 0	0 0	0 0	0 0	0 0	0 0	0 0	0 0	0 0	0 0	0 0	0 0	0 0	0 0	0 0	0 0	0 0	0 0
preferred source of info	0 0	0 0	0 0	0 0	0 0	0 0	0 0	0 0	0 0	0 0	0 0	0 0	0 0	0 0	0 0	0 0	0 0	0 0

Proportions/Means: Columns Tested (5% risk level) - A/B/D - C/D - E/F/G - H/I/J/K/L/M/N - P/Q
* small base; ** very small base (under 30) ineligible for sig testing

Table 110
Page 327

Outsell/Digital Library Federation Study (2002)
Weighted Tables

TABLE 92, continued

R7D/E_7. Print abstracts and indexes SUMMARY TABLE

		RESPONDENT TYPE				INSTITUTION TYPE			DISCIPLINE									GENDER	
	TOTAL SAMPLE	FACULTY MEMBER	GRAD. STUDENT	FACULTY /GRAD	UNDER GRAD. STUDENT	PUBLIC	PRIVATE	LIBERAL ARTS	BIOLOGIAL SCIENCES	PHYSICAL SCIENCES /MATH	SOCIAL SCIENCES	ARTS AND HUMAN.	ENGI-NEERING	BUSINESS	LAW	UNDEC. MAJOR	MALE	FEMALE
		(A)	(B)	(C)	(D)	(E)	(F)	(G)	(H)	(I)	(J)	(K)	(L)	(M)	(N)		(P)	(Q)
Base - Use Print abstracts and indexes for research	292	156	136	292	0**	129*	115*	49*	49*	60*	102*	30**	17*	32*	3**	0*	189	104*
Other (NET)	14	11	2	14	0	1	11	2	0	1	8	4	1	0	0	0	11	3
	4.7%	7.3%	1.8%	4.7%	0	0.5%	10.0%E	3.8%	0	1.7%	7.4%	14.8%	5.2%H	0	0	0	5.8%	2.9%
All sources of info	11	8	2	11	0	1	8	2	0	1	6	3	1	0	0	0	8	3
	3.7%	5.4%	1.8%	3.7%	0	0.5%	7.3%E	3.8%	0	1.7%	5.6%	11.1%	5.2%H	0	0	0	4.2%	2.9%
preferred source of info	3	3	*	3	0	*	3	0	0	0	2	1	*	0	0	0	3	0
	1.1%	1.9%	0.2%	1.1%	0	0.2%	2.6%	0	0	0	1.9%	3.7%	1.7%	0	0	0	1.7%	0
DK/Refused	4	4	0	4	0	4	0	*	0	0	4	0	*	0	0	0	4	0
	1.4%	2.6%	0	1.4%	0	2.9%	0	0.6%	0	0	3.7%	0	1.7%	0	0	0	2.1%	0

Proportions/Means: Columns Tested (5% risk level) - A/B/D - C/D - E/F/G - H/I/J/K/L/M/N - P/Q
* small base; ** very small base (under 30) ineligible for sig testing

Table 110
Page 328

TABLE 93

R7D/E_8. Online abstracts and indexes SUMMARY TABLE

		RESPONDENT TYPE				INSTITUTION TYPE			DISCIPLINE									GENDER	
	TOTAL SAMPLE	FACULTY MEMBER	GRAD. STUDENT	FACULTY /GRAD	UNDER GRAD. STUDENT	PUBLIC	PRIVATE	LIBERAL ARTS	BIOLOGIAL SCIENCES	PHYSICAL SCIENCES /MATH	SOCIAL SCIENCES	ARTS AND HUMAN.	ENGI- NEERING	BUSINESS	LAW	UNDEC. MAJOR	MALE	FEMALE
		(A)	(B)	(C)	(D)	(E)	(F)	(G)	(H)	(I)	(J)	(K)	(L)	(M)	(N)		(P)	(Q)
Base - Use Online abstracts and indexes for research	348	171	178	348	0**	151	130	68*	63*	75*	109*	47*	17*	32*	5*	0*	222	126*
Access online (NET)	282 80.9%	144 84.0%	138 77.9%	282 80.9%	0 0	119 79.0%	105 81.0%	58 85.1%	53 83.3%	63 84.0%	85 77.6%	37 78.6%	13 78.0%	27 85.3%	4 80.6%	0 0	183 82.4%	99 78.2%
All sources of info	282 80.9%	144 84.0%	138 77.9%	282 80.9%	0 0	119 79.0%	105 81.0%	58 85.1%	53 83.3%	63 84.0%	85 77.6%	37 78.6%	13 78.0%	27 85.3%	4 80.6%	0 0	183 82.4%	99 78.2%
preferred source of info	259 74.2%	133 77.7%	126 70.8%	259 74.2%	0 0	105 69.4%	99 76.1%	55 81.1%	50 79.2%	59 78.7%	77 70.7%	32 69.0%	12 69.5%	24 76.5%	4 71.0%	0 0	170 76.5%	89 70.1%
Borrow from or use in campus library (NET)	121 34.8%	49 28.8%	72 40.5%A	121 34.8%	0 0	63 41.6%	39 30.2%	19 28.4%	24 37.5%	22 29.3%	43 39.7%	17 35.7%	6 33.9%	7 23.5%	2 41.9%	0 0	66 29.7%	55 43.8%P
All sources of info	121 34.8%	49 28.8%	72 40.5%A	121 34.8%	0 0	63 41.6%	39 30.2%	19 28.4%	24 37.5%	22 29.3%	43 39.7%	17 35.7%	6 33.9%	7 23.5%	2 41.9%	0 0	66 29.7%	55 43.8%P
preferred source of info	56 16.2%	18 10.6%	38 21.6%A	56 16.2%	0 0	33 22.1%G	17 13.3%	6 8.6%	11 16.7%	5 6.7%	23 20.7%I	10 21.4%I	3 15.3%	5 14.7%	1 19.4%I	0 0	30 13.6%	26 20.8%
Borrow from or use in other libraries (NET)	15 4.4%	12 7.0%B	3 1.8%	15 4.4%	0 0	4 2.6%	7 5.7%	4 5.5%	2 2.8%	6 8.0%	4 3.4%	1 2.4%	1 8.5%	1 2.9%	* 3.2%	0 0	9 4.2%	6 4.6%
All sources of info	15 4.4%	12 7.0%B	3 1.8%	15 4.4%	0 0	4 2.6%	7 5.7%	4 5.5%	2 2.8%	6 8.0%	4 3.4%	1 2.4%	1 8.5%	1 2.9%	* 3.2%	0 0	9 4.2%	6 4.6%

Proportions/Means: Columns Tested (5% risk level) - A/B/D - C/D - E/F/G - H/I/J/K/L/M/N - P/Q
* small base; ** very small base (under 30) ineligible for sig testing

Table 117
Page 357

Outsell/Digital Library Federation Study (2002)
Weighted Tables

TABLE 93, continued

R7D/E_8. Online abstracts and indexes SUMMARY TABLE

		RESPONDENT TYPE				INSTITUTION TYPE			DISCIPLINE									GENDER	
	TOTAL SAMPLE	FACULTY MEMBER	GRAD. STUDENT	FACULTY /GRAD	UNDER GRAD. STUDENT	PUBLIC	PRIVATE	LIBERAL ARTS	BIOLOGIAL SCIENCES	PHYSICAL SCIENCES /MATH	SOCIAL SCIENCES	ARTS AND HUMAN.	ENGI-NEERING	BUSINESS	LAW	UNDEC. MAJOR	MALE	FEMALE
		(A)	(B)	(C)	(D)	(E)	(F)	(G)	(H)	(I)	(J)	(K)	(L)	(M)	(N)		(P)	(Q)
Base - Use Online abstracts and indexes for research	348	171	178	348	0**	151	130	68*	63*	75*	109*	47*	17*	32*	5*	0*	222	126*
preferred source of info	7 2.0%	5 2.9%	2 1.1%	7 2.0%	0 0	4 2.4%	3 2.4%	0 0	0 0	3 4.0%	2 1.7%	0 0	1 5.1%HK	1 2.9%	* 3.2%HK	0 0	6 2.6%	1 0.9%
Personal holdings (NET)	10 2.9%	9 5.2%B	1 0.6%	10 2.9%	0 0	3 1.8%	3 2.4%	4 6.1%	2 2.8%	3 4.0%	2 1.7%	2 4.8%	0 0	1 2.9%	* 3.2%	0 0	9 4.1%	1 0.7%
All sources of info	10 2.9%	9 5.2%B	1 0.6%	10 2.9%	0 0	3 1.8%	3 2.4%	4 6.1%	2 2.8%	3 4.0%	2 1.7%	2 4.8%	0 0	1 2.9%	* 3.2%	0 0	9 4.1%	1 0.7%
preferred source of info	4 1.2%	3 1.8%	1 0.6%	4 1.2%	0 0	1 0.6%	* 0.1%	3 4.6%F	1 1.4%	2 2.7%	0 0	1 2.4%	0 0	0 0	* 3.2%J	0 0	3 1.5%	1 0.7%
Interlibrary loan (NET)	9 2.5%	9 5.0%B	* 0.2%	9 2.5%	0 0	2 1.0%	4 3.1%	3 4.8%	4 5.6%J	1 1.3%	0 0	2 4.8%	1 6.8%IJ	1 2.9%	0 0	0 0	5 2.2%	4 3.1%
All sources of info	9 2.5%	9 5.0%B	* 0.2%	9 2.5%	0 0	2 1.0%	4 3.1%	3 4.8%	4 5.6%J	1 1.3%	0 0	2 4.8%	1 6.8%IJ	1 2.9%	0 0	0 0	5 2.2%	4 3.1%
preferred source of info	1 0.3%	1 0.7%	0 0	1 0.3%	0 0	0 0	1 0.9%	0 0	0 0	0 0	0 0	1 2.4%	0 0	0 0	0 0	0 0	0 0	1 0.9%
Printed material (NET)	7 1.9%	4 2.2%	3 1.6%	7 1.9%	0 0	4 2.5%	2 1.4%	1 1.4%	1 1.4%	1 1.3%	4 3.4%	0 0	0 0	1 2.9%	0 0	0 0	5 2.1%	2 1.5%
All sources of info	7 1.9%	4 2.2%	3 1.6%	7 1.9%	0 0	4 2.5%	2 1.4%	1 1.4%	1 1.4%	1 1.3%	4 3.4%	0 0	0 0	1 2.9%	0 0	0 0	5 2.1%	2 1.5%

Proportions/Means: Columns Tested (5% risk level) - A/B/D - C/D - E/F/G - H/I/J/K/L/M/N - P/Q
* small base; ** very small base (under 30) ineligible for sig testing

Table 117
Page 358

Outsell/Digital Library Federation Study (2002)
Weighted Tables

TABLE 93, continued

R7D/E_8. Online abstracts and indexes SUMMARY TABLE

		RESPONDENT TYPE				INSTITUTION TYPE			DISCIPLINE								GENDER	
	TOTAL SAMPLE	FACULTY MEMBER	GRAD. STUDENT	FACULTY /GRAD	UNDER GRAD. STUDENT	PUBLIC	PRIVATE	LIBERAL ARTS	BIOLOGICAL SCIENCES	PHYSICAL SCIENCES /MATH	SOCIAL SCIENCES	ARTS AND HUMAN.	ENGI-NEERING	BUSINESS	LAW	UNDEC. MAJOR	MALE	FEMALE
		(A)	(B)	(C)	(D)	(E)	(F)	(G)	(H)	(I)	(J)	(K)	(L)	(M)	(N)		(P)	(Q)
Base - Use Online abstracts and indexes for research	348	171	178	348	0**	151	130	68*	63*	75*	109*	47*	17*	32*	5*	0*	222	126*
preferred source of info	5 1.4%	3 1.7%	2 1.1%	5 1.4%	0 0	3 1.9%	2 1.4%	0 0	0 0	1 1.3%	4 3.4%	0 0	0 0	0 0	0 0	0 0	3 1.3%	2 1.5%
Office (NET)	4 1.0%	3 1.6%	1 0.5%	4 1.0%	0 0	1 0.6%	2 1.4%	1 1.3%	2 2.8%	0 0	0 0	0 0	0 0	2 5.9%IJ	0 0	0 0	2 0.8%	2 1.4%
All sources of info	4 1.0%	3 1.6%	1 0.5%	4 1.0%	0 0	1 0.6%	2 1.4%	1 1.3%	2 2.8%	0 0	0 0	0 0	0 0	2 5.9%IJ	0 0	0 0	2 0.8%	2 1.4%
preferred source of info	3 0.8%	2 1.1%	1 0.5%	3 0.8%	0 0	1 0.6%	2 1.4%	0 0	1 1.4%	0 0	0 0	0 0	0 0	2 5.9%IJ	0 0	0 0	2 0.8%	1 0.7%
Purchase from online bookstore (NET)	2 0.7%	1 0.8%	1 0.6%	2 0.7%	0 0	0 0	1 0.8%	1 1.9%	0 0	2 2.7%	0 0	0 0	* 1.7%	0 0	0 0	0 0	2 1.0%	0 0
All sources of info	2 0.7%	1 0.8%	1 0.6%	2 0.7%	0 0	0 0	1 0.8%	1 1.9%	0 0	2 2.7%	0 0	0 0	* 1.7%	0 0	0 0	0 0	2 1.0%	0 0
preferred source of info	2 0.6%	1 0.6%	1 0.6%	2 0.6%	0 0	0 0	1 0.8%	1 1.5%	0 0	2 2.7%	0 0	0 0	0 0	0 0	0 0	0 0	2 0.9%	0 0
Order from on demand document delivery service (NET)	2 0.6%	2 1.0%	* 0.2%	2 0.6%	0 0	0 0	2 1.6%	0 0	2 2.8%	0 0	0 0	0 0	* 1.7%	0 0	0 0	0 0	2 0.9%	0 0
All sources of info	2 0.6%	2 1.0%	* 0.2%	2 0.6%	0 0	0 0	2 1.6%	0 0	2 2.8%	0 0	0 0	0 0	* 1.7%	0 0	0 0	0 0	2 0.9%	0 0

Proportions/Means: Columns Tested (5% risk level) - A/B/D - C/D - E/F/G - H/I/J/K/L/M/N - P/Q
* small base; ** very small base (under 30) ineligible for sig testing

Table 117
Page 359

Outsell/Digital Library Federation Study (2002)
Weighted Tables

TABLE 93, continued

R7D/E_8. Online abstracts and indexes SUMMARY TABLE

		RESPONDENT TYPE				INSTITUTION TYPE			DISCIPLINE									GENDER	
	TOTAL SAMPLE	FACULTY MEMBER	GRAD. STUDENT	FACULTY /GRAD	UNDER GRAD. STUDENT	PUBLIC	PRIVATE	LIBERAL ARTS	BIOLOGIAL SCIENCES	PHYSICAL SCIENCES /MATH	SOCIAL SCIENCES	ARTS AND HUMAN.	ENGI-NEERING	BUSINESS	LAW	UNDEC. MAJOR	MALE	FEMALE
		(A)	(B)	(C)	(D)	(E)	(F)	(G)	(H)	(I)	(J)	(K)	(L)	(M)	(N)		(P)	(Q)
Base - Use Online abstracts and indexes for research	348	171	178	348	0**	151	130	68*	63*	75*	109*	47*	17*	32*	5*	0*	222	126*
preferred source of info	0 0	0 0	0 0	0 0	0 0	0 0	0 0	0 0	0 0	0 0	0 0	0 0	0 0	0 0	0 0	0 0	0 0	0 0
Sources (NET)	2 0.6%	2 1.2%	0 0	2 0.6%	0 0	* 0.2%	2 1.4%	0 0	2 2.8%	0 0	0 0	0 0	* 1.7%	0 0	0 0	0 0	1 0.5%	1 0.7%
All sources of info	2 0.6%	2 1.2%	0 0	2 0.6%	0 0	* 0.2%	2 1.4%	0 0	2 2.8%	0 0	0 0	0 0	* 1.7%	0 0	0 0	0 0	1 0.5%	1 0.7%
preferred source of info	* 0.1%	* 0.2%	0 0	* 0.1%	0 0	* 0.2%	0 0	0 0	0 0	0 0	0 0	0 0	* 1.7%	0 0	0 0	0 0	* 0.1%	0 0
Faculty (NET)	2 0.5%	0 0	2 1.1%	2 0.5%	0 0	2 1.2%	0 0	0 0	0 0	0 0	2 1.7%	0 0	0 0	0 0	0 0	0 0	0 0	2 1.5%
All sources of info	2 0.5%	0 0	2 1.1%	2 0.5%	0 0	2 1.2%	0 0	0 0	0 0	0 0	2 1.7%	0 0	0 0	0 0	0 0	0 0	0 0	2 1.5%
preferred source of info	2 0.5%	0 0	2 1.1%	2 0.5%	0 0	2 1.2%	0 0	0 0	0 0	0 0	2 1.7%	0 0	0 0	0 0	0 0	0 0	0 0	2 1.5%
Purchase from physical book store (NET)	2 0.5%	1 0.3%	1 0.6%	2 0.5%	0 0	* 0.2%	1 0.8%	* 0.4%	0 0	1 1.3%	0 0	0 0	1 3.4%HJ	0 0	0 0	0 0	2 0.7%	0 0
All sources of info	2 0.5%	1 0.3%	1 0.6%	2 0.5%	0 0	* 0.2%	1 0.8%	* 0.4%	0 0	1 1.3%	0 0	0 0	1 3.4%HJ	0 0	0 0	0 0	2 0.7%	0 0

Proportions/Means: Columns Tested (5% risk level) - A/B/D - C/D - E/F/G - H/I/J/K/L/M/N - P/Q
* small base; ** very small base (under 30) ineligible for sig testing

Table 117
Page 360

Outsell/Digital Library Federation Study (2002)
Weighted Tables

TABLE 93, continued

R7D/E_8. Online abstracts and indexes SUMMARY TABLE

	TOTAL SAMPLE	RESPONDENT TYPE: FACULTY MEMBER	GRAD. STUDENT	FACULTY /GRAD	UNDER GRAD. STUDENT	INSTITUTION TYPE: PUBLIC	PRIVATE	LIBERAL ARTS	DISCIPLINE: BIOLOGIAL SCIENCES	PHYSICAL SCIENCES /MATH	SOCIAL SCIENCES	ARTS AND HUMAN.	ENGI-NEERING	BUSINESS	LAW	UNDEC. MAJOR	GENDER: MALE	FEMALE
		(A)	(B)	(C)	(D)	(E)	(F)	(G)	(H)	(I)	(J)	(K)	(L)	(M)	(N)		(P)	(Q)
Base - Use Online abstracts and indexes for research	348	171	178	348	0**	151	130	68*	63*	75*	109*	47*	17*	32*	5*	0*	222	126*
preferred source of info	0 0	0 0	0 0	0 0	0 0	0 0	0 0	0 0	0 0	0 0	0 0	0 0	0 0	0 0	0 0	0 0	0 0	0 0
Ask library to purchase source (NET)	1 0.4%	1 0.7%	0 0	1 0.4%	0 0	1 0.8%	0 0	0 0	0 0	0 0	0 0	0 0	* 1.7%	1 2.9%	0 0	0 0	* 0.1%	1 0.7%
All sources of info	1 0.4%	1 0.7%	0 0	1 0.4%	0 0	1 0.8%	0 0	0 0	0 0	0 0	0 0	0 0	* 1.7%	1 2.9%	0 0	0 0	* 0.1%	1 0.7%
preferred source of info	0 0	0 0	0 0	0 0	0 0	0 0	0 0	0 0	0 0	0 0	0 0	0 0	0 0	0 0	0 0	0 0	0 0	0 0
Colleague (NET)	1 0.3%	0 0	1 0.5%	1 0.3%	0 0	0 0	1 0.7%	0 0	0 0	0 0	0 0	0 0	0 0	1 2.9%	0 0	0 0	1 0.4%	0 0
All sources of info	1 0.3%	0 0	1 0.5%	1 0.3%	0 0	0 0	1 0.7%	0 0	0 0	0 0	0 0	0 0	0 0	1 2.9%	0 0	0 0	1 0.4%	0 0
preferred source of info	0 0	0 0	0 0	0 0	0 0	0 0	0 0	0 0	0 0	0 0	0 0	0 0	0 0	0 0	0 0	0 0	0 0	0 0
E-journals (NET)	0 0	0 0	0 0	0 0	0 0	0 0	0 0	0 0	0 0	0 0	0 0	0 0	0 0	0 0	0 0	0 0	0 0	0 0
All sources of info	0 0	0 0	0 0	0 0	0 .0	0 0	0 0	0 0	0 0	0 0	0 0	0 0	0 0	0 0	0 0	0 0	0 0	0 0

Proportions/Means: Columns Tested (5% risk level) - A/B/D - C/D - E/F/G - H/I/J/K/L/M/N - P/Q
* small base; ** very small base (under 30) ineligible for sig testing

Table 117
Page 361

Outsell/Digital Library Federation Study (2002)
Weighted Tables

TABLE 93, continued

R7D/E_8. Online abstracts and indexes SUMMARY TABLE

		RESPONDENT TYPE				INSTITUTION TYPE			DISCIPLINE								GENDER	
	TOTAL SAMPLE	FACULTY MEMBER	GRAD. STUDENT	FACULTY /GRAD	UNDER GRAD. STUDENT	PUBLIC	PRIVATE	LIBERAL ARTS	BIOLOGIAL SCIENCES	PHYSICAL SCIENCES /MATH	SOCIAL SCIENCES	ARTS AND HUMAN.	ENGI-NEERING	BUSINESS	LAW	UNDEC. MAJOR	MALE	FEMALE
		(A)	(B)	(C)	(D)	(E)	(F)	(G)	(H)	(I)	(J)	(K)	(L)	(M)	(N)		(P)	(Q)
Base - Use Online abstracts and indexes for research	348	171	178	348	0**	151	130	68*	63*	75*	109*	47*	17*	32*	5*	0*	222	126*
preferred source of info	0 0	0 0	0 0	0 0	0 0	0 0	0 0	0 0	0 0	0 0	0 0	0 0	0 0	0 0	0 0	0 0	0 0	0 0
Access book/journal/ journal article elsewhere online (NET)	0 0	0 0	0 0	0 0	0 0	0 0	0 0	0 0	0 0	0 0	0 0	0 0	0 0	0 0	0 0	0 0	0 0	0 0
All sources of info	0 0	0 0	0 0	0 0	0 0	0 0	0 0	0 0	0 0	0 0	0 0	0 0	0 0	0 0	0 0	0 0	0 0	0 0
preferred source of info	0 0	0 0	0 0	0 0	0 0	0 0	0 0	0 0	0 0	0 0	0 0	0 0	0 0	0 0	0 0	0 0	0 0	0 0
Meetings/conferences (NET)	0 0	0 0	0 0	0 0	0 0	0 0	0 0	0 0	0 0	0 0	0 0	0 0	0 0	0 0	0 0	0 0	0 0	0 0
All sources of info	0 0	0 0	0 0	0 0	0 0	0 0	0 0	0 0	0 0	0 0	0 0	0 0	0 0	0 0	0 0	0 0	0 0	0 0
preferred source of info	0 0	0 0	0 0	0 0	0 0	0 0	0 0	0 0	0 0	0 0	0 0	0 0	0 0	0 0	0 0	0 0	0 0	0 0
Access from course website (NET)	0 0	0 0	0 0	0 0	0 0	0 0	0 0	0 0	0 0	0 0	0 0	0 0	0 0	0 0	0 0	0 0	0 0	0 0
All sources of info	0 0	0 0	0 0	0 0	0 0	0 0	0 0	0 0	0 0	0 0	0 0	0 0	0 0	0 0	0 0	0 0	0 0	0 0

Proportions/Means: Columns Tested (5% risk level) - A/B/D - C/D - E/F/G - H/I/J/K/L/M/N - P/Q
* small base; ** very small base (under 30) ineligible for sig testing

Table 117
Page 362

Outsell/Digital Library Federation Study (2002)
Weighted Tables

TABLE 93, continued

R7D/E_8. Online abstracts and indexes SUMMARY TABLE

		RESPONDENT TYPE				INSTITUTION TYPE			DISCIPLINE									GENDER	
	TOTAL SAMPLE	FACULTY MEMBER	GRAD. STUDENT	FACULTY /GRAD	UNDER GRAD. STUDENT	PUBLIC	PRIVATE	LIBERAL ARTS	BIOLOGIAL SCIENCES	PHYSICAL SCIENCES /MATH	SOCIAL SCIENCES	ARTS AND HUMAN.	ENGI-NEERING	BUSINESS	LAW	UNDEC. MAJOR	MALE	FEMALE
		(A)	(B)	(C)	(D)	(E)	(F)	(G)	(H)	(I)	(J)	(K)	(L)	(M)	(N)		(P)	(Q)
Base - Use Online abstracts and indexes for research	348	171	178	348	0**	151	130	68*	63*	75*	109*	47*	17*	32*	5*	0*	222	126*
preferred source of info	0 0	0 0	0 0	0 0	0 0	0 0	0 0	0 0	0 0	0 0	0 0	0 0	0 0	0 0	0 0	0 0	0 0	0 0
Other (NET)	18 5.1%	15 8.8%B	3 1.5%	18 5.1%	0 0	2 1.0%	11 8.6%E	5 7.4%E	2 2.8%	4 5.3%	8 6.9%	3 7.1%	1 5.1%	0 0	* 3.2%	0 0	14 6.3%	4 2.9%
All sources of info	17 4.8%	14 8.3%B	2 1.4%	17 4.8%	0 0	2 1.0%	11 8.4%E	4 6.1%E	1 1.4%	4 5.3%	8 6.9%	3 7.1%	1 5.1%	0 0	0 0	0 0	14 6.2%	3 2.2%
preferred source of info	7 2.0%	4 2.5%	3 1.5%	7 2.0%	0 0	1 0.4%	3 2.7%	3 4.2%	1 1.4%	2 2.7%	2 1.7%	1 2.4%	1 5.1%	0 0	* 3.2%	0 0	4 1.9%	3 2.2%
DK/Refused	3 0.8%	1 0.3%	2 1.2%	3 0.8%	0 0	2 1.0%	1 0.9%	0 0	0 0	1 1.3%	0 0	1 2.4%	1 3.4%HJ	0 0	0 0	0 0	2 0.8%	1 0.8%

Proportions/Means: Columns Tested (5% risk level) - A/B/D - C/D - E/F/G - H/I/J/K/L/M/N - P/Q
* small base; ** very small base (under 30) ineligible for sig testing

Table 117
Page 363

TABLE 94

R7D/E_9. Online databases, data sets or data sources SUMMARY TABLE

	RESPONDENT TYPE				INSTITUTION TYPE			DISCIPLINE									GENDER	
	TOTAL SAMPLE	FACULTY MEMBER	GRAD. STUDENT	FACULTY /GRAD	UNDER GRAD. STUDENT	PUBLIC	PRIVATE	LIBERAL ARTS	BIOLOGIAL SCIENCES	PHYSICAL SCIENCES /MATH	SOCIAL SCIENCES	ARTS AND HUMAN.	ENGI-NEERING	BUSINESS	LAW	UNDEC. MAJOR	MALE	FEMALE
		(A)	(B)	(C)	(D)	(E)	(F)	(G)	(H)	(I)	(J)	(K)	(L)	(M)	(N)		(P)	(Q)
Base - Use Online databases, data sets or data sources for research	324	162	162	324	0**	143	131	50*	49*	63*	98*	62*	15*	33*	5**	0*	200	124*
Access online (NET)	249 76.8%	137 84.8%B	112 68.9%	249 76.8%	0 0	101 70.8%	104 79.6%	43 87.1%E	41 83.9%J	58 92.1%JKL	62 63.5%	43 69.1%	12 80.4%	29 88.6%JK	4 85.7%	0 0	162 81.2%Q	86 69.7%
All sources of info	249 76.8%	137 84.8%B	112 68.9%	249 76.8%	0 0	101 70.8%	104 79.6%	43 87.1%E	41 83.9%J	58 92.1%JKL	62 63.5%	43 69.1%	12 80.4%	29 88.6%JK	4 85.7%	0 0	162 81.2%Q	86 69.7%
preferred source of info	227 70.2%	126 77.7%B	101 62.6%	227 70.2%	0 0	91 63.2%	95 72.9%	41 83.3%E	40 82.1%JK	56 88.9%JKL	55 55.8%	36 58.2%	10 70.6%	26 80.0%JK	4 82.1%	0 0	150 75.1%Q	77 62.2%
Borrow from or use in campus library (NET)	102 31.6%	44 27.4%	58 35.8%	102 31.6%	0 0	56 39.1%F	32 24.2%	15 29.3%	15 30.4%	17 27.0%	32 32.7%	21 34.5%	7 45.1%I	9 28.6%	1 21.4%	0 0	62 30.8%	41 32.8%
All sources of info	102 31.6%	44 27.4%	58 35.8%	102 31.6%	0 0	56 39.1%F	32 24.2%	15 29.3%	15 30.4%	17 27.0%	32 32.7%	21 34.5%	7 45.1%I	9 28.6%	1 21.4%	0 0	62 30.8%	41 32.8%
preferred source of info	59 18.3%	17 10.3%	43 26.4%A	59 18.3%	0 0	35 24.7%G	19 14.4%	5 10.4%	5 10.7%	7 11.1%	26 26.9%HI M	13 21.8%	4 27.5%HIM	3 8.6%	1 10.7%	0 0	28 14.1%	31 25.2%P
Borrow from or use in other libraries (NET)	16 4.9%	7 4.4%	9 5.4%	16 4.9%	0 0	6 4.1%	8 6.3%	2 3.5%	2 3.6%	1 1.6%	8 7.7%	4 7.3%	0 0	1 2.9%	* 3.6%	0 0	7 3.5%	9 7.2%
All sources of info	16 4.9%	7 4.4%	9 5.4%	16 4.9%	0 0	6 4.1%	8 6.3%	2 3.5%	2 3.6%	1 1.6%	8 7.7%	4 7.3%	0 0	1 2.9%	* 3.6%	0 0	7 3.5%	9 7.2%

Proportions/Means: Columns Tested (5% risk level) - A/B/D - C/D - E/F/G - H/I/J/K/L/M/N - P/Q
* small base; ** very small base (under 30) ineligible for sig testing

Table 124
Page 393

Outsell/Digital Library Federation Study (2002)
Weighted Tables

TABLE 94, continued

R7D/E_9. Online databases, data sets or data sources SUMMARY TABLE

		RESPONDENT TYPE				INSTITUTION TYPE			DISCIPLINE									GENDER	
	TOTAL SAMPLE	FACULTY MEMBER	GRAD. STUDENT	FACULTY /GRAD	UNDER GRAD. STUDENT	PUBLIC	PRIVATE	LIBERAL ARTS	BIOLOGIAL SCIENCES	PHYSICAL SCIENCES /MATH	SOCIAL SCIENCES	ARTS AND HUMAN.	ENGI-NEERING	BUSINESS	LAW	UNDEC. MAJOR	MALE	FEMALE
		(A)	(B)	(C)	(D)	(E)	(F)	(G)	(H)	(I)	(J)	(K)	(L)	(M)	(N)		(P)	(Q)
Base - Use Online databases, data sets or data sources for research	324	162	162	324	0**	143	131	50*	49*	63*	98*	62*	15*	33*	5**	0*	200	124*
preferred source of info	7 2.2%	1 0.7%	6 3.7%	7 2.2%	0 0	4 2.6%	3 2.6%	0 0	0 0	0 0	4 3.8%	3 5.5%	0 0	0 0	0 0	0 0	2 1.1%	5 3.9%
Interlibrary loan (NET)	14 4.4%	8 4.7%	7 4.2%	14 4.4%	0 0	8 5.3%	5 3.8%	2 3.5%	4 7.1%	2 3.2%	6 5.8%	2 3.6%	0 0	1 2.9%	0 0	0 0	8 4.2%	6 4.8%
All sources of info	14 4.4%	8 4.7%	7 4.2%	14 4.4%	0 0	8 5.3%	5 3.8%	2 3.5%	4 7.1%	2 3.2%	6 5.8%	2 3.6%	0 0	1 2.9%	0 0	0 0	8 4.2%	6 4.8%
preferred source of info	4 1.2%	0 0	4 2.3%	4 1.2%	0 0	4 2.6%	0 0	0 0	0 0	0 0	4 3.8%	0 0	0 0	0 0	0 0	0 0	2 0.9%	2 1.5%
Office (NET)	10 3.2%	10 6.3%B	0 0	10 3.2%	0 0	0 0	8 6.1%E	2 4.5%E	1 1.8%	0 0	4 3.8%	6 9.1%I	0 0	0 0	0 0	0 0	9 4.6%	1 0.9%
All sources of info	10 3.2%	10 6.3%B	0 0	10 3.2%	0 0	0 0	8 6.1%E	2 4.5%E	1 1.8%	0 0	4 3.8%	6 9.1%I	0 0	0 0	0 0	0 0	9 4.6%	1 0.9%
preferred source of info	10 3.2%	10 6.3%B	0 0	10 3.2%	0 0	0 0	8 6.1%E	2 4.5%E	1 1.8%	0 0	4 3.8%	6 9.1%I	0 0	0 0	0 0	0 0	9 4.6%	1 0.9%
Purchase from online bookstore (NET)	6 1.8%	3 1.7%	3 1.9%	6 1.8%	0 0	3 2.1%	3 2.1%	0 0	1 1.8%	0 0	4 3.8%	1 1.8%	0 0	0 0	0 0	0 0	3 1.5%	3 2.2%
All sources of info	6 1.8%	3 1.7%	3 1.9%	6 1.8%	0 0	3 2.1%	3 2.1%	0 0	1 1.8%	0 0	4 3.8%	1 1.8%	0 0	0 0	0 0	0 0	3 1.5%	3 2.2%

Proportions/Means: Columns Tested (5% risk level) - A/B/D - C/D - E/F/G - H/I/J/K/L/M/N - P/Q
* small base; ** very small base (under 30) ineligible for sig testing

Table 124
Page 394

Outsell/Digital Library Federation Study (2002)
Weighted Tables

TABLE 94, continued

R7D/E_9. Online databases, data sets or data sources SUMMARY TABLE

		RESPONDENT TYPE				INSTITUTION TYPE			DISCIPLINE								GENDER	
	TOTAL SAMPLE	FACULTY MEMBER	GRAD. STUDENT	FACULTY /GRAD	UNDER GRAD. STUDENT	PUBLIC	PRIVATE	LIBERAL ARTS	BIOLOGIAL SCIENCES	PHYSICAL SCIENCES /MATH	SOCIAL SCIENCES	ARTS AND HUMAN.	ENGI- NEERING	BUSINESS	LAW	UNDEC. MAJOR	MALE	FEMALE
		(A)	(B)	(C)	(D)	(E)	(F)	(G)	(H)	(I)	(J)	(K)	(L)	(M)	(N)		(P)	(Q)
Base - Use Online databases, data sets or data sources for research	324	162	162	324	0**	143	131	50*	49*	63*	98*	62*	15*	33*	5**	0*	200	124*
preferred source of info	2 0.6%	0 0	2 1.2%	2 0.6%	0 0	2 1.3%	0 0	0 0	0 0	0 0	2 1.9%	0 0	0 0	0 0	0 0	0 0	0 0	2 1.5%
Personal holdings (NET)	5 1.5%	3 1.7%	2 1.3%	5 1.5%	0 0	2 1.4%	2 1.3%	1 1.9%	2 3.6%	0 0	2 1.9%	0 0	0 0	1 2.9%	* 3.6%	0 0	3 1.4%	2 1.5%
All sources of info	5 1.5%	3 1.7%	2 1.3%	5 1.5%	0 0	2 1.4%	2 1.3%	1 1.9%	2 3.6%	0 0	2 1.9%	0 0	0 0	1 2.9%	* 3.6%	0 0	3 1.4%	2 1.5%
preferred source of info	1 0.3%	1 0.6%	0 0	1 0.3%	0 0	0 0	0 0	1 1.9%	0 0	0 0	0 0	0 0	0 0	1 2.9%	0 0	0 0	1 0.5%	0 0
Purchase from physical book store (NET)	5 1.4%	1 0.5%	4 2.2%	5 1.4%	0 0	4 2.5%	1 0.7%	0 0	3 5.4%	0 0	2 1.9%	0 0	0 0	0 0	0 0	0 0	2 0.9%	3 2.2%
All sources of info	5 1.4%	1 0.5%	4 2.2%	5 1.4%	0 0	4 2.5%	1 0.7%	0 0	3 5.4%	0 0	2 1.9%	0 0	0 0	0 0	0 0	0 0	2 0.9%	3 2.2%
preferred source of info	1 0.3%	0 0	1 0.5%	1 0.3%	0 0	1 0.6%	0 0	0 0	1 1.8%	0 0	0 0	0 0	0 0	0 0	0 0	0 0	1 0.4%	0 0
Faculty (NET)	2 0.6%	0 0	2 1.2%	2 0.6%	0 0	2 1.3%	0 0	0 0	0 0	0 0	2 1.9%	0 0	0 0	0 0	0 0	0 0	0 0	2 1.5%
All sources of info	2 0.6%	0 0	2 1.2%	2 0.6%	0 0	2 1.3%	0 0	0 0	0 0	0 0	2 1.9%	0 0	0 0	0 0	0 0	0 0	0 0	2 1.5%

Proportions/Means: Columns Tested (5% risk level) - A/B/D - C/D - E/F/G - H/I/J/K/L/M/N - P/Q
* small base; ** very small base (under 30) ineligible for sig testing

Table 124
Page 395

Outsell/Digital Library Federation Study (2002)
Weighted Tables

TABLE 94, continued

R7D/E_9. Online databases, data sets or data sources SUMMARY TABLE

		RESPONDENT TYPE				INSTITUTION TYPE			DISCIPLINE									GENDER	
	TOTAL SAMPLE	FACULTY MEMBER	GRAD. STUDENT	FACULTY /GRAD	UNDER GRAD. STUDENT	PUBLIC	PRIVATE	LIBERAL ARTS	BIOLOGIAL SCIENCES	PHYSICAL SCIENCES /MATH	SOCIAL SCIENCES	ARTS AND HUMAN.	ENGI-NEERING	BUSINESS	LAW	UNDEC. MAJOR	MALE	FEMALE
		(A)	(B)	(C)	(D)	(E)	(F)	(G)	(H)	(I)	(J)	(K)	(L)	(M)	(N)		(P)	(Q)
Base - Use Online databases, data sets or data sources for research	324	162	162	324	0**	143	131	50*	49*	63*	98*	62*	15*	33*	5**	0*	200	124*
preferred source of info	2 0.6%	0 0	2 1.2%	2 0.6%	0 0	2 1.3%	0 0	0 0	0 0	0 0	2 1.9%	0 0	0 0	0 0	0 0	0 0	0 0	2 1.5%
Colleague (NET)	1 0.3%	1 0.6%	0 0	1 0.3%	0 0	1 0.6%	0 0	0 0	0 0	0 0	0 0	0 0	0 0	1 2.9%	0 0	0 0	1 0.5%	0 0
All sources of info	1 0.3%	1 0.6%	0 0	1 0.3%	0 0	1 0.6%	0 0	0 0	0 0	0 0	0 0	0 0	0 0	1 2.9%	0 0	0 0	1 0.5%	0 0
preferred source of info	1 0.3%	1 0.6%	0 0	1 0.3%	0 0	1 0.6%	0 0	0 0	0 0	0 0	0 0	0 0	0 0	1 2.9%	0 0	0 0	1 0.5%	0 0
Order from on demand document delivery service (NET)	1 0.3%	1 0.6%	0 0	1 0.3%	0 0	1 0.6%	0 0	0 0	0 0	0 0	0 0	0 0	0 0	1 2.9%	0 0	0 0	0 0	1 0.8%
All sources of info	1 0.3%	1 0.6%	0 0	1 0.3%	0 0	1 0.6%	0 0	0 0	0 0	0 0	0 0	0 0	0 0	1 2.9%	0 0	0 0	0 0	1 0.8%
preferred source of info	0 0	0 0	0 0	0 0	0 0	0 0	0 0	0 0	0 0	0 0	0 0	0 0	0 0	0 0	0 0	0 0	0 0	0 0
Ask library to purchase source (NET)	1 0.3%	0 0	1 0.5%	1 0.3%	0 0	1 0.6%	0 0	0 0	1 1.8%	0 0	0 0	0 0	0 0	0 0	0 0	0 0	1 0.4%	0 0

Proportions/Means: Columns Tested (5% risk level) - A/B/D - C/D - E/F/G - H/I/J/K/L/M/N - P/Q
* small base; ** very small base (under 30) ineligible for sig testing

Table 124
Page 396

Outsell/Digital Library Federation Study (2002)
Weighted Tables

TABLE 94, continued

R7D/E_9. Online databases, data sets or data sources SUMMARY TABLE

		RESPONDENT TYPE				INSTITUTION TYPE			DISCIPLINE								GENDER	
	TOTAL SAMPLE	FACULTY MEMBER	GRAD. STUDENT	FACULTY /GRAD	UNDER GRAD. STUDENT	PUBLIC	PRIVATE	LIBERAL ARTS	BIOLOGIAL SCIENCES	PHYSICAL SCIENCES /MATH	SOCIAL SCIENCES	ARTS AND HUMAN.	ENGI-NEERING	BUSINESS	LAW	UNDEC. MAJOR	MALE	FEMALE
		(A)	(B)	(C)	(D)	(E)	(F)	(G)	(H)	(I)	(J)	(K)	(L)	(M)	(N)		(P)	(Q)
Base - Use Online databases, data sets or data sources for research	324	162	162	324	0**	143	131	50*	49*	63*	98*	62*	15*	33*	5**	0*	200	124*
All sources of info	1 0.3%	0 0	1 0.5%	1 0.3%	0 0	1 0.6%	0 0	0 0	1 1.8%	0 0	0 0	0 0	0 0	0 0	0 0	0 0	1 0.4%	0 0
preferred source of info	0 0	0 0	0 0	0 0	0 0	0 0	0 0	0 0	0 0	0 0	0 0	0 0	0 0	0 0	0 0	0 0	0 0	0 0
E-journals (NET)	1 0.3%	1 0.5%	0 0	1 0.3%	0 0	0 0	0 0	1 1.8%	1 1.8%	0 0	0 0	0 0	0 0	0 0	0 0	0 0	1 0.4%	0 0
All sources of info	1 0.3%	1 0.5%	0 0	1 0.3%	0 0	0 0	0 0	1 1.8%	1 1.8%	0 0	0 0	0 0	0 0	0 0	0 0	0 0	1 0.4%	0 0
preferred source of info	0 0	0 0	0 0	0 0	0 0	0 0	0 0	0 0	0 0	0 0	0 0	0 0	0 0	0 0	0 0	0 0	0 0	0 0
Printed material (NET)	1 0.3%	0 0	1 0.5%	1 0.3%	0 0	1 0.6%	0 0	0 0	1 1.8%	0 0	0 0	0 0	0 0	0 0	0 0	0 0	0 0	1 0.7%
All sources of info	1 0.3%	0 0	1 0.5%	1 0.3%	0 0	1 0.6%	0 0	0 0	1 1.8%	0 0	0 0	0 0	0 0	0 0	0 0	0 0	0 0	1 0.7%
preferred source of info	1 0.3%	0 0	1 0.5%	1 0.3%	0 0	1 0.6%	0 0	0 0	1 1.8%	0 0	0 0	0 0	0 0	0 0	0 0	0 0	0 0	1 0.7%
Access from course website (NET)	0 0	0 0	0 0	0 0	0 0	0 0	0 0	0 0	0 0	0 0	0 0	0 0	0 0	0 0	0 0	0 0	0 0	0 0

Proportions/Means: Columns Tested (5% risk level) - A/B/D - C/D - E/F/G - H/I/J/K/L/M/N - P/Q
* small base; ** very small base (under 30) ineligible for sig testing

Table 124
Page 397

Outsell/Digital Library Federation Study (2002)
Weighted Tables

TABLE 94, continued

R7D/E_9. Online databases, data sets or data sources SUMMARY TABLE

		RESPONDENT TYPE				INSTITUTION TYPE			DISCIPLINE								GENDER	
	TOTAL SAMPLE	FACULTY MEMBER	GRAD. STUDENT	FACULTY /GRAD	UNDER GRAD. STUDENT	PUBLIC	PRIVATE	LIBERAL ARTS	BIOLOGIAL SCIENCES	PHYSICAL SCIENCES /MATH	SOCIAL SCIENCES	ARTS AND HUMAN.	ENGI-NEERING	BUSINESS	LAW	UNDEC. MAJOR	MALE	FEMALE
		(A)	(B)	(C)	(D)	(E)	(F)	(G)	(H)	(I)	(J)	(K)	(L)	(M)	(N)		(P)	(Q)
Base - Use Online databases, data sets or data sources for research	324	162	162	324	0**	143	131	50*	49*	63*	98*	62*	15*	33*	5**	0*	200	124*
All sources of info	0 0	0 0	0 0	0 0	0 0	0 0	0 0	0 0	0 0	0 0	0 0	0 0	0 0	0 0	0 0	0 0	0 0	0 0
preferred source of info	0 0	0 0	0 0	0 0	0 0	0 0	0 0	0 0	0 0	0 0	0 0	0 0	0 0	0 0	0 0	0 0	0 0	0 0
Access book/journal/ journal article elsewhere online (NET)	0 0	0 0	0 0	0 0	0 0	0 0	0 0	0 0	0 0	0 0	0 0	0 0	0 0	0 0	0 0	0 0	0 0	0 0
All sources of info	0 0	0 0	0 0	0 0	0 0	0 0	0 0	0 0	0 0	0 0	0 0	0 0	0 0	0 0	0 0	0 0	0 0	0 0
preferred source of info	0 0	0 0	0 0	0 0	0 0	0 0	0 0	0 0	0 0	0 0	0 0	0 0	0 0	0 0	0 0	0 0	0 0	0 0
Meetings/conferences (NET)	0 0	0 0	0 0	0 0	0 0	0 0	0 0	0 0	0 0	0 0	0 0	0 0	0 0	0 0	0 0	0 0	0 0	0 0
All sources of info	0 0	0 0	0 0	0 0	0 0	0 0	0 0	0 0	0 0	0 0	0 0	0 0	0 0	0 0	0 0	0 0	0 0	0 0
preferred source of info	0 0	0 0	0 0	0 0	0 0	0 0	0 0	0 0	0 0	0 0	0 0	0 0	0 0	0 0	0 0	0 0	0 0	0 0

Proportions/Means: Columns Tested (5% risk level) - A/B/D - C/D - E/F/G - H/I/J/K/L/M/N - P/Q
* small base; ** very small base (under 30) ineligible for sig testing

Table 124
Page 398

TABLE 94, continued

R7D/E_9. Online databases, data sets or data sources SUMMARY TABLE

		RESPONDENT TYPE				INSTITUTION TYPE			DISCIPLINE								GENDER	
	TOTAL SAMPLE	FACULTY MEMBER	GRAD. STUDENT	FACULTY /GRAD	UNDER GRAD. STUDENT	PUBLIC	PRIVATE	LIBERAL ARTS	BIOLOGIAL SCIENCES	PHYSICAL SCIENCES /MATH	SOCIAL SCIENCES	ARTS AND HUMAN.	ENGI- NEERING	BUSINESS	LAW	UNDEC. MAJOR	MALE	FEMALE
		(A)	(B)	(C)	(D)	(E)	(F)	(G)	(H)	(I)	(J)	(K)	(L)	(M)	(N)		(P)	(Q)
Base - Use Online databases, data sets or data sources for research	324	162	162	324	0**	143	131	50*	49*	63*	98*	62*	15*	33*	5**	0*	200	124*
Sources (NET)	0 0	0 0	0 0	0 0	0 0	0 0	0 0	0 0	0 0	0 0	0 0	0 0	0 0	0 0	0 0	0 0	0 0	0 0
All sources of info	0 0	0 0	0 0	0 0	0 0	0 0	0 0	0 0	0 0	0 0	0 0	0 0	0 0	0 0	0 0	0 0	0 0	0 0
preferred source of info	0 0	0 0	0 0	0 0	0 0	0 0	0 0	0 0	0 0	0 0	0 0	0 0	0 0	0 0	0 0	0 0	0 0	0 0
Other (NET)	11 3.4%	5 3.3%	6 3.5%	11 3.4%	0 0	6 4.1%	4 3.1%	1 2.2%	0 0	0 0	6 5.8%	3 5.5%	1 3.9%HI	1 2.9%	1 10.7%	0 0	6 3.1%	5 4.0%
All sources of info	10 3.1%	4 2.6%	6 3.5%	10 3.1%	0 0	5 3.3%	4 3.1%	1 2.2%	0 0	0 0	6 5.8%	2 3.6%	1 3.9%HI	1 2.9%	1 10.7%	0 0	6 3.1%	4 3.1%
preferred source of info	3 0.8%	2 1.3%	* 0.3%	3 0.8%	0 0	2 1.4%	* 0.4%	0 0	0 0	0 0	0 0	1 1.8%	* 2.0%	1 2.9%	* 3.6%	0 0	1 0.6%	1 1.0%
DK/Refused	6 1.9%	4 2.5%	2 1.2%	6 1.9%	0 0	1 0.9%	5 3.7%	0 0	1 1.8%	0 0	2 1.9%	2 3.6%	0 0	1 2.9%	* 3.6%	0 0	4 2.1%	2 1.5%

Proportions/Means: Columns Tested (5% risk level) - A/B/D - C/D - E/F/G - H/I/J/K/L/M/N - P/Q
* small base; ** very small base (under 30) ineligible for sig testing

Table 124
Page 399

Outsell/Digital Library Federation Study (2002)
Weighted Tables

TABLE 95

R7D/E_10. Manuscripts and other primary source documents SUMMARY TABLE

		RESPONDENT TYPE				INSTITUTION TYPE			DISCIPLINE								GENDER	
	TOTAL SAMPLE	FACULTY MEMBER	GRAD. STUDENT	FACULTY /GRAD	UNDER GRAD. STUDENT	PUBLIC	PRIVATE	LIBERAL ARTS	BIOLOGIAL SCIENCES	PHYSICAL SCIENCES /MATH	SOCIAL SCIENCES	ARTS AND HUMAN.	ENGI- NEERING	BUSINESS	LAW	UNDEC. MAJOR	MALE	FEMALE
		(A)	(B)	(C)	(D)	(E)	(F)	(G)	(H)	(I)	(J)	(K)	(L)	(M)	(N)		(P)	(Q)
Base - Use Manuscripts and other primary source documents for research	343	224	119*	343	0**	135	147	61*	73*	63*	117*	47*	14*	25**	5**	0*	233	110*
Borrow from or use in campus library (NET)	258 75.2%	167 74.4%	91 76.6%	258 75.2%	0 0	101 75.1%	111 75.8%	45 74.1%	51 69.9%	50 79.4%	90 77.4%	32 69.0%	10 74.5%	20 81.5%	4 77.8%	0 0	179 76.6%	79 72.2%
All sources of info	258 75.2%	167 74.4%	91 76.6%	258 75.2%	0 0	101 75.1%	111 75.8%	45 74.1%	51 69.9%	50 79.4%	90 77.4%	32 69.0%	10 74.5%	20 81.5%	4 77.8%	0 0	179 76.6%	79 72.2%
preferred source of info	155 45.1%	97 43.1%	58 48.8%	155 45.1%	0 0	60 44.7%	68 46.2%	27 43.4%	22 30.1%	31 49.2%HL	60 51.6%HL	26 54.8%HL	4 29.8%	9 37.0%	2 51.9%	0 0	107 45.9%	48 43.4%
Access online (NET)	169 49.2%	118 52.7%	51 42.5%	169 49.2%	0 0	67 49.8%	68 46.2%	34 54.9%	48 66.3%JK	34 54.0%K	43 37.1%	15 31.0%	9 68.1%JK	17 66.7%	2 51.9%	0 0	122 52.5%	46 42.0%
All sources of info	169 49.2%	118 52.7%	51 42.5%	169 49.2%	0 0	67 49.8%	68 46.2%	34 54.9%	48 66.3%JK	34 54.0%K	43 37.1%	15 31.0%	9 68.1%JK	17 66.7%	2 51.9%	0 0	122 52.5%	46 42.0%
preferred source of info	128 37.4%	81 36.3%	47 39.6%	128 37.4%	0 0	52 38.2%	52 35.5%	25 40.3%	42 57.8%JK	26 41.3%K	32 27.4%	9 19.0%	7 53.2%JK	10 40.7%	2 37.0%	0 0	89 38.1%	39 35.9%
Interlibrary loan (NET)	50 14.6%	45 20.3%B	5 4.0%	50 14.6%	0 0	7 5.2%	20 13.8%E	23 37.4%EF	12 16.9%	10 15.9%	15 12.9%	7 14.3%	2 12.8%	4 14.8%	1 14.8%	0 0	40 17.1%	10 9.5%
All sources of info	50 14.6%	45 20.3%B	5 4.0%	50 14.6%	0 0	7 5.2%	20 13.8%E	23 37.4%EF	12 16.9%	10 15.9%	15 12.9%	7 14.3%	2 12.8%	4 14.8%	1 14.8%	0 0	40 17.1%	10 9.5%

Proportions/Means: Columns Tested (5% risk level) - A/B/D - C/D - E/F/G - H/I/J/K/L/M/N - P/Q
* small base; ** very small base (under 30) ineligible for sig testing

Table 131
Page 429

Outsell/Digital Library Federation Study (2002)
Weighted Tables

TABLE 95, continued

R7D/E_10. Manuscripts and other primary source documents SUMMARY TABLE

		RESPONDENT TYPE				INSTITUTION TYPE			DISCIPLINE								GENDER	
	TOTAL SAMPLE	FACULTY MEMBER (A)	GRAD. STUDENT (B)	FACULTY /GRAD (C)	UNDER GRAD. STUDENT (D)	PUBLIC (E)	PRIVATE (F)	LIBERAL ARTS (G)	BIOLOGIAL SCIENCES (H)	PHYSICAL SCIENCES /MATH (I)	SOCIAL SCIENCES (J)	ARTS AND HUMAN. (K)	ENGI-NEERING (L)	BUSINESS (M)	LAW (N)	UNDEC. MAJOR	MALE (P)	FEMALE (Q)
Base - Use Manuscripts and other primary source documents for research	343	224	119*	343	0**	135	147	61*	73*	63*	117*	47*	14*	25**	5**	0*	233	110*
preferred source of info	10 2.8%	9 3.9%	1 0.8%	10 2.8%	0 0	1 0.7%	4 2.8%	5 7.6%E	1 1.2%	1 1.6%	6 4.8%	2 4.8%	0 0	0 0	0 0	0 0	5 2.1%	5 4.4%
Borrow from or use in other libraries (NET)	42 12.2%	33 14.6%	9 7.7%	42 12.2%	0 0	11 8.1%	18 12.5%	13 20.6%E	4 4.8%	7 11.1%	19 16.1%HL	9 19.0%HL	* 2.1%	3 11.1%	1 11.1%	0 0	25 10.9%	17 15.1%
All sources of info	42 12.2%	33 14.6%	9 7.7%	42 12.2%	0 0	11 8.1%	18 12.5%	13 20.6%E	4 4.8%	7 11.1%	19 16.1%HL	9 19.0%HL	* 2.1%	3 11.1%	1 11.1%	0 0	25 10.9%	17 15.1%
preferred source of info	12 3.4%	8 3.4%	4 3.4%	12 3.4%	0 0	3 2.5%	7 4.8%	1 1.8%	1 1.2%	1 1.6%	6 4.8%	3 7.1%	* 2.1%	0 0	* 7.4%	0 0	8 3.2%	4 3.6%
Sources (NET)	13 3.7%	11 4.9%	2 1.3%	13 3.7%	0 0	8 5.6%	4 2.7%	1 1.6%	3 3.6%	3 4.8%J	0 0	2 4.8%J	2 12.8%HJ	3 11.1%	* 3.7%	0 0	9 3.9%	4 3.3%
All sources of info	13 3.7%	11 4.9%	2 1.3%	13 3.7%	0 0	8 5.6%	4 2.7%	1 1.6%	3 3.6%	3 4.8%J	0 0	2 4.8%J	2 12.8%HJ	3 11.1%	* 3.7%	0 0	9 3.9%	4 3.3%
preferred source of info	4 1.3%	4 1.9%	* 0.2%	4 1.3%	0 0	2 1.5%	1 1.0%	1 1.6%	2 2.4%	1 1.6%	0 0	0 0	1 4.3%JK	1 3.7%	* 3.7%	0 0	3 1.1%	2 1.7%
Order from on demand document delivery service (NET)	11 3.2%	7 3.0%	4 3.5%	11 3.2%	0 0	4 2.9%	7 4.7%	0 0	2 2.4%	0 0	6 4.8%	2 4.8%	* 2.1%	1 3.7%	0 0	0 0	8 3.4%	3 2.6%

Proportions/Means: Columns Tested (5% risk level) - A/B/D - C/D - E/F/G - H/I/J/K/L/M/N - P/Q
* small base; ** very small base (under 30) ineligible for sig testing

Table 131
Page 430

Outsell/Digital Library Federation Study (2002)
Weighted Tables

TABLE 95, continued

R7D/E_10. Manuscripts and other primary source documents SUMMARY TABLE

		RESPONDENT TYPE				INSTITUTION TYPE			DISCIPLINE									GENDER	
	TOTAL SAMPLE	FACULTY MEMBER	GRAD. STUDENT	FACULTY /GRAD	UNDER GRAD. STUDENT	PUBLIC	PRIVATE	LIBERAL ARTS	BIOLOGIAL SCIENCES	PHYSICAL SCIENCES /MATH	SOCIAL SCIENCES	ARTS AND HUMAN.	ENGI-NEERING	BUSINESS	LAW	UNDEC. MAJOR	MALE	FEMALE
		(A)	(B)	(C)	(D)	(E)	(F)	(G)	(H)	(I)	(J)	(K)	(L)	(M)	(N)		(P)	(Q)
Base - Use Manuscripts and other primary source documents for research	343	224	119*	343	0**	135	147	61*	73*	63*	117*	47*	14*	25**	5**	0*	233	110*
All sources of info	11 3.2%	7 3.0%	4 3.5%	11 3.2%	0 0	4 2.9%	7 4.7%	0 0	2 2.4%	0 0	6 4.8%	2 4.8%	* 2.1%	1 3.7%	0 0	0 0	8 3.4%	3 2.6%
preferred source of info	3 0.9%	0 0	3 2.5%A	3 0.9%	0 0	3 2.2%	0 0	0 0	0 0	0 0	2 1.6%	1 2.4%	0 0	0 0	0 0	0 0	2 0.8%	1 1.0%
Colleague (NET)	7 2.1%	5 2.3%	2 1.8%	7 2.1%	0 0	2 1.4%	4 3.0%	1 1.6%	0 0	1 1.6%	6 4.8%	0 0	1 4.3%HK	0 0	0 0	0 0	5 2.2%	2 2.0%
All sources of info	7 2.1%	5 2.3%	2 1.8%	7 2.1%	0 0	2 1.4%	4 3.0%	1 1.6%	0 0	1 1.6%	6 4.8%	0 0	1 4.3%HK	0 0	0 0	0 0	5 2.2%	2 2.0%
preferred source of info	4 1.2%	2 0.8%	2 1.8%	4 1.2%	0 0	2 1.4%	2 1.5%	0 0	0 0	0 0	4 3.2%	0 0	* 2.1%H	0 0	0 0	0 0	2 0.8%	2 2.0%
Personal holdings (NET)	7 2.0%	6 2.6%	1 0.8%	7 2.0%	0 0	3 2.3%	2 1.3%	2 3.1%	0 0	1 1.6%	4 3.2%	0 0	* 2.1%H	2 7.4%	0 0	0 0	6 2.6%	1 0.8%
All sources of info	7 2.0%	6 2.6%	1 0.8%	7 2.0%	0 0	3 2.3%	2 1.3%	2 3.1%	0 0	1 1.6%	4 3.2%	0 0	* 2.1%H	2 7.4%	0 0	0 0	6 2.6%	1 0.8%
preferred source of info	4 1.1%	4 1.7%	0 0	4 1.1%	0 0	3 2.1%	1 0.6%	0 0	0 0	0 0	2 1.6%	0 0	0 0	2 7.4%	0 0	0 0	3 1.2%	1 0.8%

Proportions/Means: Columns Tested (5% risk level) - A/B/D - C/D - E/F/G - H/I/J/K/L/M/N - P/Q
* small base; ** very small base (under 30) ineligible for sig testing

Table 131
Page 431

Outsell/Digital Library Federation Study (2002)
Weighted Tables

TABLE 95, continued

R7D/E_10. Manuscripts and other primary source documents SUMMARY TABLE

		RESPONDENT TYPE				INSTITUTION TYPE			DISCIPLINE								GENDER	
	TOTAL SAMPLE	FACULTY MEMBER	GRAD. STUDENT	FACULTY /GRAD	UNDER GRAD. STUDENT	PUBLIC	PRIVATE	LIBERAL ARTS	BIOLOGIAL SCIENCES	PHYSICAL SCIENCES /MATH	SOCIAL SCIENCES	ARTS AND HUMAN.	ENGI-NEERING	BUSINESS	LAW	UNDEC. MAJOR	MALE	FEMALE
		(A)	(B)	(C)	(D)	(E)	(F)	(G)	(H)	(I)	(J)	(K)	(L)	(M)	(N)		(P)	(Q)
Base - Use Manuscripts and other primary source documents for research	343	224	119*	343	0**	135	147	61*	73*	63*	117*	47*	14*	25**	5**	0*	233	110*
Printed material (NET)	5 1.4%	3 1.3%	2 1.6%	5 1.4%	0 0	3 2.1%	1 0.6%	1 1.6%	2 2.4%	3 4.8%J	0 0	0 0	0 0	0 0	0 0	0 0	5 2.0%	0 0
All sources of info	5 1.4%	3 1.3%	2 1.6%	5 1.4%	0 0	3 2.1%	1 0.6%	1 1.6%	2 2.4%	3 4.8%J	0 0	0 0	0 0	0 0	0 0	0 0	5 2.0%	0 0
preferred source of info	0 0	0 0	0 0	0 0	0 0	0 0	0 0	0 0	0 0	0 0	0 0	0 0	0 0	0 0	0 0	0 0	0 0	0 0
Purchase from physical book store (NET)	3 0.9%	1 0.5%	2 1.7%	3 0.9%	0 0	2 1.7%	1 0.6%	0 0	1 1.2%	0 0	0 0	2 4.8%J	0 0	0 0	0 0	0 0	2 1.0%	1 0.8%
All sources of info	3 0.9%	1 0.5%	2 1.7%	3 0.9%	0 0	2 1.7%	1 0.6%	0 0	1 1.2%	0 0	0 0	2 4.8%J	0 0	0 0	0 0	0 0	2 1.0%	1 0.8%
preferred source of info	0 0	0 0	0 0	0 0	0 0	0 0	0 0	0 0	0 0	0 0	0 0	0 0	0 0	0 0	0 0	0 0	0 0	0 0
Ask library to purchase source (NET)	3 0.9%	3 1.4%	0 0	3 0.9%	0 0	0 0	2 1.4%	1 1.6%	0 0	1 1.6%	0 0	1 2.4%	0 0	1 3.7%	0 0	0 0	2 0.8%	1 1.0%
All sources of info	3 0.9%	3 1.4%	0 0	3 0.9%	0 0	0 0	2 1.4%	1 1.6%	0 0	1 1.6%	0 0	1 2.4%	0 0	1 3.7%	0 0	0 0	2 0.8%	1 1.0%

Proportions/Means: Columns Tested (5% risk level) - A/B/D - C/D - E/F/G - H/I/J/K/L/M/N - P/Q
* small base; ** very small base (under 30) ineligible for sig testing

Table 131
Page 432

Outsell/Digital Library Federation Study (2002)
Weighted Tables

TABLE 95, continued

R7D/E_10. Manuscripts and other primary source documents SUMMARY TABLE

	TOTAL SAMPLE	RESPONDENT TYPE FACULTY MEMBER (A)	GRAD. STUDENT (B)	FACULTY /GRAD (C)	UNDER GRAD. STUDENT (D)	INSTITUTION TYPE PUBLIC (E)	PRIVATE (F)	LIBERAL ARTS (G)	DISCIPLINE BIOLOGIAL SCIENCES (H)	PHYSICAL SCIENCES /MATH (I)	SOCIAL SCIENCES (J)	ARTS AND HUMAN. (K)	ENGI- NEERING (L)	BUSINESS (M)	LAW (N)	UNDEC. MAJOR	GENDER MALE (P)	FEMALE (Q)
Base - Use Manuscripts and other primary source documents for research	343	224	119*	343	0**	135	147	61*	73*	63*	117*	47*	14*	25**	5**	0*	233	110*
preferred source of info	0 0	0 0	0 0	0 0	0 0	0 0	0 0	0 0	0 0	0 0	0 0	0 0	0 0	0 0	0 0	0 0	0 0	0 0
Purchase from online bookstore (NET)	3 0.9%	* 0.1%	3 2.3%	3 0.9%	0 0	2 1.4%	1 0.8%	0 0	1 1.2%	0 0	2 1.6%	0 0	* 2.1%	0 0	0 0	0 0	* 0.1%	3 2.5%
All sources of info	3 0.9%	* 0.1%	3 2.3%	3 0.9%	0 0	2 1.4%	1 0.8%	0 0	1 1.2%	0 0	2 1.6%	0 0	* 2.1%	0 0	0 0	0 0	* 0.1%	3 2.5%
preferred source of info	0 0	0 0	0 0	0 0	0 0	0 0	0 0	0 0	0 0	0 0	0 0	0 0	0 0	0 0	0 0	0 0	0 0	0 0
Office (NET)	2 0.5%	2 0.8%	0 0	2 0.5%	0 0	0 0	2 1.2%	0 0	2 2.4%	0 0	0 0	0 0	0 0	0 0	0 0	0 0	2 0.8%	0 0
All sources of info	2 0.5%	2 0.8%	0 0	2 0.5%	0 0	0 0	2 1.2%	0 0	2 2.4%	0 0	0 0	0 0	0 0	0 0	0 0	0 0	2 0.8%	0 0
preferred source of info	2 0.5%	2 0.8%	0 0	2 0.5%	0 0	0 0	2 1.2%	0 0	2 2.4%	0 0	0 0	0 0	0 0	0 0	0 0	0 0	2 0.8%	0 0
E-journals (NET)	1 0.3%	1 0.4%	0 0	1 0.3%	0 0	1 0.7%	0 0	0 0	0 0	1 1.6%	0 0	0 0	0 0	0 0	0 0	0 0	1 0.4%	0 0
All sources of info	1 0.3%	1 0.4%	0 0	1 0.3%	0 0	1 0.7%	0 0	0 0	0 0	1 1.6%	0 0	0 0	0 0	0 0	0 0	0 0	1 0.4%	0 0

Proportions/Means: Columns Tested (5% risk level) - A/B/D - C/D - E/F/G - H/I/J/K/L/M/N - P/Q
* small base; ** very small base (under 30) ineligible for sig testing

Table 131
Page 433

Outsell/Digital Library Federation Study (2002)
Weighted Tables

TABLE 95, continued

R7D/E_10. Manuscripts and other primary source documents SUMMARY TABLE

		RESPONDENT TYPE				INSTITUTION TYPE			DISCIPLINE								GENDER	
	TOTAL SAMPLE	FACULTY MEMBER	GRAD. STUDENT	FACULTY /GRAD	UNDER GRAD. STUDENT	PUBLIC	PRIVATE	LIBERAL ARTS	BIOLOGIAL SCIENCES	PHYSICAL SCIENCES /MATH	SOCIAL SCIENCES	ARTS AND HUMAN.	ENGI-NEERING	BUSINESS	LAW	UNDEC. MAJOR	MALE	FEMALE
		(A)	(B)	(C)	(D)	(E)	(F)	(G)	(H)	(I)	(J)	(K)	(L)	(M)	(N)		(P)	(Q)
Base - Use Manuscripts and other primary source documents for research	343	224	119*	343	0**	135	147	61*	73*	63*	117*	47*	14*	25**	5**	0*	233	110*
preferred source of info	1 0.3%	1 0.4%	0 0	1 0.3%	0 0	1 0.7%	0 0	0 0	0 0	1 1.6%	0 0	0 0	0 0	0 0	0 0	0 0	1 0.4%	0 0
Faculty (NET)	* 0.1%	0 0	* 0.2%	* 0.1%	0 0	0 0	* 0.2%	0 0	0 0	0 0	0 0	0 0	* 2.1%HJ	0 0	0 0	0 0	* 0.1%	0 0
All sources of info	* 0.1%	0 0	* 0.2%	* 0.1%	0 0	0 0	* 0.2%	0 0	0 0	0 0	0 0	0 0	* 2.1%HJ	0 0	0 0	0 0	* 0.1%	0 0
preferred source of info	0 0	0 0	0 0	0 0	0 0	0 0	0 0	0 0	0 0	0 0	0 0	0 0	0 0	0 0	0 0	0 0	0 0	0 0
Meetings/conferences (NET)	0 0	0 0	0 0	0 0	0 0	0 0	0 0	0 0	0 0	0 0	0 0	0 0	0 0	0 0	0 0	0 0	0 0	0 0
All sources of info	0 0	0 0	0 0	0 0	0 0	0 0	0 0	0 0	0 0	0 0	0 0	0 0	0 0	0 0	0 0	0 0	0 0	0 0
preferred source of info	0 0	0 0	0 0	0 0	0 0	0 0	0 0	0 0	0 0	0 0	0 0	0 0	0 0	0 0	0 0	0 0	0 0	0 0
Access from course website (NET)	0 0	0 0	0 0	0 0	0 0	0 0	0 0	0 0	0 0	0 0	0 0	0 0	0 0	0 0	0 0	0 0	0 0	0 0
All sources of info	0 0	0 0	0 0	0 0	0 0	0 0	0 0	0 0	0 0	0 0	0 0	0 0	0 0	0 0	0 0	0 0	0 0	0 0

Proportions/Means: Columns Tested (5% risk level) - A/B/D - C/D - E/F/G - H/I/J/K/L/M/N - P/Q
* small base; ** very small base (under 30) ineligible for sig testing

Table 131
Page 434

Outsell/Digital Library Federation Study (2002)
Weighted Tables

TABLE 95, continued

R7D/E_10. Manuscripts and other primary source documents SUMMARY TABLE

	RESPONDENT TYPE					INSTITUTION TYPE			DISCIPLINE								GENDER	
	TOTAL SAMPLE	FACULTY MEMBER	GRAD. STUDENT	FACULTY /GRAD	UNDER GRAD. STUDENT	PUBLIC	PRIVATE	LIBERAL ARTS	BIOLOGIAL SCIENCES	PHYSICAL SCIENCES /MATH	SOCIAL SCIENCES	ARTS AND HUMAN.	ENGI-NEERING	BUSINESS	LAW	UNDEC. MAJOR	MALE	FEMALE
		(A)	(B)	(C)	(D)	(E)	(F)	(G)	(H)	(I)	(J)	(K)	(L)	(M)	(N)		(P)	(Q)
Base - Use Manuscripts and other primary source documents for research	343	224	119*	343	0**	135	147	61*	73*	63*	117*	47*	14*	25**	5**	0*	233	110*
preferred source of info	0 0	0 0	0 0	0 0	0 0	0 0	0 0	0 0	0 0	0 0	0 0	0 0	0 0	0 0	0 0	0 0	0 0	0 0
Access book/journal/ journal article elsewhere online (NET)	0 0	0 0	0 0	0 0	0 0	0 0	0 0	0 0	0 0	0 0	0 0	0 0	0 0	0 0	0 0	0 0	0 0	0 0
All sources of info	0 0	0 0	0 0	0 0	0 0	0 0	0 0	0 0	0 0	0 0	0 0	0 0	0 0	0 0	0 0	0 0	0 0	0 0
preferred source of info	0 0	0 0	0 0	0 0	0 0	0 0	0 0	0 0	0 0	0 0	0 0	0 0	0 0	0 0	0 0	0 0	0 0	0 0
Other (NET)	31 9.1%	24 10.8%	7 6.1%	31 9.1%	0 0	14 10.1%	13 8.7%	5 8.1%	4 6.0%	1 1.6%	13 11.3%I	10 21.4%HI	1 6.4%	2 7.4%	0 0	0 0	22 9.3%	10 8.8%
All sources of info	29 8.4%	22 9.7%	7 6.1%	29 8.4%	0 0	12 9.2%	13 8.7%	4 6.0%	4 6.0%I	0 0	13 11.3%I	10 21.4%HIL	* 2.1%	1 3.7%	0 0	0 0	20 8.6%	9 8.0%
preferred source of info	14 4.0%	11 5.1%	2 1.9%	14 4.0%	0 0	5 3.6%	7 4.5%	2 3.6%	3 3.6%	1 1.6%	4 3.2%	4 9.5%	1 6.4%	1 3.7%	0 0	0 0	9 3.8%	5 4.4%
DK/Refused	7 2.0%	6 2.6%	1 1.0%	7 2.0%	0 0	3 2.4%	3 1.9%	1 1.6%	1 1.2%	1 1.6%	2 1.6%	1 2.4%	* 2.1%	2 7.4%	0 0	0 0	4 1.8%	3 2.6%

Proportions/Means: Columns Tested (5% risk level) - A/B/D - C/D - E/F/G - H/I/J/K/L/M/N - P/Q
* small base; ** very small base (under 30) ineligible for sig testing

Table 131
Page 435

Outsell/Digital Library Federation Study (2002)
Weighted Tables

TABLE 96

R7D/E_11. Proprietary software or application SUMMARY TABLE

		RESPONDENT TYPE				INSTITUTION TYPE			DISCIPLINE									GENDER	
	TOTAL SAMPLE	FACULTY MEMBER	GRAD. STUDENT	FACULTY /GRAD	UNDER GRAD. STUDENT	PUBLIC	PRIVATE	LIBERAL ARTS	BIOLOGIAL SCIENCES	PHYSICAL SCIENCES /MATH	SOCIAL SCIENCES	ARTS AND HUMAN.	ENGI-NEERING	BUSINESS	LAW	UNDEC. MAJOR	MALE	FEMALE
		(A)	(B)	(C)	(D)	(E)	(F)	(G)	(H)	(I)	(J)	(K)	(L)	(M)	(N)		(P)	(Q)
Base - Use Proprietary software or application for research	253	137	116	253	0**	113*	97*	44*	49*	72*	58*	32**	12*	26**	2**	0*	174	79*
Access online (NET)	142 56.3%	85 62.2%	57 49.4%	142 56.3%	0 0	62 55.3%	48 50.0%	32 73.1%F	29 58.9%	51 70.8%J	24 41.9%	18 55.2%	8 60.5%	11 42.9%	1 57.1%	0 0	99 57.0%	43 54.8%
All sources of info	142 56.3%	85 62.2%	57 49.4%	142 56.3%	0 0	62 55.3%	48 50.0%	32 73.1%F	29 58.9%	51 70.8%J	24 41.9%	18 55.2%	8 60.5%	11 42.9%	1 57.1%	0 0	99 57.0%	43 54.8%
preferred source of info	125 49.4%	70 51.4%	55 47.0%	125 49.4%	0 0	55 48.9%	45 46.5%	25 56.9%	25 50.0%	45 62.5%	24 41.9%	15 44.8%	7 53.5%	8 32.1%	1 50.0%	0 0	86 49.6%	39 48.8%
Borrow from or use in campus library (NET)	70 27.8%	27 20.0%	43 36.9%A	70 27.8%	0 0	33 29.1%G	34 35.6%G	3 7.0%	15 30.4%I	10 13.9%	21 35.5%I	13 41.4%	3 25.6%	7 28.6%	1 21.4%	0 0	44 25.3%	26 33.2%
All sources of info	70 27.8%	27 20.0%	43 36.9%A	70 27.8%	0 0	33 29.1%G	34 35.6%G	3 7.0%	15 30.4%I	10 13.9%	21 35.5%I	13 41.4%	3 25.6%	7 28.6%	1 21.4%	0 0	44 25.3%	26 33.2%
preferred source of info	47 18.4%	18 12.8%	29 25.0%A	47 18.4%	0 0	21 18.6%G	24 24.4%G	2 4.7%	11 21.4%I	3 4.2%	15 25.8%I	10 31.0%	2 14.0%I	6 21.4%	1 21.4%	0 0	30 17.5%	16 20.3%
Purchase from physical book store (NET)	17 6.9%	6 4.5%	11 9.7%	17 6.9%	0 0	9 7.8%	9 8.9%	0 0	4 8.9%	4 5.6%	4 6.5%	2 6.9%	1 9.3%	2 7.1%	0 0	0 0	11 6.1%	7 8.5%
All sources of info	17 6.9%	6 4.5%	11 9.7%	17 6.9%	0 0	9 7.8%	9 8.9%	0 0	4 8.9%	4 5.6%	4 6.5%	2 6.9%	1 9.3%	2 7.1%	0 0	0 0	11 6.1%	7 8.5%

Proportions/Means: Columns Tested (5% risk level) - A/B/D - C/D - E/F/G - H/I/J/K/L/M/N - P/Q
* small base; ** very small base (under 30) ineligible for sig testing

Table 138
Page 465

Outsell/Digital Library Federation Study (2002)
Weighted Tables

TABLE 96, continued

R7D/E_11. Proprietary software or application SUMMARY TABLE

		RESPONDENT TYPE				INSTITUTION TYPE			DISCIPLINE									GENDER	
	TOTAL SAMPLE	FACULTY MEMBER	GRAD. STUDENT	FACULTY /GRAD	UNDER GRAD. STUDENT	PUBLIC	PRIVATE	LIBERAL ARTS	BIOLOGIAL SCIENCES	PHYSICAL SCIENCES /MATH	SOCIAL SCIENCES	ARTS AND HUMAN.	ENGI-NEERING	BUSINESS	LAW	UNDEC. MAJOR	MALE	FEMALE
		(A)	(B)	(C)	(D)	(E)	(F)	(G)	(H)	(I)	(J)	(K)	(L)	(M)	(N)		(P)	(Q)
Base - Use Proprietary software or application for research	253	137	116	253	0**	113*	97*	44*	49*	72*	58*	32**	12*	26**	2**	0*	174	79*
preferred source of info	8 3.3%	3 2.3%	5 4.5%	8 3.3%	0 0	6 5.1%	3 2.7%	0 0	2 3.6%	3 4.2%	2 3.2%	1 3.4%	1 4.7%	0 0	0 0	0 0	6 3.7%	2 2.4%
Purchase from online bookstore (NET)	17 6.6%	10 7.6%	6 5.4%	17 6.6%	0 0	6 5.2%	6 6.3%	5 11.0%	4 8.9%	4 5.6%	2 3.2%	2 6.9%	* 2.3%	4 14.3%	* 7.1%	0 0	12 6.8%	5 6.2%
All sources of info	17 6.6%	10 7.6%	6 5.4%	17 6.6%	0 0	6 5.2%	6 6.3%	5 11.0%	4 8.9%	4 5.6%	2 3.2%	2 6.9%	* 2.3%	4 14.3%	* 7.1%	0 0	12 6.8%	5 6.2%
preferred source of info	4 1.7%	1 0.8%	3 2.8%	4 1.7%	0 0	1 1.1%	3 3.1%	0 0	1 1.8%	1 1.4%	0 0	2 6.9%	0 0	0 0	* 7.1%	0 0	3 1.8%	1 1.4%
Colleague (NET)	10 4.0%	6 4.1%	4 3.8%	10 4.0%	0 0	4 3.7%	4 4.0%	2 4.6%	2 3.6%	5 6.9%	2 3.2%	1 3.4%	* 2.3%	0 0	0 0	0 0	6 3.3%	4 5.4%
All sources of info	10 4.0%	6 4.1%	4 3.8%	10 4.0%	0 0	4 3.7%	4 4.0%	2 4.6%	2 3.6%	5 6.9%	2 3.2%	1 3.4%	* 2.3%	0 0	0 0	0 0	6 3.3%	4 5.4%
preferred source of info	6 2.5%	3 2.1%	3 2.9%	6 2.5%	0 0	3 2.9%	1 1.0%	2 4.6%	1 1.8%	4 5.6%	0 0	1 3.4%	* 2.3%	0 0	0 0	0 0	3 1.7%	3 4.1%
Order from on demand document delivery service (NET)	9 3.6%	5 3.6%	4 3.5%	9 3.6%	0 0	1 1.0%	3 3.0%	5 11.3%E	1 1.8%	5 6.9%	2 3.2%	0 0	* 2.3%	1 3.6%	0 0	0 0	5 3.0%	4 4.7%

Proportions/Means: Columns Tested (5% risk level) - A/B/D - C/D - E/F/G - H/I/J/K/L/M/N - P/Q
* small base; ** very small base (under 30) ineligible for sig testing

Table 138
Page 466

Outsell/Digital Library Federation Study (2002)
Weighted Tables

TABLE 96, continued

R7D/E_11. Proprietary software or application SUMMARY TABLE

		RESPONDENT TYPE				INSTITUTION TYPE			DISCIPLINE									GENDER	
	TOTAL SAMPLE	FACULTY MEMBER	GRAD. STUDENT	FACULTY /GRAD	UNDER GRAD. STUDENT	PUBLIC	PRIVATE	LIBERAL ARTS	BIOLOGIAL SCIENCES	PHYSICAL SCIENCES /MATH	SOCIAL SCIENCES	ARTS AND HUMAN.	ENGI-NEERING	BUSINESS	LAW	UNDEC. MAJOR	MALE	FEMALE
		(A)	(B)	(C)	(D)	(E)	(F)	(G)	(H)	(I)	(J)	(K)	(L)	(M)	(N)		(P)	(Q)
Base - Use Proprietary software or application for research	253	137	116	253	0**	113*	97*	44*	49*	72*	58*	32**	12*	26**	2**	0*	174	79*
All sources of info	9 3.6%	5 3.6%	4 3.5%	9 3.6%	0 0	1 1.0%	3 3.0%	5 11.3%E	1 1.8%	5 6.9%	2 3.2%	0 0	* 2.3%	1 3.6%	0 0	0 0	5 3.0%	4 4.7%
preferred source of info	6 2.4%	3 2.2%	3 2.7%	6 2.4%	0 0	* 0.3%	3 3.0%	3 6.9%E	0 0	4 5.6%	2 3.2%	0 0	* 2.3%	0 0	0 0	0 0	3 1.9%	3 3.6%
Ask library to purchase source (NET)	7 2.8%	5 3.7%	2 1.7%	7 2.8%	0 0	2 2.1%	2 1.9%	3 6.3%	2 3.6%	2 2.8%	2 3.2%	0 0	* 2.3%	1 3.6%	* 7.1%	0 0	6 3.3%	1 1.7%
All sources of info	7 2.8%	5 3.7%	2 1.7%	7 2.8%	0 0	2 2.1%	2 1.9%	3 6.3%	2 3.6%	2 2.8%	2 3.2%	0 0	* 2.3%	1 3.6%	* 7.1%	0 0	6 3.3%	1 1.7%
preferred source of info	2 0.8%	1 0.8%	1 0.9%	2 0.8%	0 0	2 1.9%	0 0	0 0	0 0	1 1.4%	0 0	0 0	0 0	1 3.6%	* 7.1%	0 0	2 1.1%	* 0.2%
Office (NET)	5 2.0%	4 2.8%	1 1.1%	5 2.0%	0 0	* 0.3%	4 3.9%	1 2.6%	1 1.8%	1 1.4%	2 3.2%	1 3.4%	* 2.3%	0 0	0 0	0 0	5 2.8%	* 0.4%
All sources of info	5 2.0%	4 2.8%	1 1.1%	5 2.0%	0 0	* 0.3%	4 3.9%	1 2.6%	1 1.8%	1 1.4%	2 3.2%	1 3.4%	* 2.3%	0 0	0 0	0 0	5 2.8%	* 0.4%
preferred source of info	5 2.0%	4 2.8%	1 1.1%	5 2.0%	0 0	* 0.3%	4 3.9%	1 2.6%	1 1.8%	1 1.4%	2 3.2%	1 3.4%	* 2.3%	0 0	0 0	0 0	5 2.8%	* 0.4%

Proportions/Means: Columns Tested (5% risk level) - A/B/D - C/D - E/F/G - H/I/J/K/L/M/N - P/Q
* small base; ** very small base (under 30) ineligible for sig testing

Table 138
Page 467

Outsell/Digital Library Federation Study (2002)
Weighted Tables

TABLE 96, continued

R7D/E_11. Proprietary software or application SUMMARY TABLE

	RESPONDENT TYPE				INSTITUTION TYPE			DISCIPLINE									GENDER	
	TOTAL SAMPLE	FACULTY MEMBER	GRAD. STUDENT	FACULTY /GRAD	UNDER GRAD. STUDENT	PUBLIC	PRIVATE	LIBERAL ARTS	BIOLOGIAL SCIENCES	PHYSICAL SCIENCES /MATH	SOCIAL SCIENCES	ARTS AND HUMAN.	ENGI-NEERING	BUSINESS	LAW	UNDEC. MAJOR	MALE	FEMALE
		(A)	(B)	(C)	(D)	(E)	(F)	(G)	(H)	(I)	(J)	(K)	(L)	(M)	(N)		(P)	(Q)
Base - Use Proprietary software or application for research	253	137	116	253	0**	113*	97*	44*	49*	72*	58*	32**	12*	26**	2**	0*	174	79*
Faculty (NET)	5	0	5	5	0	4	1	0	0	0	4	0	1	0	0	0	1	4
	1.9%	0	4.2%A	1.9%	0	3.6%	0.9%	0	0	0	6.5%	0	9.3%HI	0	0	0	0.3%	5.5%P
All sources of info	5	0	5	5	0	4	1	0	0	0	4	0	1	0	0	0	1	4
	1.9%	0	4.2%A	1.9%	0	3.6%	0.9%	0	0	0	6.5%	0	9.3%HI	0	0	0	0.3%	5.5%P
preferred source of info	3	0	3	3	0	2	1	0	0	0	2	0	1	0	0	0	*	2
	1.1%	0	2.4%	1.1%	0	1.9%	0.6%	0	0	0	3.2%	0	7.0%HI	0	0	0	0.2%	3.1%
Sources (NET)	4	3	1	4	0	0	1	3	0	3	0	0	*	1	0	0	4	0
	1.7%	2.1%	1.1%	1.7%	0	0	1.3%	6.7%E	0	4.2%	0	0	2.3%	3.6%	0	0	2.4%	0
All sources of info	4	3	1	4	0	0	1	3	0	3	0	0	*	1	0	0	4	0
	1.7%	2.1%	1.1%	1.7%	0	0	1.3%	6.7%E	0	4.2%	0	0	2.3%	3.6%	0	0	2.4%	0
preferred source of info	3	2	1	3	0	0	1	2	0	3	0	0	*	0	0	0	3	0
	1.3%	1.5%	1.1%	1.3%	0	0	1.3%	4.6%E	0	4.2%	0	0	2.3%	0	0	0	1.9%	0
Borrow from or use in other libraries (NET)	1	*	1	1	0	1	*	0	1	0	0	0	0	0	*	0	1	*
	0.5%	0.1%	0.9%	0.5%	0	0.9%	0.2%	0	1.8%	0	0	0	0	0	14.3%	0	0.6%	0.2%
All sources of info	1	*	1	1	0	1	*	0	1	0	0	0	0	0	*	0	1	*
	0.5%	0.1%	0.9%	0.5%	0	0.9%	0.2%	0	1.8%	0	0	0	0	0	14.3%	0	0.6%	0.2%
preferred source of info	0	0	0	0	0	0	0	0	0	0	0	0	0	0	0	0	0	0
	0	0	0	0	0	0	0	0	0	0	0	0	0	0	0	0	0	0

Proportions/Means: Columns Tested (5% risk level) - A/B/D - C/D - E/F/G - H/I/J/K/L/M/N - P/Q
* small base; ** very small base (under 30) ineligible for sig testing

Table 138
Page 468

Outsell/Digital Library Federation Study (2002)
Weighted Tables

TABLE 96, continued

R7D/E_11. Proprietary software or application SUMMARY TABLE

		RESPONDENT TYPE				INSTITUTION TYPE			DISCIPLINE								GENDER	
	TOTAL SAMPLE	FACULTY MEMBER	GRAD. STUDENT	FACULTY /GRAD	UNDER GRAD. STUDENT	PUBLIC	PRIVATE	LIBERAL ARTS	BIOLOGIAL SCIENCES	PHYSICAL SCIENCES /MATH	SOCIAL SCIENCES	ARTS AND HUMAN.	ENGI-NEERING	BUSINESS	LAW	UNDEC. MAJOR	MALE	FEMALE
		(A)	(B)	(C)	(D)	(E)	(F)	(G)	(H)	(I)	(J)	(K)	(L)	(M)	(N)		(P)	(Q)
Base - Use Proprietary software or application for research	253	137	116	253	0**	113*	97*	44*	49*	72*	58*	32**	12*	26**	2**	0*	174	79*
Meetings/conferences (NET)	1 0.4%	1 0.7%	0 0	1 0.4%	0 0	1 0.9%	0 0	0 0	0 0	1 1.4%	0 0	0 0	0 0	0 0	0 0	0 0	1 0.6%	0 0
All sources of info	1 0.4%	1 0.7%	0 0	1 0.4%	0 0	1 0.9%	0 0	0 0	0 0	1 1.4%	0 0	0 0	0 0	0 0	0 0	0 0	1 0.6%	0 0
preferred source of info	1 0.4%	1 0.7%	0 0	1 0.4%	0 0	1 0.9%	0 0	0 0	0 0	1 1.4%	0 0	0 0	0 0	0 0	0 0	0 0	1 0.6%	0 0
Printed material (NET)	1 0.4%	1 0.7%	0 0	1 0.4%	0 0	0 0	0 0	1 2.3%	0 0	1 1.4%	0 0	0 0	0 0	0 0	0 0	0 0	1 0.6%	0 0
All sources of info	1 0.4%	1 0.7%	0 0	1 0.4%	0 0	0 0	0 0	1 2.3%	0 0	1 1.4%	0 0	0 0	0 0	0 0	0 0	0 0	1 0.6%	0 0
preferred source of info	1 0.4%	1 0.7%	0 0	1 0.4%	0 0	0 0	0 0	1 2.3%	0 0	1 1.4%	0 0	0 0	0 0	0 0	0 0	0 0	1 0.6%	0 0
Interlibrary loan (NET)	1 0.3%	0 0	1 0.8%	1 0.3%	0 0	0 0	1 0.9%	0 0	1 1.8%	0 0	0 0	0 0	0 0	0 0	0 0	0 0	0 0	1 1.1%
All sources of info	1 0.3%	0 0	1 0.8%	1 0.3%	0 0	0 0	1 0.9%	0 0	1 1.8%	0 0	0 0	0 0	0 0	0 0	0 0	0 0	0 0	1 1.1%
preferred source of info	1 0.3%	0 0	1 0.8%	1 0.3%	0 0	0 0	1 0.9%	0 0	1 1.8%	0 0	0 0	0 0	0 0	0 0	0 0	0 0	0 0	1 1.1%

Proportions/Means: Columns Tested (5% risk level) - A/B/D - C/D - E/F/G - H/I/J/K/L/M/N - P/Q
* small base; ** very small base (under 30) ineligible for sig testing

Table 138
Page 469

Outsell/Digital Library Federation Study (2002)
Weighted Tables

TABLE 96, continued

R7D/E_11. Proprietary software or application SUMMARY TABLE

		RESPONDENT TYPE				INSTITUTION TYPE			DISCIPLINE								GENDER	
	TOTAL SAMPLE	FACULTY MEMBER	GRAD. STUDENT	FACULTY /GRAD	UNDER GRAD. STUDENT	PUBLIC	PRIVATE	LIBERAL ARTS	BIOLOGIAL SCIENCES	PHYSICAL SCIENCES /MATH	SOCIAL SCIENCES	ARTS AND HUMAN.	ENGI- NEERING	BUSINESS	LAW	UNDEC. MAJOR	MALE	FEMALE
		(A)	(B)	(C)	(D)	(E)	(F)	(G)	(H)	(I)	(J)	(K)	(L)	(M)	(N)		(P)	(Q)
Base - Use Proprietary software or application for research	253	137	116	253	0**	113*	97*	44*	49*	72*	58*	32**	12*	26**	2**	0*	174	79*
E-journals (NET)	0	0	0	0	0	0	0	0	0	0	0	0	0	0	0	0	0	0
	0	0	0	0	0	0	0	0	0	0	0	0	0	0	0	0	0	0
All sources of info	0	0	0	0	0	0	0	0	0	0	0	0	0	0	0	0	0	0
	0	0	0	0	0	0	0	0	0	0	0	0	0	0	0	0	0	0
preferred source of info	0	0	0	0	0	0	0	0	0	0	0	0	0	0	0	0	0	0
	0	0	0	0	0	0	0	0	0	0	0	0	0	0	0	0	0	0
Access from course website (NET)	0	0	0	0	0	0	0	0	0	0	0	0	0	0	0	0	0	0
	0	0	0	0	0	0	0	0	0	0	0	0	0	0	0	0	0	0
All sources of info	0	0	0	0	0	0	0	0	0	0	0	0	0	0	0	0	0	0
	0	0	0	0	0	0	0	0	0	0	0	0	0	0	0	0	0	0
preferred source of info	0	0	0	0	0	0	0	0	0	0	0	0	0	0	0	0	0	0
	0	0	0	0	0	0	0	0	0	0	0	0	0	0	0	0	0	0
Personal holdings (NET)	0	0	0	0	0	0	0	0	0	0	0	0	0	0	0	0	0	0
	0	0	0	0	0	0	0	0	0	0	0	0	0	0	0	0	0	0
All sources of info	0	0	0	0	0	0	0	0	0	0	0	0	0	0	0	0	0	0
	0	0	0	0	0	0	0	0	0	0	0	0	0	0	0	0	0	0
preferred source of info	0	0	0	0	0	0	0	0	0	0	0	0	0	0	0	0	0	0
	0	0	0	0	0	0	0	0	0	0	0	0	0	0	0	0	0	0

Proportions/Means: Columns Tested (5% risk level) - A/B/D - C/D - E/F/G - H/I/J/K/L/M/N - P/Q
* small base; ** very small base (under 30) ineligible for sig testing

Table 138
Page 470

Outsell/Digital Library Federation Study (2002)
Weighted Tables

TABLE 96, continued

R7D/E_11. Proprietary software or application SUMMARY TABLE

		RESPONDENT TYPE				INSTITUTION TYPE			DISCIPLINE									GENDER	
	TOTAL SAMPLE	FACULTY MEMBER	GRAD. STUDENT	FACULTY /GRAD	UNDER GRAD. STUDENT	PUBLIC	PRIVATE	LIBERAL ARTS	BIOLOGIAL SCIENCES	PHYSICAL SCIENCES /MATH	SOCIAL SCIENCES	ARTS AND HUMAN.	ENGI-NEERING	BUSINESS	LAW	UNDEC. MAJOR	MALE	FEMALE
		(A)	(B)	(C)	(D)	(E)	(F)	(G)	(H)	(I)	(J)	(K)	(L)	(M)	(N)		(P)	(Q)
Base - Use Proprietary software or application for research	253	137	116	253	0**	113*	97*	44*	49*	72*	58*	32**	12*	26**	2**	0*	174	79*
Access book/journal/ journal article elsewhere online (NET)	0 0	0 0	0 0	0 0	0 0	0 0	0 0	0 0	0 0	0 0	0 0	0 0	0 0	0 0	0 0	0 0	0 0	0 0
All sources of info	0 0	0 0	0 0	0 0	0 0	0 0	0 0	0 0	0 0	0 0	0 0	0 0	0 0	0 0	0 0	0 0	0 0	0 0
preferred source of info	0 0	0 0	0 0	0 0	0 0	0 0	0 0	0 0	0 0	0 0	0 0	0 0	0 0	0 0	0 0	0 0	0 0	0 0
Other (NET)	62 24.5%	40 29.0%	22 19.1%	62 24.5%	0 0	24 21.5%	25 26.3%	12 28.2%	11 21.4%	16 22.2%	17 29.0%	3 10.3%	3 20.9%	12 46.4%	* 14.3%	0 0	40 22.9%	22 27.8%
All sources of info	60 23.7%	40 29.0%B	20 17.5%	60 23.7%	0 0	23 20.7%	24 25.2%	12 28.2%	10 19.6%	15 20.8%	17 29.0%	3 10.3%	3 20.9%	12 46.4%	* 14.3%	0 0	40 22.9%	20 25.4%
preferred source of info	30 11.8%	22 16.3%B	8 6.5%	30 11.8%	0 0	13 11.5%	10 10.7%	7 15.2%	6 12.5%	4 5.6%	8 12.9%	1 3.4%	1 11.6%	9 35.7%	* 14.3%	0 0	22 12.6%	8 10.0%
DK/Refused	10 4.1%	8 5.6%	3 2.4%	10 4.1%	0 0	7 6.6%	2 1.9%	1 2.3%	3 5.4%	1 1.4%	4 6.5%	1 3.4%	0 0	2 7.1%	0 0	0 0	7 3.9%	4 4.6%

Proportions/Means: Columns Tested (5% risk level) - A/B/D - C/D - E/F/G - H/I/J/K/L/M/N - P/Q
* small base; ** very small base (under 30) ineligible for sig testing

Table 138
Page 471

Outsell/Digital Library Federation Study (2002)
Weighted Tables

TABLE 97

R7D/E_12. Data SUMMARY TABLE

	TOTAL SAMPLE	RESPONDENT TYPE: FACULTY MEMBER	GRAD. STUDENT	FACULTY /GRAD	UNDER GRAD. STUDENT	INSTITUTION TYPE: PUBLIC	PRIVATE	LIBERAL ARTS	DISCIPLINE: BIOLOGIAL SCIENCES	PHYSICAL SCIENCES /MATH	SOCIAL SCIENCES	ARTS AND HUMAN.	ENGI-NEERING	BUSINESS	LAW	UNDEC. MAJOR	GENDER: MALE	FEMALE
		(A)	(B)	(C)	(D)	(E)	(F)	(G)	(H)	(I)	(J)	(K)	(L)	(M)	(N)		(P)	(Q)
Base - Use Data for research	337	156	181	337	0**	153	135	49*	60*	61*	115*	45*	18*	36*	3**	0*	210	127*
Access online (NET)	224 66.4%	112 71.5%	112 62.1%	224 66.4%	0 0	92 59.9%	94 69.8%	38 77.5%E	42 70.6%K	44 72.1%K	75 65.6%K	17 37.5%	13 72.1%K	31 84.6%JK	2 81.2%	0 0	150 71.5%Q	74 58.1%
All sources of info	224 66.4%	112 71.5%	112 62.1%	224 66.4%	0 0	92 59.9%	94 69.8%	38 77.5%E	42 70.6%K	44 72.1%K	75 65.6%K	17 37.5%	13 72.1%K	31 84.6%JK	2 81.2%	0 0	150 71.5%Q	74 58.1%
preferred source of info	190 56.4%	94 59.8%	96 53.3%	190 56.4%	0 0	73 47.8%	86 64.0%E	30 62.0%	36 60.3%K	42 68.9%K	62 54.1%K	9 20.0%	11 60.7%K	28 76.9%JK	2 81.2%	0 0	125 59.3%	65 51.5%
Borrow from or use in campus library (NET)	166 49.2%	72 45.9%	94 52.1%	166 49.2%	0 0	80 52.0%	62 46.1%	24 49.4%	26 42.6%	36 59.0%M	53 45.9%	30 67.5%HJ LM	8 47.5%	12 33.3%	1 37.5%	0 0	100 47.7%	66 51.8%
All sources of info	166 49.2%	72 45.9%	94 52.1%	166 49.2%	0 0	80 52.0%	62 46.1%	24 49.4%	26 42.6%	36 59.0%M	53 45.9%	30 67.5%HJ LM	8 47.5%	12 33.3%	1 37.5%	0 0	100 47.7%	66 51.8%
preferred source of info	81 23.9%	20 13.1%	60 33.3%A	81 23.9%	0 0	48 31.4%G	27 19.9%	6 12.0%	11 19.1%	13 21.3%	26 23.0%	22 50.0%HI JLM	3 19.7%	4 10.3%	* 12.5%	0 0	42 19.9%	39 30.7%P
Borrow from or use in other libraries (NET)	25 7.5%	15 9.8%	10 5.5%	25 7.5%	0 0	8 5.3%	11 8.4%	6 12.0%	4 5.9%	4 6.6%	9 8.2%	8 17.5%LM	1 3.3%	0 0	0 0	0 0	17 8.3%	8 6.3%
All sources of info	25 7.5%	15 9.8%	10 5.5%	25 7.5%	0 0	8 5.3%	11 8.4%	6 12.0%	4 5.9%	4 6.6%	9 8.2%	8 17.5%LM	1 3.3%	0 0	0 0	0 0	17 8.3%	8 6.3%

Proportions/Means: Columns Tested (5% risk level) - A/B/D - C/D - E/F/G - H/I/J/K/L/M/N - P/Q
* small base; ** very small base (under 30) ineligible for sig testing

Table 145
Page 500

Outsell/Digital Library Federation Study (2002)
Weighted Tables

TABLE 97, continued

R7D/E_12. Data SUMMARY TABLE

		RESPONDENT TYPE				INSTITUTION TYPE			DISCIPLINE								GENDER	
	TOTAL SAMPLE	FACULTY MEMBER	GRAD. STUDENT	FACULTY /GRAD	UNDER GRAD. STUDENT	PUBLIC	PRIVATE	LIBERAL ARTS	BIOLOGIAL SCIENCES	PHYSICAL SCIENCES /MATH	SOCIAL SCIENCES	ARTS AND HUMAN.	ENGI- NEERING	BUSINESS	LAW	UNDEC. MAJOR	MALE	FEMALE
		(A)	(B)	(C)	(D)	(E)	(F)	(G)	(H)	(I)	(J)	(K)	(L)	(M)	(N)		(P)	(Q)
Base - Use Data for research	337	156	181	337	0**	153	135	49*	60*	61*	115*	45*	18*	36*	3**	0*	210	127*
preferred source of info	14 4.0%	8 5.0%	6 3.3%	14 4.0%	0 0	5 3.2%	5 3.6%	4 7.9%	2 2.9%	1 1.6%	8 6.6%	3 7.5%	0 0	0 0	0 0	0 0	11 5.1%	3 2.3%
Interlibrary loan (NET)	20 6.1%	15 9.8%B	5 2.8%	20 6.1%	0 0	6 4.0%	10 7.3%	5 9.2%	4 5.9%	4 6.6%	4 3.3%	6 12.5%	2 9.8%	2 5.1%	0 0	0 0	14 6.6%	7 5.1%
All sources of info	20 6.1%	15 9.8%B	5 2.8%	20 6.1%	0 0	6 4.0%	10 7.3%	5 9.2%	4 5.9%	4 6.6%	4 3.3%	6 12.5%	2 9.8%	2 5.1%	0 0	0 0	14 6.6%	7 5.1%
preferred source of info	0 0	0 0	0 0	0 0	0 0	0 0	0 0	0 0	0 0	0 0	0 0	0 0	0 0	0 0	0 0	0 0	0 0	0 0
Personal holdings (NET)	12 3.5%	12 7.4%B	* 0.1%	12 3.5%	0 0	3 2.3%	3 2.4%	5 10.2%EF	3 4.4%	2 3.3%	2 1.6%	4 10.0%J	1 3.3%	0 0	* 6.3%	0 0	10 4.6%	2 1.7%
All sources of info	12 3.5%	12 7.4%B	* 0.1%	12 3.5%	0 0	3 2.3%	3 2.4%	5 10.2%EF	3 4.4%	2 3.3%	2 1.6%	4 10.0%J	1 3.3%	0 0	* 6.3%	0 0	10 4.6%	2 1.7%
preferred source of info	7 2.2%	7 4.7%B	0 0	7 2.2%	0 0	2 1.5%	2 1.4%	3 6.4%	2 2.9%	0 0	2 1.6%	3 7.5%I	* 1.6%	0 0	0 0	0 0	5 2.5%	2 1.6%
Printed material (NET)	11 3.1%	8 4.9%	3 1.6%	11 3.1%	0 0	4 2.5%	3 2.1%	4 7.7%	3 4.4%	3 4.9%	4 3.3%	1 2.5%	0 0	0 0	0 0	0 0	6 2.8%	5 3.7%
All sources of info	11 3.1%	8 4.9%	3 1.6%	11 3.1%	0 0	4 2.5%	3 2.1%	4 7.7%	3 4.4%	3 4.9%	4 3.3%	1 2.5%	0 0	0 0	0 0	0 0	6 2.8%	5 3.7%
preferred source of info	5 1.4%	4 2.5%	1 0.6%	5 1.4%	0 0	2 1.3%	1 0.7%	2 3.8%	2 2.9%	2 3.3%	0 0	1 2.5%	0 0	0 0	0 0	0 0	2 1.0%	3 2.2%

Proportions/Means: Columns Tested (5% risk level) - A/B/D - C/D - E/F/G - H/I/J/K/L/M/N - P/Q
* small base; ** very small base (under 30) ineligible for sig testing

Table 145
Page 501

Outsell/Digital Library Federation Study (2002)
Weighted Tables

TABLE 97, continued

R7D/E_12. Data SUMMARY TABLE

		RESPONDENT TYPE				INSTITUTION TYPE			DISCIPLINE								GENDER	
	TOTAL SAMPLE	FACULTY MEMBER	GRAD. STUDENT	FACULTY /GRAD	UNDER GRAD. STUDENT	PUBLIC	PRIVATE	LIBERAL ARTS	BIOLOGIAL SCIENCES	PHYSICAL SCIENCES /MATH	SOCIAL SCIENCES	ARTS AND HUMAN.	ENGI-NEERING	BUSINESS	LAW	UNDEC. MAJOR	MALE	FEMALE
		(A)	(B)	(C)	(D)	(E)	(F)	(G)	(H)	(I)	(J)	(K)	(L)	(M)	(N)		(P)	(Q)
Base - Use Data for research	337	156	181	337	0**	153	135	49*	60*	61*	115*	45*	18*	36*	3**	0*	210	127*
Sources (NET)	5 1.6%	3 2.2%	2 1.0%	5 1.6%	0 0	4 2.9%	0 0	1 1.9%	0 0	1 1.6%	2 1.6%	0 0	1 3.3%H	2 5.1%	0 0	0 0	4 2.1%	1 0.8%
All sources of info	5 1.6%	3 2.2%	2 1.0%	5 1.6%	0 0	4 2.9%	0 0	1 1.9%	0 0	1 1.6%	2 1.6%	0 0	1 3.3%H	2 5.1%	0 0	0 0	4 2.1%	1 0.8%
preferred source of info	3 0.9%	1 0.8%	2 1.0%	3 0.9%	0 0	2 1.4%	0 0	1 1.9%	0 0	0 0	2 1.6%	0 0	* 1.6%	1 2.6%	0 0	0 0	3 1.5%	0 0
Colleague (NET)	5 1.4%	2 1.2%	3 1.7%	5 1.4%	0 0	1 0.7%	4 2.9%	0 0	1 1.5%	1 1.6%	0 0	1 2.5%	0 0	2 5.1%J	0 0	0 0	3 1.3%	2 1.7%
All sources of info	5 1.4%	2 1.2%	3 1.7%	5 1.4%	0 0	1 0.7%	4 2.9%	0 0	1 1.5%	1 1.6%	0 0	1 2.5%	0 0	2 5.1%J	0 0	0 0	3 1.3%	2 1.7%
preferred source of info	1 0.3%	1 0.6%	0 0	1 0.3%	0 0	0 0	1 0.7%	0 0	1 1.5%	0 0	0 0	0 0	0 0	0 0	0 0	0 0	1 0.4%	0 0
Purchase from physical book store (NET)	5 1.4%	2 1.5%	2 1.2%	5 1.4%	0 0	5 3.0%	0 0	0 0	0 0	0 0	0 0	3 7.5%HIJ	* 1.6%	1 2.6%	0 0	0 0	2 1.0%	3 2.0%
All sources of info	5 1.4%	2 1.5%	2 1.2%	5 1.4%	0 0	5 3.0%	0 0	0 0	0 0	0 0	0 0	3 7.5%HIJ	* 1.6%	1 2.6%	0 0	0 0	2 1.0%	3 2.0%
preferred source of info	0 0	0 0	0 0	0 0	0 0	0 0	0 0	0 0	0 0	0 0	0 0	0 0	0 0	0 0	0 0	0 0	0 0	0 0

Proportions/Means: Columns Tested (5% risk level) - A/B/D - C/D - E/F/G - H/I/J/K/L/M/N - P/Q
* small base; ** very small base (under 30) ineligible for sig testing

Table 145
Page 502

Outsell/Digital Library Federation Study (2002)
Weighted Tables

TABLE 97, continued

R7D/E_12. Data SUMMARY TABLE

		RESPONDENT TYPE				INSTITUTION TYPE			DISCIPLINE									GENDER	
	TOTAL SAMPLE	FACULTY MEMBER	GRAD. STUDENT	FACULTY /GRAD	UNDER GRAD. STUDENT	PUBLIC	PRIVATE	LIBERAL ARTS	BIOLOGIAL SCIENCES	PHYSICAL SCIENCES /MATH	SOCIAL SCIENCES	ARTS AND HUMAN.	ENGI- NEERING	BUSINESS	LAW	UNDEC. MAJOR	MALE	FEMALE
		(A)	(B)	(C)	(D)	(E)	(F)	(G)	(H)	(I)	(J)	(K)	(L)	(M)	(N)		(P)	(Q)
Base - Use Data for research	337	156	181	337	0**	153	135	49*	60*	61*	115*	45*	18*	36*	3**	0*	210	127*
Office (NET)	3 1.0%	2 1.6%	1 0.6%	3 1.0%	0 0	0 0	3 2.6%	0 0	0 0	1 1.6%	2 1.6%	0 0	1 3.3%H	0 0	0 0	0 0	3 1.6%	0 0
All sources of info	3 1.0%	2 1.6%	1 0.6%	3 1.0%	0 0	0 0	3 2.6%	0 0	0 0	1 1.6%	2 1.6%	0 0	1 3.3%H	0 0	0 0	0 0	3 1.6%	0 0
preferred source of info	3 1.0%	2 1.6%	1 0.6%	3 1.0%	0 0	0 0	3 2.6%	0 0	0 0	1 1.6%	2 1.6%	0 0	1 3.3%H	0 0	0 0	0 0	3 1.6%	0 0
Order from on demand document delivery service (NET)	3 0.9%	2 1.3%	1 0.5%	3 0.9%	0 0	1 0.6%	1 0.9%	1 1.8%	2 2.9%	0 0	0 0	0 0	* 1.6%	1 2.6%	0 0	0 0	2 1.0%	1 0.7%
All sources of info	3 0.9%	2 1.3%	1 0.5%	3 0.9%	0 0	1 0.6%	1 0.9%	1 1.8%	2 2.9%	0 0	0 0	0 0	* 1.6%	1 2.6%	0 0	0 0	2 1.0%	1 0.7%
preferred source of info	0 0	0 0	0 0	0 0	0 0	0 0	0 0	0 0	0 0	0 0	0 0	0 0	0 0	0 0	0 0	0 0	0 0	0 0
Purchase from online bookstore (NET)	1 0.4%	1 0.8%	0 0	1 0.4%	0 0	1 0.8%	0 0	0 0	0 0	0 0	0 0	0 0	* 1.6%	1 2.6%	0 0	0 0	1 0.4%	* 0.2%
All sources of info	1 0.4%	1 0.8%	0 0	1 0.4%	0 0	1 0.8%	0 0	0 0	0 0	0 0	0 0	0 0	* 1.6%	1 2.6%	0 0	0 0	1 0.4%	* 0.2%
preferred source of info	0 0	0 0	0 0	0 0	0 0	0 0	0 0	0 0	0 0	0 0	0 0	0 0	0 0	0 0	0 0	0 0	0 0	0 0

Proportions/Means: Columns Tested (5% risk level) - A/B/D - C/D - E/F/G - H/I/J/K/L/M/N - P/Q
* small base; ** very small base (under 30) ineligible for sig testing

Table 145
Page 503

Outsell/Digital Library Federation Study (2002)
Weighted Tables

TABLE 97, continued

R7D/E_12. Data SUMMARY TABLE

	RESPONDENT TYPE					INSTITUTION TYPE			DISCIPLINE								GENDER	
	TOTAL SAMPLE	FACULTY MEMBER	GRAD. STUDENT	FACULTY /GRAD	UNDER GRAD. STUDENT	PUBLIC	PRIVATE	LIBERAL ARTS	BIOLOGIAL SCIENCES	PHYSICAL SCIENCES /MATH	SOCIAL SCIENCES	ARTS AND HUMAN.	ENGI-NEERING	BUSINESS	LAW	UNDEC. MAJOR	MALE	FEMALE
		(A)	(B)	(C)	(D)	(E)	(F)	(G)	(H)	(I)	(J)	(K)	(L)	(M)	(N)		(P)	(Q)
Base - Use Data for research	337	156	181	337	0**	153	135	49*	60*	61*	115*	45*	18*	36*	3**	0*	210	127*
Ask library to purchase source (NET)	1	1	0	1	0	0	*	1	1	0	0	0	*	0	0	0	1	0
	0.3%	0.7%	0	0.3%	0	0	0.2%	1.8%	1.5%	0	0	0	1.6%	0	0	0	0.6%	0
All sources of info	1	1	0	1	0	0	*	1	1	0	0	0	*	0	0	0	1	0
	0.3%	0.7%	0	0.3%	0	0	0.2%	1.8%	1.5%	0	0	0	1.6%	0	0	0	0.6%	0
preferred source of info	*	*	0	*	0	0	*	0	0	0	0	0	*	0	0	0	*	0
	0.1%	0.2%	0	0.1%	0	0	0.2%	0	0	0	0	0	1.6%	0	0	0	0.1%	0
Faculty (NET)	1	0	1	1	0	0	1	0	0	0	0	1	0	0	0	0	0	1
	0.3%	0	0.6%	0.3%	0	0	0.8%	0	0	0	0	2.5%	0	0	0	0	0	0.9%
All sources of info	1	0	1	1	0	0	1	0	0	0	0	1	0	0	0	0	0	1
	0.3%	0	0.6%	0.3%	0	0	0.8%	0	0	0	0	2.5%	0	0	0	0	0	0.9%
preferred source of info	0	0	0	0	0	0	0	0	0	0	0	0	0	0	0	0	0	0
	0	0	0	0	0	0	0	0	0	0	0	0	0	0	0	0	0	0
E-journals (NET)	1	1	0	1	0	0	1	0	1	0	0	0	0	0	0	0	1	0
	0.3%	0.6%	0	0.3%	0	0	0.7%	0	1.5%	0	0	0	0	0	0	0	0.4%	0
All sources of info	1	1	0	1	0	0	1	0	1	0	0	0	0	0	0	0	1	0
	0.3%	0.6%	0	0.3%	0	0	0.7%	0	1.5%	0	0	0	0	0	0	0	0.4%	0
preferred source of info	0	0	0	0	0	0	0	0	0	0	0	0	0	0	0	0	0	0
	0	0	0	0	0	0	0	0	0	0	0	0	0	0	0	0	0	0

Proportions/Means: Columns Tested (5% risk level) - A/B/D - C/D - E/F/G - H/I/J/K/L/M/N - P/Q
* small base; ** very small base (under 30) ineligible for sig testing

Table 145
Page 504

Outsell/Digital Library Federation Study (2002)
Weighted Tables

TABLE 97, continued

R7D/E_12. Data SUMMARY TABLE

		RESPONDENT TYPE				INSTITUTION TYPE			DISCIPLINE								GENDER	
	TOTAL SAMPLE	FACULTY MEMBER	GRAD. STUDENT	FACULTY /GRAD	UNDER GRAD. STUDENT	PUBLIC	PRIVATE	LIBERAL ARTS	BIOLOGIAL SCIENCES	PHYSICAL SCIENCES /MATH	SOCIAL SCIENCES	ARTS AND HUMAN.	ENGI- NEERING	BUSINESS	LAW	UNDEC. MAJOR	MALE	FEMALE
		(A)	(B)	(C)	(D)	(E)	(F)	(G)	(H)	(I)	(J)	(K)	(L)	(M)	(N)		(P)	(Q)
Base - Use Data for research	337	156	181	337	0**	153	135	49*	60*	61*	115*	45*	18*	36*	3**	0*	210	127*
Meetings/conferences (NET)	* 0.1%	* 0.2%	0 0	* 0.1%	0 0	* 0.2%	0 0	0 0	0 0	0 0	0 0	0 0	* 1.6%	0 0	0 0	0 0	* 0.1%	0 0
All sources of info	* 0.1%	* 0.2%	0 0	* 0.1%	0 0	* 0.2%	0 0	0 0	0 0	0 0	0 0	0 0	* 1.6%	0 0	0 0	0 0	* 0.1%	0 0
preferred source of info	0 0	0 0	0 0	0 0	0 0	0 0	0 0	0 0	0 0	0 0	0 0	0 0	0 0	0 0	0 0	0 0	0 0	0 0
Access from course website (NET)	0 0	0 0	0 0	0 0	0 0	0 0	0 0	0 0	0 0	0 0	0 0	0 0	0 0	0 0	0 0	0 0	0 0	0 0
All sources of info	0 0	0 0	0 0	0 0	0 0	0 0	0 0	0 0	0 0	0 0	0 0	0 0	0 0	0 0	0 0	0 0	0 0	0 0
preferred source of info	0 0	0 0	0 0	0 0	0 0	0 0	0 0	0 0	0 0	0 0	0 0	0 0	0 0	0 0	0 0	0 0	0 0	0 0
Access book/journal/ journal article elsewhere online (NET)	0 0	0 0	0 0	0 0	0 0	0 0	0 0	0 0	0 0	0 0	0 0	0 0	0 0	0 0	0 0	0 0	0 0	0 0
All sources of info	0 0	0 0	0 0	0 0	0 0	0 0	0 0	0 0	0 0	0 0	0 0	0 0	0 0	0 0	0 0	0 0	0 0	0 0
preferred source of info	0 0	0 0	0 0	0 0	0 0	0 0	0 0	0 0	0 0	0 0	0 0	0 0	0 0	0 0	0 0	0 0	0 0	0 0

Proportions/Means: Columns Tested (5% risk level) - A/B/D - C/D - E/F/G - H/I/J/K/L/M/N - P/Q
* small base; ** very small base (under 30) ineligible for sig testing

Table 145
Page 505

Outsell/Digital Library Federation Study (2002)
Weighted Tables

TABLE 97, continued

R7D/E_12. Data SUMMARY TABLE

		RESPONDENT TYPE				INSTITUTION TYPE			DISCIPLINE								GENDER	
	TOTAL SAMPLE	FACULTY MEMBER	GRAD. STUDENT	FACULTY /GRAD	UNDER GRAD. STUDENT	PUBLIC	PRIVATE	LIBERAL ARTS	BIOLOGIAL SCIENCES	PHYSICAL SCIENCES /MATH	SOCIAL SCIENCES	ARTS AND HUMAN.	ENGI-NEERING	BUSINESS	LAW	UNDEC. MAJOR	MALE	FEMALE
		(A)	(B)	(C)	(D)	(E)	(F)	(G)	(H)	(I)	(J)	(K)	(L)	(M)	(N)		(P)	(Q)
Base - Use Data for research	337	156	181	337	0**	153	135	49*	60*	61*	115*	45*	18*	36*	3**	0*	210	127*
Other (NET)	35 10.3%	21 13.2%	14 7.7%	35 10.3%	0 0	20 13.4%F	7 4.9%	8 15.4%F	11 17.6%I	3 4.9%	11 9.8%	2 5.0%	2 9.8%	6 15.4%	* 6.3%	0 0	20 9.6%	14 11.3%
All sources of info	35 10.3%	21 13.2%	14 7.7%	35 10.3%	0 0	20 13.4%F	7 4.9%	8 15.4%F	11 17.6%I	3 4.9%	11 9.8%	2 5.0%	2 9.8%	6 15.4%	* 6.3%	0 0	20 9.6%	14 11.3%
preferred source of info	19 5.5%	9 6.0%	9 5.1%	19 5.5%	0 0	13 8.4%F	3 2.0%	3 6.1%	5 8.8%	1 1.6%	8 6.6%	1 2.5%	2 9.8%I	2 5.1%	0 0	0 0	10 4.7%	9 6.8%
DK/Refused	14 4.2%	9 5.9%	5 2.9%	14 4.2%	0 0	8 5.0%	7 5.0%	0 0	1 1.5%	1 1.6%	6 4.9%	4 10.0%	* 1.6%	2 5.1%	* 6.3%	0 0	8 3.8%	6 5.0%

Proportions/Means: Columns Tested (5% risk level) - A/B/D - C/D - E/F/G - H/I/J/K/L/M/N - P/Q
* small base; ** very small base (under 30) ineligible for sig testing

Table 145
Page 506

TABLE 98

R7D/E_13. Photographs, prints and other visual resources SUMMARY TABLE

		RESPONDENT TYPE				INSTITUTION TYPE			DISCIPLINE									GENDER	
	TOTAL SAMPLE	FACULTY MEMBER	GRAD. STUDENT	FACULTY /GRAD	UNDER GRAD. STUDENT	PUBLIC	PRIVATE	LIBERAL ARTS	BIOLOGIAL SCIENCES	PHYSICAL SCIENCES /MATH	SOCIAL SCIENCES	ARTS AND HUMAN.	ENGI- NEERING	BUSINESS	LAW	UNDEC. MAJOR	MALE	FEMALE
		(A)	(B)	(C)	(D)	(E)	(F)	(G)	(H)	(I)	(J)	(K)	(L)	(M)	(N)		(P)	(Q)
Base - Use Photographs, prints and other visual resources for research	205	94*	111*	205	0**	88*	83*	34*	48*	28**	55**	49*	12*	12**	1**	0*	127	77*
Access online (NET)	127 62.3%	57 60.8%	70 63.5%	127 62.3%	0 0	54 60.9%	48 57.5%	26 77.6%	30 61.8%K	19 67.9%	41 75.9%	19 38.6%	8 70.0%K	9 76.9%	1 100.0%	0 0	82 64.7%	45 58.4%
All sources of info	127 62.3%	57 60.8%	70 63.5%	127 62.3%	0 0	54 60.9%	48 57.5%	26 77.6%	30 61.8%K	19 67.9%	41 75.9%	19 38.6%	8 70.0%K	9 76.9%	1 100.0%	0 0	82 64.7%	45 58.4%
preferred source of info	97 47.3%	40 42.5%	57 51.3%	97 47.3%	0 0	44 50.4%	31 37.8%	21 62.4%F	24 49.1%K	17 60.7%	34 62.1%	7 13.6%	7 62.5%K	7 61.5%	1 100.0%	0 0	60 47.1%	37 47.5%
Borrow from or use in campus library (NET)	117 57.1%	46 49.1%	71 63.9%	117 57.1%	0 0	54 61.4%	49 59.2%	14 40.8%	21 43.6%	17 60.7%	32 58.6%	34 68.2%H	7 57.5%	7 53.8%	0 0	0 0	67 52.5%	50 64.7%
All sources of info	117 57.1%	46 49.1%	71 63.9%	117 57.1%	0 0	54 61.4%	49 59.2%	14 40.8%	21 43.6%	17 60.7%	32 58.6%	34 68.2%H	7 57.5%	7 53.8%	0 0	0 0	67 52.5%	50 64.7%
preferred source of info	71 34.6%	26 27.8%	45 40.4%	71 34.6%	0 0	31 35.3%	34 41.1%G	6 17.1%	11 23.6%	9 32.1%	15 27.6%	29 59.1%HL	3 30.0%	3 23.1%	0 0	0 0	41 32.0%	30 38.9%
Borrow from or use in other libraries (NET)	18 8.7%	13 13.6%B	5 4.5%	18 8.7%	0 0	3 3.2%	13 15.8%E	2 5.6%	5 10.9%	3 10.7%	4 6.9%	4 9.1%	* 2.5%	1 7.7%	0 0	0 0	12 9.6%	6 7.1%
All sources of info	18 8.7%	13 13.6%B	5 4.5%	18 8.7%	0 0	3 3.2%	13 15.8%E	2 5.6%	5 10.9%	3 10.7%	4 6.9%	4 9.1%	* 2.5%	1 7.7%	0 0	0 0	12 9.6%	6 7.1%

Proportions/Means: Columns Tested (5% risk level) - A/B/D - C/D - E/F/G - H/I/J/K/L/M/N - P/Q
* small base; ** very small base (under 30) ineligible for sig testing

Table 152
Page 536

Outsell/Digital Library Federation Study (2002)
Weighted Tables

TABLE 98, continued

R7D/E_13. Photographs, prints and other visual resources SUMMARY TABLE

		RESPONDENT TYPE				INSTITUTION TYPE			DISCIPLINE									GENDER	
	TOTAL SAMPLE	FACULTY MEMBER	GRAD. STUDENT	FACULTY /GRAD	UNDER GRAD. STUDENT	PUBLIC	PRIVATE	LIBERAL ARTS	BIOLOGIAL SCIENCES	PHYSICAL SCIENCES /MATH	SOCIAL SCIENCES	ARTS AND HUMAN.	ENGI- NEERING	BUSINESS	LAW	UNDEC. MAJOR	MALE	FEMALE
		(A)	(B)	(C)	(D)	(E)	(F)	(G)	(H)	(I)	(J)	(K)	(L)	(M)	(N)		(P)	(Q)
Base - Use Photographs, prints and other visual resources for research	205	94*	111*	205	0**	88*	83*	34*	48*	28**	55**	49*	12*	12**	1**	0*	127	77*
preferred source of info	6 3.0%	1 1.2%	5 4.5%	6 3.0%	0 0	0 0	6 7.5%E	0 0	3 5.5%	1 3.6%	0 0	2 4.5%	* 2.5%	0 0	0 0	0 0	4 3.5%	2 2.3%
Personal holdings (NET)	10 4.9%	8 8.8%B	2 1.6%	10 4.9%	0 0	4 4.4%	1 1.7%	5 14.2%F	4 7.3%	0 0	2 3.4%	2 4.5%	1 5.0%	2 15.4%	0 0	0 0	7 5.7%	3 3.7%
All sources of info	10 4.9%	8 8.8%B	2 1.6%	10 4.9%	0 0	4 4.4%	1 1.7%	5 14.2%F	4 7.3%	0 0	2 3.4%	2 4.5%	1 5.0%	2 15.4%	0 0	0 0	7 5.7%	3 3.7%
preferred source of info	6 2.9%	4 4.3%	2 1.6%	6 2.9%	0 0	4 4.1%	1 1.4%	1 3.3%	2 3.6%	0 0	0 0	2 4.5%	0 0	2 15.4%	0 0	0 0	4 3.0%	2 2.6%
Interlibrary loan (NET)	7 3.3%	5 5.2%	2 1.7%	7 3.3%	0 0	1 1.3%	3 3.5%	3 8.2%	1 1.8%	1 3.6%	4 6.9%	1 2.3%	0 0	0 0	0 0	0 0	3 2.3%	4 5.0%
All sources of info	7 3.3%	5 5.2%	2 1.7%	7 3.3%	0 0	1 1.3%	3 3.5%	3 8.2%	1 1.8%	1 3.6%	4 6.9%	1 2.3%	0 0	0 0	0 0	0 0	3 2.3%	4 5.0%
preferred source of info	0 0	0 0	0 0	0 0	0 0	0 0	0 0	0 0	0 0	0 0	0 0	0 0	0 0	0 0	0 0	0 0	0 0	0 0
Colleague (NET)	4 1.9%	3 2.9%	1 1.1%	4 1.9%	0 0	1 1.0%	3 3.7%	0 0	2 3.6%	0 0	2 3.4%	0 0	* 2.5%	0 0	0 0	0 0	4 3.1%	0 0
All sources of info	4 1.9%	3 2.9%	1 1.1%	4 1.9%	0 0	1 1.0%	3 3.7%	0 0	2 3.6%	0 0	2 3.4%	0 0	* 2.5%	0 0	0 0	0 0	4 3.1%	0 0

Proportions/Means: Columns Tested (5% risk level) - A/B/D - C/D - E/F/G - H/I/J/K/L/M/N - P/Q
* small base; ** very small base (under 30) ineligible for sig testing

Table 152
Page 537

Outsell/Digital Library Federation Study (2002)
Weighted Tables

TABLE 98, continued

R7D/E_13. Photographs, prints and other visual resources SUMMARY TABLE

		RESPONDENT TYPE				INSTITUTION TYPE			DISCIPLINE									GENDER	
	TOTAL SAMPLE	FACULTY MEMBER	GRAD. STUDENT	FACULTY /GRAD	UNDER GRAD. STUDENT	PUBLIC	PRIVATE	LIBERAL ARTS	BIOLOGIAL SCIENCES	PHYSICAL SCIENCES /MATH	SOCIAL SCIENCES	ARTS AND HUMAN.	ENGI- NEERING	BUSINESS	LAW	UNDEC. MAJOR	MALE	FEMALE
		(A)	(B)	(C)	(D)	(E)	(F)	(G)	(H)	(I)	(J)	(K)	(L)	(M)	(N)		(P)	(Q)
Base - Use Photographs, prints and other visual resources for research	205	94*	111*	205	0**	88*	83*	34*	48*	28**	55**	49*	12*	12**	1**	0*	127	77*
preferred source of info	3 1.5%	2 2.0%	1 1.1%	3 1.5%	0 0	1 1.0%	2 2.6%	0 0	1 1.8%	0 0	2 3.4%	0 0	* 2.5%	0 0	0 0	0 0	3 2.4%	0 0
Purchase from physical book store (NET)	4 1.8%	4 3.9%	0 0	4 1.8%	0 0	1 1.6%	1 1.4%	1 3.3%	0 0	0 0	0 0	3 6.8%	* 2.5%	0 0	0 0	0 0	3 2.0%	1 1.4%
All sources of info	4 1.8%	4 3.9%	0 0	4 1.8%	0 0	1 1.6%	1 1.4%	1 3.3%	0 0	0 0	0 0	3 6.8%	* 2.5%	0 0	0 0	0 0	3 2.0%	1 1.4%
preferred source of info	1 0.5%	1 1.2%	0 0	1 0.5%	0 0	0 0	1 1.4%	0 0	0 0	0 0	0 0	1 2.3%	0 0	0 0	0 0	0 0	1 0.9%	0 0
Order from on demand document delivery service (NET)	3 1.3%	3 2.9%	0 0	3 1.3%	0 0	1 1.0%	2 2.3%	0 0	2 3.6%	1 3.6%	0 0	0 0	0 0	0 0	0 0	0 0	3 2.2%	0 0
All sources of info	3 1.3%	3 2.9%	0 0	3 1.3%	0 0	1 1.0%	2 2.3%	0 0	2 3.6%	1 3.6%	0 0	0 0	0 0	0 0	0 0	0 0	3 2.2%	0 0
preferred source of info	0 0	0 0	0 0	0 0	0 0	0 0	0 0	0 0	0 0	0 0	0 0	0 0	0 0	0 0	0 0	0 0	0 0	0 0
Purchase from online bookstore (NET)	3 1.2%	3 2.7%	0 0	3 1.2%	0 0	1 1.6%	0 0	1 3.3%	0 0	0 0	0 0	2 4.5%	* 2.5%	0 0	0 0	0 0	* 0.2%	2 2.9%

Proportions/Means: Columns Tested (5% risk level) - A/B/D - C/D - E/F/G - H/I/J/K/L/M/N - P/Q
* small base; ** very small base (under 30) ineligible for sig testing

Table 152
Page 538

TABLE 98, continued

R7D/E_13. Photographs, prints and other visual resources SUMMARY TABLE

		RESPONDENT TYPE				INSTITUTION TYPE			DISCIPLINE									GENDER	
	TOTAL SAMPLE	FACULTY MEMBER	GRAD. STUDENT	FACULTY /GRAD	UNDER GRAD. STUDENT	PUBLIC	PRIVATE	LIBERAL ARTS	BIOLOGIAL SCIENCES	PHYSICAL SCIENCES /MATH	SOCIAL SCIENCES	ARTS AND HUMAN.	ENGI-NEERING	BUSINESS	LAW	UNDEC. MAJOR	MALE	FEMALE
		(A)	(B)	(C)	(D)	(E)	(F)	(G)	(H)	(I)	(J)	(K)	(L)	(M)	(N)		(P)	(Q)
Base - Use Photographs, prints and other visual resources for research	205	94*	111*	205	0**	88*	83*	34*	48*	28**	55**	49*	12*	12**	1**	0*	127	77*
All sources of info	3 1.2%	3 2.7%	0 0	3 1.2%	0 0	1 1.6%	0 0	1 3.3%	0 0	0 0	0 0	2 4.5%	* 2.5%	0 0	0 0	0 0	* 0.2%	2 2.9%
preferred source of info	0 0	0 0	0 0	0 0	0 0	0 0	0 0	0 0	0 0	0 0	0 0	0 0	0 0	0 0	0 0	0 0	0 0	0 0
Printed material (NET)	2 0.9%	1 0.9%	1 0.9%	2 0.9%	0 0	1 1.1%	0 0	1 2.6%	1 1.8%	1 3.6%	0 0	0 0	0 0	0 0	0 0	0 0	1 0.8%	1 1.1%
All sources of info	2 0.9%	1 0.9%	1 0.9%	2 0.9%	0 0	1 1.1%	0 0	1 2.6%	1 1.8%	1 3.6%	0 0	0 0	0 0	0 0	0 0	0 0	1 0.8%	1 1.1%
preferred source of info	0 0	0 0	0 0	0 0	0 0	0 0	0 0	0 0	0 0	0 0	0 0	0 0	0 0	0 0	0 0	0 0	0 0	0 0
E-journals (NET)	1 0.4%	0 0	1 0.8%	1 0.4%	0 0	1 1.0%	0 0	0 0	1 1.8%	0 0	0 0	0 0	0 0	0 0	0 0	0 0	0 0	1 1.1%
All sources of info	1 0.4%	0 0	1 0.8%	1 0.4%	0 0	1 1.0%	0 0	0 0	1 1.8%	0 0	0 0	0 0	0 0	0 0	0 0	0 0	0 0	1 1.1%
preferred source of info	1 0.4%	0 0	1 0.8%	1 0.4%	0 0	1 1.0%	0 0	0 0	1 1.8%	0 0	0 0	0 0	0 0	0 0	0 0	0 0	0 0	1 1.1%
Office (NET)	1 0.4%	1 0.9%	0 0	1 0.4%	0 0	0 0	1 1.1%	0 0	1 1.8%	0 0	0 0	0 0	0 0	0 0	0 0	0 0	1 0.7%	0 0

Proportions/Means: Columns Tested (5% risk level) - A/B/D - C/D - E/F/G - H/I/J/K/L/M/N - P/Q
* small base; ** very small base (under 30) ineligible for sig testing

Table 152
Page 539

Outsell/Digital Library Federation Study (2002)
Weighted Tables

TABLE 98, continued

R7D/E_13. Photographs, prints and other visual resources SUMMARY TABLE

		RESPONDENT TYPE				INSTITUTION TYPE			DISCIPLINE									GENDER	
	TOTAL SAMPLE	FACULTY MEMBER	GRAD. STUDENT	FACULTY /GRAD	UNDER GRAD. STUDENT	PUBLIC	PRIVATE	LIBERAL ARTS	BIOLOGIAL SCIENCES	PHYSICAL SCIENCES /MATH	SOCIAL SCIENCES	ARTS AND HUMAN.	ENGI-NEERING	BUSINESS	LAW	UNDEC. MAJOR	MALE	FEMALE
		(A)	(B)	(C)	(D)	(E)	(F)	(G)	(H)	(I)	(J)	(K)	(L)	(M)	(N)		(P)	(Q)
Base - Use Photographs, prints and other visual resources for research	205	94*	111*	205	0**	88*	83*	34*	48*	28**	55**	49*	12*	12**	1**	0*	127	77*
All sources of info	1 0.4%	1 0.9%	0 0	1 0.4%	0 0	0 0	1 1.1%	0 0	1 1.8%	0 0	0 0	0 0	0 0	0 0	0 0	0 0	1 0.7%	0 0
preferred source of info	1 0.4%	1 0.9%	0 0	1 0.4%	0 0	0 0	1 1.1%	0 0	1 1.8%	0 0	0 0	0 0	0 0	0 0	0 0	0 0	1 0.7%	0 0
Sources (NET)	1 0.4%	1 0.9%	0 0	1 0.4%	0 0	0 0	0 0	1 2.6%	1 1.8%	0 0	0 0	0 0	0 0	0 0	0 0	0 0	0 0	1 1.1%
All sources of info	1 0.4%	1 0.9%	0 0	1 0.4%	0 0	0 0	0 0	1 2.6%	1 1.8%	0 0	0 0	0 0	0 0	0 0	0 0	0 0	0 0	1 1.1%
preferred source of info	1 0.4%	1 0.9%	0 0	1 0.4%	0 0	0 0	0 0	1 2.6%	1 1.8%	0 0	0 0	0 0	0 0	0 0	0 0	0 0	0 0	1 1.1%
Ask library to purchase source (NET)	* 0.1%	* 0.3%	0 0	* 0.1%	0 0	* 0.3%	0 0	0 0	0 0	0 0	0 0	0 0	* 2.5%	0 0	0 0	0 0	* 0.2%	0 0
All sources of info	* 0.1%	* 0.3%	0 0	* 0.1%	0 0	* 0.3%	0 0	0 0	0 0	0 0	0 0	0 0	* 2.5%	0 0	0 0	0 0	* 0.2%	0 0
preferred source of info	0 0	0 0	0 0	0 0	0 0	0 0	0 0	0 0	0 0	0 0	0 0	0 0	0 0	0 0	0 0	0 0	0 0	0 0

Proportions/Means: Columns Tested (5% risk level) - A/B/D - C/D - E/F/G - H/I/J/K/L/M/N - P/Q
* small base; ** very small base (under 30) ineligible for sig testing

Table 152
Page 540

Outsell/Digital Library Federation Study (2002)
Weighted Tables

TABLE 98, continued

R7D/E_13. Photographs, prints and other visual resources SUMMARY TABLE

		RESPONDENT TYPE				INSTITUTION TYPE			DISCIPLINE									GENDER	
	TOTAL SAMPLE	FACULTY MEMBER	GRAD. STUDENT	FACULTY /GRAD	UNDER GRAD. STUDENT	PUBLIC	PRIVATE	LIBERAL ARTS	BIOLOGIAL SCIENCES	PHYSICAL SCIENCES /MATH	SOCIAL SCIENCES	ARTS AND HUMAN.	ENGI-NEERING	BUSINESS	LAW	UNDEC. MAJOR	MALE	FEMALE
		(A)	(B)	(C)	(D)	(E)	(F)	(G)	(H)	(I)	(J)	(K)	(L)	(M)	(N)		(P)	(Q)
Base - Use Photographs, prints and other visual resources for research	205	94*	111*	205	0**	88*	83*	34*	48*	28**	55**	49*	12*	12**	1**	0*	127	77*
Faculty (NET)	* 0.1%	0 0	* 0.3%	* 0.1%	0 0	* 0.3%	0 0	0 0	0 0	0 0	0 0	0 0	* 2.5%	0 0	0 0	0 0	* 0.2%	0 0
All sources of info	* 0.1%	0 0	* 0.3%	* 0.1%	0 0	* 0.3%	0 0	0 0	0 0	0 0	0 0	0 0	* 2.5%	0 0	0 0	0 0	* 0.2%	0 0
preferred source of info	0 0	0 0	0 0	0 0	0 0	0 0	0 0	0 0	0 0	0 0	0 0	0 0	0 0	0 0	0 0	0 0	0 0	0 0
Meetings/conferences (NET)	0 0	0 0	0 0	0 0	0 0	0 0	0 0	0 0	0 0	0 0	0 0	0 0	0 0	0 0	0 0	0 0	0 0	0 0
All sources of info	0 0	0 0	0 0	0 0	0 0	0 0	0 0	0 0	0 0	0 0	0 0	0 0	0 0	0 0	0 0	0 0	0 0	0 0
preferred source of info	0 0	0 0	0 0	0 0	0 0	0 0	0 0	0 0	0 0	0 0	0 0	0 0	0 0	0 0	0 0	0 0	0 0	0 0
Access from course website (NET)	0 0	0 0	0 0	0 0	0 0	0 0	0 0	0 0	0 0	0 0	0 0	0 0	0 0	0 0	0 0	0 0	0 0	0 0
All sources of info	0 0	0 0	0 0	0 0	0 0	0 0	0 0	0 0	0 0	0 0	0 0	0 0	0 0	0 0	0 0	0 0	0 0	0 0
preferred source of info	0 0	0 0	0 0	0 0	0 0	0 0	0 0	0 0	0 0	0 0	0 0	0 0	0 0	0 0	0 0	0 0	0 0	0 0

Proportions/Means: Columns Tested (5% risk level) - A/B/D - C/D - E/F/G - H/I/J/K/L/M/N - P/Q
* small base; ** very small base (under 30) ineligible for sig testing

Table 152
Page 541

Outsell/Digital Library Federation Study (2002)
Weighted Tables

TABLE 98, continued

R7D/E_13. Photographs, prints and other visual resources SUMMARY TABLE

		RESPONDENT TYPE				INSTITUTION TYPE			DISCIPLINE									GENDER	
	TOTAL SAMPLE	FACULTY MEMBER	GRAD. STUDENT	FACULTY /GRAD	UNDER GRAD. STUDENT	PUBLIC	PRIVATE	LIBERAL ARTS	BIOLOGIAL SCIENCES	PHYSICAL SCIENCES /MATH	SOCIAL SCIENCES	ARTS AND HUMAN.	ENGI-NEERING	BUSINESS	LAW	UNDEC. MAJOR	MALE	FEMALE
		(A)	(B)	(C)	(D)	(E)	(F)	(G)	(H)	(I)	(J)	(K)	(L)	(M)	(N)		(P)	(Q)
Base - Use Photographs, prints and other visual resources for research	205	94*	111*	205	0**	88*	83*	34*	48*	28**	55**	49*	12*	12**	1**	0*	127	77*
Access book/journal/ journal article elsewhere online (NET)	0 0	0 0	0 0	0 0	0 0	0 0	0 0	0 0	0 0	0 0	0 0	0 0	0 0	0 0	0 0	0 0	0 0	0 0
All sources of info	0 0	0 0	0 0	0 0	0 0	0 0	0 0	0 0	0 0	0 0	0 0	0 0	0 0	0 0	0 0	0 0	0 0	0 0
preferred source of info	0 0	0 0	0 0	0 0	0 0	0 0	0 0	0 0	0 0	0 0	0 0	0 0	0 0	0 0	0 0	0 0	0 0	0 0
Other (NET)	22 10.8%	17 17.7%B	6 5.0%	22 10.8%	0 0	9 10.1%	6 7.1%	7 21.7%F	12 25.5%L	2 7.1%	2 3.4%	6 11.4%	* 2.5%	0 0	0 0	0 0	12 9.7%	10 12.7%
All sources of info	18 9.0%	13 13.8%B	6 5.0%	18 9.0%	0 0	6 7.0%	5 6.0%	7 21.7%EF	11 21.8%L	2 7.1%	0 0	6 11.4%	* 2.5%	0 0	0 0	0 0	11 8.3%	8 10.2%
preferred source of info	12 5.7%	12 12.4%B	0 0	12 5.7%	0 0	6 6.7%	2 2.4%	4 11.2%	5 10.9%	0 0	2 3.4%	4 9.1%	0 0	0 0	0 0	0 0	8 6.1%	4 5.0%
DK/Refused	7 3.2%	6 6.7%B	* 0.3%	7 3.2%	0 0	1 1.6%	4 4.8%	1 3.3%	0 0	1 3.6%	2 3.4%	3 6.8%	* 2.5%	0 0	0 0	0 0	5 4.3%	1 1.4%

Proportions/Means: Columns Tested (5% risk level) - A/B/D - C/D - E/F/G - H/I/J/K/L/M/N - P/Q
* small base; ** very small base (under 30) ineligible for sig testing

TABLE 99

R7D/E_14. Technical Reports SUMMARY TABLE

		RESPONDENT TYPE				INSTITUTION TYPE			DISCIPLINE									GENDER	
	TOTAL SAMPLE	FACULTY MEMBER	GRAD. STUDENT	FACULTY /GRAD	UNDER GRAD. STUDENT	PUBLIC	PRIVATE	LIBERAL ARTS	BIOLOGIAL SCIENCES	PHYSICAL SCIENCES /MATH	SOCIAL SCIENCES	ARTS AND HUMAN.	ENGI-NEERING	BUSINESS	LAW	UNDEC. MAJOR	MALE	FEMALE
		(A)	(B)	(C)	(D)	(E)	(F)	(G)	(H)	(I)	(J)	(K)	(L)	(M)	(N)		(P)	(Q)
Base - Use Technical Reports for research	242	128	114*	242	0**	117*	83*	41*	50*	53*	73*	19**	17*	28*	1**	0*	148	93*
Access online (NET)	156 64.6%	84 66.0%	72 63.0%	156 64.6%	0 0	73 62.1%	57 68.4%	26 64.1%	32 63.2%	36 67.9%	47 64.1%	11 58.8%	9 51.7%	20 73.3%L	1 75.0%	0 0	95 64.3%	61 65.1%
All sources of info	156 64.6%	84 66.0%	72 63.0%	156 64.6%	0 0	73 62.1%	57 68.4%	26 64.1%	32 63.2%	36 67.9%	47 64.1%	11 58.8%	9 51.7%	20 73.3%L	1 75.0%	0 0	95 64.3%	61 65.1%
preferred source of info	119 49.3%	67 52.7%	52 45.6%	119 49.3%	0 0	48 41.1%	45 54.8%	25 61.6%E	26 50.9%	27 50.9%	38 51.3%	6 29.4%	8 44.8%	15 53.3%	1 75.0%	0 0	74 50.0%	45 48.2%
Borrow from or use in campus library (NET)	144 59.7%	71 55.6%	73 64.4%	144 59.7%	0 0	76 64.6%	47 57.2%	21 51.1%	25 49.1%	34 64.2%	45 61.5%	10 52.9%	11 65.5%	19 66.7%	1 62.5%	0 0	94 63.4%	50 54.0%
All sources of info	144 59.7%	71 55.6%	73 64.4%	144 59.7%	0 0	76 64.6%	47 57.2%	21 51.1%	25 49.1%	34 64.2%	45 61.5%	10 52.9%	11 65.5%	19 66.7%	1 62.5%	0 0	94 63.4%	50 54.0%
preferred source of info	75 31.1%	35 27.1%	40 35.5%	75 31.1%	0 0	43 36.2%	24 28.9%	9 21.0%	15 29.8%	20 37.7%	17 23.1%	8 41.2%	7 39.7%	8 30.0%	* 25.0%	0 0	50 33.5%	25 27.3%
Interlibrary loan (NET)	16 6.7%	12 9.5%	4 3.7%	16 6.7%	0 0	6 5.2%	4 5.1%	6 14.3%	3 5.3%	7 13.2%M	4 5.1%	1 5.9%	2 10.3%M	0 0	0 0	0 0	9 6.3%	7 7.4%
All sources of info	16 6.7%	12 9.5%	4 3.7%	16 6.7%	0 0	6 5.2%	4 5.1%	6 14.3%	3 5.3%	7 13.2%M	4 5.1%	1 5.9%	2 10.3%M	0 0	0 0	0 0	9 6.3%	7 7.4%
preferred source of info	3 1.4%	0 0	3 2.9%	3 1.4%	0 0	3 2.8%	0 0	0 0	0 0	0 0	2 2.6%	1 5.9%	* 1.7%	0 0	0 0	0 0	* 0.2%	3 3.2%

Proportions/Means: Columns Tested (5% risk level) - A/B/D - C/D - E/F/G - H/I/J/K/L/M/N - P/Q
* small base; ** very small base (under 30) ineligible for sig testing

Table 159
Page 571

Outsell/Digital Library Federation Study (2002)
Weighted Tables

TABLE 99, continued

R7D/E_14. Technical Reports SUMMARY TABLE

		RESPONDENT TYPE				INSTITUTION TYPE			DISCIPLINE									GENDER	
	TOTAL SAMPLE	FACULTY MEMBER	GRAD. STUDENT	FACULTY /GRAD	UNDER GRAD. STUDENT	PUBLIC	PRIVATE	LIBERAL ARTS	BIOLOGIAL SCIENCES	PHYSICAL SCIENCES /MATH	SOCIAL SCIENCES	ARTS AND HUMAN.	ENGI- NEERING	BUSINESS	LAW	UNDEC. MAJOR	MALE	FEMALE
		(A)	(B)	(C)	(D)	(E)	(F)	(G)	(H)	(I)	(J)	(K)	(L)	(M)	(N)		(P)	(Q)
Base - Use Technical Reports for research	242	128	114*	242	0**	117*	83*	41*	50*	53*	73*	19**	17*	28*	1**	0*	148	93*
Borrow from or use in other libraries (NET)	11 4.5%	6 4.8%	5 4.1%	11 4.5%	0 0	4 3.7%	3 3.2%	4 9.1%	3 5.3%	2 3.8%	4 5.1%	0 0	1 8.6%	1 3.3%	0 0	0 0	4 2.8%	7 7.0%
All sources of info	11 4.5%	6 4.8%	5 4.1%	11 4.5%	0 0	4 3.7%	3 3.2%	4 9.1%	3 5.3%	2 3.8%	4 5.1%	0 0	1 8.6%	1 3.3%	0 0	0 0	4 2.8%	7 7.0%
preferred source of info	5 2.2%	2 1.9%	3 2.4%	5 2.2%	0 0	3 2.3%	1 0.7%	2 4.6%	1 1.8%	0 0	4 5.1%	0 0	1 3.4%I	0 0	0 0	0 0	1 1.0%	4 4.0%
Colleague (NET)	8 3.2%	3 2.6%	4 3.9%	8 3.2%	0 0	6 5.3%	2 1.9%	0 0	0 0	2 3.8%	4 5.1%	1 5.9%	1 5.2%H	0 0	0 0	0 0	6 3.8%	2 2.3%
All sources of info	8 3.2%	3 2.6%	4 3.9%	8 3.2%	0 0	6 5.3%	2 1.9%	0 0	0 0	2 3.8%	4 5.1%	1 5.9%	1 5.2%H	0 0	0 0	0 0	6 3.8%	2 2.3%
preferred source of info	3 1.3%	1 0.9%	2 1.8%	3 1.3%	0 0	2 1.8%	1 1.2%	0 0	0 0	2 3.8%	0 0	1 5.9%	0 0	0 0	0 0	0 0	3 2.1%	0 0
Order from on demand document delivery service (NET)	7 3.0%	7 5.6%B	0 0	7 3.0%	0 0	1 1.1%	4 4.4%	2 5.4%	2 3.5%	2 3.8%	2 2.6%	0 0	1 3.4%	1 3.3%	0 0	0 0	4 2.4%	4 3.9%
All sources of info	7 3.0%	7 5.6%B	0 0	7 3.0%	0 0	1 1.1%	4 4.4%	2 5.4%	2 3.5%	2 3.8%	2 2.6%	0 0	1 3.4%	1 3.3%	0 0	0 0	4 2.4%	4 3.9%
preferred source of info	2 0.9%	2 1.7%	0 0	2 0.9%	0 0	* 0.2%	1 1.1%	1 2.4%	1 1.8%	1 1.9%	0 0	0 0	* 1.7%	0 0	0 0	0 0	1 0.9%	1 0.9%

Proportions/Means: Columns Tested (5% risk level) - A/B/D - C/D - E/F/G - H/I/J/K/L/M/N - P/Q
* small base; ** very small base (under 30) ineligible for sig testing

Table 159
Page 572

Outsell/Digital Library Federation Study (2002)
Weighted Tables

TABLE 99, continued

R7D/E_14. Technical Reports SUMMARY TABLE

	TOTAL SAMPLE	RESPONDENT TYPE: FACULTY MEMBER	GRAD. STUDENT	FACULTY /GRAD	UNDER GRAD. STUDENT	INSTITUTION TYPE: PUBLIC	PRIVATE	LIBERAL ARTS	DISCIPLINE: BIOLOGIAL SCIENCES	PHYSICAL SCIENCES /MATH	SOCIAL SCIENCES	ARTS AND HUMAN.	ENGI-NEERING	BUSINESS	LAW	UNDEC. MAJOR	GENDER: MALE	FEMALE
		(A)	(B)	(C)	(D)	(E)	(F)	(G)	(H)	(I)	(J)	(K)	(L)	(M)	(N)		(P)	(Q)
Base - Use Technical Reports for research	242	128	114*	242	0**	117*	83*	41*	50*	53*	73*	19**	17*	28*	1**	0*	148	93*
Sources (NET)	6 2.7%	6 4.3%	1 0.8%	6 2.7%	0 0	2 1.7%	3 4.1%	1 2.4%	2 3.5%	1 1.9%	2 2.6%	0 0	1 5.2%	1 3.3%	0 0	0 0	6 3.7%	1 0.9%
All sources of info	6 2.7%	6 4.3%	1 0.8%	6 2.7%	0 0	2 1.7%	3 4.1%	1 2.4%	2 3.5%	1 1.9%	2 2.6%	0 0	1 5.2%	1 3.3%	0 0	0 0	6 3.7%	1 0.9%
preferred source of info	2 0.9%	2 1.7%	0 0	2 0.9%	0 0	* 0.2%	2 2.3%	0 0	0 0	0 0	2 2.6%	0 0	* 1.7%	0 0	0 0	0 0	2 1.5%	0 0
Personal holdings (NET)	6 2.4%	3 2.4%	3 2.4%	6 2.4%	0 0	2 1.5%	1 1.1%	3 7.6%	2 3.5%	2 3.8%	0 0	1 5.9%	0 0	1 3.3%	0 0	0 0	6 3.9%	0 0
All sources of info	6 2.4%	3 2.4%	3 2.4%	6 2.4%	0 0	2 1.5%	1 1.1%	3 7.6%	2 3.5%	2 3.8%	0 0	1 5.9%	0 0	1 3.3%	0 0	0 0	6 3.9%	0 0
preferred source of info	4 1.6%	2 1.7%	2 1.6%	4 1.6%	0 0	2 1.5%	0 0	2 5.1%	1 1.8%	1 1.9%	0 0	1 5.9%	0 0	1 3.3%	0 0	0 0	4 2.7%	0 0
Purchase from online bookstore (NET)	3 1.2%	2 1.4%	1 1.0%	3 1.2%	0 0	2 1.7%	0 0	1 2.1%	2 3.5%	0 0	0 0	1 5.9%	0 0	0 0	0 0	0 0	3 1.9%	0 0
All sources of info	3 1.2%	2 1.4%	1 1.0%	3 1.2%	0 0	2 1.7%	0 0	1 2.1%	2 3.5%	0 0	0 0	1 5.9%	0 0	0 0	0 0	0 0	3 1.9%	0 0
preferred source of info	2 0.7%	2 1.4%	0 0	2 0.7%	0 0	1 0.7%	0 0	1 2.1%	2 3.5%	0 0	0 0	0 0	0 0	0 0	0 0	0 0	2 1.2%	0 0
Printed material (NET)	3 1.2%	2 1.6%	1 0.8%	3 1.2%	0 0	2 1.7%	1 1.1%	0 0	2 3.5%	0 0	0 0	1 5.9%	0 0	0 0	0 0	0 0	2 1.3%	1 0.9%

Proportions/Means: Columns Tested (5% risk level) - A/B/D - C/D - E/F/G - H/I/J/K/L/M/N - P/Q
* small base; ** very small base (under 30) ineligible for sig testing

Table 159
Page 573

Outsell/Digital Library Federation Study (2002)
Weighted Tables

TABLE 99, continued

R7D/E_14. Technical Reports SUMMARY TABLE

	TOTAL SAMPLE	RESPONDENT TYPE: FACULTY MEMBER	GRAD. STUDENT	FACULTY /GRAD	UNDER GRAD. STUDENT	INSTITUTION TYPE: PUBLIC	PRIVATE	LIBERAL ARTS	DISCIPLINE: BIOLOGIAL SCIENCES	PHYSICAL SCIENCES /MATH	SOCIAL SCIENCES	ARTS AND HUMAN.	ENGI-NEERING	BUSINESS	LAW	UNDEC. MAJOR	GENDER: MALE	FEMALE
		(A)	(B)	(C)	(D)	(E)	(F)	(G)	(H)	(I)	(J)	(K)	(L)	(M)	(N)		(P)	(Q)
Base - Use Technical Reports for research	242	128	114*	242	0**	117*	83*	41*	50*	53*	73*	19**	17*	28*	1**	0*	148	93*
All sources of info	3 1.2%	2 1.6%	1 0.8%	3 1.2%	0 0	2 1.7%	1 1.1%	0 0	2 3.5%	0 0	0 0	1 5.9%	0 0	0 0	0 0	0 0	2 1.3%	1 0.9%
preferred source of info	3 1.2%	2 1.6%	1 0.8%	3 1.2%	0 0	2 1.7%	1 1.1%	0 0	2 3.5%	0 0	0 0	1 5.9%	0 0	0 0	0 0	0 0	2 1.3%	1 0.9%
Ask library to purchase source (NET)	3 1.1%	1 0.9%	1 1.2%	3 1.1%	0 0	1 1.2%	1 1.4%	0 0	1 1.8%	0 0	0 0	1 5.9%	1 3.4%IJ	0 0	0 0	0 0	2 1.1%	1 0.9%
All sources of info	3 1.1%	1 0.9%	1 1.2%	3 1.1%	0 0	1 1.2%	1 1.4%	0 0	1 1.8%	0 0	0 0	1 5.9%	1 3.4%IJ	0 0	0 0	0 0	2 1.1%	1 0.9%
preferred source of info	1 0.5%	0 0	1 1.0%	1 0.5%	0 0	1 1.0%	0 0	0 0	0 0	0 0	0 0	1 5.9%	0 0	0 0	0 0	0 0	1 0.8%	0 0
Office (NET)	1 0.5%	1 1.0%	0 0	1 0.5%	0 0	0 0	1 1.5%	0 0	0 0	0 0	0 0	0 0	* 1.7%	1 3.3%	0 0	0 0	1 0.8%	0 0
All sources of info	1 0.5%	1 1.0%	0 0	1 0.5%	0 0	0 0	1 1.5%	0 0	0 0	0 0	0 0	0 0	* 1.7%	1 3.3%	0 0	0 0	1 0.8%	0 0
preferred source of info	1 0.5%	1 1.0%	0 0	1 0.5%	0 0	0 0	1 1.5%	0 0	0 0	0 0	0 0	0 0	* 1.7%	1 3.3%	0 0	0 0	1 0.8%	0 0
Faculty (NET)	1 0.4%	0 0	1 0.8%	1 0.4%	0 0	1 0.8%	0 0	0 0	0 0	0 0	0 0	0 0	0 0	1 3.3%	0 0	0 0	0 0	1 1.0%

Proportions/Means: Columns Tested (5% risk level) - A/B/D - C/D - E/F/G - H/I/J/K/L/M/N - P/Q
* small base; ** very small base (under 30) ineligible for sig testing

Table 159
Page 574

Outsell/Digital Library Federation Study (2002)
Weighted Tables

TABLE 99, continued

R7D/E_14. Technical Reports SUMMARY TABLE

	RESPONDENT TYPE					INSTITUTION TYPE			DISCIPLINE									GENDER	
	TOTAL SAMPLE	FACULTY MEMBER	GRAD. STUDENT	FACULTY /GRAD	UNDER GRAD. STUDENT	PUBLIC	PRIVATE	LIBERAL ARTS	BIOLOGIAL SCIENCES	PHYSICAL SCIENCES /MATH	SOCIAL SCIENCES	ARTS AND HUMAN.	ENGI-NEERING	BUSINESS	LAW	UNDEC. MAJOR	MALE	FEMALE
		(A)	(B)	(C)	(D)	(E)	(F)	(G)	(H)	(I)	(J)	(K)	(L)	(M)	(N)		(P)	(Q)
Base - Use Technical Reports for research	242	128	114*	242	0**	117*	83*	41*	50*	53*	73*	19**	17*	28*	1**	0*	148	93*
All sources of info	1 0.4%	0 0	1 0.8%	1 0.4%	0 0	1 0.8%	0 0	0 0	0 0	0 0	0 0	0 0	0 0	1 3.3%	0 0	0 0	0 0	1 1.0%
preferred source of info	1 0.4%	0 0	1 0.8%	1 0.4%	0 0	1 0.8%	0 0	0 0	0 0	0 0	0 0	0 0	0 0	1 3.3%	0 0	0 0	0 0	1 1.0%
E-journals (NET)	1 0.4%	0 0	1 0.8%	1 0.4%	0 0	1 0.7%	0 0	0 0	1 1.8%	0 0	0 0	0 0	0 0	0 0	0 0	0 0	0 0	1 0.9%
All sources of info	1 0.4%	0 0	1 0.8%	1 0.4%	0 0	1 0.7%	0 0	0 0	1 1.8%	0 0	0 0	0 0	0 0	0 0	0 0	0 0	0 0	1 0.9%
preferred source of info	1 0.4%	0 0	1 0.8%	1 0.4%	0 0	1 0.7%	0 0	0 0	1 1.8%	0 0	0 0	0 0	0 0	0 0	0 0	0 0	0 0	1 0.9%
Meetings/conferences (NET)	1 0.4%	1 0.7%	0 0	1 0.4%	0 0	0 0	1 1.1%	0 0	1 1.8%	0 0	0 0	0 0	0 0	0 0	0 0	0 0	1 0.6%	0 0
All sources of info	1 0.4%	1 0.7%	0 0	1 0.4%	0 0	0 0	1 1.1%	0 0	1 1.8%	0 0	0 0	0 0	0 0	0 0	0 0	0 0	1 0.6%	0 0
preferred source of info	1 0.4%	1 0.7%	0 0	1 0.4%	0 0	0 0	1 1.1%	0 0	1 1.8%	0 0	0 0	0 0	0 0	0 0	0 0	0 0	1 0.6%	0 0
Purchase from physical book store (NET)	0 0	0 0	0 0	0 0	0 0	0 0	0 0	0 0	0 0	0 0	0 0	0 0	0 0	0 0	0 0	0 0	0 0	0 0

Proportions/Means: Columns Tested (5% risk level) - A/B/D - C/D - E/F/G - H/I/J/K/L/M/N - P/Q
* small base; ** very small base (under 30) ineligible for sig testing

Table 159
Page 575

Outsell/Digital Library Federation Study (2002)
Weighted Tables

TABLE 99, continued

R7D/E_14. Technical Reports SUMMARY TABLE

		RESPONDENT TYPE				INSTITUTION TYPE			DISCIPLINE								GENDER	
	TOTAL SAMPLE	FACULTY MEMBER	GRAD. STUDENT	FACULTY /GRAD	UNDER GRAD. STUDENT	PUBLIC	PRIVATE	LIBERAL ARTS	BIOLOGIAL SCIENCES	PHYSICAL SCIENCES /MATH	SOCIAL SCIENCES	ARTS AND HUMAN.	ENGI-NEERING	BUSINESS	LAW	UNDEC. MAJOR	MALE	FEMALE
		(A)	(B)	(C)	(D)	(E)	(F)	(G)	(H)	(I)	(J)	(K)	(L)	(M)	(N)		(P)	(Q)
Base - Use Technical Reports for research	242	128	114*	242	0**	117*	83*	41*	50*	53*	73*	19**	17*	28*	1**	0*	148	93*
All sources of info	0 0	0 0	0 0	0 0	0 0	0 0	0 0	0 0	0 0	0 0	0 0	0 0	0 0	0 0	0 0	0 0	0 0	0 0
preferred source of info	0 0	0 0	0 0	0 0	0 0	0 0	0 0	0 0	0 0	0 0	0 0	0 0	0 0	0 0	0 0	0 0	0 0	0 0
Access book/journal/ journal article elsewhere online (NET)	0 0	0 0	0 0	0 0	0 0	0 0	0 0	0 0	0 0	0 0	0 0	0 0	0 0	0 0	0 0	0 0	0 0	0 0
All sources of info	0 0	0 0	0 0	0 0	0 0	0 0	0 0	0 0	0 0	0 0	0 0	0 0	0 0	0 0	0 0	0 0	0 0	0 0
preferred source of info	0 0	0 0	0 0	0 0	0 0	0 0	0 0	0 0	0 0	0 0	0 0	0 0	0 0	0 0	0 0	0 0	0 0	0 0
Access from course website (NET)	0 0	0 0	0 0	0 0	0 0	0 0	0 0	0 0	0 0	0 0	0 0	0 0	0 0	0 0	0 0	0 0	0 0	0 0
All sources of info	0 0	0 0	0 0	0 0	0 0	0 0	0 0	0 0	0 0	0 0	0 0	0 0	0 0	0 0	0 0	0 0	0 0	0 0
preferred source of info	0 0	0 0	0 0	0 0	0 0	0 0	0 0	0 0	0 0	0 0	0 0	0 0	0 0	0 0	0 0	0 0	0 0	0 0
Other (NET)	24 9.9%	14 11.1%	10 8.5%	24 9.9%	0 0	14 11.9%	7 8.1%	3 7.7%	4 8.8%	3 5.7%	11 15.4%	3 17.6%	1 5.2%	1 3.3%	0 0	0 0	10 6.5%	14 15.2%P

Proportions/Means: Columns Tested (5% risk level) - A/B/D - C/D - E/F/G - H/I/J/K/L/M/N - P/Q
* small base; ** very small base (under 30) ineligible for sig testing

Table 159
Page 576

Outsell/Digital Library Federation Study (2002)
Weighted Tables

TABLE 99, continued

R7D/E_14. Technical Reports SUMMARY TABLE

		RESPONDENT TYPE				INSTITUTION TYPE			DISCIPLINE								GENDER	
	TOTAL SAMPLE	FACULTY MEMBER	GRAD. STUDENT	FACULTY /GRAD	UNDER GRAD. STUDENT	PUBLIC	PRIVATE	LIBERAL ARTS	BIOLOGIAL SCIENCES	PHYSICAL SCIENCES /MATH	SOCIAL SCIENCES	ARTS AND HUMAN.	ENGI-NEERING	BUSINESS	LAW	UNDEC. MAJOR	MALE	FEMALE
		(A)	(B)	(C)	(D)	(E)	(F)	(G)	(H)	(I)	(J)	(K)	(L)	(M)	(N)		(P)	(Q)
Base - Use Technical Reports for research	242	128	114*	242	0**	117*	83*	41*	50*	53*	73*	19**	17*	28*	1**	0*	148	93*
All sources of info	24 9.7%	14 10.9%	10 8.5%	24 9.7%	0 0	14 11.9%	6 7.8%	3 7.7%	4 8.8%	3 5.7%	11 15.4%	3 17.6%	1 3.4%	1 3.3%	0 0	0 0	9 6.3%	14 15.2%P
preferred source of info	4 1.7%	1 1.1%	3 2.4%	4 1.7%	0 0	3 2.3%	1 1.4%	* 0.7%	2 3.5%	0 0	2 2.6%	0 0	1 3.4%I	0 0	0 0	0 0	1 1.0%	3 3.0%
DK/Refused	14 5.6%	9 6.6%	5 4.4%	14 5.6%	0 0	8 6.4%	5 6.1%	1 2.4%	0 0	2 3.8%	9 12.8%H	0 0	* 1.7%	2 6.7%	0 0	0 0	4 2.6%	10 10.4%P

Proportions/Means: Columns Tested (5% risk level) - A/B/D - C/D - E/F/G - H/I/J/K/L/M/N - P/Q
* small base; ** very small base (under 30) ineligible for sig testing

Table 159
Page 577

TABLE 100

R7D/E_15. Pre-prints SUMMARY TABLE

		RESPONDENT TYPE				INSTITUTION TYPE			DISCIPLINE								GENDER	
	TOTAL SAMPLE	FACULTY MEMBER	GRAD. STUDENT	FACULTY /GRAD	UNDER GRAD. STUDENT	PUBLIC	PRIVATE	LIBERAL ARTS	BIOLOGIAL SCIENCES	PHYSICAL SCIENCES /MATH	SOCIAL SCIENCES	ARTS AND HUMAN.	ENGI-NEERING	BUSINESS	LAW	UNDEC. MAJOR	MALE	FEMALE
		(A)	(B)	(C)	(D)	(E)	(F)	(G)	(H)	(I)	(J)	(K)	(L)	(M)	(N)		(P)	(Q)
Base - Use Pre-prints for research	158	91*	67*	158	0**	65*	65*	29**	38*	57*	30**	11**	7**	15**	1**	0*	111	48*
Access online (NET)	87 54.7%	47 51.2%	40 59.5%	87 54.7%	0 0	27 42.5%	40 61.1%E	20 68.0%	15 39.5%	39 68.4%H	11 37.5%	6 50.0%	4 65.2%	11 75.0%	* 50.0%	0 0	63 56.5%	24 50.8%
All sources of info	87 54.7%	47 51.2%	40 59.5%	87 54.7%	0 0	27 42.5%	40 61.1%E	20 68.0%	15 39.5%	39 68.4%H	11 37.5%	6 50.0%	4 65.2%	11 75.0%	* 50.0%	0 0	63 56.5%	24 50.8%
preferred source of info	75 47.4%	41 45.4%	34 50.2%	75 47.4%	0 0	23 34.9%	35 54.0%E	18 60.7%	12 32.6%	37 64.9%H	9 31.3%	1 10.0%	4 56.5%	11 75.0%	* 50.0%	0 0	56 50.7%	19 39.7%
Borrow from or use in campus library (NET)	58 36.8%	27 29.8%	31 46.2%A	58 36.8%	0 0	26 40.0%	24 36.9%	9 29.5%	15 39.5%	13 22.8%	15 50.0%	4 40.0%	3 47.8%	7 50.0%	* 25.0%	0 0	38 34.4%	20 42.5%
All sources of info	58 36.8%	27 29.8%	31 46.2%A	58 36.8%	0 0	26 40.0%	24 36.9%	9 29.5%	15 39.5%	13 22.8%	15 50.0%	4 40.0%	3 47.8%	7 50.0%	* 25.0%	0 0	38 34.4%	20 42.5%
preferred source of info	29 18.5%	15 16.6%	14 21.1%	29 18.5%	0 0	17 26.3%	10 16.1%	2 6.5%	10 25.6%I	5 8.8%	8 25.0%	3 30.0%	2 26.1%	2 12.5%	* 25.0%	0 0	18 15.9%	12 24.7%
Sources (NET)	22 13.9%	18 20.1%B	4 5.6%	22 13.9%	0 0	8 11.8%	8 12.3%	6 22.1%	11 30.2%I	4 7.0%	4 12.5%	1 10.0%	1 8.7%	1 6.2%	* 25.0%	0 0	12 10.8%	10 21.1%
All sources of info	22 13.9%	18 20.1%B	4 5.6%	22 13.9%	0 0	8 11.8%	8 12.3%	6 22.1%	11 30.2%I	4 7.0%	4 12.5%	1 10.0%	1 8.7%	1 6.2%	* 25.0%	0 0	12 10.8%	10 21.1%
preferred source of info	15 9.4%	12 13.4%	3 3.9%	15 9.4%	0 0	6 9.0%	5 8.3%	4 12.6%	9 23.3%I	4 7.0%	2 6.3%	0 0	0 0	0 0	* 25.0%	0 0	8 7.0%	7 14.8%

Proportions/Means: Columns Tested (5% risk level) - A/B/D - C/D - E/F/G - H/I/J/K/L/M/N - P/Q
* small base; ** very small base (under 30) ineligible for sig testing

Table 166
Page 606

Outsell/Digital Library Federation Study (2002)
Weighted Tables

TABLE 100, continued

R7D/E_15. Pre-prints SUMMARY TABLE

		RESPONDENT TYPE				INSTITUTION TYPE			DISCIPLINE									GENDER	
	TOTAL SAMPLE	FACULTY MEMBER	GRAD. STUDENT	FACULTY /GRAD	UNDER GRAD. STUDENT	PUBLIC	PRIVATE	LIBERAL ARTS	BIOLOGIAL SCIENCES	PHYSICAL SCIENCES /MATH	SOCIAL SCIENCES	ARTS AND HUMAN.	ENGI- NEERING	BUSINESS	LAW	UNDEC. MAJOR	MALE	FEMALE
		(A)	(B)	(C)	(D)	(E)	(F)	(G)	(H)	(I)	(J)	(K)	(L)	(M)	(N)		(P)	(Q)
Base - Use Pre-prints for research	158	91*	67*	158	0**	65*	65*	29**	38*	57*	30**	11**	7**	15**	1**	0*	111	48*
Colleague (NET)	12 7.8%	7 7.5%	6 8.4%	12 7.8%	0 0	6 9.4%	6 9.8%	0 0	5 14.0%	5 8.8%	0 0	0 0	* 4.3%	2 12.5%	0 0	0 0	9 8.0%	4 7.5%
All sources of info	12 7.8%	7 7.5%	6 8.4%	12 7.8%	0 0	6 9.4%	6 9.8%	0 0	5 14.0%	5 8.8%	0 0	0 0	* 4.3%	2 12.5%	0 0	0 0	9 8.0%	4 7.5%
preferred source of info	8 4.8%	4 4.2%	4 5.6%	8 4.8%	0 0	6 9.0%	2 2.7%	0 0	3 7.0%	4 7.0%	0 0	0 0	0 0	1 6.2%	0 0	0 0	7 6.0%	1 1.9%
Interlibrary loan (NET)	11 7.0%	7 7.7%	4 6.0%	11 7.0%	0 0	5 8.4%	2 2.7%	4 13.1%	3 7.0%	2 3.5%	4 12.5%	1 10.0%	1 8.7%	1 6.2%	0 0	0 0	5 4.9%	6 11.9%
All sources of info	11 7.0%	7 7.7%	4 6.0%	11 7.0%	0 0	5 8.4%	2 2.7%	4 13.1%	3 7.0%	2 3.5%	4 12.5%	1 10.0%	1 8.7%	1 6.2%	0 0	0 0	5 4.9%	6 11.9%
preferred source of info	5 3.3%	3 3.3%	2 3.2%	5 3.3%	0 0	3 5.1%	0 0	2 6.5%	0 0	0 0	4 12.5%	1 10.0%	* 4.3%	0 0	0 0	0 0	1 1.3%	4 7.9%P
Order from on demand document delivery service (NET)	8 4.9%	7 7.4%	1 1.5%	8 4.9%	0 0	2 2.8%	3 4.6%	3 9.9%	1 2.3%	4 7.0%	2 6.3%	0 0	0 0	1 6.2%	0 0	0 0	8 6.9%	0 0
All sources of info	8 4.9%	7 7.4%	1 1.5%	8 4.9%	0 0	2 2.8%	3 4.6%	3 9.9%	1 2.3%	4 7.0%	2 6.3%	0 0	0 0	1 6.2%	0 0	0 0	8 6.9%	0 0
preferred source of info	6 3.7%	5 5.3%	1 1.5%	6 3.7%	0 0	1 1.4%	3 4.6%	2 6.5%	0 0	3 5.3%	2 6.3%	0 0	0 0	1 6.2%	0 0	0 0	6 5.2%	0 0

Proportions/Means: Columns Tested (5% risk level) - A/B/D - C/D - E/F/G - H/I/J/K/L/M/N - P/Q
* small base; ** very small base (under 30) ineligible for sig testing

Table 166
Page 607

Outsell/Digital Library Federation Study (2002)
Weighted Tables

TABLE 100, continued

R7D/E_15. Pre-prints SUMMARY TABLE

		RESPONDENT TYPE				INSTITUTION TYPE			DISCIPLINE									GENDER	
	TOTAL SAMPLE	FACULTY MEMBER	GRAD. STUDENT	FACULTY /GRAD	UNDER GRAD. STUDENT	PUBLIC	PRIVATE	LIBERAL ARTS	BIOLOGIAL SCIENCES	PHYSICAL SCIENCES /MATH	SOCIAL SCIENCES	ARTS AND HUMAN.	ENGI-NEERING	BUSINESS	LAW	UNDEC. MAJOR	MALE	FEMALE
		(A)	(B)	(C)	(D)	(E)	(F)	(G)	(H)	(I)	(J)	(K)	(L)	(M)	(N)		(P)	(Q)
Base - Use Pre-prints for research	158	91*	67*	158	0**	65*	65*	29**	38*	57*	30**	11**	7**	15**	1**	0*	111	48*
Borrow from or use in other libraries (NET)	5 3.2%	4 4.6%	1 1.3%	5 3.2%	0 0	1 1.8%	2 2.9%	2 7.1%	1 2.3%	0 0	2 6.3%	1 10.0%	* 4.3%	1 6.2%	0 0	0 0	4 3.6%	1 2.4%
All sources of info	5 3.2%	4 4.6%	1 1.3%	5 3.2%	0 0	1 1.8%	2 2.9%	2 7.1%	1 2.3%	0 0	2 6.3%	1 10.0%	* 4.3%	1 6.2%	0 0	0 0	4 3.6%	1 2.4%
preferred source of info	3 2.1%	3 3.6%	0 0	3 2.1%	0 0	* 0.4%	2 2.9%	1 3.9%	0 0	0 0	2 6.3%	1 10.0%	* 4.3%	0 0	0 0	0 0	2 2.0%	1 2.4%
Faculty (NET)	4 2.4%	0 0	4 5.6%A	4 2.4%	0 0	4 5.8%	0 0	0 0	1 2.3%	1 1.8%	2 6.3%	0 0	0 0	0 0	0 0	0 0	4 3.4%	0 0
All sources of info	4 2.4%	0 0	4 5.6%A	4 2.4%	0 0	4 5.8%	0 0	0 0	1 2.3%	1 1.8%	2 6.3%	0 0	0 0	0 0	0 0	0 0	4 3.4%	0 0
preferred source of info	4 2.4%	0 0	4 5.6%A	4 2.4%	0 0	4 5.8%	0 0	0 0	1 2.3%	1 1.8%	2 6.3%	0 0	0 0	0 0	0 0	0 0	4 3.4%	0 0
Purchase from physical book store (NET)	2 1.2%	2 2.1%	0 0	2 1.2%	0 0	1 1.5%	1 1.4%	0 0	1 2.3%	1 1.8%	0 0	0 0	0 0	0 0	0 0	0 0	2 1.7%	0 0
All sources of info	2 1.2%	2 2.1%	0 0	2 1.2%	0 0	1 1.5%	1 1.4%	0 0	1 2.3%	1 1.8%	0 0	0 0	0 0	0 0	0 0	0 0	2 1.7%	0 0
preferred source of info	1 0.6%	1 1.0%	0 0	1 0.6%	0 0	0 0	1 1.4%	0 0	1 2.3%	0 0	0 0	0 0	0 0	0 0	0 0	0 0	1 0.8%	0 0

Proportions/Means: Columns Tested (5% risk level) - A/B/D - C/D - E/F/G - H/I/J/K/L/M/N - P/Q
* small base; ** very small base (under 30) ineligible for sig testing

Table 166
Page 608

Outsell/Digital Library Federation Study (2002)
Weighted Tables

TABLE 100, continued

R7D/E_15. Pre-prints SUMMARY TABLE

		RESPONDENT TYPE				INSTITUTION TYPE			DISCIPLINE									GENDER	
	TOTAL SAMPLE	FACULTY MEMBER	GRAD. STUDENT	FACULTY /GRAD	UNDER GRAD. STUDENT	PUBLIC	PRIVATE	LIBERAL ARTS	BIOLOGIAL SCIENCES	PHYSICAL SCIENCES /MATH	SOCIAL SCIENCES	ARTS AND HUMAN.	ENGI-NEERING	BUSINESS	LAW	UNDEC. MAJOR	MALE	FEMALE
		(A)	(B)	(C)	(D)	(E)	(F)	(G)	(H)	(I)	(J)	(K)	(L)	(M)	(N)		(P)	(Q)
Base - Use Pre-prints for research	158	91*	67*	158	0**	65*	65*	29**	38*	57*	30**	11**	7**	15**	1**	0*	111	48*
Printed material (NET)	1 0.7%	1 1.2%	0 0	1 0.7%	0 0	0 0	0 0	1 3.9%	0 0	0 0	0 0	1 10.0%	0 0	0 0	0 0	0 0	0 0	1 2.4%
All sources of info	1 0.7%	1 1.2%	0 0	1 0.7%	0 0	0 0	0 0	1 3.9%	0 0	0 0	0 0	1 10.0%	0 0	0 0	0 0	0 0	0 0	1 2.4%
preferred source of info	0 0	0 0	0 0	0 0	0 0	0 0	0 0	0 0	0 0	0 0	0 0	0 0	0 0	0 0	0 0	0 0	0 0	0 0
Purchase from online bookstore (NET)	1 0.6%	1 1.1%	0 0	1 0.6%	0 0	0 0	0 0	1 3.4%	0 0	1 1.8%	0 0	0 0	0 0	0 0	0 0	0 0	1 0.9%	0 0
All sources of info	1 0.6%	1 1.1%	0 0	1 0.6%	0 0	0 0	0 0	1 3.4%	0 0	1 1.8%	0 0	0 0	0 0	0 0	0 0	0 0	1 0.9%	0 0
preferred source of info	1 0.6%	1 1.1%	0 0	1 0.6%	0 0	0 0	0 0	1 3.4%	0 0	1 1.8%	0 0	0 0	0 0	0 0	0 0	0 0	1 0.9%	0 0
E-journals (NET)	1 0.6%	0 0	1 1.3%	1 0.6%	0 0	0 0	1 1.4%	0 0	1 2.3%	0 0	0 0	0 0	0 0	0 0	0 0	0 0	0 0	1 1.9%
All sources of info	1 0.6%	0 0	1 1.3%	1 0.6%	0 0	0 0	1 1.4%	0 0	1 2.3%	0 0	0 0	0 0	0 0	0 0	0 0	0 0	0 0	1 1.9%
preferred source of info	1 0.6%	0 0	1 1.3%	1 0.6%	0 0	0 0	1 1.4%	0 0	1 2.3%	0 0	0 0	0 0	0 0	0 0	0 0	0 0	0 0	1 1.9%
Meetings/conferences (NET)	1 0.5%	1 0.6%	* 0.4%	1 0.5%	0 0	1 0.9%	* 0.4%	0 0	0 0	0 0	0 0	0 0	1 13.0%	0 0	0 0	0 0	1 0.8%	0 0

Proportions/Means: Columns Tested (5% risk level) - A/B/D - C/D - E/F/G - H/I/J/K/L/M/N - P/Q
* small base; ** very small base (under 30) ineligible for sig testing

Table 166
Page 609

Outsell/Digital Library Federation Study (2002)
Weighted Tables

TABLE 100, continued

R7D/E_15. Pre-prints SUMMARY TABLE

	RESPONDENT TYPE				INSTITUTION TYPE			DISCIPLINE									GENDER	
	TOTAL SAMPLE	FACULTY MEMBER	GRAD. STUDENT	FACULTY /GRAD	UNDER GRAD. STUDENT	PUBLIC	PRIVATE	LIBERAL ARTS	BIOLOGIAL SCIENCES	PHYSICAL SCIENCES /MATH	SOCIAL SCIENCES	ARTS AND HUMAN.	ENGI-NEERING	BUSINESS	LAW	UNDEC. MAJOR	MALE	FEMALE
		(A)	(B)	(C)	(D)	(E)	(F)	(G)	(H)	(I)	(J)	(K)	(L)	(M)	(N)		(P)	(Q)
Base - Use Pre-prints for research	158	91*	67*	158	0**	65*	65*	29**	38*	57*	30**	11**	7**	15**	1**	0*	111	48*
All sources of info	1 0.5%	1 0.6%	* 0.4%	1 0.5%	0 0	1 0.9%	* 0.4%	0 0	0 0	0 0	0 0	0 0	1 13.0%	0 0	0 0	0 0	1 0.8%	0 0
preferred source of info	* 0.2%	* 0.3%	0 0	* 0.2%	0 0	* 0.4%	0 0	0 0	0 0	0 0	0 0	0 0	* 4.3%	0 0	0 0	0 0	* 0.3%	0 0
Personal holdings (NET)	1 0.4%	* 0.3%	* 0.4%	1 0.4%	0 0	* 0.4%	* 0.4%	0 0	0 0	0 0	0 0	0 0	1 8.7%	0 0	0 0	0 0	1 0.5%	0 0
All sources of info	1 0.4%	* 0.3%	* 0.4%	1 0.4%	0 0	* 0.4%	* 0.4%	0 0	0 0	0 0	0 0	0 0	1 8.7%	0 0	0 0	0 0	1 0.5%	0 0
preferred source of info	0 0	0 0	0 0	0 0	0 0	0 0	0 0	0 0	0 0	0 0	0 0	0 0	0 0	0 0	0 0	0 0	0 0	0 0
Access book/journal/ journal article elsewhere online (NET)	0 0	0 0	0 0	0 0	0 0	0 0	0 0	0 0	0 0	0 0	0 0	0 0	0 0	0 0	0 0	0 0	0 0	0 0
All sources of info	0 0	0 0	0 0	0 0	0 0	0 0	0 0	0 0	0 0	0 0	0 0	0 0	0 0	0 0	0 0	0 0	0 0	0 0
preferred source of info	0 0	0 0	0 0	0 0	0 0	0 0	0 0	0 0	0 0	0 0	0 0	0 0	0 0	0 0	0 0	0 0	0 0	0 0
Office (NET)	0 0	0 0	0 0	0 0	0 0	0 0	0 0	0 0	0 0	0 0	0 0	0 0	0 0	0 0	0 0	0 0	0 0	0 0

Proportions/Means: Columns Tested (5% risk level) - A/B/D - C/D - E/F/G - H/I/J/K/L/M/N - P/Q
* small base; ** very small base (under 30) ineligible for sig testing

Table 166
Page 610

Outsell/Digital Library Federation Study (2002)
Weighted Tables

TABLE 100, continued

R7D/E_15. Pre-prints SUMMARY TABLE

	RESPONDENT TYPE				INSTITUTION TYPE			DISCIPLINE								GENDER	
	TOTAL SAMPLE	FACULTY MEMBER	GRAD. STUDENT	FACULTY /GRAD	UNDER GRAD. STUDENT	PUBLIC	PRIVATE	LIBERAL ARTS	BIOLOGIAL SCIENCES	PHYSICAL SCIENCES /MATH	SOCIAL SCIENCES	ARTS AND HUMAN.	ENGI-NEERING	BUSINESS	LAW	UNDEC. MAJOR	MALE	FEMALE
		(A)	(B)	(C)	(D)	(E)	(F)	(G)	(H)	(I)	(J)	(K)	(L)	(M)	(N)		(P)	(Q)
Base - Use Pre-prints for research	158	91*	67*	158	0**	65*	65*	29**	38*	57*	30**	11**	7**	15**	1**	0*	111	48*
All sources of info	0 0	0 0	0 0	0 0	0 0	0 0	0 0	0 0	0 0	0 0	0 0	0 0	0 0	0 0	0 0	0 0	0 0	0 0
preferred source of info	0 0	0 0	0 0	0 0	0 0	0 0	0 0	0 0	0 0	0 0	0 0	0 0	0 0	0 0	0 0	0 0	0 0	0 0
Access from course website (NET)	0 0	0 0	0 0	0 0	0 0	0 0	0 0	0 0	0 0	0 0	0 0	0 0	0 0	0 0	0 0	0 0	0 0	0 0
All sources of info	0 0	0 0	0 0	0 0	0 0	0 0	0 0	0 0	0 0	0 0	0 0	0 0	0 0	0 0	0 0	0 0	0 0	0 0
preferred source of info	0 0	0 0	0 0	0 0	0 0	0 0	0 0	0 0	0 0	0 0	0 0	0 0	0 0	0 0	0 0	0 0	0 0	0 0
Ask library to purchase source (NET)	0 0	0 0	0 0	0 0	0 0	0 0	0 0	0 0	0 0	0 0	0 0	0 0	0 0	0 0	0 0	0 0	0 0	0 0
All sources of info	0 0	0 0	0 0	0 0	0 0	0 0	0 0	0 0	0 0	0 0	0 0	0 0	0 0	0 0	0 0	0 0	0 0	0 0
preferred source of info	0 0	0 0	0 0	0 0	0 0	0 0	0 0	0 0	0 0	0 0	0 0	0 0	0 0	0 0	0 0	0 0	0 0	0 0
Other (NET)	13 7.9%	11 11.6%	2 3.0%	13 7.9%	0 0	3 4.1%	7 11.1%	3 9.5%	4 11.6%	3 5.3%	2 6.3%	2 20.0%	1 13.0%	0 0	* 25.0%	0 0	8 7.1%	5 9.8%

Proportions/Means: Columns Tested (5% risk level) - A/B/D - C/D - E/F/G - H/I/J/K/L/M/N - P/Q
* small base; ** very small base (under 30) ineligible for sig testing

Table 166
Page 611

Outsell/Digital Library Federation Study (2002)
Weighted Tables

TABLE 100, continued

R7D/E_15. Pre-prints SUMMARY TABLE

		RESPONDENT TYPE				INSTITUTION TYPE			DISCIPLINE									GENDER	
	TOTAL SAMPLE	FACULTY MEMBER	GRAD. STUDENT	FACULTY /GRAD	UNDER GRAD. STUDENT	PUBLIC	PRIVATE	LIBERAL ARTS	BIOLOGIAL SCIENCES	PHYSICAL SCIENCES /MATH	SOCIAL SCIENCES	ARTS AND HUMAN.	ENGI- NEERING	BUSINESS	LAW	UNDEC. MAJOR	MALE	FEMALE
		(A)	(B)	(C)	(D)	(E)	(F)	(G)	(H)	(I)	(J)	(K)	(L)	(M)	(N)		(P)	(Q)
Base - Use Pre-prints for research	158	91*	67*	158	0**	65*	65*	29**	38*	57*	30**	11**	7**	15**	1**	0*	111	48*
All sources of info	10 6.5%	9 10.3%B	1 1.3%	10 6.5%	0 0	3 4.1%	5 7.5%	3 9.5%	4 9.3%	3 5.3%	2 6.3%	1 10.0%	1 8.7%	0 0	* 25.0%	0 0	7 6.1%	4 7.4%
preferred source of info	5 3.3%	4 4.6%	1 1.7%	5 3.3%	0 0	2 2.9%	3 5.3%	0 0	1 2.3%	0 0	2 6.3%	2 20.0%	* 4.3%	0 0	0 0	0 0	4 3.8%	1 2.4%
DK/Refused	5 3.2%	1 1.2%	4 5.9%	5 3.2%	0 0	3 4.6%	2 3.3%	0 0	1 2.3%	2 3.5%	0 0	2 20.0%	0 0	0 0	0 0	0 0	3 2.7%	2 4.5%

Proportions/Means: Columns Tested (5% risk level) - A/B/D - C/D - E/F/G - H/I/J/K/L/M/N - P/Q
* small base; ** very small base (under 30) ineligible for sig testing

Table 166
Page 612

Outsell/Digital Library Federation Study (2002)
Weighted Tables

TABLE 101

R7D/E_16. Dissertations SUMMARY TABLE

	RESPONDENT TYPE				INSTITUTION TYPE			DISCIPLINE								GENDER	
	TOTAL SAMPLE	FACULTY MEMBER	GRAD. STUDENT	FACULTY /GRAD	UNDER GRAD. STUDENT	PUBLIC	PRIVATE	LIBERAL ARTS	BIOLOGIAL SCIENCES	PHYSICAL SCIENCES /MATH	SOCIAL SCIENCES	ARTS AND HUMAN.	ENGI-NEERING	BUSINESS	LAW	UNDEC. MAJOR	MALE	FEMALE
		(A)	(B)	(C)	(D)	(E)	(F)	(G)	(H)	(I)	(J)	(K)	(L)	(M)	(N)		(P)	(Q)
Base - Use Dissertations for research	290	140	150	290	0**	133	121*	37*	36*	68*	100*	49*	15*	20**	2**	0*	193	97*
Borrow from or use in campus library (NET)	164 56.4%	63 45.2%	101 66.9%A	164 56.4%	0 0	86 65.1%G	63 51.8%	15 39.9%	22 61.0%	32 47.1%	60 60.4%	28 56.8%	8 56.9%	12 59.1%	1 54.5%	0 0	101 52.3%	63 64.6%
All sources of info	164 56.4%	63 45.2%	101 66.9%A	164 56.4%	0 0	86 65.1%G	63 51.8%	15 39.9%	22 61.0%	32 47.1%	60 60.4%	28 56.8%	8 56.9%	12 59.1%	1 54.5%	0 0	101 52.3%	63 64.6%
preferred source of info	113 38.8%	40 28.6%	73 48.3%A	113 38.8%	0 0	60 45.2%G	44 36.0%	9 24.4%	9 24.4%	20 29.4%	47 47.2%H	21 43.2%	6 43.1%	8 40.9%	1 36.4%	0 0	68 35.2%	45 45.9%
Access online (NET)	90 30.9%	40 28.5%	50 33.1%	90 30.9%	0 0	43 32.5%	35 29.0%	11 31.3%	16 43.9%K	20 29.4%	28 28.3%	11 22.7%	4 29.4%	9 45.5%	1 36.4%	0 0	59 30.4%	31 31.8%
All sources of info	90 30.9%	40 28.5%	50 33.1%	90 30.9%	0 0	43 32.5%	35 29.0%	11 31.3%	16 43.9%K	20 29.4%	28 28.3%	11 22.7%	4 29.4%	9 45.5%	1 36.4%	0 0	59 30.4%	31 31.8%
preferred source of info	74 25.6%	36 25.6%	39 25.6%	74 25.6%	0 0	34 25.8%	30 24.5%	11 28.9%	14 39.0%	16 23.5%	23 22.6%	10 20.5%	3 23.5%	7 36.4%	1 36.4%	0 0	50 25.9%	24 25.0%
Interlibrary loan (NET)	75 25.8%	49 34.9%B	26 17.3%	75 25.8%	0 0	29 21.6%	33 27.1%	13 36.2%	10 26.8%	15 22.1%	23 22.6%	21 43.2%IJ L	3 19.6%	3 13.6%	1 27.3%	0 0	52 27.0%	23 23.3%
All sources of info	75 25.8%	49 34.9%B	26 17.3%	75 25.8%	0 0	29 21.6%	33 27.1%	13 36.2%	10 26.8%	15 22.1%	23 22.6%	21 43.2%IJ L	3 19.6%	3 13.6%	1 27.3%	0 0	52 27.0%	23 23.3%

Proportions/Means: Columns Tested (5% risk level) - A/B/D - C/D - E/F/G - H/I/J/K/L/M/N - P/Q
* small base; ** very small base (under 30) ineligible for sig testing

Table 173
Page 641

Outsell/Digital Library Federation Study (2002)
Weighted Tables

TABLE 101, continued

R7D/E_16. Dissertations SUMMARY TABLE

		RESPONDENT TYPE				INSTITUTION TYPE			DISCIPLINE									GENDER	
	TOTAL SAMPLE	FACULTY MEMBER	GRAD. STUDENT	FACULTY /GRAD	UNDER GRAD. STUDENT	PUBLIC	PRIVATE	LIBERAL ARTS	BIOLOGIAL SCIENCES	PHYSICAL SCIENCES /MATH	SOCIAL SCIENCES	ARTS AND HUMAN.	ENGI-NEERING	BUSINESS	LAW	UNDEC. MAJOR	MALE	FEMALE
		(A)	(B)	(C)	(D)	(E)	(F)	(G)	(H)	(I)	(J)	(K)	(L)	(M)	(N)		(P)	(Q)
Base - Use Dissertations for research	290	140	150	290	0**	133	121*	37*	36*	68*	100*	49*	15*	20**	2**	0*	193	97*
preferred source of info	48 16.7%	39 27.6%B	10 6.5%	48 16.7%	0 0	14 10.6%	23 19.1%	11 30.7%E	5 14.6%	12 17.6%L	15 15.1%	13 27.3%L	1 3.9%	2 9.1%	* 9.1%	0 0	36 18.6%	12 12.8%
Borrow from or use in other libraries (NET)	18 6.2%	8 5.8%	10 6.6%	18 6.2%	0 0	7 5.3%	8 6.8%	3 7.5%	2 4.9%	3 4.4%	8 7.5%	4 9.1%	1 7.8%	0 0	* 9.1%	0 0	10 5.2%	8 8.3%
All sources of info	18 6.2%	8 5.8%	10 6.6%	18 6.2%	0 0	7 5.3%	8 6.8%	3 7.5%	2 4.9%	3 4.4%	8 7.5%	4 9.1%	1 7.8%	0 0	* 9.1%	0 0	10 5.2%	8 8.3%
preferred source of info	9 3.0%	2 1.6%	7 4.4%	9 3.0%	0 0	5 3.7%	4 3.2%	0 0	0 0	1 1.5%	6 5.7%	1 2.3%	1 5.9%H	0 0	* 9.1%	0 0	5 2.5%	4 4.0%
Order from on demand document delivery service (NET)	10 3.4%	9 6.8%B	* 0.2%	10 3.4%	0 0	2 1.7%	3 2.9%	4 10.9%E	1 2.4%	2 2.9%	4 3.8%	2 4.5%	1 5.9%	0 0	0 0	0 0	9 4.6%	1 0.9%
All sources of info	10 3.4%	9 6.8%B	* 0.2%	10 3.4%	0 0	2 1.7%	3 2.9%	4 10.9%E	1 2.4%	2 2.9%	4 3.8%	2 4.5%	1 5.9%	0 0	0 0	0 0	9 4.6%	1 0.9%
preferred source of info	6 2.1%	6 4.3%B	0 0	6 2.1%	0 0	2 1.5%	2 1.8%	2 5.1%	1 2.4%	0 0	4 3.8%	1 2.3%	* 2.0%	0 0	0 0	0 0	5 2.7%	1 0.9%
Colleague (NET)	8 2.8%	4 2.9%	4 2.7%	8 2.8%	0 0	3 2.4%	4 3.4%	1 2.5%	1 2.4%	4 5.9%J	0 0	2 4.5%	0 0	1 4.5%	* 9.1%	0 0	6 3.2%	2 2.1%

Proportions/Means: Columns Tested (5% risk level) - A/B/D - C/D - E/F/G - H/I/J/K/L/M/N - P/Q
* small base; ** very small base (under 30) ineligible for sig testing

Table 173
Page 642

Outsell/Digital Library Federation Study (2002)
Weighted Tables

TABLE 101, continued

R7D/E_16. Dissertations SUMMARY TABLE

		RESPONDENT TYPE				INSTITUTION TYPE			DISCIPLINE									GENDER	
	TOTAL SAMPLE	FACULTY MEMBER	GRAD. STUDENT	FACULTY /GRAD	UNDER GRAD. STUDENT	PUBLIC	PRIVATE	LIBERAL ARTS	BIOLOGIAL SCIENCES	PHYSICAL SCIENCES /MATH	SOCIAL SCIENCES	ARTS AND HUMAN.	ENGI- NEERING	BUSINESS	LAW	UNDEC. MAJOR	MALE	FEMALE
		(A)	(B)	(C)	(D)	(E)	(F)	(G)	(H)	(I)	(J)	(K)	(L)	(M)	(N)		(P)	(Q)
Base - Use Dissertations for research	290	140	150	290	0**	133	121*	37*	36*	68*	100*	49*	15*	20**	2**	0*	193	97*
All sources of info	8 2.8%	4 2.9%	4 2.7%	8 2.8%	0 0	3 2.4%	4 3.4%	1 2.5%	1 2.4%	4 5.9%J	0 0	2 4.5%	0 0	1 4.5%	* 9.1%	0 0	6 3.2%	2 2.1%
preferred source of info	7 2.4%	4 2.8%	3 2.0%	7 2.4%	0 0	3 2.3%	3 2.5%	1 2.5%	1 2.4%	4 5.9%J	0 0	1 2.3%	0 0	1 4.5%	0 0	0 0	5 2.6%	2 2.1%
Sources (NET)	7 2.3%	6 4.0%	1 0.7%	7 2.3%	0 0	4 3.0%	2 1.8%	* 0.8%	1 2.4%	2 2.9%	0 0	0 0	1 5.9%JK	3 13.6%	0 0	0 0	7 3.4%	0 0
All sources of info	7 2.3%	6 4.0%	1 0.7%	7 2.3%	0 0	4 3.0%	2 1.8%	* 0.8%	1 2.4%	2 2.9%	0 0	0 0	1 5.9%JK	3 13.6%	0 0	0 0	7 3.4%	0 0
preferred source of info	5 1.8%	4 3.1%	1 0.7%	5 1.8%	0 0	3 2.3%	2 1.6%	* 0.8%	1 2.4%	2 2.9%	0 0	0 0	1 3.9%JK	2 9.1%	0 0	0 0	5 2.8%	0 0
Purchase from physical book store (NET)	2 0.8%	1 1.0%	1 0.6%	2 0.8%	0 0	2 1.5%	* 0.2%	0 0	1 2.4%	0 0	0 0	1 2.3%	* 2.0%	0 0	0 0	0 0	2 1.2%	0 0
All sources of info	2 0.8%	1 1.0%	1 0.6%	2 0.8%	0 0	2 1.5%	* 0.2%	0 0	1 2.4%	0 0	0 0	1 2.3%	* 2.0%	0 0	0 0	0 0	2 1.2%	0 0
preferred source of info	0 0	0 0	0 0	0 0	0 0	0 0	0 0	0 0	0 0	0 0	0 0	0 0	0 0	0 0	0 0	0 0	0 0	0 0
Faculty (NET)	2 0.8%	* 0.2%	2 1.3%	2 0.8%	0 0	2 1.7%	0 0	0 0	0 0	2 2.9%	0 0	0 0	* 2.0%	0 0	0 0	0 0	2 1.2%	0 0

Proportions/Means: Columns Tested (5% risk level) - A/B/D - C/D - E/F/G - H/I/J/K/L/M/N - P/Q
* small base; ** very small base (under 30) ineligible for sig testing

Table 173
Page 643

Outsell/Digital Library Federation Study (2002)
Weighted Tables

TABLE 101, continued

R7D/E_16. Dissertations SUMMARY TABLE

		RESPONDENT TYPE				INSTITUTION TYPE			DISCIPLINE									GENDER	
	TOTAL SAMPLE	FACULTY MEMBER	GRAD. STUDENT	FACULTY /GRAD	UNDER GRAD. STUDENT	PUBLIC	PRIVATE	LIBERAL ARTS	BIOLOGIAL SCIENCES	PHYSICAL SCIENCES /MATH	SOCIAL SCIENCES	ARTS AND HUMAN.	ENGI-NEERING	BUSINESS	LAW	UNDEC. MAJOR	MALE	FEMALE
		(A)	(B)	(C)	(D)	(E)	(F)	(G)	(H)	(I)	(J)	(K)	(L)	(M)	(N)		(P)	(Q)
Base - Use Dissertations for research	290	140	150	290	0**	133	121*	37*	36*	68*	100*	49*	15*	20**	2**	0*	193	97*
All sources of info	2 0.8%	* 0.2%	2 1.3%	2 0.8%	0 0	2 1.7%	0 0	0 0	0 0	2 2.9%	0 0	0 0	* 2.0%	0 0	0 0	0 0	2 1.2%	0 0
preferred source of info	2 0.7%	0 0	2 1.3%	2 0.7%	0 0	2 1.5%	0 0	0 0	0 0	2 2.9%	0 0	0 0	0 0	0 0	0 0	0 0	2 1.0%	0 0
Ask library to purchase source (NET)	2 0.6%	0 0	2 1.3%	2 0.6%	0 0	2 1.4%	0 0	0 0	0 0	0 0	2 1.9%	0 0	0 0	0 0	0 0	0 0	2 1.0%	0 0
All sources of info	2 0.6%	0 0	2 1.3%	2 0.6%	0 0	2 1.4%	0 0	0 0	0 0	0 0	2 1.9%	0 0	0 0	0 0	0 0	0 0	2 1.0%	0 0
preferred source of info	2 0.6%	0 0	2 1.3%	2 0.6%	0 0	2 1.4%	0 0	0 0	0 0	0 0	2 1.9%	0 0	0 0	0 0	0 0	0 0	2 1.0%	0 0
Office (NET)	1 0.4%	0 0	1 0.7%	1 0.4%	0 0	0 0	1 0.9%	0 0	0 0	0 0	0 0	0 0	1 5.9%HIJK	0 0	* 9.1%	0 0	* 0.2%	1 0.6%
All sources of info	1 0.4%	0 0	1 0.7%	1 0.4%	0 0	0 0	1 0.9%	0 0	0 0	0 0	0 0	0 0	1 5.9%HIJK	0 0	* 9.1%	0 0	* 0.2%	1 0.6%
preferred source of info	1 0.4%	0 0	1 0.7%	1 0.4%	0 0	0 0	1 0.9%	0 0	0 0	0 0	0 0	0 0	1 5.9%HIJK	0 0	* 9.1%	0 0	* 0.2%	1 0.6%
Personal holdings (NET)	1 0.3%	1 0.6%	0 0	1 0.3%	0 0	0 0	0 0	1 2.4%	1 2.4%	0 0	0 0	0 0	0 0	0 0	0 0	0 0	1 0.5%	0 0

Proportions/Means: Columns Tested (5% risk level) - A/B/D - C/D - E/F/G - H/I/J/K/L/M/N - P/Q
* small base; ** very small base (under 30) ineligible for sig testing

Table 173
Page 644

Outsell/Digital Library Federation Study (2002)
Weighted Tables

TABLE 101, continued

R7D/E_16. Dissertations SUMMARY TABLE

		RESPONDENT TYPE				INSTITUTION TYPE			DISCIPLINE								GENDER	
	TOTAL SAMPLE	FACULTY MEMBER	GRAD. STUDENT	FACULTY /GRAD	UNDER GRAD. STUDENT	PUBLIC	PRIVATE	LIBERAL ARTS	BIOLOGIAL SCIENCES	PHYSICAL SCIENCES /MATH	SOCIAL SCIENCES	ARTS AND HUMAN.	ENGI- NEERING	BUSINESS	LAW	UNDEC. MAJOR	MALE	FEMALE
		(A)	(B)	(C)	(D)	(E)	(F)	(G)	(H)	(I)	(J)	(K)	(L)	(M)	(N)		(P)	(Q)
Base - Use Dissertations for research	290	140	150	290	0**	133	121*	37*	36*	68*	100*	49*	15*	20**	2**	0*	193	97*
All sources of info	1 0.3%	1 0.6%	0 0	1 0.3%	0 0	0 0	0 0	1 2.4%	1 2.4%	0 0	0 0	0 0	0 0	0 0	0 0	0 0	1 0.5%	0 0
preferred source of info	0 0	0 0	0 0	0 0	0 0	0 0	0 0	0 0	0 0	0 0	0 0	0 0	0 0	0 0	0 0	0 0	0 0	0 0
Purchase from online bookstore (NET)	* 0.1%	* 0.2%	0 0	* 0.1%	0 0	0 0	* 0.2%	0 0	0 0	0 0	0 0	0 0	* 2.0%	0 0	0 0	0 0	* 0.2%	0 0
All sources of info	* 0.1%	* 0.2%	0 0	* 0.1%	0 0	0 0	* 0.2%	0 0	0 0	0 0	0 0	0 0	* 2.0%	0 0	0 0	0 0	* 0.2%	0 0
preferred source of info	* 0.1%	* 0.2%	0 0	* 0.1%	0 0	0 0	* 0.2%	0 0	0 0	0 0	0 0	0 0	* 2.0%	0 0	0 0	0 0	* 0.2%	0 0
Printed material (NET)	* 0.1%	0 0	* 0.1%	* 0.1%	0 0	0 0	* 0.1%	0 0	0 0	0 0	0 0	0 0	0 0	0 0	* 9.1%	0 0	* 0.1%	0 0
All sources of info	* 0.1%	0 0	* 0.1%	* 0.1%	0 0	0 0	* 0.1%	0 0	0 0	0 0	0 0	0 0	0 0	0 0	* 9.1%	0 0	* 0.1%	0 0
preferred source of info	0 0	0 0	0 0	0 0	0 0	0 0	0 0	0 0	0 0	0 0	0 0	0 0	0 0	0 0	0 0	0 0	0 0	0 0
E-journals (NET)	0 0	0 0	0 0	0 0	0 0	0 0	0 0	0 0	0 0	0 0	0 0	0 0	0 0	0 0	0 0	0 0	0 0	0 0

Proportions/Means: Columns Tested (5% risk level) - A/B/D - C/D - E/F/G - H/I/J/K/L/M/N - P/Q
* small base; ** very small base (under 30) ineligible for sig testing

Table 173
Page 645

Outsell/Digital Library Federation Study (2002)
Weighted Tables

TABLE 101, continued

R7D/E_16. Dissertations SUMMARY TABLE

		RESPONDENT TYPE				INSTITUTION TYPE			DISCIPLINE								GENDER	
	TOTAL SAMPLE	FACULTY MEMBER	GRAD. STUDENT	FACULTY /GRAD	UNDER GRAD. STUDENT	PUBLIC	PRIVATE	LIBERAL ARTS	BIOLOGIAL SCIENCES	PHYSICAL SCIENCES /MATH	SOCIAL SCIENCES	ARTS AND HUMAN.	ENGI-NEERING	BUSINESS	LAW	UNDEC. MAJOR	MALE	FEMALE
		(A)	(B)	(C)	(D)	(E)	(F)	(G)	(H)	(I)	(J)	(K)	(L)	(M)	(N)		(P)	(Q)
Base - Use Dissertations for research	290	140	150	290	0**	133	121*	37*	36*	68*	100*	49*	15*	20**	2**	0*	193	97*
All sources of info	0 0	0 0	0 0	0 0	0 0	0 0	0 0	0 0	0 0	0 0	0 0	0 0	0 0	0 0	0 0	0 0	0 0	0 0
preferred source of info	0 0	0 0	0 0	0 0	0 0	0 0	0 0	0 0	0 0	0 0	0 0	0 0	0 0	0 0	0 0	0 0	0 0	0 0
Access book/journal/ journal article elsewhere online (NET)	0 0	0 0	0 0	0 0	0 0	0 0	0 0	0 0	0 0	0 0	0 0	0 0	0 0	0 0	0 0	0 0	0 0	0 0
All sources of info	0 0	0 0	0 0	0 0	0 0	0 0	0 0	0 0	0 0	0 0	0 0	0 0	0 0	0 0	0 0	0 0	0 0	0 0
preferred source of info	0 0	0 0	0 0	0 0	0 0	0 0	0 0	0 0	0 0	0 0	0 0	0 0	0 0	0 0	0 0	0 0	0 0	0 0
Meetings/conferences (NET)	0 0	0 0	0 0	0 0	0 0	0 0	0 0	0 0	0 0	0 0	0 0	0 0	0 0	0 0	0 0	0 0	0 0	0 0
All sources of info	0 0	0 0	0 0	0 0	0 0	0 0	0 0	0 0	0 0	0 0	0 0	0 0	0 0	0 0	0 0	0 0	0 0	0 0
preferred source of info	0 0	0 0	0 0	0 0	0 0	0 0	0 0	0 0	0 0	0 0	0 0	0 0	0 0	0 0	0 0	0 0	0 0	0 0
Access from course website (NET)	0 0	0 0	0 0	0 0	0 0	0 0	0 0	0 0	0 0	0 0	0 0	0 0	0 0	0 0	0 0	0 0	0 0	0 0

Proportions/Means: Columns Tested (5% risk level) - A/B/D - C/D - E/F/G - H/I/J/K/L/M/N - P/Q
* small base; ** very small base (under 30) ineligible for sig testing

Table 173
Page 646

Outsell/Digital Library Federation Study (2002)
Weighted Tables

TABLE 101, continued

R7D/E_16. Dissertations SUMMARY TABLE

	RESPONDENT TYPE					INSTITUTION TYPE			DISCIPLINE									GENDER	
	TOTAL SAMPLE	FACULTY MEMBER	GRAD. STUDENT	FACULTY /GRAD	UNDER GRAD. STUDENT	PUBLIC	PRIVATE	LIBERAL ARTS	BIOLOGIAL SCIENCES	PHYSICAL SCIENCES /MATH	SOCIAL SCIENCES	ARTS AND HUMAN.	ENGI-NEERING	BUSINESS	LAW	UNDEC. MAJOR	MALE	FEMALE
		(A)	(B)	(C)	(D)	(E)	(F)	(G)	(H)	(I)	(J)	(K)	(L)	(M)	(N)		(P)	(Q)
Base - Use Dissertations for research	290	140	150	290	0**	133	121*	37*	36*	68*	100*	49*	15*	20**	2**	0*	193	97*
All sources of info	0	0	0	0	0	0	0	0	0	0	0	0	0	0	0	0	0	0
	0	0	0	0	0	0	0	0	0	0	0	0	0	0	0	0	0	0
preferred source of info	0	0	0	0	0	0	0	0	0	0	0	0	0	0	0	0	0	0
	0	0	0	0	0	0	0	0	0	0	0	0	0	0	0	0	0	0
Other (NET)	34	19	15	34	0	8	20	6	4	13	9	6	2	0	0	0	23	12
	11.9%	13.6%	10.3%	11.9%	0	6.2%	16.8%E	16.1%	12.2%	19.1%	9.4%	11.4%	13.7%	0	0	0	11.8%	12.0%
All sources of info	32	17	14	32	0	8	18	5	4	11	9	6	2	0	0	0	20	12
	10.9%	12.2%	9.6%	10.9%	0	6.2%	15.2%E	13.7%	9.8%	16.2%	9.4%	11.4%	13.7%	0	0	0	10.3%	12.0%
preferred source of info	17	8	10	17	0	5	9	3	4	8	4	0	1	0	0	0	10	7
	6.0%	5.4%	6.5%	6.0%	0	3.9%	7.7%	7.5%	12.2%K	11.8%K	3.8%	0	7.8%K	0	0	0	5.1%	7.6%
DK/Refused	5	1	4	5	0	2	3	0	1	3	0	1	*	0	0	0	4	1
	1.8%	0.8%	2.7%	1.8%	0	1.7%	2.5%	0	2.4%	4.4%	0	2.3%	2.0%	0	0	0	2.2%	1.0%

Proportions/Means: Columns Tested (5% risk level) - A/B/D - C/D - E/F/G - H/I/J/K/L/M/N - P/Q
* small base; ** very small base (under 30) ineligible for sig testing

Table 173
Page 647

TABLE 102

R7D/E_17. News SUMMARY TABLE

		RESPONDENT TYPE				INSTITUTION TYPE			DISCIPLINE									GENDER	
	TOTAL SAMPLE	FACULTY MEMBER	GRAD. STUDENT	FACULTY /GRAD	UNDER GRAD. STUDENT	PUBLIC	PRIVATE	LIBERAL ARTS	BIOLOGIAL SCIENCES	PHYSICAL SCIENCES /MATH	SOCIAL SCIENCES	ARTS AND HUMAN.	ENGI-NEERING	BUSINESS	LAW	UNDEC. MAJOR		MALE	FEMALE
		(A)	(B)	(C)	(D)	(E)	(F)	(G)	(H)	(I)	(J)	(K)	(L)	(M)	(N)			(P)	(Q)
Base - Use News for research	207	116*	90*	207	0**	91*	62*	54*	26**	24**	77*	41*	9**	24**	5**	0*		147	60*
Access online (NET)	153 74.2%	91 78.1%	62 69.1%	153 74.2%	0 0	66 73.3%	46 75.0%	41 74.7%	22 83.3%	16 66.7%	58 75.6%	26 62.2%	7 80.0%	20 84.6%	4 78.6%	0 0		111 75.8%	42 70.2%
All sources of info	153 74.2%	91 78.1%	62 69.1%	153 74.2%	0 0	66 73.3%	46 75.0%	41 74.7%	22 83.3%	16 66.7%	58 75.6%	26 62.2%	7 80.0%	20 84.6%	4 78.6%	0 0		111 75.8%	42 70.2%
preferred source of info	118 57.2%	62 52.9%	57 62.8%	118 57.2%	0 0	56 62.2%	33 53.8%	29 52.8%	20 76.7%	10 41.7%	47 61.0%	17 40.5%	6 70.0%	15 61.5%	3 67.9%	0 0		84 56.9%	35 58.0%
Borrow from or use in campus library (NET)	102 49.2%	57 49.0%	45 49.5%	102 49.2%	0 0	46 51.1%	33 53.1%	23 41.6%	11 43.3%	17 70.8%	36 46.3%	25 59.5%	3 36.7%	7 30.8%	2 46.4%	0 0		69 47.1%	32 54.3%
All sources of info	102 49.2%	57 49.0%	45 49.5%	102 49.2%	0 0	46 51.1%	33 53.1%	23 41.6%	11 43.3%	17 70.8%	36 46.3%	25 59.5%	3 36.7%	7 30.8%	2 46.4%	0 0		69 47.1%	32 54.3%
preferred source of info	49 23.7%	22 19.3%	27 29.4%	49 23.7%	0 0	22 24.5%	18 29.2%	9 16.2%	3 10.0%	6 25.0%	21 26.8%	16 37.8%	1 16.7%	2 7.7%	1 14.3%	0 0		34 23.1%	15 25.2%
Personal holdings (NET)	15 7.1%	13 11.5%B	1 1.4%	15 7.1%	0 0	3 3.0%	5 8.4%	7 12.4%	2 6.7%	4 16.7%	4 4.9%	1 2.7%	* 3.3%	4 15.4%	0 0	0 0		14 9.3%	1 1.7%
All sources of info	15 7.1%	13 11.5%B	1 1.4%	15 7.1%	0 0	3 3.0%	5 8.4%	7 12.4%	2 6.7%	4 16.7%	4 4.9%	1 2.7%	* 3.3%	4 15.4%	0 0	0 0		14 9.3%	1 1.7%
preferred source of info	10 4.8%	9 7.5%	1 1.4%	10 4.8%	0 0	2 2.0%	2 3.9%	6 10.6%	1 3.3%	3 12.5%	2 2.4%	1 2.7%	* 3.3%	3 11.5%	0 0	0 0		9 6.1%	1 1.7%

Proportions/Means: Columns Tested (5% risk level) - A/B/D - C/D - E/F/G - H/I/J/K/L/M/N - P/Q
* small base; ** very small base (under 30) ineligible for sig testing

Table 180
Page 676

Outsell/Digital Library Federation Study (2002)
Weighted Tables

TABLE 102, continued

R7D/E_17. News SUMMARY TABLE

		RESPONDENT TYPE				INSTITUTION TYPE			DISCIPLINE									GENDER	
	TOTAL SAMPLE	FACULTY MEMBER	GRAD. STUDENT	FACULTY /GRAD	UNDER GRAD. STUDENT	PUBLIC	PRIVATE	LIBERAL ARTS	BIOLOGIAL SCIENCES	PHYSICAL SCIENCES /MATH	SOCIAL SCIENCES	ARTS AND HUMAN.	ENGI-NEERING	BUSINESS	LAW	UNDEC. MAJOR	MALE	FEMALE
		(A)	(B)	(C)	(D)	(E)	(F)	(G)	(H)	(I)	(J)	(K)	(L)	(M)	(N)		(P)	(Q)
Base - Use News for research	207	116*	90*	207	0**	91*	62*	54*	26**	24**	77*	41*	9**	24**	5**	0*	147	60*
Borrow from or use in other libraries (NET)	10 5.1%	6 5.3%	4 4.7%	10 5.1%	0 0	2 2.4%	4 7.2%	4 6.9%	0 0	1 4.2%	6 7.3%	2 5.4%	* 3.3%	1 3.8%	* 7.1%	0 0	10 7.0%	* 0.3%
All sources of info	10 5.1%	6 5.3%	4 4.7%	10 5.1%	0 0	2 2.4%	4 7.2%	4 6.9%	0 0	1 4.2%	6 7.3%	2 5.4%	* 3.3%	1 3.8%	* 7.1%	0 0	10 7.0%	* 0.3%
preferred source of info	3 1.5%	1 1.0%	2 2.1%	3 1.5%	0 0	2 2.1%	1 1.8%	0 0	0 0	0 0	2 2.4%	1 2.7%	0 0	0 0	0 0	0 0	3 2.0%	0 0
Printed material (NET)	10 4.9%	9 7.6%	1 1.4%	10 4.9%	0 0	4 4.3%	2 3.8%	4 7.0%	0 0	1 4.2%	4 4.9%	2 5.4%	* 3.3%	3 11.5%	0 0	0 0	10 6.9%	0 0
All sources of info	10 4.9%	9 7.6%	1 1.4%	10 4.9%	0 0	4 4.3%	2 3.8%	4 7.0%	0 0	1 4.2%	4 4.9%	2 5.4%	* 3.3%	3 11.5%	0 0	0 0	10 6.9%	0 0
preferred source of info	4 1.9%	4 3.4%	0 0	4 1.9%	0 0	2 2.1%	1 1.8%	1 1.7%	0 0	0 0	2 2.4%	1 2.7%	0 0	1 3.8%	0 0	0 0	4 2.7%	0 0
Interlibrary loan (NET)	5 2.6%	4 3.7%	1 1.2%	5 2.6%	0 0	2 2.7%	1 1.8%	2 3.4%	1 3.3%	0 0	0 0	2 5.4%	* 3.3%	2 7.7%	* 3.6%	0 0	4 2.4%	2 3.1%
All sources of info	5 2.6%	4 3.7%	1 1.2%	5 2.6%	0 0	2 2.7%	1 1.8%	2 3.4%	1 3.3%	0 0	0 0	2 5.4%	* 3.3%	2 7.7%	* 3.6%	0 0	4 2.4%	2 3.1%
preferred source of info	0 0	0 0	0 0	0 0	0 0	0 0	0 0	0 0	0 0	0 0	0 0	0 0	0 0	0 0	0 0	0 0	0 0	0 0

Proportions/Means: Columns Tested (5% risk level) - A/B/D - C/D - E/F/G - H/I/J/K/L/M/N - P/Q
* small base; ** very small base (under 30) ineligible for sig testing

Table 180
Page 677

Outsell/Digital Library Federation Study (2002)
Weighted Tables

TABLE 102, continued

R7D/E_17. News SUMMARY TABLE

		RESPONDENT TYPE				INSTITUTION TYPE			DISCIPLINE								GENDER	
	TOTAL SAMPLE	FACULTY MEMBER	GRAD. STUDENT	FACULTY /GRAD	UNDER GRAD. STUDENT	PUBLIC	PRIVATE	LIBERAL ARTS	BIOLOGIAL SCIENCES	PHYSICAL SCIENCES /MATH	SOCIAL SCIENCES	ARTS AND HUMAN.	ENGI-NEERING	BUSINESS	LAW	UNDEC. MAJOR	MALE	FEMALE
		(A)	(B)	(C)	(D)	(E)	(F)	(G)	(H)	(I)	(J)	(K)	(L)	(M)	(N)		(P)	(Q)
Base - Use News for research	207	116*	90*	207	0**	91*	62*	54*	26**	24**	77*	41*	9**	24**	5**	0*	147	60*
Order from on demand document delivery service (NET)	4	4	0	4	0	2	0	2	0	1	2	1	0	0	*	0	3	1
	2.0%	3.6%	0	2.0%	0	2.3%	0	3.9%	0	4.2%	2.4%	2.7%	0	0	3.6%	0	2.2%	1.7%
All sources of info	4	4	0	4	0	2	0	2	0	1	2	1	0	0	*	0	3	1
	2.0%	3.6%	0	2.0%	0	2.3%	0	3.9%	0	4.2%	2.4%	2.7%	0	0	3.6%	0	2.2%	1.7%
preferred source of info	2	2	0	2	0	0	0	2	0	1	0	1	0	0	0	0	1	1
	1.0%	1.8%	0	1.0%	0	0	0	3.9%	0	4.2%	0	2.7%	0	0	0	0	0.8%	1.7%
Colleague (NET)	3	3	0	3	0	1	1	1	0	1	0	1	*	1	0	0	2	1
	1.6%	2.9%	0	1.6%	0	1.6%	1.5%	1.8%	0	4.2%	0	2.7%	3.3%	3.8%	0	0	1.5%	1.9%
All sources of info	3	3	0	3	0	1	1	1	0	1	0	1	*	1	0	0	2	1
	1.6%	2.9%	0	1.6%	0	1.6%	1.5%	1.8%	0	4.2%	0	2.7%	3.3%	3.8%	0	0	1.5%	1.9%
preferred source of info	3	3	0	3	0	1	1	1	0	1	0	1	0	1	0	0	2	1
	1.5%	2.6%	0	1.5%	0	1.2%	1.5%	1.8%	0	4.2%	0	2.7%	0	3.8%	0	0	1.3%	1.9%
Purchase from physical book store (NET)	3	3	0	3	0	1	1	1	0	1	0	2	0	0	0	0	3	0
	1.6%	2.8%	0	1.6%	0	1.2%	1.6%	2.1%	0	4.2%	0	5.4%	0	0	0	0	2.2%	0
All sources of info	3	3	0	3	0	1	1	1	0	1	0	2	0	0	0	0	3	0
	1.6%	2.8%	0	1.6%	0	1.2%	1.6%	2.1%	0	4.2%	0	5.4%	0	0	0	0	2.2%	0
preferred source of info	3	3	0	3	0	1	1	1	0	1	0	2	0	0	0	0	3	0
	1.6%	2.8%	0	1.6%	0	1.2%	1.6%	2.1%	0	4.2%	0	5.4%	0	0	0	0	2.2%	0

Proportions/Means: Columns Tested (5% risk level) - A/B/D - C/D - E/F/G - H/I/J/K/L/M/N - P/Q
* small base; ** very small base (under 30) ineligible for sig testing

Table 180
Page 678

Outsell/Digital Library Federation Study (2002)
Weighted Tables

TABLE 102, continued

R7D/E_17. News SUMMARY TABLE

	RESPONDENT TYPE					INSTITUTION TYPE			DISCIPLINE									GENDER	
	TOTAL SAMPLE	FACULTY MEMBER	GRAD. STUDENT	FACULTY /GRAD	UNDER GRAD. STUDENT	PUBLIC	PRIVATE	LIBERAL ARTS	BIOLOGIAL SCIENCES	PHYSICAL SCIENCES /MATH	SOCIAL SCIENCES	ARTS AND HUMAN.	ENGI- NEERING	BUSINESS	LAW	UNDEC. MAJOR	MALE	FEMALE
		(A)	(B)	(C)	(D)	(E)	(F)	(G)	(H)	(I)	(J)	(K)	(L)	(M)	(N)		(P)	(Q)
Base - Use News for research	207	116*	90*	207	0**	91*	62*	54*	26**	24**	77*	41*	9**	24**	5**	0*	147	60*
Meetings/conferences (NET)	2 0.9%	2 1.6%	0 0	2 0.9%	0 0	0 0	0 0	2 3.5%	0 0	0 0	2 2.4%	0 0	0 0	0 0	0 0	0 0	0 0	2 3.1%
All sources of info	2 0.9%	2 1.6%	0 0	2 0.9%	0 0	0 0	0 0	2 3.5%	0 0	0 0	2 2.4%	0 0	0 0	0 0	0 0	0 0	0 0	2 3.1%
preferred source of info	2 0.9%	2 1.6%	0 0	2 0.9%	0 0	0 0	0 0	2 3.5%	0 0	0 0	2 2.4%	0 0	0 0	0 0	0 0	0 0	0 0	2 3.1%
Faculty (NET)	1 0.5%	0 0	1 1.1%	1 0.5%	0 0	0 0	1 1.6%	0 0	0 0	1 4.2%	0 0	0 0	0 0	0 0	0 0	0 0	1 0.7%	0 0
All sources of info	1 0.5%	0 0	1 1.1%	1 0.5%	0 0	0 0	1 1.6%	0 0	0 0	1 4.2%	0 0	0 0	0 0	0 0	0 0	0 0	1 0.7%	0 0
preferred source of info	0 0	0 0	0 0	0 0	0 0	0 0	0 0	0 0	0 0	0 0	0 0	0 0	0 0	0 0	0 0	0 0	0 0	0 0
Office (NET)	1 0.4%	1 0.8%	0 0	1 0.4%	0 0	0 0	0 0	1 1.6%	1 3.3%	0 0	0 0	0 0	0 0	0 0	0 0	0 0	0 0	1 1.5%
All sources of info	1 0.4%	1 0.8%	0 0	1 0.4%	0 0	0 0	0 0	1 1.6%	1 3.3%	0 0	0 0	0 0	0 0	0 0	0 0	0 0	0 0	1 1.5%
preferred source of info	1 0.4%	1 0.8%	0 0	1 0.4%	0 0	0 0	0 0	1 1.6%	1 3.3%	0 0	0 0	0 0	0 0	0 0	0 0	0 0	0 0	1 1.5%
E-journals (NET)	* 0.1%	0 0	* 0.3%	* 0.1%	0 0	0 0	* 0.5%	0 0	0 0	0 0	0 0	0 0	* 3.3%	0 0	0 0	0 0	* 0.2%	0 0

Proportions/Means: Columns Tested (5% risk level) - A/B/D - C/D - E/F/G - H/I/J/K/L/M/N - P/Q
* small base; ** very small base (under 30) ineligible for sig testing

Table 180
Page 679

Outsell/Digital Library Federation Study (2002)
Weighted Tables

TABLE 102, continued

R7D/E_17. News SUMMARY TABLE

	RESPONDENT TYPE					INSTITUTION TYPE			DISCIPLINE								GENDER	
	TOTAL SAMPLE	FACULTY MEMBER	GRAD. STUDENT	FACULTY /GRAD	UNDER GRAD. STUDENT	PUBLIC	PRIVATE	LIBERAL ARTS	BIOLOGIAL SCIENCES	PHYSICAL SCIENCES /MATH	SOCIAL SCIENCES	ARTS AND HUMAN.	ENGI-NEERING	BUSINESS	LAW	UNDEC. MAJOR	MALE	FEMALE
		(A)	(B)	(C)	(D)	(E)	(F)	(G)	(H)	(I)	(J)	(K)	(L)	(M)	(N)		(P)	(Q)
Base - Use News for research	207	116*	90*	207	0**	91*	62*	54*	26**	24**	77*	41*	9**	24**	5**	0*	147	60*
All sources of info	* 0.1%	0 0	* 0.3%	* 0.1%	0 0	0 0	* 0.5%	0 0	0 0	0 0	0 0	0 0	* 3.3%	0 0	0 0	0 0	* 0.2%	0 0
preferred source of info	0 0	0 0	0 0	0 0	0 0	0 0	0 0	0 0	0 0	0 0	0 0	0 0	0 0	0 0	0 0	0 0	0 0	0 0
Sources (NET)	* 0.1%	* 0.1%	0 0	* 0.1%	0 0	* 0.2%	0 0	0 0	0 0	0 0	0 0	0 0	0 0	0 0	* 3.6%	0 0	* 0.1%	0 0
All sources of info	* 0.1%	* 0.1%	0 0	* 0.1%	0 0	* 0.2%	0 0	0 0	0 0	0 0	0 0	0 0	0 0	0 0	* 3.6%	0 0	* 0.1%	0 0
preferred source of info	* 0.1%	* 0.1%	0 0	* 0.1%	0 0	* 0.2%	0 0	0 0	0 0	0 0	0 0	0 0	0 0	0 0	* 3.6%	0 0	* 0.1%	0 0
Ask library to purchase source (NET)	0 0	0 0	0 0	0 0	0 0	0 0	0 0	0 0	0 0	0 0	0 0	0 0	0 0	0 0	0 0	0 0	0 0	0 0
All sources of info	0 0	0 0	0 0	0 0	0 0	0 0	0 0	0 0	0 0	0 0	0 0	0 0	0 0	0 0	0 0	0 0	0 0	0 0
preferred source of info	0 0	0 0	0 0	0 0	0 0	0 0	0 0	0 0	0 0	0 0	0 0	0 0	0 0	0 0	0 0	0 0	0 0	0 0
Access book/journal/ journal article elsewhere online (NET)	0 0	0 0	0 0	0 0	0 0	0 0	0 0	0 0	0 0	0 0	0 0	0 0	0 0	0 0	0 0	0 0	0 0	0 0

Proportions/Means: Columns Tested (5% risk level) - A/B/D - C/D - E/F/G - H/I/J/K/L/M/N - P/Q
* small base; ** very small base (under 30) ineligible for sig testing

Table 180
Page 680

Outsell/Digital Library Federation Study (2002)
Weighted Tables

TABLE 102, continued
R7D/E_17. News SUMMARY TABLE

		RESPONDENT TYPE				INSTITUTION TYPE			DISCIPLINE									GENDER	
	TOTAL SAMPLE	FACULTY MEMBER	GRAD. STUDENT	FACULTY /GRAD	UNDER GRAD. STUDENT	PUBLIC	PRIVATE	LIBERAL ARTS	BIOLOGIAL SCIENCES	PHYSICAL SCIENCES /MATH	SOCIAL SCIENCES	ARTS AND HUMAN.	ENGI-NEERING	BUSINESS	LAW	UNDEC. MAJOR	MALE	FEMALE
		(A)	(B)	(C)	(D)	(E)	(F)	(G)	(H)	(I)	(J)	(K)	(L)	(M)	(N)		(P)	(Q)
Base - Use News for research	207	116*	90*	207	0**	91*	62*	54*	26**	24**	77*	41*	9**	24**	5**	0*	147	60*
All sources of info	0 0	0 0	0 0	0 0	0 0	0 0	0 0	0 0	0 0	0 0	0 0	0 0	0 0	0 0	0 0	0 0	0 0	0 0
preferred source of info	0 0	0 0	0 0	0 0	0 0	0 0	0 0	0 0	0 0	0 0	0 0	0 0	0 0	0 0	0 0	0 0	0 0	0 0
Access from course website (NET)	0 0	0 0	0 0	0 0	0 0	0 0	0 0	0 0	0 0	0 0	0 0	0 0	0 0	0 0	0 0	0 0	0 0	0 0
All sources of info	0 0	0 0	0 0	0 0	0 0	0 0	0 0	0 0	0 0	0 0	0 0	0 0	0 0	0 0	0 0	0 0	0 0	0 0
preferred source of info	0 0	0 0	0 0	0 0	0 0	0 0	0 0	0 0	0 0	0 0	0 0	0 0	0 0	0 0	0 0	0 0	0 0	0 0
Purchase from online bookstore (NET)	0 0	0 0	0 0	0 0	0 0	0 0	0 0	0 0	0 0	0 0	0 0	0 0	0 0	0 0	0 0	0 0	0 0	0 0
All sources of info	0 0	0 0	0 0	0 0	0 0	0 0	0 0	0 0	0 0	0 0	0 0	0 0	0 0	0 0	0 0	0 0	0 0	0 0
preferred source of info	0 0	0 0	0 0	0 0	0 0	0 0	0 0	0 0	0 0	0 0	0 0	0 0	0 0	0 0	0 0	0 0	0 0	0 0
Other (NET)	24 11.7%	15 13.1%	9 9.9%	24 11.7%	0 0	9 9.5%	8 12.9%	8 13.9%	3 10.0%	3 12.5%	8 9.8%	7 16.2%	1 13.3%	2 7.7%	1 25.0%	0 0	14 9.5%	10 16.9%
All sources of info	21 10.4%	14 12.1%	7 8.1%	21 10.4%	0 0	7 7.2%	7 12.0%	8 13.9%	3 10.0%	2 8.3%	8 9.8%	7 16.2%	1 6.7%	1 3.8%	1 21.4%	0 0	12 8.4%	9 15.2%

Proportions/Means: Columns Tested (5% risk level) - A/B/D - C/D - E/F/G - H/I/J/K/L/M/N - P/Q
* small base; ** very small base (under 30) ineligible for sig testing

Table 180
Page 681

Outsell/Digital Library Federation Study (2002)
Weighted Tables

TABLE 102, continued

R7D/E_17. News SUMMARY TABLE

		RESPONDENT TYPE				INSTITUTION TYPE			DISCIPLINE									GENDER	
	TOTAL SAMPLE	FACULTY MEMBER	GRAD. STUDENT	FACULTY /GRAD	UNDER GRAD. STUDENT	PUBLIC	PRIVATE	LIBERAL ARTS	BIOLOGIAL SCIENCES	PHYSICAL SCIENCES /MATH	SOCIAL SCIENCES	ARTS AND HUMAN.	ENGI- NEERING	BUSINESS	LAW	UNDEC. MAJOR	MALE	FEMALE
		(A)	(B)	(C)	(D)	(E)	(F)	(G)	(H)	(I)	(J)	(K)	(L)	(M)	(N)		(P)	(Q)
Base - Use News for research	207	116*	90*	207	0**	91*	62*	54*	26**	24**	77*	41*	9**	24**	5**	0*	147	60*
preferred source of info	6 3.0%	3 2.6%	3 3.4%	6 3.0%	0 0	3 3.5%	2 3.3%	1 1.6%	1 3.3%	2 8.3%	0 0	0 0	1 10.0%	2 7.7%	1 10.7%	0 0	4 2.7%	2 3.5%
DK/Refused	5 2.4%	4 3.5%	1 1.0%	5 2.4%	0 0	1 1.0%	2 3.0%	2 4.1%	1 3.3%	0 0	2 2.4%	1 2.7%	0 0	1 3.8%	* 3.6%	0 0	3 2.0%	2 3.4%

Proportions/Means: Columns Tested (5% risk level) - A/B/D - C/D - E/F/G - H/I/J/K/L/M/N - P/Q
* small base; ** very small base (under 30) ineligible for sig testing

Table 180
Page 682

TABLE 103

T7sum_3. e-books SUMMARY TABLE

		RESPONDENT TYPE				INSTITUTION TYPE			DISCIPLINE								GENDER	
	TOTAL SAMPLE	FACULTY MEMBER	GRAD. STUDENT	FACULTY /GRAD	UNDER GRAD. STUDENT	PUBLIC	PRIVATE	LIBERAL ARTS	BIOLOGIAL SCIENCES	PHYSICAL SCIENCES /MATH	SOCIAL SCIENCES	ARTS AND HUMAN.	ENGI-NEERING	BUSINESS	LAW	UNDEC. MAJOR	MALE	FEMALE
		(A)	(B)	(C)	(D)	(E)	(F)	(G)	(H)	(I)	(J)	(K)	(L)	(M)	(N)		(P)	(Q)
Base - USe e-books for teaching	40*	27**	13**	40*	0**	16**	14**	10**	6**	5**	11**	12**	3**	2**	***	0*	30**	11**
ONLINE	33 83.1%	24 87.4%	9 73.8%	33 83.1%	0 0	13 79.3%	12 89.5%	8 80.1%	6 100.0%	4 80.0%	9 83.3%	10 81.8%	3 81.8%	1 50.0%	* 50.0%	0 0	26 87.5%	7 70.5%
Search engine	10 25.3%	7 27.0%	3 21.7%	10 25.3%	0 0	4 26.2%	5 34.9%	1 10.9%	4 57.1%	0 0	2 16.7%	3 27.3%	* 9.1%	1 50.0%	* 50.0%	0 0	7 24.5%	3 27.4%
All sources of info	10 25.3%	7 27.0%	3 21.7%	10 25.3%	0 0	4 26.2%	5 34.9%	1 10.9%	4 57.1%	0 0	2 16.7%	3 27.3%	* 9.1%	1 50.0%	* 50.0%	0 0	7 24.5%	3 27.4%
preferred source of info	9 23.0%	6 23.6%	3 21.7%	9 23.0%	0 0	4 26.2%	4 28.2%	1 10.9%	4 57.1%	0 0	2 16.7%	3 27.3%	* 9.1%	0 0	* 50.0%	0 0	6 21.4%	3 27.4%
Online library catalogues and finding aids	9 21.8%	5 19.3%	3 27.2%	9 21.8%	0 0	4 26.9%	2 17.6%	2 19.4%	1 14.3%	1 20.0%	4 33.3%	2 18.2%	1 27.3%	0 0	0 0	0 0	7 24.8%	1 13.4%
All sources of info	9 21.8%	5 19.3%	3 27.2%	9 21.8%	0 0	4 26.9%	2 17.6%	2 19.4%	1 14.3%	1 20.0%	4 33.3%	2 18.2%	1 27.3%	0 0	0 0	0 0	7 24.8%	1 13.4%
preferred source of info	8 20.3%	5 19.3%	3 22.6%	8 20.3%	0 0	4 26.9%	2 13.5%	2 19.4%	1 14.3%	1 20.0%	4 33.3%	2 18.2%	* 9.1%	0 0	0 0	0 0	7 22.8%	1 13.4%
Web directory/ subject related web site	8 19.9%	7 27.0%	1 4.6%	8 19.9%	0 0	2 11.8%	2 14.3%	4 40.0%	0 0	0 0	4 33.3%	3 27.3%	1 27.3%	0 0	0 0	0 0	8 27.0%	0 0
All sources of info	8 19.9%	7 27.0%	1 4.6%	8 19.9%	0 0	2 11.8%	2 14.3%	4 40.0%	0 0	0 0	4 33.3%	3 27.3%	1 27.3%	0 0	0 0	0 0	8 27.0%	0 0

Proportions/Means: Columns Tested (5% risk level) - A/B/D - C/D - E/F/G - H/I/J/K/L/M/N - P/Q
* small base; ** very small base (under 30) ineligible for sig testing

Table 207
Page 776

Outsell/Digital Library Federation Study (2002)
Weighted Tables

TABLE 103, continued

T7sum_3. e-books SUMMARY TABLE

		RESPONDENT TYPE				INSTITUTION TYPE			DISCIPLINE								GENDER	
	TOTAL SAMPLE	FACULTY MEMBER	GRAD. STUDENT	FACULTY /GRAD	UNDER GRAD. STUDENT	PUBLIC	PRIVATE	LIBERAL ARTS	BIOLOGIAL SCIENCES	PHYSICAL SCIENCES /MATH	SOCIAL SCIENCES	ARTS AND HUMAN.	ENGI- NEERING	BUSINESS	LAW	UNDEC. MAJOR	MALE	FEMALE
		(A)	(B)	(C)	(D)	(E)	(F)	(G)	(H)	(I)	(J)	(K)	(L)	(M)	(N)		(P)	(Q)
Base - USe e-books for teaching	40*	27**	13**	40*	0**	16**	14**	10**	6**	5**	11**	12**	3**	2**	***	0*	30**	11**
preferred source of info	4 11.0%	4 16.1%	0 0	4 11.0%	0 0	0 0	1 10.1%	3 29.2%	0 0	0 0	2 16.7%	2 18.2%	* 9.1%	0 0	0 0	0 0	4 14.9%	0 0
Online databases	6 14.6%	6 20.4%	* 2.3%	6 14.6%	0 0	1 8.1%	2 17.6%	2 20.6%	0 0	2 40.0%	2 16.7%	1 9.1%	1 27.3%	0 0	0 0	0 0	5 16.0%	1 10.7%
All sources of info	6 14.6%	6 20.4%	* 2.3%	6 14.6%	0 0	1 8.1%	2 17.6%	2 20.6%	0 0	2 40.0%	2 16.7%	1 9.1%	1 27.3%	0 0	0 0	0 0	5 16.0%	1 10.7%
preferred source of info	3 6.7%	2 8.8%	* 2.3%	3 6.7%	0 0	1 6.3%	1 4.2%	1 10.9%	0 0	1 20.0%	0 0	1 9.1%	1 18.2%	0 0	0 0	0 0	2 5.3%	1 10.7%
Internet searches	5 12.0%	3 9.2%	2 18.0%	5 12.0%	0 0	2 12.6%	3 20.1%	0 0	1 14.3%	1 20.0%	0 0	1 9.1%	1 27.3%	1 50.0%	0 0	0 0	3 9.4%	2 19.0%
All sources of info	5 12.0%	3 9.2%	2 18.0%	5 12.0%	0 0	2 12.6%	3 20.1%	0 0	1 14.3%	1 20.0%	0 0	1 9.1%	1 27.3%	1 50.0%	0 0	0 0	3 9.4%	2 19.0%
preferred source of info	4 10.5%	2 7.0%	2 18.0%	4 10.5%	0 0	2 12.6%	2 15.9%	0 0	1 14.3%	1 20.0%	0 0	1 9.1%	* 9.1%	1 50.0%	0 0	0 0	2 7.5%	2 19.0%
Your own institution's web site	1 2.9%	0 0	1 9.2%	1 2.9%	0 0	1 5.5%	* 2.1%	0 0	1 14.3%	0 0	0 0	0 0	* 9.1%	0 0	0 0	0 0	1 3.9%	0 0
All sources of info	1 2.9%	0 0	1 9.2%	1 2.9%	0 0	1 5.5%	* 2.1%	0 0	1 14.3%	0 0	0 0	0 0	* 9.1%	0 0	0 0	0 0	1 3.9%	0 0
preferred source of info	1 2.2%	0 0	1 6.9%	1 2.2%	.0 0	1 5.5%	0 0	0 0	1 14.3%	0 0	0 0	0 0	0 0	0 0	0 0	0 0	1 3.0%	0 0

Proportions/Means: Columns Tested (5% risk level) - A/B/D - C/D - E/F/G - H/I/J/K/L/M/N - P/Q
* small base; ** very small base (under 30) ineligible for sig testing

Table 207
Page 777

Outsell/Digital Library Federation Study (2002)
Weighted Tables

TABLE 103, continued

T7sum_3. e-books SUMMARY TABLE

		RESPONDENT TYPE				INSTITUTION TYPE			DISCIPLINE									GENDER	
	TOTAL SAMPLE	FACULTY MEMBER	GRAD. STUDENT	FACULTY /GRAD	UNDER GRAD. STUDENT	PUBLIC	PRIVATE	LIBERAL ARTS	BIOLOGIAL SCIENCES	PHYSICAL SCIENCES /MATH	SOCIAL SCIENCES	ARTS AND HUMAN.	ENGI-NEERING	BUSINESS	LAW	UNDEC. MAJOR	MALE	FEMALE
		(A)	(B)	(C)	(D)	(E)	(F)	(G)	(H)	(I)	(J)	(K)	(L)	(M)	(N)		(P)	(Q)
Base - USe e-books for teaching	40*	27**	13**	40*	0**	16**	14**	10**	6**	5**	11**	12**	3**	2**	***	0*	30**	11**
Department web page	1 2.8%	1 4.1%	0 0	1 2.8%	0 0	1 7.0%	0 0	0 0	0 0	0 0	0 0	1 9.1%	0 0	0 0	0 0	0 0	1 3.8%	0 0
All sources of info	1 2.8%	1 4.1%	0 0	1 2.8%	0 0	1 7.0%	0 0	0 0	0 0	0 0	0 0	1 9.1%	0 0	0 0	0 0	0 0	1 3.8%	0 0
preferred source of info	0 0	0 0	0 0	0 0	0 0	0 0	0 0	0 0	0 0	0 0	0 0	0 0	0 0	0 0	0 0	0 0	0 0	0 0
Online reference service	0 0	0 0	0 0	0 0	0 0	0 0	0 0	0 0	0 0	0 0	0 0	0 0	0 0	0 0	0 0	0 0	0 0	0 0
All sources of info	0 0	0 0	0 0	0 0	0 0	0 0	0 0	0 0	0 0	0 0	0 0	0 0	0 0	0 0	0 0	0 0	0 0	0 0
preferred source of info	0 0	0 0	0 0	0 0	0 0	0 0	0 0	0 0	0 0	0 0	0 0	0 0	0 0	0 0	0 0	0 0	0 0	0 0
Online bookstore	0 0	0 0	0 0	0 0	0 0	0 0	0 0	0 0	0 0	0 0	0 0	0 0	0 0	0 0	0 0	0 0	0 0	0 0
All sources of info	0 0	0 0	0 0	0 0	0 0	0 0	0 0	0 0	0 0	0 0	0 0	0 0	0 0	0 0	0 0	0 0	0 0	0 0
preferred source of info	0 0	0 0	0 0	0 0	0 0	0 0	0 0	0 0	0 0	0 0	0 0	0 0	0 0	0 0	0 0	0 0	0 0	0 0
Online abstracting and indexing services	0 0	0 0	0 0	0 0	0 0	0 0	0 0	0 0	0 0	0 0	0 0	0 0	0 0	0 0	0 0	0 0	0 0	0 0

Proportions/Means: Columns Tested (5% risk level) - A/B/D - C/D - E/F/G - H/I/J/K/L/M/N - P/Q
* small base; ** very small base (under 30) ineligible for sig testing

Table 207
Page 778

Outsell/Digital Library Federation Study (2002)
Weighted Tables

TABLE 103, continued

T7sum_3. e-books SUMMARY TABLE

		RESPONDENT TYPE				INSTITUTION TYPE			DISCIPLINE								GENDER	
	TOTAL SAMPLE	FACULTY MEMBER	GRAD. STUDENT	FACULTY /GRAD	UNDER GRAD. STUDENT	PUBLIC	PRIVATE	LIBERAL ARTS	BIOLOGIAL SCIENCES	PHYSICAL SCIENCES /MATH	SOCIAL SCIENCES	ARTS AND HUMAN.	ENGI-NEERING	BUSINESS	LAW	UNDEC. MAJOR	MALE	FEMALE
		(A)	(B)	(C)	(D)	(E)	(F)	(G)	(H)	(I)	(J)	(K)	(L)	(M)	(N)		(P)	(Q)
Base - USe e-books for teaching	40*	27**	13**	40*	0**	16**	14**	10**	6**	5**	11**	12**	3**	2**	***	0*	30**	11**
All sources of info	0	0	0	0	0	0	0	0	0	0	0	0	0	0	0	0	0	0
	0	0	0	0	0	0	0	0	0	0	0	0	0	0	0	0	0	0
preferred source of info	0	0	0	0	0	0	0	0	0	0	0	0	0	0	0	0	0	0
	0	0	0	0	0	0	0	0	0	0	0	0	0	0	0	0	0	0
E-mail listservs	0	0	0	0	0	0	0	0	0	0	0	0	0	0	0	0	0	0
	0	0	0	0	0	0	0	0	0	0	0	0	0	0	0	0	0	0
All sources of info	0	0	0	0	0	0	0	0	0	0	0	0	0	0	0	0	0	0
	0	0	0	0	0	0	0	0	0	0	0	0	0	0	0	0	0	0
preferred source of info	0	0	0	0	0	0	0	0	0	0	0	0	0	0	0	0	0	0
	0	0	0	0	0	0	0	0	0	0	0	0	0	0	0	0	0	0
Your own personal electronic library/files	0	0	0	0	0	0	0	0	0	0	0	0	0	0	0	0	0	0
	0	0	0	0	0	0	0	0	0	0	0	0	0	0	0	0	0	0
All sources of info	0	0	0	0	0	0	0	0	0	0	0	0	0	0	0	0	0	0
	0	0	0	0	0	0	0	0	0	0	0	0	0	0	0	0	0	0
preferred source of info	0	0	0	0	0	0	0	0	0	0	0	0	0	0	0	0	0	0
	0	0	0	0	0	0	0	0	0	0	0	0	0	0	0	0	0	0
PERSONAL ASSISTANCE	13	8	5	13	0	6	4	3	2	4	2	4	1	0	0	0	11	2
	32.4%	27.9%	41.9%	32.4%	0	37.7%	26.9%	31.5%	28.6%	80.0%	16.7%	36.4%	27.3%	0	0	0	37.5%	17.9%
Colleagues inside your institution	7	4	2	7	0	2	4	1	2	3	0	1	1	0	0	0	7	0
	16.8%	15.6%	19.3%	16.8%	0	12.6%	26.9%	9.7%	28.6%	60.0%	0	9.1%	27.3%	0	0	0	22.8%	0

Proportions/Means: Columns Tested (5% risk level) - A/B/D - C/D - E/F/G - H/I/J/K/L/M/N - P/Q
* small base; ** very small base (under 30) ineligible for sig testing

Table 207
Page 779

Outsell/Digital Library Federation Study (2002)
Weighted Tables

TABLE 103, continued

T7sum_3. e-books SUMMARY TABLE

	RESPONDENT TYPE				INSTITUTION TYPE			DISCIPLINE								GENDER	
	TOTAL SAMPLE	FACULTY MEMBER	GRAD. STUDENT	FACULTY /GRAD	UNDER GRAD. STUDENT	PUBLIC	PRIVATE	LIBERAL ARTS	BIOLOGIAL SCIENCES	PHYSICAL SCIENCES /MATH	SOCIAL SCIENCES	ARTS AND HUMAN.	ENGI- NEERING	BUSINESS	LAW	UNDEC. MAJOR	MALE	FEMALE
		(A)	(B)	(C)	(D)	(E)	(F)	(G)	(H)	(I)	(J)	(K)	(L)	(M)	(N)		(P)	(Q)
Base - USe e-books for teaching	40*	27**	13**	40*	0**	16**	14**	10**	6**	5**	11**	12**	3**	2**	***	0*	30**	11**
All sources of info	7 16.8%	4 15.6%	2 19.3%	7 16.8%	0 0	2 12.6%	4 26.9%	1 9.7%	2 28.6%	3 60.0%	0 0	1 9.1%	1 27.3%	0 0	0 0	0 0	7 22.8%	0 0
preferred source of info	1 3.2%	0 0	1 10.1%	1 3.2%	0 0	0 0	1 9.3%	0 0	0 0	1 20.0%	0 0	0 0	* 9.1%	0 0	0 0	0 0	1 4.4%	0 0
A librarian in your institution	6 15.5%	3 12.3%	3 22.6%	6 15.5%	0 0	4 25.1%	0 0	2 21.8%	0 0	1 20.0%	2 16.7%	3 27.3%	0 0	0 0	0 0	0 0	4 14.7%	2 17.9%
All sources of info	6 15.5%	3 12.3%	3 22.6%	6 15.5%	0 0	4 25.1%	0 0	2 21.8%	0 0	1 20.0%	2 16.7%	3 27.3%	0 0	0 0	0 0	0 0	4 14.7%	2 17.9%
preferred source of info	3 7.5%	1 4.1%	2 14.8%	3 7.5%	0 0	2 11.8%	0 0	1 10.9%	0 0	0 0	2 16.7%	1 9.1%	0 0	0 0	0 0	0 0	1 3.8%	2 17.9%
Colleagues outside your institution	2 6.0%	2 8.8%	0 0	2 6.0%	0 0	1 7.0%	1 9.3%	0 0	0 0	1 20.0%	0 0	1 9.1%	* 9.1%	0 0	0 0	0 0	2 8.1%	0 0
All sources of info	2 6.0%	2 8.8%	0 0	2 6.0%	0 0	1 7.0%	1 9.3%	0 0	0 0	1 20.0%	0 0	1 9.1%	* 9.1%	0 0	0 0	0 0	2 8.1%	0 0
preferred source of info	0 0	0 0	0 0	0 0	0 0	0 0	0 0	0 0	0 0	0 0	0 0	0 0	0 0	0 0	0 0	0 0	0 0	0 0
Another institution's librarian	1 2.8%	1 4.1%	0 0	1 2.8%	0 0	0 0	0 0	1 10.9%	0 0	0 0	0 0	1 9.1%	0 0	0 0	0 0	0 0	1 3.8%	0 0
All sources of info	1 2.8%	1 4.1%	0 0	1 2.8%	0 0	0 0	0 0	1 10.9%	0 0	0 0	0 0	1 9.1%	0 0	0 0	0 0	0 0	1 3.8%	0 0

Proportions/Means: Columns Tested (5% risk level) - A/B/D - C/D - E/F/G - H/I/J/K/L/M/N - P/Q
* small base; ** very small base (under 30) ineligible for sig testing

Table 207
Page 780

Outsell/Digital Library Federation Study (2002)
Weighted Tables

TABLE 103, continued

T7sum_3. e-books SUMMARY TABLE

		RESPONDENT TYPE				INSTITUTION TYPE			DISCIPLINE								GENDER	
	TOTAL SAMPLE	FACULTY MEMBER	GRAD. STUDENT	FACULTY /GRAD	UNDER GRAD. STUDENT	PUBLIC	PRIVATE	LIBERAL ARTS	BIOLOGIAL SCIENCES	PHYSICAL SCIENCES /MATH	SOCIAL SCIENCES	ARTS AND HUMAN.	ENGI- NEERING	BUSINESS	LAW	UNDEC. MAJOR	MALE	FEMALE
		(A)	(B)	(C)	(D)	(E)	(F)	(G)	(H)	(I)	(J)	(K)	(L)	(M)	(N)		(P)	(Q)
Base - USe e-books for teaching	40*	27**	13**	40*	0**	16**	14**	10**	6**	5**	11**	12**	3**	2**	***	0*	30**	11**
preferred source of info	0 0	0 0	0 0	0 0	0 0	0 0	0 0	0 0	0 0	0 0	0 0	0 0	0 0	0 0	0 0	0 0	0 0	0 0
Professional meetings	0 0	0 0	0 0	0 0	0 0	0 0	0 0	0 0	0 0	0 0	0 0	0 0	0 0	0 0	0 0	0 0	0 0	0 0
All sources of info	0 0	0 0	0 0	0 0	0 0	0 0	0 0	0 0	0 0	0 0	0 0	0 0	0 0	0 0	0 0	0 0	0 0	0 0
preferred source of info	0 0	0 0	0 0	0 0	0 0	0 0	0 0	0 0	0 0	0 0	0 0	0 0	0 0	0 0	0 0	0 0	0 0	0 0
LIBRARY/PRINT	10 24.8%	8 30.0%	2 13.7%	10 24.8%	0 0	3 17.0%	2 16.8%	5 47.9%	0 0	2 40.0%	4 33.3%	2 18.2%	1 27.3%	1 50.0%	* 50.0%	0 0	9 29.5%	1 11.6%
Campus library	7 17.8%	5 19.7%	2 13.7%	7 17.8%	0 0	3 17.0%	* 3.3%	4 38.9%	0 0	2 40.0%	2 16.7%	2 18.2%	1 27.3%	0 0	* 50.0%	0 0	7 23.2%	* 2.8%
All sources of info	7 17.8%	5 19.7%	2 13.7%	7 17.8%	0 0	3 17.0%	* 3.3%	4 38.9%	0 0	2 40.0%	2 16.7%	2 18.2%	1 27.3%	0 0	* 50.0%	0 0	7 23.2%	* 2.8%
preferred source of info	2 4.4%	1 4.7%	* 3.6%	2 4.4%	0 0	1 3.6%	* 1.2%	1 9.7%	0 0	1 20.0%	0 0	0 0	1 18.2%	0 0	* 50.0%	0 0	1 4.9%	* 2.8%
Personal subscriptions to newspapers, magazines and journals	4 9.4%	4 13.7%	0 0	4 9.4%	0 0	0 0	2 13.5%	2 18.3%	0 0	0 0	4 33.3%	0 0	0 0	0 0	0 0	0 0	4 12.7%	0 0

Proportions/Means: Columns Tested (5% risk level) - A/B/D - C/D - E/F/G - H/I/J/K/L/M/N - P/Q
* small base; ** very small base (under 30) ineligible for sig testing

Table 207
Page 781

Outsell/Digital Library Federation Study (2002)
Weighted Tables

TABLE 103, continued

T7sum_3. e-books SUMMARY TABLE

	TOTAL SAMPLE	FACULTY MEMBER (A)	GRAD. STUDENT (B)	FACULTY /GRAD (C)	UNDER GRAD. STUDENT (D)	PUBLIC (E)	PRIVATE (F)	LIBERAL ARTS (G)	BIOLOGIAL SCIENCES (H)	PHYSICAL SCIENCES /MATH (I)	SOCIAL SCIENCES (J)	ARTS AND HUMAN. (K)	ENGI- NEERING (L)	BUSINESS (M)	LAW (N)	UNDEC. MAJOR	MALE (P)	FEMALE (Q)
		RESPONDENT TYPE				INSTITUTION TYPE			DISCIPLINE								GENDER	
Base - USe e-books for teaching	40*	27**	13**	40*	0**	16**	14**	10**	6**	5**	11**	12**	3**	2**	***	0*	30**	11**
All sources of info	4 9.4%	4 13.7%	0 0	4 9.4%	0 0	0 0	2 13.5%	2 18.3%	0 0	0 0	4 33.3%	0 0	0 0	0 0	0 0	0 0	4 12.7%	0 0
preferred source of info	2 4.7%	2 6.9%	0 0	2 4.7%	0 0	0 0	2 13.5%	0 0	0 0	0 0	2 16.7%	0 0	0 0	0 0	0 0	0 0	2 6.3%	0 0
Another library	1 3.5%	1 5.1%	0 0	1 3.5%	0 0	* 1.8%	0 0	1 10.9%	0 0	0 0	0 0	1 9.1%	* 9.1%	0 0	0 0	0 0	1 4.8%	0 0
All sources of info	1 3.5%	1 5.1%	0 0	1 3.5%	0 0	* 1.8%	0 0	1 10.9%	0 0	0 0	0 0	1 9.1%	* 9.1%	0 0	0 0	0 0	1 4.8%	0 0
preferred source of info	0 0	0 0	0 0	0 0	0 0	0 0	0 0	0 0	0 0	0 0	0 0	0 0	0 0	0 0	0 0	0 0	0 0	0 0
Physical bookstore	1 2.5%	1 3.6%	0 0	1 2.5%	0 0	0 0	0 0	1 9.7%	0 0	1 20.0%	0 0	0 0	0 0	0 0	0 0	0 0	1 3.4%	0 0
All sources of info	1 2.5%	1 3.6%	0 0	1 2.5%	0 0	0 0	0 0	1 9.7%	0 0	1 20.0%	0 0	0 0	0 0	0 0	0 0	0 0	1 3.4%	0 0
preferred source of info	0 0	0 0	0 0	0 0	0 0	0 0	0 0	0 0	0 0	0 0	0 0	0 0	0 0	0 0	0 0	0 0	0 0	0 0
Your own personal physical library/ files/bookshelves	1 2.3%	1 3.4%	0 0	1 2.3%	0 0	0 0	0 0	1 9.0%	0 0	0 0	0 0	0 0	0 0	1 50.0%	0 0	0 0	0 0	1 8.8%
All sources of info	1 2.3%	1 3.4%	0 0	1 2.3%	0 0	0 0	0 0	1 9.0%	0 0	0 0	0 0	0 0	0 0	1 50.0%	0 0	0 0	0 0	1 8.8%

Proportions/Means: Columns Tested (5% risk level) - A/B/D - C/D - E/F/G - H/I/J/K/L/M/N - P/Q
* small base; ** very small base (under 30) ineligible for sig testing

Table 207
Page 782

Outsell/Digital Library Federation Study (2002)
Weighted Tables

TABLE 103, continued

T7sum_3. e-books SUMMARY TABLE

		RESPONDENT TYPE				INSTITUTION TYPE			DISCIPLINE								GENDER	
	TOTAL SAMPLE	FACULTY MEMBER	GRAD. STUDENT	FACULTY /GRAD	UNDER GRAD. STUDENT	PUBLIC	PRIVATE	LIBERAL ARTS	BIOLOGIAL SCIENCES	PHYSICAL SCIENCES /MATH	SOCIAL SCIENCES	ARTS AND HUMAN.	ENGI-NEERING	BUSINESS	LAW	UNDEC. MAJOR	MALE	FEMALE
		(A)	(B)	(C)	(D)	(E)	(F)	(G)	(H)	(I)	(J)	(K)	(L)	(M)	(N)		(P)	(Q)
Base - USe e-books for teaching	40*	27**	13**	40*	0**	16**	14**	10**	6**	5**	11**	12**	3**	2**	***	0*	30**	11**
preferred source of info	1 2.3%	1 3.4%	0 0	1 2.3%	0 0	0 0	0 0	1 9.0%	0 0	0 0	0 0	0 0	0 0	1 50.0%	0 0	0 0	0 0	1 8.8%
Printed library catalogues and finding aids	0 0	0 0	0 0	0 0	0 0	0 0	0 0	0 0	0 0	0 0	0 0	0 0	0 0	0 0	0 0	0 0	0 0	0 0
All sources of info	0 0	0 0	0 0	0 0	0 0	0 0	0 0	0 0	0 0	0 0	0 0	0 0	0 0	0 0	0 0	0 0	0 0	0 0
preferred source of info	0 0	0 0	0 0	0 0	0 0	0 0	0 0	0 0	0 0	0 0	0 0	0 0	0 0	0 0	0 0	0 0	0 0	0 0
Printed abstracting and indexing services	0 0	0 0	0 0	0 0	0 0	0 0	0 0	0 0	0 0	0 0	0 0	0 0	0 0	0 0	0 0	0 0	0 0	0 0
All sources of info	0 0	0 0	0 0	0 0	0 0	0 0	0 0	0 0	0 0	0 0	0 0	0 0	0 0	0 0	0 0	0 0	0 0	0 0
preferred source of info	0 0	0 0	0 0	0 0	0 0	0 0	0 0	0 0	0 0	0 0	0 0	0 0	0 0	0 0	0 0	0 0	0 0	0 0
References cited in books or journal articles	0 0	0 0	0 0	0 0	0 0	0 0	0 0	0 0	0 0	0 0	0 0	0 0	0 0	0 0	0 0	0 0	0 0	0 0
All sources of info	0 0	0 0	0 0	0 0	0 0	0 0	0 0	0 0	0 0	0 0	0 0	0 0	0 0	0 0	0 0	0 0	0 0	0 0

Proportions/Means: Columns Tested (5% risk level) - A/B/D - C/D - E/F/G - H/I/J/K/L/M/N - P/Q
* small base; ** very small base (under 30) ineligible for sig testing

Table 207
Page 783

Outsell/Digital Library Federation Study (2002)
Weighted Tables

TABLE 103, continued

T7sum_3. e-books SUMMARY TABLE

		RESPONDENT TYPE				INSTITUTION TYPE			DISCIPLINE								GENDER	
	TOTAL SAMPLE	FACULTY MEMBER	GRAD. STUDENT	FACULTY /GRAD	UNDER GRAD. STUDENT	PUBLIC	PRIVATE	LIBERAL ARTS	BIOLOGIAL SCIENCES	PHYSICAL SCIENCES /MATH	SOCIAL SCIENCES	ARTS AND HUMAN.	ENGI- NEERING	BUSINESS	LAW	UNDEC. MAJOR	MALE	FEMALE
		(A)	(B)	(C)	(D)	(E)	(F)	(G)	(H)	(I)	(J)	(K)	(L)	(M)	(N)		(P)	(Q)
Base - USe e-books for teaching	40*	27**	13**	40*	0**	16**	14**	10**	6**	5**	11**	12**	3**	2**	***	0*	30**	11**
preferred source	0	0	0	0	0	0	0	0	0	0	0	0	0	0	0	0	0	0
of info	0	0	0	0	0	0	0	0	0	0	0	0	0	0	0	0	0	0
Students	*	*	0	*	0	0	*	0	0	0	0	0	*	0	0	0	*	0
	0.7%	1.1%	0	0.7%	0	0	2.1%	0	0	0	0	0	9.1%	0	0	0	1.0%	0
All sources of	*	*	0	*	0	0	*	0	0	0	0	0	*	0	0	0	*	0
info	0.7%	1.1%	0	0.7%	0	0	2.1%	0	0	0	0	0	9.1%	0	0	0	1.0%	0
preferred source	*	*	0	*	0	0	*	0	0	0	0	0	*	0	0	0	*	0
of info	0.7%	1.1%	0	0.7%	0	0	2.1%	0	0	0	0	0	9.1%	0	0	0	1.0%	0
Online (unspecified)	0	0	0	0	0	0	0	0	0	0	0	0	0	0	0	0	0	0
	0	0	0	0	0	0	0	0	0	0	0	0	0	0	0	0	0	0
All sources of	0	0	0	0	0	0	0	0	0	0	0	0	0	0	0	0	0	0
info	0	0	0	0	0	0	0	0	0	0	0	0	0	0	0	0	0	0
preferred source	0	0	0	0	0	0	0	0	0	0	0	0	0	0	0	0	0	0
of info	0	0	0	0	0	0	0	0	0	0	0	0	0	0	0	0	0	0
Personal office/lab	0	0	0	0	0	0	0	0	0	0	0	0	0	0	0	0	0	0
	0	0	0	0	0	0	0	0	0	0	0	0	0	0	0	0	0	0
All sources of	0	0	0	0	0	0	0	0	0	0	0	0	0	0	0	0	0	0
info	0	0	0	0	0	0	0	0	0	0	0	0	0	0	0	0	0	0
preferred source	0	0	0	0	0	0	0	0	0	0	0	0	0	0	0	0	0	0
of info	0	0	0	0	0	0	0	0	0	0	0	0	0	0	0	0	0	0

Proportions/Means: Columns Tested (5% risk level) - A/B/D - C/D - E/F/G - H/I/J/K/L/M/N - P/Q
* small base; ** very small base (under 30) ineligible for sig testing

Table 207
Page 784

Outsell/Digital Library Federation Study (2002)
Weighted Tables

TABLE 103, continued

T7sum_3. e-books SUMMARY TABLE

		RESPONDENT TYPE				INSTITUTION TYPE			DISCIPLINE								GENDER	
	TOTAL SAMPLE	FACULTY MEMBER	GRAD. STUDENT	FACULTY /GRAD	UNDER GRAD. STUDENT	PUBLIC	PRIVATE	LIBERAL ARTS	BIOLOGIAL SCIENCES	PHYSICAL SCIENCES /MATH	SOCIAL SCIENCES	ARTS AND HUMAN.	ENGI- NEERING	BUSINESS	LAW	UNDEC. MAJOR	MALE	FEMALE
		(A)	(B)	(C)	(D)	(E)	(F)	(G)	(H)	(I)	(J)	(K)	(L)	(M)	(N)		(P)	(Q)
Base - USe e-books for teaching	40*	27**	13**	40*	0**	16**	14**	10**	6**	5**	11**	12**	3**	2**	***	0*	30**	11**
Author	0 0	0 0	0 0	0 0	0 0	0 0	0 0	0 0	0 0	0 0	0 0	0 0	0 0	0 0	0 0	0 0	0 0	0 0
All sources of info	0 0	0 0	0 0	0 0	0 0	0 0	0 0	0 0	0 0	0 0	0 0	0 0	0 0	0 0	0 0	0 0	0 0	0 0
preferred source of info	0 0	0 0	0 0	0 0	0 0	0 0	0 0	0 0	0 0	0 0	0 0	0 0	0 0	0 0	0 0	0 0	0 0	0 0
Other	2 4.7%	1 3.6%	1 6.9%	2 4.7%	0 0	1 5.5%	1 7.2%	0 0	1 14.3%	1 20.0%	0 0	0 0	0 0	0 0	0 0	0 0	2 6.3%	0 0
All sources of info	2 4.7%	1 3.6%	1 6.9%	2 4.7%	0 0	1 5.5%	1 7.2%	0 0	1 14.3%	1 20.0%	0 0	0 0	0 0	0 0	0 0	0 0	2 6.3%	0 0
preferred source of info	0 0	0 0	0 0	0 0	0 0	0 0	0 0	0 0	0 0	0 0	0 0	0 0	0 0	0 0	0 0	0 0	0 0	0 0
DK/Refused	1 3.5%	1 5.1%	0 0	1 3.5%	0 0	1 7.0%	* 2.1%	0 0	0 0	0 0	0 0	1 9.1%	* 9.1%	0 0	0 0	0 0	1 4.8%	0 0

Proportions/Means: Columns Tested (5% risk level) - A/B/D - C/D - E/F/G - H/I/J/K/L/M/N - P/Q
* small base; ** very small base (under 30) ineligible for sig testing

Table 207
Page 785

Outsell/Digital Library Federation Study (2002)
Weighted Tables

TABLE 104

T7D/E_3. e-books SUMMARY TABLE

	RESPONDENT TYPE				INSTITUTION TYPE			DISCIPLINE								GENDER	
	TOTAL SAMPLE	FACULTY MEMBER	GRAD. STUDENT	FACULTY /GRAD	UNDER GRAD. STUDENT	PUBLIC	PRIVATE	LIBERAL ARTS	BIOLOGIAL SCIENCES	PHYSICAL SCIENCES /MATH	SOCIAL SCIENCES	ARTS AND HUMAN.	ENGI-NEERING	BUSINESS	LAW	UNDEC. MAJOR	MALE	FEMALE
		(A)	(B)	(C)	(D)	(E)	(F)	(G)	(H)	(I)	(J)	(K)	(L)	(M)	(N)		(P)	(Q)
Base - Use e-books for teaching	40*	27**	13**	40*	0**	16**	14**	10**	6**	5**	11**	12**	3**	2**	***	0*	30**	11**
Access online (NET)	32 80.5%	24 88.9%	8 62.6%	32 80.5%	0 0	10 64.6%	13 90.7%	9 91.4%	5 85.7%	4 80.0%	6 50.0%	12 100.0%	3 90.9%	2 100.0%	* 100.0%	0 0	24 80.0%	9 82.1%
All sources of info	32 80.5%	24 88.9%	8 62.6%	32 80.5%	0 0	10 64.6%	13 90.7%	9 91.4%	5 85.7%	4 80.0%	6 50.0%	12 100.0%	3 90.9%	2 100.0%	* 100.0%	0 0	24 80.0%	9 82.1%
preferred source of info	30 75.3%	23 85.5%	7 53.4%	30 75.3%	0 0	9 59.0%	12 88.7%	8 82.4%	4 71.4%	4 80.0%	6 50.0%	12 100.0%	3 81.8%	1 50.0%	* 100.0%	0 0	23 76.0%	8 73.3%
Borrow from or use in campus library (NET)	8 20.3%	5 18.2%	3 24.9%	8 20.3%	0 0	4 23.6%	2 17.6%	2 18.8%	1 14.3%	2 40.0%	4 33.3%	0 0	1 18.2%	1 50.0%	0 0	0 0	5 18.0%	3 26.7%
All sources of info	8 20.3%	5 18.2%	3 24.9%	8 20.3%	0 0	4 23.6%	2 17.6%	2 18.8%	1 14.3%	2 40.0%	4 33.3%	0 0	1 18.2%	1 50.0%	0 0	0 0	5 18.0%	3 26.7%
preferred source of info	6 14.9%	3 11.3%	3 22.6%	6 14.9%	0 0	4 23.6%	1 9.3%	1 9.0%	0 0	1 20.0%	4 33.3%	0 0	* 9.1%	1 50.0%	0 0	0 0	3 10.7%	3 26.7%
Purchase from online bookstore (NET)	2 4.7%	0 0	2 14.8%	2 4.7%	0 0	2 11.8%	0 0	0 0	0 0	0 0	2 16.7%	0 0	0 0	0 0	0 0	0 0	2 6.3%	0 0
All sources of info	2 4.7%	0 0	2 14.8%	2 4.7%	0 0	2 11.8%	0 0	0 0	0 0	0 0	2 16.7%	0 0	0 0	0 0	0 0	0 0	2 6.3%	0 0
preferred source of info	2 4.7%	0 0	2 14.8%	2 4.7%	0 0	2 11.8%	0 0	0 0	0 0	0 0	2 16.7%	0 0	0 0	0 0	0 0	0 0	2 6.3%	0 0

Proportions/Means: Columns Tested (5% risk level) - A/B/D - C/D - E/F/G - H/I/J/K/L/M/N - P/Q
* small base; ** very small base (under 30) ineligible for sig testing

Table 210
Page 792

Outsell/Digital Library Federation Study (2002)
Weighted Tables

TABLE 104, continued

T7D/E_3. e-books SUMMARY TABLE

		RESPONDENT TYPE				INSTITUTION TYPE			DISCIPLINE									GENDER	
	TOTAL SAMPLE	FACULTY MEMBER	GRAD. STUDENT	FACULTY /GRAD	UNDER GRAD. STUDENT	PUBLIC	PRIVATE	LIBERAL ARTS	BIOLOGIAL SCIENCES	PHYSICAL SCIENCES /MATH	SOCIAL SCIENCES	ARTS AND HUMAN.	ENGI-NEERING	BUSINESS	LAW	UNDEC. MAJOR	MALE	FEMALE
		(A)	(B)	(C)	(D)	(E)	(F)	(G)	(H)	(I)	(J)	(K)	(L)	(M)	(N)		(P)	(Q)
Base - Use e-books for teaching	40*	27**	13**	40*	0**	16**	14**	10**	6**	5**	11**	12**	3**	2**	***	0*	30**	11**
Access book/journal/ journal article elsewhere online (NET)	1 2.2%	0 0	1 6.9%	1 2.2%	0 0	1 5.5%	0 0	0 0	1 14.3%	0 0	0 0	0 0	0 0	0 0	0 0	0 0	1 3.0%	0 0
All sources of info	1 2.2%	0 0	1 6.9%	1 2.2%	0 0	1 5.5%	0 0	0 0	1 14.3%	0 0	0 0	0 0	0 0	0 0	0 0	0 0	1 3.0%	0 0
preferred source of info	1 2.2%	0 0	1 6.9%	1 2.2%	0 0	1 5.5%	0 0	0 0	1 14.3%	0 0	0 0	0 0	0 0	0 0	0 0	0 0	1 3.0%	0 0
Borrow from or use in other libraries (NET)	1 2.2%	1 3.2%	0 0	1 2.2%	0 0	0 0	0 0	1 8.6%	1 14.3%	0 0	0 0	0 0	0 0	0 0	0 0	0 0	1 3.0%	0 0
All sources of info	1 2.2%	1 3.2%	0 0	1 2.2%	0 0	0 0	0 0	1 8.6%	1 14.3%	0 0	0 0	0 0	0 0	0 0	0 0	0 0	1 3.0%	0 0
preferred source of info	1 2.2%	1 3.2%	0 0	1 2.2%	0 0	0 0	0 0	1 8.6%	1 14.3%	0 0	0 0	0 0	0 0	0 0	0 0	0 0	1 3.0%	0 0
Interlibrary loan (NET)	0 0	0 0	0 0	0 0	0 0	0 0	0 0	0 0	0 0	0 0	0 0	0 0	0 0	0 0	0 0	0 0	0 0	0 0
All sources of info	0 0	0 0	0 0	0 0	0 0	0 0	0 0	0 0	0 0	0 0	0 0	0 0	0 0	0 0	0 0	0 0	0 0	0 0
preferred source of info	0 0	0 0	0 0	0 0	0 0	0 0	0 0	0 0	0 0	0 0	0 0	0 0	0 0	0 0	0 0	0 0	0 0	0 0

Proportions/Means: Columns Tested (5% risk level) - A/B/D - C/D - E/F/G - H/I/J/K/L/M/N - P/Q
* small base; ** very small base (under 30) ineligible for sig testing

Table 210
Page 793

Outsell/Digital Library Federation Study (2002)
Weighted Tables

TABLE 104, continued

T7D/E_3. e-books SUMMARY TABLE

		RESPONDENT TYPE				INSTITUTION TYPE			DISCIPLINE									GENDER	
	TOTAL SAMPLE	FACULTY MEMBER	GRAD. STUDENT	FACULTY /GRAD	UNDER GRAD. STUDENT	PUBLIC	PRIVATE	LIBERAL ARTS	BIOLOGIAL SCIENCES	PHYSICAL SCIENCES /MATH	SOCIAL SCIENCES	ARTS AND HUMAN.	ENGI-NEERING	BUSINESS	LAW	UNDEC. MAJOR	MALE	FEMALE
		(A)	(B)	(C)	(D)	(E)	(F)	(G)	(H)	(I)	(J)	(K)	(L)	(M)	(N)		(P)	(Q)
Base - Use e-books for teaching	40*	27**	13**	40*	0**	16**	14**	10**	6**	5**	11**	12**	3**	2**	***	0*	30**	11**
Order from on demand document delivery service (NET)	0 0	0 0	0 0	0 0	0 0	0 0	0 0	0 0	0 0	0 0	0 0	0 0	0 0	0 0	0 0	0 0	0 0	0 0
All sources of info	0 0	0 0	0 0	0 0	0 0	0 0	0 0	0 0	0 0	0 0	0 0	0 0	0 0	0 0	0 0	0 0	0 0	0 0
preferred source of info	0 0	0 0	0 0	0 0	0 0	0 0	0 0	0 0	0 0	0 0	0 0	0 0	0 0	0 0	0 0	0 0	0 0	0 0
Ask library to purchase source (NET)	0 0	0 0	0 0	0 0	0 0	0 0	0 0	0 0	0 0	0 0	0 0	0 0	0 0	0 0	0 0	0 0	0 0	0 0
All sources of info	0 0	0 0	0 0	0 0	0 0	0 0	0 0	0 0	0 0	0 0	0 0	0 0	0 0	0 0	0 0	0 0	0 0	0 0
preferred source of info	0 0	0 0	0 0	0 0	0 0	0 0	0 0	0 0	0 0	0 0	0 0	0 0	0 0	0 0	0 0	0 0	0 0	0 0
Access from course website (NET)	0 0	0 0	0 0	0 0	0 0	0 0	0 0	0 0	0 0	0 0	0 0	0 0	0 0	0 0	0 0	0 0	0 0	0 0
All sources of info	0 0	0 0	0 0	0 0	0 0	0 0	0 0	0 0	0 0	0 0	0 0	0 0	0 0	0 0	0 0	0 0	0 0	0 0
preferred source of info	0 0	0 0	0 0	0 0	0 0	0 0	0 0	0 0	0 0	0 0	0 0	0 0	0 0	0 0	0 0	0 0	0 0	0 0

Proportions/Means: Columns Tested (5% risk level) - A/B/D - C/D - E/F/G - H/I/J/K/L/M/N - P/Q
* small base; ** very small base (under 30) ineligible for sig testing

Table 210
Page 794

Outsell/Digital Library Federation Study (2002)
Weighted Tables

TABLE 104, continued

T7D/E_3. e-books SUMMARY TABLE

		RESPONDENT TYPE				INSTITUTION TYPE			DISCIPLINE								GENDER	
	TOTAL SAMPLE	FACULTY MEMBER	GRAD. STUDENT	FACULTY /GRAD	UNDER GRAD. STUDENT	PUBLIC	PRIVATE	LIBERAL ARTS	BIOLOGIAL SCIENCES	PHYSICAL SCIENCES /MATH	SOCIAL SCIENCES	ARTS AND HUMAN.	ENGI-NEERING	BUSINESS	LAW	UNDEC. MAJOR	MALE	FEMALE
		(A)	(B)	(C)	(D)	(E)	(F)	(G)	(H)	(I)	(J)	(K)	(L)	(M)	(N)		(P)	(Q)
Base - Use e-books for teaching	40*	27**	13**	40*	0**	16**	14**	10**	6**	5**	11**	12**	3**	2**	***	0*	30**	11**
Purchase from physical book store (NET)	0 0	0 0	0 0	0 0	0 0	0 0	0 0	0 0	0 0	0 0	0 0	0 0	0 0	0 0	0 0	0 0	0 0	0 0
All sources of info	0 0	0 0	0 0	0 0	0 0	0 0	0 0	0 0	0 0	0 0	0 0	0 0	0 0	0 0	0 0	0 0	0 0	0 0
preferred source of info	0 0	0 0	0 0	0 0	0 0	0 0	0 0	0 0	0 0	0 0	0 0	0 0	0 0	0 0	0 0	0 0	0 0	0 0
Office (NET)	0 0	0 0	0 0	0 0	0 0	0 0	0 0	0 0	0 0	0 0	0 0	0 0	0 0	0 0	0 0	0 0	0 0	0 0
All sources of info	0 0	0 0	0 0	0 0	0 0	0 0	0 0	0 0	0 0	0 0	0 0	0 0	0 0	0 0	0 0	0 0	0 0	0 0
preferred source of info	0 0	0 0	0 0	0 0	0 0	0 0	0 0	0 0	0 0	0 0	0 0	0 0	0 0	0 0	0 0	0 0	0 0	0 0
Home (NET)	0 0	0 0	0 0	0 0	0 0	0 0	0 0	0 0	0 0	0 0	0 0	0 0	0 0	0 0	0 0	0 0	0 0	0 0
All sources of info	0 0	0 0	0 0	0 0	0 0	0 0	0 0	0 0	0 0	0 0	0 0	0 0	0 0	0 0	0 0	0 0	0 0	0 0
preferred source of info	0 0	0 0	0 0	0 0	0 0	0 0	0 0	0 0	0 0	0 0	0 0	0 0	0 0	0 0	0 0	0 0	0 0	0 0

Proportions/Means: Columns Tested (5% risk level) - A/B/D - C/D - E/F/G - H/I/J/K/L/M/N - P/Q
* small base; ** very small base (under 30) ineligible for sig testing

Table 210
Page 795

Outsell/Digital Library Federation Study (2002)
Weighted Tables

TABLE 104, continued

T7D/E_3. e-books SUMMARY TABLE

	TOTAL SAMPLE	RESPONDENT TYPE: FACULTY MEMBER	GRAD. STUDENT	FACULTY /GRAD	UNDER GRAD. STUDENT	INSTITUTION TYPE: PUBLIC	PRIVATE	LIBERAL ARTS	DISCIPLINE: BIOLOGIAL SCIENCES	PHYSICAL SCIENCES /MATH	SOCIAL SCIENCES	ARTS AND HUMAN.	ENGI- NEERING	BUSINESS	LAW	UNDEC. MAJOR	GENDER: MALE	FEMALE
		(A)	(B)	(C)	(D)	(E)	(F)	(G)	(H)	(I)	(J)	(K)	(L)	(M)	(N)		(P)	(Q)
Base - Use e-books for teaching	40*	27**	13**	40*	0**	16**	14**	10**	6**	5**	11**	12**	3**	2**	***	0*	30**	11**
Faculty (NET)	0 0	0 0	0 0	0 0	0 0	0 0	0 0	0 0	0 0	0 0	0 0	0 0	0 0	0 0	0 0	0 0	0 0	0 0
All sources of info	0 0	0 0	0 0	0 0	0 0	0 0	0 0	0 0	0 0	0 0	0 0	0 0	0 0	0 0	0 0	0 0	0 0	0 0
preferred source of info	0 0	0 0	0 0	0 0	0 0	0 0	0 0	0 0	0 0	0 0	0 0	0 0	0 0	0 0	0 0	0 0	0 0	0 0
Meeting/Conferences (NET)	0 0	0 0	0 0	0 0	0 0	0 0	0 0	0 0	0 0	0 0	0 0	0 0	0 0	0 0	0 0	0 0	0 0	0 0
All sources of info	0 0	0 0	0 0	0 0	0 0	0 0	0 0	0 0	0 0	0 0	0 0	0 0	0 0	0 0	0 0	0 0	0 0	0 0
preferred source of info	0 0	0 0	0 0	0 0	0 0	0 0	0 0	0 0	0 0	0 0	0 0	0 0	0 0	0 0	0 0	0 0	0 0	0 0
Colleagues (NET)	0 0	0 0	0 0	0 0	0 0	0 0	0 0	0 0	0 0	0 0	0 0	0 0	0 0	0 0	0 0	0 0	0 0	0 0
All sources of info	0 0	0 0	0 0	0 0	0 0	0 0	0 0	0 0	0 0	0 0	0 0	0 0	0 0	0 0	0 0	0 0	0 0	0 0
preferred source of info	0 0	0 0	0 0	0 0	0 0	0 0	0 0	0 0	0 0	0 0	0 0	0 0	0 0	0 0	0 0	0 0	0 0	0 0
Department (NET)	0 0	0 0	0 0	0 0	0 0	0 0	0 0	0 0	0 0	0 0	0 0	0 0	0 0	0 0	0 0	0 0	0 0	0 0

Proportions/Means: Columns Tested (5% risk level) - A/B/D - C/D - E/F/G - H/I/J/K/L/M/N - P/Q
* small base; ** very small base (under 30) ineligible for sig testing

Table 210
Page 796

Outsell/Digital Library Federation Study (2002)
Weighted Tables

TABLE 104, continued

T7D/E_3. e-books SUMMARY TABLE

		RESPONDENT TYPE				INSTITUTION TYPE			DISCIPLINE								GENDER	
	TOTAL SAMPLE	FACULTY MEMBER	GRAD. STUDENT	FACULTY /GRAD	UNDER GRAD. STUDENT	PUBLIC	PRIVATE	LIBERAL ARTS	BIOLOGIAL SCIENCES	PHYSICAL SCIENCES /MATH	SOCIAL SCIENCES	ARTS AND HUMAN.	ENGI-NEERING	BUSINESS	LAW	UNDEC. MAJOR	MALE	FEMALE
		(A)	(B)	(C)	(D)	(E)	(F)	(G)	(H)	(I)	(J)	(K)	(L)	(M)	(N)		(P)	(Q)
Base - Use e-books for teaching	40*	27**	13**	40*	0**	16**	14**	10**	6**	5**	11**	12**	3**	2**	***	0*	30**	11**
All sources of info	0 0	0 0	0 0	0 0	0 0	0 0	0 0	0 0	0 0	0 0	0 0	0 0	0 0	0 0	0 0	0 0	0 0	0 0
preferred source of info	0 0	0 0	0 0	0 0	0 0	0 0	0 0	0 0	0 0	0 0	0 0	0 0	0 0	0 0	0 0	0 0	0 0	0 0
Author	0 0	0 0	0 0	0 0	0 0	0 0	0 0	0 0	0 0	0 0	0 0	0 0	0 0	0 0	0 0	0 0	0 0	0 0
All sources of info	0 0	0 0	0 0	0 0	0 0	0 0	0 0	0 0	0 0	0 0	0 0	0 0	0 0	0 0	0 0	0 0	0 0	0 0
preferred source of info	0 0	0 0	0 0	0 0	0 0	0 0	0 0	0 0	0 0	0 0	0 0	0 0	0 0	0 0	0 0	0 0	0 0	0 0
Publisher (NET)	0 0	0 0	0 0	0 0	0 0	0 0	0 0	0 0	0 0	0 0	0 0	0 0	0 0	0 0	0 0	0 0	0 0	0 0
All sources of info	0 0	0 0	0 0	0 0	0 0	0 0	0 0	0 0	0 0	0 0	0 0	0 0	0 0	0 0	0 0	0 0	0 0	0 0
preferred source of info	0 0	0 0	0 0	0 0	0 0	0 0	0 0	0 0	0 0	0 0	0 0	0 0	0 0	0 0	0 0	0 0	0 0	0 0
Personal Collection/ Holdings (NET)	0 0	0 0	0 0	0 0	0 0	0 0	0 0	0 0	0 0	0 0	0 0	0 0	0 0	0 0	0 0	0 0	0 0	0 0
All sources of info	0 0	0 0	0 0	0 0	0 0	0 0	0 0	0 0	0 0	0 0	0 0	0 0	0 0	0 0	0 0	0 0	0 0	0 0

Proportions/Means: Columns Tested (5% risk level) - A/B/D - C/D - E/F/G - H/I/J/K/L/M/N - P/Q
* small base; ** very small base (under 30) ineligible for sig testing

Table 210
Page 797

Outsell/Digital Library Federation Study (2002)
Weighted Tables

TABLE 104, continued

T7D/E_3. e-books SUMMARY TABLE

		RESPONDENT TYPE				INSTITUTION TYPE			DISCIPLINE									GENDER	
	TOTAL SAMPLE	FACULTY MEMBER	GRAD. STUDENT	FACULTY /GRAD	UNDER GRAD. STUDENT	PUBLIC	PRIVATE	LIBERAL ARTS	BIOLOGIAL SCIENCES	PHYSICAL SCIENCES /MATH	SOCIAL SCIENCES	ARTS AND HUMAN.	ENGI- NEERING	BUSINESS	LAW	UNDEC. MAJOR	MALE	FEMALE
		(A)	(B)	(C)	(D)	(E)	(F)	(G)	(H)	(I)	(J)	(K)	(L)	(M)	(N)		(P)	(Q)
Base - Use e-books for teaching	40*	27**	13**	40*	0**	16**	14**	10**	6**	5**	11**	12**	3**	2**	***	0*	30**	11**
preferred source of info	0	0	0	0	0	0	0	0	0	0	0	0	0	0	0	0	0	0
	0	0	0	0	0	0	0	0	0	0	0	0	0	0	0	0	0	0
Other (NET)	1	1	*	1	0	0	*	1	0	0	0	1	*	0	0	0	1	0
	3.5%	4.1%	2.3%	3.5%	0	0	2.1%	10.9%	0	0	0	9.1%	9.1%	0	0	0	4.8%	0
All sources of info	1	1	*	1	0	0	*	1	0	0	0	1	*	0	0	0	1	0
	3.5%	4.1%	2.3%	3.5%	0	0	2.1%	10.9%	0	0	0	9.1%	9.1%	0	0	0	4.8%	0
preferred source of info	*	0	*	*	0	0	*	0	0	0	0	0	*	0	0	0	*	0
	0.7%	0	2.3%	0.7%	0	0	2.1%	0	0	0	0	0	9.1%	0	0	0	1.0%	0
DK/Refused	0	0	0	0	0	0	0	0	0	0	0	0	0	0	0	0	0	0
	0	0	0	0	0	0	0	0	0	0	0	0	0	0	0	0	0	0

Proportions/Means: Columns Tested (5% risk level) - A/B/D - C/D - E/F/G - H/I/J/K/L/M/N - P/Q
* small base; ** very small base (under 30) ineligible for sig testing

Table 210
Page 798

Outsell/Digital Library Federation Study (2002)
Weighted Tables

TABLE 105

T7sum_5. Magazines SUMMARY TABLE

		RESPONDENT TYPE				INSTITUTION TYPE			DISCIPLINE								GENDER	
	TOTAL SAMPLE	FACULTY MEMBER	GRAD. STUDENT	FACULTY /GRAD	UNDER GRAD. STUDENT	PUBLIC	PRIVATE	LIBERAL ARTS	BIOLOGIAL SCIENCES	PHYSICAL SCIENCES /MATH	SOCIAL SCIENCES	ARTS AND HUMAN.	ENGI- NEERING	BUSINESS	LAW	UNDEC. MAJOR	MALE	FEMALE
		(A)	(B)	(C)	(D)	(E)	(F)	(G)	(H)	(I)	(J)	(K)	(L)	(M)	(N)		(P)	(Q)
Base - USe Magazines for teaching	244	194	50*	244	0**	92*	80*	72*	27*	43*	68*	56*	6**	42*	2**	0*	170	74*
ONLINE	151 61.8%	124 63.6%	27 54.7%	151 61.8%	0 0	55 60.0%	48 59.7%	48 66.5%	19 71.0%	25 58.1%	41 61.1%	30 54.0%	3 52.4%	31 73.3%	1 45.5%	0 0	104 61.5%	46 62.4%
Search engine	56 23.2%	47 24.0%	10 20.0%	56 23.2%	0 0	22 23.8%	15 18.5%	20 27.6%	9 32.3%	13 30.2%	9 13.9%	9 16.0%	1 23.8%	15 35.6%JK	0 0	0 0	38 22.5%	18 24.8%
All sources of info	56 23.2%	47 24.0%	10 20.0%	56 23.2%	0 0	22 23.8%	15 18.5%	20 27.6%	9 32.3%	13 30.2%	9 13.9%	9 16.0%	1 23.8%	15 35.6%JK	0 0	0 0	38 22.5%	18 24.8%
preferred source of info	27 11.0%	21 10.7%	6 12.2%	27 11.0%	0 0	13 14.6%	4 5.1%	9 13.1%	4 16.1%	7 16.3%	4 5.6%	6 10.0%	1 9.5%	6 13.3%	0 0	0 0	17 10.2%	10 13.0%
Web directory/ subject related web site	30 12.2%	28 14.5%	2 3.6%	30 12.2%	0 0	6 6.0%	11 13.3%	14 18.9%E	5 19.4%	4 9.3%	6 8.3%	7 12.0%	1 9.5%	7 17.8%	* 9.1%	0 0	19 11.4%	11 14.2%
All sources of info	30 12.2%	28 14.5%	2 3.6%	30 12.2%	0 0	6 6.0%	11 13.3%	14 18.9%E	5 19.4%	4 9.3%	6 8.3%	7 12.0%	1 9.5%	7 17.8%	* 9.1%	0 0	19 11.4%	11 14.2%
preferred source of info	11 4.3%	10 5.0%	1 1.8%	11 4.3%	0 0	3 3.1%	5 6.1%	3 3.9%	2 6.5%	0 0	4 5.6%	2 4.0%	0 0	3 6.7%	0 0	0 0	6 3.4%	5 6.4%
Internet searches	28 11.5%	23 11.6%	6 11.1%	28 11.5%	0 0	12 13.0%	10 12.9%	6 8.1%	3 9.7%	5 11.6%	11 16.7%	2 4.0%	* 4.8%	7 15.6%	* 9.1%	0 0	20 11.6%	8 11.4%
All sources of info	28 11.5%	23 11.6%	6 11.1%	28 11.5%	0 0	12 13.0%	10 12.9%	6 8.1%	3 9.7%	5 11.6%	11 16.7%	2 4.0%	* 4.8%	7 15.6%	* 9.1%	0 0	20 11.6%	8 11.4%
preferred source of info	17 7.2%	13 6.6%	5 9.4%	17 7.2%	0 0	7 7.5%	6 7.1%	5 6.8%	2 6.5%	3 7.0%	9 13.9%	1 2.0%	* 4.8%	2 4.4%	0 0	0 0	13 7.5%	5 6.3%

Proportions/Means: Columns Tested (5% risk level) - A/B/D - C/D - E/F/G - H/I/J/K/L/M/N - P/Q
* small base; ** very small base (under 30) ineligible for sig testing

Table 221
Page 845

Outsell/Digital Library Federation Study (2002)
Weighted Tables

TABLE 105, continued

T7sum_5. Magazines SUMMARY TABLE

		RESPONDENT TYPE				INSTITUTION TYPE			DISCIPLINE								GENDER	
	TOTAL SAMPLE	FACULTY MEMBER	GRAD. STUDENT	FACULTY /GRAD	UNDER GRAD. STUDENT	PUBLIC	PRIVATE	LIBERAL ARTS	BIOLOGIAL SCIENCES	PHYSICAL SCIENCES /MATH	SOCIAL SCIENCES	ARTS AND HUMAN.	ENGI-NEERING	BUSINESS	LAW	UNDEC. MAJOR	MALE	FEMALE
		(A)	(B)	(C)	(D)	(E)	(F)	(G)	(H)	(I)	(J)	(K)	(L)	(M)	(N)		(P)	(Q)
Base - USe Magazines for teaching	244	194	50*	244	0**	92*	80*	72*	27*	43*	68*	56*	6**	42*	2**	0*	170	74*
Your own institution's web site	28	22	6	28	0	11	13	4	3	2	9	8	1	6	0	0	22	6
	11.5%	11.2%	12.8%	11.5%	0	12.5%	16.2%	5.0%	9.7%	4.7%	13.9%	14.0%	9.5%	13.3%	0	0	12.9%	8.4%
All sources of info	28	22	6	28	0	11	13	4	3	2	9	8	1	6	0	0	22	6
	11.5%	11.2%	12.8%	11.5%	0	12.5%	16.2%	5.0%	9.7%	4.7%	13.9%	14.0%	9.5%	13.3%	0	0	12.9%	8.4%
preferred source of info	18	11	6	18	0	9	7	2	2	1	6	4	*	5	0	0	14	4
	7.3%	5.9%	12.8%	7.3%	0	10.0%	8.7%	2.4%	6.5%	2.3%	8.3%	8.0%	4.8%	11.1%	0	0	8.1%	5.5%
Online library catalogues and finding aids	22	16	6	22	0	8	8	7	1	1	11	4	0	5	0	0	15	8
	9.1%	8.4%	12.2%	9.1%	0	8.8%	9.6%	9.1%	3.2%	2.3%	16.7%I	8.0%	0	11.1%	0	0	8.7%	10.3%
All sources of info	22	16	6	22	0	8	8	7	1	1	11	4	0	5	0	0	15	8
	9.1%	8.4%	12.2%	9.1%	0	8.8%	9.6%	9.1%	3.2%	2.3%	16.7%I	8.0%	0	11.1%	0	0	8.7%	10.3%
preferred source of info	17	11	6	17	0	8	5	5	1	1	9	3	0	3	0	0	13	5
	7.2%	5.9%	12.2%	7.2%	0	8.8%	5.8%	6.5%	3.2%	2.3%	13.9%	6.0%	0	6.7%	0	0	7.4%	6.5%
Online databases	20	17	3	20	0	7	4	10	4	4	6	3	*	2	1	0	12	8
	8.3%	8.9%	6.1%	8.3%	0	7.6%	4.6%	13.3%	16.1%	9.3%	8.3%	6.0%	4.8%	4.4%	36.4%	0	7.4%	10.4%
All sources of info	20	17	3	20	0	7	4	10	4	4	6	3	*	2	1	0	12	8
	8.3%	8.9%	6.1%	8.3%	0	7.6%	4.6%	13.3%	16.1%	9.3%	8.3%	6.0%	4.8%	4.4%	36.4%	0	7.4%	10.4%
preferred source of info	9	8	1	9	0	2	3	5	3	1	4	1	*	0	*	0	5	5
	3.8%	4.1%	2.3%	3.8%	0	1.9%	3.5%	6.4%	9.7%M	2.3%	5.6%	2.0%	4.8%	0	18.2%	0	2.7%	6.1%

Proportions/Means: Columns Tested (5% risk level) - A/B/D - C/D - E/F/G - H/I/J/K/L/M/N - P/Q
* small base; ** very small base (under 30) ineligible for sig testing

Table 221
Page 846

Outsell/Digital Library Federation Study (2002)
Weighted Tables

TABLE 105, continued

T7sum_5. Magazines SUMMARY TABLE

		RESPONDENT TYPE				INSTITUTION TYPE			DISCIPLINE								GENDER	
	TOTAL SAMPLE	FACULTY MEMBER	GRAD. STUDENT	FACULTY /GRAD	UNDER GRAD. STUDENT	PUBLIC	PRIVATE	LIBERAL ARTS	BIOLOGIAL SCIENCES	PHYSICAL SCIENCES /MATH	SOCIAL SCIENCES	ARTS AND HUMAN.	ENGI-NEERING	BUSINESS	LAW	UNDEC. MAJOR	MALE	FEMALE
		(A)	(B)	(C)	(D)	(E)	(F)	(G)	(H)	(I)	(J)	(K)	(L)	(M)	(N)		(P)	(Q)
Base - USe Magazines for teaching	244	194	50*	244	0**	92*	80*	72*	27*	43*	68*	56*	6**	42*	2**	0*	170	74*
Online reference service	8 3.2%	8 4.0%	0 0	8 3.2%	0 0	2 2.3%	5 5.9%	1 1.3%	1 3.2%	1 2.3%	2 2.8%	0 0	* 4.8%	4 8.9%K	0 0	0 0	4 2.4%	4 5.0%
All sources of info	8 3.2%	8 4.0%	0 0	8 3.2%	0 0	2 2.3%	5 5.9%	1 1.3%	1 3.2%	1 2.3%	2 2.8%	0 0	* 4.8%	4 8.9%K	0 0	0 0	4 2.4%	4 5.0%
preferred source of info	5 2.0%	5 2.5%	0 0	5 2.0%	0 0	2 2.3%	3 3.5%	0 0	1 3.2%	0 0	2 2.8%	0 0	* 4.8%	2 4.4%	0 0	0 0	1 0.7%	4 5.0%
Online abstracting and indexing services	2 0.7%	2 0.9%	0 0	2 0.7%	0 0	1 0.9%	0 0	1 1.2%	1 3.2%	0 0	0 0	0 0	1 14.3%	0 0	0 0	0 0	2 1.0%	0 0
All sources of info	2 0.7%	2 0.9%	0 0	2 0.7%	0 0	1 0.9%	0 0	1 1.2%	1 3.2%	0 0	0 0	0 0	1 14.3%	0 0	0 0	0 0	2 1.0%	0 0
preferred source of info	1 0.5%	1 0.6%	0 0	1 0.5%	0 0	* 0.3%	0 0	1 1.2%	1 3.2%	0 0	0 0	0 0	* 4.8%	0 0	0 0	0 0	1 0.7%	0 0
E-mail listservs	1 0.5%	1 0.7%	0 0	1 0.5%	0 0	* 0.3%	0 0	1 1.4%	0 0	1 2.3%	0 0	0 0	* 4.8%	0 0	0 0	0 0	1 0.8%	0 0
All sources of info	1 0.5%	1 0.7%	0 0	1 0.5%	0 0	* 0.3%	0 0	1 1.4%	0 0	1 2.3%	0 0	0 0	* 4.8%	0 0	0 0	0 0	1 0.8%	0 0
preferred source of info	0 0	0 0	0 0	0 0	0 0	0 0	0 0	0 0	0 0	0 0	0 0	0 0	0 0	0 0	0 0	0 0	0 0	0 0
Department web page	1 0.4%	1 0.5%	0 0	1 0.4%	0 0	0 0	1 1.3%	0 0	0 0	1 2.3%	0 0	0 0	0 0	0 0	0 0	0 0	1 0.6%	0 0

Proportions/Means: Columns Tested (5% risk level) - A/B/D - C/D - E/F/G - H/I/J/K/L/M/N - P/Q
* small base; ** very small base (under 30) ineligible for sig testing

Table 221
Page 847

Outsell/Digital Library Federation Study (2002)
Weighted Tables

TABLE 105, continued

T7sum_5. Magazines SUMMARY TABLE

		RESPONDENT TYPE				INSTITUTION TYPE			DISCIPLINE								GENDER	
	TOTAL SAMPLE	FACULTY MEMBER	GRAD. STUDENT	FACULTY /GRAD	UNDER GRAD. STUDENT	PUBLIC	PRIVATE	LIBERAL ARTS	BIOLOGIAL SCIENCES	PHYSICAL SCIENCES /MATH	SOCIAL SCIENCES	ARTS AND HUMAN.	ENGI-NEERING	BUSINESS	LAW	UNDEC. MAJOR	MALE	FEMALE
		(A)	(B)	(C)	(D)	(E)	(F)	(G)	(H)	(I)	(J)	(K)	(L)	(M)	(N)		(P)	(Q)
Base - USe Magazines for teaching	244	194	50*	244	0**	92*	80*	72*	27*	43*	68*	56*	6**	42*	2**	0*	170	74*
All sources of info	1 0.4%	1 0.5%	0 0	1 0.4%	0 0	0 0	1 1.3%	0 0	0 0	1 2.3%	0 0	0 0	0 0	0 0	0 0	0 0	1 0.6%	0 0
preferred source of info	0 0	0 0	0 0	0 0	0 0	0 0	0 0	0 0	0 0	0 0	0 0	0 0	0 0	0 0	0 0	0 0	0 0	0 0
Your own personal electronic library/files	1 0.4%	1 0.5%	0 0	1 0.4%	0 0	0 0	1 1.2%	0 0	0 0	0 0	0 0	0 0	0 0	1 2.2%	0 0	0 0	1 0.5%	0 0
All sources of info	1 0.4%	1 0.5%	0 0	1 0.4%	0 0	0 0	1 1.2%	0 0	0 0	0 0	0 0	0 0	0 0	1 2.2%	0 0	0 0	1 0.5%	0 0
preferred source of info	1 0.4%	1 0.5%	0 0	1 0.4%	0 0	0 0	1 1.2%	0 0	0 0	0 0	0 0	0 0	0 0	1 2.2%	0 0	0 0	1 0.5%	0 0
Online bookstore	0 0	0 0	0 0	0 0	0 0	0 0	0 0	0 0	0 0	0 0	0 0	0 0	0 0	0 0	0 0	0 0	0 0	0 0
All sources of info	0 0	0 0	0 0	0 0	0 0	0 0	0 0	0 0	0 0	0 0	0 0	0 0	0 0	0 0	0 0	0 0	0 0	0 0
preferred source of info	0 0	0 0	0 0	0 0	0 0	0 0	0 0	0 0	0 0	0 0	0 0	0 0	0 0	0 0	0 0	0 0	0 0	0 0
LIBRARY/PRINT	140 57.5%	123 63.2%B	17 35.1%	140 57.5%	0 0	42 45.9%	49 60.8%	49 68.5%E	15 54.8%	28 65.1%	34 50.0%	34 60.0%	3 52.4%	25 60.0%	1 72.7%	0 0	99 58.5%	41 55.0%
Campus library	89 36.7%	75 38.6%	14 29.1%	89 36.7%	0 0	26 28.8%	32 40.5%	31 42.5%	11 41.9%	18 41.9%	21 30.6%	26 46.0%	2 28.6%	11 26.7%	1 36.4%	0 0	65 38.2%	25 33.2%

Proportions/Means: Columns Tested (5% risk level) - A/B/D - C/D - E/F/G - H/I/J/K/L/M/N - P/Q
* small base; ** very small base (under 30) ineligible for sig testing

Table 221
Page 848

Outsell/Digital Library Federation Study (2002)
Weighted Tables

TABLE 105, continued

T7sum_5. Magazines SUMMARY TABLE

		RESPONDENT TYPE				INSTITUTION TYPE			DISCIPLINE								GENDER	
	TOTAL SAMPLE	FACULTY MEMBER	GRAD. STUDENT	FACULTY /GRAD	UNDER GRAD. STUDENT	PUBLIC	PRIVATE	LIBERAL ARTS	BIOLOGIAL SCIENCES	PHYSICAL SCIENCES /MATH	SOCIAL SCIENCES	ARTS AND HUMAN.	ENGI-NEERING	BUSINESS	LAW	UNDEC. MAJOR	MALE	FEMALE
		(A)	(B)	(C)	(D)	(E)	(F)	(G)	(H)	(I)	(J)	(K)	(L)	(M)	(N)		(P)	(Q)
Base - USe Magazines for teaching	244	194	50*	244	0**	92*	80*	72*	27*	43*	68*	56*	6**	42*	2**	0*	170	74*
All sources of info	89 36.7%	75 38.6%	14 29.1%	89 36.7%	0 0	26 28.8%	32 40.5%	31 42.5%	11 41.9%	18 41.9%	21 30.6%	26 46.0%	2 28.6%	11 26.7%	1 36.4%	0 0	65 38.2%	25 33.2%
preferred source of info	44 18.1%	34 17.5%	10 20.4%	44 18.1%	0 0	15 16.2%	15 18.8%	14 19.7%	6 22.6%	9 20.9%	11 16.7%	12 22.0%	* 4.8%	5 11.1%	* 18.2%	0 0	31 18.2%	13 17.8%
Personal subscriptions to newspapers, magazines and journals	60 24.7%	57 29.5%B	3 6.1%	60 24.7%	0 0	14 15.7%	17 21.8%	28 39.2%EF	6 22.6%	15 34.9%K	11 16.7%	8 14.0%	2 28.6%	18 42.2%JK	1 27.3%	0 0	45 26.7%	15 20.1%
All sources of info	60 24.7%	57 29.5%B	3 6.1%	60 24.7%	0 0	14 15.7%	17 21.8%	28 39.2%EF	6 22.6%	15 34.9%K	11 16.7%	8 14.0%	2 28.6%	18 42.2%JK	1 27.3%	0 0	45 26.7%	15 20.1%
preferred source of info	36 14.7%	33 16.9%	3 6.1%	36 14.7%	0 0	7 7.7%	14 17.2%	15 20.9%E	4 12.9%	9 20.9%	8 11.1%	6 10.0%	1 23.8%	8 20.0%	* 18.2%	0 0	31 18.2%Q	5 6.7%
Your own personal physical library/ files/bookshelves	22 8.8%	20 10.5%	1 2.3%	22 8.8%	0 0	8 8.4%	5 6.6%	9 11.9%	2 6.5%	7 16.3%J	2 2.8%	7 12.0%	* 4.8%	4 8.9%	* 9.1%	0 0	16 9.5%	5 7.2%
All sources of info	22 8.8%	20 10.5%	1 2.3%	22 8.8%	0 0	8 8.4%	5 6.6%	9 11.9%	2 6.5%	7 16.3%J	2 2.8%	7 12.0%	* 4.8%	4 8.9%	* 9.1%	0 0	16 9.5%	5 7.2%
preferred source of info	9 3.9%	9 4.8%	0 0	9 3.9%	0 0	4 4.8%	3 3.8%	2 2.8%	0 0	4 9.3%M	2 2.8%	3 6.0%	0 0	0 0	* 9.1%	0 0	6 3.6%	3 4.4%

Proportions/Means: Columns Tested (5% risk level) - A/B/D - C/D - E/F/G - H/I/J/K/L/M/N - P/Q
* small base; ** very small base (under 30) ineligible for sig testing

Table 221
Page 849

Outsell/Digital Library Federation Study (2002)
Weighted Tables

TABLE 105, continued

T7sum_5. Magazines SUMMARY TABLE

		RESPONDENT TYPE				INSTITUTION TYPE			DISCIPLINE								GENDER	
	TOTAL SAMPLE	FACULTY MEMBER	GRAD. STUDENT	FACULTY /GRAD	UNDER GRAD. STUDENT	PUBLIC	PRIVATE	LIBERAL ARTS	BIOLOGIAL SCIENCES	PHYSICAL SCIENCES /MATH	SOCIAL SCIENCES	ARTS AND HUMAN.	ENGI-NEERING	BUSINESS	LAW	UNDEC. MAJOR	MALE	FEMALE
		(A)	(B)	(C)	(D)	(E)	(F)	(G)	(H)	(I)	(J)	(K)	(L)	(M)	(N)		(P)	(Q)
Base - USe Magazines for teaching	244	194	50*	244	0**	92*	80*	72*	27*	43*	68*	56*	6**	42*	2**	0*	170	74*
Physical bookstore	7 3.1%	6 3.3%	1 2.3%	7 3.1%	0 0	3 2.8%	4 4.8%	1 1.6%	2 6.5%	0 0	0 0	4 8.0%	* 4.8%	1 2.2%	0 0	0 0	2 1.4%	5 7.0%P
All sources of info	7 3.1%	6 3.3%	1 2.3%	7 3.1%	0 0	3 2.8%	4 4.8%	1 1.6%	2 6.5%	0 0	0 0	4 8.0%	* 4.8%	1 2.2%	0 0	0 0	2 1.4%	5 7.0%P
preferred source of info	2 1.0%	1 0.6%	1 2.3%	2 1.0%	0 0	1 1.5%	1 1.2%	0 0	0 0	0 0	0 0	1 2.0%	* 4.8%	1 2.2%	0 0	0 0	* 0.2%	2 2.8%
References cited in books or journal articles	6 2.5%	6 3.1%	0 0	6 2.5%	0 0	3 3.6%	0 0	3 3.9%	0 0	0 0	2 2.8%	1 2.0%	* 4.8%	3 6.7%	0 0	0 0	3 1.8%	3 4.0%
All sources of info	6 2.5%	6 3.1%	0 0	6 2.5%	0 0	3 3.6%	0 0	3 3.9%	0 0	0 0	2 2.8%	1 2.0%	* 4.8%	3 6.7%	0 0	0 0	3 1.8%	3 4.0%
preferred source of info	1 0.4%	1 0.5%	0 0	1 0.4%	0 0	0 0	0 0	1 1.3%	0 0	0 0	0 0	0 0	0 0	1 2.2%	0 0	0 0	1 0.5%	0 0
Another library	4 1.7%	4 2.1%	0 0	4 1.7%	0 0	0 0	1 1.3%	3 4.2%	0 0	2 4.7%	0 0	1 2.0%	0 0	1 2.2%	0 0	0 0	4 2.4%	0 0
All sources of info	4 1.7%	4 2.1%	0 0	4 1.7%	0 0	0 0	1 1.3%	3 4.2%	0 0	2 4.7%	0 0	1 2.0%	0 0	1 2.2%	0 0	0 0	4 2.4%	0 0
preferred source of info	0 0	0 0	0 0	0 0	0 0	0 0	0 0	0 0	0 0	0 0	0 0	0 0	0 0	0 0	0 0	0 0	0 0	0 0

Proportions/Means: Columns Tested (5% risk level) - A/B/D - C/D - E/F/G - H/I/J/K/L/M/N - P/Q
* small base; ** very small base (under 30) ineligible for sig testing

Table 221
Page 850

Outsell/Digital Library Federation Study (2002)
Weighted Tables

TABLE 105, continued

T7sum_5. Magazines SUMMARY TABLE

		RESPONDENT TYPE				INSTITUTION TYPE			DISCIPLINE									GENDER	
	TOTAL SAMPLE	FACULTY MEMBER	GRAD. STUDENT	FACULTY /GRAD	UNDER GRAD. STUDENT	PUBLIC	PRIVATE	LIBERAL ARTS	BIOLOGICAL SCIENCES	PHYSICAL SCIENCES /MATH	SOCIAL SCIENCES	ARTS AND HUMAN.	ENGI-NEERING	BUSINESS	LAW	UNDEC. MAJOR	MALE	FEMALE
		(A)	(B)	(C)	(D)	(E)	(F)	(G)	(H)	(I)	(J)	(K)	(L)	(M)	(N)		(P)	(Q)
Base - USe Magazines for teaching	244	194	50*	244	0**	92*	80*	72*	27*	43*	68*	56*	6**	42*	2**	0*	170	74*
Printed abstracting and indexing services	* 0.1%	* 0.1%	0 0	* 0.1%	0 0	* 0.2%	0 0	0 0	0 0	0 0	0 0	0 0	0 0	0 0	* 9.1%	0 0	* 0.1%	0 0
All sources of info	* 0.1%	* 0.1%	0 0	* 0.1%	0 0	* 0.2%	0 0	0 0	0 0	0 0	0 0	0 0	0 0	0 0	* 9.1%	0 0	* 0.1%	0 0
preferred source of info	* 0.1%	* 0.1%	0 0	* 0.1%	0 0	* 0.2%	0 0	0 0	0 0	0 0	0 0	0 0	0 0	0 0	* 9.1%	0 0	* 0.1%	0 0
Printed library catalogues and finding aids	0 0	0 0	0 0	0 0	0 0	0 0	0 0	0 0	0 0	0 0	0 0	0 0	0 0	0 0	0 0	0 0	0 0	0 0
All sources of info	0 0	0 0	0 0	0 0	0 0	0 0	0 0	0 0	0 0	0 0	0 0	0 0	0 0	0 0	0 0	0 0	0 0	0 0
preferred source of info	0 0	0 0	0 0	0 0	0 0	0 0	0 0	0 0	0 0	0 0	0 0	0 0	0 0	0 0	0 0	0 0	0 0	0 0
PERSONAL ASSISTANCE	41 16.9%	31 15.7%	11 21.6%	41 16.9%	0 0	16 17.8%	15 18.9%	10 13.6%	4 16.1%	9 20.9%	8 11.1%	11 20.0%	1 19.0%	7 17.8%	1 27.3%	0 0	29 17.2%	12 16.2%
Colleagues inside your institution	27 10.9%	18 9.3%	9 17.3%	27 10.9%	0 0	12 12.9%	9 11.1%	6 8.2%	4 12.9%	3 7.0%	6 8.3%	7 12.0%	1 14.3%	7 15.6%	* 18.2%	0 0	17 9.9%	10 13.2%
All sources of info	27 10.9%	18 9.3%	9 17.3%	27 10.9%	0 0	12 12.9%	9 11.1%	6 8.2%	4 12.9%	3 7.0%	6 8.3%	7 12.0%	1 14.3%	7 15.6%	* 18.2%	0 0	17 9.9%	10 13.2%

Proportions/Means: Columns Tested (5% risk level) - A/B/D - C/D - E/F/G - H/I/J/K/L/M/N - P/Q
* small base; ** very small base (under 30) ineligible for sig testing

Table 221
Page 851

Outsell/Digital Library Federation Study (2002)
Weighted Tables

TABLE 105, continued

T7sum_5. Magazines SUMMARY TABLE

		RESPONDENT TYPE				INSTITUTION TYPE			DISCIPLINE								GENDER	
	TOTAL SAMPLE	FACULTY MEMBER	GRAD. STUDENT	FACULTY /GRAD	UNDER GRAD. STUDENT	PUBLIC	PRIVATE	LIBERAL ARTS	BIOLOGIAL SCIENCES	PHYSICAL SCIENCES /MATH	SOCIAL SCIENCES	ARTS AND HUMAN.	ENGI- NEERING	BUSINESS	LAW	UNDEC. MAJOR	MALE	FEMALE
		(A)	(B)	(C)	(D)	(E)	(F)	(G)	(H)	(I)	(J)	(K)	(L)	(M)	(N)		(P)	(Q)
Base - USe Magazines for teaching	244	194	50*	244	0**	92*	80*	72*	27*	43*	68*	56*	6**	42*	2**	0*	170	74*
preferred source of info	15	7	8	15	0	8	5	2	2	2	4	4	1	2	*	0	10	5
	6.1%	3.7%	15.5%A	6.1%	0	8.7%	6.2%	2.8%	6.5%	4.7%	5.6%	8.0%	14.3%	4.4%	9.1%	0	5.8%	6.8%
A librarian in your institution	17	13	4	17	0	7	5	5	2	6	2	6	1	1	*	0	15	2
	7.0%	6.5%	8.9%	7.0%	0	7.3%	6.7%	6.9%	6.5%	14.0%M	2.8%	10.0%	9.5%	2.2%	18.2%	0	8.8%	3.0%
All sources of info	17	13	4	17	0	7	5	5	2	6	2	6	1	1	*	0	15	2
	7.0%	6.5%	8.9%	7.0%	0	7.3%	6.7%	6.9%	6.5%	14.0%M	2.8%	10.0%	9.5%	2.2%	18.2%	0	8.8%	3.0%
preferred source of info	6	4	1	6	0	4	2	0	1	1	0	3	*	0	0	0	4	1
	2.3%	2.3%	2.3%	2.3%	0	3.8%	2.5%	0	3.2%	2.3%	0	6.0%	4.8%	0	0	0	2.6%	1.5%
Colleagues outside your institution	8	8	0	8	0	2	4	2	0	1	4	2	0	1	0	0	8	0
	3.3%	4.1%	0	3.3%	0	2.0%	4.9%	2.9%	0	2.3%	5.6%	4.0%	0	2.2%	0	0	4.7%	0
All sources of info	8	8	0	8	0	2	4	2	0	1	4	2	0	1	0	0	8	0
	3.3%	4.1%	0	3.3%	0	2.0%	4.9%	2.9%	0	2.3%	5.6%	4.0%	0	2.2%	0	0	4.7%	0
preferred source of info	1	1	0	1	0	0	1	0	0	0	0	1	0	0	0	0	1	0
	0.5%	0.6%	0	0.5%	0	0	1.4%	0	0	0	0	2.0%	0	0	0	0	0.7%	0
Another institution's librarian	1	1	0	1	0	1	0	0	0	1	0	0	0	0	0	0	1	0
	0.4%	0.5%	0	0.4%	0	1.1%	0	0	0	2.3%	0	0	0	0	0	0	0.6%	0
All sources of info	1	1	0	1	0	1	0	0	0	1	0	0	0	0	0	0	1	0
	0.4%	0.5%	0	0.4%	0	1.1%	0	0	0	2.3%	0	0	0	0	0	0	0.6%	0
preferred source of info	0	0	0	0	0	0	0	0	0	0	0	0	0	0	0	0	0	0
	0	0	0	0	0	0	0	0	0	0	0	0	0	0	0	0	0	0

Proportions/Means: Columns Tested (5% risk level) - A/B/D - C/D - E/F/G - H/I/J/K/L/M/N - P/Q
* small base; ** very small base (under 30) ineligible for sig testing

Table 221
Page 852

Outsell/Digital Library Federation Study (2002)
Weighted Tables

TABLE 105, continued

T7sum_5. Magazines SUMMARY TABLE

		RESPONDENT TYPE				INSTITUTION TYPE			DISCIPLINE									GENDER	
	TOTAL SAMPLE	FACULTY MEMBER	GRAD. STUDENT	FACULTY /GRAD	UNDER GRAD. STUDENT	PUBLIC	PRIVATE	LIBERAL ARTS	BIOLOGIAL SCIENCES	PHYSICAL SCIENCES /MATH	SOCIAL SCIENCES	ARTS AND HUMAN.	ENGI-NEERING	BUSINESS	LAW	UNDEC. MAJOR	MALE	FEMALE
		(A)	(B)	(C)	(D)	(E)	(F)	(G)	(H)	(I)	(J)	(K)	(L)	(M)	(N)		(P)	(Q)
Base - USe Magazines for teaching	244	194	50*	244	0**	92*	80*	72*	27*	43*	68*	56*	6**	42*	2**	0*	170	74*
Professional meetings	0 0	0 0	0 0	0 0	0 0	0 0	0 0	0 0	0 0	0 0	0 0	0 0	0 0	0 0	0 0	0 0	0 0	0 0
All sources of info	0 0	0 0	0 0	0 0	0 0	0 0	0 0	0 0	0 0	0 0	0 0	0 0	0 0	0 0	0 0	0 0	0 0	0 0
preferred source of info	0 0	0 0	0 0	0 0	0 0	0 0	0 0	0 0	0 0	0 0	0 0	0 0	0 0	0 0	0 0	0 0	0 0	0 0
Students	3 1.3%	3 1.6%	0 0	3 1.3%	0 0	* 0.3%	1 1.2%	2 2.6%	0 0	0 0	2 2.8%	0 0	* 4.8%	1 2.2%	0 0	0 0	2 1.3%	1 1.3%
All sources of info	3 1.3%	3 1.6%	0 0	3 1.3%	0 0	* 0.3%	1 1.2%	2 2.6%	0 0	0 0	2 2.8%	0 0	* 4.8%	1 2.2%	0 0	0 0	2 1.3%	1 1.3%
preferred source of info	2 0.8%	2 1.0%	0 0	2 0.8%	0 0	0 0	0 0	2 2.6%	0 0	0 0	2 2.8%	0 0	0 0	0 0	0 0	0 0	2 1.1%	0 0
Online (unspecified)	3 1.2%	3 1.5%	0 0	3 1.2%	0 0	2 2.0%	1 1.4%	0 0	0 0	0 0	2 2.8%	1 2.0%	0 0	0 0	0 0	0 0	1 0.7%	2 2.5%
All sources of info	3 1.2%	3 1.5%	0 0	3 1.2%	0 0	2 2.0%	1 1.4%	0 0	0 0	0 0	2 2.8%	1 2.0%	0 0	0 0	0 0	0 0	1 0.7%	2 2.5%
preferred source of info	2 0.8%	2 1.0%	0 0	2 0.8%	0 0	2 2.0%	0 0	0 0	0 0	0 0	2 2.8%	0 0	0 0	0 0	0 0	0 0	0 0	2 2.5%
Personal office/lab	3 1.2%	3 1.5%	0 0	3 1.2%	0 .0	2 2.0%	0 0	1 1.6%	0 0	0 0	2 2.8%	1 2.0%	0 0	0 0	0 0	0 0	1 0.7%	2 2.5%

Proportions/Means: Columns Tested (5% risk level) - A/B/D - C/D - E/F/G - H/I/J/K/L/M/N - P/Q
* small base; ** very small base (under 30) ineligible for sig testing

Table 221
Page 853

Outsell/Digital Library Federation Study (2002)
Weighted Tables

TABLE 105, continued

T7sum_5. Magazines SUMMARY TABLE

		RESPONDENT TYPE				INSTITUTION TYPE			DISCIPLINE									GENDER	
	TOTAL SAMPLE	FACULTY MEMBER	GRAD. STUDENT	FACULTY /GRAD	UNDER GRAD. STUDENT	PUBLIC	PRIVATE	LIBERAL ARTS	BIOLOGIAL SCIENCES	PHYSICAL SCIENCES /MATH	SOCIAL SCIENCES	ARTS AND HUMAN.	ENGI-NEERING	BUSINESS	LAW	UNDEC. MAJOR	MALE	FEMALE
		(A)	(B)	(C)	(D)	(E)	(F)	(G)	(H)	(I)	(J)	(K)	(L)	(M)	(N)		(P)	(Q)
Base - USe Magazines for teaching	244	194	50*	244	0**	92*	80*	72*	27*	43*	68*	56*	6**	42*	2**	0*	170	74*
All sources of info	3	3	0	3	0	2	0	1	0	0	2	1	0	0	0	0	1	2
	1.2%	1.5%	0	1.2%	0	2.0%	0	1.6%	0	0	2.8%	2.0%	0	0	0	0	0.7%	2.5%
preferred source of info	0	0	0	0	0	0	0	0	0	0	0	0	0	0	0	0	0	0
	0	0	0	0	0	0	0	0	0	0	0	0	0	0	0	0	0	0
Author	0	0	0	0	0	0	0	0	0	0	0	0	0	0	0	0	0	0
	0	0	0	0	0	0	0	0	0	0	0	0	0	0	0	0	0	0
All sources of info	0	0	0	0	0	0	0	0	0	0	0	0	0	0	0	0	0	0
	0	0	0	0	0	0	0	0	0	0	0	0	0	0	0	0	0	0
preferred source of info	0	0	0	0	0	0	0	0	0	0	0	0	0	0	0	0	0	0
	0	0	0	0	0	0	0	0	0	0	0	0	0	0	0	0	0	0
Other	19	18	1	19	0	9	2	8	2	3	0	7	1	7	*	0	14	5
	8.0%	9.3%	2.8%	8.0%	0	9.8%	2.8%	11.5%	6.5%	7.0%	0	12.0%J	19.0%	15.6%J	18.2%	0	8.4%	7.0%
All sources of info	17	16	1	17	0	9	1	7	2	3	0	4	1	7	*	0	13	4
	7.1%	8.2%	2.8%	7.1%	0	9.8%F	1.4%	9.9%F	6.5%	7.0%	0	8.0%	19.0%	15.6%J	18.2%	0	7.8%	5.5%
preferred source of info	7	7	*	7	0	2	2	3	0	2	0	3	1	1	*	0	6	1
	2.9%	3.5%	0.6%	2.9%	0	1.8%	2.8%	4.3%	0	4.7%	0	6.0%	9.5%	2.2%	9.1%	0	3.5%	1.5%
DK/Refused	15	12	2	15	0	5	4	5	0	3	2	6	*	4	*	0	7	8
	6.0%	6.4%	4.5%	6.0%	0	6.0%	5.3%	6.8%	0	7.0%	2.8%	10.0%	4.8%	8.9%	9.1%	0	4.2%	10.2%

Proportions/Means: Columns Tested (5% risk level) - A/B/D - C/D - E/F/G - H/I/J/K/L/M/N - P/Q
* small base; ** very small base (under 30) ineligible for sig testing

Table 221
Page 854

Outsell/Digital Library Federation Study (2002)
Weighted Tables

TABLE 106

T7D/E_5. Magazines SUMMARY TABLE

		RESPONDENT TYPE				INSTITUTION TYPE			DISCIPLINE									GENDER	
	TOTAL SAMPLE	FACULTY MEMBER	GRAD. STUDENT	FACULTY /GRAD	UNDER GRAD. STUDENT	PUBLIC	PRIVATE	LIBERAL ARTS	BIOLOGIAL SCIENCES	PHYSICAL SCIENCES /MATH	SOCIAL SCIENCES	ARTS AND HUMAN.	ENGI- NEERING	BUSINESS	LAW	UNDEC. MAJOR	MALE	FEMALE
		(A)	(B)	(C)	(D)	(E)	(F)	(G)	(H)	(I)	(J)	(K)	(L)	(M)	(N)		(P)	(Q)
Base - Use Magazines for teaching	244	194	50*	244	0**	92*	80*	72*	27*	43*	68*	56*	6**	42*	2**	0*	170	74*
Borrow from or use in campus library (NET)	170 69.6%	135 69.3%	35 70.8%	170 69.6%	0 0	64 70.2%	55 68.4%	51 70.1%	18 67.7%	32 74.4%	45 66.7%	41 74.0%	4 71.4%	28 66.7%	* 18.2%	0 0	122 72.2%	47 63.6%
All sources of info	170 69.6%	135 69.3%	35 70.8%	170 69.6%	0 0	64 70.2%	55 68.4%	51 70.1%	18 67.7%	32 74.4%	45 66.7%	41 74.0%	4 71.4%	28 66.7%	* 18.2%	0 0	122 72.2%	47 63.6%
preferred source of info	116 47.6%	87 44.8%	29 58.5%	116 47.6%	0 0	47 50.9%	38 48.0%	31 42.9%	12 45.2%	21 48.8%	34 50.0%	34 60.0%M	2 33.3%	13 31.1%	* 9.1%	0 0	81 48.0%	35 46.7%
Access online (NET)	80 32.8%	68 35.1%	12 23.7%	80 32.8%	0 0	35 37.9%	22 27.8%	23 31.7%	12 45.2%K	16 37.2%	19 27.8%	11 20.0%	2 28.6%	19 44.4%K	1 63.6%	0 0	57 33.6%	23 30.9%
All sources of info	80 32.8%	68 35.1%	12 23.7%	80 32.8%	0 0	35 37.9%	22 27.8%	23 31.7%	12 45.2%K	16 37.2%	19 27.8%	11 20.0%	2 28.6%	19 44.4%K	1 63.6%	0 0	57 33.6%	23 30.9%
preferred source of info	56 23.1%	48 24.6%	9 17.6%	56 23.1%	0 0	24 26.2%	14 17.8%	18 25.2%	10 35.5%K	10 23.3%	11 16.7%	7 12.0%	1 19.0%	17 40.0%JK	1 45.5%	0 0	39 22.9%	18 23.7%
Access from course website (NET)	29 12.0%	25 13.1%	4 7.6%	29 12.0%	0 0	9 9.7%	6 7.8%	14 19.5%	3 9.7%	6 14.0%	6 8.3%	7 12.0%	1 19.0%	7 15.6%	1 27.3%	0 0	24 14.3%	5 6.7%
All sources of info	29 12.0%	25 13.1%	4 7.6%	29 12.0%	0 0	9 9.7%	6 7.8%	14 19.5%	3 9.7%	6 14.0%	6 8.3%	7 12.0%	1 19.0%	7 15.6%	1 27.3%	0 0	24 14.3%	5 6.7%
preferred source of info	19 8.0%	18 9.0%	2 3.8%	19 8.0%	0 0	7 7.4%	3 4.0%	9 13.0%	1 3.2%	3 7.0%	4 5.6%	6 10.0%	1 19.0%	5 11.1%	* 18.2%	0 0	16 9.7%	3 4.0%

Proportions/Means: Columns Tested (5% risk level) - A/B/D - C/D - E/F/G - H/I/J/K/L/M/N - P/Q
* small base; ** very small base (under 30) ineligible for sig testing

Table 224
Page 861

Outsell/Digital Library Federation Study (2002)
Weighted Tables

TABLE 106, continued

T7D/E_5. Magazines SUMMARY TABLE

	RESPONDENT TYPE				INSTITUTION TYPE			DISCIPLINE								GENDER	
	TOTAL SAMPLE	FACULTY MEMBER	GRAD. STUDENT	FACULTY /GRAD	UNDER GRAD. STUDENT	PUBLIC	PRIVATE	LIBERAL ARTS	BIOLOGIAL SCIENCES	PHYSICAL SCIENCES /MATH	SOCIAL SCIENCES	ARTS AND HUMAN.	ENGI- NEERING	BUSINESS	LAW	UNDEC. MAJOR	MALE	FEMALE
		(A)	(B)	(C)	(D)	(E)	(F)	(G)	(H)	(I)	(J)	(K)	(L)	(M)	(N)		(P)	(Q)
Base - Use Magazines for teaching	244	194	50*	244	0**	92*	80*	72*	27*	43*	68*	56*	6**	42*	2**	0*	170	74*
Purchase from physical book store (NET)	29 11.7%	22 11.3%	7 13.3%	29 11.7%	0 0	12 13.1%	10 13.0%	6 8.6%	4 12.9%	1 2.3%	9 13.9%	12 22.0%IM	1 23.8%	1 2.2%	0 0	0 0	19 11.5%	9 12.4%
All sources of info	29 11.7%	22 11.3%	7 13.3%	29 11.7%	0 0	12 13.1%	10 13.0%	6 8.6%	4 12.9%	1 2.3%	9 13.9%	12 22.0%IM	1 23.8%	1 2.2%	0 0	0 0	19 11.5%	9 12.4%
preferred source of info	13 5.3%	10 5.0%	3 6.6%	13 5.3%	0 0	7 7.6%	3 3.8%	3 4.0%	2 6.5%	1 2.3%	6 8.3%	3 6.0%	1 19.0%	0 0	0 0	0 0	9 5.3%	4 5.4%
Borrow from or use in other libraries (NET)	14 5.6%	11 5.5%	3 6.1%	14 5.6%	0 0	6 6.5%	2 2.7%	6 7.7%	2 6.5%	4 9.3%	6 8.3%	1 2.0%	0 0	1 2.2%	* 9.1%	0 0	8 4.6%	6 7.8%
All sources of info	14 5.6%	11 5.5%	3 6.1%	14 5.6%	0 0	6 6.5%	2 2.7%	6 7.7%	2 6.5%	4 9.3%	6 8.3%	1 2.0%	0 0	1 2.2%	* 9.1%	0 0	8 4.6%	6 7.8%
preferred source of info	5 2.1%	2 1.1%	3 6.1%	5 2.1%	0 0	2 2.2%	1 1.4%	2 2.6%	0 0	0 0	4 5.6%	1 2.0%	0 0	0 0	* 9.1%	0 0	* 0.1%	5 6.6%P
Interlibrary loan (NET)	12 4.9%	10 5.1%	2 3.8%	12 4.9%	0 0	2 2.0%	6 7.6%	4 5.4%	2 6.5%	1 2.3%	4 5.6%	2 4.0%	* 4.8%	3 6.7%	0 0	0 0	8 4.8%	4 5.0%
All sources of info	12 4.9%	10 5.1%	2 3.8%	12 4.9%	0 0	2 2.0%	6 7.6%	4 5.4%	2 6.5%	1 2.3%	4 5.6%	2 4.0%	* 4.8%	3 6.7%	0 0	0 0	8 4.8%	4 5.0%
preferred source of info	3 1.1%	3 1.4%	0 0	3 1.1%	0 0	0 0	3 3.5%	0 0	1 3.2%	0 0	2 2.8%	0 0	0 0	0 0	0 0	0 0	2 1.1%	1 1.2%

Proportions/Means: Columns Tested (5% risk level) - A/B/D - C/D - E/F/G - H/I/J/K/L/M/N - P/Q
* small base; ** very small base (under 30) ineligible for sig testing

Table 224
Page 862

Outsell/Digital Library Federation Study (2002)
Weighted Tables

TABLE 106, continued

T7D/E_5. Magazines SUMMARY TABLE

		RESPONDENT TYPE				INSTITUTION TYPE			DISCIPLINE								GENDER	
	TOTAL SAMPLE	FACULTY MEMBER	GRAD. STUDENT	FACULTY /GRAD	UNDER GRAD. STUDENT	PUBLIC	PRIVATE	LIBERAL ARTS	BIOLOGIAL SCIENCES	PHYSICAL SCIENCES /MATH	SOCIAL SCIENCES	ARTS AND HUMAN.	ENGI-NEERING	BUSINESS	LAW	UNDEC. MAJOR	MALE	FEMALE
		(A)	(B)	(C)	(D)	(E)	(F)	(G)	(H)	(I)	(J)	(K)	(L)	(M)	(N)		(P)	(Q)
Base - Use Magazines for teaching	244	194	50*	244	0**	92*	80*	72*	27*	43*	68*	56*	6**	42*	2**	0*	170	74*
Personal Collection/ Holdings (NET)	10 4.3%	9 4.8%	1 2.3%	10 4.3%	0 0	1 1.0%	8 9.8%E	2 2.5%	2 6.5%	2 4.7%	2 2.8%	1 2.0%	0 0	4 8.9%	0 0	0 0	8 4.5%	3 3.9%
All sources of info	10 4.3%	9 4.8%	1 2.3%	10 4.3%	0 0	1 1.0%	8 9.8%E	2 2.5%	2 6.5%	2 4.7%	2 2.8%	1 2.0%	0 0	4 8.9%	0 0	0 0	8 4.5%	3 3.9%
preferred source of info	6 2.3%	6 2.9%	0 0	6 2.3%	0 0	1 1.0%	5 6.0%	0 0	1 3.2%	2 4.7%	2 2.8%	0 0	0 0	1 2.2%	0 0	0 0	6 3.4%	0 0
Publisher (NET)	5 2.2%	5 2.8%	0 0	5 2.2%	0 0	1 0.6%	5 6.0%	0 0	1 3.2%	0 0	2 2.8%	1 2.0%	1 9.5%	1 2.2%	0 0	0 0	5 3.2%	0 0
All sources of info	5 2.2%	5 2.8%	0 0	5 2.2%	0 0	1 0.6%	5 6.0%	0 0	1 3.2%	0 0	2 2.8%	1 2.0%	1 9.5%	1 2.2%	0 0	0 0	5 3.2%	0 0
preferred source of info	2 0.8%	2 1.0%	0 0	2 0.8%	0 0	0 0	2 2.4%	0 0	0 0	0 0	2 2.8%	0 0	0 0	0 0	0 0	0 0	2 1.1%	0 0
Order from on demand document delivery service (NET)	5 2.0%	5 2.5%	0 0	5 2.0%	0 0	0 0	2 2.3%	3 4.1%	0 0	2 4.7%	0 0	0 0	0 0	3 6.7%	0 0	0 0	5 2.8%	0 0
All sources of info	5 2.0%	5 2.5%	0 0	5 2.0%	0 0	0 0	2 2.3%	3 4.1%	0 0	2 4.7%	0 0	0 0	0 0	3 6.7%	0 0	0 0	5 2.8%	0 0
preferred source of info	4 1.6%	4 2.0%	0 0	4 1.6%	0 0	0 0	2 2.3%	2 2.8%	0 0	2 4.7%	0 0	0 0	0 0	2 4.4%	0 0	0 0	4 2.3%	0 0

Proportions/Means: Columns Tested (5% risk level) - A/B/D - C/D - E/F/G - H/I/J/K/L/M/N - P/Q
* small base; ** very small base (under 30) ineligible for sig testing

Table 224
Page 863

Outsell/Digital Library Federation Study (2002)
Weighted Tables

TABLE 106, continued

T7D/E_5. Magazines SUMMARY TABLE

	TOTAL SAMPLE	RESPONDENT TYPE: FACULTY MEMBER	RESPONDENT TYPE: GRAD. STUDENT	RESPONDENT TYPE: FACULTY /GRAD	RESPONDENT TYPE: UNDER GRAD. STUDENT	INSTITUTION TYPE: PUBLIC	INSTITUTION TYPE: PRIVATE	INSTITUTION TYPE: LIBERAL ARTS	DISCIPLINE: BIOLOGIAL SCIENCES	DISCIPLINE: PHYSICAL SCIENCES /MATH	DISCIPLINE: SOCIAL SCIENCES	DISCIPLINE: ARTS AND HUMAN.	DISCIPLINE: ENGI-NEERING	DISCIPLINE: BUSINESS	DISCIPLINE: LAW	DISCIPLINE: UNDEC. MAJOR	GENDER: MALE	GENDER: FEMALE
		(A)	(B)	(C)	(D)	(E)	(F)	(G)	(H)	(I)	(J)	(K)	(L)	(M)	(N)		(P)	(Q)
Base - Use Magazines for teaching	244	194	50*	244	0**	92*	80*	72*	27*	43*	68*	56*	6**	42*	2**	0*	170	74*
Colleagues (NET)	3	2	1	3	0	1	1	1	1	0	0	1	*	1	0	0	2	1
	1.3%	0.9%	2.8%	1.3%	0	1.2%	1.5%	1.2%	3.2%	0	0	2.0%	4.8%	2.2%	0	0	1.2%	1.5%
All sources of info	3	2	1	3	0	1	1	1	1	0	0	1	*	1	0	0	2	1
	1.3%	0.9%	2.8%	1.3%	0	1.2%	1.5%	1.2%	3.2%	0	0	2.0%	4.8%	2.2%	0	0	1.2%	1.5%
preferred source of info	1	1	*	1	0	0	1	0	0	0	0	0	*	1	0	0	1	0
	0.5%	0.5%	0.6%	0.5%	0	0	1.5%	0	0	0	0	0	4.8%	2.2%	0	0	0.7%	0
Home (NET)	3	2	1	3	0	0	1	2	0	0	2	1	0	0	0	0	3	0
	1.2%	1.0%	2.3%	1.2%	0	0	1.4%	2.6%	0	0	2.8%	2.0%	0	0	0	0	1.8%	0
All sources of info	3	2	1	3	0	0	1	2	0	0	2	1	0	0	0	0	3	0
	1.2%	1.0%	2.3%	1.2%	0	0	1.4%	2.6%	0	0	2.8%	2.0%	0	0	0	0	1.8%	0
preferred source of info	3	2	1	3	0	0	1	2	0	0	2	1	0	0	0	0	3	0
	1.2%	1.0%	2.3%	1.2%	0	0	1.4%	2.6%	0	0	2.8%	2.0%	0	0	0	0	1.8%	0
Purchase from online bookstore (NET)	2	2	0	2	0	1	0	1	0	0	0	1	0	1	0	0	2	0
	0.8%	1.1%	0	0.8%	0	1.0%	0	1.6%	0	0	0	2.0%	0	2.2%	0	0	1.2%	0
All sources of info	2	2	0	2	0	1	0	1	0	0	0	1	0	1	0	0	2	0
	0.8%	1.1%	0	0.8%	0	1.0%	0	1.6%	0	0	0	2.0%	0	2.2%	0	0	1.2%	0
preferred source of info	1	1	0	1	0	1	0	0	0	0	0	0	0	1	0	0	1	0
	0.4%	0.5%	0	0.4%	0	1.0%	0	0	0	0	0	0	0	2.2%	0	0	0.5%	0
Department (NET)	2	1	1	2	0	0	2	0	0	0	0	1	0	1	0	0	0	2
	0.8%	0.5%	2.3%	0.8%	0	0	2.6%	0	0	0	0	2.0%	0	2.2%	0	0	0	2.8%

Proportions/Means: Columns Tested (5% risk level) - A/B/D - C/D - E/F/G - H/I/J/K/L/M/N - P/Q
* small base; ** very small base (under 30) ineligible for sig testing

Table 224
Page 864

Outsell/Digital Library Federation Study (2002)
Weighted Tables

TABLE 106, continued

T7D/E_5. Magazines SUMMARY TABLE

		RESPONDENT TYPE				INSTITUTION TYPE			DISCIPLINE								GENDER	
	TOTAL SAMPLE	FACULTY MEMBER	GRAD. STUDENT	FACULTY /GRAD	UNDER GRAD. STUDENT	PUBLIC	PRIVATE	LIBERAL ARTS	BIOLOGIAL SCIENCES	PHYSICAL SCIENCES /MATH	SOCIAL SCIENCES	ARTS AND HUMAN.	ENGI-NEERING	BUSINESS	LAW	UNDEC. MAJOR	MALE	FEMALE
		(A)	(B)	(C)	(D)	(E)	(F)	(G)	(H)	(I)	(J)	(K)	(L)	(M)	(N)		(P)	(Q)
Base - Use Magazines for teaching	244	194	50*	244	0**	92*	80*	72*	27*	43*	68*	56*	6**	42*	2**	0*	170	74*
All sources of info	2 0.8%	1 0.5%	1 2.3%	2 0.8%	0 0	0 0	2 2.6%	0 0	0 0	0 0	0 0	1 2.0%	0 0	1 2.2%	0 0	0 0	0 0	2 2.8%
preferred source of info	1 0.5%	0 0	1 2.3%	1 0.5%	0 0	0 0	1 1.4%	0 0	0 0	0 0	0 0	1 2.0%	0 0	0 0	0 0	0 0	0 0	1 1.5%
Office (NET)	2 0.8%	2 1.0%	0 0	2 0.8%	0 0	1 1.1%	0 0	1 1.3%	0 0	1 2.3%	0 0	0 0	0 0	1 2.2%	0 0	0 0	2 1.1%	0 0
All sources of info	2 0.8%	2 1.0%	0 0	2 0.8%	0 0	1 1.1%	0 0	1 1.3%	0 0	1 2.3%	0 0	0 0	0 0	1 2.2%	0 0	0 0	2 1.1%	0 0
preferred source of info	2 0.8%	2 1.0%	0 0	2 0.8%	0 0	1 1.1%	0 0	1 1.3%	0 0	1 2.3%	0 0	0 0	0 0	1 2.2%	0 0	0 0	2 1.1%	0 0
Faculty (NET)	1 0.5%	0 0	1 2.3%	1 0.5%	0 0	0 0	1 1.4%	0 0	0 0	0 0	0 0	1 2.0%	0 0	0 0	0 0	0 0	0 0	1 1.5%
All sources of info	1 0.5%	0 0	1 2.3%	1 0.5%	0 0	0 0	1 1.4%	0 0	0 0	0 0	0 0	1 2.0%	0 0	0 0	0 0	0 0	0 0	1 1.5%
preferred source of info	1 0.5%	0 0	1 2.3%	1 0.5%	0 0	0 0	1 1.4%	0 0	0 0	0 0	0 0	1 2.0%	0 0	0 0	0 0	0 0	0 0	1 1.5%
Ask library to purchase source (NET)	* 0.2%	* 0.1%	* 0.6%	* 0.2%	0 0	* 0.5%	0 0	0 0	0 0	0 0	0 0	0 0	* 4.8%	0 0	* 9.1%	0 0	* 0.3%	0 0

Proportions/Means: Columns Tested (5% risk level) - A/B/D - C/D - E/F/G - H/I/J/K/L/M/N - P/Q
* small base; ** very small base (under 30) ineligible for sig testing

Table 224
Page 865

Outsell/Digital Library Federation Study (2002)
Weighted Tables

TABLE 106, continued

T7D/E_5. Magazines SUMMARY TABLE

		RESPONDENT TYPE				INSTITUTION TYPE			DISCIPLINE								GENDER	
	TOTAL SAMPLE	FACULTY MEMBER	GRAD. STUDENT	FACULTY /GRAD	UNDER GRAD. STUDENT	PUBLIC	PRIVATE	LIBERAL ARTS	BIOLOGIAL SCIENCES	PHYSICAL SCIENCES /MATH	SOCIAL SCIENCES	ARTS AND HUMAN.	ENGI- NEERING	BUSINESS	LAW	UNDEC. MAJOR	MALE	FEMALE
		(A)	(B)	(C)	(D)	(E)	(F)	(G)	(H)	(I)	(J)	(K)	(L)	(M)	(N)		(P)	(Q)
Base - Use Magazines for teaching	244	194	50*	244	0**	92*	80*	72*	27*	43*	68*	56*	6**	42*	2**	0*	170	74*
All sources of info	* 0.2%	* 0.1%	* 0.6%	* 0.2%	0 0	* 0.5%	0 0	0 0	0 0	0 0	0 0	0 0	* 4.8%	0 0	* 9.1%	0 0	* 0.3%	0 0
preferred source of info	* 0.1%	* 0.1%	0 0	* 0.1%	0 0	* 0.2%	0 0	0 0	0 0	0 0	0 0	0 0	0 0	0 0	* 9.1%	0 0	* 0.1%	0 0
Author	0 0	0 0	0 0	0 0	0 0	0 0	0 0	0 0	0 0	0 0	0 0	0 0	0 0	0 0	0 0	0 0	0 0	0 0
All sources of info	0 0	0 0	0 0	0 0	0 0	0 0	0 0	0 0	0 0	0 0	0 0	0 0	0 0	0 0	0 0	0 0	0 0	0 0
preferred source of info	0 0	0 0	0 0	0 0	0 0	0 0	0 0	0 0	0 0	0 0	0 0	0 0	0 0	0 0	0 0	0 0	0 0	0 0
Access book/journal/ journal article elsewhere online (NET)	0 0	0 0	0 0	0 0	0 0	0 0	0 0	0 0	0 0	0 0	0 0	0 0	0 0	0 0	0 0	0 0	0 0	0 0
All sources of info	0 0	0 0	0 0	0 0	0 0	0 0	0 0	0 0	0 0	0 0	0 0	0 0	0 0	0 0	0 0	0 0	0 0	0 0
preferred source of info	0 0	0 0	0 0	0 0	0 0	0 0	0 0	0 0	0 0	0 0	0 0	0 0	0 0	0 0	0 0	0 0	0 0	0 0
Meeting/Conferences (NET)	0 0	0 0	0 0	0 0	0 0	0 0	0 0	0 0	0 0	0 0	0 0	0 0	0 0	0 0	0 0	0 0	0 0	0 0

Proportions/Means: Columns Tested (5% risk level) - A/B/D - C/D - E/F/G - H/I/J/K/L/M/N - P/Q
* small base; ** very small base (under 30) ineligible for sig testing

Table 224
Page 866

Outsell/Digital Library Federation Study (2002)
Weighted Tables

TABLE 106, continued

T7D/E_5. Magazines SUMMARY TABLE

		RESPONDENT TYPE				INSTITUTION TYPE			DISCIPLINE								GENDER	
	TOTAL SAMPLE	FACULTY MEMBER	GRAD. STUDENT	FACULTY /GRAD	UNDER GRAD. STUDENT	PUBLIC	PRIVATE	LIBERAL ARTS	BIOLOGIAL SCIENCES	PHYSICAL SCIENCES /MATH	SOCIAL SCIENCES	ARTS AND HUMAN.	ENGI-NEERING	BUSINESS	LAW	UNDEC. MAJOR	MALE	FEMALE
		(A)	(B)	(C)	(D)	(E)	(F)	(G)	(H)	(I)	(J)	(K)	(L)	(M)	(N)		(P)	(Q)
Base - Use Magazines for teaching	244	194	50*	244	0**	92*	80*	72*	27*	43*	68*	56*	6**	42*	2**	0*	170	74*
All sources of info	0	0	0	0	0	0	0	0	0	0	0	0	0	0	0	0	0	0
	0	0	0	0	0	0	0	0	0	0	0	0	0	0	0	0	0	0
preferred source of info	0	0	0	0	0	0	0	0	0	0	0	0	0	0	0	0	0	0
	0	0	0	0	0	0	0	0	0	0	0	0	0	0	0	0	0	0
Other (NET)	8	8	0	8	0	2	2	4	1	2	2	1	1	1	*	0	4	4
	3.2%	4.0%	0	3.2%	0	1.9%	2.4%	5.8%	3.2%	4.7%	2.8%	2.0%	14.3%	2.2%	9.1%	0	2.3%	5.3%
All sources of info	8	8	0	8	0	2	2	4	1	2	2	1	1	1	*	0	4	4
	3.2%	4.0%	0	3.2%	0	1.9%	2.4%	5.8%	3.2%	4.7%	2.8%	2.0%	14.3%	2.2%	9.1%	0	2.3%	5.3%
preferred source of info	4	4	0	4	0	*	2	2	1	0	2	1	0	0	*	0	1	3
	1.7%	2.1%	0	1.7%	0	0.2%	2.4%	2.8%	3.2%	0	2.8%	2.0%	0	0	9.1%	0	0.6%	4.0%
DK/Refused	6	6	0	6	0	2	2	2	0	3	0	1	*	2	0	0	2	4
	2.6%	3.2%	0	2.6%	0	2.2%	2.8%	2.8%	0	7.0%	0	2.0%	4.8%	4.4%	0	0	1.4%	5.4%

Proportions/Means: Columns Tested (5% risk level) - A/B/D - C/D - E/F/G - H/I/J/K/L/M/N - P/Q
* small base; ** very small base (under 30) ineligible for sig testing

Table 224
Page 867

TABLE 107

T7sum_6. Papers delivered at professional meetings SUMMARY TABLE

		RESPONDENT TYPE				INSTITUTION TYPE			DISCIPLINE									GENDER	
	TOTAL SAMPLE	FACULTY MEMBER	GRAD. STUDENT	FACULTY /GRAD	UNDER GRAD. STUDENT	PUBLIC	PRIVATE	LIBERAL ARTS	BIOLOGIAL SCIENCES	PHYSICAL SCIENCES /MATH	SOCIAL SCIENCES	ARTS AND HUMAN.	ENGI-NEERING	BUSINESS	LAW	UNDEC. MAJOR	MALE	FEMALE
		(A)	(B)	(C)	(D)	(E)	(F)	(G)	(H)	(I)	(J)	(K)	(L)	(M)	(N)		(P)	(Q)
Base - USe Papers delivered at professional meetings for teaching	192	149	42*	192	0**	64*	78*	50*	26**	35*	43**	55*	9**	23**	1**	0*	129	63*
ONLINE	112 58.4%	85 56.9%	27 63.8%	112 58.4%	0 0	39 61.4%	39 50.7%	33 66.7%	12 48.3%	22 62.9%	26 60.9%	34 61.2%	6 66.7%	11 48.0%	1 71.4%	0 0	78 60.1%	34 55.0%
Web directory/ subject related web site	35 18.4%	31 20.6%	4 10.5%	35 18.4%	0 0	9 14.1%	17 21.6%	9 18.8%	3 10.3%	9 25.7%	9 21.7%	8 14.3%	3 30.0%	4 16.0%	0 0	0 0	22 16.7%	14 21.8%
All sources of info	35 18.4%	31 20.6%	4 10.5%	35 18.4%	0 0	9 14.1%	17 21.6%	9 18.8%	3 10.3%	9 25.7%	9 21.7%	8 14.3%	3 30.0%	4 16.0%	0 0	0 0	22 16.7%	14 21.8%
preferred source of info	27 13.9%	23 15.4%	4 8.4%	27 13.9%	0 0	7 10.2%	14 18.1%	6 12.1%	3 10.3%	7 20.0%	8 17.4%	7 12.2%	1 10.0%	2 8.0%	0 0	0 0	15 11.5%	12 18.7%
Search engine	29 14.9%	22 15.0%	6 14.4%	29 14.9%	0 0	7 10.2%	11 14.4%	11 21.6%	6 24.1%	6 17.1%	8 17.4%	6 10.2%	1 10.0%	2 8.0%	1 42.9%	0 0	25 19.2%Q	4 5.9%
All sources of info	29 14.9%	22 15.0%	6 14.4%	29 14.9%	0 0	7 10.2%	11 14.4%	11 21.6%	6 24.1%	6 17.1%	8 17.4%	6 10.2%	1 10.0%	2 8.0%	1 42.9%	0 0	25 19.2%Q	4 5.9%
preferred source of info	20 10.3%	14 9.3%	6 13.7%	20 10.3%	0 0	5 8.0%	9 11.6%	6 11.3%	5 20.7%	4 11.4%	6 13.0%	2 4.1%	1 6.7%	2 8.0%	* 14.3%	0 0	17 13.3%	3 4.2%
Internet searches	20 10.5%	17 11.2%	3 8.0%	20 10.5%	0 0	7 10.4%	6 8.1%	7 14.4%	4 17.2%	2 5.7%	2 4.3%	9 16.3%	1 10.0%	2 8.0%	* 14.3%	0 0	16 12.4%	4 6.7%
All sources of info	20 10.5%	17 11.2%	3 8.0%	20 10.5%	0 0	7 10.4%	6 8.1%	7 14.4%	4 17.2%	2 5.7%	2 4.3%	9 16.3%	1 10.0%	2 8.0%	* 14.3%	0 0	16 12.4%	4 6.7%

Proportions/Means: Columns Tested (5% risk level) - A/B/D - C/D - E/F/G - H/I/J/K/L/M/N - P/Q
* small base; ** very small base (under 30) ineligible for sig testing

Table 228
Page 879

Outsell/Digital Library Federation Study (2002)
Weighted Tables

TABLE 107, continued

T7sum_6. Papers delivered at professional meetings SUMMARY TABLE

		RESPONDENT TYPE				INSTITUTION TYPE			DISCIPLINE								GENDER	
	TOTAL SAMPLE	FACULTY MEMBER	GRAD. STUDENT	FACULTY /GRAD	UNDER GRAD. STUDENT	PUBLIC	PRIVATE	LIBERAL ARTS	BIOLOGIAL SCIENCES	PHYSICAL SCIENCES /MATH	SOCIAL SCIENCES	ARTS AND HUMAN.	ENGI-NEERING	BUSINESS	LAW	UNDEC. MAJOR	MALE	FEMALE
		(A)	(B)	(C)	(D)	(E)	(F)	(G)	(H)	(I)	(J)	(K)	(L)	(M)	(N)		(P)	(Q)
Base - USe Papers delivered at professional meetings for teaching	192	149	42*	192	0**	64*	78*	50*	26**	35*	43**	55*	9**	23**	1**	0*	129	63*
preferred source of info	11 5.8%	8 5.4%	3 7.3%	11 5.8%	0 0	6 8.6%	1 1.4%	4 9.0%	1 3.4%	1 2.9%	0 0	8 14.3%	* 3.3%	1 4.0%	* 14.3%	0 0	9 6.7%	2 3.8%
Online databases	18 9.3%	12 7.9%	6 14.1%	18 9.3%	0 0	6 10.0%	6 7.1%	6 11.9%	3 10.3%	4 11.4%	2 4.3%	7 12.2%	1 6.7%	2 8.0%	* 14.3%	0 0	12 9.1%	6 9.7%
All sources of info	18 9.3%	12 7.9%	6 14.1%	18 9.3%	0 0	6 10.0%	6 7.1%	6 11.9%	3 10.3%	4 11.4%	2 4.3%	7 12.2%	1 6.7%	2 8.0%	* 14.3%	0 0	12 9.1%	6 9.7%
preferred source of info	10 5.2%	7 4.9%	3 6.5%	10 5.2%	0 0	4 6.1%	1 1.4%	5 10.1%F	1 3.4%	3 8.6%	2 4.3%	3 6.1%	0 0	1 4.0%	0 0	0 0	6 4.7%	4 6.4%
Your own institution's web site	10 5.5%	6 4.3%	4 9.7%	10 5.5%	0 0	6 9.3%	2 2.0%	3 5.9%	0 0	2 5.7%	2 4.3%	3 6.1%	* 3.3%	3 12.0%	* 14.3%	0 0	7 5.5%	3 5.4%
All sources of info	10 5.5%	6 4.3%	4 9.7%	10 5.5%	0 0	6 9.3%	2 2.0%	3 5.9%	0 0	2 5.7%	2 4.3%	3 6.1%	* 3.3%	3 12.0%	* 14.3%	0 0	7 5.5%	3 5.4%
preferred source of info	7 3.8%	3 2.2%	4 9.7%A	7 3.8%	0 0	5 7.6%	2 2.0%	1 1.9%	0 0	0 0	2 4.3%	2 4.1%	* 3.3%	3 12.0%	* 14.3%	0 0	5 4.0%	2 3.6%
Department web page	10 5.0%	7 5.0%	2 5.3%	10 5.0%	0 0	3 4.9%	4 4.8%	3 5.5%	2 6.9%	0 0	6 13.0%	2 4.1%	0 0	0 0	0 0	0 0	5 3.6%	5 8.0%
All sources of info	10 5.0%	7 5.0%	2 5.3%	10 5.0%	0 0	3 4.9%	4 4.8%	3 5.5%	2 6.9%	0 0	6 13.0%	2 4.1%	0 0	0 0	0 0	0 0	5 3.6%	5 8.0%

Proportions/Means: Columns Tested (5% risk level) - A/B/D - C/D - E/F/G - H/I/J/K/L/M/N - P/Q
* small base; ** very small base (under 30) ineligible for sig testing

Table 228
Page 880

Outsell/Digital Library Federation Study (2002)
Weighted Tables

TABLE 107, continued

T7sum_6. Papers delivered at professional meetings SUMMARY TABLE

		RESPONDENT TYPE				INSTITUTION TYPE			DISCIPLINE								GENDER	
	TOTAL SAMPLE	FACULTY MEMBER	GRAD. STUDENT	FACULTY /GRAD	UNDER GRAD. STUDENT	PUBLIC	PRIVATE	LIBERAL ARTS	BIOLOGIAL SCIENCES	PHYSICAL SCIENCES /MATH	SOCIAL SCIENCES	ARTS AND HUMAN.	ENGI-NEERING	BUSINESS	LAW	UNDEC. MAJOR	MALE	FEMALE
		(A)	(B)	(C)	(D)	(E)	(F)	(G)	(H)	(I)	(J)	(K)	(L)	(M)	(N)		(P)	(Q)
Base - USe Papers delivered at professional meetings for teaching	192	149	42*	192	0**	64*	78*	50*	26**	35*	43**	55*	9**	23**	1**	0*	129	63*
preferred source of info	3 1.5%	2 1.2%	1 2.6%	3 1.5%	0 0	2 3.1%	0 0	1 1.8%	2 6.9%	0 0	0 0	1 2.0%	0 0	0 0	0 0	0 0	1 0.7%	2 3.2%
Online library catalogues and finding aids	7 3.9%	3 2.2%	4 9.5%	7 3.9%	0 0	5 8.5%F	0 0	2 3.9%	0 0	1 2.9%	4 8.7%	1 2.0%	1 6.7%	1 4.0%	0 0	0 0	4 3.3%	3 5.1%
All sources of info	7 3.9%	3 2.2%	4 9.5%	7 3.9%	0 0	5 8.5%F	0 0	2 3.9%	0 0	1 2.9%	4 8.7%	1 2.0%	1 6.7%	1 4.0%	0 0	0 0	4 3.3%	3 5.1%
preferred source of info	4 2.2%	2 1.4%	2 5.1%	4 2.2%	0 0	3 5.1%	0 0	1 1.9%	0 0	0 0	2 4.3%	1 2.0%	* 3.3%	1 4.0%	0 0	0 0	2 1.6%	2 3.5%
Online reference service	6 3.4%	6 4.1%	* 0.7%	6 3.4%	0 0	1 2.2%	4 5.2%	1 2.0%	0 0	1 2.9%	4 8.7%	1 2.0%	1 6.7%	0 0	0 0	0 0	5 3.9%	1 2.3%
All sources of info	6 3.4%	6 4.1%	* 0.7%	6 3.4%	0 0	1 2.2%	4 5.2%	1 2.0%	0 0	1 2.9%	4 8.7%	1 2.0%	1 6.7%	0 0	0 0	0 0	5 3.9%	1 2.3%
preferred source of info	4 2.2%	4 2.9%	0 0	4 2.2%	0 0	1 1.7%	2 2.8%	1 2.0%	0 0	1 2.9%	2 4.3%	1 2.0%	* 3.3%	0 0	0 0	0 0	3 2.2%	1 2.3%
Online abstracting and indexing services	4 2.3%	4 2.9%	0 0	4 2.3%	0 0	2 2.7%	2 2.2%	1 2.0%	0 0	1 2.9%	0 0	2 4.1%	1 13.3%	0 0	0 0	0 0	4 3.4%	0 0

Proportions/Means: Columns Tested (5% risk level) - A/B/D - C/D - E/F/G - H/I/J/K/L/M/N - P/Q
* small base; ** very small base (under 30) ineligible for sig testing

Table 228
Page 881

Outsell/Digital Library Federation Study (2002)
Weighted Tables

TABLE 107, continued

T7sum_6. Papers delivered at professional meetings SUMMARY TABLE

	RESPONDENT TYPE				INSTITUTION TYPE			DISCIPLINE								GENDER	
	TOTAL SAMPLE	FACULTY MEMBER (A)	GRAD. STUDENT (B)	FACULTY /GRAD (C)	UNDER GRAD. STUDENT (D)	PUBLIC (E)	PRIVATE (F)	LIBERAL ARTS (G)	BIOLOGIAL SCIENCES (H)	PHYSICAL SCIENCES /MATH (I)	SOCIAL SCIENCES (J)	ARTS AND HUMAN. (K)	ENGI-NEERING (L)	BUSINESS (M)	LAW (N)	UNDEC. MAJOR	MALE (P)	FEMALE (Q)
Base - USe Papers delivered at professional meetings for teaching	192	149	42*	192	0**	64*	78*	50*	26**	35*	43**	55*	9**	23**	1**	0*	129	63*
All sources of info	4 2.3%	4 2.9%	0 0	4 2.3%	0 0	2 2.7%	2 2.2%	1 2.0%	0 0	1 2.9%	0 0	2 4.1%	1 13.3%	0 0	0 0	0 0	4 3.4%	0 0
preferred source of info	1 0.7%	1 0.9%	0 0	1 0.7%	0 0	1 2.2%	0 0	0 0	0 0	0 0	0 0	1 2.0%	* 3.3%	0 0	0 0	0 0	1 1.1%	0 0
Online bookstore	1 0.6%	1 0.8%	0 0	1 0.6%	0 0	0 0	0 0	1 2.2%	0 0	0 0	0 0	1 2.0%	0 0	0 0	0 0	0 0	1 0.9%	0 0
All sources of info	1 0.6%	1 0.8%	0 0	1 0.6%	0 0	0 0	0 0	1 2.2%	0 0	0 0	0 0	1 2.0%	0 0	0 0	0 0	0 0	1 0.9%	0 0
preferred source of info	0 0	0 0	0 0	0 0	0 0	0 0	0 0	0 0	0 0	0 0	0 0	0 0	0 0	0 0	0 0	0 0	0 0	0 0
E-mail listservs	0 0	0 0	0 0	0 0	0 0	0 0	0 0	0 0	0 0	0 0	0 0	0 0	0 0	0 0	0 0	0 0	0 0	0 0
All sources of info	0 0	0 0	0 0	0 0	0 0	0 0	0 0	0 0	0 0	0 0	0 0	0 0	0 0	0 0	0 0	0 0	0 0	0 0
preferred source of info	0 0	0 0	0 0	0 0	0 0	0 0	0 0	0 0	0 0	0 0	0 0	0 0	0 0	0 0	0 0	0 0	0 0	0 0
Your own personal electronic library/files	0 0	0 0	0 0	0 0	0 0	0 0	0 0	0 0	0 0	0 0	0 0	0 0	0 0	0 0	0 0	0 0	0 0	0 0

Proportions/Means: Columns Tested (5% risk level) - A/B/D - C/D - E/F/G - H/I/J/K/L/M/N - P/Q
* small base; ** very small base (under 30) ineligible for sig testing

Table 228
Page 882

Outsell/Digital Library Federation Study (2002)
Weighted Tables

TABLE 107, continued

T7sum_6. Papers delivered at professional meetings SUMMARY TABLE

		RESPONDENT TYPE				INSTITUTION TYPE			DISCIPLINE								GENDER	
	TOTAL SAMPLE	FACULTY MEMBER	GRAD. STUDENT	FACULTY /GRAD	UNDER GRAD. STUDENT	PUBLIC	PRIVATE	LIBERAL ARTS	BIOLOGIAL SCIENCES	PHYSICAL SCIENCES /MATH	SOCIAL SCIENCES	ARTS AND HUMAN.	ENGI-NEERING	BUSINESS	LAW	UNDEC. MAJOR	MALE	FEMALE
		(A)	(B)	(C)	(D)	(E)	(F)	(G)	(H)	(I)	(J)	(K)	(L)	(M)	(N)		(P)	(Q)
Base - USe Papers delivered at professional meetings for teaching	192	149	42*	192	0**	64*	78*	50*	26**	35*	43**	55*	9**	23**	1**	0*	129	63*
All sources of info	0 0	0 0	0 0	0 0	0 0	0 0	0 0	0 0	0 0	0 0	0 0	0 0	0 0	0 0	0 0	0 0	0 0	0 0
preferred source of info	0 0	0 0	0 0	0 0	0 0	0 0	0 0	0 0	0 0	0 0	0 0	0 0	0 0	0 0	0 0	0 0	0 0	0 0
LIBRARY/PRINT	84 43.9%	73 48.6%B	12 27.5%	84 43.9%	0 0	22 34.5%	38 49.2%	24 47.8%	10 37.9%	14 40.0%	15 34.8%	30 55.1%	4 43.3%	11 48.0%	* 28.6%	0 0	65 50.5%Q	19 30.3%
Campus library	57 29.7%	45 30.3%	12 27.5%	57 29.7%	0 0	18 27.4%	26 33.8%	13 26.0%	9 34.5%	7 20.0%	8 17.4%	25 44.9%I	3 36.7%	6 24.0%	* 14.3%	0 0	40 30.8%	17 27.2%
All sources of info	57 29.7%	45 30.3%	12 27.5%	57 29.7%	0 0	18 27.4%	26 33.8%	13 26.0%	9 34.5%	7 20.0%	8 17.4%	25 44.9%I	3 36.7%	6 24.0%	* 14.3%	0 0	40 30.8%	17 27.2%
preferred source of info	21 10.8%	16 10.5%	5 11.7%	21 10.8%	0 0	8 12.2%	11 13.8%	2 4.3%	3 10.3%	2 5.7%	2 4.3%	11 20.4%	2 23.3%	1 4.0%	0 0	0 0	17 12.9%	4 6.4%
Your own personal physical library/ files/bookshelves	21 10.8%	18 12.4%	2 5.3%	21 10.8%	0 0	5 7.1%	12 15.8%	4 7.8%	2 6.9%	2 5.7%	6 13.0%	7 12.2%	1 10.0%	4 16.0%	0 0	0 0	17 12.9%	4 6.5%
All sources of info	21 10.8%	18 12.4%	2 5.3%	21 10.8%	0 0	5 7.1%	12 15.8%	4 7.8%	2 6.9%	2 5.7%	6 13.0%	7 12.2%	1 10.0%	4 16.0%	0 0	0 0	17 12.9%	4 6.5%
preferred source of info	7 3.8%	7 4.8%	0 0	7 3.8%	0 0	1 1.5%	6 8.1%	0 0	2 6.9%	0 0	2 4.3%	1 2.0%	1 6.7%	2 8.0%	0 0	0 0	6 4.9%	1 1.5%

Proportions/Means: Columns Tested (5% risk level) - A/B/D - C/D - E/F/G - H/I/J/K/L/M/N - P/Q
* small base; ** very small base (under 30) ineligible for sig testing

Table 228
Page 883

Outsell/Digital Library Federation Study (2002)
Weighted Tables

TABLE 107, continued

T7sum_6. Papers delivered at professional meetings SUMMARY TABLE

		RESPONDENT TYPE				INSTITUTION TYPE			DISCIPLINE								GENDER	
	TOTAL SAMPLE	FACULTY MEMBER	GRAD. STUDENT	FACULTY /GRAD	UNDER GRAD. STUDENT	PUBLIC	PRIVATE	LIBERAL ARTS	BIOLOGIAL SCIENCES	PHYSICAL SCIENCES /MATH	SOCIAL SCIENCES	ARTS AND HUMAN.	ENGI-NEERING	BUSINESS	LAW	UNDEC. MAJOR	MALE	FEMALE
		(A)	(B)	(C)	(D)	(E)	(F)	(G)	(H)	(I)	(J)	(K)	(L)	(M)	(N)		(P)	(Q)
Base - USe Papers delivered at professional meetings for teaching	192	149	42*	192	0**	64*	78*	50*	26**	35*	43**	55*	9**	23**	1**	0*	129	63*
Personal subscriptions to newspapers, magazines and journals	18 9.2%	18 11.8%B	0 0	18 9.2%	0 0	6 8.7%	7 8.5%	5 10.7%	0 0	4 11.4%	2 4.3%	9 16.3%	1 10.0%	2 8.0%	0 0	0 0	17 12.8%Q	1 1.6%
All sources of info	18 9.2%	18 11.8%B	0 0	18 9.2%	0 0	6 8.7%	7 8.5%	5 10.7%	0 0	4 11.4%	2 4.3%	9 16.3%	1 10.0%	2 8.0%	0 0	0 0	17 12.8%Q	1 1.6%
preferred source of info	5 2.5%	5 3.1%	0 0	5 2.5%	0 0	1 2.0%	0 0	3 6.8%F	0 0	3 8.6%	0 0	1 2.0%	1 6.7%	0 0	0 0	0 0	4 2.9%	1 1.6%
References cited in books or journal articles	10 5.4%	10 6.8%	* 0.7%	10 5.4%	0 0	3 5.3%	4 5.3%	3 5.7%	0 0	3 8.6%	2 4.3%	2 4.1%	* 3.3%	3 12.0%	* 14.3%	0 0	10 8.0%Q	0 0
All sources of info	10 5.4%	10 6.8%	* 0.7%	10 5.4%	0 0	3 5.3%	4 5.3%	3 5.7%	0 0	3 8.6%	2 4.3%	2 4.1%	* 3.3%	3 12.0%	* 14.3%	0 0	10 8.0%Q	0 0
preferred source of info	5 2.6%	5 3.3%	0 0	5 2.6%	0 0	* 0.3%	4 4.9%	1 1.9%	0 0	1 2.9%	2 4.3%	0 0	0 0	2 8.0%	* 14.3%	0 0	5 3.8%	0 0
Printed abstracting and indexing services	7 3.5%	7 4.4%	0 0	7 3.5%	0 0	0 0	4 4.8%	3 5.8%	1 3.4%	2 5.7%	4 8.7%	0 0	0 0	0 0	0 0	0 0	6 4.4%	1 1.6%

Proportions/Means: Columns Tested (5% risk level) - A/B/D - C/D - E/F/G - H/I/J/K/L/M/N - P/Q
* small base; ** very small base (under 30) ineligible for sig testing

Table 228
Page 884

Outsell/Digital Library Federation Study (2002)
Weighted Tables

TABLE 107, continued

T7sum_6. Papers delivered at professional meetings SUMMARY TABLE

		RESPONDENT TYPE				INSTITUTION TYPE			DISCIPLINE								GENDER	
	TOTAL SAMPLE	FACULTY MEMBER	GRAD. STUDENT	FACULTY /GRAD	UNDER GRAD. STUDENT	PUBLIC	PRIVATE	LIBERAL ARTS	BIOLOGIAL SCIENCES	PHYSICAL SCIENCES /MATH	SOCIAL SCIENCES	ARTS AND HUMAN.	ENGI-NEERING	BUSINESS	LAW	UNDEC. MAJOR	MALE	FEMALE
		(A)	(B)	(C)	(D)	(E)	(F)	(G)	(H)	(I)	(J)	(K)	(L)	(M)	(N)		(P)	(Q)
Base - USe Papers delivered at professional meetings for teaching	192	149	42*	192	0**	64*	78*	50*	26**	35*	43**	55*	9**	23**	1**	0*	129	63*
All sources of info	7 3.5%	7 4.4%	0 0	7 3.5%	0 0	0 0	4 4.8%	3 5.8%	1 3.4%	2 5.7%	4 8.7%	0 0	0 0	0 0	0 0	0 0	6 4.4%	1 1.6%
preferred source of info	1 0.5%	1 0.6%	0 0	1 0.5%	0 0	0 0	0 0	1 1.8%	1 3.4%	0 0	0 0	0 0	0 0	0 0	0 0	0 0	1 0.7%	0 0
Printed library catalogues and finding aids	1 0.7%	1 0.9%	0 0	1 0.7%	0 0	* 0.5%	0 0	1 2.2%	0 0	0 0	0 0	1 2.0%	* 3.3%	0 0	0 0	0 0	1 1.1%	0 0
All sources of info	1 0.7%	1 0.9%	0 0	1 0.7%	0 0	* 0.5%	0 0	1 2.2%	0 0	0 0	0 0	1 2.0%	* 3.3%	0 0	0 0	0 0	1 1.1%	0 0
preferred source of info	1 0.6%	1 0.8%	0 0	1 0.6%	0 0	0 0	0 0	1 2.2%	0 0	0 0	0 0	1 2.0%	0 0	0 0	0 0	0 0	1 0.9%	0 0
Another library	1 0.5%	1 0.7%	0 0	1 0.5%	0 0	1 1.6%	0 0	0 0	0 0	1 2.9%	0 0	0 0	0 0	0 0	0 0	0 0	1 0.8%	0 0
All sources of info	1 0.5%	1 0.7%	0 0	1 0.5%	0 0	1 1.6%	0 0	0 0	0 0	1 2.9%	0 0	0 0	0 0	0 0	0 0	0 0	1 0.8%	0 0
preferred source of info	0 0	0 0	0 0	0 0	0 0	0 0	0 0	0 0	0 0	0 0	0 0	0 0	0 0	0 0	0 0	0 0	0 0	0 0
Physical bookstore	0 0	0 0	0 0	0 0	0 0	0 0	0 0	0 0	0 0	0 0	0 0	0 0	0 0	0 0	0 0	0 0	0 0	0 0

Proportions/Means: Columns Tested (5% risk level) - A/B/D - C/D - E/F/G - H/I/J/K/L/M/N - P/Q
* small base; ** very small base (under 30) ineligible for sig testing

Table 228
Page 885

Outsell/Digital Library Federation Study (2002)
Weighted Tables

TABLE 107, continued

T7sum_6. Papers delivered at professional meetings SUMMARY TABLE

		RESPONDENT TYPE				INSTITUTION TYPE			DISCIPLINE									GENDER	
	TOTAL SAMPLE	FACULTY MEMBER	GRAD. STUDENT	FACULTY /GRAD	UNDER GRAD. STUDENT	PUBLIC	PRIVATE	LIBERAL ARTS	BIOLOGIAL SCIENCES	PHYSICAL SCIENCES /MATH	SOCIAL SCIENCES	ARTS AND HUMAN.	ENGI- NEERING	BUSINESS	LAW	UNDEC. MAJOR	MALE	FEMALE
		(A)	(B)	(C)	(D)	(E)	(F)	(G)	(H)	(I)	(J)	(K)	(L)	(M)	(N)		(P)	(Q)
Base - USe Papers delivered at professional meetings for teaching	192	149	42*	192	0**	64*	78*	50*	26**	35*	43**	55*	9**	23**	1**	0*	129	63*
All sources of info	0 0	0 0	0 0	0 0	0 0	0 0	0 0	0 0	0 0	0 0	0 0	0 0	0 0	0 0	0 0	0 0	0 0	0 0
preferred source of info	0 0	0 0	0 0	0 0	0 0	0 0	0 0	0 0	0 0	0 0	0 0	0 0	0 0	0 0	0 0	0 0	0 0	0 0
PERSONAL ASSISTANCE	71 37.1%	55 36.9%	16 38.1%	71 37.1%	0 0	23 35.7%	30 38.2%	19 37.2%	11 44.8%	11 31.4%	9 21.7%	26 46.9%	3 36.7%	10 44.0%	* 14.3%	0 0	45 35.2%	26 41.2%
Professional meetings	37 19.1%	36 23.8%B	1 2.6%	37 19.1%	0 0	11 16.7%	14 18.2%	12 23.6%	4 17.2%	8 22.9%	4 8.7%	11 20.4%	2 20.0%	7 32.0%	* 14.3%	0 0	25 19.0%	12 19.5%
All sources of info	37 19.1%	36 23.8%B	1 2.6%	37 19.1%	0 0	11 16.7%	14 18.2%	12 23.6%	4 17.2%	8 22.9%	4 8.7%	11 20.4%	2 20.0%	7 32.0%	* 14.3%	0 0	25 19.0%	12 19.5%
preferred source of info	28 14.6%	27 17.9%B	1 2.6%	28 14.6%	0 0	6 9.2%	11 14.5%	11 21.6%	4 13.8%	7 20.0%	4 8.7%	7 12.2%	1 13.3%	6 24.0%	* 14.3%	0 0	16 12.2%	12 19.5%
Colleagues inside your institution	24 12.5%	12 8.0%	12 28.6%A	24 12.5%	0 0	8 12.4%	14 18.2%G	2 3.9%	4 13.8%	3 8.6%	6 13.0%	7 12.2%	1 16.7%	4 16.0%	0 0	0 0	17 13.3%	7 11.1%
All sources of info	24 12.5%	12 8.0%	12 28.6%A	24 12.5%	0 0	8 12.4%	14 18.2%G	2 3.9%	4 13.8%	3 8.6%	6 13.0%	7 12.2%	1 16.7%	4 16.0%	0 0	0 0	17 13.3%	7 11.1%
preferred source of info	11 5.7%	5 3.1%	6 14.8%A	11 5.7%	0 0	5 7.3%	6 8.0%	0 0	2 6.9%	1 2.9%	4 8.7%	2 4.1%	* 3.3%	2 8.0%	0 0	0 0	9 6.9%	2 3.2%

Proportions/Means: Columns Tested (5% risk level) - A/B/D - C/D - E/F/G - H/I/J/K/L/M/N - P/Q
* small base; ** very small base (under 30) ineligible for sig testing

Table 228
Page 886

Outsell/Digital Library Federation Study (2002)
Weighted Tables

TABLE 107, continued

T7sum_6. Papers delivered at professional meetings SUMMARY TABLE

		RESPONDENT TYPE				INSTITUTION TYPE			DISCIPLINE								GENDER	
	TOTAL SAMPLE	FACULTY MEMBER	GRAD. STUDENT	FACULTY /GRAD	UNDER GRAD. STUDENT	PUBLIC	PRIVATE	LIBERAL ARTS	BIOLOGIAL SCIENCES	PHYSICAL SCIENCES /MATH	SOCIAL SCIENCES	ARTS AND HUMAN.	ENGI-NEERING	BUSINESS	LAW	UNDEC. MAJOR	MALE	FEMALE
		(A)	(B)	(C)	(D)	(E)	(F)	(G)	(H)	(I)	(J)	(K)	(L)	(M)	(N)		(P)	(Q)
Base - USe Papers delivered at professional meetings for teaching	192	149	42*	192	0**	64*	78*	50*	26**	35*	43**	55*	9**	23**	1**	0*	129	63*
A librarian in your institution	16 8.2%	13 8.4%	3 7.3%	16 8.2%	0 0	5 8.2%	6 7.3%	5 9.7%	3 10.3%	1 2.9%	2 4.3%	9 16.3%	* 3.3%	1 4.0%	0 0	0 0	9 6.9%	7 10.8%
All sources of info	16 8.2%	13 8.4%	3 7.3%	16 8.2%	0 0	5 8.2%	6 7.3%	5 9.7%	3 10.3%	1 2.9%	2 4.3%	9 16.3%	* 3.3%	1 4.0%	0 0	0 0	9 6.9%	7 10.8%
preferred source of info	2 1.1%	1 0.8%	1 2.1%	2 1.1%	0 0	1 1.4%	1 1.5%	0 0	2 6.9%	0 0	0 0	0 0	* 3.3%	0 0	0 0	0 0	* 0.2%	2 2.8%
Colleagues outside your institution	9 4.6%	5 3.5%	4 8.6%	9 4.6%	0 0	3 4.3%	4 5.2%	2 4.0%	4 17.2%	3 8.6%	0 0	1 2.0%	* 3.3%	0 0	0 0	0 0	5 4.0%	4 5.8%
All sources of info	9 4.6%	5 3.5%	4 8.6%	9 4.6%	0 0	3 4.3%	4 5.2%	2 4.0%	4 17.2%	3 8.6%	0 0	1 2.0%	* 3.3%	0 0	0 0	0 0	5 4.0%	4 5.8%
preferred source of info	3 1.5%	1 0.7%	2 4.4%	3 1.5%	0 0	2 2.9%	0 0	1 2.0%	1 3.4%	2 5.7%	0 0	0 0	0 0	0 0	0 0	0 0	2 1.5%	1 1.6%
Another institution's librarian	0 0	0 0	0 0	0 0	0 0	0 0	0 0	0 0	0 0	0 0	0 0	0 0	0 0	0 0	0 0	0 0	0 0	0 0
All sources of info	0 0	0 0	0 0	0 0	0 0	0 0	0 0	0 0	0 0	0 0	0 0	0 0	0 0	0 0	0 0	0 0	0 0	0 0
preferred source of info	0 0	0 0	0 0	0 0	0 0	0 0	0 0	0 0	0 0	0 0	0 0	0 0	0 0	0 0	0 0	0 0	0 0	0 0

Proportions/Means: Columns Tested (5% risk level) - A/B/D - C/D - E/F/G - H/I/J/K/L/M/N - P/Q
* small base; ** very small base (under 30) ineligible for sig testing

Table 228
Page 887

Outsell/Digital Library Federation Study (2002)
Weighted Tables

TABLE 107, continued

T7sum_6. Papers delivered at professional meetings SUMMARY TABLE

	RESPONDENT TYPE					INSTITUTION TYPE			DISCIPLINE									GENDER	
	TOTAL SAMPLE	FACULTY MEMBER	GRAD. STUDENT	FACULTY /GRAD	UNDER GRAD. STUDENT	PUBLIC	PRIVATE	LIBERAL ARTS	BIOLOGIAL SCIENCES	PHYSICAL SCIENCES /MATH	SOCIAL SCIENCES	ARTS AND HUMAN.	ENGI-NEERING	BUSINESS	LAW	UNDEC. MAJOR	MALE	FEMALE
		(A)	(B)	(C)	(D)	(E)	(F)	(G)	(H)	(I)	(J)	(K)	(L)	(M)	(N)		(P)	(Q)
Base - USe Papers delivered at professional meetings for teaching	192	149	42*	192	0**	64*	78*	50*	26**	35*	43**	55*	9**	23**	1**	0*	129	63*
Online (unspecified)	2 1.0%	1 0.6%	1 2.4%	2 1.0%	0 0	0 0	2 2.4%	0 0	1 3.4%	1 2.9%	0 0	0 0	0 0	0 0	0 0	0 0	0 0	2 3.0%
All sources of info	2 1.0%	1 0.6%	1 2.4%	2 1.0%	0 0	0 0	2 2.4%	0 0	1 3.4%	1 2.9%	0 0	0 0	0 0	0 0	0 0	0 0	0 0	2 3.0%
preferred source of info	1 0.5%	0 0	1 2.4%	1 0.5%	0 0	0 0	1 1.3%	0 0	0 0	1 2.9%	0 0	0 0	0 0	0 0	0 0	0 0	0 0	1 1.6%
Personal office/lab	1 0.6%	1 0.8%	0 0	1 0.6%	0 0	0 0	1 1.4%	0 0	0 0	0 0	0 0	1 2.0%	0 0	0 0	0 0	0 0	0 0	1 1.8%
All sources of info	1 0.6%	1 0.8%	0 0	1 0.6%	0 0	0 0	1 1.4%	0 0	0 0	0 0	0 0	1 2.0%	0 0	0 0	0 0	0 0	0 0	1 1.8%
preferred source of info	0 0	0 0	0 0	0 0	0 0	0 0	0 0	0 0	0 0	0 0	0 0	0 0	0 0	0 0	0 0	0 0	0 0	0 0
Author	1 0.6%	1 0.8%	0 0	1 0.6%	0 0	1 1.7%	0 0	0 0	0 0	0 0	0 0	1 2.0%	0 0	0 0	0 0	0 0	0 0	1 1.8%
All sources of info	1 0.6%	1 0.8%	0 0	1 0.6%	0 0	1 1.7%	0 0	0 0	0 0	0 0	0 0	1 2.0%	0 0	0 0	0 0	0 0	0 0	1 1.8%
preferred source of info	1 0.6%	1 0.8%	0 0	1 0.6%	0 0	1 1.7%	0 0	0 0	0 0	0 0	0 0	1 2.0%	0 0	0 0	0 0	0 0	0 0	1 1.8%

Proportions/Means: Columns Tested (5% risk level) - A/B/D - C/D - E/F/G - H/I/J/K/L/M/N - P/Q
* small base; ** very small base (under 30) ineligible for sig testing

Table 228
Page 888

Outsell/Digital Library Federation Study (2002)
Weighted Tables

TABLE 107, continued

T7sum_6. Papers delivered at professional meetings SUMMARY TABLE

		RESPONDENT TYPE				INSTITUTION TYPE			DISCIPLINE								GENDER	
	TOTAL SAMPLE	FACULTY MEMBER	GRAD. STUDENT	FACULTY /GRAD	UNDER GRAD. STUDENT	PUBLIC	PRIVATE	LIBERAL ARTS	BIOLOGIAL SCIENCES	PHYSICAL SCIENCES /MATH	SOCIAL SCIENCES	ARTS AND HUMAN.	ENGI-NEERING	BUSINESS	LAW	UNDEC. MAJOR	MALE	FEMALE
		(A)	(B)	(C)	(D)	(E)	(F)	(G)	(H)	(I)	(J)	(K)	(L)	(M)	(N)		(P)	(Q)
Base - USe Papers delivered at professional meetings for teaching	192	149	42*	192	0**	64*	78*	50*	26**	35*	43**	55*	9**	23**	1**	0*	129	63*
Students	1 0.5%	1 0.7%	0 0	1 0.5%	0 0	0 0	0 0	1 2.0%	0 0	1 2.9%	0 0	0 0	0 0	0 0	0 0	0 0	0 0	1 1.6%
All sources of info	1 0.5%	1 0.7%	0 0	1 0.5%	0 0	0 0	0 0	1 2.0%	0 0	1 2.9%	0 0	0 0	0 0	0 0	0 0	0 0	0 0	1 1.6%
preferred source of info	0 0	0 0	0 0	0 0	0 0	0 0	0 0	0 0	0 0	0 0	0 0	0 0	0 0	0 0	0 0	0 0	0 0	0 0
Other	24 12.3%	21 13.9%	3 6.6%	24 12.3%	0 0	7 10.2%	10 12.8%	7 14.2%	2 6.9%	6 17.1%	4 8.7%	6 10.2%	1 16.7%	5 20.0%	* 28.6%	0 0	17 13.0%	7 10.7%
All sources of info	21 10.8%	18 12.0%	3 6.6%	21 10.8%	0 0	7 10.2%	8 10.4%	6 12.2%	2 6.9%	5 14.3%	2 4.3%	6 10.2%	1 16.7%	5 20.0%	* 28.6%	0 0	14 10.8%	7 10.7%
preferred source of info	9 4.8%	7 4.7%	2 5.2%	9 4.8%	0 0	3 5.2%	3 4.0%	3 5.6%	1 3.4%	2 5.7%	4 8.7%	0 0	1 6.7%	2 8.0%	* 14.3%	0 0	5 3.5%	5 7.6%
DK/Refused	11 5.5%	9 6.1%	1 3.3%	11 5.5%	0 0	2 3.8%	5 6.6%	3 6.0%	0 0	0 0	6 13.0%	4 8.2%	* 3.3%	0 0	* 14.3%	0 0	6 4.9%	4 6.9%

Proportions/Means: Columns Tested (5% risk level) - A/B/D - C/D - E/F/G - H/I/J/K/L/M/N - P/Q
* small base; ** very small base (under 30) ineligible for sig testing

Table 228
Page 889

Outsell/Digital Library Federation Study (2002)
Weighted Tables

TABLE 108

T7D/E_6. Papers delivered at professional meetings SUMMARY TABLE

		RESPONDENT TYPE				INSTITUTION TYPE			DISCIPLINE									GENDER	
	TOTAL SAMPLE	FACULTY MEMBER	GRAD. STUDENT	FACULTY /GRAD	UNDER GRAD. STUDENT	PUBLIC	PRIVATE	LIBERAL ARTS	BIOLOGIAL SCIENCES	PHYSICAL SCIENCES /MATH	SOCIAL SCIENCES	ARTS AND HUMAN.	ENGI-NEERING	BUSINESS	LAW	UNDEC. MAJOR	MALE	FEMALE
		(A)	(B)	(C)	(D)	(E)	(F)	(G)	(H)	(I)	(J)	(K)	(L)	(M)	(N)		(P)	(Q)
Base - Use Papers delivered at professional meetings for teaching	192	149	42*	192	0**	64*	78*	50*	26**	35*	43**	55*	9**	23**	1**	0*	129	63*
Access online (NET)	79 41.4%	60 40.2%	19 45.5%	79 41.4%	0 0	33 50.8%	26 33.3%	21 42.0%	10 37.9%	19 54.3%	19 43.5%	18 32.7%	4 50.0%	9 40.0%	* 28.6%	0 0	52 40.1%	28 44.2%
All sources of info	79 41.4%	60 40.2%	19 45.5%	79 41.4%	0 0	33 50.8%	26 33.3%	21 42.0%	10 37.9%	19 54.3%	19 43.5%	18 32.7%	4 50.0%	9 40.0%	* 28.6%	0 0	52 40.1%	28 44.2%
preferred source of info	65 33.7%	47 31.6%	18 41.3%	65 33.7%	0 0	28 43.7%	22 27.9%	15 29.9%	8 31.0%	14 40.0%	17 39.1%	15 26.5%	3 40.0%	7 32.0%	* 28.6%	0 0	43 33.0%	22 35.3%
Borrow from or use in campus library (NET)	62 32.4%	43 28.8%	19 45.0%	62 32.4%	0 0	22 34.5%	25 31.7%	15 30.8%	12 48.3%	14 40.0%	9 21.7%	17 30.6%	6 63.3%	4 16.0%	* 28.6%	0 0	46 35.7%	16 25.4%
All sources of info	62 32.4%	43 28.8%	19 45.0%	62 32.4%	0 0	22 34.5%	25 31.7%	15 30.8%	12 48.3%	14 40.0%	9 21.7%	17 30.6%	6 63.3%	4 16.0%	* 28.6%	0 0	46 35.7%	16 25.4%
preferred source of info	42 21.6%	28 18.7%	14 32.1%	42 21.6%	0 0	15 24.1%	19 24.3%	7 14.3%	10 37.9%	8 22.9%	6 13.0%	12 22.4%	3 33.3%	3 12.0%	* 14.3%	0 0	29 22.2%	13 20.6%
Meeting/Conferences (NET)	37 19.3%	30 20.1%	7 16.5%	37 19.3%	0 0	15 23.5%	8 10.8%	14 27.3%F	4 13.8%	5 14.3%	9 21.7%	11 20.4%	1 10.0%	7 28.0%	1 42.9%	0 0	20 15.4%	17 27.3%
All sources of info	37 19.3%	30 20.1%	7 16.5%	37 19.3%	0 0	15 23.5%	8 10.8%	14 27.3%F	4 13.8%	5 14.3%	9 21.7%	11 20.4%	1 10.0%	7 28.0%	1 42.9%	0 0	20 15.4%	17 27.3%

Proportions/Means: Columns Tested (5% risk level) - A/B/D - C/D - E/F/G - H/I/J/K/L/M/N - P/Q
* small base; ** very small base (under 30) ineligible for sig testing

Table 231
Page 896

Outsell/Digital Library Federation Study (2002)
Weighted Tables

TABLE 108, continued

T7D/E_6. Papers delivered at professional meetings SUMMARY TABLE

		RESPONDENT TYPE				INSTITUTION TYPE			DISCIPLINE									GENDER	
	TOTAL SAMPLE	FACULTY MEMBER	GRAD. STUDENT	FACULTY /GRAD	UNDER GRAD. STUDENT	PUBLIC	PRIVATE	LIBERAL ARTS	BIOLOGIAL SCIENCES	PHYSICAL SCIENCES /MATH	SOCIAL SCIENCES	ARTS AND HUMAN.	ENGI-NEERING	BUSINESS	LAW	UNDEC. MAJOR	MALE	FEMALE
		(A)	(B)	(C)	(D)	(E)	(F)	(G)	(H)	(I)	(J)	(K)	(L)	(M)	(N)		(P)	(Q)
Base - Use Papers delivered at professional meetings for teaching	192	149	42*	192	0**	64*	78*	50*	26**	35*	43**	55*	9**	23**	1**	0*	129	63*
preferred source of info	30 15.6%	25 16.6%	5 12.1%	30 15.6%	0 0	10 15.4%	8 9.6%	12 25.0%F	2 6.9%	5 14.3%	8 17.4%	8 14.3%	1 10.0%	7 28.0%	* 28.6%	0 0	17 13.2%	13 20.4%
Author	21 11.2%	21 14.3%B	0 0	21 11.2%	0 0	5 7.2%	14 17.9%	3 5.7%	2 6.9%	2 5.7%	6 13.0%	8 14.3%	* 3.3%	4 16.0%	* 14.3%	0 0	17 13.2%	4 7.0%
All sources of info	21 11.2%	21 14.3%B	0 0	21 11.2%	0 0	5 7.2%	14 17.9%	3 5.7%	2 6.9%	2 5.7%	6 13.0%	8 14.3%	* 3.3%	4 16.0%	* 14.3%	0 0	17 13.2%	4 7.0%
preferred source of info	15 8.0%	15 10.3%	0 0	15 8.0%	0 0	1 2.0%	11 14.3%E	3 5.7%	1 3.4%	1 2.9%	4 8.7%	7 12.2%	0 0	3 12.0%	* 14.3%	0 0	11 8.7%	4 6.5%
Colleagues (NET)	15 7.8%	8 5.4%	7 16.5%A	15 7.8%	0 0	5 7.4%	8 10.6%	2 4.0%	0 0	3 8.6%	8 17.4%	4 8.2%	0 0	0 0	0 0	0 0	13 10.0%	2 3.4%
All sources of info	15 7.8%	8 5.4%	7 16.5%A	15 7.8%	0 0	5 7.4%	8 10.6%	2 4.0%	0 0	3 8.6%	8 17.4%	4 8.2%	0 0	0 0	0 0	0 0	13 10.0%	2 3.4%
preferred source of info	3 1.6%	2 1.3%	1 2.4%	3 1.6%	0 0	1 1.6%	0 0	2 4.0%	0 0	3 8.6%K	0 0	0 0	0 0	0 0	0 0	0 0	2 1.5%	1 1.6%
Access from course website (NET)	11 5.9%	10 7.0%	1 2.1%	11 5.9%	0 0	2 3.3%	5 6.6%	4 8.0%	2 6.9%	3 8.6%	0 0	6 10.2%	0 0	1 4.0%	0 0	0 0	8 6.4%	3 4.8%
All sources of info	11 5.9%	10 7.0%	1 2.1%	11 5.9%	0 0	2 3.3%	5 6.6%	4 8.0%	2 6.9%	3 8.6%	0 0	6 10.2%	0 0	1 4.0%	0 0	0 0	8 6.4%	3 4.8%

Proportions/Means: Columns Tested (5% risk level) - A/B/D - C/D - E/F/G - H/I/J/K/L/M/N - P/Q
* small base; ** very small base (under 30) ineligible for sig testing

Table 231
Page 897

Outsell/Digital Library Federation Study (2002)
Weighted Tables

TABLE 108, continued

T7D/E_6. Papers delivered at professional meetings SUMMARY TABLE

		RESPONDENT TYPE				INSTITUTION TYPE			DISCIPLINE									GENDER	
	TOTAL SAMPLE	FACULTY MEMBER	GRAD. STUDENT	FACULTY /GRAD	UNDER GRAD. STUDENT	PUBLIC	PRIVATE	LIBERAL ARTS	BIOLOGIAL SCIENCES	PHYSICAL SCIENCES /MATH	SOCIAL SCIENCES	ARTS AND HUMAN.	ENGI-NEERING	BUSINESS	LAW	UNDEC. MAJOR	MALE	FEMALE
		(A)	(B)	(C)	(D)	(E)	(F)	(G)	(H)	(I)	(J)	(K)	(L)	(M)	(N)		(P)	(Q)
Base - Use Papers delivered at professional meetings for teaching	192	149	42*	192	0**	64*	78*	50*	26**	35*	43**	55*	9**	23**	1**	0*	129	63*
preferred source of info	6 3.2%	6 4.1%	0 0	6 3.2%	0 0	1 1.6%	2 2.6%	3 6.0%	1 3.4%	2 5.7%	0 0	2 4.1%	0 0	1 4.0%	0 0	0 0	5 3.9%	1 1.6%
Personal Collection/ Holdings (NET)	9 4.5%	9 5.7%	0 0	9 4.5%	0 0	2 2.8%	5 6.6%	2 3.2%	1 3.4%	1 2.9%	4 8.7%	1 2.0%	1 10.0%	1 4.0%	0 0	0 0	9 6.6%	0 0
All sources of info	9 4.5%	9 5.7%	0 0	9 4.5%	0 0	2 2.8%	5 6.6%	2 3.2%	1 3.4%	1 2.9%	4 8.7%	1 2.0%	1 10.0%	1 4.0%	0 0	0 0	9 6.6%	0 0
preferred source of info	2 1.1%	2 1.4%	0 0	2 1.1%	0 0	2 2.8%	0 0	* 0.6%	1 3.4%	0 0	0 0	0 0	* 3.3%	1 4.0%	0 0	0 0	2 1.6%	0 0
Order from on demand document delivery service (NET)	6 3.2%	6 4.1%	0 0	6 3.2%	0 0	2 3.3%	2 2.4%	2 4.3%	0 0	2 5.7%	2 4.3%	2 4.1%	0 0	0 0	0 0	0 0	6 4.7%	0 0
All sources of info	6 3.2%	6 4.1%	0 0	6 3.2%	0 0	2 3.3%	2 2.4%	2 4.3%	0 0	2 5.7%	2 4.3%	2 4.1%	0 0	0 0	0 0	0 0	6 4.7%	0 0
preferred source of info	4 2.1%	4 2.7%	0 0	4 2.1%	0 0	0 0	2 2.4%	2 4.3%	0 0	1 2.9%	2 4.3%	1 2.0%	0 0	0 0	0 0	0 0	4 3.1%	0 0
Interlibrary loan (NET)	6 3.2%	5 3.3%	1 2.6%	6 3.2%	0 0	0 0	2 2.9%	4 7.7%E	2 6.9%	2 5.7%	0 0	1 2.0%	* 3.3%	1 4.0%	0 0	0 0	3 2.3%	3 5.0%

Proportions/Means: Columns Tested (5% risk level) - A/B/D - C/D - E/F/G - H/I/J/K/L/M/N - P/Q
* small base; ** very small base (under 30) ineligible for sig testing

Table 231
Page 898

Outsell/Digital Library Federation Study (2002)
Weighted Tables

TABLE 108, continued

T7D/E_6. Papers delivered at professional meetings SUMMARY TABLE

		RESPONDENT TYPE				INSTITUTION TYPE			DISCIPLINE									GENDER	
	TOTAL SAMPLE	FACULTY MEMBER	GRAD. STUDENT	FACULTY /GRAD	UNDER GRAD. STUDENT	PUBLIC	PRIVATE	LIBERAL ARTS	BIOLOGIAL SCIENCES	PHYSICAL SCIENCES /MATH	SOCIAL SCIENCES	ARTS AND HUMAN.	ENGI- NEERING	BUSINESS	LAW	UNDEC. MAJOR	MALE	FEMALE
		(A)	(B)	(C)	(D)	(E)	(F)	(G)	(H)	(I)	(J)	(K)	(L)	(M)	(N)		(P)	(Q)
Base - Use Papers delivered at professional meetings for teaching	192	149	42*	192	0**	64*	78*	50*	26**	35*	43**	55*	9**	23**	1**	0*	129	63*
All sources of info	6 3.2%	5 3.3%	1 2.6%	6 3.2%	0 0	0 0	2 2.9%	4 7.7%E	2 6.9%	2 5.7%	0 0	1 2.0%	* 3.3%	1 4.0%	0 0	0 0	3 2.3%	3 5.0%
preferred source of info	3 1.4%	3 1.8%	0 0	3 1.4%	0 0	0 0	1 1.1%	2 3.8%	2 6.9%	1 2.9%	0 0	0 0	0 0	0 0	0 0	0 0	2 1.4%	1 1.6%
Publisher (NET)	6 3.1%	4 2.7%	2 4.4%	6 3.1%	0 0	4 6.1%	1 1.4%	1 1.9%	0 0	0 0	2 4.3%	2 4.1%	0 0	2 8.0%	0 0	0 0	4 3.2%	2 3.0%
All sources of info	6 3.1%	4 2.7%	2 4.4%	6 3.1%	0 0	4 6.1%	1 1.4%	1 1.9%	0 0	0 0	2 4.3%	2 4.1%	0 0	2 8.0%	0 0	0 0	4 3.2%	2 3.0%
preferred source of info	3 1.5%	1 0.6%	2 4.4%	3 1.5%	0 0	2 2.9%	0 0	1 1.9%	0 0	0 0	2 4.3%	0 0	0 0	1 4.0%	0 0	0 0	1 0.7%	2 3.0%
Borrow from or use in other libraries (NET)	5 2.4%	2 1.6%	2 5.3%	5 2.4%	0 0	1 2.2%	2 2.9%	1 2.0%	0 0	1 2.9%	0 0	3 6.1%	* 3.3%	0 0	0 0	0 0	3 2.5%	1 2.3%
All sources of info	5 2.4%	2 1.6%	2 5.3%	5 2.4%	0 0	1 2.2%	2 2.9%	1 2.0%	0 0	1 2.9%	0 0	3 6.1%	* 3.3%	0 0	0 0	0 0	3 2.5%	1 2.3%
preferred source of info	3 1.3%	1 0.9%	1 2.6%	3 1.3%	0 0	* 0.5%	2 2.9%	0 0	0 0	0 0	0 0	2 4.1%	* 3.3%	0 0	0 0	0 0	2 1.7%	* 0.5%

Proportions/Means: Columns Tested (5% risk level) - A/B/D - C/D - E/F/G - H/I/J/K/L/M/N - P/Q
* small base; ** very small base (under 30) ineligible for sig testing

Table 231
Page 899

Outsell/Digital Library Federation Study (2002)
Weighted Tables

TABLE 108, continued

T7D/E_6. Papers delivered at professional meetings SUMMARY TABLE

		RESPONDENT TYPE				INSTITUTION TYPE			DISCIPLINE								GENDER	
	TOTAL SAMPLE	FACULTY MEMBER	GRAD. STUDENT	FACULTY /GRAD	UNDER GRAD. STUDENT	PUBLIC	PRIVATE	LIBERAL ARTS	BIOLOGIAL SCIENCES	PHYSICAL SCIENCES /MATH	SOCIAL SCIENCES	ARTS AND HUMAN.	ENGI-NEERING	BUSINESS	LAW	UNDEC. MAJOR	MALE	FEMALE
		(A)	(B)	(C)	(D)	(E)	(F)	(G)	(H)	(I)	(J)	(K)	(L)	(M)	(N)		(P)	(Q)
Base - Use Papers delivered at professional meetings for teaching	192	149	42*	192	0**	64*	78*	50*	26**	35*	43**	55*	9**	23**	1**	0*	129	63*
Purchase from online bookstore (NET)	3 1.7%	3 2.2%	0 0	3 1.7%	0 0	0 0	2 2.7%	1 2.2%	1 3.4%	0 0	0 0	1 2.0%	* 3.3%	1 4.0%	0 0	0 0	1 0.9%	2 3.3%
All sources of info	3 1.7%	3 2.2%	0 0	3 1.7%	0 0	0 0	2 2.7%	1 2.2%	1 3.4%	0 0	0 0	1 2.0%	* 3.3%	1 4.0%	0 0	0 0	1 0.9%	2 3.3%
preferred source of info	3 1.5%	3 2.0%	0 0	3 1.5%	0 0	0 0	2 2.3%	1 2.2%	1 3.4%	0 0	0 0	1 2.0%	0 0	1 4.0%	0 0	0 0	1 0.7%	2 3.3%
Office (NET)	3 1.7%	3 2.1%	0 0	3 1.7%	0 0	0 0	1 1.4%	2 4.1%	0 0	0 0	0 0	2 4.1%	0 0	1 4.0%	0 0	0 0	2 1.6%	1 1.8%
All sources of info	3 1.7%	3 2.1%	0 0	3 1.7%	0 0	0 0	1 1.4%	2 4.1%	0 0	0 0	0 0	2 4.1%	0 0	1 4.0%	0 0	0 0	2 1.6%	1 1.8%
preferred source of info	2 1.2%	2 1.5%	0 0	2 1.2%	0 0	0 0	1 1.4%	1 2.2%	0 0	0 0	0 0	2 4.1%	0 0	0 0	0 0	0 0	1 0.9%	1 1.8%
Purchase from physical book store (NET)	1 0.5%	1 0.6%	0 0	1 0.5%	0 0	0 0	1 1.1%	0 0	1 3.4%	0 0	0 0	0 0	0 0	0 0	0 0	0 0	1 0.7%	0 0
All sources of info	1 0.5%	1 0.6%	0 0	1 0.5%	0 0	0 0	1 1.1%	0 0	1 3.4%	0 0	0 0	0 0	0 0	0 0	0 0	0 0	1 0.7%	0 0

Proportions/Means: Columns Tested (5% risk level) - A/B/D - C/D - E/F/G - H/I/J/K/L/M/N - P/Q
* small base; ** very small base (under 30) ineligible for sig testing

Table 231
Page 900

Outsell/Digital Library Federation Study (2002)
Weighted Tables

TABLE 108, continued

T7D/E_6. Papers delivered at professional meetings SUMMARY TABLE

		RESPONDENT TYPE				INSTITUTION TYPE			DISCIPLINE									GENDER	
	TOTAL SAMPLE	FACULTY MEMBER	GRAD. STUDENT	FACULTY /GRAD	UNDER GRAD. STUDENT	PUBLIC	PRIVATE	LIBERAL ARTS	BIOLOGIAL SCIENCES	PHYSICAL SCIENCES /MATH	SOCIAL SCIENCES	ARTS AND HUMAN.	ENGI-NEERING	BUSINESS	LAW	UNDEC. MAJOR	MALE	FEMALE
		(A)	(B)	(C)	(D)	(E)	(F)	(G)	(H)	(I)	(J)	(K)	(L)	(M)	(N)		(P)	(Q)
Base - Use Papers delivered at professional meetings for teaching	192	149	42*	192	0**	64*	78*	50*	26**	35*	43**	55*	9**	23**	1**	0*	129	63*
preferred source of info	1 0.5%	1 0.6%	0 0	1 0.5%	0 0	0 0	1 1.1%	0 0	1 3.4%	0 0	0 0	0 0	0 0	0 0	0 0	0 0	1 0.7%	0 0
Faculty (NET)	1 0.3%	0 0	1 1.4%	1 0.3%	0 0	0 0	1 0.7%	0 0	0 0	0 0	0 0	0 0	1 6.7%	0 0	0 0	0 0	1 0.4%	0 0
All sources of info	1 0.3%	0 0	1 1.4%	1 0.3%	0 0	0 0	1 0.7%	0 0	0 0	0 0	0 0	0 0	1 6.7%	0 0	0 0	0 0	1 0.4%	0 0
preferred source of info	* 0.2%	0 0	* 0.7%	* 0.2%	0 0	0 0	* 0.4%	0 0	0 0	0 0	0 0	0 0	* 3.3%	0 0	0 0	0 0	* 0.2%	0 0
Department (NET)	0 0	0 0	0 0	0 0	0 0	0 0	0 0	0 0	0 0	0 0	0 0	0 0	0 0	0 0	0 0	0 0	0 0	0 0
All sources of info	0 0	0 0	0 0	0 0	0 0	0 0	0 0	0 0	0 0	0 0	0 0	0 0	0 0	0 0	0 0	0 0	0 0	0 0
preferred source of info	0 0	0 0	0 0	0 0	0 0	0 0	0 0	0 0	0 0	0 0	0 0	0 0	0 0	0 0	0 0	0 0	0 0	0 0
Access book/journal/ journal article elsewhere online (NET)	0 0	0 0	0 0	0 0	0 0	0 0	0 0	0 0	0 0	0 0	0 0	0 0	0 0	0 0	0 0	0 0	0 0	0 0

Proportions/Means: Columns Tested (5% risk level) - A/B/D - C/D - E/F/G - H/I/J/K/L/M/N - P/Q
* small base; ** very small base (under 30) ineligible for sig testing

Table 231
Page 901

TABLE 108, continued

T7D/E_6. Papers delivered at professional meetings SUMMARY TABLE

		RESPONDENT TYPE				INSTITUTION TYPE			DISCIPLINE									GENDER	
	TOTAL SAMPLE	FACULTY MEMBER	GRAD. STUDENT	FACULTY /GRAD	UNDER GRAD. STUDENT	PUBLIC	PRIVATE	LIBERAL ARTS	BIOLOGIAL SCIENCES	PHYSICAL SCIENCES /MATH	SOCIAL SCIENCES	ARTS AND HUMAN.	ENGI- NEERING	BUSINESS	LAW	UNDEC. MAJOR	MALE	FEMALE
		(A)	(B)	(C)	(D)	(E)	(F)	(G)	(H)	(I)	(J)	(K)	(L)	(M)	(N)		(P)	(Q)
Base - Use Papers delivered at professional meetings for teaching	192	149	42*	192	0**	64*	78*	50*	26**	35*	43**	55*	9**	23**	1**	0*	129	63*
All sources of info	0	0	0	0	0	0	0	0	0	0	0	0	0	0	0	0	0	0
	0	0	0	0	0	0	0	0	0	0	0	0	0	0	0	0	0	0
preferred source of info	0	0	0	0	0	0	0	0	0	0	0	0	0	0	0	0	0	0
	0	0	0	0	0	0	0	0	0	0	0	0	0	0	0	0	0	0
Ask library to purchase source (NET)	0	0	0	0	0	0	0	0	0	0	0	0	0	0	0	0	0	0
	0	0	0	0	0	0	0	0	0	0	0	0	0	0	0	0	0	0
All sources of info	0	0	0	0	0	0	0	0	0	0	0	0	0	0	0	0	0	0
	0	0	0	0	0	0	0	0	0	0	0	0	0	0	0	0	0	0
preferred source of info	0	0	0	0	0	0	0	0	0	0	0	0	0	0	0	0	0	0
	0	0	0	0	0	0	0	0	0	0	0	0	0	0	0	0	0	0
Home (NET)	0	0	0	0	0	0	0	0	0	0	0	0	0	0	0	0	0	0
	0	0	0	0	0	0	0	0	0	0	0	0	0	0	0	0	0	0
All sources of info	0	0	0	0	0	0	0	0	0	0	0	0	0	0	0	0	0	0
	0	0	0	0	0	0	0	0	0	0	0	0	0	0	0	0	0	0
preferred source of info	0	0	0	0	0	0	0	0	0	0	0	0	0	0	0	0	0	0
	0	0	0	0	0	0	0	0	0	0	0	0	0	0	0	0	0	0

Proportions/Means: Columns Tested (5% risk level) - A/B/D - C/D - E/F/G - H/I/J/K/L/M/N - P/Q
* small base; ** very small base (under 30) ineligible for sig testing

Table 231
Page 902

Outsell/Digital Library Federation Study (2002)
Weighted Tables

TABLE 108, continued

T7D/E_6. Papers delivered at professional meetings SUMMARY TABLE

		RESPONDENT TYPE				INSTITUTION TYPE			DISCIPLINE									GENDER	
	TOTAL SAMPLE	FACULTY MEMBER	GRAD. STUDENT	FACULTY /GRAD	UNDER GRAD. STUDENT	PUBLIC	PRIVATE	LIBERAL ARTS	BIOLOGIAL SCIENCES	PHYSICAL SCIENCES /MATH	SOCIAL SCIENCES	ARTS AND HUMAN.	ENGI-NEERING	BUSINESS	LAW	UNDEC. MAJOR	MALE	FEMALE
		(A)	(B)	(C)	(D)	(E)	(F)	(G)	(H)	(I)	(J)	(K)	(L)	(M)	(N)		(P)	(Q)
Base - Use Papers delivered at professional meetings for teaching	192	149	42*	192	0**	64*	78*	50*	26**	35*	43**	55*	9**	23**	1**	0*	129	63*
Other (NET)	13 6.6%	11 7.2%	2 4.4%	13 6.6%	0 0	4 6.5%	5 6.9%	3 6.3%	1 3.4%	2 5.7%	4 8.7%	4 8.2%	1 6.7%	1 4.0%	0 0	0 0	10 8.0%	2 3.6%
All sources of info	11 5.6%	9 5.9%	2 4.4%	11 5.6%	0 0	4 6.5%	3 4.4%	3 6.3%	1 3.4%	2 5.7%	2 4.3%	4 8.2%	1 6.7%	1 4.0%	0 0	0 0	9 6.6%	2 3.6%
preferred source of info	5 2.8%	4 2.4%	2 4.4%	5 2.8%	0 0	2 3.4%	3 4.2%	0 0	0 0	0 0	4 8.7%	1 2.0%	1 6.7%	0 0	0 0	0 0	4 3.4%	1 1.8%
DK/Refused	5 2.8%	5 3.6%	0 0	5 2.8%	0 0	1 2.0%	4 5.3%	0 0	0 0	0 0	2 4.3%	3 6.1%	0 0	0 0	* 14.3%	0 0	4 3.2%	1 2.1%

Proportions/Means: Columns Tested (5% risk level) - A/B/D - C/D - E/F/G - H/I/J/K/L/M/N - P/Q
* small base; ** very small base (under 30) ineligible for sig testing

Table 231
Page 903

Outsell/Digital Library Federation Study (2002)
Weighted Tables

TABLE 109

T7sum_7. Print abstracts and indexes SUMMARY TABLE

		RESPONDENT TYPE				INSTITUTION TYPE			DISCIPLINE									GENDER	
	TOTAL SAMPLE	FACULTY MEMBER	GRAD. STUDENT	FACULTY /GRAD	UNDER GRAD. STUDENT	PUBLIC	PRIVATE	LIBERAL ARTS	BIOLOGIAL SCIENCES	PHYSICAL SCIENCES /MATH	SOCIAL SCIENCES	ARTS AND HUMAN.	ENGI-NEERING	BUSINESS	LAW	UNDEC. MAJOR	MALE	FEMALE
		(A)	(B)	(C)	(D)	(E)	(F)	(G)	(H)	(I)	(J)	(K)	(L)	(M)	(N)		(P)	(Q)
Base - USe Print abstracts and indexes for teaching	154	110*	44*	154	0**	58*	53*	43*	37*	25**	43**	29**	6**	13**	1**	0*	107*	47*
ONLINE	119 76.9%	88 79.9%	31 69.6%	119 76.9%	0 0	44 75.7%	34 64.8%	41 93.5%EF	27 73.8%	20 80.0%	36 82.6%	19 65.4%	5 77.3%	11 85.7%	1 100.0%	0 0	80 74.9%	39 81.6%
Your own institution's web site	27 17.7%	21 19.0%	6 14.7%	27 17.7%	0 0	10 17.3%	9 17.0%	8 19.2%	4 9.5%	2 8.0%	13 30.4%	4 15.4%	1 22.7%	3 21.4%	0 0	0 0	16 15.0%	11 24.0%
All sources of info	27 17.7%	21 19.0%	6 14.7%	27 17.7%	0 0	10 17.3%	9 17.0%	8 19.2%	4 9.5%	2 8.0%	13 30.4%	4 15.4%	1 22.7%	3 21.4%	0 0	0 0	16 15.0%	11 24.0%
preferred source of info	19 12.1%	13 11.8%	6 12.7%	19 12.1%	0 0	8 13.9%	6 11.8%	4 10.0%	2 4.8%	1 4.0%	9 21.7%	2 7.7%	1 22.7%	3 21.4%	0 0	0 0	8 7.6%	10 22.1%P
Online databases	26 16.6%	20 18.0%	6 13.2%	26 16.6%	0 0	8 13.2%	9 17.4%	9 20.3%	8 21.4%	5 20.0%	6 13.0%	4 15.4%	* 4.5%	2 14.3%	1 75.0%	0 0	20 18.4%	6 12.6%
All sources of info	26 16.6%	20 18.0%	6 13.2%	26 16.6%	0 0	8 13.2%	9 17.4%	9 20.3%	8 21.4%	5 20.0%	6 13.0%	4 15.4%	* 4.5%	2 14.3%	1 75.0%	0 0	20 18.4%	6 12.6%
preferred source of info	16 10.2%	10 9.1%	6 12.8%	16 10.2%	0 0	5 8.3%	8 14.7%	3 7.2%	5 14.3%	3 12.0%	4 8.7%	3 11.5%	0 0	0 0	* 50.0%	0 0	11 10.1%	5 10.4%
Search engine	21 13.3%	17 15.6%	3 7.6%	21 13.3%	0 0	8 14.1%	7 13.2%	5 12.3%	7 19.0%	4 16.0%	4 8.7%	2 7.7%	1 22.7%	2 14.3%	* 25.0%	0 0	16 15.4%	4 8.6%
All sources of info	21 13.3%	17 15.6%	3 7.6%	21 13.3%	0 0	8 14.1%	7 13.2%	5 12.3%	7 19.0%	4 16.0%	4 8.7%	2 7.7%	1 22.7%	2 14.3%	* 25.0%	0 0	16 15.4%	4 8.6%

Proportions/Means: Columns Tested (5% risk level) - A/B/D - C/D - E/F/G - H/I/J/K/L/M/N - P/Q
* small base; ** very small base (under 30) ineligible for sig testing

Table 235
Page 915

Outsell/Digital Library Federation Study (2002)
Weighted Tables

TABLE 109, continued

T7sum_7. Print abstracts and indexes SUMMARY TABLE

	TOTAL SAMPLE	RESPONDENT TYPE: FACULTY MEMBER (A)	GRAD. STUDENT (B)	FACULTY /GRAD (C)	UNDER GRAD. STUDENT (D)	INSTITUTION TYPE: PUBLIC (E)	PRIVATE (F)	LIBERAL ARTS (G)	DISCIPLINE: BIOLOGIAL SCIENCES (H)	PHYSICAL SCIENCES /MATH (I)	SOCIAL SCIENCES (J)	ARTS AND HUMAN. (K)	ENGI-NEERING (L)	BUSINESS (M)	LAW (N)	UNDEC. MAJOR	GENDER: MALE (P)	FEMALE (Q)
Base - USe Print abstracts and indexes for teaching	154	110*	44*	154	0**	58*	53*	43*	37*	25**	43**	29**	6**	13**	1**	0*	107*	47*
preferred source of info	11 6.9%	9 8.0%	2 4.0%	11 6.9%	0 0	6 10.1%	2 3.3%	3 6.9%	5 14.3%	3 12.0%	0 0	1 3.8%	* 4.5%	1 7.1%	0 0	0 0	9 8.0%	2 4.3%
Online library catalogues and finding aids	19 12.6%	13 11.6%	7 15.2%	19 12.6%	0 0	5 8.8%	6 12.1%	8 18.2%	4 11.9%	2 8.0%	6 13.0%	2 7.7%	1 22.7%	4 28.6%	0 0	0 0	14 12.7%	6 12.3%
All sources of info	19 12.6%	13 11.6%	7 15.2%	19 12.6%	0 0	5 8.8%	6 12.1%	8 18.2%	4 11.9%	2 8.0%	6 13.0%	2 7.7%	1 22.7%	4 28.6%	0 0	0 0	14 12.7%	6 12.3%
preferred source of info	12 7.8%	8 7.4%	4 8.8%	12 7.8%	0 0	3 5.7%	3 5.1%	6 14.1%	2 4.8%	1 4.0%	4 8.7%	2 7.7%	1 22.7%	2 14.3%	0 0	0 0	9 8.4%	3 6.6%
Web directory/ subject related web site	19 12.2%	14 12.7%	5 11.1%	19 12.2%	0 0	7 12.2%	6 11.6%	6 13.1%	6 16.7%	5 20.0%	2 4.3%	4 15.4%	* 4.5%	1 7.1%	* 25.0%	0 0	12 11.2%	7 14.7%
All sources of info	19 12.2%	14 12.7%	5 11.1%	19 12.2%	0 0	7 12.2%	6 11.6%	6 13.1%	6 16.7%	5 20.0%	2 4.3%	4 15.4%	* 4.5%	1 7.1%	* 25.0%	0 0	12 11.2%	7 14.7%
preferred source of info	11 7.1%	7 6.3%	4 9.1%	11 7.1%	0 0	3 5.2%	3 6.0%	5 11.0%	4 9.5%	3 12.0%	2 4.3%	2 7.7%	* 4.5%	0 0	0 0	0 0	6 5.4%	5 10.9%
Internet searches	14 8.9%	11 9.6%	3 7.2%	14 8.9%	0 0	8 13.6%	5 9.1%	1 2.3%	2 4.8%	6 24.0%	2 4.3%	0 0	1 18.2%	3 21.4%	* 25.0%	0 0	12 10.9%	2 4.4%
All sources of info	14 8.9%	11 9.6%	3 7.2%	14 8.9%	0 0	8 13.6%	5 9.1%	1 2.3%	2 4.8%	6 24.0%	2 4.3%	0 0	1 18.2%	3 21.4%	* 25.0%	0 0	12 10.9%	2 4.4%

Proportions/Means: Columns Tested (5% risk level) - A/B/D - C/D - E/F/G - H/I/J/K/L/M/N - P/Q
* small base; ** very small base (under 30) ineligible for sig testing

Table 235
Page 916

Outsell/Digital Library Federation Study (2002)
Weighted Tables

TABLE 109, continued

T7sum_7. Print abstracts and indexes SUMMARY TABLE

	RESPONDENT TYPE				INSTITUTION TYPE			DISCIPLINE								GENDER	
	TOTAL SAMPLE	FACULTY MEMBER	GRAD. STUDENT	FACULTY /GRAD	UNDER GRAD. STUDENT	PUBLIC	PRIVATE	LIBERAL ARTS	BIOLOGIAL SCIENCES	PHYSICAL SCIENCES /MATH	SOCIAL SCIENCES	ARTS AND HUMAN.	ENGI- NEERING	BUSINESS	LAW	UNDEC. MAJOR	MALE	FEMALE
		(A)	(B)	(C)	(D)	(E)	(F)	(G)	(H)	(I)	(J)	(K)	(L)	(M)	(N)		(P)	(Q)
Base - USe Print abstracts and indexes for teaching	154	110*	44*	154	0**	58*	53*	43*	37*	25**	43**	29**	6**	13**	1**	0*	107*	47*
preferred source of info	3 1.9%	2 1.6%	1 2.7%	3 1.9%	0 0	2 3.6%	1 1.7%	0 0	1 2.4%	1 4.0%	0 0	0 0	0 0	1 7.1%	* 25.0%	0 0	2 2.0%	1 1.9%
Online abstracting and indexing services	12 7.7%	12 10.8%B	0 0	12 7.7%	0 0	* 0.5%	1 1.7%	11 24.8%EF	3 7.1%	3 12.0%	2 4.3%	2 7.7%	* 4.5%	2 14.3%	0 0	0 0	8 7.7%	4 7.7%
All sources of info	12 7.7%	12 10.8%B	0 0	12 7.7%	0 0	* 0.5%	1 1.7%	11 24.8%EF	3 7.1%	3 12.0%	2 4.3%	2 7.7%	* 4.5%	2 14.3%	0 0	0 0	8 7.7%	4 7.7%
preferred source of info	7 4.5%	7 6.3%	0 0	7 4.5%	0 0	* 0.5%	1 1.7%	6 13.4%EF	2 4.8%	1 4.0%	2 4.3%	1 3.8%	* 4.5%	1 7.1%	0 0	0 0	5 4.9%	2 3.7%
Online reference service	7 4.2%	5 4.2%	2 4.3%	7 4.2%	0 0	4 6.5%	0 0	3 6.4%	3 7.1%	2 8.0%	2 4.3%	0 0	0 0	0 0	0 0	0 0	4 3.5%	3 5.8%
All sources of info	7 4.2%	5 4.2%	2 4.3%	7 4.2%	0 0	4 6.5%	0 0	3 6.4%	3 7.1%	2 8.0%	2 4.3%	0 0	0 0	0 0	0 0	0 0	4 3.5%	3 5.8%
preferred source of info	1 0.6%	1 0.8%	0 0	1 0.6%	0 0	1 1.5%	0 0	0 0	1 2.4%	0 0	0 0	0 0	0 0	0 0	0 0	0 0	1 0.8%	0 0
Online bookstore	4 2.4%	4 3.3%	0 0	4 2.4%	0 0	1 1.5%	0 0	3 6.5%	1 2.4%	0 0	2 4.3%	0 0	0 0	1 7.1%	0 0	0 0	2 1.7%	2 4.0%
All sources of info	4 2.4%	4 3.3%	0 0	4 2.4%	0 0	1 1.5%	0 0	3 6.5%	1 2.4%	0 0	2 4.3%	0 0	0 0	1 7.1%	0 0	0 0	2 1.7%	2 4.0%

Proportions/Means: Columns Tested (5% risk level) - A/B/D - C/D - E/F/G - H/I/J/K/L/M/N - P/Q
* small base; ** very small base (under 30) ineligible for sig testing

Table 235
Page 917

Outsell/Digital Library Federation Study (2002)
Weighted Tables

TABLE 109, continued

T7sum_7. Print abstracts and indexes SUMMARY TABLE

		RESPONDENT TYPE				INSTITUTION TYPE			DISCIPLINE									GENDER	
	TOTAL SAMPLE	FACULTY MEMBER	GRAD. STUDENT	FACULTY /GRAD	UNDER GRAD. STUDENT	PUBLIC	PRIVATE	LIBERAL ARTS	BIOLOGIAL SCIENCES	PHYSICAL SCIENCES /MATH	SOCIAL SCIENCES	ARTS AND HUMAN.	ENGI-NEERING	BUSINESS	LAW	UNDEC. MAJOR	MALE	FEMALE
		(A)	(B)	(C)	(D)	(E)	(F)	(G)	(H)	(I)	(J)	(K)	(L)	(M)	(N)		(P)	(Q)
Base - USe Print abstracts and indexes for teaching	154	110*	44*	154	0**	58*	53*	43*	37*	25**	43**	29**	6**	13**	1**	.0*	107*	47*
preferred source of info	3 1.8%	3 2.5%	0 0	3 1.8%	0 0	0 0	0 0	3 6.5%	0 0	0 0	2 4.3%	0 0	0 0	1 7.1%	0 0	0 0	1 0.9%	2 4.0%
Department web page	3 2.1%	* 0.3%	3 6.6%A	3 2.1%	0 0	2 3.2%	1 2.4%	0 0	0 0	1 4.0%	2 4.3%	0 0	* 4.5%	0 0	0 0	0 0	1 1.2%	2 4.0%
All sources of info	3 2.1%	* 0.3%	3 6.6%A	3 2.1%	0 0	2 3.2%	1 2.4%	0 0	0 0	1 4.0%	2 4.3%	0 0	* 4.5%	0 0	0 0	0 0	1 1.2%	2 4.0%
preferred source of info	2 1.4%	* 0.3%	2 4.3%	2 1.4%	0 0	2 3.2%	* 0.5%	0 0	0 0	0 0	2 4.3%	0 0	* 4.5%	0 0	0 0	0 0	* 0.3%	2 4.0%
E-mail listservs	2 1.1%	2 1.6%	0 0	2 1.1%	0 0	1 1.5%	1 1.7%	0 0	2 4.8%	0 0	0 0	0 0	0 0	0 0	0 0	0 0	1 0.8%	1 1.9%
All sources of info	2 1.1%	2 1.6%	0 0	2 1.1%	0 0	1 1.5%	1 1.7%	0 0	2 4.8%	0 0	0 0	0 0	0 0	0 0	0 0	0 0	1 0.8%	1 1.9%
preferred source of info	1 0.6%	1 0.8%	0 0	1 0.6%	0 0	0 0	1 1.7%	0 0	1 2.4%	0 0	0 0	0 0	0 0	0 0	0 0	0 0	0 0	1 1.9%
Your own personal electronic library/files	1 0.8%	1 1.2%	0 0	1 0.8%	0 0	1 2.2%	0 0	0 0	0 0	0 0	0 0	1 3.8%	0 0	0 0	* 25.0%	0 0	1 1.2%	0 0
All sources of info	1 0.8%	1 1.2%	0 0	1 0.8%	0 0	1 2.2%	0 0	0 0	0 0	0 0	0 0	1 3.8%	0 0	0 0	* 25.0%	0 0	1 1.2%	0 0

Proportions/Means: Columns Tested (5% risk level) - A/B/D - C/D - E/F/G - H/I/J/K/L/M/N - P/Q
* small base; ** very small base (under 30) ineligible for sig testing

Table 235
Page 918

Outsell/Digital Library Federation Study (2002)
Weighted Tables

TABLE 109, continued

T7sum_7. Print abstracts and indexes SUMMARY TABLE

		RESPONDENT TYPE				INSTITUTION TYPE			DISCIPLINE								GENDER	
	TOTAL SAMPLE	FACULTY MEMBER	GRAD. STUDENT	FACULTY /GRAD	UNDER GRAD. STUDENT	PUBLIC	PRIVATE	LIBERAL ARTS	BIOLOGIAL SCIENCES	PHYSICAL SCIENCES /MATH	SOCIAL SCIENCES	ARTS AND HUMAN.	ENGI-NEERING	BUSINESS	LAW	UNDEC. MAJOR	MALE	FEMALE
		(A)	(B)	(C)	(D)	(E)	(F)	(G)	(H)	(I)	(J)	(K)	(L)	(M)	(N)		(P)	(Q)
Base - USe Print abstracts and indexes for teaching	154	110*	44*	154	0**	58*	53*	43*	37*	25**	43**	29**	6**	13**	1**	0*	107*	47*
preferred source of info	1 0.8%	1 1.2%	0 0	1 0.8%	0 0	1 2.2%	0 0	0 0	0 0	0 0	0 0	1 3.8%	0 0	0 0	* 25.0%	0 0	1 1.2%	0 0
LIBRARY/PRINT	84 54.3%	71 64.5%B	13 28.8%	84 54.3%	0 0	26 44.9%	30 56.5%	28 64.2%	18 50.0%	16 64.0%	21 47.8%	18 61.5%	4 59.1%	7 50.0%	1 75.0%	0 0	65 60.8%Q	19 39.6%
Campus library	73 47.2%	61 55.5%B	12 26.2%	73 47.2%	0 0	23 39.4%	26 48.8%	24 55.5%	18 47.6%	15 60.0%	17 39.1%	13 46.2%	4 59.1%	6 42.9%	1 75.0%	0 0	57 53.1%	16 33.7%
All sources of info	73 47.2%	61 55.5%B	12 26.2%	73 47.2%	0 0	23 39.4%	26 48.8%	24 55.5%	18 47.6%	15 60.0%	17 39.1%	13 46.2%	4 59.1%	6 42.9%	1 75.0%	0 0	57 53.1%	16 33.7%
preferred source of info	37 23.8%	29 26.0%	8 18.3%	37 23.8%	0 0	11 18.8%	16 30.4%	10 22.5%	7 19.0%	5 20.0%	11 26.1%	9 30.8%	2 27.3%	3 21.4%	0 0	0 0	32 29.7%Q	5 10.6%
Your own personal physical library/ files/bookshelves	12 7.8%	12 10.6%	* 0.7%	12 7.8%	0 0	3 5.1%	6 11.6%	3 6.8%	4 9.5%	0 0	2 4.3%	4 15.4%	* 4.5%	2 14.3%	0 0	0 0	9 8.5%	3 6.1%
All sources of info	12 7.8%	12 10.6%	* 0.7%	12 7.8%	0 0	3 5.1%	6 11.6%	3 6.8%	4 9.5%	0 0	2 4.3%	4 15.4%	* 4.5%	2 14.3%	0 0	0 0	9 8.5%	3 6.1%
preferred source of info	3 2.0%	3 2.8%	0 0	3 2.0%	0 0	0 0	3 5.9%	0 0	1 2.4%	0 0	0 0	2 7.7%	0 0	0 0	0 0	0 0	3 2.9%	0 0

Proportions/Means: Columns Tested (5% risk level) - A/B/D - C/D - E/F/G - H/I/J/K/L/M/N - P/Q
* small base; ** very small base (under 30) ineligible for sig testing

Table 235
Page 919

Outsell/Digital Library Federation Study (2002)
Weighted Tables

TABLE 109, continued

T7sum_7. Print abstracts and indexes SUMMARY TABLE

		RESPONDENT TYPE				INSTITUTION TYPE			DISCIPLINE								GENDER	
	TOTAL SAMPLE	FACULTY MEMBER	GRAD. STUDENT	FACULTY /GRAD	UNDER GRAD. STUDENT	PUBLIC	PRIVATE	LIBERAL ARTS	BIOLOGIAL SCIENCES	PHYSICAL SCIENCES /MATH	SOCIAL SCIENCES	ARTS AND HUMAN.	ENGI- NEERING	BUSINESS	LAW	UNDEC. MAJOR	MALE	FEMALE
		(A)	(B)	(C)	(D)	(E)	(F)	(G)	(H)	(I)	(J)	(K)	(L)	(M)	(N)		(P)	(Q)
Base - USe Print abstracts and indexes for teaching	154	110*	44*	154	0**	58*	53*	43*	37*	25**	43**	29**	6**	13**	1**	0*	107*	47*
Personal subscriptions to newspapers, magazines and journals	9 5.7%	9 8.0%	0 0	9 5.7%	0 0	2 3.9%	4 7.1%	3 6.5%	1 2.4%	1 4.0%	4 8.7%	2 7.7%	0 0	1 7.1%	0 0	0 0	7 6.4%	2 4.2%
All sources of info	9 5.7%	9 8.0%	0 0	9 5.7%	0 0	2 3.9%	4 7.1%	3 6.5%	1 2.4%	1 4.0%	4 8.7%	2 7.7%	0 0	1 7.1%	0 0	0 0	7 6.4%	2 4.2%
preferred source of info	1 0.6%	1 0.9%	0 0	1 0.6%	0 0	0 0	1 1.9%	0 0	0 0	1 4.0%	0 0	0 0	0 0	0 0	0 0	0 0	1 0.9%	0 0
Another library	6 4.0%	6 5.6%	0 0	6 4.0%	0 0	1 2.2%	0 0	5 11.4%F	1 2.4%	2 8.0%	0 0	1 3.8%	0 0	2 14.3%	* 50.0%	0 0	5 5.0%	1 1.9%
All sources of info	6 4.0%	6 5.6%	0 0	6 4.0%	0 0	1 2.2%	0 0	5 11.4%F	1 2.4%	2 8.0%	0 0	1 3.8%	0 0	2 14.3%	* 50.0%	0 0	5 5.0%	1 1.9%
preferred source of info	0 0	0 0	0 0	0 0	0 0	0 0	0 0	0 0	0 0	0 0	0 0	0 0	0 0	0 0	0 0	0 0	0 0	0 0
Printed abstracting and indexing services	3 2.1%	3 2.7%	* 0.7%	3 2.1%	0 0	2 3.2%	1 2.7%	0 0	0 0	0 0	0 0	1 3.8%	* 4.5%	2 14.3%	0 0	0 0	2 2.2%	1 2.0%
All sources of info	3 2.1%	3 2.7%	* 0.7%	3 2.1%	0 0	2 3.2%	1 2.7%	0 0	0 0	0 0	0 0	1 3.8%	* 4.5%	2 14.3%	0 0	0 0	2 2.2%	1 2.0%

Proportions/Means: Columns Tested (5% risk level) - A/B/D - C/D - E/F/G - H/I/J/K/L/M/N - P/Q
* small base; ** very small base (under 30) ineligible for sig testing

Table 235
Page 920

Outsell/Digital Library Federation Study (2002)
Weighted Tables

TABLE 109, continued

T7sum_7. Print abstracts and indexes SUMMARY TABLE

		RESPONDENT TYPE				INSTITUTION TYPE			DISCIPLINE									GENDER	
	TOTAL SAMPLE	FACULTY MEMBER	GRAD. STUDENT	FACULTY /GRAD	UNDER GRAD. STUDENT	PUBLIC	PRIVATE	LIBERAL ARTS	BIOLOGIAL SCIENCES	PHYSICAL SCIENCES /MATH	SOCIAL SCIENCES	ARTS AND HUMAN.	ENGI- NEERING	BUSINESS	LAW	UNDEC. MAJOR	MALE	FEMALE
		(A)	(B)	(C)	(D)	(E)	(F)	(G)	(H)	(I)	(J)	(K)	(L)	(M)	(N)		(P)	(Q)
Base - USe Print abstracts and indexes for teaching	154	110*	44*	154	0**	58*	53*	43*	37*	25**	43**	29**	6**	13**	1**	0*	107*	47*
preferred source of info	0 0	0 0	0 0	0 0	0 0	0 0	0 0	0 0	0 0	0 0	0 0	0 0	0 0	0 0	0 0	0 0	0 0	0 0
Physical bookstore	3 2.0%	3 2.8%	0 0	3 2.0%	0 0	2 3.9%	1 1.7%	0 0	1 2.4%	0 0	0 0	2 7.7%	0 0	0 0	0 0	0 0	3 2.9%	0 0
All sources of info	3 2.0%	3 2.8%	0 0	3 2.0%	0 0	2 3.9%	1 1.7%	0 0	1 2.4%	0 0	0 0	2 7.7%	0 0	0 0	0 0	0 0	3 2.9%	0 0
preferred source of info	0 0	0 0	0 0	0 0	0 0	0 0	0 0	0 0	0 0	0 0	0 0	0 0	0 0	0 0	0 0	0 0	0 0	0 0
References cited in books or journal articles	3 1.9%	2 1.7%	1 2.5%	3 1.9%	0 0	1 1.9%	0 0	2 4.3%	0 0	0 0	2 4.3%	1 3.8%	0 0	0 0	0 0	0 0	1 1.0%	2 4.0%
All sources of info	3 1.9%	2 1.7%	1 2.5%	3 1.9%	0 0	1 1.9%	0 0	2 4.3%	0 0	0 0	2 4.3%	1 3.8%	0 0	0 0	0 0	0 0	1 1.0%	2 4.0%
preferred source of info	0 0	0 0	0 0	0 0	0 0	0 0	0 0	0 0	0 0	0 0	0 0	0 0	0 0	0 0	0 0	0 0	0 0	0 0
Printed library catalogues and finding aids	2 1.4%	2 2.0%	0 0	2 1.4%	0 0	0 0	0 0	2 5.0%	0 0	0 0	2 4.3%	0 0	* 4.5%	0 0	0 0	0 0	* 0.3%	2 4.0%
All sources of info	2 1.4%	2 2.0%	0 0	2 1.4%	0 0	0 0	0 0	2 5.0%	0 0	0 0	2 4.3%	0 0	* 4.5%	0 0	0 0	0 0	* 0.3%	2 4.0%

Proportions/Means: Columns Tested (5% risk level) - A/B/D - C/D - E/F/G - H/I/J/K/L/M/N - P/Q
* small base; ** very small base (under 30) ineligible for sig testing

Table 235
Page 921

Outsell/Digital Library Federation Study (2002)
Weighted Tables

TABLE 109, continued

T7sum_7. Print abstracts and indexes SUMMARY TABLE

		RESPONDENT TYPE				INSTITUTION TYPE			DISCIPLINE									GENDER	
	TOTAL SAMPLE	FACULTY MEMBER	GRAD. STUDENT	FACULTY /GRAD	UNDER GRAD. STUDENT	PUBLIC	PRIVATE	LIBERAL ARTS	BIOLOGIAL SCIENCES	PHYSICAL SCIENCES /MATH	SOCIAL SCIENCES	ARTS AND HUMAN.	ENGI- NEERING	BUSINESS	LAW	UNDEC. MAJOR	MALE	FEMALE
		(A)	(B)	(C)	(D)	(E)	(F)	(G)	(H)	(I)	(J)	(K)	(L)	(M)	(N)		(P)	(Q)
Base - USe Print abstracts and indexes for teaching	154	110*	44*	154	0**	58*	53*	43*	37*	25**	43**	29**	6**	13**	1**	0*	107*	47*
preferred source of info	0 0	0 0	0 0	0 0	0 0	0 0	0 0	0 0	0 0	0 0	0 0	0 0	0 0	0 0	0 0	0 0	0 0	0 0
PERSONAL ASSISTANCE	53 34.2%	37 33.1%	16 37.0%	53 34.2%	0 0	24 41.0%	13 24.7%	16 36.8%	11 31.0%	7 28.0%	13 30.4%	12 42.3%	1 22.7%	7 57.1%	0 0	0 0	34 31.7%	19 39.9%
A librarian in your institution	28 18.4%	23 21.1%	5 11.5%	28 18.4%	0 0	7 12.5%	7 13.2%	14 32.6%EF	4 11.9%	3 12.0%	6 13.0%	10 34.6%	1 9.1%	5 35.7%	0 0	0 0	17 15.9%	11 23.9%
All sources of info	28 18.4%	23 21.1%	5 11.5%	28 18.4%	0 0	7 12.5%	7 13.2%	14 32.6%EF	4 11.9%	3 12.0%	6 13.0%	10 34.6%	1 9.1%	5 35.7%	0 0	0 0	17 15.9%	11 23.9%
preferred source of info	4 2.8%	2 1.9%	2 5.1%	4 2.8%	0 0	2 3.9%	1 2.1%	1 2.1%	0 0	0 0	0 0	3 11.5%	0 0	1 7.1%	0 0	0 0	3 3.1%	1 2.0%
Colleagues inside your institution	27 17.8%	15 13.9%	12 27.7%	27 17.8%	0 0	17 30.2%FG	5 9.6%	5 11.3%	8 21.4%	4 16.0%	8 17.4%	2 7.7%	1 18.2%	5 35.7%	0 0	0 0	17 16.0%	10 21.9%
All sources of info	27 17.8%	15 13.9%	12 27.7%	27 17.8%	0 0	17 30.2%FG	5 9.6%	5 11.3%	8 21.4%	4 16.0%	8 17.4%	2 7.7%	1 18.2%	5 35.7%	0 0	0 0	17 16.0%	10 21.9%
preferred source of info	16 10.4%	7 6.6%	9 19.9%A	16 10.4%	0 0	11 18.1%	4 6.9%	2 4.3%	6 16.7%	3 12.0%	6 13.0%	0 0	* 4.5%	1 7.1%	0 0	0 0	9 8.0%	7 15.8%
Colleagues outside your institution	7 4.4%	6 5.3%	1 2.0%	7 4.4%	0 0	4 6.5%	1 1.7%	2 4.8%	3 7.1%	1 4.0%	0 0	0 0	* 4.5%	3 21.4%	0 0	0 0	5 4.6%	2 3.7%
All sources of info	7 4.4%	6 5.3%	1 2.0%	7 4.4%	·0 0	4 6.5%	1 1.7%	2 4.8%	3 7.1%	1 4.0%	0 0	0 0	* 4.5%	3 21.4%	0 0	0 0	5 4.6%	2 3.7%

Proportions/Means: Columns Tested (5% risk level) - A/B/D - C/D - E/F/G - H/I/J/K/L/M/N - P/Q
* small base; ** very small base (under 30) ineligible for sig testing

Table 235
Page 922

Outsell/Digital Library Federation Study (2002)
Weighted Tables

TABLE 109, continued

T7sum_7. Print abstracts and indexes SUMMARY TABLE

	TOTAL SAMPLE	FACULTY MEMBER	GRAD. STUDENT	FACULTY /GRAD	UNDER GRAD. STUDENT	PUBLIC	PRIVATE	LIBERAL ARTS	BIOLOGIAL SCIENCES	PHYSICAL SCIENCES /MATH	SOCIAL SCIENCES	ARTS AND HUMAN.	ENGI-NEERING	BUSINESS	LAW	UNDEC. MAJOR	MALE	FEMALE
		RESPONDENT TYPE				INSTITUTION TYPE			DISCIPLINE								GENDER	
		(A)	(B)	(C)	(D)	(E)	(F)	(G)	(H)	(I)	(J)	(K)	(L)	(M)	(N)		(P)	(Q)
Base - USe Print abstracts and indexes for teaching	154	110*	44*	154	0**	58*	53*	43*	37*	25**	43**	29**	6**	13**	1**	0*	107*	47*
preferred source of info	0	0	0	0	0	0	0	0	0	0	0	0	0	0	0	0	0	0
	0	0	0	0	0	0	0	0	0	0	0	0	0	0	0	0	0	0
Professional meetings	2	2	0	2	0	1	1	0	0	2	0	0	0	0	0	0	2	0
	1.3%	1.8%	0	1.3%	0	1.7%	1.9%	0	0	8.0%	0	0	0	0	0	0	1.9%	0
All sources of info	2	2	0	2	0	1	1	0	0	2	0	0	0	0	0	0	2	0
	1.3%	1.8%	0	1.3%	0	1.7%	1.9%	0	0	8.0%	0	0	0	0	0	0	1.9%	0
preferred source of info	1	1	0	1	0	0	1	0	0	1	0	0	0	0	0	0	1	0
	0.6%	0.9%	0	0.6%	0	0	1.9%	0	0	4.0%	0	0	0	0	0	0	0.9%	0
Another institution's librarian	1	1	0	1	0	0	0	1	1	0	0	0	0	0	0	0	0	1
	0.6%	0.8%	0	0.6%	0	0	0	2.0%	2.4%	0	0	0	0	0	0	0	0	1.9%
All sources of info	1	1	0	1	0	0	0	1	1	0	0	0	0	0	0	0	0	1
	0.6%	0.8%	0	0.6%	0	0	0	2.0%	2.4%	0	0	0	0	0	0	0	0	1.9%
preferred source of info	0	0	0	0	0	0	0	0	0	0	0	0	0	0	0	0	0	0
	0	0	0	0	0	0	0	0	0	0	0	0	0	0	0	0	0	0
Online (unspecified)	3	1	2	3	0	0	3	0	0	0	2	1	0	0	0	0	1	2
	1.9%	1.0%	4.3%	1.9%	0	0	5.7%	0	0	0	4.3%	3.8%	0	0	0	0	1.0%	4.0%
All sources of info	3	1	2	3	0	0	3	0	0	0	2	1	0	0	0	0	1	2
	1.9%	1.0%	4.3%	1.9%	0	0	5.7%	0	0	0	4.3%	3.8%	0	0	0	0	1.0%	4.0%

Proportions/Means: Columns Tested (5% risk level) - A/B/D - C/D - E/F/G - H/I/J/K/L/M/N - P/Q
* small base; ** very small base (under 30) ineligible for sig testing

Table 235
Page 923

Outsell/Digital Library Federation Study (2002)
Weighted Tables

TABLE 109, continued

T7sum_7. Print abstracts and indexes SUMMARY TABLE

	TOTAL SAMPLE	RESPONDENT TYPE FACULTY MEMBER	GRAD. STUDENT	FACULTY /GRAD	UNDER GRAD. STUDENT	INSTITUTION TYPE PUBLIC	PRIVATE	LIBERAL ARTS	DISCIPLINE BIOLOGIAL SCIENCES	PHYSICAL SCIENCES /MATH	SOCIAL SCIENCES	ARTS AND HUMAN.	ENGI- NEERING	BUSINESS	LAW	UNDEC. MAJOR	GENDER MALE	FEMALE
		(A)	(B)	(C)	(D)	(E)	(F)	(G)	(H)	(I)	(J)	(K)	(L)	(M)	(N)		(P)	(Q)
Base - USe Print abstracts and indexes for teaching	154	110*	44*	154	0**	58*	53*	43*	37*	25**	43**	29**	6**	13**	1**	0*	107*	47*
preferred source of info	0 0	0 0	0 0	0 0	0 0	0 0	0 0	0 0	0 0	0 0	0 0	0 0	0 0	0 0	0 0	0 0	0 0	0 0
Personal office/lab	1 0.8%	1 1.1%	0 0	1 0.8%	0 0	0 0	* 0.5%	1 2.0%	1 2.4%	0 0	0 0	0 0	* 4.5%	0 0	0 0	0 0	* 0.3%	1 1.9%
All sources of info	1 0.8%	1 1.1%	0 0	1 0.8%	0 0	0 0	* 0.5%	1 2.0%	1 2.4%	0 0	0 0	0 0	* 4.5%	0 0	0 0	0 0	* 0.3%	1 1.9%
preferred source of info	1 0.6%	1 0.8%	0 0	1 0.6%	0 0	0 0	0 0	1 2.0%	1 2.4%	0 0	0 0	0 0	0 0	0 0	0 0	0 0	0 0	1 1.9%
Students	1 0.8%	1 1.1%	0 0	1 0.8%	0 0	0 0	* 0.5%	1 2.0%	1 2.4%	0 0	0 0	0 0	* 4.5%	0 0	0 0	0 0	* 0.3%	1 1.9%
All sources of info	1 0.8%	1 1.1%	0 0	1 0.8%	0 0	0 0	* 0.5%	1 2.0%	1 2.4%	0 0	0 0	0 0	* 4.5%	0 0	0 0	0 0	* 0.3%	1 1.9%
preferred source of info	0 0	0 0	0 0	0 0	0 0	0 0	0 0	0 0	0 0	0 0	0 0	0 0	0 0	0 0	0 0	0 0	0 0	0 0
Author	0 0	0 0	0 0	0 0	0 0	0 0	0 0	0 0	0 0	0 0	0 0	0 0	0 0	0 0	0 0	0 0	0 0	0 0
All sources of info	0 0	0 0	0 0	0 0	0 0	0 0	0 0	0 0	0 0	0 0	0 0	0 0	0 0	0 0	0 0	0 0	0 0	0 0
preferred source of info	0 0	0 0	0 0	0 0	0 0	0 0	0 0	0 0	0 0	0 0	0 0	0 0	0 0	0 0	0 0	0 0	0 0	0 0

Proportions/Means: Columns Tested (5% risk level) - A/B/D - C/D - E/F/G - H/I/J/K/L/M/N - P/Q
* small base; ** very small base (under 30) ineligible for sig testing

Table 235
Page 924

Outsell/Digital Library Federation Study (2002)
Weighted Tables

TABLE 109, continued

T7sum_7. Print abstracts and indexes SUMMARY TABLE

		RESPONDENT TYPE				INSTITUTION TYPE			DISCIPLINE								GENDER	
	TOTAL SAMPLE	FACULTY MEMBER	GRAD. STUDENT	FACULTY /GRAD	UNDER GRAD. STUDENT	PUBLIC	PRIVATE	LIBERAL ARTS	BIOLOGIAL SCIENCES	PHYSICAL SCIENCES /MATH	SOCIAL SCIENCES	ARTS AND HUMAN.	ENGI-NEERING	BUSINESS	LAW	UNDEC. MAJOR	MALE	FEMALE
		(A)	(B)	(C)	(D)	(E)	(F)	(G)	(H)	(I)	(J)	(K)	(L)	(M)	(N)		(P)	(Q)
Base - USe Print abstracts and indexes for teaching	154	110*	44*	154	0**	58*	53*	43*	37*	25**	43**	29**	6**	13**	1**	0*	107*	47*
Other	10 6.5%	9 8.2%	1 2.3%	10 6.5%	0 0	3 5.5%	3 6.0%	4 8.6%	1 2.4%	3 12.0%	4 8.7%	0 0	1 9.1%	2 14.3%	0 0	0 0	9 8.6%	1 1.9%
All sources of info	10 6.3%	9 8.0%	1 2.3%	10 6.3%	0 0	3 5.5%	3 5.4%	4 8.6%	1 2.4%	3 12.0%	4 8.7%	0 0	* 4.5%	2 14.3%	0 0	0 0	9 8.3%	1 1.9%
preferred source of info	1 0.8%	1 1.2%	0 0	1 0.8%	0 0	1 1.7%	* 0.5%	0 0	0 0	1 4.0%	0 0	0 0	* 4.5%	0 0	0 0	0 0	1 1.2%	0 0
DK/Refused	2 1.4%	1 1.0%	1 2.3%	2 1.4%	0 0	0 0	2 4.0%	0 0	0 0	1 4.0%	0 0	1 3.8%	0 0	0 0	0 0	0 0	2 2.0%	0 0

Proportions/Means: Columns Tested (5% risk level) - A/B/D - C/D - E/F/G - H/I/J/K/L/M/N - P/Q
* small base; ** very small base (under 30) ineligible for sig testing

TABLE 110

T7D/E_7. Print abstracts and indexes SUMMARY TABLE

		RESPONDENT TYPE				INSTITUTION TYPE			DISCIPLINE									GENDER	
	TOTAL SAMPLE	FACULTY MEMBER	GRAD. STUDENT	FACULTY /GRAD	UNDER GRAD. STUDENT	PUBLIC	PRIVATE	LIBERAL ARTS	BIOLOGIAL SCIENCES	PHYSICAL SCIENCES /MATH	SOCIAL SCIENCES	ARTS AND HUMAN.	ENGI- NEERING	BUSINESS	LAW	UNDEC. MAJOR	MALE	FEMALE
		(A)	(B)	(C)	(D)	(E)	(F)	(G)	(H)	(I)	(J)	(K)	(L)	(M)	(N)		(P)	(Q)
Base - Use Print abstracts and indexes for teaching	154	110*	44*	154	0**	58*	53*	43*	37*	25**	43**	29**	6**	13**	1**	0*	107*	47*
Borrow from or use in campus library (NET)	117 75.5%	89 80.7%B	27 62.6%	117 75.5%	0 0	39 67.2%	42 79.3%	36 82.0%	29 78.6%	18 72.0%	34 78.3%	21 73.1%	5 72.7%	9 71.4%	1 75.0%	0 0	86 80.6%	30 64.1%
All sources of info	117 75.5%	89 80.7%B	27 62.6%	117 75.5%	0 0	39 67.2%	42 79.3%	36 82.0%	29 78.6%	18 72.0%	34 78.3%	21 73.1%	5 72.7%	9 71.4%	1 75.0%	0 0	86 80.6%	30 64.1%
preferred source of info	85 54.8%	61 55.3%	23 53.4%	85 54.8%	0 0	32 55.2%	26 49.9%	26 60.2%	20 54.8%	12 48.0%	24 56.5%	17 57.7%	3 54.5%	7 57.1%	* 25.0%	0 0	57 53.5%	27 57.6%
Access online (NET)	62 40.1%	46 41.5%	16 36.5%	62 40.1%	0 0	21 36.1%	23 44.2%	17 40.3%	16 42.9%	11 44.0%	15 34.8%	9 30.8%	3 45.5%	7 57.1%	1 100.0%	0 0	47 43.5%	15 32.4%
All sources of info	62 40.1%	46 41.5%	16 36.5%	62 40.1%	0 0	21 36.1%	23 44.2%	17 40.3%	16 42.9%	11 44.0%	15 34.8%	9 30.8%	3 45.5%	7 57.1%	1 100.0%	0 0	47 43.5%	15 32.4%
preferred source of info	48 31.3%	35 31.6%	13 30.6%	48 31.3%	0 0	18 30.7%	18 34.0%	13 28.8%	13 35.7%	8 32.0%	13 30.4%	6 19.2%	2 36.4%	6 42.9%	1 75.0%	0 0	35 32.6%	13 28.4%
Personal Collection/ Holdings (NET)	8 4.9%	8 6.9%	0 0	8 4.9%	0 0	1 1.5%	5 9.2%	2 4.3%	3 7.1%	2 8.0%	2 4.3%	1 3.8%	0 0	0 0	0 0	0 0	7 6.3%	1 1.9%
All sources of info	8 4.9%	8 6.9%	0 0	8 4.9%	0 0	1 1.5%	5 9.2%	2 4.3%	3 7.1%	2 8.0%	2 4.3%	1 3.8%	0 0	0 0	0 0	0 0	7 6.3%	1 1.9%
preferred source of info	3 1.9%	3 2.7%	0 0	3 1.9%	0 0	1 1.5%	1 2.1%	1 2.3%	1 2.4%	1 4.0%	0 0	1 3.8%	0 0	0 0	0 0	0 0	3 2.8%	0 0

Proportions/Means: Columns Tested (5% risk level) - A/B/D - C/D - E/F/G - H/I/J/K/L/M/N - P/Q
* small base; ** very small base (under 30) ineligible for sig testing

Table 238
Page 932

Outsell/Digital Library Federation Study (2002)
Weighted Tables

TABLE 110, continued

T7D/E_7. Print abstracts and indexes SUMMARY TABLE

		RESPONDENT TYPE				INSTITUTION TYPE			DISCIPLINE								GENDER	
	TOTAL SAMPLE	FACULTY MEMBER	GRAD. STUDENT	FACULTY /GRAD	UNDER GRAD. STUDENT	PUBLIC	PRIVATE	LIBERAL ARTS	BIOLOGIAL SCIENCES	PHYSICAL SCIENCES /MATH	SOCIAL SCIENCES	ARTS AND HUMAN.	ENGI- NEERING	BUSINESS	LAW	UNDEC. MAJOR	MALE	FEMALE
		(A)	(B)	(C)	(D)	(E)	(F)	(G)	(H)	(I)	(J)	(K)	(L)	(M)	(N)		(P)	(Q)
Base - Use Print abstracts and indexes for teaching	154	110*	44*	154	0**	58*	53*	43*	37*	25**	43**	29**	6**	13**	1**	0*	107*	47*
Borrow from or use in other libraries (NET)	7 4.3%	4 3.6%	3 6.3%	7 4.3%	0 0	2 3.2%	2 3.8%	3 6.5%	1 2.4%	0 0	4 8.7%	1 3.8%	0 0	1 7.1%	0 0	0 0	2 1.9%	5 9.8%
All sources of info	7 4.3%	4 3.6%	3 6.3%	7 4.3%	0 0	2 3.2%	2 3.8%	3 6.5%	1 2.4%	0 0	4 8.7%	1 3.8%	0 0	1 7.1%	0 0	0 0	2 1.9%	5 9.8%
preferred source of info	3 1.9%	1 1.0%	2 4.3%	3 1.9%	0 0	2 3.2%	1 2.1%	0 0	0 0	0 0	2 4.3%	1 3.8%	0 0	0 0	0 0	0 0	1 1.0%	2 4.0%
Purchase from physical book store (NET)	5 3.2%	5 4.4%	0 0	5 3.2%	0 0	1 1.9%	2 3.5%	2 4.3%	1 2.4%	1 4.0%	2 4.3%	1 3.8%	0 0	0 0	0 0	0 0	3 2.8%	2 4.0%
All sources of info	5 3.2%	5 4.4%	0 0	5 3.2%	0 0	1 1.9%	2 3.5%	2 4.3%	1 2.4%	1 4.0%	2 4.3%	1 3.8%	0 0	0 0	0 0	0 0	3 2.8%	2 4.0%
preferred source of info	1 0.6%	1 0.9%	0 0	1 0.6%	0 0	0 0	1 1.9%	0 0	0 0	1 4.0%	0 0	0 0	0 0	0 0	0 0	0 0	1 0.9%	0 0
Publisher (NET)	4 2.4%	2 1.6%	2 4.3%	4 2.4%	0 0	3 4.8%	0 0	1 2.0%	2 4.8%	0 0	2 4.3%	0 0	0 0	0 0	0 0	0 0	2 1.6%	2 4.0%
All sources of info	4 2.4%	2 1.6%	2 4.3%	4 2.4%	0 0	3 4.8%	0 0	1 2.0%	2 4.8%	0 0	2 4.3%	0 0	0 0	0 0	0 0	0 0	2 1.6%	2 4.0%
preferred source of info	3 1.8%	1 0.8%	2 4.3%	3 1.8%	0 0	2 3.2%	0 0	1 2.0%	1 2.4%	0 0	2 4.3%	0 0	0 0	0 0	0 0	0 0	1 0.8%	2 4.0%

Proportions/Means: Columns Tested (5% risk level) - A/B/D - C/D - E/F/G - H/I/J/K/L/M/N - P/Q
* small base; ** very small base (under 30) ineligible for sig testing

Table 238
Page 933

Outsell/Digital Library Federation Study (2002)
Weighted Tables

TABLE 110, continued

T7D/E_7. Print abstracts and indexes SUMMARY TABLE

		RESPONDENT TYPE				INSTITUTION TYPE			DISCIPLINE								GENDER	
	TOTAL SAMPLE	FACULTY MEMBER	GRAD. STUDENT	FACULTY /GRAD	UNDER GRAD. STUDENT	PUBLIC	PRIVATE	LIBERAL ARTS	BIOLOGIAL SCIENCES	PHYSICAL SCIENCES /MATH	SOCIAL SCIENCES	ARTS AND HUMAN.	ENGI-NEERING	BUSINESS	LAW	UNDEC. MAJOR	MALE	FEMALE
		(A)	(B)	(C)	(D)	(E)	(F)	(G)	(H)	(I)	(J)	(K)	(L)	(M)	(N)		(P)	(Q)
Base - Use Print abstracts and indexes for teaching	154	110*	44*	154	0**	58*	53*	43*	37*	25**	43**	29**	6**	13**	1**	0*	107*	47*
Interlibrary loan (NET)	3 2.0%	3 2.8%	0 0	3 2.0%	0 0	1 1.9%	1 1.7%	1 2.6%	1 2.4%	0 0	0 0	2 7.7%	0 0	0 0	0 0	0 0	3 2.9%	0 0
All sources of info	3 2.0%	3 2.8%	0 0	3 2.0%	0 0	1 1.9%	1 1.7%	1 2.6%	1 2.4%	0 0	0 0	2 7.7%	0 0	0 0	0 0	0 0	3 2.9%	0 0
preferred source of info	1 0.6%	1 0.8%	0 0	1 0.6%	0 0	0 0	1 1.7%	0 0	1 2.4%	0 0	0 0	0 0	0 0	0 0	0 0	0 0	1 0.8%	0 0
Purchase from online bookstore (NET)	2 1.4%	2 2.0%	0 0	2 1.4%	0 0	0 0	* 0.5%	2 4.3%	0 0	0 0	2 4.3%	0 0	* 4.5%	0 0	0 0	0 0	* 0.3%	2 4.0%
All sources of info	2 1.4%	2 2.0%	0 0	2 1.4%	0 0	0 0	* 0.5%	2 4.3%	0 0	0 0	2 4.3%	0 0	* 4.5%	0 0	0 0	0 0	* 0.3%	2 4.0%
preferred source of info	2 1.4%	2 2.0%	0 0	2 1.4%	0 0	0 0	* 0.5%	2 4.3%	0 0	0 0	2 4.3%	0 0	* 4.5%	0 0	0 0	0 0	* 0.3%	2 4.0%
Colleagues (NET)	2 1.3%	1 0.9%	1 2.3%	2 1.3%	0 0	0 0	1 1.9%	1 2.3%	0 0	2 8.0%	0 0	0 0	0 0	0 0	0 0	0 0	1 0.9%	1 2.1%
All sources of info	2 1.3%	1 0.9%	1 2.3%	2 1.3%	0 0	0 0	1 1.9%	1 2.3%	0 0	2 8.0%	0 0	0 0	0 0	0 0	0 0	0 0	1 0.9%	1 2.1%
preferred source of info	1 0.6%	0 0	1 2.3%	1 0.6%	0 0	0 0	1 1.9%	0 0	0 0	1 4.0%	0 0	0 0	0 0	0 0	0 0	0 0	1 0.9%	0 0

Proportions/Means: Columns Tested (5% risk level) - A/B/D - C/D - E/F/G - H/I/J/K/L/M/N - P/Q
* small base; ** very small base (under 30) ineligible for sig testing

Table 238
Page 934

Outsell/Digital Library Federation Study (2002)
Weighted Tables

TABLE 110, continued

T7D/E_7. Print abstracts and indexes SUMMARY TABLE

	RESPONDENT TYPE					INSTITUTION TYPE			DISCIPLINE								GENDER	
	TOTAL SAMPLE	FACULTY MEMBER	GRAD. STUDENT	FACULTY /GRAD	UNDER GRAD. STUDENT	PUBLIC	PRIVATE	LIBERAL ARTS	BIOLOGIAL SCIENCES	PHYSICAL SCIENCES /MATH	SOCIAL SCIENCES	ARTS AND HUMAN.	ENGI-NEERING	BUSINESS	LAW	UNDEC. MAJOR	MALE	FEMALE
		(A)	(B)	(C)	(D)	(E)	(F)	(G)	(H)	(I)	(J)	(K)	(L)	(M)	(N)		(P)	(Q)
Base - Use Print abstracts and indexes for teaching	154	110*	44*	154	0**	58*	53*	43*	37*	25**	43**	29**	6**	13**	1**	0*	107*	47*
Order from on demand document delivery service (NET)	2 1.2%	0 0	2 4.3%	2 1.2%	0 0	2 3.2%	0 0	0 0	0 0	0 0	2 4.3%	0 0	0 0	0 0	0 0	0 0	0 0	2 4.0%
All sources of info	2 1.2%	0 0	2 4.3%	2 1.2%	0 0	2 3.2%	0 0	0 0	0 0	0 0	2 4.3%	0 0	0 0	0 0	0 0	0 0	0 0	2 4.0%
preferred source of info	0 0	0 0	0 0	0 0	0 0	0 0	0 0	0 0	0 0	0 0	0 0	0 0	0 0	0 0	0 0	0 0	0 0	0 0
Home (NET)	1 0.7%	1 1.0%	0 0	1 0.7%	0 0	0 0	1 2.1%	0 0	0 0	0 0	0 0	1 3.8%	0 0	0 0	0 0	0 0	1 1.0%	0 0
All sources of info	1 0.7%	1 1.0%	0 0	1 0.7%	0 0	0 0	1 2.1%	0 0	0 0	0 0	0 0	1 3.8%	0 0	0 0	0 0	0 0	1 1.0%	0 0
preferred source of info	1 0.7%	1 1.0%	0 0	1 0.7%	0 0	0 0	1 2.1%	0 0	0 0	0 0	0 0	1 3.8%	0 0	0 0	0 0	0 0	1 1.0%	0 0
Department (NET)	1 0.7%	0 0	1 2.5%	1 0.7%	0 0	1 1.9%	0 0	0 0	0 0	0 0	0 0	1 3.8%	0 0	0 0	0 0	0 0	1 1.0%	0 0
All sources of info	1 0.7%	0 0	1 2.5%	1 0.7%	0 0	1 1.9%	0 0	0 0	0 0	0 0	0 0	1 3.8%	0 0	0 0	0 0	0 0	1 1.0%	0 0
preferred source of info	1 0.7%	0 0	1 2.5%	1 0.7%	0 0	1 1.9%	0 0	0 0	0 0	0 0	0 0	1 3.8%	0 0	0 0	0 0	0 0	1 1.0%	0 0

Proportions/Means: Columns Tested (5% risk level) - A/B/D - C/D - E/F/G - H/I/J/K/L/M/N - P/Q
* small base; ** very small base (under 30) ineligible for sig testing

Table 238
Page 935

Outsell/Digital Library Federation Study (2002)
Weighted Tables

TABLE 110, continued

T7D/E_7. Print abstracts and indexes SUMMARY TABLE

		RESPONDENT TYPE				INSTITUTION TYPE			DISCIPLINE								GENDER	
	TOTAL SAMPLE	FACULTY MEMBER	GRAD. STUDENT	FACULTY /GRAD	UNDER GRAD. STUDENT	PUBLIC	PRIVATE	LIBERAL ARTS	BIOLOGIAL SCIENCES	PHYSICAL SCIENCES /MATH	SOCIAL SCIENCES	ARTS AND HUMAN.	ENGI- NEERING	BUSINESS	LAW	UNDEC. MAJOR	MALE	FEMALE
		(A)	(B)	(C)	(D)	(E)	(F)	(G)	(H)	(I)	(J)	(K)	(L)	(M)	(N)		(P)	(Q)
Base - Use Print abstracts and indexes for teaching	154	110*	44*	154	0**	58*	53*	43*	37*	25**	43**	29**	6**	13**	1**	0*	107*	47*
Access from course website (NET)	1 0.6%	1 0.9%	0 0	1 0.6%	0 0	0 0	0 0	1 2.3%	0 0	1 4.0%	0 0	0 0	0 0	0 0	0 0	0 0	0 0	1 2.1%
All sources of info	1 0.6%	1 0.9%	0 0	1 0.6%	0 0	0 0	0 0	1 2.3%	0 0	1 4.0%	0 0	0 0	0 0	0 0	0 0	0 0	0 0	1 2.1%
preferred source of info	1 0.6%	1 0.9%	0 0	1 0.6%	0 0	0 0	0 0	1 2.3%	0 0	1 4.0%	0 0	0 0	0 0	0 0	0 0	0 0	0 0	1 2.1%
Office (NET)	1 0.6%	0 0	1 2.0%	1 0.6%	0 0	0 0	1 1.7%	0 0	1 2.4%	0 0	0 0	0 0	0 0	0 0	0 0	0 0	1 0.8%	0 0
All sources of info	1 0.6%	0 0	1 2.0%	1 0.6%	0 0	0 0	1 1.7%	0 0	1 2.4%	0 0	0 0	0 0	0 0	0 0	0 0	0 0	1 0.8%	0 0
preferred source of info	1 0.6%	0 0	1 2.0%	1 0.6%	0 0	0 0	1 1.7%	0 0	1 2.4%	0 0	0 0	0 0	0 0	0 0	0 0	0 0	1 0.8%	0 0
Faculty (NET)	1 0.6%	0 0	1 2.0%	1 0.6%	0 0	1 1.5%	0 0	0 0	1 2.4%	0 0	0 0	0 0	0 0	0 0	0 0	0 0	0 0	1 1.9%
All sources of info	1 0.6%	0 0	1 2.0%	1 0.6%	0 0	1 1.5%	0 0	0 0	1 2.4%	0 0	0 0	0 0	0 0	0 0	0 0	0 0	0 0	1 1.9%
preferred source of info	0 0	0 0	0 0	0 0	0 0	0 0	0 0	0 0	0 0	0 0	0 0	0 0	0 0	0 0	0 0	0 0	0 0	0 0

Proportions/Means: Columns Tested (5% risk level) - A/B/D - C/D - E/F/G - H/I/J/K/L/M/N - P/Q
* small base; ** very small base (under 30) ineligible for sig testing

Table 238
Page 936

Outsell/Digital Library Federation Study (2002)
Weighted Tables

TABLE 110, continued

T7D/E_7. Print abstracts and indexes SUMMARY TABLE

		RESPONDENT TYPE				INSTITUTION TYPE			DISCIPLINE									GENDER	
	TOTAL SAMPLE	FACULTY MEMBER	GRAD. STUDENT	FACULTY /GRAD	UNDER GRAD. STUDENT	PUBLIC	PRIVATE	LIBERAL ARTS	BIOLOGIAL SCIENCES	PHYSICAL SCIENCES /MATH	SOCIAL SCIENCES	ARTS AND HUMAN.	ENGI-NEERING	BUSINESS	LAW	UNDEC. MAJOR	MALE	FEMALE
		(A)	(B)	(C)	(D)	(E)	(F)	(G)	(H)	(I)	(J)	(K)	(L)	(M)	(N)		(P)	(Q)
Base - Use Print abstracts and indexes for teaching	154	110*	44*	154	0**	58*	53*	43*	37*	25**	43**	29**	6**	13**	1**	0*	107*	47*
Ask library to purchase source (NET)	0 0	0 0	0 0	0 0	0 0	0 0	0 0	0 0	0 0	0 0	0 0	0 0	0 0	0 0	0 0	0 0	0 0	0 0
All sources of info	0 0	0 0	0 0	0 0	0 0	0 0	0 0	0 0	0 0	0 0	0 0	0 0	0 0	0 0	0 0	0 0	0 0	0 0
preferred source of info	0 0	0 0	0 0	0 0	0 0	0 0	0 0	0 0	0 0	0 0	0 0	0 0	0 0	0 0	0 0	0 0	0 0	0 0
Author	0 0	0 0	0 0	0 0	0 0	0 0	0 0	0 0	0 0	0 0	0 0	0 0	0 0	0 0	0 0	0 0	0 0	0 0
All sources of info	0 0	0 0	0 0	0 0	0 0	0 0	0 0	0 0	0 0	0 0	0 0	0 0	0 0	0 0	0 0	0 0	0 0	0 0
preferred source of info	0 0	0 0	0 0	0 0	0 0	0 0	0 0	0 0	0 0	0 0	0 0	0 0	0 0	0 0	0 0	0 0	0 0	0 0
Meeting/Conferences (NET)	0 0	0 0	0 0	0 0	0 0	0 0	0 0	0 0	0 0	0 0	0 0	0 0	0 0	0 0	0 0	0 0	0 0	0 0
All sources of info	0 0	0 0	0 0	0 0	0 0	0 0	0 0	0 0	0 0	0 0	0 0	0 0	0 0	0 0	0 0	0 0	0 0	0 0
preferred source of info	0 0	0 0	0 0	0 0	0 0	0 0	0 0	0 0	0 0	0 0	0 0	0 0	0 0	0 0	0 0	0 0	0 0	0 0

Proportions/Means: Columns Tested (5% risk level) - A/B/D - C/D - E/F/G - H/I/J/K/L/M/N - P/Q
* small base; ** very small base (under 30) ineligible for sig testing

Table 238
Page 937

Outsell/Digital Library Federation Study (2002)
Weighted Tables

TABLE 110, continued

T7D/E_7. Print abstracts and indexes SUMMARY TABLE

	TOTAL SAMPLE	RESPONDENT TYPE: FACULTY MEMBER	GRAD. STUDENT	FACULTY /GRAD	UNDER GRAD. STUDENT	INSTITUTION TYPE: PUBLIC	PRIVATE	LIBERAL ARTS	DISCIPLINE: BIOLOGIAL SCIENCES	PHYSICAL SCIENCES /MATH	SOCIAL SCIENCES	ARTS AND HUMAN.	ENGI-NEERING	BUSINESS	LAW	UNDEC. MAJOR	GENDER: MALE	FEMALE
		(A)	(B)	(C)	(D)	(E)	(F)	(G)	(H)	(I)	(J)	(K)	(L)	(M)	(N)		(P)	(Q)
Base - Use Print abstracts and indexes for teaching	154	110*	44*	154	0**	58*	53*	43*	37*	25**	43**	29**	6**	13**	1**	0*	107*	47*
Access book/journal/ journal article elsewhere online (NET)	0 0	0 0	0 0	0 0	0 0	0 0	0 0	0 0	0 0	0 0	0 0	0 0	0 0	0 0	0 0	0 0	0 0	0 0
All sources of info	0 0	0 0	0 0	0 0	0 0	0 0	0 0	0 0	0 0	0 0	0 0	0 0	0 0	0 0	0 0	0 0	0 0	0 0
preferred source of info	0 0	0 0	0 0	0 0	0 0	0 0	0 0	0 0	0 0	0 0	0 0	0 0	0 0	0 0	0 0	0 0	0 0	0 0
Other (NET)	5 3.1%	4 3.8%	1 1.3%	5 3.1%	0 0	3 4.7%	2 4.0%	0 0	0 0	2 8.0%	0 0	2 7.7%	1 9.1%	0 0	0 0	0 0	5 4.5%	0 0
All sources of info	3 2.2%	3 2.8%	* 0.7%	3 2.2%	0 0	2 4.2%	1 1.9%	0 0	0 0	2 8.0%	0 0	1 3.8%	* 4.5%	0 0	0 0	0 0	3 3.2%	0 0
preferred source of info	2 1.6%	2 1.9%	* 0.7%	2 1.6%	0 0	1 2.2%	1 2.1%	0 0	0 0	1 4.0%	0 0	1 3.8%	* 4.5%	0 0	0 0	0 0	2 2.2%	0 0
DK/Refused	1 0.7%	1 1.0%	0 0	1 0.7%	0 0	1 1.9%	0 0	0 0	0 0	0 0	0 0	1 3.8%	0 0	0 0	0 0	0 0	1 1.0%	0 0

Proportions/Means: Columns Tested (5% risk level) - A/B/D - C/D - E/F/G - H/I/J/K/L/M/N - P/Q
* small base; ** very small base (under 30) ineligible for sig testing

Table 238
Page 938

TABLE 111

T7sum_8. Online abstracts and indexes SUMMARY TABLE

		RESPONDENT TYPE				INSTITUTION TYPE			DISCIPLINE								GENDER	
	TOTAL SAMPLE	FACULTY MEMBER	GRAD. STUDENT	FACULTY /GRAD	UNDER GRAD. STUDENT	PUBLIC	PRIVATE	LIBERAL ARTS	BIOLOGIAL SCIENCES	PHYSICAL SCIENCES /MATH	SOCIAL SCIENCES	ARTS AND HUMAN.	ENGI-NEERING	BUSINESS	LAW	UNDEC. MAJOR	MALE	FEMALE
		(A)	(B)	(C)	(D)	(E)	(F)	(G)	(H)	(I)	(J)	(K)	(L)	(M)	(N)		(P)	(Q)
Base - USe Online abstracts and indexes for teaching	173	126	47*	173	0**	68*	58*	47*	26**	29**	58*	32**	5**	20**	2**	0*	120*	53*
ONLINE	152 87.6%	108 85.5%	44 93.0%	152 87.6%	0 0	64 92.8%	48 83.0%	40 85.7%	25 93.3%	25 86.2%	53 90.3%	26 79.3%	4 88.2%	18 86.4%	2 100.0%	0 0	104 86.1%	48 90.9%
Online databases	37 21.6%	27 21.8%	10 21.0%	37 21.6%	0 0	13 18.5%	8 14.2%	16 35.2%F	6 23.3%	8 27.6%	9 16.1%	8 24.1%	1 11.8%	5 22.7%	1 44.4%	0 0	20 16.3%	18 33.6%P
All sources of info	37 21.6%	27 21.8%	10 21.0%	37 21.6%	0 0	13 18.5%	8 14.2%	16 35.2%F	6 23.3%	8 27.6%	9 16.1%	8 24.1%	1 11.8%	5 22.7%	1 44.4%	0 0	20 16.3%	18 33.6%P
preferred source of info	28 16.0%	22 17.2%	6 12.7%	28 16.0%	0 0	8 11.8%	7 12.2%	12 26.6%	4 16.7%	8 27.6%	8 12.9%	3 10.3%	* 5.9%	4 18.2%	* 22.2%	0 0	13 10.7%	15 28.0%P
Your own institution's web site	32 18.3%	18 14.2%	14 29.3%	32 18.3%	0 0	18 26.1%	7 12.1%	7 14.7%	5 20.0%	3 10.3%	11 19.4%	6 17.2%	2 35.3%	5 22.7%	* 11.1%	0 0	20 16.7%	12 22.1%
All sources of info	32 18.3%	18 14.2%	14 29.3%	32 18.3%	0 0	18 26.1%	7 12.1%	7 14.7%	5 20.0%	3 10.3%	11 19.4%	6 17.2%	2 35.3%	5 22.7%	* 11.1%	0 0	20 16.7%	12 22.1%
preferred source of info	28 16.4%	16 12.5%	13 26.8%	28 16.4%	0 0	16 23.5%	7 11.6%	6 11.9%	4 13.3%	2 6.9%	11 19.4%	6 17.2%	1 23.5%	5 22.7%	* 11.1%	0 0	18 14.6%	11 20.4%
Search engine	31 17.7%	24 18.8%	7 14.5%	31 17.7%	0 0	15 22.4%	9 14.7%	7 14.3%	4 16.7%	4 13.8%	8 12.9%	8 24.1%	1 17.6%	6 27.3%	* 22.2%	0 0	27 22.8%Q	3 5.9%
All sources of info	31 17.7%	24 18.8%	7 14.5%	31 17.7%	0 0	15 22.4%	9 14.7%	7 14.3%	4 16.7%	4 13.8%	8 12.9%	8 24.1%	1 17.6%	6 27.3%	* 22.2%	0 0	27 22.8%Q	3 5.9%

Proportions/Means: Columns Tested (5% risk level) - A/B/D - C/D - E/F/G - H/I/J/K/L/M/N - P/Q
* small base; ** very small base (under 30) ineligible for sig testing

Table 242
Page 950

Outsell/Digital Library Federation Study (2002)
Weighted Tables

TABLE 111, continued

T7sum_8. Online abstracts and indexes SUMMARY TABLE

	RESPONDENT TYPE				INSTITUTION TYPE			DISCIPLINE									GENDER	
	TOTAL SAMPLE	FACULTY MEMBER	GRAD. STUDENT	FACULTY /GRAD	UNDER GRAD. STUDENT	PUBLIC	PRIVATE	LIBERAL ARTS	BIOLOGIAL SCIENCES	PHYSICAL SCIENCES /MATH	SOCIAL SCIENCES	ARTS AND HUMAN.	ENGI- NEERING	BUSINESS	LAW	UNDEC. MAJOR	MALE	FEMALE
		(A)	(B)	(C)	(D)	(E)	(F)	(G)	(H)	(I)	(J)	(K)	(L)	(M)	(N)		(P)	(Q)
Base - USe Online abstracts and indexes for teaching	173	126	47*	173	0**	68*	58*	47*	26**	29**	58*	32**	5**	20**	2**	0*	120*	53*
preferred source of info	21 12.2%	17 13.7%	4 8.2%	21 12.2%	0 0	11 16.3%	5 9.0%	5 10.2%	4 16.7%	3 10.3%	4 6.5%	6 17.2%	* 5.9%	4 18.2%	* 22.2%	0 0	19 15.9%	2 3.8%
Web directory/ subject related web site	29 16.9%	25 20.2%	4 8.3%	29 16.9%	0 0	8 11.5%	14 23.4%	8 17.0%	6 23.3%	5 17.2%	11 19.4%	2 6.9%	1 11.8%	4 18.2%	* 22.2%	0 0	17 14.5%	12 22.5%
All sources of info	29 16.9%	25 20.2%	4 8.3%	29 16.9%	0 0	8 11.5%	14 23.4%	8 17.0%	6 23.3%	5 17.2%	11 19.4%	2 6.9%	1 11.8%	4 18.2%	* 22.2%	0 0	17 14.5%	12 22.5%
preferred source of info	23 13.1%	20 15.7%	3 5.9%	23 13.1%	0 0	6 9.4%	12 20.9%	4 8.6%	6 23.3%	2 6.9%	11 19.4%	1 3.4%	0 0	2 9.1%	* 11.1%	0 0	13 10.8%	10 18.2%
Online library catalogues and finding aids	23 13.2%	8 6.5%	15 31.1%A	23 13.2%	0 0	11 16.0%	7 12.2%	5 10.6%	1 3.3%	3 10.3%	11 19.4%	6 17.2%	* 5.9%	2 9.1%	0 0	0 0	17 14.3%	6 10.9%
All sources of info	23 13.2%	8 6.5%	15 31.1%A	23 13.2%	0 0	11 16.0%	7 12.2%	5 10.6%	1 3.3%	3 10.3%	11 19.4%	6 17.2%	* 5.9%	2 9.1%	0 0	0 0	17 14.3%	6 10.9%
preferred source of info	17 9.8%	6 5.0%	11 22.6%A	17 9.8%	0 0	10 14.3%	2 3.9%	5 10.6%	1 3.3%	2 6.9%	8 12.9%	4 13.8%	* 5.9%	2 9.1%	0 0	0 0	14 11.9%	3 5.2%
Internet searches	19 11.2%	15 11.6%	5 10.3%	19 11.2%	0 0	6 8.7%	10 17.6%	3 7.1%	4 16.7%	3 10.3%	6 9.7%	3 10.3%	1 23.5%	2 9.1%	0 0	0 0	14 11.4%	6 10.9%
All sources of info	19 11.2%	15 11.6%	5 10.3%	19 11.2%	0 .0	6 8.7%	10 17.6%	3 7.1%	4 16.7%	3 10.3%	6 9.7%	3 10.3%	1 23.5%	2 9.1%	0 0	0 0	14 11.4%	6 10.9%

Proportions/Means: Columns Tested (5% risk level) - A/B/D - C/D - E/F/G - H/I/J/K/L/M/N - P/Q
* small base; ** very small base (under 30) ineligible for sig testing

Table 242
Page 951

Outsell/Digital Library Federation Study (2002)
Weighted Tables

TABLE 111, continued

T7sum_8. Online abstracts and indexes SUMMARY TABLE

	TOTAL SAMPLE	RESPONDENT TYPE: FACULTY MEMBER (A)	GRAD. STUDENT (B)	FACULTY /GRAD (C)	UNDER GRAD. STUDENT (D)	INSTITUTION TYPE: PUBLIC (E)	PRIVATE (F)	LIBERAL ARTS (G)	DISCIPLINE: BIOLOGIAL SCIENCES (H)	PHYSICAL SCIENCES /MATH (I)	SOCIAL SCIENCES (J)	ARTS AND HUMAN. (K)	ENGI- NEERING (L)	BUSINESS (M)	LAW (N)	UNDEC. MAJOR	GENDER: MALE (P)	FEMALE (Q)
Base - USe Online abstracts and indexes for teaching	173	126	47*	173	0**	68*	58*	47*	26**	29**	58*	32**	5**	20**	2**	0*	120*	53*
preferred source of info	5 2.7%	3 2.2%	2 4.0%	5 2.7%	0 0	2 2.9%	2 4.0%	* 0.6%	2 6.7%	2 6.9%	0 0	0 0	1 17.6%	0 0	0 0	0 0	5 3.9%	0 0
Online abstracting and indexing services	15 8.5%	12 9.3%	3 6.3%	15 8.5%	0 0	5 7.5%	7 11.7%	3 6.2%	1 3.3%	3 10.3%	8 12.9%	2 6.9%	0 0	1 4.5%	* 11.1%	0 0	9 7.2%	6 11.4%
All sources of info	15 8.5%	12 9.3%	3 6.3%	15 8.5%	0 0	5 7.5%	7 11.7%	3 6.2%	1 3.3%	3 10.3%	8 12.9%	2 6.9%	0 0	1 4.5%	* 11.1%	0 0	9 7.2%	6 11.4%
preferred source of info	8 4.5%	8 6.2%	0 0	8 4.5%	0 0	2 3.2%	4 6.5%	2 4.0%	1 3.3%	1 3.4%	4 6.5%	1 3.4%	0 0	1 4.5%	* 11.1%	0 0	5 4.0%	3 5.8%
E-mail listservs	5 2.6%	5 3.6%	0 0	5 2.6%	0 0	4 5.4%	0 0	1 1.9%	2 6.7%	0 0	2 3.2%	0 0	0 0	1 4.5%	0 0	0 0	5 3.8%	0 0
All sources of info	5 2.6%	5 3.6%	0 0	5 2.6%	0 0	4 5.4%	0 0	1 1.9%	2 6.7%	0 0	2 3.2%	0 0	0 0	1 4.5%	0 0	0 0	5 3.8%	0 0
preferred source of info	2 1.1%	2 1.5%	0 0	2 1.1%	0 0	2 2.7%	0 0	0 0	0 0	0 0	2 3.2%	0 0	0 0	0 0	0 0	0 0	2 1.6%	0 0
Online reference service	4 2.3%	4 3.1%	0 0	4 2.3%	0 0	1 1.6%	1 1.5%	2 4.1%	1 3.3%	1 3.4%	0 0	1 3.4%	0 0	1 4.5%	0 0	0 0	3 2.3%	1 2.1%
All sources of info	4 2.3%	4 3.1%	0 0	4 2.3%	0 0	1 1.6%	1 1.5%	2 4.1%	1 3.3%	1 3.4%	0 0	1 3.4%	0 0	1 4.5%	0 0	0 0	3 2.3%	1 2.1%

Proportions/Means: Columns Tested (5% risk level) - A/B/D - C/D - E/F/G - H/I/J/K/L/M/N - P/Q
* small base; ** very small base (under 30) ineligible for sig testing

Table 242
Page 952

Outsell/Digital Library Federation Study (2002)
Weighted Tables

TABLE 111, continued

T7sum_8. Online abstracts and indexes SUMMARY TABLE

		RESPONDENT TYPE				INSTITUTION TYPE			DISCIPLINE								GENDER	
	TOTAL SAMPLE	FACULTY MEMBER	GRAD. STUDENT	FACULTY /GRAD	UNDER GRAD. STUDENT	PUBLIC	PRIVATE	LIBERAL ARTS	BIOLOGIAL SCIENCES	PHYSICAL SCIENCES /MATH	SOCIAL SCIENCES	ARTS AND HUMAN.	ENGI- NEERING	BUSINESS	LAW	UNDEC. MAJOR	MALE	FEMALE
		(A)	(B)	(C)	(D)	(E)	(F)	(G)	(H)	(I)	(J)	(K)	(L)	(M)	(N)		(P)	(Q)
Base - USe Online abstracts and indexes for teaching	173	126	47*	173	0**	68*	58*	47*	26**	29**	58*	32**	5**	20**	2**	0*	120*	53*
preferred source of info	3 1.7%	3 2.4%	0 0	3 1.7%	0 0	1 1.6%	1 1.5%	1 2.1%	1 3.3%	1 3.4%	0 0	1 3.4%	0 0	0 0	0 0	0 0	2 1.6%	1 2.1%
Department web page	3 1.7%	1 0.8%	2 4.0%	3 1.7%	0 0	2 2.7%	0 0	1 2.1%	0 0	1 3.4%	2 3.2%	0 0	0 0	0 0	0 0	0 0	3 2.4%	0 0
All sources of info	3 1.7%	1 0.8%	2 4.0%	3 1.7%	0 0	2 2.7%	0 0	1 2.1%	0 0	1 3.4%	2 3.2%	0 0	0 0	0 0	0 0	0 0	3 2.4%	0 0
preferred source of info	2 1.1%	0 0	2 4.0%	2 1.1%	0 0	2 2.7%	0 0	0 0	0 0	0 0	2 3.2%	0 0	0 0	0 0	0 0	0 0	2 1.6%	0 0
Online bookstore	2 1.1%	2 1.5%	0 0	2 1.1%	0 0	0 0	0 0	2 4.0%	0 0	0 0	2 3.2%	0 0	0 0	0 0	0 0	0 0	0 0	2 3.6%
All sources of info	2 1.1%	2 1.5%	0 0	2 1.1%	0 0	0 0	0 0	2 4.0%	0 0	0 0	2 3.2%	0 0	0 0	0 0	0 0	0 0	0 0	2 3.6%
preferred source of info	0 0	0 0	0 0	0 0	0 0	0 0	0 0	0 0	0 0	0 0	0 0	0 0	0 0	0 0	0 0	0 0	0 0	0 0
Your own personal electronic library/files	0 0	0 0	0 0	0 0	0 0	0 0	0 0	0 0	0 0	0 0	0 0	0 0	0 0	0 0	0 0	0 0	0 0	0 0
All sources of info	0 0	0 0	0 0	0 0	0 0	0 0	0 0	0 0	0 0	0 0	0 0	0 0	0 0	0 0	0 0	0 0	0 0	0 0

Proportions/Means: Columns Tested (5% risk level) - A/B/D - C/D - E/F/G - H/I/J/K/L/M/N - P/Q
* small base; ** very small base (under 30) ineligible for sig testing

Table 242
Page 953

Outsell/Digital Library Federation Study (2002)
Weighted Tables

TABLE 111, continued

T7sum_8. Online abstracts and indexes SUMMARY TABLE

	TOTAL SAMPLE	RESPONDENT TYPE: FACULTY MEMBER (A)	GRAD. STUDENT (B)	FACULTY /GRAD (C)	UNDER GRAD. STUDENT (D)	INSTITUTION TYPE: PUBLIC (E)	PRIVATE (F)	LIBERAL ARTS (G)	DISCIPLINE: BIOLOGIAL SCIENCES (H)	PHYSICAL SCIENCES /MATH (I)	SOCIAL SCIENCES (J)	ARTS AND HUMAN. (K)	ENGI-NEERING (L)	BUSINESS (M)	LAW (N)	UNDEC. MAJOR	GENDER: MALE (P)	FEMALE (Q)
Base - USe Online abstracts and indexes for teaching	173	126	47*	173	0**	68*	58*	47*	26**	29**	58*	32**	5**	20**	2**	0*	120*	53*
preferred source of info	0 0	0 0	0 0	0 0	0 0	0 0	0 0	0 0	0 0	0 0	0 0	0 0	0 0	0 0	0 0	0 0	0 0	0 0
LIBRARY/PRINT	58 33.5%	50 40.1%B	7 15.8%	58 33.5%	0 0	18 26.4%	18 31.5%	22 46.3%	5 20.0%	13 44.8%	13 22.6%	13 41.4%	2 47.1%	10 50.0%	1 33.3%	0 0	47 39.0%Q	11 21.0%
Campus library	50 28.7%	43 34.5%B	6 13.4%	50 28.7%	0 0	14 20.1%	16 28.0%	20 42.2%E	5 20.0%	11 37.9%	11 19.4%	12 37.9%	2 41.2%	7 36.4%	* 22.2%	0 0	41 33.9%Q	9 16.8%
All sources of info	50 28.7%	43 34.5%B	6 13.4%	50 28.7%	0 0	14 20.1%	16 28.0%	20 42.2%E	5 20.0%	11 37.9%	11 19.4%	12 37.9%	2 41.2%	7 36.4%	* 22.2%	0 0	41 33.9%Q	9 16.8%
preferred source of info	14 8.3%	11 8.7%	3 7.3%	14 8.3%	0 0	1 2.1%	8 13.5%E	5 11.0%	1 3.3%	2 6.9%	6 9.7%	3 10.3%	1 29.4%	1 4.5%	* 11.1%	0 0	10 7.9%	5 9.2%
References cited in books or journal articles	5 2.8%	4 2.9%	1 2.4%	5 2.8%	0 0	2 2.7%	2 3.4%	1 2.0%	1 3.3%	0 0	2 3.2%	1 3.4%	0 0	1 4.5%	0 0	0 0	4 3.1%	1 2.1%
All sources of info	5 2.8%	4 2.9%	1 2.4%	5 2.8%	0 0	2 2.7%	2 3.4%	1 2.0%	1 3.3%	0 0	2 3.2%	1 3.4%	0 0	1 4.5%	0 0	0 0	4 3.1%	1 2.1%
preferred source of info	0 0	0 0	0 0	0 0	0 0	0 0	0 0	0 0	0 0	0 0	0 0	0 0	0 0	0 0	0 0	0 0	0 0	0 0
Printed abstracting and indexing services	4 2.3%	4 3.2%	0 0	4 2.3%	0 0	2 3.1%	0 0	2 4.1%	0 0	2 6.9%	0 0	1 3.4%	0 0	1 4.5%	0 0	0 0	4 3.4%	0 0

Proportions/Means: Columns Tested (5% risk level) - A/B/D - C/D - E/F/G - H/I/J/K/L/M/N - P/Q
* small base; ** very small base (under 30) ineligible for sig testing

Table 242
Page 954

Outsell/Digital Library Federation Study (2002)
Weighted Tables

TABLE 111, continued

T7sum_8. Online abstracts and indexes SUMMARY TABLE

	TOTAL SAMPLE	RESPONDENT TYPE: FACULTY MEMBER	GRAD. STUDENT	FACULTY /GRAD	UNDER GRAD. STUDENT	INSTITUTION TYPE: PUBLIC	PRIVATE	LIBERAL ARTS	DISCIPLINE: BIOLOGIAL SCIENCES	PHYSICAL SCIENCES /MATH	SOCIAL SCIENCES	ARTS AND HUMAN.	ENGI-NEERING	BUSINESS	LAW	UNDEC. MAJOR	GENDER: MALE	FEMALE
		(A)	(B)	(C)	(D)	(E)	(F)	(G)	(H)	(I)	(J)	(K)	(L)	(M)	(N)		(P)	(Q)
Base - USe Online abstracts and indexes for teaching	173	126	47*	173	0**	68*	58*	47*	26**	29**	58*	32**	5**	20**	2**	0*	120*	53*
All sources of info	4 2.3%	4 3.2%	0 0	4 2.3%	0 0	2 3.1%	0 0	2 4.1%	0 0	2 6.9%	0 0	1 3.4%	0 0	1 4.5%	0 0	0 0	4 3.4%	0 0
preferred source of info	0 0	0 0	0 0	0 0	0 0	0 0	0 0	0 0	0 0	0 0	0 0	0 0	0 0	0 0	0 0	0 0	0 0	0 0
Another library	4 2.0%	4 2.8%	0 0	4 2.0%	0 0	1 1.9%	1 1.9%	1 2.4%	0 0	0 0	0 0	3 10.3%	0 0	0 0	* 11.1%	0 0	4 2.9%	0 0
All sources of info	4 2.0%	4 2.8%	0 0	4 2.0%	0 0	1 1.9%	1 1.9%	1 2.4%	0 0	0 0	0 0	3 10.3%	0 0	0 0	* 11.1%	0 0	4 2.9%	0 0
preferred source of info	0 0	0 0	0 0	0 0	0 0	0 0	0 0	0 0	0 0	0 0	0 0	0 0	0 0	0 0	0 0	0 0	0 0	0 0
Personal subscriptions to newspapers, magazines and journals	3 1.8%	3 2.5%	0 0	3 1.8%	0 0	1 1.8%	1 1.5%	1 2.1%	1 3.3%	1 3.4%	0 0	0 0	* 5.9%	1 4.5%	0 0	0 0	3 2.6%	0 0
All sources of info	3 1.8%	3 2.5%	0 0	3 1.8%	0 0	1 1.8%	1 1.5%	1 2.1%	1 3.3%	1 3.4%	0 0	0 0	* 5.9%	1 4.5%	0 0	0 0	3 2.6%	0 0
preferred source of info	0 0	0 0	0 0	0 0	0 0	0 0	0 0	0 0	0 0	0 0	0 0	0 0	0 0	0 0	0 0	0 0	0 0	0 0

Proportions/Means: Columns Tested (5% risk level) - A/B/D - C/D - E/F/G - H/I/J/K/L/M/N - P/Q
* small base; ** very small base (under 30) ineligible for sig testing

Table 242
Page 955

Outsell/Digital Library Federation Study (2002)
Weighted Tables

TABLE 111, continued

T7sum_8. Online abstracts and indexes SUMMARY TABLE

		RESPONDENT TYPE				INSTITUTION TYPE			DISCIPLINE								GENDER	
	TOTAL SAMPLE	FACULTY MEMBER	GRAD. STUDENT	FACULTY /GRAD	UNDER GRAD. STUDENT	PUBLIC	PRIVATE	LIBERAL ARTS	BIOLOGIAL SCIENCES	PHYSICAL SCIENCES /MATH	SOCIAL SCIENCES	ARTS AND HUMAN.	ENGI- NEERING	BUSINESS	LAW	UNDEC. MAJOR	MALE	FEMALE
		(A)	(B)	(C)	(D)	(E)	(F)	(G)	(H)	(I)	(J)	(K)	(L)	(M)	(N)		(P)	(Q)
Base - USe Online abstracts and indexes for teaching	173	126	47*	173	0**	68*	58*	47*	26**	29**	58*	32**	5**	20**	2**	0*	120*	53*
Your own personal physical library/ files/bookshelves	3 1.8%	3 2.4%	0 0	3 1.8%	0 0	1 1.6%	1 1.6%	1 2.1%	0 0	1 3.4%	0 0	0 0	0 0	2 9.1%	* 11.1%	0 0	2 1.6%	1 2.1%
All sources of info	3 1.8%	3 2.4%	0 0	3 1.8%	0 0	1 1.6%	1 1.6%	1 2.1%	0 0	1 3.4%	0 0	0 0	0 0	2 9.1%	* 11.1%	0 0	2 1.6%	1 2.1%
preferred source of info	* 0.1%	* 0.1%	0 0	* 0.1%	0 0	* 0.2%	0 0	0 0	0 0	0 0	0 0	0 0	0 0	0 0	* 11.1%	0 0	0 0	* 0.3%
Printed library catalogues and finding aids	0 0	0 0	0 0	0 0	0 0	0 0	0 0	0 0	0 0	0 0	0 0	0 0	0 0	0 0	0 0	0 0	0 0	0 0
All sources of info	0 0	0 0	0 0	0 0	0 0	0 0	0 0	0 0	0 0	0 0	0 0	0 0	0 0	0 0	0 0	0 0	0 0	0 0
preferred source of info	0 0	0 0	0 0	0 0	0 0	0 0	0 0	0 0	0 0	0 0	0 0	0 0	0 0	0 0	0 0	0 0	0 0	0 0
Physical bookstore	0 0	0 0	0 0	0 0	0 0	0 0	0 0	0 0	0 0	0 0	0 0	0 0	0 0	0 0	0 0	0 0	0 0	0 0
All sources of info	0 0	0 0	0 0	0 0	0 0	0 0	0 0	0 0	0 0	0 0	0 0	0 0	0 0	0 0	0 0	0 0	0 0	0 0
preferred source of info	0 0	0 0	0 0	0 0	0 0	0 0	0 0	0 0	0 0	0 0	0 0	0 0	0 0	0 0	0 0	0 0	0 0	0 0

Proportions/Means: Columns Tested (5% risk level) - A/B/D - C/D - E/F/G - H/I/J/K/L/M/N - P/Q
* small base; ** very small base (under 30) ineligible for sig testing

Table 242
Page 956

Outsell/Digital Library Federation Study (2002)
Weighted Tables

TABLE 111, continued

T7sum_8. Online abstracts and indexes SUMMARY TABLE

	TOTAL SAMPLE	RESPONDENT TYPE: FACULTY MEMBER	GRAD. STUDENT	FACULTY /GRAD	UNDER GRAD. STUDENT	INSTITUTION TYPE: PUBLIC	PRIVATE	LIBERAL ARTS	DISCIPLINE: BIOLOGICAL SCIENCES	PHYSICAL SCIENCES /MATH	SOCIAL SCIENCES	ARTS AND HUMAN.	ENGI-NEERING	BUSINESS	LAW	UNDEC. MAJOR	GENDER: MALE	FEMALE
		(A)	(B)	(C)	(D)	(E)	(F)	(G)	(H)	(I)	(J)	(K)	(L)	(M)	(N)		(P)	(Q)
Base - USe Online abstracts and indexes for teaching	173	126	47*	173	0**	68*	58*	47*	26**	29**	58*	32**	5**	20**	2**	0*	120*	53*
PERSONAL ASSISTANCE	39 22.6%	32 25.3%	7 15.2%	39 22.6%	0 0	13 18.5%	16 28.3%	10 21.4%	4 16.7%	9 31.0%	8 12.9%	11 34.5%	1 23.5%	6 27.3%	* 11.1%	0 0	29 24.0%	10 19.3%
A librarian in your institution	30 17.5%	24 19.4%	6 12.4%	30 17.5%	0 0	7 10.9%	15 25.3%	8 17.4%	4 13.3%	7 24.1%	8 12.9%	9 27.6%	* 5.9%	3 13.6%	* 11.1%	0 0	21 17.5%	9 17.4%
All sources of info	30 17.5%	24 19.4%	6 12.4%	30 17.5%	0 0	7 10.9%	15 25.3%	8 17.4%	4 13.3%	7 24.1%	8 12.9%	9 27.6%	* 5.9%	3 13.6%	* 11.1%	0 0	21 17.5%	9 17.4%
preferred source of info	9 5.4%	7 5.7%	2 4.5%	9 5.4%	0 0	3 4.5%	5 9.2%	1 1.9%	1 3.3%	3 10.3%	0 0	4 13.8%	0 0	1 4.5%	0 0	0 0	7 6.2%	2 3.4%
Colleagues inside your institution	14 8.3%	13 10.4%	1 2.7%	14 8.3%	0 0	9 12.5%	2 2.9%	4 8.9%	1 3.3%	4 13.8%	0 0	6 17.2%	1 23.5%	3 13.6%	0 0	0 0	13 11.2%	1 1.9%
All sources of info	14 8.3%	13 10.4%	1 2.7%	14 8.3%	0 0	9 12.5%	2 2.9%	4 8.9%	1 3.3%	4 13.8%	0 0	6 17.2%	1 23.5%	3 13.6%	0 0	0 0	13 11.2%	1 1.9%
preferred source of info	1 0.5%	1 0.7%	0 0	1 0.5%	0 0	0 0	0 0	1 1.9%	1 3.3%	0 0	0 0	0 0	0 0	0 0	0 0	0 0	1 0.7%	0 0
Colleagues outside your institution	8 4.5%	8 6.2%	0 0	8 4.5%	0 0	4 6.4%	* 0.5%	3 6.8%	1 3.3%	2 6.9%	0 0	2 6.9%	1 17.6%	2 9.1%	0 0	0 0	7 5.7%	1 1.9%
All sources of info	8 4.5%	8 6.2%	0 0	8 4.5%	0 0	4 6.4%	* 0.5%	3 6.8%	1 3.3%	2 6.9%	0 0	2 6.9%	1 17.6%	2 9.1%	0 0	0 0	7 5.7%	1 1.9%
preferred source of info	* 0.2%	* 0.2%	0 0	* 0.2%	0 0	* 0.4%	0 0	0 0	0 0	0 0	0 0	0 0	* 5.9%	0 0	0 0	0 0	* 0.2%	0 0

Proportions/Means: Columns Tested (5% risk level) - A/B/D - C/D - E/F/G - H/I/J/K/L/M/N - P/Q
* small base; ** very small base (under 30) ineligible for sig testing

Table 242
Page 957

Outsell/Digital Library Federation Study (2002)
Weighted Tables

TABLE 111, continued

T7sum_8. Online abstracts and indexes SUMMARY TABLE

		RESPONDENT TYPE				INSTITUTION TYPE			DISCIPLINE								GENDER	
	TOTAL SAMPLE	FACULTY MEMBER	GRAD. STUDENT	FACULTY /GRAD	UNDER GRAD. STUDENT	PUBLIC	PRIVATE	LIBERAL ARTS	BIOLOGIAL SCIENCES	PHYSICAL SCIENCES /MATH	SOCIAL SCIENCES	ARTS AND HUMAN.	ENGI-NEERING	BUSINESS	LAW	UNDEC. MAJOR	MALE	FEMALE
		(A)	(B)	(C)	(D)	(E)	(F)	(G)	(H)	(I)	(J)	(K)	(L)	(M)	(N)		(P)	(Q)
Base - USe Online abstracts and indexes for teaching	173	126	47*	173	0**	68*	58*	47*	26**	29**	58*	32**	5**	20**	2**	0*	120*	53*
Professional meetings	1	1	0	1	0	0	0	1	0	1	0	0	0	0	0	0	0	1
	0.6%	0.8%	0	0.6%	0	0	0	2.1%	0	3.4%	0	0	0	0	0	0	0	1.9%
All sources of info	1	1	0	1	0	0	0	1	0	1	0	0	0	0	0	0	0	1
	0.6%	0.8%	0	0.6%	0	0	0	2.1%	0	3.4%	0	0	0	0	0	0	0	1.9%
preferred source of info	0	0	0	0	0	0	0	0	0	0	0	0	0	0	0	0	0	0
	0	0	0	0	0	0	0	0	0	0	0	0	0	0	0	0	0	0
Another institution's librarian	0	0	0	0	0	0	0	0	0	0	0	0	0	0	0	0	0	0
	0	0	0	0	0	0	0	0	0	0	0	0	0	0	0	0	0	0
All sources of info	0	0	0	0	0	0	0	0	0	0	0	0	0	0	0	0	0	0
	0	0	0	0	0	0	0	0	0	0	0	0	0	0	0	0	0	0
preferred source of info	0	0	0	0	0	0	0	0	0	0	0	0	0	0	0	0	0	0
	0	0	0	0	0	0	0	0	0	0	0	0	0	0	0	0	0	0
Personal office/lab	3	3	0	3	0	1	1	1	2	0	0	1	0	0	0	0	3	0
	1.7%	2.3%	0	1.7%	0	1.6%	1.5%	1.9%	6.7%	0	0	3.4%	0	0	0	0	2.4%	0
All sources of info	3	3	0	3	0	1	1	1	2	0	0	1	0	0	0	0	3	0
	1.7%	2.3%	0	1.7%	0	1.6%	1.5%	1.9%	6.7%	0	0	3.4%	0	0	0	0	2.4%	0
preferred source of info	0	0	0	0	0	0	0	0	0	0	0	0	0	0	0	0	0	0
	0	0	0	0	0	0	0	0	0	0	0	0	0	0	0	0	0	0

Proportions/Means: Columns Tested (5% risk level) - A/B/D - C/D - E/F/G - H/I/J/K/L/M/N - P/Q
* small base; ** very small base (under 30) ineligible for sig testing

Table 242
Page 958

Outsell/Digital Library Federation Study (2002)
Weighted Tables

TABLE 111, continued

T7sum_8. Online abstracts and indexes SUMMARY TABLE

		RESPONDENT TYPE				INSTITUTION TYPE			DISCIPLINE									GENDER	
	TOTAL SAMPLE	FACULTY MEMBER	GRAD. STUDENT	FACULTY /GRAD	UNDER GRAD. STUDENT	PUBLIC	PRIVATE	LIBERAL ARTS	BIOLOGIAL SCIENCES	PHYSICAL SCIENCES /MATH	SOCIAL SCIENCES	ARTS AND HUMAN.	ENGI- NEERING	BUSINESS	LAW	UNDEC. MAJOR	MALE	FEMALE
		(A)	(B)	(C)	(D)	(E)	(F)	(G)	(H)	(I)	(J)	(K)	(L)	(M)	(N)		(P)	(Q)
Base - USe Online abstracts and indexes for teaching	173	126	47*	173	0**	68*	58*	47*	26**	29**	58*	32**	5**	20**	2**	0*	120*	53*
Online (unspecified)	3 1.6%	1 0.7%	2 4.0%	3 1.6%	0 0	0 0	3 4.8%	0 0	1 3.3%	0 0	2 3.2%	0 0	0 0	0 0	0 0	0 0	1 0.7%	2 3.6%
All sources of info	3 1.6%	1 0.7%	2 4.0%	3 1.6%	0 0	0 0	3 4.8%	0 0	1 3.3%	0 0	2 3.2%	0 0	0 0	0 0	0 0	0 0	1 0.7%	2 3.6%
preferred source of info	0 0	0 0	0 0	0 0	0 0	0 0	0 0	0 0	0 0	0 0	0 0	0 0	0 0	0 0	0 0	0 0	0 0	0 0
Students	2 1.1%	2 1.5%	0 0	2 1.1%	0 0	0 0	0 0	2 4.0%	0 0	0 0	2 3.2%	0 0	0 0	0 0	0 0	0 0	2 1.6%	0 0
All sources of info	2 1.1%	2 1.5%	0 0	2 1.1%	0 0	0 0	0 0	2 4.0%	0 0	0 0	2 3.2%	0 0	0 0	0 0	0 0	0 0	2 1.6%	0 0
preferred source of info	0 0	0 0	0 0	0 0	0 0	0 0	0 0	0 0	0 0	0 0	0 0	0 0	0 0	0 0	0 0	0 0	0 0	0 0
Author	0 0	0 0	0 0	0 0	0 0	0 0	0 0	0 0	0 0	0 0	0 0	0 0	0 0	0 0	0 0	0 0	0 0	0 0
All sources of info	0 0	0 0	0 0	0 0	0 0	0 0	0 0	0 0	0 0	0 0	0 0	0 0	0 0	0 0	0 0	0 0	0 0	0 0
preferred source of info	0 0	0 0	0 0	0 0	0 0	0 0	0 0	0 0	0 0	0 0	0 0	0 0	0 0	0 0	0 0	0 0	0 0	0 0
Other	16 9.1%	13 10.1%	3 6.3%	16 9.1%	0 0	4 5.7%	7 12.0%	5 10.3%	3 10.0%	4 13.8%	4 6.5%	2 6.9%	* 5.9%	3 13.6%	0 0	0 0	11 9.1%	5 9.0%

Proportions/Means: Columns Tested (5% risk level) - A/B/D - C/D - E/F/G - H/I/J/K/L/M/N - P/Q
* small base; ** very small base (under 30) ineligible for sig testing

Table 242
Page 959

Outsell/Digital Library Federation Study (2002)
Weighted Tables

TABLE 111, continued

T7sum_8. Online abstracts and indexes SUMMARY TABLE

		RESPONDENT TYPE				INSTITUTION TYPE			DISCIPLINE									GENDER	
	TOTAL SAMPLE	FACULTY MEMBER	GRAD. STUDENT	FACULTY /GRAD	UNDER GRAD. STUDENT	PUBLIC	PRIVATE	LIBERAL ARTS	BIOLOGIAL SCIENCES	PHYSICAL SCIENCES /MATH	SOCIAL SCIENCES	ARTS AND HUMAN.	ENGI- NEERING	BUSINESS	LAW	UNDEC. MAJOR	MALE	FEMALE
		(A)	(B)	(C)	(D)	(E)	(F)	(G)	(H)	(I)	(J)	(K)	(L)	(M)	(N)		(P)	(Q)
Base - USe Online abstracts and indexes for teaching	173	126	47*	173	0**	68*	58*	47*	26**	29**	58*	32**	5**	20**	2**	0*	120*	53*
All sources of info	12 6.9%	9 7.1%	3 6.3%	12 6.9%	0 0	3 4.4%	5 8.8%	4 8.2%	3 10.0%	3 10.3%	2 3.2%	2 6.9%	* 5.9%	2 9.1%	0 0	0 0	7 5.9%	5 9.0%
preferred source of info	10 5.7%	8 6.3%	2 4.0%	10 5.7%	0 0	3 4.1%	3 5.5%	4 8.2%	1 3.3%	3 10.3%	4 6.5%	0 0	* 5.9%	2 9.1%	0 0	0 0	8 6.6%	2 3.6%
DK/Refused	4 2.4%	3 2.5%	1 2.4%	4 2.4%	0 0	0 0	2 3.9%	2 4.3%	1 3.3%	0 0	0 0	3 10.3%	0 0	0 0	0 0	0 0	2 1.9%	2 3.8%

Proportions/Means: Columns Tested (5% risk level) - A/B/D - C/D - E/F/G - H/I/J/K/L/M/N - P/Q
* small base; ** very small base (under 30) ineligible for sig testing

TABLE 112

T7D/E_8. Online abstracts and indexes SUMMARY TABLE

		RESPONDENT TYPE				INSTITUTION TYPE			DISCIPLINE								GENDER	
	TOTAL SAMPLE	FACULTY MEMBER	GRAD. STUDENT	FACULTY /GRAD	UNDER GRAD. STUDENT	PUBLIC	PRIVATE	LIBERAL ARTS	BIOLOGIAL SCIENCES	PHYSICAL SCIENCES /MATH	SOCIAL SCIENCES	ARTS AND HUMAN.	ENGI-NEERING	BUSINESS	LAW	UNDEC. MAJOR	MALE	FEMALE
		(A)	(B)	(C)	(D)	(E)	(F)	(G)	(H)	(I)	(J)	(K)	(L)	(M)	(N)		(P)	(Q)
Base - Use Online abstracts and indexes for teaching	173	126	47*	173	0**	68*	58*	47*	26**	29**	58*	32**	5**	20**	2**	0*	120*	53*
Access online (NET)	138 79.5%	101 80.2%	37 77.8%	138 79.5%	0 0	55 80.9%	43 74.8%	39 83.4%	19 73.3%	23 79.3%	47 80.6%	24 72.4%	5 94.1%	19 90.9%	2 100.0%	0 0	100 83.3%	38 71.0%
All sources of info	138 79.5%	101 80.2%	37 77.8%	138 79.5%	0 0	55 80.9%	43 74.8%	39 83.4%	19 73.3%	23 79.3%	47 80.6%	24 72.4%	5 94.1%	19 90.9%	2 100.0%	0 0	100 83.3%	38 71.0%
preferred source of info	125 72.4%	92 73.3%	33 69.8%	125 72.4%	0 0	53 77.7%	38 66.1%	34 72.4%	18 70.0%	20 69.0%	45 77.4%	19 58.6%	4 76.5%	18 86.4%	1 77.8%	0 0	91 75.6%	34 65.0%
Borrow from or use in campus library (NET)	69 40.1%	50 39.8%	19 40.8%	69 40.1%	0 0	27 39.5%	23 39.1%	20 42.2%	11 40.0%	11 37.9%	23 38.7%	16 48.3%	1 17.6%	8 40.9%	* 22.2%	0 0	47 39.2%	22 42.1%
All sources of info	69 40.1%	50 39.8%	19 40.8%	69 40.1%	0 0	27 39.5%	23 39.1%	20 42.2%	11 40.0%	11 37.9%	23 38.7%	16 48.3%	1 17.6%	8 40.9%	* 22.2%	0 0	47 39.2%	22 42.1%
preferred source of info	33 19.1%	21 17.1%	12 24.6%	33 19.1%	0 0	13 19.6%	15 25.4%	5 10.7%	4 16.7%	6 20.7%	9 16.1%	10 31.0%	* 5.9%	3 13.6%	* 11.1%	0 0	20 16.3%	14 25.7%
Interlibrary loan (NET)	9 5.1%	7 5.5%	2 4.0%	9 5.1%	0 0	4 5.7%	0 0	5 10.5%F	1 3.3%	4 13.8%	2 3.2%	1 3.4%	0 0	1 4.5%	0 0	0 0	8 6.5%	1 1.9%
All sources of info	9 5.1%	7 5.5%	2 4.0%	9 5.1%	0 0	4 5.7%	0 0	5 10.5%F	1 3.3%	4 13.8%	2 3.2%	1 3.4%	0 0	1 4.5%	0 0	0 0	8 6.5%	1 1.9%
preferred source of info	0 0	0 0	0 0	0 0	0 0	0 0	0 0	0 0	0 0	0 0	0 0	0 0	0 0	0 0	0 0	0 0	0 0	0 0

Proportions/Means: Columns Tested (5% risk level) - A/B/D - C/D - E/F/G - H/I/J/K/L/M/N - P/Q
* small base; ** very small base (under 30) ineligible for sig testing

Table 245
Page 967

Outsell/Digital Library Federation Study (2002)
Weighted Tables

TABLE 112, continued

T7D/E_8. Online abstracts and indexes SUMMARY TABLE

		RESPONDENT TYPE				INSTITUTION TYPE			DISCIPLINE									GENDER	
	TOTAL SAMPLE	FACULTY MEMBER	GRAD. STUDENT	FACULTY /GRAD	UNDER GRAD. STUDENT	PUBLIC	PRIVATE	LIBERAL ARTS	BIOLOGIAL SCIENCES	PHYSICAL SCIENCES /MATH	SOCIAL SCIENCES	ARTS AND HUMAN.	ENGI-NEERING	BUSINESS	LAW	UNDEC. MAJOR	MALE	FEMALE
		(A)	(B)	(C)	(D)	(E)	(F)	(G)	(H)	(I)	(J)	(K)	(L)	(M)	(N)		(P)	(Q)
Base - Use Online abstracts and indexes for teaching	173	126	47*	173	0**	68*	58*	47*	26**	29**	58*	32**	5**	20**	2**	0*	120*	53*
Access from course website (NET)	6 3.3%	5 3.8%	1 1.9%	6 3.3%	0 0	2 2.7%	2 3.0%	2 4.3%	2 6.7%	2 6.9%	2 3.2%	0 0	0 0	0 0	0 0	0 0	6 4.7%	0 0
All sources of info	6 3.3%	5 3.8%	1 1.9%	6 3.3%	0 0	2 2.7%	2 3.0%	2 4.3%	2 6.7%	2 6.9%	2 3.2%	0 0	0 0	0 0	0 0	0 0	6 4.7%	0 0
preferred source of info	2 1.1%	2 1.5%	0 0	2 1.1%	0 0	0 0	1 1.5%	1 2.1%	1 3.3%	1 3.4%	0 0	0 0	0 0	0 0	0 0	0 0	2 1.6%	0 0
Office (NET)	3 1.8%	3 2.5%	0 0	3 1.8%	0 0	1 1.6%	1 1.9%	1 1.9%	1 3.3%	0 0	0 0	2 6.9%	0 0	0 0	0 0	0 0	1 0.9%	2 3.8%
All sources of info	3 1.8%	3 2.5%	0 0	3 1.8%	0 0	1 1.6%	1 1.9%	1 1.9%	1 3.3%	0 0	0 0	2 6.9%	0 0	0 0	0 0	0 0	1 0.9%	2 3.8%
preferred source of info	2 1.2%	2 1.6%	0 0	2 1.2%	0 0	0 0	1 1.9%	1 1.9%	1 3.3%	0 0	0 0	1 3.4%	0 0	0 0	0 0	0 0	0 0	2 3.8%
Home (NET)	3 1.6%	3 2.2%	0 0	3 1.6%	0 0	0 0	1 1.5%	2 4.0%	1 3.3%	0 0	2 3.2%	0 0	0 0	0 0	0 0	0 0	2 1.6%	1 1.7%
All sources of info	3 1.6%	3 2.2%	0 0	3 1.6%	0 0	0 0	1 1.5%	2 4.0%	1 3.3%	0 0	2 3.2%	0 0	0 0	0 0	0 0	0 0	2 1.6%	1 1.7%
preferred source of info	2 1.1%	2 1.5%	0 0	2 1.1%	0 0	0 0	0 0	2 4.0%	0 0	0 0	2 3.2%	0 0	0 0	0 0	0 0	0 0	2 1.6%	0 0

Proportions/Means: Columns Tested (5% risk level) - A/B/D - C/D - E/F/G - H/I/J/K/L/M/N - P/Q
* small base; ** very small base (under 30) ineligible for sig testing

Table 245
Page 968

Outsell/Digital Library Federation Study (2002)
Weighted Tables

TABLE 112, continued

T7D/E_8. Online abstracts and indexes SUMMARY TABLE

		RESPONDENT TYPE				INSTITUTION TYPE			DISCIPLINE									GENDER	
	TOTAL SAMPLE	FACULTY MEMBER	GRAD. STUDENT	FACULTY /GRAD	UNDER GRAD. STUDENT	PUBLIC	PRIVATE	LIBERAL ARTS	BIOLOGIAL SCIENCES	PHYSICAL SCIENCES /MATH	SOCIAL SCIENCES	ARTS AND HUMAN.	ENGI- NEERING	BUSINESS	LAW	UNDEC. MAJOR	MALE	FEMALE
		(A)	(B)	(C)	(D)	(E)	(F)	(G)	(H)	(I)	(J)	(K)	(L)	(M)	(N)		(P)	(Q)
Base - Use Online abstracts and indexes for teaching	173	126	47*	173	0**	68*	58*	47*	26**	29**	58*	32**	5**	20**	2**	0*	120*	53*
Publisher (NET)	2 1.1%	2 1.5%	0 0	2 1.1%	0 0	0 0	1 1.5%	1 2.1%	1 3.3%	1 3.4%	0 0	0 0	0 0	0 0	0 0	0 0	1 0.8%	1 1.7%
All sources of info	2 1.1%	2 1.5%	0 0	2 1.1%	0 0	0 0	1 1.5%	1 2.1%	1 3.3%	1 3.4%	0 0	0 0	0 0	0 0	0 0	0 0	1 0.8%	1 1.7%
preferred source of info	1 0.5%	1 0.7%	0 0	1 0.5%	0 0	0 0	1 1.5%	0 0	1 3.3%	0 0	0 0	0 0	0 0	0 0	0 0	0 0	0 0	1 1.7%
Meeting/Conferences (NET)	2 1.0%	2 1.4%	0 0	2 1.0%	0 0	0 0	1 1.5%	1 1.9%	2 6.7%	0 0	0 0	0 0	0 0	0 0	0 0	0 0	2 1.5%	0 0
All sources of info	2 1.0%	2 1.4%	0 0	2 1.0%	0 0	0 0	1 1.5%	1 1.9%	2 6.7%	0 0	0 0	0 0	0 0	0 0	0 0	0 0	2 1.5%	0 0
preferred source of info	1 0.5%	1 0.7%	0 0	1 0.5%	0 0	0 0	0 0	1 1.9%	1 3.3%	0 0	0 0	0 0	0 0	0 0	0 0	0 0	1 0.7%	0 0
Borrow from or use in other libraries (NET)	2 0.9%	1 1.0%	* 0.6%	2 0.9%	0 0	0 0	1 1.0%	1 2.1%	0 0	1 3.4%	0 0	0 0	1 11.8%	0 0	0 0	0 0	2 1.3%	0 0
All sources of info	2 0.9%	1 1.0%	* 0.6%	2 0.9%	0 0	0 0	1 1.0%	1 2.1%	0 0	1 3.4%	0 0	0 0	1 11.8%	0 0	0 0	0 0	2 1.3%	0 0
preferred source of info	2 0.9%	1 1.0%	* 0.6%	2 0.9%	0 0	0 0	1 1.0%	1 2.1%	0 0	1 3.4%	0 0	0 0	1 11.8%	0 0	0 0	0 0	2 1.3%	0 0

Proportions/Means: Columns Tested (5% risk level) - A/B/D - C/D - E/F/G - H/I/J/K/L/M/N - P/Q
* small base; ** very small base (under 30) ineligible for sig testing

Table 245
Page 969

Outsell/Digital Library Federation Study (2002)
Weighted Tables

TABLE 112, continued

T7D/E_8. Online abstracts and indexes SUMMARY TABLE

	RESPONDENT TYPE					INSTITUTION TYPE			DISCIPLINE								GENDER	
	TOTAL SAMPLE	FACULTY MEMBER	GRAD. STUDENT	FACULTY /GRAD	UNDER GRAD. STUDENT	PUBLIC	PRIVATE	LIBERAL ARTS	BIOLOGIAL SCIENCES	PHYSICAL SCIENCES /MATH	SOCIAL SCIENCES	ARTS AND HUMAN.	ENGI-NEERING	BUSINESS	LAW	UNDEC. MAJOR	MALE	FEMALE
		(A)	(B)	(C)	(D)	(E)	(F)	(G)	(H)	(I)	(J)	(K)	(L)	(M)	(N)		(P)	(Q)
Base - Use Online abstracts and indexes for teaching	173	126	47*	173	0**	68*	58*	47*	26**	29**	58*	32**	5**	20**	2**	0*	120*	53*
Purchase from physical book store (NET)	1 0.7%	1 0.8%	* 0.6%	1 0.7%	0 0	0 0	1 2.2%	0 0	0 0	1 3.4%	0 0	0 0	* 5.9%	0 0	0 0	0 0	1 1.1%	0 0
All sources of info	1 0.7%	1 0.8%	* 0.6%	1 0.7%	0 0	0 0	1 2.2%	0 0	0 0	1 3.4%	0 0	0 0	* 5.9%	0 0	0 0	0 0	1 1.1%	0 0
preferred source of info	1 0.6%	1 0.8%	0 0	1 0.6%	0 0	0 0	1 1.7%	0 0	0 0	1 3.4%	0 0	0 0	0 0	0 0	0 0	0 0	1 0.8%	0 0
Purchase from online bookstore (NET)	1 0.7%	1 0.8%	* 0.4%	1 0.7%	0 0	0 0	* 0.3%	1 2.1%	0 0	1 3.4%	0 0	0 0	0 0	0 0	* 11.1%	0 0	0 0	1 2.2%
All sources of info	1 0.7%	1 0.8%	* 0.4%	1 0.7%	0 0	0 0	* 0.3%	1 2.1%	0 0	1 3.4%	0 0	0 0	0 0	0 0	* 11.1%	0 0	0 0	1 2.2%
preferred source of info	* 0.1%	0 0	* 0.4%	* 0.1%	0 0	0 0	* 0.3%	0 0	0 0	0 0	0 0	0 0	0 0	0 0	* 11.1%	0 0	0 0	* 0.3%
Personal Collection/ Holdings (NET)	1 0.6%	1 0.8%	0 0	1 0.6%	0 0	0 0	0 0	1 2.1%	0 0	1 3.4%	0 0	0 0	0 0	0 0	0 0	0 0	1 0.8%	0 0
All sources of info	1 0.6%	1 0.8%	0 0	1 0.6%	0 0	0 0	0 0	1 2.1%	0 0	1 3.4%	0 0	0 0	0 0	0 0	0 0	0 0	1 0.8%	0 0
preferred source of info	0 0	0 0	0 0	0 0	0 0	0 0	0 0	0 0	0 0	0 0	0 0	0 0	0 0	0 0	0 0	0 0	0 0	0 0

Proportions/Means: Columns Tested (5% risk level) - A/B/D - C/D - E/F/G - H/I/J/K/L/M/N - P/Q
* small base; ** very small base (under 30) ineligible for sig testing

Table 245
Page 970

Outsell/Digital Library Federation Study (2002)
Weighted Tables

TABLE 112, continued

T7D/E_8. Online abstracts and indexes SUMMARY TABLE

		RESPONDENT TYPE				INSTITUTION TYPE			DISCIPLINE									GENDER	
	TOTAL SAMPLE	FACULTY MEMBER	GRAD. STUDENT	FACULTY /GRAD	UNDER GRAD. STUDENT	PUBLIC	PRIVATE	LIBERAL ARTS	BIOLOGIAL SCIENCES	PHYSICAL SCIENCES /MATH	SOCIAL SCIENCES	ARTS AND HUMAN.	ENGI-NEERING	BUSINESS	LAW	UNDEC. MAJOR	MALE	FEMALE
		(A)	(B)	(C)	(D)	(E)	(F)	(G)	(H)	(I)	(J)	(K)	(L)	(M)	(N)		(P)	(Q)
Base - Use Online abstracts and indexes for teaching	173	126	47*	173	0**	68*	58*	47*	26**	29**	58*	32**	5**	20**	2**	0*	120*	53*
Faculty (NET)	*	0	*	*	0	0	*	0	0	0	0	0	*	0	0	0	*	0
	0.2%	0	0.6%	0.2%	0	0	0.5%	0	0	0	0	0	5.9%	0	0	0	0.2%	0
All sources of info	*	0	*	*	0	0	*	0	0	0	0	0	*	0	0	0	*	0
	0.2%	0	0.6%	0.2%	0	0	0.5%	0	0	0	0	0	5.9%	0	0	0	0.2%	0
preferred source of info	*	0	*	*	0	0	*	0	0	0	0	0	*	0	0	0	*	0
	0.2%	0	0.6%	0.2%	0	0	0.5%	0	0	0	0	0	5.9%	0	0	0	0.2%	0
Access book/journal/ journal article elsewhere online (NET)	0	0	0	0	0	0	0	0	0	0	0	0	0	0	0	0	0	0
	0	0	0	0	0	0	0	0	0	0	0	0	0	0	0	0	0	0
All sources of info	0	0	0	0	0	0	0	0	0	0	0	0	0	0	0	0	0	0
	0	0	0	0	0	0	0	0	0	0	0	0	0	0	0	0	0	0
preferred source of info	0	0	0	0	0	0	0	0	0	0	0	0	0	0	0	0	0	0
	0	0	0	0	0	0	0	0	0	0	0	0	0	0	0	0	0	0
Colleagues (NET)	0	0	0	0	0	0	0	0	0	0	0	0	0	0	0	0	0	0
	0	0	0	0	0	0	0	0	0	0	0	0	0	0	0	0	0	0
All sources of info	0	0	0	0	0	0	0	0	0	0	0	0	0	0	0	0	0	0
	0	0	0	0	0	0	0	0	0	0	0	0	0	0	0	0	0	0
preferred source of info	0	0	0	0	0	0	0	0	0	0	0	0	0	0	0	0	0	0
	0	0	0	0	0	0	0	0	0	0	0	0	0	0	0	0	0	0

Proportions/Means: Columns Tested (5% risk level) - A/B/D - C/D - E/F/G - H/I/J/K/L/M/N - P/Q
* small base; ** very small base (under 30) ineligible for sig testing

Table 245
Page 971

Outsell/Digital Library Federation Study (2002)
Weighted Tables

TABLE 112, continued

T7D/E_8. Online abstracts and indexes SUMMARY TABLE

		RESPONDENT TYPE				INSTITUTION TYPE			DISCIPLINE								GENDER	
	TOTAL SAMPLE	FACULTY MEMBER	GRAD. STUDENT	FACULTY /GRAD	UNDER GRAD. STUDENT	PUBLIC	PRIVATE	LIBERAL ARTS	BIOLOGIAL SCIENCES	PHYSICAL SCIENCES /MATH	SOCIAL SCIENCES	ARTS AND HUMAN.	ENGI- NEERING	BUSINESS	LAW	UNDEC. MAJOR	MALE	FEMALE
		(A)	(B)	(C)	(D)	(E)	(F)	(G)	(H)	(I)	(J)	(K)	(L)	(M)	(N)		(P)	(Q)
Base - Use Online abstracts and indexes for teaching	173	126	47*	173	0**	68*	58*	47*	26**	29**	58*	32**	5**	20**	2**	0*	120*	53*
Department (NET)	0 0	0 0	0 0	0 0	0 0	0 0	0 0	0 0	0 0	0 0	0 0	0 0	0 0	0 0	0 0	0 0	0 0	0 0
All sources of info	0 0	0 0	0 0	0 0	0 0	0 0	0 0	0 0	0 0	0 0	0 0	0 0	0 0	0 0	0 0	0 0	0 0	0 0
preferred source of info	0 0	0 0	0 0	0 0	0 0	0 0	0 0	0 0	0 0	0 0	0 0	0 0	0 0	0 0	0 0	0 0	0 0	0 0
Author	0 0	0 0	0 0	0 0	0 0	0 0	0 0	0 0	0 0	0 0	0 0	0 0	0 0	0 0	0 0	0 0	0 0	0 0
All sources of info	0 0	0 0	0 0	0 0	0 0	0 0	0 0	0 0	0 0	0 0	0 0	0 0	0 0	0 0	0 0	0 0	0 0	0 0
preferred source of info	0 0	0 0	0 0	0 0	0 0	0 0	0 0	0 0	0 0	0 0	0 0	0 0	0 0	0 0	0 0	0 0	0 0	0 0
Ask library to purchase source (NET)	0 0	0 0	0 0	0 0	0 0	0 0	0 0	0 0	0 0	0 0	0 0	0 0	0 0	0 0	0 0	0 0	0 0	0 0
All sources of info	0 0	0 0	0 0	0 0	0 0	0 0	0 0	0 0	0 0	0 0	0 0	0 0	0 0	0 0	0 0	0 0	0 0	0 0
preferred source of info	0 0	0 0	0 0	0 0	0 0	0 0	0 0	0 0	0 0	0 0	0 0	0 0	0 0	0 0	0 0	0 0	0 0	0 0

Proportions/Means: Columns Tested (5% risk level) - A/B/D - C/D - E/F/G - H/I/J/K/L/M/N - P/Q
* small base; ** very small base (under 30) ineligible for sig testing

Table 245
Page 972

Outsell/Digital Library Federation Study (2002)
Weighted Tables

TABLE 112, continued

T7D/E_8. Online abstracts and indexes SUMMARY TABLE

	TOTAL SAMPLE	RESPONDENT TYPE: FACULTY MEMBER (A)	GRAD. STUDENT (B)	FACULTY /GRAD (C)	UNDER GRAD. STUDENT (D)	INSTITUTION TYPE: PUBLIC (E)	PRIVATE (F)	LIBERAL ARTS (G)	DISCIPLINE: BIOLOGIAL SCIENCES (H)	PHYSICAL SCIENCES /MATH (I)	SOCIAL SCIENCES (J)	ARTS AND HUMAN. (K)	ENGI-NEERING (L)	BUSINESS (M)	LAW (N)	UNDEC. MAJOR	GENDER: MALE (P)	FEMALE (Q)
Base - Use Online abstracts and indexes for teaching	173	126	47*	173	0**	68*	58*	47*	26**	29**	58*	32**	5**	20**	2**	0*	120*	53*
Order from on demand document delivery service (NET)	0 0	0 0	0 0	0 0	0 0	0 0	0 0	0 0	0 0	0 0	0 0	0 0	0 0	0 0	0 0	0 0	0 0	0 0
All sources of info	0 0	0 0	0 0	0 0	0 0	0 0	0 0	0 0	0 0	0 0	0 0	0 0	0 0	0 0	0 0	0 0	0 0	0 0
preferred source of info	0 0	0 0	0 0	0 0	0 0	0 0	0 0	0 0	0 0	0 0	0 0	0 0	0 0	0 0	0 0	0 0	0 0	0 0
Other (NET)	3 1.7%	1 0.9%	2 4.0%	3 1.7%	0 0	2 2.7%	1 1.9%	0 0	0 0	0 0	2 3.2%	1 3.4%	0 0	0 0	0 0	0 0	0 0	3 5.7%P
All sources of info	3 1.7%	1 0.9%	2 4.0%	3 1.7%	0 0	2 2.7%	1 1.9%	0 0	0 0	0 0	2 3.2%	1 3.4%	0 0	0 0	0 0	0 0	0 0	3 5.7%P
preferred source of info	2 1.1%	0 0	2 4.0%	2 1.1%	0 0	2 2.7%	0 0	0 0	0 0	0 0	2 3.2%	0 0	0 0	0 0	0 0	0 0	0 0	2 3.6%
DK/Refused	2 1.3%	2 1.8%	0 0	2 1.3%	0 0	0 0	0 0	2 4.8%	0 0	0 0	0 0	2 6.9%	0 0	0 0	0 0	0 0	2 1.9%	0 0

Proportions/Means: Columns Tested (5% risk level) - A/B/D - C/D - E/F/G - H/I/J/K/L/M/N - P/Q
* small base; ** very small base (under 30) ineligible for sig testing

Table 245
Page 973

Outsell/Digital Library Federation Study (2002)
Weighted Tables

TABLE 113

T7sum_9. Online databases, data sets or data sources SUMMARY TABLE

		RESPONDENT TYPE				INSTITUTION TYPE			DISCIPLINE								GENDER	
	TOTAL SAMPLE	FACULTY MEMBER	GRAD. STUDENT	FACULTY /GRAD	UNDER GRAD. STUDENT	PUBLIC	PRIVATE	LIBERAL ARTS	BIOLOGIAL SCIENCES	PHYSICAL SCIENCES /MATH	SOCIAL SCIENCES	ARTS AND HUMAN.	ENGI- NEERING	BUSINESS	LAW	UNDEC. MAJOR	MALE	FEMALE
		(A)	(B)	(C)	(D)	(E)	(F)	(G)	(H)	(I)	(J)	(K)	(L)	(M)	(N)		(P)	(Q)
Base - USe Online databases, data sets or data sources for teaching	296	222	74*	296	0**	110*	117*	68*	36*	68*	88*	62*	8**	31*	3**	0*	217	79*
ONLINE	247 83.5%	196 88.4%B	51 68.8%	247 83.5%	0 0	87 79.0%	98 83.8%	62 90.2%	29 80.5%	55 80.9%	73 83.0%	53 85.5%	8 89.7%	27 87.9%	2 93.3%	0 0	186 85.8%	61 77.2%
Search engine	82 27.6%	69 31.2%B	12 16.7%	82 27.6%	0 0	32 28.6%	24 20.8%	26 37.4%F	11 31.7%	22 32.4%	17 19.1%	19 30.9%	3 34.5%	8 27.3%	1 33.3%	0 0	64 29.5%	18 22.3%
All sources of info	82 27.6%	69 31.2%B	12 16.7%	82 27.6%	0 0	32 28.6%	24 20.8%	26 37.4%F	11 31.7%	22 32.4%	17 19.1%	19 30.9%	3 34.5%	8 27.3%	1 33.3%	0 0	64 29.5%	18 22.3%
preferred source of info	47 15.7%	36 16.4%	10 13.8%	47 15.7%	0 0	22 20.0%	12 10.6%	12 17.7%	4 12.2%	16 23.5%J	6 6.4%	13 21.8%J	2 24.1%	5 15.2%	* 13.3%	0 0	37 16.9%	10 12.5%
Online databases	59 20.0%	48 21.8%	11 14.4%	59 20.0%	0 0	21 18.8%	18 15.2%	21 30.0%F	9 24.4%	17 25.0%	15 17.0%	11 18.2%	1 6.9%	6 18.2%	1 33.3%	0 0	46 21.4%	13 15.9%
All sources of info	59 20.0%	48 21.8%	11 14.4%	59 20.0%	0 0	21 18.8%	18 15.2%	21 30.0%F	9 24.4%	17 25.0%	15 17.0%	11 18.2%	1 6.9%	6 18.2%	1 33.3%	0 0	46 21.4%	13 15.9%
preferred source of info	36 12.2%	27 12.4%	9 11.7%	36 12.2%	0 0	16 14.6%	11 9.5%	9 12.9%	4 12.2%	11 16.2%	9 10.6%	7 10.9%	* 3.4%	4 12.1%	1 20.0%	0 0	24 11.2%	12 14.8%
Web directory/ subject related web site	49 16.5%	41 18.3%	8 11.3%	49 16.5%	0 0	12 10.8%	27 23.1%E	10 14.4%	4 12.2%	10 14.7%	19 21.3%	10 16.4%	1 13.8%	4 12.1%	1 26.7%	0 0	34 15.8%	15 18.6%
All sources of info	49 16.5%	41 18.3%	8 11.3%	49 16.5%	0 0	12 10.8%	27 23.1%E	10 14.4%	4 12.2%	10 14.7%	19 21.3%	10 16.4%	1 13.8%	4 12.1%	1 26.7%	0 0	34 15.8%	15 18.6%

Proportions/Means: Columns Tested (5% risk level) - A/B/D - C/D - E/F/G - H/I/J/K/L/M/N - P/Q
* small base; ** very small base (under 30) ineligible for sig testing

Table 249
Page 985

Outsell/Digital Library Federation Study (2002)
Weighted Tables

TABLE 113, continued

T7sum_9. Online databases, data sets or data sources SUMMARY TABLE

		RESPONDENT TYPE				INSTITUTION TYPE			DISCIPLINE									GENDER	
	TOTAL SAMPLE	FACULTY MEMBER	GRAD. STUDENT	FACULTY /GRAD	UNDER GRAD. STUDENT	PUBLIC	PRIVATE	LIBERAL ARTS	BIOLOGIAL SCIENCES	PHYSICAL SCIENCES /MATH	SOCIAL SCIENCES	ARTS AND HUMAN.	ENGI-NEERING	BUSINESS	LAW	UNDEC. MAJOR	MALE	FEMALE
		(A)	(B)	(C)	(D)	(E)	(F)	(G)	(H)	(I)	(J)	(K)	(L)	(M)	(N)		(P)	(Q)
Base - USe Online databases, data sets or data sources for teaching	296	222	74*	296	0**	110*	117*	68*	36*	68*	88*	62*	8**	31*	3**	0*	217	79*
preferred source of info	31 10.5%	28 12.5%	3 4.5%	31 10.5%	0 0	8 6.9%	19 16.2%	5 6.8%	4 9.8%	4 5.9%	17 19.1%IK	2 3.6%	1 13.8%	3 9.1%	1 20.0%	0 0	24 10.9%	8 9.5%
Your own institution's web site	40 13.5%	27 12.3%	13 17.2%	40 13.5%	0 0	19 17.0%	15 13.2%	6 8.5%	5 14.6%	5 7.4%	15 17.0%	10 16.4%	1 17.2%	3 9.1%	* 13.3%	0 0	26 12.2%	14 17.2%
All sources of info	40 13.5%	27 12.3%	13 17.2%	40 13.5%	0 0	19 17.0%	15 13.2%	6 8.5%	5 14.6%	5 7.4%	15 17.0%	10 16.4%	1 17.2%	3 9.1%	* 13.3%	0 0	26 12.2%	14 17.2%
preferred source of info	34 11.5%	23 10.6%	11 14.3%	34 11.5%	0 0	14 13.0%	14 11.8%	6 8.5%	5 14.6%	5 7.4%	13 14.9%	7 10.9%	1 10.3%	3 9.1%	* 6.7%	0 0	25 11.4%	9 11.8%
Internet searches	37 12.4%	30 13.5%	7 9.0%	37 12.4%	0 0	12 10.9%	17 14.3%	8 11.8%	3 7.3%	7 10.3%	11 12.8%	8 12.7%	2 24.1%	6 18.2%	* 13.3%	0 0	29 13.3%	8 10.0%
All sources of info	37 12.4%	30 13.5%	7 9.0%	37 12.4%	0 0	12 10.9%	17 14.3%	8 11.8%	3 7.3%	7 10.3%	11 12.8%	8 12.7%	2 24.1%	6 18.2%	* 13.3%	0 0	29 13.3%	8 10.0%
preferred source of info	21 7.2%	16 7.1%	5 7.3%	21 7.2%	0 0	6 5.4%	10 8.8%	5 7.3%	3 7.3%	4 5.9%	8 8.5%	3 5.5%	1 10.3%	3 9.1%	0 0	0 0	16 7.4%	5 6.4%
Online library catalogues and finding aids	29 9.7%	21 9.5%	8 10.2%	29 9.7%	0 0	9 8.1%	9 8.1%	10 15.0%	2 4.9%	0 0	11 12.8%I	9 14.5%I	1 10.3%	6 18.2%I	* 6.7%	0 0	20 9.4%	8 10.5%

Proportions/Means: Columns Tested (5% risk level) - A/B/D - C/D - E/F/G - H/I/J/K/L/M/N - P/Q
* small base; ** very small base (under 30) ineligible for sig testing

Table 249
Page 986

Outsell/Digital Library Federation Study (2002)
Weighted Tables

TABLE 113, continued

T7sum_9. Online databases, data sets or data sources SUMMARY TABLE

	RESPONDENT TYPE					INSTITUTION TYPE			DISCIPLINE									GENDER	
	TOTAL SAMPLE	FACULTY MEMBER	GRAD. STUDENT	FACULTY /GRAD	UNDER GRAD. STUDENT	PUBLIC	PRIVATE	LIBERAL ARTS	BIOLOGIAL SCIENCES	PHYSICAL SCIENCES /MATH	SOCIAL SCIENCES	ARTS AND HUMAN.	ENGI- NEERING	BUSINESS	LAW	UNDEC. MAJOR	MALE	FEMALE
		(A)	(B)	(C)	(D)	(E)	(F)	(G)	(H)	(I)	(J)	(K)	(L)	(M)	(N)		(P)	(Q)
Base - USe Online databases, data sets or data sources for teaching	296	222	74*	296	0**	110*	117*	68*	36*	68*	88*	62*	8**	31*	3**	0*	217	79*
All sources of info	29 9.7%	21 9.5%	8 10.2%	29 9.7%	0 0	9 8.1%	9 8.1%	10 15.0%	2 4.9%	0 0	11 12.8%I	9 14.5%I	1 10.3%	6 18.2%I	* 6.7%	0 0	20 9.4%	8 10.5%
preferred source of info	17 5.9%	14 6.3%	3 4.6%	17 5.9%	0 0	7 6.1%	4 3.6%	7 9.6%	2 4.9%	0 0	8 8.5%I	4 7.3%I	1 10.3%	3 9.1%I	0 0	0 0	14 6.5%	3 4.2%
Online reference service	9 3.1%	9 4.1%	0 0	9 3.1%	0 0	* 0.3%	7 6.0%E	2 2.7%	0 0	2 2.9%	4 4.3%	0 0	* 3.4%	3 9.1%K	* 13.3%	0 0	8 3.8%	1 1.2%
All sources of info	9 3.1%	9 4.1%	0 0	9 3.1%	0 0	* 0.3%	7 6.0%E	2 2.7%	0 0	2 2.9%	4 4.3%	0 0	* 3.4%	3 9.1%K	* 13.3%	0 0	8 3.8%	1 1.2%
preferred source of info	5 1.8%	5 2.3%	0 0	5 1.8%	0 0	* 0.2%	4 3.5%	1 1.4%	0 0	1 1.5%	2 2.1%	0 0	* 3.4%	2 6.1%	* 6.7%	0 0	4 2.0%	1 1.2%
Online abstracting and indexing services	7 2.3%	7 3.0%	0 0	7 2.3%	0 0	1 0.7%	1 1.0%	5 7.1%EF	2 4.9%	2 2.9%	0 0	2 3.6%	1 6.9%	0 0	* 6.7%	0 0	5 2.1%	2 2.7%
All sources of info	7 2.3%	7 3.0%	0 0	7 2.3%	0 0	1 0.7%	1 1.0%	5 7.1%EF	2 4.9%	2 2.9%	0 0	2 3.6%	1 6.9%	0 0	* 6.7%	0 0	5 2.1%	2 2.7%
preferred source of info	2 0.5%	2 0.7%	0 0	2 0.5%	0 0	* 0.4%	1 1.0%	0 0	0 0	0 0	0 0	1 1.8%	* 3.4%	0 0	* 6.7%	0 0	* 0.1%	1 1.6%
Department web page	6 2.0%	0 0	6 8.2%A	6 2.0%	0 0	4 3.4%	2 1.9%	0 0	0 0	2 2.9%	2 2.1%	0 0	* 3.4%	2 6.1%	0 0	0 0	3 1.5%	3 3.5%

Proportions/Means: Columns Tested (5% risk level) - A/B/D - C/D - E/F/G - H/I/J/K/L/M/N - P/Q
* small base; ** very small base (under 30) ineligible for sig testing

Table 249
Page 987

Outsell/Digital Library Federation Study (2002)
Weighted Tables

TABLE 113, continued

T7sum_9. Online databases, data sets or data sources SUMMARY TABLE

		RESPONDENT TYPE				INSTITUTION TYPE			DISCIPLINE									GENDER	
	TOTAL SAMPLE	FACULTY MEMBER	GRAD. STUDENT	FACULTY /GRAD	UNDER GRAD. STUDENT	PUBLIC	PRIVATE	LIBERAL ARTS	BIOLOGIAL SCIENCES	PHYSICAL SCIENCES /MATH	SOCIAL SCIENCES	ARTS AND HUMAN.	ENGI- NEERING	BUSINESS	LAW	UNDEC. MAJOR	MALE	FEMALE
		(A)	(B)	(C)	(D)	(E)	(F)	(G)	(H)	(I)	(J)	(K)	(L)	(M)	(N)		(P)	(Q)
Base - USe Online databases, data sets or data sources for teaching	296	222	74*	296	0**	110*	117*	68*	36*	68*	88*	62*	8**	31*	3**	0*	217	79*
All sources of info	6 2.0%	0 0	6 8.2%A	6 2.0%	0 0	4 3.4%	2 1.9%	0 0	0 0	2 2.9%	2 2.1%	0 0	* 3.4%	2 6.1%	0 0	0 0	3 1.5%	3 3.5%
preferred source of info	2 0.8%	0 0	2 3.0%A	2 0.8%	0 0	2 1.7%	* 0.2%	0 0	0 0	1 1.5%	0 0	0 0	* 3.4%	1 3.0%	0 0	0 0	1 0.6%	1 1.2%
Your own personal electronic library/files	5 1.7%	5 2.3%	0 0	5 1.7%	0 0	2 2.0%	3 2.5%	0 0	0 0	2 2.9%	2 2.1%	0 0	* 3.4%	1 3.0%	0 0	0 0	4 1.8%	1 1.6%
All sources of info	5 1.7%	5 2.3%	0 0	5 1.7%	0 0	2 2.0%	3 2.5%	0 0	0 0	2 2.9%	2 2.1%	0 0	* 3.4%	1 3.0%	0 0	0 0	4 1.8%	1 1.6%
preferred source of info	* 0.1%	* 0.1%	0 0	* 0.1%	0 0	* 0.3%	0 0	0 0	0 0	0 0	0 0	0 0	* 3.4%	0 0	0 0	0 0	0 0	* 0.4%
Online bookstore	3 1.0%	3 1.3%	0 0	3 1.0%	0 0	0 0	2 1.6%	1 1.4%	0 0	0 0	2 2.1%	0 0	0 0	1 3.0%	0 0	0 0	3 1.3%	0 0
All sources of info	3 1.0%	3 1.3%	0 0	3 1.0%	0 0	0 0	2 1.6%	1 1.4%	0 0	0 0	2 2.1%	0 0	0 0	1 3.0%	0 0	0 0	3 1.3%	0 0
preferred source of info	0 0	0 0	0 0	0 0	0 0	0 0	0 0	0 0	0 0	0 0	0 0	0 0	0 0	0 0	0 0	0 0	0 0	0 0
E-mail listservs	0 0	0 0	0 0	0 0	0 0	0 0	0 0	0 0	0 0	0 0	0 0	0 0	0 0	0 0	0 0	0 0	0 0	0 0

Proportions/Means: Columns Tested (5% risk level) - A/B/D - C/D - E/F/G - H/I/J/K/L/M/N - P/Q
* small base; ** very small base (under 30) ineligible for sig testing

Table 249
Page 988

Outsell/Digital Library Federation Study (2002)
Weighted Tables

TABLE 113, continued

T7sum_9. Online databases, data sets or data sources SUMMARY TABLE

		RESPONDENT TYPE				INSTITUTION TYPE			DISCIPLINE									GENDER	
	TOTAL SAMPLE	FACULTY MEMBER	GRAD. STUDENT	FACULTY /GRAD	UNDER GRAD. STUDENT	PUBLIC	PRIVATE	LIBERAL ARTS	BIOLOGIAL SCIENCES	PHYSICAL SCIENCES /MATH	SOCIAL SCIENCES	ARTS AND HUMAN.	ENGI-NEERING	BUSINESS	LAW	UNDEC. MAJOR	MALE	FEMALE
		(A)	(B)	(C)	(D)	(E)	(F)	(G)	(H)	(I)	(J)	(K)	(L)	(M)	(N)		(P)	(Q)
Base - USe Online databases, data sets or data sources for teaching	296	222	74*	296	0**	110*	117*	68*	36*	68*	88*	62*	8**	31*	3**	0*	217	79*
All sources of info	0 0	0 0	0 0	0 0	0 0	0 0	0 0	0 0	0 0	0 0	0 0	0 0	0 0	0 0	0 0	0 0	0 0	0 0
preferred source of info	0 0	0 0	0 0	0 0	0 0	0 0	0 0	0 0	0 0	0 0	0 0	0 0	0 0	0 0	0 0	0 0	0 0	0 0
LIBRARY/PRINT	115 39.0%	94 42.3%	21 28.9%	115 39.0%	0 0	40 36.2%	42 35.6%	34 49.3%	14 39.0%	27 39.7%	30 34.0%	30 49.1%	3 31.0%	10 33.3%	1 40.0%	0 0	91 42.1%	24 30.3%
Campus library	86 29.0%	69 31.0%	17 23.2%	86 29.0%	0 0	30 27.5%	32 27.1%	24 34.8%	12 34.1%	18 26.5%	24 27.7%	21 34.5%	3 31.0%	7 21.2%	1 26.7%	0 0	64 29.5%	22 27.8%
All sources of info	86 29.0%	69 31.0%	17 23.2%	86 29.0%	0 0	30 27.5%	32 27.1%	24 34.8%	12 34.1%	18 26.5%	24 27.7%	21 34.5%	3 31.0%	7 21.2%	1 26.7%	0 0	64 29.5%	22 27.8%
preferred source of info	25 8.5%	17 7.8%	8 10.3%	25 8.5%	0 0	9 8.2%	9 7.4%	7 10.7%	4 9.8%	7 10.3%	8 8.5%	6 9.1%	* 3.4%	1 3.0%	* 6.7%	0 0	19 8.8%	6 7.6%
Your own personal physical library/ files/bookshelves	19 6.5%	19 8.7%B	0 0	19 6.5%	0 0	7 6.7%	5 4.2%	7 10.1%	3 7.3%	4 5.9%	4 4.3%	6 9.1%	* 3.4%	3 9.1%	* 6.7%	0 0	14 6.6%	5 6.3%
All sources of info	19 6.5%	19 8.7%B	0 0	19 6.5%	0 0	7 6.7%	5 4.2%	7 10.1%	3 7.3%	4 5.9%	4 4.3%	6 9.1%	* 3.4%	3 9.1%	* 6.7%	0 0	14 6.6%	5 6.3%
preferred source of info	5 1.6%	5 2.2%	0 0	5 1.6%	0 0	1 0.8%	1 1.0%	3 4.1%	0 0	0 0	2 2.1%	1 1.8%	0 0	2 6.1%I	0 0	0 0	3 1.4%	2 2.3%

Proportions/Means: Columns Tested (5% risk level) - A/B/D - C/D - E/F/G - H/I/J/K/L/M/N - P/Q
* small base; ** very small base (under 30) ineligible for sig testing

Table 249
Page 989

Outsell/Digital Library Federation Study (2002)
Weighted Tables

TABLE 113, continued

T7sum_9. Online databases, data sets or data sources SUMMARY TABLE

		RESPONDENT TYPE				INSTITUTION TYPE			DISCIPLINE									GENDER	
	TOTAL SAMPLE	FACULTY MEMBER	GRAD. STUDENT	FACULTY /GRAD	UNDER GRAD. STUDENT	PUBLIC	PRIVATE	LIBERAL ARTS	BIOLOGIAL SCIENCES	PHYSICAL SCIENCES /MATH	SOCIAL SCIENCES	ARTS AND HUMAN.	ENGI-NEERING	BUSINESS	LAW	UNDEC. MAJOR	MALE	FEMALE
		(A)	(B)	(C)	(D)	(E)	(F)	(G)	(H)	(I)	(J)	(K)	(L)	(M)	(N)		(P)	(Q)
Base - USe Online databases, data sets or data sources for teaching	296	222	74*	296	0**	110*	117*	68*	36*	68*	88*	62*	8**	31*	3**	0*	217	79*
References cited in books or journal articles	17 5.8%	14 6.3%	3 4.4%	17 5.8%	0 0	8 7.4%	4 3.5%	5 7.3%	1 2.4%	7 10.3%	4 4.3%	6 9.1%	0 0	0 0	0 0	0 0	16 7.6%	1 1.1%
All sources of info	17 5.8%	14 6.3%	3 4.4%	17 5.8%	0 0	8 7.4%	4 3.5%	5 7.3%	1 2.4%	7 10.3%	4 4.3%	6 9.1%	0 0	0 0	0 0	0 0	16 7.6%	1 1.1%
preferred source of info	5 1.8%	3 1.4%	2 2.9%	5 1.8%	0 0	2 1.9%	2 1.8%	1 1.5%	0 0	3 4.4%	0 0	2 3.6%	0 0	0 0	0 0	0 0	5 2.4%	0 0
Personal subscriptions to newspapers, magazines and journals	16 5.5%	15 6.8%	1 1.4%	16 5.5%	0 0	6 5.6%	6 4.9%	4 6.1%	1 2.4%	5 7.4%	4 4.3%	4 7.3%	0 0	2 6.1%	* 6.7%	0 0	14 6.5%	2 2.5%
All sources of info	16 5.5%	15 6.8%	1 1.4%	16 5.5%	0 0	6 5.6%	6 4.9%	4 6.1%	1 2.4%	5 7.4%	4 4.3%	4 7.3%	0 0	2 6.1%	* 6.7%	0 0	14 6.5%	2 2.5%
preferred source of info	2 0.7%	1 0.5%	1 1.4%	2 0.7%	0 0	0 0	2 1.7%	0 0	0 0	2 2.9%	0 0	0 0	0 0	0 0	0 0	0 0	2 0.9%	0 0
Another library	7 2.3%	7 3.0%	0 0	7 2.3%	0 0	2 1.7%	5 4.2%	0 0	0 0	0 0	6 6.4%	1 1.8%	0 0	0 0	0 0	0 0	7 3.1%	0 0
All sources of info	7 2.3%	7 3.0%	0 0	7 2.3%	0 0	2 1.7%	5 4.2%	0 0	0 0	0 0	6 6.4%	1 1.8%	0 0	0 0	0 0	0 0	7 3.1%	0 0

Proportions/Means: Columns Tested (5% risk level) - A/B/D - C/D - E/F/G - H/I/J/K/L/M/N - P/Q
* small base; ** very small base (under 30) ineligible for sig testing

Table 249
Page 990

Outsell/Digital Library Federation Study (2002)
Weighted Tables

TABLE 113, continued

T7sum_9. Online databases, data sets or data sources SUMMARY TABLE

		RESPONDENT TYPE				INSTITUTION TYPE			DISCIPLINE									GENDER	
	TOTAL SAMPLE	FACULTY MEMBER	GRAD. STUDENT	FACULTY /GRAD	UNDER GRAD. STUDENT	PUBLIC	PRIVATE	LIBERAL ARTS	BIOLOGIAL SCIENCES	PHYSICAL SCIENCES /MATH	SOCIAL SCIENCES	ARTS AND HUMAN.	ENGI-NEERING	BUSINESS	LAW	UNDEC. MAJOR	MALE	FEMALE
		(A)	(B)	(C)	(D)	(E)	(F)	(G)	(H)	(I)	(J)	(K)	(L)	(M)	(N)		(P)	(Q)
Base - USe Online databases, data sets or data sources for teaching	296	222	74*	296	0**	110*	117*	68*	36*	68*	88*	62*	8**	31*	3**	0*	217	79*
preferred source of info	0 0	0 0	0 0	0 0	0 0	0 0	0 0	0 0	0 0	0 0	0 0	0 0	0 0	0 0	0 0	0 0	0 0	0 0
Physical bookstore	4 1.3%	3 1.3%	1 1.5%	4 1.3%	0 0	0 0	3 2.6%	1 1.4%	0 0	0 0	2 2.1%	1 1.8%	0 0	1 3.0%	0 0	0 0	4 1.8%	0 0
All sources of info	4 1.3%	3 1.3%	1 1.5%	4 1.3%	0 0	0 0	3 2.6%	1 1.4%	0 0	0 0	2 2.1%	1 1.8%	0 0	1 3.0%	0 0	0 0	4 1.8%	0 0
preferred source of info	1 0.4%	0 0	1 1.5%	1 0.4%	0 0	0 0	1 1.0%	0 0	0 0	0 0	0 0	1 1.8%	0 0	0 0	0 0	0 0	1 0.5%	0 0
Printed abstracting and indexing services	3 1.0%	3 1.4%	0 0	3 1.0%	0 0	* 0.2%	2 1.6%	1 1.5%	1 2.4%	2 2.9%	0 0	0 0	0 0	0 0	* 6.7%	0 0	3 1.3%	* 0.2%
All sources of info	3 1.0%	3 1.4%	0 0	3 1.0%	0 0	* 0.2%	2 1.6%	1 1.5%	1 2.4%	2 2.9%	0 0	0 0	0 0	0 0	* 6.7%	0 0	3 1.3%	* 0.2%
preferred source of info	2 0.6%	2 0.8%	0 0	2 0.6%	0 0	0 0	2 1.6%	0 0	1 2.4%	1 1.5%	0 0	0 0	0 0	0 0	0 0	0 0	2 0.9%	0 0
Printed library catalogues and finding aids	1 0.4%	1 0.6%	0 0	1 0.4%	0 0	* 0.3%	0 0	1 1.4%	0 0	0 0	0 0	0 0	0 0	1 3.0%	* 13.3%	0 0	1 0.5%	* 0.2%
All sources of info	1 0.4%	1 0.6%	0 0	1 0.4%	0 0	* 0.3%	0 0	1 1.4%	0 0	0 0	0 0	0 0	0 0	1 3.0%	* 13.3%	0 0	1 0.5%	* 0.2%

Proportions/Means: Columns Tested (5% risk level) - A/B/D - C/D - E/F/G - H/I/J/K/L/M/N - P/Q
* small base; ** very small base (under 30) ineligible for sig testing

Table 249
Page 991

Outsell/Digital Library Federation Study (2002)
Weighted Tables

TABLE 113, continued

T7sum_9. Online databases, data sets or data sources SUMMARY TABLE

		RESPONDENT TYPE				INSTITUTION TYPE			DISCIPLINE								GENDER	
	TOTAL SAMPLE	FACULTY MEMBER	GRAD. STUDENT	FACULTY /GRAD	UNDER GRAD. STUDENT	PUBLIC	PRIVATE	LIBERAL ARTS	BIOLOGIAL SCIENCES	PHYSICAL SCIENCES /MATH	SOCIAL SCIENCES	ARTS AND HUMAN.	ENGI- NEERING	BUSINESS	LAW	UNDEC. MAJOR	MALE	FEMALE
		(A)	(B)	(C)	(D)	(E)	(F)	(G)	(H)	(I)	(J)	(K)	(L)	(M)	(N)		(P)	(Q)
Base - USe Online databases, data sets or data sources for teaching	296	222	74*	296	0**	110*	117*	68*	36*	68*	88*	62*	8**	31*	3**	0*	217	79*
preferred source of info	* 0.1%	* 0.1%	0 0	* 0.1%	0 0	* 0.2%	0 0	0 0	0 0	0 0	0 0	0 0	0 0	0 0	* 6.7%	0 0	* 0.1%	0 0
PERSONAL ASSISTANCE	76 25.6%	56 25.4%	19 26.1%	76 25.6%	0 0	26 24.0%	27 22.7%	23 32.9%	9 24.4%	13 19.1%	17 19.1%	22 36.4%I	3 31.0%	11 36.4%	1 26.7%	0 0	56 25.8%	20 24.9%
Colleagues inside your institution	52 17.7%	35 15.6%	18 24.2%	52 17.7%	0 0	21 19.2%	19 15.9%	13 18.5%	6 17.1%	10 14.7%	11 12.8%	16 25.5%	2 20.7%	7 24.2%	* 6.7%	0 0	35 16.1%	18 22.1%
All sources of info	52 17.7%	35 15.6%	18 24.2%	52 17.7%	0 0	21 19.2%	19 15.9%	13 18.5%	6 17.1%	10 14.7%	11 12.8%	16 25.5%	2 20.7%	7 24.2%	* 6.7%	0 0	35 16.1%	18 22.1%
preferred source of info	14 4.8%	6 2.8%	8 11.0%A	14 4.8%	0 0	7 6.2%	6 4.8%	2 2.7%	3 7.3%	3 4.4%	2 2.1%	6 9.1%	* 3.4%	1 3.0%	0 0	0 0	7 3.3%	7 9.1%
A librarian in your institution	35 12.0%	32 14.3%	4 4.9%	35 12.0%	0 0	8 7.5%	13 11.4%	14 20.1%E	3 7.3%	5 7.4%	8 8.5%	12 20.0%I	1 10.3%	7 21.2%I	1 20.0%	0 0	30 13.8%	5 6.8%
All sources of info	35 12.0%	32 14.3%	4 4.9%	35 12.0%	0 0	8 7.5%	13 11.4%	14 20.1%E	3 7.3%	5 7.4%	8 8.5%	12 20.0%I	1 10.3%	7 21.2%I	1 20.0%	0 0	30 13.8%	5 6.8%
preferred source of info	6 2.1%	4 1.7%	2 3.0%	6 2.1%	0 0	2 2.2%	1 0.8%	3 4.0%	1 2.4%	0 0	2 2.1%	2 3.6%	0 0	1 3.0%	* 6.7%	0 0	4 1.8%	2 2.8%
Colleagues outside your institution	15 5.2%	14 6.5%	1 1.4%	15 5.2%	0 0	3 2.9%	5 4.4%	7 10.1%	2 4.9%	5 7.4%J	0 0	6 9.1%J	0 0	3 9.1%J	* 6.7%	0 0	13 6.2%	2 2.4%

Proportions/Means: Columns Tested (5% risk level) - A/B/D - C/D - E/F/G - H/I/J/K/L/M/N - P/Q
* small base; ** very small base (under 30) ineligible for sig testing

Table 249
Page 992

Outsell/Digital Library Federation Study (2002)
Weighted Tables

TABLE 113, continued

T7sum_9. Online databases, data sets or data sources SUMMARY TABLE

		RESPONDENT TYPE				INSTITUTION TYPE			DISCIPLINE									GENDER	
	TOTAL SAMPLE	FACULTY MEMBER	GRAD. STUDENT	FACULTY /GRAD	UNDER GRAD. STUDENT	PUBLIC	PRIVATE	LIBERAL ARTS	BIOLOGIAL SCIENCES	PHYSICAL SCIENCES /MATH	SOCIAL SCIENCES	ARTS AND HUMAN.	ENGI-NEERING	BUSINESS	LAW	UNDEC. MAJOR	MALE	FEMALE
		(A)	(B)	(C)	(D)	(E)	(F)	(G)	(H)	(I)	(J)	(K)	(L)	(M)	(N)		(P)	(Q)
Base - USe Online databases, data sets or data sources for teaching	296	222	74*	296	0**	110*	117*	68*	36*	68*	88*	62*	8**	31*	3**	0*	217	79*
All sources of info	15 5.2%	14 6.5%	1 1.4%	15 5.2%	0 0	3 2.9%	5 4.4%	7 10.1%	2 4.9%	5 7.4%J	0 0	6 9.1%J	0 0	3 9.1%J	* 6.7%	0 0	13 6.2%	2 2.4%
preferred source of info	2 0.7%	2 1.0%	0 0	2 0.7%	0 0	0 0	1 0.9%	1 1.6%	0 0	1 1.5%	0 0	1 1.8%	0 0	0 0	0 0	0 0	2 1.0%	0 0
Professional meetings	4 1.3%	4 1.7%	0 0	4 1.3%	0 0	3 2.7%	1 0.8%	0 0	1 2.4%	2 2.9%	0 0	0 0	0 0	1 3.0%	0 0	0 0	4 1.8%	0 0
All sources of info	4 1.3%	4 1.7%	0 0	4 1.3%	0 0	3 2.7%	1 0.8%	0 0	1 2.4%	2 2.9%	0 0	0 0	0 0	1 3.0%	0 0	0 0	4 1.8%	0 0
preferred source of info	1 0.3%	1 0.5%	0 0	1 0.3%	0 0	1 0.9%	0 0	0 0	0 0	1 1.5%	0 0	0 0	0 0	0 0	0 0	0 0	1 0.5%	0 0
Another institution's librarian	0 0	0 0	0 0	0 0	0 0	0 0	0 0	0 0	0 0	0 0	0 0	0 0	0 0	0 0	0 0	0 0	0 0	0 0
All sources of info	0 0	0 0	0 0	0 0	0 0	0 0	0 0	0 0	0 0	0 0	0 0	0 0	0 0	0 0	0 0	0 0	0 0	0 0
preferred source of info	0 0	0 0	0 0	0 0	0 0	0 0	0 0	0 0	0 0	0 0	0 0	0 0	0 0	0 0	0 0	0 0	0 0	0 0
Online (unspecified)	3 0.9%	3 1.2%	0 0	3 0.9%	0 0	0 0	3 2.4%	0 0	1 2.4%	0 0	2 2.1%	0 0	0 0	0 0	0 0	0 0	2 0.9%	1 1.1%

Proportions/Means: Columns Tested (5% risk level) - A/B/D - C/D - E/F/G - H/I/J/K/L/M/N - P/Q
* small base; ** very small base (under 30) ineligible for sig testing

Table 249
Page 993

Outsell/Digital Library Federation Study (2002)
Weighted Tables

TABLE 113, continued

T7sum_9. Online databases, data sets or data sources SUMMARY TABLE

		RESPONDENT TYPE				INSTITUTION TYPE			DISCIPLINE								GENDER	
	TOTAL SAMPLE	FACULTY MEMBER	GRAD. STUDENT	FACULTY /GRAD	UNDER GRAD. STUDENT	PUBLIC	PRIVATE	LIBERAL ARTS	BIOLOGIAL SCIENCES	PHYSICAL SCIENCES /MATH	SOCIAL SCIENCES	ARTS AND HUMAN.	ENGI-NEERING	BUSINESS	LAW	UNDEC. MAJOR	MALE	FEMALE
		(A)	(B)	(C)	(D)	(E)	(F)	(G)	(H)	(I)	(J)	(K)	(L)	(M)	(N)		(P)	(Q)
Base - USe Online databases, data sets or data sources for teaching	296	222	74*	296	0**	110*	117*	68*	36*	68*	88*	62*	8**	31*	3**	0*	217	79*
All sources of info	3 0.9%	3 1.2%	0 0	3 0.9%	0 0	0 0	3 2.4%	0 0	1 2.4%	0 0	2 2.1%	0 0	0 0	0 0	0 0	0 0	2 0.9%	1 1.1%
preferred source of info	0 0	0 0	0 0	0 0	0 0	0 0	0 0	0 0	0 0	0 0	0 0	0 0	0 0	0 0	0 0	0 0	0 0	0 0
Personal office/lab	2 0.8%	2 1.0%	0 0	2 0.8%	0 0	0 0	1 1.0%	1 1.6%	0 0	0 0	0 0	2 3.6%	0 0	0 0	0 0	0 0	2 1.0%	0 0
All sources of info	2 0.8%	2 1.0%	0 0	2 0.8%	0 0	0 0	1 1.0%	1 1.6%	0 0	0 0	0 0	2 3.6%	0 0	0 0	0 0	0 0	2 1.0%	0 0
preferred source of info	1 0.4%	1 0.5%	0 0	1 0.4%	0 0	0 0	1 1.0%	0 0	0 0	0 0	0 0	1 1.8%	0 0	0 0	0 0	0 0	1 0.5%	0 0
Students	0 0	0 0	0 0	0 0	0 0	0 0	0 0	0 0	0 0	0 0	0 0	0 0	0 0	0 0	0 0	0 0	0 0	0 0
All sources of info	0 0	0 0	0 0	0 0	0 0	0 0	0 0	0 0	0 0	0 0	0 0	0 0	0 0	0 0	0 0	0 0	0 0	0 0
preferred source of info	0 0	0 0	0 0	0 0	0 0	0 0	0 0	0 0	0 0	0 0	0 0	0 0	0 0	0 0	0 0	0 0	0 0	0 0
Author	0 0	0 0	0 0	0 0	0 0	0 0	0 0	0 0	0 0	0 0	0 0	0 0	0 0	0 0	0 0	0 0	0 0	0 0

Proportions/Means: Columns Tested (5% risk level) - A/B/D - C/D - E/F/G - H/I/J/K/L/M/N - P/Q
* small base; ** very small base (under 30) ineligible for sig testing

Table 249
Page 994

Outsell/Digital Library Federation Study (2002)
Weighted Tables

TABLE 113, continued

T7sum_9. Online databases, data sets or data sources SUMMARY TABLE

		RESPONDENT TYPE				INSTITUTION TYPE			DISCIPLINE								GENDER	
	TOTAL SAMPLE	FACULTY MEMBER	GRAD. STUDENT	FACULTY /GRAD	UNDER GRAD. STUDENT	PUBLIC	PRIVATE	LIBERAL ARTS	BIOLOGIAL SCIENCES	PHYSICAL SCIENCES /MATH	SOCIAL SCIENCES	ARTS AND HUMAN.	ENGI-NEERING	BUSINESS	LAW	UNDEC. MAJOR	MALE	FEMALE
		(A)	(B)	(C)	(D)	(E)	(F)	(G)	(H)	(I)	(J)	(K)	(L)	(M)	(N)		(P)	(Q)
Base - USe Online databases, data sets or data sources for teaching	296	222	74*	296	0**	110*	117*	68*	36*	68*	88*	62*	8**	31*	3**	0*	217	79*
All sources of info	0 0	0 0	0 0	0 0	0 0	0 0	0 0	0 0	0 0	0 0	0 0	0 0	0 0	0 0	0 0	0 0	0 0	0 0
preferred source of info	0 0	0 0	0 0	0 0	0 0	0 0	0 0	0 0	0 0	0 0	0 0	0 0	0 0	0 0	0 0	0 0	0 0	0 0
Other	33 11.2%	23 10.3%	10 14.0%	33 11.2%	0 0	13 11.7%	16 13.3%	5 6.8%	2 4.9%	7 10.3%	13 14.9%	6 9.1%	1 6.9%	5 15.2%	* 13.3%	0 0	23 10.7%	10 12.6%
All sources of info	29 9.9%	23 10.3%	7 8.9%	29 9.9%	0 0	11 10.0%	14 11.7%	5 6.8%	2 4.9%	7 10.3%	9 10.6%	6 9.1%	1 6.9%	5 15.2%	* 13.3%	0 0	23 10.7%	6 7.9%
preferred source of info	14 4.6%	8 3.4%	6 8.2%	14 4.6%	0 0	4 3.8%	7 5.7%	3 4.1%	2 4.9%	3 4.4%	8 8.5%	0 0	* 3.4%	1 3.0%	* 6.7%	0 0	9 4.1%	5 6.0%
DK/Refused	25 8.5%	21 9.7%	4 5.1%	25 8.5%	0 0	10 8.9%	9 7.3%	7 10.0%	4 12.2%	5 7.4%	9 10.6%	3 5.5%	* 3.4%	3 9.1%	0 0	0 0	17 7.6%	9 11.0%

Proportions/Means: Columns Tested (5% risk level) - A/B/D - C/D - E/F/G - H/I/J/K/L/M/N - P/Q
* small base; ** very small base (under 30) ineligible for sig testing

Table 249
Page 995

TABLE 114

T7D/E_9. Online databases, data sets or data sources SUMMARY TABLE

	RESPONDENT TYPE				INSTITUTION TYPE			DISCIPLINE								GENDER	
	TOTAL SAMPLE	FACULTY MEMBER	GRAD. STUDENT	FACULTY /GRAD	UNDER GRAD. STUDENT	PUBLIC	PRIVATE	LIBERAL ARTS	BIOLOGIAL SCIENCES	PHYSICAL SCIENCES /MATH	SOCIAL SCIENCES	ARTS AND HUMAN.	ENGI- NEERING	BUSINESS	LAW	UNDEC. MAJOR	MALE	FEMALE
		(A)	(B)	(C)	(D)	(E)	(F)	(G)	(H)	(I)	(J)	(K)	(L)	(M)	(N)		(P)	(Q)
Base - Use Online databases, data sets or data sources for teaching	296	222	74*	296	0**	110*	117*	68*	36*	68*	88*	62*	8**	31*	3**	0*	217	79*
Access online (NET)	235 79.5%	185 83.6%B	50 67.5%	235 79.5%	0 0	88 79.4%	93 79.7%	54 79.5%	29 80.5%	57 83.8%	71 80.9%	44 70.9%	8 93.1%	24 78.8%	2 80.0%	0 0	173 79.8%	62 78.9%
All sources of info	235 79.5%	185 83.6%B	50 67.5%	235 79.5%	0 0	88 79.4%	93 79.7%	54 79.5%	29 80.5%	57 83.8%	71 80.9%	44 70.9%	8 93.1%	24 78.8%	2 80.0%	0 0	173 79.8%	62 78.9%
preferred source of info	216 73.0%	171 77.3%B	45 60.2%	216 73.0%	0 0	76 68.4%	90 77.2%	50 73.4%	28 78.0%	50 73.5%	70 78.7%K	37 60.0%	7 82.8%	22 72.7%	2 80.0%	0 0	162 74.7%	54 68.6%
Borrow from or use in campus library (NET)	86 29.2%	57 25.8%	29 39.6%A	86 29.2%	0 0	38 34.4%	26 21.9%	23 33.5%	10 26.8%	20 29.4%	23 25.5%	22 36.4%	3 31.0%	8 27.3%	1 33.3%	0 0	59 27.0%	28 35.2%
All sources of info	86 29.2%	57 25.8%	29 39.6%A	86 29.2%	0 0	38 34.4%	26 21.9%	23 33.5%	10 26.8%	20 29.4%	23 25.5%	22 36.4%	3 31.0%	8 27.3%	1 33.3%	0 0	59 27.0%	28 35.2%
preferred source of info	40 13.5%	23 10.5%	17 22.7%A	40 13.5%	0 0	15 13.8%	13 10.8%	12 17.8%	4 12.2%	10 14.7%	9 10.6%	12 20.0%	0 0	4 12.1%	* 6.7%	0 0	27 12.5%	13 16.3%
Personal Collection/ Holdings (NET)	5 1.8%	5 2.4%	0 0	5 1.8%	0 0	1 1.0%	2 1.7%	2 3.1%	0 0	3 4.4%	0 0	2 3.6%	0 0	0 0	0 0	0 0	3 1.4%	2 2.8%
All sources of info	5 1.8%	5 2.4%	0 0	5 1.8%	0 0	1 1.0%	2 1.7%	2 3.1%	0 0	3 4.4%	0 0	2 3.6%	0 0	0 0	0 0	0 0	3 1.4%	2 2.8%
preferred source of info	1 0.3%	1 0.5%	0 0	1 0.3%	0 0	0 0	1 0.9%	0 0	0 0	1 1.5%	0 0	0 0	0 0	0 0	0 0	0 0	1 0.5%	0 0

Proportions/Means: Columns Tested (5% risk level) - A/B/D - C/D - E/F/G - H/I/J/K/L/M/N - P/Q
* small base; ** very small base (under 30) ineligible for sig testing

Table 252
Page 1002

Outsell/Digital Library Federation Study (2002)
Weighted Tables

TABLE 114, continued

T7D/E_9. Online databases, data sets or data sources SUMMARY TABLE

		RESPONDENT TYPE				INSTITUTION TYPE			DISCIPLINE								GENDER	
	TOTAL SAMPLE	FACULTY MEMBER	GRAD. STUDENT	FACULTY /GRAD	UNDER GRAD. STUDENT	PUBLIC	PRIVATE	LIBERAL ARTS	BIOLOGIAL SCIENCES	PHYSICAL SCIENCES /MATH	SOCIAL SCIENCES	ARTS AND HUMAN.	ENGI-NEERING	BUSINESS	LAW	UNDEC. MAJOR	MALE	FEMALE
		(A)	(B)	(C)	(D)	(E)	(F)	(G)	(H)	(I)	(J)	(K)	(L)	(M)	(N)		(P)	(Q)
Base - Use Online databases, data sets or data sources for teaching	296	222	74*	296	0**	110*	117*	68*	36*	68*	88*	62*	8**	31*	3**	0*	217	79*
Colleagues (NET)	4 1.4%	1 0.4%	3 4.4%A	4 1.4%	0 0	1 1.0%	3 2.6%	0 0	0 0	1 1.5%	0 0	2 3.6%	0 0	1 3.0%	0 0	0 0	2 0.9%	2 2.8%
All sources of info	4 1.4%	1 0.4%	3 4.4%A	4 1.4%	0 0	1 1.0%	3 2.6%	0 0	0 0	1 1.5%	0 0	2 3.6%	0 0	1 3.0%	0 0	0 0	2 0.9%	2 2.8%
preferred source of info	4 1.4%	1 0.4%	3 4.4%A	4 1.4%	0 0	1 1.0%	3 2.6%	0 0	0 0	1 1.5%	0 0	2 3.6%	0 0	1 3.0%	0 0	0 0	2 0.9%	2 2.8%
Publisher (NET)	4 1.4%	4 1.9%	0 0	4 1.4%	0 0	1 1.1%	1 0.8%	2 3.0%	1 2.4%	0 0	0 0	1 1.8%	* 3.4%	2 6.1%IJ	0 0	0 0	3 1.5%	1 1.2%
All sources of info	4 1.4%	4 1.9%	0 0	4 1.4%	0 0	1 1.1%	1 0.8%	2 3.0%	1 2.4%	0 0	0 0	1 1.8%	* 3.4%	2 6.1%IJ	0 0	0 0	3 1.5%	1 1.2%
preferred source of info	4 1.4%	4 1.9%	0 0	4 1.4%	0 0	1 1.1%	1 0.8%	2 3.0%	1 2.4%	0 0	0 0	1 1.8%	* 3.4%	2 6.1%IJ	0 0	0 0	3 1.5%	1 1.2%
Borrow from or use in other libraries (NET)	4 1.4%	1 0.5%	3 3.9%	4 1.4%	0 0	3 2.6%	* 0.1%	1 1.5%	0 0	2 2.9%	2 2.1%	0 0	0 0	0 0	* 6.7%	0 0	2 0.9%	2 2.6%
All sources of info	4 1.4%	1 0.5%	3 3.9%	4 1.4%	0 0	3 2.6%	* 0.1%	1 1.5%	0 0	2 2.9%	2 2.1%	0 0	0 0	0 0	* 6.7%	0 0	2 0.9%	2 2.6%

Proportions/Means: Columns Tested (5% risk level) - A/B/D - C/D - E/F/G - H/I/J/K/L/M/N - P/Q
* small base; ** very small base (under 30) ineligible for sig testing

Table 252
Page 1003

Outsell/Digital Library Federation Study (2002)
Weighted Tables

TABLE 114, continued

T7D/E_9. Online databases, data sets or data sources SUMMARY TABLE

		RESPONDENT TYPE				INSTITUTION TYPE			DISCIPLINE								GENDER	
	TOTAL SAMPLE	FACULTY MEMBER	GRAD. STUDENT	FACULTY /GRAD	UNDER GRAD. STUDENT	PUBLIC	PRIVATE	LIBERAL ARTS	BIOLOGIAL SCIENCES	PHYSICAL SCIENCES /MATH	SOCIAL SCIENCES	ARTS AND HUMAN.	ENGI-NEERING	BUSINESS	LAW	UNDEC. MAJOR	MALE	FEMALE
		(A)	(B)	(C)	(D)	(E)	(F)	(G)	(H)	(I)	(J)	(K)	(L)	(M)	(N)		(P)	(Q)
Base - Use Online databases, data sets or data sources for teaching	296	222	74*	296	0**	110*	117*	68*	36*	68*	88*	62*	8**	31*	3**	0*	217	79*
preferred source of info	3 1.0%	0 0	3 3.9%A	3 1.0%	0 0	3 2.6%	0 0	0 0	0 0	1 1.5%	2 2.1%	0 0	0 0	0 0	0 0	0 0	1 0.5%	2 2.4%
Purchase from online bookstore (NET)	4 1.3%	4 1.8%	0 0	4 1.3%	0 0	* 0.2%	4 3.2%	0 0	0 0	0 0	4 4.3%	0 0	0 0	0 0	* 6.7%	0 0	4 1.8%	0 0
All sources of info	4 1.3%	4 1.8%	0 0	4 1.3%	0 0	* 0.2%	4 3.2%	0 0	0 0	0 0	4 4.3%	0 0	0 0	0 0	* 6.7%	0 0	4 1.8%	0 0
preferred source of info	0 0	0 0	0 0	0 0	0 0	0 0	0 0	0 0	0 0	0 0	0 0	0 0	0 0	0 0	0 0	0 0	0 0	0 0
Interlibrary loan (NET)	3 1.2%	3 1.6%	0 0	3 1.2%	0 0	1 1.1%	1 1.1%	1 1.4%	0 0	0 0	0 0	1 1.8%	* 3.4%	2 6.1%IJ	* 6.7%	0 0	3 1.5%	* 0.2%
All sources of info	3 1.2%	3 1.6%	0 0	3 1.2%	0 0	1 1.1%	1 1.1%	1 1.4%	0 0	0 0	0 0	1 1.8%	* 3.4%	2 6.1%IJ	* 6.7%	0 0	3 1.5%	* 0.2%
preferred source of info	1 0.4%	1 0.5%	0 0	1 0.4%	0 0	0 0	1 1.0%	0 0	0 0	0 0	0 0	1 1.8%	0 0	0 0	0 0	0 0	1 0.5%	0 0
Access from course website (NET)	3 1.0%	2 0.9%	1 1.3%	3 1.0%	0 0	1 0.9%	1 0.8%	1 1.5%	0 0	2 2.9%	0 0	0 0	0 0	1 3.0%	0 0	0 0	3 1.4%	0 0
All sources of info	3 1.0%	2 0.9%	1 1.3%	3 1.0%	0 0	1 0.9%	1 0.8%	1 1.5%	0 0	2 2.9%	0 0	0 0	0 0	1 3.0%	0 0	0 0	3 1.4%	0 0

Proportions/Means: Columns Tested (5% risk level) - A/B/D - C/D - E/F/G - H/I/J/K/L/M/N - P/Q
* small base; ** very small base (under 30) ineligible for sig testing

Table 252
Page 1004

Outsell/Digital Library Federation Study (2002)
Weighted Tables

TABLE 114, continued

T7D/E_9. Online databases, data sets or data sources SUMMARY TABLE

		RESPONDENT TYPE				INSTITUTION TYPE			DISCIPLINE									GENDER	
	TOTAL SAMPLE	FACULTY MEMBER	GRAD. STUDENT	FACULTY /GRAD	UNDER GRAD. STUDENT	PUBLIC	PRIVATE	LIBERAL ARTS	BIOLOGIAL SCIENCES	PHYSICAL SCIENCES /MATH	SOCIAL SCIENCES	ARTS AND HUMAN.	ENGI- NEERING	BUSINESS	LAW	UNDEC. MAJOR	MALE	FEMALE
		(A)	(B)	(C)	(D)	(E)	(F)	(G)	(H)	(I)	(J)	(K)	(L)	(M)	(N)		(P)	(Q)
Base - Use Online databases, data sets or data sources for teaching	296	222	74*	296	0**	110*	117*	68*	36*	68*	88*	62*	8**	31*	3**	0*	217	79*
preferred source of info	1 0.3%	1 0.5%	0 0	1 0.3%	0 0	0 0	0 0	1 1.5%	0 0	1 1.5%	0 0	0 0	0 0	0 0	0 0	0 0	1 0.5%	0 0
Office (NET)	3 1.0%	3 1.3%	0 0	3 1.0%	0 0	1 1.0%	1 0.8%	1 1.4%	1 2.4%	0 0	0 0	1 1.8%	0 0	1 3.0%	0 0	0 0	3 1.4%	0 0
All sources of info	3 1.0%	3 1.3%	0 0	3 1.0%	0 0	1 1.0%	1 0.8%	1 1.4%	1 2.4%	0 0	0 0	1 1.8%	0 0	1 3.0%	0 0	0 0	3 1.4%	0 0
preferred source of info	1 0.4%	1 0.5%	0 0	1 0.4%	0 0	1 1.0%	0 0	0 0	0 0	0 0	0 0	1 1.8%	0 0	0 0	0 0	0 0	1 0.5%	0 0
Purchase from physical book store (NET)	3 0.9%	1 0.6%	1 1.7%	3 0.9%	0 0	1 1.3%	1 1.0%	0 0	0 0	1 1.5%	0 0	1 1.8%	* 3.4%	0 0	* 6.7%	0 0	3 1.2%	0 0
All sources of info	3 0.9%	1 0.6%	1 1.7%	3 0.9%	0 0	1 1.3%	1 1.0%	0 0	0 0	1 1.5%	0 0	1 1.8%	* 3.4%	0 0	* 6.7%	0 0	3 1.2%	0 0
preferred source of info	1 0.4%	0 0	1 1.7%	1 0.4%	0 0	1 1.2%	0 0	0 0	0 0	1 1.5%	0 0	0 0	* 3.4%	0 0	0 0	0 0	1 0.6%	0 0
Meeting/Conferences (NET)	2 0.7%	2 0.9%	0 0	2 0.7%	0 0	2 1.7%	0 0	0 0	0 0	1 1.5%	0 0	0 0	0 0	1 3.0%	0 0	0 0	2 0.9%	0 0
All sources of info	2 0.7%	2 0.9%	0 0	2 0.7%	0 0	2 1.7%	0 0	0 0	0 0	1 1.5%	0 0	0 0	0 0	1 3.0%	0 0	0 0	2 0.9%	0 0

Proportions/Means: Columns Tested (5% risk level) - A/B/D - C/D - E/F/G - H/I/J/K/L/M/N - P/Q
* small base; ** very small base (under 30) ineligible for sig testing

Table 252
Page 1005

Outsell/Digital Library Federation Study (2002)
Weighted Tables

TABLE 114, continued

T7D/E_9. Online databases, data sets or data sources SUMMARY TABLE

		RESPONDENT TYPE				INSTITUTION TYPE			DISCIPLINE									GENDER	
	TOTAL SAMPLE	FACULTY MEMBER	GRAD. STUDENT	FACULTY /GRAD	UNDER GRAD. STUDENT	PUBLIC	PRIVATE	LIBERAL ARTS	BIOLOGIAL SCIENCES	PHYSICAL SCIENCES /MATH	SOCIAL SCIENCES	ARTS AND HUMAN.	ENGI-NEERING	BUSINESS	LAW	UNDEC. MAJOR	MALE	FEMALE
		(A)	(B)	(C)	(D)	(E)	(F)	(G)	(H)	(I)	(J)	(K)	(L)	(M)	(N)		(P)	(Q)
Base - Use Online databases, data sets or data sources for teaching	296	222	74*	296	0**	110*	117*	68*	36*	68*	88*	62*	8**	31*	3**	0*	217	79*
preferred source of info	1 0.3%	1 0.4%	0 0	1 0.3%	0 0	1 0.8%	0 0	0 0	0 0	0 0	0 0	0 0	0 0	1 3.0%	0 0	0 0	1 0.4%	0 0
Home (NET)	2 0.6%	0 0	2 2.5%A	2 0.6%	0 0	2 1.7%	0 0	0 0	0 0	0 0	2 2.1%	0 0	0 0	0 0	0 0	0 0	0 0	2 2.4%P
All sources of info	2 0.6%	0 0	2 2.5%A	2 0.6%	0 0	2 1.7%	0 0	0 0	0 0	0 0	2 2.1%	0 0	0 0	0 0	0 0	0 0	0 0	2 2.4%P
preferred source of info	2 0.6%	0 0	2 2.5%A	2 0.6%	0 0	2 1.7%	0 0	0 0	0 0	0 0	2 2.1%	0 0	0 0	0 0	0 0	0 0	0 0	2 2.4%P
Author	2 0.6%	2 0.8%	0 0	2 0.6%	0 0	0 0	2 1.6%	0 0	0 0	0 0	2 2.1%	0 0	0 0	0 0	0 0	0 0	0 0	2 2.4%P
All sources of info	2 0.6%	2 0.8%	0 0	2 0.6%	0 0	0 0	2 1.6%	0 0	0 0	0 0	2 2.1%	0 0	0 0	0 0	0 0	0 0	0 0	2 2.4%P
preferred source of info	2 0.6%	2 0.8%	0 0	2 0.6%	0 0	0 0	2 1.6%	0 0	0 0	0 0	2 2.1%	0 0	0 0	0 0	0 0	0 0	0 0	2 2.4%P
Ask library to purchase source (NET)	1 0.4%	1 0.4%	* 0.4%	1 0.4%	0 0	1 1.1%	0 0	0 0	0 0	0 0	0 0	0 0	* 3.4%	1 3.0%	0 0	0 0	1 0.6%	0 0
All sources of info	1 0.4%	1 0.4%	* 0.4%	1 0.4%	0 0	1 1.1%	0 0	0 0	0 0	0 0	0 0	0 0	* 3.4%	1 3.0%	0 0	0 0	1 0.6%	0 0

Proportions/Means: Columns Tested (5% risk level) - A/B/D - C/D - E/F/G - H/I/J/K/L/M/N - P/Q
* small base; ** very small base (under 30) ineligible for sig testing

Table 252
Page 1006

Outsell/Digital Library Federation Study (2002)
Weighted Tables

TABLE 114, continued

T7D/E_9. Online databases, data sets or data sources SUMMARY TABLE

	RESPONDENT TYPE				INSTITUTION TYPE			DISCIPLINE									GENDER	
	TOTAL SAMPLE	FACULTY MEMBER	GRAD. STUDENT	FACULTY /GRAD	UNDER GRAD. STUDENT	PUBLIC	PRIVATE	LIBERAL ARTS	BIOLOGIAL SCIENCES	PHYSICAL SCIENCES /MATH	SOCIAL SCIENCES	ARTS AND HUMAN.	ENGI-NEERING	BUSINESS	LAW	UNDEC. MAJOR	MALE	FEMALE
		(A)	(B)	(C)	(D)	(E)	(F)	(G)	(H)	(I)	(J)	(K)	(L)	(M)	(N)		(P)	(Q)
Base - Use Online databases, data sets or data sources for teaching	296	222	74*	296	0**	110*	117*	68*	36*	68*	88*	62*	8**	31*	3**	0*	217	79*
preferred source of info	* 0.1%	0 0	* 0.4%	* 0.1%	0 0	* 0.3%	0 0	0 0	0 0	0 0	0 0	0 0	* 3.4%	0 0	0 0	0 0	* 0.1%	0 0
Order from on demand document delivery service (NET)	1 0.3%	1 0.4%	0 0	1 0.3%	0 0	0 0	1 0.8%	0 0	0 0	0 0	0 0	0 0	0 0	1 3.0%	0 0	0 0	1 0.4%	0 0
All sources of info	1 0.3%	1 0.4%	0 0	1 0.3%	0 0	0 0	1 0.8%	0 0	0 0	0 0	0 0	0 0	0 0	1 3.0%	0 0	0 0	1 0.4%	0 0
preferred source of info	1 0.3%	1 0.4%	0 0	1 0.3%	0 0	0 0	1 0.8%	0 0	0 0	0 0	0 0	0 0	0 0	1 3.0%	0 0	0 0	1 0.4%	0 0
Access book/journal/ journal article elsewhere online (NET)	0 0	0 0	0 0	0 0	0 0	0 0	0 0	0 0	0 0	0 0	0 0	0 0	0 0	0 0	0 0	0 0	0 0	0 0
All sources of info	0 0	0 0	0 0	0 0	0 0	0 0	0 0	0 0	0 0	0 0	0 0	0 0	0 0	0 0	0 0	0 0	0 0	0 0
preferred source of info	0 0	0 0	0 0	0 0	0 0	0 0	0 0	0 0	0 0	0 0	0 0	0 0	0 0	0 0	0 0	0 0	0 0	0 0
Faculty (NET)	0 0	0 0	0 0	0 0	0 0	0 0	0 0	0 0	0 0	0 0	0 0	0 0	0 0	0 0	0 0	0 0	0 0	0 0

Proportions/Means: Columns Tested (5% risk level) - A/B/D - C/D - E/F/G - H/I/J/K/L/M/N - P/Q
* small base; ** very small base (under 30) ineligible for sig testing

Table 252
Page 1007

Outsell/Digital Library Federation Study (2002)
Weighted Tables

TABLE 114, continued

T7D/E_9. Online databases, data sets or data sources SUMMARY TABLE

		RESPONDENT TYPE				INSTITUTION TYPE			DISCIPLINE								GENDER	
	TOTAL SAMPLE	FACULTY MEMBER	GRAD. STUDENT	FACULTY /GRAD	UNDER GRAD. STUDENT	PUBLIC	PRIVATE	LIBERAL ARTS	BIOLOGIAL SCIENCES	PHYSICAL SCIENCES /MATH	SOCIAL SCIENCES	ARTS AND HUMAN.	ENGI-NEERING	BUSINESS	LAW	UNDEC. MAJOR	MALE	FEMALE
		(A)	(B)	(C)	(D)	(E)	(F)	(G)	(H)	(I)	(J)	(K)	(L)	(M)	(N)		(P)	(Q)
Base - Use Online databases, data sets or data sources for teaching	296	222	74*	296	0**	110*	117*	68*	36*	68*	88*	62*	8**	31*	3**	0*	217	79*
All sources of info	0 0	0 0	0 0	0 0	0 0	0 0	0 0	0 0	0 0	0 0	0 0	0 0	0 0	0 0	0 0	0 0	0 0	0 0
preferred source of info	0 0	0 0	0 0	0 0	0 0	0 0	0 0	0 0	0 0	0 0	0 0	0 0	0 0	0 0	0 0	0 0	0 0	0 0
Department (NET)	0 0	0 0	0 0	0 0	0 0	0 0	0 0	0 0	0 0	0 0	0 0	0 0	0 0	0 0	0 0	0 0	0 0	0 0
All sources of info	0 0	0 0	0 0	0 0	0 0	0 0	0 0	0 0	0 0	0 0	0 0	0 0	0 0	0 0	0 0	0 0	0 0	0 0
preferred source of info	0 0	0 0	0 0	0 0	0 0	0 0	0 0	0 0	0 0	0 0	0 0	0 0	0 0	0 0	0 0	0 0	0 0	0 0
Other (NET)	7 2.5%	4 1.9%	3 4.2%	7 2.5%	0 0	5 4.9%F	0 0	2 2.9%	1 2.4%	3 4.4%	0 0	2 3.6%	0 0	1 3.0%	* 13.3%	0 0	4 1.9%	3 4.0%
All sources of info	7 2.5%	4 1.9%	3 4.2%	7 2.5%	0 0	5 4.9%F	0 0	2 2.9%	1 2.4%	3 4.4%	0 0	2 3.6%	0 0	1 3.0%	* 13.3%	0 0	4 1.9%	3 4.0%
preferred source of info	4 1.5%	1 0.6%	3 4.2%	4 1.5%	0 0	4 4.0%	0 0	0 0	1 2.4%	1 1.5%	0 0	2 3.6%	0 0	0 0	* 13.3%	0 0	2 1.0%	2 2.8%
DK/Refused	13 4.3%	13 5.7%	0 0	13 4.3%	0 0	4 4.0%	5 4.4%	3 4.4%	2 4.9%	2 2.9%	4 4.3%	4 7.3%	1 6.9%	0 0	0 0	0 0	12 5.4%	1 1.1%

Proportions/Means: Columns Tested (5% risk level) - A/B/D - C/D - E/F/G - H/I/J/K/L/M/N - P/Q
* small base; ** very small base (under 30) ineligible for sig testing

Table 252
Page 1008

Outsell/Digital Library Federation Study (2002)
Weighted Tables

TABLE 115

T7sum_10. Manuscripts and other primary source documents SUMMARY TABLE

	RESPONDENT TYPE				INSTITUTION TYPE			DISCIPLINE									GENDER	
	TOTAL SAMPLE	FACULTY MEMBER	GRAD. STUDENT	FACULTY /GRAD	UNDER GRAD. STUDENT	PUBLIC	PRIVATE	LIBERAL ARTS	BIOLOGIAL SCIENCES	PHYSICAL SCIENCES /MATH	SOCIAL SCIENCES	ARTS AND HUMAN.	ENGI-NEERING	BUSINESS	LAW	UNDEC. MAJOR	MALE	FEMALE
		(A)	(B)	(C)	(D)	(E)	(F)	(G)	(H)	(I)	(J)	(K)	(L)	(M)	(N)		(P)	(Q)
Base - USe Manuscripts and other primary source documents for teaching	283	189	94*	283	0**	133	90*	59*	50*	61*	68*	73*	8**	21**	1**	0*	208	75*
ONLINE	195 68.8%	140 73.9%B	55 58.6%	195 68.8%	0 0	85 63.9%	60 66.5%	49 83.4%EF	40 80.7%JK	45 73.8%	38 55.6%	46 63.1%	7 79.3%	18 82.6%	1 87.5%	0 0	148 71.0%	47 62.6%
Web directory/ subject related web site	55 19.6%	45 23.9%B	10 10.9%	55 19.6%	0 0	16 11.6%	22 24.1%E	18 30.5%E	11 21.1%	10 16.4%	17 25.0%	10 13.8%	3 31.0%	5 21.7%	1 37.5%	0 0	44 21.0%	12 15.7%
All sources of info	55 19.6%	45 23.9%B	10 10.9%	55 19.6%	0 0	16 11.6%	22 24.1%E	18 30.5%E	11 21.1%	10 16.4%	17 25.0%	10 13.8%	3 31.0%	5 21.7%	1 37.5%	0 0	44 21.0%	12 15.7%
preferred source of info	25 8.8%	18 9.6%	7 7.2%	25 8.8%	0 0	2 1.5%	15 16.1%E	8 14.1%E	4 8.8%	3 4.9%	9 13.9%	6 7.7%	1 17.2%	1 4.3%	* 12.5%	0 0	21 10.2%	4 5.0%
Search engine	52 18.5%	41 21.9%	11 11.8%	52 18.5%	0 0	29 21.8%	12 12.8%	12 19.8%	11 22.8%	17 27.9%J	6 8.3%	11 15.4%	1 13.8%	6 26.1%	* 25.0%	0 0	39 18.9%	13 17.4%
All sources of info	52 18.5%	41 21.9%	11 11.8%	52 18.5%	0 0	29 21.8%	12 12.8%	12 19.8%	11 22.8%	17 27.9%J	6 8.3%	11 15.4%	1 13.8%	6 26.1%	* 25.0%	0 0	39 18.9%	13 17.4%
preferred source of info	25 8.9%	19 10.0%	6 6.7%	25 8.9%	0 0	13 9.7%	7 7.2%	6 9.8%	6 12.3%	10 16.4%J	2 2.8%	4 6.2%	1 10.3%	2 8.7%	0 0	0 0	20 9.8%	5 6.5%
Online databases	38 13.4%	27 14.3%	11 11.5%	38 13.4%	0 0	13 10.1%	11 12.0%	13 22.7%E	11 22.8%K	14 23.0%K	6 8.3%	4 6.2%	0 0	2 8.7%	* 25.0%	0 0	28 13.5%	10 12.9%

Proportions/Means: Columns Tested (5% risk level) - A/B/D - C/D - E/F/G - H/I/J/K/L/M/N - P/Q
* small base; ** very small base (under 30) ineligible for sig testing

Table 256
Page 1020

Outsell/Digital Library Federation Study (2002)
Weighted Tables

TABLE 115, continued

T7sum_10. Manuscripts and other primary source documents SUMMARY TABLE

	TOTAL SAMPLE	RESPONDENT TYPE: FACULTY MEMBER (A)	GRAD. STUDENT (B)	FACULTY /GRAD (C)	UNDER GRAD. STUDENT (D)	INSTITUTION TYPE: PUBLIC (E)	PRIVATE (F)	LIBERAL ARTS (G)	DISCIPLINE: BIOLOGIAL SCIENCES (H)	PHYSICAL SCIENCES /MATH (I)	SOCIAL SCIENCES (J)	ARTS AND HUMAN. (K)	ENGI-NEERING (L)	BUSINESS (M)	LAW (N)	UNDEC. MAJOR	GENDER: MALE (P)	FEMALE (Q)
Base - USe Manuscripts and other primary source documents for teaching	283	189	94*	283	0**	133	90*	59*	50*	61*	68*	73*	8**	21**	1**	0*	208	75*
All sources of info	38 13.4%	27 14.3%	11 11.5%	38 13.4%	0 0	13 10.1%	11 12.0%	13 22.7%E	11 22.8%K	14 23.0%K	6 8.3%	4 6.2%	0 0	2 8.7%	* 25.0%	0 0	28 13.5%	10 12.9%
preferred source of info	23 8.2%	14 7.6%	9 9.3%	23 8.2%	0 0	7 5.0%	11 12.0%	6 9.5%	8 15.8%K	8 13.1%	4 5.6%	3 4.6%	0 0	0 0	* 12.5%	0 0	14 6.9%	9 11.7%
Your own institution's web site	26 9.2%	21 11.3%	5 4.8%	26 9.2%	0 0	8 5.8%	10 10.7%	9 14.4%	4 8.8%	4 6.6%	6 8.3%	6 7.7%	1 17.2%	5 21.7%	* 12.5%	0 0	20 9.4%	6 8.4%
All sources of info	26 9.2%	21 11.3%	5 4.8%	26 9.2%	0 0	8 5.8%	10 10.7%	9 14.4%	4 8.8%	4 6.6%	6 8.3%	6 7.7%	1 17.2%	5 21.7%	* 12.5%	0 0	20 9.4%	6 8.4%
preferred source of info	17 6.1%	14 7.3%	3 3.6%	17 6.1%	0 0	6 4.4%	4 4.1%	8 12.9%E	2 3.5%	3 4.9%	4 5.6%	3 4.6%	1 17.2%	4 17.4%	* 12.5%	0 0	12 5.7%	5 7.3%
Internet searches	26 9.1%	17 9.2%	9 9.1%	26 9.1%	0 0	13 10.0%	6 7.2%	6 10.1%	7 14.0%	6 9.8%	4 5.6%	4 6.2%	1 17.2%	3 13.0%	* 25.0%	0 0	18 8.9%	7 9.9%
All sources of info	26 9.1%	17 9.2%	9 9.1%	26 9.1%	0 0	13 10.0%	6 7.2%	6 10.1%	7 14.0%	6 9.8%	4 5.6%	4 6.2%	1 17.2%	3 13.0%	* 25.0%	0 0	18 8.9%	7 9.9%
preferred source of info	14 5.0%	8 4.2%	6 6.7%	14 5.0%	0 0	8 6.3%	4 4.3%	2 3.4%	4 8.8%	3 4.9%	4 5.6%	2 3.1%	1 10.3%	0 0	0 0	0 0	10 5.0%	4 5.2%

Proportions/Means: Columns Tested (5% risk level) - A/B/D - C/D - E/F/G - H/I/J/K/L/M/N - P/Q
* small base; ** very small base (under 30) ineligible for sig testing

Table 256
Page 1021

Outsell/Digital Library Federation Study (2002)
Weighted Tables

TABLE 115, continued

T7sum_10. Manuscripts and other primary source documents SUMMARY TABLE

		RESPONDENT TYPE				INSTITUTION TYPE			DISCIPLINE									GENDER	
	TOTAL SAMPLE	FACULTY MEMBER	GRAD. STUDENT	FACULTY /GRAD	UNDER GRAD. STUDENT	PUBLIC	PRIVATE	LIBERAL ARTS	BIOLOGICAL SCIENCES	PHYSICAL SCIENCES /MATH	SOCIAL SCIENCES	ARTS AND HUMAN.	ENGI-NEERING	BUSINESS	LAW	UNDEC. MAJOR	MALE	FEMALE
		(A)	(B)	(C)	(D)	(E)	(F)	(G)	(H)	(I)	(J)	(K)	(L)	(M)	(N)		(P)	(Q)
Base - USe Manuscripts and other primary source documents for teaching	283	189	94*	283	0**	133	90*	59*	50*	61*	68*	73*	8**	21**	1**	0*	208	75*
Online library catalogues and finding aids	26 9.0%	15 8.1%	10 10.9%	26 9.0%	0 0	12 8.7%	12 13.0%	2 3.6%	5 10.5%	2 3.3%	6 8.3%	9 12.3%	1 10.3%	3 13.0%	0 0	0 0	19 9.4%	6 8.1%
All sources of info	26 9.0%	15 8.1%	10 10.9%	26 9.0%	0 0	12 8.7%	12 13.0%	2 3.6%	5 10.5%	2 3.3%	6 8.3%	9 12.3%	1 10.3%	3 13.0%	0 0	0 0	19 9.4%	6 8.1%
preferred source of info	14 4.9%	7 3.5%	7 7.6%	14 4.9%	0 0	5 4.1%	7 8.0%	1 1.7%	4 7.0%	1 1.6%	6 8.3%	1 1.5%	1 6.9%	2 8.7%	0 0	0 0	11 5.2%	3 4.0%
Online reference service	14 5.1%	14 7.4%B	* 0.3%	14 5.1%	0 0	3 2.6%	3 3.6%	8 13.1%EF	3 5.3%	2 3.3%	2 2.8%	4 6.2%	1 6.9%	3 13.0%	0 0	0 0	10 5.0%	4 5.3%
All sources of info	14 5.1%	14 7.4%B	* 0.3%	14 5.1%	0 0	3 2.6%	3 3.6%	8 13.1%EF	3 5.3%	2 3.3%	2 2.8%	4 6.2%	1 6.9%	3 13.0%	0 0	0 0	10 5.0%	4 5.3%
preferred source of info	4 1.6%	4 2.3%	0 0	4 1.6%	0 0	1 0.8%	2 2.6%	1 1.6%	0 0	0 0	0 0	2 3.1%	* 3.4%	2 8.7%	0 0	0 0	3 1.6%	1 1.5%
Online abstracting and indexing services	8 2.9%	7 3.7%	1 1.2%	8 2.9%	0 0	4 3.3%	0 0	4 6.4%F	2 3.5%	4 6.6%	0 0	2 3.1%	0 0	0 0	* 12.5%	0 0	5 2.6%	3 3.7%
All sources of info	8 2.9%	7 3.7%	1 1.2%	8 2.9%	0 0	4 3.3%	0 0	4 6.4%F	2 3.5%	4 6.6%	0 0	2 3.1%	0 0	0 0	* 12.5%	0 0	5 2.6%	3 3.7%

Proportions/Means: Columns Tested (5% risk level) - A/B/D - C/D - E/F/G - H/I/J/K/L/M/N - P/Q
* small base; ** very small base (under 30) ineligible for sig testing

Table 256
Page 1022

Outsell/Digital Library Federation Study (2002)
Weighted Tables

TABLE 115, continued

T7sum_10. Manuscripts and other primary source documents SUMMARY TABLE

		RESPONDENT TYPE				INSTITUTION TYPE			DISCIPLINE									GENDER	
	TOTAL SAMPLE	FACULTY MEMBER	GRAD. STUDENT	FACULTY /GRAD	UNDER GRAD. STUDENT	PUBLIC	PRIVATE	LIBERAL ARTS	BIOLOGIAL SCIENCES	PHYSICAL SCIENCES /MATH	SOCIAL SCIENCES	ARTS AND HUMAN.	ENGI- NEERING	BUSINESS	LAW	UNDEC. MAJOR	MALE	FEMALE
		(A)	(B)	(C)	(D)	(E)	(F)	(G)	(H)	(I)	(J)	(K)	(L)	(M)	(N)		(P)	(Q)
Base - USe Manuscripts and other primary source documents for teaching	283	189	94*	283	0**	133	90*	59*	50*	61*	68*	73*	8**	21**	1**	0*	208	75*
preferred source of info	4 1.4%	4 2.1%	0 0	4 1.4%	0 0	2 1.6%	0 0	2 3.2%	1 1.8%	3 4.9%	0 0	0 0	0 0	0 0	* 12.5%	0 0	2 1.0%	2 2.5%
Online bookstore	6 2.1%	6 3.2%	0 0	6 2.1%	0 0	2 1.4%	3 3.3%	1 1.9%	0 0	0 0	4 5.6%	2 3.1%	0 0	0 0	0 0	0 0	6 2.9%	0 0
All sources of info	6 2.1%	6 3.2%	0 0	6 2.1%	0 0	2 1.4%	3 3.3%	1 1.9%	0 0	0 0	4 5.6%	2 3.1%	0 0	0 0	0 0	0 0	6 2.9%	0 0
preferred source of info	1 0.4%	1 0.6%	0 0	1 0.4%	0 0	0 0	1 1.2%	0 0	0 0	0 0	0 0	1 1.5%	0 0	0 0	0 0	0 0	1 0.5%	0 0
Department web page	6 2.0%	2 0.9%	4 4.3%	6 2.0%	0 0	5 3.7%	0 0	1 1.5%	4 7.0%I	0 0	0 0	2 3.1%	0 0	0 0	0 0	0 0	3 1.4%	3 3.8%
All sources of info	6 2.0%	2 0.9%	4 4.3%	6 2.0%	0 0	5 3.7%	0 0	1 1.5%	4 7.0%I	0 0	0 0	2 3.1%	0 0	0 0	0 0	0 0	3 1.4%	3 3.8%
preferred source of info	4 1.3%	1 0.5%	3 3.1%	4 1.3%	0 0	4 2.8%	0 0	0 0	3 5.3%	0 0	0 0	1 1.5%	0 0	0 0	0 0	0 0	1 0.4%	3 3.8%P
Your own personal electronic library/files	2 0.8%	1 0.6%	1 1.2%	2 0.8%	0 0	2 1.7%	0 0	0 0	0 0	0 0	0 0	2 3.1%	0 0	0 0	0 0	0 0	2 1.1%	0 0
All sources of info	2 0.8%	1 0.6%	1 1.2%	2 0.8%	0 0	2 1.7%	0 0	0 0	0 0	0 0	0 0	2 3.1%	0 0	0 0	0 0	0 0	2 1.1%	0 0

Proportions/Means: Columns Tested (5% risk level) - A/B/D - C/D - E/F/G - H/I/J/K/L/M/N - P/Q
* small base; ** very small base (under 30) ineligible for sig testing

Table 256
Page 1023

Outsell/Digital Library Federation Study (2002)
Weighted Tables

TABLE 115, continued

T7sum_10. Manuscripts and other primary source documents SUMMARY TABLE

		RESPONDENT TYPE				INSTITUTION TYPE			DISCIPLINE									GENDER	
	TOTAL SAMPLE	FACULTY MEMBER	GRAD. STUDENT	FACULTY /GRAD	UNDER GRAD. STUDENT	PUBLIC	PRIVATE	LIBERAL ARTS	BIOLOGIAL SCIENCES	PHYSICAL SCIENCES /MATH	SOCIAL SCIENCES	ARTS AND HUMAN.	ENGI-NEERING	BUSINESS	LAW	UNDEC. MAJOR	MALE	FEMALE
		(A)	(B)	(C)	(D)	(E)	(F)	(G)	(H)	(I)	(J)	(K)	(L)	(M)	(N)		(P)	(Q)
Base - USe Manuscripts and other primary source documents for teaching	283	189	94*	283	0**	133	90*	59*	50*	61*	68*	73*	8**	21**	1**	0*	208	75*
preferred source of info	1 0.4%	0 0	1 1.2%	1 0.4%	0 0	1 0.8%	0 0	0 0	0 0	0 0	0 0	1 1.5%	0 0	0 0	0 0	0 0	1 0.5%	0 0
E-mail listservs	2 0.7%	2 1.0%	0 0	2 0.7%	0 0	1 0.8%	0 0	1 1.5%	1 1.8%	0 0	0 0	0 0	0 0	1 4.3%	* 12.5%	0 0	2 1.0%	0 0
All sources of info	2 0.7%	2 1.0%	0 0	2 0.7%	0 0	1 0.8%	0 0	1 1.5%	1 1.8%	0 0	0 0	0 0	0 0	1 4.3%	* 12.5%	0 0	2 1.0%	0 0
preferred source of info	0 0	0 0	0 0	0 0	0 0	0 0	0 0	0 0	0 0	0 0	0 0	0 0	0 0	0 0	0 0	0 0	0 0	0 0
LIBRARY/PRINT	170 60.1%	129 68.4%B	41 43.4%	170 60.1%	0 0	82 61.7%	49 54.1%	39 65.8%	24 47.4%	36 59.0%	36 52.8%	56 76.9%HI J	4 44.8%	14 65.2%	1 62.5%	0 0	136 65.5%Q	34 45.2%
Campus library	132 46.7%	98 52.0%B	34 35.9%	132 46.7%	0 0	60 45.4%	40 44.2%	32 53.5%	21 42.1%	27 44.3%	28 41.7%	43 58.5%	3 31.0%	10 47.8%	* 25.0%	0 0	106 50.9%Q	26 35.1%
All sources of info	132 46.7%	98 52.0%B	34 35.9%	132 46.7%	0 0	60 45.4%	40 44.2%	32 53.5%	21 42.1%	27 44.3%	28 41.7%	43 58.5%	3 31.0%	10 47.8%	* 25.0%	0 0	106 50.9%Q	26 35.1%
preferred source of info	57 20.1%	35 18.4%	22 23.4%	57 20.1%	0 0	28 20.8%	20 21.9%	9 15.7%	5 10.5%	7 11.5%	17 25.0%	24 32.3%HI	1 13.8%	3 13.0%	* 12.5%	0 0	41 19.5%	16 21.7%

Proportions/Means: Columns Tested (5% risk level) - A/B/D - C/D - E/F/G - H/I/J/K/L/M/N - P/Q
* small base; ** very small base (under 30) ineligible for sig testing

Table 256
Page 1024

Outsell/Digital Library Federation Study (2002)
Weighted Tables

TABLE 115, continued

T7sum_10. Manuscripts and other primary source documents SUMMARY TABLE

	TOTAL SAMPLE	RESPONDENT TYPE: FACULTY MEMBER	GRAD. STUDENT	FACULTY /GRAD	UNDER GRAD. STUDENT	INSTITUTION TYPE: PUBLIC	PRIVATE	LIBERAL ARTS	DISCIPLINE: BIOLOGIAL SCIENCES	PHYSICAL SCIENCES /MATH	SOCIAL SCIENCES	ARTS AND HUMAN.	ENGI-NEERING	BUSINESS	LAW	UNDEC. MAJOR	GENDER: MALE	FEMALE
		(A)	(B)	(C)	(D)	(E)	(F)	(G)	(H)	(I)	(J)	(K)	(L)	(M)	(N)		(P)	(Q)
Base - USe Manuscripts and other primary source documents for teaching	283	189	94*	283	0**	133	90*	59*	50*	61*	68*	73*	8**	21**	1**	0*	208	75*
Your own personal physical library/ files/bookshelves	38 13.4%	35 18.5%B	3 3.1%	38 13.4%	0 0	20 14.7%	10 10.9%	8 14.1%	3 5.3%	12 19.7%H	8 11.1%	9 12.3%	1 13.8%	6 26.1%	0 0	0 0	32 15.5%	6 7.5%
All sources of info	38 13.4%	35 18.5%B	3 3.1%	38 13.4%	0 0	20 14.7%	10 10.9%	8 14.1%	3 5.3%	12 19.7%H	8 11.1%	9 12.3%	1 13.8%	6 26.1%	0 0	0 0	32 15.5%	6 7.5%
preferred source of info	18 6.3%	15 7.9%	3 3.1%	18 6.3%	0 0	8 5.8%	7 7.6%	3 5.3%	0 0	6 9.8%H	8 11.1%H	3 4.6%	1 10.3%	0 0	0 0	0 0	15 7.3%	3 3.4%
References cited in books or journal articles	15 5.2%	14 7.2%	1 1.2%	15 5.2%	0 0	5 4.0%	4 4.7%	5 8.8%	1 1.8%	4 6.6%	0 0	8 10.8%J	0 0	2 8.7%	* 12.5%	0 0	13 6.1%	2 2.7%
All sources of info	15 5.2%	14 7.2%	1 1.2%	15 5.2%	0 0	5 4.0%	4 4.7%	5 8.8%	1 1.8%	4 6.6%	0 0	8 10.8%J	0 0	2 8.7%	* 12.5%	0 0	13 6.1%	2 2.7%
preferred source of info	8 3.0%	7 3.9%	1 1.2%	8 3.0%	0 0	4 3.3%	2 2.3%	2 3.3%	1 1.8%	2 3.3%	0 0	4 6.2%	0 0	1 4.3%	* 12.5%	0 0	8 3.6%	1 1.2%
Personal subscriptions to newspapers, magazines and journals	12 4.2%	11 5.9%	1 1.0%	12 4.2%	0 0	6 4.8%	4 4.2%	2 3.0%	4 8.8%J	2 3.3%	0 0	2 3.1%	1 6.9%	3 13.0%	0 0	0 0	10 4.9%	2 2.4%

Proportions/Means: Columns Tested (5% risk level) - A/B/D - C/D - E/F/G - H/I/J/K/L/M/N - P/Q
* small base; ** very small base (under 30) ineligible for sig testing

Table 256
Page 1025

Outsell/Digital Library Federation Study (2002)
Weighted Tables

TABLE 115, continued

T7sum_10. Manuscripts and other primary source documents SUMMARY TABLE

		RESPONDENT TYPE				INSTITUTION TYPE			DISCIPLINE									GENDER	
	TOTAL SAMPLE	FACULTY MEMBER	GRAD. STUDENT	FACULTY /GRAD	UNDER GRAD. STUDENT	PUBLIC	PRIVATE	LIBERAL ARTS	BIOLOGIAL SCIENCES	PHYSICAL SCIENCES /MATH	SOCIAL SCIENCES	ARTS AND HUMAN.	ENGI- NEERING	BUSINESS	LAW	UNDEC. MAJOR	MALE	FEMALE
		(A)	(B)	(C)	(D)	(E)	(F)	(G)	(H)	(I)	(J)	(K)	(L)	(M)	(N)		(P)	(Q)
Base - USe Manuscripts and other primary source documents for teaching	283	189	94*	283	0**	133	90*	59*	50*	61*	68*	73*	8**	21**	1**	0*	208	75*
All sources of info	12 4.2%	11 5.9%	1 1.0%	12 4.2%	0 0	6 4.8%	4 4.2%	2 3.0%	4 8.8%J	2 3.3%	0 0	2 3.1%	1 6.9%	3 13.0%	0 0	0 0	10 4.9%	2 2.4%
preferred source of info	3 1.0%	3 1.4%	0 0	3 1.0%	0 0	1 0.7%	1 1.0%	1 1.5%	2 3.5%	0 0	0 0	0 0	0 0	1 4.3%	0 0	0 0	3 1.3%	0 0
Another library	11 3.8%	10 5.2%	1 1.2%	11 3.8%	0 0	1 0.7%	5 5.5%E	5 8.5%E	3 5.3%	3 4.9%	2 2.8%	2 3.1%	0 0	1 4.3%	* 12.5%	0 0	10 4.7%	1 1.3%
All sources of info	11 3.8%	10 5.2%	1 1.2%	11 3.8%	0 0	1 0.7%	5 5.5%E	5 8.5%E	3 5.3%	3 4.9%	2 2.8%	2 3.1%	0 0	1 4.3%	* 12.5%	0 0	10 4.7%	1 1.3%
preferred source of info	1 0.4%	1 0.5%	0 0	1 0.4%	0 0	0 0	0 0	1 1.7%	0 0	1 1.6%	0 0	0 0	0 0	0 0	0 0	0 0	0 0	1 1.3%
Physical bookstore	9 3.2%	8 4.3%	1 1.1%	9 3.2%	0 0	5 3.9%	2 2.2%	2 3.2%	2 3.5%	4 6.6%	0 0	3 4.6%	0 0	0 0	0 0	0 0	8 4.0%	1 1.2%
All sources of info	9 3.2%	8 4.3%	1 1.1%	9 3.2%	0 0	5 3.9%	2 2.2%	2 3.2%	2 3.5%	4 6.6%	0 0	3 4.6%	0 0	0 0	0 0	0 0	8 4.0%	1 1.2%
preferred source of info	2 0.7%	1 0.5%	1 1.1%	2 0.7%	0 0	1 0.8%	0 0	1 1.7%	0 0	2 3.3%	0 0	0 0	0 0	0 0	0 0	0 0	2 1.0%	0 0
Printed abstracting and indexing services	6 2.1%	6 3.2%	0 0	6 2.1%	0 .0	3 2.4%	2 2.1%	1 1.7%	0 0	1 1.6%	4 5.6%	1 1.5%	0 0	0 0	* 12.5%	0 0	6 2.9%	0 0

Proportions/Means: Columns Tested (5% risk level) - A/B/D - C/D - E/F/G - H/I/J/K/L/M/N - P/Q
* small base; ** very small base (under 30) ineligible for sig testing

Table 256
Page 1026

Outsell/Digital Library Federation Study (2002)
Weighted Tables

TABLE 115, continued

T7sum_10. Manuscripts and other primary source documents SUMMARY TABLE

		RESPONDENT TYPE				INSTITUTION TYPE			DISCIPLINE								GENDER	
	TOTAL SAMPLE	FACULTY MEMBER	GRAD. STUDENT	FACULTY /GRAD	UNDER GRAD. STUDENT	PUBLIC	PRIVATE	LIBERAL ARTS	BIOLOGIAL SCIENCES	PHYSICAL SCIENCES /MATH	SOCIAL SCIENCES	ARTS AND HUMAN.	ENGI- NEERING	BUSINESS	LAW	UNDEC. MAJOR	MALE	FEMALE
		(A)	(B)	(C)	(D)	(E)	(F)	(G)	(H)	(I)	(J)	(K)	(L)	(M)	(N)		(P)	(Q)
Base - USe Manuscripts and other primary source documents for teaching	283	189	94*	283	0**	133	90*	59*	50*	61*	68*	73*	8**	21**	1**	0*	208	75*
All sources of info	6 2.1%	6 3.2%	0 0	6 2.1%	0 0	3 2.4%	2 2.1%	1 1.7%	0 0	1 1.6%	4 5.6%	1 1.5%	0 0	0 0	* 12.5%	0 0	6 2.9%	0 0
preferred source of info	3 1.1%	3 1.7%	0 0	3 1.1%	0 0	3 2.4%	0 0	0 0	0 0	0 0	2 2.8%	1 1.5%	0 0	0 0	* 12.5%	0 0	3 1.5%	0 0
Printed library catalogues and finding aids	5 1.9%	4 2.2%	1 1.2%	5 1.9%	0 0	3 2.5%	0 0	2 3.4%	1 1.8%	0 0	0 0	3 4.6%	0 0	1 4.3%	* 12.5%	0 0	3 1.6%	2 2.7%
All sources of info	5 1.9%	4 2.2%	1 1.2%	5 1.9%	0 0	3 2.5%	0 0	2 3.4%	1 1.8%	0 0	0 0	3 4.6%	0 0	1 4.3%	* 12.5%	0 0	3 1.6%	2 2.7%
preferred source of info	1 0.3%	1 0.5%	0 0	1 0.3%	0 0	0 0	0 0	1 1.5%	1 1.8%	0 0	0 0	0 0	0 0	0 0	0 0	0 0	0 0	1 1.2%
PERSONAL ASSISTANCE	79 27.8%	46 24.6%	32 34.3%	79 27.8%	0 0	49 36.6%F	16 17.2%	14 24.2%	9 17.5%	18 29.5%	13 19.4%	29 40.0%HJ	2 20.7%	7 34.8%	* 25.0%	0 0	58 28.0%	20 27.3%
Colleagues inside your institution	50 17.6%	28 14.9%	22 23.0%	50 17.6%	0 0	30 22.7%	12 13.6%	7 12.0%	8 15.8%	13 21.3%	8 11.1%	16 21.5%	1 10.3%	5 21.7%	0 0	0 0	35 17.0%	14 19.1%
All sources of info	50 17.6%	28 14.9%	22 23.0%	50 17.6%	0 0	30 22.7%	12 13.6%	7 12.0%	8 15.8%	13 21.3%	8 11.1%	16 21.5%	1 10.3%	5 21.7%	0 0	0 0	35 17.0%	14 19.1%

Proportions/Means: Columns Tested (5% risk level) - A/B/D - C/D - E/F/G - H/I/J/K/L/M/N - P/Q
* small base; ** very small base (under 30) ineligible for sig testing

Table 256
Page 1027

Outsell/Digital Library Federation Study (2002)
Weighted Tables

TABLE 115, continued

T7sum_10. Manuscripts and other primary source documents SUMMARY TABLE

		RESPONDENT TYPE				INSTITUTION TYPE			DISCIPLINE								GENDER	
	TOTAL SAMPLE	FACULTY MEMBER	GRAD. STUDENT	FACULTY /GRAD	UNDER GRAD. STUDENT	PUBLIC	PRIVATE	LIBERAL ARTS	BIOLOGIAL SCIENCES	PHYSICAL SCIENCES /MATH	SOCIAL SCIENCES	ARTS AND HUMAN.	ENGI- NEERING	BUSINESS	LAW	UNDEC. MAJOR	MALE	FEMALE
		(A)	(B)	(C)	(D)	(E)	(F)	(G)	(H)	(I)	(J)	(K)	(L)	(M)	(N)		(P)	(Q)
Base - USe Manuscripts and other primary source documents for teaching	283	189	94*	283	0**	133	90*	59*	50*	61*	68*	73*	8**	21**	1**	0*	208	75*
preferred source of info	19 6.8%	5 2.6%	14 15.2%A	19 6.8%	0 0	13 9.5%	5 6.0%	1 1.9%	4 7.0%	4 6.6%	2 2.8%	7 9.2%	* 3.4%	3 13.0%	0 0	0 0	11 5.3%	8 11.0%
A librarian in your institution	36 12.8%	24 12.7%	12 13.2%	36 12.8%	0 0	24 18.0%F	3 3.6%	9 15.5%F	4 7.0%	7 11.5%	8 11.1%	15 20.0%H	1 6.9%	3 13.0%	* 25.0%	0 0	29 14.1%	7 9.3%
All sources of info	36 12.8%	24 12.7%	12 13.2%	36 12.8%	0 0	24 18.0%F	3 3.6%	9 15.5%F	4 7.0%	7 11.5%	8 11.1%	15 20.0%H	1 6.9%	3 13.0%	* 25.0%	0 0	29 14.1%	7 9.3%
preferred source of info	12 4.2%	6 3.3%	6 6.0%	12 4.2%	0 0	9 6.8%	1 1.0%	2 3.4%	1 1.8%	0 0	6 8.3%	4 6.2%	0 0	1 4.3%	0 0	0 0	8 3.9%	4 5.2%
Colleagues outside your institution	25 8.9%	22 11.8%B	3 2.9%	25 8.9%	0 0	18 13.5%F	3 3.3%	4 7.0%	1 1.8%	4 6.6%	8 11.1%	9 12.3%H	0 0	4 17.4%	0 0	0 0	19 9.2%	6 8.0%
All sources of info	25 8.9%	22 11.8%B	3 2.9%	25 8.9%	0 0	18 13.5%F	3 3.3%	4 7.0%	1 1.8%	4 6.6%	8 11.1%	9 12.3%H	0 0	4 17.4%	0 0	0 0	19 9.2%	6 8.0%
preferred source of info	2 0.7%	2 1.0%	0 0	2 0.7%	0 0	2 1.4%	0 0	0 0	0 0	1 1.6%	0 0	0 0	0 0	1 4.3%	0 0	0 0	2 0.9%	0 0
Professional meetings	2 0.9%	2 1.3%	0 0	2 0.9%	0 0	1 1.1%	1 1.1%	0 0	0 0	1 1.6%	0 0	1 1.5%	* 3.4%	0 0	0 0	0 0	2 1.2%	0 0
All sources of info	2 0.9%	2 1.3%	0 0	2 0.9%	0 0	1 1.1%	1 1.1%	0 0	0 0	1 1.6%	0 0	1 1.5%	* 3.4%	0 0	0 0	0 0	2 1.2%	0 0

Proportions/Means: Columns Tested (5% risk level) - A/B/D - C/D - E/F/G - H/I/J/K/L/M/N - P/Q
* small base; ** very small base (under 30) ineligible for sig testing

Table 256
Page 1028

Outsell/Digital Library Federation Study (2002)
Weighted Tables

TABLE 115, continued

T7sum_10. Manuscripts and other primary source documents SUMMARY TABLE

		RESPONDENT TYPE				INSTITUTION TYPE			DISCIPLINE									GENDER	
	TOTAL SAMPLE	FACULTY MEMBER	GRAD. STUDENT	FACULTY /GRAD	UNDER GRAD. STUDENT	PUBLIC	PRIVATE	LIBERAL ARTS	BIOLOGIAL SCIENCES	PHYSICAL SCIENCES /MATH	SOCIAL SCIENCES	ARTS AND HUMAN.	ENGI-NEERING	BUSINESS	LAW	UNDEC. MAJOR	MALE	FEMALE
		(A)	(B)	(C)	(D)	(E)	(F)	(G)	(H)	(I)	(J)	(K)	(L)	(M)	(N)		(P)	(Q)
Base - USe Manuscripts and other primary source documents for teaching	283	189	94*	283	0**	133	90*	59*	50*	61*	68*	73*	8**	21**	1**	0*	208	75*
preferred source of info	* 0.1%	* 0.2%	0 0	* 0.1%	0 0	* 0.2%	0 0	0 0	0 0	0 0	0 0	0 0	* 3.4%	0 0	0 0	0 0	* 0.1%	0 0
Another institution's librarian	1 0.5%	1 0.7%	0 0	1 0.5%	0 0	0 0	* 0.2%	1 1.9%	0 0	0 0	0 0	1 1.5%	0 0	0 0	* 12.5%	0 0	1 0.6%	0 0
All sources of info	1 0.5%	1 0.7%	0 0	1 0.5%	0 0	0 0	* 0.2%	1 1.9%	0 0	0 0	0 0	1 1.5%	0 0	0 0	* 12.5%	0 0	1 0.6%	0 0
preferred source of info	0 0	0 0	0 0	0 0	0 0	0 0	0 0	0 0	0 0	0 0	0 0	0 0	0 0	0 0	0 0	0 0	0 0	0 0
Personal office/lab	2 0.7%	2 1.0%	0 0	2 0.7%	0 0	2 1.4%	0 0	0 0	0 0	0 0	2 2.8%	0 0	0 0	0 0	0 0	0 0	2 0.9%	0 0
All sources of info	2 0.7%	2 1.0%	0 0	2 0.7%	0 0	2 1.4%	0 0	0 0	0 0	0 0	2 2.8%	0 0	0 0	0 0	0 0	0 0	2 0.9%	0 0
preferred source of info	0 0	0 0	0 0	0 0	0 0	0 0	0 0	0 0	0 0	0 0	0 0	0 0	0 0	0 0	0 0	0 0	0 0	0 0
Online (unspecified)	2 0.7%	2 1.0%	0 0	2 0.7%	0 0	2 1.4%	0 0	0 0	1 1.8%	1 1.6%	0 0	0 0	0 0	0 0	0 0	0 0	2 0.9%	0 0
All sources of info	2 0.7%	2 1.0%	0 0	2 0.7%	0 0	2 1.4%	0 0	0 0	1 1.8%	1 1.6%	0 0	0 0	0 0	0 0	0 0	0 0	2 0.9%	0 0

Proportions/Means: Columns Tested (5% risk level) - A/B/D - C/D - E/F/G - H/I/J/K/L/M/N - P/Q
* small base; ** very small base (under 30) ineligible for sig testing

Table 256
Page 1029

Outsell/Digital Library Federation Study (2002)
Weighted Tables

TABLE 115, continued

T7sum_10. Manuscripts and other primary source documents SUMMARY TABLE

		RESPONDENT TYPE				INSTITUTION TYPE			DISCIPLINE								GENDER	
	TOTAL SAMPLE	FACULTY MEMBER	GRAD. STUDENT	FACULTY /GRAD	UNDER GRAD. STUDENT	PUBLIC	PRIVATE	LIBERAL ARTS	BIOLOGIAL SCIENCES	PHYSICAL SCIENCES /MATH	SOCIAL SCIENCES	ARTS AND HUMAN.	ENGI-NEERING	BUSINESS	LAW	UNDEC. MAJOR	MALE	FEMALE
		(A)	(B)	(C)	(D)	(E)	(F)	(G)	(H)	(I)	(J)	(K)	(L)	(M)	(N)		(P)	(Q)
Base - USe Manuscripts and other primary source documents for teaching	283	189	94*	283	0**	133	90*	59*	50*	61*	68*	73*	8**	21**	1**	0*	208	75*
preferred source of info	2 0.7%	2 1.0%	0 0	2 0.7%	0 0	2 1.4%	0 0	0 0	1 1.8%	1 1.6%	0 0	0 0	0 0	0 0	0 0	0 0	2 0.9%	0 0
Author	1 0.4%	1 0.6%	0 0	1 0.4%	0 0	0 0	1 1.2%	0 0	0 0	0 0	0 0	1 1.5%	0 0	0 0	0 0	0 0	1 0.5%	0 0
All sources of info	1 0.4%	1 0.6%	0 0	1 0.4%	0 0	0 0	1 1.2%	0 0	0 0	0 0	0 0	1 1.5%	0 0	0 0	0 0	0 0	1 0.5%	0 0
preferred source of info	0 0	0 0	0 0	0 0	0 0	0 0	0 0	0 0	0 0	0 0	0 0	0 0	0 0	0 0	0 0	0 0	0 0	0 0
Students	* 0.1%	0 0	* 0.3%	* 0.1%	0 0	0 0	* 0.3%	0 0	0 0	0 0	0 0	0 0	* 3.4%	0 0	0 0	0 0	0 0	* 0.4%
All sources of info	* 0.1%	0 0	* 0.3%	* 0.1%	0 0	0 0	* 0.3%	0 0	0 0	0 0	0 0	0 0	* 3.4%	0 0	0 0	0 0	0 0	* 0.4%
preferred source of info	0 0	0 0	0 0	0 0	0 0	0 0	0 0	0 0	0 0	0 0	0 0	0 0	0 0	0 0	0 0	0 0	0 0	0 0
Other	25 8.8%	19 10.1%	6 6.3%	25 8.8%	0 0	14 10.3%	6 6.5%	5 8.9%	4 7.0%	8 13.1%	6 8.3%	4 6.2%	* 3.4%	3 13.0%	* 12.5%	0 0	18 8.7%	7 9.2%
All sources of info	24 8.5%	18 9.6%	6 6.3%	24 8.5%	0 0	13 9.7%	6 6.5%	5 8.9%	4 7.0%	8 13.1%	6 8.3%	4 6.2%	* 3.4%	2 8.7%	* 12.5%	0 0	17 8.2%	7 9.2%

Proportions/Means: Columns Tested (5% risk level) - A/B/D - C/D - E/F/G - H/I/J/K/L/M/N - P/Q
* small base; ** very small base (under 30) ineligible for sig testing

Table 256
Page 1030

Outsell/Digital Library Federation Study (2002)
Weighted Tables

TABLE 115, continued

T7sum_10. Manuscripts and other primary source documents SUMMARY TABLE

		RESPONDENT TYPE				INSTITUTION TYPE			DISCIPLINE									GENDER	
	TOTAL SAMPLE	FACULTY MEMBER	GRAD. STUDENT	FACULTY /GRAD	UNDER GRAD. STUDENT	PUBLIC	PRIVATE	LIBERAL ARTS	BIOLOGIAL SCIENCES	PHYSICAL SCIENCES /MATH	SOCIAL SCIENCES	ARTS AND HUMAN.	ENGI-NEERING	BUSINESS	LAW	UNDEC. MAJOR	MALE	FEMALE
		(A)	(B)	(C)	(D)	(E)	(F)	(G)	(H)	(I)	(J)	(K)	(L)	(M)	(N)		(P)	(Q)
Base - USe Manuscripts and other primary source documents for teaching	283	189	94*	283	0**	133	90*	59*	50*	61*	68*	73*	8**	21**	1**	0*	208	75*
preferred source of info	6 2.0%	4 2.0%	2 2.0%	6 2.0%	0 0	5 3.5%	1 1.0%	0 0	2 3.5%	1 1.6%	2 2.8%	0 0	0 0	1 4.3%	0 0	0 0	3 1.4%	3 3.7%
DK/Refused	15 5.3%	13 6.7%	2 2.3%	15 5.3%	0 0	6 4.8%	3 3.2%	6 9.3%	4 7.0%	5 8.2%	2 2.8%	3 4.6%	0 0	1 4.3%	* 12.5%	0 0	11 5.3%	4 5.1%

Proportions/Means: Columns Tested (5% risk level) - A/B/D - C/D - E/F/G - H/I/J/K/L/M/N - P/Q
* small base; ** very small base (under 30) ineligible for sig testing

TABLE 116

T7D/E_10. Manuscripts and other primary source documents SUMMARY TABLE

		RESPONDENT TYPE				INSTITUTION TYPE			DISCIPLINE								GENDER	
	TOTAL SAMPLE	FACULTY MEMBER	GRAD. STUDENT	FACULTY /GRAD	UNDER GRAD. STUDENT	PUBLIC	PRIVATE	LIBERAL ARTS	BIOLOGIAL SCIENCES	PHYSICAL SCIENCES /MATH	SOCIAL SCIENCES	ARTS AND HUMAN.	ENGI-NEERING	BUSINESS	LAW	UNDEC. MAJOR	MALE	FEMALE
		(A)	(B)	(C)	(D)	(E)	(F)	(G)	(H)	(I)	(J)	(K)	(L)	(M)	(N)		(P)	(Q)
Base - Use Manuscripts and other primary source documents for teaching	283	189	94*	283	0**	133	90*	59*	50*	61*	68*	73*	8**	21**	1**	0*	208	75*
Borrow from or use in campus library (NET)	190 67.1%	123 64.9%	67 71.7%	190 67.1%	0 0	90 67.8%	59 65.8%	40 67.6%	33 66.7%	34 55.7%	49 72.2%	54 73.8%I	4 48.3%	15 69.6%	1 62.5%	0 0	138 66.3%	52 69.4%
All sources of info	190 67.1%	123 64.9%	67 71.7%	190 67.1%	0 0	90 67.8%	59 65.8%	40 67.6%	33 66.7%	34 55.7%	49 72.2%	54 73.8%I	4 48.3%	15 69.6%	1 62.5%	0 0	138 66.3%	52 69.4%
preferred source of info	131 46.2%	76 40.3%	54 58.0%A	131 46.2%	0 0	64 47.7%	41 45.8%	26 43.4%	15 29.8%	22 36.1%	39 58.3%HI	45 61.5%HI	2 27.6%	7 30.4%	1 37.5%	0 0	89 42.6%	42 56.0%
Access online (NET)	118 41.9%	92 48.8%B	26 28.0%	118 41.9%	0 0	53 39.4%	36 39.8%	30 50.7%	32 63.2%IJK	25 41.0%	21 30.6%	21 29.2%	5 62.1%	14 65.2%	1 50.0%	0 0	92 44.4%	26 34.9%
All sources of info	118 41.9%	92 48.8%B	26 28.0%	118 41.9%	0 0	53 39.4%	36 39.8%	30 50.7%	32 63.2%IJK	25 41.0%	21 30.6%	21 29.2%	5 62.1%	14 65.2%	1 50.0%	0 0	92 44.4%	26 34.9%
preferred source of info	89 31.3%	67 35.3%	22 23.2%	89 31.3%	0 0	39 29.4%	27 30.1%	22 37.4%	24 47.4%JK	22 36.1%K	15 22.2%	12 16.9%	5 55.2%	10 47.8%	1 37.5%	0 0	69 33.4%	19 25.6%
Interlibrary loan (NET)	24 8.4%	21 11.0%B	3 3.2%	24 8.4%	0 0	5 3.7%	9 10.0%	10 16.5%E	4 8.8%	6 9.8%	8 11.1%	3 4.6%	1 6.9%	2 8.7%	0 0	0 0	20 9.5%	4 5.2%
All sources of info	24 8.4%	21 11.0%B	3 3.2%	24 8.4%	0 0	5 3.7%	9 10.0%	10 16.5%E	4 8.8%	6 9.8%	8 11.1%	3 4.6%	1 6.9%	2 8.7%	0 0	0 0	20 9.5%	4 5.2%

Proportions/Means: Columns Tested (5% risk level) - A/B/D - C/D - E/F/G - H/I/J/K/L/M/N - P/Q
* small base; ** very small base (under 30) ineligible for sig testing

Table 259
Page 1038

Outsell/Digital Library Federation Study (2002)
Weighted Tables

TABLE 116, continued

T7D/E_10. Manuscripts and other primary source documents SUMMARY TABLE

		RESPONDENT TYPE				INSTITUTION TYPE			DISCIPLINE									GENDER	
	TOTAL SAMPLE	FACULTY MEMBER	GRAD. STUDENT	FACULTY /GRAD	UNDER GRAD. STUDENT	PUBLIC	PRIVATE	LIBERAL ARTS	BIOLOGIAL SCIENCES	PHYSICAL SCIENCES /MATH	SOCIAL SCIENCES	ARTS AND HUMAN.	ENGI-NEERING	BUSINESS	LAW	UNDEC. MAJOR	MALE	FEMALE
		(A)	(B)	(C)	(D)	(E)	(F)	(G)	(H)	(I)	(J)	(K)	(L)	(M)	(N)		(P)	(Q)
Base - Use Manuscripts and other primary source documents for teaching	283	189	94*	283	0**	133	90*	59*	50*	61*	68*	73*	8**	21**	1**	0*	208	75*
preferred source of info	8 2.7%	8 4.1%	0 0	8 2.7%	0 0	0 0	4 4.2%E	4 6.8%E	1 1.8%	2 3.3%	4 5.6%	1 1.5%	0 0	0 0	0 0	0 0	8 3.7%	0 0
Borrow from or use in other libraries (NET)	19 6.8%	17 9.0%	2 2.3%	19 6.8%	0 0	3 2.5%	12 13.3%E	4 6.6%	4 8.8%	5 8.2%	4 5.6%	6 7.7%	0 0	0 0	1 37.5%	0 0	13 6.4%	6 7.8%
All sources of info	19 6.8%	17 9.0%	2 2.3%	19 6.8%	0 0	3 2.5%	12 13.3%E	4 6.6%	4 8.8%	5 8.2%	4 5.6%	6 7.7%	0 0	0 0	1 37.5%	0 0	13 6.4%	6 7.8%
preferred source of info	6 2.1%	5 2.6%	1 1.1%	6 2.1%	0 0	2 1.5%	4 4.3%	0 0	2 3.5%	1 1.6%	2 2.8%	1 1.5%	0 0	0 0	* 12.5%	0 0	4 1.9%	2 2.7%
Personal Collection/ Holdings (NET)	19 6.7%	19 10.0%B	0 0	19 6.7%	0 0	12 9.1%	2 1.9%	5 8.5%	5 10.5%J	6 9.8%J	0 0	4 6.2%	* 3.4%	3 13.0%	0 0	0 0	15 7.1%	4 5.5%
All sources of info	19 6.7%	19 10.0%B	0 0	19 6.7%	0 0	12 9.1%	2 1.9%	5 8.5%	5 10.5%J	6 9.8%J	0 0	4 6.2%	* 3.4%	3 13.0%	0 0	0 0	15 7.1%	4 5.5%
preferred source of info	10 3.4%	10 5.1%B	0 0	10 3.4%	0 0	7 5.3%	2 1.9%	1 1.5%	4 8.8%J	2 3.3%	0 0	1 1.5%	* 3.4%	2 8.7%	0 0	0 0	8 3.7%	2 2.7%
Access from course website (NET)	10 3.4%	7 3.5%	3 3.3%	10 3.4%	0 0	4 3.0%	5 5.4%	1 1.5%	3 5.3%	3 4.9%	0 0	2 3.1%	0 0	2 8.7%	0 0	0 0	8 3.8%	2 2.4%

Proportions/Means: Columns Tested (5% risk level) - A/B/D - C/D - E/F/G - H/I/J/K/L/M/N - P/Q
* small base; ** very small base (under 30) ineligible for sig testing

Table 259
Page 1039

Outsell/Digital Library Federation Study (2002)
Weighted Tables

TABLE 116, continued

T7D/E_10. Manuscripts and other primary source documents SUMMARY TABLE

		RESPONDENT TYPE				INSTITUTION TYPE			DISCIPLINE									GENDER	
	TOTAL SAMPLE	FACULTY MEMBER	GRAD. STUDENT	FACULTY /GRAD	UNDER GRAD. STUDENT	PUBLIC	PRIVATE	LIBERAL ARTS	BIOLOGIAL SCIENCES	PHYSICAL SCIENCES /MATH	SOCIAL SCIENCES	ARTS AND HUMAN.	ENGI-NEERING	BUSINESS	LAW	UNDEC. MAJOR	MALE	FEMALE
		(A)	(B)	(C)	(D)	(E)	(F)	(G)	(H)	(I)	(J)	(K)	(L)	(M)	(N)		(P)	(Q)
Base - Use Manuscripts and other primary source documents for teaching	283	189	94*	283	0**	133	90*	59*	50*	61*	68*	73*	8**	21**	1**	0*	208	75*
All sources of info	10 3.4%	7 3.5%	3 3.3%	10 3.4%	0 0	4 3.0%	5 5.4%	1 1.5%	3 5.3%	3 4.9%	0 0	2 3.1%	0 0	2 8.7%	0 0	0 0	8 3.8%	2 2.4%
preferred source of info	5 1.8%	2 1.1%	3 3.3%	5 1.8%	0 0	2 1.6%	3 3.4%	0 0	0 0	2 3.3%	0 0	2 3.1%	0 0	1 4.3%	0 0	0 0	4 2.0%	1 1.2%
Purchase from physical book store (NET)	10 3.4%	8 4.0%	2 2.0%	10 3.4%	0 0	4 2.7%	4 4.3%	2 3.4%	2 3.5%	2 3.3%	4 5.6%	1 1.5%	1 10.3%	0 0	0 0	0 0	9 4.2%	1 1.2%
All sources of info	10 3.4%	8 4.0%	2 2.0%	10 3.4%	0 0	4 2.7%	4 4.3%	2 3.4%	2 3.5%	2 3.3%	4 5.6%	1 1.5%	1 10.3%	0 0	0 0	0 0	9 4.2%	1 1.2%
preferred source of info	4 1.3%	2 1.0%	2 2.0%	4 1.3%	0 0	2 1.4%	1 1.0%	1 1.7%	1 1.8%	1 1.6%	2 2.8%	0 0	0 0	0 0	0 0	0 0	3 1.4%	1 1.2%
Author	9 3.1%	7 3.7%	2 2.0%	9 3.1%	0 0	3 2.3%	3 2.9%	3 5.5%	1 1.8%	1 1.6%	2 2.8%	4 6.2%	1 6.9%	0 0	0 0	0 0	6 2.9%	3 3.7%
All sources of info	9 3.1%	7 3.7%	2 2.0%	9 3.1%	0 0	3 2.3%	3 2.9%	3 5.5%	1 1.8%	1 1.6%	2 2.8%	4 6.2%	1 6.9%	0 0	0 0	0 0	6 2.9%	3 3.7%
preferred source of info	6 2.2%	4 2.3%	2 2.0%	6 2.2%	0 0	2 1.4%	1 1.3%	3 5.5%	1 1.8%	1 1.6%	2 2.8%	2 3.1%	* 3.4%	0 0	0 0	0 0	4 1.7%	3 3.7%

Proportions/Means: Columns Tested (5% risk level) - A/B/D - C/D - E/F/G - H/I/J/K/L/M/N - P/Q
* small base; ** very small base (under 30) ineligible for sig testing

Table 259
Page 1040

Outsell/Digital Library Federation Study (2002)
Weighted Tables

TABLE 116, continued

T7D/E_10. Manuscripts and other primary source documents SUMMARY TABLE

		RESPONDENT TYPE				INSTITUTION TYPE			DISCIPLINE									GENDER	
	TOTAL SAMPLE	FACULTY MEMBER	GRAD. STUDENT	FACULTY /GRAD	UNDER GRAD. STUDENT	PUBLIC	PRIVATE	LIBERAL ARTS	BIOLOGIAL SCIENCES	PHYSICAL SCIENCES /MATH	SOCIAL SCIENCES	ARTS AND HUMAN.	ENGI-NEERING	BUSINESS	LAW	UNDEC. MAJOR	MALE	FEMALE
		(A)	(B)	(C)	(D)	(E)	(F)	(G)	(H)	(I)	(J)	(K)	(L)	(M)	(N)		(P)	(Q)
Base - Use Manuscripts and other primary source documents for teaching	283	189	94*	283	0**	133	90*	59*	50*	61*	68*	73*	8**	21**	1**	0*	208	75*
Office (NET)	8 2.7%	8 4.1%	0 0	8 2.7%	0 0	4 3.0%	3 3.1%	1 1.7%	2 3.5%	3 4.9%	2 2.8%	1 1.5%	0 0	0 0	0 0	0 0	7 3.3%	1 1.2%
All sources of info	8 2.7%	8 4.1%	0 0	8 2.7%	0 0	4 3.0%	3 3.1%	1 1.7%	2 3.5%	3 4.9%	2 2.8%	1 1.5%	0 0	0 0	0 0	0 0	7 3.3%	1 1.2%
preferred source of info	5 1.7%	5 2.5%	0 0	5 1.7%	0 0	3 2.3%	2 1.9%	0 0	2 3.5%	0 0	2 2.8%	1 1.5%	0 0	0 0	0 0	0 0	4 1.9%	1 1.2%
Colleagues (NET)	4 1.4%	2 1.1%	2 2.1%	4 1.4%	0 0	3 2.3%	1 1.0%	0 0	1 1.8%	2 3.3%	0 0	1 1.5%	0 0	0 0	0 0	0 0	3 1.4%	1 1.3%
All sources of info	4 1.4%	2 1.1%	2 2.1%	4 1.4%	0 0	3 2.3%	1 1.0%	0 0	1 1.8%	2 3.3%	0 0	1 1.5%	0 0	0 0	0 0	0 0	3 1.4%	1 1.3%
preferred source of info	2 0.7%	0 0	2 2.1%	2 0.7%	0 0	2 1.5%	0 0	0 0	0 0	2 3.3%	0 0	0 0	0 0	0 0	0 0	0 0	1 0.5%	1 1.3%
Publisher (NET)	4 1.3%	4 1.9%	0 0	4 1.3%	0 0	1 1.0%	2 2.2%	* 0.5%	1 1.8%	0 0	0 0	2 3.1%	* 3.4%	0 0	* 12.5%	0 0	2 1.2%	1 1.5%
All sources of info	4 1.3%	4 1.9%	0 0	4 1.3%	0 0	1 1.0%	2 2.2%	* 0.5%	1 1.8%	0 0	0 0	2 3.1%	* 3.4%	0 0	* 12.5%	0 0	2 1.2%	1 1.5%
preferred source of info	2 0.6%	2 0.8%	0 0	2 0.6%	.0 0	1 1.0%	0 0	* 0.5%	0 0	0 0	0 0	1 1.5%	* 3.4%	0 0	* 12.5%	0 0	* 0.2%	1 1.5%

Proportions/Means: Columns Tested (5% risk level) - A/B/D - C/D - E/F/G - H/I/J/K/L/M/N - P/Q
* small base; ** very small base (under 30) ineligible for sig testing

Table 259
Page 1041

Outsell/Digital Library Federation Study (2002)
Weighted Tables

TABLE 116, continued

T7D/E_10. Manuscripts and other primary source documents SUMMARY TABLE

	RESPONDENT TYPE				INSTITUTION TYPE			DISCIPLINE									GENDER	
	TOTAL SAMPLE	FACULTY MEMBER	GRAD. STUDENT	FACULTY /GRAD	UNDER GRAD. STUDENT	PUBLIC	PRIVATE	LIBERAL ARTS	BIOLOGIAL SCIENCES	PHYSICAL SCIENCES /MATH	SOCIAL SCIENCES	ARTS AND HUMAN.	ENGI-NEERING	BUSINESS	LAW	UNDEC. MAJOR	MALE	FEMALE
		(A)	(B)	(C)	(D)	(E)	(F)	(G)	(H)	(I)	(J)	(K)	(L)	(M)	(N)		(P)	(Q)
Base - Use Manuscripts and other primary source documents for teaching	283	189	94*	283	0**	133	90*	59*	50*	61*	68*	73*	8**	21**	1**	0*	208	75*
Department (NET)	3	0	3	3	0	2	1	0	1	1	0	1	0	0	0	0	2	1
	1.1%	0	3.2%A	1.1%	0	1.5%	1.1%	0	1.8%	1.6%	0	1.5%	0	0	0	0	1.0%	1.3%
All sources of info	3	0	3	3	0	2	1	0	1	1	0	1	0	0	0	0	2	1
	1.1%	0	3.2%A	1.1%	0	1.5%	1.1%	0	1.8%	1.6%	0	1.5%	0	0	0	0	1.0%	1.3%
preferred source of info	3	0	3	3	0	2	1	0	1	1	0	1	0	0	0	0	2	1
	1.1%	0	3.2%A	1.1%	0	1.5%	1.1%	0	1.8%	1.6%	0	1.5%	0	0	0	0	1.0%	1.3%
Home (NET)	2	1	1	2	0	1	1	0	0	0	0	2	0	0	0	0	1	1
	0.8%	0.6%	1.2%	0.8%	0	0.8%	1.2%	0	0	0	0	3.1%	0	0	0	0	0.5%	1.5%
All sources of info	2	1	1	2	0	1	1	0	0	0	0	2	0	0	0	0	1	1
	0.8%	0.6%	1.2%	0.8%	0	0.8%	1.2%	0	0	0	0	3.1%	0	0	0	0	0.5%	1.5%
preferred source of info	1	0	1	1	0	1	0	0	0	0	0	1	0	0	0	0	1	0
	0.4%	0	1.2%	0.4%	0	0.8%	0	0	0	0	0	1.5%	0	0	0	0	0.5%	0
Order from on demand document delivery service (NET)	2	2	0	2	0	*	0	2	0	1	0	0	0	1	*	0	2	0
	0.7%	1.1%	0	0.7%	0	0.1%	0	3.3%	0	1.6%	0	0	0	4.3%	12.5%	0	1.0%	0
All sources of info	2	2	0	2	0	*	0	2	0	1	0	0	0	1	*	0	2	0
	0.7%	1.1%	0	0.7%	0	0.1%	0	3.3%	0	1.6%	0	0	0	4.3%	12.5%	0	1.0%	0

Proportions/Means: Columns Tested (5% risk level) - A/B/D - C/D - E/F/G - H/I/J/K/L/M/N - P/Q
* small base; ** very small base (under 30) ineligible for sig testing

Table 259
Page 1042

Outsell/Digital Library Federation Study (2002)
Weighted Tables

TABLE 116, continued

T7D/E_10. Manuscripts and other primary source documents SUMMARY TABLE

		RESPONDENT TYPE				INSTITUTION TYPE			DISCIPLINE									GENDER	
	TOTAL SAMPLE	FACULTY MEMBER	GRAD. STUDENT	FACULTY /GRAD	UNDER GRAD. STUDENT	PUBLIC	PRIVATE	LIBERAL ARTS	BIOLOGICAL SCIENCES	PHYSICAL SCIENCES /MATH	SOCIAL SCIENCES	ARTS AND HUMAN.	ENGI-NEERING	BUSINESS	LAW	UNDEC. MAJOR	MALE	FEMALE
		(A)	(B)	(C)	(D)	(E)	(F)	(G)	(H)	(I)	(J)	(K)	(L)	(M)	(N)		(P)	(Q)
Base - Use Manuscripts and other primary source documents for teaching	283	189	94*	283	0**	133	90*	59*	50*	61*	68*	73*	8**	21**	1**	0*	208	75*
preferred source of info	1 0.3%	1 0.5%	0 0	1 0.3%	0 0	0 0	0 0	1 1.6%	0 0	0 0	0 0	0 0	0 0	1 4.3%	0 0	0 0	1 0.4%	0 0
Faculty (NET)	2 0.7%	0 0	2 2.1%	2 0.7%	0 0	2 1.5%	0 0	0 0	0 0	2 3.3%	0 0	0 0	0 0	0 0	0 0	0 0	1 0.5%	1 1.3%
All sources of info	2 0.7%	0 0	2 2.1%	2 0.7%	0 0	2 1.5%	0 0	0 0	0 0	2 3.3%	0 0	0 0	0 0	0 0	0 0	0 0	1 0.5%	1 1.3%
preferred source of info	1 0.4%	0 0	1 1.1%	1 0.4%	0 0	1 0.8%	0 0	0 0	0 0	1 1.6%	0 0	0 0	0 0	0 0	0 0	0 0	0 0	1 1.3%
Purchase from online bookstore (NET)	1 0.4%	1 0.6%	0 0	1 0.4%	0 0	0 0	1 1.2%	0 0	0 0	0 0	0 0	1 1.5%	0 0	0 0	0 0	0 0	1 0.5%	0 0
All sources of info	1 0.4%	1 0.6%	0 0	1 0.4%	0 0	0 0	1 1.2%	0 0	0 0	0 0	0 0	1 1.5%	0 0	0 0	0 0	0 0	1 0.5%	0 0
preferred source of info	1 0.4%	1 0.6%	0 0	1 0.4%	0 0	0 0	1 1.2%	0 0	0 0	0 0	0 0	1 1.5%	0 0	0 0	0 0	0 0	1 0.5%	0 0
Ask library to purchase source (NET)	1 0.4%	1 0.6%	0 0	1 0.4%	0 0	0 0	1 1.2%	0 0	0 0	0 0	0 0	1 1.5%	0 0	0 0	0 0	0 0	1 0.5%	0 0

Proportions/Means: Columns Tested (5% risk level) - A/B/D - C/D - E/F/G - H/I/J/K/L/M/N - P/Q
* small base; ** very small base (under 30) ineligible for sig testing

Table 259
Page 1043

Outsell/Digital Library Federation Study (2002)
Weighted Tables

TABLE 116, continued

T7D/E_10. Manuscripts and other primary source documents SUMMARY TABLE

		RESPONDENT TYPE				INSTITUTION TYPE			DISCIPLINE								GENDER	
	TOTAL SAMPLE	FACULTY MEMBER	GRAD. STUDENT	FACULTY /GRAD	UNDER GRAD. STUDENT	PUBLIC	PRIVATE	LIBERAL ARTS	BIOLOGIAL SCIENCES	PHYSICAL SCIENCES /MATH	SOCIAL SCIENCES	ARTS AND HUMAN.	ENGI-NEERING	BUSINESS	LAW	UNDEC. MAJOR	MALE	FEMALE
		(A)	(B)	(C)	(D)	(E)	(F)	(G)	(H)	(I)	(J)	(K)	(L)	(M)	(N)		(P)	(Q)
Base - Use Manuscripts and other primary source documents for teaching	283	189	94*	283	0**	133	90*	59*	50*	61*	68*	73*	8**	21**	1**	0*	208	75*
All sources of info	1 0.4%	1 0.6%	0 0	1 0.4%	0 0	0 0	1 1.2%	0 0	0 0	0 0	0 0	1 1.5%	0 0	0 0	0 0	0 0	1 0.5%	0 0
preferred source of info	0 0	0 0	0 0	0 0	0 0	0 0	0 0	0 0	0 0	0 0	0 0	0 0	0 0	0 0	0 0	0 0	0 0	0 0
Meeting/Conferences (NET)	0 0	0 0	0 0	0 0	0 0	0 0	0 0	0 0	0 0	0 0	0 0	0 0	0 0	0 0	0 0	0 0	0 0	0 0
All sources of info	0 0	0 0	0 0	0 0	0 0	0 0	0 0	0 0	0 0	0 0	0 0	0 0	0 0	0 0	0 0	0 0	0 0	0 0
preferred source of info	0 0	0 0	0 0	0 0	0 0	0 0	0 0	0 0	0 0	0 0	0 0	0 0	0 0	0 0	0 0	0 0	0 0	0 0
Access book/journal/ journal article elsewhere online (NET)	0 0	0 0	0 0	0 0	0 0	0 0	0 0	0 0	0 0	0 0	0 0	0 0	0 0	0 0	0 0	0 0	0 0	0 0
All sources of info	0 0	0 0	0 0	0 0	0 0	0 0	0 0	0 0	0 0	0 0	0 0	0 0	0 0	0 0	0 0	0 0	0 0	0 0
preferred source of info	0 0	0 0	0 0	0 0	0 0	0 0	0 0	0 0	0 0	0 0	0 0	0 0	0 0	0 0	0 0	0 0	0 0	0 0

Proportions/Means: Columns Tested (5% risk level) - A/B/D - C/D - E/F/G - H/I/J/K/L/M/N - P/Q
* small base; ** very small base (under 30) ineligible for sig testing

Table 259
Page 1044

Outsell/Digital Library Federation Study (2002)
Weighted Tables

TABLE 116, continued

T7D/E_10. Manuscripts and other primary source documents SUMMARY TABLE

		RESPONDENT TYPE				INSTITUTION TYPE			DISCIPLINE								GENDER	
	TOTAL SAMPLE	FACULTY MEMBER	GRAD. STUDENT	FACULTY /GRAD	UNDER GRAD. STUDENT	PUBLIC	PRIVATE	LIBERAL ARTS	BIOLOGIAL SCIENCES	PHYSICAL SCIENCES /MATH	SOCIAL SCIENCES	ARTS AND HUMAN.	ENGI-NEERING	BUSINESS	LAW	UNDEC. MAJOR	MALE	FEMALE
		(A)	(B)	(C)	(D)	(E)	(F)	(G)	(H)	(I)	(J)	(K)	(L)	(M)	(N)		(P)	(Q)
Base - Use Manuscripts and other primary source documents for teaching	283	189	94*	283	0**	133	90*	59*	50*	61*	68*	73*	8**	21**	1**	0*	208	75*
Other (NET)	7 2.6%	5 2.6%	2 2.6%	7 2.6%	0 0	3 2.5%	2 2.4%	2 3.4%	1 1.8%	3 4.9%	2 2.8%	1 1.5%	1 6.9%	0 0	0 0	0 0	4 2.0%	3 4.4%
All sources of info	7 2.6%	5 2.6%	2 2.6%	7 2.6%	0 0	3 2.5%	2 2.4%	2 3.4%	1 1.8%	3 4.9%	2 2.8%	1 1.5%	1 6.9%	0 0	0 0	0 0	4 2.0%	3 4.4%
preferred source of info	1 0.5%	1 0.5%	* 0.3%	1 0.5%	0 0	0 0	* 0.3%	1 1.7%	0 0	1 1.6%	0 0	0 0	* 3.4%	0 0	0 0	0 0	1 0.5%	* 0.4%
DK/Refused	8 2.9%	6 3.1%	2 2.6%	8 2.9%	0 0	5 3.9%	3 3.5%	0 0	0 0	3 4.9%	2 2.8%	2 3.1%	* 3.4%	1 4.3%	0 0	0 0	8 4.0%	0 0

Proportions/Means: Columns Tested (5% risk level) - A/B/D - C/D - E/F/G - H/I/J/K/L/M/N - P/Q
* small base; ** very small base (under 30) ineligible for sig testing

Table 259
Page 1045

Outsell/Digital Library Federation Study (2002)
Weighted Tables

TABLE 117

T7sum_11. Proprietary software or application SUMMARY TABLE

		RESPONDENT TYPE				INSTITUTION TYPE			DISCIPLINE								GENDER	
	TOTAL SAMPLE	FACULTY MEMBER	GRAD. STUDENT	FACULTY /GRAD	UNDER GRAD. STUDENT	PUBLIC	PRIVATE	LIBERAL ARTS	BIOLOGIAL SCIENCES	PHYSICAL SCIENCES /MATH	SOCIAL SCIENCES	ARTS AND HUMAN.	ENGI-NEERING	BUSINESS	LAW	UNDEC. MAJOR	MALE	FEMALE
		(A)	(B)	(C)	(D)	(E)	(F)	(G)	(H)	(I)	(J)	(K)	(L)	(M)	(N)		(P)	(Q)
Base - USe Proprietary software or application for teaching	190	129	61*	190	0**	65*	62*	63*	29*	61*	34**	31**	14*	20**	1**	0*	144	46*
ONLINE	114 59.8%	86 66.9%B	28 44.9%	114 59.8%	0 0	35 54.2%	30 48.0%	49 77.3%EF	19 66.7%	36 59.0%	23 66.7%	17 53.6%	7 49.0%	11 57.1%	1 80.0%	0 0	88 61.1%	26 55.7%
Search engine	35 18.5%	29 22.8%B	6 9.5%	35 18.5%	0 0	6 8.4%	7 11.4%	23 36.0%EF	5 18.2%	14 23.0%	4 11.1%	6 17.9%	3 18.4%	4 19.0%	* 20.0%	0 0	27 18.7%	8 18.0%
All sources of info	35 18.5%	29 22.8%B	6 9.5%	35 18.5%	0 0	6 8.4%	7 11.4%	23 36.0%EF	5 18.2%	14 23.0%	4 11.1%	6 17.9%	3 18.4%	4 19.0%	* 20.0%	0 0	27 18.7%	8 18.0%
preferred source of info	20 10.4%	16 12.6%	4 5.8%	20 10.4%	0 0	2 2.7%	4 5.7%	15 23.1%EF	3 9.1%	7 11.5%	4 11.1%	3 10.7%	1 8.2%	2 9.5%	0 0	0 0	14 9.5%	6 13.3%
Web directory/ subject related web site	34 17.8%	28 22.1%B	5 8.9%	34 17.8%	0 0	8 12.6%	9 13.8%	17 27.2%E	5 18.2%	13 21.3%	8 22.2%	3 10.7%	3 18.4%	2 9.5%	* 20.0%	0 0	25 17.7%	8 18.0%
All sources of info	34 17.8%	28 22.1%B	5 8.9%	34 17.8%	0 0	8 12.6%	9 13.8%	17 27.2%E	5 18.2%	13 21.3%	8 22.2%	3 10.7%	3 18.4%	2 9.5%	* 20.0%	0 0	25 17.7%	8 18.0%
preferred source of info	17 9.2%	15 11.9%	2 3.5%	17 9.2%	0 0	4 5.9%	5 8.4%	8 13.3%	3 9.1%	5 8.2%	4 11.1%	2 7.1%	2 12.2%	2 9.5%	* 20.0%	0 0	14 9.6%	4 7.7%
Internet searches	23 12.2%	18 13.8%	5 8.7%	23 12.2%	0 0	9 13.7%	6 10.1%	8 12.6%	6 21.2%	6 9.8%	2 5.6%	3 10.7%	1 6.1%	5 23.8%	* 20.0%	0 0	16 11.4%	7 14.4%
All sources of info	23 12.2%	18 13.8%	5 8.7%	23 12.2%	0 0	9 13.7%	6 10.1%	8 12.6%	6 21.2%	6 9.8%	2 5.6%	3 10.7%	1 6.1%	5 23.8%	* 20.0%	0 0	16 11.4%	7 14.4%

Proportions/Means: Columns Tested (5% risk level) - A/B/D - C/D - E/F/G - H/I/J/K/L/M/N - P/Q
* small base; ** very small base (under 30) ineligible for sig testing

Table 263
Page 1057

TABLE 117, continued

T7sum_11. Proprietary software or application SUMMARY TABLE

	TOTAL SAMPLE	RESPONDENT TYPE: FACULTY MEMBER	GRAD. STUDENT	FACULTY /GRAD	UNDER GRAD. STUDENT	INSTITUTION TYPE: PUBLIC	PRIVATE	LIBERAL ARTS	DISCIPLINE: BIOLOGIAL SCIENCES	PHYSICAL SCIENCES /MATH	SOCIAL SCIENCES	ARTS AND HUMAN.	ENGI-NEERING	BUSINESS	LAW	UNDEC. MAJOR	GENDER: MALE	FEMALE
		(A)	(B)	(C)	(D)	(E)	(F)	(G)	(H)	(I)	(J)	(K)	(L)	(M)	(N)		(P)	(Q)
Base - USe Proprietary software or application for teaching	190	129	61*	190	0**	65*	62*	63*	29*	61*	34**	31**	14*	20**	1**	0*	144	46*
preferred source of info	12 6.3%	8 6.2%	4 6.6%	12 6.3%	0 0	6 9.0%	2 3.8%	4 6.1%	4 15.2%I	2 3.3%	2 5.6%	1 3.6%	1 4.1%	2 9.5%	* 20.0%	0 0	8 5.7%	4 8.2%
Your own institution's web site	17 9.0%	8 6.2%	9 15.0%	17 9.0%	0 0	7 10.0%	6 9.7%	5 7.4%	3 9.1%	4 6.6%	6 16.7%	3 10.7%	1 4.1%	1 4.8%	0 0	0 0	13 9.2%	4 8.6%
All sources of info	17 9.0%	8 6.2%	9 15.0%	17 9.0%	0 0	7 10.0%	6 9.7%	5 7.4%	3 9.1%	4 6.6%	6 16.7%	3 10.7%	1 4.1%	1 4.8%	0 0	0 0	13 9.2%	4 8.6%
preferred source of info	6 3.4%	3 2.5%	3 5.4%	6 3.4%	0 0	2 2.4%	3 4.8%	2 3.0%	2 6.1%	3 4.9%	0 0	1 3.6%	1 4.1%	0 0	0 0	0 0	6 4.5%	0 0
Online reference service	9 4.5%	9 6.7%	0 0	9 4.5%	0 0	4 6.6%	0 0	4 6.8%	1 3.0%	3 4.9%	0 0	2 7.1%	1 4.1%	2 9.5%	0 0	0 0	9 6.0%	0 0
All sources of info	9 4.5%	9 6.7%	0 0	9 4.5%	0 0	4 6.6%	0 0	4 6.8%	1 3.0%	3 4.9%	0 0	2 7.1%	1 4.1%	2 9.5%	0 0	0 0	9 6.0%	0 0
preferred source of info	3 1.5%	3 2.2%	0 0	3 1.5%	0 0	3 4.3%	0 0	0 0	1 3.0%	1 1.6%	0 0	0 0	0 0	1 4.8%	0 0	0 0	3 2.0%	0 0
Online databases	8 4.3%	6 4.9%	2 3.1%	8 4.3%	0 0	4 6.5%	0 0	4 6.3%	2 6.1%	2 3.3%	2 5.6%	1 3.6%	* 2.0%	1 4.8%	* 20.0%	0 0	7 5.0%	1 2.2%
All sources of info	8 4.3%	6 4.9%	2 3.1%	8 4.3%	0 0	4 6.5%	0 0	4 6.3%	2 6.1%	2 3.3%	2 5.6%	1 3.6%	* 2.0%	1 4.8%	* 20.0%	0 0	7 5.0%	1 2.2%

Proportions/Means: Columns Tested (5% risk level) - A/B/D - C/D - E/F/G - H/I/J/K/L/M/N - P/Q
* small base; ** very small base (under 30) ineligible for sig testing

Table 263
Page 1058

Outsell/Digital Library Federation Study (2002)
Weighted Tables

TABLE 117, continued

T7sum_11. Proprietary software or application SUMMARY TABLE

		RESPONDENT TYPE				INSTITUTION TYPE			DISCIPLINE								GENDER	
	TOTAL SAMPLE	FACULTY MEMBER	GRAD. STUDENT	FACULTY /GRAD	UNDER GRAD. STUDENT	PUBLIC	PRIVATE	LIBERAL ARTS	BIOLOGIAL SCIENCES	PHYSICAL SCIENCES /MATH	SOCIAL SCIENCES	ARTS AND HUMAN.	ENGI-NEERING	BUSINESS	LAW	UNDEC. MAJOR	MALE	FEMALE
		(A)	(B)	(C)	(D)	(E)	(F)	(G)	(H)	(I)	(J)	(K)	(L)	(M)	(N)		(P)	(Q)
Base - USe Proprietary software or application for teaching	190	129	61*	190	0**	65*	62*	63*	29*	61*	34**	31**	14*	20**	1**	0*	144	46*
preferred source of info	6 3.2%	4 3.3%	2 3.1%	6 3.2%	0 0	3 5.1%	0 0	3 4.5%	1 3.0%	2 3.3%	2 5.6%	0 0	* 2.0%	1 4.8%	* 20.0%	0 0	5 3.6%	1 2.2%
Department web page	8 4.0%	4 2.9%	4 6.3%	8 4.0%	0 0	4 6.0%	4 6.1%	0 0	1 3.0%	0 0	6 16.7%	1 3.6%	0 0	0 0	0 0	0 0	4 2.6%	4 8.4%
All sources of info	8 4.0%	4 2.9%	4 6.3%	8 4.0%	0 0	4 6.0%	4 6.1%	0 0	1 3.0%	0 0	6 16.7%	1 3.6%	0 0	0 0	0 0	0 0	4 2.6%	4 8.4%
preferred source of info	4 2.0%	2 1.5%	2 3.3%	4 2.0%	0 0	2 3.1%	2 3.0%	0 0	1 3.0%	0 0	2 5.6%	1 3.6%	0 0	0 0	0 0	0 0	2 1.3%	2 4.3%
Online library catalogues and finding aids	5 2.7%	5 3.8%	* 0.5%	5 2.7%	0 0	1 1.7%	2 3.5%	2 3.0%	0 0	0 0	4 11.1%	1 3.6%	* 2.0%	0 0	0 0	0 0	5 3.6%	0 0
All sources of info	5 2.7%	5 3.8%	* 0.5%	5 2.7%	0 0	1 1.7%	2 3.5%	2 3.0%	0 0	0 0	4 11.1%	1 3.6%	* 2.0%	0 0	0 0	0 0	5 3.6%	0 0
preferred source of info	* 0.2%	0 0	* 0.5%	* 0.2%	0 0	0 0	* 0.5%	0 0	0 0	0 0	0 0	0 0	* 2.0%	0 0	0 0	0 0	* 0.2%	0 0
Your own personal electronic library/files	3 1.6%	1 0.9%	2 3.1%	3 1.6%	0 0	2 3.3%	1 1.5%	0 0	0 0	0 0	2 5.6%	0 0	* 2.0%	1 4.8%	0 0	0 0	2 1.3%	1 2.6%
All sources of info	3 1.6%	1 0.9%	2 3.1%	3 1.6%	0 0	2 3.3%	1 1.5%	0 0	0 0	0 0	2 5.6%	0 0	* 2.0%	1 4.8%	0 0	0 0	2 1.3%	1 2.6%

Proportions/Means: Columns Tested (5% risk level) - A/B/D - C/D - E/F/G - H/I/J/K/L/M/N - P/Q
* small base; ** very small base (under 30) ineligible for sig testing

Table 263
Page 1059

Outsell/Digital Library Federation Study (2002)
Weighted Tables

TABLE 117, continued

T7sum_11. Proprietary software or application SUMMARY TABLE

		RESPONDENT TYPE				INSTITUTION TYPE			DISCIPLINE								GENDER	
	TOTAL SAMPLE	FACULTY MEMBER	GRAD. STUDENT	FACULTY /GRAD	UNDER GRAD. STUDENT	PUBLIC	PRIVATE	LIBERAL ARTS	BIOLOGIAL SCIENCES	PHYSICAL SCIENCES /MATH	SOCIAL SCIENCES	ARTS AND HUMAN.	ENGI- NEERING	BUSINESS	LAW	UNDEC. MAJOR	MALE	FEMALE
		(A)	(B)	(C)	(D)	(E)	(F)	(G)	(H)	(I)	(J)	(K)	(L)	(M)	(N)		(P)	(Q)
Base - USe Proprietary software or application for teaching	190	129	61*	190	0**	65*	62*	63*	29*	61*	34**	31**	14*	20**	1**	0*	144	46*
preferred source of info	3 1.6%	1 0.9%	2 3.1%	3 1.6%	0 0	2 3.3%	1 1.5%	0 0	0 0	0 0	2 5.6%	0 0	* 2.0%	1 4.8%	0 0	0 0	2 1.3%	1 2.6%
Online abstracting and indexing services	3 1.5%	3 2.2%	0 0	3 1.5%	0 0	0 0	2 3.0%	1 1.6%	0 0	1 1.6%	2 5.6%	0 0	0 0	0 0	0 0	0 0	3 2.0%	0 0
All sources of info	3 1.5%	3 2.2%	0 0	3 1.5%	0 0	0 0	2 3.0%	1 1.6%	0 0	1 1.6%	2 5.6%	0 0	0 0	0 0	0 0	0 0	3 2.0%	0 0
preferred source of info	3 1.5%	3 2.2%	0 0	3 1.5%	0 0	0 0	2 3.0%	1 1.6%	0 0	1 1.6%	2 5.6%	0 0	0 0	0 0	0 0	0 0	3 2.0%	0 0
Online bookstore	1 0.6%	1 0.9%	0 0	1 0.6%	0 0	1 1.7%	0 0	0 0	0 0	0 0	0 0	1 3.6%	0 0	0 0	0 0	0 0	1 0.8%	0 0
All sources of info	1 0.6%	1 0.9%	0 0	1 0.6%	0 0	1 1.7%	0 0	0 0	0 0	0 0	0 0	1 3.6%	0 0	0 0	0 0	0 0	1 0.8%	0 0
preferred source of info	0 0	0 0	0 0	0 0	0 0	0 0	0 0	0 0	0 0	0 0	0 0	0 0	0 0	0 0	0 0	0 0	0 0	0 0
E-mail listservs	1 0.5%	1 0.8%	0 0	1 0.5%	0 0	0 0	0 0	1 1.6%	0 0	1 1.6%	0 0	0 0	0 0	0 0	0 0	0 0	1 0.7%	0 0
All sources of info	1 0.5%	1 0.8%	0 0	1 0.5%	0 0	0 0	0 0	1 1.6%	0 0	1 1.6%	0 0	0 0	0 0	0 0	0 0	0 0	1 0.7%	0 0

Proportions/Means: Columns Tested (5% risk level) - A/B/D - C/D - E/F/G - H/I/J/K/L/M/N - P/Q
* small base; ** very small base (under 30) ineligible for sig testing

Table 263
Page 1060

Outsell/Digital Library Federation Study (2002)
Weighted Tables

TABLE 117, continued

T7sum_11. Proprietary software or application SUMMARY TABLE

	TOTAL SAMPLE	RESPONDENT TYPE FACULTY MEMBER	GRAD. STUDENT	FACULTY /GRAD	UNDER GRAD. STUDENT	INSTITUTION TYPE PUBLIC	PRIVATE	LIBERAL ARTS	DISCIPLINE BIOLOGIAL SCIENCES	PHYSICAL SCIENCES /MATH	SOCIAL SCIENCES	ARTS AND HUMAN.	ENGI-NEERING	BUSINESS	LAW	UNDEC. MAJOR	GENDER MALE	FEMALE
		(A)	(B)	(C)	(D)	(E)	(F)	(G)	(H)	(I)	(J)	(K)	(L)	(M)	(N)		(P)	(Q)
Base - USe Proprietary software or application for teaching	190	129	61*	190	0**	65*	62*	63*	29*	61*	34**	31**	14*	20**	1**	0*	144	46*
preferred source of info	0 0	0 0	0 0	0 0	0 0	0 0	0 0	0 0	0 0	0 0	0 0	0 0	0 0	0 0	0 0	0 0	0 0	0 0
PERSONAL ASSISTANCE	90 47.4%	55 42.5%	35 57.6%	90 47.4%	0 0	32 49.3%	31 49.8%	27 42.9%	10 33.3%	34 55.7%H	15 44.4%	18 57.1%	6 42.9%	7 33.3%	1 80.0%	0 0	72 49.9%	18 39.6%
Colleagues inside your institution	79 41.4%	47 36.2%	32 52.4%	79 41.4%	0 0	29 44.1%	25 40.5%	25 39.5%	9 30.3%	31 50.8%	13 38.9%	15 46.4%	5 36.7%	6 28.6%	* 40.0%	0 0	61 42.8%	17 37.2%
All sources of info	79 41.4%	47 36.2%	32 52.4%	79 41.4%	0 0	29 44.1%	25 40.5%	25 39.5%	9 30.3%	31 50.8%	13 38.9%	15 46.4%	5 36.7%	6 28.6%	* 40.0%	0 0	61 42.8%	17 37.2%
preferred source of info	51 27.1%	27 20.8%	25 40.2%A	51 27.1%	0 0	18 27.5%	18 29.6%	15 24.2%	7 24.2%	21 34.4%	6 16.7%	11 35.7%	3 18.4%	4 19.0%	* 20.0%	0 0	42 29.0%	10 21.1%
Colleagues outside your institution	22 11.8%	20 15.9%B	2 3.1%	22 11.8%	0 0	6 9.6%	5 8.5%	11 17.1%	4 12.1%	11 18.0%	2 5.6%	3 10.7%	1 10.2%	1 4.8%	* 20.0%	0 0	15 10.2%	8 16.6%
All sources of info	22 11.8%	20 15.9%B	2 3.1%	22 11.8%	0 0	6 9.6%	5 8.5%	11 17.1%	4 12.1%	11 18.0%	2 5.6%	3 10.7%	1 10.2%	1 4.8%	* 20.0%	0 0	15 10.2%	8 16.6%
preferred source of info	4 1.9%	4 2.8%	0 0	4 1.9%	0 0	1 2.2%	2 3.5%	0 0	1 3.0%	1 1.6%	0 0	1 3.6%	1 4.1%	0 0	0 0	0 0	4 2.5%	0 0
A librarian in your institution	15 7.7%	11 8.9%	3 5.2%	15 7.7%	0 0	6 8.5%	3 4.8%	6 9.7%	0 0	4 6.6%	4 11.1%	6 17.9%	0 0	1 4.8%	* 40.0%	0 0	14 9.4%	1 2.4%

Proportions/Means: Columns Tested (5% risk level) - A/B/D - C/D - E/F/G - H/I/J/K/L/M/N - P/Q
* small base; ** very small base (under 30) ineligible for sig testing

TABLE 117, continued

T7sum_11. Proprietary software or application SUMMARY TABLE

		RESPONDENT TYPE				INSTITUTION TYPE			DISCIPLINE								GENDER	
	TOTAL SAMPLE	FACULTY MEMBER	GRAD. STUDENT	FACULTY /GRAD	UNDER GRAD. STUDENT	PUBLIC	PRIVATE	LIBERAL ARTS	BIOLOGIAL SCIENCES	PHYSICAL SCIENCES /MATH	SOCIAL SCIENCES	ARTS AND HUMAN.	ENGI-NEERING	BUSINESS	LAW	UNDEC. MAJOR	MALE	FEMALE
		(A)	(B)	(C)	(D)	(E)	(F)	(G)	(H)	(I)	(J)	(K)	(L)	(M)	(N)		(P)	(Q)
Base - USe	190	129	61*	190	0**	65*	62*	63*	29*	61*	34**	31**	14*	20**	1**	0*	144	46*
Proprietary software or application for teaching																		
All sources of info	15	11	3	15	0	6	3	6	0	4	4	6	0	1	*	0	14	1
	7.7%	8.9%	5.2%	7.7%	0	8.5%	4.8%	9.7%	0	6.6%	11.1%	17.9%	0	4.8%	40.0%	0	9.4%	2.4%
preferred source of info	3	2	1	3	0	1	2	0	0	0	2	0	0	1	0	0	3	0
	1.5%	1.5%	1.5%	1.5%	0	1.4%	3.0%	0	0	0	5.6%	0	0	4.8%	0	0	2.0%	0
Professional meetings	3	3	0	3	0	*	1	2	0	1	0	1	1	0	0	0	3	0
	1.6%	2.3%	0	1.6%	0	0.4%	0.9%	3.4%	0	1.6%	0	3.6%	6.1%	0	0	0	2.1%	0
All sources of info	3	3	0	3	0	*	1	2	0	1	0	1	1	0	0	0	3	0
	1.6%	2.3%	0	1.6%	0	0.4%	0.9%	3.4%	0	1.6%	0	3.6%	6.1%	0	0	0	2.1%	0
preferred source of info	2	2	0	2	0	0	1	1	0	0	0	1	1	0	0	0	2	0
	0.9%	1.3%	0	0.9%	0	0	0.9%	1.8%	0	0	0	3.6%	4.1%I	0	0	0	1.2%	0
Another institution's librarian	0	0	0	0	0	0	0	0	0	0	0	0	0	0	0	0	0	0
	0	0	0	0	0	0	0	0	0	0	0	0	0	0	0	0	0	0
All sources of info	0	0	0	0	0	0	0	0	0	0	0	0	0	0	0	0	0	0
	0	0	0	0	0	0	0	0	0	0	0	0	0	0	0	0	0	0
preferred source of info	0	0	0	0	0	0	0	0	0	0	0	0	0	0	0	0	0	0
	0	0	0	0	0	0	0	0	0	0	0	0	0	0	0	0	0	0
LIBRARY/PRINT	52	40	12	52	0	18	11	23	4	21	8	8	5	7	*	0	42	10
	27.5%	31.2%	19.8%	27.5%	0	28.2%	17.1%	37.1%F	15.2%	34.4%	22.2%	25.0%	32.7%	33.3%	40.0%	0	29.3%	21.9%

Proportions/Means: Columns Tested (5% risk level) - A/B/D - C/D - E/F/G - H/I/J/K/L/M/N - P/Q
* small base; ** very small base (under 30) ineligible for sig testing

Table 263
Page 1062

Outsell/Digital Library Federation Study (2002)
Weighted Tables

TABLE 117, continued

T7sum_11. Proprietary software or application SUMMARY TABLE

		RESPONDENT TYPE				INSTITUTION TYPE			DISCIPLINE								GENDER	
	TOTAL SAMPLE	FACULTY MEMBER	GRAD. STUDENT	FACULTY /GRAD	UNDER GRAD. STUDENT	PUBLIC	PRIVATE	LIBERAL ARTS	BIOLOGIAL SCIENCES	PHYSICAL SCIENCES /MATH	SOCIAL SCIENCES	ARTS AND HUMAN.	ENGI-NEERING	BUSINESS	LAW	UNDEC. MAJOR	MALE	FEMALE
		(A)	(B)	(C)	(D)	(E)	(F)	(G)	(H)	(I)	(J)	(K)	(L)	(M)	(N)		(P)	(Q)
Base - USe Proprietary software or application for teaching	190	129	61*	190	0**	65*	62*	63*	29*	61*	34**	31**	14*	20**	1**	0*	144	46*
Campus library	35	23	12	35	0	11	6	17	3	16	6	8	2	1	*	0	28	7
	18.4%	18.0%	19.4%	18.4%	0	17.6%	10.1%	27.5%F	9.1%	26.2%	16.7%	25.0%	12.2%	4.8%	20.0%	0	19.4%	15.4%
All sources of info	35	23	12	35	0	11	6	17	3	16	6	8	2	1	*	0	28	7
	18.4%	18.0%	19.4%	18.4%	0	17.6%	10.1%	27.5%F	9.1%	26.2%	16.7%	25.0%	12.2%	4.8%	20.0%	0	19.4%	15.4%
preferred source of info	9	*	8	9	0	6	3	0	0	3	4	1	1	0	*	0	5	3
	4.5%	0.1%	13.8%A	4.5%	0	8.8%G	4.7%	0	0	4.9%	11.1%	3.6%	4.1%	0	20.0%	0	3.8%	6.9%
Your own personal physical library/ files/bookshelves	20	19	*	20	0	6	4	10	2	7	4	2	1	4	0	0	17	2
	10.3%	15.1%B	0.5%	10.3%	0	8.9%	6.9%	15.2%	6.1%	11.5%	11.1%	7.1%	8.2%	19.0%	0	0	12.2%	4.7%
All sources of info	20	19	*	20	0	6	4	10	2	7	4	2	1	4	0	0	17	2
	10.3%	15.1%B	0.5%	10.3%	0	8.9%	6.9%	15.2%	6.1%	11.5%	11.1%	7.1%	8.2%	19.0%	0	0	12.2%	4.7%
preferred source of info	9	9	*	9	0	4	4	1	0	2	2	1	1	3	0	0	9	*
	4.7%	6.7%	0.5%	4.7%	0	5.6%	6.9%	1.6%	0	3.3%	5.6%	3.6%	8.2%H	14.3%	0	0	6.0%	0.6%
References cited in books or journal articles	6	6	0	6	0	1	1	4	2	3	0	0	*	1	*	0	3	3
	3.2%	4.8%	0	3.2%	0	2.1%	1.4%	6.2%	6.1%	4.9%	0	0	2.0%	4.8%	20.0%	0	2.4%	6.0%
All sources of info	6	6	0	6	0	1	1	4	2	3	0	0	*	1	*	0	3	3
	3.2%	4.8%	0	3.2%	0	2.1%	1.4%	6.2%	6.1%	4.9%	0	0	2.0%	4.8%	20.0%	0	2.4%	6.0%
preferred source of info	1	1	0	1	0	*	0	1	0	1	0	0	*	0	0	0	*	1
	0.7%	1.0%	0	0.7%	0	0.4%	0	1.6%	0	1.6%	0	0	2.0%	0	0	0	0.2%	2.2%

Proportions/Means: Columns Tested (5% risk level) - A/B/D - C/D - E/F/G - H/I/J/K/L/M/N - P/Q
* small base; ** very small base (under 30) ineligible for sig testing

Table 263
Page 1063

Outsell/Digital Library Federation Study (2002)
Weighted Tables

TABLE 117, continued

T7sum_11. Proprietary software or application SUMMARY TABLE

		RESPONDENT TYPE				INSTITUTION TYPE			DISCIPLINE								GENDER	
	TOTAL SAMPLE	FACULTY MEMBER	GRAD. STUDENT	FACULTY /GRAD	UNDER GRAD. STUDENT	PUBLIC	PRIVATE	LIBERAL ARTS	BIOLOGIAL SCIENCES	PHYSICAL SCIENCES /MATH	SOCIAL SCIENCES	ARTS AND HUMAN.	ENGI-NEERING	BUSINESS	LAW	UNDEC. MAJOR	MALE	FEMALE
		(A)	(B)	(C)	(D)	(E)	(F)	(G)	(H)	(I)	(J)	(K)	(L)	(M)	(N)		(P)	(Q)
Base - USe Proprietary software or application for teaching	190	129	61*	190	0**	65*	62*	63*	29*	61*	34**	31**	14*	20**	1**	0*	144	46*
Personal subscriptions to newspapers, magazines and journals	6 3.1%	6 4.5%	0 0	6 3.1%	0 0	2 3.2%	* 0.5%	3 5.5%	1 3.0%	2 3.3%	0 0	0 0	2 14.3%I	1 4.8%	0 0	0 0	6 3.9%	* 0.6%
All sources of info	6 3.1%	6 4.5%	0 0	6 3.1%	0 0	2 3.2%	* 0.5%	3 5.5%	1 3.0%	2 3.3%	0 0	0 0	2 14.3%I	1 4.8%	0 0	0 0	6 3.9%	* 0.6%
preferred source of info	1 0.6%	1 0.9%	0 0	1 0.6%	0 0	0 0	0 0	1 1.9%	1 3.0%	0 0	0 0	0 0	* 2.0%	0 0	0 0	0 0	1 0.8%	0 0
Printed abstracting and indexing services	2 1.0%	2 1.4%	0 0	2 1.0%	0 0	1 1.4%	0 0	1 1.5%	0 0	0 0	0 0	0 0	0 0	2 9.5%	0 0	0 0	2 1.3%	0 0
All sources of info	2 1.0%	2 1.4%	0 0	2 1.0%	0 0	1 1.4%	0 0	1 1.5%	0 0	0 0	0 0	0 0	0 0	2 9.5%	0 0	0 0	2 1.3%	0 0
preferred source of info	0 0	0 0	0 0	0 0	0 0	0 0	0 0	0 0	0 0	0 0	0 0	0 0	0 0	0 0	0 0	0 0	0 0	0 0
Another library	1 0.8%	1 0.7%	1 0.9%	1 0.8%	0 0	1 0.9%	0 0	1 1.4%	1 3.0%	0 0	0 0	0 0	1 4.1%I	0 0	0 0	0 0	1 0.4%	1 1.9%
All sources of info	1 0.8%	1 0.7%	1 0.9%	1 0.8%	0 ·0	1 0.9%	0 0	1 1.4%	1 3.0%	0 0	0 0	0 0	1 4.1%I	0 0	0 0	0 0	1 0.4%	1 1.9%

Proportions/Means: Columns Tested (5% risk level) - A/B/D - C/D - E/F/G - H/I/J/K/L/M/N - P/Q
* small base; ** very small base (under 30) ineligible for sig testing

Table 263
Page 1064

Outsell/Digital Library Federation Study (2002)
Weighted Tables

TABLE 117, continued

T7sum_11. Proprietary software or application SUMMARY TABLE

	TOTAL SAMPLE	RESPONDENT TYPE: FACULTY MEMBER (A)	GRAD. STUDENT (B)	FACULTY /GRAD (C)	UNDER GRAD. STUDENT (D)	INSTITUTION TYPE: PUBLIC (E)	PRIVATE (F)	LIBERAL ARTS (G)	DISCIPLINE: BIOLOGIAL SCIENCES (H)	PHYSICAL SCIENCES /MATH (I)	SOCIAL SCIENCES (J)	ARTS AND HUMAN. (K)	ENGI-NEERING (L)	BUSINESS (M)	LAW (N)	UNDEC. MAJOR	GENDER: MALE (P)	FEMALE (Q)
Base - USe Proprietary software or application for teaching	190	129	61*	190	0**	65*	62*	63*	29*	61*	34**	31**	14*	20**	1**	0*	144	46*
preferred source of info	0 0	0 0	0 0	0 0	0 0	0 0	0 0	0 0	0 0	0 0	0 0	0 0	0 0	0 0	0 0	0 0	0 0	0 0
Physical bookstore	1 0.5%	1 0.7%	0 0	1 0.5%	0 0	0 0	0 0	1 1.4%	1 3.0%	0 0	0 0	0 0	0 0	0 0	0 0	0 0	0 0	1 1.9%
All sources of info	1 0.5%	1 0.7%	0 0	1 0.5%	0 0	0 0	0 0	1 1.4%	1 3.0%	0 0	0 0	0 0	0 0	0 0	0 0	0 0	0 0	1 1.9%
preferred source of info	0 0	0 0	0 0	0 0	0 0	0 0	0 0	0 0	0 0	0 0	0 0	0 0	0 0	0 0	0 0	0 0	0 0	0 0
Printed library catalogues and finding aids	* 0.1%	* 0.1%	0 0	* 0.1%	0 0	* 0.3%	0 0	0 0	0 0	0 0	0 0	0 0	0 0	0 0	* 20.0%	0 0	* 0.1%	0 0
All sources of info	* 0.1%	* 0.1%	0 0	* 0.1%	0 0	* 0.3%	0 0	0 0	0 0	0 0	0 0	0 0	0 0	0 0	* 20.0%	0 0	* 0.1%	0 0
preferred source of info	0 0	0 0	0 0	0 0	0 0	0 0	0 0	0 0	0 0	0 0	0 0	0 0	0 0	0 0	0 0	0 0	0 0	0 0
Personal office/lab	0 0	0 0	0 0	0 0	0 0	0 0	0 0	0 0	0 0	0 0	0 0	0 0	0 0	0 0	0 0	0 0	0 0	0 0
All sources of info	0 0	0 0	0 0	0 0	0 0	0 0	0 0	0 0	0 0	0 0	0 0	0 0	0 0	0 0	0 0	0 0	0 0	0 0

Proportions/Means: Columns Tested (5% risk level) - A/B/D - C/D - E/F/G - H/I/J/K/L/M/N - P/Q
* small base; ** very small base (under 30) ineligible for sig testing

Table 263
Page 1065

Outsell/Digital Library Federation Study (2002)
Weighted Tables

TABLE 117, continued

T7sum_11. Proprietary software or application SUMMARY TABLE

		RESPONDENT TYPE				INSTITUTION TYPE			DISCIPLINE								GENDER	
	TOTAL SAMPLE	FACULTY MEMBER	GRAD. STUDENT	FACULTY /GRAD	UNDER GRAD. STUDENT	PUBLIC	PRIVATE	LIBERAL ARTS	BIOLOGIAL SCIENCES	PHYSICAL SCIENCES /MATH	SOCIAL SCIENCES	ARTS AND HUMAN.	ENGI-NEERING	BUSINESS	LAW	UNDEC. MAJOR	MALE	FEMALE
		(A)	(B)	(C)	(D)	(E)	(F)	(G)	(H)	(I)	(J)	(K)	(L)	(M)	(N)		(P)	(Q)
Base - USe	190	129	61*	190	0**	65*	62*	63*	29*	61*	34**	31**	14*	20**	1**	0*	144	46*
Proprietary software or application for teaching																		
preferred source	0	0	0	0	0	0	0	0	0	0	0	0	0	0	0	0	0	0
of info	0	0	0	0	0	0	0	0	0	0	0	0	0	0	0	0	0	0
Online (unspecified)	0	0	0	0	0	0	0	0	0	0	0	0	0	0	0	0	0	0
	0	0	0	0	0	0	0	0	0	0	0	0	0	0	0	0	0	0
All sources of	0	0	0	0	0	0	0	0	0	0	0	0	0	0	0	0	0	0
info	0	0	0	0	0	0	0	0	0	0	0	0	0	0	0	0	0	0
preferred source	0	0	0	0	0	0	0	0	0	0	0	0	0	0	0	0	0	0
of info	0	0	0	0	0	0	0	0	0	0	0	0	0	0	0	0	0	0
Students	0	0	0	0	0	0	0	0	0	0	0	0	0	0	0	0	0	0
	0	0	0	0	0	0	0	0	0	0	0	0	0	0	0	0	0	0
All sources of	0	0	0	0	0	0	0	0	0	0	0	0	0	0	0	0	0	0
info	0	0	0	0	0	0	0	0	0	0	0	0	0	0	0	0	0	0
preferred source	0	0	0	0	0	0	0	0	0	0	0	0	0	0	0	0	0	0
of info	0	0	0	0	0	0	0	0	0	0	0	0	0	0	0	0	0	0
Author	0	0	0	0	0	0	0	0	0	0	0	0	0	0	0	0	0	0
	0	0	0	0	0	0	0	0	0	0	0	0	0	0	0	0	0	0
All sources of	0	0	0	0	0	0	0	0	0	0	0	0	0	0	0	0	0	0
info	0	0	0	0	0	0	0	0	0	0	0	0	0	0	0	0	0	0

Proportions/Means: Columns Tested (5% risk level) - A/B/D - C/D - E/F/G - H/I/J/K/L/M/N - P/Q
* small base; ** very small base (under 30) ineligible for sig testing

Table 263
Page 1066

Outsell/Digital Library Federation Study (2002)
Weighted Tables

TABLE 117, continued

T7sum_11. Proprietary software or application SUMMARY TABLE

		RESPONDENT TYPE				INSTITUTION TYPE			DISCIPLINE								GENDER	
	TOTAL SAMPLE	FACULTY MEMBER	GRAD. STUDENT	FACULTY /GRAD	UNDER GRAD. STUDENT	PUBLIC	PRIVATE	LIBERAL ARTS	BIOLOGIAL SCIENCES	PHYSICAL SCIENCES /MATH	SOCIAL SCIENCES	ARTS AND HUMAN.	ENGI- NEERING	BUSINESS	LAW	UNDEC. MAJOR	MALE	FEMALE
		(A)	(B)	(C)	(D)	(E)	(F)	(G)	(H)	(I)	(J)	(K)	(L)	(M)	(N)		(P)	(Q)
Base - USe Proprietary software or application for teaching	190	129	61*	190	0**	65*	62*	63*	29*	61*	34**	31**	14*	20**	1**	0*	144	46*
preferred source of info	0 0	0 0	0 0	0 0	0 0	0 0	0 0	0 0	0 0	0 0	0 0	0 0	0 0	0 0	0 0	0 0	0 0	0 0
Other	37 19.6%	31 24.5%B	6 9.6%	37 19.6%	0 0	8 12.9%	12 19.7%	17 26.6%	8 27.3%	14 23.0%	4 11.1%	4 14.3%	4 30.6%	3 14.3%	0 0	0 0	26 18.0%	11 24.8%
All sources of info	37 19.5%	31 24.2%B	6 9.6%	37 19.5%	0 0	8 12.5%	12 19.7%	17 26.6%	8 27.3%	14 23.0%	4 11.1%	4 14.3%	4 28.6%	3 14.3%	0 0	0 0	26 17.8%	11 24.8%
preferred source of info	23 12.2%	19 14.7%	4 7.0%	23 12.2%	0 0	7 10.3%	8 13.7%	8 12.9%	4 15.2%	8 13.1%	2 5.6%	4 14.3%	3 18.4%	2 9.5%	0 0	0 0	13 9.0%	10 22.3%P
DK/Refused	16 8.2%	11 8.5%	5 7.7%	16 8.2%	0 0	7 10.1%	4 6.9%	5 7.7%	2 6.1%	5 8.2%	2 5.6%	3 10.7%	1 6.1%	3 14.3%	0 0	0 0	9 6.0%	7 15.1%

Proportions/Means: Columns Tested (5% risk level) - A/B/D - C/D - E/F/G - H/I/J/K/L/M/N - P/Q
* small base; ** very small base (under 30) ineligible for sig testing

TABLE 118

T7D/E_11. Proprietary software or application SUMMARY TABLE

		RESPONDENT TYPE				INSTITUTION TYPE			DISCIPLINE								GENDER	
	TOTAL SAMPLE	FACULTY MEMBER	GRAD. STUDENT	FACULTY /GRAD	UNDER GRAD. STUDENT	PUBLIC	PRIVATE	LIBERAL ARTS	BIOLOGIAL SCIENCES	PHYSICAL SCIENCES /MATH	SOCIAL SCIENCES	ARTS AND HUMAN.	ENGI-NEERING	BUSINESS	LAW	UNDEC. MAJOR	MALE	FEMALE
		(A)	(B)	(C)	(D)	(E)	(F)	(G)	(H)	(I)	(J)	(K)	(L)	(M)	(N)		(P)	(Q)
Base - Use Proprietary software or application for teaching	190	129	61*	190	0**	65*	62*	63*	29*	61*	34**	31**	14*	20**	1**	0*	144	46*
Access online (NET)	87 45.8%	65 50.2%	22 36.5%	87 45.8%	0 0	24 37.3%	25 40.4%	38 59.8%EF	16 54.5%	31 50.8%	11 33.3%	11 35.7%	7 46.9%	10 52.4%	1 80.0%	0 0	71 49.8%	15 33.4%
All sources of info	87 45.8%	65 50.2%	22 36.5%	87 45.8%	0 0	24 37.3%	25 40.4%	38 59.8%EF	16 54.5%	31 50.8%	11 33.3%	11 35.7%	7 46.9%	10 52.4%	1 80.0%	0 0	71 49.8%	15 33.4%
preferred source of info	73 38.3%	54 42.3%	18 29.8%	73 38.3%	0 0	18 27.9%	23 36.9%	32 50.4%E	12 42.4%	27 44.3%	9 27.8%	9 28.6%	6 42.9%	8 42.9%	1 60.0%	0 0	63 43.9%Q	10 20.8%
Borrow from or use in campus library (NET)	22 11.4%	7 5.8%	14 23.1%A	22 11.4%	0 0	12 19.1%G	6 9.9%	3 4.9%	2 6.1%	5 8.2%	6 16.7%	4 14.3%	1 6.1%	4 19.0%	* 20.0%	0 0	16 11.4%	5 11.3%
All sources of info	22 11.4%	7 5.8%	14 23.1%A	22 11.4%	0 0	12 19.1%G	6 9.9%	3 4.9%	2 6.1%	5 8.2%	6 16.7%	4 14.3%	1 6.1%	4 19.0%	* 20.0%	0 0	16 11.4%	5 11.3%
preferred source of info	15 7.7%	3 2.1%	12 19.5%A	15 7.7%	0 0	11 16.1%G	3 4.9%	1 1.8%	1 3.0%	2 3.3%	6 16.7%	4 14.3%	1 4.1%	1 4.8%	* 20.0%	0 0	10 7.2%	4 9.3%
Publisher (NET)	19 9.9%	19 14.7%B	0 0	19 9.9%	0 0	6 8.8%	7 11.5%	6 9.6%	5 18.2%	6 9.8%	0 0	3 10.7%	1 10.2%	3 14.3%	0 0	0 0	14 9.5%	5 11.3%
All sources of info	19 9.9%	19 14.7%B	0 0	19 9.9%	0 0	6 8.8%	7 11.5%	6 9.6%	5 18.2%	6 9.8%	0 0	3 10.7%	1 10.2%	3 14.3%	0 0	0 0	14 9.5%	5 11.3%

Proportions/Means: Columns Tested (5% risk level) - A/B/D - C/D - E/F/G - H/I/J/K/L/M/N - P/Q
* small base; ** very small base (under 30) ineligible for sig testing

Table 266
Page 1074

TABLE 118, continued

T7D/E_11. Proprietary software or application SUMMARY TABLE

	RESPONDENT TYPE				INSTITUTION TYPE			DISCIPLINE									GENDER	
	TOTAL SAMPLE	FACULTY MEMBER	GRAD. STUDENT	FACULTY /GRAD	UNDER GRAD. STUDENT	PUBLIC	PRIVATE	LIBERAL ARTS	BIOLOGIAL SCIENCES	PHYSICAL SCIENCES /MATH	SOCIAL SCIENCES	ARTS AND HUMAN.	ENGI-NEERING	BUSINESS	LAW	UNDEC. MAJOR	MALE	FEMALE
		(A)	(B)	(C)	(D)	(E)	(F)	(G)	(H)	(I)	(J)	(K)	(L)	(M)	(N)		(P)	(Q)
Base - Use Proprietary software or application for teaching	190	129	61*	190	0**	65*	62*	63*	29*	61*	34**	31**	14*	20**	1**	0*	144	46*
preferred source of info	14 7.6%	14 11.2%B	0 0	14 7.6%	0 0	3 4.9%	6 9.9%	5 8.0%	5 18.2%I	3 4.9%	0 0	3 10.7%	1 6.1%	2 9.5%	0 0	0 0	9 6.4%	5 11.3%
Department (NET)	14 7.5%	8 6.1%	6 10.3%	14 7.5%	0 0	9 13.1%F	0 0	6 9.1%F	4 12.1%	7 11.5%	2 5.6%	0 0	1 6.1%	1 4.8%	0 0	0 0	10 7.3%	4 8.1%
All sources of info	14 7.5%	8 6.1%	6 10.3%	14 7.5%	0 0	9 13.1%F	0 0	6 9.1%F	4 12.1%	7 11.5%	2 5.6%	0 0	1 6.1%	1 4.8%	0 0	0 0	10 7.3%	4 8.1%
preferred source of info	11 5.7%	6 4.3%	5 8.7%	11 5.7%	0 0	7 11.1%F	0 0	4 5.9%	4 12.1%	4 6.6%	2 5.6%	0 0	1 4.1%	1 4.8%	0 0	0 0	9 6.4%	2 3.8%
Purchase from physical book store (NET)	11 6.1%	9 7.4%	2 3.3%	11 6.1%	0 0	4 5.8%	4 6.0%	4 6.4%	0 0	7 11.5%	2 5.6%	0 0	1 4.1%	2 9.5%	* 20.0%	0 0	11 7.4%	1 2.0%
All sources of info	11 6.1%	9 7.4%	2 3.3%	11 6.1%	0 0	4 5.8%	4 6.0%	4 6.4%	0 0	7 11.5%	2 5.6%	0 0	1 4.1%	2 9.5%	* 20.0%	0 0	11 7.4%	1 2.0%
preferred source of info	8 4.1%	6 4.5%	2 3.3%	8 4.1%	0 0	3 4.6%	3 4.5%	2 3.2%	0 0	5 8.2%	2 5.6%	0 0	0 0	1 4.8%	0 0	0 0	7 4.8%	1 2.0%
Colleagues (NET)	9 4.6%	5 3.9%	4 6.1%	9 4.6%	0 0	4 6.1%	1 1.4%	4 6.2%	2 6.1%	4 6.6%	2 5.6%	1 3.6%	0 0	0 0	0 0	0 0	4 2.7%	5 10.6%P

Proportions/Means: Columns Tested (5% risk level) - A/B/D - C/D - E/F/G - H/I/J/K/L/M/N - P/Q
* small base; ** very small base (under 30) ineligible for sig testing

Table 266
Page 1075

Outsell/Digital Library Federation Study (2002)
Weighted Tables

TABLE 118, continued

T7D/E_11. Proprietary software or application SUMMARY TABLE

		RESPONDENT TYPE				INSTITUTION TYPE			DISCIPLINE									GENDER	
	TOTAL SAMPLE	FACULTY MEMBER	GRAD. STUDENT	FACULTY /GRAD	UNDER GRAD. STUDENT	PUBLIC	PRIVATE	LIBERAL ARTS	BIOLOGIAL SCIENCES	PHYSICAL SCIENCES /MATH	SOCIAL SCIENCES	ARTS AND HUMAN.	ENGI-NEERING	BUSINESS	LAW	UNDEC. MAJOR	MALE	FEMALE
		(A)	(B)	(C)	(D)	(E)	(F)	(G)	(H)	(I)	(J)	(K)	(L)	(M)	(N)		(P)	(Q)
Base - Use Proprietary software or application for teaching	190	129	61*	190	0**	65*	62*	63*	29*	61*	34**	31**	14*	20**	1**	0*	144	46*
All sources of info	9 4.6%	5 3.9%	4 6.1%	9 4.6%	0 0	4 6.1%	1 1.4%	4 6.2%	2 6.1%	4 6.6%	2 5.6%	1 3.6%	0 0	0 0	0 0	0 0	4 2.7%	5 10.6%P
preferred source of info	8 4.2%	4 3.2%	4 6.1%	8 4.2%	0 0	4 6.1%	1 1.4%	3 4.8%	1 3.0%	4 6.6%	2 5.6%	1 3.6%	0 0	0 0	0 0	0 0	4 2.7%	4 8.6%
Order from on demand document delivery service (NET)	9 4.5%	7 5.2%	2 3.1%	9 4.5%	0 0	2 2.9%	4 6.1%	3 4.6%	2 6.1%	3 4.9%	4 11.1%	0 0	0 0	0 0	0 0	0 0	8 5.3%	1 1.9%
All sources of info	9 4.5%	7 5.2%	2 3.1%	9 4.5%	0 0	2 2.9%	4 6.1%	3 4.6%	2 6.1%	3 4.9%	4 11.1%	0 0	0 0	0 0	0 0	0 0	8 5.3%	1 1.9%
preferred source of info	5 2.5%	5 3.7%	0 0	5 2.5%	0 0	0 0	2 3.0%	3 4.6%	0 0	1 1.6%	4 11.1%	0 0	0 0	0 0	0 0	0 0	5 3.3%	0 0
Office (NET)	7 3.6%	3 2.0%	4 6.7%	7 3.6%	0 0	3 4.6%	2 2.7%	2 3.3%	0 0	0 0	2 5.6%	3 10.7%	1 4.1%I	1 4.8%	0 0	0 0	2 1.5%	5 9.9%P
All sources of info	7 3.6%	3 2.0%	4 6.7%	7 3.6%	0 0	3 4.6%	2 2.7%	2 3.3%	0 0	0 0	2 5.6%	3 10.7%	1 4.1%I	1 4.8%	0 0	0 0	2 1.5%	5 9.9%P
preferred source of info	6 3.1%	2 1.3%	4 6.7%	6 3.1%	0 0	3 4.6%	2 2.7%	1 1.8%	0 0	0 0	2 5.6%	3 10.7%	1 4.1%I	0 0	0 0	0 0	2 1.5%	4 7.9%P
Purchase from online bookstore (NET)	7 3.5%	6 4.5%	1 1.4%	7 3.5%	0 0	1 1.4%	2 3.0%	4 6.2%	2 6.1%	3 4.9%	2 5.6%	0 0	0 0	0 0	0 0	0 0	6 3.9%	1 2.2%

Proportions/Means: Columns Tested (5% risk level) - A/B/D - C/D - E/F/G - H/I/J/K/L/M/N - P/Q
* small base; ** very small base (under 30) ineligible for sig testing

Table 266
Page 1076

Outsell/Digital Library Federation Study (2002)
Weighted Tables

TABLE 118, continued

T7D/E_11. Proprietary software or application SUMMARY TABLE

		RESPONDENT TYPE				INSTITUTION TYPE			DISCIPLINE								GENDER	
	TOTAL SAMPLE	FACULTY MEMBER	GRAD. STUDENT	FACULTY /GRAD	UNDER GRAD. STUDENT	PUBLIC	PRIVATE	LIBERAL ARTS	BIOLOGIAL SCIENCES	PHYSICAL SCIENCES /MATH	SOCIAL SCIENCES	ARTS AND HUMAN.	ENGI-NEERING	BUSINESS	LAW	UNDEC. MAJOR	MALE	FEMALE
		(A)	(B)	(C)	(D)	(E)	(F)	(G)	(H)	(I)	(J)	(K)	(L)	(M)	(N)		(P)	(Q)
Base - Use Proprietary software or application for teaching	190	129	61*	190	0**	65*	62*	63*	29*	61*	34**	31**	14*	20**	1**	0*	144	46*
All sources of info	7 3.5%	6 4.5%	1 1.4%	7 3.5%	0 0	1 1.4%	2 3.0%	4 6.2%	2 6.1%	3 4.9%	2 5.6%	0 0	0 0	0 0	0 0	0 0	6 3.9%	1 2.2%
preferred source of info	5 2.4%	4 2.9%	1 1.4%	5 2.4%	0 0	1 1.4%	2 3.0%	2 3.0%	2 6.1%	1 1.6%	2 5.6%	0 0	0 0	0 0	0 0	0 0	4 2.5%	1 2.2%
Faculty (NET)	5 2.4%	1 0.7%	4 5.8%A	5 2.4%	0 0	1 1.4%	4 5.8%	0 0	1 3.0%	1 1.6%	0 0	1 3.6%	1 4.1%	1 4.8%	0 0	0 0	3 2.4%	1 2.4%
All sources of info	5 2.4%	1 0.7%	4 5.8%A	5 2.4%	0 0	1 1.4%	4 5.8%	0 0	1 3.0%	1 1.6%	0 0	1 3.6%	1 4.1%	1 4.8%	0 0	0 0	3 2.4%	1 2.4%
preferred source of info	5 2.4%	1 0.7%	4 5.8%A	5 2.4%	0 0	1 1.4%	4 5.8%	0 0	1 3.0%	1 1.6%	0 0	1 3.6%	1 4.1%	1 4.8%	0 0	0 0	3 2.4%	1 2.4%
Interlibrary loan (NET)	4 1.9%	3 2.0%	1 1.8%	4 1.9%	0 0	2 3.4%	1 0.9%	1 1.4%	1 3.0%	0 0	0 0	2 7.1%	1 4.1%I	0 0	0 0	0 0	3 1.8%	1 2.4%
All sources of info	4 1.9%	3 2.0%	1 1.8%	4 1.9%	0 0	2 3.4%	1 0.9%	1 1.4%	1 3.0%	0 0	0 0	2 7.1%	1 4.1%I	0 0	0 0	0 0	3 1.8%	1 2.4%
preferred source of info	2 0.9%	1 0.5%	1 1.8%	2 0.9%	0 0	1 1.7%	1 0.9%	0 0	0 0	0 0	0 0	1 3.6%	1 4.1%I	0 0	0 0	0 0	1 0.4%	1 2.4%
Ask library to purchase source (NET)	2 1.3%	1 1.0%	1 1.8%	2 1.3%	0 0	1 2.0%	0 0	1 1.8%	0 0	0 0	0 0	2 7.1%	0 0	0 0	* 20.0%	0 0	1 0.9%	1 2.4%

Proportions/Means: Columns Tested (5% risk level) - A/B/D - C/D - E/F/G - H/I/J/K/L/M/N - P/Q
* small base; ** very small base (under 30) ineligible for sig testing

Table 266
Page 1077

Outsell/Digital Library Federation Study (2002)
Weighted Tables

TABLE 118, continued

T7D/E_11. Proprietary software or application SUMMARY TABLE

		RESPONDENT TYPE				INSTITUTION TYPE			DISCIPLINE									GENDER	
	TOTAL SAMPLE	FACULTY MEMBER	GRAD. STUDENT	FACULTY /GRAD	UNDER GRAD. STUDENT	PUBLIC	PRIVATE	LIBERAL ARTS	BIOLOGIAL SCIENCES	PHYSICAL SCIENCES /MATH	SOCIAL SCIENCES	ARTS AND HUMAN.	ENGI-NEERING	BUSINESS	LAW	UNDEC. MAJOR	MALE	FEMALE
		(A)	(B)	(C)	(D)	(E)	(F)	(G)	(H)	(I)	(J)	(K)	(L)	(M)	(N)		(P)	(Q)
Base - Use Proprietary software or application for teaching	190	129	61*	190	0**	65*	62*	63*	29*	61*	34**	31**	14*	20**	1**	0*	144	46*
All sources of info	2	1	1	2	0	1	0	1	0	0	0	2	0	0	*	0	1	1
	1.3%	1.0%	1.8%	1.3%	0	2.0%	0	1.8%	0	0	0	7.1%	0	0	20.0%	0	0.9%	2.4%
preferred source of info	1	*	1	1	0	1	0	0	0	0	0	1	0	0	*	0	1	0
	0.7%	0.1%	1.8%	0.7%	0	2.0%	0	0	0	0	0	3.6%	0	0	20.0%	0	0.9%	0
Author	2	2	0	2	0	*	1	1	0	2	0	0	*	0	0	0	2	*
	1.2%	1.8%	0	1.2%	0	0.4%	1.6%	1.6%	0	3.3%	0	0	2.0%	0	0	0	1.4%	0.6%
All sources of info	2	2	0	2	0	*	1	1	0	2	0	0	*	0	0	0	2	*
	1.2%	1.8%	0	1.2%	0	0.4%	1.6%	1.6%	0	3.3%	0	0	2.0%	0	0	0	1.4%	0.6%
preferred source of info	2	2	0	2	0	*	1	1	0	2	0	0	*	0	0	0	2	*
	1.2%	1.8%	0	1.2%	0	0.4%	1.6%	1.6%	0	3.3%	0	0	2.0%	0	0	0	1.4%	0.6%
Personal Collection/ Holdings (NET)	2	2	0	2	0	1	0	1	0	1	0	0	*	1	0	0	2	0
	1.2%	1.7%	0	1.2%	0	1.9%	0	1.6%	0	1.6%	0	0	2.0%	4.8%	0	0	1.5%	0
All sources of info	2	2	0	2	0	1	0	1	0	1	0	0	*	1	0	0	2	0
	1.2%	1.7%	0	1.2%	0	1.9%	0	1.6%	0	1.6%	0	0	2.0%	4.8%	0	0	1.5%	0
preferred source of info	2	2	0	2	0	1	0	1	0	1	0	0	*	1	0	0	2	0
	1.2%	1.7%	0	1.2%	0	1.9%	0	1.6%	0	1.6%	0	0	2.0%	4.8%	0	0	1.5%	0
Borrow from or use in other libraries (NET)	1	0	1	1	0	1	0	0	0	1	0	0	0	0	0	0	1	0
	0.5%	0	1.6%	0.5%	0	1.5%	0	0	0	1.6%	0	0	0	0	0	0	0.7%	0

Proportions/Means: Columns Tested (5% risk level) - A/B/D - C/D - E/F/G - H/I/J/K/L/M/N - P/Q
* small base; ** very small base (under 30) ineligible for sig testing

Table 266
Page 1078

Outsell/Digital Library Federation Study (2002)
Weighted Tables

TABLE 118, continued

T7D/E_11. Proprietary software or application SUMMARY TABLE

		RESPONDENT TYPE				INSTITUTION TYPE			DISCIPLINE								GENDER	
	TOTAL SAMPLE	FACULTY MEMBER	GRAD. STUDENT	FACULTY /GRAD	UNDER GRAD. STUDENT	PUBLIC	PRIVATE	LIBERAL ARTS	BIOLOGIAL SCIENCES	PHYSICAL SCIENCES /MATH	SOCIAL SCIENCES	ARTS AND HUMAN.	ENGI-NEERING	BUSINESS	LAW	UNDEC. MAJOR	MALE	FEMALE
		(A)	(B)	(C)	(D)	(E)	(F)	(G)	(H)	(I)	(J)	(K)	(L)	(M)	(N)		(P)	(Q)
Base - Use Proprietary software or application for teaching	190	129	61*	190	0**	65*	62*	63*	29*	61*	34**	31**	14*	20**	1**	0*	144	46*
All sources of info	1 0.5%	0 0	1 1.6%	1 0.5%	0 0	1 1.5%	0 0	0 0	0 0	1 1.6%	0 0	0 0	0 0	0 0	0 0	0 0	1 0.7%	0 0
preferred source of info	0 0	0 0	0 0	0 0	0 0	0 0	0 0	0 0	0 0	0 0	0 0	0 0	0 0	0 0	0 0	0 0	0 0	0 0
Access from course website (NET)	1 0.5%	1 0.8%	0 0	1 0.5%	0 0	0 0	0 0	1 1.6%	0 0	1 1.6%	0 0	0 0	0 0	0 0	0 0	0 0	1 0.7%	0 0
All sources of info	1 0.5%	1 0.8%	0 0	1 0.5%	0 0	0 0	0 0	1 1.6%	0 0	1 1.6%	0 0	0 0	0 0	0 0	0 0	0 0	1 0.7%	0 0
preferred source of info	0 0	0 0	0 0	0 0	0 0	0 0	0 0	0 0	0 0	0 0	0 0	0 0	0 0	0 0	0 0	0 0	0 0	0 0
Meeting/Conferences (NET)	0 0	0 0	0 0	0 0	0 0	0 0	0 0	0 0	0 0	0 0	0 0	0 0	0 0	0 0	0 0	0 0	0 0	0 0
All sources of info	0 0	0 0	0 0	0 0	0 0	0 0	0 0	0 0	0 0	0 0	0 0	0 0	0 0	0 0	0 0	0 0	0 0	0 0
preferred source of info	0 0	0 0	0 0	0 0	0 0	0 0	0 0	0 0	0 0	0 0	0 0	0 0	0 0	0 0	0 0	0 0	0 0	0 0
Home (NET)	0 0	0 0	0 0	0 0	0 0	0 0	0 0	0 0	0 0	0 0	0 0	0 0	0 0	0 0	0 0	0 0	0 0	0 0

Proportions/Means: Columns Tested (5% risk level) - A/B/D - C/D - E/F/G - H/I/J/K/L/M/N - P/Q
* small base; ** very small base (under 30) ineligible for sig testing

Table 266
Page 1079

Outsell/Digital Library Federation Study (2002)
Weighted Tables

TABLE 118, continued

T7D/E_11. Proprietary software or application SUMMARY TABLE

		RESPONDENT TYPE				INSTITUTION TYPE			DISCIPLINE								GENDER	
	TOTAL SAMPLE	FACULTY MEMBER	GRAD. STUDENT	FACULTY /GRAD	UNDER GRAD. STUDENT	PUBLIC	PRIVATE	LIBERAL ARTS	BIOLOGIAL SCIENCES	PHYSICAL SCIENCES /MATH	SOCIAL SCIENCES	ARTS AND HUMAN.	ENGI- NEERING	BUSINESS	LAW	UNDEC. MAJOR	MALE	FEMALE
		(A)	(B)	(C)	(D)	(E)	(F)	(G)	(H)	(I)	(J)	(K)	(L)	(M)	(N)		(P)	(Q)
Base - Use Proprietary software or application for teaching	190	129	61*	190	0**	65*	62*	63*	29*	61*	34**	31**	14*	20**	1**	0*	144	46*
All sources of info	0 0	0 0	0 0	0 0	0 0	0 0	0 0	0 0	0 0	0 0	0 0	0 0	0 0	0 0	0 0	0 0	0 0	0 0
preferred source of info	0 0	0 0	0 0	0 0	0 0	0 0	0 0	0 0	0 0	0 0	0 0	0 0	0 0	0 0	0 0	0 0	0 0	0 0
Access book/journal/ journal article elsewhere online (NET)	0 0	0 0	0 0	0 0	0 0	0 0	0 0	0 0	0 0	0 0	0 0	0 0	0 0	0 0	0 0	0 0	0 0	0 0
All sources of info	0 0	0 0	0 0	0 0	0 0	0 0	0 0	0 0	0 0	0 0	0 0	0 0	0 0	0 0	0 0	0 0	0 0	0 0
preferred source of info	0 0	0 0	0 0	0 0	0 0	0 0	0 0	0 0	0 0	0 0	0 0	0 0	0 0	0 0	0 0	0 0	0 0	0 0
Other (NET)	34 17.8%	25 19.2%	9 14.9%	34 17.8%	0 0	11 16.7%	14 23.0%	9 13.7%	6 21.2%	11 18.0%	4 11.1%	8 25.0%	4 28.6%	1 4.8%	0 0	0 0	25 17.5%	9 18.6%
All sources of info	33 17.6%	24 18.9%	9 14.9%	33 17.6%	0 0	11 16.3%	14 23.0%	9 13.7%	6 21.2%	11 18.0%	4 11.1%	8 25.0%	4 26.5%	1 4.8%	0 0	0 0	25 17.3%	9 18.6%
preferred source of info	25 13.0%	17 13.5%	7 12.1%	25 13.0%	0 0	9 13.0%	11 17.4%	5 8.7%	4 12.1%	8 13.1%	4 11.1%	6 17.9%	3 20.4%	1 4.8%	0 0	0 0	17 11.9%	8 16.4%

Proportions/Means: Columns Tested (5% risk level) - A/B/D - C/D - E/F/G - H/I/J/K/L/M/N - P/Q
* small base; ** very small base (under 30) ineligible for sig testing

Table 266
Page 1080

Outsell/Digital Library Federation Study (2002)
Weighted Tables

TABLE 118, continued

T7D/E_11. Proprietary software or application SUMMARY TABLE

		RESPONDENT TYPE				INSTITUTION TYPE			DISCIPLINE								GENDER	
	TOTAL SAMPLE	FACULTY MEMBER	GRAD. STUDENT	FACULTY /GRAD	UNDER GRAD. STUDENT	PUBLIC	PRIVATE	LIBERAL ARTS	BIOLOGIAL SCIENCES	PHYSICAL SCIENCES /MATH	SOCIAL SCIENCES	ARTS AND HUMAN.	ENGI-NEERING	BUSINESS	LAW	UNDEC. MAJOR	MALE	FEMALE
		(A)	(B)	(C)	(D)	(E)	(F)	(G)	(H)	(I)	(J)	(K)	(L)	(M)	(N)		(P)	(Q)
Base - Use Proprietary software or application for teaching	190	129	61*	190	0**	65*	62*	63*	29*	61*	34**	31**	14*	20**	1**	0*	144	46*
DK/Refused	10	8	2	10	0	2	5	3	0	2	2	1	1	4	0	0	4	6
	5.1%	6.1%	2.8%	5.1%	0	2.8%	7.9%	4.7%	0	3.3%	5.6%	3.6%	6.1%	19.0%	0	0	2.7%	12.3%P

Proportions/Means: Columns Tested (5% risk level) - A/B/D - C/D - E/F/G - H/I/J/K/L/M/N - P/Q
* small base; ** very small base (under 30) ineligible for sig testing

Table 266
Page 1081

TABLE 119

T7sum_12. Data SUMMARY TABLE

		RESPONDENT TYPE				INSTITUTION TYPE			DISCIPLINE								GENDER	
	TOTAL SAMPLE	FACULTY MEMBER	GRAD. STUDENT	FACULTY /GRAD	UNDER GRAD. STUDENT	PUBLIC	PRIVATE	LIBERAL ARTS	BIOLOGIAL SCIENCES	PHYSICAL SCIENCES /MATH	SOCIAL SCIENCES	ARTS AND HUMAN.	ENGI-NEERING	BUSINESS	LAW	UNDEC. MAJOR	MALE	FEMALE
		(A)	(B)	(C)	(D)	(E)	(F)	(G)	(H)	(I)	(J)	(K)	(L)	(M)	(N)		(P)	(Q)
Base - USe Data for teaching	264	186	79*	264	0**	112*	85*	68*	48*	63*	75*	37*	8**	32*	1**	0*	174	91*
ONLINE	188 71.1%	144 77.9%B	44 55.1%	188 71.1%	0 0	68 60.9%	63 74.2%	57 84.0%E	35 72.7%	47 74.6%	56 75.0%	21 57.6%	5 57.1%	22 70.6%	1 100.0%	0 0	129 74.1%	59 65.3%
Search engine	53 20.1%	44 23.7%B	9 11.4%	53 20.1%	0 0	20 17.6%	18 21.6%	15 22.2%	9 18.2%	15 23.8%	15 20.0%	10 27.3%	1 14.3%	3 8.8%	* 14.3%	0 0	41 23.4%	12 13.6%
All sources of info	53 20.1%	44 23.7%B	9 11.4%	53 20.1%	0 0	20 17.6%	18 21.6%	15 22.2%	9 18.2%	15 23.8%	15 20.0%	10 27.3%	1 14.3%	3 8.8%	* 14.3%	0 0	41 23.4%	12 13.6%
preferred source of info	25 9.4%	19 10.3%	6 7.4%	25 9.4%	0 0	13 11.8%	5 5.7%	7 10.2%	4 9.1%	8 12.7%	8 10.0%	3 9.1%	1 7.1%	1 2.9%	* 14.3%	0 0	19 11.1%	6 6.3%
Web directory/ subject related web site	48 18.0%	45 24.0%B	3 4.0%	48 18.0%	0 0	12 11.0%	15 17.8%	20 29.9%E	4 9.1%	15 23.8%H	11 15.0%	3 9.1%	1 14.3%	12 38.2%HJ K	* 28.6%	0 0	32 18.6%	15 16.9%
All sources of info	48 18.0%	45 24.0%B	3 4.0%	48 18.0%	0 0	12 11.0%	15 17.8%	20 29.9%E	4 9.1%	15 23.8%H	11 15.0%	3 9.1%	1 14.3%	12 38.2%HJ K	* 28.6%	0 0	32 18.6%	15 16.9%
preferred source of info	19 7.1%	17 9.0%	2 2.7%	19 7.1%	0 0	5 4.6%	7 8.2%	7 9.8%	2 3.6%	5 7.9%	2 2.5%	1 3.0%	* 3.6%	8 26.5%HI JK	* 28.6%	0 0	12 7.0%	7 7.4%
Online databases	38 14.4%	32 17.0%	7 8.3%	38 14.4%	0 0	14 12.4%	11 13.0%	13 19.4%	13 27.3%JK	10 15.9%	6 7.5%	3 9.1%	1 10.7%	5 14.7%	* 28.6%	0 0	27 15.6%	11 12.1%
All sources of info	38 14.4%	32 17.0%	7 8.3%	38 14.4%	0 ·0	14 12.4%	11 13.0%	13 19.4%	13 27.3%JK	10 15.9%	6 7.5%	3 9.1%	1 10.7%	5 14.7%	* 28.6%	0 0	27 15.6%	11 12.1%

Proportions/Means: Columns Tested (5% risk level) - A/B/D - C/D - E/F/G - H/I/J/K/L/M/N - P/Q
* small base; ** very small base (under 30) ineligible for sig testing

Table 270
Page 1092

Outsell/Digital Library Federation Study (2002)
Weighted Tables

TABLE 119, continued

T7sum_12. Data SUMMARY TABLE

		RESPONDENT TYPE				INSTITUTION TYPE			DISCIPLINE									GENDER	
	TOTAL SAMPLE	FACULTY MEMBER	GRAD. STUDENT	FACULTY /GRAD	UNDER GRAD. STUDENT	PUBLIC	PRIVATE	LIBERAL ARTS	BIOLOGIAL SCIENCES	PHYSICAL SCIENCES /MATH	SOCIAL SCIENCES	ARTS AND HUMAN.	ENGI- NEERING	BUSINESS	LAW	UNDEC. MAJOR	MALE	FEMALE
		(A)	(B)	(C)	(D)	(E)	(F)	(G)	(H)	(I)	(J)	(K)	(L)	(M)	(N)		(P)	(Q)
Base - USe Data for teaching	264	186	79*	264	0**	112*	85*	68*	48*	63*	75*	37*	8**	32*	1**	0*	174	91*
preferred source of info	25 9.3%	19 10.2%	6 7.1%	25 9.3%	0 0	10 8.5%	7 7.8%	8 12.5%	9 18.2%JK	8 12.7%	2 2.5%	1 3.0%	0 0	5 14.7%J	* 14.3%	0 0	16 9.5%	8 9.0%
Internet searches	32 12.0%	24 12.9%	8 9.9%	32 12.0%	0 0	10 9.3%	15 17.2%	7 10.1%	8 16.4%	7 11.1%	11 15.0%	2 6.1%	1 7.1%	3 8.8%	0 0	0 0	23 13.3%	9 9.6%
All sources of info	32 12.0%	24 12.9%	8 9.9%	32 12.0%	0 0	10 9.3%	15 17.2%	7 10.1%	8 16.4%	7 11.1%	11 15.0%	2 6.1%	1 7.1%	3 8.8%	0 0	0 0	23 13.3%	9 9.6%
preferred source of info	19 7.3%	13 7.2%	6 7.4%	19 7.3%	0 0	8 6.8%	9 10.3%	3 4.3%	4 9.1%	3 4.8%	9 12.5%	0 0	1 7.1%	2 5.9%	0 0	0 0	16 9.3%	3 3.4%
Your own institution's web site	26 9.9%	21 11.4%	5 6.4%	26 9.9%	0 0	9 7.9%	11 12.8%	7 9.7%	7 14.5%	6 9.5%	8 10.0%	2 6.1%	* 3.6%	3 8.8%	* 28.6%	0 0	17 9.8%	9 10.2%
All sources of info	26 9.9%	21 11.4%	5 6.4%	26 9.9%	0 0	9 7.9%	11 12.8%	7 9.7%	7 14.5%	6 9.5%	8 10.0%	2 6.1%	* 3.6%	3 8.8%	* 28.6%	0 0	17 9.8%	9 10.2%
preferred source of info	17 6.6%	14 7.3%	4 4.9%	17 6.6%	0 0	6 5.2%	6 7.0%	6 8.4%	4 7.3%	5 7.9%	6 7.5%	1 3.0%	0 0	2 5.9%	* 28.6%	0 0	14 7.9%	4 4.2%
Online library catalogues and finding aids	22 8.3%	13 7.0%	9 11.2%	22 8.3%	0 0	8 7.3%	10 11.4%	4 5.9%	3 5.5%	1 1.6%	13 17.5%IM	4 12.1%I	1 7.1%	0 0	0 0	0 0	13 7.8%	8 9.2%
All sources of info	22 8.3%	13 7.0%	9 11.2%	22 8.3%	0 0	8 7.3%	10 11.4%	4 5.9%	3 5.5%	1 1.6%	13 17.5%IM	4 12.1%I	1 7.1%	0 0	0 0	0 0	13 7.8%	8 9.2%

Proportions/Means: Columns Tested (5% risk level) - A/B/D - C/D - E/F/G - H/I/J/K/L/M/N - P/Q
* small base; ** very small base (under 30) ineligible for sig testing

Table 270
Page 1093

Outsell/Digital Library Federation Study (2002)
Weighted Tables

TABLE 119, continued

T7sum_12. Data SUMMARY TABLE

		RESPONDENT TYPE				INSTITUTION TYPE			DISCIPLINE									GENDER	
	TOTAL SAMPLE	FACULTY MEMBER	GRAD. STUDENT	FACULTY /GRAD	UNDER GRAD. STUDENT	PUBLIC	PRIVATE	LIBERAL ARTS	BIOLOGIAL SCIENCES	PHYSICAL SCIENCES /MATH	SOCIAL SCIENCES	ARTS AND HUMAN.	ENGI- NEERING	BUSINESS	LAW	UNDEC. MAJOR	MALE	FEMALE
		(A)	(B)	(C)	(D)	(E)	(F)	(G)	(H)	(I)	(J)	(K)	(L)	(M)	(N)		(P)	(Q)
Base - USe Data for teaching	264	186	79*	264	0**	112*	85*	68*	48*	63*	75*	37*	8**	32*	1**	0*	174	91*
preferred source of info	8 3.0%	5 2.6%	3 3.9%	8 3.0%	0 0	4 3.4%	3 3.7%	1 1.5%	2 3.6%	1 1.6%	4 5.0%	1 3.0%	* 3.6%	0 0	0 0	0 0	5 3.0%	3 3.0%
Department web page	9 3.6%	3 1.6%	6 8.0%A	9 3.6%	0 0	7 5.9%F	0 0	3 4.1%	1 1.8%	1 1.6%	4 5.0%	2 6.1%	1 7.1%	1 2.9%	0 0	0 0	2 1.0%	8 8.5%P
All sources of info	9 3.6%	3 1.6%	6 8.0%A	9 3.6%	0 0	7 5.9%F	0 0	3 4.1%	1 1.8%	1 1.6%	4 5.0%	2 6.1%	1 7.1%	1 2.9%	0 0	0 0	2 1.0%	8 8.5%P
preferred source of info	4 1.6%	2 1.2%	2 2.6%	4 1.6%	0 0	2 2.1%	0 0	2 2.8%	0 0	0 0	2 2.5%	1 3.0%	* 3.6%	1 2.9%	0 0	0 0	* 0.2%	4 4.3%P
Online reference service	8 2.9%	4 2.0%	4 5.1%	8 2.9%	0 0	2 1.9%	5 5.5%	1 1.3%	1 1.8%	1 1.6%	4 5.0%	1 3.0%	0 0	1 2.9%	0 0	0 0	7 3.9%	1 1.0%
All sources of info	8 2.9%	4 2.0%	4 5.1%	8 2.9%	0 0	2 1.9%	5 5.5%	1 1.3%	1 1.8%	1 1.6%	4 5.0%	1 3.0%	0 0	1 2.9%	0 0	0 0	7 3.9%	1 1.0%
preferred source of info	4 1.4%	2 1.0%	2 2.4%	4 1.4%	0 0	0 0	4 4.4%E	0 0	0 0	0 0	4 5.0%	0 0	0 0	0 0	0 0	0 0	4 2.2%	0 0
Online abstracting and indexing services	7 2.8%	7 4.0%	0 0	7 2.8%	0 0	3 2.7%	1 0.7%	4 5.6%	2 3.6%	2 3.2%	2 2.5%	1 3.0%	1 7.1%	0 0	0 0	0 0	6 3.6%	1 1.3%
All sources of info	7 2.8%	7 4.0%	0 0	7 2.8%	0 0	3 2.7%	1 0.7%	4 5.6%	2 3.6%	2 3.2%	2 2.5%	1 3.0%	1 7.1%	0 0	0 0	0 0	6 3.6%	1 1.3%
preferred source of info	1 0.4%	1 0.6%	0 0	1 0.4%	0 0	0 0	* 0.3%	1 1.3%	1 1.8%	0 0	0 0	0 0	* 3.6%	0 0	0 0	0 0	1 0.5%	* 0.3%

Proportions/Means: Columns Tested (5% risk level) - A/B/D - C/D - E/F/G - H/I/J/K/L/M/N - P/Q
* small base; ** very small base (under 30) ineligible for sig testing

Table 270
Page 1094

Outsell/Digital Library Federation Study (2002)
Weighted Tables

TABLE 119, continued

T7sum_12. Data SUMMARY TABLE

	TOTAL SAMPLE	RESPONDENT TYPE: FACULTY MEMBER (A)	GRAD. STUDENT (B)	FACULTY /GRAD (C)	UNDER GRAD. STUDENT (D)	INSTITUTION TYPE: PUBLIC (E)	PRIVATE (F)	LIBERAL ARTS (G)	DISCIPLINE: BIOLOGIAL SCIENCES (H)	PHYSICAL SCIENCES /MATH (I)	SOCIAL SCIENCES (J)	ARTS AND HUMAN. (K)	ENGI-NEERING (L)	BUSINESS (M)	LAW (N)	UNDEC. MAJOR	GENDER: MALE (P)	FEMALE (Q)
Base - USe Data for teaching	264	186	79*	264	0**	112*	85*	68*	48*	63*	75*	37*	8**	32*	1**	0*	174	91*
Your own personal electronic library/files	4 1.4%	2 1.0%	2 2.4%	4 1.4%	0 0	1 0.9%	2 2.2%	1 1.3%	1 1.8%	1 1.6%	2 2.5%	0 0	0 0	0 0	0 0	0 0	1 0.5%	3 3.2%
All sources of info	4 1.4%	2 1.0%	2 2.4%	4 1.4%	0 0	1 0.9%	2 2.2%	1 1.3%	1 1.8%	1 1.6%	2 2.5%	0 0	0 0	0 0	0 0	0 0	1 0.5%	3 3.2%
preferred source of info	1 0.4%	1 0.5%	0 0	1 0.4%	0 0	1 0.9%	0 0	0 0	0 0	1 1.6%	0 0	0 0	0 0	0 0	0 0	0 0	0 0	1 1.1%
Online bookstore	3 1.3%	3 1.9%	0 0	3 1.3%	0 0	1 1.0%	* 0.3%	2 3.0%	0 0	0 0	0 0	2 6.1%	* 3.6%	1 2.9%	0 0	0 0	1 0.7%	2 2.5%
All sources of info	3 1.3%	3 1.9%	0 0	3 1.3%	0 0	1 1.0%	* 0.3%	2 3.0%	0 0	0 0	0 0	2 6.1%	* 3.6%	1 2.9%	0 0	0 0	1 0.7%	2 2.5%
preferred source of info	1 0.4%	1 0.5%	0 0	1 0.4%	0 0	0 0	0 0	1 1.4%	0 0	0 0	0 0	0 0	0 0	1 2.9%	0 0	0 0	1 0.5%	0 0
E-mail listservs	0 0	0 0	0 0	0 0	0 0	0 0	0 0	0 0	0 0	0 0	0 0	0 0	0 0	0 0	0 0	0 0	0 0	0 0
All sources of info	0 0	0 0	0 0	0 0	0 0	0 0	0 0	0 0	0 0	0 0	0 0	0 0	0 0	0 0	0 0	0 0	0 0	0 0
preferred source of info	0 0	0 0	0 0	0 0	0 0	0 0	0 0	0 0	0 0	0 0	0 0	0 0	0 0	0 0	0 0	0 0	0 0	0 0

Proportions/Means: Columns Tested (5% risk level) - A/B/D - C/D - E/F/G - H/I/J/K/L/M/N - P/Q
* small base; ** very small base (under 30) ineligible for sig testing

Table 270
Page 1095

Outsell/Digital Library Federation Study (2002)
Weighted Tables

TABLE 119, continued

T7sum_12. Data SUMMARY TABLE

		RESPONDENT TYPE				INSTITUTION TYPE			DISCIPLINE								GENDER	
	TOTAL SAMPLE	FACULTY MEMBER	GRAD. STUDENT	FACULTY /GRAD	UNDER GRAD. STUDENT	PUBLIC	PRIVATE	LIBERAL ARTS	BIOLOGIAL SCIENCES	PHYSICAL SCIENCES /MATH	SOCIAL SCIENCES	ARTS AND HUMAN.	ENGI-NEERING	BUSINESS	LAW	UNDEC. MAJOR	MALE	FEMALE
		(A)	(B)	(C)	(D)	(E)	(F)	(G)	(H)	(I)	(J)	(K)	(L)	(M)	(N)		(P)	(Q)
Base - USe Data for teaching	264	186	79*	264	0**	112*	85*	68*	48*	63*	75*	37*	8**	32*	1**	0*	174	91*
LIBRARY/PRINT	156 58.8%	121 65.2%B	35 43.7%	156 58.8%	0 0	61 54.7%	46 53.7%	49 72.1%EF	25 50.9%	38 60.3%	49 65.0%	24 63.6%	5 60.7%	15 47.1%	1 57.1%	0 0	106 61.1%	50 54.5%
Campus library	116 43.8%	89 48.0%	27 34.1%	116 43.8%	0 0	44 39.6%	31 36.1%	41 60.6%EF	20 41.8%	30 47.6%M	34 45.0%	20 54.5%M	4 46.4%	7 23.5%	1 42.9%	0 0	79 45.3%	37 41.0%
All sources of info	116 43.8%	89 48.0%	27 34.1%	116 43.8%	0 0	44 39.6%	31 36.1%	41 60.6%EF	20 41.8%	30 47.6%M	34 45.0%	20 54.5%M	4 46.4%	7 23.5%	1 42.9%	0 0	79 45.3%	37 41.0%
preferred source of info	44 16.7%	30 16.1%	14 18.1%	44 16.7%	0 0	17 15.6%	13 15.0%	14 20.5%	7 14.5%	8 12.7%	17 22.5%M	9 24.2%M	2 25.0%	1 2.9%	* 14.3%	0 0	24 13.9%	20 21.9%
Your own personal physical library/ files/bookshelves	40 15.2%	33 18.0%	7 8.7%	40 15.2%	0 0	18 16.3%	9 10.4%	13 19.6%	7 14.5%	12 19.0%	8 10.0%	10 27.3%J	1 10.7%	3 8.8%	0 0	0 0	28 15.9%	13 14.0%
All sources of info	40 15.2%	33 18.0%	7 8.7%	40 15.2%	0 0	18 16.3%	9 10.4%	13 19.6%	7 14.5%	12 19.0%	8 10.0%	10 27.3%J	1 10.7%	3 8.8%	0 0	0 0	28 15.9%	13 14.0%
preferred source of info	19 7.2%	16 8.8%	3 3.5%	19 7.2%	0 0	10 8.8%	5 5.8%	4 6.3%	4 7.3%	5 7.9%	4 5.0%	3 9.1%	1 7.1%	3 8.8%	0 0	0 0	15 8.8%	4 4.1%
Personal subscriptions to newspapers, magazines and journals	22 8.3%	20 10.7%	2 2.6%	22 8.3%	0 0	11 10.1%	4 4.8%	7 9.8%	3 5.5%	5 7.9%	6 7.5%	2 6.1%	1 10.7%	6 17.6%	0 0	0 0	16 9.3%	6 6.4%
All sources of info	22 8.3%	20 10.7%	2 2.6%	22 8.3%	0 0	11 10.1%	4 4.8%	7 9.8%	3 5.5%	5 7.9%	6 7.5%	2 6.1%	1 10.7%	6 17.6%	0 0	0 0	16 9.3%	6 6.4%

Proportions/Means: Columns Tested (5% risk level) - A/B/D - C/D - E/F/G - H/I/J/K/L/M/N - P/Q
* small base; ** very small base (under 30) ineligible for sig testing

Table 270
Page 1096

Outsell/Digital Library Federation Study (2002)
Weighted Tables

TABLE 119, continued

T7sum_12. Data SUMMARY TABLE

		RESPONDENT TYPE				INSTITUTION TYPE			DISCIPLINE								GENDER	
	TOTAL SAMPLE	FACULTY MEMBER	GRAD. STUDENT	FACULTY /GRAD	UNDER GRAD. STUDENT	PUBLIC	PRIVATE	LIBERAL ARTS	BIOLOGIAL SCIENCES	PHYSICAL SCIENCES /MATH	SOCIAL SCIENCES	ARTS AND HUMAN.	ENGI-NEERING	BUSINESS	LAW	UNDEC. MAJOR	MALE	FEMALE
		(A)	(B)	(C)	(D)	(E)	(F)	(G)	(H)	(I)	(J)	(K)	(L)	(M)	(N)		(P)	(Q)
Base - USe Data for teaching	264	186	79*	264	0**	112*	85*	68*	48*	63*	75*	37*	8**	32*	1**	0*	174	91*
preferred source of info	6 2.2%	5 2.7%	1 1.2%	6 2.2%	0 0	2 1.9%	1 1.1%	3 4.2%	1 1.8%	1 1.6%	2 2.5%	0 0	* 3.6%	2 5.9%	0 0	0 0	4 2.4%	2 2.0%
References cited in books or journal articles	18 6.7%	15 8.0%	3 3.6%	18 6.7%	0 0	8 7.4%	8 8.8%	2 2.8%	2 3.6%	3 4.8%	8 10.0%	1 3.0%	1 7.1%	4 11.8%	0 0	0 0	11 6.4%	7 7.3%
All sources of info	18 6.7%	15 8.0%	3 3.6%	18 6.7%	0 0	8 7.4%	8 8.8%	2 2.8%	2 3.6%	3 4.8%	8 10.0%	1 3.0%	1 7.1%	4 11.8%	0 0	0 0	11 6.4%	7 7.3%
preferred source of info	7 2.5%	6 3.0%	1 1.3%	7 2.5%	0 0	1 0.9%	5 5.6%	1 1.3%	1 1.8%	2 3.2%	2 2.5%	0 0	0 0	2 5.9%	0 0	0 0	4 2.2%	3 3.0%
Printed library catalogues and finding aids	7 2.8%	7 3.5%	1 1.1%	7 2.8%	0 0	4 3.3%	0 0	4 5.6%F	2 3.6%	1 1.6%	4 5.0%	0 0	0 0	1 2.9%	0 0	0 0	7 3.8%	1 1.0%
All sources of info	7 2.8%	7 3.5%	1 1.1%	7 2.8%	0 0	4 3.3%	0 0	4 5.6%F	2 3.6%	1 1.6%	4 5.0%	0 0	0 0	1 2.9%	0 0	0 0	7 3.8%	1 1.0%
preferred source of info	2 0.7%	2 1.0%	0 0	2 0.7%	0 0	0 0	0 0	2 2.8%	0 0	0 0	2 2.5%	0 0	0 0	0 0	0 0	0 0	2 1.1%	0 0
Another library	7 2.7%	5 2.8%	2 2.4%	7 2.7%	0 0	1 1.0%	5 5.7%	1 1.5%	0 0	2 3.2%	4 5.0%	1 3.0%	0 0	0 0	* 14.3%	0 0	5 3.0%	2 2.1%
All sources of info	7 2.7%	5 2.8%	2 2.4%	7 2.7%	0 0	1 1.0%	5 5.7%	1 1.5%	0 0	2 3.2%	4 5.0%	1 3.0%	0 0	0 0	* 14.3%	0 0	5 3.0%	2 2.1%

Proportions/Means: Columns Tested (5% risk level) - A/B/D - C/D - E/F/G - H/I/J/K/L/M/N - P/Q
* small base; ** very small base (under 30) ineligible for sig testing

Table 270
Page 1097

Outsell/Digital Library Federation Study (2002)
Weighted Tables

TABLE 119, continued

T7sum_12. Data SUMMARY TABLE

	RESPONDENT TYPE				INSTITUTION TYPE			DISCIPLINE									GENDER	
	TOTAL SAMPLE	FACULTY MEMBER	GRAD. STUDENT	FACULTY /GRAD	UNDER GRAD. STUDENT	PUBLIC	PRIVATE	LIBERAL ARTS	BIOLOGIAL SCIENCES	PHYSICAL SCIENCES /MATH	SOCIAL SCIENCES	ARTS AND HUMAN.	ENGI- NEERING	BUSINESS	LAW	UNDEC. MAJOR	MALE	FEMALE
		(A)	(B)	(C)	(D)	(E)	(F)	(G)	(H)	(I)	(J)	(K)	(L)	(M)	(N)		(P)	(Q)
Base - USe Data for teaching	264	186	79*	264	0**	112*	85*	68*	48*	63*	75*	37*	8**	32*	1**	0*	174	91*
preferred source of info	0 0	0 0	0 0	0 0	0 0	0 0	0 0	0 0	0 0	0 0	0 0	0 0	0 0	0 0	0 0	0 0	0 0	0 0
Physical bookstore	5 2.0%	3 1.8%	2 2.4%	5 2.0%	0 0	3 2.7%	1 1.4%	1 1.5%	1 1.8%	2 3.2%	0 0	1 3.0%	* 3.6%	1 2.9%	0 0	0 0	4 2.5%	1 1.0%
All sources of info	5 2.0%	3 1.8%	2 2.4%	5 2.0%	0 0	3 2.7%	1 1.4%	1 1.5%	1 1.8%	2 3.2%	0 0	1 3.0%	* 3.6%	1 2.9%	0 0	0 0	4 2.5%	1 1.0%
preferred source of info	4 1.6%	2 1.2%	2 2.4%	4 1.6%	0 0	2 1.7%	1 1.4%	1 1.5%	1 1.8%	2 3.2%	0 0	0 0	* 3.6%	1 2.9%	0 0	0 0	3 1.9%	1 1.0%
Printed abstracting and indexing services	0 0	0 0	0 0	0 0	0 0	0 0	0 0	0 0	0 0	0 0	0 0	0 0	0 0	0 0	0 0	0 0	0 0	0 0
All sources of info	0 0	0 0	0 0	0 0	0 0	0 0	0 0	0 0	0 0	0 0	0 0	0 0	0 0	0 0	0 0	0 0	0 0	0 0
preferred source of info	0 0	0 0	0 0	0 0	0 0	0 0	0 0	0 0	0 0	0 0	0 0	0 0	0 0	0 0	0 0	0 0	0 0	0 0
PERSONAL ASSISTANCE	77 29.0%	49 26.5%	27 34.7%	77 29.0%	0 0	35 31.2%	20 24.0%	21 31.6%	11 23.6%	19 30.2%	19 25.0%	17 45.5%HM	4 46.4%	7 20.6%	* 28.6%	0 0	49 28.3%	28 30.3%
Colleagues inside your institution	54 20.5%	32 17.4%	22 27.7%	54 20.5%	0 0	29 25.6%	14 16.0%	12 17.6%	7 14.5%	15 23.8%	11 15.0%	12 33.3%H	3 32.1%	6 17.6%	* 28.6%	0 0	31 18.0%	23 25.2%

Proportions/Means: Columns Tested (5% risk level) - A/B/D - C/D - E/F/G - H/I/J/K/L/M/N - P/Q
* small base; ** very small base (under 30) ineligible for sig testing

Table 270
Page 1098

Outsell/Digital Library Federation Study (2002)
Weighted Tables

TABLE 119, continued

T7sum_12. Data SUMMARY TABLE

		RESPONDENT TYPE				INSTITUTION TYPE			DISCIPLINE								GENDER	
	TOTAL SAMPLE	FACULTY MEMBER	GRAD. STUDENT	FACULTY /GRAD	UNDER GRAD. STUDENT	PUBLIC	PRIVATE	LIBERAL ARTS	BIOLOGIAL SCIENCES	PHYSICAL SCIENCES /MATH	SOCIAL SCIENCES	ARTS AND HUMAN.	ENGI- NEERING	BUSINESS	LAW	UNDEC. MAJOR	MALE	FEMALE
		(A)	(B)	(C)	(D)	(E)	(F)	(G)	(H)	(I)	(J)	(K)	(L)	(M)	(N)		(P)	(Q)
Base - USe Data for teaching	264	186	79*	264	0**	112*	85*	68*	48*	63*	75*	37*	8**	32*	1**	0*	174	91*
All sources of info	54 20.5%	32 17.4%	22 27.7%	54 20.5%	0 0	29 25.6%	14 16.0%	12 17.6%	7 14.5%	15 23.8%	11 15.0%	12 33.3%H	3 32.1%	6 17.6%	* 28.6%	0 0	31 18.0%	23 25.2%
preferred source of info	21 8.1%	6 3.2%	15 19.5%A	21 8.1%	0 0	13 12.0%G	7 8.0%	1 1.7%	4 9.1%J	7 11.1%J	0 0	8 21.2%JM	1 14.3%	1 2.9%	0 0	0 0	13 7.5%	8 9.1%
A librarian in your institution	32 12.1%	24 12.8%	8 10.5%	32 12.1%	0 0	12 10.8%	9 10.0%	11 16.9%	4 7.3%	4 6.3%	15 20.0%	7 18.2%	1 10.7%	2 5.9%	0 0	0 0	24 14.1%	8 8.3%
All sources of info	32 12.1%	24 12.8%	8 10.5%	32 12.1%	0 0	12 10.8%	9 10.0%	11 16.9%	4 7.3%	4 6.3%	15 20.0%	7 18.2%	1 10.7%	2 5.9%	0 0	0 0	24 14.1%	8 8.3%
preferred source of info	7 2.5%	3 1.7%	3 4.2%	7 2.5%	0 0	3 2.3%	3 3.5%	1 1.5%	0 0	1 1.6%	2 2.5%	3 9.1%H	* 3.6%	0 0	0 0	0 0	5 2.7%	2 2.1%
Colleagues outside your institution	19 7.2%	16 8.6%	3 3.8%	19 7.2%	0 0	6 5.5%	5 6.1%	8 11.4%	2 3.6%	5 7.9%	6 7.5%	4 12.1%	* 3.6%	2 5.9%	0 0	0 0	10 5.9%	9 9.7%
All sources of info	19 7.2%	16 8.6%	3 3.8%	19 7.2%	0 0	6 5.5%	5 6.1%	8 11.4%	2 3.6%	5 7.9%	6 7.5%	4 12.1%	* 3.6%	2 5.9%	0 0	0 0	10 5.9%	9 9.7%
preferred source of info	0 0	0 0	0 0	0 0	0 0	0 0	0 0	0 0	0 0	0 0	0 0	0 0	0 0	0 0	0 0	0 0	0 0	0 0
Professional meetings	7 2.8%	6 3.2%	1 1.8%	7 2.8%	0 0	5 4.0%	1 1.2%	2 2.8%	1 1.8%	2 3.2%	2 2.5%	1 3.0%	1 7.1%	1 2.9%	0 0	0 0	5 2.6%	3 3.2%
All sources of info	7 2.8%	6 3.2%	1 1.8%	7 2.8%	0 0	5 4.0%	1 1.2%	2 2.8%	1 1.8%	2 3.2%	2 2.5%	1 3.0%	1 7.1%	1 2.9%	0 0	0 0	5 2.6%	3 3.2%

Proportions/Means: Columns Tested (5% risk level) - A/B/D - C/D - E/F/G - H/I/J/K/L/M/N - P/Q
* small base; ** very small base (under 30) ineligible for sig testing

Table 270
Page 1099

Outsell/Digital Library Federation Study (2002)
Weighted Tables

TABLE 119, continued

T7sum_12. Data SUMMARY TABLE

	TOTAL SAMPLE	RESPONDENT TYPE: FACULTY MEMBER (A)	GRAD. STUDENT (B)	FACULTY /GRAD (C)	UNDER GRAD. STUDENT (D)	INSTITUTION TYPE: PUBLIC (E)	PRIVATE (F)	LIBERAL ARTS (G)	DISCIPLINE: BIOLOGIAL SCIENCES (H)	PHYSICAL SCIENCES /MATH (I)	SOCIAL SCIENCES (J)	ARTS AND HUMAN. (K)	ENGI-NEERING (L)	BUSINESS (M)	LAW (N)	UNDEC. MAJOR	GENDER: MALE (P)	FEMALE (Q)
Base - USe Data for teaching	264	186	79*	264	0**	112*	85*	68*	48*	63*	75*	37*	8**	32*	1**	0*	174	91*
preferred source of info	* 0.1%	0 0	* 0.4%	* 0.1%	0 0	* 0.3%	0 0	0 0	0 0	0 0	0 0	0 0	* 3.6%	0 0	0 0	0 0	* 0.2%	0 0
Another institution's librarian	4 1.4%	1 0.5%	3 3.5%	4 1.4%	0 0	1 0.8%	3 3.2%	0 0	2 3.6%	0 0	2 2.5%	0 0	0 0	0 0	0 0	0 0	1 0.5%	3 3.0%
All sources of info	4 1.4%	1 0.5%	3 3.5%	4 1.4%	0 0	1 0.8%	3 3.2%	0 0	2 3.6%	0 0	2 2.5%	0 0	0 0	0 0	0 0	0 0	1 0.5%	3 3.0%
preferred source of info	1 0.3%	0 0	1 1.1%	1 0.3%	0 0	1 0.8%	0 0	0 0	1 1.8%	0 0	0 0	0 0	0 0	0 0	0 0	0 0	0 0	1 1.0%
Online (unspecified)	5 1.8%	3 1.6%	2 2.4%	5 1.8%	0 0	1 0.9%	4 4.4%	0 0	0 0	1 1.6%	4 5.0%	0 0	0 0	0 0	0 0	0 0	3 1.7%	2 2.1%
All sources of info	5 1.8%	3 1.6%	2 2.4%	5 1.8%	0 0	1 0.9%	4 4.4%	0 0	0 0	1 1.6%	4 5.0%	0 0	0 0	0 0	0 0	0 0	3 1.7%	2 2.1%
preferred source of info	0 0	0 0	0 0	0 0	0 0	0 0	0 0	0 0	0 0	0 0	0 0	0 0	0 0	0 0	0 0	0 0	0 0	0 0
Personal office/lab	2 0.7%	2 0.9%	0 0	2 0.7%	0 0	0 0	1 1.0%	1 1.3%	2 3.6%	0 0	0 0	0 0	0 0	0 0	0 0	0 0	2 1.0%	0 0
All sources of info	2 0.7%	2 0.9%	0 0	2 0.7%	0 0	0 0	1 1.0%	1 1.3%	2 3.6%	0 0	0 0	0 0	0 0	0 0	0 0	0 0	2 1.0%	0 0
preferred source of info	1 0.3%	1 0.5%	0 0	1 0.3%	0 0	0 0	0 0	1 1.3%	1 1.8%	0 0	0 0	0 0	0 0	0 0	0 0	0 0	1 0.5%	0 0

Proportions/Means: Columns Tested (5% risk level) - A/B/D - C/D - E/F/G - H/I/J/K/L/M/N - P/Q
* small base; ** very small base (under 30) ineligible for sig testing

Table 270
Page 1100

Outsell/Digital Library Federation Study (2002)
Weighted Tables

TABLE 119, continued

T7sum_12. Data SUMMARY TABLE

	RESPONDENT TYPE				INSTITUTION TYPE			DISCIPLINE									GENDER	
	TOTAL SAMPLE	FACULTY MEMBER	GRAD. STUDENT	FACULTY /GRAD	UNDER GRAD. STUDENT	PUBLIC	PRIVATE	LIBERAL ARTS	BIOLOGIAL SCIENCES	PHYSICAL SCIENCES /MATH	SOCIAL SCIENCES	ARTS AND HUMAN.	ENGI-NEERING	BUSINESS	LAW	UNDEC. MAJOR	MALE	FEMALE
		(A)	(B)	(C)	(D)	(E)	(F)	(G)	(H)	(I)	(J)	(K)	(L)	(M)	(N)		(P)	(Q)
Base - USe Data for teaching	264	186	79*	264	0**	112*	85*	68*	48*	63*	75*	37*	8**	32*	1**	0*	174	91*
Students	0 0	0 0	0 0	0 0	0 0	0 0	0 0	0 0	0 0	0 0	0 0	0 0	0 0	0 0	0 0	0 0	0 0	0 0
All sources of info	0 0	0 0	0 0	0 0	0 0	0 0	0 0	0 0	0 0	0 0	0 0	0 0	0 0	0 0	0 0	0 0	0 0	0 0
preferred source of info	0 0	0 0	0 0	0 0	0 0	0 0	0 0	0 0	0 0	0 0	0 0	0 0	0 0	0 0	0 0	0 0	0 0	0 0
Author	0 0	0 0	0 0	0 0	0 0	0 0	0 0	0 0	0 0	0 0	0 0	0 0	0 0	0 0	0 0	0 0	0 0	0 0
All sources of info	0 0	0 0	0 0	0 0	0 0	0 0	0 0	0 0	0 0	0 0	0 0	0 0	0 0	0 0	0 0	0 0	0 0	0 0
preferred source of info	0 0	0 0	0 0	0 0	0 0	0 0	0 0	0 0	0 0	0 0	0 0	0 0	0 0	0 0	0 0	0 0	0 0	0 0
Other	28 10.6%	18 10.0%	10 12.3%	28 10.6%	0 0	14 12.7%	7 8.5%	7 9.9%	5 10.9%	9 14.3%	8 10.0%	1 3.0%	1 7.1%	5 14.7%	0 0	0 0	18 10.3%	10 11.3%
All sources of info	27 10.2%	17 9.3%	10 12.3%	27 10.2%	0 0	14 12.7%	6 7.1%	7 9.9%	4 9.1%	9 14.3%	8 10.0%	1 3.0%	* 3.6%	5 14.7%	0 0	0 0	17 9.6%	10 11.3%
preferred source of info	15 5.6%	10 5.3%	5 6.2%	15 5.6%	0 0	8 6.9%	4 5.1%	3 4.2%	3 5.5%	3 4.8%	6 7.5%	1 3.0%	1 7.1%	2 5.9%	0 0	0 0	8 4.8%	7 7.1%
DK/Refused	15 5.7%	12 6.5%	3 3.8%	15 5.7%	0 0	6 5.6%	7 8.0%	2 2.9%	2 3.6%	3 4.8%	6 7.5%	3 9.1%	* 3.6%	1 2.9%	0 0	0 0	6 3.6%	9 9.7%

Proportions/Means: Columns Tested (5% risk level) - A/B/D - C/D - E/F/G - H/I/J/K/L/M/N - P/Q
* small base; ** very small base (under 30) ineligible for sig testing

Table 270
Page 1101

Outsell/Digital Library Federation Study (2002)
Weighted Tables

TABLE 120

T7D/E_12. Data SUMMARY TABLE

	TOTAL SAMPLE	RESPONDENT TYPE: FACULTY MEMBER	GRAD. STUDENT	FACULTY /GRAD	UNDER GRAD. STUDENT	INSTITUTION TYPE: PUBLIC	PRIVATE	LIBERAL ARTS	DISCIPLINE: BIOLOGIAL SCIENCES	PHYSICAL SCIENCES /MATH	SOCIAL SCIENCES	ARTS AND HUMAN.	ENGI-NEERING	BUSINESS	LAW	UNDEC. MAJOR	GENDER: MALE	FEMALE
		(A)	(B)	(C)	(D)	(E)	(F)	(G)	(H)	(I)	(J)	(K)	(L)	(M)	(N)		(P)	(Q)
Base - Use Data for teaching	264	186	79*	264	0**	112*	85*	68*	48*	63*	75*	37*	8**	32*	1**	0*	174	91*
Access online (NET)	160 60.4%	120 64.6%	40 50.7%	160 60.4%	0 0	62 55.2%	52 61.2%	46 68.1%	31 63.6%	43 68.3%K	38 50.0%	17 45.5%	3 42.9%	27 85.3%H JK	1 100.0%	0 0	109 63.1%	50 55.4%
All sources of info	160 60.4%	120 64.6%	40 50.7%	160 60.4%	0 0	62 55.2%	52 61.2%	46 68.1%	31 63.6%	43 68.3%K	38 50.0%	17 45.5%	3 42.9%	27 85.3%H JK	1 100.0%	0 0	109 63.1%	50 55.4%
preferred source of info	122 46.2%	88 47.7%	34 42.6%	122 46.2%	0 0	46 41.2%	43 50.8%	33 48.5%	22 45.5%	34 54.0%K	32 42.5%	10 27.3%	1 17.9%	21 67.6%H JK	1 100.0%	0 0	83 48.0%	39 42.6%
Borrow from or use in campus library (NET)	127 48.2%	89 48.1%	38 48.3%	127 48.2%	0 0	47 42.0%	41 47.9%	40 58.9%E	20 41.8%M	37 58.7%M	41 55.0%M	19 51.5%M	4 46.4%	6 17.6%	1 42.9%	0 0	83 47.6%	45 49.4%
All sources of info	127 48.2%	89 48.1%	38 48.3%	127 48.2%	0 0	47 42.0%	41 47.9%	40 58.9%E	20 41.8%M	37 58.7%M	41 55.0%M	19 51.5%M	4 46.4%	6 17.6%	1 42.9%	0 0	83 47.6%	45 49.4%
preferred source of info	74 27.9%	48 26.0%	26 32.4%	74 27.9%	0 0	30 26.9%	22 25.5%	22 32.7%	13 27.3%M	15 23.8%M	26 35.0%M	15 39.4%M	3 35.7%	2 5.9%	0 0	0 0	47 27.2%	27 29.3%
Access from course website (NET)	20 7.7%	18 9.5%	3 3.6%	20 7.7%	0 0	11 10.0%	2 2.1%	7 10.9%F	4 9.1%	3 4.8%	8 10.0%	0 0	1 10.7%	5 14.7%K	0 0	0 0	12 7.0%	8 9.2%
All sources of info	20 7.7%	18 9.5%	3 3.6%	20 7.7%	0 0	11 10.0%	2 2.1%	7 10.9%F	4 9.1%	3 4.8%	8 10.0%	0 0	1 10.7%	5 14.7%K	0 0	0 0	12 7.0%	8 9.2%

Proportions/Means: Columns Tested (5% risk level) - A/B/D - C/D - E/F/G - H/I/J/K/L/M/N - P/Q
* small base; ** very small base (under 30) ineligible for sig testing

Table 273
Page 1108

Outsell/Digital Library Federation Study (2002)
Weighted Tables

TABLE 120, continued

T7D/E_12. Data SUMMARY TABLE

		RESPONDENT TYPE				INSTITUTION TYPE			DISCIPLINE									GENDER	
	TOTAL SAMPLE	FACULTY MEMBER	GRAD. STUDENT	FACULTY /GRAD	UNDER GRAD. STUDENT	PUBLIC	PRIVATE	LIBERAL ARTS	BIOLOGIAL SCIENCES	PHYSICAL SCIENCES /MATH	SOCIAL SCIENCES	ARTS AND HUMAN.	ENGI- NEERING	BUSINESS	LAW	UNDEC. MAJOR	MALE	FEMALE
		(A)	(B)	(C)	(D)	(E)	(F)	(G)	(H)	(I)	(J)	(K)	(L)	(M)	(N)		(P)	(Q)
Base - Use Data for teaching	264	186	79*	264	0**	112*	85*	68*	48*	63*	75*	37*	8**	32*	1**	0*	174	91*
preferred source of info	14 5.2%	11 5.8%	3 3.6%	14 5.2%	0 0	8 7.3%F	0 0	6 8.2%F	3 5.5%	2 3.2%	6 7.5%	0 0	1 7.1%	3 8.8%	0 0	0 0	9 5.2%	5 5.2%
Personal Collection/ Holdings (NET)	20 7.4%	16 8.6%	4 4.8%	20 7.4%	0 0	14 12.8%F	1 1.5%	4 6.0%	4 7.3%	6 9.5%	4 5.0%	3 9.1%	1 14.3%	2 5.9%	0 0	0 0	15 8.5%	5 5.4%
All sources of info	20 7.4%	16 8.6%	4 4.8%	20 7.4%	0 0	14 12.8%F	1 1.5%	4 6.0%	4 7.3%	6 9.5%	4 5.0%	3 9.1%	1 14.3%	2 5.9%	0 0	0 0	15 8.5%	5 5.4%
preferred source of info	15 5.7%	12 6.5%	3 3.6%	15 5.7%	0 0	12 10.6%F	0 0	3 4.6%	3 5.5%	4 6.3%	4 5.0%	3 9.1%	* 3.6%	1 2.9%	0 0	0 0	11 6.4%	4 4.3%
Interlibrary loan (NET)	17 6.4%	15 8.0%	2 2.5%	17 6.4%	0 0	7 6.3%	6 7.1%	4 5.6%	4 9.1%	4 6.3%	4 5.0%	2 6.1%	1 7.1%	2 5.9%	0 0	0 0	14 8.1%	3 3.0%
All sources of info	17 6.4%	15 8.0%	2 2.5%	17 6.4%	0 0	7 6.3%	6 7.1%	4 5.6%	4 9.1%	4 6.3%	4 5.0%	2 6.1%	1 7.1%	2 5.9%	0 0	0 0	14 8.1%	3 3.0%
preferred source of info	1 0.4%	1 0.6%	0 0	1 0.4%	0 0	* 0.3%	1 1.0%	0 0	1 1.8%	0 0	0 0	0 0	* 3.6%	0 0	0 0	0 0	1 0.7%	0 0
Faculty (NET)	10 3.8%	0 0	10 12.7%A	10 3.8%	0 0	7 6.1%	3 3.8%	0 0	1 1.8%	4 6.3%	2 2.5%	1 3.0%	* 3.6%	2 5.9%	0 0	0 0	7 4.2%	3 3.1%
All sources of info	10 3.8%	0 0	10 12.7%A	10 3.8%	0 0	7 6.1%	3 3.8%	0 0	1 1.8%	4 6.3%	2 2.5%	1 3.0%	* 3.6%	2 5.9%	0 0	0 0	7 4.2%	3 3.1%

Proportions/Means: Columns Tested (5% risk level) - A/B/D - C/D - E/F/G - H/I/J/K/L/M/N - P/Q
* small base; ** very small base (under 30) ineligible for sig testing

Table 273
Page 1109

Outsell/Digital Library Federation Study (2002)
Weighted Tables

TABLE 120, continued

T7D/E_12. Data SUMMARY TABLE

		RESPONDENT TYPE				INSTITUTION TYPE			DISCIPLINE									GENDER	
	TOTAL SAMPLE	FACULTY MEMBER	GRAD. STUDENT	FACULTY /GRAD	UNDER GRAD. STUDENT	PUBLIC	PRIVATE	LIBERAL ARTS	BIOLOGIAL SCIENCES	PHYSICAL SCIENCES /MATH	SOCIAL SCIENCES	ARTS AND HUMAN.	ENGI-NEERING	BUSINESS	LAW	UNDEC. MAJOR	MALE	FEMALE
		(A)	(B)	(C)	(D)	(E)	(F)	(G)	(H)	(I)	(J)	(K)	(L)	(M)	(N)		(P)	(Q)
Base - Use Data for teaching	264	186	79*	264	0**	112*	85*	68*	48*	63*	75*	37*	8**	32*	1**	0*	174	91*
preferred source of info	4	0	4	4	0	2	2	0	1	2	0	0	*	1	0	0	2	2
	1.6%	0	5.2%A	1.6%	0	1.7%	2.6%	0	1.8%	3.2%	0	0	3.6%	2.9%	0	0	1.3%	2.0%
Colleagues (NET)	9	6	3	9	0	4	4	1	1	5	0	3	0	0	0	0	6	3
	3.5%	3.4%	3.8%	3.5%	0	3.7%	4.7%	1.7%	1.8%	7.9%J	0	9.1%J	0	0	0	0	3.5%	3.4%
All sources of info	9	6	3	9	0	4	4	1	1	5	0	3	0	0	0	0	6	3
	3.5%	3.4%	3.8%	3.5%	0	3.7%	4.7%	1.7%	1.8%	7.9%J	0	9.1%J	0	0	0	0	3.5%	3.4%
preferred source of info	7	4	3	7	0	2	4	1	0	5	0	2	0	0	0	0	4	3
	2.7%	2.3%	3.8%	2.7%	0	1.9%	4.7%	1.7%	0	7.9%HJ	0	6.1%	0	0	0	0	2.4%	3.4%
Borrow from or use in other libraries (NET)	8	5	3	8	0	2	4	2	1	3	0	3	1	0	0	0	6	2
	3.0%	2.7%	3.6%	3.0%	0	1.9%	4.4%	3.0%	1.8%	4.8%	0	9.1%J	7.1%	0	0	0	3.3%	2.3%
All sources of info	8	5	3	8	0	2	4	2	1	3	0	3	1	0	0	0	6	2
	3.0%	2.7%	3.6%	3.0%	0	1.9%	4.4%	3.0%	1.8%	4.8%	0	9.1%J	7.1%	0	0	0	3.3%	2.3%
preferred source of info	3	0	3	3	0	1	2	0	0	0	0	2	1	0	0	0	2	1
	1.1%	0	3.6%A	1.1%	0	1.0%	2.0%	0	0	0	0	6.1%	7.1%	0	0	0	1.0%	1.2%
Purchase from physical book store (NET)	8	8	0	8	0	4	2	1	2	0	2	2	1	1	0	0	7	1
	2.9%	4.1%	0	2.9%	0	3.9%	2.9%	1.3%	3.6%	0	2.5%	6.1%	10.7%	2.9%	0	0	3.9%	1.0%
All sources of info	8	8	0	8	0	4	2	1	2	0	2	2	1	1	0	0	7	1
	2.9%	4.1%	0	2.9%	0	3.9%	2.9%	1.3%	3.6%	0	2.5%	6.1%	10.7%	2.9%	0	0	3.9%	1.0%

Proportions/Means: Columns Tested (5% risk level) - A/B/D - C/D - E/F/G - H/I/J/K/L/M/N - P/Q
* small base; ** very small base (under 30) ineligible for sig testing

Table 273
Page 1110

Outsell/Digital Library Federation Study (2002)
Weighted Tables

TABLE 120, continued

T7D/E_12. Data SUMMARY TABLE

		RESPONDENT TYPE				INSTITUTION TYPE			DISCIPLINE								GENDER	
	TOTAL SAMPLE	FACULTY MEMBER	GRAD. STUDENT	FACULTY /GRAD	UNDER GRAD. STUDENT	PUBLIC	PRIVATE	LIBERAL ARTS	BIOLOGIAL SCIENCES	PHYSICAL SCIENCES /MATH	SOCIAL SCIENCES	ARTS AND HUMAN.	ENGI- NEERING	BUSINESS	LAW	UNDEC. MAJOR	MALE	FEMALE
		(A)	(B)	(C)	(D)	(E)	(F)	(G)	(H)	(I)	(J)	(K)	(L)	(M)	(N)		(P)	(Q)
Base - Use Data for teaching	264	186	79*	264	0**	112*	85*	68*	48*	63*	75*	37*	8**	32*	1**	0*	174	91*
preferred source of info	3 1.0%	3 1.4%	0 0	3 1.0%	0 0	2 1.8%	1 0.7%	0 0	0 0	0 0	0 0	1 3.0%	1 7.1%	1 2.9%	0 0	0 0	3 1.5%	0 0
Office (NET)	5 1.8%	5 2.6%	0 0	5 1.8%	0 0	0 0	5 5.7%E	0 0	2 3.6%	0 0	2 2.5%	0 0	* 3.6%	1 2.9%	0 0	0 0	5 2.6%	* 0.3%
All sources of info	5 1.8%	5 2.6%	0 0	5 1.8%	0 0	0 0	5 5.7%E	0 0	2 3.6%	0 0	2 2.5%	0 0	* 3.6%	1 2.9%	0 0	0 0	5 2.6%	* 0.3%
preferred source of info	5 1.7%	5 2.5%	0 0	5 1.7%	0 0	0 0	5 5.4%E	0 0	2 3.6%	0 0	2 2.5%	0 0	0 0	1 2.9%	0 0	0 0	5 2.6%	0 0
Order from on demand document delivery service (NET)	3 1.1%	3 1.6%	0 0	3 1.1%	0 0	2 1.7%	0 0	1 1.7%	0 0	0 0	0 0	1 3.0%	0 0	2 5.9%	0 0	0 0	1 0.5%	2 2.3%
All sources of info	3 1.1%	3 1.6%	0 0	3 1.1%	0 0	2 1.7%	0 0	1 1.7%	0 0	0 0	0 0	1 3.0%	0 0	2 5.9%	0 0	0 0	1 0.5%	2 2.3%
preferred source of info	2 0.8%	2 1.1%	0 0	2 0.8%	0 0	1 0.8%	0 0	1 1.7%	0 0	0 0	0 0	1 3.0%	0 0	1 2.9%	0 0	0 0	0 0	2 2.3%
Home (NET)	3 1.0%	0 0	3 3.5%A	3 1.0%	0 0	1 0.8%	2 2.2%	0 0	1 1.8%	0 0	2 2.5%	0 0	0 0	0 0	0 0	0 0	1 0.5%	2 2.1%
All sources of info	3 1.0%	0 0	3 3.5%A	3 1.0%	0 0	1 0.8%	2 2.2%	0 0	1 1.8%	0 0	2 2.5%	0 0	0 0	0 0	0 0	0 0	1 0.5%	2 2.1%

Proportions/Means: Columns Tested (5% risk level) - A/B/D - C/D - E/F/G - H/I/J/K/L/M/N - P/Q
* small base; ** very small base (under 30) ineligible for sig testing

Table 273
Page 1111

Outsell/Digital Library Federation Study (2002)
Weighted Tables

TABLE 120, continued

T7D/E_12. Data SUMMARY TABLE

		RESPONDENT TYPE				INSTITUTION TYPE			DISCIPLINE									GENDER	
	TOTAL SAMPLE	FACULTY MEMBER	GRAD. STUDENT	FACULTY /GRAD	UNDER GRAD. STUDENT	PUBLIC	PRIVATE	LIBERAL ARTS	BIOLOGIAL SCIENCES	PHYSICAL SCIENCES /MATH	SOCIAL SCIENCES	ARTS AND HUMAN.	ENGI-NEERING	BUSINESS	LAW	UNDEC. MAJOR	MALE	FEMALE
		(A)	(B)	(C)	(D)	(E)	(F)	(G)	(H)	(I)	(J)	(K)	(L)	(M)	(N)		(P)	(Q)
Base - Use Data for teaching	264	186	79*	264	0**	112*	85*	68*	48*	63*	75*	37*	8**	32*	1**	0*	174	91*
preferred source of info	3 1.0%	0 0	3 3.5%A	3 1.0%	0 0	1 0.8%	2 2.2%	0 0	1 1.8%	0 0	2 2.5%	0 0	0 0	0 0	0 0	0 0	1 0.5%	2 2.1%
Purchase from online bookstore (NET)	3 1.0%	3 1.4%	0 0	3 1.0%	0 0	1 1.1%	1 0.7%	1 1.3%	1 1.8%	0 0	0 0	0 0	1 10.7%	1 2.9%	0 0	0 0	2 1.0%	1 1.0%
All sources of info	3 1.0%	3 1.4%	0 0	3 1.0%	0 0	1 1.1%	1 0.7%	1 1.3%	1 1.8%	0 0	0 0	0 0	1 10.7%	1 2.9%	0 0	0 0	2 1.0%	1 1.0%
preferred source of info	* 0.1%	* 0.2%	0 0	* 0.1%	0 0	0 0	* 0.3%	0 0	0 0	0 0	0 0	0 0	* 3.6%	0 0	0 0	0 0	* 0.2%	0 0
Meeting/Conferences (NET)	2 0.8%	1 0.6%	1 1.3%	2 0.8%	0 0	1 1.0%	1 1.2%	0 0	0 0	1 1.6%	0 0	1 3.0%	0 0	0 0	0 0	0 0	1 0.6%	1 1.2%
All sources of info	2 0.8%	1 0.6%	1 1.3%	2 0.8%	0 0	1 1.0%	1 1.2%	0 0	0 0	1 1.6%	0 0	1 3.0%	0 0	0 0	0 0	0 0	1 0.6%	1 1.2%
preferred source of info	0 0	0 0	0 0	0 0	0 0	0 0	0 0	0 0	0 0	0 0	0 0	0 0	0 0	0 0	0 0	0 0	0 0	0 0
Publisher (NET)	2 0.8%	2 1.1%	0 0	2 0.8%	0 0	0 0	1 1.2%	1 1.5%	0 0	2 3.2%	0 0	0 0	0 0	0 0	0 0	0 0	2 1.2%	0 0
All sources of info	2 0.8%	2 1.1%	0 0	2 0.8%	0 0	0 0	1 1.2%	1 1.5%	0 0	2 3.2%	0 0	0 0	0 0	0 0	0 0	0 0	2 1.2%	0 0
preferred source of info	1 0.4%	1 0.5%	0 0	1 0.4%	0 0	0 0	0 0	1 1.5%	0 0	1 1.6%	0 0	0 0	0 0	0 0	0 0	0 0	1 0.6%	0 0

Proportions/Means: Columns Tested (5% risk level) - A/B/D - C/D - E/F/G - H/I/J/K/L/M/N - P/Q
* small base; ** very small base (under 30) ineligible for sig testing

Table 273
Page 1112

Outsell/Digital Library Federation Study (2002)
Weighted Tables

TABLE 120, continued

T7D/E_12. Data SUMMARY TABLE

		RESPONDENT TYPE				INSTITUTION TYPE			DISCIPLINE								GENDER	
	TOTAL SAMPLE	FACULTY MEMBER	GRAD. STUDENT	FACULTY /GRAD	UNDER GRAD. STUDENT	PUBLIC	PRIVATE	LIBERAL ARTS	BIOLOGIAL SCIENCES	PHYSICAL SCIENCES /MATH	SOCIAL SCIENCES	ARTS AND HUMAN.	ENGI- NEERING	BUSINESS	LAW	UNDEC. MAJOR	MALE	FEMALE
		(A)	(B)	(C)	(D)	(E)	(F)	(G)	(H)	(I)	(J)	(K)	(L)	(M)	(N)		(P)	(Q)
Base - Use Data for teaching	264	186	79*	264	0**	112*	85*	68*	48*	63*	75*	37*	8**	32*	1**	0*	174	91*
Department (NET)	1 0.5%	* 0.1%	1 1.4%	1 0.5%	0 0	* 0.2%	1 1.3%	0 0	0 0	0 0	0 0	1 3.0%	0 0	0 0	* 14.3%	0 0	* 0.1%	1 1.2%
All sources of info	1 0.5%	* 0.1%	1 1.4%	1 0.5%	0 0	* 0.2%	1 1.3%	0 0	0 0	0 0	0 0	1 3.0%	0 0	0 0	* 14.3%	0 0	* 0.1%	1 1.2%
preferred source of info	0 0	0 0	0 0	0 0	0 0	0 0	0 0	0 0	0 0	0 0	0 0	0 0	0 0	0 0	0 0	0 0	0 0	0 0
Ask library to purchase source (NET)	1 0.4%	1 0.5%	0 0	1 0.4%	0 0	1 0.9%	0 0	0 0	0 0	1 1.6%	0 0	0 0	0 0	0 0	0 0	0 0	1 0.6%	0 0
All sources of info	1 0.4%	1 0.5%	0 0	1 0.4%	0 0	1 0.9%	0 0	0 0	0 0	1 1.6%	0 0	0 0	0 0	0 0	0 0	0 0	1 0.6%	0 0
preferred source of info	0 0	0 0	0 0	0 0	0 0	0 0	0 0	0 0	0 0	0 0	0 0	0 0	0 0	0 0	0 0	0 0	0 0	0 0
Access book/journal/ journal article elsewhere online (NET)	0 0	0 0	0 0	0 0	0 0	0 0	0 0	0 0	0 0	0 0	0 0	0 0	0 0	0 0	0 0	0 0	0 0	0 0
All sources of info	0 0	0 0	0 0	0 0	0 0	0 0	0 0	0 0	0 0	0 0	0 0	0 0	0 0	0 0	0 0	0 0	0 0	0 0
preferred source of info	0 0	0 0	0 0	0 0	0 0	0 0	0 0	0 0	0 0	0 0	0 0	0 0	0 0	0 0	0 0	0 0	0 0	0 0

Proportions/Means: Columns Tested (5% risk level) - A/B/D - C/D - E/F/G - H/I/J/K/L/M/N - P/Q
* small base; ** very small base (under 30) ineligible for sig testing

Table 273
Page 1113

Outsell/Digital Library Federation Study (2002)
Weighted Tables

TABLE 120, continued

T7D/E_12. Data SUMMARY TABLE

		RESPONDENT TYPE				INSTITUTION TYPE			DISCIPLINE									GENDER	
	TOTAL SAMPLE	FACULTY MEMBER	GRAD. STUDENT	FACULTY /GRAD	UNDER GRAD. STUDENT	PUBLIC	PRIVATE	LIBERAL ARTS	BIOLOGIAL SCIENCES	PHYSICAL SCIENCES /MATH	SOCIAL SCIENCES	ARTS AND HUMAN.	ENGI-NEERING	BUSINESS	LAW	UNDEC. MAJOR	MALE	FEMALE
		(A)	(B)	(C)	(D)	(E)	(F)	(G)	(H)	(I)	(J)	(K)	(L)	(M)	(N)		(P)	(Q)
Base - Use Data for teaching	264	186	79*	264	0**	112*	85*	68*	48*	63*	75*	37*	8**	32*	1**	0*	174	91*
Author	0 0	0 0	0 0	0 0	0 0	0 0	0 0	0 0	0 0	0 0	0 0	0 0	0 0	0 0	0 0	0 0	0 0	0 0
All sources of info	0 0	0 0	0 0	0 0	0 0	0 0	0 0	0 0	0 0	0 0	0 0	0 0	0 0	0 0	0 0	0 0	0 0	0 0
preferred source of info	0 0	0 0	0 0	0 0	0 0	0 0	0 0	0 0	0 0	0 0	0 0	0 0	0 0	0 0	0 0	0 0	0 0	0 0
Other (NET)	13 4.9%	9 4.8%	4 5.1%	13 4.9%	0 0	6 5.3%	4 4.7%	3 4.3%	4 7.3%J	2 3.2%	0 0	3 9.1%J	1 14.3%	3 8.8%J	0 0	0 0	6 3.2%	7 7.9%
All sources of info	10 3.7%	7 3.7%	3 3.6%	10 3.7%	0 0	4 3.3%	3 3.6%	3 4.3%	4 7.3%J	2 3.2%	0 0	1 3.0%	1 14.3%	2 5.9%	0 0	0 0	4 2.1%	6 6.7%
preferred source of info	7 2.6%	6 3.0%	1 1.8%	7 2.6%	0 0	4 3.6%	2 2.5%	1 1.3%	4 7.3%IJ	0 0	0 0	2 6.1%	* 3.6%	1 2.9%	0 0	0 0	4 2.2%	3 3.5%
DK/Refused	4 1.6%	4 2.3%	0 0	4 1.6%	0 0	2 2.2%	2 2.2%	0 0	0 0	0 0	4 5.0%	0 0	1 7.1%	0 0	0 0	0 0	1 0.3%	4 4.1%P

Proportions/Means: Columns Tested (5% risk level) - A/B/D - C/D - E/F/G - H/I/J/K/L/M/N - P/Q
* small base; ** very small base (under 30) ineligible for sig testing

Table 273
Page 1114

Outsell/Digital Library Federation Study (2002)
Weighted Tables

TABLE 121

T7sum_13. Photographs, prints and other visual resources SUMMARY TABLE

	RESPONDENT TYPE				INSTITUTION TYPE			DISCIPLINE								GENDER	
	TOTAL SAMPLE	FACULTY MEMBER	GRAD. STUDENT	FACULTY /GRAD	UNDER GRAD. STUDENT	PUBLIC	PRIVATE	LIBERAL ARTS	BIOLOGIAL SCIENCES	PHYSICAL SCIENCES /MATH	SOCIAL SCIENCES	ARTS AND HUMAN.	ENGI-NEERING	BUSINESS	LAW	UNDEC. MAJOR	MALE	FEMALE
		(A)	(B)	(C)	(D)	(E)	(F)	(G)	(H)	(I)	(J)	(K)	(L)	(M)	(N)		(P)	(Q)
Base - USe Photographs, prints and other visual resources for teaching	290	195	95*	290	0**	105*	116*	69*	64*	53*	62*	72*	12*	26**	1**	0*	208	82*
ONLINE	188	136	52	188	0	66	69	54	47	36	39	43	9	14	1	0	133	56
	64.9%	69.5%B	55.4%	64.9%	0	62.7%	59.2%	77.8%F	72.6%	67.9%	63.6%	59.4%	73.8%	53.6%	80.0%	0	63.8%	67.8%
Search engine	65	51	14	65	0	21	28	16	12	15	8	18	5	7	*	0	51	14
	22.5%	26.1%	15.1%	22.5%	0	20.0%	24.3%	23.2%	19.2%	28.3%	12.1%	25.0%	40.5%HJ	28.6%	20.0%	0	24.7%	17.0%
All sources of info	65	51	14	65	0	21	28	16	12	15	8	18	5	7	*	0	51	14
	22.5%	26.1%	15.1%	22.5%	0	20.0%	24.3%	23.2%	19.2%	28.3%	12.1%	25.0%	40.5%HJ	28.6%	20.0%	0	24.7%	17.0%
preferred source of info	35	24	11	35	0	13	13	9	7	10	6	7	3	3	*	0	29	6
	12.2%	12.3%	11.8%	12.2%	0	12.5%	11.3%	13.1%	11.0%	18.9%	9.1%	9.4%	23.8%K	10.7%	20.0%	0	14.1%	7.4%
Internet searches	53	35	18	53	0	21	15	17	18	8	13	9	1	4	*	0	33	20
	18.3%	18.1%	18.6%	18.3%	0	19.9%	12.8%	24.8%	27.4%KL	15.1%	21.2%	12.5%	9.5%	14.3%	40.0%	0	15.7%	24.8%
All sources of info	53	35	18	53	0	21	15	17	18	8	13	9	1	4	*	0	33	20
	18.3%	18.1%	18.6%	18.3%	0	19.9%	12.8%	24.8%	27.4%KL	15.1%	21.2%	12.5%	9.5%	14.3%	40.0%	0	15.7%	24.8%
preferred source of info	30	22	8	30	0	10	9	12	12	6	8	1	1	3	0	0	21	9
	10.5%	11.5%	8.4%	10.5%	0	9.2%	7.4%	17.4%	19.2%K	11.3%K	12.1%K	1.6%	4.8%	10.7%	0	0	10.0%	11.5%
Web directory/ subject related web site	47	36	11	47	0	11	19	17	11	8	11	12	3	2	0	0	31	16
	16.1%	18.3%	11.4%	16.1%	0	10.3%	16.3%	24.3%E	16.4%	15.1%	18.2%	17.2%	21.4%	7.1%	0	0	14.9%	19.1%

Proportions/Means: Columns Tested (5% risk level) - A/B/D - C/D - E/F/G - H/I/J/K/L/M/N - P/Q
* small base; ** very small base (under 30) ineligible for sig testing

Table 277
Page 1126

Outsell/Digital Library Federation Study (2002)
Weighted Tables

TABLE 121, continued

T7sum_13. Photographs, prints and other visual resources SUMMARY TABLE

		RESPONDENT TYPE				INSTITUTION TYPE			DISCIPLINE									GENDER	
	TOTAL SAMPLE	FACULTY MEMBER	GRAD. STUDENT	FACULTY /GRAD	UNDER GRAD. STUDENT	PUBLIC	PRIVATE	LIBERAL ARTS	BIOLOGIAL SCIENCES	PHYSICAL SCIENCES /MATH	SOCIAL SCIENCES	ARTS AND HUMAN.	ENGI- NEERING	BUSINESS	LAW	UNDEC. MAJOR		MALE	FEMALE
		(A)	(B)	(C)	(D)	(E)	(F)	(G)	(H)	(I)	(J)	(K)	(L)	(M)	(N)			(P)	(Q)
Base - USe Photographs, prints and other visual resources for teaching	290	195	95*	290	0**	105*	116*	69*	64*	53*	62*	72*	12*	26**	1**	0*		208	82*
All sources of info	47 16.1%	36 18.3%	11 11.4%	47 16.1%	0 0	11 10.3%	19 16.3%	17 24.3%E	11 16.4%	8 15.1%	11 18.2%	12 17.2%	3 21.4%	2 7.1%	0 0	0 0		31 14.9%	16 19.1%
preferred source of info	31 10.8%	25 12.6%	7 7.3%	31 10.8%	0 0	6 5.7%	14 11.7%	12 17.1%E	8 12.3%	5 9.4%	9 15.2%	7 9.4%	1 11.9%	1 3.6%	0 0	0 0		21 9.9%	11 13.1%
Online databases	19 6.4%	14 7.4%	4 4.4%	19 6.4%	0 0	4 4.2%	7 5.7%	8 11.0%	7 11.0%J	7 13.2%JK	0 0	2 3.1%	* 2.4%	2 7.1%	* 20.0%	0 0		14 6.6%	5 5.9%
All sources of info	19 6.4%	14 7.4%	4 4.4%	19 6.4%	0 0	4 4.2%	7 5.7%	8 11.0%	7 11.0%J	7 13.2%JK	0 0	2 3.1%	* 2.4%	2 7.1%	* 20.0%	0 0		14 6.6%	5 5.9%
preferred source of info	10 3.4%	8 3.9%	2 2.3%	10 3.4%	0 0	3 3.1%	4 3.1%	3 4.2%	4 6.8%K	4 7.5%K	0 0	0 0	* 2.4%K	1 3.6%	* 20.0%	0 0		8 3.8%	2 2.3%
Online library catalogues and finding aids	13 4.3%	11 5.7%	1 1.5%	13 4.3%	0 0	6 6.0%	3 2.2%	4 5.4%	2 2.7%	1 1.9%	4 6.1%	4 6.3%	1 4.8%	1 3.6%	0 0	0 0		12 5.5%	1 1.2%
All sources of info	13 4.3%	11 5.7%	1 1.5%	13 4.3%	0 0	6 6.0%	3 2.2%	4 5.4%	2 2.7%	1 1.9%	4 6.1%	4 6.3%	1 4.8%	1 3.6%	0 0	0 0		12 5.5%	1 1.2%
preferred source of info	5 1.8%	5 2.6%	* 0.3%	5 1.8%	0 0	1 1.1%	1 1.2%	3 4.0%	2 2.7%	0 0	2 3.0%	1 1.6%	1 4.8%I	0 0	0 0	0 0		5 2.6%	0 0

Proportions/Means: Columns Tested (5% risk level) - A/B/D - C/D - E/F/G - H/I/J/K/L/M/N - P/Q
* small base; ** very small base (under 30) ineligible for sig testing

Table 277
Page 1127

Outsell/Digital Library Federation Study (2002)
Weighted Tables

TABLE 121, continued

T7sum_13. Photographs, prints and other visual resources SUMMARY TABLE

	RESPONDENT TYPE					INSTITUTION TYPE			DISCIPLINE									GENDER	
	TOTAL SAMPLE	FACULTY MEMBER	GRAD. STUDENT	FACULTY /GRAD	UNDER GRAD. STUDENT	PUBLIC	PRIVATE	LIBERAL ARTS	BIOLOGIAL SCIENCES	PHYSICAL SCIENCES /MATH	SOCIAL SCIENCES	ARTS AND HUMAN.	ENGI-NEERING	BUSINESS	LAW	UNDEC. MAJOR	MALE	FEMALE
		(A)	(B)	(C)	(D)	(E)	(F)	(G)	(H)	(I)	(J)	(K)	(L)	(M)	(N)		(P)	(Q)
Base - USe Photographs, prints and other visual resources for teaching	290	195	95*	290	0**	105*	116*	69*	64*	53*	62*	72*	12*	26**	1**	0*	208	82*
Your own institution's web site	12 4.0%	4 1.8%	8 8.7%A	12 4.0%	0 0	6 6.1%	4 3.6%	1 1.7%	4 6.8%I	0 0	4 6.1%	2 3.1%	1 9.5%I	0 0	* 20.0%	0 0	6 2.9%	6 6.9%
All sources of info	12 4.0%	4 1.8%	8 8.7%A	12 4.0%	0 0	6 6.1%	4 3.6%	1 1.7%	4 6.8%I	0 0	4 6.1%	2 3.1%	1 9.5%I	0 0	* 20.0%	0 0	6 2.9%	6 6.9%
preferred source of info	9 3.2%	3 1.6%	6 6.3%	9 3.2%	0 0	4 3.9%	4 3.4%	1 1.7%	4 5.5%	0 0	4 6.1%	1 1.6%	1 4.8%I	0 0	* 20.0%	0 0	4 2.1%	5 5.8%
Online reference service	5 1.6%	5 2.4%	0 0	5 1.6%	0 0	2 1.7%	2 1.7%	1 1.3%	2 2.7%	0 0	0 0	1 1.6%	0 0	2 7.1%	0 0	0 0	3 1.4%	2 2.2%
All sources of info	5 1.6%	5 2.4%	0 0	5 1.6%	0 0	2 1.7%	2 1.7%	1 1.3%	2 2.7%	0 0	0 0	1 1.6%	0 0	2 7.1%	0 0	0 0	3 1.4%	2 2.2%
preferred source of info	3 0.9%	3 1.4%	0 0	3 0.9%	0 0	2 1.7%	0 0	1 1.3%	1 1.4%	0 0	0 0	0 0	0 0	2 7.1%	0 0	0 0	1 0.4%	2 2.2%
Department web page	4 1.4%	2 1.2%	2 1.7%	4 1.4%	0 0	0 0	4 3.4%	0 0	0 0	2 3.8%	0 0	1 1.6%	1 7.1%HJ	0 0	0 0	0 0	3 1.4%	1 1.4%
All sources of info	4 1.4%	2 1.2%	2 1.7%	4 1.4%	0 0	0 0	4 3.4%	0 0	0 0	2 3.8%	0 0	1 1.6%	1 7.1%HJ	0 0	0 0	0 0	3 1.4%	1 1.4%

Proportions/Means: Columns Tested (5% risk level) - A/B/D - C/D - E/F/G - H/I/J/K/L/M/N - P/Q
* small base; ** very small base (under 30) ineligible for sig testing

Table 277
Page 1128

Outsell/Digital Library Federation Study (2002)
Weighted Tables

TABLE 121, continued

T7sum_13. Photographs, prints and other visual resources SUMMARY TABLE

		RESPONDENT TYPE				INSTITUTION TYPE			DISCIPLINE								GENDER	
	TOTAL SAMPLE	FACULTY MEMBER	GRAD. STUDENT	FACULTY /GRAD	UNDER GRAD. STUDENT	PUBLIC	PRIVATE	LIBERAL ARTS	BIOLOGIAL SCIENCES	PHYSICAL SCIENCES /MATH	SOCIAL SCIENCES	ARTS AND HUMAN.	ENGI-NEERING	BUSINESS	LAW	UNDEC. MAJOR	MALE	FEMALE
		(A)	(B)	(C)	(D)	(E)	(F)	(G)	(H)	(I)	(J)	(K)	(L)	(M)	(N)		(P)	(Q)
Base - USe Photographs, prints and other visual resources for teaching	290	195	95*	290	0**	105*	116*	69*	64*	53*	62*	72*	12*	26**	1**	0*	208	82*
preferred source of info	2 0.8%	1 0.5%	1 1.4%	2 0.8%	0 0	0 0	2 2.0%	0 0	0 0	2 3.8%	0 0	0 0	* 2.4%HK	0 0	0 0	0 0	2 1.1%	0 0
Online bookstore	2 0.8%	2 1.1%	0 0	2 0.8%	0 0	0 0	1 1.0%	1 1.6%	0 0	0 0	0 0	2 3.1%	0 0	0 0	0 0	0 0	2 1.1%	0 0
All sources of info	2 0.8%	2 1.1%	0 0	2 0.8%	0 0	0 0	1 1.0%	1 1.6%	0 0	0 0	0 0	2 3.1%	0 0	0 0	0 0	0 0	2 1.1%	0 0
preferred source of info	1 0.4%	1 0.6%	0 0	1 0.4%	0 0	0 0	0 0	1 1.6%	0 0	0 0	0 0	1 1.6%	0 0	0 0	0 0	0 0	1 0.5%	0 0
E-mail listservs	1 0.3%	0 0	1 0.9%	1 0.3%	0 0	1 0.8%	0 0	0 0	1 1.4%	0 0	0 0	0 0	0 0	0 0	0 0	0 0	0 0	1 1.1%
All sources of info	1 0.3%	0 0	1 0.9%	1 0.3%	0 0	1 0.8%	0 0	0 0	1 1.4%	0 0	0 0	0 0	0 0	0 0	0 0	0 0	0 0	1 1.1%
preferred source of info	1 0.3%	0 0	1 0.9%	1 0.3%	0 0	1 0.8%	0 0	0 0	1 1.4%	0 0	0 0	0 0	0 0	0 0	0 0	0 0	0 0	1 1.1%
Online abstracting and indexing services	* 0.1%	* 0.1%	0 0	* 0.1%	0 0	* 0.3%	0 0	0 0	0 0	0 0	0 0	0 0	* 2.4%HK	0 0	0 0	0 0	* 0.1%	0 0

Proportions/Means: Columns Tested (5% risk level) - A/B/D - C/D - E/F/G - H/I/J/K/L/M/N - P/Q
* small base; ** very small base (under 30) ineligible for sig testing

Table 277
Page 1129

Outsell/Digital Library Federation Study (2002)
Weighted Tables

TABLE 121, continued

T7sum_13. Photographs, prints and other visual resources SUMMARY TABLE

		RESPONDENT TYPE				INSTITUTION TYPE			DISCIPLINE								GENDER	
	TOTAL SAMPLE	FACULTY MEMBER	GRAD. STUDENT	FACULTY /GRAD	UNDER GRAD. STUDENT	PUBLIC	PRIVATE	LIBERAL ARTS	BIOLOGIAL SCIENCES	PHYSICAL SCIENCES /MATH	SOCIAL SCIENCES	ARTS AND HUMAN.	ENGI-NEERING	BUSINESS	LAW	UNDEC. MAJOR	MALE	FEMALE
		(A)	(B)	(C)	(D)	(E)	(F)	(G)	(H)	(I)	(J)	(K)	(L)	(M)	(N)		(P)	(Q)
Base - USe Photographs, prints and other visual resources for teaching	290	195	95*	290	0**	105*	116*	69*	64*	53*	62*	72*	12*	26**	1**	0*	208	82*
All sources of info	* 0.1%	* 0.1%	0 0	* 0.1%	0 0	* 0.3%	0 0	0 0	0 0	0 0	0 0	0 0	* 2.4%HK	0 0	0 0	0 0	* 0.1%	0 0
preferred source of info	0 0	0 0	0 0	0 0	0 0	0 0	0 0	0 0	0 0	0 0	0 0	0 0	0 0	0 0	0 0	0 0	0 0	0 0
Your own personal electronic library/files	0 0	0 0	0 0	0 0	0 0	0 0	0 0	0 0	0 0	0 0	0 0	0 0	0 0	0 0	0 0	0 0	0 0	0 0
All sources of info	0 0	0 0	0 0	0 0	0 0	0 0	0 0	0 0	0 0	0 0	0 0	0 0	0 0	0 0	0 0	0 0	0 0	0 0
preferred source of info	0 0	0 0	0 0	0 0	0 0	0 0	0 0	0 0	0 0	0 0	0 0	0 0	0 0	0 0	0 0	0 0	0 0	0 0
LIBRARY/PRINT	152 52.4%	111 56.7%	41 43.4%	152 52.4%	0 0	54 51.9%	63 54.4%	35 49.7%	27 42.5%	28 52.8%	28 45.5%	48 67.2%HJ	7 54.8%	13 50.0%	1 60.0%	0 0	113 54.5%	39 47.0%
Campus library	103 35.6%	75 38.5%	28 29.7%	103 35.6%	0 0	38 36.6%	40 34.6%	25 35.8%	16 24.7%	20 37.7%	19 30.3%	35 48.4%H	6 45.2%H	8 32.1%	0 0	0 0	77 36.8%	27 32.5%
All sources of info	103 35.6%	75 38.5%	28 29.7%	103 35.6%	0 0	38 36.6%	40 34.6%	25 35.8%	16 24.7%	20 37.7%	19 30.3%	35 48.4%H	6 45.2%H	8 32.1%	0 0	0 0	77 36.8%	27 32.5%

Proportions/Means: Columns Tested (5% risk level) - A/B/D - C/D - E/F/G - H/I/J/K/L/M/N - P/Q
* small base; ** very small base (under 30) ineligible for sig testing

Table 277
Page 1130

Outsell/Digital Library Federation Study (2002)
Weighted Tables

TABLE 121, continued

T7sum_13. Photographs, prints and other visual resources SUMMARY TABLE

		RESPONDENT TYPE				INSTITUTION TYPE			DISCIPLINE									GENDER	
	TOTAL SAMPLE	FACULTY MEMBER	GRAD. STUDENT	FACULTY /GRAD	UNDER GRAD. STUDENT	PUBLIC	PRIVATE	LIBERAL ARTS	BIOLOGIAL SCIENCES	PHYSICAL SCIENCES /MATH	SOCIAL SCIENCES	ARTS AND HUMAN.	ENGI- NEERING	BUSINESS	LAW	UNDEC. MAJOR	MALE	FEMALE
		(A)	(B)	(C)	(D)	(E)	(F)	(G)	(H)	(I)	(J)	(K)	(L)	(M)	(N)		(P)	(Q)
Base - USe Photographs, prints and other visual resources for teaching	290	195	95*	290	0**	105*	116*	69*	64*	53*	62*	72*	12*	26**	1**	0*	208	82*
preferred source of info	45 15.7%	29 14.9%	16 17.3%	45 15.7%	0 0	19 18.0%	20 16.9%	7 10.2%	4 5.5%	6 11.3%	11 18.2%	20 28.1%HI	2 14.3%	3 10.7%	0 0	0 0	32 15.6%	13 15.8%
Your own personal physical library/ files/bookshelves	51 17.7%	42 21.7%B	9 9.4%	51 17.7%	0 0	21 19.8%	18 15.7%	12 17.9%	11 17.8%	13 24.5%	9 15.2%	11 15.6%	1 9.5%	5 17.9%	1 60.0%	0 0	39 18.8%	12 14.8%
All sources of info	51 17.7%	42 21.7%B	9 9.4%	51 17.7%	0 0	21 19.8%	18 15.7%	12 17.9%	11 17.8%	13 24.5%	9 15.2%	11 15.6%	1 9.5%	5 17.9%	1 60.0%	0 0	39 18.8%	12 14.8%
preferred source of info	22 7.5%	15 7.7%	7 7.3%	22 7.5%	0 0	10 9.1%	6 5.1%	6 9.2%	4 6.8%	7 13.2%	2 3.0%	7 9.4%	1 4.8%	1 3.6%	* 40.0%	0 0	15 7.0%	7 8.9%
Personal subscriptions to newspapers, magazines and journals	30 10.3%	30 15.3%B	0 0	30 10.3%	0 0	5 4.8%	18 15.5%E	7 10.0%	5 8.2%	5 9.4%	8 12.1%	6 7.8%	1 7.1%	6 21.4%	0 0	0 0	27 12.9%Q	3 3.6%
All sources of info	30 10.3%	30 15.3%B	0 0	30 10.3%	0 0	5 4.8%	18 15.5%E	7 10.0%	5 8.2%	5 9.4%	8 12.1%	6 7.8%	1 7.1%	6 21.4%	0 0	0 0	27 12.9%Q	3 3.6%
preferred source of info	16 5.4%	16 8.0%B	0 0	16 5.4%	0 0	3 3.3%	12 10.6%G	0 0	3 4.1%	1 1.9%	6 9.1%	3 4.7%	* 2.4%	3 10.7%	0 0	0 0	15 7.1%	1 1.2%

Proportions/Means: Columns Tested (5% risk level) - A/B/D - C/D - E/F/G - H/I/J/K/L/M/N - P/Q
* small base; ** very small base (under 30) ineligible for sig testing

Table 277
Page 1131

Outsell/Digital Library Federation Study (2002)
Weighted Tables

TABLE 121, continued

T7sum_13. Photographs, prints and other visual resources SUMMARY TABLE

		RESPONDENT TYPE				INSTITUTION TYPE			DISCIPLINE									GENDER	
	TOTAL SAMPLE	FACULTY MEMBER	GRAD. STUDENT	FACULTY /GRAD	UNDER GRAD. STUDENT	PUBLIC	PRIVATE	LIBERAL ARTS	BIOLOGIAL SCIENCES	PHYSICAL SCIENCES /MATH	SOCIAL SCIENCES	ARTS AND HUMAN.	ENGI-NEERING	BUSINESS	LAW	UNDEC. MAJOR	MALE	FEMALE
		(A)	(B)	(C)	(D)	(E)	(F)	(G)	(H)	(I)	(J)	(K)	(L)	(M)	(N)		(P)	(Q)
Base - USe Photographs, prints and other visual resources for teaching	290	195	95*	290	0**	105*	116*	69*	64*	53*	62*	72*	12*	26**	1**	0*	208	82*
Physical bookstore	9	9	0	9	0	4	2	3	1	0	0	8	*	0	0	0	6	3
	3.1%	4.6%	0	3.1%	0	3.5%	1.9%	4.5%	1.4%	0	0	10.9%HIJ	2.4%	0	0	0	2.7%	4.1%
All sources of info	9	9	0	9	0	4	2	3	1	0	0	8	*	0	0	0	6	3
	3.1%	4.6%	0	3.1%	0	3.5%	1.9%	4.5%	1.4%	0	0	10.9%HIJ	2.4%	0	0	0	2.7%	4.1%
preferred source of info	1	1	0	1	0	0	0	1	1	0	0	0	0	0	0	0	1	0
	0.3%	0.5%	0	0.3%	0	0	0	1.3%	1.4%	0	0	0	0	0	0	0	0.4%	0
Another library	8	7	1	8	0	1	3	4	3	3	0	2	0	0	0	0	5	3
	2.7%	3.6%	0.9%	2.7%	0	0.8%	2.5%	5.9%	4.1%	5.7%	0	3.1%	0	0	0	0	2.3%	3.6%
All sources of info	8	7	1	8	0	1	3	4	3	3	0	2	0	0	0	0	5	3
	2.7%	3.6%	0.9%	2.7%	0	0.8%	2.5%	5.9%	4.1%	5.7%	0	3.1%	0	0	0	0	2.3%	3.6%
preferred source of info	0	0	0	0	0	0	0	0	0	0	0	0	0	0	0	0	0	0
	0	0	0	0	0	0	0	0	0	0	0	0	0	0	0	0	0	0
References cited in books or journal articles	5	3	2	5	0	1	2	2	3	1	0	1	*	0	0	0	3	2
	1.7%	1.7%	1.9%	1.7%	0	1.1%	1.5%	3.1%	4.1%	1.9%	0	1.6%	2.4%	0	0	0	1.6%	2.1%
All sources of info	5	3	2	5	0	1	2	2	3	1	0	1	*	0	0	0	3	2
	1.7%	1.7%	1.9%	1.7%	0	1.1%	1.5%	3.1%	4.1%	1.9%	0	1.6%	2.4%	0	0	0	1.6%	2.1%
preferred source of info	2	1	1	2	0	1	0	1	1	0	0	1	0	0	0	0	2	0
	0.7%	0.6%	0.9%	0.7%	0	0.8%	0	1.6%	1.4%	0	0	1.6%	0	0	0	0	1.0%	0

Proportions/Means: Columns Tested (5% risk level) - A/B/D - C/D - E/F/G - H/I/J/K/L/M/N - P/Q
* small base; ** very small base (under 30) ineligible for sig testing

Table 277
Page 1132

Outsell/Digital Library Federation Study (2002)
Weighted Tables

TABLE 121, continued

T7sum_13. Photographs, prints and other visual resources SUMMARY TABLE

		RESPONDENT TYPE				INSTITUTION TYPE			DISCIPLINE								GENDER	
	TOTAL SAMPLE	FACULTY MEMBER	GRAD. STUDENT	FACULTY /GRAD	UNDER GRAD. STUDENT	PUBLIC	PRIVATE	LIBERAL ARTS	BIOLOGIAL SCIENCES	PHYSICAL SCIENCES /MATH	SOCIAL SCIENCES	ARTS AND HUMAN.	ENGI- NEERING	BUSINESS	LAW	UNDEC. MAJOR	MALE	FEMALE
		(A)	(B)	(C)	(D)	(E)	(F)	(G)	(H)	(I)	(J)	(K)	(L)	(M)	(N)		(P)	(Q)
Base - USe Photographs, prints and other visual resources for teaching	290	195	95*	290	0**	105*	116*	69*	64*	53*	62*	72*	12*	26**	1**	0*	208	82*
Printed library catalogues and finding aids	5 1.7%	1 0.5%	4 4.4%A	5 1.7%	0 0	3 2.9%	2 1.7%	0 0	1 1.4%	0 0	2 3.0%	2 3.1%	0 0	0 0	0 0	0 0	4 2.0%	1 1.1%
All sources of info	5 1.7%	1 0.5%	4 4.4%A	5 1.7%	0 0	3 2.9%	2 1.7%	0 0	1 1.4%	0 0	2 3.0%	2 3.1%	0 0	0 0	0 0	0 0	4 2.0%	1 1.1%
preferred source of info	2 0.8%	0 0	2 2.4%A	2 0.8%	0 0	1 1.1%	1 1.0%	0 0	0 0	0 0	0 0	2 3.1%	0 0	0 0	0 0	0 0	2 1.1%	0 0
Printed abstracting and indexing services	1 0.4%	1 0.6%	0 0	1 0.4%	0 0	1 1.1%	0 0	0 0	0 0	0 0	0 0	1 1.6%	0 0	0 0	0 0	0 0	1 0.5%	0 0
All sources of info	1 0.4%	1 0.6%	0 0	1 0.4%	0 0	1 1.1%	0 0	0 0	0 0	0 0	0 0	1 1.6%	0 0	0 0	0 0	0 0	1 0.5%	0 0
preferred source of info	0 0	0 0	0 0	0 0	0 0	0 0	0 0	0 0	0 0	0 0	0 0	0 0	0 0	0 0	0 0	0 0	0 0	0 0
PERSONAL ASSISTANCE	83 28.8%	52 26.7%	31 33.2%	83 28.8%	0 0	31 29.2%	35 30.0%	18 26.0%	13 20.5%	15 28.3%	15 24.2%	27 37.5%H	4 33.3%	9 35.7%	0 0	0 0	59 28.3%	25 29.9%
Colleagues inside your institution	60 20.6%	35 18.0%	25 26.0%	60 20.6%	0 0	23 22.3%	26 22.0%	11 15.8%	10 15.1%	13 24.5%	9 15.2%	17 23.4%	3 28.6%	7 28.6%	0 0	0 0	44 21.3%	15 18.8%

Proportions/Means: Columns Tested (5% risk level) - A/B/D - C/D - E/F/G - H/I/J/K/L/M/N - P/Q
* small base; ** very small base (under 30) ineligible for sig testing

Table 277
Page 1133

Outsell/Digital Library Federation Study (2002)
Weighted Tables

TABLE 121, continued

T7sum_13. Photographs, prints and other visual resources SUMMARY TABLE

	TOTAL SAMPLE	RESPONDENT TYPE: FACULTY MEMBER	GRAD. STUDENT	FACULTY /GRAD	UNDER GRAD. STUDENT	INSTITUTION TYPE: PUBLIC	PRIVATE	LIBERAL ARTS	DISCIPLINE: BIOLOGIAL SCIENCES	PHYSICAL SCIENCES /MATH	SOCIAL SCIENCES	ARTS AND HUMAN.	ENGI-NEERING	BUSINESS	LAW	UNDEC. MAJOR	GENDER: MALE	FEMALE
		(A)	(B)	(C)	(D)	(E)	(F)	(G)	(H)	(I)	(J)	(K)	(L)	(M)	(N)		(P)	(Q)
Base - USe Photographs, prints and other visual resources for teaching	290	195	95*	290	0**	105*	116*	69*	64*	53*	62*	72*	12*	26**	1**	0*	208	82*
All sources of info	60 20.6%	35 18.0%	25 26.0%	60 20.6%	0 0	23 22.3%	26 22.0%	11 15.8%	10 15.1%	13 24.5%	9 15.2%	17 23.4%	3 28.6%	7 28.6%	0 0	0 0	44 21.3%	15 18.8%
preferred source of info	27 9.4%	9 4.7%	18 19.0%A	27 9.4%	0 0	10 9.4%	14 12.4%	3 4.2%	5 8.2%	7 13.2%	2 3.0%	8 10.9%	1 4.8%	5 17.9%	0 0	0 0	17 8.2%	10 12.5%
A librarian in your institution	30 10.5%	22 11.0%	9 9.4%	30 10.5%	0 0	11 10.5%	13 11.6%	6 8.6%	6 9.6%	4 7.5%	9 15.2%	8 10.9%	1 9.5%	2 7.1%	0 0	0 0	24 11.4%	7 8.2%
All sources of info	30 10.5%	22 11.0%	9 9.4%	30 10.5%	0 0	11 10.5%	13 11.6%	6 8.6%	6 9.6%	4 7.5%	9 15.2%	8 10.9%	1 9.5%	2 7.1%	0 0	0 0	24 11.4%	7 8.2%
preferred source of info	12 4.0%	6 3.0%	6 6.0%	12 4.0%	0 0	5 4.7%	4 3.2%	3 4.3%	1 1.4%	1 1.9%	6 9.1%	2 3.1%	0 0	2 7.1%	0 0	0 0	9 4.2%	3 3.5%
Colleagues outside your institution	13 4.4%	12 6.0%	1 1.2%	13 4.4%	0 0	6 6.0%	3 2.7%	3 4.9%	2 2.7%	2 3.8%	0 0	8 10.9%J	* 2.4%	1 3.6%	0 0	0 0	5 2.5%	8 9.2%P
All sources of info	13 4.4%	12 6.0%	1 1.2%	13 4.4%	0 0	6 6.0%	3 2.7%	3 4.9%	2 2.7%	2 3.8%	0 0	8 10.9%J	* 2.4%	1 3.6%	0 0	0 0	5 2.5%	8 9.2%P
preferred source of info	1 0.4%	0 0	1 1.2%	1 0.4%	0 0	0 0	1 1.0%	0 0	0 0	0 0	0 0	1 1.6%	0 0	0 0	0 0	0 0	0 0	1 1.4%
Another institution's librarian	1 0.4%	1 0.6%	0 0	1 0.4%	0 0	0 0	1 1.0%	0 0	0 0	0 0	0 0	1 1.6%	0 0	0 0	0 0	0 0	1 0.5%	0 0

Proportions/Means: Columns Tested (5% risk level) - A/B/D - C/D - E/F/G - H/I/J/K/L/M/N - P/Q
* small base; ** very small base (under 30) ineligible for sig testing

Table 277
Page 1134

Outsell/Digital Library Federation Study (2002)
Weighted Tables

TABLE 121, continued

T7sum_13. Photographs, prints and other visual resources SUMMARY TABLE

		RESPONDENT TYPE				INSTITUTION TYPE			DISCIPLINE									GENDER	
	TOTAL SAMPLE	FACULTY MEMBER	GRAD. STUDENT	FACULTY /GRAD	UNDER GRAD. STUDENT	PUBLIC	PRIVATE	LIBERAL ARTS	BIOLOGIAL SCIENCES	PHYSICAL SCIENCES /MATH	SOCIAL SCIENCES	ARTS AND HUMAN.	ENGI-NEERING	BUSINESS	LAW	UNDEC. MAJOR		MALE	FEMALE
		(A)	(B)	(C)	(D)	(E)	(F)	(G)	(H)	(I)	(J)	(K)	(L)	(M)	(N)			(P)	(Q)
Base - USe Photographs, prints and other visual resources for teaching	290	195	95*	290	0**	105*	116*	69*	64*	53*	62*	72*	12*	26**	1**	0*		208	82*
All sources of info	1	1	0	1	0	0	1	0	0	0	0	1	0	0	0	0		1	0
	0.4%	0.6%	0	0.4%	0	0	1.0%	0	0	0	0	1.6%	0	0	0	0		0.5%	0
preferred source of info	0	0	0	0	0	0	0	0	0	0	0	0	0	0	0	0		0	0
	0	0	0	0	0	0	0	0	0	0	0	0	0	0	0	0		0	0
Professional meetings	0	0	0	0	0	0	0	0	0	0	0	0	0	0	0	0		0	0
	0	0	0	0	0	0	0	0	0	0	0	0	0	0	0	0		0	0
All sources of info	0	0	0	0	0	0	0	0	0	0	0	0	0	0	0	0		0	0
	0	0	0	0	0	0	0	0	0	0	0	0	0	0	0	0		0	0
preferred source of info	0	0	0	0	0	0	0	0	0	0	0	0	0	0	0	0		0	0
	0	0	0	0	0	0	0	0	0	0	0	0	0	0	0	0		0	0
Online (unspecified)	5	4	*	5	0	2	2	0	0	1	2	1	1	0	0	0		5	0
	1.6%	2.2%	0.3%	1.6%	0	2.4%	1.8%	0	0	1.9%	3.0%	1.6%	4.8%H	0	0	0		2.2%	0
All sources of info	5	4	*	5	0	2	2	0	0	1	2	1	1	0	0	0		5	0
	1.6%	2.2%	0.3%	1.6%	0	2.4%	1.8%	0	0	1.9%	3.0%	1.6%	4.8%H	0	0	0		2.2%	0
preferred source of info	2	2	*	2	0	2	0	0	0	0	2	0	1	0	0	0		2	0
	0.8%	1.1%	0.3%	0.8%	0	2.4%	0	0	0	0	3.0%	0	4.8%HIK	0	0	0		1.2%	0
Students	2	2	0	2	0	1	1	0	1	0	0	1	0	0	0	0		2	0
	0.7%	1.0%	0	0.7%	0	0.8%	1.0%	0	1.4%	0	0	1.6%	0	0	0	0		1.0%	0

Proportions/Means: Columns Tested (5% risk level) - A/B/D - C/D - E/F/G - H/I/J/K/L/M/N - P/Q
* small base; ** very small base (under 30) ineligible for sig testing

Table 277
Page 1135

Outsell/Digital Library Federation Study (2002)
Weighted Tables

TABLE 121, continued

T7sum_13. Photographs, prints and other visual resources SUMMARY TABLE

		RESPONDENT TYPE				INSTITUTION TYPE			DISCIPLINE								GENDER	
	TOTAL SAMPLE	FACULTY MEMBER	GRAD. STUDENT	FACULTY /GRAD	UNDER GRAD. STUDENT	PUBLIC	PRIVATE	LIBERAL ARTS	BIOLOGIAL SCIENCES	PHYSICAL SCIENCES /MATH	SOCIAL SCIENCES	ARTS AND HUMAN.	ENGI- NEERING	BUSINESS	LAW	UNDEC. MAJOR	MALE	FEMALE
		(A)	(B)	(C)	(D)	(E)	(F)	(G)	(H)	(I)	(J)	(K)	(L)	(M)	(N)		(P)	(Q)
Base - USe Photographs, prints and other visual resources for teaching	290	195	95*	290	0**	105*	116*	69*	64*	53*	62*	72*	12*	26**	1**	0*	208	82*
All sources of info	2 0.7%	2 1.0%	0 0	2 0.7%	0 0	1 0.8%	1 1.0%	0 0	1 1.4%	0 0	0 0	1 1.6%	0 0	0 0	0 0	0 0	2 1.0%	0 0
preferred source of info	0 0	0 0	0 0	0 0	0 0	0 0	0 0	0 0	0 0	0 0	0 0	0 0	0 0	0 0	0 0	0 0	0 0	0 0
Personal office/lab	1 0.3%	1 0.5%	0 0	1 0.3%	0 0	0 0	0 0	1 1.4%	0 0	1 1.9%	0 0	0 0	0 0	0 0	0 0	0 0	1 0.5%	0 0
All sources of info	1 0.3%	1 0.5%	0 0	1 0.3%	0 0	0 0	0 0	1 1.4%	0 0	1 1.9%	0 0	0 0	0 0	0 0	0 0	0 0	1 0.5%	0 0
preferred source of info	0 0	0 0	0 0	0 0	0 0	0 0	0 0	0 0	0 0	0 0	0 0	0 0	0 0	0 0	0 0	0 0	0 0	0 0
Author	* 0.1%	* 0.1%	0 0	* 0.1%	0 0	0 0	0 0	* 0.4%	0 0	0 0	0 0	0 0	* 2.4%HK	0 0	0 0	0 0	* 0.1%	0 0
All sources of info	* 0.1%	* 0.1%	0 0	* 0.1%	0 0	0 0	0 0	* 0.4%	0 0	0 0	0 0	0 0	* 2.4%HK	0 0	0 0	0 0	* 0.1%	0 0
preferred source of info	0 0	0 0	0 0	0 0	0 0	0 0	0 0	0 0	0 0	0 0	0 0	0 0	0 0	0 0	0 0	0 0	0 0	0 0
Other	22 7.7%	18 9.3%	4 4.5%	22 7.7%	0 0	10 9.9%	7 5.8%	5 7.6%	5 8.2%	6 11.3%	2 3.0%	6 7.8%	1 7.1%	3 10.7%	0 0	0 0	13 6.5%	9 10.9%

Proportions/Means: Columns Tested (5% risk level) - A/B/D - C/D - E/F/G - H/I/J/K/L/M/N - P/Q
* small base; ** very small base (under 30) ineligible for sig testing

Table 277
Page 1136

Outsell/Digital Library Federation Study (2002)
Weighted Tables

TABLE 121, continued

T7sum_13. Photographs, prints and other visual resources SUMMARY TABLE

	RESPONDENT TYPE				INSTITUTION TYPE			DISCIPLINE									GENDER	
	TOTAL SAMPLE	FACULTY MEMBER	GRAD. STUDENT	FACULTY /GRAD	UNDER GRAD. STUDENT	PUBLIC	PRIVATE	LIBERAL ARTS	BIOLOGIAL SCIENCES	PHYSICAL SCIENCES /MATH	SOCIAL SCIENCES	ARTS AND HUMAN.	ENGI-NEERING	BUSINESS	LAW	UNDEC. MAJOR	MALE	FEMALE
		(A)	(B)	(C)	(D)	(E)	(F)	(G)	(H)	(I)	(J)	(K)	(L)	(M)	(N)		(P)	(Q)
Base - USe Photographs, prints and other visual resources for teaching	290	195	95*	290	0**	105*	116*	69*	64*	53*	62*	72*	12*	26**	1**	0*	208	82*
All sources of info	20 7.0%	16 8.4%	4 4.2%	20 7.0%	0 0	9 9.1%	6 4.8%	5 7.6%	4 6.8%	6 11.3%	2 3.0%	6 7.8%	1 4.8%	2 7.1%	0 0	0 0	11 5.4%	9 10.9%
preferred source of info	11 3.9%	8 4.0%	3 3.5%	11 3.9%	0 0	5 4.9%	4 3.4%	2 3.1%	4 5.5%	3 5.7%	0 0	2 3.1%	1 4.8%J	2 7.1%	0 0	0 0	6 3.1%	5 5.8%
DK/Refused	17 5.7%	13 6.7%	3 3.5%	17 5.7%	0 0	8 7.6%	7 5.7%	2 2.9%	3 4.1%	1 1.9%	4 6.1%	7 9.4%	1 11.9%I	1 3.6%	0 0	0 0	10 5.0%	6 7.5%

Proportions/Means: Columns Tested (5% risk level) - A/B/D - C/D - E/F/G - H/I/J/K/L/M/N - P/Q
* small base; ** very small base (under 30) ineligible for sig testing

Table 277
Page 1137

Outsell/Digital Library Federation Study (2002)
Weighted Tables

TABLE 122

T7D/E_13. Photographs, prints and other visual resources SUMMARY TABLE

		RESPONDENT TYPE				INSTITUTION TYPE			DISCIPLINE								GENDER	
	TOTAL SAMPLE	FACULTY MEMBER	GRAD. STUDENT	FACULTY /GRAD	UNDER GRAD. STUDENT	PUBLIC	PRIVATE	LIBERAL ARTS	BIOLOGIAL SCIENCES	PHYSICAL SCIENCES /MATH	SOCIAL SCIENCES	ARTS AND HUMAN.	ENGI-NEERING	BUSINESS	LAW	UNDEC. MAJOR	MALE	FEMALE
		(A)	(B)	(C)	(D)	(E)	(F)	(G)	(H)	(I)	(J)	(K)	(L)	(M)	(N)		(P)	(Q)
Base - Use Photographs, prints and other visual resources for teaching	290	195	95*	290	0**	105*	116*	69*	64*	53*	62*	72*	12*	26**	1**	0*	208	82*
Access online (NET)	166 57.3%	123 63.0%B	43 45.5%	166 57.3%	0 0	53 51.1%	61 52.4%	52 74.7%EF	42 65.8%K	33 62.3%K	36 57.6%	30 42.2%	8 69.0%K	16 60.7%	1 80.0%	0 0	113 54.4%	53 64.4%
All sources of info	166 57.3%	123 63.0%B	43 45.5%	166 57.3%	0 0	53 51.1%	61 52.4%	52 74.7%EF	42 65.8%K	33 62.3%K	36 57.6%	30 42.2%	8 69.0%K	16 60.7%	1 80.0%	0 0	113 54.4%	53 64.4%
preferred source of info	120 41.3%	85 43.3%	35 37.0%	120 41.3%	0 0	38 36.2%	43 37.3%	39 55.5%EF	32 49.3%K	29 54.7%K	24 39.4%	17 23.4%	6 50.0%K	11 42.9%	1 60.0%	0 0	84 40.2%	36 43.9%
Borrow from or use in campus library (NET)	124 42.7%	80 41.0%	44 46.3%	124 42.7%	0 0	42 40.4%	52 44.8%	30 42.7%	21 32.9%	22 41.5%	24 39.4%	40 56.3%H	6 47.6%	10 39.3%	0 0	0 0	91 43.9%	33 39.7%
All sources of info	124 42.7%	80 41.0%	44 46.3%	124 42.7%	0 0	42 40.4%	52 44.8%	30 42.7%	21 32.9%	22 41.5%	24 39.4%	40 56.3%H	6 47.6%	10 39.3%	0 0	0 0	91 43.9%	33 39.7%
preferred source of info	74 25.7%	39 19.8%	36 37.9%A	74 25.7%	0 0	31 30.0%	31 26.4%	12 17.9%	7 11.0%	9 17.0%	19 30.3%H	34 46.9%HI L	2 19.0%	4 14.3%	0 0	0 0	54 25.8%	21 25.4%
Personal Collection/ Holdings (NET)	35 11.9%	30 15.2%B	5 5.2%	35 11.9%	0 0	12 11.7%	9 7.6%	13 19.3%F	6 9.6%	9 17.0%	4 6.1%	10 14.1%	1 11.9%	4 14.3%	* 40.0%	0 0	25 12.2%	9 11.2%
All sources of info	35 11.9%	30 15.2%B	5 5.2%	35 11.9%	0 0	12 11.7%	9 7.6%	13 19.3%F	6 9.6%	9 17.0%	4 6.1%	10 14.1%	1 11.9%	4 14.3%	* 40.0%	0 0	25 12.2%	9 11.2%

Proportions/Means: Columns Tested (5% risk level) - A/B/D - C/D - E/F/G - H/I/J/K/L/M/N - P/Q
* small base; ** very small base (under 30) ineligible for sig testing

Table 280
Page 1144

Outsell/Digital Library Federation Study (2002)
Weighted Tables

TABLE 122, continued

T7D/E_13. Photographs, prints and other visual resources SUMMARY TABLE

		RESPONDENT TYPE				INSTITUTION TYPE			DISCIPLINE								GENDER	
	TOTAL SAMPLE	FACULTY MEMBER	GRAD. STUDENT	FACULTY /GRAD	UNDER GRAD. STUDENT	PUBLIC	PRIVATE	LIBERAL ARTS	BIOLOGIAL SCIENCES	PHYSICAL SCIENCES /MATH	SOCIAL SCIENCES	ARTS AND HUMAN.	ENGI-NEERING	BUSINESS	LAW	UNDEC. MAJOR	MALE	FEMALE
		(A)	(B)	(C)	(D)	(E)	(F)	(G)	(H)	(I)	(J)	(K)	(L)	(M)	(N)		(P)	(Q)
Base - Use Photographs, prints and other visual resources for teaching	290	195	95*	290	0**	105*	116*	69*	64*	53*	62*	72*	12*	26**	1**	0*	208	82*
preferred source of info	19 6.5%	15 7.6%	4 4.2%	19 6.5%	0 0	6 5.5%	8 6.6%	5 7.8%	4 5.5%	2 3.8%	4 6.1%	7 9.4%	1 7.1%	2 7.1%	* 20.0%	0 0	14 6.6%	5 6.2%
Borrow from or use in other libraries (NET)	14 4.9%	8 3.9%	7 7.0%	14 4.9%	0 0	9 8.2%F	1 0.8%	5 7.0%F	4 5.5%	1 1.9%	8 12.1%	2 3.1%	0 0	0 0	0 0	0 0	8 4.0%	6 7.2%
All sources of info	14 4.9%	8 3.9%	7 7.0%	14 4.9%	0 0	9 8.2%F	1 0.8%	5 7.0%F	4 5.5%	1 1.9%	8 12.1%	2 3.1%	0 0	0 0	0 0	0 0	8 4.0%	6 7.2%
preferred source of info	7 2.3%	2 1.1%	5 4.9%	7 2.3%	0 0	5 4.4%F	0 0	2 3.1%	1 1.4%	1 1.9%	4 6.1%	1 1.6%	0 0	0 0	0 0	0 0	4 1.8%	3 3.6%
Access from course website (NET)	13 4.6%	10 5.2%	3 3.3%	13 4.6%	0 0	5 5.0%	4 3.4%	4 6.0%	3 4.1%	5 9.4%J	0 0	2 3.1%	1 11.9%JK	2 7.1%	* 20.0%	0 0	10 4.9%	3 3.9%
All sources of info	13 4.6%	10 5.2%	3 3.3%	13 4.6%	0 0	5 5.0%	4 3.4%	4 6.0%	3 4.1%	5 9.4%J	0 0	2 3.1%	1 11.9%JK	2 7.1%	* 20.0%	0 0	10 4.9%	3 3.9%
preferred source of info	9 3.1%	6 3.0%	3 3.3%	9 3.1%	0 0	5 4.7%	4 3.2%	* 0.4%	2 2.7%	2 3.8%	0 0	2 3.1%	1 7.1%J	2 7.1%	* 20.0%	0 0	7 3.2%	2 2.8%
Purchase from physical book store (NET)	12 4.2%	12 6.2%B	0 0	12 4.2%	0 0	5 4.9%	3 2.7%	4 5.6%	3 4.1%	0 0	2 3.0%	7 9.4%I	0 0	1 3.6%	0 0	0 0	9 4.3%	3 3.9%

Proportions/Means: Columns Tested (5% risk level) - A/B/D - C/D - E/F/G - H/I/J/K/L/M/N - P/Q
* small base; ** very small base (under 30) ineligible for sig testing

Table 280
Page 1145

Outsell/Digital Library Federation Study (2002)
Weighted Tables

TABLE 122, continued

T7D/E_13. Photographs, prints and other visual resources SUMMARY TABLE

		RESPONDENT TYPE				INSTITUTION TYPE			DISCIPLINE									GENDER	
	TOTAL SAMPLE	FACULTY MEMBER	GRAD. STUDENT	FACULTY /GRAD	UNDER GRAD. STUDENT	PUBLIC	PRIVATE	LIBERAL ARTS	BIOLOGIAL SCIENCES	PHYSICAL SCIENCES /MATH	SOCIAL SCIENCES	ARTS AND HUMAN.	ENGI-NEERING	BUSINESS	LAW	UNDEC. MAJOR	MALE	FEMALE
		(A)	(B)	(C)	(D)	(E)	(F)	(G)	(H)	(I)	(J)	(K)	(L)	(M)	(N)		(P)	(Q)
Base - Use Photographs, prints and other visual resources for teaching	290	195	95*	290	0**	105*	116*	69*	64*	53*	62*	72*	12*	26**	1**	0*	208	82*
All sources of info	12 4.2%	12 6.2%B	0 0	12 4.2%	0 0	5 4.9%	3 2.7%	4 5.6%	3 4.1%	0 0	2 3.0%	7 9.4%I	0 0	1 3.6%	0 0	0 0	9 4.3%	3 3.9%
preferred source of info	6 2.1%	6 3.1%	0 0	6 2.1%	0 0	2 1.9%	3 2.7%	1 1.3%	3 4.1%	0 0	0 0	3 4.7%	0 0	0 0	0 0	0 0	4 1.8%	2 2.7%
Interlibrary loan (NET)	12 4.1%	7 3.5%	5 5.2%	12 4.1%	0 0	4 4.1%	6 4.9%	2 2.7%	5 8.2%	3 5.7%	2 3.0%	1 1.6%	1 4.8%	0 0	0 0	0 0	7 3.4%	5 5.9%
All sources of info	12 4.1%	7 3.5%	5 5.2%	12 4.1%	0 0	4 4.1%	6 4.9%	2 2.7%	5 8.2%	3 5.7%	2 3.0%	1 1.6%	1 4.8%	0 0	0 0	0 0	7 3.4%	5 5.9%
preferred source of info	5 1.7%	4 1.9%	1 1.2%	5 1.7%	0 0	0 0	5 4.1%	0 0	4 5.5%K	1 1.9%	0 0	0 0	* 2.4%K	0 0	0 0	0 0	3 1.4%	2 2.3%
Colleagues (NET)	12 4.0%	7 3.6%	5 4.9%	12 4.0%	0 0	4 3.5%	7 5.9%	1 1.6%	5 8.2%	2 3.8%	0 0	2 3.1%	* 2.4%	2 7.1%	0 0	0 0	8 3.7%	4 4.8%
All sources of info	12 4.0%	7 3.6%	5 4.9%	12 4.0%	0 0	4 3.5%	7 5.9%	1 1.6%	5 8.2%	2 3.8%	0 0	2 3.1%	* 2.4%	2 7.1%	0 0	0 0	8 3.7%	4 4.8%
preferred source of info	5 1.8%	3 1.6%	2 2.0%	5 1.8%	0 0	2 1.7%	3 2.8%	0 0	2 2.7%	1 1.9%	0 0	1 1.6%	* 2.4%	1 3.6%	0 0	0 0	5 2.5%	0 0

Proportions/Means: Columns Tested (5% risk level) - A/B/D - C/D - E/F/G - H/I/J/K/L/M/N - P/Q
* small base; ** very small base (under 30) ineligible for sig testing

TABLE 122, continued

T7D/E_13. Photographs, prints and other visual resources SUMMARY TABLE

		RESPONDENT TYPE				INSTITUTION TYPE			DISCIPLINE									GENDER	
	TOTAL SAMPLE	FACULTY MEMBER	GRAD. STUDENT	FACULTY /GRAD	UNDER GRAD. STUDENT	PUBLIC	PRIVATE	LIBERAL ARTS	BIOLOGIAL SCIENCES	PHYSICAL SCIENCES /MATH	SOCIAL SCIENCES	ARTS AND HUMAN.	ENGI- NEERING	BUSINESS	LAW	UNDEC. MAJOR		MALE	FEMALE
		(A)	(B)	(C)	(D)	(E)	(F)	(G)	(H)	(I)	(J)	(K)	(L)	(M)	(N)			(P)	(Q)
Base - Use Photographs, prints and other visual resources for teaching	290	195	95*	290	0**	105*	116*	69*	64*	53*	62*	72*	12*	26**	1**	0*		208	82*
Publisher (NET)	8 2.8%	8 4.1%	0 0	8 2.8%	0 0	4 3.7%	0 0	4 6.1%F	0 0	5 9.4%HJK	0 0	0 0	* 2.4%HK	3 10.7%	0 0	0 0		6 3.0%	2 2.3%
All sources of info	8 2.8%	8 4.1%	0 0	8 2.8%	0 0	4 3.7%	0 0	4 6.1%F	0 0	5 9.4%HJK	0 0	0 0	* 2.4%HK	3 10.7%	0 0	0 0		6 3.0%	2 2.3%
preferred source of info	5 1.8%	5 2.6%	0 0	5 1.8%	0 0	3 2.8%	0 0	2 3.2%	0 0	3 5.7%	0 0	0 0	* 2.4%HK	2 7.1%	0 0	0 0		4 2.0%	1 1.1%
Office (NET)	7 2.3%	6 2.9%	1 0.9%	7 2.3%	0 0	1 1.0%	5 4.0%	1 1.3%	3 4.1%	1 1.9%	0 0	1 1.6%	0 0	2 7.1%	0 0	0 0		6 2.7%	1 1.2%
All sources of info	7 2.3%	6 2.9%	1 0.9%	7 2.3%	0 0	1 1.0%	5 4.0%	1 1.3%	3 4.1%	1 1.9%	0 0	1 1.6%	0 0	2 7.1%	0 0	0 0		6 2.7%	1 1.2%
preferred source of info	6 2.0%	5 2.5%	1 0.9%	6 2.0%	0 0	1 1.0%	5 4.0%	0 0	3 4.1%	1 1.9%	0 0	1 1.6%	0 0	1 3.6%	0 0	0 0		5 2.3%	1 1.2%
Department (NET)	5 1.8%	2 1.1%	3 3.2%	5 1.8%	0 0	4 3.8%	* 0.2%	1 1.4%	0 0	2 3.8%	0 0	1 1.6%	* 2.4%H	2 7.1%	0 0	0 0		3 1.6%	2 2.3%
All sources of info	5 1.8%	2 1.1%	3 3.2%	5 1.8%	0 0	4 3.8%	* 0.2%	1 1.4%	0 0	2 3.8%	0 0	1 1.6%	* 2.4%H	2 7.1%	0 0	0 0		3 1.6%	2 2.3%
preferred source of info	2 0.7%	1 0.5%	1 1.1%	2 0.7%	0 0	1 1.0%	0 0	1 1.4%	0 0	2 3.8%	0 0	0 0	0 0	0 0	0 0	0 0		1 0.5%	1 1.2%

Proportions/Means: Columns Tested (5% risk level) - A/B/D - C/D - E/F/G - H/I/J/K/L/M/N - P/Q
* small base; ** very small base (under 30) ineligible for sig testing

Table 280
Page 1147

Outsell/Digital Library Federation Study (2002)
Weighted Tables

TABLE 122, continued

T7D/E_13. Photographs, prints and other visual resources SUMMARY TABLE

		RESPONDENT TYPE				INSTITUTION TYPE			DISCIPLINE									GENDER	
	TOTAL SAMPLE	FACULTY MEMBER	GRAD. STUDENT	FACULTY /GRAD	UNDER GRAD. STUDENT	PUBLIC	PRIVATE	LIBERAL ARTS	BIOLOGIAL SCIENCES	PHYSICAL SCIENCES /MATH	SOCIAL SCIENCES	ARTS AND HUMAN.	ENGI-NEERING	BUSINESS	LAW	UNDEC. MAJOR	MALE	FEMALE
		(A)	(B)	(C)	(D)	(E)	(F)	(G)	(H)	(I)	(J)	(K)	(L)	(M)	(N)		(P)	(Q)
Base - Use Photographs, prints and other visual resources for teaching	290	195	95*	290	0**	105*	116*	69*	64*	53*	62*	72*	12*	26**	1**	0*	208	82*
Faculty (NET)	4	0	4	4	0	0	4	0	0	0	2	2	0	0	0	0	0	4
	1.4%	0	4.4%A	1.4%	0	0	3.6%	0	0	0	3.0%	3.1%	0	0	0	0	0	5.0%P
All sources of info	4	0	4	4	0	0	4	0	0	0	2	2	0	0	0	0	0	4
	1.4%	0	4.4%A	1.4%	0	0	3.6%	0	0	0	3.0%	3.1%	0	0	0	0	0	5.0%P
preferred source of info	2	0	2	2	0	0	2	0	0	0	0	2	0	0	0	0	0	2
	0.8%	0	2.4%A	0.8%	0	0	1.9%	0	0	0	0	3.1%	0	0	0	0	0	2.7%P
Purchase from online bookstore (NET)	4	4	0	4	0	3	1	0	2	0	0	1	0	1	0	0	3	1
	1.3%	1.9%	0	1.3%	0	2.8%	0.8%	0	2.7%	0	0	1.6%	0	3.6%	0	0	1.4%	1.1%
All sources of info	4	4	0	4	0	3	1	0	2	0	0	1	0	1	0	0	3	1
	1.3%	1.9%	0	1.3%	0	2.8%	0.8%	0	2.7%	0	0	1.6%	0	3.6%	0	0	1.4%	1.1%
preferred source of info	1	1	0	1	0	1	0	0	1	0	0	0	0	0	0	0	1	0
	0.3%	0.5%	0	0.3%	0	0.8%	0	0	1.4%	0	0	0	0	0	0	0	0.4%	0
Home (NET)	3	2	1	3	0	1	2	0	1	0	2	0	0	0	0	0	3	0
	1.0%	1.0%	0.9%	1.0%	0	0.8%	1.6%	0	1.4%	0	3.0%	0	0	0	0	0	1.3%	0
All sources of info	3	2	1	3	0	1	2	0	1	0	2	0	0	0	0	0	3	0
	1.0%	1.0%	0.9%	1.0%	0	0.8%	1.6%	0	1.4%	0	3.0%	0	0	0	0	0	1.3%	0
preferred source of info	3	2	1	3	0	1	2	0	1	0	2	0	0	0	0	0	3	0
	1.0%	1.0%	0.9%	1.0%	0	0.8%	1.6%	0	1.4%	0	3.0%	0	0	0	0	0	1.3%	0

Proportions/Means: Columns Tested (5% risk level) - A/B/D - C/D - E/F/G - H/I/J/K/L/M/N - P/Q
* small base; ** very small base (under 30) ineligible for sig testing

Table 280
Page 1148

Outsell/Digital Library Federation Study (2002)
Weighted Tables

TABLE 122, continued

T7D/E_13. Photographs, prints and other visual resources SUMMARY TABLE

		RESPONDENT TYPE				INSTITUTION TYPE			DISCIPLINE								GENDER	
	TOTAL SAMPLE	FACULTY MEMBER	GRAD. STUDENT	FACULTY /GRAD	UNDER GRAD. STUDENT	PUBLIC	PRIVATE	LIBERAL ARTS	BIOLOGIAL SCIENCES	PHYSICAL SCIENCES /MATH	SOCIAL SCIENCES	ARTS AND HUMAN.	ENGI-NEERING	BUSINESS	LAW	UNDEC. MAJOR	MALE	FEMALE
		(A)	(B)	(C)	(D)	(E)	(F)	(G)	(H)	(I)	(J)	(K)	(L)	(M)	(N)		(P)	(Q)
Base - Use Photographs, prints and other visual resources for teaching	290	195	95*	290	0**	105*	116*	69*	64*	53*	62*	72*	12*	26**	1**	0*	208	82*
Order from on demand document delivery service (NET)	3 1.0%	3 1.4%	0 0	3 1.0%	0 0	0 0	1 0.8%	2 2.7%	1 1.4%	0 0	2 3.0%	0 0	0 0	0 0	0 0	0 0	3 1.3%	0 0
All sources of info	3 1.0%	3 1.4%	0 0	3 1.0%	0 0	0 0	1 0.8%	2 2.7%	1 1.4%	0 0	2 3.0%	0 0	0 0	0 0	0 0	0 0	3 1.3%	0 0
preferred source of info	2 0.6%	2 1.0%	0 0	2 0.6%	0 0	0 0	0 0	2 2.7%	0 0	0 0	2 3.0%	0 0	0 0	0 0	0 0	0 0	2 0.9%	0 0
Ask library to purchase source (NET)	0 0	0 0	0 0	0 0	0 0	0 0	0 0	0 0	0 0	0 0	0 0	0 0	0 0	0 0	0 0	0 0	0 0	0 0
All sources of info	0 0	0 0	0 0	0 0	0 0	0 0	0 0	0 0	0 0	0 0	0 0	0 0	0 0	0 0	0 0	0 0	0 0	0 0
preferred source of info	0 0	0 0	0 0	0 0	0 0	0 0	0 0	0 0	0 0	0 0	0 0	0 0	0 0	0 0	0 0	0 0	0 0	0 0
Author	0 0	0 0	0 0	0 0	0 0	0 0	0 0	0 0	0 0	0 0	0 0	0 0	0 0	0 0	0 0	0 0	0 0	0 0
All sources of info	0 0	0 0	0 0	0 0	0 0	0 0	0 0	0 0	0 0	0 0	0 0	0 0	0 0	0 0	0 0	0 0	0 0	0 0

Proportions/Means: Columns Tested (5% risk level) - A/B/D - C/D - E/F/G - H/I/J/K/L/M/N - P/Q
* small base; ** very small base (under 30) ineligible for sig testing

Table 280
Page 1149

Outsell/Digital Library Federation Study (2002)
Weighted Tables

TABLE 122, continued

T7D/E_13. Photographs, prints and other visual resources SUMMARY TABLE

		RESPONDENT TYPE				INSTITUTION TYPE			DISCIPLINE									GENDER	
	TOTAL SAMPLE	FACULTY MEMBER	GRAD. STUDENT	FACULTY /GRAD	UNDER GRAD. STUDENT	PUBLIC	PRIVATE	LIBERAL ARTS	BIOLOGIAL SCIENCES	PHYSICAL SCIENCES /MATH	SOCIAL SCIENCES	ARTS AND HUMAN.	ENGI-NEERING	BUSINESS	LAW	UNDEC. MAJOR	MALE	FEMALE
		(A)	(B)	(C)	(D)	(E)	(F)	(G)	(H)	(I)	(J)	(K)	(L)	(M)	(N)		(P)	(Q)
Base - Use Photographs, prints and other visual resources for teaching	290	195	95*	290	0**	105*	116*	69*	64*	53*	62*	72*	12*	26**	1**	0*	208	82*
preferred source of info	0 0	0 0	0 0	0 0	0 0	0 0	0 0	0 0	0 0	0 0	0 0	0 0	0 0	0 0	0 0	0 0	0 0	0 0
Meeting/Conferences (NET)	0 0	0 0	0 0	0 0	0 0	0 0	0 0	0 0	0 0	0 0	0 0	0 0	0 0	0 0	0 0	0 0	0 0	0 0
All sources of info	0 0	0 0	0 0	0 0	0 0	0 0	0 0	0 0	0 0	0 0	0 0	0 0	0 0	0 0	0 0	0 0	0 0	0 0
preferred source of info	0 0	0 0	0 0	0 0	0 0	0 0	0 0	0 0	0 0	0 0	0 0	0 0	0 0	0 0	0 0	0 0	0 0	0 0
Access book/journal/ journal article elsewhere online (NET)	0 0	0 0	0 0	0 0	0 0	0 0	0 0	0 0	0 0	0 0	0 0	0 0	0 0	0 0	0 0	0 0	0 0	0 0
All sources of info	0 0	0 0	0 0	0 0	0 0	0 0	0 0	0 0	0 0	0 0	0 0	0 0	0 0	0 0	0 0	0 0	0 0	0 0
preferred source of info	0 0	0 0	0 0	0 0	0 0	0 0	0 0	0 0	0 0	0 0	0 0	0 0	0 0	0 0	0 0	0 0	0 0	0 0
Other (NET)	24 8.3%	19 9.7%	5 5.5%	24 8.3%	0 0	6 6.0%	13 11.1%	5 7.2%	7 11.0%	4 7.5%	4 6.1%	4 6.3%	1 9.5%	4 14.3%	0 0	0 0	21 10.0%	3 4.0%

Proportions/Means: Columns Tested (5% risk level) - A/B/D - C/D - E/F/G - H/I/J/K/L/M/N - P/Q
* small base; ** very small base (under 30) ineligible for sig testing

Table 280
Page 1150

Outsell/Digital Library Federation Study (2002)
Weighted Tables

TABLE 122, continued

T7D/E_13. Photographs, prints and other visual resources SUMMARY TABLE

		RESPONDENT TYPE				INSTITUTION TYPE			DISCIPLINE									GENDER	
	TOTAL SAMPLE	FACULTY MEMBER	GRAD. STUDENT	FACULTY /GRAD	UNDER GRAD. STUDENT	PUBLIC	PRIVATE	LIBERAL ARTS	BIOLOGIAL SCIENCES	PHYSICAL SCIENCES /MATH	SOCIAL SCIENCES	ARTS AND HUMAN.	ENGI- NEERING	BUSINESS	LAW	UNDEC. MAJOR	MALE	FEMALE
		(A)	(B)	(C)	(D)	(E)	(F)	(G)	(H)	(I)	(J)	(K)	(L)	(M)	(N)		(P)	(Q)
Base - Use Photographs, prints and other visual resources for teaching	290	195	95*	290	0**	105*	116*	69*	64*	53*	62*	72*	12*	26**	1**	0*	208	82*
All sources of info	23 8.0%	18 9.3%	5 5.5%	23 8.0%	0 0	6 6.0%	12 10.3%	5 7.2%	6 9.6%	4 7.5%	4 6.1%	4 6.3%	1 9.5%	4 14.3%	0 0	0 0	21 10.0%	2 2.9%
preferred source of info	13 4.6%	13 6.4%	1 0.9%	13 4.6%	0 0	3 2.8%	9 7.4%	2 2.8%	4 6.8%	1 1.9%	2 3.0%	3 4.7%	0 0	3 10.7%	0 0	0 0	12 5.6%	2 2.3%
DK/Refused	11 3.9%	8 4.3%	3 3.2%	11 3.9%	0 0	7 6.2%	2 1.8%	3 4.0%	3 4.1%	1 1.9%	6 9.1%K	0 0	1 9.5%IK	1 3.6%	0 0	0 0	8 3.7%	4 4.5%

Proportions/Means: Columns Tested (5% risk level) - A/B/D - C/D - E/F/G - H/I/J/K/L/M/N - P/Q
* small base; ** very small base (under 30) ineligible for sig testing

Table 280
Page 1151

TABLE 123

T7sum_14. Technical Reports SUMMARY TABLE

	TOTAL SAMPLE	RESPONDENT TYPE: FACULTY MEMBER	GRAD. STUDENT	FACULTY /GRAD	UNDER GRAD. STUDENT	INSTITUTION TYPE: PUBLIC	PRIVATE	LIBERAL ARTS	DISCIPLINE: BIOLOGIAL SCIENCES	PHYSICAL SCIENCES /MATH	SOCIAL SCIENCES	ARTS AND HUMAN.	ENGI-NEERING	BUSINESS	LAW	UNDEC. MAJOR	GENDER: MALE	FEMALE
		(A)	(B)	(C)	(D)	(E)	(F)	(G)	(H)	(I)	(J)	(K)	(L)	(M)	(N)		(P)	(Q)
Base - USe Technical Reports for teaching	137	109*	28**	137	0**	58*	50*	29**	26**	27**	39**	12**	9*	21**	1**	0*	101*	36**
ONLINE	106 77.4%	85 77.9%	21 75.7%	106 77.4%	0 0	41 70.0%	38 77.0%	27 93.4%	21 80.0%	20 74.1%	32 81.0%	10 81.8%	6 67.7%	16 73.9%	1 71.4%	0 0	74 73.6%	31 88.2%
Search engine	36 26.1%	29 26.2%	7 25.4%	36 26.1%	0 0	15 26.0%	10 19.6%	11 37.5%	4 13.3%	8 29.6%	15 38.1%	2 18.2%	3 29.0%	4 17.4%	1 42.9%	0 0	29 29.1%	6 17.6%
All sources of info	36 26.1%	29 26.2%	7 25.4%	36 26.1%	0 0	15 26.0%	10 19.6%	11 37.5%	4 13.3%	8 29.6%	15 38.1%	2 18.2%	3 29.0%	4 17.4%	1 42.9%	0 0	29 29.1%	6 17.6%
preferred source of info	21 15.2%	15 13.7%	6 21.2%	21 15.2%	0 0	11 18.7%	3 5.8%	7 24.4%	1 3.3%	7 25.9%	9 23.8%	0 0	1 12.9%	2 8.7%	1 42.9%	0 0	18 18.3%	2 6.6%
Web directory/ subject related web site	28 20.7%	27 25.2%	1 3.2%	28 20.7%	0 0	8 14.0%	12 23.6%	8 29.3%	8 30.0%	4 14.8%	8 19.0%	2 18.2%	1 9.7%	6 26.1%	* 14.3%	0 0	20 19.9%	8 23.0%
All sources of info	28 20.7%	27 25.2%	1 3.2%	28 20.7%	0 0	8 14.0%	12 23.6%	8 29.3%	8 30.0%	4 14.8%	8 19.0%	2 18.2%	1 9.7%	6 26.1%	* 14.3%	0 0	20 19.9%	8 23.0%
preferred source of info	16 11.4%	15 13.5%	1 3.2%	16 11.4%	0 0	6 10.1%	8 15.6%	2 6.6%	4 13.3%	2 7.4%	6 14.3%	2 18.2%	* 3.2%	2 8.7%	0 0	0 0	12 11.7%	4 10.5%
Online databases	26 18.7%	21 19.1%	5 17.4%	26 18.7%	0 0	8 13.4%	11 22.8%	6 22.5%	9 33.3%	4 14.8%	6 14.3%	2 18.2%	1 9.7%	4 17.4%	* 28.6%	0 0	15 14.6%	11 30.5%
All sources of info	26 18.7%	21 19.1%	5 17.4%	26 18.7%	0 0	8 13.4%	11 22.8%	6 22.5%	9 33.3%	4 14.8%	6 14.3%	2 18.2%	1 9.7%	4 17.4%	* 28.6%	0 0	15 14.6%	11 30.5%
preferred source of info	16 12.0%	14 12.4%	3 10.1%	16 12.0%	0 0	5 8.6%	8 15.6%	4 12.5%	6 23.3%	3 11.1%	4 9.5%	1 9.1%	* 3.2%	2 8.7%	* 14.3%	0 0	8 8.1%	8 23.0%

Proportions/Means: Columns Tested (5% risk level) - A/B/D - C/D - E/F/G - H/I/J/K/L/M/N - P/Q
* small base; ** very small base (under 30) ineligible for sig testing

Table 284
Page 1163

Outsell/Digital Library Federation Study (2002)
Weighted Tables

TABLE 123, continued

T7sum_14. Technical Reports SUMMARY TABLE

		RESPONDENT TYPE				INSTITUTION TYPE			DISCIPLINE									GENDER	
	TOTAL SAMPLE	FACULTY MEMBER	GRAD. STUDENT	FACULTY /GRAD	UNDER GRAD. STUDENT	PUBLIC	PRIVATE	LIBERAL ARTS	BIOLOGIAL SCIENCES	PHYSICAL SCIENCES /MATH	SOCIAL SCIENCES	ARTS AND HUMAN.	ENGI-NEERING	BUSINESS	LAW	UNDEC. MAJOR	MALE	FEMALE
		(A)	(B)	(C)	(D)	(E)	(F)	(G)	(H)	(I)	(J)	(K)	(L)	(M)	(N)		(P)	(Q)
Base - USe Technical Reports for teaching	137	109*	28**	137	0**	58*	50*	29**	26**	27**	39**	12**	9*	21**	1**	0*	101*	36**
Internet searches	24 17.3%	18 16.7%	5 19.5%	24 17.3%	0 0	8 13.0%	10 20.3%	6 20.9%	1 3.3%	3 11.1%	11 28.6%	3 27.3%	1 16.1%	4 17.4%	0 0	0 0	16 15.8%	8 21.7%
All sources of info	24 17.3%	18 16.7%	5 19.5%	24 17.3%	0 0	8 13.0%	10 20.3%	6 20.9%	1 3.3%	3 11.1%	11 28.6%	3 27.3%	1 16.1%	4 17.4%	0 0	0 0	16 15.8%	8 21.7%
preferred source of info	14 10.5%	11 10.0%	4 12.8%	14 10.5%	0 0	5 9.3%	5 9.9%	4 14.2%	1 3.3%	2 7.4%	6 14.3%	2 18.2%	1 9.7%	3 13.0%	0 0	0 0	11 11.3%	3 8.4%
Your own institution's web site	12 9.1%	9 7.9%	4 13.9%	12 9.1%	0 0	4 7.6%	7 13.5%	1 4.5%	4 16.7%	4 14.8%	0 0	2 18.2%	1 9.7%	1 4.3%	0 0	0 0	8 7.6%	5 13.3%
All sources of info	12 9.1%	9 7.9%	4 13.9%	12 9.1%	0 0	4 7.6%	7 13.5%	1 4.5%	4 16.7%	4 14.8%	0 0	2 18.2%	1 9.7%	1 4.3%	0 0	0 0	8 7.6%	5 13.3%
preferred source of info	7 5.1%	5 4.8%	2 6.3%	7 5.1%	0 0	3 5.7%	4 7.4%	0 0	4 13.3%	2 7.4%	0 0	0 0	1 6.5%	1 4.3%	0 0	0 0	4 4.2%	3 7.7%
Online reference service	6 4.2%	6 5.3%	0 0	6 4.2%	0 0	1 1.6%	3 6.0%	2 6.3%	1 3.3%	0 0	2 4.8%	1 9.1%	0 0	2 8.7%	0 0	0 0	6 5.7%	0 0
All sources of info	6 4.2%	6 5.3%	0 0	6 4.2%	0 0	1 1.6%	3 6.0%	2 6.3%	1 3.3%	0 0	2 4.8%	1 9.1%	0 0	2 8.7%	0 0	0 0	6 5.7%	0 0
preferred source of info	3 2.0%	3 2.5%	0 0	3 2.0%	0 0	0 0	2 3.8%	1 3.1%	1 3.3%	0 0	2 4.8%	0 0	0 0	0 0	0 0	0 0	3 2.7%	0 0

Proportions/Means: Columns Tested (5% risk level) - A/B/D - C/D - E/F/G - H/I/J/K/L/M/N - P/Q
* small base; ** very small base (under 30) ineligible for sig testing

Table 284
Page 1164

Outsell/Digital Library Federation Study (2002)
Weighted Tables

TABLE 123, continued

T7sum_14. Technical Reports SUMMARY TABLE

		RESPONDENT TYPE				INSTITUTION TYPE			DISCIPLINE									GENDER	
	TOTAL SAMPLE	FACULTY MEMBER	GRAD. STUDENT	FACULTY /GRAD	UNDER GRAD. STUDENT	PUBLIC	PRIVATE	LIBERAL ARTS	BIOLOGIAL SCIENCES	PHYSICAL SCIENCES /MATH	SOCIAL SCIENCES	ARTS AND HUMAN.	ENGI- NEERING	BUSINESS	LAW	UNDEC. MAJOR	MALE	FEMALE
		(A)	(B)	(C)	(D)	(E)	(F)	(G)	(H)	(I)	(J)	(K)	(L)	(M)	(N)		(P)	(Q)
Base - USe Technical Reports for teaching	137	109*	28**	137	0**	58*	50*	29**	26**	27**	39**	12**	9*	21**	1**	0*	101*	36**
Online library catalogues and finding aids	5 3.5%	5 4.2%	* 1.0%	5 3.5%	0 0	2 3.4%	0 0	3 10.1%	0 0	1 3.7%	2 4.8%	0 0	1 9.7%	1 4.3%	* 14.3%	0 0	3 2.9%	2 5.3%
All sources of info	5 3.5%	5 4.2%	* 1.0%	5 3.5%	0 0	2 3.4%	0 0	3 10.1%	0 0	1 3.7%	2 4.8%	0 0	1 9.7%	1 4.3%	* 14.3%	0 0	3 2.9%	2 5.3%
preferred source of info	3 2.5%	3 3.1%	0 0	3 2.5%	0 0	2 2.6%	0 0	2 6.6%	0 0	0 0	2 4.8%	0 0	1 6.5%	1 4.3%	0 0	0 0	2 1.5%	2 5.3%
Online abstracting and indexing services	4 3.0%	3 2.9%	1 3.6%	4 3.0%	0 0	* 0.5%	3 5.9%	1 3.3%	0 0	2 7.4%	0 0	0 0	* 3.2%	2 8.7%	0 0	0 0	4 4.1%	0 0
All sources of info	4 3.0%	3 2.9%	1 3.6%	4 3.0%	0 0	* 0.5%	3 5.9%	1 3.3%	0 0	2 7.4%	0 0	0 0	* 3.2%	2 8.7%	0 0	0 0	4 4.1%	0 0
preferred source of info	2 1.4%	1 0.9%	1 3.6%	2 1.4%	0 0	0 0	2 3.9%	0 0	0 0	1 3.7%	0 0	0 0	0 0	1 4.3%	0 0	0 0	2 1.9%	0 0
Department web page	3 2.4%	3 3.1%	0 0	3 2.4%	0 0	3 5.7%	0 0	0 0	0 0	1 3.7%	0 0	1 9.1%	* 3.2%	1 4.3%	0 0	0 0	2 2.4%	1 2.6%
All sources of info	3 2.4%	3 3.1%	0 0	3 2.4%	0 0	3 5.7%	0 0	0 0	0 0	1 3.7%	0 0	1 9.1%	* 3.2%	1 4.3%	0 0	0 0	2 2.4%	1 2.6%
preferred source of info	1 0.9%	1 1.1%	0 0	1 0.9%	0 0	1 2.1%	0 0	0 0	0 0	0 0	0 0	0 0	* 3.2%	1 4.3%	0 0	0 0	* 0.3%	1 2.6%

Proportions/Means: Columns Tested (5% risk level) - A/B/D - C/D - E/F/G - H/I/J/K/L/M/N - P/Q
* small base; ** very small base (under 30) ineligible for sig testing

Table 284
Page 1165

Outsell/Digital Library Federation Study (2002)
Weighted Tables

TABLE 123, continued

T7sum_14. Technical Reports SUMMARY TABLE

		RESPONDENT TYPE				INSTITUTION TYPE			DISCIPLINE									GENDER	
	TOTAL SAMPLE	FACULTY MEMBER	GRAD. STUDENT	FACULTY /GRAD	UNDER GRAD. STUDENT	PUBLIC	PRIVATE	LIBERAL ARTS	BIOLOGIAL SCIENCES	PHYSICAL SCIENCES /MATH	SOCIAL SCIENCES	ARTS AND HUMAN.	ENGI-NEERING	BUSINESS	LAW	UNDEC. MAJOR	MALE	FEMALE
		(A)	(B)	(C)	(D)	(E)	(F)	(G)	(H)	(I)	(J)	(K)	(L)	(M)	(N)		(P)	(Q)
Base - USe Technical Reports for teaching	137	109*	28**	137	0**	58*	50*	29**	26**	27**	39**	12**	9*	21**	1**	0*	101*	36**
Online bookstore	3 2.3%	3 2.8%	0 0	3 2.3%	0 0	* 0.5%	3 5.7%	0 0	0 0	0 0	2 4.8%	0 0	* 3.2%	1 4.3%	0 0	0 0	1 1.2%	2 5.3%
All sources of info	3 2.3%	3 2.8%	0 0	3 2.3%	0 0	* 0.5%	3 5.7%	0 0	0 0	0 0	2 4.8%	0 0	* 3.2%	1 4.3%	0 0	0 0	1 1.2%	2 5.3%
preferred source of info	* 0.2%	* 0.3%	0 0	* 0.2%	0 0	* 0.5%	0 0	0 0	0 0	0 0	0 0	0 0	* 3.2%	0 0	0 0	0 0	* 0.3%	0 0
E-mail listservs	0 0	0 0	0 0	0 0	0 0	0 0	0 0	0 0	0 0	0 0	0 0	0 0	0 0	0 0	0 0	0 0	0 0	0 0
All sources of info	0 0	0 0	0 0	0 0	0 0	0 0	0 0	0 0	0 0	0 0	0 0	0 0	0 0	0 0	0 0	0 0	0 0	0 0
preferred source of info	0 0	0 0	0 0	0 0	0 0	0 0	0 0	0 0	0 0	0 0	0 0	0 0	0 0	0 0	0 0	0 0	0 0	0 0
Your own personal electronic library/files	0 0	0 0	0 0	0 0	0 0	0 0	0 0	0 0	0 0	0 0	0 0	0 0	0 0	0 0	0 0	0 0	0 0	0 0
All sources of info	0 0	0 0	0 0	0 0	0 0	0 0	0 0	0 0	0 0	0 0	0 0	0 0	0 0	0 0	0 0	0 0	0 0	0 0
preferred source of info	0 0	0 0	0 0	0 0	0 0	0 0	0 0	0 0	0 0	0 0	0 0	0 0	0 0	0 0	0 0	0 0	0 0	0 0
LIBRARY/PRINT	70 51.5%	60 55.0%	11 37.8%	70 51.5%	0 0	26 44.6%	29 59.3%	15 52.0%	12 46.7%	12 44.4%	21 52.4%	7 54.5%	5 51.6%	13 60.9%	1 85.7%	0 0	53 52.5%	17 48.5%

Proportions/Means: Columns Tested (5% risk level) - A/B/D - C/D - E/F/G - H/I/J/K/L/M/N - P/Q
* small base; ** very small base (under 30) ineligible for sig testing

Table 284
Page 1166

Outsell/Digital Library Federation Study (2002)
Weighted Tables

TABLE 123, continued

T7sum_14. Technical Reports SUMMARY TABLE

		RESPONDENT TYPE				INSTITUTION TYPE			DISCIPLINE								GENDER	
	TOTAL SAMPLE	FACULTY MEMBER	GRAD. STUDENT	FACULTY /GRAD	UNDER GRAD. STUDENT	PUBLIC	PRIVATE	LIBERAL ARTS	BIOLOGIAL SCIENCES	PHYSICAL SCIENCES /MATH	SOCIAL SCIENCES	ARTS AND HUMAN.	ENGI-NEERING	BUSINESS	LAW	UNDEC. MAJOR	MALE	FEMALE
		(A)	(B)	(C)	(D)	(E)	(F)	(G)	(H)	(I)	(J)	(K)	(L)	(M)	(N)		(P)	(Q)
Base - USe Technical Reports for teaching	137	109*	28**	137	0**	58*	50*	29**	26**	27**	39**	12**	9*	21**	1**	0*	101*	36**
Campus library	56 41.1%	49 44.9%	7 26.5%	56 41.1%	0 0	22 37.5%	21 42.9%	13 45.5%	12 46.7%	11 40.7%	15 38.1%	7 54.5%	3 32.3%	7 34.8%	1 71.4%	0 0	43 42.5%	13 37.2%
All sources of info	56 41.1%	49 44.9%	7 26.5%	56 41.1%	0 0	22 37.5%	21 42.9%	13 45.5%	12 46.7%	11 40.7%	15 38.1%	7 54.5%	3 32.3%	7 34.8%	1 71.4%	0 0	43 42.5%	13 37.2%
preferred source of info	18 12.9%	15 13.4%	3 11.1%	18 12.9%	0 0	8 13.9%	7 13.3%	3 10.1%	4 16.7%	6 22.2%	2 4.8%	1 9.1%	1 16.1%	3 13.0%	0 0	0 0	17 16.5%	1 2.8%
Your own personal physical library/ files/bookshelves	14 10.4%	14 13.1%	0 0	14 10.4%	0 0	4 6.2%	7 13.8%	4 13.3%	0 0	2 7.4%	8 19.0%	0 0	1 9.7%	4 17.4%	* 14.3%	0 0	13 12.9%	1 3.4%
All sources of info	14 10.4%	14 13.1%	0 0	14 10.4%	0 0	4 6.2%	7 13.8%	4 13.3%	0 0	2 7.4%	8 19.0%	0 0	1 9.7%	4 17.4%	* 14.3%	0 0	13 12.9%	1 3.4%
preferred source of info	6 4.6%	6 5.8%	0 0	6 4.6%	0 0	* 0.5%	4 8.2%	2 6.7%	0 0	1 3.7%	4 9.5%	0 0	1 6.5%	1 4.3%	0 0	0 0	6 5.9%	* 0.8%
References cited in books or journal articles	11 7.7%	8 7.7%	2 7.8%	11 7.7%	0 0	5 7.7%	5 10.3%	1 3.3%	1 3.3%	0 0	6 14.3%	1 9.1%	1 9.7%	2 8.7%	* 14.3%	0 0	9 8.6%	2 5.3%
All sources of info	11 7.7%	8 7.7%	2 7.8%	11 7.7%	0 0	5 7.7%	5 10.3%	1 3.3%	1 3.3%	0 0	6 14.3%	1 9.1%	1 9.7%	2 8.7%	* 14.3%	0 0	9 8.6%	2 5.3%
preferred source of info	3 1.9%	* 0.4%	2 7.8%	3 1.9%	0 0	2 4.0%	* 0.6%	0 0	0 0	0 0	2 4.8%	0 0	1 6.5%	0 0	* 14.3%	0 0	1 0.7%	2 5.3%

Proportions/Means: Columns Tested (5% risk level) - A/B/D - C/D - E/F/G - H/I/J/K/L/M/N - P/Q
* small base; ** very small base (under 30) ineligible for sig testing

Table 284
Page 1167

Outsell/Digital Library Federation Study (2002)
Weighted Tables

TABLE 123, continued

T7sum_14. Technical Reports SUMMARY TABLE

	TOTAL SAMPLE	RESPONDENT TYPE: FACULTY MEMBER	GRAD. STUDENT	FACULTY /GRAD	UNDER GRAD. STUDENT	INSTITUTION TYPE: PUBLIC	PRIVATE	LIBERAL ARTS	DISCIPLINE: BIOLOGIAL SCIENCES	PHYSICAL SCIENCES /MATH	SOCIAL SCIENCES	ARTS AND HUMAN.	ENGI-NEERING	BUSINESS	LAW	UNDEC. MAJOR	GENDER: MALE	FEMALE
		(A)	(B)	(C)	(D)	(E)	(F)	(G)	(H)	(I)	(J)	(K)	(L)	(M)	(N)		(P)	(Q)
Base - USe Technical Reports for teaching	137	109*	28**	137	0**	58*	50*	29**	26**	27**	39**	12**	9*	21**	1**	0*	101*	36**
Personal subscriptions to newspapers, magazines and journals	9 6.6%	9 8.3%	0 0	9 6.6%	0 0	4 6.9%	3 6.2%	2 6.5%	1 3.3%	1 3.7%	0 0	1 9.1%	1 12.9%	5 21.7%	* 14.3%	0 0	8 8.0%	1 2.6%
All sources of info	9 6.6%	9 8.3%	0 0	9 6.6%	0 0	4 6.9%	3 6.2%	2 6.5%	1 3.3%	1 3.7%	0 0	1 9.1%	1 12.9%	5 21.7%	* 14.3%	0 0	8 8.0%	1 2.6%
preferred source of info	1 0.9%	1 1.1%	0 0	1 0.9%	0 0	* 0.5%	1 1.9%	0 0	0 0	0 0	0 0	0 0	* 3.2%	1 4.3%	0 0	0 0	1 1.2%	0 0
Another library	6 4.4%	6 5.5%	0 0	6 4.4%	0 0	* 0.8%	3 5.6%	3 9.7%	2 6.7%	0 0	4 9.5%	0 0	* 3.2%	0 0	* 14.3%	0 0	4 4.2%	2 4.9%
All sources of info	6 4.4%	6 5.5%	0 0	6 4.4%	0 0	* 0.8%	3 5.6%	3 9.7%	2 6.7%	0 0	4 9.5%	0 0	* 3.2%	0 0	* 14.3%	0 0	4 4.2%	2 4.9%
preferred source of info	0 0	0 0	0 0	0 0	0 0	0 0	0 0	0 0	0 0	0 0	0 0	0 0	0 0	0 0	0 0	0 0	0 0	0 0
Physical bookstore	1 0.7%	0 0	1 3.6%	1 0.7%	0 0	0 0	1 2.0%	0 0	0 0	1 3.7%	0 0	0 0	0 0	0 0	0 0	0 0	1 1.0%	0 0
All sources of info	1 0.7%	0 0	1 3.6%	1 0.7%	0 0	0 0	1 2.0%	0 0	0 0	1 3.7%	0 0	0 0	0 0	0 0	0 0	0 0	1 1.0%	0 0
preferred source of info	1 0.7%	0 0	1 3.6%	1 0.7%	0 0	0 0	1 2.0%	0 0	0 0	1 3.7%	0 0	0 0	0 0	0 0	0 0	0 0	1 1.0%	0 0

Proportions/Means: Columns Tested (5% risk level) - A/B/D - C/D - E/F/G - H/I/J/K/L/M/N - P/Q
* small base; ** very small base (under 30) ineligible for sig testing

Table 284
Page 1168

Outsell/Digital Library Federation Study (2002)
Weighted Tables

TABLE 123, continued

T7sum_14. Technical Reports SUMMARY TABLE

		RESPONDENT TYPE				INSTITUTION TYPE			DISCIPLINE									GENDER	
	TOTAL SAMPLE	FACULTY MEMBER	GRAD. STUDENT	FACULTY /GRAD	UNDER GRAD. STUDENT	PUBLIC	PRIVATE	LIBERAL ARTS	BIOLOGIAL SCIENCES	PHYSICAL SCIENCES /MATH	SOCIAL SCIENCES	ARTS AND HUMAN.	ENGI- NEERING	BUSINESS	LAW	UNDEC. MAJOR	MALE	FEMALE
		(A)	(B)	(C)	(D)	(E)	(F)	(G)	(H)	(I)	(J)	(K)	(L)	(M)	(N)		(P)	(Q)
Base - USe Technical Reports for teaching	137	109*	28**	137	0**	58*	50*	29**	26**	27**	39**	12**	9*	21**	1**	0*	101*	36**
Printed library catalogues and finding aids	* 0.2%	* 0.3%	0 0	* 0.2%	0 0	0 0	* 0.6%	0 0	0 0	0 0	0 0	0 0	* 3.2%	0 0	0 0	0 0	* 0.3%	0 0
All sources of info	* 0.2%	* 0.3%	0 0	* 0.2%	0 0	0 0	* 0.6%	0 0	0 0	0 0	0 0	0 0	* 3.2%	0 0	0 0	0 0	* 0.3%	0 0
preferred source of info	0 0	0 0	0 0	0 0	0 0	0 0	0 0	0 0	0 0	0 0	0 0	0 0	0 0	0 0	0 0	0 0	0 0	0 0
Printed abstracting and indexing services	* 0.2%	* 0.3%	0 0	* 0.2%	0 0	* 0.5%	0 0	0 0	0 0	0 0	0 0	0 0	* 3.2%	0 0	0 0	0 0	* 0.3%	0 0
All sources of info	* 0.2%	* 0.3%	0 0	* 0.2%	0 0	* 0.5%	0 0	0 0	0 0	0 0	0 0	0 0	* 3.2%	0 0	0 0	0 0	* 0.3%	0 0
preferred source of info	0 0	0 0	0 0	0 0	0 0	0 0	0 0	0 0	0 0	0 0	0 0	0 0	0 0	0 0	0 0	0 0	0 0	0 0
PERSONAL ASSISTANCE	31 22.7%	23 21.4%	8 27.7%	31 22.7%	0 0	12 21.0%	15 29.9%	4 13.7%	6 23.3%	7 25.9%	8 19.0%	6 45.5%	3 29.0%	2 8.7%	* 28.6%	0 0	22 21.9%	9 25.1%
A librarian in your institution	18 13.3%	14 12.7%	4 15.5%	18 13.3%	0 0	7 11.6%	8 17.0%	3 10.2%	4 13.3%	2 7.4%	8 19.0%	3 27.3%	1 16.1%	0 0	* 28.6%	0 0	11 10.6%	8 21.1%
All sources of info	18 13.3%	14 12.7%	4 15.5%	18 13.3%	0 0	7 11.6%	8 17.0%	3 10.2%	4 13.3%	2 7.4%	8 19.0%	3 27.3%	1 16.1%	0 0	* 28.6%	0 0	11 10.6%	8 21.1%

Proportions/Means: Columns Tested (5% risk level) - A/B/D - C/D - E/F/G - H/I/J/K/L/M/N - P/Q
* small base; ** very small base (under 30) ineligible for sig testing

Table 284
Page 1169

Outsell/Digital Library Federation Study (2002)
Weighted Tables

TABLE 123, continued

T7sum_14. Technical Reports SUMMARY TABLE

	TOTAL SAMPLE	RESPONDENT TYPE: FACULTY MEMBER	GRAD. STUDENT	FACULTY /GRAD	UNDER GRAD. STUDENT	INSTITUTION TYPE: PUBLIC	PRIVATE	LIBERAL ARTS	DISCIPLINE: BIOLOGIAL SCIENCES	PHYSICAL SCIENCES /MATH	SOCIAL SCIENCES	ARTS AND HUMAN.	ENGI- NEERING	BUSINESS	LAW	UNDEC. MAJOR	GENDER: MALE	FEMALE
		(A)	(B)	(C)	(D)	(E)	(F)	(G)	(H)	(I)	(J)	(K)	(L)	(M)	(N)		(P)	(Q)
Base - USe Technical Reports for teaching	137	109*	28**	137	0**	58*	50*	29**	26**	27**	39**	12**	9*	21**	1**	0*	101*	36**
preferred source of info	5 3.8%	4 3.6%	1 4.6%	5 3.8%	0 0	1 2.2%	2 4.4%	2 6.2%	2 6.7%	0 0	2 4.8%	1 9.1%	* 3.2%	0 0	* 14.3%	0 0	2 2.3%	3 8.1%
Colleagues inside your institution	13 9.6%	9 7.9%	5 16.4%	13 9.6%	0 0	5 7.7%	8 15.1%	1 4.1%	4 13.3%	3 11.1%	0 0	3 27.3%	1 16.1%	2 8.7%	0 0	0 0	10 9.9%	3 9.0%
All sources of info	13 9.6%	9 7.9%	5 16.4%	13 9.6%	0 0	5 7.7%	8 15.1%	1 4.1%	4 13.3%	3 11.1%	0 0	3 27.3%	1 16.1%	2 8.7%	0 0	0 0	10 9.9%	3 9.0%
preferred source of info	4 2.9%	1 0.9%	3 10.7%	4 2.9%	0 0	4 6.7%	0 0	0 0	1 3.3%	1 3.7%	0 0	1 9.1%	0 0	1 4.3%	0 0	0 0	3 3.0%	1 2.5%
Colleagues outside your institution	5 3.3%	5 4.2%	0 0	5 3.3%	0 0	* 0.5%	3 6.0%	1 4.5%	1 3.3%	2 7.4%	0 0	1 9.1%	1 6.5%	0 0	0 0	0 0	4 4.2%	* 0.8%
All sources of info	5 3.3%	5 4.2%	0 0	5 3.3%	0 0	* 0.5%	3 6.0%	1 4.5%	1 3.3%	2 7.4%	0 0	1 9.1%	1 6.5%	0 0	0 0	0 0	4 4.2%	* 0.8%
preferred source of info	0 0	0 0	0 0	0 0	0 0	0 0	0 0	0 0	0 0	0 0	0 0	0 0	0 0	0 0	0 0	0 0	0 0	0 0
Professional meetings	3 2.4%	3 3.1%	0 0	3 2.4%	0 0	2 3.5%	1 2.6%	0 0	1 3.3%	2 7.4%	0 0	0 0	* 3.2%	0 0	* 14.3%	0 0	3 3.3%	0 0
All sources of info	3 2.4%	3 3.1%	0 0	3 2.4%	0 0	2 3.5%	1 2.6%	0 0	1 3.3%	2 7.4%	0 0	0 0	* 3.2%	0 0	* 14.3%	0 0	3 3.3%	0 0
preferred source of info	2 1.6%	2 2.0%	0 0	2 1.6%	0 0	2 3.2%	* 0.6%	0 0	1 3.3%	1 3.7%	0 0	0 0	* 3.2%	0 0	0 0	0 0	2 2.1%	0 0

Proportions/Means: Columns Tested (5% risk level) - A/B/D - C/D - E/F/G - H/I/J/K/L/M/N - P/Q
* small base; ** very small base (under 30) ineligible for sig testing

Table 284
Page 1170

Outsell/Digital Library Federation Study (2002)
Weighted Tables

TABLE 123, continued

T7sum_14. Technical Reports SUMMARY TABLE

		RESPONDENT TYPE				INSTITUTION TYPE			DISCIPLINE								GENDER	
	TOTAL SAMPLE	FACULTY MEMBER	GRAD. STUDENT	FACULTY /GRAD	UNDER GRAD. STUDENT	PUBLIC	PRIVATE	LIBERAL ARTS	BIOLOGIAL SCIENCES	PHYSICAL SCIENCES /MATH	SOCIAL SCIENCES	ARTS AND HUMAN.	ENGI-NEERING	BUSINESS	LAW	UNDEC. MAJOR	MALE	FEMALE
		(A)	(B)	(C)	(D)	(E)	(F)	(G)	(H)	(I)	(J)	(K)	(L)	(M)	(N)		(P)	(Q)
Base - USe Technical Reports for teaching	137	109*	28**	137	0**	58*	50*	29**	26**	27**	39**	12**	9*	21**	1**	0*	101*	36**
Another institution's librarian	* 0.1%	* 0.2%	0 0	* 0.1%	0 0	* 0.3%	0 0	0 0	0 0	0 0	0 0	0 0	0 0	0 0	* 14.3%	0 0	* 0.2%	0 0
All sources of info	* 0.1%	* 0.2%	0 0	* 0.1%	0 0	* 0.3%	0 0	0 0	0 0	0 0	0 0	0 0	0 0	0 0	* 14.3%	0 0	* 0.2%	0 0
preferred source of info	0 0	0 0	0 0	0 0	0 0	0 0	0 0	0 0	0 0	0 0	0 0	0 0	0 0	0 0	0 0	0 0	0 0	0 0
Online (unspecified)	2 1.6%	1 1.0%	1 4.0%	2 1.6%	0 0	1 1.9%	1 2.3%	0 0	0 0	0 0	0 0	2 18.2%	0 0	0 0	0 0	0 0	1 1.1%	1 3.1%
All sources of info	2 1.6%	1 1.0%	1 4.0%	2 1.6%	0 0	1 1.9%	1 2.3%	0 0	0 0	0 0	0 0	2 18.2%	0 0	0 0	0 0	0 0	1 1.1%	1 3.1%
preferred source of info	1 0.8%	0 0	1 4.0%	1 0.8%	0 0	1 1.9%	0 0	0 0	0 0	0 0	0 0	1 9.1%	0 0	0 0	0 0	0 0	0 0	1 3.1%
Author	2 1.4%	2 1.7%	0 0	2 1.4%	0 0	2 3.2%	0 0	0 0	0 0	0 0	2 4.8%	0 0	0 0	0 0	0 0	0 0	2 1.9%	0 0
All sources of info	2 1.4%	2 1.7%	0 0	2 1.4%	0 0	2 3.2%	0 0	0 0	0 0	0 0	2 4.8%	0 0	0 0	0 0	0 0	0 0	2 1.9%	0 0
preferred source of info	2 1.4%	2 1.7%	0 0	2 1.4%	0 0	2 3.2%	0 0	0 0	0 0	0 0	2 4.8%	0 0	0 0	0 0	0 0	0 0	2 1.9%	0 0
Students	1 0.7%	1 0.9%	0 0	1 0.7%	0 0	0 0	0 0	1 3.3%	0 0	0 0	0 0	0 0	0 0	1 4.3%	0 0	0 0	1 0.9%	0 0

Proportions/Means: Columns Tested (5% risk level) - A/B/D - C/D - E/F/G - H/I/J/K/L/M/N - P/Q
* small base; ** very small base (under 30) ineligible for sig testing

Table 284
Page 1171

Outsell/Digital Library Federation Study (2002)
Weighted Tables

TABLE 123, continued

T7sum_14. Technical Reports SUMMARY TABLE

	TOTAL SAMPLE	RESPONDENT TYPE: FACULTY MEMBER	RESPONDENT TYPE: GRAD. STUDENT	RESPONDENT TYPE: FACULTY /GRAD	RESPONDENT TYPE: UNDER GRAD. STUDENT	INSTITUTION TYPE: PUBLIC	INSTITUTION TYPE: PRIVATE	INSTITUTION TYPE: LIBERAL ARTS	DISCIPLINE: BIOLOGIAL SCIENCES	DISCIPLINE: PHYSICAL SCIENCES /MATH	DISCIPLINE: SOCIAL SCIENCES	DISCIPLINE: ARTS AND HUMAN.	DISCIPLINE: ENGI-NEERING	DISCIPLINE: BUSINESS	DISCIPLINE: LAW	DISCIPLINE: UNDEC. MAJOR	GENDER: MALE	GENDER: FEMALE
		(A)	(B)	(C)	(D)	(E)	(F)	(G)	(H)	(I)	(J)	(K)	(L)	(M)	(N)		(P)	(Q)
Base - USe Technical Reports for teaching	137	109*	28**	137	0**	58*	50*	29**	26**	27**	39**	12**	9*	21**	1**	0*	101*	36**
All sources of info	1	1	0	1	0	0	0	1	0	0	0	0	0	1	0	0	1	0
	0.7%	0.9%	0	0.7%	0	0	0	3.3%	0	0	0	0	0	4.3%	0	0	0.9%	0
preferred source of info	0	0	0	0	0	0	0	0	0	0	0	0	0	0	0	0	0	0
	0	0	0	0	0	0	0	0	0	0	0	0	0	0	0	0	0	0
Personal office/lab	*	*	0	*	0	*	0	0	0	0	0	0	0	0	*	0	*	0
	0.1%	0.2%	0	0.1%	0	0.3%	0	0	0	0	0	0	0	0	14.3%	0	0.2%	0
All sources of info	*	*	0	*	0	*	0	0	0	0	0	0	0	0	*	0	*	0
	0.1%	0.2%	0	0.1%	0	0.3%	0	0	0	0	0	0	0	0	14.3%	0	0.2%	0
preferred source of info	0	0	0	0	0	0	0	0	0	0	0	0	0	0	0	0	0	0
	0	0	0	0	0	0	0	0	0	0	0	0	0	0	0	0	0	0
Other	14	13	1	14	0	4	7	3	3	2	0	1	1	7	0	0	11	3
	10.0%	12.1%	2.1%	10.0%	0	6.6%	14.2%	9.8%	10.0%	7.4%	0	9.1%	16.1%	30.4%	0	0	10.6%	8.5%
All sources of info	13	12	1	13	0	4	7	2	3	2	0	1	1	6	0	0	10	3
	9.4%	11.2%	2.1%	9.4%	0	6.6%	14.2%	6.5%	10.0%	7.4%	0	9.1%	16.1%	26.1%	0	0	9.7%	8.5%
preferred source of info	6	5	*	6	0	1	3	2	1	0	0	1	1	3	0	0	4	2
	4.1%	4.9%	1.0%	4.1%	0	2.0%	5.3%	6.5%	3.3%	0	0	9.1%	9.7%	13.0%	0	0	3.5%	5.9%
DK/Refused	4	4	0	4	0	2	1	1	2	0	0	1	*	1	*	0	2	3
	3.1%	3.9%	0	3.1%	0	4.2%	1.8%	3.3%	6.7%	0	0	9.1%	3.2%	4.3%	14.3%	0	1.6%	7.5%

Proportions/Means: Columns Tested (5% risk level) - A/B/D - C/D - E/F/G - H/I/J/K/L/M/N - P/Q
* small base; ** very small base (under 30) ineligible for sig testing

Table 284
Page 1172

Outsell/Digital Library Federation Study (2002)
Weighted Tables

TABLE 124

T7D/E_14. Technical Reports SUMMARY TABLE

	RESPONDENT TYPE				INSTITUTION TYPE			DISCIPLINE								GENDER	
	TOTAL SAMPLE	FACULTY MEMBER	GRAD. STUDENT	FACULTY /GRAD	UNDER GRAD. STUDENT	PUBLIC	PRIVATE	LIBERAL ARTS	BIOLOGIAL SCIENCES	PHYSICAL SCIENCES /MATH	SOCIAL SCIENCES	ARTS AND HUMAN.	ENGI- NEERING	BUSINESS	LAW	UNDEC. MAJOR	MALE	FEMALE
		(A)	(B)	(C)	(D)	(E)	(F)	(G)	(H)	(I)	(J)	(K)	(L)	(M)	(N)		(P)	(Q)
Base - Use Technical Reports for teaching	137	109*	28**	137	0**	58*	50*	29**	26**	27**	39**	12**	9*	21**	1**	0*	101*	36**
Access online (NET)	94 68.5%	76 69.9%	18 63.1%	94 68.5%	0 0	38 65.1%	34 67.6%	22 77.0%	17 63.3%	18 66.7%	28 71.4%	8 63.6%	6 61.3%	17 78.3%	1 57.1%	0 0	69 68.3%	25 69.1%
All sources of info	94 68.5%	76 69.9%	18 63.1%	94 68.5%	0 0	38 65.1%	34 67.6%	22 77.0%	17 63.3%	18 66.7%	28 71.4%	8 63.6%	6 61.3%	17 78.3%	1 57.1%	0 0	69 68.3%	25 69.1%
preferred source of info	78 57.1%	65 59.9%	13 46.4%	78 57.1%	0 0	28 48.4%	29 57.8%	21 73.8%	13 50.0%	15 55.6%	24 61.9%	6 45.5%	4 48.4%	15 69.6%	1 57.1%	0 0	55 54.1%	24 65.8%
Borrow from or use in campus library (NET)	70 51.2%	55 50.5%	15 54.0%	70 51.2%	0 0	33 57.2%	22 45.2%	14 49.4%	15 56.7%	13 48.1%	23 57.1%	9 72.7%	4 48.4%	6 26.1%	1 57.1%	0 0	52 51.4%	18 50.8%
All sources of info	70 51.2%	55 50.5%	15 54.0%	70 51.2%	0 0	33 57.2%	22 45.2%	14 49.4%	15 56.7%	13 48.1%	23 57.1%	9 72.7%	4 48.4%	6 26.1%	1 57.1%	0 0	52 51.4%	18 50.8%
preferred source of info	37 27.4%	27 25.2%	10 35.9%	37 27.4%	0 0	20 34.2%	13 25.9%	5 16.0%	7 26.7%	8 29.6%	9 23.8%	6 45.5%	3 38.7%	4 17.4%	* 14.3%	0 0	29 28.8%	8 23.2%
Personal Collection/ Holdings (NET)	9 6.3%	9 7.9%	0 0	9 6.3%	0 0	1 1.7%	5 9.6%	3 10.1%	0 0	3 11.1%	6 14.3%	0 0	0 0	0 0	0 0	0 0	9 8.6%	0 0
All sources of info	9 6.3%	9 7.9%	0 0	9 6.3%	0 0	1 1.7%	5 9.6%	3 10.1%	0 0	3 11.1%	6 14.3%	0 0	0 0	0 0	0 0	0 0	9 8.6%	0 0
preferred source of info	5 3.5%	5 4.4%	0 0	5 3.5%	0 0	0 0	4 7.6%	1 3.5%	0 0	1 3.7%	4 9.5%	0 0	0 0	0 0	0 0	0 0	5 4.7%	0 0

Proportions/Means: Columns Tested (5% risk level) - A/B/D - C/D - E/F/G - H/I/J/K/L/M/N - P/Q
* small base; ** very small base (under 30) ineligible for sig testing

Table 287
Page 1179

Outsell/Digital Library Federation Study (2002)
Weighted Tables

TABLE 124, continued

T7D/E_14. Technical Reports SUMMARY TABLE

	TOTAL SAMPLE	RESPONDENT TYPE: FACULTY MEMBER	GRAD. STUDENT	FACULTY /GRAD	UNDER GRAD. STUDENT	INSTITUTION TYPE: PUBLIC	PRIVATE	LIBERAL ARTS	DISCIPLINE: BIOLOGIAL SCIENCES	PHYSICAL SCIENCES /MATH	SOCIAL SCIENCES	ARTS AND HUMAN.	ENGI- NEERING	BUSINESS	LAW	UNDEC. MAJOR	GENDER: MALE	FEMALE
		(A)	(B)	(C)	(D)	(E)	(F)	(G)	(H)	(I)	(J)	(K)	(L)	(M)	(N)		(P)	(Q)
Base - Use Technical Reports for teaching	137	109*	28**	137	0**	58*	50*	29**	26**	27**	39**	12**	9*	21**	1**	0*	101*	36**
Access from course website (NET)	5	3	2	5	0	2	3	1	0	1	2	0	1	2	0	0	5	0
	3.9%	2.9%	7.8%	3.9%	0	3.2%	5.1%	3.3%	0	3.7%	4.8%	0	6.5%	8.7%	0	0	5.3%	0
All sources of info	5	3	2	5	0	2	3	1	0	1	2	0	1	2	0	0	5	0
	3.9%	2.9%	7.8%	3.9%	0	3.2%	5.1%	3.3%	0	3.7%	4.8%	0	6.5%	8.7%	0	0	5.3%	0
preferred source of info	4	2	2	4	0	2	1	1	0	1	2	0	0	1	0	0	4	0
	2.8%	1.8%	6.7%	2.8%	0	3.2%	2.0%	3.3%	0	3.7%	4.8%	0	0	4.3%	0	0	3.8%	0
Purchase from physical book store (NET)	5	5	0	5	0	1	3	1	1	1	2	0	*	1	0	0	2	3
	3.6%	4.6%	0	3.6%	0	2.1%	5.8%	3.1%	3.3%	3.7%	4.8%	0	3.2%	4.3%	0	0	2.2%	7.7%
All sources of info	5	5	0	5	0	1	3	1	1	1	2	0	*	1	0	0	2	3
	3.6%	4.6%	0	3.6%	0	2.1%	5.8%	3.1%	3.3%	3.7%	4.8%	0	3.2%	4.3%	0	0	2.2%	7.7%
preferred source of info	1	1	0	1	0	1	0	0	0	0	0	0	0	1	0	0	1	0
	0.7%	0.9%	0	0.7%	0	1.6%	0	0	0	0	0	0	0	4.3%	0	0	0.9%	0
Interlibrary loan (NET)	4	4	0	4	0	1	1	2	1	2	0	1	*	0	*	0	3	2
	3.3%	4.1%	0	3.3%	0	2.3%	2.3%	7.0%	3.3%	7.4%	0	9.1%	3.2%	0	14.3%	0	2.6%	5.3%
All sources of info	4	4	0	4	0	1	1	2	1	2	0	1	*	0	*	0	3	2
	3.3%	4.1%	0	3.3%	0	2.3%	2.3%	7.0%	3.3%	7.4%	0	9.1%	3.2%	0	14.3%	0	2.6%	5.3%
preferred source of info	1	1	0	1	0	*	0	1	0	1	0	0	0	0	*	0	*	1
	0.9%	1.1%	0	0.9%	0	0.3%	0	3.5%	0	3.7%	0	0	0	0	14.3%	0	0.2%	2.8%

Proportions/Means: Columns Tested (5% risk level) - A/B/D - C/D - E/F/G - H/I/J/K/L/M/N - P/Q
* small base; ** very small base (under 30) ineligible for sig testing

Table 287
Page 1180

Outsell/Digital Library Federation Study (2002)
Weighted Tables

TABLE 124, continued

T7D/E_14. Technical Reports SUMMARY TABLE

		RESPONDENT TYPE				INSTITUTION TYPE			DISCIPLINE									GENDER	
	TOTAL SAMPLE	FACULTY MEMBER	GRAD. STUDENT	FACULTY /GRAD	UNDER GRAD. STUDENT	PUBLIC	PRIVATE	LIBERAL ARTS	BIOLOGIAL SCIENCES	PHYSICAL SCIENCES /MATH	SOCIAL SCIENCES	ARTS AND HUMAN.	ENGI- NEERING	BUSINESS	LAW	UNDEC. MAJOR	MALE	FEMALE
		(A)	(B)	(C)	(D)	(E)	(F)	(G)	(H)	(I)	(J)	(K)	(L)	(M)	(N)		(P)	(Q)
Base - Use Technical Reports for teaching	137	109*	28**	137	0**	58*	50*	29**	26**	27**	39**	12**	9*	21**	1**	0*	101*	36**
Borrow from or use in other libraries (NET)	4 3.0%	4 3.7%	* 0.6%	4 3.0%	0 0	2 3.7%	1 2.3%	1 3.1%	2 6.7%	0 0	0 0	1 9.1%	0 0	1 4.3%	* 28.6%	0 0	3 3.2%	1 2.5%
All sources of info	4 3.0%	4 3.7%	* 0.6%	4 3.0%	0 0	2 3.7%	1 2.3%	1 3.1%	2 6.7%	0 0	0 0	1 9.1%	0 0	1 4.3%	* 28.6%	0 0	3 3.2%	1 2.5%
preferred source of info	1 0.8%	1 0.8%	* 0.6%	1 0.8%	0 0	1 1.8%	0 0	0 0	1 3.3%	0 0	0 0	0 0	0 0	0 0	* 14.3%	0 0	1 1.0%	0 0
Colleagues (NET)	2 1.6%	2 2.0%	0 0	2 1.6%	0 0	* 0.5%	2 3.8%	0 0	1 3.3%	1 3.7%	0 0	0 0	* 3.2%	0 0	0 0	0 0	1 1.0%	1 3.3%
All sources of info	2 1.6%	2 2.0%	0 0	2 1.6%	0 0	* 0.5%	2 3.8%	0 0	1 3.3%	1 3.7%	0 0	0 0	* 3.2%	0 0	0 0	0 0	1 1.0%	1 3.3%
preferred source of info	2 1.4%	2 1.7%	0 0	2 1.4%	0 0	0 0	2 3.8%	0 0	1 3.3%	1 3.7%	0 0	0 0	0 0	0 0	0 0	0 0	1 1.0%	1 2.5%
Publisher (NET)	2 1.3%	2 1.7%	0 0	2 1.3%	0 0	2 3.1%	0 0	0 0	1 3.3%	0 0	0 0	0 0	0 0	1 4.3%	0 0	0 0	1 0.9%	1 2.5%
All sources of info	2 1.3%	2 1.7%	0 0	2 1.3%	0 0	2 3.1%	0 0	0 0	1 3.3%	0 0	0 0	0 0	0 0	1 4.3%	0 0	0 0	1 0.9%	1 2.5%
preferred source of info	1 0.6%	1 0.8%	0 0	1 0.6%	0 0	1 1.5%	0 0	0 0	1 3.3%	0 0	0 0	0 0	0 0	0 0	0 0	0 0	0 0	1 2.5%

Proportions/Means: Columns Tested (5% risk level) - A/B/D - C/D - E/F/G - H/I/J/K/L/M/N - P/Q
* small base; ** very small base (under 30) ineligible for sig testing

Table 287
Page 1181

Outsell/Digital Library Federation Study (2002)
Weighted Tables

TABLE 124, continued

T7D/E_14. Technical Reports SUMMARY TABLE

	RESPONDENT TYPE				INSTITUTION TYPE			DISCIPLINE									GENDER	
	TOTAL SAMPLE	FACULTY MEMBER	GRAD. STUDENT	FACULTY /GRAD	UNDER GRAD. STUDENT	PUBLIC	PRIVATE	LIBERAL ARTS	BIOLOGIAL SCIENCES	PHYSICAL SCIENCES /MATH	SOCIAL SCIENCES	ARTS AND HUMAN.	ENGI-NEERING	BUSINESS	LAW	UNDEC. MAJOR	MALE	FEMALE
		(A)	(B)	(C)	(D)	(E)	(F)	(G)	(H)	(I)	(J)	(K)	(L)	(M)	(N)		(P)	(Q)
Base - Use Technical Reports for teaching	137	109*	28**	137	0**	58*	50*	29**	26**	27**	39**	12**	9*	21**	1**	0*	101*	36**
Order from on demand document delivery service (NET)	2 1.1%	2 1.4%	0 0	2 1.1%	0 0	1 1.6%	1 1.2%	0 0	0 0	0 0	0 0	0 0	1 6.5%	1 4.3%	0 0	0 0	1 0.6%	1 2.6%
All sources of info	2 1.1%	2 1.4%	0 0	2 1.1%	0 0	1 1.6%	1 1.2%	0 0	0 0	0 0	0 0	0 0	1 6.5%	1 4.3%	0 0	0 0	1 0.6%	1 2.6%
preferred source of info	* 0.2%	* 0.3%	0 0	* 0.2%	0 0	0 0	* 0.6%	0 0	0 0	0 0	0 0	0 0	* 3.2%	0 0	0 0	0 0	* 0.3%	0 0
Author	1 1.0%	1 1.3%	0 0	1 1.0%	0 0	* 0.3%	1 2.5%	0 0	0 0	0 0	0 0	0 0	* 3.2%	1 4.3%	* 14.3%	0 0	1 1.4%	0 0
All sources of info	1 1.0%	1 1.3%	0 0	1 1.0%	0 0	* 0.3%	1 2.5%	0 0	0 0	0 0	0 0	0 0	* 3.2%	1 4.3%	* 14.3%	0 0	1 1.4%	0 0
preferred source of info	0 0	0 0	0 0	0 0	0 0	0 0	0 0	0 0	0 0	0 0	0 0	0 0	0 0	0 0	0 0	0 0	0 0	0 0
Ask library to purchase source (NET)	1 0.7%	1 0.9%	0 0	1 0.7%	0 0	1 1.6%	0 0	0 0	0 0	0 0	0 0	0 0	0 0	1 4.3%	0 0	0 0	1 0.9%	0 0
All sources of info	1 0.7%	1 0.9%	0 0	1 0.7%	0 0	1 1.6%	0 0	0 0	0 0	0 0	0 0	0 0	0 0	1 4.3%	0 0	0 0	1 0.9%	0 0
preferred source of info	1 0.7%	1 0.9%	0 0	1 0.7%	0 0	1 1.6%	0 0	0 0	0 0	0 0	0 0	0 0	0 0	1 4.3%	0 0	0 0	1 0.9%	0 0

Proportions/Means: Columns Tested (5% risk level) - A/B/D - C/D - E/F/G - H/I/J/K/L/M/N - P/Q
* small base; ** very small base (under 30) ineligible for sig testing

Table 287
Page 1182

Outsell/Digital Library Federation Study (2002)
Weighted Tables

TABLE 124, continued

T7D/E_14. Technical Reports SUMMARY TABLE

		RESPONDENT TYPE				INSTITUTION TYPE			DISCIPLINE								GENDER	
	TOTAL SAMPLE	FACULTY MEMBER	GRAD. STUDENT	FACULTY /GRAD	UNDER GRAD. STUDENT	PUBLIC	PRIVATE	LIBERAL ARTS	BIOLOGIAL SCIENCES	PHYSICAL SCIENCES /MATH	SOCIAL SCIENCES	ARTS AND HUMAN.	ENGI-NEERING	BUSINESS	LAW	UNDEC. MAJOR	MALE	FEMALE
		(A)	(B)	(C)	(D)	(E)	(F)	(G)	(H)	(I)	(J)	(K)	(L)	(M)	(N)		(P)	(Q)
Base - Use Technical Reports for teaching	137	109*	28**	137	0**	58*	50*	29**	26**	27**	39**	12**	9*	21**	1**	0*	101*	36**
Meeting/Conferences (NET)	1 0.6%	1 0.8%	0 0	1 0.6%	0 0	1 1.5%	0 0	0 0	1 3.3%	0 0	0 0	0 0	0 0	0 0	0 0	0 0	1 0.9%	0 0
All sources of info	1 0.6%	1 0.8%	0 0	1 0.6%	0 0	1 1.5%	0 0	0 0	1 3.3%	0 0	0 0	0 0	0 0	0 0	0 0	0 0	1 0.9%	0 0
preferred source of info	1 0.6%	1 0.8%	0 0	1 0.6%	0 0	1 1.5%	0 0	0 0	1 3.3%	0 0	0 0	0 0	0 0	0 0	0 0	0 0	1 0.9%	0 0
Purchase from online bookstore (NET)	1 0.6%	1 0.8%	0 0	1 0.6%	0 0	0 0	0 0	1 3.1%	1 3.3%	0 0	0 0	0 0	0 0	0 0	0 0	0 0	0 0	1 2.5%
All sources of info	1 0.6%	1 0.8%	0 0	1 0.6%	0 0	0 0	0 0	1 3.1%	1 3.3%	0 0	0 0	0 0	0 0	0 0	0 0	0 0	0 0	1 2.5%
preferred source of info	0 0	0 0	0 0	0 0	0 0	0 0	0 0	0 0	0 0	0 0	0 0	0 0	0 0	0 0	0 0	0 0	0 0	0 0
Department (NET)	1 0.6%	1 0.8%	0 0	1 0.6%	0 0	1 1.5%	0 0	0 0	1 3.3%	0 0	0 0	0 0	0 0	0 0	0 0	0 0	0 0	1 2.5%
All sources of info	1 0.6%	1 0.8%	0 0	1 0.6%	0 0	1 1.5%	0 0	0 0	1 3.3%	0 0	0 0	0 0	0 0	0 0	0 0	0 0	0 0	1 2.5%
preferred source of info	0 0	0 0	0 0	0 0	0 0	0 0	0 0	0 0	0 0	0 0	0 0	0 0	0 0	0 0	0 0	0 0	0 0	0 0
Faculty (NET)	* 0.2%	0 0	* 1.0%	* 0.2%	0 0	0 0	* 0.6%	0 0	0 0	0 0	0 0	0 0	* 3.2%	0 0	0 0	0 0	* 0.3%	0 0

Proportions/Means: Columns Tested (5% risk level) - A/B/D - C/D - E/F/G - H/I/J/K/L/M/N - P/Q
* small base; ** very small base (under 30) ineligible for sig testing

Table 287
Page 1183

Outsell/Digital Library Federation Study (2002)
Weighted Tables

TABLE 124, continued

T7D/E_14. Technical Reports SUMMARY TABLE

		RESPONDENT TYPE				INSTITUTION TYPE			DISCIPLINE								GENDER	
	TOTAL SAMPLE	FACULTY MEMBER	GRAD. STUDENT	FACULTY /GRAD	UNDER GRAD. STUDENT	PUBLIC	PRIVATE	LIBERAL ARTS	BIOLOGIAL SCIENCES	PHYSICAL SCIENCES /MATH	SOCIAL SCIENCES	ARTS AND HUMAN.	ENGI- NEERING	BUSINESS	LAW	UNDEC. MAJOR	MALE	FEMALE
		(A)	(B)	(C)	(D)	(E)	(F)	(G)	(H)	(I)	(J)	(K)	(L)	(M)	(N)		(P)	(Q)
Base - Use Technical Reports for teaching	137	109*	28**	137	0**	58*	50*	29**	26**	27**	39**	12**	9*	21**	1**	0*	101*	36**
All sources of info	* 0.2%	0 0	* 1.0%	* 0.2%	0 0	0 0	* 0.6%	0 0	0 0	0 0	0 0	0 0	* 3.2%	0 0	0 0	0 0	* 0.3%	0 0
preferred source of info	0 0	0 0	0 0	0 0	0 0	0 0	0 0	0 0	0 0	0 0	0 0	0 0	0 0	0 0	0 0	0 0	0 0	0 0
Office (NET)	0 0	0 0	0 0	0 0	0 0	0 0	0 0	0 0	0 0	0 0	0 0	0 0	0 0	0 0	0 0	0 0	0 0	0 0
All sources of info	0 0	0 0	0 0	0 0	0 0	0 0	0 0	0 0	0 0	0 0	0 0	0 0	0 0	0 0	0 0	0 0	0 0	0 0
preferred source of info	0 0	0 0	0 0	0 0	0 0	0 0	0 0	0 0	0 0	0 0	0 0	0 0	0 0	0 0	0 0	0 0	0 0	0 0
Home (NET)	0 0	0 0	0 0	0 0	0 0	0 0	0 0	0 0	0 0	0 0	0 0	0 0	0 0	0 0	0 0	0 0	0 0	0 0
All sources of info	0 0	0 0	0 0	0 0	0 0	0 0	0 0	0 0	0 0	0 0	0 0	0 0	0 0	0 0	0 0	0 0	0 0	0 0
preferred source of info	0 0	0 0	0 0	0 0	0 0	0 0	0 0	0 0	0 0	0 0	0 0	0 0	0 0	0 0	0 0	0 0	0 0	0 0
Access book/journal/ journal article elsewhere online (NET)	0 0	0 0	0 0	0 0	0 0	0 0	0 0	0 0	0 0	0 0	0 0	0 0	0 0	0 0	0 0	0 0	0 0	0 0

Proportions/Means: Columns Tested (5% risk level) - A/B/D - C/D - E/F/G - H/I/J/K/L/M/N - P/Q
* small base; ** very small base (under 30) ineligible for sig testing

Table 287
Page 1184

Outsell/Digital Library Federation Study (2002)
Weighted Tables

TABLE 124, continued

T7D/E_14. Technical Reports SUMMARY TABLE

		RESPONDENT TYPE				INSTITUTION TYPE			DISCIPLINE								GENDER	
	TOTAL SAMPLE	FACULTY MEMBER	GRAD. STUDENT	FACULTY /GRAD	UNDER GRAD. STUDENT	PUBLIC	PRIVATE	LIBERAL ARTS	BIOLOGIAL SCIENCES	PHYSICAL SCIENCES /MATH	SOCIAL SCIENCES	ARTS AND HUMAN.	ENGI-NEERING	BUSINESS	LAW	UNDEC. MAJOR	MALE	FEMALE
		(A)	(B)	(C)	(D)	(E)	(F)	(G)	(H)	(I)	(J)	(K)	(L)	(M)	(N)		(P)	(Q)
Base - Use Technical Reports for teaching	137	109*	28**	137	0**	58*	50*	29**	26**	27**	39**	12**	9*	21**	1**	0*	101*	36**
All sources of info	0 0	0 0	0 0	0 0	0 0	0 0	0 0	0 0	0 0	0 0	0 0	0 0	0 0	0 0	0 0	0 0	0 0	0 0
preferred source of info	0 0	0 0	0 0	0 0	0 0	0 0	0 0	0 0	0 0	0 0	0 0	0 0	0 0	0 0	0 0	0 0	0 0	0 0
Other (NET)	5 3.6%	2 1.6%	3 11.3%	5 3.6%	0 0	3 5.9%	1 1.2%	1 3.1%	3 10.0%	0 0	0 0	1 9.1%	1 12.9%	0 0	0 0	0 0	3 3.1%	2 4.9%
All sources of info	5 3.6%	2 1.6%	3 11.3%	5 3.6%	0 0	3 5.9%	1 1.2%	1 3.1%	3 10.0%	0 0	0 0	1 9.1%	1 12.9%	0 0	0 0	0 0	3 3.1%	2 4.9%
preferred source of info	3 2.3%	* 0.3%	3 10.3%	3 2.3%	0 0	3 5.4%	0 0	0 0	2 6.7%	0 0	0 0	1 9.1%	* 3.2%	0 0	0 0	0 0	2 2.3%	1 2.5%
DK/Refused	1 1.1%	1 1.3%	0 0	1 1.1%	0 0	* 0.5%	1 2.4%	0 0	1 3.3%	0 0	0 0	0 0	1 6.5%	0 0	0 0	0 0	1 1.2%	* 0.8%

Proportions/Means: Columns Tested (5% risk level) - A/B/D - C/D - E/F/G - H/I/J/K/L/M/N - P/Q
* small base; ** very small base (under 30) ineligible for sig testing

Table 287
Page 1185

TABLE 125

T7sum_15. Pre-prints SUMMARY TABLE

	TOTAL SAMPLE	RESPONDENT TYPE: FACULTY MEMBER	GRAD. STUDENT	FACULTY /GRAD	UNDER GRAD. STUDENT	INSTITUTION TYPE: PUBLIC	PRIVATE	LIBERAL ARTS	DISCIPLINE: BIOLOGIAL SCIENCES	PHYSICAL SCIENCES /MATH	SOCIAL SCIENCES	ARTS AND HUMAN.	ENGI-NEERING	BUSINESS	LAW	UNDEC. MAJOR	GENDER: MALE	FEMALE
		(A)	(B)	(C)	(D)	(E)	(F)	(G)	(H)	(I)	(J)	(K)	(L)	(M)	(N)		(P)	(Q)
Base - USe Pre-prints for teaching	84*	71*	13**	84*	0**	32**	34**	18**	16**	21**	21**	11**	3**	12**	1**	0*	62*	22**
ONLINE	50 59.9%	43 59.8%	8 60.4%	50 59.9%	0 0	24 75.9%	15 42.9%	12 63.5%	8 50.0%	14 66.7%	11 54.5%	9 80.0%	1 50.0%	7 53.8%	* 66.7%	0 0	39 62.6%	11 52.3%
Web directory/ subject related web site	18 21.1%	16 22.3%	2 14.7%	18 21.1%	0 0	7 21.6%	5 14.4%	6 32.7%	2 11.1%	6 28.6%	6 27.3%	2 20.0%	* 10.0%	2 15.4%	0 0	0 0	15 24.1%	3 12.6%
All sources of info	18 21.1%	16 22.3%	2 14.7%	18 21.1%	0 0	7 21.6%	5 14.4%	6 32.7%	2 11.1%	6 28.6%	6 27.3%	2 20.0%	* 10.0%	2 15.4%	0 0	0 0	15 24.1%	3 12.6%
preferred source of info	11 13.0%	11 15.4%	0 0	11 13.0%	0 0	3 9.4%	4 11.4%	4 22.2%	2 11.1%	2 9.5%	4 18.2%	2 20.0%	* 10.0%	1 7.7%	0 0	0 0	10 16.2%	1 4.0%
Search engine	13 15.3%	12 16.6%	1 7.8%	13 15.3%	0 0	7 22.1%	5 14.4%	1 5.0%	2 11.1%	4 19.0%	4 18.2%	2 20.0%	0 0	1 7.7%	* 33.3%	0 0	11 17.4%	2 9.1%
All sources of info	13 15.3%	12 16.6%	1 7.8%	13 15.3%	0 0	7 22.1%	5 14.4%	1 5.0%	2 11.1%	4 19.0%	4 18.2%	2 20.0%	0 0	1 7.7%	* 33.3%	0 0	11 17.4%	2 9.1%
preferred source of info	6 7.2%	5 7.1%	1 7.8%	6 7.2%	0 0	3 10.3%	2 5.5%	1 5.0%	1 5.6%	3 14.3%	0 0	1 10.0%	0 0	1 7.7%	* 33.3%	0 0	4 6.6%	2 9.1%
Your own institution's web site	12 14.4%	7 9.7%	5 41.1%	12 14.4%	0 0	9 28.9%	2 5.9%	1 5.0%	1 5.6%	1 4.8%	2 9.1%	6 50.0%	0 0	3 23.1%	0 0	0 0	7 11.8%	5 22.0%
All sources of info	12 14.4%	7 9.7%	5 41.1%	12 14.4%	0 0	9 28.9%	2 5.9%	1 5.0%	1 5.6%	1 4.8%	2 9.1%	6 50.0%	0 0	3 23.1%	0 0	0 0	7 11.8%	5 22.0%

Proportions/Means: Columns Tested (5% risk level) - A/B/D - C/D - E/F/G - H/I/J/K/L/M/N - P/Q
* small base; ** very small base (under 30) ineligible for sig testing

Table 291
Page 1196

TABLE 125, continued

T7sum_15. Pre-prints SUMMARY TABLE

	RESPONDENT TYPE					INSTITUTION TYPE			DISCIPLINE								GENDER	
	TOTAL SAMPLE	FACULTY MEMBER	GRAD. STUDENT	FACULTY /GRAD	UNDER GRAD. STUDENT	PUBLIC	PRIVATE	LIBERAL ARTS	BIOLOGIAL SCIENCES	PHYSICAL SCIENCES /MATH	SOCIAL SCIENCES	ARTS AND HUMAN.	ENGI- NEERING	BUSINESS	LAW	UNDEC. MAJOR	MALE	FEMALE
		(A)	(B)	(C)	(D)	(E)	(F)	(G)	(H)	(I)	(J)	(K)	(L)	(M)	(N)		(P)	(Q)
Base - USe Pre-prints for teaching	84*	71*	13**	84*	0**	32**	34**	18**	16**	21**	21**	11**	3**	12**	1**	0*	62*	22**
preferred source of info	6 7.0%	4 5.1%	2 17.6%	6 7.0%	0 0	4 12.9%	1 2.6%	1 5.0%	1 5.6%	0 0	0 0	2 20.0%	0 0	3 23.1%	0 0	0 0	3 4.8%	3 13.4%
Online databases	6 7.3%	6 8.2%	* 2.3%	6 7.3%	0 0	2 6.7%	* 0.9%	4 20.4%	2 11.1%	3 14.3%	0 0	1 10.0%	* 10.0%	0 0	0 0	0 0	6 9.9%	0 0
All sources of info	6 7.3%	6 8.2%	* 2.3%	6 7.3%	0 0	2 6.7%	* 0.9%	4 20.4%	2 11.1%	3 14.3%	0 0	1 10.0%	* 10.0%	0 0	0 0	0 0	6 9.9%	0 0
preferred source of info	2 2.6%	2 2.6%	* 2.3%	2 2.6%	0 0	0 0	* 0.9%	2 10.2%	1 5.6%	1 4.8%	0 0	0 0	* 10.0%	0 0	0 0	0 0	2 3.5%	0 0
Internet searches	5 5.8%	4 5.6%	1 6.9%	5 5.8%	0 0	4 11.7%	1 3.5%	0 0	2 11.1%	1 4.8%	0 0	0 0	* 10.0%	2 15.4%	0 0	0 0	3 4.9%	2 8.6%
All sources of info	5 5.8%	4 5.6%	1 6.9%	5 5.8%	0 0	4 11.7%	1 3.5%	0 0	2 11.1%	1 4.8%	0 0	0 0	* 10.0%	2 15.4%	0 0	0 0	3 4.9%	2 8.6%
preferred source of info	4 4.4%	3 4.0%	1 6.9%	4 4.4%	0 0	4 11.7%	0 0	0 0	1 5.6%	1 4.8%	0 0	0 0	0 0	2 15.4%	0 0	0 0	3 4.4%	1 4.6%
Online reference service	3 3.3%	3 3.9%	0 0	3 3.3%	0 0	1 2.9%	2 5.5%	0 0	0 0	0 0	2 9.1%	0 0	0 0	1 7.7%	0 0	0 0	1 1.5%	2 8.6%
All sources of info	3 3.3%	3 3.9%	0 0	3 3.3%	0 0	1 2.9%	2 5.5%	0 0	0 0	0 0	2 9.1%	0 0	0 0	1 7.7%	0 0	0 0	1 1.5%	2 8.6%
preferred source of info	2 2.2%	2 2.6%	0 0	2 2.2%	0 0	0 0	2 5.5%	0 0	0 0	0 0	2 9.1%	0 0	0 0	0 0	0 0	0 0	0 0	2 8.6%

Proportions/Means: Columns Tested (5% risk level) - A/B/D - C/D - E/F/G - H/I/J/K/L/M/N - P/Q
* small base; ** very small base (under 30) ineligible for sig testing

Table 291
Page 1197

Outsell/Digital Library Federation Study (2002)
Weighted Tables

TABLE 125, continued

T7sum_15. Pre-prints SUMMARY TABLE

	TOTAL SAMPLE	RESPONDENT TYPE: FACULTY MEMBER	GRAD. STUDENT	FACULTY /GRAD	UNDER GRAD. STUDENT	INSTITUTION TYPE: PUBLIC	PRIVATE	LIBERAL ARTS	DISCIPLINE: BIOLOGIAL SCIENCES	PHYSICAL SCIENCES /MATH	SOCIAL SCIENCES	ARTS AND HUMAN.	ENGI-NEERING	BUSINESS	LAW	UNDEC. MAJOR	GENDER: MALE	FEMALE
		(A)	(B)	(C)	(D)	(E)	(F)	(G)	(H)	(I)	(J)	(K)	(L)	(M)	(N)		(P)	(Q)
Base - USe Pre-prints for teaching	84*	71*	13**	84*	0**	32**	34**	18**	16**	21**	21**	11**	3**	12**	1**	0*	62*	22**
Online library catalogues and finding aids	3 3.1%	2 3.2%	* 2.3%	3 3.1%	0 0	0 0	3 7.6%	0 0	1 5.6%	0 0	0 0	1 10.0%	1 20.0%	0 0	0 0	0 0	2 2.7%	1 4.0%
All sources of info	3 3.1%	2 3.2%	* 2.3%	3 3.1%	0 0	0 0	3 7.6%	0 0	1 5.6%	0 0	0 0	1 10.0%	1 20.0%	0 0	0 0	0 0	2 2.7%	1 4.0%
preferred source of info	1 1.7%	1 1.6%	* 2.3%	1 1.7%	0 0	0 0	1 4.3%	0 0	1 5.6%	0 0	0 0	0 0	1 20.0%	0 0	0 0	0 0	1 0.9%	1 4.0%
Department web page	2 2.2%	0 0	2 14.7%	2 2.2%	0 0	2 5.9%	0 0	0 0	0 0	0 0	2 9.1%	0 0	0 0	0 0	0 0	0 0	0 0	2 8.6%
All sources of info	2 2.2%	0 0	2 14.7%	2 2.2%	0 0	2 5.9%	0 0	0 0	0 0	0 0	2 9.1%	0 0	0 0	0 0	0 0	0 0	0 0	2 8.6%
preferred source of info	0 0	0 0	0 0	0 0	0 0	0 0	0 0	0 0	0 0	0 0	0 0	0 0	0 0	0 0	0 0	0 0	0 0	0 0
Your own personal electronic library/files	1 1.5%	* 0.2%	1 8.8%	1 1.5%	0 0	1 4.1%	0 0	0 0	0 0	0 0	0 0	1 10.0%	0 0	0 0	* 33.3%	0 0	1 2.1%	0 0
All sources of info	1 1.5%	* 0.2%	1 8.8%	1 1.5%	0 0	1 4.1%	0 0	0 0	0 0	0 0	0 0	1 10.0%	0 0	0 0	* 33.3%	0 0	1 2.1%	0 0
preferred source of info	* 0.2%	* 0.2%	0 0	* 0.2%	0 0	* 0.5%	0 0	0 0	0 0	0 0	0 0	0 0	0 0	0 0	* 33.3%	0 0	* 0.3%	0 0

Proportions/Means: Columns Tested (5% risk level) - A/B/D - C/D - E/F/G - H/I/J/K/L/M/N - P/Q
* small base; ** very small base (under 30) ineligible for sig testing

Table 291
Page 1198

Outsell/Digital Library Federation Study (2002)
Weighted Tables

TABLE 125, continued

T7sum_15. Pre-prints SUMMARY TABLE

		RESPONDENT TYPE				INSTITUTION TYPE			DISCIPLINE								GENDER	
	TOTAL SAMPLE	FACULTY MEMBER	GRAD. STUDENT	FACULTY /GRAD	UNDER GRAD. STUDENT	PUBLIC	PRIVATE	LIBERAL ARTS	BIOLOGIAL SCIENCES	PHYSICAL SCIENCES /MATH	SOCIAL SCIENCES	ARTS AND HUMAN.	ENGI-NEERING	BUSINESS	LAW	UNDEC. MAJOR	MALE	FEMALE
		(A)	(B)	(C)	(D)	(E)	(F)	(G)	(H)	(I)	(J)	(K)	(L)	(M)	(N)		(P)	(Q)
Base - USe Pre-prints for teaching	84*	71*	13**	84*	0**	32**	34**	18**	16**	21**	21**	11**	3**	12**	1**	0*	62*	22**
Online abstracting and indexing services	1 1.2%	1 1.4%	0 0	1 1.2%	0 0	0 0	0 0	1 5.4%	0 0	1 4.8%	0 0	0 0	0 0	0 0	0 0	0 0	1 1.6%	0 0
All sources of info	1 1.2%	1 1.4%	0 0	1 1.2%	0 0	0 0	0 0	1 5.4%	0 0	1 4.8%	0 0	0 0	0 0	0 0	0 0	0 0	1 1.6%	0 0
preferred source of info	1 1.2%	1 1.4%	0 0	1 1.2%	0 0	0 0	0 0	1 5.4%	0 0	1 4.8%	0 0	0 0	0 0	0 0	0 0	0 0	1 1.6%	0 0
E-mail listservs	0 0	0 0	0 0	0 0	0 0	0 0	0 0	0 0	0 0	0 0	0 0	0 0	0 0	0 0	0 0	0 0	0 0	0 0
All sources of info	0 0	0 0	0 0	0 0	0 0	0 0	0 0	0 0	0 0	0 0	0 0	0 0	0 0	0 0	0 0	0 0	0 0	0 0
preferred source of info	0 0	0 0	0 0	0 0	0 0	0 0	0 0	0 0	0 0	0 0	0 0	0 0	0 0	0 0	0 0	0 0	0 0	0 0
Online bookstore	0 0	0 0	0 0	0 0	0 0	0 0	0 0	0 0	0 0	0 0	0 0	0 0	0 0	0 0	0 0	0 0	0 0	0 0
All sources of info	0 0	0 0	0 0	0 0	0 0	0 0	0 0	0 0	0 0	0 0	0 0	0 0	0 0	0 0	0 0	0 0	0 0	0 0
preferred source of info	0 0	0 0	0 0	0 0	0 0	0 0	0 0	0 0	0 0	0 0	0 0	0 0	0 0	0 0	0 0	0 0	0 0	0 0
LIBRARY/PRINT	44 52.4%	41 57.1%	3 25.8%	44 52.4%	0 0	15 46.9%	18 51.9%	12 62.6%	5 33.3%	12 57.1%	13 63.6%	8 70.0%	1 40.0%	5 38.5%	0 0	0 0	37 58.6%	8 34.6%

Proportions/Means: Columns Tested (5% risk level) - A/B/D - C/D - E/F/G - H/I/J/K/L/M/N - P/Q
* small base; ** very small base (under 30) ineligible for sig testing

Table 291
Page 1199

Outsell/Digital Library Federation Study (2002)
Weighted Tables

TABLE 125, continued

T7sum_15. Pre-prints SUMMARY TABLE

		RESPONDENT TYPE				INSTITUTION TYPE			DISCIPLINE									GENDER	
	TOTAL SAMPLE	FACULTY MEMBER	GRAD. STUDENT	FACULTY /GRAD	UNDER GRAD. STUDENT	PUBLIC	PRIVATE	LIBERAL ARTS	BIOLOGIAL SCIENCES	PHYSICAL SCIENCES /MATH	SOCIAL SCIENCES	ARTS AND HUMAN.	ENGI-NEERING	BUSINESS	LAW	UNDEC. MAJOR	MALE	FEMALE
		(A)	(B)	(C)	(D)	(E)	(F)	(G)	(H)	(I)	(J)	(K)	(L)	(M)	(N)		(P)	(Q)
Base - USe Pre-prints for teaching	84*	71*	13**	84*	0**	32**	34**	18**	16**	21**	21**	11**	3**	12**	1**	0*	62*	22**
Campus library	28 33.6%	25 35.0%	3 25.8%	28 33.6%	0 0	12 37.5%	9 25.6%	8 41.5%	4 22.2%	8 38.1%	6 27.3%	6 50.0%	1 30.0%	5 38.5%	0 0	0 0	23 36.4%	6 25.4%
All sources of info	28 33.6%	25 35.0%	3 25.8%	28 33.6%	0 0	12 37.5%	9 25.6%	8 41.5%	4 22.2%	8 38.1%	6 27.3%	6 50.0%	1 30.0%	5 38.5%	0 0	0 0	23 36.4%	6 25.4%
preferred source of info	12 14.4%	10 14.4%	2 14.7%	12 14.4%	0 0	5 15.3%	4 13.2%	3 15.2%	2 11.1%	3 14.3%	2 9.1%	3 30.0%	* 10.0%	2 15.4%	0 0	0 0	9 15.0%	3 12.8%
Personal subscriptions to newspapers, magazines and journals	11 12.8%	10 13.5%	1 8.8%	11 12.8%	0 0	4 12.9%	6 16.6%	1 5.4%	1 5.6%	2 9.5%	6 27.3%	2 20.0%	0 0	0 0	0 0	0 0	10 15.9%	1 4.0%
All sources of info	11 12.8%	10 13.5%	1 8.8%	11 12.8%	0 0	4 12.9%	6 16.6%	1 5.4%	1 5.6%	2 9.5%	6 27.3%	2 20.0%	0 0	0 0	0 0	0 0	10 15.9%	1 4.0%
preferred source of info	3 3.3%	3 3.9%	0 0	3 3.3%	0 0	1 2.8%	2 5.5%	0 0	1 5.6%	0 0	2 9.1%	0 0	0 0	0 0	0 0	0 0	2 3.0%	1 4.0%
Your own personal physical library/ files/bookshelves	7 8.5%	6 8.5%	1 8.8%	7 8.5%	0 0	1 3.5%	2 6.4%	4 21.0%	0 0	2 9.5%	4 18.2%	1 10.0%	* 10.0%	0 0	0 0	0 0	7 11.5%	0 0
All sources of info	7 8.5%	6 8.5%	1 8.8%	7 8.5%	0 0	1 3.5%	2 6.4%	4 21.0%	0 0	2 9.5%	4 18.2%	1 10.0%	* 10.0%	0 0	0 0	0 0	7 11.5%	0 0
preferred source of info	* 0.3%	* 0.4%	0 0	* 0.3%	0 0	0 0	* 0.9%	0 0	0 0	0 0	0 0	0 0	* 10.0%	0 0	0 0	0 0	* 0.5%	0 0

Proportions/Means: Columns Tested (5% risk level) - A/B/D - C/D - E/F/G - H/I/J/K/L/M/N - P/Q
* small base; ** very small base (under 30) ineligible for sig testing

Table 291
Page 1200

Outsell/Digital Library Federation Study (2002)
Weighted Tables

TABLE 125, continued

T7sum_15. Pre-prints SUMMARY TABLE

	TOTAL SAMPLE	RESPONDENT TYPE: FACULTY MEMBER	GRAD. STUDENT	FACULTY /GRAD	UNDER GRAD. STUDENT	INSTITUTION TYPE: PUBLIC	PRIVATE	LIBERAL ARTS	DISCIPLINE: BIOLOGIAL SCIENCES	PHYSICAL SCIENCES /MATH	SOCIAL SCIENCES	ARTS AND HUMAN.	ENGI-NEERING	BUSINESS	LAW	UNDEC. MAJOR	GENDER: MALE	FEMALE
		(A)	(B)	(C)	(D)	(E)	(F)	(G)	(H)	(I)	(J)	(K)	(L)	(M)	(N)		(P)	(Q)
Base - USe Pre-prints for teaching	84*	71*	13**	84*	0**	32**	34**	18**	16**	21**	21**	11**	3**	12**	1**	0*	62*	22**
References cited in books or journal articles	3 3.7%	3 4.4%	0 0	3 3.7%	0 0	1 3.1%	1 3.3%	1 5.4%	0 0	2 9.5%	0 0	1 10.0%	0 0	0 0	0 0	0 0	3 5.0%	0 0
All sources of info	3 3.7%	3 4.4%	0 0	3 3.7%	0 0	1 3.1%	1 3.3%	1 5.4%	0 0	2 9.5%	0 0	1 10.0%	0 0	0 0	0 0	0 0	3 5.0%	0 0
preferred source of info	1 1.2%	1 1.4%	0 0	1 1.2%	0 0	0 0	0 0	1 5.4%	0 0	1 4.8%	0 0	0 0	0 0	0 0	0 0	0 0	1 1.6%	0 0
Printed library catalogues and finding aids	3 3.3%	3 3.9%	0 0	3 3.3%	0 0	0 0	3 8.1%	0 0	1 5.6%	0 0	2 9.1%	0 0	0 0	0 0	0 0	0 0	3 4.4%	0 0
All sources of info	3 3.3%	3 3.9%	0 0	3 3.3%	0 0	0 0	3 8.1%	0 0	1 5.6%	0 0	2 9.1%	0 0	0 0	0 0	0 0	0 0	3 4.4%	0 0
preferred source of info	1 1.0%	1 1.2%	0 0	1 1.0%	0 0	0 0	1 2.6%	0 0	1 5.6%	0 0	0 0	0 0	0 0	0 0	0 0	0 0	1 1.4%	0 0
Physical bookstore	1 1.3%	1 1.6%	0 0	1 1.3%	0 0	1 3.5%	0 0	0 0	0 0	0 0	0 0	1 10.0%	0 0	0 0	0 0	0 0	0 0	1 5.1%
All sources of info	1 1.3%	1 1.6%	0 0	1 1.3%	0 0	1 3.5%	0 0	0 0	0 0	0 0	0 0	1 10.0%	0 0	0 0	0 0	0 0	0 0	1 5.1%
preferred source of info	0 0	0 0	0 0	0 0	0 0	0 0	0 0	0 0	0 0	0 0	0 0	0 0	0 0	0 0	0 0	0 0	0 0	0 0

Proportions/Means: Columns Tested (5% risk level) - A/B/D - C/D - E/F/G - H/I/J/K/L/M/N - P/Q
* small base; ** very small base (under 30) ineligible for sig testing

Table 291
Page 1201

Outsell/Digital Library Federation Study (2002)
Weighted Tables

TABLE 125, continued

T7sum_15. Pre-prints SUMMARY TABLE

	TOTAL SAMPLE	RESPONDENT TYPE: FACULTY MEMBER	GRAD. STUDENT	FACULTY /GRAD	UNDER GRAD. STUDENT	INSTITUTION TYPE: PUBLIC	PRIVATE	LIBERAL ARTS	DISCIPLINE: BIOLOGIAL SCIENCES	PHYSICAL SCIENCES /MATH	SOCIAL SCIENCES	ARTS AND HUMAN.	ENGI-NEERING	BUSINESS	LAW	UNDEC. MAJOR	GENDER: MALE	FEMALE
		(A)	(B)	(C)	(D)	(E)	(F)	(G)	(H)	(I)	(J)	(K)	(L)	(M)	(N)		(P)	(Q)
Base - USe Pre-prints for teaching	84*	71*	13**	84*	0**	32**	34**	18**	16**	21**	21**	11**	3**	12**	1**	0*	62*	22**
Another library	1	1	0	1	0	0	0	1	0	1	0	0	0	0	0	0	1	0
	1.2%	1.4%	0	1.2%	0	0	0	5.4%	0	4.8%	0	0	0	0	0	0	1.6%	0
All sources of info	1	1	0	1	0	0	0	1	0	1	0	0	0	0	0	0	1	0
	1.2%	1.4%	0	1.2%	0	0	0	5.4%	0	4.8%	0	0	0	0	0	0	1.6%	0
preferred source of info	0	0	0	0	0	0	0	0	0	0	0	0	0	0	0	0	0	0
	0	0	0	0	0	0	0	0	0	0	0	0	0	0	0	0	0	0
Printed abstracting and indexing services	1	1	0	1	0	0	1	0	0	1	0	0	0	0	0	0	1	0
	1.2%	1.4%	0	1.2%	0	0	2.9%	0	0	4.8%	0	0	0	0	0	0	1.6%	0
All sources of info	1	1	0	1	0	0	1	0	0	1	0	0	0	0	0	0	1	0
	1.2%	1.4%	0	1.2%	0	0	2.9%	0	0	4.8%	0	0	0	0	0	0	1.6%	0
preferred source of info	0	0	0	0	0	0	0	0	0	0	0	0	0	0	0	0	0	0
	0	0	0	0	0	0	0	0	0	0	0	0	0	0	0	0	0	0
PERSONAL ASSISTANCE	35	26	9	35	0	13	15	8	5	7	13	6	1	3	*	0	27	9
	42.1%	36.7%	72.3%	42.1%	0	40.2%	43.9%	41.9%	33.3%	33.3%	63.6%	50.0%	50.0%	23.1%	33.3%	0	42.8%	40.0%
Colleagues inside your institution	23	14	9	23	0	11	7	5	5	3	9	3	1	1	0	0	15	8
	27.1%	19.1%	72.3%	27.1%	0	33.4%	21.8%	26.1%	33.3%	14.3%	45.5%	30.0%	30.0%	7.7%	0	0	24.2%	35.4%
All sources of info	23	14	9	23	0	11	7	5	5	3	9	3	1	1	0	0	15	8
	27.1%	19.1%	72.3%	27.1%	0	33.4%	21.8%	26.1%	33.3%	14.3%	45.5%	30.0%	30.0%	7.7%	0	0	24.2%	35.4%
preferred source of info	12	6	6	12	0	5	5	2	4	2	2	2	1	1	0	0	8	4
	14.3%	8.2%	48.4%	14.3%	0	15.3%	15.4%	10.5%	27.8%	9.5%	9.1%	20.0%	20.0%	7.7%	0	0	12.9%	18.3%

Proportions/Means: Columns Tested (5% risk level) - A/B/D - C/D - E/F/G - H/I/J/K/L/M/N - P/Q
* small base; ** very small base (under 30) ineligible for sig testing

Table 291
Page 1202

Outsell/Digital Library Federation Study (2002)
Weighted Tables

TABLE 125, continued

T7sum_15. Pre-prints SUMMARY TABLE

		RESPONDENT TYPE				INSTITUTION TYPE			DISCIPLINE								GENDER	
	TOTAL SAMPLE	FACULTY MEMBER	GRAD. STUDENT	FACULTY /GRAD	UNDER GRAD. STUDENT	PUBLIC	PRIVATE	LIBERAL ARTS	BIOLOGIAL SCIENCES	PHYSICAL SCIENCES /MATH	SOCIAL SCIENCES	ARTS AND HUMAN.	ENGI-NEERING	BUSINESS	LAW	UNDEC. MAJOR	MALE	FEMALE
		(A)	(B)	(C)	(D)	(E)	(F)	(G)	(H)	(I)	(J)	(K)	(L)	(M)	(N)		(P)	(Q)
Base - USe Pre-prints for teaching	84*	71*	13**	84*	0**	32**	34**	18**	16**	21**	21**	11**	3**	12**	1**	0*	62*	22**
A librarian in your institution	12 14.2%	11 15.2%	1 8.8%	12 14.2%	0 0	3 10.7%	6 16.6%	3 15.9%	0 0	3 14.3%	2 9.1%	4 40.0%	1 20.0%	2 15.4%	* 33.3%	0 0	12 19.2%	0 0
All sources of info	12 14.2%	11 15.2%	1 8.8%	12 14.2%	0 0	3 10.7%	6 16.6%	3 15.9%	0 0	3 14.3%	2 9.1%	4 40.0%	1 20.0%	2 15.4%	* 33.3%	0 0	12 19.2%	0 0
preferred source of info	4 4.9%	4 5.7%	0 0	4 4.9%	0 0	0 0	3 9.1%	1 5.4%	0 0	1 4.8%	2 9.1%	0 0	* 10.0%	1 7.7%	0 0	0 0	4 6.6%	0 0
Colleagues outside your institution	12 13.7%	12 16.1%	0 0	12 13.7%	0 0	6 18.1%	4 11.1%	2 10.8%	0 0	4 19.0%	8 36.4%	0 0	0 0	0 0	0 0	0 0	9 13.9%	3 13.2%
All sources of info	12 13.7%	12 16.1%	0 0	12 13.7%	0 0	6 18.1%	4 11.1%	2 10.8%	0 0	4 19.0%	8 36.4%	0 0	0 0	0 0	0 0	0 0	9 13.9%	3 13.2%
preferred source of info	4 4.6%	4 5.4%	0 0	4 4.6%	0 0	1 3.1%	2 5.5%	1 5.4%	0 0	2 9.5%	2 9.1%	0 0	0 0	0 0	0 0	0 0	3 4.6%	1 4.6%
Professional meetings	3 3.8%	3 4.4%	0 0	3 3.8%	0 0	1 3.1%	2 6.4%	0 0	0 0	1 4.8%	2 9.1%	0 0	* 10.0%	0 0	0 0	0 0	3 5.1%	0 0
All sources of info	3 3.8%	3 4.4%	0 0	3 3.8%	0 0	1 3.1%	2 6.4%	0 0	0 0	1 4.8%	2 9.1%	0 0	* 10.0%	0 0	0 0	0 0	3 5.1%	0 0
preferred source of info	1 1.5%	1 1.8%	0 0	1 1.5%	0 0	1 3.1%	* 0.9%	0 0	0 0	1 4.8%	0 0	0 0	* 10.0%	0 0	0 0	0 0	1 2.1%	0 0
Another institution's librarian	0 0	0 0	0 0	0 0	0 0	0 0	0 0	0 0	0 0	0 0	0 0	0 0	0 0	0 0	0 0	0 0	0 0	0 0

Proportions/Means: Columns Tested (5% risk level) - A/B/D - C/D - E/F/G - H/I/J/K/L/M/N - P/Q
* small base; ** very small base (under 30) ineligible for sig testing

Table 291
Page 1203

Outsell/Digital Library Federation Study (2002)
Weighted Tables

TABLE 125, continued

T7sum_15. Pre-prints SUMMARY TABLE

		RESPONDENT TYPE				INSTITUTION TYPE			DISCIPLINE								GENDER	
	TOTAL SAMPLE	FACULTY MEMBER	GRAD. STUDENT	FACULTY /GRAD	UNDER GRAD. STUDENT	PUBLIC	PRIVATE	LIBERAL ARTS	BIOLOGIAL SCIENCES	PHYSICAL SCIENCES /MATH	SOCIAL SCIENCES	ARTS AND HUMAN.	ENGI- NEERING	BUSINESS	LAW	UNDEC. MAJOR	MALE	FEMALE
		(A)	(B)	(C)	(D)	(E)	(F)	(G)	(H)	(I)	(J)	(K)	(L)	(M)	(N)		(P)	(Q)
Base - USe Pre-prints for teaching	84*	71*	13**	84*	0**	32**	34**	18**	16**	21**	21**	11**	3**	12**	1**	0*	62*	22**
All sources of info	0 0	0 0	0 0	0 0	0 0	0 0	0 0	0 0	0 0	0 0	0 0	0 0	0 0	0 0	0 0	0 0	0 0	0 0
preferred source of info	0 0	0 0	0 0	0 0	0 0	0 0	0 0	0 0	0 0	0 0	0 0	0 0	0 0	0 0	0 0	0 0	0 0	0 0
Online (unspecified)	1 1.3%	1 1.6%	0 0	1 1.3%	0 0	0 0	1 3.3%	0 0	0 0	0 0	0 0	1 10.0%	0 0	0 0	0 0	0 0	1 1.8%	0 0
All sources of info	1 1.3%	1 1.6%	0 0	1 1.3%	0 0	0 0	1 3.3%	0 0	0 0	0 0	0 0	1 10.0%	0 0	0 0	0 0	0 0	1 1.8%	0 0
preferred source of info	0 0	0 0	0 0	0 0	0 0	0 0	0 0	0 0	0 0	0 0	0 0	0 0	0 0	0 0	0 0	0 0	0 0	0 0
Students	* 0.2%	* 0.2%	0 0	* 0.2%	0 0	* 0.5%	0 0	0 0	0 0	0 0	0 0	0 0	0 0	0 0	* 33.3%	0 0	* 0.3%	0 0
All sources of info	* 0.2%	* 0.2%	0 0	* 0.2%	0 0	* 0.5%	0 0	0 0	0 0	0 0	0 0	0 0	0 0	0 0	* 33.3%	0 0	* 0.3%	0 0
preferred source of info	0 0	0 0	0 0	0 0	0 0	0 0	0 0	0 0	0 0	0 0	0 0	0 0	0 0	0 0	0 0	0 0	0 0	0 0
Personal office/lab	0 0	0 0	0 0	0 0	0 0	0 0	0 0	0 0	0 0	0 0	0 0	0 0	0 0	0 0	0 0	0 0	0 0	0 0
All sources of info	0 0	0 0	0 0	0 0	0 0	0 0	0 0	0 0	0 0	0 0	0 0	0 0	0 0	0 0	0 0	0 0	0 0	0 0

Proportions/Means: Columns Tested (5% risk level) - A/B/D - C/D - E/F/G - H/I/J/K/L/M/N - P/Q
* small base; ** very small base (under 30) ineligible for sig testing

Table 291
Page 1204

Outsell/Digital Library Federation Study (2002)
Weighted Tables

TABLE 125, continued

T7sum_15. Pre-prints SUMMARY TABLE

		RESPONDENT TYPE				INSTITUTION TYPE			DISCIPLINE									GENDER	
	TOTAL SAMPLE	FACULTY MEMBER	GRAD. STUDENT	FACULTY /GRAD	UNDER GRAD. STUDENT	PUBLIC	PRIVATE	LIBERAL ARTS	BIOLOGIAL SCIENCES	PHYSICAL SCIENCES /MATH	SOCIAL SCIENCES	ARTS AND HUMAN.	ENGI-NEERING	BUSINESS	LAW	UNDEC. MAJOR	MALE	FEMALE
		(A)	(B)	(C)	(D)	(E)	(F)	(G)	(H)	(I)	(J)	(K)	(L)	(M)	(N)		(P)	(Q)
Base - USe Pre-prints for teaching	84*	71*	13**	84*	0**	32**	34**	18**	16**	21**	21**	11**	3**	12**	1**	0*	62*	22**
preferred source of info	0 0	0 0	0 0	0 0	0 0	0 0	0 0	0 0	0 0	0 0	0 0	0 0	0 0	0 0	0 0	0 0	0 0	0 0
Author	0 0	0 0	0 0	0 0	0 0	0 0	0 0	0 0	0 0	0 0	0 0	0 0	0 0	0 0	0 0	0 0	0 0	0 0
All sources of info	0 0	0 0	0 0	0 0	0 0	0 0	0 0	0 0	0 0	0 0	0 0	0 0	0 0	0 0	0 0	0 0	0 0	0 0
preferred source of info	0 0	0 0	0 0	0 0	0 0	0 0	0 0	0 0	0 0	0 0	0 0	0 0	0 0	0 0	0 0	0 0	0 0	0 0
Other	12 14.2%	10 14.0%	2 15.7%	12 14.2%	0 0	5 16.4%	5 14.0%	2 10.8%	2 11.1%	5 23.8%	2 9.1%	2 20.0%	0 0	1 7.7%	* 33.3%	0 0	10 16.0%	2 9.1%
All sources of info	12 14.2%	10 14.0%	2 15.7%	12 14.2%	0 0	5 16.4%	5 14.0%	2 10.8%	2 11.1%	5 23.8%	2 9.1%	2 20.0%	0 0	1 7.7%	* 33.3%	0 0	10 16.0%	2 9.1%
preferred source of info	5 5.9%	5 7.0%	0 0	5 5.9%	0 0	2 6.6%	2 5.5%	1 5.4%	1 5.6%	3 14.3%	0 0	0 0	0 0	1 7.7%	* 33.3%	0 0	4 6.6%	1 4.0%
DK/Refused	8 9.9%	7 10.4%	1 6.9%	8 9.9%	0 0	4 11.6%	4 11.1%	1 4.8%	2 11.1%	0 0	6 27.3%	0 0	0 0	1 7.7%	0 0	0 0	5 7.5%	4 16.6%

Proportions/Means: Columns Tested (5% risk level) - A/B/D - C/D - E/F/G - H/I/J/K/L/M/N - P/Q
* small base; ** very small base (under 30) ineligible for sig testing

Table 291
Page 1205

Outsell/Digital Library Federation Study (2002)
Weighted Tables

TABLE 126

T7D/E_15. Pre-prints SUMMARY TABLE

		RESPONDENT TYPE				INSTITUTION TYPE			DISCIPLINE								GENDER	
	TOTAL SAMPLE	FACULTY MEMBER	GRAD. STUDENT	FACULTY /GRAD	UNDER GRAD. STUDENT	PUBLIC	PRIVATE	LIBERAL ARTS	BIOLOGIAL SCIENCES	PHYSICAL SCIENCES /MATH	SOCIAL SCIENCES	ARTS AND HUMAN.	ENGI- NEERING	BUSINESS	LAW	UNDEC. MAJOR	MALE	FEMALE
		(A)	(B)	(C)	(D)	(E)	(F)	(G)	(H)	(I)	(J)	(K)	(L)	(M)	(N)		(P)	(Q)
Base - Use Pre-prints for teaching	84*	71*	13**	84*	0**	32**	34**	18**	16**	21**	21**	11**	3**	12**	1**	0*	62*	22**
Borrow from or use in campus library (NET)	32 38.3%	26 36.1%	6 50.3%	32 38.3%	0 0	12 38.8%	15 43.5%	5 27.6%	7 44.4%	5 23.8%	8 36.4%	8 70.0%	2 70.0%	3 23.1%	0 0	0 0	23 36.2%	10 44.2%
All sources of info	32 38.3%	26 36.1%	6 50.3%	32 38.3%	0 0	12 38.8%	15 43.5%	5 27.6%	7 44.4%	5 23.8%	8 36.4%	8 70.0%	2 70.0%	3 23.1%	0 0	0 0	23 36.2%	10 44.2%
preferred source of info	23 27.7%	18 25.3%	5 41.5%	23 27.7%	0 0	8 25.1%	11 31.1%	5 26.1%	5 33.3%	4 19.0%	6 27.3%	4 40.0%	1 40.0%	3 23.1%	0 0	0 0	16 25.3%	8 34.6%
Access online (NET)	30 36.0%	29 40.6%	1 10.1%	30 36.0%	0 0	12 37.5%	9 25.8%	10 52.0%	4 22.2%	11 52.4%	4 18.2%	3 30.0%	1 30.0%	7 61.5%	* 66.7%	0 0	26 41.2%	5 21.1%
All sources of info	30 36.0%	29 40.6%	1 10.1%	30 36.0%	0 0	12 37.5%	9 25.8%	10 52.0%	4 22.2%	11 52.4%	4 18.2%	3 30.0%	1 30.0%	7 61.5%	* 66.7%	0 0	26 41.2%	5 21.1%
preferred source of info	24 28.7%	23 32.0%	1 10.1%	24 28.7%	0 0	9 28.4%	6 19.1%	9 47.0%	3 16.7%	10 47.6%	2 9.1%	2 20.0%	1 20.0%	7 53.8%	* 66.7%	0 0	21 34.3%	3 12.8%
Colleagues (NET)	15 18.2%	12 17.4%	3 22.6%	15 18.2%	0 0	7 21.2%	6 16.6%	3 15.9%	4 22.2%	3 14.3%	6 27.3%	2 20.0%	0 0	1 7.7%	0 0	0 0	13 21.6%	2 8.6%
All sources of info	15 18.2%	12 17.4%	3 22.6%	15 18.2%	0 0	7 21.2%	6 16.6%	3 15.9%	4 22.2%	3 14.3%	6 27.3%	2 20.0%	0 0	1 7.7%	0 0	0 0	13 21.6%	2 8.6%
preferred source of info	12 13.7%	10 13.4%	2 15.7%	12 13.7%	0 0	5 15.3%	5 14.0%	2 10.5%	3 16.7%	2 9.5%	4 18.2%	2 20.0%	0 0	1 7.7%	0 0	0 0	10 15.5%	2 8.6%

Proportions/Means: Columns Tested (5% risk level) - A/B/D - C/D - E/F/G - H/I/J/K/L/M/N - P/Q
* small base; ** very small base (under 30) ineligible for sig testing

Table 294
Page 1212

Outsell/Digital Library Federation Study (2002)
Weighted Tables

TABLE 126, continued

T7D/E_15. Pre-prints SUMMARY TABLE

	RESPONDENT TYPE				INSTITUTION TYPE			DISCIPLINE									GENDER	
	TOTAL SAMPLE	FACULTY MEMBER	GRAD. STUDENT	FACULTY /GRAD	UNDER GRAD. STUDENT	PUBLIC	PRIVATE	LIBERAL ARTS	BIOLOGIAL SCIENCES	PHYSICAL SCIENCES /MATH	SOCIAL SCIENCES	ARTS AND HUMAN.	ENGI-NEERING	BUSINESS	LAW	UNDEC. MAJOR	MALE	FEMALE
		(A)	(B)	(C)	(D)	(E)	(F)	(G)	(H)	(I)	(J)	(K)	(L)	(M)	(N)		(P)	(Q)
Base - Use Pre-prints for teaching	84*	71*	13**	84*	0**	32**	34**	18**	16**	21**	21**	11**	3**	12**	1**	0*	62*	22**
Order from on demand document delivery service (NET)	5 5.6%	5 6.6%	0 0	5 5.6%	0 0	1 2.9%	2 5.5%	2 10.2%	0 0	0 0	4 18.2%	0 0	0 0	1 7.7%	0 0	0 0	3 4.5%	2 8.6%
All sources of info	5 5.6%	5 6.6%	0 0	5 5.6%	0 0	1 2.9%	2 5.5%	2 10.2%	0 0	0 0	4 18.2%	0 0	0 0	1 7.7%	0 0	0 0	3 4.5%	2 8.6%
preferred source of info	5 5.6%	5 6.6%	0 0	5 5.6%	0 0	1 2.9%	2 5.5%	2 10.2%	0 0	0 0	4 18.2%	0 0	0 0	1 7.7%	0 0	0 0	3 4.5%	2 8.6%
Purchase from physical book store (NET)	4 4.7%	4 5.6%	0 0	4 4.7%	0 0	2 6.7%	2 5.5%	0 0	0 0	1 4.8%	2 9.1%	1 10.0%	0 0	0 0	0 0	0 0	3 4.6%	1 5.1%
All sources of info	4 4.7%	4 5.6%	0 0	4 4.7%	0 0	2 6.7%	2 5.5%	0 0	0 0	1 4.8%	2 9.1%	1 10.0%	0 0	0 0	0 0	0 0	3 4.6%	1 5.1%
preferred source of info	2 2.5%	2 3.0%	0 0	2 2.5%	0 0	2 6.7%	0 0	0 0	0 0	1 4.8%	0 0	1 10.0%	0 0	0 0	0 0	0 0	1 1.6%	1 5.1%
Faculty (NET)	3 3.8%	0 0	3 24.9%	3 3.8%	0 0	0 0	3 9.3%	0 0	2 11.1%	0 0	0 0	1 10.0%	* 10.0%	0 0	0 0	0 0	2 3.3%	1 5.1%
All sources of info	3 3.8%	0 0	3 24.9%	3 3.8%	0 0	0 0	3 9.3%	0 0	2 11.1%	0 0	0 0	1 10.0%	* 10.0%	0 0	0 0	0 0	2 3.3%	1 5.1%
preferred source of info	3 3.4%	0 0	3 22.6%	3 3.4%	0 0	0 0	3 8.5%	0 0	2 11.1%	0 0	0 0	1 10.0%	0 0	0 0	0 0	0 0	2 2.8%	1 5.1%

Proportions/Means: Columns Tested (5% risk level) - A/B/D - C/D - E/F/G - H/I/J/K/L/M/N - P/Q
* small base; ** very small base (under 30) ineligible for sig testing

Table 294
Page 1213

Outsell/Digital Library Federation Study (2002)
Weighted Tables

TABLE 126, continued

T7D/E_15. Pre-prints SUMMARY TABLE

	TOTAL SAMPLE	RESPONDENT TYPE: FACULTY MEMBER	GRAD. STUDENT	FACULTY /GRAD	UNDER GRAD. STUDENT	INSTITUTION TYPE: PUBLIC	PRIVATE	LIBERAL ARTS	DISCIPLINE: BIOLOGIAL SCIENCES	PHYSICAL SCIENCES /MATH	SOCIAL SCIENCES	ARTS AND HUMAN.	ENGI- NEERING	BUSINESS	LAW	UNDEC. MAJOR	GENDER: MALE	FEMALE
		(A)	(B)	(C)	(D)	(E)	(F)	(G)	(H)	(I)	(J)	(K)	(L)	(M)	(N)		(P)	(Q)
Base - Use Pre-prints for teaching	84*	71*	13**	84*	0**	32**	34**	18**	16**	21**	21**	11**	3**	12**	1**	0*	62*	22**
Author	3 3.3%	3 3.9%	0 0	3 3.3%	0 0	1 3.3%	2 5.2%	0 0	3 16.7%	0 0	0 0	0 0	0 0	0 0	* 33.3%	0 0	1 1.7%	2 8.0%
All sources of info	3 3.3%	3 3.9%	0 0	3 3.3%	0 0	1 3.3%	2 5.2%	0 0	3 16.7%	0 0	0 0	0 0	0 0	0 0	* 33.3%	0 0	1 1.7%	2 8.0%
preferred source of info	1 1.2%	1 1.5%	0 0	1 1.2%	0 0	1 3.3%	0 0	0 0	1 5.6%	0 0	0 0	0 0	0 0	0 0	* 33.3%	0 0	* 0.3%	1 4.0%
Interlibrary loan (NET)	2 2.3%	2 2.7%	0 0	2 2.3%	0 0	1 2.9%	0 0	1 5.4%	0 0	1 4.8%	0 0	0 0	0 0	1 7.7%	0 0	0 0	2 3.1%	0 0
All sources of info	2 2.3%	2 2.7%	0 0	2 2.3%	0 0	1 2.9%	0 0	1 5.4%	0 0	1 4.8%	0 0	0 0	0 0	1 7.7%	0 0	0 0	2 3.1%	0 0
preferred source of info	0 0	0 0	0 0	0 0	0 0	0 0	0 0	0 0	0 0	0 0	0 0	0 0	0 0	0 0	0 0	0 0	0 0	0 0
Purchase from online bookstore (NET)	2 2.2%	2 2.6%	0 0	2 2.2%	0 0	0 0	0 0	2 10.2%	0 0	0 0	2 9.1%	0 0	0 0	0 0	0 0	0 0	2 3.0%	0 0
All sources of info	2 2.2%	2 2.6%	0 0	2 2.2%	0 0	0 0	0 0	2 10.2%	0 0	0 0	2 9.1%	0 0	0 0	0 0	0 0	0 0	2 3.0%	0 0
preferred source of info	0 0	0 0	0 0	0 0	0 0	0 0	0 0	0 0	0 0	0 0	0 0	0 0	0 0	0 0	0 0	0 0	0 0	0 0
Office (NET)	2 2.1%	2 2.5%	0 0	2 2.1%	0 0	0 0	2 5.2%	0 0	2 11.1%	0 0	0 0	0 0	0 0	0 0	0 0	0 0	1 1.4%	1 4.0%

Proportions/Means: Columns Tested (5% risk level) - A/B/D - C/D - E/F/G - H/I/J/K/L/M/N - P/Q
* small base; ** very small base (under 30) ineligible for sig testing

Table 294
Page 1214

Outsell/Digital Library Federation Study (2002)
Weighted Tables

TABLE 126, continued

T7D/E_15. Pre-prints SUMMARY TABLE

	RESPONDENT TYPE					INSTITUTION TYPE			DISCIPLINE								GENDER	
	TOTAL SAMPLE	FACULTY MEMBER	GRAD. STUDENT	FACULTY /GRAD	UNDER GRAD. STUDENT	PUBLIC	PRIVATE	LIBERAL ARTS	BIOLOGIAL SCIENCES	PHYSICAL SCIENCES /MATH	SOCIAL SCIENCES	ARTS AND HUMAN.	ENGI-NEERING	BUSINESS	LAW	UNDEC. MAJOR	MALE	FEMALE
		(A)	(B)	(C)	(D)	(E)	(F)	(G)	(H)	(I)	(J)	(K)	(L)	(M)	(N)		(P)	(Q)
Base - Use Pre-prints for teaching	84*	71*	13**	84*	0**	32**	34**	18**	16**	21**	21**	11**	3**	12**	1**	0*	62*	22**
All sources of info	2 2.1%	2 2.5%	0 0	2 2.1%	0 0	0 0	2 5.2%	0 0	2 11.1%	0 0	0 0	0 0	0 0	0 0	0 0	0 0	1 1.4%	1 4.0%
preferred source of info	2 2.1%	2 2.5%	0 0	2 2.1%	0 0	0 0	2 5.2%	0 0	2 11.1%	0 0	0 0	0 0	0 0	0 0	0 0	0 0	1 1.4%	1 4.0%
Access from course website (NET)	1 1.4%	1 1.2%	* 2.3%	1 1.4%	0 0	0 0	1 3.5%	0 0	1 5.6%	0 0	0 0	0 0	* 10.0%	0 0	0 0	0 0	* 0.5%	1 4.0%
All sources of info	1 1.4%	1 1.2%	* 2.3%	1 1.4%	0 0	0 0	1 3.5%	0 0	1 5.6%	0 0	0 0	0 0	* 10.0%	0 0	0 0	0 0	* 0.5%	1 4.0%
preferred source of info	* 0.3%	0 0	* 2.3%	* 0.3%	0 0	0 0	* 0.9%	0 0	0 0	0 0	0 0	0 0	* 10.0%	0 0	0 0	0 0	* 0.5%	0 0
Home (NET)	1 1.3%	0 0	1 8.8%	1 1.3%	0 0	1 3.5%	0 0	0 0	0 0	0 0	0 0	1 10.0%	0 0	0 0	0 0	0 0	1 1.8%	0 0
All sources of info	1 1.3%	0 0	1 8.8%	1 1.3%	0 0	1 3.5%	0 0	0 0	0 0	0 0	0 0	1 10.0%	0 0	0 0	0 0	0 0	1 1.8%	0 0
preferred source of info	0 0	0 0	0 0	0 0	0 0	0 0	0 0	0 0	0 0	0 0	0 0	0 0	0 0	0 0	0 0	0 0	0 0	0 0
Department (NET)	1 1.2%	0 0	1 7.8%	1 1.2%	0 0	1 3.1%	0 0	0 0	0 0	1 4.8%	0 0	0 0	0 0	0 0	0 0	0 0	0 0	1 4.6%
All sources of info	1 1.2%	0 0	1 7.8%	1 1.2%	0 0	1 3.1%	0 0	0 0	0 0	1 4.8%	0 0	0 0	0 0	0 0	0 0	0 0	0 0	1 4.6%

Proportions/Means: Columns Tested (5% risk level) - A/B/D - C/D - E/F/G - H/I/J/K/L/M/N - P/Q
* small base; ** very small base (under 30) ineligible for sig testing

Table 294
Page 1215

Outsell/Digital Library Federation Study (2002)
Weighted Tables

TABLE 126, continued

T7D/E_15. Pre-prints SUMMARY TABLE

		RESPONDENT TYPE				INSTITUTION TYPE			DISCIPLINE									GENDER	
	TOTAL SAMPLE	FACULTY MEMBER	GRAD. STUDENT	FACULTY /GRAD	UNDER GRAD. STUDENT	PUBLIC	PRIVATE	LIBERAL ARTS	BIOLOGIAL SCIENCES	PHYSICAL SCIENCES /MATH	SOCIAL SCIENCES	ARTS AND HUMAN.	ENGI-NEERING	BUSINESS	LAW	UNDEC. MAJOR	MALE	FEMALE
		(A)	(B)	(C)	(D)	(E)	(F)	(G)	(H)	(I)	(J)	(K)	(L)	(M)	(N)		(P)	(Q)
Base - Use Pre-prints for teaching	84*	71*	13**	84*	0**	32**	34**	18**	16**	21**	21**	11**	3**	12**	1**	0*	62*	22**
preferred source of info	1	0	1	1	0	1	0	0	0	1	0	0	0	0	0	0	0	1
	1.2%	0	7.8%	1.2%	0	3.1%	0	0	0	4.8%	0	0	0	0	0	0	0	4.6%
Publisher (NET)	1	1	0	1	0	1	0	0	0	1	0	0	0	0	0	0	1	0
	1.2%	1.4%	0	1.2%	0	3.1%	0	0	0	4.8%	0	0	0	0	0	0	1.6%	0
All sources of info	1	1	0	1	0	1	0	0	0	1	0	0	0	0	0	0	1	0
	1.2%	1.4%	0	1.2%	0	3.1%	0	0	0	4.8%	0	0	0	0	0	0	1.6%	0
preferred source of info	0	0	0	0	0	0	0	0	0	0	0	0	0	0	0	0	0	0
	0	0	0	0	0	0	0	0	0	0	0	0	0	0	0	0	0	0
Personal Collection/ Holdings (NET)	1	1	0	1	0	0	*	*	0	0	0	0	1	0	0	0	1	0
	0.7%	0.8%	0	0.7%	0	0	0.9%	1.6%	0	0	0	0	20.0%	0	0	0	0.9%	0
All sources of info	1	1	0	1	0	0	*	*	0	0	0	0	1	0	0	0	1	0
	0.7%	0.8%	0	0.7%	0	0	0.9%	1.6%	0	0	0	0	20.0%	0	0	0	0.9%	0
preferred source of info	1	1	0	1	0	0	*	*	0	0	0	0	1	0	0	0	1	0
	0.7%	0.8%	0	0.7%	0	0	0.9%	1.6%	0	0	0	0	20.0%	0	0	0	0.9%	0
Meeting/Conferences (NET)	*	*	0	*	0	0	*	0	0	0	0	0	*	0	0	0	*	0
	0.3%	0.4%	0	0.3%	0	0	0.9%	0	0	0	0	0	10.0%	0	0	0	0.5%	0
All sources of info	*	*	0	*	0	0	*	0	0	0	0	0	*	0	0	0	*	0
	0.3%	0.4%	0	0.3%	0	0	0.9%	0	0	0	0	0	10.0%	0	0	0	0.5%	0
preferred source of info	*	*	0	*	0	0	*	0	0	0	0	0	*	0	0	0	*	0
	0.3%	0.4%	0	0.3%	0	0	0.9%	0	0	0	0	0	10.0%	0	0	0	0.5%	0

Proportions/Means: Columns Tested (5% risk level) - A/B/D - C/D - E/F/G - H/I/J/K/L/M/N - P/Q
* small base; ** very small base (under 30) ineligible for sig testing

Table 294
Page 1216

Outsell/Digital Library Federation Study (2002)
Weighted Tables

TABLE 126, continued

T7D/E_15. Pre-prints SUMMARY TABLE

		RESPONDENT TYPE				INSTITUTION TYPE			DISCIPLINE									GENDER	
	TOTAL SAMPLE	FACULTY MEMBER	GRAD. STUDENT	FACULTY /GRAD	UNDER GRAD. STUDENT	PUBLIC	PRIVATE	LIBERAL ARTS	BIOLOGIAL SCIENCES	PHYSICAL SCIENCES /MATH	SOCIAL SCIENCES	ARTS AND HUMAN.	ENGI-NEERING	BUSINESS	LAW	UNDEC. MAJOR	MALE	FEMALE
		(A)	(B)	(C)	(D)	(E)	(F)	(G)	(H)	(I)	(J)	(K)	(L)	(M)	(N)		(P)	(Q)
Base - Use Pre-prints for teaching	84*	71*	13**	84*	0**	32**	34**	18**	16**	21**	21**	11**	3**	12**	1**	0*	62*	22**
Access book/journal/ journal article elsewhere online (NET)	0 0	0 0	0 0	0 0	0 0	0 0	0 0	0 0	0 0	0 0	0 0	0 0	0 0	0 0	0 0	0 0	0 0	0 0
All sources of info	0 0	0 0	0 0	0 0	0 0	0 0	0 0	0 0	0 0	0 0	0 0	0 0	0 0	0 0	0 0	0 0	0 0	0 0
preferred source of info	0 0	0 0	0 0	0 0	0 0	0 0	0 0	0 0	0 0	0 0	0 0	0 0	0 0	0 0	0 0	0 0	0 0	0 0
Ask library to purchase source (NET)	0 0	0 0	0 0	0 0	0 0	0 0	0 0	0 0	0 0	0 0	0 0	0 0	0 0	0 0	0 0	0 0	0 0	0 0
All sources of info	0 0	0 0	0 0	0 0	0 0	0 0	0 0	0 0	0 0	0 0	0 0	0 0	0 0	0 0	0 0	0 0	0 0	0 0
preferred source of info	0 0	0 0	0 0	0 0	0 0	0 0	0 0	0 0	0 0	0 0	0 0	0 0	0 0	0 0	0 0	0 0	0 0	0 0
Borrow from or use in other libraries (NET)	0 0	0 0	0 0	0 0	0 0	0 0	0 0	0 0	0 0	0 0	0 0	0 0	0 0	0 0	0 0	0 0	0 0	0 0
All sources of info	0 0	0 0	0 0	0 0	0 0	0 0	0 0	0 0	0 0	0 0	0 0	0 0	0 0	0 0	0 0	0 0	0 0	0 0

Proportions/Means: Columns Tested (5% risk level) - A/B/D - C/D - E/F/G - H/I/J/K/L/M/N - P/Q
* small base; ** very small base (under 30) ineligible for sig testing

Table 294
Page 1217

Outsell/Digital Library Federation Study (2002)
Weighted Tables

TABLE 126, continued

T7D/E_15. Pre-prints SUMMARY TABLE

		RESPONDENT TYPE				INSTITUTION TYPE			DISCIPLINE									GENDER	
	TOTAL SAMPLE	FACULTY MEMBER	GRAD. STUDENT	FACULTY /GRAD	UNDER GRAD. STUDENT	PUBLIC	PRIVATE	LIBERAL ARTS	BIOLOGIAL SCIENCES	PHYSICAL SCIENCES /MATH	SOCIAL SCIENCES	ARTS AND HUMAN.	ENGI-NEERING	BUSINESS	LAW	UNDEC. MAJOR	MALE	FEMALE
		(A)	(B)	(C)	(D)	(E)	(F)	(G)	(H)	(I)	(J)	(K)	(L)	(M)	(N)		(P)	(Q)
Base - Use Pre-prints for teaching	84*	71*	13**	84*	0**	32**	34**	18**	16**	21**	21**	11**	3**	12**	1**	0*	62*	22**
preferred source of info	0 0	0 0	0 0	0 0	0 0	0 0	0 0	0 0	0 0	0 0	0 0	0 0	0 0	0 0	0 0	0 0	0 0	0 0
Other (NET)	9 10.3%	9 12.1%	0 0	9 10.3%	0 0	3 9.0%	5 14.0%	1 5.4%	0 0	3 14.3%	6 27.3%	0 0	0 0	0 0	0 0	0 0	7 10.8%	2 8.6%
preferred source of info	8 9.1%	8 10.7%	0 0	8 9.1%	0 0	3 9.0%	5 14.0%	0 0	0 0	2 9.5%	6 27.3%	0 0	0 0	0 0	0 0	0 0	6 9.2%	2 8.6%
All sources of info	6 6.8%	6 8.1%	0 0	6 6.8%	0 0	0 0	5 14.0%	1 5.4%	0 0	2 9.5%	4 18.2%	0 0	0 0	0 0	0 0	0 0	4 6.2%	2 8.6%
DK/Refused	3 3.3%	3 3.9%	0 0	3 3.3%	0 0	2 6.1%	0 0	1 4.8%	1 5.6%	1 4.8%	0 0	0 0	0 0	1 7.7%	0 0	0 0	2 3.1%	1 4.0%

Proportions/Means: Columns Tested (5% risk level) - A/B/D - C/D - E/F/G - H/I/J/K/L/M/N - P/Q
* small base; ** very small base (under 30) ineligible for sig testing

Table 294
Page 1218

TABLE 127

T7sum_16. Dissertations SUMMARY TABLE

		RESPONDENT TYPE				INSTITUTION TYPE			DISCIPLINE									GENDER	
	TOTAL SAMPLE	FACULTY MEMBER	GRAD. STUDENT	FACULTY /GRAD	UNDER GRAD. STUDENT	PUBLIC	PRIVATE	LIBERAL ARTS	BIOLOGIAL SCIENCES	PHYSICAL SCIENCES /MATH	SOCIAL SCIENCES	ARTS AND HUMAN.	ENGI- NEERING	BUSINESS	LAW	UNDEC. MAJOR	MALE	FEMALE
		(A)	(B)	(C)	(D)	(E)	(F)	(G)	(H)	(I)	(J)	(K)	(L)	(M)	(N)		(P)	(Q)
Base - USe Dissertations for teaching	83*	60*	23**	83*	0**	33**	34**	16**	11**	14**	23**	25**	4**	7**	***	0*	60*	23**
ONLINE	49 59.4%	37 61.8%	12 53.0%	49 59.4%	0 0	18 56.3%	17 51.8%	13 81.3%	6 58.3%	10 71.4%	13 58.3%	16 63.6%	2 53.3%	2 28.6%	0 0	0 0	35 58.7%	14 61.3%
Online databases	15 17.7%	10 16.1%	5 22.0%	15 17.7%	0 0	6 19.6%	5 14.8%	3 19.8%	1 8.3%	3 21.4%	4 16.7%	7 27.3%	* 6.7%	0 0	0 0	0 0	11 19.0%	3 14.5%
All sources of info	15 17.7%	10 16.1%	5 22.0%	15 17.7%	0 0	6 19.6%	5 14.8%	3 19.8%	1 8.3%	3 21.4%	4 16.7%	7 27.3%	* 6.7%	0 0	0 0	0 0	11 19.0%	3 14.5%
preferred source of info	13 15.1%	8 12.5%	5 22.0%	13 15.1%	0 0	4 13.1%	5 14.8%	3 19.8%	1 8.3%	2 14.3%	4 16.7%	6 22.7%	* 6.7%	0 0	0 0	0 0	9 15.4%	3 14.5%
Search engine	8 10.2%	6 10.8%	2 8.8%	8 10.2%	0 0	4 12.7%	1 3.0%	3 20.1%	1 8.3%	3 21.4%	0 0	3 13.6%	* 6.7%	1 14.3%	0 0	0 0	7 12.5%	1 4.3%
All sources of info	8 10.2%	6 10.8%	2 8.8%	8 10.2%	0 0	4 12.7%	1 3.0%	3 20.1%	1 8.3%	3 21.4%	0 0	3 13.6%	* 6.7%	1 14.3%	0 0	0 0	7 12.5%	1 4.3%
preferred source of info	4 4.8%	3 5.0%	1 4.4%	4 4.8%	0 0	1 3.1%	0 0	3 18.4%	1 8.3%	2 14.3%	0 0	1 4.5%	0 0	0 0	0 0	0 0	4 6.7%	0 0
Your own institution's web site	8 9.9%	6 9.8%	2 10.1%	8 9.9%	0 0	3 8.6%	3 7.7%	3 16.9%	2 16.7%	0 0	2 8.3%	3 13.6%	1 26.7%	0 0	0 0	0 0	7 11.8%	1 4.8%
All sources of info	8 9.9%	6 9.8%	2 10.1%	8 9.9%	0 0	3 8.6%	3 7.7%	3 16.9%	2 16.7%	0 0	2 8.3%	3 13.6%	1 26.7%	0 0	0 0	0 0	7 11.8%	1 4.8%

Proportions/Means: Columns Tested (5% risk level) - A/B/D - C/D - E/F/G - H/I/J/K/L/M/N - P/Q
* small base; ** very small base (under 30) ineligible for sig testing

Table 298
Page 1230

Outsell/Digital Library Federation Study (2002)
Weighted Tables

TABLE 127, continued

T7sum_16. Dissertations SUMMARY TABLE

		RESPONDENT TYPE				INSTITUTION TYPE			DISCIPLINE									GENDER	
	TOTAL SAMPLE	FACULTY MEMBER	GRAD. STUDENT	FACULTY /GRAD	UNDER GRAD. STUDENT	PUBLIC	PRIVATE	LIBERAL ARTS	BIOLOGIAL SCIENCES	PHYSICAL SCIENCES /MATH	SOCIAL SCIENCES	ARTS AND HUMAN.	ENGI- NEERING	BUSINESS	LAW	UNDEC. MAJOR	MALE	FEMALE
		(A)	(B)	(C)	(D)	(E)	(F)	(G)	(H)	(I)	(J)	(K)	(L)	(M)	(N)		(P)	(Q)
Base - USe Dissertations for teaching	83*	60*	23**	83*	0**	33**	34**	16**	11**	14**	23**	25**	4**	7**	***	0*	60*	23**
preferred source of info	6 6.7%	3 5.5%	2 10.1%	6 6.7%	0 0	1 4.3%	2 6.8%	2 11.5%	1 8.3%	0 0	2 8.3%	2 9.1%	1 13.3%	0 0	0 0	0 0	4 7.5%	1 4.8%
Online library catalogues and finding aids	8 9.2%	6 9.5%	2 8.3%	8 9.2%	0 0	3 9.3%	2 5.9%	3 15.5%	2 16.7%	0 0	2 8.3%	3 13.6%	1 13.3%	0 0	0 0	0 0	6 9.4%	2 8.6%
All sources of info	8 9.2%	6 9.5%	2 8.3%	8 9.2%	0 0	3 9.3%	2 5.9%	3 15.5%	2 16.7%	0 0	2 8.3%	3 13.6%	1 13.3%	0 0	0 0	0 0	6 9.4%	2 8.6%
preferred source of info	5 6.5%	3 5.8%	2 8.3%	5 6.5%	0 0	3 9.3%	1 2.6%	1 8.6%	2 16.7%	0 0	2 8.3%	1 4.5%	1 13.3%	0 0	0 0	0 0	3 5.6%	2 8.6%
Internet searches	5 6.1%	5 8.4%	0 0	5 6.1%	0 0	3 8.9%	2 6.3%	0 0	0 0	3 21.4%	0 0	1 4.5%	0 0	1 14.3%	0 0	0 0	3 4.9%	2 9.1%
All sources of info	5 6.1%	5 8.4%	0 0	5 6.1%	0 0	3 8.9%	2 6.3%	0 0	0 0	3 21.4%	0 0	1 4.5%	0 0	1 14.3%	0 0	0 0	3 4.9%	2 9.1%
preferred source of info	4 4.7%	4 6.5%	0 0	4 4.7%	0 0	3 8.9%	1 3.0%	0 0	0 0	3 21.4%	0 0	0 0	0 0	1 14.3%	0 0	0 0	3 4.9%	1 4.3%
Web directory/ subject related web site	4 5.0%	4 6.9%	0 0	4 5.0%	0 0	2 7.0%	0 0	2 11.5%	0 0	2 14.3%	2 8.3%	0 0	* 6.7%	0 0	0 0	0 0	2 3.8%	2 8.1%
All sources of info	4 5.0%	4 6.9%	0 0	4 5.0%	0 0	2 7.0%	0 0	2 11.5%	0 0	2 14.3%	2 8.3%	0 0	* 6.7%	0 0	0 0	0 0	2 3.8%	2 8.1%

Proportions/Means: Columns Tested (5% risk level) - A/B/D - C/D - E/F/G - H/I/J/K/L/M/N - P/Q
* small base; ** very small base (under 30) ineligible for sig testing

Table 298
Page 1231

Outsell/Digital Library Federation Study (2002)
Weighted Tables

TABLE 127, continued

T7sum_16. Dissertations SUMMARY TABLE

		RESPONDENT TYPE				INSTITUTION TYPE			DISCIPLINE									GENDER	
	TOTAL SAMPLE	FACULTY MEMBER	GRAD. STUDENT	FACULTY /GRAD	UNDER GRAD. STUDENT	PUBLIC	PRIVATE	LIBERAL ARTS	BIOLOGIAL SCIENCES	PHYSICAL SCIENCES /MATH	SOCIAL SCIENCES	ARTS AND HUMAN.	ENGI- NEERING	BUSINESS	LAW	UNDEC. MAJOR	MALE	FEMALE
		(A)	(B)	(C)	(D)	(E)	(F)	(G)	(H)	(I)	(J)	(K)	(L)	(M)	(N)		(P)	(Q)
Base - USe Dissertations for teaching	83*	60*	23**	83*	0**	33**	34**	16**	11**	14**	23**	25**	4**	7**	***	0*	60*	23**
preferred source of info	3 3.5%	3 4.8%	0 0	3 3.5%	0 0	1 3.1%	0 0	2 11.5%	0 0	1 7.1%	2 8.3%	0 0	0 0	0 0	0 0	0 0	1 1.7%	2 8.1%
Online abstracting and indexing services	3 3.7%	3 5.1%	0 0	3 3.7%	0 0	* 0.9%	3 8.2%	0 0	1 8.3%	0 0	2 8.3%	0 0	* 6.7%	0 0	0 0	0 0	3 5.1%	0 0
All sources of info	3 3.7%	3 5.1%	0 0	3 3.7%	0 0	* 0.9%	3 8.2%	0 0	1 8.3%	0 0	2 8.3%	0 0	* 6.7%	0 0	0 0	0 0	3 5.1%	0 0
preferred source of info	1 1.4%	1 1.9%	0 0	1 1.4%	0 0	* 0.9%	1 2.6%	0 0	1 8.3%	0 0	0 0	0 0	* 6.7%	0 0	0 0	0 0	1 2.0%	0 0
Department web page	3 3.3%	2 3.1%	1 3.9%	3 3.3%	0 0	0 0	1 2.6%	2 11.5%	1 8.3%	0 0	2 8.3%	0 0	0 0	0 0	0 0	0 0	0 0	3 11.9%
All sources of info	3 3.3%	2 3.1%	1 3.9%	3 3.3%	0 0	0 0	1 2.6%	2 11.5%	1 8.3%	0 0	2 8.3%	0 0	0 0	0 0	0 0	0 0	0 0	3 11.9%
preferred source of info	1 1.1%	0 0	1 3.9%	1 1.1%	0 0	0 0	1 2.6%	0 0	1 8.3%	0 0	0 0	0 0	0 0	0 0	0 0	0 0	0 0	1 3.8%
Your own personal electronic library/files	1 1.4%	1 1.9%	0 0	1 1.4%	0 0	0 0	1 3.3%	0 0	0 0	0 0	0 0	1 4.5%	0 0	0 0	0 0	0 0	1 1.9%	0 0
All sources of info	1 1.4%	1 1.9%	0 0	1 1.4%	0 0	0 0	1 3.3%	0 0	0 0	0 0	0 0	1 4.5%	0 0	0 0	0 0	0 0	1 1.9%	0 0

Proportions/Means: Columns Tested (5% risk level) - A/B/D - C/D - E/F/G - H/I/J/K/L/M/N - P/Q
* small base; ** very small base (under 30) ineligible for sig testing

Table 298
Page 1232

Outsell/Digital Library Federation Study (2002)
Weighted Tables

TABLE 127, continued

T7sum_16. Dissertations SUMMARY TABLE

		RESPONDENT TYPE				INSTITUTION TYPE			DISCIPLINE								GENDER	
	TOTAL SAMPLE	FACULTY MEMBER	GRAD. STUDENT	FACULTY /GRAD	UNDER GRAD. STUDENT	PUBLIC	PRIVATE	LIBERAL ARTS	BIOLOGIAL SCIENCES	PHYSICAL SCIENCES /MATH	SOCIAL SCIENCES	ARTS AND HUMAN.	ENGI- NEERING	BUSINESS	LAW	UNDEC. MAJOR	MALE	FEMALE
		(A)	(B)	(C)	(D)	(E)	(F)	(G)	(H)	(I)	(J)	(K)	(L)	(M)	(N)		(P)	(Q)
Base - USe Dissertations for teaching	83*	60*	23**	83*	0**	33**	34**	16**	11**	14**	23**	25**	4**	7**	***	0*	60*	23**
preferred source of info	1 1.4%	1 1.9%	0 0	1 1.4%	0 0	0 0	1 3.3%	0 0	0 0	0 0	0 0	1 4.5%	0 0	0 0	0 0	0 0	1 1.9%	0 0
Online reference service	* 0.4%	* 0.5%	0 0	* 0.4%	0 0	* 0.9%	0 0	0 0	0 0	0 0	0 0	0 0	* 6.7%	0 0	0 0	0 0	* 0.5%	0 0
All sources of info	* 0.4%	* 0.5%	0 0	* 0.4%	0 0	* 0.9%	0 0	0 0	0 0	0 0	0 0	0 0	* 6.7%	0 0	0 0	0 0	* 0.5%	0 0
preferred source of info	0 0	0 0	0 0	0 0	0 0	0 0	0 0	0 0	0 0	0 0	0 0	0 0	0 0	0 0	0 0	0 0	0 0	0 0
E-mail listservs	0 0	0 0	0 0	0 0	0 0	0 0	0 0	0 0	0 0	0 0	0 0	0 0	0 0	0 0	0 0	0 0	0 0	0 0
All sources of info	0 0	0 0	0 0	0 0	0 0	0 0	0 0	0 0	0 0	0 0	0 0	0 0	0 0	0 0	0 0	0 0	0 0	0 0
preferred source of info	0 0	0 0	0 0	0 0	0 0	0 0	0 0	0 0	0 0	0 0	0 0	0 0	0 0	0 0	0 0	0 0	0 0	0 0
Online bookstore	0 0	0 0	0 0	0 0	0 0	0 0	0 0	0 0	0 0	0 0	0 0	0 0	0 0	0 0	0 0	0 0	0 0	0 0
All sources of info	0 0	0 0	0 0	0 0	0 0	0 0	0 0	0 0	0 0	0 0	0 0	0 0	0 0	0 0	0 0	0 0	0 0	0 0
preferred source of info	0 0	0 0	0 0	0 0	0 0	0 0	0 0	0 0	0 0	0 0	0 0	0 0	0 0	0 0	0 0	0 0	0 0	0 0

Proportions/Means: Columns Tested (5% risk level) - A/B/D - C/D - E/F/G - H/I/J/K/L/M/N - P/Q
* small base; ** very small base (under 30) ineligible for sig testing

Table 298
Page 1233

Outsell/Digital Library Federation Study (2002)
Weighted Tables

TABLE 127, continued

T7sum_16. Dissertations SUMMARY TABLE

		RESPONDENT TYPE				INSTITUTION TYPE			DISCIPLINE								GENDER	
	TOTAL SAMPLE	FACULTY MEMBER	GRAD. STUDENT	FACULTY /GRAD	UNDER GRAD. STUDENT	PUBLIC	PRIVATE	LIBERAL ARTS	BIOLOGIAL SCIENCES	PHYSICAL SCIENCES /MATH	SOCIAL SCIENCES	ARTS AND HUMAN.	ENGI- NEERING	BUSINESS	LAW	UNDEC. MAJOR	MALE	FEMALE
		(A)	(B)	(C)	(D)	(E)	(F)	(G)	(H)	(I)	(J)	(K)	(L)	(M)	(N)		(P)	(Q)
Base - USe Dissertations for teaching	83*	60*	23**	83*	0**	33**	34**	16**	11**	14**	23**	25**	4**	7**	***	0*	60*	23**
LIBRARY/PRINT	36 42.9%	31 51.6%	5 19.9%	36 42.9%	0 0	15 45.0%	14 40.7%	7 43.1%	4 41.7%	6 42.9%	6 25.0%	12 50.0%	2 53.3%	5 71.4%	* 100.0%	0 0	24 39.8%	12 50.9%
Campus library	25 30.6%	22 36.5%	3 15.0%	25 30.6%	0 0	10 29.7%	9 27.9%	6 37.8%	3 25.0%	4 28.6%	6 25.0%	9 36.4%	2 46.7%	2 28.6%	* 100.0%	0 0	13 22.6%	12 50.9%
All sources of info	25 30.6%	22 36.5%	3 15.0%	25 30.6%	0 0	10 29.7%	9 27.9%	6 37.8%	3 25.0%	4 28.6%	6 25.0%	9 36.4%	2 46.7%	2 28.6%	* 100.0%	0 0	13 22.6%	12 50.9%
preferred source of info	9 10.4%	6 10.1%	3 11.1%	9 10.4%	0 0	4 12.9%	2 7.3%	2 11.5%	1 8.3%	1 7.1%	2 8.3%	3 13.6%	1 33.3%	0 0	0 0	0 0	4 7.5%	4 17.7%
Another library	5 6.3%	5 8.7%	0 0	5 6.3%	0 0	2 6.3%	1 2.6%	2 14.0%	2 16.7%	0 0	0 0	2 9.1%	* 6.7%	1 14.3%	0 0	0 0	5 8.8%	0 0
All sources of info	5 6.3%	5 8.7%	0 0	5 6.3%	0 0	2 6.3%	1 2.6%	2 14.0%	2 16.7%	0 0	0 0	2 9.1%	* 6.7%	1 14.3%	0 0	0 0	5 8.8%	0 0
preferred source of info	2 2.2%	2 3.0%	0 0	2 2.2%	0 0	1 2.8%	1 2.6%	0 0	1 8.3%	0 0	0 0	0 0	0 0	1 14.3%	0 0	0 0	2 3.0%	0 0
Your own personal physical library/ files/bookshelves	5 6.2%	5 8.6%	0 0	5 6.2%	0 0	3 9.2%	2 6.4%	0 0	1 8.3%	1 7.1%	2 8.3%	1 4.5%	* 6.7%	0 0	0 0	0 0	2 4.0%	3 11.9%
All sources of info	5 6.2%	5 8.6%	0 0	5 6.2%	0 0	3 9.2%	2 6.4%	0 0	1 8.3%	1 7.1%	2 8.3%	1 4.5%	* 6.7%	0 0	0 0	0 0	2 4.0%	3 11.9%

Proportions/Means: Columns Tested (5% risk level) - A/B/D - C/D - E/F/G - H/I/J/K/L/M/N - P/Q
* small base; ** very small base (under 30) ineligible for sig testing

Table 298
Page 1234

Outsell/Digital Library Federation Study (2002)
Weighted Tables

TABLE 127, continued

T7sum_16. Dissertations SUMMARY TABLE

		RESPONDENT TYPE				INSTITUTION TYPE			DISCIPLINE									GENDER	
	TOTAL SAMPLE	FACULTY MEMBER	GRAD. STUDENT	FACULTY /GRAD	UNDER GRAD. STUDENT	PUBLIC	PRIVATE	LIBERAL ARTS	BIOLOGIAL SCIENCES	PHYSICAL SCIENCES /MATH	SOCIAL SCIENCES	ARTS AND HUMAN.	ENGI-NEERING	BUSINESS	LAW	UNDEC. MAJOR	MALE	FEMALE
		(A)	(B)	(C)	(D)	(E)	(F)	(G)	(H)	(I)	(J)	(K)	(L)	(M)	(N)		(P)	(Q)
Base - USe Dissertations for teaching	83*	60*	23**	83*	0**	33**	34**	16**	11**	14**	23**	25**	4**	7**	***	0*	60*	23**
preferred source of info	3 3.8%	3 5.3%	0 0	3 3.8%	0 0	1 3.1%	2 6.4%	0 0	0 0	1 7.1%	2 8.3%	0 0	* 6.7%	0 0	0 0	0 0	1 2.2%	2 8.1%
References cited in books or journal articles	3 3.8%	3 5.3%	0 0	3 3.8%	0 0	1 3.4%	2 6.1%	0 0	0 0	0 0	0 0	2 9.1%	0 0	1 14.3%	0 0	0 0	3 5.3%	0 0
All sources of info	3 3.8%	3 5.3%	0 0	3 3.8%	0 0	1 3.4%	2 6.1%	0 0	0 0	0 0	0 0	2 9.1%	0 0	1 14.3%	0 0	0 0	3 5.3%	0 0
preferred source of info	2 2.5%	2 3.4%	0 0	2 2.5%	0 0	0 0	2 6.1%	0 0	0 0	0 0	0 0	1 4.5%	0 0	1 14.3%	0 0	0 0	2 3.4%	0 0
Personal subscriptions to newspapers, magazines and journals	2 2.9%	2 4.0%	0 0	2 2.9%	0 0	2 7.4%	0 0	0 0	0 0	1 7.1%	0 0	1 4.5%	* 6.7%	0 0	0 0	0 0	2 4.0%	0 0
All sources of info	2 2.9%	2 4.0%	0 0	2 2.9%	0 0	2 7.4%	0 0	0 0	0 0	1 7.1%	0 0	1 4.5%	* 6.7%	0 0	0 0	0 0	2 4.0%	0 0
preferred source of info	0 0	0 0	0 0	0 0	0 0	0 0	0 0	0 0	0 0	0 0	0 0	0 0	0 0	0 0	0 0	0 0	0 0	0 0
Printed abstracting and indexing services	2 2.5%	1 1.5%	1 4.9%	2 2.5%	0 0	1 2.8%	1 3.3%	0 0	0 0	0 0	0 0	1 4.5%	0 0	1 14.3%	0 0	0 0	2 3.4%	0 0

Proportions/Means: Columns Tested (5% risk level) - A/B/D - C/D - E/F/G - H/I/J/K/L/M/N - P/Q
* small base; ** very small base (under 30) ineligible for sig testing

Table 298
Page 1235

Outsell/Digital Library Federation Study (2002)
Weighted Tables

TABLE 127, continued

T7sum_16. Dissertations SUMMARY TABLE

		RESPONDENT TYPE				INSTITUTION TYPE			DISCIPLINE								GENDER	
	TOTAL SAMPLE	FACULTY MEMBER	GRAD. STUDENT	FACULTY /GRAD	UNDER GRAD. STUDENT	PUBLIC	PRIVATE	LIBERAL ARTS	BIOLOGIAL SCIENCES	PHYSICAL SCIENCES /MATH	SOCIAL SCIENCES	ARTS AND HUMAN.	ENGI-NEERING	BUSINESS	LAW	UNDEC. MAJOR	MALE	FEMALE
		(A)	(B)	(C)	(D)	(E)	(F)	(G)	(H)	(I)	(J)	(K)	(L)	(M)	(N)		(P)	(Q)
Base - USe Dissertations for teaching	83*	60*	23**	83*	0**	33**	34**	16**	11**	14**	23**	25**	4**	7**	***	0*	60*	23**
All sources of info	2 2.5%	1 1.5%	1 4.9%	2 2.5%	0 0	1 2.8%	1 3.3%	0 0	0 0	0 0	0 0	1 4.5%	0 0	1 14.3%	0 0	0 0	2 3.4%	0 0
preferred source of info	2 2.5%	1 1.5%	1 4.9%	2 2.5%	0 0	1 2.8%	1 3.3%	0 0	0 0	0 0	0 0	1 4.5%	0 0	1 14.3%	0 0	0 0	2 3.4%	0 0
Printed library catalogues and finding aids	1 1.4%	1 1.9%	0 0	1 1.4%	0 0	1 3.4%	0 0	0 0	0 0	0 0	0 0	1 4.5%	0 0	0 0	0 0	0 0	1 1.9%	0 0
All sources of info	1 1.4%	1 1.9%	0 0	1 1.4%	0 0	1 3.4%	0 0	0 0	0 0	0 0	0 0	1 4.5%	0 0	0 0	0 0	0 0	1 1.9%	0 0
preferred source of info	1 1.4%	1 1.9%	0 0	1 1.4%	0 0	1 3.4%	0 0	0 0	0 0	0 0	0 0	1 4.5%	0 0	0 0	0 0	0 0	1 1.9%	0 0
Physical bookstore	1 1.4%	1 1.9%	0 0	1 1.4%	0 0	1 3.4%	0 0	0 0	0 0	0 0	0 0	1 4.5%	0 0	0 0	0 0	0 0	1 1.9%	0 0
All sources of info	1 1.4%	1 1.9%	0 0	1 1.4%	0 0	1 3.4%	0 0	0 0	0 0	0 0	0 0	1 4.5%	0 0	0 0	0 0	0 0	1 1.9%	0 0
preferred source of info	0 0	0 0	0 0	0 0	0 0	0 0	0 0	0 0	0 0	0 0	0 0	0 0	0 0	0 0	0 0	0 0	0 0	0 0
PERSONAL ASSISTANCE	30 36.4%	23 38.1%	7 31.7%	30 36.4%	0 0	12 37.2%	15 43.4%	3 20.1%	3 25.0%	4 28.6%	13 58.3%	6 22.7%	2 40.0%	3 42.9%	* 100.0%	0 0	20 34.0%	10 42.5%

Proportions/Means: Columns Tested (5% risk level) - A/B/D - C/D - E/F/G - H/I/J/K/L/M/N - P/Q
* small base; ** very small base (under 30) ineligible for sig testing

Table 298
Page 1236

Outsell/Digital Library Federation Study (2002)
Weighted Tables

TABLE 127, continued

T7sum_16. Dissertations SUMMARY TABLE

		RESPONDENT TYPE				INSTITUTION TYPE			DISCIPLINE									GENDER	
	TOTAL SAMPLE	FACULTY MEMBER	GRAD. STUDENT	FACULTY /GRAD	UNDER GRAD. STUDENT	PUBLIC	PRIVATE	LIBERAL ARTS	BIOLOGIAL SCIENCES	PHYSICAL SCIENCES /MATH	SOCIAL SCIENCES	ARTS AND HUMAN.	ENGI-NEERING	BUSINESS	LAW	UNDEC. MAJOR	MALE	FEMALE
		(A)	(B)	(C)	(D)	(E)	(F)	(G)	(H)	(I)	(J)	(K)	(L)	(M)	(N)		(P)	(Q)
Base - USe Dissertations for teaching	83*	60*	23**	83*	0**	33**	34**	16**	11**	14**	23**	25**	4**	7**	***	0*	60*	23**
Colleagues inside your institution	17 20.0%	11 18.6%	5 23.5%	17 20.0%	0 0	8 24.1%	9 25.6%	0 0	3 25.0%	3 21.4%	6 25.0%	1 4.5%	1 26.7%	3 42.9%	* 100.0%	0 0	10 16.2%	7 29.5%
All sources of info	17 20.0%	11 18.6%	5 23.5%	17 20.0%	0 0	8 24.1%	9 25.6%	0 0	3 25.0%	3 21.4%	6 25.0%	1 4.5%	1 26.7%	3 42.9%	* 100.0%	0 0	10 16.2%	7 29.5%
preferred source of info	7 8.6%	3 5.2%	4 17.8%	7 8.6%	0 0	3 10.4%	4 11.2%	0 0	1 8.3%	1 7.1%	4 16.7%	0 0	1 13.3%	1 14.3%	0 0	0 0	3 5.2%	4 17.4%
A librarian in your institution	16 18.7%	14 22.7%	2 8.3%	16 18.7%	0 0	4 13.1%	8 23.5%	3 20.1%	1 8.3%	1 7.1%	9 41.7%	3 13.6%	1 20.0%	0 0	0 0	0 0	12 19.7%	4 16.2%
All sources of info	16 18.7%	14 22.7%	2 8.3%	16 18.7%	0 0	4 13.1%	8 23.5%	3 20.1%	1 8.3%	1 7.1%	9 41.7%	3 13.6%	1 20.0%	0 0	0 0	0 0	12 19.7%	4 16.2%
preferred source of info	6 7.2%	4 6.9%	2 8.3%	6 7.2%	0 0	2 5.7%	3 8.9%	1 6.9%	0 0	0 0	4 16.7%	2 9.1%	0 0	0 0	0 0	0 0	6 10.1%	0 0
Colleagues outside your institution	8 9.6%	8 13.2%	0 0	8 9.6%	0 0	3 9.5%	5 14.3%	0 0	1 8.3%	2 14.3%	2 8.3%	2 9.1%	0 0	1 14.3%	0 0	0 0	6 9.9%	2 8.8%
All sources of info	8 9.6%	8 13.2%	0 0	8 9.6%	0 0	3 9.5%	5 14.3%	0 0	1 8.3%	2 14.3%	2 8.3%	2 9.1%	0 0	1 14.3%	0 0	0 0	6 9.9%	2 8.8%
preferred source of info	4 4.8%	4 6.7%	0 0	4 4.8%	0 0	1 3.1%	3 8.9%	0 0	0 0	1 7.1%	2 8.3%	1 4.5%	0 0	0 0	0 0	0 0	3 4.8%	1 4.8%
Professional meetings	2 2.3%	2 3.1%	0 0	2 2.3%	0 0	0 0	2 5.6%	0 0	0 0	0 0	2 8.3%	0 0	0 0	0 0	0 0	0 0	2 3.2%	0 0

Proportions/Means: Columns Tested (5% risk level) - A/B/D - C/D - E/F/G - H/I/J/K/L/M/N - P/Q
* small base; ** very small base (under 30) ineligible for sig testing

Table 298
Page 1237

Outsell/Digital Library Federation Study (2002)
Weighted Tables

TABLE 127, continued

T7sum_16. Dissertations SUMMARY TABLE

	TOTAL SAMPLE	RESPONDENT TYPE: FACULTY MEMBER	GRAD. STUDENT	FACULTY /GRAD	UNDER GRAD. STUDENT	INSTITUTION TYPE: PUBLIC	PRIVATE	LIBERAL ARTS	DISCIPLINE: BIOLOGIAL SCIENCES	PHYSICAL SCIENCES /MATH	SOCIAL SCIENCES	ARTS AND HUMAN.	ENGI-NEERING	BUSINESS	LAW	UNDEC. MAJOR	GENDER: MALE	FEMALE
		(A)	(B)	(C)	(D)	(E)	(F)	(G)	(H)	(I)	(J)	(K)	(L)	(M)	(N)		(P)	(Q)
Base - USe Dissertations for teaching	83*	60*	23**	83*	0**	33**	34**	16**	11**	14**	23**	25**	4**	7**	***	0*	60*	23**
All sources of info	2 2.3%	2 3.1%	0 0	2 2.3%	0 0	0 0	2 5.6%	0 0	0 0	0 0	2 8.3%	0 0	0 0	0 0	0 0	0 0	2 3.2%	0 0
preferred source of info	0 0	0 0	0 0	0 0	0 0	0 0	0 0	0 0	0 0	0 0	0 0	0 0	0 0	0 0	0 0	0 0	0 0	0 0
Another institution's librarian	1 1.2%	0 0	1 4.4%	1 1.2%	0 0	1 3.1%	0 0	0 0	0 0	1 7.1%	0 0	0 0	0 0	0 0	0 0	0 0	1 1.7%	0 0
All sources of info	1 1.2%	0 0	1 4.4%	1 1.2%	0 0	1 3.1%	0 0	0 0	0 0	1 7.1%	0 0	0 0	0 0	0 0	0 0	0 0	1 1.7%	0 0
preferred source of info	0 0	0 0	0 0	0 0	0 0	0 0	0 0	0 0	0 0	0 0	0 0	0 0	0 0	0 0	0 0	0 0	0 0	0 0
Personal office/lab	* 0.4%	* 0.5%	0 0	* 0.4%	0 0	0 0	* 0.9%	0 0	0 0	0 0	0 0	0 0	* 6.7%	0 0	0 0	0 0	* 0.5%	0 0
All sources of info	* 0.4%	* 0.5%	0 0	* 0.4%	0 0	0 0	* 0.9%	0 0	0 0	0 0	0 0	0 0	* 6.7%	0 0	0 0	0 0	* 0.5%	0 0
preferred source of info	0 0	0 0	0 0	0 0	0 0	0 0	0 0	0 0	0 0	0 0	0 0	0 0	0 0	0 0	0 0	0 0	0 0	0 0
Students	* 0.4%	* 0.5%	0 0	* 0.4%	0 0	0 0	* 0.9%	0 0	0 0	0 0	0 0	0 0	* 6.7%	0 0	0 0	0 0	* 0.5%	0 0

Proportions/Means: Columns Tested (5% risk level) - A/B/D - C/D - E/F/G - H/I/J/K/L/M/N - P/Q
* small base; ** very small base (under 30) ineligible for sig testing

Table 298
Page 1238

Outsell/Digital Library Federation Study (2002)
Weighted Tables

TABLE 127, continued

T7sum_16. Dissertations SUMMARY TABLE

		RESPONDENT TYPE				INSTITUTION TYPE			DISCIPLINE								GENDER	
	TOTAL SAMPLE	FACULTY MEMBER	GRAD. STUDENT	FACULTY /GRAD	UNDER GRAD. STUDENT	PUBLIC	PRIVATE	LIBERAL ARTS	BIOLOGIAL SCIENCES	PHYSICAL SCIENCES /MATH	SOCIAL SCIENCES	ARTS AND HUMAN.	ENGI- NEERING	BUSINESS	LAW	UNDEC. MAJOR	MALE	FEMALE
		(A)	(B)	(C)	(D)	(E)	(F)	(G)	(H)	(I)	(J)	(K)	(L)	(M)	(N)		(P)	(Q)
Base - USe Dissertations for teaching	83*	60*	23**	83*	0**	33**	34**	16**	11**	14**	23**	25**	4**	7**	***	0*	60*	23**
All sources of info	*	*	0	*	0	0	*	0	0	0	0	0	*	0	0	0	*	0
	0.4%	0.5%	0	0.4%	0	0	0.9%	0	0	0	0	0	6.7%	0	0	0	0.5%	0
preferred source of info	0	0	0	0	0	0	0	0	0	0	0	0	0	0	0	0	0	0
	0	0	0	0	0	0	0	0	0	0	0	0	0	0	0	0	0	0
Online (unspecified)	0	0	0	0	0	0	0	0	0	0	0	0	0	0	0	0	0	0
	0	0	0	0	0	0	0	0	0	0	0	0	0	0	0	0	0	0
All sources of info	0	0	0	0	0	0	0	0	0	0	0	0	0	0	0	0	0	0
	0	0	0	0	0	0	0	0	0	0	0	0	0	0	0	0	0	0
preferred source of info	0	0	0	0	0	0	0	0	0	0	0	0	0	0	0	0	0	0
	0	0	0	0	0	0	0	0	0	0	0	0	0	0	0	0	0	0
Author	0	0	0	0	0	0	0	0	0	0	0	0	0	0	0	0	0	0
	0	0	0	0	0	0	0	0	0	0	0	0	0	0	0	0	0	0
All sources of info	0	0	0	0	0	0	0	0	0	0	0	0	0	0	0	0	0	0
	0	0	0	0	0	0	0	0	0	0	0	0	0	0	0	0	0	0
preferred source of info	0	0	0	0	0	0	0	0	0	0	0	0	0	0	0	0	0	0
	0	0	0	0	0	0	0	0	0	0	0	0	0	0	0	0	0	0
Other	4	2	1	4	0	*	3	1	0	1	0	2	1	0	0	0	3	1
	4.6%	4.0%	6.2%	4.6%	0	0.9%	7.5%	6.1%	0	7.1%	0	9.1%	13.3%	0	0	0	4.5%	4.8%
All sources of info	4	2	1	4	0	*	3	1	0	1	0	2	1	0	0	0	3	1
	4.6%	4.0%	6.2%	4.6%	0	0.9%	7.5%	6.1%	0	7.1%	0	9.1%	13.3%	0	0	0	4.5%	4.8%

Proportions/Means: Columns Tested (5% risk level) - A/B/D - C/D - E/F/G - H/I/J/K/L/M/N - P/Q
* small base; ** very small base (under 30) ineligible for sig testing

Table 298
Page 1239

Outsell/Digital Library Federation Study (2002)
Weighted Tables

TABLE 127, continued

T7sum_16. Dissertations SUMMARY TABLE

		RESPONDENT TYPE				INSTITUTION TYPE			DISCIPLINE								GENDER	
	TOTAL SAMPLE	FACULTY MEMBER	GRAD. STUDENT	FACULTY /GRAD	UNDER GRAD. STUDENT	PUBLIC	PRIVATE	LIBERAL ARTS	BIOLOGIAL SCIENCES	PHYSICAL SCIENCES /MATH	SOCIAL SCIENCES	ARTS AND HUMAN.	ENGI-NEERING	BUSINESS	LAW	UNDEC. MAJOR	MALE	FEMALE
		(A)	(B)	(C)	(D)	(E)	(F)	(G)	(H)	(I)	(J)	(K)	(L)	(M)	(N)		(P)	(Q)
Base - USe Dissertations for teaching	83*	60*	23**	83*	0**	33**	34**	16**	11**	14**	23**	25**	4**	7**	***	0*	60*	23**
preferred source of info	2 2.9%	1 2.1%	1 4.9%	2 2.9%	0 0	0 0	1 4.2%	1 6.1%	0 0	1 7.1%	0 0	1 4.5%	* 6.7%	0 0	0 0	0 0	2 4.0%	0 0
DK/Refused	7 8.5%	6 10.0%	1 4.4%	7 8.5%	0 0	4 13.1%	2 5.4%	1 5.7%	2 16.7%	1 7.1%	0 0	2 9.1%	0 0	2 28.6%	* 100.0%	0 0	5 8.8%	2 7.8%

Proportions/Means: Columns Tested (5% risk level) - A/B/D - C/D - E/F/G - H/I/J/K/L/M/N - P/Q
* small base; ** very small base (under 30) ineligible for sig testing

Table 298
Page 1240

Outsell/Digital Library Federation Study (2002)
Weighted Tables

TABLE 128

T7D/E_16. Dissertations SUMMARY TABLE

		RESPONDENT TYPE				INSTITUTION TYPE			DISCIPLINE								GENDER	
	TOTAL SAMPLE	FACULTY MEMBER	GRAD. STUDENT	FACULTY /GRAD	UNDER GRAD. STUDENT	PUBLIC	PRIVATE	LIBERAL ARTS	BIOLOGIAL SCIENCES	PHYSICAL SCIENCES /MATH	SOCIAL SCIENCES	ARTS AND HUMAN.	ENGI- NEERING	BUSINESS	LAW	UNDEC. MAJOR	MALE	FEMALE
		(A)	(B)	(C)	(D)	(E)	(F)	(G)	(H)	(I)	(J)	(K)	(L)	(M)	(N)		(P)	(Q)
Base - Use Dissertations for teaching	83*	60*	23**	83*	0**	33**	34**	16**	11**	14**	23**	25**	4**	7**	***	0*	60*	23**
Borrow from or use in campus library (NET)	45 54.0%	32 53.9%	12 54.2%	45 54.0%	0 0	17 52.5%	19 57.0%	8 50.7%	6 58.3%	7 50.0%	13 58.3%	13 54.5%	3 66.7%	2 28.6%	* 100.0%	0 0	33 55.1%	12 51.1%
All sources of info	45 54.0%	32 53.9%	12 54.2%	45 54.0%	0 0	17 52.5%	19 57.0%	8 50.7%	6 58.3%	7 50.0%	13 58.3%	13 54.5%	3 66.7%	2 28.6%	* 100.0%	0 0	33 55.1%	12 51.1%
preferred source of info	30 36.6%	22 36.2%	9 37.7%	30 36.6%	0 0	11 33.3%	13 39.2%	6 37.8%	3 25.0%	4 28.6%	11 50.0%	9 36.4%	2 53.3%	1 14.3%	* 100.0%	0 0	20 34.0%	10 43.3%
Access online (NET)	26 31.0%	18 29.5%	8 34.9%	26 31.0%	0 0	10 30.7%	10 30.5%	5 32.8%	4 33.3%	6 42.9%	6 25.0%	8 31.8%	2 40.0%	1 14.3%	0 0	0 0	21 34.4%	5 22.3%
All sources of info	26 31.0%	18 29.5%	8 34.9%	26 31.0%	0 0	10 30.7%	10 30.5%	5 32.8%	4 33.3%	6 42.9%	6 25.0%	8 31.8%	2 40.0%	1 14.3%	0 0	0 0	21 34.4%	5 22.3%
preferred source of info	24 29.2%	17 27.5%	8 33.6%	24 29.2%	0 0	10 29.8%	9 26.8%	5 32.8%	4 33.3%	6 42.9%	6 25.0%	8 31.8%	1 26.7%	0 0	0 0	0 0	20 33.4%	4 18.3%
Interlibrary loan (NET)	15 18.6%	13 22.0%	2 9.8%	15 18.6%	0 0	4 11.7%	4 12.9%	7 44.3%	1 8.3%	2 14.3%	2 8.3%	10 40.9%	1 13.3%	0 0	0 0	0 0	10 16.6%	6 23.8%
All sources of info	15 18.6%	13 22.0%	2 9.8%	15 18.6%	0 0	4 11.7%	4 12.9%	7 44.3%	1 8.3%	2 14.3%	2 8.3%	10 40.9%	1 13.3%	0 0	0 0	0 0	10 16.6%	6 23.8%
preferred source of info	6 7.4%	4 6.5%	2 9.8%	6 7.4%	0 0	0 0	2 6.6%	4 23.7%	1 8.3%	0 0	2 8.3%	3 13.6%	0 0	0 0	0 0	0 0	4 7.1%	2 8.1%

Proportions/Means: Columns Tested (5% risk level) - A/B/D - C/D - E/F/G - H/I/J/K/L/M/N - P/Q
* small base; ** very small base (under 30) ineligible for sig testing

Table 301
Page 1247

Outsell/Digital Library Federation Study (2002)
Weighted Tables

TABLE 128, continued

T7D/E_16. Dissertations SUMMARY TABLE

	TOTAL SAMPLE	RESPONDENT TYPE: FACULTY MEMBER	GRAD. STUDENT	FACULTY /GRAD	UNDER GRAD. STUDENT	INSTITUTION TYPE: PUBLIC	PRIVATE	LIBERAL ARTS	DISCIPLINE: BIOLOGIAL SCIENCES	PHYSICAL SCIENCES /MATH	SOCIAL SCIENCES	ARTS AND HUMAN.	ENGI-NEERING	BUSINESS	LAW	UNDEC. MAJOR	GENDER: MALE	FEMALE
		(A)	(B)	(C)	(D)	(E)	(F)	(G)	(H)	(I)	(J)	(K)	(L)	(M)	(N)		(P)	(Q)
Base - Use Dissertations for teaching	83*	60*	23**	83*	0**	33**	34**	16**	11**	14**	23**	25**	4**	7**	***	0*	60*	23**
Borrow from or use in other libraries (NET)	9	8	1	9	0	5	3	1	2	3	0	2	*	2	0	0	9	0
	11.1%	13.1%	5.7%	11.1%	0	16.1%	8.9%	5.4%	16.7%	21.4%	0	9.1%	6.7%	28.6%	0	0	15.4%	0
All sources of info	9	8	1	9	0	5	3	1	2	3	0	2	*	2	0	0	9	0
	11.1%	13.1%	5.7%	11.1%	0	16.1%	8.9%	5.4%	16.7%	21.4%	0	9.1%	6.7%	28.6%	0	0	15.4%	0
preferred source of info	2	2	*	2	0	2	0	0	0	0	0	0	*	2	0	0	2	0
	2.6%	3.1%	1.3%	2.6%	0	6.6%	0	0	0	0	0	0	6.7%	28.6%	0	0	3.6%	0
Colleagues (NET)	8	6	2	8	0	4	4	0	1	1	4	0	0	2	0	0	6	2
	9.1%	9.4%	8.3%	9.1%	0	11.6%	10.9%	0	8.3%	7.1%	16.7%	0	0	28.6%	0	0	9.4%	8.1%
All sources of info	8	6	2	8	0	4	4	0	1	1	4	0	0	2	0	0	6	2
	9.1%	9.4%	8.3%	9.1%	0	11.6%	10.9%	0	8.3%	7.1%	16.7%	0	0	28.6%	0	0	9.4%	8.1%
preferred source of info	5	5	0	5	0	2	3	0	0	1	2	0	0	2	0	0	5	0
	5.7%	7.9%	0	5.7%	0	5.9%	8.3%	0	0	7.1%	8.3%	0	0	28.6%	0	0	8.0%	0
Personal Collection/ Holdings (NET)	2	2	0	2	0	2	*	0	1	1	0	0	*	0	0	0	1	1
	2.6%	3.6%	0	2.6%	0	5.7%	0.9%	0	8.3%	7.1%	0	0	6.7%	0	0	0	2.2%	3.8%
All sources of info	2	2	0	2	0	2	*	0	1	1	0	0	*	0	0	0	1	1
	2.6%	3.6%	0	2.6%	0	5.7%	0.9%	0	8.3%	7.1%	0	0	6.7%	0	0	0	2.2%	3.8%
preferred source of info	1	1	0	1	0	1	*	0	0	1	0	0	*	0	0	0	1	0
	1.6%	2.1%	0	1.6%	0	3.1%	0.9%	0	0	7.1%	0	0	6.7%	0	0	0	2.2%	0

Proportions/Means: Columns Tested (5% risk level) - A/B/D - C/D - E/F/G - H/I/J/K/L/M/N - P/Q
* small base; ** very small base (under 30) ineligible for sig testing

Table 301
Page 1248

Outsell/Digital Library Federation Study (2002)
Weighted Tables

TABLE 128, continued

T7D/E_16. Dissertations SUMMARY TABLE

		RESPONDENT TYPE				INSTITUTION TYPE			DISCIPLINE									GENDER	
	TOTAL SAMPLE	FACULTY MEMBER	GRAD. STUDENT	FACULTY /GRAD	UNDER GRAD. STUDENT	PUBLIC	PRIVATE	LIBERAL ARTS	BIOLOGIAL SCIENCES	PHYSICAL SCIENCES /MATH	SOCIAL SCIENCES	ARTS AND HUMAN.	ENGI- NEERING	BUSINESS	LAW	UNDEC. MAJOR	MALE	FEMALE
		(A)	(B)	(C)	(D)	(E)	(F)	(G)	(H)	(I)	(J)	(K)	(L)	(M)	(N)		(P)	(Q)
Base - Use Dissertations for teaching	83*	60*	23**	83*	0**	33**	34**	16**	11**	14**	23**	25**	4**	7**	***	0*	60*	23**
Order from on demand document delivery service (NET)	2 2.4%	2 3.3%	0 0	2 2.4%	0 0	0 0	2 5.9%	0 0	1 8.3%	0 0	0 0	1 4.5%	0 0	0 0	0 0	0 0	1 1.5%	1 4.8%
All sources of info	2 2.4%	2 3.3%	0 0	2 2.4%	0 0	0 0	2 5.9%	0 0	1 8.3%	0 0	0 0	1 4.5%	0 0	0 0	0 0	0 0	1 1.5%	1 4.8%
preferred source of info	0 0	0 0	0 0	0 0	0 0	0 0	0 0	0 0	0 0	0 0	0 0	0 0	0 0	0 0	0 0	0 0	0 0	0 0
Purchase from physical book store (NET)	2 2.4%	2 3.3%	0 0	2 2.4%	0 0	0 0	2 5.9%	0 0	1 8.3%	0 0	0 0	1 4.5%	0 0	0 0	0 0	0 0	1 1.5%	1 4.8%
All sources of info	2 2.4%	2 3.3%	0 0	2 2.4%	0 0	0 0	2 5.9%	0 0	1 8.3%	0 0	0 0	1 4.5%	0 0	0 0	0 0	0 0	1 1.5%	1 4.8%
preferred source of info	2 2.4%	2 3.3%	0 0	2 2.4%	0 0	0 0	2 5.9%	0 0	1 8.3%	0 0	0 0	1 4.5%	0 0	0 0	0 0	0 0	1 1.5%	1 4.8%
Meeting/Conferences (NET)	2 2.3%	0 0	2 8.3%	2 2.3%	0 0	2 5.7%	0 0	0 0	0 0	0 0	2 8.3%	0 0	0 0	0 0	0 0	0 0	0 0	2 8.1%
All sources of info	2 2.3%	0 0	2 8.3%	2 2.3%	0 0	2 5.7%	0 0	0 0	0 0	0 0	2 8.3%	0 0	0 0	0 0	0 0	0 0	0 0	2 8.1%
preferred source of info	2 2.3%	0 0	2 8.3%	2 2.3%	0 0	2 5.7%	0 0	0 0	0 0	0 0	2 8.3%	0 0	0 0	0 0	0 0	0 0	0 0	2 8.1%

Proportions/Means: Columns Tested (5% risk level) - A/B/D - C/D - E/F/G - H/I/J/K/L/M/N - P/Q
* small base; ** very small base (under 30) ineligible for sig testing

Table 301
Page 1249

Outsell/Digital Library Federation Study (2002)
Weighted Tables

TABLE 128, continued

T7D/E_16. Dissertations SUMMARY TABLE

		RESPONDENT TYPE				INSTITUTION TYPE			DISCIPLINE								GENDER	
	TOTAL SAMPLE	FACULTY MEMBER	GRAD. STUDENT	FACULTY /GRAD	UNDER GRAD. STUDENT	PUBLIC	PRIVATE	LIBERAL ARTS	BIOLOGIAL SCIENCES	PHYSICAL SCIENCES /MATH	SOCIAL SCIENCES	ARTS AND HUMAN.	ENGI- NEERING	BUSINESS	LAW	UNDEC. MAJOR	MALE	FEMALE
		(A)	(B)	(C)	(D)	(E)	(F)	(G)	(H)	(I)	(J)	(K)	(L)	(M)	(N)		(P)	(Q)
Base - Use Dissertations for teaching	83*	60*	23**	83*	0**	33**	34**	16**	11**	14**	23**	25**	4**	7**	***	0*	60*	23**
Publisher (NET)	1	1	0	1	0	0	1	0	0	0	0	1	0	0	0	0	0	1
	1.4%	1.9%	0	1.4%	0	0	3.3%	0	0	0	0	4.5%	0	0	0	0	0	4.8%
All sources of info	1	1	0	1	0	0	1	0	0	0	0	1	0	0	0	0	0	1
	1.4%	1.9%	0	1.4%	0	0	3.3%	0	0	0	0	4.5%	0	0	0	0	0	4.8%
preferred source of info	1	1	0	1	0	0	1	0	0	0	0	1	0	0	0	0	0	1
	1.4%	1.9%	0	1.4%	0	0	3.3%	0	0	0	0	4.5%	0	0	0	0	0	4.8%
Faculty (NET)	1	0	1	1	0	1	0	0	0	0	0	1	0	0	0	0	0	1
	1.4%	0	4.9%	1.4%	0	3.4%	0	0	0	0	0	4.5%	0	0	0	0	0	4.8%
All sources of info	1	0	1	1	0	1	0	0	0	0	0	1	0	0	0	0	0	1
	1.4%	0	4.9%	1.4%	0	3.4%	0	0	0	0	0	4.5%	0	0	0	0	0	4.8%
preferred source of info	1	0	1	1	0	1	0	0	0	0	0	1	0	0	0	0	0	1
	1.4%	0	4.9%	1.4%	0	3.4%	0	0	0	0	0	4.5%	0	0	0	0	0	4.8%
Author	1	1	0	1	0	1	0	0	0	1	0	0	0	0	0	0	1	0
	1.2%	1.7%	0	1.2%	0	3.1%	0	0	0	7.1%	0	0	0	0	0	0	1.7%	0
All sources of info	1	1	0	1	0	1	0	0	0	1	0	0	0	0	0	0	1	0
	1.2%	1.7%	0	1.2%	0	3.1%	0	0	0	7.1%	0	0	0	0	0	0	1.7%	0
preferred source of info	1	1	0	1	0	1	0	0	0	1	0	0	0	0	0	0	1	0
	1.2%	1.7%	0	1.2%	0	3.1%	0	0	0	7.1%	0	0	0	0	0	0	1.7%	0

Proportions/Means: Columns Tested (5% risk level) - A/B/D - C/D - E/F/G - H/I/J/K/L/M/N - P/Q
* small base; ** very small base (under 30) ineligible for sig testing

Table 301
Page 1250

Outsell/Digital Library Federation Study (2002)
Weighted Tables

TABLE 128, continued

T7D/E_16. Dissertations SUMMARY TABLE

		RESPONDENT TYPE				INSTITUTION TYPE			DISCIPLINE								GENDER	
	TOTAL SAMPLE	FACULTY MEMBER	GRAD. STUDENT	FACULTY /GRAD	UNDER GRAD. STUDENT	PUBLIC	PRIVATE	LIBERAL ARTS	BIOLOGIAL SCIENCES	PHYSICAL SCIENCES /MATH	SOCIAL SCIENCES	ARTS AND HUMAN.	ENGI- NEERING	BUSINESS	LAW	UNDEC. MAJOR	MALE	FEMALE
		(A)	(B)	(C)	(D)	(E)	(F)	(G)	(H)	(I)	(J)	(K)	(L)	(M)	(N)		(P)	(Q)
Base - Use Dissertations for teaching	83*	60*	23**	83*	0**	33**	34**	16**	11**	14**	23**	25**	4**	7**	***	0*	60*	23**
Access from course website (NET)	1 1.1%	1 1.5%	0 0	1 1.1%	0 0	1 2.8%	0 0	0 0	0 0	0 0	0 0	0 0	0 0	1 14.3%	0 0	0 0	1 1.6%	0 0
All sources of info	1 1.1%	1 1.5%	0 0	1 1.1%	0 0	1 2.8%	0 0	0 0	0 0	0 0	0 0	0 0	0 0	1 14.3%	0 0	0 0	1 1.6%	0 0
preferred source of info	0 0	0 0	0 0	0 0	0 0	0 0	0 0	0 0	0 0	0 0	0 0	0 0	0 0	0 0	0 0	0 0	0 0	0 0
Purchase from online bookstore (NET)	0 0	0 0	0 0	0 0	0 0	0 0	0 0	0 0	0 0	0 0	0 0	0 0	0 0	0 0	0 0	0 0	0 0	0 0
All sources of info	0 0	0 0	0 0	0 0	0 0	0 0	0 0	0 0	0 0	0 0	0 0	0 0	0 0	0 0	0 0	0 0	0 0	0 0
preferred source of info	0 0	0 0	0 0	0 0	0 0	0 0	0 0	0 0	0 0	0 0	0 0	0 0	0 0	0 0	0 0	0 0	0 0	0 0
Ask library to purchase source (NET)	0 0	0 0	0 0	0 0	0 0	0 0	0 0	0 0	0 0	0 0	0 0	0 0	0 0	0 0	0 0	0 0	0 0	0 0
All sources of info	0 0	0 0	0 0	0 0	0 0	0 0	0 0	0 0	0 0	0 0	0 0	0 0	0 0	0 0	0 0	0 0	0 0	0 0
preferred source of info	0 0	0 0	0 0	0 0	0 0	0 0	0 0	0 0	0 0	0 0	0 0	0 0	0 0	0 0	0 0	0 0	0 0	0 0

Proportions/Means: Columns Tested (5% risk level) - A/B/D - C/D - E/F/G - H/I/J/K/L/M/N - P/Q
* small base; ** very small base (under 30) ineligible for sig testing

Table 301
Page 1251

Outsell/Digital Library Federation Study (2002)
Weighted Tables

TABLE 128, continued

T7D/E_16. Dissertations SUMMARY TABLE

		RESPONDENT TYPE				INSTITUTION TYPE			DISCIPLINE									GENDER	
	TOTAL SAMPLE	FACULTY MEMBER	GRAD. STUDENT	FACULTY /GRAD	UNDER GRAD. STUDENT	PUBLIC	PRIVATE	LIBERAL ARTS	BIOLOGIAL SCIENCES	PHYSICAL SCIENCES /MATH	SOCIAL SCIENCES	ARTS AND HUMAN.	ENGI-NEERING	BUSINESS	LAW	UNDEC. MAJOR	MALE	FEMALE
		(A)	(B)	(C)	(D)	(E)	(F)	(G)	(H)	(I)	(J)	(K)	(L)	(M)	(N)		(P)	(Q)
Base - Use Dissertations for teaching	83*	60*	23**	83*	0**	33**	34**	16**	11**	14**	23**	25**	4**	7**	***	0*	60*	23**
Department (NET)	0 0	0 0	0 0	0 0	0 0	0 0	0 0	0 0	0 0	0 0	0 0	0 0	0 0	0 0	0 0	0 0	0 0	0 0
All sources of info	0 0	0 0	0 0	0 0	0 0	0 0	0 0	0 0	0 0	0 0	0 0	0 0	0 0	0 0	0 0	0 0	0 0	0 0
preferred source of info	0 0	0 0	0 0	0 0	0 0	0 0	0 0	0 0	0 0	0 0	0 0	0 0	0 0	0 0	0 0	0 0	0 0	0 0
Office (NET)	0 0	0 0	0 0	0 0	0 0	0 0	0 0	0 0	0 0	0 0	0 0	0 0	0 0	0 0	0 0	0 0	0 0	0 0
All sources of info	0 0	0 0	0 0	0 0	0 0	0 0	0 0	0 0	0 0	0 0	0 0	0 0	0 0	0 0	0 0	0 0	0 0	0 0
preferred source of info	0 0	0 0	0 0	0 0	0 0	0 0	0 0	0 0	0 0	0 0	0 0	0 0	0 0	0 0	0 0	0 0	0 0	0 0
Home (NET)	0 0	0 0	0 0	0 0	0 0	0 0	0 0	0 0	0 0	0 0	0 0	0 0	0 0	0 0	0 0	0 0	0 0	0 0
All sources of info	0 0	0 0	0 0	0 0	0 0	0 0	0 0	0 0	0 0	0 0	0 0	0 0	0 0	0 0	0 0	0 0	0 0	0 0
preferred source of info	0 0	0 0	0 0	0 0	0 0	0 0	0 0	0 0	0 0	0 0	0 0	0 0	0 0	0 0	0 0	0 0	0 0	0 0

Proportions/Means: Columns Tested (5% risk level) - A/B/D - C/D - E/F/G - H/I/J/K/L/M/N - P/Q
* small base; ** very small base (under 30) ineligible for sig testing

Table 301
Page 1252

Outsell/Digital Library Federation Study (2002)
Weighted Tables

TABLE 128, continued

T7D/E_16. Dissertations SUMMARY TABLE

		RESPONDENT TYPE				INSTITUTION TYPE			DISCIPLINE									GENDER	
	TOTAL SAMPLE	FACULTY MEMBER	GRAD. STUDENT	FACULTY /GRAD	UNDER GRAD. STUDENT	PUBLIC	PRIVATE	LIBERAL ARTS	BIOLOGIAL SCIENCES	PHYSICAL SCIENCES /MATH	SOCIAL SCIENCES	ARTS AND HUMAN.	ENGI-NEERING	BUSINESS	LAW	UNDEC. MAJOR	MALE	FEMALE
		(A)	(B)	(C)	(D)	(E)	(F)	(G)	(H)	(I)	(J)	(K)	(L)	(M)	(N)		(P)	(Q)
Base - Use Dissertations for teaching	83*	60*	23**	83*	0**	33**	34**	16**	11**	14**	23**	25**	4**	7**	***	0*	60*	23**
Access book/journal/ journal article elsewhere online (NET)	0 0	0 0	0 0	0 0	0 0	0 0	0 0	0 0	0 0	0 0	0 0	0 0	0 0	0 0	0 0	0 0	0 0	0 0
All sources of info	0 0	0 0	0 0	0 0	0 0	0 0	0 0	0 0	0 0	0 0	0 0	0 0	0 0	0 0	0 0	0 0	0 0	0 0
preferred source of info	0 0	0 0	0 0	0 0	0 0	0 0	0 0	0 0	0 0	0 0	0 0	0 0	0 0	0 0	0 0	0 0	0 0	0 0
Other (NET)	1 1.7%	1 2.3%	0 0	1 1.7%	0 0	1 3.4%	* 0.9%	0 0	0 0	0 0	0 0	1 4.5%	* 6.7%	0 0	0 0	0 0	1 2.4%	0 0
All sources of info	1 1.7%	1 2.3%	0 0	1 1.7%	0 0	1 3.4%	* 0.9%	0 0	0 0	0 0	0 0	1 4.5%	* 6.7%	0 0	0 0	0 0	1 2.4%	0 0
preferred source of info	* 0.4%	* 0.5%	0 0	* 0.4%	0 0	0 0	* 0.9%	0 0	0 0	0 0	0 0	0 0	* 6.7%	0 0	0 0	0 0	* 0.5%	0 0
DK/Refused	7 8.0%	6 9.4%	1 4.4%	7 8.0%	0 0	3 9.2%	3 8.0%	1 5.7%	3 25.0%	1 7.1%	0 0	1 4.5%	0 0	2 28.6%	0 0	0 0	5 8.1%	2 7.8%

Proportions/Means: Columns Tested (5% risk level) - A/B/D - C/D - E/F/G - H/I/J/K/L/M/N - P/Q
* small base; ** very small base (under 30) ineligible for sig testing

TABLE 129

T7sum_17. News SUMMARY TABLE

	RESPONDENT TYPE				INSTITUTION TYPE			DISCIPLINE								GENDER	
	TOTAL SAMPLE	FACULTY MEMBER	GRAD. STUDENT	FACULTY /GRAD	UNDER GRAD. STUDENT	PUBLIC	PRIVATE	LIBERAL ARTS	BIOLOGIAL SCIENCES	PHYSICAL SCIENCES /MATH	SOCIAL SCIENCES	ARTS AND HUMAN.	ENGI-NEERING	BUSINESS	LAW	UNDEC. MAJOR	MALE	FEMALE
		(A)	(B)	(C)	(D)	(E)	(F)	(G)	(H)	(I)	(J)	(K)	(L)	(M)	(N)		(P)	(Q)
Base - USe News for teaching	291	214	76*	291	0**	116*	101*	74*	33*	47*	90*	50*	6**	62*	3**	0*	200	91*
ONLINE	198 68.2%	150 69.9%	49 63.4%	198 68.2%	0 0	73 63.2%	71 70.4%	54 73.1%	24 73.0%	31 66.0%	64 70.8%	31 62.2%	5 80.0%	42 67.2%	2 73.3%	0 0	137 68.7%	61 67.2%
Web directory/ subject related web site	75 25.9%	59 27.7%	16 21.1%	75 25.9%	0 0	17 14.6%	33 33.1%E	25 34.0%E	12 37.8%J	12 25.5%	17 18.8%	13 26.7%	3 55.0%	17 26.9%	1 33.3%	0 0	48 24.1%	27 30.0%
All sources of info	75 25.9%	59 27.7%	16 21.1%	75 25.9%	0 0	17 14.6%	33 33.1%E	25 34.0%E	12 37.8%J	12 25.5%	17 18.8%	13 26.7%	3 55.0%	17 26.9%	1 33.3%	0 0	48 24.1%	27 30.0%
preferred source of info	44 15.1%	32 15.1%	11 14.8%	44 15.1%	0 0	10 8.6%	18 18.1%	15 21.0%E	7 21.6%	7 14.9%	9 10.4%	9 17.8%	2 30.0%	9 14.9%	* 13.3%	0 0	24 12.3%	19 21.2%
Search engine	59 20.4%	50 23.4%	9 12.1%	59 20.4%	0 0	28 24.2%	14 13.5%	18 23.9%	6 18.9%	15 31.9%M	19 20.8%	9 17.8%	1 15.0%	9 14.9%	* 13.3%	0 0	46 23.0%	14 14.9%
All sources of info	59 20.4%	50 23.4%	9 12.1%	59 20.4%	0 0	28 24.2%	14 13.5%	18 23.9%	6 18.9%	15 31.9%M	19 20.8%	9 17.8%	1 15.0%	9 14.9%	* 13.3%	0 0	46 23.0%	14 14.9%
preferred source of info	36 12.5%	28 13.2%	8 10.6%	36 12.5%	0 0	18 15.3%	9 8.6%	10 13.5%	2 5.4%	10 21.3%HM	15 16.7%	6 11.1%	* 5.0%	4 6.0%	0 0	0 0	28 14.3%	8 8.7%
Internet searches	39 13.4%	25 11.5%	14 18.6%	39 13.4%	0 0	18 15.7%	14 13.9%	7 9.0%	4 10.8%	1 2.1%	15 16.7%I	8 15.6%I	1 10.0%	10 16.4%I	1 26.7%	0 0	24 12.1%	15 16.1%
All sources of info	39 13.4%	25 11.5%	14 18.6%	39 13.4%	0 0	18 15.7%	14 13.9%	7 9.0%	4 10.8%	1 2.1%	15 16.7%I	8 15.6%I	1 10.0%	10 16.4%I	1 26.7%	0 0	24 12.1%	15 16.1%
preferred source of info	17 5.9%	9 4.4%	8 10.1%	17 5.9%	0 0	8 7.1%	6 6.0%	3 3.8%	2 5.4%	0 0	8 8.3%	2 4.4%	* 5.0%	5 7.5%	1 26.7%	0 0	10 5.2%	7 7.4%

Proportions/Means: Columns Tested (5% risk level) - A/B/D - C/D - E/F/G - H/I/J/K/L/M/N - P/Q
* small base; ** very small base (under 30) ineligible for sig testing

Table 305
Page 1264

Outsell/Digital Library Federation Study (2002)
Weighted Tables

TABLE 129, continued

T7sum_17. News SUMMARY TABLE

		RESPONDENT TYPE				INSTITUTION TYPE			DISCIPLINE									GENDER	
	TOTAL SAMPLE	FACULTY MEMBER	GRAD. STUDENT	FACULTY /GRAD	UNDER GRAD. STUDENT	PUBLIC	PRIVATE	LIBERAL ARTS	BIOLOGIAL SCIENCES	PHYSICAL SCIENCES /MATH	SOCIAL SCIENCES	ARTS AND HUMAN.	ENGI- NEERING	BUSINESS	LAW	UNDEC. MAJOR	MALE	FEMALE
		(A)	(B)	(C)	(D)	(E)	(F)	(G)	(H)	(I)	(J)	(K)	(L)	(M)	(N)		(P)	(Q)
Base - USe News for teaching	291	214	76*	291	0**	116*	101*	74*	33*	47*	90*	50*	6**	62*	3**	0*	200	91*
Online databases	33 11.4%	25 11.8%	8 10.5%	33 11.4%	0 0	12 10.5%	14 13.4%	8 10.3%	7 21.6%KM	6 12.8%	11 12.5%	3 6.7%	1 10.0%	5 7.5%	* 13.3%	0 0	27 13.6%	6 6.7%
All sources of info	33 11.4%	25 11.8%	8 10.5%	33 11.4%	0 0	12 10.5%	14 13.4%	8 10.3%	7 21.6%KM	6 12.8%	11 12.5%	3 6.7%	1 10.0%	5 7.5%	* 13.3%	0 0	27 13.6%	6 6.7%
preferred source of info	20 7.0%	15 7.2%	5 6.4%	20 7.0%	0 0	5 4.2%	11 10.4%	5 6.6%	3 8.1%	4 8.5%	9 10.4%	1 2.2%	* 5.0%	3 4.5%	0 0	0 0	17 8.3%	4 4.0%
Your own institution's web site	17 5.7%	13 5.9%	4 5.4%	17 5.7%	0 0	7 5.8%	8 8.1%	2 2.4%	2 5.4%	0 0	9 10.4%I	3 6.7%	* 5.0%	2 3.0%	0 0	0 0	11 5.3%	6 6.7%
All sources of info	17 5.7%	13 5.9%	4 5.4%	17 5.7%	0 0	7 5.8%	8 8.1%	2 2.4%	2 5.4%	0 0	9 10.4%I	3 6.7%	* 5.0%	2 3.0%	0 0	0 0	11 5.3%	6 6.7%
preferred source of info	11 3.7%	8 3.6%	3 3.9%	11 3.7%	0 0	6 4.9%	4 4.2%	1 1.2%	1 2.7%	0 0	8 8.3%	1 2.2%	* 5.0%	1 1.5%	0 0	0 0	8 3.9%	3 3.3%
Online library catalogues and finding aids	8 2.7%	2 1.0%	6 7.8%A	8 2.7%	0 0	1 0.8%	7 7.0%EG	0 0	1 2.7%	0 0	2 2.1%	3 6.7%	0 0	2 3.0%	0 0	0 0	4 2.0%	4 4.3%
All sources of info	8 2.7%	2 1.0%	6 7.8%A	8 2.7%	0 0	1 0.8%	7 7.0%EG	0 0	1 2.7%	0 0	2 2.1%	3 6.7%	0 0	2 3.0%	0 0	0 0	4 2.0%	4 4.3%
preferred source of info	2 0.7%	1 0.4%	1 1.5%	2 0.7%	0 0	1 0.8%	1 1.1%	0 0	0 0	0 0	0 0	1 2.2%	0 0	1 1.5%	0 0	0 0	2 1.0%	0 0

Proportions/Means: Columns Tested (5% risk level) - A/B/D - C/D - E/F/G - H/I/J/K/L/M/N - P/Q
* small base; ** very small base (under 30) ineligible for sig testing

Table 305
Page 1265

Outsell/Digital Library Federation Study (2002)
Weighted Tables

TABLE 129, continued

T7sum_17. News SUMMARY TABLE

		RESPONDENT TYPE				INSTITUTION TYPE			DISCIPLINE								GENDER	
	TOTAL SAMPLE	FACULTY MEMBER	GRAD. STUDENT	FACULTY /GRAD	UNDER GRAD. STUDENT	PUBLIC	PRIVATE	LIBERAL ARTS	BIOLOGIAL SCIENCES	PHYSICAL SCIENCES /MATH	SOCIAL SCIENCES	ARTS AND HUMAN.	ENGI-NEERING	BUSINESS	LAW	UNDEC. MAJOR	MALE	FEMALE
		(A)	(B)	(C)	(D)	(E)	(F)	(G)	(H)	(I)	(J)	(K)	(L)	(M)	(N)		(P)	(Q)
Base - USe News for teaching	291	214	76*	291	0**	116*	101*	74*	33*	47*	90*	50*	6**	62*	3**	0*	200	91*
Online reference service	7 2.6%	7 3.5%	0 0	7 2.6%	0 0	4 3.2%	1 0.9%	3 3.8%	2 5.4%J	2 4.3%	0 0	0 0	0 0	4 6.0%J	0 0	0 0	6 2.8%	2 2.0%
All sources of info	7 2.6%	7 3.5%	0 0	7 2.6%	0 0	4 3.2%	1 0.9%	3 3.8%	2 5.4%J	2 4.3%	0 0	0 0	0 0	4 6.0%J	0 0	0 0	6 2.8%	2 2.0%
preferred source of info	3 1.0%	3 1.3%	0 0	3 1.0%	0 0	2 1.7%	0 0	1 1.2%	1 2.7%	1 2.1%	0 0	0 0	0 0	1 1.5%	0 0	0 0	3 1.4%	0 0
Online abstracting and indexing services	4 1.5%	3 1.5%	1 1.5%	4 1.5%	0 0	* 0.2%	1 1.1%	3 3.9%	0 0	1 2.1%	2 2.1%	1 2.2%	* 5.0%	0 0	0 0	0 0	1 0.6%	3 3.3%
All sources of info	4 1.5%	3 1.5%	1 1.5%	4 1.5%	0 0	* 0.2%	1 1.1%	3 3.9%	0 0	1 2.1%	2 2.1%	1 2.2%	* 5.0%	0 0	0 0	0 0	1 0.6%	3 3.3%
preferred source of info	* 0.1%	* 0.1%	0 0	* 0.1%	0 0	* 0.2%	0 0	0 0	0 0	0 0	0 0	0 0	* 5.0%	0 0	0 0	0 0	* 0.1%	0 0
Your own personal electronic library/files	3 1.0%	1 0.5%	2 2.5%	3 1.0%	0 0	2 1.6%	0 0	1 1.4%	0 0	1 2.1%	2 2.1%	0 0	0 0	0 0	0 0	0 0	1 0.5%	2 2.1%
All sources of info	3 1.0%	1 0.5%	2 2.5%	3 1.0%	0 0	2 1.6%	0 0	1 1.4%	0 0	1 2.1%	2 2.1%	0 0	0 0	0 0	0 0	0 0	1 0.5%	2 2.1%
preferred source of info	0 0	0 0	0 0	0 0	0 0	0 0	0 0	0 0	0 0	0 0	0 0	0 0	0 0	0 0	0 0	0 0	0 0	0 0

Proportions/Means: Columns Tested (5% risk level) - A/B/D - C/D - E/F/G - H/I/J/K/L/M/N - P/Q
* small base; ** very small base (under 30) ineligible for sig testing

Table 305
Page 1266

Outsell/Digital Library Federation Study (2002)
Weighted Tables

TABLE 129, continued

T7sum_17. News SUMMARY TABLE

		RESPONDENT TYPE				INSTITUTION TYPE			DISCIPLINE								GENDER	
	TOTAL SAMPLE	FACULTY MEMBER	GRAD. STUDENT	FACULTY /GRAD	UNDER GRAD. STUDENT	PUBLIC	PRIVATE	LIBERAL ARTS	BIOLOGIAL SCIENCES	PHYSICAL SCIENCES /MATH	SOCIAL SCIENCES	ARTS AND HUMAN.	ENGI-NEERING	BUSINESS	LAW	UNDEC. MAJOR	MALE	FEMALE
		(A)	(B)	(C)	(D)	(E)	(F)	(G)	(H)	(I)	(J)	(K)	(L)	(M)	(N)		(P)	(Q)
Base - USe News for teaching	291	214	76*	291	0**	116*	101*	74*	33*	47*	90*	50*	6**	62*	3**	0*	200	91*
E-mail listservs	3	3	0	3	0	2	1	0	0	1	0	0	1	1	0	0	3	*
	1.0%	1.3%	0	1.0%	0	1.3%	1.3%	0	0	2.1%	0	0	15.0%	1.5%	0	0	1.3%	0.3%
All sources of info	3	3	0	3	0	2	1	0	0	1	0	0	1	1	0	0	3	*
	1.0%	1.3%	0	1.0%	0	1.3%	1.3%	0	0	2.1%	0	0	15.0%	1.5%	0	0	1.3%	0.3%
preferred source of info	1	1	0	1	0	1	0	0	0	0	0	0	*	1	0	0	1	*
	0.4%	0.6%	0	0.4%	0	1.1%	0	0	0	0	0	0	5.0%	1.5%	0	0	0.5%	0.3%
Department web page	1	1	0	1	0	0	*	1	0	0	0	0	*	1	0	0	1	0
	0.4%	0.6%	0	0.4%	0	0	0.3%	1.3%	0	0	0	0	5.0%	1.5%	0	0	0.6%	0
All sources of info	1	1	0	1	0	0	*	1	0	0	0	0	*	1	0	0	1	0
	0.4%	0.6%	0	0.4%	0	0	0.3%	1.3%	0	0	0	0	5.0%	1.5%	0	0	0.6%	0
preferred source of info	*	*	0	*	0	0	*	0	0	0	0	0	*	0	0	0	*	0
	0.1%	0.1%	0	0.1%	0	0	0.3%	0	0	0	0	0	5.0%	0	0	0	0.1%	0
Online bookstore	0	0	0	0	0	0	0	0	0	0	0	0	0	0	0	0	0	0
	0	0	0	0	0	0	0	0	0	0	0	0	0	0	0	0	0	0
All sources of info	0	0	0	0	0	0	0	0	0	0	0	0	0	0	0	0	0	0
	0	0	0	0	0	0	0	0	0	0	0	0	0	0	0	0	0	0
preferred source of info	0	0	0	0	0	0	0	0	0	0	0	0	0	0	0	0	0	0
	0	0	0	0	0	0	0	0	0	0	0	0	0	0	0	0	0	0
LIBRARY/PRINT	179	146	32	179	0	67	58	54	22	32	47	32	3	41	2	0	128	50
	61.4%	68.3%B	42.0%	61.4%	0	57.7%	57.5%	72.6%	67.6%	68.1%	52.1%	64.4%	45.0%	65.7%	60.0%	0	64.2%	55.2%

Proportions/Means: Columns Tested (5% risk level) - A/B/D - C/D - E/F/G - H/I/J/K/L/M/N - P/Q
* small base; ** very small base (under 30) ineligible for sig testing

Table 305
Page 1267

Outsell/Digital Library Federation Study (2002)
Weighted Tables

TABLE 129, continued

T7sum_17. News SUMMARY TABLE

	RESPONDENT TYPE					INSTITUTION TYPE			DISCIPLINE								GENDER	
	TOTAL SAMPLE	FACULTY MEMBER	GRAD. STUDENT	FACULTY /GRAD	UNDER GRAD. STUDENT	PUBLIC	PRIVATE	LIBERAL ARTS	BIOLOGIAL SCIENCES	PHYSICAL SCIENCES /MATH	SOCIAL SCIENCES	ARTS AND HUMAN.	ENGI- NEERING	BUSINESS	LAW	UNDEC. MAJOR	MALE	FEMALE
		(A)	(B)	(C)	(D)	(E)	(F)	(G)	(H)	(I)	(J)	(K)	(L)	(M)	(N)		(P)	(Q)
Base - USe News for teaching	291	214	76*	291	0**	116*	101*	74*	33*	47*	90*	50*	6**	62*	3**	0*	200	91*
Personal subscriptions to newspapers, magazines and journals	110 37.8%	96 44.7%B	14 18.5%	110 37.8%	0 0	45 39.1%	30 29.9%	34 46.5%F	10 29.7%	17 36.2%	32 35.4%	19 37.8%	2 35.0%	29 46.3%	1 53.3%	0 0	80 39.9%	30 33.2%
All sources of info	110 37.8%	96 44.7%B	14 18.5%	110 37.8%	0 0	45 39.1%	30 29.9%	34 46.5%F	10 29.7%	17 36.2%	32 35.4%	19 37.8%	2 35.0%	29 46.3%	1 53.3%	0 0	80 39.9%	30 33.2%
preferred source of info	49 16.7%	46 21.3%B	3 3.9%	49 16.7%	0 0	18 15.4%	15 14.8%	16 21.4%	4 10.8%	9 19.1%	13 14.6%	4 8.9%	1 15.0%	17 26.9%K	1 33.3%	0 0	37 18.6%	12 12.7%
Campus library	90 31.0%	73 34.1%	17 22.3%	90 31.0%	0 0	32 27.6%	30 29.8%	28 38.0%	15 45.9%M	18 38.3%	24 27.1%	17 33.3%	1 25.0%	14 22.4%	1 20.0%	0 0	66 33.2%	24 26.0%
All sources of info	90 31.0%	73 34.1%	17 22.3%	90 31.0%	0 0	32 27.6%	30 29.8%	28 38.0%	15 45.9%M	18 38.3%	24 27.1%	17 33.3%	1 25.0%	14 22.4%	1 20.0%	0 0	66 33.2%	24 26.0%
preferred source of info	30 10.1%	21 10.0%	8 10.6%	30 10.1%	0 0	11 9.8%	12 11.4%	7 9.0%	4 13.5%	4 8.5%	6 6.3%	10 20.0%J	1 10.0%	5 7.5%	* 6.7%	0 0	19 9.7%	10 11.1%
Your own personal physical library/ files/bookshelves	15 5.3%	14 6.3%	2 2.5%	15 5.3%	0 0	5 4.2%	6 5.5%	5 6.9%	1 2.7%	1 2.1%	2 2.1%	3 6.7%	0 0	8 13.4%IJ	0 0	0 0	12 6.3%	3 3.3%
All sources of info	15 5.3%	14 6.3%	2 2.5%	15 5.3%	0 0	5 4.2%	6 5.5%	5 6.9%	1 2.7%	1 2.1%	2 2.1%	3 6.7%	0 0	8 13.4%IJ	0 0	0 0	12 6.3%	3 3.3%
preferred source of info	7 2.4%	5 2.3%	2 2.5%	7 2.4%	0 0	2 1.8%	4 3.7%	1 1.5%	1 2.7%	0 0	2 2.1%	2 4.4%	0 0	2 3.0%	0 0	0 0	5 2.5%	2 2.1%

Proportions/Means: Columns Tested (5% risk level) - A/B/D - C/D - E/F/G - H/I/J/K/L/M/N - P/Q
* small base; ** very small base (under 30) ineligible for sig testing

Table 305
Page 1268

Outsell/Digital Library Federation Study (2002)
Weighted Tables

TABLE 129, continued

T7sum_17. News SUMMARY TABLE

		RESPONDENT TYPE				INSTITUTION TYPE			DISCIPLINE								GENDER	
	TOTAL SAMPLE	FACULTY MEMBER	GRAD. STUDENT	FACULTY /GRAD	UNDER GRAD. STUDENT	PUBLIC	PRIVATE	LIBERAL ARTS	BIOLOGIAL SCIENCES	PHYSICAL SCIENCES /MATH	SOCIAL SCIENCES	ARTS AND HUMAN.	ENGI-NEERING	BUSINESS	LAW	UNDEC. MAJOR	MALE	FEMALE
		(A)	(B)	(C)	(D)	(E)	(F)	(G)	(H)	(I)	(J)	(K)	(L)	(M)	(N)		(P)	(Q)
Base - USe News for teaching	291	214	76*	291	0**	116*	101*	74*	33*	47*	90*	50*	6**	62*	3**	0*	200	91*
References cited in books or journal articles	13 4.4%	12 5.5%	1 1.5%	13 4.4%	0 0	5 4.2%	2 2.1%	6 8.0%	0 0	6 12.8%HJ	2 2.1%	2 4.4%	0 0	3 4.5%	0 0	0 0	12 5.9%	1 1.2%
All sources of info	13 4.4%	12 5.5%	1 1.5%	13 4.4%	0 0	5 4.2%	2 2.1%	6 8.0%	0 0	6 12.8%HJ	2 2.1%	2 4.4%	0 0	3 4.5%	0 0	0 0	12 5.9%	1 1.2%
preferred source of info	1 0.3%	1 0.4%	0 0	1 0.3%	0 0	1 0.8%	0 0	0 0	0 0	0 0	0 0	0 0	0 0	1 1.5%	0 0	0 0	1 0.5%	0 0
Another library	6 2.0%	6 2.7%	0 0	6 2.0%	0 0	2 1.8%	2 1.9%	2 2.6%	0 0	1 2.1%	4 4.2%	0 0	0 0	1 1.5%	* 6.7%	0 0	6 2.9%	0 0
All sources of info	6 2.0%	6 2.7%	0 0	6 2.0%	0 0	2 1.8%	2 1.9%	2 2.6%	0 0	1 2.1%	4 4.2%	0 0	0 0	1 1.5%	* 6.7%	0 0	6 2.9%	0 0
preferred source of info	0 0	0 0	0 0	0 0	0 0	0 0	0 0	0 0	0 0	0 0	0 0	0 0	0 0	0 0	0 0	0 0	0 0	0 0
Physical bookstore	5 1.6%	4 1.8%	1 1.2%	5 1.6%	0 0	2 1.6%	3 2.9%	0 0	0 0	1 2.1%	2 2.1%	0 0	0 0	2 3.0%	0 0	0 0	5 2.4%	0 0
All sources of info	5 1.6%	4 1.8%	1 1.2%	5 1.6%	0 0	2 1.6%	3 2.9%	0 0	0 0	1 2.1%	2 2.1%	0 0	0 0	2 3.0%	0 0	0 0	5 2.4%	0 0
preferred source of info	1 0.3%	1 0.5%	0 0	1 0.3%	0 0	0 0	1 1.0%	0 0	0 0	1 2.1%	0 0	0 0	0 0	0 0	0 0	0 0	1 0.5%	0 0

Proportions/Means: Columns Tested (5% risk level) - A/B/D - C/D - E/F/G - H/I/J/K/L/M/N - P/Q
* small base; ** very small base (under 30) ineligible for sig testing

Table 305
Page 1269

Outsell/Digital Library Federation Study (2002)
Weighted Tables

TABLE 129, continued

T7sum_17. News SUMMARY TABLE

		RESPONDENT TYPE				INSTITUTION TYPE			DISCIPLINE								GENDER	
	TOTAL SAMPLE	FACULTY MEMBER	GRAD. STUDENT	FACULTY /GRAD	UNDER GRAD. STUDENT	PUBLIC	PRIVATE	LIBERAL ARTS	BIOLOGIAL SCIENCES	PHYSICAL SCIENCES /MATH	SOCIAL SCIENCES	ARTS AND HUMAN.	ENGI- NEERING	BUSINESS	LAW	UNDEC. MAJOR	MALE	FEMALE
		(A)	(B)	(C)	(D)	(E)	(F)	(G)	(H)	(I)	(J)	(K)	(L)	(M)	(N)		(P)	(Q)
Base - USe News for teaching	291	214	76*	291	0**	116*	101*	74*	33*	47*	90*	50*	6**	62*	3**	0*	200	91*
Printed abstracting and indexing services	1 0.4%	1 0.6%	0 0	1 0.4%	0 0	* 0.2%	1 0.9%	0 0	0 0	0 0	0 0	0 0	* 5.0%	1 1.5%	0 0	0 0	* 0.1%	1 1.0%
All sources of info	1 0.4%	1 0.6%	0 0	1 0.4%	0 0	* 0.2%	1 0.9%	0 0	0 0	0 0	0 0	0 0	* 5.0%	1 1.5%	0 0	0 0	* 0.1%	1 1.0%
preferred source of info	1 0.3%	1 0.4%	0 0	1 0.3%	0 0	0 0	1 0.9%	0 0	0 0	0 0	0 0	0 0	0 0	1 1.5%	0 0	0 0	0 0	1 1.0%
Printed library catalogues and finding aids	0 0	0 0	0 0	0 0	0 0	0 0	0 0	0 0	0 0	0 0	0 0	0 0	0 0	0 0	0 0	0 0	0 0	0 0
All sources of info	0 0	0 0	0 0	0 0	0 0	0 0	0 0	0 0	0 0	0 0	0 0	0 0	0 0	0 0	0 0	0 0	0 0	0 0
preferred source of info	0 0	0 0	0 0	0 0	0 0	0 0	0 0	0 0	0 0	0 0	0 0	0 0	0 0	0 0	0 0	0 0	0 0	0 0
PERSONAL ASSISTANCE	42 14.6%	24 11.3%	18 23.8%A	42 14.6%	0 0	22 18.8%	13 12.8%	8 10.5%	4 13.5%	7 14.9%	15 16.7%	8 15.6%	1 10.0%	7 11.9%	* 6.7%	0 0	31 15.7%	11 12.2%
Colleagues inside your institution	28 9.7%	18 8.2%	11 13.7%	28 9.7%	0 0	16 13.8%G	9 9.2%	3 3.9%	3 8.1%	4 8.5%	9 10.4%	7 13.3%	1 10.0%	5 7.5%	* 6.7%	0 0	22 10.9%	6 7.0%
All sources of info	28 9.7%	18 8.2%	11 13.7%	28 9.7%	0 0	16 13.8%G	9 9.2%	3 3.9%	3 8.1%	4 8.5%	9 10.4%	7 13.3%	1 10.0%	5 7.5%	* 6.7%	0 0	22 10.9%	6 7.0%

Proportions/Means: Columns Tested (5% risk level) - A/B/D - C/D - E/F/G - H/I/J/K/L/M/N - P/Q
* small base; ** very small base (under 30) ineligible for sig testing

Table 305
Page 1270

Outsell/Digital Library Federation Study (2002)
Weighted Tables

TABLE 129, continued

T7sum_17. News SUMMARY TABLE

	TOTAL SAMPLE	RESPONDENT TYPE: FACULTY MEMBER	GRAD. STUDENT	FACULTY /GRAD	UNDER GRAD. STUDENT	INSTITUTION TYPE: PUBLIC	PRIVATE	LIBERAL ARTS	DISCIPLINE: BIOLOGIAL SCIENCES	PHYSICAL SCIENCES /MATH	SOCIAL SCIENCES	ARTS AND HUMAN.	ENGI- NEERING	BUSINESS	LAW	UNDEC. MAJOR	GENDER: MALE	FEMALE
		(A)	(B)	(C)	(D)	(E)	(F)	(G)	(H)	(I)	(J)	(K)	(L)	(M)	(N)		(P)	(Q)
Base - USe News for teaching	291	214	76*	291	0**	116*	101*	74*	33*	47*	90*	50*	6**	62*	3**	0*	200	91*
preferred source of info	15 5.3%	5 2.2%	11 13.7%A	15 5.3%	0 0	9 7.9%	5 5.1%	1 1.4%	1 2.7%	2 4.3%	4 4.2%	6 11.1%	* 5.0%	3 4.5%	0 0	0 0	10 4.9%	6 6.1%
A librarian in your institution	17 6.0%	10 4.5%	8 10.1%	17 6.0%	0 0	9 7.6%	4 3.7%	5 6.6%	2 5.4%	4 8.5%	8 8.3%	1 2.2%	0 0	3 4.5%	* 6.7%	0 0	13 6.3%	5 5.1%
All sources of info	17 6.0%	10 4.5%	8 10.1%	17 6.0%	0 0	9 7.6%	4 3.7%	5 6.6%	2 5.4%	4 8.5%	8 8.3%	1 2.2%	0 0	3 4.5%	* 6.7%	0 0	13 6.3%	5 5.1%
preferred source of info	9 3.0%	2 0.9%	7 8.8%A	9 3.0%	0 0	5 4.2%	2 1.9%	2 2.6%	0 0	1 2.1%	6 6.3%	1 2.2%	0 0	1 1.5%	0 0	0 0	5 2.5%	4 4.1%
Colleagues outside your institution	9 2.9%	9 4.0%	0 0	9 2.9%	0 0	4 3.2%	3 2.9%	2 2.7%	1 2.7%	3 6.4%	4 4.2%	0 0	0 0	1 1.5%	0 0	0 0	9 4.3%	0 0
All sources of info	9 2.9%	9 4.0%	0 0	9 2.9%	0 0	4 3.2%	3 2.9%	2 2.7%	1 2.7%	3 6.4%	4 4.2%	0 0	0 0	1 1.5%	0 0	0 0	9 4.3%	0 0
preferred source of info	0 0	0 0	0 0	0 0	0 0	0 0	0 0	0 0	0 0	0 0	0 0	0 0	0 0	0 0	0 0	0 0	0 0	0 0
Professional meetings	1 0.3%	1 0.4%	0 0	1 0.3%	0 0	0 0	0 0	1 1.2%	1 2.7%	0 0	0 0	0 0	0 0	0 0	0 0	0 0	1 0.4%	0 0
All sources of info	1 0.3%	1 0.4%	0 0	1 0.3%	0 0	0 0	0 0	1 1.2%	1 2.7%	0 0	0 0	0 0	0 0	0 0	0 0	0 0	1 0.4%	0 0
preferred source of info	1 0.3%	1 0.4%	0 0	1 0.3%	0 0	0 0	0 0	1 1.2%	1 2.7%	0 0	0 0	0 0	0 0	0 0	0 0	0 0	1 0.4%	0 0

Proportions/Means: Columns Tested (5% risk level) - A/B/D - C/D - E/F/G - H/I/J/K/L/M/N - P/Q
* small base; ** very small base (under 30) ineligible for sig testing

Table 305
Page 1271

Outsell/Digital Library Federation Study (2002)
Weighted Tables

TABLE 129, continued

T7sum_17. News SUMMARY TABLE

		RESPONDENT TYPE				INSTITUTION TYPE			DISCIPLINE								GENDER	
	TOTAL SAMPLE	FACULTY MEMBER	GRAD. STUDENT	FACULTY /GRAD	UNDER GRAD. STUDENT	PUBLIC	PRIVATE	LIBERAL ARTS	BIOLOGIAL SCIENCES	PHYSICAL SCIENCES /MATH	SOCIAL SCIENCES	ARTS AND HUMAN.	ENGI-NEERING	BUSINESS	LAW	UNDEC. MAJOR	MALE	FEMALE
		(A)	(B)	(C)	(D)	(E)	(F)	(G)	(H)	(I)	(J)	(K)	(L)	(M)	(N)		(P)	(Q)
Base - USe News for teaching	291	214	76*	291	0**	116*	101*	74*	33*	47*	90*	50*	6**	62*	3**	0*	200	91*
Another institution's librarian	0	0	0	0	0	0	0	0	0	0	0	0	0	0	0	0	0	0
	0	0	0	0	0	0	0	0	0	0	0	0	0	0	0	0	0	0
All sources of info	0	0	0	0	0	0	0	0	0	0	0	0	0	0	0	0	0	0
	0	0	0	0	0	0	0	0	0	0	0	0	0	0	0	0	0	0
preferred source of info	0	0	0	0	0	0	0	0	0	0	0	0	0	0	0	0	0	0
	0	0	0	0	0	0	0	0	0	0	0	0	0	0	0	0	0	0
Online (unspecified)	5	3	2	5	0	2	3	0	0	0	4	0	0	1	0	0	2	3
	1.6%	1.3%	2.5%	1.6%	0	1.6%	2.8%	0	0	0	4.2%	0	0	1.5%	0	0	0.9%	3.1%
All sources of info	5	3	2	5	0	2	3	0	0	0	4	0	0	1	0	0	2	3
	1.6%	1.3%	2.5%	1.6%	0	1.6%	2.8%	0	0	0	4.2%	0	0	1.5%	0	0	0.9%	3.1%
preferred source of info	5	3	2	5	0	2	3	0	0	0	4	0	0	1	0	0	2	3
	1.6%	1.3%	2.5%	1.6%	0	1.6%	2.8%	0	0	0	4.2%	0	0	1.5%	0	0	0.9%	3.1%
Personal office/lab	1	0	1	1	0	0	1	0	1	0	0	0	0	0	0	0	0	1
	0.3%	0	1.2%	0.3%	0	0	0.9%	0	2.7%	0	0	0	0	0	0	0	0	1.0%
All sources of info	1	0	1	1	0	0	1	0	1	0	0	0	0	0	0	0	0	1
	0.3%	0	1.2%	0.3%	0	0	0.9%	0	2.7%	0	0	0	0	0	0	0	0	1.0%
preferred source of info	1	0	1	1	0	0	1	0	1	0	0	0	0	0	0	0	0	1
	0.3%	0	1.2%	0.3%	0	0	0.9%	0	2.7%	0	0	0	0	0	0	0	0	1.0%
Students	0	0	0	0	0	0	0	0	0	0	0	0	0	0	0	0	0	0
	0	0	0	0	0	0	0	0	0	0	0	0	0	0	0	0	0	0

Proportions/Means: Columns Tested (5% risk level) - A/B/D - C/D - E/F/G - H/I/J/K/L/M/N - P/Q
* small base; ** very small base (under 30) ineligible for sig testing

Table 305
Page 1272

Outsell/Digital Library Federation Study (2002)
Weighted Tables

TABLE 129, continued

T7sum_17. News SUMMARY TABLE

		RESPONDENT TYPE				INSTITUTION TYPE			DISCIPLINE									GENDER	
	TOTAL SAMPLE	FACULTY MEMBER	GRAD. STUDENT	FACULTY /GRAD	UNDER GRAD. STUDENT	PUBLIC	PRIVATE	LIBERAL ARTS	BIOLOGIAL SCIENCES	PHYSICAL SCIENCES /MATH	SOCIAL SCIENCES	ARTS AND HUMAN.	ENGI- NEERING	BUSINESS	LAW	UNDEC. MAJOR	MALE	FEMALE
		(A)	(B)	(C)	(D)	(E)	(F)	(G)	(H)	(I)	(J)	(K)	(L)	(M)	(N)		(P)	(Q)
Base - USe News for teaching	291	214	76*	291	0**	116*	101*	74*	33*	47*	90*	50*	6**	62*	3**	0*	200	91*
All sources of info	0 0	0 0	0 0	0 0	0 0	0 0	0 0	0 0	0 0	0 0	0 0	0 0	0 0	0 0	0 0	0 0	0 0	0 0
preferred source of info	0 0	0 0	0 0	0 0	0 0	0 0	0 0	0 0	0 0	0 0	0 0	0 0	0 0	0 0	0 0	0 0	0 0	0 0
Author	0 0	0 0	0 0	0 0	0 0	0 0	0 0	0 0	0 0	0 0	0 0	0 0	0 0	0 0	0 0	0 0	0 0	0 0
All sources of info	0 0	0 0	0 0	0 0	0 0	0 0	0 0	0 0	0 0	0 0	0 0	0 0	0 0	0 0	0 0	0 0	0 0	0 0
preferred source of info	0 0	0 0	0 0	0 0	0 0	0 0	0 0	0 0	0 0	0 0	0 0	0 0	0 0	0 0	0 0	0 0	0 0	0 0
Other	37 12.9%	30 14.0%	7 9.8%	37 12.9%	0 0	19 16.2%	12 11.8%	7 9.1%	3 8.1%	8 17.0%	8 8.3%	8 15.6%	1 15.0%	10 16.4%	* 13.3%	0 0	24 12.0%	13 14.7%
All sources of info	36 12.2%	28 13.1%	7 9.8%	36 12.2%	0 0	19 16.2%	10 9.9%	7 9.1%	3 8.1%	8 17.0%	6 6.3%	8 15.6%	1 15.0%	10 16.4%	* 13.3%	0 0	24 12.0%	12 12.7%
preferred source of info	17 5.9%	14 6.4%	3 4.4%	17 5.9%	0 0	9 7.9%	4 4.2%	4 5.1%	3 8.1%	3 6.4%	2 2.1%	4 8.9%	* 5.0%	5 7.5%	* 6.7%	0 0	12 6.0%	5 5.6%
DK/Refused	21 7.4%	17 8.1%	4 5.1%	21 7.4%	0 0	8 6.8%	5 4.8%	9 11.8%	4 10.8%	5 10.6%	6 6.3%	2 4.4%	0 0	5 7.5%	* 13.3%	0 0	14 6.9%	8 8.4%

Proportions/Means: Columns Tested (5% risk level) - A/B/D - C/D - E/F/G - H/I/J/K/L/M/N - P/Q
* small base; ** very small base (under 30) ineligible for sig testing

Table 305
Page 1273

Outsell/Digital Library Federation Study (2002)
Weighted Tables

TABLE 130

T7D/E_17. News SUMMARY TABLE

		RESPONDENT TYPE				INSTITUTION TYPE			DISCIPLINE									GENDER	
	TOTAL SAMPLE	FACULTY MEMBER	GRAD. STUDENT	FACULTY /GRAD	UNDER GRAD. STUDENT	PUBLIC	PRIVATE	LIBERAL ARTS	BIOLOGIAL SCIENCES	PHYSICAL SCIENCES /MATH	SOCIAL SCIENCES	ARTS AND HUMAN.	ENGI-NEERING	BUSINESS	LAW	UNDEC. MAJOR	MALE	FEMALE
		(A)	(B)	(C)	(D)	(E)	(F)	(G)	(H)	(I)	(J)	(K)	(L)	(M)	(N)		(P)	(Q)
Base - Use News for teaching	291	214	76*	291	0**	116*	101*	74*	33*	47*	90*	50*	6**	62*	3**	0*	200	91*
Access online (NET)	198 68.0%	155 72.2%B	43 56.1%	198 68.0%	0 0	77 66.6%	62 61.1%	59 79.7%F	20 62.2%	36 76.6%K	64 70.8%	28 55.6%	4 70.0%	44 70.1%	2 73.3%	0 0	145 72.4%Q	53 58.4%
All sources of info	198 68.0%	155 72.2%B	43 56.1%	198 68.0%	0 0	77 66.6%	62 61.1%	59 79.7%F	20 62.2%	36 76.6%K	64 70.8%	28 55.6%	4 70.0%	44 70.1%	2 73.3%	0 0	145 72.4%Q	53 58.4%
preferred source of info	158 54.3%	119 55.7%	39 50.4%	158 54.3%	0 0	64 54.8%	50 49.2%	45 60.3%	18 54.1%	30 63.8%K	51 56.3%	20 40.0%	3 55.0%	34 55.2%	2 66.7%	0 0	114 57.1%	44 48.1%
Borrow from or use in campus library (NET)	98 33.6%	67 31.0%	31 40.6%	98 33.6%	0 0	39 33.4%	34 33.8%	25 33.5%	15 45.9%M	14 29.8%	30 33.3%	22 44.4%M	2 35.0%	14 22.4%	* 6.7%	0 0	70 34.9%	28 30.6%
All sources of info	98 33.6%	67 31.0%	31 40.6%	98 33.6%	0 0	39 33.4%	34 33.8%	25 33.5%	15 45.9%M	14 29.8%	30 33.3%	22 44.4%M	2 35.0%	14 22.4%	* 6.7%	0 0	70 34.9%	28 30.6%
preferred source of info	40 13.9%	19 8.9%	21 27.6%A	40 13.9%	0 0	16 14.2%	17 16.9%	7 9.1%	5 16.2%M	4 8.5%	13 14.6%	13 26.7%IM	1 25.0%	3 4.5%	* 6.7%	0 0	26 13.1%	14 15.6%
Access from course website (NET)	66 22.8%	58 26.9%B	9 11.6%	66 22.8%	0 0	29 25.0%	18 17.6%	20 26.7%	9 27.0%	12 25.5%	17 18.8%	8 15.6%	1 25.0%	19 29.9%	1 33.3%	0 0	42 21.0%	25 27.0%
All sources of info	66 22.8%	58 26.9%B	9 11.6%	66 22.8%	0 0	29 25.0%	18 17.6%	20 26.7%	9 27.0%	12 25.5%	17 18.8%	8 15.6%	1 25.0%	19 29.9%	1 33.3%	0 0	42 21.0%	25 27.0%
preferred source of info	42 14.6%	39 18.0%B	4 4.8%	42 14.6%	0 0	18 15.5%	13 13.3%	11 14.8%	7 21.6%	5 10.6%	9 10.4%	4 8.9%	1 15.0%	15 23.9%K	1 26.7%	0 0	29 14.5%	13 14.6%

Proportions/Means: Columns Tested (5% risk level) - A/B/D - C/D - E/F/G - H/I/J/K/L/M/N - P/Q
* small base; ** very small base (under 30) ineligible for sig testing

Table 308
Page 1280

Outsell/Digital Library Federation Study (2002)
Weighted Tables

TABLE 130, continued

T7D/E_17. News SUMMARY TABLE

	TOTAL SAMPLE	RESPONDENT TYPE FACULTY MEMBER	GRAD. STUDENT	FACULTY /GRAD	UNDER GRAD. STUDENT	INSTITUTION TYPE PUBLIC	PRIVATE	LIBERAL ARTS	DISCIPLINE BIOLOGIAL SCIENCES	PHYSICAL SCIENCES /MATH	SOCIAL SCIENCES	ARTS AND HUMAN.	ENGI-NEERING	BUSINESS	LAW	UNDEC. MAJOR	GENDER MALE	FEMALE
		(A)	(B)	(C)	(D)	(E)	(F)	(G)	(H)	(I)	(J)	(K)	(L)	(M)	(N)		(P)	(Q)
Base - Use News for teaching	291	214	76*	291	0**	116*	101*	74*	33*	47*	90*	50*	6**	62*	3**	0*	200	91*
Personal Collection/ Holdings (NET)	25 8.4%	21 9.7%	4 4.9%	25 8.4%	0 0	9 7.7%	8 7.8%	8 10.5%	1 2.7%	5 10.6%	6 6.3%	6 11.1%	0 0	7 11.9%	0 0	0 0	17 8.5%	8 8.3%
All sources of info	25 8.4%	21 9.7%	4 4.9%	25 8.4%	0 0	9 7.7%	8 7.8%	8 10.5%	1 2.7%	5 10.6%	6 6.3%	6 11.1%	0 0	7 11.9%	0 0	0 0	17 8.5%	8 8.3%
preferred source of info	13 4.5%	11 5.2%	2 2.5%	13 4.5%	0 0	5 4.4%	6 6.0%	2 2.6%	0 0	2 4.3%	4 4.2%	4 8.9%	0 0	3 4.5%	0 0	0 0	9 4.7%	4 4.1%
Order from on demand document delivery service (NET)	9 3.1%	9 4.2%	0 0	9 3.1%	0 0	1 0.8%	3 3.0%	5 6.7%E	0 0	2 4.3%	2 2.1%	2 4.4%	0 0	3 4.5%	0 0	0 0	8 4.0%	1 1.0%
All sources of info	9 3.1%	9 4.2%	0 0	9 3.1%	0 0	1 0.8%	3 3.0%	5 6.7%E	0 0	2 4.3%	2 2.1%	2 4.4%	0 0	3 4.5%	0 0	0 0	8 4.0%	1 1.0%
preferred source of info	3 1.0%	3 1.4%	0 0	3 1.0%	0 0	0 0	1 0.9%	2 2.8%	0 0	0 0	0 0	1 2.2%	0 0	2 3.0%	0 0	0 0	2 1.0%	1 1.0%
Purchase from physical book store (NET)	7 2.5%	7 3.4%	0 0	7 2.5%	0 0	2 1.9%	5 5.2%	0 0	1 2.7%	2 4.3%	2 2.1%	1 2.2%	1 10.0%	1 1.5%	0 0	0 0	6 3.1%	1 1.2%
All sources of info	7 2.5%	7 3.4%	0 0	7 2.5%	0 0	2 1.9%	5 5.2%	0 0	1 2.7%	2 4.3%	2 2.1%	1 2.2%	1 10.0%	1 1.5%	0 0	0 0	6 3.1%	1 1.2%
preferred source of info	5 1.7%	5 2.3%	0 0	5 1.7%	0 0	2 1.6%	3 3.1%	0 0	0 0	2 4.3%	2 2.1%	1 2.2%	0 0	0 0	0 0	0 0	4 1.9%	1 1.2%

Proportions/Means: Columns Tested (5% risk level) - A/B/D - C/D - E/F/G - H/I/J/K/L/M/N - P/Q
* small base; ** very small base (under 30) ineligible for sig testing

Table 308
Page 1281

Outsell/Digital Library Federation Study (2002)
Weighted Tables

TABLE 130, continued

T7D/E_17. News SUMMARY TABLE

		RESPONDENT TYPE				INSTITUTION TYPE			DISCIPLINE								GENDER	
	TOTAL SAMPLE	FACULTY MEMBER	GRAD. STUDENT	FACULTY /GRAD	UNDER GRAD. STUDENT	PUBLIC	PRIVATE	LIBERAL ARTS	BIOLOGIAL SCIENCES	PHYSICAL SCIENCES /MATH	SOCIAL SCIENCES	ARTS AND HUMAN.	ENGI-NEERING	BUSINESS	LAW	UNDEC. MAJOR	MALE	FEMALE
		(A)	(B)	(C)	(D)	(E)	(F)	(G)	(H)	(I)	(J)	(K)	(L)	(M)	(N)		(P)	(Q)
Base - Use News for teaching	291	214	76*	291	0**	116*	101*	74*	33*	47*	90*	50*	6**	62*	3**	0*	200	91*
Interlibrary loan (NET)	4 1.4%	2 0.9%	2 2.9%	4 1.4%	0 0	0 0	4 4.1%	0 0	0 0	0 0	2 2.1%	2 4.4%	0 0	0 0	0 0	0 0	3 1.5%	1 1.2%
All sources of info	4 1.4%	2 0.9%	2 2.9%	4 1.4%	0 0	0 0	4 4.1%	0 0	0 0	0 0	2 2.1%	2 4.4%	0 0	0 0	0 0	0 0	3 1.5%	1 1.2%
preferred source of info	0 0	0 0	0 0	0 0	0 0	0 0	0 0	0 0	0 0	0 0	0 0	0 0	0 0	0 0	0 0	0 0	0 0	0 0
Office (NET)	4 1.3%	4 1.8%	0 0	4 1.3%	0 0	0 0	3 2.7%	1 1.4%	1 2.7%	1 2.1%	2 2.1%	0 0	0 0	0 0	0 0	0 0	3 1.4%	1 1.0%
All sources of info	4 1.3%	4 1.8%	0 0	4 1.3%	0 0	0 0	3 2.7%	1 1.4%	1 2.7%	1 2.1%	2 2.1%	0 0	0 0	0 0	0 0	0 0	3 1.4%	1 1.0%
preferred source of info	3 1.0%	3 1.3%	0 0	3 1.0%	0 0	0 0	2 1.9%	1 1.4%	0 0	1 2.1%	2 2.1%	0 0	0 0	0 0	0 0	0 0	3 1.4%	0 0
Department (NET)	3 1.1%	2 1.0%	1 1.5%	3 1.1%	0 0	1 1.0%	2 2.0%	0 0	0 0	0 0	0 0	2 4.4%	0 0	1 1.5%	0 0	0 0	1 0.6%	2 2.2%
All sources of info	3 1.1%	2 1.0%	1 1.5%	3 1.1%	0 0	1 1.0%	2 2.0%	0 0	0 0	0 0	0 0	2 4.4%	0 0	1 1.5%	0 0	0 0	1 0.6%	2 2.2%
preferred source of info	2 0.7%	1 0.4%	1 1.5%	2 0.7%	0 0	0 0	2 2.0%	0 0	0 0	0 0	0 0	1 2.2%	0 0	1 1.5%	0 0	0 0	0 0	2 2.2%

Proportions/Means: Columns Tested (5% risk level) - A/B/D - C/D - E/F/G - H/I/J/K/L/M/N - P/Q
* small base; ** very small base (under 30) ineligible for sig testing

Table 308
Page 1282

Outsell/Digital Library Federation Study (2002)
Weighted Tables

TABLE 130, continued

T7D/E_17. News SUMMARY TABLE

	TOTAL SAMPLE	RESPONDENT TYPE: FACULTY MEMBER	GRAD. STUDENT	FACULTY /GRAD	UNDER GRAD. STUDENT	INSTITUTION TYPE: PUBLIC	PRIVATE	LIBERAL ARTS	DISCIPLINE: BIOLOGIAL SCIENCES	PHYSICAL SCIENCES /MATH	SOCIAL SCIENCES	ARTS AND HUMAN.	ENGI-NEERING	BUSINESS	LAW	UNDEC. MAJOR	GENDER: MALE	FEMALE
		(A)	(B)	(C)	(D)	(E)	(F)	(G)	(H)	(I)	(J)	(K)	(L)	(M)	(N)		(P)	(Q)
Base - Use News for teaching	291	214	76*	291	0**	116*	101*	74*	33*	47*	90*	50*	6**	62*	3**	0*	200	91*
Borrow from or use in other libraries (NET)	3	0	3	3	0	2	1	0	1	0	2	0	0	0	0	0	1	2
	0.9%	0	3.6%A	0.9%	0	1.6%	0.9%	0	2.7%	0	2.1%	0	0	0	0	0	0.4%	2.1%
All sources of info	3	0	3	3	0	2	1	0	1	0	2	0	0	0	0	0	1	2
	0.9%	0	3.6%A	0.9%	0	1.6%	0.9%	0	2.7%	0	2.1%	0	0	0	0	0	0.4%	2.1%
preferred source of info	3	0	3	3	0	2	1	0	1	0	2	0	0	0	0	0	1	2
	0.9%	0	3.6%A	0.9%	0	1.6%	0.9%	0	2.7%	0	2.1%	0	0	0	0	0	0.4%	2.1%
Colleagues (NET)	2	0	2	2	0	2	0	0	0	0	0	2	0	0	0	0	0	2
	0.8%	0	2.9%A	0.8%	0	1.9%	0	0	0	0	0	4.4%	0	0	0	0	0	2.5%
All sources of info	2	0	2	2	0	2	0	0	0	0	0	2	0	0	0	0	0	2
	0.8%	0	2.9%A	0.8%	0	1.9%	0	0	0	0	0	4.4%	0	0	0	0	0	2.5%
preferred source of info	2	0	2	2	0	2	0	0	0	0	0	2	0	0	0	0	0	2
	0.8%	0	2.9%A	0.8%	0	1.9%	0	0	0	0	0	4.4%	0	0	0	0	0	2.5%
Home (NET)	1	1	0	1	0	0	1	0	1	0	0	0	0	0	0	0	0	1
	0.3%	0.4%	0	0.3%	0	0	0.9%	0	2.7%	0	0	0	0	0	0	0	0	1.0%
All sources of info	1	1	0	1	0	0	1	0	1	0	0	0	0	0	0	0	0	1
	0.3%	0.4%	0	0.3%	0	0	0.9%	0	2.7%	0	0	0	0	0	0	0	0	1.0%
preferred source of info	1	1	0	1	0	0	1	0	1	0	0	0	0	0	0	0	0	1
	0.3%	0.4%	0	0.3%	0	0	0.9%	0	2.7%	0	0	0	0	0	0	0	0	1.0%

Proportions/Means: Columns Tested (5% risk level) - A/B/D - C/D - E/F/G - H/I/J/K/L/M/N - P/Q
* small base; ** very small base (under 30) ineligible for sig testing

Table 308
Page 1283

Outsell/Digital Library Federation Study (2002)
Weighted Tables

TABLE 130, continued

T7D/E_17. News SUMMARY TABLE

		RESPONDENT TYPE				INSTITUTION TYPE			DISCIPLINE									GENDER	
	TOTAL SAMPLE	FACULTY MEMBER	GRAD. STUDENT	FACULTY /GRAD	UNDER GRAD. STUDENT	PUBLIC	PRIVATE	LIBERAL ARTS	BIOLOGIAL SCIENCES	PHYSICAL SCIENCES /MATH	SOCIAL SCIENCES	ARTS AND HUMAN.	ENGI-NEERING	BUSINESS	LAW	UNDEC. MAJOR	MALE	FEMALE
		(A)	(B)	(C)	(D)	(E)	(F)	(G)	(H)	(I)	(J)	(K)	(L)	(M)	(N)		(P)	(Q)
Base - Use News for teaching	291	214	76*	291	0**	116*	101*	74*	33*	47*	90*	50*	6**	62*	3**	0*	200	91*
Purchase from online bookstore (NET)	1 0.3%	1 0.4%	0 0	1 0.3%	0 0	0 0	0 0	1 1.2%	1 2.7%	0 0	0 0	0 0	0 0	0 0	0 0	0 0	1 0.4%	0 0
All sources of info	1 0.3%	1 0.4%	0 0	1 0.3%	0 0	0 0	0 0	1 1.2%	1 2.7%	0 0	0 0	0 0	0 0	0 0	0 0	0 0	1 0.4%	0 0
preferred source of info	0 0	0 0	0 0	0 0	0 0	0 0	0 0	0 0	0 0	0 0	0 0	0 0	0 0	0 0	0 0	0 0	0 0	0 0
Meeting/Conferences (NET)	0 0	0 0	0 0	0 0	0 0	0 0	0 0	0 0	0 0	0 0	0 0	0 0	0 0	0 0	0 0	0 0	0 0	0 0
All sources of info	0 0	0 0	0 0	0 0	0 0	0 0	0 0	0 0	0 0	0 0	0 0	0 0	0 0	0 0	0 0	0 0	0 0	0 0
preferred source of info	0 0	0 0	0 0	0 0	0 0	0 0	0 0	0 0	0 0	0 0	0 0	0 0	0 0	0 0	0 0	0 0	0 0	0 0
Ask library to purchase source (NET)	0 0	0 0	0 0	0 0	0 0	0 0	0 0	0 0	0 0	0 0	0 0	0 0	0 0	0 0	0 0	0 0	0 0	0 0
All sources of info	0 0	0 0	0 0	0 0	0 0	0 0	0 0	0 0	0 0	0 0	0 0	0 0	0 0	0 0	0 0	0 0	0 0	0 0
preferred source of info	0 0	0 0	0 0	0 0	0 0	0 0	0 0	0 0	0 0	0 0	0 0	0 0	0 0	0 0	0 0	0 0	0 0	0 0

Proportions/Means: Columns Tested (5% risk level) - A/B/D - C/D - E/F/G - H/I/J/K/L/M/N - P/Q
* small base; ** very small base (under 30) ineligible for sig testing

Table 308
Page 1284

Outsell/Digital Library Federation Study (2002)
Weighted Tables

TABLE 130, continued

T7D/E_17. News SUMMARY TABLE

		RESPONDENT TYPE				INSTITUTION TYPE			DISCIPLINE									GENDER	
	TOTAL SAMPLE	FACULTY MEMBER	GRAD. STUDENT	FACULTY /GRAD	UNDER GRAD. STUDENT	PUBLIC	PRIVATE	LIBERAL ARTS	BIOLOGIAL SCIENCES	PHYSICAL SCIENCES /MATH	SOCIAL SCIENCES	ARTS AND HUMAN.	ENGI-NEERING	BUSINESS	LAW	UNDEC. MAJOR	MALE	FEMALE
		(A)	(B)	(C)	(D)	(E)	(F)	(G)	(H)	(I)	(J)	(K)	(L)	(M)	(N)		(P)	(Q)
Base - Use News for teaching	291	214	76*	291	0**	116*	101*	74*	33*	47*	90*	50*	6**	62*	3**	0*	200	91*
Access book/journal/ journal article elsewhere online (NET)	0 0	0 0	0 0	0 0	0 0	0 0	0 0	0 0	0 0	0 0	0 0	0 0	0 0	0 0	0 0	0 0	0 0	0 0
All sources of info	0 0	0 0	0 0	0 0	0 0	0 0	0 0	0 0	0 0	0 0	0 0	0 0	0 0	0 0	0 0	0 0	0 0	0 0
preferred source of info	0 0	0 0	0 0	0 0	0 0	0 0	0 0	0 0	0 0	0 0	0 0	0 0	0 0	0 0	0 0	0 0	0 0	0 0
Author	0 0	0 0	0 0	0 0	0 0	0 0	0 0	0 0	0 0	0 0	0 0	0 0	0 0	0 0	0 0	0 0	0 0	0 0
All sources of info	0 0	0 0	0 0	0 0	0 0	0 0	0 0	0 0	0 0	0 0	0 0	0 0	0 0	0 0	0 0	0 0	0 0	0 0
preferred source of info	0 0	0 0	0 0	0 0	0 0	0 0	0 0	0 0	0 0	0 0	0 0	0 0	0 0	0 0	0 0	0 0	0 0	0 0
Publisher (NET)	0 0	0 0	0 0	0 0	0 0	0 0	0 0	0 0	0 0	0 0	0 0	0 0	0 0	0 0	0 0	0 0	0 0	0 0
All sources of info	0 0	0 0	0 0	0 0	0 0	0 0	0 0	0 0	0 0	0 0	0 0	0 0	0 0	0 0	0 0	0 0	0 0	0 0
preferred source of info	0 0	0 0	0 0	0 0	0 0	0 0	0 0	0 0	0 0	0 0	0 0	0 0	0 0	0 0	0 0	0 0	0 0	0 0

Proportions/Means: Columns Tested (5% risk level) - A/B/D - C/D - E/F/G - H/I/J/K/L/M/N - P/Q
* small base; ** very small base (under 30) ineligible for sig testing

Table 308
Page 1285

Outsell/Digital Library Federation Study (2002)
Weighted Tables

TABLE 130, continued

T7D/E_17. News SUMMARY TABLE

	RESPONDENT TYPE					INSTITUTION TYPE			DISCIPLINE								GENDER	
	TOTAL SAMPLE	FACULTY MEMBER	GRAD. STUDENT	FACULTY /GRAD	UNDER GRAD. STUDENT	PUBLIC	PRIVATE	LIBERAL ARTS	BIOLOGIAL SCIENCES	PHYSICAL SCIENCES /MATH	SOCIAL SCIENCES	ARTS AND HUMAN.	ENGI-NEERING	BUSINESS	LAW	UNDEC. MAJOR	MALE	FEMALE
		(A)	(B)	(C)	(D)	(E)	(F)	(G)	(H)	(I)	(J)	(K)	(L)	(M)	(N)		(P)	(Q)
Base - Use News for teaching	291	214	76*	291	0**	116*	101*	74*	33*	47*	90*	50*	6**	62*	3**	0*	200	91*
Faculty (NET)	0 0	0 0	0 0	0 0	0 0	0 0	0 0	0 0	0 0	0 0	0 0	0 0	0 0	0 0	0 0	0 0	0 0	0 0
All sources of info	0 0	0 0	0 0	0 0	0 0	0 0	0 0	0 0	0 0	0 0	0 0	0 0	0 0	0 0	0 0	0 0	0 0	0 0
preferred source of info	0 0	0 0	0 0	0 0	0 0	0 0	0 0	0 0	0 0	0 0	0 0	0 0	0 0	0 0	0 0	0 0	0 0	0 0
Other (NET)	11 3.9%	9 4.1%	3 3.3%	11 3.9%	0 0	5 4.5%	3 3.2%	3 3.9%	0 0	1 2.1%	4 4.2%	3 6.7%	* 5.0%	3 4.5%	* 6.7%	0 0	7 3.5%	4 4.8%
All sources of info	9 3.3%	7 3.2%	3 3.3%	9 3.3%	0 0	5 4.5%	3 3.2%	1 1.4%	0 0	1 2.1%	2 2.1%	3 6.7%	* 5.0%	3 4.5%	* 6.7%	0 0	5 2.5%	4 4.8%
preferred source of info	4 1.5%	3 1.3%	1 1.8%	4 1.5%	0 0	1 1.0%	1 1.2%	2 2.5%	0 0	0 0	2 2.1%	1 2.2%	* 5.0%	1 1.5%	0 0	0 0	4 2.0%	* 0.3%
DK/Refused	14 4.9%	11 4.9%	4 4.9%	14 4.9%	0 0	6 5.0%	4 3.8%	5 6.5%	1 2.7%	3 6.4%	6 6.3%	1 2.2%	0 0	4 6.0%	0 0	0 0	8 3.8%	7 7.3%

Proportions/Means: Columns Tested (5% risk level) - A/B/D - C/D - E/F/G - H/I/J/K/L/M/N - P/Q
* small base; ** very small base (under 30) ineligible for sig testing

Table 308
Page 1286

TABLE 131

S7sum_3. e-books SUMMARY TABLE

		RESPONDENT TYPE				INSTITUTION TYPE			DISCIPLINE								GENDER	
	TOTAL SAMPLE	FACULTY MEMBER	GRAD. STUDENT	FACULTY /GRAD	UNDER GRAD. STUDENT	PUBLIC	PRIVATE	LIBERAL ARTS	BIOLOGIAL SCIENCES	PHYSICAL SCIENCES /MATH	SOCIAL SCIENCES	ARTS AND HUMAN.	ENGI- NEERING	BUSINESS	LAW	UNDEC. MAJOR	MALE	FEMALE
		(A)	(B)	(C)	(D)	(E)	(F)	(G)	(H)	(I)	(J)	(K)	(L)	(M)	(N)		(P)	(Q)
Base - Use e-books for coursework	131	0**	46*	46*	85*	54*	34**	43*	18**	15**	45**	22**	7**	12**	1**	10*	58*	73*
ONLINE	106	0	37	37	69	38	32	36	14	10	38	17	6	10	1	10	44	62
	80.7%	0	79.7%	79.7%	81.2%	71.5%	92.0%	83.0%	76.2%	66.7%	83.3%	75.0%	87.5%	84.6%	87.5%	100.0%	75.5%	84.7%
Search engine (NET)	37	0	9	9	28	8	13	16	2	4	8	8	3	6	*	7	20	17
	28.0%	0	19.1%	19.1%	32.8%	15.4%	37.0%	36.4%E	9.5%	26.7%	16.7%	35.0%	41.7%	46.2%	12.5%	70.0%	34.7%	22.6%
All sources of info	37	0	9	9	28	8	13	16	2	4	8	8	3	6	*	7	20	17
	28.0%	0	19.1%	19.1%	32.8%	15.4%	37.0%	36.4%E	9.5%	26.7%	16.7%	35.0%	41.7%	46.2%	12.5%	70.0%	34.7%	22.6%
preferred source of info	30	0	8	8	21	6	12	11	2	4	8	4	2	4	0	6	18	12
	22.5%	0	17.8%	17.8%	24.9%	11.0%	36.2%	25.8%	9.5%	26.7%	16.7%	20.0%	29.2%	30.8%	0	60.0%	30.7%	15.9%
Your own institution's web site (NET)	24	0	8	8	16	5	12	6	4	1	11	3	1	2	*	1	5	19
	18.0%	0	17.1%	17.1%	18.5%	9.2%	35.9%	14.7%	19.0%	6.7%	25.0%	15.0%	20.8%	15.4%	12.5%	10.0%	8.2%	25.8%P
All sources of info	24	0	8	8	16	5	12	6	4	1	11	3	1	2	*	1	5	19
	18.0%	0	17.1%	17.1%	18.5%	9.2%	35.9%	14.7%	19.0%	6.7%	25.0%	15.0%	20.8%	15.4%	12.5%	10.0%	8.2%	25.8%P
preferred source of info	21	0	5	5	16	5	9	6	4	0	11	2	1	1	*	1	4	17
	15.7%	0	10.5%	10.5%	18.5%	9.2%	27.0%	14.7%	19.0%	0	25.0%	10.0%	20.8%	7.7%	12.5%	10.0%	6.5%	23.0%P
Online library catalogues and finding aids (NET)	17	0	6	6	12	8	5	5	3	1	6	4	1	3	0	0	5	12
	13.3%	0	12.0%	12.0%	13.9%	14.6%	13.1%	11.6%	14.3%	6.7%	12.5%	20.0%	12.5%	23.1%	0	0	9.3%	16.4%
All sources of info	17	0	6	6	12	8	5	5	3	1	6	4	1	3	0	0	5	12
	13.3%	0	12.0%	12.0%	13.9%	14.6%	13.1%	11.6%	14.3%	6.7%	12.5%	20.0%	12.5%	23.1%	0	0	9.3%	16.4%

Proportions/Means: Columns Tested (5% risk level) - A/B/D - C/D - E/F/G - H/I/J/K/L/M/N - P/Q
* small base; ** very small base (under 30) ineligible for sig testing

Table 335
Page 1377

Outsell/Digital Library Federation Study (2002)
Weighted Tables

TABLE 131, continued

S7sum_3. e-books SUMMARY TABLE

		RESPONDENT TYPE				INSTITUTION TYPE			DISCIPLINE									GENDER	
	TOTAL SAMPLE	FACULTY MEMBER	GRAD. STUDENT	FACULTY /GRAD	UNDER GRAD. STUDENT	PUBLIC	PRIVATE	LIBERAL ARTS	BIOLOGIAL SCIENCES	PHYSICAL SCIENCES /MATH	SOCIAL SCIENCES	ARTS AND HUMAN.	ENGI-NEERING	BUSINESS	LAW	UNDEC. MAJOR	MALE	FEMALE
		(A)	(B)	(C)	(D)	(E)	(F)	(G)	(H)	(I)	(J)	(K)	(L)	(M)	(N)		(P)	(Q)
Base - Use e-books for coursework	131	0**	46*	46*	85*	54*	34**	43*	18**	15**	45**	22**	7**	12**	1**	10*	58*	73*
preferred source of info	13 9.8%	0 0	5 10.7%	5 10.7%	8 9.3%	6 10.6%	2 6.3%	5 11.6%	3 14.3%	1 6.7%	4 8.3%	3 15.0%	* 4.2%	2 15.4%	0 0	0 0	5 8.8%	8 10.7%
Internet searches (NET)	15 11.4%	0 0	7 14.8%	7 14.8%	8 9.6%	11 19.8%	* 0.8%	4 9.5%	2 9.5%	2 13.3%	6 12.5%	2 10.0%	1 20.8%	1 7.7%	0 0	1 10.0%	10 17.1%	5 6.9%
All sources of info	15 11.4%	0 0	7 14.8%	7 14.8%	8 9.6%	11 19.8%	* 0.8%	4 9.5%	2 9.5%	2 13.3%	6 12.5%	2 10.0%	1 20.8%	1 7.7%	0 0	1 10.0%	10 17.1%	5 6.9%
preferred source of info	11 8.1%	0 0	5 10.1%	5 10.1%	6 7.1%	8 15.7%	0 0	2 5.2%	1 4.8%	2 13.3%	4 8.3%	2 10.0%	1 12.5%	1 7.7%	0 0	0 0	7 11.7%	4 5.3%
Online databases (NET)	12 9.3%	0 0	5 10.7%	5 10.7%	7 8.5%	4 6.5%	3 8.2%	6 13.6%	2 9.5%	1 6.7%	4 8.3%	2 10.0%	1 16.7%	1 7.7%	* 25.0%	1 10.0%	3 5.3%	9 12.4%
All sources of info	12 9.3%	0 0	5 10.7%	5 10.7%	7 8.5%	4 6.5%	3 8.2%	6 13.6%	2 9.5%	1 6.7%	4 8.3%	2 10.0%	1 16.7%	1 7.7%	* 25.0%	1 10.0%	3 5.3%	9 12.4%
preferred source of info	8 5.8%	0 0	4 9.4%	4 9.4%	3 3.8%	4 6.5%	2 6.5%	2 4.3%	2 9.5%	1 6.7%	2 4.2%	1 5.0%	1 8.3%	1 7.7%	* 25.0%	0 0	1 2.4%	6 8.5%
Web directory/ subject related web site (NET)	10 7.8%	0 0	4 8.6%	4 8.6%	6 7.4%	3 5.1%	3 8.9%	4 10.3%	4 19.0%	2 13.3%	2 4.2%	2 10.0%	* 4.2%	0 0	* 25.0%	0 0	4 6.4%	7 9.0%
All sources of info	10 7.8%	0 0	4 8.6%	4 8.6%	6 7.4%	3 5.1%	3 8.9%	4 10.3%	4 19.0%	2 13.3%	2 4.2%	2 10.0%	* 4.2%	0 0	* 25.0%	0 0	4 6.4%	7 9.0%
preferred source of info	6 4.5%	0 0	1 1.9%	1 1.9%	5 5.9%	2 3.5%	1 2.6%	3 7.3%	2 9.5%	1 6.7%	2 4.2%	1 5.0%	0 0	0 0	* 12.5%	0 0	1 1.9%	5 6.6%

Proportions/Means: Columns Tested (5% risk level) - A/B/D - C/D - E/F/G - H/I/J/K/L/M/N - P/Q
* small base; ** very small base (under 30) ineligible for sig testing

Table 335
Page 1378

Outsell/Digital Library Federation Study (2002)
Weighted Tables

TABLE 131, continued

S7sum_3. e-books SUMMARY TABLE

	TOTAL SAMPLE	RESPONDENT TYPE: FACULTY MEMBER	GRAD. STUDENT	FACULTY /GRAD	UNDER GRAD. STUDENT	INSTITUTION TYPE: PUBLIC	PRIVATE	LIBERAL ARTS	DISCIPLINE: BIOLOGIAL SCIENCES	PHYSICAL SCIENCES /MATH	SOCIAL SCIENCES	ARTS AND HUMAN.	ENGI-NEERING	BUSINESS	LAW	UNDEC. MAJOR	GENDER: MALE	FEMALE
		(A)	(B)	(C)	(D)	(E)	(F)	(G)	(H)	(I)	(J)	(K)	(L)	(M)	(N)		(P)	(Q)
Base - Use e-books for coursework	131	0**	46*	46*	85*	54*	34**	43*	18**	15**	45**	22**	7**	12**	1**	10*	58*	73*
Online abstracting and indexing services (NET)	4 3.0%	0 0	2 4.1%	2 4.1%	2 2.5%	2 3.5%	0 0	2 4.9%	0 0	0 0	2 4.2%	1 5.0%	0 0	0 0	0 0	1 10.0%	1 1.7%	3 4.1%
All sources of info	4 3.0%	0 0	2 4.1%	2 4.1%	2 2.5%	2 3.5%	0 0	2 4.9%	0 0	0 0	2 4.2%	1 5.0%	0 0	0 0	0 0	1 10.0%	1 1.7%	3 4.1%
preferred source of info	3 2.2%	0 0	2 4.1%	2 4.1%	1 1.2%	2 3.5%	0 0	1 2.3%	0 0	0 0	2 4.2%	0 0	0 0	0 0	0 0	1 10.0%	1 1.7%	2 2.6%
Department web page (NET)	4 3.0%	0 0	2 4.1%	2 4.1%	2 2.4%	0 0	2 5.5%	2 4.7%	1 4.8%	1 6.7%	2 4.2%	0 0	0 0	0 0	* 12.5%	0 0	3 4.9%	1 1.4%
All sources of info	4 3.0%	0 0	2 4.1%	2 4.1%	2 2.4%	0 0	2 5.5%	2 4.7%	1 4.8%	1 6.7%	2 4.2%	0 0	0 0	0 0	* 12.5%	0 0	3 4.9%	1 1.4%
preferred source of info	4 3.0%	0 0	2 4.1%	2 4.1%	2 2.4%	0 0	2 5.5%	2 4.7%	1 4.8%	1 6.7%	2 4.2%	0 0	0 0	0 0	* 12.5%	0 0	3 4.9%	1 1.4%
Online reference service (NET)	2 1.2%	0 0	1 1.4%	1 1.4%	1 1.2%	1 2.7%	* 0.5%	0 0	0 0	0 0	0 0	0 0	* 4.2%	0 0	* 25.0%	1 10.0%	1 1.1%	1 1.4%
All sources of info	2 1.2%	0 0	1 1.4%	1 1.4%	1 1.2%	1 2.7%	* 0.5%	0 0	0 0	0 0	0 0	0 0	* 4.2%	0 0	* 25.0%	1 10.0%	1 1.1%	1 1.4%
preferred source of info	1 0.9%	0 0	* 0.4%	* 0.4%	1 1.2%	1 2.2%	0 0	0 0	0 0	0 0	0 0	0 0	0 0	0 0	* 12.5%	1 10.0%	* 0.3%	1 1.4%

Proportions/Means: Columns Tested (5% risk level) - A/B/D - C/D - E/F/G - H/I/J/K/L/M/N - P/Q
* small base; ** very small base (under 30) ineligible for sig testing

Table 335
Page 1379

Outsell/Digital Library Federation Study (2002)
Weighted Tables

TABLE 131, continued

S7sum_3. e-books SUMMARY TABLE

		RESPONDENT TYPE				INSTITUTION TYPE			DISCIPLINE								GENDER	
	TOTAL SAMPLE	FACULTY MEMBER	GRAD. STUDENT	FACULTY /GRAD	UNDER GRAD. STUDENT	PUBLIC	PRIVATE	LIBERAL ARTS	BIOLOGIAL SCIENCES	PHYSICAL SCIENCES /MATH	SOCIAL SCIENCES	ARTS AND HUMAN.	ENGI- NEERING	BUSINESS	LAW	UNDEC. MAJOR	MALE	FEMALE
		(A)	(B)	(C)	(D)	(E)	(F)	(G)	(H)	(I)	(J)	(K)	(L)	(M)	(N)		(P)	(Q)
Base - Use e-books for coursework	131	0**	46*	46*	85*	54*	34**	43*	18**	15**	45**	22**	7**	12**	1**	10*	58*	73*
Your own personal electronic library/files (NET)	* 0.2%	0 0	* 0.6%	* 0.6%	0 0	0 0	* 0.8%	0 0	0 0	0 0	0 0	0 0	* 4.2%	0 0	0 0	0 0	* 0.5%	0 0
All sources of info	* 0.2%	0 0	* 0.6%	* 0.6%	0 0	0 0	* 0.8%	0 0	0 0	0 0	0 0	0 0	* 4.2%	0 0	0 0	0 0	* 0.5%	0 0
preferred source of info	0 0	0 0	0 0	0 0	0 0	0 0	0 0	0 0	0 0	0 0	0 0	0 0	0 0	0 0	0 0	0 0	0 0	0 0
E-mail listservs (NET)	0 0	0 0	0 0	0 0	0 0	0 0	0 0	0 0	0 0	0 0	0 0	0 0	0 0	0 0	0 0	0 0	0 0	0 0
All sources of info	0 0	0 0	0 0	0 0	0 0	0 0	0 0	0 0	0 0	0 0	0 0	0 0	0 0	0 0	0 0	0 0	0 0	0 0
preferred source of info	0 0	0 0	0 0	0 0	0 0	0 0	0 0	0 0	0 0	0 0	0 0	0 0	0 0	0 0	0 0	0 0	0 0	0 0
Online bookstore (NET)	0 0	0 0	0 0	0 0	0 0	0 0	0 0	0 0	0 0	0 0	0 0	0 0	0 0	0 0	0 0	0 0	0 0	0 0
All sources of info	0 0	0 0	0 0	0 0	0 0	0 0	0 0	0 0	0 0	0 0	0 0	0 0	0 0	0 0	0 0	0 0	0 0	0 0
preferred source of info	0 0	0 0	0 0	0 0	0 0	0 0	0 0	0 0	0 0	0 0	0 0	0 0	0 0	0 0	0 0	0 0	0 0	0 0

Proportions/Means: Columns Tested (5% risk level) - A/B/D - C/D - E/F/G - H/I/J/K/L/M/N - P/Q
* small base; ** very small base (under 30) ineligible for sig testing

Table 335
Page 1380

TABLE 131, continued

S7sum_3. e-books SUMMARY TABLE

		RESPONDENT TYPE				INSTITUTION TYPE			DISCIPLINE								GENDER	
	TOTAL SAMPLE	FACULTY MEMBER	GRAD. STUDENT	FACULTY /GRAD	UNDER GRAD. STUDENT	PUBLIC	PRIVATE	LIBERAL ARTS	BIOLOGIAL SCIENCES	PHYSICAL SCIENCES /MATH	SOCIAL SCIENCES	ARTS AND HUMAN.	ENGI-NEERING	BUSINESS	LAW	UNDEC. MAJOR	MALE	FEMALE
		(A)	(B)	(C)	(D)	(E)	(F)	(G)	(H)	(I)	(J)	(K)	(L)	(M)	(N)		(P)	(Q)
Base - Use e-books for coursework	131	0**	46*	46*	85*	54*	34**	43*	18**	15**	45**	22**	7**	12**	1**	10*	58*	73*
PERSONAL ASSISTANCE	34 25.9%	0 0	14 30.6%	14 30.6%	20 23.4%	16 30.4%	4 12.6%	13 31.0%	5 28.6%	5 33.3%	8 16.7%	9 40.0%	1 20.8%	4 30.8%	* 12.5%	2 20.0%	20 34.2%	14 19.4%
A librarian in your institution (NET)	19 14.6%	0 0	5 11.4%	5 11.4%	14 16.4%	9 17.6%	* 0.8%	9 21.8%	4 19.0%	1 6.7%	6 12.5%	6 25.0%	1 8.3%	2 15.4%	0 0	1 10.0%	12 20.7%	7 9.7%
All sources of info	19 14.6%	0 0	5 11.4%	5 11.4%	14 16.4%	9 17.6%	* 0.8%	9 21.8%	4 19.0%	1 6.7%	6 12.5%	6 25.0%	1 8.3%	2 15.4%	0 0	1 10.0%	12 20.7%	7 9.7%
preferred source of info	13 9.8%	0 0	3 6.6%	3 6.6%	10 11.6%	8 14.1%	0 0	5 12.4%	4 19.0%	1 6.7%	4 8.3%	3 15.0%	* 4.2%	0 0	0 0	1 10.0%	7 11.9%	6 8.2%
Faculty members inside your institution (NET)	16 12.4%	0 0	9 19.9%	9 19.9%	7 8.4%	7 12.8%	4 12.6%	5 11.8%	2 9.5%	4 26.7%	2 4.2%	4 20.0%	1 16.7%	2 15.4%	* 12.5%	1 10.0%	8 14.0%	8 11.2%
All sources of info	16 12.4%	0 0	9 19.9%	9 19.9%	7 8.4%	7 12.8%	4 12.6%	5 11.8%	2 9.5%	4 26.7%	2 4.2%	4 20.0%	1 16.7%	2 15.4%	* 12.5%	1 10.0%	8 14.0%	8 11.2%
preferred source of info	10 7.4%	0 0	6 12.6%	6 12.6%	4 4.6%	5 9.2%	3 8.5%	2 4.3%	2 9.5%	3 20.0%	2 4.2%	1 5.0%	1 12.5%	1 7.7%	* 12.5%	0 0	5 8.2%	5 6.7%
Other students inside your institution (NET)	5 3.6%	0 0	2 3.4%	2 3.4%	3 3.7%	2 3.8%	2 4.6%	1 2.6%	0 0	1 6.7%	0 0	2 10.0%	1 8.3%	1 7.7%	0 0	0 0	5 8.2%Q	0 0
All sources of info	5 3.6%	0 0	2 3.4%	2 3.4%	3 3.7%	2 3.8%	2 4.6%	1 2.6%	0 0	1 6.7%	0 0	2 10.0%	1 8.3%	1 7.7%	0 0	0 0	5 8.2%Q	0 0

Proportions/Means: Columns Tested (5% risk level) - A/B/D - C/D - E/F/G - H/I/J/K/L/M/N - P/Q
* small base; ** very small base (under 30) ineligible for sig testing

Table 335
Page 1381

Outsell/Digital Library Federation Study (2002)
Weighted Tables

TABLE 131, continued

S7sum_3. e-books SUMMARY TABLE

		RESPONDENT TYPE				INSTITUTION TYPE			DISCIPLINE								GENDER	
	TOTAL SAMPLE	FACULTY MEMBER	GRAD. STUDENT	FACULTY /GRAD	UNDER GRAD. STUDENT	PUBLIC	PRIVATE	LIBERAL ARTS	BIOLOGIAL SCIENCES	PHYSICAL SCIENCES /MATH	SOCIAL SCIENCES	ARTS AND HUMAN.	ENGI-NEERING	BUSINESS	LAW	UNDEC. MAJOR	MALE	FEMALE
		(A)	(B)	(C)	(D)	(E)	(F)	(G)	(H)	(I)	(J)	(K)	(L)	(M)	(N)		(P)	(Q)
Base - Use e-books for coursework	131	0**	46*	46*	85*	54*	34**	43*	18**	15**	45**	22**	7**	12**	1**	10*	58*	73*
preferred source of info	0 0	0 0	0 0	0 0	0 0	0 0	0 0	0 0	0 0	0 0	0 0	0 0	0 0	0 0	0 0	0 0	0 0	0 0
Faculty members outside your institution (NET)	1 0.7%	0 0	1 2.0%	1 2.0%	0 0	1 1.7%	0 0	0 0	0 0	0 0	0 0	0 0	0 0	1 7.7%	0 0	0 0	1 1.6%	0 0
All sources of info	1 0.7%	0 0	1 2.0%	1 2.0%	0 0	1 1.7%	0 0	0 0	0 0	0 0	0 0	0 0	0 0	1 7.7%	0 0	0 0	1 1.6%	0 0
preferred source of info	0 0	0 0	0 0	0 0	0 0	0 0	0 0	0 0	0 0	0 0	0 0	0 0	0 0	0 0	0 0	0 0	0 0	0 0
Another institution's librarian (NET)	0 0	0 0	0 0	0 0	0 0	0 0	0 0	0 0	0 0	0 0	0 0	0 0	0 0	0 0	0 0	0 0	0 0	0 0
All sources of info	0 0	0 0	0 0	0 0	0 0	0 0	0 0	0 0	0 0	0 0	0 0	0 0	0 0	0 0	0 0	0 0	0 0	0 0
preferred source of info	0 0	0 0	0 0	0 0	0 0	0 0	0 0	0 0	0 0	0 0	0 0	0 0	0 0	0 0	0 0	0 0	0 0	0 0
Other students outside your institution (NET)	0 0	0 0	0 0	0 0	0 0	0 0	0 0	0 0	0 0	0 0	0 0	0 0	0 0	0 0	0 0	0 0	0 0	0 0
All sources of info	0 0	0 0	0 0	0 0	0 0	0 0	0 0	0 0	0 0	0 0	0 0	0 0	0 0	0 0	0 0	0 0	0 0	0 0

Proportions/Means: Columns Tested (5% risk level) - A/B/D - C/D - E/F/G - H/I/J/K/L/M/N - P/Q
* small base; ** very small base (under 30) ineligible for sig testing

Table 335
Page 1382

Outsell/Digital Library Federation Study (2002)
Weighted Tables

TABLE 131, continued

S7sum_3. e-books SUMMARY TABLE

		RESPONDENT TYPE				INSTITUTION TYPE			DISCIPLINE									GENDER	
	TOTAL SAMPLE	FACULTY MEMBER	GRAD. STUDENT	FACULTY /GRAD	UNDER GRAD. STUDENT	PUBLIC	PRIVATE	LIBERAL ARTS	BIOLOGIAL SCIENCES	PHYSICAL SCIENCES /MATH	SOCIAL SCIENCES	ARTS AND HUMAN.	ENGI-NEERING	BUSINESS	LAW	UNDEC. MAJOR	MALE	FEMALE
		(A)	(B)	(C)	(D)	(E)	(F)	(G)	(H)	(I)	(J)	(K)	(L)	(M)	(N)		(P)	(Q)
Base - Use e-books for coursework	131	0**	46*	46*	85*	54*	34**	43*	18**	15**	45**	22**	7**	12**	1**	10*	58*	73*
preferred source of info	0 0	0 0	0 0	0 0	0 0	0 0	0 0	0 0	0 0	0 0	0 0	0 0	0 0	0 0	0 0	0 0	0 0	0 0
Professional meetings (NET)	0 0	0 0	0 0	0 0	0 0	0 0	0 0	0 0	0 0	0 0	0 0	0 0	0 0	0 0	0 0	0 0	0 0	0 0
All sources of info	0 0	0 0	0 0	0 0	0 0	0 0	0 0	0 0	0 0	0 0	0 0	0 0	0 0	0 0	0 0	0 0	0 0	0 0
preferred source of info	0 0	0 0	0 0	0 0	0 0	0 0	0 0	0 0	0 0	0 0	0 0	0 0	0 0	0 0	0 0	0 0	0 0	0 0
LIBRARY FACILITIES/ PRINT	17 13.0%	0 0	7 15.7%	7 15.7%	10 11.6%	8 15.7%	3 10.0%	5 12.1%	0 0	3 20.0%	8 16.7%	3 15.0%	1 16.7%	1 7.7%	* 12.5%	1 10.0%	9 15.4%	8 11.2%
Campus library (NET)	15 11.6%	0 0	7 15.7%	7 15.7%	8 9.4%	7 12.2%	3 10.0%	5 12.1%	0 0	3 20.0%	6 12.5%	3 15.0%	1 16.7%	1 7.7%	* 12.5%	1 10.0%	7 12.2%	8 11.2%
All sources of info	15 11.6%	0 0	7 15.7%	7 15.7%	8 9.4%	7 12.2%	3 10.0%	5 12.1%	0 0	3 20.0%	6 12.5%	3 15.0%	1 16.7%	1 7.7%	* 12.5%	1 10.0%	7 12.2%	8 11.2%
preferred source of info	7 5.0%	0 0	4 9.7%	4 9.7%	2 2.4%	3 5.2%	3 7.5%	1 2.6%	0 0	1 6.7%	2 4.2%	2 10.0%	* 4.2%	1 7.7%	* 12.5%	0 0	2 4.0%	4 5.7%
Your own personal physical library/ files/bookshelves (NET)	2 1.4%	0 0	0 0	0 0	2 2.2%	2 3.5%	0 0	0 0	0 0	0 0	2 4.2%	0 0	0 0	0 0	0 0	0 0	2 3.2%	0 0

Proportions/Means: Columns Tested (5% risk level) - A/B/D - C/D - E/F/G - H/I/J/K/L/M/N - P/Q
* small base; ** very small base (under 30) ineligible for sig testing

Table 335
Page 1383

Outsell/Digital Library Federation Study (2002)
Weighted Tables

TABLE 131, continued

S7sum_3. e-books SUMMARY TABLE

		RESPONDENT TYPE				INSTITUTION TYPE			DISCIPLINE									GENDER	
	TOTAL SAMPLE	FACULTY MEMBER	GRAD. STUDENT	FACULTY /GRAD	UNDER GRAD. STUDENT	PUBLIC	PRIVATE	LIBERAL ARTS	BIOLOGIAL SCIENCES	PHYSICAL SCIENCES /MATH	SOCIAL SCIENCES	ARTS AND HUMAN.	ENGI-NEERING	BUSINESS	LAW	UNDEC. MAJOR	MALE	FEMALE
		(A)	(B)	(C)	(D)	(E)	(F)	(G)	(H)	(I)	(J)	(K)	(L)	(M)	(N)		(P)	(Q)
Base - Use e-books for coursework	131	0**	46*	46*	85*	54*	34**	43*	18**	15**	45**	22**	7**	12**	1**	10*	58*	73*
All sources of info	2 1.4%	0 0	0 0	0 0	2 2.2%	2 3.5%	0 0	0 0	0 0	0 0	2 4.2%	0 0	0 0	0 0	0 0	0 0	2 3.2%	0 0
preferred source of info	2 1.4%	0 0	0 0	0 0	2 2.2%	2 3.5%	0 0	0 0	0 0	0 0	2 4.2%	0 0	0 0	0 0	0 0	0 0	2 3.2%	0 0
Physical bookstore (NET)	1 0.9%	0 0	0 0	0 0	1 1.3%	0 0	0 0	1 2.6%	0 0	0 0	0 0	1 5.0%	0 0	0 0	0 0	0 0	0 0	1 1.5%
All sources of info	1 0.9%	0 0	0 0	0 0	1 1.3%	0 0	0 0	1 2.6%	0 0	0 0	0 0	1 5.0%	0 0	0 0	0 0	0 0	0 0	1 1.5%
preferred source of info	0 0	0 0	0 0	0 0	0 0	0 0	0 0	0 0	0 0	0 0	0 0	0 0	0 0	0 0	0 0	0 0	0 0	0 0
Printed abstracting and indexing services (NET)	0 0	0 0	0 0	0 0	0 0	0 0	0 0	0 0	0 0	0 0	0 0	0 0	0 0	0 0	0 0	0 0	0 0	0 0
All sources of info	0 0	0 0	0 0	0 0	0 0	0 0	0 0	0 0	0 0	0 0	0 0	0 0	0 0	0 0	0 0	0 0	0 0	0 0
preferred source of info	0 0	0 0	0 0	0 0	0 0	0 0	0 0	0 0	0 0	0 0	0 0	0 0	0 0	0 0	0 0	0 0	0 0	0 0
References cited in books or journal articles (NET)	0 0	0 0	0 0	0 0	0 0	0 0	0 0	0 0	0 0	0 0	0 0	0 0	0 0	0 0	0 0	0 0	0 0	0 0

Proportions/Means: Columns Tested (5% risk level) - A/B/D - C/D - E/F/G - H/I/J/K/L/M/N - P/Q
* small base; ** very small base (under 30) ineligible for sig testing

Table 335
Page 1384

Outsell/Digital Library Federation Study (2002)
Weighted Tables

TABLE 131, continued

S7sum_3. e-books SUMMARY TABLE

	TOTAL SAMPLE	RESPONDENT TYPE: FACULTY MEMBER	RESPONDENT TYPE: GRAD. STUDENT	RESPONDENT TYPE: FACULTY /GRAD	RESPONDENT TYPE: UNDER GRAD. STUDENT	INSTITUTION TYPE: PUBLIC	INSTITUTION TYPE: PRIVATE	INSTITUTION TYPE: LIBERAL ARTS	DISCIPLINE: BIOLOGIAL SCIENCES	DISCIPLINE: PHYSICAL SCIENCES /MATH	DISCIPLINE: SOCIAL SCIENCES	DISCIPLINE: ARTS AND HUMAN.	DISCIPLINE: ENGI-NEERING	DISCIPLINE: BUSINESS	DISCIPLINE: LAW	DISCIPLINE: UNDEC. MAJOR	GENDER: MALE	GENDER: FEMALE
		(A)	(B)	(C)	(D)	(E)	(F)	(G)	(H)	(I)	(J)	(K)	(L)	(M)	(N)		(P)	(Q)
Base - Use e-books for coursework	131	0**	46*	46*	85*	54*	34**	43*	18**	15**	45**	22**	7**	12**	1**	10*	58*	73*
All sources of info	0 0	0 0	0 0	0 0	0 0	0 0	0 0	0 0	0 0	0 0	0 0	0 0	0 0	0 0	0 0	0 0	0 0	0 0
preferred source of info	0 0	0 0	0 0	0 0	0 0	0 0	0 0	0 0	0 0	0 0	0 0	0 0	0 0	0 0	0 0	0 0	0 0	0 0
Another library (NET)	0 0	0 0	0 0	0 0	0 0	0 0	0 0	0 0	0 0	0 0	0 0	0 0	0 0	0 0	0 0	0 0	0 0	0 0
All sources of info	0 0	0 0	0 0	0 0	0 0	0 0	0 0	0 0	0 0	0 0	0 0	0 0	0 0	0 0	0 0	0 0	0 0	0 0
preferred source of info	0 0	0 0	0 0	0 0	0 0	0 0	0 0	0 0	0 0	0 0	0 0	0 0	0 0	0 0	0 0	0 0	0 0	0 0
Personal subscriptions to newspapers, magazines and journals (NET)	0 0	0 0	0 0	0 0	0 0	0 0	0 0	0 0	0 0	0 0	0 0	0 0	0 0	0 0	0 0	0 0	0 0	0 0
All sources of info	0 0	0 0	0 0	0 0	0 0	0 0	0 0	0 0	0 0	0 0	0 0	0 0	0 0	0 0	0 0	0 0	0 0	0 0
preferred source of info	0 0	0 0	0 0	0 0	0 0	0 0	0 0	0 0	0 0	0 0	0 0	0 0	0 0	0 0	0 0	0 0	0 0	0 0
Printed library catalogues and finding aids (NET)	0 0	0 0	0 0	0 0	0 0	0 0	0 0	0 0	0 0	0 0	0 0	0 0	0 0	0 0	0 0	0 0	0 0	0 0

Proportions/Means: Columns Tested (5% risk level) - A/B/D - C/D - E/F/G - H/I/J/K/L/M/N - P/Q
* small base; ** very small base (under 30) ineligible for sig testing

Table 335
Page 1385

Outsell/Digital Library Federation Study (2002)
Weighted Tables

TABLE 131, continued

S7sum_3. e-books SUMMARY TABLE

	TOTAL SAMPLE	RESPONDENT TYPE: FACULTY MEMBER	GRAD. STUDENT	FACULTY /GRAD	UNDER GRAD. STUDENT	INSTITUTION TYPE: PUBLIC	PRIVATE	LIBERAL ARTS	DISCIPLINE: BIOLOGIAL SCIENCES	PHYSICAL SCIENCES /MATH	SOCIAL SCIENCES	ARTS AND HUMAN.	ENGI-NEERING	BUSINESS	LAW	UNDEC. MAJOR	GENDER: MALE	FEMALE
		(A)	(B)	(C)	(D)	(E)	(F)	(G)	(H)	(I)	(J)	(K)	(L)	(M)	(N)		(P)	(Q)
Base - Use e-books for coursework	131	0**	46*	46*	85*	54*	34**	43*	18**	15**	45**	22**	7**	12**	1**	10*	58*	73*
All sources of info	0	0	0	0	0	0	0	0	0	0	0	0	0	0	0	0	0	0
	0	0	0	0	0	0	0	0	0	0	0	0	0	0	0	0	0	0
preferred source of info	0	0	0	0	0	0	0	0	0	0	0	0	0	0	0	0	0	0
	0	0	0	0	0	0	0	0	0	0	0	0	0	0	0	0	0	0
Other (NET)	2	0	*	*	2	2	*	0	0	0	2	0	0	0	*	0	*	2
	1.6%	0	0.4%	0.4%	2.2%	3.5%	0.5%	0	0	0	4.2%	0	0	0	12.5%	0	0.3%	2.6%
All sources of info	2	0	*	*	2	2	*	0	0	0	2	0	0	0	*	0	*	2
	1.6%	0	0.4%	0.4%	2.2%	3.5%	0.5%	0	0	0	4.2%	0	0	0	12.5%	0	0.3%	2.6%
preferred source of info	2	0	0	0	2	2	0	0	0	0	2	0	0	0	0	0	0	2
	1.4%	0	0	0	2.2%	3.5%	0	0	0	0	4.2%	0	0	0	0	0	0	2.6%
Online (unspecified)	1	0	1	1	0	1	0	0	0	0	0	0	0	1	0	0	1	0
	0.7%	0	2.0%	2.0%	0	1.7%	0	0	0	0	0	0	0	7.7%	0	0	1.6%	0
All sources of info	1	0	1	1	0	1	0	0	0	0	0	0	0	1	0	0	1	0
	0.7%	0	2.0%	2.0%	0	1.7%	0	0	0	0	0	0	0	7.7%	0	0	1.6%	0
preferred source of info	1	0	1	1	0	1	0	0	0	0	0	0	0	1	0	0	1	0
	0.7%	0	2.0%	2.0%	0	1.7%	0	0	0	0	0	0	0	7.7%	0	0	1.6%	0
E-journals	*	0	*	*	0	0	*	0	0	0	0	0	*	0	0	0	*	0
	0.2%	0	0.6%	0.6%	0	0	0.8%	0	0	0	0	0	4.2%	0	0	0	0.5%	0
All sources of info	*	0	*	*	0	0	*	0	0	0	0	0	*	0	0	0	*	0
	0.2%	0	0.6%	0.6%	0	0	0.8%	0	0	0	0	0	4.2%	0	0	0	0.5%	0

Proportions/Means: Columns Tested (5% risk level) - A/B/D - C/D - E/F/G - H/I/J/K/L/M/N - P/Q
* small base; ** very small base (under 30) ineligible for sig testing

Table 335
Page 1386

Outsell/Digital Library Federation Study (2002)
Weighted Tables

TABLE 131, continued

S7sum_3. e-books SUMMARY TABLE

		RESPONDENT TYPE				INSTITUTION TYPE			DISCIPLINE									GENDER	
	TOTAL SAMPLE	FACULTY MEMBER	GRAD. STUDENT	FACULTY /GRAD	UNDER GRAD. STUDENT	PUBLIC	PRIVATE	LIBERAL ARTS	BIOLOGIAL SCIENCES	PHYSICAL SCIENCES /MATH	SOCIAL SCIENCES	ARTS AND HUMAN.	ENGI- NEERING	BUSINESS	LAW	UNDEC. MAJOR	MALE	FEMALE
		(A)	(B)	(C)	(D)	(E)	(F)	(G)	(H)	(I)	(J)	(K)	(L)	(M)	(N)		(P)	(Q)
Base - Use e-books for coursework	131	0**	46*	46*	85*	54*	34**	43*	18**	15**	45**	22**	7**	12**	1**	10*	58*	73*
preferred source of info	0 0	0 0	0 0	0 0	0 0	0 0	0 0	0 0	0 0	0 0	0 0	0 0	0 0	0 0	0 0	0 0	0 0	0 0
DK/Refused	5 4.2%	0 0	1 2.2%	1 2.2%	4 5.2%	2 4.5%	0 0	3 7.0%	0 0	2 13.3%	0 0	2 10.0%	* 4.2%	1 7.7%	0 0	0 0	3 5.7%	2 2.9%

Proportions/Means: Columns Tested (5% risk level) - A/B/D - C/D - E/F/G - H/I/J/K/L/M/N - P/Q
* small base; ** very small base (under 30) ineligible for sig testing

Table 335
Page 1387

Outsell/Digital Library Federation Study (2002)
Weighted Tables

TABLE 132

S7D/E_3. e-books SUMMARY TABLE

		RESPONDENT TYPE				INSTITUTION TYPE			DISCIPLINE								GENDER	
	TOTAL SAMPLE	FACULTY MEMBER	GRAD. STUDENT	FACULTY /GRAD	UNDER GRAD. STUDENT	PUBLIC	PRIVATE	LIBERAL ARTS	BIOLOGIAL SCIENCES	PHYSICAL SCIENCES /MATH	SOCIAL SCIENCES	ARTS AND HUMAN.	ENGI-NEERING	BUSINESS	LAW	UNDEC. MAJOR	MALE	FEMALE
		(A)	(B)	(C)	(D)	(E)	(F)	(G)	(H)	(I)	(J)	(K)	(L)	(M)	(N)		(P)	(Q)
Base - Use e-books for coursework	131	0**	46*	46*	85*	54*	34**	43*	18**	15**	45**	22**	7**	12**	1**	10*	58*	73*
Access online (NET)	93 70.5%	0 0	27 58.3%	27 58.3%	66 77.0%B C	29 54.1%	27 79.8%	36 83.3%E	12 66.7%	11 73.3%	30 66.7%	17 75.0%	6 83.3%	7 61.5%	1 87.5%	8 80.0%	39 66.2%	54 73.9%
All sources of info	93 70.5%	0 0	27 58.3%	27 58.3%	66 77.0%B C	29 54.1%	27 79.8%	36 83.3%E	12 66.7%	11 73.3%	30 66.7%	17 75.0%	6 83.3%	7 61.5%	1 87.5%	8 80.0%	39 66.2%	54 73.9%
preferred source of info	81 61.4%	0 0	23 50.8%	23 50.8%	57 67.1%	24 44.2%	27 78.1%	30 69.5%E	11 61.9%	8 53.3%	26 58.3%	16 70.0%	5 66.7%	7 61.5%	1 87.5%	6 60.0%	33 56.5%	48 65.3%
Borrow from or use in campus library (NET)	46 34.6%	0 0	18 40.2%	18 40.2%	27 31.7%	23 43.6%	9 26.6%	13 29.9%	7 38.1%	6 40.0%	15 33.3%	7 30.0%	3 41.7%	5 38.5%	* 12.5%	3 30.0%	24 40.4%	22 30.1%
All sources of info	46 34.6%	0 0	18 40.2%	18 40.2%	27 31.7%	23 43.6%	9 26.6%	13 29.9%	7 38.1%	6 40.0%	15 33.3%	7 30.0%	3 41.7%	5 38.5%	* 12.5%	3 30.0%	24 40.4%	22 30.1%
preferred source of info	39 29.7%	0 0	17 36.9%	17 36.9%	22 25.8%	22 40.1%	7 19.0%	11 25.3%	6 33.3%	6 40.0%	13 29.2%	4 20.0%	2 33.3%	4 30.8%	* 12.5%	3 30.0%	21 36.6%	18 24.2%
Purchase from online bookstore (NET)	3 2.2%	0 0	3 6.3%D	3 6.3%D	0 0	2 3.5%	1 2.9%	0 0	0 0	1 6.7%	2 4.2%	0 0	0 0	0 0	0 0	0 0	3 4.9%	0 0
All sources of info	3 2.2%	0 0	3 6.3%D	3 6.3%D	0 0	2 3.5%	1 2.9%	0 0	0 0	1 6.7%	2 4.2%	0 0	0 0	0 0	0 0	0 0	3 4.9%	0 0
preferred source of info	3 2.2%	0 0	3 6.3%D	3 6.3%D	0 0	2 3.5%	1 2.9%	0 0	0 0	1 6.7%	2 4.2%	0 0	0 0	0 0	0 0	0 0	3 4.9%	0 0

Proportions/Means: Columns Tested (5% risk level) - A/B/D - C/D - E/F/G - H/I/J/K/L/M/N - P/Q
* small base; ** very small base (under 30) ineligible for sig testing

Table 338
Page 1392

Outsell/Digital Library Federation Study (2002)
Weighted Tables

TABLE 132, continued

S7D/E_3. e-books SUMMARY TABLE

		RESPONDENT TYPE				INSTITUTION TYPE			DISCIPLINE									GENDER	
	TOTAL SAMPLE	FACULTY MEMBER	GRAD. STUDENT	FACULTY /GRAD	UNDER GRAD. STUDENT	PUBLIC	PRIVATE	LIBERAL ARTS	BIOLOGIAL SCIENCES	PHYSICAL SCIENCES /MATH	SOCIAL SCIENCES	ARTS AND HUMAN.	ENGI-NEERING	BUSINESS	LAW	UNDEC. MAJOR	MALE	FEMALE
		(A)	(B)	(C)	(D)	(E)	(F)	(G)	(H)	(I)	(J)	(K)	(L)	(M)	(N)		(P)	(Q)
Base - Use e-books for coursework	131	0**	46*	46*	85*	54*	34**	43*	18**	15**	45**	22**	7**	12**	1**	10*	58*	73*
Purchase from physical book store (NET)	2 1.5%	0 0	0 0	0 0	2 2.3%	2 3.6%	0 0	0 0	0 0	0 0	0 0	0 0	0 0	1 7.7%	0 0	1 10.0%	0 0	2 2.6%
All sources of info	2 1.5%	0 0	0 0	0 0	2 2.3%	2 3.6%	0 0	0 0	0 0	0 0	0 0	0 0	0 0	1 7.7%	0 0	1 10.0%	0 0	2 2.6%
preferred source of info	2 1.5%	0 0	0 0	0 0	2 2.3%	2 3.6%	0 0	0 0	0 0	0 0	0 0	0 0	0 0	1 7.7%	0 0	1 10.0%	0 0	2 2.6%
Home (NET)	2 1.4%	0 0	2 4.1%	2 4.1%	0 0	2 3.5%	0 0	0 0	0 0	0 0	2 4.2%	0 0	0 0	0 0	0 0	0 0	0 0	2 2.6%
All sources of info	2 1.4%	0 0	2 4.1%	2 4.1%	0 0	2 3.5%	0 0	0 0	0 0	0 0	2 4.2%	0 0	0 0	0 0	0 0	0 0	0 0	2 2.6%
preferred source of info	2 1.4%	0 0	2 4.1%	2 4.1%	0 0	2 3.5%	0 0	0 0	0 0	0 0	2 4.2%	0 0	0 0	0 0	0 0	0 0	0 0	2 2.6%
Interlibrary loan (NET)	1 0.9%	0 0	0 0	0 0	1 1.3%	0 0	0 0	1 2.6%	0 0	0 0	0 0	1 5.0%	0 0	0 0	0 0	0 0	0 0	1 1.5%
All sources of info	1 0.9%	0 0	0 0	0 0	1 1.3%	0 0	0 0	1 2.6%	0 0	0 0	0 0	1 5.0%	0 0	0 0	0 0	0 0	0 0	1 1.5%
preferred source of info	0 0	0 0	0 0	0 0	0 0	0 0	0 0	0 0	0 0	0 0	0 0	0 0	0 0	0 0	0 0	0 0	0 0	0 0

Proportions/Means: Columns Tested (5% risk level) - A/B/D - C/D - E/F/G - H/I/J/K/L/M/N - P/Q
* small base; ** very small base (under 30) ineligible for sig testing

Table 338
Page 1393

Outsell/Digital Library Federation Study (2002)
Weighted Tables

TABLE 132, continued

S7D/E_3. e-books SUMMARY TABLE

		RESPONDENT TYPE				INSTITUTION TYPE			DISCIPLINE								GENDER	
	TOTAL SAMPLE	FACULTY MEMBER	GRAD. STUDENT	FACULTY /GRAD	UNDER GRAD. STUDENT	PUBLIC	PRIVATE	LIBERAL ARTS	BIOLOGIAL SCIENCES	PHYSICAL SCIENCES /MATH	SOCIAL SCIENCES	ARTS AND HUMAN.	ENGI- NEERING	BUSINESS	LAW	UNDEC. MAJOR	MALE	FEMALE
		(A)	(B)	(C)	(D)	(E)	(F)	(G)	(H)	(I)	(J)	(K)	(L)	(M)	(N)		(P)	(Q)
Base - Use e-books for coursework	131	0**	46*	46*	85*	54*	34**	43*	18**	15**	45**	22**	7**	12**	1**	10*	58*	73*
Order from on demand document delivery service (NET)	0 0	0 0	0 0	0 0	0 0	0 0	0 0	0 0	0 0	0 0	0 0	0 0	0 0	0 0	0 0	0 0	0 0	0 0
All sources of info	0 0	0 0	0 0	0 0	0 0	0 0	0 0	0 0	0 0	0 0	0 0	0 0	0 0	0 0	0 0	0 0	0 0	0 0
preferred source of info	0 0	0 0	0 0	0 0	0 0	0 0	0 0	0 0	0 0	0 0	0 0	0 0	0 0	0 0	0 0	0 0	0 0	0 0
Access from course website (NET)	0 0	0 0	0 0	0 0	0 0	0 0	0 0	0 0	0 0	0 0	0 0	0 0	0 0	0 0	0 0	0 0	0 0	0 0
All sources of info	0 0	0 0	0 0	0 0	0 0	0 0	0 0	0 0	0 0	0 0	0 0	0 0	0 0	0 0	0 0	0 0	0 0	0 0
preferred source of info	0 0	0 0	0 0	0 0	0 0	0 0	0 0	0 0	0 0	0 0	0 0	0 0	0 0	0 0	0 0	0 0	0 0	0 0
Access book/journal/ journal article elsewhere online (NET)	0 0	0 0	0 0	0 0	0 0	0 0	0 0	0 0	0 0	0 0	0 0	0 0	0 0	0 0	0 0	0 0	0 0	0 0
All sources of info	0 0	0 0	0 0	0 0	0 0	0 0	0 0	0 0	0 0	0 0	0 0	0 0	0 0	0 0	0 0	0 0	0 0	0 0
preferred source of info	0 0	0 0	0 0	0 0	0 0	0 0	0 0	0 0	0 0	0 0	0 0	0 0	0 0	0 0	0 0	0 0	0 0	0 0

Proportions/Means: Columns Tested (5% risk level) - A/B/D - C/D - E/F/G - H/I/J/K/L/M/N - P/Q
* small base; ** very small base (under 30) ineligible for sig testing

Table 338
Page 1394

Outsell/Digital Library Federation Study (2002)
Weighted Tables

TABLE 132, continued
S7D/E_3. e-books SUMMARY TABLE

		RESPONDENT TYPE				INSTITUTION TYPE			DISCIPLINE								GENDER	
	TOTAL SAMPLE	FACULTY MEMBER	GRAD. STUDENT	FACULTY /GRAD	UNDER GRAD. STUDENT	PUBLIC	PRIVATE	LIBERAL ARTS	BIOLOGIAL SCIENCES	PHYSICAL SCIENCES /MATH	SOCIAL SCIENCES	ARTS AND HUMAN.	ENGI-NEERING	BUSINESS	LAW	UNDEC. MAJOR	MALE	FEMALE
		(A)	(B)	(C)	(D)	(E)	(F)	(G)	(H)	(I)	(J)	(K)	(L)	(M)	(N)		(P)	(Q)
Base - Use e-books for coursework	131	0**	46*	46*	85*	54*	34**	43*	18**	15**	45**	22**	7**	12**	1**	10*	58*	73*
Borrow from or use in other libraries (NET)	0 0	0 0	0 0	0 0	0 0	0 0	0 0	0 0	0 0	0 0	0 0	0 0	0 0	0 0	0 0	0 0	0 0	0 0
All sources of info	0 0	0 0	0 0	0 0	0 0	0 0	0 0	0 0	0 0	0 0	0 0	0 0	0 0	0 0	0 0	0 0	0 0	0 0
preferred source of info	0 0	0 0	0 0	0 0	0 0	0 0	0 0	0 0	0 0	0 0	0 0	0 0	0 0	0 0	0 0	0 0	0 0	0 0
Ask library to purchase source (NET)	0 0	0 0	0 0	0 0	0 0	0 0	0 0	0 0	0 0	0 0	0 0	0 0	0 0	0 0	0 0	0 0	0 0	0 0
All sources of info	0 0	0 0	0 0	0 0	0 0	0 0	0 0	0 0	0 0	0 0	0 0	0 0	0 0	0 0	0 0	0 0	0 0	0 0
preferred source of info	0 0	0 0	0 0	0 0	0 0	0 0	0 0	0 0	0 0	0 0	0 0	0 0	0 0	0 0	0 0	0 0	0 0	0 0
Faculty (NET)	0 0	0 0	0 0	0 0	0 0	0 0	0 0	0 0	0 0	0 0	0 0	0 0	0 0	0 0	0 0	0 0	0 0	0 0
All sources of info	0 0	0 0	0 0	0 0	0 0	0 0	0 0	0 0	0 0	0 0	0 0	0 0	0 0	0 0	0 0	0 0	0 0	0 0
preferred source of info	0 0	0 0	0 0	0 0	0 0	0 0	0 0	0 0	0 0	0 0	0 0	0 0	0 0	0 0	0 0	0 0	0 0	0 0

Proportions/Means: Columns Tested (5% risk level) - A/B/D - C/D - E/F/G - H/I/J/K/L/M/N - P/Q
* small base; ** very small base (under 30) ineligible for sig testing

Table 338
Page 1395

Outsell/Digital Library Federation Study (2002)
Weighted Tables

TABLE 132, continued

S7D/E_3. e-books SUMMARY TABLE

		RESPONDENT TYPE				INSTITUTION TYPE			DISCIPLINE								GENDER	
	TOTAL SAMPLE	FACULTY MEMBER	GRAD. STUDENT	FACULTY /GRAD	UNDER GRAD. STUDENT	PUBLIC	PRIVATE	LIBERAL ARTS	BIOLOGIAL SCIENCES	PHYSICAL SCIENCES /MATH	SOCIAL SCIENCES	ARTS AND HUMAN.	ENGI-NEERING	BUSINESS	LAW	UNDEC. MAJOR	MALE	FEMALE
		(A)	(B)	(C)	(D)	(E)	(F)	(G)	(H)	(I)	(J)	(K)	(L)	(M)	(N)		(P)	(Q)
Base - Use e-books for coursework	131	0**	46*	46*	85*	54*	34**	43*	18**	15**	45**	22**	7**	12**	1**	10*	58*	73*
Colleagues (NET)	0	0	0	0	0	0	0	0	0	0	0	0	0	0	0	0	0	0
	0	0	0	0	0	0	0	0	0	0	0	0	0	0	0	0	0	0
All sources of info	0	0	0	0	0	0	0	0	0	0	0	0	0	0	0	0	0	0
	0	0	0	0	0	0	0	0	0	0	0	0	0	0	0	0	0	0
preferred source of info	0	0	0	0	0	0	0	0	0	0	0	0	0	0	0	0	0	0
	0	0	0	0	0	0	0	0	0	0	0	0	0	0	0	0	0	0
In class (NET)	0	0	0	0	0	0	0	0	0	0	0	0	0	0	0	0	0	0
	0	0	0	0	0	0	0	0	0	0	0	0	0	0	0	0	0	0
All sources of info	0	0	0	0	0	0	0	0	0	0	0	0	0	0	0	0	0	0
	0	0	0	0	0	0	0	0	0	0	0	0	0	0	0	0	0	0
preferred source of info	0	0	0	0	0	0	0	0	0	0	0	0	0	0	0	0	0	0
	0	0	0	0	0	0	0	0	0	0	0	0	0	0	0	0	0	0
Dorm room (NET)	0	0	0	0	0	0	0	0	0	0	0	0	0	0	0	0	0	0
	0	0	0	0	0	0	0	0	0	0	0	0	0	0	0	0	0	0
All sources of info	0	0	0	0	0	0	0	0	0	0	0	0	0	0	0	0	0	0
	0	0	0	0	0	0	0	0	0	0	0	0	0	0	0	0	0	0
preferred source of info	0	0	0	0	0	0	0	0	0	0	0	0	0	0	0	0	0	0
	0	0	0	0	0	0	0	0	0	0	0	0	0	0	0	0	0	0
Personal Holdings (NET)	0	0	0	0	0	0	0	0	0	0	0	0	0	0	0	0	0	0
	0	0	0	0	0	0	0	0	0	0	0	0	0	0	0	0	0	0

Proportions/Means: Columns Tested (5% risk level) - A/B/D - C/D - E/F/G - H/I/J/K/L/M/N - P/Q
* small base; ** very small base (under 30) ineligible for sig testing

Table 338
Page 1396

Outsell/Digital Library Federation Study (2002)
Weighted Tables

TABLE 132, continued

S7D/E_3. e-books SUMMARY TABLE

		RESPONDENT TYPE				INSTITUTION TYPE			DISCIPLINE								GENDER	
	TOTAL SAMPLE	FACULTY MEMBER	GRAD. STUDENT	FACULTY /GRAD	UNDER GRAD. STUDENT	PUBLIC	PRIVATE	LIBERAL ARTS	BIOLOGIAL SCIENCES	PHYSICAL SCIENCES /MATH	SOCIAL SCIENCES	ARTS AND HUMAN.	ENGI-NEERING	BUSINESS	LAW	UNDEC. MAJOR	MALE	FEMALE
		(A)	(B)	(C)	(D)	(E)	(F)	(G)	(H)	(I)	(J)	(K)	(L)	(M)	(N)		(P)	(Q)
Base - Use e-books for coursework	131	0**	46*	46*	85*	54*	34**	43*	18**	15**	45**	22**	7**	12**	1**	10*	58*	73*
All sources of info	0	0	0	0	0	0	0	0	0	0	0	0	0	0	0	0	0	0
	0	0	0	0	0	0	0	0	0	0	0	0	0	0	0	0	0	0
preferred source of info	0	0	0	0	0	0	0	0	0	0	0	0	0	0	0	0	0	0
	0	0	0	0	0	0	0	0	0	0	0	0	0	0	0	0	0	0
Other (NET)	3	0	0	0	3	3	0	0	0	0	2	0	0	0	0	1	0	3
	2.2%	0	0	0	3.4%	5.4%	0	0	0	0	4.2%	0	0	0	0	10.0%	0	3.9%
All sources of info	3	0	0	0	3	3	0	0	0	0	2	0	0	0	0	1	0	3
	2.2%	0	0	0	3.4%	5.4%	0	0	0	0	4.2%	0	0	0	0	10.0%	0	3.9%
preferred source of info	2	0	0	0	2	2	0	0	0	0	2	0	0	0	0	0	0	2
	1.4%	0	0	0	2.2%	3.5%	0	0	0	0	4.2%	0	0	0	0	0	0	2.6%
DK/Refused	3	0	1	1	2	1	0	2	1	0	0	2	0	0	0	0	1	2
	2.4%	0	1.9%	1.9%	2.6%	1.6%	0	5.2%	4.8%	0	0	10.0%	0	0	0	0	1.9%	2.7%

Proportions/Means: Columns Tested (5% risk level) - A/B/D - C/D - E/F/G - H/I/J/K/L/M/N - P/Q
* small base; ** very small base (under 30) ineligible for sig testing

Table 338
Page 1397

Outsell/Digital Library Federation Study (2002)
Weighted Tables

TABLE 133

S7sum_5. Magazines SUMMARY TABLE

	TOTAL SAMPLE	RESPONDENT TYPE: FACULTY MEMBER	GRAD. STUDENT	FACULTY /GRAD	UNDER GRAD. STUDENT	INSTITUTION TYPE: PUBLIC	PRIVATE	LIBERAL ARTS	DISCIPLINE: BIOLOGIAL SCIENCES	PHYSICAL SCIENCES /MATH	SOCIAL SCIENCES	ARTS AND HUMAN.	ENGI-NEERING	BUSINESS	LAW	UNDEC. MAJOR	GENDER: MALE	FEMALE
		(A)	(B)	(C)	(D)	(E)	(F)	(G)	(H)	(I)	(J)	(K)	(L)	(M)	(N)		(P)	(Q)
Base - Use Magazines for coursework	408	0**	125	125	283	183	72*	152	41*	36*	135*	106*	11*	53*	2**	23*	209	199
ONLINE	308 75.5%	0 0	102 81.8%	102 81.8%	206 72.7%	134 73.1%	59 81.2%	115 75.6%	33 80.9%	29 80.6%	102 75.0%	77 72.6%	8 66.7%	42 78.9%	1 80.0%	16 69.6%	158 75.7%	150 75.2%
Search engine (NET)	92 22.5%	0 0	20 16.0%	20 16.0%	72 25.4%	25 13.5%	22 30.3%E	45 29.6%E	8 19.1%	6 16.7%	34 25.0%	18 16.8%	3 25.6%	15 28.1%	* 20.0%	8 34.8%	53 25.3%	39 19.6%
All sources of info	92 22.5%	0 0	20 16.0%	20 16.0%	72 25.4%	25 13.5%	22 30.3%E	45 29.6%E	8 19.1%	6 16.7%	34 25.0%	18 16.8%	3 25.6%	15 28.1%	* 20.0%	8 34.8%	53 25.3%	39 19.6%
preferred source of info	58 14.1%	0 0	11 9.1%	11 9.1%	46 16.3%	16 8.8%	17 23.5%E	24 16.0%	5 12.8%	3 8.3%	23 16.7%	8 7.4%	1 12.8%	10 19.3%K	* 10.0%	7 30.4%	33 15.8%	25 12.3%
Your own institution's web site (NET)	72 17.5%	0 0	24 19.3%	24 19.3%	48 16.8%	31 17.0%	11 14.8%	30 19.5%	5 12.8%	8 22.2%	36 26.4%KM	13 12.6%	1 10.3%	5 8.8%	* 20.0%	3 13.0%	24 11.7%	47 23.6%P
All sources of info	72 17.5%	0 0	24 19.3%	24 19.3%	48 16.8%	31 17.0%	11 14.8%	30 19.5%	5 12.8%	8 22.2%	36 26.4%KM	13 12.6%	1 10.3%	5 8.8%	* 20.0%	3 13.0%	24 11.7%	47 23.6%P
preferred source of info	44 10.9%	0 0	14 11.4%	14 11.4%	30 10.6%	16 8.7%	9 12.2%	20 12.8%	2 4.3%	6 16.7%M	23 16.7%M	10 9.5%	1 7.7%	2 3.5%	* 10.0%	1 4.3%	16 7.4%	29 14.4%P
Online library catalogues and finding aids (NET)	66 16.1%	0 0	24 19.2%	24 19.2%	42 14.8%	24 13.0%	16 21.9%	26 17.1%	9 21.3%	13 36.1%JK	13 9.7%	16 14.7%	2 15.4%	10 19.3%	* 10.0%	3 13.0%	29 13.7%	37 18.7%
All sources of info	66 16.1%	0 0	24 19.2%	24 19.2%	42 14.8%	24 13.0%	16 21.9%	26 17.1%	9 21.3%	13 36.1%JK	13 9.7%	16 14.7%	2 15.4%	10 19.3%	* 10.0%	3 13.0%	29 13.7%	37 18.7%

Proportions/Means: Columns Tested (5% risk level) - A/B/D - C/D - E/F/G - H/I/J/K/L/M/N - P/Q
* small base; ** very small base (under 30) ineligible for sig testing

Table 349
Page 1443

Outsell/Digital Library Federation Study (2002)
Weighted Tables

TABLE 133, continued

S7sum_5. Magazines SUMMARY TABLE

	TOTAL SAMPLE	RESPONDENT TYPE: FACULTY MEMBER	GRAD. STUDENT	FACULTY /GRAD	UNDER GRAD. STUDENT	INSTITUTION TYPE: PUBLIC	PRIVATE	LIBERAL ARTS	DISCIPLINE: BIOLOGIAL SCIENCES	PHYSICAL SCIENCES /MATH	SOCIAL SCIENCES	ARTS AND HUMAN.	ENGI-NEERING	BUSINESS	LAW	UNDEC. MAJOR	GENDER: MALE	FEMALE
		(A)	(B)	(C)	(D)	(E)	(F)	(G)	(H)	(I)	(J)	(K)	(L)	(M)	(N)		(P)	(Q)
Base - Use Magazines for coursework	408	0**	125	125	283	183	72*	152	41*	36*	135*	106*	11*	53*	2**	23*	209	199
preferred source of info	44 10.8%	0 0	18 14.6%	18 14.6%	26 9.2%	14 7.7%	12 16.6%	18 11.8%	7 17.0%J	8 22.2%J	8 5.6%	12 11.6%	1 7.7%	7 12.3%	0 0	2 8.7%	18 8.7%	26 13.1%
Internet searches (NET)	50 12.2%	0 0	21 16.9%	21 16.9%	29 10.1%	32 17.5%G	7 9.4%	11 7.1%	4 8.5%	3 8.3%	15 11.1%	15 13.7%	2 17.9%	9 17.5%	* 10.0%	2 8.7%	27 12.9%	23 11.4%
All sources of info	50 12.2%	0 0	21 16.9%	21 16.9%	29 10.1%	32 17.5%G	7 9.4%	11 7.1%	4 8.5%	3 8.3%	15 11.1%	15 13.7%	2 17.9%	9 17.5%	* 10.0%	2 8.7%	27 12.9%	23 11.4%
preferred source of info	24 5.8%	0 0	7 5.7%	7 5.7%	16 5.8%	16 8.9%G	3 4.8%	4 2.6%	2 4.3%	1 2.8%	8 5.6%	8 7.4%	1 7.7%	5 8.8%	0 0	0 0	14 6.6%	10 4.9%
Online databases (NET)	49 11.9%	0 0	22 18.0%D	22 18.0%D	26 9.2%	24 13.1%	7 10.0%	17 11.4%	5 12.8%	4 11.1%	11 8.3%	18 16.8%	1 5.1%	8 15.8%	* 10.0%	1 4.3%	28 13.4%	21 10.3%
All sources of info	49 11.9%	0 0	22 18.0%D	22 18.0%D	26 9.2%	24 13.1%	7 10.0%	17 11.4%	5 12.8%	4 11.1%	11 8.3%	18 16.8%	1 5.1%	8 15.8%	* 10.0%	1 4.3%	28 13.4%	21 10.3%
preferred source of info	39 9.6%	0 0	17 13.8%	17 13.8%	22 7.8%	21 11.5%	4 5.6%	14 9.3%	3 6.4%	4 11.1%	11 8.3%	13 12.6%	* 2.6%	7 12.3%	* 10.0%	1 4.3%	23 10.8%	17 8.4%
Web directory/ subject related web site (NET)	34 8.3%	0 0	9 7.5%	9 7.5%	25 8.7%	15 8.4%	4 5.6%	15 9.6%	5 12.8%	2 5.6%	11 8.3%	7 6.3%	1 5.1%	5 8.8%	1 30.0%	3 13.0%	22 10.8%	12 5.8%
All sources of info	34 8.3%	0 0	9 7.5%	9 7.5%	25 8.7%	15 8.4%	4 5.6%	15 9.6%	5 12.8%	2 5.6%	11 8.3%	7 6.3%	1 5.1%	5 8.8%	1 30.0%	3 13.0%	22 10.8%	12 5.8%
preferred source of info	18 4.4%	0 0	2 2.0%	2 2.0%	16 5.5%	9 4.7%	2 2.8%	8 4.9%	4 8.5%	1 2.8%	8 5.6%	2 2.1%	1 5.1%	2 3.5%	* 20.0%	1 4.3%	9 4.5%	9 4.3%

Proportions/Means: Columns Tested (5% risk level) - A/B/D - C/D - E/F/G - H/I/J/K/L/M/N - P/Q
* small base; ** very small base (under 30) ineligible for sig testing

Table 349
Page 1444

TABLE 133, continued

S7sum_5. Magazines SUMMARY TABLE

		RESPONDENT TYPE				INSTITUTION TYPE			DISCIPLINE									GENDER	
	TOTAL SAMPLE	FACULTY MEMBER	GRAD. STUDENT	FACULTY /GRAD	UNDER GRAD. STUDENT	PUBLIC	PRIVATE	LIBERAL ARTS	BIOLOGIAL SCIENCES	PHYSICAL SCIENCES /MATH	SOCIAL SCIENCES	ARTS AND HUMAN.	ENGI- NEERING	BUSINESS	LAW	UNDEC. MAJOR	MALE	FEMALE
		(A)	(B)	(C)	(D)	(E)	(F)	(G)	(H)	(I)	(J)	(K)	(L)	(M)	(N)		(P)	(Q)
Base - Use Magazines for coursework	408	0**	125	125	283	183	72*	152	41*	36*	135*	106*	11*	53*	2**	23*	209	199
Online reference service (NET)	20 4.8%	0 0	10 7.6%	10 7.6%	10 3.6%	11 5.8%	5 6.9%	4 2.7%	5 12.8%IK	0 0	6 4.2%	3 3.2%	1 5.1%I	3 5.3%	0 0	2 8.7%	13 6.2%	7 3.4%
All sources of info	20 4.8%	0 0	10 7.6%	10 7.6%	10 3.6%	11 5.8%	5 6.9%	4 2.7%	5 12.8%IK	0 0	6 4.2%	3 3.2%	1 5.1%I	3 5.3%	0 0	2 8.7%	13 6.2%	7 3.4%
preferred source of info	6 1.6%	0 0	5 3.7%D	5 3.7%D	2 0.7%	3 1.5%	3 3.7%	1 0.6%	2 4.3%K	0 0	2 1.4%	0 0	0 0	3 5.3%K	0 0	0 0	4 1.7%	3 1.4%
Department web page (NET)	10 2.5%	0 0	5 4.2%	5 4.2%	5 1.7%	9 5.0%G	0 0	1 0.6%	3 6.4%	0 0	4 2.8%	3 3.2%	* 2.6%	0 0	0 0	0 0	7 3.5%	3 1.4%
All sources of info	10 2.5%	0 0	5 4.2%	5 4.2%	5 1.7%	9 5.0%G	0 0	1 0.6%	3 6.4%	0 0	4 2.8%	3 3.2%	* 2.6%	0 0	0 0	0 0	7 3.5%	3 1.4%
preferred source of info	4 1.1%	0 0	2 1.8%	2 1.8%	2 0.7%	3 1.9%	0 0	1 0.6%	2 4.3%J	0 0	0 0	2 2.1%	* 2.6%J	0 0	0 0	0 0	4 2.1%	0 0
Online abstracting and indexing services (NET)	7 1.7%	0 0	3 2.0%	3 2.0%	4 1.5%	1 0.6%	1 1.9%	4 2.8%	1 2.1%	0 0	0 0	4 4.2%J	* 2.6%J	0 0	* 10.0%	1 4.3%	6 2.8%	1 0.5%
All sources of info	7 1.7%	0 0	3 2.0%	3 2.0%	4 1.5%	1 0.6%	1 1.9%	4 2.8%	1 2.1%	0 0	0 0	4 4.2%J	* 2.6%J	0 0	* 10.0%	1 4.3%	6 2.8%	1 0.5%
preferred source of info	5 1.1%	0 0	1 0.9%	1 0.9%	3 1.2%	0 0	1 1.5%	3 2.2%	0 0	0 0	0 0	3 3.2%	0 0	0 0	* 10.0%	1 4.3%	4 2.1%	* 0.1%
Online bookstore (NET)	2 0.5%	0 0	2 1.6%	2 1.6%	0 0	1 0.6%	1 1.3%	0 0	0 0	0 0	0 0	1 1.1%	0 0	1 1.8%	0 0	0 0	0 0	2 1.0%

Proportions/Means: Columns Tested (5% risk level) - A/B/D - C/D - E/F/G - H/I/J/K/L/M/N - P/Q
* small base; ** very small base (under 30) ineligible for sig testing

Table 349
Page 1445

Outsell/Digital Library Federation Study (2002)
Weighted Tables

TABLE 133, continued

S7sum_5. Magazines SUMMARY TABLE

		RESPONDENT TYPE				INSTITUTION TYPE			DISCIPLINE									GENDER	
	TOTAL SAMPLE	FACULTY MEMBER	GRAD. STUDENT	FACULTY /GRAD	UNDER GRAD. STUDENT	PUBLIC	PRIVATE	LIBERAL ARTS	BIOLOGIAL SCIENCES	PHYSICAL SCIENCES /MATH	SOCIAL SCIENCES	ARTS AND HUMAN.	ENGI-NEERING	BUSINESS	LAW	UNDEC. MAJOR	MALE	FEMALE
		(A)	(B)	(C)	(D)	(E)	(F)	(G)	(H)	(I)	(J)	(K)	(L)	(M)	(N)		(P)	(Q)
Base - Use Magazines for coursework	408	0**	125	125	283	183	72*	152	41*	36*	135*	106*	11*	53*	2**	23*	209	199
All sources of info	2 0.5%	0 0	2 1.6%	2 1.6%	0 0	1 0.6%	1 1.3%	0 0	0 0	0 0	0 0	1 1.1%	0 0	1 1.8%	0 0	0 0	0 0	2 1.0%
preferred source of info	0 0	0 0	0 0	0 0	0 0	0 0	0 0	0 0	0 0	0 0	0 0	0 0	0 0	0 0	0 0	0 0	0 0	0 0
Your own personal electronic library/files (NET)	1 0.3%	0 0	* 0.1%	* 0.1%	1 0.4%	* 0.1%	0 0	1 0.7%	0 0	1 2.8%	0 0	0 0	0 0	0 0	* 10.0%	0 0	* 0.1%	1 0.5%
All sources of info	1 0.3%	0 0	* 0.1%	* 0.1%	1 0.4%	* 0.1%	0 0	1 0.7%	0 0	1 2.8%	0 0	0 0	0 0	0 0	* 10.0%	0 0	* 0.1%	1 0.5%
preferred source of info	1 0.2%	0 0	0 0	0 0	1 0.4%	0 0	0 0	1 0.7%	0 0	1 2.8%	0 0	0 0	0 0	0 0	0 0	0 0	0 0	1 0.5%
E-mail listservs (NET)	0 0	0 0	0 0	0 0	0 0	0 0	0 0	0 0	0 0	0 0	0 0	0 0	0 0	0 0	0 0	0 0	0 0	0 0
All sources of info	0 0	0 0	0 0	0 0	0 0	0 0	0 0	0 0	0 0	0 0	0 0	0 0	0 0	0 0	0 0	0 0	0 0	0 0
preferred source of info	0 0	0 0	0 0	0 0	0 0	0 0	0 0	0 0	0 0	0 0	0 0	0 0	0 0	0 0	0 0	0 0	0 0	0 0
LIBRARY FACILITIES/ PRINT	129 31.5%	0 0	43 34.5%	43 34.5%	86 30.2%	59 32.0%	21 29.0%	49 32.1%	15 36.2%	7 19.4%	43 31.9%	34 31.6%	5 41.0%I	16 29.8%	* 20.0%	9 39.1%	68 32.6%	60 30.3%

Proportions/Means: Columns Tested (5% risk level) - A/B/D - C/D - E/F/G - H/I/J/K/L/M/N - P/Q
* small base; ** very small base (under 30) ineligible for sig testing

Table 349
Page 1446

Outsell/Digital Library Federation Study (2002)
Weighted Tables

TABLE 133, continued

S7sum_5. Magazines SUMMARY TABLE

		RESPONDENT TYPE				INSTITUTION TYPE			DISCIPLINE								GENDER	
	TOTAL SAMPLE	FACULTY MEMBER	GRAD. STUDENT	FACULTY /GRAD	UNDER GRAD. STUDENT	PUBLIC	PRIVATE	LIBERAL ARTS	BIOLOGIAL SCIENCES	PHYSICAL SCIENCES /MATH	SOCIAL SCIENCES	ARTS AND HUMAN.	ENGI-NEERING	BUSINESS	LAW	UNDEC. MAJOR	MALE	FEMALE
		(A)	(B)	(C)	(D)	(E)	(F)	(G)	(H)	(I)	(J)	(K)	(L)	(M)	(N)		(P)	(Q)
Base - Use Magazines for coursework	408	0**	125	125	283	183	72*	152	41*	36*	135*	106*	11*	53*	2**	23*	209	199
Campus library (NET)	112 27.4%	0 0	37 29.9%	37 29.9%	74 26.3%	50 27.0%	17 23.5%	45 29.6%	12 29.8%	6 16.7%	38 27.8%	31 29.5%	4 35.9%I	12 22.8%	* 20.0%	8 34.8%	61 29.1%	51 25.6%
All sources of info	112 27.4%	0 0	37 29.9%	37 29.9%	74 26.3%	50 27.0%	17 23.5%	45 29.6%	12 29.8%	6 16.7%	38 27.8%	31 29.5%	4 35.9%I	12 22.8%	* 20.0%	8 34.8%	61 29.1%	51 25.6%
preferred source of info	73 17.8%	0 0	21 16.5%	21 16.5%	52 18.4%	32 17.4%	11 15.7%	30 19.4%	6 14.9%	3 8.3%	24 18.1%	25 23.2%	3 23.1%	7 12.3%	* 20.0%	5 21.7%	37 17.8%	35 17.8%
Physical bookstore (NET)	10 2.6%	0 0	4 3.4%	4 3.4%	6 2.2%	5 2.5%	2 2.8%	4 2.5%	0 0	0 0	2 1.4%	4 4.2%	* 2.6%	3 5.3%	0 0	1 4.3%	6 3.0%	4 2.1%
All sources of info	10 2.6%	0 0	4 3.4%	4 3.4%	6 2.2%	5 2.5%	2 2.8%	4 2.5%	0 0	0 0	2 1.4%	4 4.2%	* 2.6%	3 5.3%	0 0	1 4.3%	6 3.0%	4 2.1%
preferred source of info	3 0.7%	0 0	1 0.7%	1 0.7%	2 0.7%	1 0.6%	1 1.3%	1 0.7%	0 0	0 0	0 0	1 1.1%	0 0	1 1.8%	0 0	1 4.3%	2 1.0%	1 0.5%
Personal subscriptions to newspapers, magazines and journals (NET)	9 2.2%	0 0	6 5.0%D	6 5.0%D	3 1.0%	2 1.1%	4 5.8%E	3 1.8%	1 2.1%	0 0	0 0	2 2.1%	* 2.6%J	6 10.5%IJK	0 0	0 0	3 1.4%	6 3.0%
All sources of info	9 2.2%	0 0	6 5.0%D	6 5.0%D	3 1.0%	2 1.1%	4 5.8%E	3 1.8%	1 2.1%	0 0	0 0	2 2.1%	* 2.6%J	6 10.5%IJK	0 0	0 0	3 1.4%	6 3.0%
preferred source of info	2 0.5%	0 0	2 1.7%D	2 1.7%D	0 0	1 0.5%	1 1.7%	0 0	0 0	0 0	0 0	0 0	* 2.6%JK	2 3.5%J	0 0	0 0	0 0	2 1.1%

Proportions/Means: Columns Tested (5% risk level) - A/B/D - C/D - E/F/G - H/I/J/K/L/M/N - P/Q
* small base; ** very small base (under 30) ineligible for sig testing

Table 349
Page 1447

Outsell/Digital Library Federation Study (2002)
Weighted Tables

TABLE 133, continued

S7sum_5. Magazines SUMMARY TABLE

		RESPONDENT TYPE				INSTITUTION TYPE			DISCIPLINE								GENDER	
	TOTAL SAMPLE	FACULTY MEMBER	GRAD. STUDENT	FACULTY /GRAD	UNDER GRAD. STUDENT	PUBLIC	PRIVATE	LIBERAL ARTS	BIOLOGIAL SCIENCES	PHYSICAL SCIENCES /MATH	SOCIAL SCIENCES	ARTS AND HUMAN.	ENGI- NEERING	BUSINESS	LAW	UNDEC. MAJOR	MALE	FEMALE
		(A)	(B)	(C)	(D)	(E)	(F)	(G)	(H)	(I)	(J)	(K)	(L)	(M)	(N)		(P)	(Q)
Base - Use Magazines for coursework	408	0**	125	125	283	183	72*	152	41*	36*	135*	106*	11*	53*	2**	23*	209	199
References cited in books or journal articles (NET)	6 1.4%	0 0	0 0	0 0	6 2.0%	0 0	2 2.6%E	4 2.4%	2 4.3%K	1 2.8%	2 1.4%	0 0	0 0	1 1.8%	0 0	0 0	2 0.9%	4 1.8%
All sources of info	6 1.4%	0 0	0 0	0 0	6 2.0%	0 0	2 2.6%E	4 2.4%	2 4.3%K	1 2.8%	2 1.4%	0 0	0 0	1 1.8%	0 0	0 0	2 0.9%	4 1.8%
preferred source of info	0 0	0 0	0 0	0 0	0 0	0 0	0 0	0 0	0 0	0 0	0 0	0 0	0 0	0 0	0 0	0 0	0 0	0 0
Printed abstracting and indexing services (NET)	5 1.2%	0 0	3 2.4%	3 2.4%	2 0.7%	4 2.1%	1 1.5%	0 0	0 0	0 0	4 2.8%	1 1.1%	0 0	0 0	0 0	0 0	3 1.4%	2 0.9%
All sources of info	5 1.2%	0 0	3 2.4%	3 2.4%	2 0.7%	4 2.1%	1 1.5%	0 0	0 0	0 0	4 2.8%	1 1.1%	0 0	0 0	0 0	0 0	3 1.4%	2 0.9%
preferred source of info	2 0.5%	0 0	0 0	0 0	2 0.7%	2 1.0%	0 0	0 0	0 0	0 0	2 1.4%	0 0	0 0	0 0	0 0	0 0	2 0.9%	0 0
Another library (NET)	4 1.0%	0 0	2 1.8%	2 1.8%	2 0.7%	1 0.5%	1 1.9%	2 1.2%	2 4.3%J	1 2.8%	0 0	1 1.1%	* 2.6%J	0 0	0 0	0 0	2 1.2%	2 0.9%
All sources of info	4 1.0%	0 0	2 1.8%	2 1.8%	2 0.7%	1 0.5%	1 1.9%	2 1.2%	2 4.3%J	1 2.8%	0 0	1 1.1%	* 2.6%J	0 0	0 0	0 0	2 1.2%	2 0.9%
preferred source of info	2 0.5%	0 0	1 0.7%	1 0.7%	1 0.4%	1 0.5%	0 0	1 0.7%	1 2.1%	1 2.8%	0 0	0 0	0 0	0 0	0 0	0 0	1 0.5%	1 0.4%

Proportions/Means: Columns Tested (5% risk level) - A/B/D - C/D - E/F/G - H/I/J/K/L/M/N - P/Q
* small base; ** very small base (under 30) ineligible for sig testing

Table 349
Page 1448

Outsell/Digital Library Federation Study (2002)
Weighted Tables

TABLE 133, continued

S7sum_5. Magazines SUMMARY TABLE

	TOTAL SAMPLE	RESPONDENT TYPE: FACULTY MEMBER (A)	GRAD. STUDENT (B)	FACULTY /GRAD (C)	UNDER GRAD. STUDENT (D)	INSTITUTION TYPE: PUBLIC (E)	PRIVATE (F)	LIBERAL ARTS (G)	DISCIPLINE: BIOLOGIAL SCIENCES (H)	PHYSICAL SCIENCES /MATH (I)	SOCIAL SCIENCES (J)	ARTS AND HUMAN. (K)	ENGI-NEERING (L)	BUSINESS (M)	LAW (N)	UNDEC. MAJOR	GENDER: MALE (P)	FEMALE (Q)
Base - Use Magazines for coursework	408	0**	125	125	283	183	72*	152	41*	36*	135*	106*	11*	53*	2**	23*	209	199
Your own personal physical library/ files/bookshelves (NET)	3 0.8%	0 0	2 1.8%	2 1.8%	1 0.3%	2 1.1%	1 1.5%	0 0	1 2.1%	0 0	0 0	2 2.1%	0 0	0 0	0 0	0 0	1 0.5%	2 1.0%
All sources of info	3 0.8%	0 0	2 1.8%	2 1.8%	1 0.3%	2 1.1%	1 1.5%	0 0	1 2.1%	0 0	0 0	2 2.1%	0 0	0 0	0 0	0 0	1 0.5%	2 1.0%
preferred source of info	0 0	0 0	0 0	0 0	0 0	0 0	0 0	0 0	0 0	0 0	0 0	0 0	0 0	0 0	0 0	0 0	0 0	0 0
Printed library catalogues and finding aids (NET)	1 0.1%	0 0	0 0	0 0	1 0.2%	1 0.3%	0 0	0 0	0 0	0 0	0 0	0 0	1 5.1%HIJKM	0 0	0 0	0 0	* 0.1%	* 0.1%
All sources of info	1 0.1%	0 0	0 0	0 0	1 0.2%	1 0.3%	0 0	0 0	0 0	0 0	0 0	0 0	1 5.1%HIJKM	0 0	0 0	0 0	* 0.1%	* 0.1%
preferred source of info	1 0.1%	0 0	0 0	0 0	1 0.2%	1 0.3%	0 0	0 0	0 0	0 0	0 0	0 0	1 5.1%HIJKM	0 0	0 0	0 0	* 0.1%	* 0.1%
PERSONAL ASSISTANCE	126 30.9%	0 0	33 26.2%	33 26.2%	93 33.0%	54 29.7%	19 26.8%	52 34.3%	11 25.5%	8 22.2%	39 29.2%	40 37.9%	3 30.8%	14 26.3%	* 20.0%	10 43.5%	67 32.2%	59 29.6%
A librarian in your institution (NET)	84 20.7%	0 0	16 12.9%	16 12.9%	68 24.1%B C	35 19.2%	11 14.5%	39 25.4%	6 14.9%	6 16.7%	23 16.7%	26 24.2%	2 15.4%	12 22.8%	* 10.0%	10 43.5%	43 20.8%	41 20.6%

Proportions/Means: Columns Tested (5% risk level) - A/B/D - C/D - E/F/G - H/I/J/K/L/M/N - P/Q
* small base; ** very small base (under 30) ineligible for sig testing

Table 349
Page 1449

TABLE 133, continued

S7sum_5. Magazines SUMMARY TABLE

	RESPONDENT TYPE				INSTITUTION TYPE			DISCIPLINE								GENDER		
	TOTAL SAMPLE	FACULTY MEMBER	GRAD. STUDENT	FACULTY /GRAD	UNDER GRAD. STUDENT	PUBLIC	PRIVATE	LIBERAL ARTS	BIOLOGIAL SCIENCES	PHYSICAL SCIENCES /MATH	SOCIAL SCIENCES	ARTS AND HUMAN.	ENGI- NEERING	BUSINESS	LAW	UNDEC. MAJOR	MALE	FEMALE
		(A)	(B)	(C)	(D)	(E)	(F)	(G)	(H)	(I)	(J)	(K)	(L)	(M)	(N)		(P)	(Q)
Base - Use Magazines for coursework	408	0**	125	125	283	183	72*	152	41*	36*	135*	106*	11*	53*	2**	23*	209	199
All sources of info	84 20.7%	0 0	16 12.9%	16 12.9%	68 24.1%B C	35 19.2%	11 14.5%	39 25.4%	6 14.9%	6 16.7%	23 16.7%	26 24.2%	2 15.4%	12 22.8%	* 10.0%	10 43.5%	43 20.8%	41 20.6%
preferred source of info	30 7.4%	0 0	1 0.9%	1 0.9%	29 10.3%BC	13 7.2%	3 4.1%	14 9.3%	1 2.1%	3 8.3%	9 6.9%	7 6.3%	1 5.1%	6 10.5%	* 10.0%	4 17.4%	16 7.9%	14 6.9%
Faculty members inside your institution (NET)	55 13.5%	0 0	21 16.7%	21 16.7%	34 12.2%	24 13.2%	10 13.5%	21 14.0%	7 17.0%	4 11.1%	13 9.7%	22 21.1%JM	2 15.4%	3 5.3%	* 10.0%	4 17.4%	33 15.8%	22 11.2%
All sources of info	55 13.5%	0 0	21 16.7%	21 16.7%	34 12.2%	24 13.2%	10 13.5%	21 14.0%	7 17.0%	4 11.1%	13 9.7%	22 21.1%JM	2 15.4%	3 5.3%	* 10.0%	4 17.4%	33 15.8%	22 11.2%
preferred source of info	18 4.5%	0 0	7 5.7%	7 5.7%	11 3.9%	8 4.6%	2 2.4%	8 5.3%	3 6.4%	3 8.3%M	4 2.8%	8 7.4%M	1 7.7%M	0 0	* 10.0%	0 0	12 5.8%	6 3.1%
Other students inside your institution (NET)	27 6.7%	0 0	15 12.0%D	15 12.0%D	12 4.3%	16 8.6%	5 6.5%	7 4.4%	2 4.3%	0 0	11 8.3%	11 10.5%I	1 10.3%I	2 3.5%	0 0	0 0	16 7.6%	11 5.7%
All sources of info	27 6.7%	0 0	15 12.0%D	15 12.0%D	12 4.3%	16 8.6%	5 6.5%	7 4.4%	2 4.3%	0 0	11 8.3%	11 10.5%I	1 10.3%I	2 3.5%	0 0	0 0	16 7.6%	11 5.7%
preferred source of info	8 2.0%	0 0	4 3.2%	4 3.2%	4 1.6%	6 3.0%	1 1.3%	2 1.2%	0 0	0 0	4 2.8%	3 3.2%	* 2.6%	1 1.8%	0 0	0 0	4 2.0%	4 2.1%
Faculty members outside your institution (NET)	6 1.5%	0 0	4 3.4%	4 3.4%	2 0.7%	2 1.1%	2 3.1%	2 1.2%	1 2.1%	0 0	2 1.4%	3 3.2%	0 0	0 0	0 0	0 0	3 1.5%	3 1.5%

Proportions/Means: Columns Tested (5% risk level) - A/B/D - C/D - E/F/G - H/I/J/K/L/M/N - P/Q
* small base; ** very small base (under 30) ineligible for sig testing

Table 349
Page 1450

TABLE 133, continued

S7sum_5. Magazines SUMMARY TABLE

	TOTAL SAMPLE	RESPONDENT TYPE FACULTY MEMBER	GRAD. STUDENT	FACULTY /GRAD	UNDER GRAD. STUDENT	INSTITUTION TYPE PUBLIC	PRIVATE	LIBERAL ARTS	DISCIPLINE BIOLOGIAL SCIENCES	PHYSICAL SCIENCES /MATH	SOCIAL SCIENCES	ARTS AND HUMAN.	ENGI-NEERING	BUSINESS	LAW	UNDEC. MAJOR	GENDER MALE	FEMALE
		(A)	(B)	(C)	(D)	(E)	(F)	(G)	(H)	(I)	(J)	(K)	(L)	(M)	(N)		(P)	(Q)
Base - Use Magazines for coursework	408	0**	125	125	283	183	72*	152	41*	36*	135*	106*	11*	53*	2**	23*	209	199
All sources of info	6 1.5%	0 0	4 3.4%	4 3.4%	2 0.7%	2 1.1%	2 3.1%	2 1.2%	1 2.1%	0 0	2 1.4%	3 3.2%	0 0	0 0	0 0	0 0	3 1.5%	3 1.5%
preferred source of info	3 0.7%	0 0	1 0.9%	1 0.9%	2 0.7%	0 0	1 1.5%	2 1.2%	0 0	0 0	2 1.4%	1 1.1%	0 0	0 0	0 0	0 0	1 0.5%	2 0.9%
Other students outside your institution (NET)	3 0.8%	0 0	2 1.8%	2 1.8%	1 0.4%	1 0.6%	1 1.5%	1 0.7%	0 0	0 0	0 0	3 3.2%	0 0	0 0	0 0	0 0	1 0.5%	2 1.1%
All sources of info	3 0.8%	0 0	2 1.8%	2 1.8%	1 0.4%	1 0.6%	1 1.5%	1 0.7%	0 0	0 0	0 0	3 3.2%	0 0	0 0	0 0	0 0	1 0.5%	2 1.1%
preferred source of info	0 0	0 0	0 0	0 0	0 0	0 0	0 0	0 0	0 0	0 0	0 0	0 0	0 0	0 0	0 0	0 0	0 0	0 0
Professional meetings (NET)	1 0.2%	0 0	0 0	0 0	1 0.4%	0 0	0 0	1 0.7%	0 0	1 2.8%	0 0	0 0	0 0	0 0	0 0	0 0	1 0.5%	0 0
All sources of info	1 0.2%	0 0	0 0	0 0	1 0.4%	0 0	0 0	1 0.7%	0 0	1 2.8%	0 0	0 0	0 0	0 0	0 0	0 0	1 0.5%	0 0
preferred source of info	0 0	0 0	0 0	0 0	0 0	0 0	0 0	0 0	0 0	0 0	0 0	0 0	0 0	0 0	0 0	0 0	0 0	0 0
Another institution's librarian (NET)	0 0	0 0	0 0	0 0	0 0	0 0	0 0	0 0	0 0	0 0	0 0	0 0	0 0	0 0	0 0	0 0	0 0	0 0

Proportions/Means: Columns Tested (5% risk level) - A/B/D - C/D - E/F/G - H/I/J/K/L/M/N - P/Q
* small base; ** very small base (under 30) ineligible for sig testing

Table 349
Page 1451

Outsell/Digital Library Federation Study (2002)
Weighted Tables

TABLE 133, continued

S7sum_5. Magazines SUMMARY TABLE

	TOTAL SAMPLE	RESPONDENT TYPE: FACULTY MEMBER	GRAD. STUDENT	FACULTY /GRAD	UNDER GRAD. STUDENT	INSTITUTION TYPE: PUBLIC	PRIVATE	LIBERAL ARTS	DISCIPLINE: BIOLOGIAL SCIENCES	PHYSICAL SCIENCES /MATH	SOCIAL SCIENCES	ARTS AND HUMAN.	ENGI-NEERING	BUSINESS	LAW	UNDEC. MAJOR	GENDER: MALE	FEMALE
		(A)	(B)	(C)	(D)	(E)	(F)	(G)	(H)	(I)	(J)	(K)	(L)	(M)	(N)		(P)	(Q)
Base - Use Magazines for coursework	408	0**	125	125	283	183	72*	152	41*	36*	135*	106*	11*	53*	2**	23*	209	199
All sources of info	0	0	0	0	0	0	0	0	0	0	0	0	0	0	0	0	0	0
	0	0	0	0	0	0	0	0	0	0	0	0	0	0	0	0	0	0
preferred source of info	0	0	0	0	0	0	0	0	0	0	0	0	0	0	0	0	0	0
	0	0	0	0	0	0	0	0	0	0	0	0	0	0	0	0	0	0
Other (NET)	10	0	3	3	7	5	2	3	1	2	4	1	*	2	0	0	3	7
	2.4%	0	2.6%	2.6%	2.3%	2.8%	2.6%	1.9%	2.1%	5.6%	2.8%	1.1%	2.6%	3.5%	0	0	1.6%	3.3%
All sources of info	10	0	3	3	7	5	2	3	1	2	4	1	*	2	0	0	3	7
	2.4%	0	2.6%	2.6%	2.3%	2.8%	2.6%	1.9%	2.1%	5.6%	2.8%	1.1%	2.6%	3.5%	0	0	1.6%	3.3%
preferred source of info	3	0	*	*	3	3	0	0	1	0	2	0	*	0	0	0	*	3
	0.7%	0	0.2%	0.2%	1.0%	1.7%	0	0	2.1%	0	1.4%	0	2.6%K	0	0	0	0.1%	1.4%
Online (unspecified)	7	0	2	2	5	6	1	0	2	0	2	1	0	2	0	0	2	5
	1.6%	0	1.5%	1.5%	1.7%	3.1%	1.2%	0	4.3%	0	1.4%	1.1%	0	3.5%	0	0	1.0%	2.3%
All sources of info	7	0	2	2	5	6	1	0	2	0	2	1	0	2	0	0	2	5
	1.6%	0	1.5%	1.5%	1.7%	3.1%	1.2%	0	4.3%	0	1.4%	1.1%	0	3.5%	0	0	1.0%	2.3%
preferred source of info	4	0	2	2	2	4	0	0	1	0	2	1	0	0	0	0	1	3
	1.0%	0	1.5%	1.5%	0.7%	2.1%	0	0	2.1%	0	1.4%	1.1%	0	0	0	0	0.5%	1.4%
E-journals	0	0	0	0	0	0	0	0	0	0	0	0	0	0	0	0	0	0
	0	0	0	0	0	0	0	0	0	0	0	0	0	0	0	0	0	0
All sources of info	0	0	0	0	0	0	0	0	0	0	0	0	0	0	0	0	0	0
	0	0	0	0	0	0	0	0	0	0	0	0	0	0	0	0	0	0

Proportions/Means: Columns Tested (5% risk level) - A/B/D - C/D - E/F/G - H/I/J/K/L/M/N - P/Q
* small base; ** very small base (under 30) ineligible for sig testing

Table 349
Page 1452

Outsell/Digital Library Federation Study (2002)
Weighted Tables

TABLE 133, continued

S7sum_5. Magazines SUMMARY TABLE

		RESPONDENT TYPE				INSTITUTION TYPE			DISCIPLINE									GENDER	
	TOTAL SAMPLE	FACULTY MEMBER	GRAD. STUDENT	FACULTY /GRAD	UNDER GRAD. STUDENT	PUBLIC	PRIVATE	LIBERAL ARTS	BIOLOGIAL SCIENCES	PHYSICAL SCIENCES /MATH	SOCIAL SCIENCES	ARTS AND HUMAN.	ENGI- NEERING	BUSINESS	LAW	UNDEC. MAJOR	MALE	FEMALE
		(A)	(B)	(C)	(D)	(E)	(F)	(G)	(H)	(I)	(J)	(K)	(L)	(M)	(N)		(P)	(Q)
Base - Use Magazines for coursework	408	0**	125	125	283	183	72*	152	41*	36*	135*	106*	11*	53*	2**	23*	209	199
preferred source of info	0 0	0 0	0 0	0 0	0 0	0 0	0 0	0 0	0 0	0 0	0 0	0 0	0 0	0 0	0 0	0 0	0 0	0 0
DK/Refused	11 2.7%	0 0	1 1.0%	1 1.0%	10 3.4%	9 4.9%G	1 1.3%	1 0.7%	0 0	3 8.3%K	4 2.8%	1 1.1%	* 2.6%	3 5.3%	0 0	0 0	7 3.4%	4 1.9%

Proportions/Means: Columns Tested (5% risk level) - A/B/D - C/D - E/F/G - H/I/J/K/L/M/N - P/Q
* small base; ** very small base (under 30) ineligible for sig testing

Table 349
Page 1453

Outsell/Digital Library Federation Study (2002)
Weighted Tables

TABLE 134

S7D/E_5. Magazines SUMMARY TABLE

		RESPONDENT TYPE				INSTITUTION TYPE			DISCIPLINE									GENDER	
	TOTAL SAMPLE	FACULTY MEMBER	GRAD. STUDENT	FACULTY /GRAD	UNDER GRAD. STUDENT	PUBLIC	PRIVATE	LIBERAL ARTS	BIOLOGIAL SCIENCES	PHYSICAL SCIENCES /MATH	SOCIAL SCIENCES	ARTS AND HUMAN.	ENGI-NEERING	BUSINESS	LAW	UNDEC. MAJOR	MALE	FEMALE
		(A)	(B)	(C)	(D)	(E)	(F)	(G)	(H)	(I)	(J)	(K)	(L)	(M)	(N)		(P)	(Q)
Base - Use Magazines for coursework	408	0**	125	125	283	183	72*	152	41*	36*	135*	106*	11*	53*	2**	23*	209	199
Borrow from or use in campus library (NET)	326 79.9%	0 0	93 74.5%	93 74.5%	233 82.2%	142 77.3%	53 73.6%	131 85.9%F	29 70.2%	29 80.6%	109 80.6%	87 82.1%	11 97.4%HIJ KM	40 75.4%	2 90.0%	19 82.6%	173 82.8%	153 76.8%
All sources of info	326 79.9%	0 0	93 74.5%	93 74.5%	233 82.2%	142 77.3%	53 73.6%	131 85.9%F	29 70.2%	29 80.6%	109 80.6%	87 82.1%	11 97.4%HIJ KM	40 75.4%	2 90.0%	19 82.6%	173 82.8%	153 76.8%
preferred source of info	275 67.3%	0 0	76 60.8%	76 60.8%	199 70.1%	124 67.5%F	37 51.1%	114 74.7%F	25 59.6%	24 66.7%	90 66.7%	80 74.7%M	9 82.1%HM	29 54.4%	1 60.0%	17 73.9%	150 71.8%	125 62.5%
Access online (NET)	115 28.3%	0 0	43 34.3%	43 34.3%	73 25.6%	51 27.6%	28 38.6%G	37 24.1%	14 34.0%	12 33.3%	39 29.2%	24 22.1%	2 17.9%	19 35.1%	1 40.0%	5 21.7%	61 29.0%	55 27.5%
All sources of info	115 28.3%	0 0	43 34.3%	43 34.3%	73 25.6%	51 27.6%	28 38.6%G	37 24.1%	14 34.0%	12 33.3%	39 29.2%	24 22.1%	2 17.9%	19 35.1%	1 40.0%	5 21.7%	61 29.0%	55 27.5%
preferred source of info	85 20.8%	0 0	30 24.0%	30 24.0%	55 19.3%	35 19.1%	24 33.0%EG	26 17.0%	11 25.5%	9 25.0%	28 20.8%	17 15.8%	2 15.4%	14 26.3%	1 30.0%	4 17.4%	44 21.0%	41 20.5%
Purchase from physical book store (NET)	28 6.9%	0 0	9 6.9%	9 6.9%	20 7.0%	15 8.1%	8 10.6%	6 3.8%	1 2.1%	3 8.3%	11 8.3%	3 3.2%	* 2.6%	7 12.3%K	0 0	3 13.0%	11 5.2%	17 8.7%
All sources of info	28 6.9%	0 0	9 6.9%	9 6.9%	20 7.0%	15 8.1%	8 10.6%	6 3.8%	1 2.1%	3 8.3%	11 8.3%	3 3.2%	* 2.6%	7 12.3%K	0 0	3 13.0%	11 5.2%	17 8.7%
preferred source of info	15 3.6%	0 0	5 3.7%	5 3.7%	10 3.5%	8 4.3%	4 5.2%	3 1.9%	0 0	0 0	8 5.6%	1 1.1%	* 2.6%	5 8.8%HK	0 0	1 4.3%	4 2.0%	10 5.3%

Proportions/Means: Columns Tested (5% risk level) - A/B/D - C/D - E/F/G - H/I/J/K/L/M/N - P/Q
* small base; ** very small base (under 30) ineligible for sig testing

Table 352
Page 1460

Outsell/Digital Library Federation Study (2002)
Weighted Tables

TABLE 134, continued

S7D/E_5. Magazines SUMMARY TABLE

	RESPONDENT TYPE				INSTITUTION TYPE			DISCIPLINE								GENDER	
	TOTAL SAMPLE	FACULTY MEMBER	GRAD. STUDENT	FACULTY /GRAD	UNDER GRAD. STUDENT	PUBLIC	PRIVATE	LIBERAL ARTS	BIOLOGIAL SCIENCES	PHYSICAL SCIENCES /MATH	SOCIAL SCIENCES	ARTS AND HUMAN.	ENGI-NEERING	BUSINESS	LAW	UNDEC. MAJOR	MALE	FEMALE
		(A)	(B)	(C)	(D)	(E)	(F)	(G)	(H)	(I)	(J)	(K)	(L)	(M)	(N)		(P)	(Q)
Base - Use Magazines for coursework	408	0**	125	125	283	183	72*	152	41*	36*	135*	106*	11*	53*	2**	23*	209	199
Borrow from or use in other libraries (NET)	16 3.9%	0 0	5 4.1%	5 4.1%	11 3.9%	8 4.3%	1 1.8%	7 4.6%	4 8.5%	2 5.6%	4 2.8%	3 3.2%	0 0	1 1.8%	1 30.0%	2 8.7%	6 2.9%	10 5.0%
All sources of info	16 3.9%	0 0	5 4.1%	5 4.1%	11 3.9%	8 4.3%	1 1.8%	7 4.6%	4 8.5%	2 5.6%	4 2.8%	3 3.2%	0 0	1 1.8%	1 30.0%	2 8.7%	6 2.9%	10 5.0%
preferred source of info	8 1.9%	0 0	4 3.1%	4 3.1%	4 1.4%	5 2.5%	* 0.2%	3 2.0%	3 6.4%	1 2.8%	2 1.4%	1 1.1%	0 0	0 0	* 10.0%	1 4.3%	1 0.5%	7 3.4%
Interlibrary loan (NET)	9 2.1%	0 0	2 1.5%	2 1.5%	7 2.3%	5 2.5%	0 0	4 2.5%	2 4.3%K	2 5.6%K	4 2.8%	0 0	0 0	0 0	0 0	1 4.3%	3 1.4%	6 2.8%
All sources of info	9 2.1%	0 0	2 1.5%	2 1.5%	7 2.3%	5 2.5%	0 0	4 2.5%	2 4.3%K	2 5.6%K	4 2.8%	0 0	0 0	0 0	0 0	1 4.3%	3 1.4%	6 2.8%
preferred source of info	5 1.1%	0 0	2 1.5%	2 1.5%	3 1.0%	5 2.5%	0 0	0 0	1 2.1%	0 0	4 2.8%	0 0	0 0	0 0	0 0	0 0	2 0.9%	3 1.4%
Faculty (NET)	7 1.7%	0 0	1 0.7%	1 0.7%	6 2.2%	3 1.7%	0 0	4 2.5%	2 4.3%	0 0	2 1.4%	3 3.2%	0 0	0 0	0 0	0 0	2 1.0%	5 2.5%
All sources of info	7 1.7%	0 0	1 0.7%	1 0.7%	6 2.2%	3 1.7%	0 0	4 2.5%	2 4.3%	0 0	2 1.4%	3 3.2%	0 0	0 0	0 0	0 0	2 1.0%	5 2.5%
preferred source of info	4 1.0%	0 0	0 0	0 0	4 1.5%	2 1.2%	0 0	2 1.3%	1 2.1%	0 0	0 0	3 3.2%	0 0	0 0	0 0	0 0	2 1.0%	2 1.1%

Proportions/Means: Columns Tested (5% risk level) - A/B/D - C/D - E/F/G - H/I/J/K/L/M/N - P/Q
* small base; ** very small base (under 30) ineligible for sig testing

Table 352
Page 1461

Outsell/Digital Library Federation Study (2002)
Weighted Tables

TABLE 134, continued

S7D/E_5. Magazines SUMMARY TABLE

		RESPONDENT TYPE				INSTITUTION TYPE			DISCIPLINE									GENDER	
	TOTAL SAMPLE	FACULTY MEMBER	GRAD. STUDENT	FACULTY /GRAD	UNDER GRAD. STUDENT	PUBLIC	PRIVATE	LIBERAL ARTS	BIOLOGIAL SCIENCES	PHYSICAL SCIENCES /MATH	SOCIAL SCIENCES	ARTS AND HUMAN.	ENGI-NEERING	BUSINESS	LAW	UNDEC. MAJOR	MALE	FEMALE
		(A)	(B)	(C)	(D)	(E)	(F)	(G)	(H)	(I)	(J)	(K)	(L)	(M)	(N)		(P)	(Q)
Base - Use Magazines for coursework	408	0**	125	125	283	183	72*	152	41*	36*	135*	106*	11*	53*	2**	23*	209	199
Purchase from online bookstore (NET)	7 1.6%	0 0	5 3.9%D	5 3.9%D	2 0.7%	2 1.0%	5 6.6%EG	0 0	1 2.1%	0 0	4 2.8%	1 1.1%	0 0	1 1.8%	0 0	0 0	0 0	7 3.4%P
All sources of info	7 1.6%	0 0	5 3.9%D	5 3.9%D	2 0.7%	2 1.0%	5 6.6%EG	0 0	1 2.1%	0 0	4 2.8%	1 1.1%	0 0	1 1.8%	0 0	0 0	0 0	7 3.4%P
preferred source of info	1 0.2%	0 0	1 0.7%	1 0.7%	0 0	0 0	1 1.3%	0 0	0 0	0 0	0 0	0 0	0 0	1 1.8%	0 0	0 0	0 0	1 0.5%
Personal Holdings (NET)	4 1.0%	0 0	4 3.1%D	4 3.1%D	0 0	1 0.5%	3 4.1%G	0 0	0 0	0 0	0 0	1 1.1%	0 0	3 5.3%J	0 0	0 0	1 0.4%	3 1.5%
All sources of info	4 1.0%	0 0	4 3.1%D	4 3.1%D	0 0	1 0.5%	3 4.1%G	0 0	0 0	0 0	0 0	1 1.1%	0 0	3 5.3%J	0 0	0 0	1 0.4%	3 1.5%
preferred source of info	1 0.2%	0 0	1 0.7%	1 0.7%	0 0	0 0	1 1.3%	0 0	0 0	0 0	0 0	0 0	0 0	1 1.8%	0 0	0 0	1 0.4%	0 0
Ask library to purchase source (NET)	2 0.5%	0 0	0 0	0 0	2 0.7%	1 0.6%	0 0	1 0.7%	0 0	1 2.8%	0 0	1 1.1%	0 0	0 0	0 0	0 0	0 0	2 1.1%
All sources of info	2 0.5%	0 0	0 0	0 0	2 0.7%	1 0.6%	0 0	1 0.7%	0 0	1 2.8%	0 0	1 1.1%	0 0	0 0	0 0	0 0	0 0	2 1.1%
preferred source of info	2 0.5%	0 0	0 0	0 0	2 0.7%	1 0.6%	0 0	1 0.7%	0 0	1 2.8%	0 0	1 1.1%	0 0	0 0	0 0	0 0	0 0	2 1.1%

Proportions/Means: Columns Tested (5% risk level) - A/B/D - C/D - E/F/G - H/I/J/K/L/M/N - P/Q
* small base; ** very small base (under 30) ineligible for sig testing

Table 352
Page 1462

Outsell/Digital Library Federation Study (2002)
Weighted Tables

TABLE 134, continued

S7D/E_5. Magazines SUMMARY TABLE

		RESPONDENT TYPE				INSTITUTION TYPE			DISCIPLINE									GENDER	
	TOTAL SAMPLE	FACULTY MEMBER	GRAD. STUDENT	FACULTY /GRAD	UNDER GRAD. STUDENT	PUBLIC	PRIVATE	LIBERAL ARTS	BIOLOGIAL SCIENCES	PHYSICAL SCIENCES /MATH	SOCIAL SCIENCES	ARTS AND HUMAN.	ENGI- NEERING	BUSINESS	LAW	UNDEC. MAJOR	MALE	FEMALE
		(A)	(B)	(C)	(D)	(E)	(F)	(G)	(H)	(I)	(J)	(K)	(L)	(M)	(N)		(P)	(Q)
Base - Use Magazines for coursework	408	0**	125	125	283	183	72*	152	41*	36*	135*	106*	11*	53*	2**	23*	209	199
Home (NET)	2 0.5%	0 0	1 0.7%	1 0.7%	1 0.4%	0 0	2 2.8%E	0 0	0 0	0 0	0 0	1 1.1%	0 0	1 1.8%	0 0	0 0	1 0.5%	1 0.5%
All sources of info	2 0.5%	0 0	1 0.7%	1 0.7%	1 0.4%	0 0	2 2.8%E	0 0	0 0	0 0	0 0	1 1.1%	0 0	1 1.8%	0 0	0 0	1 0.5%	1 0.5%
preferred source of info	1 0.3%	0 0	0 0	0 0	1 0.4%	0 0	1 1.5%	0 0	0 0	0 0	0 0	1 1.1%	0 0	0 0	0 0	0 0	1 0.5%	0 0
Colleagues (NET)	2 0.5%	0 0	0 0	0 0	2 0.7%	0 0	0 0	2 1.2%	0 0	0 0	2 1.4%	0 0	0 0	0 0	0 0	0 0	2 0.9%	0 0
All sources of info	2 0.5%	0 0	0 0	0 0	2 0.7%	0 0	0 0	2 1.2%	0 0	0 0	2 1.4%	0 0	0 0	0 0	0 0	0 0	2 0.9%	0 0
preferred source of info	0 0	0 0	0 0	0 0	0 0	0 0	0 0	0 0	0 0	0 0	0 0	0 0	0 0	0 0	0 0	0 0	0 0	0 0
Access book/journal/ journal article elsewhere online (NET)	0 0	0 0	0 0	0 0	0 0	0 0	0 0	0 0	0 0	0 0	0 0	0 0	0 0	0 0	0 0	0 0	0 0	0 0
All sources of info	0 0	0 0	0 0	0 0	0 0	0 0	0 0	0 0	0 0	0 0	0 0	0 0	0 0	0 0	0 0	0 0	0 0	0 0
preferred source of info	0 0	0 0	0 0	0 0	0 0	0 0	0 0	0 0	0 0	0 0	0 0	0 0	0 0	0 0	0 0	0 0	0 0	0 0

Proportions/Means: Columns Tested (5% risk level) - A/B/D - C/D - E/F/G - H/I/J/K/L/M/N - P/Q
* small base; ** very small base (under 30) ineligible for sig testing

Table 352
Page 1463

Outsell/Digital Library Federation Study (2002)
Weighted Tables

TABLE 134, continued

S7D/E_5. Magazines SUMMARY TABLE

		RESPONDENT TYPE				INSTITUTION TYPE			DISCIPLINE									GENDER	
	TOTAL SAMPLE	FACULTY MEMBER	GRAD. STUDENT	FACULTY /GRAD	UNDER GRAD. STUDENT	PUBLIC	PRIVATE	LIBERAL ARTS	BIOLOGIAL SCIENCES	PHYSICAL SCIENCES /MATH	SOCIAL SCIENCES	ARTS AND HUMAN.	ENGI- NEERING	BUSINESS	LAW	UNDEC. MAJOR	MALE	FEMALE
		(A)	(B)	(C)	(D)	(E)	(F)	(G)	(H)	(I)	(J)	(K)	(L)	(M)	(N)		(P)	(Q)
Base - Use Magazines for coursework	408	0**	125	125	283	183	72*	152	41*	36*	135*	106*	11*	53*	2**	23*	209	199
Order from on demand document delivery service (NET)	0 0	0 0	0 0	0 0	0 0	0 0	0 0	0 0	0 0	0 0	0 0	0 0	0 0	0 0	0 0	0 0	0 0	0 0
All sources of info	0 0	0 0	0 0	0 0	0 0	0 0	0 0	0 0	0 0	0 0	0 0	0 0	0 0	0 0	0 0	0 0	0 0	0 0
preferred source of info	0 0	0 0	0 0	0 0	0 0	0 0	0 0	0 0	0 0	0 0	0 0	0 0	0 0	0 0	0 0	0 0	0 0	0 0
In class (NET)	0 0	0 0	0 0	0 0	0 0	0 0	0 0	0 0	0 0	0 0	0 0	0 0	0 0	0 0	0 0	0 0	0 0	0 0
All sources of info	0 0	0 0	0 0	0 0	0 0	0 0	0 0	0 0	0 0	0 0	0 0	0 0	0 0	0 0	0 0	0 0	0 0	0 0
preferred source of info	0 0	0 0	0 0	0 0	0 0	0 0	0 0	0 0	0 0	0 0	0 0	0 0	0 0	0 0	0 0	0 0	0 0	0 0
Dorm room (NET)	0 0	0 0	0 0	0 0	0 0	0 0	0 0	0 0	0 0	0 0	0 0	0 0	0 0	0 0	0 0	0 0	0 0	0 0
All sources of info	0 0	0 0	0 0	0 0	0 0	0 0	0 0	0 0	0 0	0 0	0 0	0 0	0 0	0 0	0 0	0 0	0 0	0 0
preferred source of info	0 0	0 0	0 0	0 0	0 0	0 0	0 0	0 0	0 0	0 0	0 0	0 0	0 0	0 0	0 0	0 0	0 0	0 0
Access from course website (NET)	0 0	0 0	0 0	0 0	0 0	0 0	0 0	0 0	0 0	0 0	0 0	0 0	0 0	0 0	0 0	0 0	0 0	0 0

Proportions/Means: Columns Tested (5% risk level) - A/B/D - C/D - E/F/G - H/I/J/K/L/M/N - P/Q
* small base; ** very small base (under 30) ineligible for sig testing

Table 352
Page 1464

Outsell/Digital Library Federation Study (2002)
Weighted Tables

TABLE 134, continued

S7D/E_5. Magazines SUMMARY TABLE

	TOTAL SAMPLE	RESPONDENT TYPE: FACULTY MEMBER	GRAD. STUDENT	FACULTY /GRAD	UNDER GRAD. STUDENT	INSTITUTION TYPE: PUBLIC	PRIVATE	LIBERAL ARTS	DISCIPLINE: BIOLOGIAL SCIENCES	PHYSICAL SCIENCES /MATH	SOCIAL SCIENCES	ARTS AND HUMAN.	ENGI- NEERING	BUSINESS	LAW	UNDEC. MAJOR	GENDER: MALE	FEMALE
		(A)	(B)	(C)	(D)	(E)	(F)	(G)	(H)	(I)	(J)	(K)	(L)	(M)	(N)		(P)	(Q)
Base - Use Magazines for coursework	408	0**	125	125	283	183	72*	152	41*	36*	135*	106*	11*	53*	2**	23*	209	199
All sources of info	0	0	0	0	0	0	0	0	0	0	0	0	0	0	0	0	0	0
	0	0	0	0	0	0	0	0	0	0	0	0	0	0	0	0	0	0
preferred source of info	0	0	0	0	0	0	0	0	0	0	0	0	0	0	0	0	0	0
	0	0	0	0	0	0	0	0	0	0	0	0	0	0	0	0	0	0
Other (NET)	13	0	5	5	8	2	6	5	2	1	4	2	*	4	0	0	6	7
	3.1%	0	4.0%	4.0%	2.8%	1.2%	7.7%E	3.2%	4.3%	2.8%	2.8%	2.1%	2.6%	7.0%	0	0	2.9%	3.3%
All sources of info	11	0	3	3	8	2	4	5	2	1	4	2	*	2	0	0	6	5
	2.7%	0	2.5%	2.5%	2.8%	1.2%	5.1%	3.2%	4.3%	2.8%	2.8%	2.1%	2.6%	3.5%	0	0	2.9%	2.4%
preferred source of info	8	0	5	5	3	2	5	1	1	1	2	1	0	3	0	0	3	5
	1.9%	0	3.7%	3.7%	1.1%	1.1%	6.5%EG	0.7%	2.1%	2.8%	1.4%	1.1%	0	5.3%	0	0	1.5%	2.3%
DK/Refused	4	0	1	1	3	1	0	3	1	0	2	0	0	1	0	0	1	3
	0.9%	0	0.7%	0.7%	1.0%	0.5%	0	1.8%	2.1%	0	1.4%	0	0	1.8%	0	0	0.4%	1.4%

Proportions/Means: Columns Tested (5% risk level) - A/B/D - C/D - E/F/G - H/I/J/K/L/M/N - P/Q
* small base; ** very small base (under 30) ineligible for sig testing

TABLE 135

S7sum_6. Papers delivered at professional meetings SUMMARY TABLE

		RESPONDENT TYPE				INSTITUTION TYPE			DISCIPLINE									GENDER	
	TOTAL SAMPLE	FACULTY MEMBER	GRAD. STUDENT	FACULTY /GRAD	UNDER GRAD. STUDENT	PUBLIC	PRIVATE	LIBERAL ARTS	BIOLOGIAL SCIENCES	PHYSICAL SCIENCES /MATH	SOCIAL SCIENCES	ARTS AND HUMAN.	ENGI-NEERING	BUSINESS	LAW	UNDEC. MAJOR	MALE	FEMALE
		(A)	(B)	(C)	(D)	(E)	(F)	(G)	(H)	(I)	(J)	(K)	(L)	(M)	(N)		(P)	(Q)
Base - Use Papers delivered at professional meetings for coursework	243	0**	150	150	93*	127*	63*	53*	36*	34*	85*	43*	9*	25**	2**	9*	103*	140
ONLINE	144 59.5%	0 0	83 55.1%	83 55.1%	62 66.7%	69 54.2%	38 61.4%	37 70.1%	24 65.9%	16 47.1%	53 62.2%	21 50.0%	6 67.7%	16 63.0%	2 78.6%	7 77.8%	60 58.3%	84 60.4%
Search engine (NET)	40 16.5%	0 0	18 12.1%	18 12.1%	22 23.7%B C	15 11.7%	10 16.1%	15 28.8%E	8 22.0%	4 11.8%	8 8.9%	7 15.8%	2 25.8%J	9 37.0%	* 14.3%	2 22.2%	18 17.6%	22 15.7%
All sources of info	40 16.5%	0 0	18 12.1%	18 12.1%	22 23.7%B C	15 11.7%	10 16.1%	15 28.8%E	8 22.0%	4 11.8%	8 8.9%	7 15.8%	2 25.8%J	9 37.0%	* 14.3%	2 22.2%	18 17.6%	22 15.7%
preferred source of info	21 8.5%	0 0	10 6.8%	10 6.8%	10 11.1%	7 5.7%	6 9.8%	7 13.5%	3 7.3%	2 5.9%	4 4.4%	3 7.9%	1 12.9%	7 29.6%	* 7.1%	0 0	12 12.0%	8 5.8%
Online databases (NET)	35 14.3%	0 0	23 15.4%	23 15.4%	12 12.5%	8 6.0%	17 27.4%E	10 18.4%E	6 17.1%	6 17.6%	11 13.3%	6 13.2%	* 3.2%	3 11.1%	1 21.4%	2 22.2%	12 11.8%	22 16.1%
All sources of info	35 14.3%	0 0	23 15.4%	23 15.4%	12 12.5%	8 6.0%	17 27.4%E	10 18.4%E	6 17.1%	6 17.6%	11 13.3%	6 13.2%	* 3.2%	3 11.1%	1 21.4%	2 22.2%	12 11.8%	22 16.1%
preferred source of info	22 9.1%	0 0	12 7.7%	12 7.7%	11 11.4%	5 3.6%	9 14.0%E	9 16.5%E	6 17.1%KL	5 14.7%	8 8.9%	1 2.6%	0 0	1 3.7%	* 14.3%	1 11.1%	7 6.6%	15 10.9%
Your own institution's web site (NET)	27 11.3%	0 0	15 9.8%	15 9.8%	13 13.7%	14 11.0%	8 13.5%	5 9.4%	4 12.2%	5 14.7%	8 8.9%	4 10.5%	1 12.9%	2 7.4%	0 0	3 33.3%	10 10.0%	17 12.2%

Proportions/Means: Columns Tested (5% risk level) - A/B/D - C/D - E/F/G - H/I/J/K/L/M/N - P/Q
* small base; ** very small base (under 30) ineligible for sig testing

Table 356
Page 1477

Outsell/Digital Library Federation Study (2002)
Weighted Tables

TABLE 135, continued

S7sum_6. Papers delivered at professional meetings SUMMARY TABLE

		RESPONDENT TYPE				INSTITUTION TYPE			DISCIPLINE									GENDER	
	TOTAL SAMPLE	FACULTY MEMBER	GRAD. STUDENT	FACULTY /GRAD	UNDER GRAD. STUDENT	PUBLIC	PRIVATE	LIBERAL ARTS	BIOLOGIAL SCIENCES	PHYSICAL SCIENCES /MATH	SOCIAL SCIENCES	ARTS AND HUMAN.	ENGI-NEERING	BUSINESS	LAW	UNDEC. MAJOR	MALE	FEMALE
		(A)	(B)	(C)	(D)	(E)	(F)	(G)	(H)	(I)	(J)	(K)	(L)	(M)	(N)		(P)	(Q)
Base - Use Papers delivered at professional meetings for coursework	243	0**	150	150	93*	127*	63*	53*	36*	34*	85*	43*	9*	25**	2**	9*	103*	140
All sources of info	27 11.3%	0 0	15 9.8%	15 9.8%	13 13.7%	14 11.0%	8 13.5%	5 9.4%	4 12.2%	5 14.7%	8 8.9%	4 10.5%	1 12.9%	2 7.4%	0 0	3 33.3%	10 10.0%	17 12.2%
preferred source of info	21 8.7%	0 0	13 8.9%	13 8.9%	8 8.5%	13 10.2%	5 8.3%	3 5.7%	4 12.2%	4 11.8%	8 8.9%	3 7.9%	1 9.7%	0 0	0 0	1 11.1%	8 8.1%	13 9.2%
Web directory/ subject related web site (NET)	27 11.1%	0 0	17 11.3%	17 11.3%	10 10.8%	16 12.5%	3 4.9%	8 14.9%	3 7.3%	2 5.9%	15 17.8%	3 7.9%	1 12.9%	2 7.4%	1 35.7%	0 0	13 12.4%	14 10.1%
All sources of info	27 11.1%	0 0	17 11.3%	17 11.3%	10 10.8%	16 12.5%	3 4.9%	8 14.9%	3 7.3%	2 5.9%	15 17.8%	3 7.9%	1 12.9%	2 7.4%	1 35.7%	0 0	13 12.4%	14 10.1%
preferred source of info	16 6.5%	0 0	13 8.4%	13 8.4%	3 3.5%	12 9.4%	1 1.3%	3 5.7%	1 2.4%	1 2.9%	9 11.1%	1 2.6%	1 9.7%	2 7.4%	1 28.6%	0 0	8 7.6%	8 5.7%
Online library catalogues and finding aids (NET)	21 8.8%	0 0	13 8.9%	13 8.9%	8 8.8%	9 6.8%	8 12.2%	5 9.7%	2 4.9%	2 5.9%	9 11.1%	6 13.2%	1 6.5%	1 3.7%	* 7.1%	1 11.1%	7 7.0%	14 10.2%
All sources of info	21 8.8%	0 0	13 8.9%	13 8.9%	8 8.8%	9 6.8%	8 12.2%	5 9.7%	2 4.9%	2 5.9%	9 11.1%	6 13.2%	1 6.5%	1 3.7%	* 7.1%	1 11.1%	7 7.0%	14 10.2%
preferred source of info	13 5.4%	0 0	10 6.6%	10 6.6%	3 3.5%	7 5.4%	4 6.7%	2 4.0%	2 4.9%	1 2.9%	6 6.7%	2 5.3%	1 6.5%	1 3.7%	0 0	1 11.1%	4 4.1%	9 6.4%

Proportions/Means: Columns Tested (5% risk level) - A/B/D - C/D - E/F/G - H/I/J/K/L/M/N - P/Q
* small base; ** very small base (under 30) ineligible for sig testing

Table 356
Page 1478

Outsell/Digital Library Federation Study (2002)
Weighted Tables

TABLE 135, continued

S7sum_6. Papers delivered at professional meetings SUMMARY TABLE

	TOTAL SAMPLE	RESPONDENT TYPE: FACULTY MEMBER	GRAD. STUDENT	FACULTY /GRAD	UNDER GRAD. STUDENT	INSTITUTION TYPE: PUBLIC	PRIVATE	LIBERAL ARTS	DISCIPLINE: BIOLOGIAL SCIENCES	PHYSICAL SCIENCES /MATH	SOCIAL SCIENCES	ARTS AND HUMAN.	ENGI-NEERING	BUSINESS	LAW	UNDEC. MAJOR	GENDER: MALE	FEMALE
		(A)	(B)	(C)	(D)	(E)	(F)	(G)	(H)	(I)	(J)	(K)	(L)	(M)	(N)		(P)	(Q)
Base - Use Papers delivered at professional meetings for coursework	243	0**	150	150	93*	127*	63*	53*	36*	34*	85*	43*	9*	25**	2**	9*	103*	140
Internet searches (NET)	20 8.3%	0 0	12 8.3%	12 8.3%	8 8.4%	11 8.7%	4 6.0%	5 10.1%	4 9.8%	2 5.9%	6 6.7%	4 10.5%	1 16.1%	1 3.7%	* 7.1%	2 22.2%	10 9.8%	10 7.2%
All sources of info	20 8.3%	0 0	12 8.3%	12 8.3%	8 8.4%	11 8.7%	4 6.0%	5 10.1%	4 9.8%	2 5.9%	6 6.7%	4 10.5%	1 16.1%	1 3.7%	* 7.1%	2 22.2%	10 9.8%	10 7.2%
preferred source of info	13 5.4%	0 0	9 5.9%	9 5.9%	4 4.7%	8 6.0%	2 3.7%	3 6.1%	3 7.3%	0 0	6 6.7%	3 7.9%	1 6.5%I	0 0	0 0	1 11.1%	7 6.4%	7 4.8%
Department web page (NET)	8 3.1%	0 0	2 1.6%	2 1.6%	5 5.4%	3 2.6%	* 0.5%	4 7.3%	2 4.9%	1 2.9%	2 2.2%	0 0	1 9.7%K	0 0	0 0	2 22.2%	2 2.2%	5 3.7%
All sources of info	8 3.1%	0 0	2 1.6%	2 1.6%	5 5.4%	3 2.6%	* 0.5%	4 7.3%	2 4.9%	1 2.9%	2 2.2%	0 0	1 9.7%K	0 0	0 0	2 22.2%	2 2.2%	5 3.7%
preferred source of info	4 1.8%	0 0	1 0.9%	1 0.9%	3 3.4%	2 1.9%	0 0	2 3.8%	1 2.4%	1 2.9%	0 0	0 0	1 6.5%JK	0 0	0 0	2 22.2%	2 1.9%	2 1.8%
Online reference service (NET)	5 2.2%	0 0	4 2.8%	4 2.8%	1 1.3%	2 1.9%	3 4.7%	0 0	1 2.4%	0 0	4 4.4%	0 0	1 6.5%IK	0 0	* 7.1%	0 0	2 1.6%	4 2.7%
All sources of info	5 2.2%	0 0	4 2.8%	4 2.8%	1 1.3%	2 1.9%	3 4.7%	0 0	1 2.4%	0 0	4 4.4%	0 0	1 6.5%IK	0 0	* 7.1%	0 0	2 1.6%	4 2.7%
preferred source of info	3 1.1%	0 0	2 1.3%	2 1.3%	1 0.9%	2 1.5%	1 1.4%	0 0	1 2.4%	0 0	2 2.2%	0 0	0 0	0 0	0 0	0 0	1 0.9%	2 1.3%

Proportions/Means: Columns Tested (5% risk level) - A/B/D - C/D - E/F/G - H/I/J/K/L/M/N - P/Q
* small base; ** very small base (under 30) ineligible for sig testing

Table 356
Page 1479

Outsell/Digital Library Federation Study (2002)
Weighted Tables

TABLE 135, continued

S7sum_6. Papers delivered at professional meetings SUMMARY TABLE

	TOTAL SAMPLE	FACULTY MEMBER (A)	GRAD. STUDENT (B)	FACULTY /GRAD (C)	UNDER GRAD. STUDENT (D)	PUBLIC (E)	PRIVATE (F)	LIBERAL ARTS (G)	BIOLOGIAL SCIENCES (H)	PHYSICAL SCIENCES /MATH (I)	SOCIAL SCIENCES (J)	ARTS AND HUMAN. (K)	ENGI- NEERING (L)	BUSINESS (M)	LAW (N)	UNDEC. MAJOR	MALE (P)	FEMALE (Q)
		RESPONDENT TYPE				INSTITUTION TYPE			DISCIPLINE								GENDER	
Base - Use Papers delivered at professional meetings for coursework	243	0**	150	150	93*	127*	63*	53*	36*	34*	85*	43*	9*	25**	2**	9*	103*	140
Online abstracting and indexing services (NET)	5 1.9%	0 0	3 1.9%	3 1.9%	2 2.0%	4 3.0%	1 1.5%	0 0	0 0	0 0	4 4.4%	0 0	0 0	1 3.7%	0 0	0 0	3 2.7%	2 1.3%
All sources of info	5 1.9%	0 0	3 1.9%	3 1.9%	2 2.0%	4 3.0%	1 1.5%	0 0	0 0	0 0	4 4.4%	0 0	0 0	1 3.7%	0 0	0 0	3 2.7%	2 1.3%
preferred source of info	3 1.2%	0 0	1 0.6%	1 0.6%	2 2.0%	2 1.5%	1 1.5%	0 0	0 0	0 0	2 2.2%	0 0	0 0	1 3.7%	0 0	0 0	1 0.9%	2 1.3%
Your own personal electronic library/files (NET)	2 0.9%	0 0	1 0.9%	1 0.9%	1 0.9%	* 0.2%	2 3.2%	0 0	1 2.4%	0 0	0 0	1 2.6%	* 3.2%J	0 0	0 0	0 0	1 1.1%	1 0.8%
All sources of info	2 0.9%	0 0	1 0.9%	1 0.9%	1 0.9%	* 0.2%	2 3.2%	0 0	1 2.4%	0 0	0 0	1 2.6%	* 3.2%J	0 0	0 0	0 0	1 1.1%	1 0.8%
preferred source of info	* 0.1%	0 0	* 0.2%	* 0.2%	0 0	* 0.2%	0 0	0 0	0 0	0 0	0 0	0 0	* 3.2%J	0 0	0 0	0 0	* 0.3%	0 0
Online bookstore (NET)	1 0.4%	0 0	0 0	0 0	1 1.0%	0 0	1 1.5%	0 0	0 0	0 0	0 0	0 0	0 0	1 3.7%	0 0	0 0	1 0.9%	0 0
All sources of info	1 0.4%	0 0	0 0	0 0	1 1.0%	0 0	1 1.5%	0 0	0 0	0 0	0 0	0 0	0 0	1 3.7%	0 0	0 0	1 0.9%	0 0

Proportions/Means: Columns Tested (5% risk level) - A/B/D - C/D - E/F/G - H/I/J/K/L/M/N - P/Q
* small base; ** very small base (under 30) ineligible for sig testing

Table 356
Page 1480

Outsell/Digital Library Federation Study (2002)
Weighted Tables

TABLE 135, continued

S7sum_6. Papers delivered at professional meetings SUMMARY TABLE

		RESPONDENT TYPE				INSTITUTION TYPE			DISCIPLINE									GENDER	
	TOTAL SAMPLE	FACULTY MEMBER	GRAD. STUDENT	FACULTY /GRAD	UNDER GRAD. STUDENT	PUBLIC	PRIVATE	LIBERAL ARTS	BIOLOGIAL SCIENCES	PHYSICAL SCIENCES /MATH	SOCIAL SCIENCES	ARTS AND HUMAN.	ENGI- NEERING	BUSINESS	LAW	UNDEC. MAJOR	MALE	FEMALE
		(A)	(B)	(C)	(D)	(E)	(F)	(G)	(H)	(I)	(J)	(K)	(L)	(M)	(N)		(P)	(Q)
Base - Use Papers delivered at professional meetings for coursework	243	0**	150	150	93*	127*	63*	53*	36*	34*	85*	43*	9*	25**	2**	9*	103*	140
preferred source of info	1 0.4%	0 0	0 0	0 0	1 1.0%	0 0	1 1.5%	0 0	0 0	0 0	0 0	0 0	0 0	1 3.7%	0 0	0 0	1 0.9%	0 0
E-mail listservs (NET)	0 0	0 0	0 0	0 0	0 0	0 0	0 0	0 0	0 0	0 0	0 0	0 0	0 0	0 0	0 0	0 0	0 0	0 0
All sources of info	0 0	0 0	0 0	0 0	0 0	0 0	0 0	0 0	0 0	0 0	0 0	0 0	0 0	0 0	0 0	0 0	0 0	0 0
preferred source of info	0 0	0 0	0 0	0 0	0 0	0 0	0 0	0 0	0 0	0 0	0 0	0 0	0 0	0 0	0 0	0 0	0 0	0 0
PERSONAL ASSISTANCE	107 44.2%	0 0	70 46.5%	70 46.5%	38 40.5%	54 42.5%	32 50.5%	22 40.8%	11 31.7%	20 58.8%H	38 44.4%	21 50.0%	4 45.2%	8 33.3%	2 64.3%	3 33.3%	44 42.2%	64 45.7%
Faculty members inside your institution (NET)	75 31.1%	0 0	54 35.8%	54 35.8%	22 23.4%	38 29.7%	25 39.4%	13 24.5%	8 22.0%	16 47.1%H	26 31.1%	15 34.2%	3 32.3%	5 18.5%	1 42.9%	2 22.2%	30 29.3%	45 32.3%
All sources of info	75 31.1%	0 0	54 35.8%	54 35.8%	22 23.4%	38 29.7%	25 39.4%	13 24.5%	8 22.0%	16 47.1%H	26 31.1%	15 34.2%	3 32.3%	5 18.5%	1 42.9%	2 22.2%	30 29.3%	45 32.3%
preferred source of info	58 23.9%	0 0	42 28.0%	42 28.0%	16 17.2%	33 25.6%	15 24.7%	10 18.8%	4 12.2%	10 29.4%	26 31.1%H	9 21.1%	2 19.4%	4 14.8%	1 35.7%	2 22.2%	26 25.3%	32 22.8%

Proportions/Means: Columns Tested (5% risk level) - A/B/D - C/D - E/F/G - H/I/J/K/L/M/N - P/Q
* small base; ** very small base (under 30) ineligible for sig testing

Table 356
Page 1481

Outsell/Digital Library Federation Study (2002)
Weighted Tables

TABLE 135, continued

S7sum_6. Papers delivered at professional meetings SUMMARY TABLE

		RESPONDENT TYPE				INSTITUTION TYPE			DISCIPLINE								GENDER	
	TOTAL SAMPLE	FACULTY MEMBER	GRAD. STUDENT	FACULTY /GRAD	UNDER GRAD. STUDENT	PUBLIC	PRIVATE	LIBERAL ARTS	BIOLOGIAL SCIENCES	PHYSICAL SCIENCES /MATH	SOCIAL SCIENCES	ARTS AND HUMAN.	ENGI-NEERING	BUSINESS	LAW	UNDEC. MAJOR	MALE	FEMALE
		(A)	(B)	(C)	(D)	(E)	(F)	(G)	(H)	(I)	(J)	(K)	(L)	(M)	(N)		(P)	(Q)
Base - Use Papers delivered at professional meetings for coursework	243	0**	150	150	93*	127*	63*	53*	36*	34*	85*	43*	9*	25**	2**	9*	103*	140
A librarian in your institution (NET)	26 10.5%	0 0	9 6.0%	9 6.0%	17 17.9%BC	9 7.3%	6 8.9%	11 20.1%E	2 4.9%	2 5.9%	9 11.1%	6 13.2%	* 3.2%	5 18.5%	1 35.7%	1 11.1%	10 9.9%	15 11.0%
All sources of info	26 10.5%	0 0	9 6.0%	9 6.0%	17 17.9%BC	9 7.3%	6 8.9%	11 20.1%E	2 4.9%	2 5.9%	9 11.1%	6 13.2%	* 3.2%	5 18.5%	1 35.7%	1 11.1%	10 9.9%	15 11.0%
preferred source of info	11 4.7%	0 0	3 2.3%	3 2.3%	8 8.6%BC	6 4.3%	1 1.8%	5 9.1%	1 2.4%	0 0	4 4.4%	4 10.5%	* 3.2%	2 7.4%	* 7.1%	0 0	3 2.5%	9 6.4%
Other students inside your institution (NET)	14 5.7%	0 0	10 6.4%	10 6.4%	4 4.5%	7 5.8%	5 8.6%	1 1.9%	3 7.3%	2 5.9%	2 2.2%	3 7.9%	2 19.4%J	1 3.7%	* 7.1%	1 11.1%	6 5.6%	8 5.7%
All sources of info	14 5.7%	0 0	10 6.4%	10 6.4%	4 4.5%	7 5.8%	5 8.6%	1 1.9%	3 7.3%	2 5.9%	2 2.2%	3 7.9%	2 19.4%J	1 3.7%	* 7.1%	1 11.1%	6 5.6%	8 5.7%
preferred source of info	4 1.5%	0 0	3 2.3%	3 2.3%	* 0.3%	2 1.7%	2 2.5%	0 0	0 0	1 2.9%	0 0	2 5.3%	* 3.2%J	0 0	* 7.1%	0 0	1 1.4%	2 1.6%
Professional meetings (NET)	10 3.9%	0 0	9 5.7%	9 5.7%	1 1.1%	4 3.0%	6 9.3%G	0 0	1 2.4%	4 11.8%K	4 4.4%	0 0	0 0	1 3.7%	0 0	0 0	3 2.9%	7 4.7%
All sources of info	10 3.9%	0 0	9 5.7%	9 5.7%	1 1.1%	4 3.0%	6 9.3%G	0 0	1 2.4%	4 11.8%K	4 4.4%	0 0	0 0	1 3.7%	0 0	0 0	3 2.9%	7 4.7%

Proportions/Means: Columns Tested (5% risk level) - A/B/D - C/D - E/F/G - H/I/J/K/L/M/N - P/Q
* small base; ** very small base (under 30) ineligible for sig testing

Table 356
Page 1482

Outsell/Digital Library Federation Study (2002)
Weighted Tables

TABLE 135, continued

S7sum_6. Papers delivered at professional meetings SUMMARY TABLE

		RESPONDENT TYPE				INSTITUTION TYPE			DISCIPLINE									GENDER	
	TOTAL SAMPLE	FACULTY MEMBER	GRAD. STUDENT	FACULTY /GRAD	UNDER GRAD. STUDENT	PUBLIC	PRIVATE	LIBERAL ARTS	BIOLOGIAL SCIENCES	PHYSICAL SCIENCES /MATH	SOCIAL SCIENCES	ARTS AND HUMAN.	ENGI- NEERING	BUSINESS	LAW	UNDEC. MAJOR	MALE	FEMALE
		(A)	(B)	(C)	(D)	(E)	(F)	(G)	(H)	(I)	(J)	(K)	(L)	(M)	(N)		(P)	(Q)
Base - Use Papers delivered at professional meetings for coursework	243	0**	150	150	93*	127*	63*	53*	36*	34*	85*	43*	9*	25**	2**	9*	103*	140
preferred source of info	5 2.0%	0 0	5 3.3%	5 3.3%	0 0	2 1.5%	3 4.8%	0 0	0 0	3 8.8%	2 2.2%	0 0	0 0	0 0	0 0	0 0	2 1.9%	3 2.1%
Another institution's librarian (NET)	2 0.8%	0 0	2 1.3%	2 1.3%	0 0	2 1.5%	0 0	0 0	0 0	0 0	2 2.2%	0 0	0 0	0 0	0 0	0 0	2 1.8%	0 0
All sources of info	2 0.8%	0 0	2 1.3%	2 1.3%	0 0	2 1.5%	0 0	0 0	0 0	0 0	2 2.2%	0 0	0 0	0 0	0 0	0 0	2 1.8%	0 0
preferred source of info	0 0	0 0	0 0	0 0	0 0	0 0	0 0	0 0	0 0	0 0	0 0	0 0	0 0	0 0	0 0	0 0	0 0	0 0
Faculty members outside your institution (NET)	1 0.4%	0 0	1 0.7%	1 0.7%	0 0	0 0	1 1.6%	0 0	0 0	1 2.9%	0 0	0 0	0 0	0 0	0 0	0 0	0 0	1 0.7%
All sources of info	1 0.4%	0 0	1 0.7%	1 0.7%	0 0	0 0	1 1.6%	0 0	0 0	1 2.9%	0 0	0 0	0 0	0 0	0 0	0 0	0 0	1 0.7%
preferred source of info	0 0	0 0	0 0	0 0	0 0	0 0	0 0	0 0	0 0	0 0	0 0	0 0	0 0	0 0	0 0	0 0	0 0	0 0
Other students outside your institution (NET)	0 0	0 0	0 0	0 0	0 0	0 0	0 0	0 0	0 0	0 0	0 0	0 0	0 0	0 0	0 0	0 0	0 0	0 0

Proportions/Means: Columns Tested (5% risk level) - A/B/D - C/D - E/F/G - H/I/J/K/L/M/N - P/Q
* small base; ** very small base (under 30) ineligible for sig testing

Table 356
Page 1483

Outsell/Digital Library Federation Study (2002)
Weighted Tables

TABLE 135, continued

S7sum_6. Papers delivered at professional meetings SUMMARY TABLE

		RESPONDENT TYPE				INSTITUTION TYPE			DISCIPLINE									GENDER	
	TOTAL SAMPLE	FACULTY MEMBER	GRAD. STUDENT	FACULTY /GRAD	UNDER GRAD. STUDENT	PUBLIC	PRIVATE	LIBERAL ARTS	BIOLOGIAL SCIENCES	PHYSICAL SCIENCES /MATH	SOCIAL SCIENCES	ARTS AND HUMAN.	ENGI- NEERING	BUSINESS	LAW	UNDEC. MAJOR	MALE	FEMALE
		(A)	(B)	(C)	(D)	(E)	(F)	(G)	(H)	(I)	(J)	(K)	(L)	(M)	(N)		(P)	(Q)
Base - Use Papers delivered at professional meetings for coursework	243	0**	150	150	93*	127*	63*	53*	36*	34*	85*	43*	9*	25**	2**	9*	103*	140
All sources of info	0 0	0 0	0 0	0 0	0 0	0 0	0 0	0 0	0 0	0 0	0 0	0 0	0 0	0 0	0 0	0 0	0 0	0 0
preferred source of info	0 0	0 0	0 0	0 0	0 0	0 0	0 0	0 0	0 0	0 0	0 0	0 0	0 0	0 0	0 0	0 0	0 0	0 0
LIBRARY FACILITIES/ PRINT	57 23.7%	0 0	36 24.0%	36 24.0%	22 23.2%	26 20.6%	18 28.0%	14 26.1%	11 29.3%	10 29.4%	13 15.6%	15 34.2%J	2 22.6%	5 18.5%	1 21.4%	2 22.2%	21 20.6%	36 25.9%
Campus library (NET)	47 19.5%	0 0	30 19.7%	30 19.7%	18 19.0%	22 17.6%	14 22.2%	11 20.9%	8 22.0%	10 29.4%J	9 11.1%	12 28.9%J	2 19.4%	4 14.8%	* 7.1%	2 22.2%	18 17.5%	29 21.0%
All sources of info	47 19.5%	0 0	30 19.7%	30 19.7%	18 19.0%	22 17.6%	14 22.2%	11 20.9%	8 22.0%	10 29.4%J	9 11.1%	12 28.9%J	2 19.4%	4 14.8%	* 7.1%	2 22.2%	18 17.5%	29 21.0%
preferred source of info	14 5.9%	0 0	12 8.2%	12 8.2%	2 2.2%	9 6.8%	4 5.8%	2 3.8%	1 2.4%	4 11.8%	2 2.2%	7 15.8%HJ	1 9.7%	0 0	0 0	0 0	6 5.7%	8 6.1%
References cited in books or journal articles (NET)	7 2.8%	0 0	6 3.9%	6 3.9%	1 0.9%	5 3.7%	1 1.8%	1 1.7%	3 7.3%	0 0	2 2.2%	2 5.3%	0 0	0 0	0 0	0 0	1 1.1%	6 4.0%
All sources of info	7 2.8%	0 0	6 3.9%	6 3.9%	1 0.9%	5 3.7%	1 1.8%	1 1.7%	3 7.3%	0 0	2 2.2%	2 5.3%	0 0	0 0	0 0	0 0	1 1.1%	6 4.0%

Proportions/Means: Columns Tested (5% risk level) - A/B/D - C/D - E/F/G - H/I/J/K/L/M/N - P/Q
* small base; ** very small base (under 30) ineligible for sig testing

Table 356
Page 1484

Outsell/Digital Library Federation Study (2002)
Weighted Tables

TABLE 135, continued

S7sum_6. Papers delivered at professional meetings SUMMARY TABLE

		RESPONDENT TYPE				INSTITUTION TYPE			DISCIPLINE									GENDER	
	TOTAL SAMPLE	FACULTY MEMBER	GRAD. STUDENT	FACULTY /GRAD	UNDER GRAD. STUDENT	PUBLIC	PRIVATE	LIBERAL ARTS	BIOLOGIAL SCIENCES	PHYSICAL SCIENCES /MATH	SOCIAL SCIENCES	ARTS AND HUMAN.	ENGI- NEERING	BUSINESS	LAW	UNDEC. MAJOR	MALE	FEMALE
		(A)	(B)	(C)	(D)	(E)	(F)	(G)	(H)	(I)	(J)	(K)	(L)	(M)	(N)		(P)	(Q)
Base - Use Papers delivered at professional meetings for coursework	243	0**	150	150	93*	127*	63*	53*	36*	34*	85*	43*	9*	25**	2**	9*	103*	140
preferred source of info	5 2.0%	0 0	4 2.6%	4 2.6%	1 0.9%	3 2.2%	1 1.8%	1 1.7%	2 4.9%	0 0	2 2.2%	1 2.6%	0 0	0 0	0 0	0 0	0 0	5 3.4%
Physical bookstore (NET)	3 1.3%	0 0	1 0.8%	1 0.8%	2 2.0%	0 0	1 1.9%	2 3.5%	0 0	0 0	2 2.2%	0 0	* 3.2%	1 3.7%	0 0	0 0	3 3.0%	0 0
All sources of info	3 1.3%	0 0	1 0.8%	1 0.8%	2 2.0%	0 0	1 1.9%	2 3.5%	0 0	0 0	2 2.2%	0 0	* 3.2%	1 3.7%	0 0	0 0	3 3.0%	0 0
preferred source of info	3 1.3%	0 0	1 0.8%	1 0.8%	2 2.0%	0 0	1 1.9%	2 3.5%	0 0	0 0	2 2.2%	0 0	* 3.2%	1 3.7%	0 0	0 0	3 3.0%	0 0
Your own personal physical library/ files/bookshelves (NET)	2 0.9%	0 0	* 0.1%	* 0.1%	2 2.2%	* 0.1%	0 0	2 3.9%	0 0	0 0	0 0	1 2.6%	0 0	1 3.7%	* 7.1%	0 0	1 1.3%	1 0.7%
All sources of info	2 0.9%	0 0	* 0.1%	* 0.1%	2 2.2%	* 0.1%	0 0	2 3.9%	0 0	0 0	0 0	1 2.6%	0 0	1 3.7%	* 7.1%	0 0	1 1.3%	1 0.7%
preferred source of info	1 0.4%	0 0	0 0	0 0	1 1.0%	0 0	0 0	1 1.8%	0 0	0 0	0 0	0 0	0 0	1 3.7%	0 0	0 0	0 0	1 0.7%
Printed library catalogues and finding aids (NET)	1 0.6%	0 0	* 0.2%	* 0.2%	1 1.2%	0 0	1 2.3%	0 0	0 0	0 0	0 0	1 2.6%	* 3.2%J	0 0	0 0	0 0	* 0.3%	1 0.8%

Proportions/Means: Columns Tested (5% risk level) - A/B/D - C/D - E/F/G - H/I/J/K/L/M/N - P/Q
* small base; ** very small base (under 30) ineligible for sig testing

Table 356
Page 1485

Outsell/Digital Library Federation Study (2002)
Weighted Tables

TABLE 135, continued

S7sum_6. Papers delivered at professional meetings SUMMARY TABLE

		RESPONDENT TYPE				INSTITUTION TYPE			DISCIPLINE								GENDER	
	TOTAL SAMPLE	FACULTY MEMBER	GRAD. STUDENT	FACULTY /GRAD	UNDER GRAD. STUDENT	PUBLIC	PRIVATE	LIBERAL ARTS	BIOLOGIAL SCIENCES	PHYSICAL SCIENCES /MATH	SOCIAL SCIENCES	ARTS AND HUMAN.	ENGI- NEERING	BUSINESS	LAW	UNDEC. MAJOR	MALE	FEMALE
		(A)	(B)	(C)	(D)	(E)	(F)	(G)	(H)	(I)	(J)	(K)	(L)	(M)	(N)		(P)	(Q)
Base - Use Papers delivered at professional meetings for coursework	243	0**	150	150	93*	127*	63*	53*	36*	34*	85*	43*	9*	25**	2**	9*	103*	140
All sources of info	1 0.6%	0 0	* 0.2%	* 0.2%	1 1.2%	0 0	1 2.3%	0 0	0 0	0 0	0 0	1 2.6%	* 3.2%J	0 0	0 0	0 0	* 0.3%	1 0.8%
preferred source of info	0 0	0 0	0 0	0 0	0 0	0 0	0 0	0 0	0 0	0 0	0 0	0 0	0 0	0 0	0 0	0 0	0 0	0 0
Printed abstracting and indexing services (NET)	1 0.4%	0 0	1 0.6%	1 0.6%	0 0	0 0	1 1.4%	0 0	1 2.4%	0 0	0 0	0 0	0 0	0 0	0 0	0 0	0 0	1 0.6%
All sources of info	1 0.4%	0 0	1 0.6%	1 0.6%	0 0	0 0	1 1.4%	0 0	1 2.4%	0 0	0 0	0 0	0 0	0 0	0 0	0 0	0 0	1 0.6%
preferred source of info	0 0	0 0	0 0	0 0	0 0	0 0	0 0	0 0	0 0	0 0	0 0	0 0	0 0	0 0	0 0	0 0	0 0	0 0
Another library (NET)	* 0.1%	0 0	* 0.1%	* 0.1%	0 0	0 0	* 0.3%	0 0	0 0	0 0	0 0	0 0	0 0	0 0	* 7.1%	0 0	0 0	* 0.1%
All sources of info	* 0.1%	0 0	* 0.1%	* 0.1%	0 0	0 0	* 0.3%	0 0	0 0	0 0	0 0	0 0	0 0	0 0	* 7.1%	0 0	0 0	* 0.1%
preferred source of info	0 0	0 0	0 0	0 0	0 0	0 0	0 0	0 0	0 0	0 0	0 0	0 0	0 0	0 0	0 0	0 0	0 0	0 0

Proportions/Means: Columns Tested (5% risk level) - A/B/D - C/D - E/F/G - H/I/J/K/L/M/N - P/Q
* small base; ** very small base (under 30) ineligible for sig testing

Table 356
Page 1486

Outsell/Digital Library Federation Study (2002)
Weighted Tables

TABLE 135, continued

S7sum_6. Papers delivered at professional meetings SUMMARY TABLE

		RESPONDENT TYPE				INSTITUTION TYPE			DISCIPLINE									GENDER	
	TOTAL SAMPLE	FACULTY MEMBER	GRAD. STUDENT	FACULTY /GRAD	UNDER GRAD. STUDENT	PUBLIC	PRIVATE	LIBERAL ARTS	BIOLOGIAL SCIENCES	PHYSICAL SCIENCES /MATH	SOCIAL SCIENCES	ARTS AND HUMAN.	ENGI- NEERING	BUSINESS	LAW	UNDEC. MAJOR	MALE	FEMALE
		(A)	(B)	(C)	(D)	(E)	(F)	(G)	(H)	(I)	(J)	(K)	(L)	(M)	(N)		(P)	(Q)
Base - Use Papers delivered at professional meetings for coursework	243	0**	150	150	93*	127*	63*	53*	36*	34*	85*	43*	9*	25**	2**	9*	103*	140
Personal subscriptions to newspapers, magazines and journals (NET)	0 0	0 0	0 0	0 0	0 0	0 0	0 0	0 0	0 0	0 0	0 0	0 0	0 0	0 0	0 0	0 0	0 0	0 0
All sources of info	0 0	0 0	0 0	0 0	0 0	0 0	0 0	0 0	0 0	0 0	0 0	0 0	0 0	0 0	0 0	0 0	0 0	0 0
preferred source of info	0 0	0 0	0 0	0 0	0 0	0 0	0 0	0 0	0 0	0 0	0 0	0 0	0 0	0 0	0 0	0 0	0 0	0 0
Other (NET)	17 6.9%	0 0	6 4.1%	6 4.1%	11 11.4%	11 8.6%	3 4.6%	3 5.4%	5 14.6%I	0 0	4 4.4%	3 7.9%	* 3.2%	2 7.4%	* 7.1%	2 22.2%	10 9.7%	7 4.8%
All sources of info	16 6.8%	0 0	6 3.9%	6 3.9%	11 11.4%BC	11 8.4%	3 4.6%	3 5.4%	5 14.6%I	0 0	4 4.4%	3 7.9%	0 0	2 7.4%	* 7.1%	2 22.2%	10 9.4%	7 4.8%
preferred source of info	6 2.4%	0 0	2 1.4%	2 1.4%	4 4.0%	5 3.8%	1 1.4%	0 0	4 9.8%JK	0 0	0 0	0 0	* 3.2%J	1 3.7%	0 0	1 11.1%	4 3.8%	2 1.3%
Online (unspecified)	5 2.0%	0 0	2 1.2%	2 1.2%	3 3.2%	3 2.1%	1 1.8%	1 1.9%	2 4.9%	1 2.9%	0 0	1 2.6%	0 0	1 3.7%	0 0	0 0	1 0.9%	4 2.8%
All sources of info	5 2.0%	0 0	2 1.2%	2 1.2%	3 3.2%	3 2.1%	1 1.8%	1 1.9%	2 4.9%	1 2.9%	0 0	1 2.6%	0 0	1 3.7%	0 0	0 0	1 0.9%	4 2.8%

Proportions/Means: Columns Tested (5% risk level) - A/B/D - C/D - E/F/G - H/I/J/K/L/M/N - P/Q
* small base; ** very small base (under 30) ineligible for sig testing

Table 356
Page 1487

Outsell/Digital Library Federation Study (2002)
Weighted Tables

TABLE 135, continued

S7sum_6. Papers delivered at professional meetings SUMMARY TABLE

		RESPONDENT TYPE				INSTITUTION TYPE			DISCIPLINE									GENDER	
	TOTAL SAMPLE	FACULTY MEMBER	GRAD. STUDENT	FACULTY /GRAD	UNDER GRAD. STUDENT	PUBLIC	PRIVATE	LIBERAL ARTS	BIOLOGIAL SCIENCES	PHYSICAL SCIENCES /MATH	SOCIAL SCIENCES	ARTS AND HUMAN.	ENGI-NEERING	BUSINESS	LAW	UNDEC. MAJOR	MALE	FEMALE
		(A)	(B)	(C)	(D)	(E)	(F)	(G)	(H)	(I)	(J)	(K)	(L)	(M)	(N)		(P)	(Q)
Base - Use Papers delivered at professional meetings for coursework	243	0**	150	150	93*	127*	63*	53*	36*	34*	85*	43*	9*	25**	2**	9*	103*	140
preferred source of info	5 2.0%	0 0	2 1.2%	2 1.2%	3 3.2%	3 2.1%	1 1.8%	1 1.9%	2 4.9%	1 2.9%	0 0	1 2.6%	0 0	1 3.7%	0 0	0 0	1 0.9%	4 2.8%
E-journals	0 0	0 0	0 0	0 0	0 0	0 0	0 0	0 0	0 0	0 0	0 0	0 0	0 0	0 0	0 0	0 0	0 0	0 0
All sources of info	0 0	0 0	0 0	0 0	0 0	0 0	0 0	0 0	0 0	0 0	0 0	0 0	0 0	0 0	0 0	0 0	0 0	0 0
preferred source of info	0 0	0 0	0 0	0 0	0 0	0 0	0 0	0 0	0 0	0 0	0 0	0 0	0 0	0 0	0 0	0 0	0 0	0 0
DK/Refused	13 5.4%	0 0	6 4.1%	6 4.1%	7 7.5%	6 4.4%	5 8.4%	2 4.2%	2 4.9%	3 8.8%	2 2.2%	3 7.9%	* 3.2%	3 11.1%	0 0	0 0	5 4.9%	8 5.7%

Proportions/Means: Columns Tested (5% risk level) - A/B/D - C/D - E/F/G - H/I/J/K/L/M/N - P/Q
* small base; ** very small base (under 30) ineligible for sig testing

Table 356
Page 1488

Outsell/Digital Library Federation Study (2002)
Weighted Tables

TABLE 136

S7D/E_6. Papers delivered at professional meetings SUMMARY TABLE

		RESPONDENT TYPE				INSTITUTION TYPE			DISCIPLINE									GENDER	
	TOTAL SAMPLE	FACULTY MEMBER	GRAD. STUDENT	FACULTY /GRAD	UNDER GRAD. STUDENT	PUBLIC	PRIVATE	LIBERAL ARTS	BIOLOGIAL SCIENCES	PHYSICAL SCIENCES /MATH	SOCIAL SCIENCES	ARTS AND HUMAN.	ENGI-NEERING	BUSINESS	LAW	UNDEC. MAJOR	MALE	FEMALE
		(A)	(B)	(C)	(D)	(E)	(F)	(G)	(H)	(I)	(J)	(K)	(L)	(M)	(N)		(P)	(Q)
Base - Use Papers delivered at professional meetings for coursework	243	0**	150	150	93*	127*	63*	53*	36*	34*	85*	43*	9*	25**	2**	9*	103*	140
Borrow from or use in campus library (NET)	112 46.3%	0 0	64 42.8%	64 42.8%	48 52.0%	61 47.6%	26 41.5%	26 48.9%	18 51.2%	13 38.2%	34 40.0%	28 65.8%IJ	5 54.8%	9 37.0%	1 35.7%	4 44.4%	48 46.3%	65 46.3%
All sources of info	112 46.3%	0 0	64 42.8%	64 42.8%	48 52.0%	61 47.6%	26 41.5%	26 48.9%	18 51.2%	13 38.2%	34 40.0%	28 65.8%IJ	5 54.8%	9 37.0%	1 35.7%	4 44.4%	48 46.3%	65 46.3%
preferred source of info	84 34.5%	0 0	45 30.2%	45 30.2%	38 41.3%	44 34.8%	22 35.5%	17 32.4%	12 34.1%	10 29.4%	21 24.4%	27 63.2%HI J	4 45.2%J	8 33.3%	* 14.3%	1 11.1%	39 37.5%	45 32.2%
Access online (NET)	111 45.8%	0 0	67 44.8%	67 44.8%	44 47.2%	57 45.0%	25 39.7%	29 54.7%	19 53.7%	14 41.2%	43 51.1%	13 31.6%	4 48.4%	9 37.0%	1 57.1%	6 66.7%	43 42.0%	68 48.5%
All sources of info	111 45.8%	0 0	67 44.8%	67 44.8%	44 47.2%	57 45.0%	25 39.7%	29 54.7%	19 53.7%	14 41.2%	43 51.1%	13 31.6%	4 48.4%	9 37.0%	1 57.1%	6 66.7%	43 42.0%	68 48.5%
preferred source of info	99 40.7%	0 0	63 41.9%	63 41.9%	36 38.8%	49 38.4%	23 37.0%	27 50.5%	16 43.9%K	14 41.2%	39 46.7%K	9 21.1%	4 41.9%	9 37.0%	1 57.1%	6 66.7%	40 38.8%	59 42.0%
Faculty (NET)	31 12.7%	0 0	28 18.7%D	28 18.7%D	3 3.1%	17 13.2%	11 18.0%	3 5.4%	4 9.8%	6 17.6%	13 15.6%	3 7.9%	1 9.7%	3 11.1%	* 7.1%	1 11.1%	15 14.6%	16 11.3%
All sources of info	31 12.7%	0 0	28 18.7%D	28 18.7%D	3 3.1%	17 13.2%	11 18.0%	3 5.4%	4 9.8%	6 17.6%	13 15.6%	3 7.9%	1 9.7%	3 11.1%	* 7.1%	1 11.1%	15 14.6%	16 11.3%

Proportions/Means: Columns Tested (5% risk level) - A/B/D - C/D - E/F/G - H/I/J/K/L/M/N - P/Q
* small base; ** very small base (under 30) ineligible for sig testing

Table 359
Page 1495

Outsell/Digital Library Federation Study (2002)
Weighted Tables

TABLE 136, continued

S7D/E_6. Papers delivered at professional meetings SUMMARY TABLE

		RESPONDENT TYPE				INSTITUTION TYPE			DISCIPLINE									GENDER	
	TOTAL SAMPLE	FACULTY MEMBER	GRAD. STUDENT	FACULTY /GRAD	UNDER GRAD. STUDENT	PUBLIC	PRIVATE	LIBERAL ARTS	BIOLOGIAL SCIENCES	PHYSICAL SCIENCES /MATH	SOCIAL SCIENCES	ARTS AND HUMAN.	ENGI-NEERING	BUSINESS	LAW	UNDEC. MAJOR	MALE	FEMALE
		(A)	(B)	(C)	(D)	(E)	(F)	(G)	(H)	(I)	(J)	(K)	(L)	(M)	(N)		(P)	(Q)
Base - Use Papers delivered at professional meetings for coursework	243	0**	150	150	93*	127*	63*	53*	36*	34*	85*	43*	9*	25**	2**	9*	103*	140
preferred source of info	23 9.4%	0 0	21 13.9%D	21 13.9%D	2 2.2%	13 10.3%	8 12.4%	2 3.8%	2 4.9%	4 11.8%	11 13.3%	3 7.9%	* 3.2%	1 3.7%	* 7.1%	1 11.1%	9 8.6%	14 10.0%
Colleagues (NET)	7 2.9%	0 0	7 4.7%	7 4.7%	0 0	2 1.5%	5 8.2%E	0 0	0 0	1 2.9%	4 4.4%	2 5.3%	0 0	0 0	0 0	0 0	2 2.1%	5 3.5%
All sources of info	7 2.9%	0 0	7 4.7%	7 4.7%	0 0	2 1.5%	5 8.2%E	0 0	0 0	1 2.9%	4 4.4%	2 5.3%	0 0	0 0	0 0	0 0	2 2.1%	5 3.5%
preferred source of info	0 0	0 0	0 0	0 0	0 0	0 0	0 0	0 0	0 0	0 0	0 0	0 0	0 0	0 0	0 0	0 0	0 0	0 0
Borrow from or use in other libraries (NET)	4 1.7%	0 0	3 2.1%	3 2.1%	1 1.2%	1 0.8%	3 5.1%	0 0	1 2.4%	0 0	2 2.2%	1 2.6%	0 0	0 0	* 14.3%	0 0	1 1.0%	3 2.3%
All sources of info	4 1.7%	0 0	3 2.1%	3 2.1%	1 1.2%	1 0.8%	3 5.1%	0 0	1 2.4%	0 0	2 2.2%	1 2.6%	0 0	0 0	* 14.3%	0 0	1 1.0%	3 2.3%
preferred source of info	3 1.4%	0 0	2 1.5%	2 1.5%	1 1.2%	* 0.1%	3 5.1%E	0 0	0 0	0 0	2 2.2%	1 2.6%	0 0	0 0	* 14.3%	0 0	* 0.2%	3 2.3%
In class (NET)	4 1.6%	0 0	1 0.6%	1 0.6%	3 3.1%	3 2.2%	0 0	1 1.9%	0 0	1 2.9%	2 2.2%	0 0	0 0	1 3.7%	0 0	0 0	2 1.9%	2 1.3%
All sources of info	4 1.6%	0 0	1 0.6%	1 0.6%	3 3.1%	3 2.2%	0 0	1 1.9%	0 0	1 2.9%	2 2.2%	0 0	0 0	1 3.7%	0 0	0 0	2 1.9%	2 1.3%

Proportions/Means: Columns Tested (5% risk level) - A/B/D - C/D - E/F/G - H/I/J/K/L/M/N - P/Q
* small base; ** very small base (under 30) ineligible for sig testing

Table 359
Page 1496

Outsell/Digital Library Federation Study (2002)
Weighted Tables

TABLE 136, continued

S7D/E_6. Papers delivered at professional meetings SUMMARY TABLE

		RESPONDENT TYPE				INSTITUTION TYPE			DISCIPLINE									GENDER	
	TOTAL SAMPLE	FACULTY MEMBER	GRAD. STUDENT	FACULTY /GRAD	UNDER GRAD. STUDENT	PUBLIC	PRIVATE	LIBERAL ARTS	BIOLOGIAL SCIENCES	PHYSICAL SCIENCES /MATH	SOCIAL SCIENCES	ARTS AND HUMAN.	ENGI- NEERING	BUSINESS	LAW	UNDEC. MAJOR	MALE	FEMALE
		(A)	(B)	(C)	(D)	(E)	(F)	(G)	(H)	(I)	(J)	(K)	(L)	(M)	(N)		(P)	(Q)
Base - Use Papers delivered at professional meetings for coursework	243	0**	150	150	93*	127*	63*	53*	36*	34*	85*	43*	9*	25**	2**	9*	103*	140
preferred source of info	4	0	1	1	3	3	0	1	0	1	2	0	0	1	0	0	2	2
	1.6%	0	0.6%	0.6%	3.1%	2.2%	0	1.9%	0	2.9%	2.2%	0	0	3.7%	0	0	1.9%	1.3%
Order from on demand document delivery service (NET)	2	0	2	2	0	2	0	0	0	0	2	0	*	0	0	0	*	2
	0.9%	0	1.4%	1.4%	0	1.7%	0	0	0	0	2.2%	0	3.2%	0	0	0	0.3%	1.3%
All sources of info	2	0	2	2	0	2	0	0	0	0	2	0	*	0	0	0	*	2
	0.9%	0	1.4%	1.4%	0	1.7%	0	0	0	0	2.2%	0	3.2%	0	0	0	0.3%	1.3%
preferred source of info	0	0	0	0	0	0	0	0	0	0	0	0	0	0	0	0	0	0
	0	0	0	0	0	0	0	0	0	0	0	0	0	0	0	0	0	0
Interlibrary loan (NET)	2	0	2	2	0	0	2	0	0	0	2	0	0	0	0	0	0	2
	0.8%	0	1.3%	1.3%	0	0	3.0%	0	0	0	2.2%	0	0	0	0	0	0	1.3%
All sources of info	2	0	2	2	0	0	2	0	0	0	2	0	0	0	0	0	0	2
	0.8%	0	1.3%	1.3%	0	0	3.0%	0	0	0	2.2%	0	0	0	0	0	0	1.3%
preferred source of info	0	0	0	0	0	0	0	0	0	0	0	0	0	0	0	0	0	0
	0	0	0	0	0	0	0	0	0	0	0	0	0	0	0	0	0	0
Purchase from physical book store (NET)	1	0	0	0	1	0	*	1	0	0	0	0	*	1	0	0	1	0
	0.5%	0	0	0	1.3%	0	0.5%	1.8%	0	0	0	0	3.2%J	3.7%	0	0	1.2%	0

Proportions/Means: Columns Tested (5% risk level) - A/B/D - C/D - E/F/G - H/I/J/K/L/M/N - P/Q
* small base; ** very small base (under 30) ineligible for sig testing

Table 359
Page 1497

Outsell/Digital Library Federation Study (2002)
Weighted Tables

TABLE 136, continued

S7D/E_6. Papers delivered at professional meetings SUMMARY TABLE

	TOTAL SAMPLE	RESPONDENT TYPE: FACULTY MEMBER (A)	GRAD. STUDENT (B)	FACULTY /GRAD (C)	UNDER GRAD. STUDENT (D)	INSTITUTION TYPE: PUBLIC (E)	PRIVATE (F)	LIBERAL ARTS (G)	DISCIPLINE: BIOLOGIAL SCIENCES (H)	PHYSICAL SCIENCES /MATH (I)	SOCIAL SCIENCES (J)	ARTS AND HUMAN. (K)	ENGI-NEERING (L)	BUSINESS (M)	LAW (N)	UNDEC. MAJOR	GENDER: MALE (P)	FEMALE (Q)
Base - Use Papers delivered at professional meetings for coursework	243	0**	150	150	93*	127*	63*	53*	36*	34*	85*	43*	9*	25**	2**	9*	103*	140
All sources of info	1 0.5%	0 0	0 0	0 0	1 1.3%	0 0	* 0.5%	1 1.8%	0 0	0 0	0 0	0 0	* 3.2%J	1 3.7%	0 0	0 0	1 1.2%	0 0
preferred source of info	0 0	0 0	0 0	0 0	0 0	0 0	0 0	0 0	0 0	0 0	0 0	0 0	0 0	0 0	0 0	0 0	0 0	0 0
Personal Holdings (NET)	1 0.4%	0 0	0 0	0 0	1 1.0%	0 0	0 0	1 1.8%	0 0	0 0	0 0	0 0	0 0	1 3.7%	0 0	0 0	0 0	1 0.7%
All sources of info	1 0.4%	0 0	0 0	0 0	1 1.0%	0 0	0 0	1 1.8%	0 0	0 0	0 0	0 0	0 0	1 3.7%	0 0	0 0	0 0	1 0.7%
preferred source of info	1 0.4%	0 0	0 0	0 0	1 1.0%	0 0	0 0	1 1.8%	0 0	0 0	0 0	0 0	0 0	1 3.7%	0 0	0 0	0 0	1 0.7%
Home (NET)	0 0	0 0	0 0	0 0	0 0	0 0	0 0	0 0	0 0	0 0	0 0	0 0	0 0	0 0	0 0	0 0	0 0	0 0
All sources of info	0 0	0 0	0 0	0 0	0 0	0 0	0 0	0 0	0 0	0 0	0 0	0 0	0 0	0 0	0 0	0 0	0 0	0 0
preferred source of info	0 0	0 0	0 0	0 0	0 0	0 0	0 0	0 0	0 0	0 0	0 0	0 0	0 0	0 0	0 0	0 0	0 0	0 0
Ask library to purchase source (NET)	0 0	0 0	0 0	0 0	0 0	0 0	0 0	0 0	0 0	0 0	0 0	0 0	0 0	0 0	0 0	0 0	0 0	0 0

Proportions/Means: Columns Tested (5% risk level) - A/B/D - C/D - E/F/G - H/I/J/K/L/M/N - P/Q
* small base; ** very small base (under 30) ineligible for sig testing

Table 359
Page 1498

Outsell/Digital Library Federation Study (2002)
Weighted Tables

TABLE 136, continued

S7D/E_6. Papers delivered at professional meetings SUMMARY TABLE

	TOTAL SAMPLE	RESPONDENT TYPE: FACULTY MEMBER	GRAD. STUDENT	FACULTY /GRAD	UNDER GRAD. STUDENT	INSTITUTION TYPE: PUBLIC	PRIVATE	LIBERAL ARTS	DISCIPLINE: BIOLOGIAL SCIENCES	PHYSICAL SCIENCES /MATH	SOCIAL SCIENCES	ARTS AND HUMAN.	ENGI-NEERING	BUSINESS	LAW	UNDEC. MAJOR	GENDER: MALE	FEMALE
		(A)	(B)	(C)	(D)	(E)	(F)	(G)	(H)	(I)	(J)	(K)	(L)	(M)	(N)		(P)	(Q)
Base - Use Papers delivered at professional meetings for coursework	243	0**	150	150	93*	127*	63*	53*	36*	34*	85*	43*	9*	25**	2**	9*	103*	140
All sources of info	0 0	0 0	0 0	0 0	0 0	0 0	0 0	0 0	0 0	0 0	0 0	0 0	0 0	0 0	0 0	0 0	0 0	0 0
preferred source of info	0 0	0 0	0 0	0 0	0 0	0 0	0 0	0 0	0 0	0 0	0 0	0 0	0 0	0 0	0 0	0 0	0 0	0 0
Access from course website (NET)	0 0	0 0	0 0	0 0	0 0	0 0	0 0	0 0	0 0	0 0	0 0	0 0	0 0	0 0	0 0	0 0	0 0	0 0
All sources of info	0 0	0 0	0 0	0 0	0 0	0 0	0 0	0 0	0 0	0 0	0 0	0 0	0 0	0 0	0 0	0 0	0 0	0 0
preferred source of info	0 0	0 0	0 0	0 0	0 0	0 0	0 0	0 0	0 0	0 0	0 0	0 0	0 0	0 0	0 0	0 0	0 0	0 0
Access book/journal/journal article elsewhere online (NET)	0 0	0 0	0 0	0 0	0 0	0 0	0 0	0 0	0 0	0 0	0 0	0 0	0 0	0 0	0 0	0 0	0 0	0 0
All sources of info	0 0	0 0	0 0	0 0	0 0	0 0	0 0	0 0	0 0	0 0	0 0	0 0	0 0	0 0	0 0	0 0	0 0	0 0
preferred source of info	0 0	0 0	0 0	0 0	0 0	0 0	0 0	0 0	0 0	0 0	0 0	0 0	0 0	0 0	0 0	0 0	0 0	0 0

Proportions/Means: Columns Tested (5% risk level) - A/B/D - C/D - E/F/G - H/I/J/K/L/M/N - P/Q
* small base; ** very small base (under 30) ineligible for sig testing

Table 359
Page 1499

Outsell/Digital Library Federation Study (2002)
Weighted Tables

TABLE 136, continued

S7D/E_6. Papers delivered at professional meetings SUMMARY TABLE

		RESPONDENT TYPE				INSTITUTION TYPE			DISCIPLINE									GENDER	
	TOTAL SAMPLE	FACULTY MEMBER	GRAD. STUDENT	FACULTY /GRAD	UNDER GRAD. STUDENT	PUBLIC	PRIVATE	LIBERAL ARTS	BIOLOGIAL SCIENCES	PHYSICAL SCIENCES /MATH	SOCIAL SCIENCES	ARTS AND HUMAN.	ENGI- NEERING	BUSINESS	LAW	UNDEC. MAJOR	MALE	FEMALE
		(A)	(B)	(C)	(D)	(E)	(F)	(G)	(H)	(I)	(J)	(K)	(L)	(M)	(N)		(P)	(Q)
Base - Use Papers delivered at professional meetings for coursework	243	0**	150	150	93*	127*	63*	53*	36*	34*	85*	43*	9*	25**	2**	9*	103*	140
Dorm room (NET)	0 0	0 0	0 0	0 0	0 0	0 0	0 0	0 0	0 0	0 0	0 0	0 0	0 0	0 0	0 0	0 0	0 0	0 0
All sources of info	0 0	0 0	0 0	0 0	0 0	0 0	0 0	0 0	0 0	0 0	0 0	0 0	0 0	0 0	0 0	0 0	0 0	0 0
preferred source of info	0 0	0 0	0 0	0 0	0 0	0 0	0 0	0 0	0 0	0 0	0 0	0 0	0 0	0 0	0 0	0 0	0 0	0 0
Purchase from online bookstore (NET)	0 0	0 0	0 0	0 0	0 0	0 0	0 0	0 0	0 0	0 0	0 0	0 0	0 0	0 0	0 0	0 0	0 0	0 0
All sources of info	0 0	0 0	0 0	0 0	0 0	0 0	0 0	0 0	0 0	0 0	0 0	0 0	0 0	0 0	0 0	0 0	0 0	0 0
preferred source of info	0 0	0 0	0 0	0 0	0 0	0 0	0 0	0 0	0 0	0 0	0 0	0 0	0 0	0 0	0 0	0 0	0 0	0 0
Other (NET)	29 11.8%	0 0	18 11.7%	18 11.7%	11 11.8%	16 12.5%	6 10.1%	6 11.9%	3 7.3%	5 14.7%	13 15.6%	3 7.9%	1 6.5%	3 11.1%	0 0	1 11.1%	14 13.8%	14 10.2%
All sources of info	29 11.8%	0 0	18 11.7%	18 11.7%	11 11.8%	16 12.5%	6 10.1%	6 11.9%	3 7.3%	5 14.7%	13 15.6%	3 7.9%	1 6.5%	3 11.1%	0 0	1 11.1%	14 13.8%	14 10.2%
preferred source of info	18 7.5%	0 0	13 8.4%	13 8.4%	6 6.1%	11 8.9%	5 8.1%	2 3.6%	2 4.9%	4 11.8%K	9 11.1%	0 0	* 3.2%	2 7.4%	0 0	1 11.1%	8 7.9%	10 7.3%

Proportions/Means: Columns Tested (5% risk level) - A/B/D - C/D - E/F/G - H/I/J/K/L/M/N - P/Q
* small base; ** very small base (under 30) ineligible for sig testing

Table 359
Page 1500

Outsell/Digital Library Federation Study (2002)
Weighted Tables

TABLE 136, continued

S7D/E_6. Papers delivered at professional meetings SUMMARY TABLE

		RESPONDENT TYPE				INSTITUTION TYPE			DISCIPLINE									GENDER	
	TOTAL SAMPLE	FACULTY MEMBER	GRAD. STUDENT	FACULTY /GRAD	UNDER GRAD. STUDENT	PUBLIC	PRIVATE	LIBERAL ARTS	BIOLOGIAL SCIENCES	PHYSICAL SCIENCES /MATH	SOCIAL SCIENCES	ARTS AND HUMAN.	ENGI-NEERING	BUSINESS	LAW	UNDEC. MAJOR	MALE	FEMALE
		(A)	(B)	(C)	(D)	(E)	(F)	(G)	(H)	(I)	(J)	(K)	(L)	(M)	(N)		(P)	(Q)
Base - Use Papers delivered at professional meetings for coursework	243	0**	150	150	93*	127*	63*	53*	36*	34*	85*	43*	9*	25**	2**	9*	103*	140
DK/Refused	9	0	4	4	5	6	1	2	4	1	0	1	1	3	*	0	4	5
	3.8%	0	2.8%	2.8%	5.4%	4.4%	1.9%	4.4%	9.8%J	2.9%	0	2.6%	6.5%J	11.1%	7.1%	0	4.4%	3.4%

Proportions/Means: Columns Tested (5% risk level) - A/B/D - C/D - E/F/G - H/I/J/K/L/M/N - P/Q
* small base; ** very small base (under 30) ineligible for sig testing

Table 359
Page 1501

Outsell/Digital Library Federation Study (2002)
Weighted Tables

TABLE 137

S7sum_7. Print abstracts and indexes SUMMARY TABLE

		RESPONDENT TYPE				INSTITUTION TYPE			DISCIPLINE								GENDER	
	TOTAL SAMPLE	FACULTY MEMBER	GRAD. STUDENT	FACULTY /GRAD	UNDER GRAD. STUDENT	PUBLIC	PRIVATE	LIBERAL ARTS	BIOLOGIAL SCIENCES	PHYSICAL SCIENCES /MATH	SOCIAL SCIENCES	ARTS AND HUMAN.	ENGI-NEERING	BUSINESS	LAW	UNDEC. MAJOR	MALE	FEMALE
		(A)	(B)	(C)	(D)	(E)	(F)	(G)	(H)	(I)	(J)	(K)	(L)	(M)	(N)		(P)	(Q)
Base - Use Print abstracts and indexes for coursework	423	0**	214	214	209	200	100*	123*	52*	47*	177*	85*	13*	35*	6*	7*	197	226
ONLINE	328 77.6%	0 0	163 76.2%	163 76.2%	165 79.0%	147 73.2%	81 81.1%	101 81.8%	38 72.9%	40 85.1%N	137 77.7%	67 78.9%N	12 87.0%N	25 71.1%	4 62.2%	5 71.4%	155 78.8%	173 76.5%
Your own institution's web site (NET)	97 23.0%	0 0	47 21.8%	47 21.8%	50 24.2%	38 19.2%	28 28.3%	31 24.9%	11 22.0%	14 29.8%M	41 23.4%M	22 26.3%M	3 19.6%	3 7.9%	1 10.8%	2 28.6%	46 23.3%	51 22.8%
All sources of info	97 23.0%	0 0	47 21.8%	47 21.8%	50 24.2%	38 19.2%	28 28.3%	31 24.9%	11 22.0%	14 29.8%M	41 23.4%M	22 26.3%M	3 19.6%	3 7.9%	1 10.8%	2 28.6%	46 23.3%	51 22.8%
preferred source of info	74 17.5%	0 0	38 17.5%	38 17.5%	36 17.4%	29 14.4%	21 20.9%	24 19.7%	10 18.6%	10 21.3%M	32 18.1%	17 19.7%M	2 15.2%	2 5.3%	1 8.1%	1 14.3%	37 18.9%	37 16.2%
Online library catalogues and finding aids (NET)	79 18.8%	0 0	42 19.5%	42 19.5%	38 18.0%	39 19.4%	16 15.7%	25 20.1%	9 16.9%	6 12.8%	41 23.4%M	17 19.7%	2 15.2%	3 7.9%	1 8.1%	1 14.3%	18 9.3%	61 27.0%P
All sources of info	79 18.8%	0 0	42 19.5%	42 19.5%	38 18.0%	39 19.4%	16 15.7%	25 20.1%	9 16.9%	6 12.8%	41 23.4%M	17 19.7%	2 15.2%	3 7.9%	1 8.1%	1 14.3%	18 9.3%	61 27.0%P
preferred source of info	55 13.0%	0 0	28 13.3%	28 13.3%	27 12.8%	30 15.0%	8 8.3%	17 13.6%	5 10.2%	4 8.5%	30 17.0%	10 11.8%	1 10.9%	3 7.9%	* 5.4%	1 14.3%	14 7.0%	41 18.2%P
Search engine (NET)	77 18.1%	0 0	20 9.3%	20 9.3%	57 27.2%B C	24 12.1%	11 11.1%	41 33.7%EF	7 13.6%	15 31.9%HJL N	24 13.8%	17 19.7%	2 13.0%	10 28.9%JN	* 5.4%	1 14.3%	43 21.8%	34 14.9%

Proportions/Means: Columns Tested (5% risk level) - A/B/D - C/D - E/F/G - H/I/J/K/L/M/N - P/Q
* small base; ** very small base (under 30) ineligible for sig testing

Table 363
Page 1513

Outsell/Digital Library Federation Study (2002)
Weighted Tables

TABLE 137, continued

S7sum_7. Print abstracts and indexes SUMMARY TABLE

		RESPONDENT TYPE				INSTITUTION TYPE			DISCIPLINE									GENDER	
	TOTAL SAMPLE	FACULTY MEMBER	GRAD. STUDENT	FACULTY /GRAD	UNDER GRAD. STUDENT	PUBLIC	PRIVATE	LIBERAL ARTS	BIOLOGIAL SCIENCES	PHYSICAL SCIENCES /MATH	SOCIAL SCIENCES	ARTS AND HUMAN.	ENGI-NEERING	BUSINESS	LAW	UNDEC. MAJOR	MALE	FEMALE
		(A)	(B)	(C)	(D)	(E)	(F)	(G)	(H)	(I)	(J)	(K)	(L)	(M)	(N)		(P)	(Q)
Base - Use Print abstracts and indexes for coursework	423	0**	214	214	209	200	100*	123*	52*	47*	177*	85*	13*	35*	6*	7*	197	226
All sources of info	77 18.1%	0 0	20 9.3%	20 9.3%	57 27.2%B C	24 12.1%	11 11.1%	41 33.7%EF	7 13.6%	15 31.9%HJL N	24 13.8%	17 19.7%	2 13.0%	10 28.9%JN	* 5.4%	1 14.3%	43 21.8%	34 14.9%
preferred source of info	37 8.7%	0 0	12 5.7%	12 5.7%	25 11.7%	16 7.9%	7 7.2%	14 11.2%	4 8.5%	7 14.9%J	9 5.3%	7 7.9%	1 10.9%	7 21.1%JK	* 5.4%	0 0	21 10.7%	16 7.0%
Online databases (NET)	62 14.6%	0 0	35 16.1%	35 16.1%	27 13.0%	25 12.5%	19 19.3%	17 14.2%	10 18.6%	6 12.8%	23 12.8%	15 17.1%	2 15.2%	5 13.2%	2 35.1%IJKLM	0 0	32 16.2%	30 13.2%
All sources of info	62 14.6%	0 0	35 16.1%	35 16.1%	27 13.0%	25 12.5%	19 19.3%	17 14.2%	10 18.6%	6 12.8%	23 12.8%	15 17.1%	2 15.2%	5 13.2%	2 35.1%IJKLM	0 0	32 16.2%	30 13.2%
preferred source of info	47 11.1%	0 0	25 11.8%	25 11.8%	22 10.3%	20 9.8%	15 15.5%	12 9.6%	6 11.9%	5 10.6%	21 11.7%	9 10.5%	1 8.7%	4 10.5%	1 18.9%	0 0	24 12.2%	23 10.1%
Internet searches (NET)	35 8.2%	0 0	19 8.7%	19 8.7%	16 7.8%	20 10.0%	8 7.9%	7 5.6%	5 10.2%	6 12.8%	13 7.4%	3 3.9%	* 2.2%	7 18.4%KL	* 2.7%	0 0	16 7.9%	19 8.5%
All sources of info	35 8.2%	0 0	19 8.7%	19 8.7%	16 7.8%	20 10.0%	8 7.9%	7 5.6%	5 10.2%	6 12.8%	13 7.4%	3 3.9%	* 2.2%	7 18.4%KL	* 2.7%	0 0	16 7.9%	19 8.5%
preferred source of info	22 5.2%	0 0	12 5.5%	12 5.5%	10 4.9%	15 7.6%	4 4.1%	3 2.3%	4 8.5%K	2 4.3%	9 5.3%	1 1.3%	* 2.2%	5 13.2%K	* 2.7%	0 0	11 5.4%	11 5.0%
Web directory/ subject related web site (NET)	29 6.8%	0 0	13 6.0%	13 6.0%	16 7.6%	9 4.6%	10 10.1%	10 7.8%	5 10.2%	2 4.3%	8 4.3%	7 7.9%	2 15.2%IJ	4 10.5%	1 8.1%	1 14.3%	17 8.8%	11 5.1%

Proportions/Means: Columns Tested (5% risk level) - A/B/D - C/D - E/F/G - H/I/J/K/L/M/N - P/Q
* small base; ** very small base (under 30) ineligible for sig testing

Table 363
Page 1514

TABLE 137, continued

S7sum_7. Print abstracts and indexes SUMMARY TABLE

	TOTAL SAMPLE	RESPONDENT TYPE: FACULTY MEMBER	GRAD. STUDENT	FACULTY /GRAD	UNDER GRAD. STUDENT	INSTITUTION TYPE: PUBLIC	PRIVATE	LIBERAL ARTS	DISCIPLINE: BIOLOGIAL SCIENCES	PHYSICAL SCIENCES /MATH	SOCIAL SCIENCES	ARTS AND HUMAN.	ENGI-NEERING	BUSINESS	LAW	UNDEC. MAJOR	GENDER: MALE	FEMALE
		(A)	(B)	(C)	(D)	(E)	(F)	(G)	(H)	(I)	(J)	(K)	(L)	(M)	(N)		(P)	(Q)
Base - Use Print abstracts and indexes for coursework	423	0**	214	214	209	200	100*	123*	52*	47*	177*	85*	13*	35*	6*	7*	197	226
All sources of info	29 6.8%	0 0	13 6.0%	13 6.0%	16 7.6%	9 4.6%	10 10.1%	10 7.8%	5 10.2%	2 4.3%	8 4.3%	7 7.9%	2 15.2%IJ	4 10.5%	1 8.1%	1 14.3%	17 8.8%	11 5.1%
preferred source of info	20 4.8%	0 0	9 4.4%	9 4.4%	11 5.1%	7 3.4%	9 8.6%	5 3.8%	4 8.5%	1 2.1%	6 3.2%	3 3.9%	1 10.9%IJ	3 7.9%	1 8.1%	1 14.3%	14 7.1%	6 2.8%
Online abstracting and indexing services (NET)	20 4.8%	0 0	8 3.9%	8 3.9%	12 5.7%	8 4.2%	2 2.5%	9 7.7%	0 0	3 6.4%	11 6.4%	4 5.3%	1 8.7%HM	0 0	* 5.4%HM	0 0	10 5.1%	10 4.5%
All sources of info	20 4.8%	0 0	8 3.9%	8 3.9%	12 5.7%	8 4.2%	2 2.5%	9 7.7%	0 0	3 6.4%	11 6.4%	4 5.3%	1 8.7%HM	0 0	* 5.4%HM	0 0	10 5.1%	10 4.5%
preferred source of info	10 2.5%	0 0	7 3.2%	7 3.2%	3 1.7%	6 3.0%	1 1.3%	3 2.6%	0 0	1 2.1%	8 4.3%	1 1.3%	1 4.3%H	0 0	* 2.7%H	0 0	4 1.8%	7 3.0%
Department web page (NET)	8 2.0%	0 0	6 3.0%	6 3.0%	2 1.0%	5 2.7%	1 0.9%	2 1.7%	0 0	3 6.4%J	2 1.1%	1 1.3%	1 4.3%H	2 5.3%	0 0	0 0	5 2.6%	3 1.4%
All sources of info	8 2.0%	0 0	6 3.0%	6 3.0%	2 1.0%	5 2.7%	1 0.9%	2 1.7%	0 0	3 6.4%J	2 1.1%	1 1.3%	1 4.3%H	2 5.3%	0 0	0 0	5 2.6%	3 1.4%
preferred source of info	6 1.3%	0 0	4 2.0%	4 2.0%	1 0.5%	4 2.2%	0 0	1 0.9%	0 0	1 2.1%	2 1.1%	1 1.3%	1 4.3%H	1 2.6%	0 0	0 0	3 1.6%	2 1.0%
Online reference service (NET)	8 2.0%	0 0	4 1.8%	4 1.8%	5 2.2%	4 2.0%	4 4.1%	* 0.2%	0 0	1 2.1%	4 2.1%	2 2.6%	1 8.7%HJM	0 0	* 2.7%H	0 0	3 1.5%	5 2.3%

Proportions/Means: Columns Tested (5% risk level) - A/B/D - C/D - E/F/G - H/I/J/K/L/M/N - P/Q
* small base; ** very small base (under 30) ineligible for sig testing

Table 363
Page 1515

Outsell/Digital Library Federation Study (2002)
Weighted Tables

TABLE 137, continued

S7sum_7. Print abstracts and indexes SUMMARY TABLE

	TOTAL SAMPLE	RESPONDENT TYPE: FACULTY MEMBER	GRAD. STUDENT	FACULTY /GRAD	UNDER GRAD. STUDENT	INSTITUTION TYPE: PUBLIC	PRIVATE	LIBERAL ARTS	DISCIPLINE: BIOLOGIAL SCIENCES	PHYSICAL SCIENCES /MATH	SOCIAL SCIENCES	ARTS AND HUMAN.	ENGI- NEERING	BUSINESS	LAW	UNDEC. MAJOR	GENDER: MALE	FEMALE
		(A)	(B)	(C)	(D)	(E)	(F)	(G)	(H)	(I)	(J)	(K)	(L)	(M)	(N)		(P)	(Q)
Base - Use Print abstracts and indexes for coursework	423	0**	214	214	209	200	100*	123*	52*	47*	177*	85*	13*	35*	6*	7*	197	226
All sources of info	8 2.0%	0 0	4 1.8%	4 1.8%	5 2.2%	4 2.0%	4 4.1%	* 0.2%	0 0	1 2.1%	4 2.1%	2 2.6%	1 8.7%HJM	0 0	* 2.7%H	0 0	3 1.5%	5 2.3%
preferred source of info	4 1.0%	0 0	2 1.0%	2 1.0%	2 1.0%	1 0.6%	3 3.0%	0 0	0 0	1 2.1%	2 1.1%	1 1.3%	0 0	0 0	* 2.7%H	0 0	2 1.0%	2 1.0%
Your own personal electronic library/files (NET)	5 1.2%	0 0	5 2.3%	5 2.3%	0 0	* 0.1%	5 4.7%EG	0 0	1 1.7%	0 0	4 2.1%	0 0	* 2.2%K	0 0	0 0	0 0	3 1.5%	2 0.8%
All sources of info	5 1.2%	0 0	5 2.3%	5 2.3%	0 0	* 0.1%	5 4.7%EG	0 0	1 1.7%	0 0	4 2.1%	0 0	* 2.2%K	0 0	0 0	0 0	3 1.5%	2 0.8%
preferred source of info	2 0.5%	0 0	2 1.0%	2 1.0%	0 0	* 0.1%	2 1.9%	0 0	0 0	0 0	2 1.1%	0 0	* 2.2%K	0 0	0 0	0 0	2 1.1%	0 0
Online bookstore (NET)	1 0.3%	0 0	1 0.5%	1 0.5%	0 0	1 0.6%	0 0	0 0	0 0	0 0	0 0	1 1.3%	0 0	0 0	0 0	0 0	1 0.6%	0 0
All sources of info	1 0.3%	0 0	1 0.5%	1 0.5%	0 0	1 0.6%	0 0	0 0	0 0	0 0	0 0	1 1.3%	0 0	0 0	0 0	0 0	1 0.6%	0 0
preferred source of info	0 0	0 0	0 0	0 0	0 0	0 0	0 0	0 0	0 0	0 0	0 0	0 0	0 0	0 0	0 0	0 0	0 0	0 0
E-mail listservs (NET)	0 0	0 0	0 0	0 0	0 0	0 0	0 0	0 0	0 0	0 0	0 0	0 0	0 0	0 0	0 0	0 0	0 0	0 0

Proportions/Means: Columns Tested (5% risk level) - A/B/D - C/D - E/F/G - H/I/J/K/L/M/N - P/Q
* small base; ** very small base (under 30) ineligible for sig testing

Table 363
Page 1516

Outsell/Digital Library Federation Study (2002)
Weighted Tables

TABLE 137, continued

S7sum_7. Print abstracts and indexes SUMMARY TABLE

		RESPONDENT TYPE				INSTITUTION TYPE			DISCIPLINE									GENDER	
	TOTAL SAMPLE	FACULTY MEMBER	GRAD. STUDENT	FACULTY /GRAD	UNDER GRAD. STUDENT	PUBLIC	PRIVATE	LIBERAL ARTS	BIOLOGIAL SCIENCES	PHYSICAL SCIENCES /MATH	SOCIAL SCIENCES	ARTS AND HUMAN.	ENGI-NEERING	BUSINESS	LAW	UNDEC. MAJOR	MALE	FEMALE
		(A)	(B)	(C)	(D)	(E)	(F)	(G)	(H)	(I)	(J)	(K)	(L)	(M)	(N)		(P)	(Q)
Base - Use Print abstracts and indexes for coursework	423	0**	214	214	209	200	100*	123*	52*	47*	177*	85*	13*	35*	6*	7*	197	226
All sources of info	0 0	0 0	0 0	0 0	0 0	0 0	0 0	0 0	0 0	0 0	0 0	0 0	0 0	0 0	0 0	0 0	0 0	0 0
preferred source of info	0 0	0 0	0 0	0 0	0 0	0 0	0 0	0 0	0 0	0 0	0 0	0 0	0 0	0 0	0 0	0 0	0 0	0 0
LIBRARY FACILITIES/ PRINT	129 30.4%	0 0	79 36.9%D	79 36.9%D	49 23.7%	58 29.0%	35 35.6%	35 28.5%	13 25.4%	17 36.2%	47 26.6%	34 39.5%	3 23.9%	9 26.3%	3 51.4%HJ LM	2 28.6%	60 30.5%	69 30.3%
Campus library (NET)	111 26.2%	0 0	70 32.7%D	70 32.7%D	41 19.5%	48 23.9%	32 32.1%	31 25.2%	10 18.6%	16 34.0%	38 21.3%	31 36.8%HJ	3 23.9%	8 23.7%	3 40.5%HJ	2 28.6%	51 25.9%	60 26.5%
All sources of info	111 26.2%	0 0	70 32.7%D	70 32.7%D	41 19.5%	48 23.9%	32 32.1%	31 25.2%	10 18.6%	16 34.0%	38 21.3%	31 36.8%HJ	3 23.9%	8 23.7%	3 40.5%HJ	2 28.6%	51 25.9%	60 26.5%
preferred source of info	64 15.0%	0 0	41 19.0%D	41 19.0%D	23 10.9%	30 14.8%	21 20.6%	13 10.9%	6 11.9%	8 17.0%	24 13.8%	16 18.4%	1 8.7%	6 15.8%	2 24.3%L	1 14.3%	28 14.3%	35 15.7%
Printed library catalogues and finding aids (NET)	11 2.6%	0 0	5 2.4%	5 2.4%	6 2.9%	6 2.8%	3 3.4%	2 1.8%	2 3.4%	0 0	6 3.2%	3 3.9%	0 0	0 0	* 5.4%IM	0 0	4 2.2%	7 3.0%
All sources of info	11 2.6%	0 0	5 2.4%	5 2.4%	6 2.9%	6 2.8%	3 3.4%	2 1.8%	2 3.4%	0 0	6 3.2%	3 3.9%	0 0	0 0	* 5.4%IM	0 0	4 2.2%	7 3.0%

Proportions/Means: Columns Tested (5% risk level) - A/B/D - C/D - E/F/G - H/I/J/K/L/M/N - P/Q
* small base; ** very small base (under 30) ineligible for sig testing

Table 363
Page 1517

Outsell/Digital Library Federation Study (2002)
Weighted Tables

TABLE 137, continued

S7sum_7. Print abstracts and indexes SUMMARY TABLE

		RESPONDENT TYPE				INSTITUTION TYPE			DISCIPLINE									GENDER	
	TOTAL SAMPLE	FACULTY MEMBER	GRAD. STUDENT	FACULTY /GRAD	UNDER GRAD. STUDENT	PUBLIC	PRIVATE	LIBERAL ARTS	BIOLOGIAL SCIENCES	PHYSICAL SCIENCES /MATH	SOCIAL SCIENCES	ARTS AND HUMAN.	ENGI- NEERING	BUSINESS	LAW	UNDEC. MAJOR	MALE	FEMALE
		(A)	(B)	(C)	(D)	(E)	(F)	(G)	(H)	(I)	(J)	(K)	(L)	(M)	(N)		(P)	(Q)
Base - Use Print abstracts and indexes for coursework	423	0**	214	214	209	200	100*	123*	52*	47*	177*	85*	13*	35*	6*	7*	197	226
preferred source of info	5 1.3%	0 0	3 1.4%	3 1.4%	2 1.1%	3 1.4%	* 0.3%	2 1.8%	1 1.7%	0 0	2 1.1%	2 2.6%	0 0	0 0	* 5.4%IJM	0 0	3 1.8%	2 0.8%
References cited in books or journal articles (NET)	10 2.3%	0 0	4 1.8%	4 1.8%	6 2.9%	2 1.1%	2 1.6%	6 5.0%	1 1.7%	1 2.1%	4 2.1%	3 3.9%	1 4.3%	0 0	* 5.4%M	0 0	7 3.3%	3 1.5%
All sources of info	10 2.3%	0 0	4 1.8%	4 1.8%	6 2.9%	2 1.1%	2 1.6%	6 5.0%	1 1.7%	1 2.1%	4 2.1%	3 3.9%	1 4.3%	0 0	* 5.4%M	0 0	7 3.3%	3 1.5%
preferred source of info	2 0.5%	0 0	* 0.1%	* 0.1%	2 1.0%	* 0.1%	0 0	2 1.6%	1 1.7%	0 0	0 0	1 1.3%	* 2.2%J	0 0	0 0	0 0	2 1.2%	0 0
Another library (NET)	8 1.9%	0 0	2 0.9%	2 0.9%	6 3.0%	2 0.9%	0 0	6 5.2%EF	0 0	3 6.4%J	2 1.1%	3 3.9%	0 0	0 0	0 0	0 0	6 3.0%	2 1.0%
All sources of info	8 1.9%	0 0	2 0.9%	2 0.9%	6 3.0%	2 0.9%	0 0	6 5.2%EF	0 0	3 6.4%J	2 1.1%	3 3.9%	0 0	0 0	0 0	0 0	6 3.0%	2 1.0%
preferred source of info	2 0.4%	0 0	2 0.9%	2 0.9%	0 0	2 0.9%	0 0	0 0	0 0	0 0	2 1.1%	0 0	0 0	0 0	0 0	0 0	2 1.0%	0 0
Printed abstracting and indexing services (NET)	8 1.8%	0 0	5 2.1%	5 2.1%	3 1.4%	3 1.5%	3 3.4%	1 0.9%	1 1.7%	0 0	4 2.1%	2 2.6%	* 2.2%	0 0	* 5.4%IM	0 0	2 1.2%	5 2.3%

Proportions/Means: Columns Tested (5% risk level) - A/B/D - C/D - E/F/G - H/I/J/K/L/M/N - P/Q
* small base; ** very small base (under 30) ineligible for sig testing

Table 363
Page 1518

Outsell/Digital Library Federation Study (2002)
Weighted Tables

TABLE 137, continued

S7sum_7. Print abstracts and indexes SUMMARY TABLE

	RESPONDENT TYPE					INSTITUTION TYPE			DISCIPLINE									GENDER	
	TOTAL SAMPLE	FACULTY MEMBER	GRAD. STUDENT	FACULTY /GRAD	UNDER GRAD. STUDENT	PUBLIC	PRIVATE	LIBERAL ARTS	BIOLOGIAL SCIENCES	PHYSICAL SCIENCES /MATH	SOCIAL SCIENCES	ARTS AND HUMAN.	ENGI-NEERING	BUSINESS	LAW	UNDEC. MAJOR	MALE	FEMALE
		(A)	(B)	(C)	(D)	(E)	(F)	(G)	(H)	(I)	(J)	(K)	(L)	(M)	(N)		(P)	(Q)
Base - Use Print abstracts and indexes for coursework	423	0**	214	214	209	200	100*	123*	52*	47*	177*	85*	13*	35*	6*	7*	197	226
All sources of info	8 1.8%	0 0	5 2.1%	5 2.1%	3 1.4%	3 1.5%	3 3.4%	1 0.9%	1 1.7%	0 0	4 2.1%	2 2.6%	* 2.2%	0 0	* 5.4%IM	0 0	2 1.2%	5 2.3%
preferred source of info	* *	0 0	* 0.1%	* 0.1%	0 0	0 0	* 0.2%	0 0	0 0	0 0	0 0	0 0	0 0	0 0	* 2.7%HIJK	0 0	0 0	* 0.1%
Personal subscriptions to newspapers, magazines and journals (NET)	3 0.8%	0 0	1 0.6%	1 0.6%	2 1.1%	0 0	1 1.2%	2 1.8%	0 0	0 0	0 0	2 2.6%	* 2.2%J	1 2.6%J	0 0	0 0	2 1.2%	1 0.5%
All sources of info	3 0.8%	0 0	1 0.6%	1 0.6%	2 1.1%	0 0	1 1.2%	2 1.8%	0 0	0 0	0 0	2 2.6%	* 2.2%J	1 2.6%J	0 0	0 0	2 1.2%	1 0.5%
preferred source of info	0 0	0 0	0 0	0 0	0 0	0 0	0 0	0 0	0 0	0 0	0 0	0 0	0 0	0 0	0 0	0 0	0 0	0 0
Your own personal physical library/ files/bookshelves (NET)	2 0.5%	0 0	1 0.5%	1 0.5%	1 0.4%	1 0.4%	1 1.1%	0 0	1 1.7%	0 0	0 0	1 1.3%	0 0	0 0	0 0	0 0	1 0.6%	1 0.4%
All sources of info	2 0.5%	0 0	1 0.5%	1 0.5%	1 0.4%	1 0.4%	1 1.1%	0 0	1 1.7%	0 0	0 0	1 1.3%	0 0	0 0	0 0	0 0	1 0.6%	1 0.4%
preferred source of info	1 0.3%	0 0	1 0.5%	1 0.5%	.0 0	0 0	1 1.1%	0 0	0 0	0 0	0 0	1 1.3%	0 0	0 0	0 0	0 0	1 0.6%	0 0

Proportions/Means: Columns Tested (5% risk level) - A/B/D - C/D - E/F/G - H/I/J/K/L/M/N - P/Q
* small base; ** very small base (under 30) ineligible for sig testing

Table 363
Page 1519

Outsell/Digital Library Federation Study (2002)
Weighted Tables

TABLE 137, continued

S7sum_7. Print abstracts and indexes SUMMARY TABLE

		RESPONDENT TYPE				INSTITUTION TYPE			DISCIPLINE								GENDER	
	TOTAL SAMPLE	FACULTY MEMBER	GRAD. STUDENT	FACULTY /GRAD	UNDER GRAD. STUDENT	PUBLIC	PRIVATE	LIBERAL ARTS	BIOLOGIAL SCIENCES	PHYSICAL SCIENCES /MATH	SOCIAL SCIENCES	ARTS AND HUMAN.	ENGI-NEERING	BUSINESS	LAW	UNDEC. MAJOR	MALE	FEMALE
		(A)	(B)	(C)	(D)	(E)	(F)	(G)	(H)	(I)	(J)	(K)	(L)	(M)	(N)		(P)	(Q)
Base - Use Print abstracts and indexes for coursework	423	0**	214	214	209	200	100*	123*	52*	47*	177*	85*	13*	35*	6*	7*	197	226
Physical bookstore (NET)	1 0.2%	0 0	1 0.5%	1 0.5%	0 0	0 0	1 1.0%	0 0	0 0	1 2.1%	0 0	0 0	0 0	0 0	0 0	0 0	1 0.5%	0 0
All sources of info	1 0.2%	0 0	1 0.5%	1 0.5%	0 0	0 0	1 1.0%	0 0	0 0	1 2.1%	0 0	0 0	0 0	0 0	0 0	0 0	1 0.5%	0 0
preferred source of info	0 0	0 0	0 0	0 0	0 0	0 0	0 0	0 0	0 0	0 0	0 0	0 0	0 0	0 0	0 0	0 0	0 0	0 0
PERSONAL ASSISTANCE	106 25.0%	0 0	45 21.0%	45 21.0%	61 29.1%	39 19.6%	20 19.9%	47 37.8%EF	13 25.4%	16 34.0%	38 21.3%	21 25.0%	2 17.4%	9 26.3%	2 29.7%	4 57.1%	49 24.7%	57 25.2%
A librarian in your institution (NET)	71 16.8%	0 0	18 8.5%	18 8.5%	53 25.2%BC	16 8.2%	14 13.8%	41 33.2%EF	11 20.3%	9 19.1%	23 12.8%	16 18.4%	1 6.5%	7 18.4%	2 27.0%JL	4 57.1%	29 14.9%	42 18.4%
All sources of info	71 16.8%	0 0	18 8.5%	18 8.5%	53 25.2%BC	16 8.2%	14 13.8%	41 33.2%EF	11 20.3%	9 19.1%	23 12.8%	16 18.4%	1 6.5%	7 18.4%	2 27.0%JL	4 57.1%	29 14.9%	42 18.4%
preferred source of info	33 7.8%	0 0	9 4.0%	9 4.0%	24 11.7%BC	12 6.1%	4 4.3%	16 13.4%F	7 13.6%	2 4.3%	11 6.4%	6 6.6%	1 6.5%	5 13.2%	1 8.1%	1 14.3%	15 7.7%	18 7.9%
Faculty members inside your institution (NET)	52 12.3%	0 0	29 13.6%	29 13.6%	23 11.0%	24 12.1%	8 8.4%	19 15.7%	3 5.1%	11 23.4%H	21 11.7%	11 13.2%	1 10.9%	4 10.5%	* 5.4%	1 14.3%	28 14.3%	24 10.6%

Proportions/Means: Columns Tested (5% risk level) - A/B/D - C/D - E/F/G - H/I/J/K/L/M/N - P/Q
* small base; ** very small base (under 30) ineligible for sig testing

Table 363
Page 1520

Outsell/Digital Library Federation Study (2002)
Weighted Tables

TABLE 137, continued

S7sum_7. Print abstracts and indexes SUMMARY TABLE

		RESPONDENT TYPE				INSTITUTION TYPE			DISCIPLINE									GENDER	
	TOTAL SAMPLE	FACULTY MEMBER	GRAD. STUDENT	FACULTY /GRAD	UNDER GRAD. STUDENT	PUBLIC	PRIVATE	LIBERAL ARTS	BIOLOGIAL SCIENCES	PHYSICAL SCIENCES /MATH	SOCIAL SCIENCES	ARTS AND HUMAN.	ENGI- NEERING	BUSINESS	LAW	UNDEC. MAJOR	MALE	FEMALE
		(A)	(B)	(C)	(D)	(E)	(F)	(G)	(H)	(I)	(J)	(K)	(L)	(M)	(N)		(P)	(Q)
Base - Use Print abstracts and indexes for coursework	423	0**	214	214	209	200	100*	123*	52*	47*	177*	85*	13*	35*	6*	7*	197	226
All sources of info	52 12.3%	0 0	29 13.6%	29 13.6%	23 11.0%	24 12.1%	8 8.4%	19 15.7%	3 5.1%	11 23.4%H	21 11.7%	11 13.2%	1 10.9%	4 10.5%	* 5.4%	1 14.3%	28 14.3%	24 10.6%
preferred source of info	16 3.7%	0 0	9 4.4%	9 4.4%	6 3.0%	12 5.8%F	* 0.3%	4 3.3%	0 0	2 4.3%	8 4.3%	4 5.3%	1 6.5%H	1 2.6%	0 0	0 0	9 4.7%	7 2.9%
Other students inside your institution (NET)	15 3.6%	0 0	6 3.0%	6 3.0%	9 4.3%	5 2.4%	3 2.8%	8 6.4%	2 3.4%	5 10.6%J	4 2.1%	2 2.6%	1 4.3%	2 5.3%	* 2.7%	0 0	9 4.3%	7 3.0%
All sources of info	15 3.6%	0 0	6 3.0%	6 3.0%	9 4.3%	5 2.4%	3 2.8%	8 6.4%	2 3.4%	5 10.6%J	4 2.1%	2 2.6%	1 4.3%	2 5.3%	* 2.7%	0 0	9 4.3%	7 3.0%
preferred source of info	2 0.4%	0 0	1 0.4%	1 0.4%	1 0.5%	1 0.4%	0 0	1 0.8%	1 1.7%	1 2.1%	0 0	0 0	0 0	0 0	0 0	0 0	1 0.5%	1 0.4%
Another institution's librarian (NET)	4 0.9%	0 0	0 0	0 0	4 1.9%	0 0	0 0	4 3.3%E	0 0	1 2.1%	2 1.1%	1 1.3%	0 0	0 0	0 0	0 0	2 1.1%	2 0.8%
All sources of info	4 0.9%	0 0	0 0	0 0	4 1.9%	0 0	0 0	4 3.3%E	0 0	1 2.1%	2 1.1%	1 1.3%	0 0	0 0	0 0	0 0	2 1.1%	2 0.8%
preferred source of info	0 0	0 0	0 0	0 0	0 0	0 0	0 0	0 0	0 0	0 0	0 0	0 0	0 0	0 0	0 0	0 0	0 0	0 0

Proportions/Means: Columns Tested (5% risk level) - A/B/D - C/D - E/F/G - H/I/J/K/L/M/N - P/Q
* small base; ** very small base (under 30) ineligible for sig testing

Table 363
Page 1521

Outsell/Digital Library Federation Study (2002)
Weighted Tables

TABLE 137, continued

S7sum_7. Print abstracts and indexes SUMMARY TABLE

		RESPONDENT TYPE				INSTITUTION TYPE			DISCIPLINE									GENDER	
	TOTAL SAMPLE	FACULTY MEMBER	GRAD. STUDENT	FACULTY /GRAD	UNDER GRAD. STUDENT	PUBLIC	PRIVATE	LIBERAL ARTS	BIOLOGIAL SCIENCES	PHYSICAL SCIENCES /MATH	SOCIAL SCIENCES	ARTS AND HUMAN.	ENGI-NEERING	BUSINESS	LAW	UNDEC. MAJOR	MALE	FEMALE
		(A)	(B)	(C)	(D)	(E)	(F)	(G)	(H)	(I)	(J)	(K)	(L)	(M)	(N)		(P)	(Q)
Base - Use Print abstracts and indexes for coursework	423	0**	214	214	209	200	100*	123*	52*	47*	177*	85*	13*	35*	6*	7*	197	226
Faculty members outside your institution (NET)	1 0.3%	0 0	1 0.5%	1 0.5%	0 0	0 0	1 1.1%	0 0	0 0	0 0	0 0	1 1.3%	0 0	0 0	0 0	0 0	0 0	1 0.5%
All sources of info	1 0.3%	0 0	1 0.5%	1 0.5%	0 0	0 0	1 1.1%	0 0	0 0	0 0	0 0	1 1.3%	0 0	0 0	0 0	0 0	0 0	1 0.5%
preferred source of info	0 0	0 0	0 0	0 0	0 0	0 0	0 0	0 0	0 0	0 0	0 0	0 0	0 0	0 0	0 0	0 0	0 0	0 0
Other students outside your institution (NET)	1 0.2%	0 0	0 0	0 0	1 0.5%	0 0	0 0	1 0.8%	0 0	1 2.1%	0 0	0 0	0 0	0 0	0 0	0 0	1 0.5%	0 0
All sources of info	1 0.2%	0 0	0 0	0 0	1 0.5%	0 0	0 0	1 0.8%	0 0	1 2.1%	0 0	0 0	0 0	0 0	0 0	0 0	1 0.5%	0 0
preferred source of info	0 0	0 0	0 0	0 0	0 0	0 0	0 0	0 0	0 0	0 0	0 0	0 0	0 0	0 0	0 0	0 0	0 0	0 0
Professional meetings (NET)	0 0	0 0	0 0	0 0	0 0	0 0	0 0	0 0	0 0	0 0	0 0	0 0	0 0	0 0	0 0	0 0	0 0	0 0
All sources of info	0 0	0 0	0 0	0 0	0 0	0 0	0 0	0 0	0 0	0 0	0 0	0 0	0 0	0 0	0 0	0 0	0 0	0 0
preferred source of info	0 0	0 0	0 0	0 0	0 0	0 0	0 0	0 0	0 0	0 0	0 0	0 0	0 0	0 0	0 0	0 0	0 0	0 0

Proportions/Means: Columns Tested (5% risk level) - A/B/D - C/D - E/F/G - H/I/J/K/L/M/N - P/Q
* small base; ** very small base (under 30) ineligible for sig testing

Table 363
Page 1522

Outsell/Digital Library Federation Study (2002)
Weighted Tables

TABLE 137, continued

S7sum_7. Print abstracts and indexes SUMMARY TABLE

	TOTAL SAMPLE	RESPONDENT TYPE: FACULTY MEMBER	GRAD. STUDENT	FACULTY /GRAD	UNDER GRAD. STUDENT	INSTITUTION TYPE: PUBLIC	PRIVATE	LIBERAL ARTS	DISCIPLINE: BIOLOGIAL SCIENCES	PHYSICAL SCIENCES /MATH	SOCIAL SCIENCES	ARTS AND HUMAN.	ENGI-NEERING	BUSINESS	LAW	UNDEC. MAJOR	GENDER: MALE	FEMALE
		(A)	(B)	(C)	(D)	(E)	(F)	(G)	(H)	(I)	(J)	(K)	(L)	(M)	(N)		(P)	(Q)
Base - Use Print abstracts and indexes for coursework	423	0**	214	214	209	200	100*	123*	52*	47*	177*	85*	13*	35*	6*	7*	197	226
Other (NET)	21	0	9	9	11	13	2	5	1	2	9	3	1	2	1	2	6	15
	4.9%	0	4.4%	4.4%	5.4%	6.5%	2.3%	4.4%	1.7%	4.3%	5.3%	3.9%	4.3%	5.3%	10.8%H	28.6%	3.0%	6.6%
All sources of info	16	0	8	8	8	8	2	5	0	2	6	3	0	2	1	2	5	10
	3.7%	0	3.5%	3.5%	3.8%	4.1%	2.3%	4.2%	0	4.3%	3.2%	3.9%	0	5.3%	10.8%HJ L	28.6%	2.7%	4.5%
preferred source of info	9	0	2	2	6	5	1	2	1	0	4	1	1	0	*	2	1	8
	2.0%	0	1.0%	1.0%	3.1%	2.5%	1.0%	2.0%	1.7%	0	2.1%	1.3%	4.3%I	0	2.7%I	28.6%	0.3%	3.5%P
Online (unspecified)	6	0	2	2	4	5	*	1	1	1	4	0	*	0	0	0	1	5
	1.4%	0	1.0%	1.0%	1.8%	2.3%	0.3%	0.8%	1.7%	2.1%	2.1%	0	2.2%K	0	0	0	0.7%	2.1%
All sources of info	6	0	2	2	4	5	*	1	1	1	4	0	*	0	0	0	1	5
	1.4%	0	1.0%	1.0%	1.8%	2.3%	0.3%	0.8%	1.7%	2.1%	2.1%	0	2.2%K	0	0	0	0.7%	2.1%
preferred source of info	2	0	*	*	2	2	*	0	0	0	2	0	*	0	0	0	*	2
	0.5%	0	0.1%	0.1%	0.9%	0.9%	0.3%	0	0	0	1.1%	0	2.2%K	0	0	0	0.1%	0.8%
E-journals	0	0	0	0	0	0	0	0	0	0	0	0	0	0	0	0	0	0
	0	0	0	0	0	0	0	0	0	0	0	0	0	0	0	0	0	0
All sources of info	0	0	0	0	0	0	0	0	0	0	0	0	0	0	0	0	0	0
	0	0	0	0	0	0	0	0	0	0	0	0	0	0	0	0	0	0
preferred source of info	0	0	0	0	0	0	0	0	0	0	0	0	0	0	0	0	0	0
	0	0	0	0	0	0	0	0	0	0	0	0	0	0	0	0	0	0

Proportions/Means: Columns Tested (5% risk level) - A/B/D - C/D - E/F/G - H/I/J/K/L/M/N - P/Q
* small base; ** very small base (under 30) ineligible for sig testing

Table 363
Page 1523

Outsell/Digital Library Federation Study (2002)
Weighted Tables

TABLE 137, continued

S7sum_7. Print abstracts and indexes SUMMARY TABLE

		RESPONDENT TYPE				INSTITUTION TYPE			DISCIPLINE								GENDER	
	TOTAL SAMPLE	FACULTY MEMBER	GRAD. STUDENT	FACULTY /GRAD	UNDER GRAD. STUDENT	PUBLIC	PRIVATE	LIBERAL ARTS	BIOLOGIAL SCIENCES	PHYSICAL SCIENCES /MATH	SOCIAL SCIENCES	ARTS AND HUMAN.	ENGI-NEERING	BUSINESS	LAW	UNDEC. MAJOR	MALE	FEMALE
		(A)	(B)	(C)	(D)	(E)	(F)	(G)	(H)	(I)	(J)	(K)	(L)	(M)	(N)		(P)	(Q)
Base - Use Print abstracts and indexes for coursework	423	0**	214	214	209	200	100*	123*	52*	47*	177*	85*	13*	35*	6*	7*	197	226
DK/Refused	13 3.1%	0 0	7 3.3%	7 3.3%	6 2.8%	6 3.0%	3 2.9%	4 3.3%	2 3.4%	3 6.4%	4 2.1%	3 3.9%	0 0	1 2.6%	* 2.7%	0 0	3 1.6%	10 4.3%

Proportions/Means: Columns Tested (5% risk level) - A/B/D - C/D - E/F/G - H/I/J/K/L/M/N - P/Q
* small base; ** very small base (under 30) ineligible for sig testing

TABLE 138

S7D/E_7. Print abstracts and indexes SUMMARY TABLE

		RESPONDENT TYPE				INSTITUTION TYPE			DISCIPLINE									GENDER	
	TOTAL SAMPLE	FACULTY MEMBER	GRAD. STUDENT	FACULTY /GRAD	UNDER GRAD. STUDENT	PUBLIC	PRIVATE	LIBERAL ARTS	BIOLOGIAL SCIENCES	PHYSICAL SCIENCES /MATH	SOCIAL SCIENCES	ARTS AND HUMAN.	ENGI-NEERING	BUSINESS	LAW	UNDEC. MAJOR	MALE	FEMALE
		(A)	(B)	(C)	(D)	(E)	(F)	(G)	(H)	(I)	(J)	(K)	(L)	(M)	(N)		(P)	(Q)
Base - Use Print abstracts and indexes for coursework	423	0**	214	214	209	200	100*	123*	52*	47*	177*	85*	13*	35*	6*	7*	197	226
Borrow from or use in campus library (NET)	307 72.6%	0 0	160 74.6%	160 74.6%	147 70.5%	140 70.0%	76 76.8%	90 73.5%	40 76.3%	33 70.2%	124 70.2%	66 77.6%	9 67.4%	24 68.4%	5 78.4%	6 85.7%	150 76.2%	157 69.4%
All sources of info	307 72.6%	0 0	160 74.6%	160 74.6%	147 70.5%	140 70.0%	76 76.8%	90 73.5%	40 76.3%	33 70.2%	124 70.2%	66 77.6%	9 67.4%	24 68.4%	5 78.4%	6 85.7%	150 76.2%	157 69.4%
preferred source of info	248 58.6%	0 0	131 61.1%	131 61.1%	117 56.0%	118 59.0%	59 58.8%	71 57.8%	31 59.3%	29 61.7%	100 56.4%	54 63.2%	8 56.5%	20 55.3%	3 54.1%	4 57.1%	122 62.0%	126 55.6%
Access online (NET)	187 44.3%	0 0	90 41.8%	90 41.8%	98 46.9%	75 37.3%	49 48.9%	64 52.1%E	20 39.0%	21 44.7%	83 46.8%	32 38.2%	6 45.7%	18 50.0%	3 51.4%	4 57.1%	89 45.1%	99 43.7%
All sources of info	187 44.3%	0 0	90 41.8%	90 41.8%	98 46.9%	75 37.3%	49 48.9%	64 52.1%E	20 39.0%	21 44.7%	83 46.8%	32 38.2%	6 45.7%	18 50.0%	3 51.4%	4 57.1%	89 45.1%	99 43.7%
preferred source of info	152 35.9%	0 0	74 34.4%	74 34.4%	78 37.6%	67 33.2%	39 38.8%	47 38.1%	18 35.6%	14 29.8%	70 39.4%	25 28.9%	5 37.0%	16 44.7%	3 40.5%	2 28.6%	68 34.8%	83 37.0%
Faculty (NET)	13 3.0%	0 0	9 4.0%	9 4.0%	4 2.0%	5 2.5%	4 3.6%	4 3.3%	2 3.4%	4 8.5%K	4 2.1%	1 1.3%	1 6.5%M	0 0	* 2.7%	1 14.3%	7 3.4%	6 2.7%
All sources of info	13 3.0%	0 0	9 4.0%	9 4.0%	4 2.0%	5 2.5%	4 3.6%	4 3.3%	2 3.4%	4 8.5%K	4 2.1%	1 1.3%	1 6.5%M	0 0	* 2.7%	1 14.3%	7 3.4%	6 2.7%
preferred source of info	6 1.5%	0 0	4 2.0%	4 2.0%	2 1.0%	4 1.9%	* 0.5%	2 1.6%	0 0	1 2.1%	4 2.1%	0 0	* 2.2%K	0 0	* 2.7%HK	1 14.3%	1 0.7%	5 2.2%

Proportions/Means: Columns Tested (5% risk level) - A/B/D - C/D - E/F/G - H/I/J/K/L/M/N - P/Q
* small base; ** very small base (under 30) ineligible for sig testing

Table 366
Page 1531

Outsell/Digital Library Federation Study (2002)
Weighted Tables

TABLE 138, continued

S7D/E_7. Print abstracts and indexes SUMMARY TABLE

		RESPONDENT TYPE				INSTITUTION TYPE			DISCIPLINE									GENDER	
	TOTAL SAMPLE	FACULTY MEMBER	GRAD. STUDENT	FACULTY /GRAD	UNDER GRAD. STUDENT	PUBLIC	PRIVATE	LIBERAL ARTS	BIOLOGIAL SCIENCES	PHYSICAL SCIENCES /MATH	SOCIAL SCIENCES	ARTS AND HUMAN.	ENGI-NEERING	BUSINESS	LAW	UNDEC. MAJOR	MALE	FEMALE
		(A)	(B)	(C)	(D)	(E)	(F)	(G)	(H)	(I)	(J)	(K)	(L)	(M)	(N)		(P)	(Q)
Base - Use Print abstracts and indexes for coursework	423	0**	214	214	209	200	100*	123*	52*	47*	177*	85*	13*	35*	6*	7*	197	226
Interlibrary loan (NET)	12 2.8%	0 0	5 2.1%	5 2.1%	7 3.4%	7 3.5%	2 2.4%	2 1.8%	1 1.7%	1 2.1%	4 2.1%	3 3.9%	* 2.2%	2 5.3%	1 8.1%HJ	0 0	3 1.7%	8 3.7%
All sources of info	12 2.8%	0 0	5 2.1%	5 2.1%	7 3.4%	7 3.5%	2 2.4%	2 1.8%	1 1.7%	1 2.1%	4 2.1%	3 3.9%	* 2.2%	2 5.3%	1 8.1%HJ	0 0	3 1.7%	8 3.7%
preferred source of info	4 0.8%	0 0	* 0.1%	* 0.1%	3 1.6%	2 1.2%	0 0	1 0.9%	0 0	1 2.1%	0 0	2 2.6%	* 2.2%J	0 0	0 0	0 0	1 0.7%	2 0.9%
Borrow from or use in other libraries (NET)	12 2.8%	0 0	4 1.9%	4 1.9%	8 3.6%	4 2.0%	2 2.2%	5 4.4%	1 1.7%	3 6.4%	4 2.1%	3 3.9%	* 2.2%	0 0	* 5.4%M	0 0	7 3.3%	5 2.2%
All sources of info	12 2.8%	0 0	4 1.9%	4 1.9%	8 3.6%	4 2.0%	2 2.2%	5 4.4%	1 1.7%	3 6.4%	4 2.1%	3 3.9%	* 2.2%	0 0	* 5.4%M	0 0	7 3.3%	5 2.2%
preferred source of info	4 1.0%	0 0	2 0.9%	2 0.9%	2 1.0%	2 1.1%	2 1.9%	0 0	1 1.7%	1 2.1%	2 1.1%	0 0	* 2.2%K	0 0	0 0	0 0	* 0.1%	4 1.7%
Purchase from online bookstore (NET)	4 0.9%	0 0	2 1.0%	2 1.0%	2 0.9%	4 2.0%	0 0	0 0	0 0	1 2.1%	2 1.1%	1 1.3%	0 0	0 0	0 0	0 0	1 0.5%	3 1.3%
All sources of info	4 0.9%	0 0	2 1.0%	2 1.0%	2 0.9%	4 2.0%	0 0	0 0	0 0	1 2.1%	2 1.1%	1 1.3%	0 0	0 0	0 0	0 0	1 0.5%	3 1.3%
preferred source of info	3 0.7%	0 0	1 0.5%	1 0.5%	2 0.9%	3 1.4%	0 0	0 0	0 0	1 2.1%	2 1.1%	0 0	0 0	0 0	0 0	0 0	1 0.5%	2 0.8%

Proportions/Means: Columns Tested (5% risk level) - A/B/D - C/D - E/F/G - H/I/J/K/L/M/N - P/Q
* small base; ** very small base (under 30) ineligible for sig testing

Table 366
Page 1532

Outsell/Digital Library Federation Study (2002)
Weighted Tables

TABLE 138, continued

S7D/E_7. Print abstracts and indexes SUMMARY TABLE

	RESPONDENT TYPE				INSTITUTION TYPE			DISCIPLINE									GENDER	
	TOTAL SAMPLE	FACULTY MEMBER	GRAD. STUDENT	FACULTY /GRAD	UNDER GRAD. STUDENT	PUBLIC	PRIVATE	LIBERAL ARTS	BIOLOGIAL SCIENCES	PHYSICAL SCIENCES /MATH	SOCIAL SCIENCES	ARTS AND HUMAN.	ENGI-NEERING	BUSINESS	LAW	UNDEC. MAJOR	MALE	FEMALE
		(A)	(B)	(C)	(D)	(E)	(F)	(G)	(H)	(I)	(J)	(K)	(L)	(M)	(N)		(P)	(Q)
Base - Use Print abstracts and indexes for coursework	423	0**	214	214	209	200	100*	123*	52*	47*	177*	85*	13*	35*	6*	7*	197	226
Purchase from physical book store (NET)	4 0.9%	0 0	0 0	0 0	4 1.8%	2 0.9%	1 0.9%	1 0.8%	0 0	0 0	2 1.1%	0 0	0 0	2 5.3%K	0 0	0 0	1 0.5%	3 1.2%
All sources of info	4 0.9%	0 0	0 0	0 0	4 1.8%	2 0.9%	1 0.9%	1 0.8%	0 0	0 0	2 1.1%	0 0	0 0	2 5.3%K	0 0	0 0	1 0.5%	3 1.2%
preferred source of info	0 0	0 0	0 0	0 0	0 0	0 0	0 0	0 0	0 0	0 0	0 0	0 0	0 0	0 0	0 0	0 0	0 0	0 0
Ask library to purchase source (NET)	2 0.5%	0 0	1 0.5%	1 0.5%	1 0.5%	1 0.6%	0 0	1 0.9%	0 0	0 0	0 0	2 2.6%	0 0	0 0	0 0	0 0	1 0.6%	1 0.5%
All sources of info	2 0.5%	0 0	1 0.5%	1 0.5%	1 0.5%	1 0.6%	0 0	1 0.9%	0 0	0 0	0 0	2 2.6%	0 0	0 0	0 0	0 0	1 0.6%	1 0.5%
preferred source of info	1 0.3%	0 0	1 0.5%	1 0.5%	0 0	1 0.6%	0 0	0 0	0 0	0 0	0 0	1 1.3%	0 0	0 0	0 0	0 0	0 0	1 0.5%
Access book/journal/ journal article elsewhere online (NET)	0 0	0 0	0 0	0 0	0 0	0 0	0 0	0 0	0 0	0 0	0 0	0 0	0 0	0 0	0 0	0 0	0 0	0 0
All sources of info	0 0	0 0	0 0	0 0	0 0	0 0	0 0	0 0	0 0	0 0	0 0	0 0	0 0	0 0	0 0	0 0	0 0	0 0

Proportions/Means: Columns Tested (5% risk level) - A/B/D - C/D - E/F/G - H/I/J/K/L/M/N - P/Q
* small base; ** very small base (under 30) ineligible for sig testing

Table 366
Page 1533

TABLE 138, continued

S7D/E_7. Print abstracts and indexes SUMMARY TABLE

	RESPONDENT TYPE					INSTITUTION TYPE			DISCIPLINE								GENDER	
	TOTAL SAMPLE	FACULTY MEMBER	GRAD. STUDENT	FACULTY /GRAD	UNDER GRAD. STUDENT	PUBLIC	PRIVATE	LIBERAL ARTS	BIOLOGIAL SCIENCES	PHYSICAL SCIENCES /MATH	SOCIAL SCIENCES	ARTS AND HUMAN.	ENGI-NEERING	BUSINESS	LAW	UNDEC. MAJOR	MALE	FEMALE
		(A)	(B)	(C)	(D)	(E)	(F)	(G)	(H)	(I)	(J)	(K)	(L)	(M)	(N)		(P)	(Q)
Base - Use Print abstracts and indexes for coursework	423	0**	214	214	209	200	100*	123*	52*	47*	177*	85*	13*	35*	6*	7*	197	226
preferred source of info	0 0	0 0	0 0	0 0	0 0	0 0	0 0	0 0	0 0	0 0	0 0	0 0	0 0	0 0	0 0	0 0	0 0	0 0
Order from on demand document delivery service (NET)	0 0	0 0	0 0	0 0	0 0	0 0	0 0	0 0	0 0	0 0	0 0	0 0	0 0	0 0	0 0	0 0	0 0	0 0
All sources of info	0 0	0 0	0 0	0 0	0 0	0 0	0 0	0 0	0 0	0 0	0 0	0 0	0 0	0 0	0 0	0 0	0 0	0 0
preferred source of info	0 0	0 0	0 0	0 0	0 0	0 0	0 0	0 0	0 0	0 0	0 0	0 0	0 0	0 0	0 0	0 0	0 0	0 0
Home (NET)	0 0	0 0	0 0	0 0	0 0	0 0	0 0	0 0	0 0	0 0	0 0	0 0	0 0	0 0	0 0	0 0	0 0	0 0
All sources of info	0 0	0 0	0 0	0 0	0 0	0 0	0 0	0 0	0 0	0 0	0 0	0 0	0 0	0 0	0 0	0 0	0 0	0 0
preferred source of info	0 0	0 0	0 0	0 0	0 0	0 0	0 0	0 0	0 0	0 0	0 0	0 0	0 0	0 0	0 0	0 0	0 0	0 0
Access from course website (NET)	0 0	0 0	0 0	0 0	0 0	0 0	0 0	0 0	0 0	0 0	0 0	0 0	0 0	0 0	0 0	0 0	0 0	0 0
All sources of info	0 0	0 0	0 0	0 0	0 0	0 0	0 0	0 0	0 0	0 0	0 0	0 0	0 0	0 0	0 0	0 0	0 0	0 0

Proportions/Means: Columns Tested (5% risk level) - A/B/D - C/D - E/F/G - H/I/J/K/L/M/N - P/Q
* small base; ** very small base (under 30) ineligible for sig testing

Table 366
Page 1534

Outsell/Digital Library Federation Study (2002)
Weighted Tables

TABLE 138, continued

S7D/E_7. Print abstracts and indexes SUMMARY TABLE

	TOTAL SAMPLE	RESPONDENT TYPE: FACULTY MEMBER	GRAD. STUDENT	FACULTY /GRAD	UNDER GRAD. STUDENT	INSTITUTION TYPE: PUBLIC	PRIVATE	LIBERAL ARTS	DISCIPLINE: BIOLOGIAL SCIENCES	PHYSICAL SCIENCES /MATH	SOCIAL SCIENCES	ARTS AND HUMAN.	ENGI- NEERING	BUSINESS	LAW	UNDEC. MAJOR	GENDER: MALE	FEMALE
		(A)	(B)	(C)	(D)	(E)	(F)	(G)	(H)	(I)	(J)	(K)	(L)	(M)	(N)		(P)	(Q)
Base - Use Print abstracts and indexes for coursework	423	0**	214	214	209	200	100*	123*	52*	47*	177*	85*	13*	35*	6*	7*	197	226
preferred source of info	0 0	0 0	0 0	0 0	0 0	0 0	0 0	0 0	0 0	0 0	0 0	0 0	0 0	0 0	0 0	0 0	0 0	0 0
Colleagues (NET)	0 0	0 0	0 0	0 0	0 0	0 0	0 0	0 0	0 0	0 0	0 0	0 0	0 0	0 0	0 0	0 0	0 0	0 0
All sources of info	0 0	0 0	0 0	0 0	0 0	0 0	0 0	0 0	0 0	0 0	0 0	0 0	0 0	0 0	0 0	0 0	0 0	0 0
preferred source of info	0 0	0 0	0 0	0 0	0 0	0 0	0 0	0 0	0 0	0 0	0 0	0 0	0 0	0 0	0 0	0 0	0 0	0 0
In class (NET)	0 0	0 0	0 0	0 0	0 0	0 0	0 0	0 0	0 0	0 0	0 0	0 0	0 0	0 0	0 0	0 0	0 0	0 0
All sources of info	0 0	0 0	0 0	0 0	0 0	0 0	0 0	0 0	0 0	0 0	0 0	0 0	0 0	0 0	0 0	0 0	0 0	0 0
preferred source of info	0 0	0 0	0 0	0 0	0 0	0 0	0 0	0 0	0 0	0 0	0 0	0 0	0 0	0 0	0 0	0 0	0 0	0 0
Dorm room (NET)	0 0	0 0	0 0	0 0	0 0	0 0	0 0	0 0	0 0	0 0	0 0	0 0	0 0	0 0	0 0	0 0	0 0	0 0
All sources of info	0 0	0 0	0 0	0 0	0 0	0 0	0 0	0 0	0 0	0 0	0 0	0 0	0 0	0 0	0 0	0 0	0 0	0 0

Proportions/Means: Columns Tested (5% risk level) - A/B/D - C/D - E/F/G - H/I/J/K/L/M/N - P/Q
* small base; ** very small base (under 30) ineligible for sig testing

Table 366
Page 1535

Outsell/Digital Library Federation Study (2002)
Weighted Tables

TABLE 138, continued

S7D/E_7. Print abstracts and indexes SUMMARY TABLE

		RESPONDENT TYPE				INSTITUTION TYPE			DISCIPLINE									GENDER	
	TOTAL SAMPLE	FACULTY MEMBER	GRAD. STUDENT	FACULTY /GRAD	UNDER GRAD. STUDENT	PUBLIC	PRIVATE	LIBERAL ARTS	BIOLOGIAL SCIENCES	PHYSICAL SCIENCES /MATH	SOCIAL SCIENCES	ARTS AND HUMAN.	ENGI-NEERING	BUSINESS	LAW	UNDEC. MAJOR	MALE	FEMALE
		(A)	(B)	(C)	(D)	(E)	(F)	(G)	(H)	(I)	(J)	(K)	(L)	(M)	(N)		(P)	(Q)
Base - Use Print abstracts and indexes for coursework	423	0**	214	214	209	200	100*	123*	52*	47*	177*	85*	13*	35*	6*	7*	197	226
preferred source of info	0 0	0 0	0 0	0 0	0 0	0 0	0 0	0 0	0 0	0 0	0 0	0 0	0 0	0 0	0 0	0 0	0 0	0 0
Personal Holdings (NET)	0 0	0 0	0 0	0 0	0 0	0 0	0 0	0 0	0 0	0 0	0 0	0 0	0 0	0 0	0 0	0 0	0 0	0 0
All sources of info	0 0	0 0	0 0	0 0	0 0	0 0	0 0	0 0	0 0	0 0	0 0	0 0	0 0	0 0	0 0	0 0	0 0	0 0
preferred source of info	0 0	0 0	0 0	0 0	0 0	0 0	0 0	0 0	0 0	0 0	0 0	0 0	0 0	0 0	0 0	0 0	0 0	0 0
Other (NET)	7 1.7%	0 0	1 0.5%	1 0.5%	6 2.8%	2 1.1%	1 1.0%	4 3.2%	3 5.1%J	1 2.1%	0 0	2 2.6%	0 0	0 0	* 2.7%J	1 14.3%	2 1.1%	5 2.2%
All sources of info	6 1.5%	0 0	1 0.5%	1 0.5%	5 2.4%	2 1.1%	1 1.0%	3 2.4%	2 3.4%J	1 2.1%	0 0	2 2.6%	0 0	0 0	* 2.7%J	1 14.3%	2 1.1%	4 1.8%
preferred source of info	2 0.5%	0 0	* 0.1%	* 0.1%	2 1.0%	1 0.6%	0 0	1 0.7%	1 1.7%	0 0	0 0	1 1.3%	0 0	0 0	* 2.7%IJ	0 0	0 0	2 1.0%
DK/Refused	3 0.7%	0 0	1 0.5%	1 0.5%	2 1.0%	2 1.0%	0 0	1 0.9%	1 1.7%	0 0	0 0	2 2.6%	0 0	0 0	0 0	0 0	2 1.1%	1 0.4%

Proportions/Means: Columns Tested (5% risk level) - A/B/D - C/D - E/F/G - H/I/J/K/L/M/N - P/Q
* small base; ** very small base (under 30) ineligible for sig testing

Table 366
Page 1536

Outsell/Digital Library Federation Study (2002)
Weighted Tables

TABLE 139

S7sum_8. Online abstracts and indexes SUMMARY TABLE

	RESPONDENT TYPE				INSTITUTION TYPE			DISCIPLINE								GENDER	
	TOTAL SAMPLE	FACULTY MEMBER	GRAD. STUDENT	FACULTY /GRAD	UNDER GRAD. STUDENT	PUBLIC	PRIVATE	LIBERAL ARTS	BIOLOGIAL SCIENCES	PHYSICAL SCIENCES /MATH	SOCIAL SCIENCES	ARTS AND HUMAN.	ENGI-NEERING	BUSINESS	LAW	UNDEC. MAJOR	MALE	FEMALE
		(A)	(B)	(C)	(D)	(E)	(F)	(G)	(H)	(I)	(J)	(K)	(L)	(M)	(N)		(P)	(Q)
Base - Use Online abstracts and indexes for coursework	481	0**	212	212	269	219	105*	157	69*	61*	162*	88*	15*	57*	5**	25*	213	268
ONLINE	412 85.5%	0 0	182 85.6%	182 85.6%	230 85.5%	183 83.4%	94 89.7%	135 85.8%	61 88.5%	57 93.4%KL	133 82.6%	72 81.0%	12 82.7%	50 88.5%	4 88.9%	22 88.0%	188 88.2%	224 83.5%
Search engine (NET)	113 23.4%	0 0	28 13.2%	28 13.2%	84 31.4%B C	37 16.9%	16 15.6%	59 37.6%EF	15 21.8%	17 27.9%J	23 14.0%	22 25.3%	6 36.5%J	19 32.8%J	2 33.3%	10 40.0%	62 29.2%Q	50 18.7%
All sources of info	113 23.4%	0 0	28 13.2%	28 13.2%	84 31.4%B C	37 16.9%	16 15.6%	59 37.6%EF	15 21.8%	17 27.9%J	23 14.0%	22 25.3%	6 36.5%J	19 32.8%J	2 33.3%	10 40.0%	62 29.2%Q	50 18.7%
preferred source of info	62 12.9%	0 0	14 6.7%	14 6.7%	48 17.7%B C	24 11.1%	9 9.0%	28 17.9%	9 12.8%	8 13.1%	13 8.1%	11 12.7%	3 21.2%J	14 24.6%J	1 14.8%	3 12.0%	33 15.6%	29 10.7%
Online library catalogues and finding aids (NET)	88 18.2%	0 0	46 21.6%	46 21.6%	42 15.6%	49 22.6%	14 13.5%	24 15.4%	11 16.7%	9 14.8%	26 16.3%	22 25.3%	2 13.5%	12 21.3%	1 11.1%	4 16.0%	39 18.4%	49 18.1%
All sources of info	88 18.2%	0 0	46 21.6%	46 21.6%	42 15.6%	49 22.6%	14 13.5%	24 15.4%	11 16.7%	9 14.8%	26 16.3%	22 25.3%	2 13.5%	12 21.3%	1 11.1%	4 16.0%	39 18.4%	49 18.1%
preferred source of info	65 13.5%	0 0	36 16.8%	36 16.8%	29 10.8%	38 17.5%	11 10.5%	15 9.8%	7 10.3%	5 8.2%	23 14.0%	17 19.0%	1 9.6%	8 14.8%	1 11.1%	3 12.0%	29 13.7%	36 13.3%
Your own institution's web site (NET)	87 18.1%	0 0	33 15.5%	33 15.5%	54 20,2%	32 14.6%	15 13.9%	41 25.9%EF	17 24.4%M	13 21.3%M	26 16.3%	16 17.7%	3 21.2%M	5 8.2%	1 14.8%	7 28.0%	34 15.7%	54 20.0%

Proportions/Means: Columns Tested (5% risk level) - A/B/D - C/D - E/F/G - H/I/J/K/L/M/N - P/Q
* small base; ** very small base (under 30) ineligible for sig testing

Table 370
Page 1548

Outsell/Digital Library Federation Study (2002)
Weighted Tables

TABLE 139, continued

S7sum_8. Online abstracts and indexes SUMMARY TABLE

	TOTAL SAMPLE	RESPONDENT TYPE: FACULTY MEMBER	GRAD. STUDENT	FACULTY /GRAD	UNDER GRAD. STUDENT	INSTITUTION TYPE: PUBLIC	PRIVATE	LIBERAL ARTS	DISCIPLINE: BIOLOGICAL SCIENCES	PHYSICAL SCIENCES /MATH	SOCIAL SCIENCES	ARTS AND HUMAN.	ENGI-NEERING	BUSINESS	LAW	UNDEC. MAJOR	GENDER: MALE	FEMALE
		(A)	(B)	(C)	(D)	(E)	(F)	(G)	(H)	(I)	(J)	(K)	(L)	(M)	(N)		(P)	(Q)
Base - Use Online abstracts and indexes for coursework	481	0**	212	212	269	219	105*	157	69*	61*	162*	88*	15*	57*	5**	25*	213	268
All sources of info	87 18.1%	0 0	33 15.5%	33 15.5%	54 20.2%	32 14.6%	15 13.9%	41 25.9%EF	17 24.4%M	13 21.3%M	26 16.3%	16 17.7%	3 21.2%M	5 8.2%	1 14.8%	7 28.0%	34 15.7%	54 20.0%
preferred source of info	73 15.2%	0 0	28 13.4%	28 13.4%	45 16.6%	27 12.5%	12 11.2%	34 21.6%E	11 16.7%	13 21.3%M	23 14.0%	12 13.9%	3 17.3%	5 8.2%	1 11.1%	6 24.0%	27 12.8%	46 17.1%
Online databases (NET)	83 17.2%	0 0	45 21.2%	45 21.2%	38 14.1%	26 11.9%	31 30.1%EG	25 16.2%	13 19.2%	12 19.7%	32 19.8%	13 15.2%	1 7.7%	7 11.5%	2 37.0%	3 12.0%	40 18.9%	43 15.9%
All sources of info	83 17.2%	0 0	45 21.2%	45 21.2%	38 14.1%	26 11.9%	31 30.1%EG	25 16.2%	13 19.2%	12 19.7%	32 19.8%	13 15.2%	1 7.7%	7 11.5%	2 37.0%	3 12.0%	40 18.9%	43 15.9%
preferred source of info	60 12.4%	0 0	37 17.2%D	37 17.2%D	23 8.6%	22 10.1%	24 23.0%EG	14 8.6%	12 17.9%	7 11.5%	23 14.0%	9 10.1%	1 5.8%	6 9.8%	2 33.3%	1 4.0%	24 11.4%	36 13.3%
Internet searches (NET)	64 13.4%	0 0	31 14.5%	31 14.5%	33 12.5%	34 15.3%	17 16.3%	14 8.7%	13 19.2%K	10 16.4%	21 12.8%	6 6.3%	2 15.4%	8 14.8%	* 3.7%	4 16.0%	33 15.3%	32 11.8%
All sources of info	64 13.4%	0 0	31 14.5%	31 14.5%	33 12.5%	34 15.3%	17 16.3%	14 8.7%	13 19.2%K	10 16.4%	21 12.8%	6 6.3%	2 15.4%	8 14.8%	* 3.7%	4 16.0%	33 15.3%	32 11.8%
preferred source of info	46 9.6%	0 0	25 11.7%	25 11.7%	22 8.0%	31 14.0%G	10 9.6%	6 3.6%	10 14.1%K	8 13.1%K	15 9.3%	2 2.5%	2 13.5%K	7 13.1%K	0 0	2 8.0%	22 10.5%	24 9.0%
Web directory/ subject related web site (NET)	37 7.7%	0 0	10 4.7%	10 4.7%	27 10.1%BC	11 4.9%	10 9.5%	16 10.3%	6 9.0%	9 14.8%K	11 7.0%	2 2.5%	2 11.5%K	3 4.9%	1 14.8%	3 12.0%	17 8.1%	20 7.3%

Proportions/Means: Columns Tested (5% risk level) - A/B/D - C/D - E/F/G - H/I/J/K/L/M/N - P/Q
* small base; ** very small base (under 30) ineligible for sig testing

Table 370
Page 1549

Outsell/Digital Library Federation Study (2002)
Weighted Tables

TABLE 139, continued

S7sum_8. Online abstracts and indexes SUMMARY TABLE

	TOTAL SAMPLE	RESPONDENT TYPE: FACULTY MEMBER	GRAD. STUDENT	FACULTY /GRAD	UNDER GRAD. STUDENT	INSTITUTION TYPE: PUBLIC	PRIVATE	LIBERAL ARTS	DISCIPLINE: BIOLOGIAL SCIENCES	PHYSICAL SCIENCES /MATH	SOCIAL SCIENCES	ARTS AND HUMAN.	ENGI-NEERING	BUSINESS	LAW	UNDEC. MAJOR	GENDER: MALE	FEMALE
		(A)	(B)	(C)	(D)	(E)	(F)	(G)	(H)	(I)	(J)	(K)	(L)	(M)	(N)		(P)	(Q)
Base - Use Online abstracts and indexes for coursework	481	0**	212	212	269	219	105*	157	69*	61*	162*	88*	15*	57*	5**	25*	213	268
All sources of info	37 7.7%	0 0	10 4.7%	10 4.7%	27 10.1%BC	11 4.9%	10 9.5%	16 10.3%	6 9.0%	9 14.8%K	11 7.0%	2 2.5%	2 11.5%K	3 4.9%	1 14.8%	3 12.0%	17 8.1%	20 7.3%
preferred source of info	25 5.3%	0 0	5 2.3%	5 2.3%	21 7.7%BC	6 2.7%	9 8.2%E	11 7.0%	4 6.4%KM	7 11.5%KM	9 5.8%	0 0	1 7.7%KM	0 0	1 11.1%	3 12.0%	10 4.7%	16 5.8%
Online abstracting and indexing services (NET)	33 6.9%	0 0	16 7.3%	16 7.3%	18 6.5%	11 5.1%	7 7.0%	15 9.2%	4 6.4%	5 8.2%	15 9.3%	6 6.3%	0 0	2 3.3%	* 3.7%	1 4.0%	19 8.8%	14 5.3%
All sources of info	33 6.9%	0 0	16 7.3%	16 7.3%	18 6.5%	11 5.1%	7 7.0%	15 9.2%	4 6.4%	5 8.2%	15 9.3%	6 6.3%	0 0	2 3.3%	* 3.7%	1 4.0%	19 8.8%	14 5.3%
preferred source of info	14 2.9%	0 0	6 2.7%	6 2.7%	8 3.0%	4 1.7%	3 3.0%	7 4.4%	1 1.3%	2 3.3%	6 3.5%	3 3.8%	0 0	1 1.6%	0 0	1 4.0%	9 4.3%	5 1.7%
Online reference service (NET)	21 4.4%	0 0	14 6.8%D	14 6.8%D	7 2.5%	14 6.4%	4 4.0%	3 1.9%	4 6.4%	1 1.6%	8 4.7%	2 2.5%	0 0	5 8.2%	* 7.4%	1 4.0%	7 3.4%	14 5.2%
All sources of info	21 4.4%	0 0	14 6.8%D	14 6.8%D	7 2.5%	14 6.4%	4 4.0%	3 1.9%	4 6.4%	1 1.6%	8 4.7%	2 2.5%	0 0	5 8.2%	* 7.4%	1 4.0%	7 3.4%	14 5.2%
preferred source of info	10 2.0%	0 0	8 3.6%	8 3.6%	2 0.8%	8 3.4%	1 1.1%	1 0.7%	2 2.6%	1 1.6%	2 1.2%	1 1.3%	0 0	3 4.9%	* 3.7%	1 4.0%	2 0.8%	8 2.9%
Department web page (NET)	16 3.4%	0 0	6 3.0%	6 3.0%	10 3.7%	8 3.5%	2 1.9%	7 4.2%	1 1.3%	3 4.9%	6 3.5%	2 2.5%	1 3.8%	2 3.3%	* 3.7%	2 8.0%	9 4.1%	8 2.9%

Proportions/Means: Columns Tested (5% risk level) - A/B/D - C/D - E/F/G - H/I/J/K/L/M/N - P/Q
* small base; ** very small base (under 30) ineligible for sig testing

Table 370
Page 1550

Outsell/Digital Library Federation Study (2002)
Weighted Tables

TABLE 139, continued

S7sum_8. Online abstracts and indexes SUMMARY TABLE

	RESPONDENT TYPE				INSTITUTION TYPE			DISCIPLINE								GENDER	
	TOTAL SAMPLE	FACULTY MEMBER	GRAD. STUDENT	FACULTY /GRAD	UNDER GRAD. STUDENT	PUBLIC	PRIVATE	LIBERAL ARTS	BIOLOGIAL SCIENCES	PHYSICAL SCIENCES /MATH	SOCIAL SCIENCES	ARTS AND HUMAN.	ENGI-NEERING	BUSINESS	LAW	UNDEC. MAJOR	MALE	FEMALE
		(A)	(B)	(C)	(D)	(E)	(F)	(G)	(H)	(I)	(J)	(K)	(L)	(M)	(N)		(P)	(Q)
Base - Use Online abstracts and indexes for coursework	481	0**	212	212	269	219	105*	157	69*	61*	162*	88*	15*	57*	5**	25*	213	268
All sources of info	16	0	6	6	10	8	2	7	1	3	6	2	1	2	*	2	9	8
	3.4%	0	3.0%	3.0%	3.7%	3.5%	1.9%	4.2%	1.3%	4.9%	3.5%	2.5%	3.8%	3.3%	3.7%	8.0%	4.1%	2.9%
preferred source of info	8	0	4	4	4	7	0	2	0	1	4	2	*	1	*	0	4	4
	1.7%	0	2.1%	2.1%	1.5%	3.0%	0	1.2%	0	1.6%	2.3%	2.5%	1.9%	1.6%	3.7%	0	2.1%	1.5%
Your own personal electronic library/files (NET)	*	0	*	*	0	0	*	0	0	0	0	0	*	0	0	0	*	0
	0.1%	0	0.1%	0.1%	0	0	0.3%	0	0	0	0	0	1.9%JK	0	0	0	0.1%	0
All sources of info	*	0	*	*	0	0	*	0	0	0	0	0	*	0	0	0	*	0
	0.1%	0	0.1%	0.1%	0	0	0.3%	0	0	0	0	0	1.9%JK	0	0	0	0.1%	0
preferred source of info	0	0	0	0	0	0	0	0	0	0	0	0	0	0	0	0	0	0
	0	0	0	0	0	0	0	0	0	0	0	0	0	0	0	0	0	0
E-mail listservs (NET)	0	0	0	0	0	0	0	0	0	0	0	0	0	0	0	0	0	0
	0	0	0	0	0	0	0	0	0	0	0	0	0	0	0	0	0	0
All sources of info	0	0	0	0	0	0	0	0	0	0	0	0	0	0	0	0	0	0
	0	0	0	0	0	0	0	0	0	0	0	0	0	0	0	0	0	0
preferred source of info	0	0	0	0	0	0	0	0	0	0	0	0	0	0	0	0	0	0
	0	0	0	0	0	0	0	0	0	0	0	0	0	0	0	0	0	0
Online bookstore (NET)	0	0	0	0	0	0	0	0	0	0	0	0	0	0	0	0	0	0
	0	0	0	0	0	0	0	0	0	0	0	0	0	0	0	0	0	0

Proportions/Means: Columns Tested (5% risk level) - A/B/D - C/D - E/F/G - H/I/J/K/L/M/N - P/Q
* small base; ** very small base (under 30) ineligible for sig testing

Table 370
Page 1551

Outsell/Digital Library Federation Study (2002)
Weighted Tables

TABLE 139, continued

S7sum_8. Online abstracts and indexes SUMMARY TABLE

		RESPONDENT TYPE				INSTITUTION TYPE			DISCIPLINE									GENDER	
	TOTAL SAMPLE	FACULTY MEMBER	GRAD. STUDENT	FACULTY /GRAD	UNDER GRAD. STUDENT	PUBLIC	PRIVATE	LIBERAL ARTS	BIOLOGIAL SCIENCES	PHYSICAL SCIENCES /MATH	SOCIAL SCIENCES	ARTS AND HUMAN.	ENGI-NEERING	BUSINESS	LAW	UNDEC. MAJOR	MALE	FEMALE
		(A)	(B)	(C)	(D)	(E)	(F)	(G)	(H)	(I)	(J)	(K)	(L)	(M)	(N)		(P)	(Q)
Base - Use Online abstracts and indexes for coursework	481	0**	212	212	269	219	105*	157	69*	61*	162*	88*	15*	57*	5**	25*	213	268
All sources of info	0 0	0 0	0 0	0 0	0 0	0 0	0 0	0 0	0 0	0 0	0 0	0 0	0 0	0 0	0 0	0 0	0 0	0 0
preferred source of info	0 0	0 0	0 0	0 0	0 0	0 0	0 0	0 0	0 0	0 0	0 0	0 0	0 0	0 0	0 0	0 0	0 0	0 0
PERSONAL ASSISTANCE	125 26.0%	0 0	52 24.4%	52 24.4%	73 27.2%	48 21.7%	25 24.0%	52 33.3%E	18 26.9%	15 24.6%	30 18.6%	34 38.0%J	5 34.6%J	13 23.0%	2 37.0%	8 32.0%	54 25.3%	71 26.5%
A librarian in your institution (NET)	76 15.8%	0 0	21 9.7%	21 9.7%	55 20.6%B C	23 10.7%	13 12.1%	40 25.4%EF	10 14.1%	4 6.6%	19 11.6%	27 30.4%HI JLM	2 13.5%	7 13.1%	1 25.9%	6 24.0%	37 17.2%	39 14.7%
All sources of info	76 15.8%	0 0	21 9.7%	21 9.7%	55 20.6%B C	23 10.7%	13 12.1%	40 25.4%EF	10 14.1%	4 6.6%	19 11.6%	27 30.4%HI JLM	2 13.5%	7 13.1%	1 25.9%	6 24.0%	37 17.2%	39 14.7%
preferred source of info	29 6.1%	0 0	9 4.3%	9 4.3%	20 7.5%	11 4.9%	5 4.9%	13 8.4%	4 6.4%	1 1.6%	8 4.7%	12 13.9%IJL	0 0	3 4.9%	* 3.7%	1 4.0%	13 6.3%	16 5.9%
Faculty members inside your institution (NET)	68 14.1%	0 0	32 14.9%	32 14.9%	36 13.4%	28 12.6%	15 14.2%	25 16.1%	12 17.9%	12 19.7%	19 11.6%	10 11.4%	3 21.2%	7 11.5%	1 18.5%	4 16.0%	26 12.4%	41 15.4%
All sources of info	68 14.1%	0 0	32 14.9%	32 14.9%	36 13.4%	28 12.6%	15 14.2%	25 16.1%	12 17.9%	12 19.7%	19 11.6%	10 11.4%	3 21.2%	7 11.5%	1 18.5%	4 16.0%	26 12.4%	41 15.4%

Proportions/Means: Columns Tested (5% risk level) - A/B/D - C/D - E/F/G - H/I/J/K/L/M/N - P/Q
* small base; ** very small base (under 30) ineligible for sig testing

Table 370
Page 1552

TABLE 139, continued

S7sum_8. Online abstracts and indexes SUMMARY TABLE

		RESPONDENT TYPE				INSTITUTION TYPE			DISCIPLINE									GENDER	
	TOTAL SAMPLE	FACULTY MEMBER	GRAD. STUDENT	FACULTY /GRAD	UNDER GRAD. STUDENT	PUBLIC	PRIVATE	LIBERAL ARTS	BIOLOGIAL SCIENCES	PHYSICAL SCIENCES /MATH	SOCIAL SCIENCES	ARTS AND HUMAN.	ENGI-NEERING	BUSINESS	LAW	UNDEC. MAJOR	MALE	FEMALE
		(A)	(B)	(C)	(D)	(E)	(F)	(G)	(H)	(I)	(J)	(K)	(L)	(M)	(N)		(P)	(Q)
Base - Use Online abstracts and indexes for coursework	481	0**	212	212	269	219	105*	157	69*	61*	162*	88*	15*	57*	5**	25*	213	268
preferred source of info	24 5.0%	0 0	12 5.4%	12 5.4%	12 4.6%	9 4.1%	7 6.3%	8 5.3%	4 6.4%	3 4.9%	8 4.7%	3 3.8%	1 9.6%	2 3.3%	* 7.4%	2 8.0%	9 4.3%	15 5.5%
Other students inside your institution (NET)	20 4.2%	0 0	11 5.0%	11 5.0%	9 3.5%	6 2.7%	8 7.6%	6 3.9%	4 5.1%	4 6.6%	4 2.3%	4 5.1%	* 1.9%	3 4.9%	* 3.7%	1 4.0%	8 3.7%	12 4.5%
All sources of info	20 4.2%	0 0	11 5.0%	11 5.0%	9 3.5%	6 2.7%	8 7.6%	6 3.9%	4 5.1%	4 6.6%	4 2.3%	4 5.1%	* 1.9%	3 4.9%	* 3.7%	1 4.0%	8 3.7%	12 4.5%
preferred source of info	6 1.2%	0 0	5 2.2%	5 2.2%	1 0.5%	3 1.4%	2 1.8%	1 0.6%	1 1.3%	1 1.6%	2 1.2%	0 0	* 1.9%K	1 1.6%	0 0	1 4.0%	3 1.5%	3 1.1%
Faculty members outside your institution (NET)	4 0.9%	0 0	4 2.0%D	4 2.0%D	0 0	3 1.3%	1 1.3%	0 0	1 1.3%	0 0	2 1.2%	0 0	* 1.9%K	1 1.6%	* 3.7%	0 0	1 0.6%	3 1.1%
All sources of info	4 0.9%	0 0	4 2.0%D	4 2.0%D	0 0	3 1.3%	1 1.3%	0 0	1 1.3%	0 0	2 1.2%	0 0	* 1.9%K	1 1.6%	* 3.7%	0 0	1 0.6%	3 1.1%
preferred source of info	2 0.4%	0 0	2 0.9%	2 0.9%	0 0	2 0.9%	0 0	0 0	0 0	0 0	2 1.2%	0 0	0 0	0 0	0 0	0 0	0 0	2 0.7%
Other students outside your institution (NET)	3 0.6%	0 0	1 0.4%	1 0.4%	2 0.7%	0 0	1 0.9%	2 1.2%	0 0	0 0	2 1.2%	0 0	0 0	1 1.6%	0 0	0 0	1 0.4%	2 0.7%

Proportions/Means: Columns Tested (5% risk level) - A/B/D - C/D - E/F/G - H/I/J/K/L/M/N - P/Q
* small base; ** very small base (under 30) ineligible for sig testing

Table 370
Page 1553

TABLE 139, continued

S7sum_8. Online abstracts and indexes SUMMARY TABLE

	RESPONDENT TYPE					INSTITUTION TYPE			DISCIPLINE									GENDER	
	TOTAL SAMPLE	FACULTY MEMBER	GRAD. STUDENT	FACULTY /GRAD	UNDER GRAD. STUDENT	PUBLIC	PRIVATE	LIBERAL ARTS	BIOLOGIAL SCIENCES	PHYSICAL SCIENCES /MATH	SOCIAL SCIENCES	ARTS AND HUMAN.	ENGI-NEERING	BUSINESS	LAW	UNDEC. MAJOR	MALE	FEMALE
		(A)	(B)	(C)	(D)	(E)	(F)	(G)	(H)	(I)	(J)	(K)	(L)	(M)	(N)		(P)	(Q)
Base - Use Online abstracts and indexes for coursework	481	0**	212	212	269	219	105*	157	69*	61*	162*	88*	15*	57*	5**	25*	213	268
All sources of info	3 0.6%	0 0	1 0.4%	1 0.4%	2 0.7%	0 0	1 0.9%	2 1.2%	0 0	0 0	2 1.2%	0 0	0 0	1 1.6%	0 0	0 0	1 0.4%	2 0.7%
preferred source of info	0 0	0 0	0 0	0 0	0 0	0 0	0 0	0 0	0 0	0 0	0 0	0 0	0 0	0 0	0 0	0 0	0 0	0 0
Another institution's librarian (NET)	0 0	0 0	0 0	0 0	0 0	0 0	0 0	0 0	0 0	0 0	0 0	0 0	0 0	0 0	0 0	0 0	0 0	0 0
All sources of info	0 0	0 0	0 0	0 0	0 0	0 0	0 0	0 0	0 0	0 0	0 0	0 0	0 0	0 0	0 0	0 0	0 0	0 0
preferred source of info	0 0	0 0	0 0	0 0	0 0	0 0	0 0	0 0	0 0	0 0	0 0	0 0	0 0	0 0	0 0	0 0	0 0	0 0
Professional meetings (NET)	0 0	0 0	0 0	0 0	0 0	0 0	0 0	0 0	0 0	0 0	0 0	0 0	0 0	0 0	0 0	0 0	0 0	0 0
All sources of info	0 0	0 0	0 0	0 0	0 0	0 0	0 0	0 0	0 0	0 0	0 0	0 0	0 0	0 0	0 0	0 0	0 0	0 0
preferred source of info	0 0	0 0	0 0	0 0	0 0	0 0	0 0	0 0	0 0	0 0	0 0	0 0	0 0	0 0	0 0	0 0	0 0	0 0
LIBRARY FACILITIES/ PRINT	91 18.9%	0 0	33 15.7%	33 15.7%	58 21.5%	30 13.7%	22 20.8%	39 25.1%E	11 16.7%	11 18.0%	28 17.4%	25 27.8%	3 23.1%	8 14.8%	1 22.2%	3 12.0%	40 19.0%	51 18.9%

Proportions/Means: Columns Tested (5% risk level) - A/B/D - C/D - E/F/G - H/I/J/K/L/M/N - P/Q
* small base; ** very small base (under 30) ineligible for sig testing

Table 370
Page 1554

TABLE 139, continued

S7sum_8. Online abstracts and indexes SUMMARY TABLE

		RESPONDENT TYPE				INSTITUTION TYPE			DISCIPLINE									GENDER	
	TOTAL SAMPLE	FACULTY MEMBER	GRAD. STUDENT	FACULTY /GRAD	UNDER GRAD. STUDENT	PUBLIC	PRIVATE	LIBERAL ARTS	BIOLOGIAL SCIENCES	PHYSICAL SCIENCES /MATH	SOCIAL SCIENCES	ARTS AND HUMAN.	ENGI- NEERING	BUSINESS	LAW	UNDEC. MAJOR	MALE	FEMALE
		(A)	(B)	(C)	(D)	(E)	(F)	(G)	(H)	(I)	(J)	(K)	(L)	(M)	(N)		(P)	(Q)
Base - Use Online abstracts and indexes for coursework	481	0**	212	212	269	219	105*	157	69*	61*	162*	88*	15*	57*	5**	25*	213	268
Campus library (NET)	72 14.9%	0 0	24 11.1%	24 11.1%	48 18.0%	20 9.3%	18 16.8%	34 21.6%E	8 11.5%	9 14.8%	26 16.3%	17 19.0%	3 21.2%M	5 8.2%	1 22.2%	3 12.0%	31 14.5%	41 15.3%
All sources of info	72 14.9%	0 0	24 11.1%	24 11.1%	48 18.0%	20 9.3%	18 16.8%	34 21.6%E	8 11.5%	9 14.8%	26 16.3%	17 19.0%	3 21.2%M	5 8.2%	1 22.2%	3 12.0%	31 14.5%	41 15.3%
preferred source of info	24 5.0%	0 0	8 3.9%	8 3.9%	16 5.8%	9 4.3%	2 2.3%	12 7.6%	1 1.3%	2 3.3%	11 7.0%	7 7.6%	1 7.7%H	2 3.3%	0 0	0 0	10 4.7%	14 5.2%
References cited in books or journal articles (NET)	9 1.9%	0 0	6 2.8%	6 2.8%	3 1.2%	4 1.8%	2 1.9%	3 2.0%	2 2.6%	1 1.6%	2 1.2%	3 3.8%	* 1.9%	1 1.6%	0 0	0 0	5 2.2%	5 1.7%
All sources of info	9 1.9%	0 0	6 2.8%	6 2.8%	3 1.2%	4 1.8%	2 1.9%	3 2.0%	2 2.6%	1 1.6%	2 1.2%	3 3.8%	* 1.9%	1 1.6%	0 0	0 0	5 2.2%	5 1.7%
preferred source of info	0 0	0 0	0 0	0 0	0 0	0 0	0 0	0 0	0 0	0 0	0 0	0 0	0 0	0 0	0 0	0 0	0 0	0 0
Printed library catalogues and finding aids (NET)	9 1.8%	0 0	4 1.8%	4 1.8%	5 1.9%	6 2.6%	2 2.0%	1 0.6%	1 1.3%	1 1.6%	2 1.2%	2 2.5%	0 0	3 4.9%	0 0	0 0	2 1.0%	7 2.5%
All sources of info	9 1.8%	0 0	4 1.8%	4 1.8%	5 1.9%	6 2.6%	2 2.0%	1 0.6%	1 1.3%	1 1.6%	2 1.2%	2 2.5%	0 0	3 4.9%	0 0	0 0	2 1.0%	7 2.5%

Proportions/Means: Columns Tested (5% risk level) - A/B/D - C/D - E/F/G - H/I/J/K/L/M/N - P/Q
* small base; ** very small base (under 30) ineligible for sig testing

Table 370
Page 1555

Outsell/Digital Library Federation Study (2002)
Weighted Tables

TABLE 139, continued

S7sum_8. Online abstracts and indexes SUMMARY TABLE

		RESPONDENT TYPE				INSTITUTION TYPE			DISCIPLINE									GENDER	
	TOTAL SAMPLE	FACULTY MEMBER	GRAD. STUDENT	FACULTY /GRAD	UNDER GRAD. STUDENT	PUBLIC	PRIVATE	LIBERAL ARTS	BIOLOGIAL SCIENCES	PHYSICAL SCIENCES /MATH	SOCIAL SCIENCES	ARTS AND HUMAN.	ENGI-NEERING	BUSINESS	LAW	UNDEC. MAJOR	MALE	FEMALE
		(A)	(B)	(C)	(D)	(E)	(F)	(G)	(H)	(I)	(J)	(K)	(L)	(M)	(N)		(P)	(Q)
Base - Use Online abstracts and indexes for coursework	481	0**	212	212	269	219	105*	157	69*	61*	162*	88*	15*	57*	5**	25*	213	268
preferred source of info	1 0.2%	0 0	0 0	0 0	1 0.3%	1 0.4%	0 0	0 0	0 0	0 0	0 0	0 0	0 0	1 1.6%	0 0	0 0	0 0	1 0.3%
Your own personal physical library/ files/bookshelves (NET)	5 1.1%	0 0	3 1.4%	3 1.4%	2 0.8%	2 0.8%	1 1.1%	2 1.4%	1 1.3%	0 0	0 0	3 3.8%J	0 0	1 1.6%	0 0	0 0	3 1.4%	2 0.8%
All sources of info	5 1.1%	0 0	3 1.4%	3 1.4%	2 0.8%	2 0.8%	1 1.1%	2 1.4%	1 1.3%	0 0	0 0	3 3.8%J	0 0	1 1.6%	0 0	0 0	3 1.4%	2 0.8%
preferred source of info	2 0.4%	0 0	2 1.0%	2 1.0%	0 0	1 0.4%	1 1.1%	0 0	0 0	0 0	0 0	1 1.3%	0 0	1 1.6%	0 0	0 0	1 0.4%	1 0.4%
Another library (NET)	3 0.6%	0 0	0 0	0 0	3 1.0%	0 0	0 0	3 1.8%	1 1.3%	0 0	2 1.2%	0 0	0 0	0 0	0 0	0 0	1 0.4%	2 0.7%
All sources of info	3 0.6%	0 0	0 0	0 0	3 1.0%	0 0	0 0	3 1.8%	1 1.3%	0 0	2 1.2%	0 0	0 0	0 0	0 0	0 0	1 0.4%	2 0.7%
preferred source of info	0 0	0 0	0 0	0 0	0 0	0 0	0 0	0 0	0 0	0 0	0 0	0 0	0 0	0 0	0 0	0 0	0 0	0 0
Printed abstracting and indexing services (NET)	2 0.4%	0 0	0 0	0 0	2 0.8%	1 0.4%	0 0	1 0.7%	0 0	0 0	0 0	1 1.3%	0 0	1 1.6%	0 0	0 0	1 0.5%	1 0.3%

Proportions/Means: Columns Tested (5% risk level) - A/B/D - C/D - E/F/G - H/I/J/K/L/M/N - P/Q
* small base; ** very small base (under 30) ineligible for sig testing

Table 370
Page 1556

TABLE 139, continued

S7sum_8. Online abstracts and indexes SUMMARY TABLE

		RESPONDENT TYPE				INSTITUTION TYPE			DISCIPLINE									GENDER	
	TOTAL SAMPLE	FACULTY MEMBER	GRAD. STUDENT	FACULTY /GRAD	UNDER GRAD. STUDENT	PUBLIC	PRIVATE	LIBERAL ARTS	BIOLOGIAL SCIENCES	PHYSICAL SCIENCES /MATH	SOCIAL SCIENCES	ARTS AND HUMAN.	ENGI-NEERING	BUSINESS	LAW	UNDEC. MAJOR	MALE	FEMALE
		(A)	(B)	(C)	(D)	(E)	(F)	(G)	(H)	(I)	(J)	(K)	(L)	(M)	(N)		(P)	(Q)
Base - Use Online abstracts and indexes for coursework	481	0**	212	212	269	219	105*	157	69*	61*	162*	88*	15*	57*	5**	25*	213	268
All sources of info	2 0.4%	0 0	0 0	0 0	2 0.8%	1 0.4%	0 0	1 0.7%	0 0	0 0	0 0	1 1.3%	0 0	1 1.6%	0 0	0 0	1 0.5%	1 0.3%
preferred source of info	0 0	0 0	0 0	0 0	0 0	0 0	0 0	0 0	0 0	0 0	0 0	0 0	0 0	0 0	0 0	0 0	0 0	0 0
Physical bookstore (NET)	2 0.4%	0 0	1 0.4%	1 0.4%	1 0.4%	0 0	1 0.8%	1 0.7%	1 1.3%	0 0	0 0	1 1.3%	0 0	0 0	0 0	0 0	0 0	2 0.7%
All sources of info	2 0.4%	0 0	1 0.4%	1 0.4%	1 0.4%	0 0	1 0.8%	1 0.7%	1 1.3%	0 0	0 0	1 1.3%	0 0	0 0	0 0	0 0	0 0	2 0.7%
preferred source of info	0 0	0 0	0 0	0 0	0 0	0 0	0 0	0 0	0 0	0 0	0 0	0 0	0 0	0 0	0 0	0 0	0 0	0 0
Personal subscriptions to newspapers, magazines and journals (NET)	0 0	0 0	0 0	0 0	0 0	0 0	0 0	0 0	0 0	0 0	0 0	0 0	0 0	0 0	0 0	0 0	0 0	0 0
All sources of info	0 0	0 0	0 0	0 0	0 0	0 0	0 0	0 0	0 0	0 0	0 0	0 0	0 0	0 0	0 0	0 0	0 0	0 0
preferred source of info	0 0	0 0	0 0	0 0	0 0	0 0	0 0	0 0	0 0	0 0	0 0	0 0	0 0	0 0	0 0	0 0	0 0	0 0

Proportions/Means: Columns Tested (5% risk level) - A/B/D - C/D - E/F/G - H/I/J/K/L/M/N - P/Q
* small base; ** very small base (under 30) ineligible for sig testing

Table 370
Page 1557

Outsell/Digital Library Federation Study (2002)
Weighted Tables

TABLE 139, continued

S7sum_8. Online abstracts and indexes SUMMARY TABLE

	TOTAL SAMPLE	RESPONDENT TYPE: FACULTY MEMBER	GRAD. STUDENT	FACULTY /GRAD	UNDER GRAD. STUDENT	INSTITUTION TYPE: PUBLIC	PRIVATE	LIBERAL ARTS	DISCIPLINE: BIOLOGIAL SCIENCES	PHYSICAL SCIENCES /MATH	SOCIAL SCIENCES	ARTS AND HUMAN.	ENGI-NEERING	BUSINESS	LAW	UNDEC. MAJOR	GENDER: MALE	FEMALE
		(A)	(B)	(C)	(D)	(E)	(F)	(G)	(H)	(I)	(J)	(K)	(L)	(M)	(N)		(P)	(Q)
Base - Use Online abstracts and indexes for coursework	481	0**	212	212	269	219	105*	157	69*	61*	162*	88*	15*	57*	5**	25*	213	268
Other (NET)	22 4.5%	0 0	8 3.8%	8 3.8%	14 5.1%	9 4.2%	5 4.8%	7 4.7%	3 3.8%	1 1.6%	8 4.7%	7 7.6%	1 5.8%	2 3.3%	0 0	1 4.0%	10 4.5%	12 4.4%
All sources of info	18 3.7%	0 0	7 3.3%	7 3.3%	11 4.0%	8 3.7%	2 2.2%	7 4.7%	2 2.6%	1 1.6%	6 3.5%	7 7.6%	1 5.8%	2 3.3%	0 0	0 0	9 4.1%	9 3.4%
preferred source of info	13 2.8%	0 0	6 2.7%	6 2.7%	8 2.8%	7 3.1%	4 3.5%	3 1.8%	2 2.6%	1 1.6%	8 4.7%	1 1.3%	0 0	1 1.6%	0 0	1 4.0%	6 2.8%	7 2.8%
Online (unspecified)	4 0.8%	0 0	2 0.9%	2 0.9%	2 0.8%	3 1.3%	0 0	1 0.7%	0 0	1 1.6%	2 1.2%	1 1.3%	0 0	0 0	0 0	0 0	1 0.5%	3 1.1%
All sources of info	4 0.8%	0 0	2 0.9%	2 0.9%	2 0.8%	3 1.3%	0 0	1 0.7%	0 0	1 1.6%	2 1.2%	1 1.3%	0 0	0 0	0 0	0 0	1 0.5%	3 1.1%
preferred source of info	4 0.8%	0 0	2 0.9%	2 0.9%	2 0.8%	3 1.3%	0 0	1 0.7%	0 0	1 1.6%	2 1.2%	1 1.3%	0 0	0 0	0 0	0 0	1 0.5%	3 1.1%
E-journals	3 0.7%	0 0	2 1.0%	2 1.0%	1 0.4%	3 1.4%	* 0.3%	0 0	0 0	0 0	2 1.2%	1 1.3%	* 1.9%	0 0	0 0	0 0	0 0	3 1.2%
All sources of info	3 0.7%	0 0	2 1.0%	2 1.0%	1 0.4%	3 1.4%	* 0.3%	0 0	0 0	0 0	2 1.2%	1 1.3%	* 1.9%	0 0	0 0	0 0	0 0	3 1.2%
preferred source of info	3 0.6%	0 0	2 0.9%	2 0.9%	1 0.4%	3 1.4%	0 0	0 0	0 0	0 0	2 1.2%	1 1.3%	0 0	0 0	0 0	0 0	0 0	3 1.1%

Proportions/Means: Columns Tested (5% risk level) - A/B/D - C/D - E/F/G - H/I/J/K/L/M/N - P/Q
* small base; ** very small base (under 30) ineligible for sig testing

Table 370
Page 1558

Outsell/Digital Library Federation Study (2002)
Weighted Tables

TABLE 139, continued

S7sum_8. Online abstracts and indexes SUMMARY TABLE

		RESPONDENT TYPE				INSTITUTION TYPE			DISCIPLINE									GENDER	
	TOTAL SAMPLE	FACULTY MEMBER	GRAD. STUDENT	FACULTY /GRAD	UNDER GRAD. STUDENT	PUBLIC	PRIVATE	LIBERAL ARTS	BIOLOGIAL SCIENCES	PHYSICAL SCIENCES /MATH	SOCIAL SCIENCES	ARTS AND HUMAN.	ENGI-NEERING	BUSINESS	LAW	UNDEC. MAJOR	MALE	FEMALE
		(A)	(B)	(C)	(D)	(E)	(F)	(G)	(H)	(I)	(J)	(K)	(L)	(M)	(N)		(P)	(Q)
Base - Use Online abstracts and indexes for coursework	481	0**	212	212	269	219	105*	157	69*	61*	162*	88*	15*	57*	5**	25*	213	268
DK/Refused	12 2.4%	0 0	3 1.3%	3 1.3%	9 3.3%	8 3.6%	3 2.7%	1 0.6%	0 0	0 0	4 2.3%	4 5.1%	1 3.8%HI	2 3.3%	0 0	1 4.0%	9 4.1%	3 1.1%

Proportions/Means: Columns Tested (5% risk level) - A/B/D - C/D - E/F/G - H/I/J/K/L/M/N - P/Q
* small base; ** very small base (under 30) ineligible for sig testing

TABLE 140

S7D/E_8. Online abstracts and indexes SUMMARY TABLE

	RESPONDENT TYPE					INSTITUTION TYPE			DISCIPLINE								GENDER	
	TOTAL SAMPLE	FACULTY MEMBER	GRAD. STUDENT	FACULTY /GRAD	UNDER GRAD. STUDENT	PUBLIC	PRIVATE	LIBERAL ARTS	BIOLOGIAL SCIENCES	PHYSICAL SCIENCES /MATH	SOCIAL SCIENCES	ARTS AND HUMAN.	ENGI-NEERING	BUSINESS	LAW	UNDEC. MAJOR	MALE	FEMALE
		(A)	(B)	(C)	(D)	(E)	(F)	(G)	(H)	(I)	(J)	(K)	(L)	(M)	(N)		(P)	(Q)
Base - Use Online abstracts and indexes for coursework	481	0**	212	212	269	219	105*	157	69*	61*	162*	88*	15*	57*	5**	25*	213	268
Access online (NET)	317 65.9%	0 0	140 65.8%	140 65.8%	177 66.0%	137 62.3%	70 66.8%	111 70.3%	45 65.4%	47 77.0%K	102 62.8%	49 55.7%	11 71.2%	41 72.1%K	4 81.5%	19 76.0%	150 70.6%	167 62.2%
All sources of info	317 65.9%	0 0	140 65.8%	140 65.8%	177 66.0%	137 62.3%	70 66.8%	111 70.3%	45 65.4%	47 77.0%K	102 62.8%	49 55.7%	11 71.2%	41 72.1%K	4 81.5%	19 76.0%	150 70.6%	167 62.2%
preferred source of info	284 59.1%	0 0	130 61.0%	130 61.0%	155 57.6%	123 55.9%	64 61.2%	98 62.2%	42 61.5%	40 65.6%	94 58.1%	45 50.6%	9 61.5%	35 62.3%	4 81.5%	15 60.0%	131 61.3%	154 57.4%
Borrow from or use in campus library (NET)	219 45.6%	0 0	91 43.0%	91 43.0%	128 47.7%	99 45.0%	48 45.8%	73 46.3%	33 48.7%	21 34.4%	77 47.7%	45 50.6%	7 48.1%	24 42.6%	2 37.0%	10 40.0%	95 44.4%	125 46.5%
All sources of info	219 45.6%	0 0	91 43.0%	91 43.0%	128 47.7%	99 45.0%	48 45.8%	73 46.3%	33 48.7%	21 34.4%	77 47.7%	45 50.6%	7 48.1%	24 42.6%	2 37.0%	10 40.0%	95 44.4%	125 46.5%
preferred source of info	163 33.8%	0 0	68 31.8%	68 31.8%	95 35.4%	77 35.0%	35 33.9%	51 32.2%	23 33.3%	14 23.0%	56 34.9%	39 44.3%I	5 34.6%	18 31.1%	1 11.1%	7 28.0%	67 31.6%	96 35.7%
Interlibrary loan (NET)	12 2.5%	0 0	4 1.9%	4 1.9%	8 2.9%	4 1.8%	1 1.1%	7 4.3%	1 1.3%	1 1.6%	6 3.5%	3 3.8%	0 0	1 1.6%	0 0	0 0	5 2.5%	7 2.4%
All sources of info	12 2.5%	0 0	4 1.9%	4 1.9%	8 2.9%	4 1.8%	1 1.1%	7 4.3%	1 1.3%	1 1.6%	6 3.5%	3 3.8%	0 0	1 1.6%	0 0	0 0	5 2.5%	7 2.4%
preferred source of info	5 1.0%	0 0	3 1.4%	3 1.4%	2 0.7%	3 1.3%	0 0	2 1.2%	0 0	1 1.6%	4 2.3%	0 0	0 0	0 0	0 0	0 0	1 0.5%	4 1.4%

Proportions/Means: Columns Tested (5% risk level) - A/B/D - C/D - E/F/G - H/I/J/K/L/M/N - P/Q
* small base; ** very small base (under 30) ineligible for sig testing

Table 373
Page 1566

TABLE 140, continued

S7D/E_8. Online abstracts and indexes SUMMARY TABLE

	TOTAL SAMPLE	RESPONDENT TYPE: FACULTY MEMBER	GRAD. STUDENT	FACULTY /GRAD	UNDER GRAD. STUDENT	INSTITUTION TYPE: PUBLIC	PRIVATE	LIBERAL ARTS	DISCIPLINE: BIOLOGIAL SCIENCES	PHYSICAL SCIENCES /MATH	SOCIAL SCIENCES	ARTS AND HUMAN.	ENGI-NEERING	BUSINESS	LAW	UNDEC. MAJOR	GENDER: MALE	FEMALE
		(A)	(B)	(C)	(D)	(E)	(F)	(G)	(H)	(I)	(J)	(K)	(L)	(M)	(N)		(P)	(Q)
Base - Use Online abstracts and indexes for coursework	481	0**	212	212	269	219	105*	157	69*	61*	162*	88*	15*	57*	5**	25*	213	268
Borrow from or use in other libraries (NET)	7 1.4%	0 0	2 0.9%	2 0.9%	5 1.9%	6 2.7%	0 0	1 0.6%	0 0	0 0	6 3.5%	0 0	* 1.9%K	1 1.6%	0 0	0 0	3 1.5%	4 1.4%
All sources of info	7 1.4%	0 0	2 0.9%	2 0.9%	5 1.9%	6 2.7%	0 0	1 0.6%	0 0	0 0	6 3.5%	0 0	* 1.9%K	1 1.6%	0 0	0 0	3 1.5%	4 1.4%
preferred source of info	4 0.8%	0 0	0 0	0 0	4 1.4%	4 1.7%	0 0	0 0	0 0	0 0	4 2.3%	0 0	0 0	0 0	0 0	0 0	2 0.9%	2 0.7%
Faculty (NET)	3 0.7%	0 0	* 0.2%	* 0.2%	3 1.1%	0 0	* 0.4%	3 1.9%	0 0	0 0	2 1.2%	1 1.3%	* 1.9%	0 0	* 3.7%	0 0	* 0.1%	3 1.2%
All sources of info	3 0.7%	0 0	* 0.2%	* 0.2%	3 1.1%	0 0	* 0.4%	3 1.9%	0 0	0 0	2 1.2%	1 1.3%	* 1.9%	0 0	* 3.7%	0 0	* 0.1%	3 1.2%
preferred source of info	2 0.5%	0 0	* 0.1%	* 0.1%	2 0.7%	0 0	* 0.3%	2 1.2%	0 0	0 0	2 1.2%	0 0	* 1.9%K	0 0	0 0	0 0	* 0.1%	2 0.7%
Ask library to purchase source (NET)	3 0.6%	0 0	2 0.9%	2 0.9%	1 0.4%	2 0.9%	0 0	1 0.6%	0 0	1 1.6%	2 1.2%	0 0	0 0	0 0	0 0	0 0	2 0.9%	1 0.4%
All sources of info	3 0.6%	0 0	2 0.9%	2 0.9%	1 0.4%	2 0.9%	0 0	1 0.6%	0 0	1 1.6%	2 1.2%	0 0	0 0	0 0	0 0	0 0	2 0.9%	1 0.4%
preferred source of info	3 0.6%	0 0	2 0.9%	2 0.9%	1 0.4%	2 0.9%	0 0	1 0.6%	0 0	1 1.6%	2 1.2%	0 0	0 0	0 0	0 0	0 0	2 0.9%	1 0.4%

Proportions/Means: Columns Tested (5% risk level) - A/B/D - C/D - E/F/G - H/I/J/K/L/M/N - P/Q
* small base; ** very small base (under 30) ineligible for sig testing

Table 373
Page 1567

Outsell/Digital Library Federation Study (2002)
Weighted Tables

TABLE 140, continued

S7D/E_8. Online abstracts and indexes SUMMARY TABLE

		RESPONDENT TYPE				INSTITUTION TYPE			DISCIPLINE									GENDER	
	TOTAL SAMPLE	FACULTY MEMBER	GRAD. STUDENT	FACULTY /GRAD	UNDER GRAD. STUDENT	PUBLIC	PRIVATE	LIBERAL ARTS	BIOLOGIAL SCIENCES	PHYSICAL SCIENCES /MATH	SOCIAL SCIENCES	ARTS AND HUMAN.	ENGI-NEERING	BUSINESS	LAW	UNDEC. MAJOR	MALE	FEMALE
		(A)	(B)	(C)	(D)	(E)	(F)	(G)	(H)	(I)	(J)	(K)	(L)	(M)	(N)		(P)	(Q)
Base - Use Online abstracts and indexes for coursework	481	0**	212	212	269	219	105*	157	69*	61*	162*	88*	15*	57*	5**	25*	213	268
Personal Holdings (NET)	2 0.4%	0 0	2 1.0%	2 1.0%	0 0	1 0.4%	1 1.1%	0 0	0 0	0 0	0 0	1 1.3%	0 0	1 1.6%	0 0	0 0	1 0.4%	1 0.4%
All sources of info	2 0.4%	0 0	2 1.0%	2 1.0%	0 0	1 0.4%	1 1.1%	0 0	0 0	0 0	0 0	1 1.3%	0 0	1 1.6%	0 0	0 0	1 0.4%	1 0.4%
preferred source of info	1 0.2%	0 0	1 0.4%	1 0.4%	0 0	1 0.4%	0 0	0 0	0 0	0 0	0 0	0 0	0 0	1 1.6%	0 0	0 0	1 0.4%	0 0
Order from on demand document delivery service (NET)	2 0.4%	0 0	0 0	0 0	2 0.7%	0 0	0 0	2 1.2%	0 0	0 0	2 1.2%	0 0	0 0	0 0	0 0	0 0	0 0	2 0.7%
All sources of info	2 0.4%	0 0	0 0	0 0	2 0.7%	0 0	0 0	2 1.2%	0 0	0 0	2 1.2%	0 0	0 0	0 0	0 0	0 0	0 0	2 0.7%
preferred source of info	0 0	0 0	0 0	0 0	0 0	0 0	0 0	0 0	0 0	0 0	0 0	0 0	0 0	0 0	0 0	0 0	0 0	0 0
Purchase from online bookstore (NET)	1 0.3%	0 0	1 0.5%	1 0.5%	* 0.1%	1 0.6%	0 0	0 0	0 0	1 1.6%	0 0	0 0	* 1.9%JK	0 0	0 0	0 0	1 0.5%	* 0.1%
All sources of info	1 0.3%	0 0	1 0.5%	1 0.5%	* 0.1%	1 0.6%	0 0	0 0	0 0	1 1.6%	0 0	0 0	* 1.9%JK	0 0	0 0	0 0	1 0.5%	* 0.1%
preferred source of info	1 0.3%	0 0	1 0.5%	1 0.5%	* 0,1%	1 0.6%	0 0	0 0	0 0	1 1.6%	0 0	0 0	* 1.9%JK	0 0	0 0	0 0	1 0.5%	* 0.1%

Proportions/Means: Columns Tested (5% risk level) - A/B/D - C/D - E/F/G - H/I/J/K/L/M/N - P/Q
* small base; ** very small base (under 30) ineligible for sig testing

Table 373
Page 1568

Outsell/Digital Library Federation Study (2002)
Weighted Tables

TABLE 140, continued

S7D/E_8. Online abstracts and indexes SUMMARY TABLE

		RESPONDENT TYPE				INSTITUTION TYPE			DISCIPLINE									GENDER	
	TOTAL SAMPLE	FACULTY MEMBER	GRAD. STUDENT	FACULTY /GRAD	UNDER GRAD. STUDENT	PUBLIC	PRIVATE	LIBERAL ARTS	BIOLOGIAL SCIENCES	PHYSICAL SCIENCES /MATH	SOCIAL SCIENCES	ARTS AND HUMAN.	ENGI-NEERING	BUSINESS	LAW	UNDEC. MAJOR	MALE	FEMALE
		(A)	(B)	(C)	(D)	(E)	(F)	(G)	(H)	(I)	(J)	(K)	(L)	(M)	(N)		(P)	(Q)
Base - Use Online abstracts and indexes for coursework	481	0**	212	212	269	219	105*	157	69*	61*	162*	88*	15*	57*	5**	25*	213	268
Purchase from physical book store (NET)	1 0.2%	0 0	0 0	0 0	1 0.4%	0 0	1 1.1%	0 0	0 0	0 0	0 0	1 1.3%	0 0	0 0	0 0	0 0	0 0	1 0.4%
All sources of info	1 0.2%	0 0	0 0	0 0	1 0.4%	0 0	1 1.1%	0 0	0 0	0 0	0 0	1 1.3%	0 0	0 0	0 0	0 0	0 0	1 0.4%
preferred source of info	0 0	0 0	0 0	0 0	0 0	0 0	0 0	0 0	0 0	0 0	0 0	0 0	0 0	0 0	0 0	0 0	0 0	0 0
Access from course website (NET)	1 0.2%	0 0	0 0	0 0	1 0.3%	0 0	1 0.9%	0 0	0 0	0 0	0 0	0 0	0 0	1 1.6%	0 0	0 0	1 0.4%	0 0
All sources of info	1 0.2%	0 0	0 0	0 0	1 0.3%	0 0	1 0.9%	0 0	0 0	0 0	0 0	0 0	0 0	1 1.6%	0 0	0 0	1 0.4%	0 0
preferred source of info	1 0.2%	0 0	0 0	0 0	1 0.3%	0 0	1 0.9%	0 0	0 0	0 0	0 0	0 0	0 0	1 1.6%	0 0	0 0	1 0.4%	0 0
Colleagues (NET)	1 0.2%	0 0	1 0.4%	1 0.4%	0 0	1 0.4%	0 0	0 0	1 1.3%	0 0	0 0	0 0	0 0	0 0	0 0	0 0	0 0	1 0.3%
All sources of info	1 0.2%	0 0	1 0.4%	1 0.4%	0 0	1 0.4%	0 0	0 0	1 1.3%	0 0	0 0	0 0	0 0	0 0	0 0	0 0	0 0	1 0.3%
preferred source of info	0 0	0 0	0 0	0 0	0 0	0 0	0 0	0 0	0 0	0 0	0 0	0 0	0 0	0 0	0 0	0 0	0 0	0 0

Proportions/Means: Columns Tested (5% risk level) - A/B/D - C/D - E/F/G - H/I/J/K/L/M/N - P/Q
* small base; ** very small base (under 30) ineligible for sig testing

Table 373
Page 1569

TABLE 140, continued

S7D/E_8. Online abstracts and indexes SUMMARY TABLE

		RESPONDENT TYPE				INSTITUTION TYPE			DISCIPLINE									GENDER	
	TOTAL SAMPLE	FACULTY MEMBER	GRAD. STUDENT	FACULTY /GRAD	UNDER GRAD. STUDENT	PUBLIC	PRIVATE	LIBERAL ARTS	BIOLOGIAL SCIENCES	PHYSICAL SCIENCES /MATH	SOCIAL SCIENCES	ARTS AND HUMAN.	ENGI-NEERING	BUSINESS	LAW	UNDEC. MAJOR	MALE	FEMALE
		(A)	(B)	(C)	(D)	(E)	(F)	(G)	(H)	(I)	(J)	(K)	(L)	(M)	(N)		(P)	(Q)
Base - Use Online abstracts and indexes for coursework	481	0**	212	212	269	219	105*	157	69*	61*	162*	88*	15*	57*	5**	25*	213	268
Home (NET)	0 0	0 0	0 0	0 0	0 0	0 0	0 0	0 0	0 0	0 0	0 0	0 0	0 0	0 0	0 0	0 0	0 0	0 0
All sources of info	0 0	0 0	0 0	0 0	0 0	0 0	0 0	0 0	0 0	0 0	0 0	0 0	0 0	0 0	0 0	0 0	0 0	0 0
preferred source of info	0 0	0 0	0 0	0 0	0 0	0 0	0 0	0 0	0 0	0 0	0 0	0 0	0 0	0 0	0 0	0 0	0 0	0 0
In class (NET)	0 0	0 0	0 0	0 0	0 0	0 0	0 0	0 0	0 0	0 0	0 0	0 0	0 0	0 0	0 0	0 0	0 0	0 0
All sources of info	0 0	0 0	0 0	0 0	0 0	0 0	0 0	0 0	0 0	0 0	0 0	0 0	0 0	0 0	0 0	0 0	0 0	0 0
preferred source of info	0 0	0 0	0 0	0 0	0 0	0 0	0 0	0 0	0 0	0 0	0 0	0 0	0 0	0 0	0 0	0 0	0 0	0 0
Dorm room (NET)	0 0	0 0	0 0	0 0	0 0	0 0	0 0	0 0	0 0	0 0	0 0	0 0	0 0	0 0	0 0	0 0	0 0	0 0
All sources of info	0 0	0 0	0 0	0 0	0 0	0 0	0 0	0 0	0 0	0 0	0 0	0 0	0 0	0 0	0 0	0 0	0 0	0 0
preferred source of info	0 0	0 0	0 0	0 0	0 0	0 0	0 0	0 0	0 0	0 0	0 0	0 0	0 0	0 0	0 0	0 0	0 0	0 0

Proportions/Means: Columns Tested (5% risk level) - A/B/D - C/D - E/F/G - H/I/J/K/L/M/N - P/Q
* small base; ** very small base (under 30) ineligible for sig testing

TABLE 140, continued

S7D/E_8. Online abstracts and indexes SUMMARY TABLE

		RESPONDENT TYPE				INSTITUTION TYPE			DISCIPLINE									GENDER	
	TOTAL SAMPLE	FACULTY MEMBER	GRAD. STUDENT	FACULTY /GRAD	UNDER GRAD. STUDENT	PUBLIC	PRIVATE	LIBERAL ARTS	BIOLOGIAL SCIENCES	PHYSICAL SCIENCES /MATH	SOCIAL SCIENCES	ARTS AND HUMAN.	ENGI- NEERING	BUSINESS	LAW	UNDEC. MAJOR	MALE	FEMALE
		(A)	(B)	(C)	(D)	(E)	(F)	(G)	(H)	(I)	(J)	(K)	(L)	(M)	(N)		(P)	(Q)
Base - Use Online abstracts and indexes for coursework	481	0**	212	212	269	219	105*	157	69*	61*	162*	88*	15*	57*	5**	25*	213	268
Access book/journal/ journal article elsewhere online (NET)	0 0	0 0	0 0	0 0	0 0	0 0	0 0	0 0	0 0	0 0	0 0	0 0	0 0	0 0	0 0	0 0	0 0	0 0
All sources of info	0 0	0 0	0 0	0 0	0 0	0 0	0 0	0 0	0 0	0 0	0 0	0 0	0 0	0 0	0 0	0 0	0 0	0 0
preferred source of info	0 0	0 0	0 0	0 0	0 0	0 0	0 0	0 0	0 0	0 0	0 0	0 0	0 0	0 0	0 0	0 0	0 0	0 0
Other (NET)	12 2.6%	0 0	8 3.6%	8 3.6%	5 1.7%	7 3.1%	3 2.8%	3 1.8%	6 9.0%JK	3 4.9%J	0 0	1 1.3%	0 0	1 1.6%	* 3.7%	1 4.0%	5 2.3%	7 2.8%
All sources of info	11 2.4%	0 0	8 3.6%	8 3.6%	4 1.4%	6 2.6%	3 2.8%	3 1.8%	6 9.0%JK	3 4.9%J	0 0	1 1.3%	0 0	1 1.6%	* 3.7%	0 0	4 1.8%	7 2.8%
preferred source of info	7 1.5%	0 0	6 2.8%D	6 2.8%D	1 0.4%	5 2.2%	2 2.0%	0 0	2 2.6%	2 3.3%J	0 0	1 1.3%	0 0	1 1.6%	* 3.7%	1 4.0%	4 1.9%	3 1.1%
DK/Refused	10 2.1%	0 0	2 1.0%	2 1.0%	8 3.0%	4 1.9%	2 1.8%	4 2.6%	2 2.6%	2 3.3%J	0 0	3 3.8%J	0 0	1 1.6%	* 3.7%	2 8.0%	3 1.5%	7 2.6%

Proportions/Means: Columns Tested (5% risk level) - A/B/D - C/D - E/F/G - H/I/J/K/L/M/N - P/Q
* small base; ** very small base (under 30) ineligible for sig testing

Table 373
Page 1571

Outsell/Digital Library Federation Study (2002)
Weighted Tables

TABLE 141

S7sum_9. Online databases, data sets or data sources SUMMARY TABLE

		RESPONDENT TYPE				INSTITUTION TYPE			DISCIPLINE								GENDER	
	TOTAL SAMPLE	FACULTY MEMBER	GRAD. STUDENT	FACULTY /GRAD	UNDER GRAD. STUDENT	PUBLIC	PRIVATE	LIBERAL ARTS	BIOLOGIAL SCIENCES	PHYSICAL SCIENCES /MATH	SOCIAL SCIENCES	ARTS AND HUMAN.	ENGI- NEERING	BUSINESS	LAW	UNDEC. MAJOR	MALE	FEMALE
		(A)	(B)	(C)	(D)	(E)	(F)	(G)	(H)	(I)	(J)	(K)	(L)	(M)	(N)		(P)	(Q)
Base - Use Online databases, data sets or data sources for coursework	565	0**	236	236	329	254	142	169	87*	61*	175*	109*	21*	68*	9*	35*	262	303
ONLINE	457 80.9%	0 0	194 82.6%	194 82.6%	263 79.8%	198 77.9%	121 85.5%	138 81.7%	72 82.8%	52 85.2%	137 78.5%	91 83.5%	17 78.1%	54 79.5%	9 92.7%JL	26 74.3%	207 79.1%	250 82.5%
Search engine (NET)	157 27.8%	0 0	40 16.8%	40 16.8%	117 35.6%B C	48 19.0%	35 24.4%	74 43.7%EF	18 20.2%	16 26.2%	41 23.7%	32 29.9%	5 23.3%	26 38.4%HJ N	2 16.4%	17 48.6%	84 32.1%	73 24.0%
All sources of info	157 27.8%	0 0	40 16.8%	40 16.8%	117 35.6%B C	48 19.0%	35 24.4%	74 43.7%EF	18 20.2%	16 26.2%	41 23.7%	32 29.9%	5 23.3%	26 38.4%HJ N	2 16.4%	17 48.6%	84 32.1%	73 24.0%
preferred source of info	103 18.3%	0 0	23 9.8%	23 9.8%	80 24.3%B C	36 14.3%	23 16.4%	44 25.9%E	16 18.2%	8 13.1%	28 16.1%	20 18.6%	3 16.4%	17 24.7%N	1 9.1%	10 28.6%	48 18.2%	55 18.3%
Your own institution's web site (NET)	105 18.7%	0 0	45 18.9%	45 18.9%	61 18.5%	47 18.4%	28 20.0%	30 17.8%	8 9.1%	15 24.6%H	39 22.6%H	22 20.6%H	3 16.4%	12 17.8%	1 10.9%	4 11.4%	46 17.4%	60 19.7%
All sources of info	105 18.7%	0 0	45 18.9%	45 18.9%	61 18.5%	47 18.4%	28 20.0%	30 17.8%	8 9.1%	15 24.6%H	39 22.6%H	22 20.6%H	3 16.4%	12 17.8%	1 10.9%	4 11.4%	46 17.4%	60 19.7%
preferred source of info	88 15.5%	0 0	34 14.3%	34 14.3%	54 16.4%	43 17.1%	20 14.3%	24 14.3%	6 7.1%	13 21.3%H	34 19.4%H	19 17.5%H	3 12.3%	9 13.7%	1 9.1%	3 8.6%	39 14.9%	49 16.1%
Internet searches (NET)	84 14.9%	0 0	32 13.4%	32 13.4%	53 16.0%	44 17.5%	18 12.6%	22 12.9%	19 22.2%IN	3 4.9%	24 14.0%	15 13.4%	5 21.9%IN	15 21.9%IN	* 3.6%	3 8.6%	30 11.6%	54 17.8%

Proportions/Means: Columns Tested (5% risk level) - A/B/D - C/D - E/F/G - H/I/J/K/L/M/N - P/Q
* small base; ** very small base (under 30) ineligible for sig testing

Table 377
Page 1583

Outsell/Digital Library Federation Study (2002)
Weighted Tables

TABLE 141, continued

S7sum_9. Online databases, data sets or data sources SUMMARY TABLE

		RESPONDENT TYPE				INSTITUTION TYPE			DISCIPLINE								GENDER	
	TOTAL SAMPLE	FACULTY MEMBER	GRAD. STUDENT	FACULTY /GRAD	UNDER GRAD. STUDENT	PUBLIC	PRIVATE	LIBERAL ARTS	BIOLOGIAL SCIENCES	PHYSICAL SCIENCES /MATH	SOCIAL SCIENCES	ARTS AND HUMAN.	ENGI- NEERING	BUSINESS	LAW	UNDEC. MAJOR	MALE	FEMALE
		(A)	(B)	(C)	(D)	(E)	(F)	(G)	(H)	(I)	(J)	(K)	(L)	(M)	(N)		(P)	(Q)
Base - Use Online databases, data sets or data sources for coursework	565	0**	236	236	329	254	142	169	87*	61*	175*	109*	21*	68*	9*	35*	262	303
All sources of info	84 14.9%	0 0	32 13.4%	32 13.4%	53 16.0%	44 17.5%	18 12.6%	22 12.9%	19 22.2%IN	3 4.9%	24 14.0%	15 13.4%	5 21.9%IN	15 21.9%IN	* 3.6%	3 8.6%	30 11.6%	54 17.8%
preferred source of info	55 9.7%	0 0	22 9.5%	22 9.5%	32 9.8%	34 13.5%G	10 7.2%	10 6.0%	16 18.2%IJN	2 3.3%	13 7.5%	10 9.3%	3 15.1%IN	9 13.7%IN	* 1.8%	1 2.9%	23 8.7%	32 10.6%
Online library catalogues and finding aids (NET)	79 14.0%	0 0	43 18.4%D	43 18.4%D	36 10.8%	38 14.9%	19 13.1%	23 13.4%	13 15.2%	8 13.1%	26 15.1%	18 16.5%	1 6.8%	7 9.6%	1 7.3%	5 14.3%	30 11.4%	49 16.2%
All sources of info	79 14.0%	0 0	43 18.4%D	43 18.4%D	36 10.8%	38 14.9%	19 13.1%	23 13.4%	13 15.2%	8 13.1%	26 15.1%	18 16.5%	1 6.8%	7 9.6%	1 7.3%	5 14.3%	30 11.4%	49 16.2%
preferred source of info	58 10.3%	0 0	33 14.1%D	33 14.1%D	25 7.6%	30 12.0%	12 8.3%	16 9.5%	11 12.1%	6 9.8%	23 12.9%	11 10.3%	1 4.1%	4 5.5%	* 3.6%	3 8.6%	18 6.9%	40 13.2%P
Online databases (NET)	76 13.4%	0 0	45 19.0%D	45 19.0%D	31 9.4%	19 7.3%	38 26.8%EG	19 11.3%	10 11.1%	12 19.7%	23 12.9%	17 15.5%	2 9.6%	7 11.0%	3 34.5%HJK LM	2 5.7%	38 14.5%	38 12.5%
All sources of info	76 13.4%	0 0	45 19.0%D	45 19.0%D	31 9.4%	19 7.3%	38 26.8%EG	19 11.3%	10 11.1%	12 19.7%	23 12.9%	17 15.5%	2 9.6%	7 11.0%	3 34.5%HJK LM	2 5.7%	38 14.5%	38 12.5%
preferred source of info	48 8.5%	0 0	29 12.3%D	29 12.3%D	19 5.8%	14 5.6%	25 17.8%EG	9 5.3%	8 9.1%	7 11.5%	15 8.6%	9 8.2%	1 4.1%	4 5.5%	3 29.1%HIJ KLM	2 5.7%	21 8.0%	27 9.0%

Proportions/Means: Columns Tested (5% risk level) - A/B/D - C/D - E/F/G - H/I/J/K/L/M/N - P/Q
* small base; ** very small base (under 30) ineligible for sig testing

Table 377
Page 1584

Outsell/Digital Library Federation Study (2002)
Weighted Tables

TABLE 141, continued

S7sum_9. Online databases, data sets or data sources SUMMARY TABLE

	TOTAL SAMPLE	RESPONDENT TYPE: FACULTY MEMBER	GRAD. STUDENT	FACULTY /GRAD	UNDER GRAD. STUDENT	INSTITUTION TYPE: PUBLIC	PRIVATE	LIBERAL ARTS	DISCIPLINE: BIOLOGIAL SCIENCES	PHYSICAL SCIENCES /MATH	SOCIAL SCIENCES	ARTS AND HUMAN.	ENGI-NEERING	BUSINESS	LAW	UNDEC. MAJOR	GENDER: MALE	FEMALE
		(A)	(B)	(C)	(D)	(E)	(F)	(G)	(H)	(I)	(J)	(K)	(L)	(M)	(N)		(P)	(Q)
Base - Use Online databases, data sets or data sources for coursework	565	0**	236	236	329	254	142	169	87*	61*	175*	109*	21*	68*	9*	35*	262	303
Web directory/ subject related web site (NET)	30 5.3%	0 0	17 7.2%	17 7.2%	13 3.9%	12 4.8%	8 6.0%	9 5.4%	6 7.1%	3 4.9%	8 4.3%	6 5.2%	2 8.2%	4 5.5%	2 21.8%HIJKL M	0 0	12 4.5%	18 5.9%
All sources of info	30 5.3%	0 0	17 7.2%	17 7.2%	13 3.9%	12 4.8%	8 6.0%	9 5.4%	6 7.1%	3 4.9%	8 4.3%	6 5.2%	2 8.2%	4 5.5%	2 21.8%HIJKL M	0 0	12 4.5%	18 5.9%
preferred source of info	24 4.2%	0 0	16 6.7%D	16 6.7%D	8 2.4%	11 4.2%	7 4.9%	6 3.6%	5 6.1%	2 3.3%	8 4.3%	4 4.1%	1 2.7%	2 2.7%	2 21.8%HIJKL M	0 0	10 3.8%	14 4.5%
Department web page (NET)	18 3.2%	0 0	8 3.4%	8 3.4%	10 3.0%	8 3.1%	5 3.6%	5 3.0%	4 4.0%K	8 13.1%HJKM	2 1.1%	0 0	1 6.8%JKM	0 0	* 1.8%KM	3 8.6%	9 3.5%	9 2.9%
All sources of info	18 3.2%	0 0	8 3.4%	8 3.4%	10 3.0%	8 3.1%	5 3.6%	5 3.0%	4 4.0%K	8 13.1%HJKM	2 1.1%	0 0	1 6.8%JKM	0 0	* 1.8%KM	3 8.6%	9 3.5%	9 2.9%
preferred source of info	15 2.6%	0 0	7 3.0%	7 3.0%	8 2.3%	7 2.6%	4 2.9%	4 2.4%	4 4.0%K	6 9.8%JKM	2 1.1%	0 0	1 5.5%JKM	0 0	* 1.8%KM	2 5.7%	6 2.3%	9 2.9%
Online reference service (NET)	13 2.4%	0 0	7 3.2%	7 3.2%	6 1.8%	5 1.9%	4 2.5%	5 2.9%	3 3.0%	1 1.6%	4 2.2%	2 2.1%	* 1.4%	2 2.7%	1 5.5%	1 2.9%	9 3.5%	4 1.4%
All sources of info	13 2.4%	0 0	7 3.2%	7 3.2%	6 1.8%	5 1.9%	4 2.5%	5 2.9%	3 3.0%	1 1.6%	4 2.2%	2 2.1%	* 1.4%	2 2.7%	1 5.5%	1 2.9%	9 3.5%	4 1.4%

Proportions/Means: Columns Tested (5% risk level) - A/B/D - C/D - E/F/G - H/I/J/K/L/M/N - P/Q
* small base; ** very small base (under 30) ineligible for sig testing

Table 377
Page 1585

Outsell/Digital Library Federation Study (2002)
Weighted Tables

TABLE 141, continued

S7sum_9. Online databases, data sets or data sources SUMMARY TABLE

	RESPONDENT TYPE					INSTITUTION TYPE			DISCIPLINE									GENDER	
	TOTAL SAMPLE	FACULTY MEMBER	GRAD. STUDENT	FACULTY /GRAD	UNDER GRAD. STUDENT	PUBLIC	PRIVATE	LIBERAL ARTS	BIOLOGIAL SCIENCES	PHYSICAL SCIENCES /MATH	SOCIAL SCIENCES	ARTS AND HUMAN.	ENGI- NEERING	BUSINESS	LAW	UNDEC. MAJOR	MALE	FEMALE
		(A)	(B)	(C)	(D)	(E)	(F)	(G)	(H)	(I)	(J)	(K)	(L)	(M)	(N)		(P)	(Q)
Base - Use Online databases, data sets or data sources for coursework	565	0**	236	236	329	254	142	169	87*	61*	175*	109*	21*	68*	9*	35*	262	303
preferred source of info	5 0.9%	0 0	3 1.4%	3 1.4%	2 0.6%	2 0.8%	2 1.5%	1 0.7%	3 3.0%J	0 0	0 0	1 1.0%	0 0	1 1.4%	1 5.5%IJKL	0 0	4 1.5%	1 0.4%
Your own personal electronic library/files (NET)	8 1.4%	0 0	6 2.5%	6 2.5%	2 0.6%	1 0.5%	5 3.4%E	2 1.1%	2 2.0%	2 3.3%	2 1.1%	0 0	* 1.4%	1 1.4%	0 0	1 2.9%	2 0.9%	6 1.8%
All sources of info	8 1.4%	0 0	6 2.5%	6 2.5%	2 0.6%	1 0.5%	5 3.4%E	2 1.1%	2 2.0%	2 3.3%	2 1.1%	0 0	* 1.4%	1 1.4%	0 0	1 2.9%	2 0.9%	6 1.8%
preferred source of info	4 0.7%	0 0	3 1.3%	3 1.3%	1 0.3%	1 0.5%	2 1.3%	1 0.6%	0 0	0 0	2 1.1%	0 0	* 1.4%	1 1.4%	0 0	1 2.9%	1 0.5%	3 0.9%
Online abstracting and indexing services (NET)	5 1.0%	0 0	3 1.3%	3 1.3%	2 0.7%	1 0.3%	3 2.2%	1 0.8%	2 2.0%	2 3.3%J	0 0	1 1.0%	1 2.7%JM	0 0	0 0	0 0	1 0.5%	4 1.4%
All sources of info	5 1.0%	0 0	3 1.3%	3 1.3%	2 0.7%	1 0.3%	3 2.2%	1 0.8%	2 2.0%	2 3.3%J	0 0	1 1.0%	1 2.7%JM	0 0	0 0	0 0	1 0.5%	4 1.4%
preferred source of info	2 0.4%	0 0	1 0.5%	1 0.5%	1 0.3%	1 0.3%	1 0.8%	0 0	2 2.0%	0 0	0 0	0 0	* 1.4%J	0 0	0 0	0 0	* 0.1%	2 0.6%
Online bookstore (NET)	2 0.4%	0 0	1 0.4%	1 0.4%	1 0.3%	2 0.8%	0 0	0 0	0 0	1 1.6%	0 0	1 1.0%	0 0	0 0	0 0	0 0	1 0.4%	1 0.3%

Proportions/Means: Columns Tested (5% risk level) - A/B/D - C/D - E/F/G - H/I/J/K/L/M/N - P/Q
* small base; ** very small base (under 30) ineligible for sig testing

Table 377
Page 1586

Outsell/Digital Library Federation Study (2002)
Weighted Tables

TABLE 141, continued

S7sum_9. Online databases, data sets or data sources SUMMARY TABLE

		RESPONDENT TYPE				INSTITUTION TYPE			DISCIPLINE									GENDER	
	TOTAL SAMPLE	FACULTY MEMBER	GRAD. STUDENT	FACULTY /GRAD	UNDER GRAD. STUDENT	PUBLIC	PRIVATE	LIBERAL ARTS	BIOLOGIAL SCIENCES	PHYSICAL SCIENCES /MATH	SOCIAL SCIENCES	ARTS AND HUMAN.	ENGI-NEERING	BUSINESS	LAW	UNDEC. MAJOR	MALE	FEMALE
		(A)	(B)	(C)	(D)	(E)	(F)	(G)	(H)	(I)	(J)	(K)	(L)	(M)	(N)		(P)	(Q)
Base - Use Online databases, data sets or data sources for coursework	565	0**	236	236	329	254	142	169	87*	61*	175*	109*	21*	68*	9*	35*	262	303
All sources of info	2 0.4%	0 0	1 0.4%	1 0.4%	1 0.3%	2 0.8%	0 0	0 0	0 0	1 1.6%	0 0	1 1.0%	0 0	0 0	0 0	0 0	1 0.4%	1 0.3%
preferred source of info	0 0	0 0	0 0	0 0	0 0	0 0	0 0	0 0	0 0	0 0	0 0	0 0	0 0	0 0	0 0	0 0	0 0	0 0
E-mail listservs (NET)	* 0.1%	0 0	0 0	0 0	* 0.1%	* 0.1%	0 0	0 0	0 0	0 0	0 0	0 0	* 1.4%J	0 0	0 0	0 0	* 0.1%	0 0
All sources of info	* 0.1%	0 0	0 0	0 0	* 0.1%	* 0.1%	0 0	0 0	0 0	0 0	0 0	0 0	* 1.4%J	0 0	0 0	0 0	* 0.1%	0 0
preferred source of info	* 0.1%	0 0	0 0	0 0	* 0.1%	* 0.1%	0 0	0 0	0 0	0 0	0 0	0 0	* 1.4%J	0 0	0 0	0 0	* 0.1%	0 0
PERSONAL ASSISTANCE	164 29.1%	0 0	59 25.2%	59 25.2%	105 31.8%	63 24.7%	39 27.2%	63 37.1%E	26 30.3%	20 32.8%	36 20.4%	37 34.0%J	7 31.5%	20 28.8%	3 30.9%	16 45.7%	84 31.9%	81 26.6%
A librarian in your institution (NET)	96 16.9%	0 0	27 11.6%	27 11.6%	68 20.7%B C	29 11.4%	20 14.2%	46 27.4%EF	13 15.2%	8 13.1%	19 10.8%	28 25.8%J	3 16.4%	12 17.8%	2 21.8%J	10 28.6%	50 19.0%	46 15.1%
All sources of info	96 16.9%	0 0	27 11.6%	27 11.6%	68 20.7%B C	29 11.4%	20 14.2%	46 27.4%EF	13 15.2%	8 13.1%	19 10.8%	28 25.8%J	3 16.4%	12 17.8%	2 21.8%J	10 28.6%	50 19.0%	46 15.1%

Proportions/Means: Columns Tested (5% risk level) - A/B/D - C/D - E/F/G - H/I/J/K/L/M/N - P/Q
* small base; ** very small base (under 30) ineligible for sig testing

Table 377
Page 1587

Outsell/Digital Library Federation Study (2002)
Weighted Tables

TABLE 141, continued

S7sum_9. Online databases, data sets or data sources SUMMARY TABLE

		RESPONDENT TYPE				INSTITUTION TYPE			DISCIPLINE									GENDER	
	TOTAL SAMPLE	FACULTY MEMBER	GRAD. STUDENT	FACULTY /GRAD	UNDER GRAD. STUDENT	PUBLIC	PRIVATE	LIBERAL ARTS	BIOLOGIAL SCIENCES	PHYSICAL SCIENCES /MATH	SOCIAL SCIENCES	ARTS AND HUMAN.	ENGI- NEERING	BUSINESS	LAW	UNDEC. MAJOR	MALE	FEMALE
		(A)	(B)	(C)	(D)	(E)	(F)	(G)	(H)	(I)	(J)	(K)	(L)	(M)	(N)		(P)	(Q)
Base - Use Online databases, data sets or data sources for coursework	565	0**	236	236	329	254	142	169	87*	61*	175*	109*	21*	68*	9*	35*	262	303
preferred source of info	39 6.9%	0 0	13 5.7%	13 5.7%	25 7.7%	17 6.7%	7 4.7%	15 9.0%	5 6.1%	3 4.9%	8 4.3%	13 12.4%JL	1 2.7%	7 11.0%	1 5.5%	1 2.9%	23 8.9%	15 5.1%
Faculty members inside your institution (NET)	93 16.4%	0 0	30 12.9%	30 12.9%	62 18.9%	34 13.4%	18 13.0%	40 23.8%EF	17 19.2%	14 23.0%J	17 9.7%	19 17.5%	4 19.2%	10 15.1%	1 9.1%	11 31.4%	48 18.4%	45 14.8%
All sources of info	93 16.4%	0 0	30 12.9%	30 12.9%	62 18.9%	34 13.4%	18 13.0%	40 23.8%EF	17 19.2%	14 23.0%J	17 9.7%	19 17.5%	4 19.2%	10 15.1%	1 9.1%	11 31.4%	48 18.4%	45 14.8%
preferred source of info	43 7.7%	0 0	16 6.7%	16 6.7%	28 8.4%	17 6.9%	9 6.2%	17 10.1%	3 3.0%	5 8.2%	13 7.5%	7 6.2%	2 9.6%H	7 11.0%H	* 3.6%	6 17.1%	21 8.1%	22 7.3%
Other students inside your institution (NET)	37 6.6%	0 0	16 6.8%	16 6.8%	21 6.4%	12 4.6%	11 7.8%	14 8.4%	7 8.1%	6 9.8%	8 4.3%	9 8.2%	1 4.1%	3 4.1%	1 9.1%	3 8.6%	18 6.7%	19 6.4%
All sources of info	37 6.6%	0 0	16 6.8%	16 6.8%	21 6.4%	12 4.6%	11 7.8%	14 8.4%	7 8.1%	6 9.8%	8 4.3%	9 8.2%	1 4.1%	3 4.1%	1 9.1%	3 8.6%	18 6.7%	19 6.4%
preferred source of info	8 1.4%	0 0	2 0.8%	2 0.8%	6 1.8%	3 1.1%	2 1.4%	3 1.8%	3 3.0%J	2 3.3%J	0 0	2 2.1%	0 0	0 0	0 0	1 2.9%	2 0.8%	6 1.9%
Other students outside your institution (NET)	3 0.5%	0 0	1 0.4%	1 0.4%	2 0.6%	2 0.7%	0 0	1 0.6%	1 1.0%	0 0	0 0	0 0	0 0	1 1.4%	0 0	1 2.9%	0 0	3 0.9%

Proportions/Means: Columns Tested (5% risk level) - A/B/D - C/D - E/F/G - H/I/J/K/L/M/N - P/Q
* small base; ** very small base (under 30) ineligible for sig testing

Table 377
Page 1588

Outsell/Digital Library Federation Study (2002)
Weighted Tables

TABLE 141, continued

S7sum_9. Online databases, data sets or data sources SUMMARY TABLE

		RESPONDENT TYPE				INSTITUTION TYPE			DISCIPLINE									GENDER	
	TOTAL SAMPLE	FACULTY MEMBER	GRAD. STUDENT	FACULTY /GRAD	UNDER GRAD. STUDENT	PUBLIC	PRIVATE	LIBERAL ARTS	BIOLOGIAL SCIENCES	PHYSICAL SCIENCES /MATH	SOCIAL SCIENCES	ARTS AND HUMAN.	ENGI- NEERING	BUSINESS	LAW	UNDEC. MAJOR	MALE	FEMALE
		(A)	(B)	(C)	(D)	(E)	(F)	(G)	(H)	(I)	(J)	(K)	(L)	(M)	(N)		(P)	(Q)
Base - Use Online databases, data sets or data sources for coursework	565	0**	236	236	329	254	142	169	87*	61*	175*	109*	21*	68*	9*	35*	262	303
All sources of info	3 0.5%	0 0	1 0.4%	1 0.4%	2 0.6%	2 0.7%	0 0	1 0.6%	1 1.0%	0 0	0 0	0 0	0 0	1 1.4%	0 0	1 2.9%	0 0	3 0.9%
preferred source of info	0 0	0 0	0 0	0 0	0 0	0 0	0 0	0 0	0 0	0 0	0 0	0 0	0 0	0 0	0 0	0 0	0 0	0 0
Another institution's librarian (NET)	0 0	0 0	0 0	0 0	0 0	0 0	0 0	0 0	0 0	0 0	0 0	0 0	0 0	0 0	0 0	0 0	0 0	0 0
All sources of info	0 0	0 0	0 0	0 0	0 0	0 0	0 0	0 0	0 0	0 0	0 0	0 0	0 0	0 0	0 0	0 0	0 0	0 0
preferred source of info	0 0	0 0	0 0	0 0	0 0	0 0	0 0	0 0	0 0	0 0	0 0	0 0	0 0	0 0	0 0	0 0	0 0	0 0
Faculty members outside your institution (NET)	0 0	0 0	0 0	0 0	0 0	0 0	0 0	0 0	0 0	0 0	0 0	0 0	0 0	0 0	0 0	0 0	0 0	0 0
All sources of info	0 0	0 0	0 0	0 0	0 0	0 0	0 0	0 0	0 0	0 0	0 0	0 0	0 0	0 0	0 0	0 0	0 0	0 0
preferred source of info	0 0	0 0	0 0	0 0	0 0	0 0	0 0	0 0	0 0	0 0	0 0	0 0	0 0	0 0	0 0	0 0	0 0	0 0
Professional meetings (NET)	0 0	0 0	0 0	0 0	0 0	0 0	0 0	0 0	0 0	0 0	0 0	0 0	0 0	0 0	0 0	0 0	0 0	0 0

Proportions/Means: Columns Tested (5% risk level) - A/B/D - C/D - E/F/G - H/I/J/K/L/M/N - P/Q
* small base; ** very small base (under 30) ineligible for sig testing

Table 377
Page 1589

Outsell/Digital Library Federation Study (2002)
Weighted Tables

TABLE 141, continued

S7sum_9. Online databases, data sets or data sources SUMMARY TABLE

		RESPONDENT TYPE				INSTITUTION TYPE			DISCIPLINE								GENDER	
	TOTAL SAMPLE	FACULTY MEMBER	GRAD. STUDENT	FACULTY /GRAD	UNDER GRAD. STUDENT	PUBLIC	PRIVATE	LIBERAL ARTS	BIOLOGIAL SCIENCES	PHYSICAL SCIENCES /MATH	SOCIAL SCIENCES	ARTS AND HUMAN.	ENGI-NEERING	BUSINESS	LAW	UNDEC. MAJOR	MALE	FEMALE
		(A)	(B)	(C)	(D)	(E)	(F)	(G)	(H)	(I)	(J)	(K)	(L)	(M)	(N)		(P)	(Q)
Base - Use Online databases, data sets or data sources for coursework	565	0**	236	236	329	254	142	169	87*	61*	175*	109*	21*	68*	9*	35*	262	303
All sources of info	0 0	0 0	0 0	0 0	0 0	0 0	0 0	0 0	0 0	0 0	0 0	0 0	0 0	0 0	0 0	0 0	0 0	0 0
preferred source of info	0 0	0 0	0 0	0 0	0 0	0 0	0 0	0 0	0 0	0 0	0 0	0 0	0 0	0 0	0 0	0 0	0 0	0 0
LIBRARY FACILITIES/ PRINT	111 19.6%	0 0	52 22.2%	52 22.2%	58 17.7%	40 16.0%	29 20.4%	41 24.3%	18 21.2%	11 18.0%	36 20.4%	20 18.6%	5 23.3%	9 13.7%	2 21.8%	9 25.7%	63 24.0%Q	48 15.8%
Campus library (NET)	100 17.7%	0 0	47 20.1%	47 20.1%	52 15.9%	34 13.5%	27 18.8%	39 22.9%E	16 18.2%	10 16.4%	34 19.4%	18 16.5%	4 17.8%	8 12.3%	2 21.8%	8 22.9%	56 21.3%	44 14.5%
All sources of info	100 17.7%	0 0	47 20.1%	47 20.1%	52 15.9%	34 13.5%	27 18.8%	39 22.9%E	16 18.2%	10 16.4%	34 19.4%	18 16.5%	4 17.8%	8 12.3%	2 21.8%	8 22.9%	56 21.3%	44 14.5%
preferred source of info	39 7.0%	0 0	20 8.3%	20 8.3%	20 6.0%	16 6.1%	11 7.4%	13 7.8%	4 4.0%	2 3.3%	15 8.6%	8 7.2%	2 11.0%H	4 5.5%	1 9.1%	4 11.4%	27 10.3%Q	12 4.0%
Another library (NET)	10 1.7%	0 0	3 1.2%	3 1.2%	7 2.1%	3 1.2%	3 1.9%	4 2.2%	2 2.0%	0 0	6 3.2%	0 0	* 1.4%	2 2.7%	0 0	0 0	8 2.9%	2 0.6%
All sources of info	10 1.7%	0 0	3 1.2%	3 1.2%	7 2.1%	3 1.2%	3 1.9%	4 2.2%	2 2.0%	0 0	6 3.2%	0 0	* 1.4%	2 2.7%	0 0	0 0	8 2.9%	2 0.6%
preferred source of info	0 0	0 0	0 0	0 0	0 0	0 0	0 0	0 0	0 0	0 0	0 0	0 0	0 0	0 0	0 0	0 0	0 0	0 0

Proportions/Means: Columns Tested (5% risk level) - A/B/D - C/D - E/F/G - H/I/J/K/L/M/N - P/Q
* small base; ** very small base (under 30) ineligible for sig testing

Table 377
Page 1590

Outsell/Digital Library Federation Study (2002)
Weighted Tables

TABLE 141, continued

S7sum_9. Online databases, data sets or data sources SUMMARY TABLE

		RESPONDENT TYPE				INSTITUTION TYPE			DISCIPLINE								GENDER	
	TOTAL SAMPLE	FACULTY MEMBER	GRAD. STUDENT	FACULTY /GRAD	UNDER GRAD. STUDENT	PUBLIC	PRIVATE	LIBERAL ARTS	BIOLOGIAL SCIENCES	PHYSICAL SCIENCES /MATH	SOCIAL SCIENCES	ARTS AND HUMAN.	ENGI-NEERING	BUSINESS	LAW	UNDEC. MAJOR	MALE	FEMALE
		(A)	(B)	(C)	(D)	(E)	(F)	(G)	(H)	(I)	(J)	(K)	(L)	(M)	(N)		(P)	(Q)
Base - Use Online databases, data sets or data sources for coursework	565	0**	236	236	329	254	142	169	87*	61*	175*	109*	21*	68*	9*	35*	262	303
Your own personal physical library/ files/bookshelves (NET)	5 0.9%	0 0	2 0.8%	2 0.8%	3 1.0%	2 0.7%	2 1.3%	1 0.8%	2 2.0%	2 3.3%J	0 0	1 1.0%	* 1.4%J	0 0	0 0	0 0	3 1.3%	2 0.6%
All sources of info	5 0.9%	0 0	2 0.8%	2 0.8%	3 1.0%	2 0.7%	2 1.3%	1 0.8%	2 2.0%	2 3.3%J	0 0	1 1.0%	* 1.4%J	0 0	0 0	0 0	3 1.3%	2 0.6%
preferred source of info	2 0.4%	0 0	1 0.4%	1 0.4%	1 0.4%	1 0.3%	1 0.7%	* 0.2%	1 1.0%	1 1.6%	0 0	0 0	* 1.4%J	0 0	0 0	0 0	2 0.8%	0 0
References cited in books or journal articles (NET)	5 0.8%	0 0	3 1.1%	3 1.1%	2 0.6%	0 0	3 1.8%	2 1.3%	0 0	0 0	0 0	2 2.1%	* 1.4%J	1 1.4%	* 1.8%HIJ	1 2.9%	2 0.9%	2 0.7%
All sources of info	5 0.8%	0 0	3 1.1%	3 1.1%	2 0.6%	0 0	3 1.8%	2 1.3%	0 0	0 0	0 0	2 2.1%	* 1.4%J	1 1.4%	* 1.8%HIJ	1 2.9%	2 0.9%	2 0.7%
preferred source of info	1 0.2%	0 0	* 0.1%	* 0.1%	1 0.3%	0 0	* 0.2%	1 0.6%	0 0	0 0	0 0	0 0	* 1.4%J	0 0	0 0	1 2.9%	1 0.5%	0 0
Printed abstracting and indexing services (NET)	3 0.5%	0 0	2 0.8%	2 0.8%	1 0.3%	2 0.7%	0 0	1 0.5%	1 1.0%	0 0	2 1.1%	0 0	0 0	0 0	0 0	0 0	0 0	3 0.9%

Proportions/Means: Columns Tested (5% risk level) - A/B/D - C/D - E/F/G - H/I/J/K/L/M/N - P/Q
* small base; ** very small base (under 30) ineligible for sig testing

Table 377
Page 1591

Outsell/Digital Library Federation Study (2002)
Weighted Tables

TABLE 141, continued

S7sum_9. Online databases, data sets or data sources SUMMARY TABLE

		RESPONDENT TYPE				INSTITUTION TYPE			DISCIPLINE									GENDER	
	TOTAL SAMPLE	FACULTY MEMBER	GRAD. STUDENT	FACULTY /GRAD	UNDER GRAD. STUDENT	PUBLIC	PRIVATE	LIBERAL ARTS	BIOLOGIAL SCIENCES	PHYSICAL SCIENCES /MATH	SOCIAL SCIENCES	ARTS AND HUMAN.	ENGI- NEERING	BUSINESS	LAW	UNDEC. MAJOR	MALE	FEMALE
		(A)	(B)	(C)	(D)	(E)	(F)	(G)	(H)	(I)	(J)	(K)	(L)	(M)	(N)		(P)	(Q)
Base - Use Online databases, data sets or data sources for coursework	565	0**	236	236	329	254	142	169	87*	61*	175*	109*	21*	68*	9*	35*	262	303
All sources of info	3 0.5%	0 0	2 0.8%	2 0.8%	1 0.3%	2 0.7%	0 0	1 0.5%	1 1.0%	0 0	2 1.1%	0 0	0 0	0 0	0 0	0 0	0 0	3 0.9%
preferred source of info	0 0	0 0	0 0	0 0	0 0	0 0	0 0	0 0	0 0	0 0	0 0	0 0	0 0	0 0	0 0	0 0	0 0	0 0
Printed library catalogues and finding aids (NET)	2 0.3%	0 0	0 0	0 0	2 0.6%	0 0	0 0	2 1.1%	0 0	0 0	2 1.1%	0 0	0 0	0 0	0 0	0 0	2 0.7%	0 0
All sources of info	2 0.3%	0 0	0 0	0 0	2 0.6%	0 0	0 0	2 1.1%	0 0	0 0	2 1.1%	0 0	0 0	0 0	0 0	0 0	2 0.7%	0 0
preferred source of info	0 0	0 0	0 0	0 0	0 0	0 0	0 0	0 0	0 0	0 0	0 0	0 0	0 0	0 0	0 0	0 0	0 0	0 0
Physical bookstore (NET)	2 0.3%	0 0	1 0.4%	1 0.4%	1 0.2%	2 0.6%	0 0	0 0	0 0	0 0	0 0	0 0	1 2.7%HJK	1 1.4%	0 0	0 0	2 0.6%	0 0
All sources of info	2 0.3%	0 0	1 0.4%	1 0.4%	1 0.2%	2 0.6%	0 0	0 0	0 0	0 0	0 0	0 0	1 2.7%HJK	1 1.4%	0 0	0 0	2 0.6%	0 0
preferred source of info	1 0.2%	0 0	1 0.4%	1 0.4%	* 0.1%	1 0.5%	0 0	0 0	0 0	0 0	0 0	0 0	* 1.4%J	1 1.4%	0 0	0 0	1 0.5%	0 0

Proportions/Means: Columns Tested (5% risk level) - A/B/D - C/D - E/F/G - H/I/J/K/L/M/N - P/Q
* small base; ** very small base (under 30) ineligible for sig testing

Table 377
Page 1592

Outsell/Digital Library Federation Study (2002)
Weighted Tables

TABLE 141, continued

S7sum_9. Online databases, data sets or data sources SUMMARY TABLE

		RESPONDENT TYPE				INSTITUTION TYPE			DISCIPLINE								GENDER	
	TOTAL SAMPLE	FACULTY MEMBER	GRAD. STUDENT	FACULTY /GRAD	UNDER GRAD. STUDENT	PUBLIC	PRIVATE	LIBERAL ARTS	BIOLOGIAL SCIENCES	PHYSICAL SCIENCES /MATH	SOCIAL SCIENCES	ARTS AND HUMAN.	ENGI-NEERING	BUSINESS	LAW	UNDEC. MAJOR	MALE	FEMALE
		(A)	(B)	(C)	(D)	(E)	(F)	(G)	(H)	(I)	(J)	(K)	(L)	(M)	(N)		(P)	(Q)
Base - Use Online databases, data sets or data sources for coursework	565	0**	236	236	329	254	142	169	87*	61*	175*	109*	21*	68*	9*	35*	262	303
Personal subscriptions to newspapers, magazines and journals (NET)	1 0.2%	0 0	0 0	0 0	1 0.3%	1 0.3%	0 0	0 0	1 1.0%	0 0	0 0	0 0	0 0	0 0	0 0	0 0	1 0.3%	0 0
All sources of info	1 0.2%	0 0	0 0	0 0	1 0.3%	1 0.3%	0 0	0 0	1 1.0%	0 0	0 0	0 0	0 0	0 0	0 0	0 0	1 0.3%	0 0
preferred source of info	0 0	0 0	0 0	0 0	0 0	0 0	0 0	0 0	0 0	0 0	0 0	0 0	0 0	0 0	0 0	0 0	0 0	0 0
Other (NET)	14 2.5%	0 0	3 1.3%	3 1.3%	11 3.3%	7 2.7%	2 1.4%	5 3.1%	2 2.0%	0 0	2 1.1%	2 2.1%	2 8.2%HIJK	3 4.1%	1 5.5%IJ	3 8.6%	11 4.1%Q	3 1.1%
All sources of info	14 2.4%	0 0	3 1.3%	3 1.3%	11 3.2%	6 2.5%	2 1.4%	5 3.1%	2 2.0%	0 0	2 1.1%	2 2.1%	1 6.8%IJ	3 4.1%	1 5.5%IJ	3 8.6%	11 4.1%Q	3 1.0%
preferred source of info	5 0.9%	0 0	1 0.4%	1 0.4%	4 1.3%	4 1.7%	0 0	1 0.7%	0 0	0 0	2 1.1%	2 2.1%	* 1.4%	1 1.4%	0 0	0 0	5 1.9%Q	* 0.1%
Online (unspecified)	7 1.2%	0 0	3 1.2%	3 1.2%	4 1.1%	6 2.5%	* 0.2%	0 0	1 1.0%	1 1.6%	4 2.2%	0 0	1 4.1%KM	0 0	0 0	0 0	* 0.1%	6 2.1%
All sources of info	7 1.2%	0 0	3 1.2%	3 1.2%	4 1.1%	6 2.5%	* 0.2%	0 0	1 1.0%	1 1.6%	4 2.2%	0 0	1 4.1%KM	0 0	0 0	0 0	* 0.1%	6 2.1%

Proportions/Means: Columns Tested (5% risk level) - A/B/D - C/D - E/F/G - H/I/J/K/L/M/N - P/Q
* small base; ** very small base (under 30) ineligible for sig testing

Table 377
Page 1593

Outsell/Digital Library Federation Study (2002)
Weighted Tables

TABLE 141, continued

S7sum_9. Online databases, data sets or data sources SUMMARY TABLE

	RESPONDENT TYPE					INSTITUTION TYPE			DISCIPLINE								GENDER	
	TOTAL SAMPLE	FACULTY MEMBER	GRAD. STUDENT	FACULTY /GRAD	UNDER GRAD. STUDENT	PUBLIC	PRIVATE	LIBERAL ARTS	BIOLOGIAL SCIENCES	PHYSICAL SCIENCES /MATH	SOCIAL SCIENCES	ARTS AND HUMAN.	ENGI- NEERING	BUSINESS	LAW	UNDEC. MAJOR	MALE	FEMALE
		(A)	(B)	(C)	(D)	(E)	(F)	(G)	(H)	(I)	(J)	(K)	(L)	(M)	(N)		(P)	(Q)
Base - Use Online databases, data sets or data sources for coursework	565	0**	236	236	329	254	142	169	87*	61*	175*	109*	21*	68*	9*	35*	262	303
preferred source of info	6 1.0%	0 0	3 1.2%	3 1.2%	3 0.9%	6 2.3%	0 0	0 0	1 1.0%	1 1.6%	4 2.2%	0 0	* 1.4%	0 0	0 0	0 0	* 0.1%	6 1.9%
E-journals	2 0.4%	0 0	2 0.8%	2 0.8%	0 0	1 0.4%	1 0.7%	0 0	0 0	2 3.3%J	0 0	0 0	0 0	0 0	0 0	0 0	1 0.4%	1 0.3%
All sources of info	2 0.4%	0 0	2 0.8%	2 0.8%	0 0	1 0.4%	1 0.7%	0 0	0 0	2 3.3%J	0 0	0 0	0 0	0 0	0 0	0 0	1 0.4%	1 0.3%
preferred source of info	0 0	0 0	0 0	0 0	0 0	0 0	0 0	0 0	0 0	0 0	0 0	0 0	0 0	0 0	0 0	0 0	0 0	0 0
DK/Refused	17 3.1%	0 0	7 3.2%	7 3.2%	10 3.0%	10 3.8%	4 2.6%	4 2.4%	3 3.0%	3 4.9%	8 4.3%	1 1.0%	1 5.5%K	1 1.4%	0 0	1 2.9%	6 2.3%	11 3.7%

Proportions/Means: Columns Tested (5% risk level) - A/B/D - C/D - E/F/G - H/I/J/K/L/M/N - P/Q
* small base; ** very small base (under 30) ineligible for sig testing

Table 377
Page 1594

Outsell/Digital Library Federation Study (2002)
Weighted Tables

TABLE 142

S7D/E_9. Online databases, data sets or data sources SUMMARY TABLE

		RESPONDENT TYPE				INSTITUTION TYPE			DISCIPLINE								GENDER	
	TOTAL SAMPLE	FACULTY MEMBER	GRAD. STUDENT	FACULTY /GRAD	UNDER GRAD. STUDENT	PUBLIC	PRIVATE	LIBERAL ARTS	BIOLOGIAL SCIENCES	PHYSICAL SCIENCES /MATH	SOCIAL SCIENCES	ARTS AND HUMAN.	ENGI-NEERING	BUSINESS	LAW	UNDEC. MAJOR	MALE	FEMALE
		(A)	(B)	(C)	(D)	(E)	(F)	(G)	(H)	(I)	(J)	(K)	(L)	(M)	(N)		(P)	(Q)
Base - Use Online databases, data sets or data sources for coursework	565	0**	236	236	329	254	142	169	87*	61*	175*	109*	21*	68*	9*	35*	262	303
Access online (NET)	416	0	177	177	239	168	112	137	62	46	126	77	16	53	8	28	190	227
	73.7%	0	75.3%	75.3%	72.5%	66.1%	78.9%E	80.6%E	71.7%	75.4%	72.0%	71.1%	74.0%	78.1%	83.6%	80.0%	72.3%	74.9%
All sources of info	416	0	177	177	239	168	112	137	62	46	126	77	16	53	8	28	190	227
	73.7%	0	75.3%	75.3%	72.5%	66.1%	78.9%E	80.6%E	71.7%	75.4%	72.0%	71.1%	74.0%	78.1%	83.6%	80.0%	72.3%	74.9%
preferred source of info	364	0	162	162	203	148	99	117	55	41	109	66	13	48	7	24	162	203
	64.5%	0	68.7%	68.7%	61.5%	58.3%	70.1%E	69.1%E	63.6%	67.2%	62.4%	60.8%	63.0%	71.2%	76.4%	68.6%	61.6%	67.0%
Borrow from or use in campus library (NET)	228	0	87	87	141	108	54	67	33	21	75	53	9	20	3	14	112	116
	40.4%	0	37.0%	37.0%	42.9%	42.5%	38.0%	39.4%	38.4%	34.4%	43.0%	48.5%MN	42.5%	30.1%	29.1%	40.0%	42.8%	38.4%
All sources of info	228	0	87	87	141	108	54	67	33	21	75	53	9	20	3	14	112	116
	40.4%	0	37.0%	37.0%	42.9%	42.5%	38.0%	39.4%	38.4%	34.4%	43.0%	48.5%MN	42.5%	30.1%	29.1%	40.0%	42.8%	38.4%
preferred source of info	153	0	55	55	98	75	34	44	26	13	51	36	5	12	2	9	82	71
	27.1%	0	23.4%	23.4%	29.7%	29.4%	24.0%	26.2%	29.3%	21.3%	29.0%	33.0%M	23.3%	17.8%	20.0%	25.7%	31.1%	23.6%
Faculty (NET)	9	0	4	4	5	6	1	2	1	1	4	1	1	1	0	1	4	5
	1.6%	0	1.7%	1.7%	1.6%	2.5%	0.6%	1.3%	1.0%	1.6%	2.2%	1.0%	2.7%	1.4%	0	2.9%	1.5%	1.8%
All sources of info	9	0	4	4	5	6	1	2	1	1	4	1	1	1	0	1	4	5
	1.6%	0	1.7%	1.7%	1.6%	2.5%	0.6%	1.3%	1.0%	1.6%	2.2%	1.0%	2.7%	1.4%	0	2.9%	1.5%	1.8%
preferred source of info	8	0	3	3	5	6	0	2	0	1	4	1	*	1	0	1	4	4
	1.4%	0	1.2%	1.2%	1.6%	2.4%	0	1.3%	0	1.6%	2.2%	1.0%	1.4%	1.4%	0	2.9%	1.5%	1.4%

Proportions/Means: Columns Tested (5% risk level) - A/B/D - C/D - E/F/G - H/I/J/K/L/M/N - P/Q
* small base; ** very small base (under 30) ineligible for sig testing

Table 380
Page 1601

Outsell/Digital Library Federation Study (2002)
Weighted Tables

TABLE 142, continued

S7D/E_9. Online databases, data sets or data sources SUMMARY TABLE

		RESPONDENT TYPE				INSTITUTION TYPE			DISCIPLINE								GENDER	
	TOTAL SAMPLE	FACULTY MEMBER	GRAD. STUDENT	FACULTY /GRAD	UNDER GRAD. STUDENT	PUBLIC	PRIVATE	LIBERAL ARTS	BIOLOGIAL SCIENCES	PHYSICAL SCIENCES /MATH	SOCIAL SCIENCES	ARTS AND HUMAN.	ENGI-NEERING	BUSINESS	LAW	UNDEC. MAJOR	MALE	FEMALE
		(A)	(B)	(C)	(D)	(E)	(F)	(G)	(H)	(I)	(J)	(K)	(L)	(M)	(N)		(P)	(Q)
Base - Use Online databases, data sets or data sources for coursework	565	0**	236	236	329	254	142	169	87*	61*	175*	109*	21*	68*	9*	35*	262	303
Interlibrary loan (NET)	8 1.4%	0 0	3 1.2%	3 1.2%	5 1.6%	3 1.2%	0 0	5 3.1%	1 1.0%	0 0	4 2.2%	1 1.0%	0 0	0 0	* 3.6%IM	2 5.7%	3 1.2%	5 1.7%
All sources of info	8 1.4%	0 0	3 1.2%	3 1.2%	5 1.6%	3 1.2%	0 0	5 3.1%	1 1.0%	0 0	4 2.2%	1 1.0%	0 0	0 0	* 3.6%IM	2 5.7%	3 1.2%	5 1.7%
preferred source of info	1 0.2%	0 0	1 0.4%	1 0.4%	0 0	1 0.4%	0 0	0 0	1 1.0%	0 0	0 0	0 0	0 0	0 0	* 1.8%IJKM	0 0	* 0.1%	1 0.3%
Borrow from or use in other libraries (NET)	7 1.3%	0 0	1 0.4%	1 0.4%	7 2.0%	7 2.6%	1 0.6%	0 0	2 2.0%	0 0	4 2.2%	0 0	0 0	2 2.7%	0 0	0 0	2 0.7%	6 1.8%
All sources of info	7 1.3%	0 0	1 0.4%	1 0.4%	7 2.0%	7 2.6%	1 0.6%	0 0	2 2.0%	0 0	4 2.2%	0 0	0 0	2 2.7%	0 0	0 0	2 0.7%	6 1.8%
preferred source of info	3 0.5%	0 0	1 0.4%	1 0.4%	2 0.6%	2 0.7%	1 0.6%	0 0	1 1.0%	0 0	2 1.1%	0 0	0 0	0 0	0 0	0 0	0 0	3 0.9%
Home (NET)	6 1.1%	0 0	2 0.9%	2 0.9%	4 1.2%	6 2.2%	0 0	* 0.2%	2 2.0%	0 0	2 1.1%	1 1.0%	* 1.4%	1 1.4%	0 0	0 0	3 1.1%	3 1.0%
All sources of info	6 1.1%	0 0	2 0.9%	2 0.9%	4 1.2%	6 2.2%	0 0	* 0.2%	2 2.0%	0 0	2 1.1%	1 1.0%	* 1.4%	1 1.4%	0 0	0 0	3 1.1%	3 1.0%
preferred source of info	5 0.9%	0 0	2 0.9%	2 0.9%	3 0.9%	5 1.9%	0 0	* 0.2%	1 1.0%	0 0	2 1.1%	1 1.0%	* 1.4%	1 1.4%	0 0	0 0	2 0.8%	3 1.0%

Proportions/Means: Columns Tested (5% risk level) - A/B/D - C/D - E/F/G - H/I/J/K/L/M/N - P/Q
* small base; ** very small base (under 30) ineligible for sig testing

Table 380
Page 1602

Outsell/Digital Library Federation Study (2002)
Weighted Tables

TABLE 142, continued

S7D/E_9. Online databases, data sets or data sources SUMMARY TABLE

		RESPONDENT TYPE				INSTITUTION TYPE			DISCIPLINE								GENDER	
	TOTAL SAMPLE	FACULTY MEMBER	GRAD. STUDENT	FACULTY /GRAD	UNDER GRAD. STUDENT	PUBLIC	PRIVATE	LIBERAL ARTS	BIOLOGIAL SCIENCES	PHYSICAL SCIENCES /MATH	SOCIAL SCIENCES	ARTS AND HUMAN.	ENGI- NEERING	BUSINESS	LAW	UNDEC. MAJOR	MALE	FEMALE
		(A)	(B)	(C)	(D)	(E)	(F)	(G)	(H)	(I)	(J)	(K)	(L)	(M)	(N)		(P)	(Q)
Base - Use Online databases, data sets or data sources for coursework	565	0**	236	236	329	254	142	169	87*	61*	175*	109*	21*	68*	9*	35*	262	303
Personal Holdings (NET)	5 0.9%	0 0	3 1.4%	3 1.4%	2 0.6%	4 1.6%	1 0.9%	0 0	1 1.0%	1 1.6%	2 1.1%	1 1.0%	* 1.4%	0 0	* 1.8%M	0 0	3 1.3%	2 0.7%
All sources of info	5 0.9%	0 0	3 1.4%	3 1.4%	2 0.6%	4 1.6%	1 0.9%	0 0	1 1.0%	1 1.6%	2 1.1%	1 1.0%	* 1.4%	0 0	* 1.8%M	0 0	3 1.3%	2 0.7%
preferred source of info	3 0.6%	0 0	3 1.4%	3 1.4%	0 0	2 0.8%	1 0.9%	0 0	0 0	1 1.6%	2 1.1%	0 0	* 1.4%	0 0	* 1.8%HKM	0 0	1 0.5%	2 0.7%
Purchase from physical book store (NET)	4 0.7%	0 0	2 0.8%	2 0.8%	2 0.6%	1 0.4%	3 2.0%	* 0.2%	2 2.0%	0 0	0 0	0 0	* 1.4%J	2 2.7%J	* 1.8%IJK	0 0	2 0.8%	2 0.6%
All sources of info	4 0.7%	0 0	2 0.8%	2 0.8%	2 0.6%	1 0.4%	3 2.0%	* 0.2%	2 2.0%	0 0	0 0	0 0	* 1.4%J	2 2.7%J	* 1.8%IJK	0 0	2 0.8%	2 0.6%
preferred source of info	3 0.5%	0 0	1 0.4%	1 0.4%	2 0.6%	1 0.4%	2 1.2%	* 0.2%	2 2.0%	0 0	0 0	0 0	* 1.4%J	1 1.4%	0 0	0 0	1 0.5%	2 0.6%
Colleagues (NET)	3 0.5%	0 0	1 0.5%	1 0.5%	2 0.6%	1 0.4%	0 0	2 1.1%	1 1.0%	0 0	0 0	1 1.0%	0 0	0 0	0 0	1 2.9%	1 0.3%	2 0.7%
All sources of info	3 0.5%	0 0	1 0.5%	1 0.5%	2 0.6%	1 0.4%	0 0	2 1.1%	1 1.0%	0 0	0 0	1 1.0%	0 0	0 0	0 0	1 2.9%	1 0.3%	2 0.7%
preferred source of info	1 0.2%	0 0	1 0.5%	1 0.5%	0 0	1 0.4%	0 0	0 0	0 0	0 0	0 0	1 1.0%	0 0	0 0	0 0	0 0	0 0	1 0.4%

Proportions/Means: Columns Tested (5% risk level) - A/B/D - C/D - E/F/G - H/I/J/K/L/M/N - P/Q
* small base; ** very small base (under 30) ineligible for sig testing

Table 380
Page 1603

Outsell/Digital Library Federation Study (2002)
Weighted Tables

TABLE 142, continued

S7D/E_9. Online databases, data sets or data sources SUMMARY TABLE

		RESPONDENT TYPE				INSTITUTION TYPE			DISCIPLINE									GENDER	
	TOTAL SAMPLE	FACULTY MEMBER	GRAD. STUDENT	FACULTY /GRAD	UNDER GRAD. STUDENT	PUBLIC	PRIVATE	LIBERAL ARTS	BIOLOGIAL SCIENCES	PHYSICAL SCIENCES /MATH	SOCIAL SCIENCES	ARTS AND HUMAN.	ENGI-NEERING	BUSINESS	LAW	UNDEC. MAJOR	MALE	FEMALE
		(A)	(B)	(C)	(D)	(E)	(F)	(G)	(H)	(I)	(J)	(K)	(L)	(M)	(N)		(P)	(Q)
Base - Use Online databases, data sets or data sources for coursework	565	0**	236	236	329	254	142	169	87*	61*	175*	109*	21*	68*	9*	35*	262	303
Dorm room (NET)	3 0.4%	0 0	0 0	0 0	3 0.8%	1 0.6%	0 0	1 0.7%	0 0	0 0	0 0	2 2.1%	* 1.4%J	0 0	0 0	0 0	0 0	3 0.8%
All sources of info	3 0.4%	0 0	0 0	0 0	3 0.8%	1 0.6%	0 0	1 0.7%	0 0	0 0	0 0	2 2.1%	* 1.4%J	0 0	0 0	0 0	0 0	3 0.8%
preferred source of info	3 0.4%	0 0	0 0	0 0	3 0.8%	1 0.6%	0 0	1 0.7%	0 0	0 0	0 0	2 2.1%	* 1.4%J	0 0	0 0	0 0	0 0	3 0.8%
Purchase from online bookstore (NET)	2 0.4%	0 0	1 0.4%	1 0.4%	1 0.3%	1 0.4%	1 0.7%	0 0	1 1.0%	0 0	0 0	0 0	0 0	1 1.4%	* 1.8%IJK	0 0	0 0	2 0.7%
All sources of info	2 0.4%	0 0	1 0.4%	1 0.4%	1 0.3%	1 0.4%	1 0.7%	0 0	1 1.0%	0 0	0 0	0 0	0 0	1 1.4%	* 1.8%IJK	0 0	0 0	2 0.7%
preferred source of info	1 0.2%	0 0	0 0	0 0	1 0.3%	1 0.4%	0 0	0 0	0 0	0 0	0 0	0 0	0 0	1 1.4%	0 0	0 0	0 0	1 0.3%
Ask library to purchase source (NET)	1 0.2%	0 0	1 0.4%	1 0.4%	0 0	0 0	1 0.7%	0 0	0 0	1 1.6%	0 0	0 0	0 0	0 0	0 0	0 0	1 0.4%	0 0
All sources of info	1 0.2%	0 0	1 0.4%	1 0.4%	0 0	0 0	1 0.7%	0 0	0 0	1 1.6%	0 0	0 0	0 0	0 0	0 0	0 0	1 0.4%	0 0
preferred source of info	1 0.2%	0 0	1 0.4%	1 0.4%	0 0	0 0	1 0.7%	0 0	0 0	1 1.6%	0 0	0 0	0 0	0 0	0 0	0 0	1 0.4%	0 0

Proportions/Means: Columns Tested (5% risk level) - A/B/D - C/D - E/F/G - H/I/J/K/L/M/N - P/Q
* small base; ** very small base (under 30) ineligible for sig testing

Table 380
Page 1604

Outsell/Digital Library Federation Study (2002)
Weighted Tables

TABLE 142, continued

S7D/E_9. Online databases, data sets or data sources SUMMARY TABLE

		RESPONDENT TYPE				INSTITUTION TYPE			DISCIPLINE									GENDER	
	TOTAL SAMPLE	FACULTY MEMBER	GRAD. STUDENT	FACULTY /GRAD	UNDER GRAD. STUDENT	PUBLIC	PRIVATE	LIBERAL ARTS	BIOLOGIAL SCIENCES	PHYSICAL SCIENCES /MATH	SOCIAL SCIENCES	ARTS AND HUMAN.	ENGI-NEERING	BUSINESS	LAW	UNDEC. MAJOR	MALE	FEMALE
		(A)	(B)	(C)	(D)	(E)	(F)	(G)	(H)	(I)	(J)	(K)	(L)	(M)	(N)		(P)	(Q)
Base - Use Online databases, data sets or data sources for coursework	565	0**	236	236	329	254	142	169	87*	61*	175*	109*	21*	68*	9*	35*	262	303
Access from course website (NET)	* 0.1%	0 0	0 0	0 0	* 0.1%	* 0.1%	0 0	0 0	0 0	0 0	0 0	0 0	* 1.4%J	0 0	0 0	0 0	* 0.1%	0 0
All sources of info	* 0.1%	0 0	0 0	0 0	* 0.1%	* 0.1%	0 0	0 0	0 0	0 0	0 0	0 0	* 1.4%J	0 0	0 0	0 0	* 0.1%	0 0
preferred source of info	* 0.1%	0 0	0 0	0 0	* 0.1%	* 0.1%	0 0	0 0	0 0	0 0	0 0	0 0	* 1.4%J	0 0	0 0	0 0	* 0.1%	0 0
In class (NET)	* *	0 0	* 0.1%	* 0.1%	0 0	0 0	* 0.1%	0 0	0 0	0 0	0 0	0 0	0 0	0 0	* 1.8%HIJKM	0 0	* 0.1%	0 0
All sources of info	* *	0 0	* 0.1%	* 0.1%	0 0	0 0	* 0.1%	0 0	0 0	0 0	0 0	0 0	0 0	0 0	* 1.8%HIJKM	0 0	* 0.1%	0 0
preferred source of info	0 0	0 0	0 0	0 0	0 0	0 0	0 0	0 0	0 0	0 0	0 0	0 0	0 0	0 0	0 0	0 0	0 0	0 0
Access book/journal/ journal article elsewhere online (NET)	0 0	0 0	0 0	0 0	0 0	0 0	0 0	0 0	0 0	0 0	0 0	0 0	0 0	0 0	0 0	0 0	0 0	0 0
All sources of info	0 0	0 0	0 0	0 0	0 0	0 0	0 0	0 0	0 0	0 0	0 0	0 0	0 0	0 0	0 0	0 0	0 0	0 0
preferred source of info	0 0	0 0	0 0	0 0	0 0	0 0	0 0	0 0	0 0	0 0	0 0	0 0	0 0	0 0	0 0	0 0	0 0	0 0

Proportions/Means: Columns Tested (5% risk level) - A/B/D - C/D - E/F/G - H/I/J/K/L/M/N - P/Q
* small base; ** very small base (under 30) ineligible for sig testing

Table 380
Page 1605

Outsell/Digital Library Federation Study (2002)
Weighted Tables

TABLE 142, continued

S7D/E_9. Online databases, data sets or data sources SUMMARY TABLE

		RESPONDENT TYPE				INSTITUTION TYPE			DISCIPLINE									GENDER	
	TOTAL SAMPLE	FACULTY MEMBER	GRAD. STUDENT	FACULTY /GRAD	UNDER GRAD. STUDENT	PUBLIC	PRIVATE	LIBERAL ARTS	BIOLOGIAL SCIENCES	PHYSICAL SCIENCES /MATH	SOCIAL SCIENCES	ARTS AND HUMAN.	ENGI- NEERING	BUSINESS	LAW	UNDEC. MAJOR	MALE	FEMALE
		(A)	(B)	(C)	(D)	(E)	(F)	(G)	(H)	(I)	(J)	(K)	(L)	(M)	(N)		(P)	(Q)
Base - Use Online databases, data sets or data sources for coursework	565	0**	236	236	329	254	142	169	87*	61*	175*	109*	21*	68*	9*	35*	262	303
Order from on demand document delivery service (NET)	0 0	0 0	0 0	0 0	0 0	0 0	0 0	0 0	0 0	0 0	0 0	0 0	0 0	0 0	0 0	0 0	0 0	0 0
All sources of info	0 0	0 0	0 0	0 0	0 0	0 0	0 0	0 0	0 0	0 0	0 0	0 0	0 0	0 0	0 0	0 0	0 0	0 0
preferred source of info	0 0	0 0	0 0	0 0	0 0	0 0	0 0	0 0	0 0	0 0	0 0	0 0	0 0	0 0	0 0	0 0	0 0	0 0
Other (NET)	9 1.6%	0 0	3 1.5%	3 1.5%	6 1.7%	4 1.6%	1 0.8%	4 2.4%	3 3.0%	1 1.6%	2 1.1%	2 2.1%	* 1.4%	0 0	* 1.8%M	1 2.9%	5 1.9%	4 1.4%
All sources of info	9 1.6%	0 0	3 1.5%	3 1.5%	6 1.7%	4 1.6%	1 0.8%	4 2.4%	3 3.0%	1 1.6%	2 1.1%	2 2.1%	* 1.4%	0 0	* 1.8%M	1 2.9%	5 1.9%	4 1.4%
preferred source of info	4 0.8%	0 0	1 0.5%	1 0.5%	3 0.9%	1 0.4%	1 0.8%	2 1.3%	1 1.0%	1 1.6%	0 0	1 1.0%	* 1.4%J	0 0	0 0	1 2.9%	2 0.8%	2 0.7%
DK/Refused	14 2.5%	0 0	4 1.7%	4 1.7%	10 3.0%	10 3.9%	2 1.6%	2 1.2%	1 1.0%	3 4.9%K	6 3.2%	0 0	1 4.1%K	4 5.5%K	0 0	0 0	7 2.7%	7 2.4%

Proportions/Means: Columns Tested (5% risk level) - A/B/D - C/D - E/F/G - H/I/J/K/L/M/N - P/Q
* small base; ** very small base (under 30) ineligible for sig testing

Table 380
Page 1606

Outsell/Digital Library Federation Study (2002)
Weighted Tables

TABLE 143

S7sum_10. Manuscripts and other primary source documents SUMMARY TABLE

		RESPONDENT TYPE				INSTITUTION TYPE			DISCIPLINE									GENDER	
	TOTAL SAMPLE	FACULTY MEMBER	GRAD. STUDENT	FACULTY /GRAD	UNDER GRAD. STUDENT	PUBLIC	PRIVATE	LIBERAL ARTS	BIOLOGIAL SCIENCES	PHYSICAL SCIENCES /MATH	SOCIAL SCIENCES	ARTS AND HUMAN.	ENGI-NEERING	BUSINESS	LAW	UNDEC. MAJOR	MALE	FEMALE
		(A)	(B)	(C)	(D)	(E)	(F)	(G)	(H)	(I)	(J)	(K)	(L)	(M)	(N)		(P)	(Q)
Base - Use Manuscripts and other primary source documents for coursework	447	0**	192	192	255	194	91*	161	58*	48*	167*	101*	10*	37*	4**	21*	182	265
ONLINE	330 73.8%	0 0	132 68.7%	132 68.7%	198 77.7%	134 68.9%	67 73.5%	129 80.0%E	44 75.8%	37 77.1%	118 70.8%	74 73.3%	8 75.0%	30 80.0%	3 75.0%	16 76.2%	128 70.2%	202 76.4%
Search engine (NET)	96 21.5%	0 0	24 12.3%	24 12.3%	73 28.5%BC	21 10.9%	20 21.7%E	55 34.3%E	8 13.6%	7 14.6%	26 15.7%	28 27.8%HJ	3 27.8%	16 42.5%HIJ	* 8.3%	8 38.1%	29 15.8%	68 25.5%P
All sources of info	96 21.5%	0 0	24 12.3%	24 12.3%	73 28.5%BC	21 10.9%	20 21.7%E	55 34.3%E	8 13.6%	7 14.6%	26 15.7%	28 27.8%HJ	3 27.8%	16 42.5%HIJ	* 8.3%	8 38.1%	29 15.8%	68 25.5%P
preferred source of info	41 9.1%	0 0	6 3.3%	6 3.3%	35 13.5%BC	12 6.3%	7 7.8%	21 13.3%	4 7.6%	5 10.4%	11 6.7%	8 7.8%	1 13.9%	5 12.5%	* 4.2%	6 28.6%	10 5.5%	31 11.6%
Online library catalogues and finding aids (NET)	75 16.8%	0 0	27 14.1%	27 14.1%	48 18.8%	39 19.8%F	8 8.5%	29 17.8%	11 18.2%	5 10.4%	30 18.0%	19 18.9%	1 5.6%	7 20.0%	* 8.3%	2 9.5%	30 16.3%	45 17.2%
All sources of info	75 16.8%	0 0	27 14.1%	27 14.1%	48 18.8%	39 19.8%F	8 8.5%	29 17.8%	11 18.2%	5 10.4%	30 18.0%	19 18.9%	1 5.6%	7 20.0%	* 8.3%	2 9.5%	30 16.3%	45 17.2%
preferred source of info	55 12.4%	0 0	24 12.6%	24 12.6%	31 12.2%	34 17.3%F	6 6.5%	16 9.8%	9 15.2%	4 8.3%	21 12.4%	17 16.7%	* 2.8%	4 10.0%	0 0	1 4.8%	23 12.4%	33 12.3%
Your own institution's web site (NET)	71 15.9%	0 0	33 17.2%	33 17.2%	38 14.8%	26 13.3%	21 23.2%	24 14.7%	12 21.2%	11 22.9%	23 13.5%	11 11.1%	3 30.6%JK	7 20.0%	* 4.2%	3 14.3%	28 15.3%	43 16.3%

Proportions/Means: Columns Tested (5% risk level) - A/B/D - C/D - E/F/G - H/I/J/K/L/M/N - P/Q
* small base; ** very small base (under 30) ineligible for sig testing

Table 384
Page 1618

Outsell/Digital Library Federation Study (2002)
Weighted Tables

TABLE 143, continued

S7sum_10. Manuscripts and other primary source documents SUMMARY TABLE

	TOTAL SAMPLE	RESPONDENT TYPE: FACULTY MEMBER	GRAD. STUDENT	FACULTY /GRAD	UNDER GRAD. STUDENT	INSTITUTION TYPE: PUBLIC	PRIVATE	LIBERAL ARTS	DISCIPLINE: BIOLOGIAL SCIENCES	PHYSICAL SCIENCES /MATH	SOCIAL SCIENCES	ARTS AND HUMAN.	ENGI-NEERING	BUSINESS	LAW	UNDEC. MAJOR	GENDER: MALE	FEMALE
		(A)	(B)	(C)	(D)	(E)	(F)	(G)	(H)	(I)	(J)	(K)	(L)	(M)	(N)		(P)	(Q)
Base - Use Manuscripts and other primary source documents for coursework	447	0**	192	192	255	194	91*	161	58*	48*	167*	101*	10*	37*	4**	21*	182	265
All sources of info	71 15.9%	0 0	33 17.2%	33 17.2%	38 14.8%	26 13.3%	21 23.2%	24 14.7%	12 21.2%	11 22.9%	23 13.5%	11 11.1%	3 30.6%JK	7 20.0%	* 4.2%	3 14.3%	28 15.3%	43 16.3%
preferred source of info	53 11.9%	0 0	24 12.5%	24 12.5%	29 11.5%	19 9.9%	15 16.8%	19 11.7%	11 19.7%K	8 16.7%	17 10.1%	8 7.8%	2 22.2%K	5 12.5%	* 4.2%	2 9.5%	21 11.3%	33 12.4%
Online databases (NET)	63 14.1%	0 0	29 14.9%	29 14.9%	34 13.4%	23 12.1%	15 16.5%	24 15.1%	7 12.1%	6 12.5%	32 19.1%	9 8.9%	1 11.1%	6 15.0%	1 29.2%	1 4.8%	39 21.6%Q	24 8.9%
All sources of info	63 14.1%	0 0	29 14.9%	29 14.9%	34 13.4%	23 12.1%	15 16.5%	24 15.1%	7 12.1%	6 12.5%	32 19.1%	9 8.9%	1 11.1%	6 15.0%	1 29.2%	1 4.8%	39 21.6%Q	24 8.9%
preferred source of info	48 10.8%	0 0	23 12.0%	23 12.0%	25 9.9%	20 10.3%	10 11.0%	18 11.3%	6 10.6%	5 10.4%	28 16.9%K	4 4.4%	* 2.8%	3 7.5%	* 8.3%	1 4.8%	30 16.7%Q	18 6.7%
Internet searches (NET)	49 11.1%	0 0	14 7.1%	14 7.1%	36 14.0%B C	25 12.7%F	3 3.3%	22 13.5%F	4 6.1%	8 16.7%	19 11.2%	9 8.9%	* 2.8%	5 12.5%	* 4.2%	5 23.8%	13 7.0%	37 13.8%P
All sources of info	49 11.1%	0 0	14 7.1%	14 7.1%	36 14.0%B C	25 12.7%F	3 3.3%	22 13.5%F	4 6.1%	8 16.7%	19 11.2%	9 8.9%	* 2.8%	5 12.5%	* 4.2%	5 23.8%	13 7.0%	37 13.8%P
preferred source of info	25 5.6%	0 0	7 3.6%	7 3.6%	18 7.0%	14 7.2%	1 1.2%	10 6.1%	2 3.0%	4 8.3%	11 6.7%	4 4.4%	* 2.8%	1 2.5%	* 4.2%	2 9.5%	4 2.3%	21 7.8%P

Proportions/Means: Columns Tested (5% risk level) - A/B/D - C/D - E/F/G - H/I/J/K/L/M/N - P/Q
* small base; ** very small base (under 30) ineligible for sig testing

Table 384
Page 1619

TABLE 143, continued

S7sum_10. Manuscripts and other primary source documents SUMMARY TABLE

		RESPONDENT TYPE				INSTITUTION TYPE			DISCIPLINE								GENDER	
	TOTAL SAMPLE	FACULTY MEMBER	GRAD. STUDENT	FACULTY /GRAD	UNDER GRAD. STUDENT	PUBLIC	PRIVATE	LIBERAL ARTS	BIOLOGIAL SCIENCES	PHYSICAL SCIENCES /MATH	SOCIAL SCIENCES	ARTS AND HUMAN.	ENGI-NEERING	BUSINESS	LAW	UNDEC. MAJOR	MALE	FEMALE
		(A)	(B)	(C)	(D)	(E)	(F)	(G)	(H)	(I)	(J)	(K)	(L)	(M)	(N)		(P)	(Q)
Base - Use Manuscripts and other primary source documents for coursework	447	0**	192	192	255	194	91*	161	58*	48*	167*	101*	10*	37*	4**	21*	182	265
Web directory/ subject related web site (NET)	29 6.6%	0 0	16 8.2%	16 8.2%	14 5.4%	6 3.1%	12 12.9%E	12 7.2%	4 6.1%	3 6.3%	6 3.4%	10 10.0%	1 5.6%	3 7.5%	1 20.8%	3 14.3%	10 5.7%	19 7.2%
All sources of info	29 6.6%	0 0	16 8.2%	16 8.2%	14 5.4%	6 3.1%	12 12.9%E	12 7.2%	4 6.1%	3 6.3%	6 3.4%	10 10.0%	1 5.6%	3 7.5%	1 20.8%	3 14.3%	10 5.7%	19 7.2%
preferred source of info	18 4.1%	0 0	10 5.3%	10 5.3%	8 3.3%	4 2.0%	6 7.0%	8 5.1%	4 6.1%	0 0	6 3.4%	6 5.6%	0 0	2 5.0%	1 20.8%	1 4.8%	7 3.6%	12 4.5%
Department web page (NET)	18 4.1%	0 0	10 5.2%	10 5.2%	8 3.2%	8 4.1%	4 4.4%	6 3.8%	2 3.0%	2 4.2%	6 3.4%	4 4.4%	1 5.6%	4 10.0%	0 0	0 0	9 5.0%	9 3.5%
All sources of info	18 4.1%	0 0	10 5.2%	10 5.2%	8 3.2%	8 4.1%	4 4.4%	6 3.8%	2 3.0%	2 4.2%	6 3.4%	4 4.4%	1 5.6%	4 10.0%	0 0	0 0	9 5.0%	9 3.5%
preferred source of info	8 1.8%	0 0	5 2.6%	5 2.6%	3 1.2%	3 1.6%	3 3.3%	2 1.3%	1 1.5%	1 2.1%	2 1.1%	2 2.2%	* 2.8%	2 5.0%	0 0	0 0	2 1.2%	6 2.3%
Online abstracting and indexing services (NET)	13 2.9%	0 0	4 2.2%	4 2.2%	9 3.4%	3 1.6%	4 4.7%	5 3.3%	3 4.5%	1 2.1%	2 1.1%	7 6.7%J	1 5.6%M	0 0	0 0	0 0	4 2.0%	9 3.5%
All sources of info	13 2.9%	0 0	4 2.2%	4 2.2%	9 3.4%	3 1.6%	4 4.7%	5 3.3%	3 4.5%	1 2.1%	2 1.1%	7 6.7%J	1 5.6%M	0 0	0 0	0 0	4 2.0%	9 3.5%

Proportions/Means: Columns Tested (5% risk level) - A/B/D - C/D - E/F/G - H/I/J/K/L/M/N - P/Q
* small base; ** very small base (under 30) ineligible for sig testing

Table 384
Page 1620

Outsell/Digital Library Federation Study (2002)
Weighted Tables

TABLE 143, continued

S7sum_10. Manuscripts and other primary source documents SUMMARY TABLE

	RESPONDENT TYPE				INSTITUTION TYPE			DISCIPLINE								GENDER	
	TOTAL SAMPLE	FACULTY MEMBER	GRAD. STUDENT	FACULTY /GRAD	UNDER GRAD. STUDENT	PUBLIC	PRIVATE	LIBERAL ARTS	BIOLOGIAL SCIENCES	PHYSICAL SCIENCES /MATH	SOCIAL SCIENCES	ARTS AND HUMAN.	ENGI-NEERING	BUSINESS	LAW	UNDEC. MAJOR	MALE	FEMALE
		(A)	(B)	(C)	(D)	(E)	(F)	(G)	(H)	(I)	(J)	(K)	(L)	(M)	(N)		(P)	(Q)
Base - Use Manuscripts and other primary source documents for coursework	447	0**	192	192	255	194	91*	161	58*	48*	167*	101*	10*	37*	4**	21*	182	265
preferred source of info	6 1.4%	0 0	2 1.0%	2 1.0%	4 1.7%	2 1.2%	3 3.1%	1 0.7%	1 1.5%	1 2.1%	2 1.1%	2 2.2%	* 2.8%	0 0	0 0	0 0	1 0.7%	5 1.9%
Online reference service (NET)	7 1.5%	0 0	4 2.0%	4 2.0%	3 1.2%	4 2.2%	2 1.7%	1 0.6%	1 1.5%	1 2.1%	0 0	2 2.2%	* 2.8%J	1 2.5%	1 12.5%	1 4.8%	4 2.1%	3 1.1%
All sources of info	7 1.5%	0 0	4 2.0%	4 2.0%	3 1.2%	4 2.2%	2 1.7%	1 0.6%	1 1.5%	1 2.1%	0 0	2 2.2%	* 2.8%J	1 2.5%	1 12.5%	1 4.8%	4 2.1%	3 1.1%
preferred source of info	2 0.3%	0 0	1 0.3%	1 0.3%	1 0.4%	* 0.2%	* 0.2%	1 0.6%	0 0	0 0	0 0	0 0	0 0	0 0	1 12.5%	1 4.8%	1 0.7%	* 0.1%
Your own personal electronic library/files (NET)	2 0.5%	0 0	1 0.6%	1 0.6%	1 0.4%	2 1.2%	0 0	0 0	0 0	0 0	0 0	2 2.2%	0 0	0 0	0 0	0 0	1 0.6%	1 0.4%
All sources of info	2 0.5%	0 0	1 0.6%	1 0.6%	1 0.4%	2 1.2%	0 0	0 0	0 0	0 0	0 0	2 2.2%	0 0	0 0	0 0	0 0	1 0.6%	1 0.4%
preferred source of info	1 0.3%	0 0	1 0.6%	1 0.6%	0 0	1 0.6%	0 0	0 0	0 0	0 0	0 0	1 1.1%	0 0	0 0	0 0	0 0	1 0.6%	0 0
Online bookstore (NET)	1 0.2%	0 0	1 0.5%	1 0.5%	0 0	1 0.5%	0 0	0 0	0 0	1 2.1%	0 0	0 0	0 0	0 0	0 0	0 0	0 0	1 0.4%

Proportions/Means: Columns Tested (5% risk level) - A/B/D - C/D - E/F/G - H/I/J/K/L/M/N - P/Q
* small base; ** very small base (under 30) ineligible for sig testing

Table 384
Page 1621

Outsell/Digital Library Federation Study (2002)
Weighted Tables

TABLE 143, continued

S7sum_10. Manuscripts and other primary source documents SUMMARY TABLE

	TOTAL SAMPLE	RESPONDENT TYPE: FACULTY MEMBER (A)	GRAD. STUDENT (B)	FACULTY /GRAD (C)	UNDER GRAD. STUDENT (D)	INSTITUTION TYPE: PUBLIC (E)	PRIVATE (F)	LIBERAL ARTS (G)	DISCIPLINE: BIOLOGIAL SCIENCES (H)	PHYSICAL SCIENCES /MATH (I)	SOCIAL SCIENCES (J)	ARTS AND HUMAN. (K)	ENGI- NEERING (L)	BUSINESS (M)	LAW (N)	UNDEC. MAJOR	GENDER: MALE (P)	FEMALE (Q)
Base - Use Manuscripts and other primary source documents for coursework	447	0**	192	192	255	194	91*	161	58*	48*	167*	101*	10*	37*	4**	21*	182	265
All sources of info	1 0.2%	0 0	1 0.5%	1 0.5%	0 0	1 0.5%	0 0	0 0	0 0	1 2.1%	0 0	0 0	0 0	0 0	0 0	0 0	0 0	1 0.4%
preferred source of info	0 0	0 0	0 0	0 0	0 0	0 0	0 0	0 0	0 0	0 0	0 0	0 0	0 0	0 0	0 0	0 0	0 0	0 0
E-mail listservs (NET)	0 0	0 0	0 0	0 0	0 0	0 0	0 0	0 0	0 0	0 0	0 0	0 0	0 0	0 0	0 0	0 0	0 0	0 0
All sources of info	0 0	0 0	0 0	0 0	0 0	0 0	0 0	0 0	0 0	0 0	0 0	0 0	0 0	0 0	0 0	0 0	0 0	0 0
preferred source of info	0 0	0 0	0 0	0 0	0 0	0 0	0 0	0 0	0 0	0 0	0 0	0 0	0 0	0 0	0 0	0 0	0 0	0 0
PERSONAL ASSISTANCE	173 38.7%	0 0	61 31.9%	61 31.9%	112 43.9%BC	65 33.3%	25 27.2%	84 51.9%EF	16 27.3%	16 33.3%	58 34.8%	54 53.3%HIJM	4 41.7%	12 32.5%	1 20.8%	12 57.1%	62 33.8%	112 42.1%
Faculty members inside your institution (NET)	106 23.8%	0 0	39 20.4%	39 20.4%	67 26.3%	41 21.1%	14 15.5%	51 31.7%F	11 19.7%	12 25.0%	36 21.3%	32 32.2%M	3 25.0%	6 15.0%	* 8.3%	6 28.6%	36 20.0%	70 26.3%
All sources of info	106 23.8%	0 0	39 20.4%	39 20.4%	67 26.3%	41 21.1%	14 15.5%	51 31.7%F	11 19.7%	12 25.0%	36 21.3%	32 32.2%M	3 25.0%	6 15.0%	* 8.3%	6 28.6%	36 20.0%	70 26.3%

Proportions/Means: Columns Tested (5% risk level) - A/B/D - C/D - E/F/G - H/I/J/K/L/M/N - P/Q
* small base; ** very small base (under 30) ineligible for sig testing

Table 384
Page 1622

Outsell/Digital Library Federation Study (2002)
Weighted Tables

TABLE 143, continued

S7sum_10. Manuscripts and other primary source documents SUMMARY TABLE

		RESPONDENT TYPE				INSTITUTION TYPE			DISCIPLINE								GENDER	
	TOTAL SAMPLE	FACULTY MEMBER	GRAD. STUDENT	FACULTY /GRAD	UNDER GRAD. STUDENT	PUBLIC	PRIVATE	LIBERAL ARTS	BIOLOGIAL SCIENCES	PHYSICAL SCIENCES /MATH	SOCIAL SCIENCES	ARTS AND HUMAN.	ENGI-NEERING	BUSINESS	LAW	UNDEC. MAJOR	MALE	FEMALE
		(A)	(B)	(C)	(D)	(E)	(F)	(G)	(H)	(I)	(J)	(K)	(L)	(M)	(N)		(P)	(Q)
Base - Use Manuscripts and other primary source documents for coursework	447	0**	192	192	255	194	91*	161	58*	48*	167*	101*	10*	37*	4**	21*	182	265
preferred source of info	51 11.3%	0 0	22 11.3%	22 11.3%	29 11.4%	21 10.6%	8 8.7%	22 13.7%	10 16.7%	7 14.6%	15 9.0%	12 12.2%	1 13.9%	3 7.5%	* 8.3%	2 9.5%	14 7.4%	37 14.0%
A librarian in your institution (NET)	103 23.1%	0 0	24 12.6%	24 12.6%	79 31.1%B C	32 16.5%	10 11.1%	61 37.9%EF	5 9.1%	6 12.5%	38 22.5%H	36 35.6%HI L	2 16.7%	8 22.5%	1 12.5%	8 38.1%	34 18.5%	70 26.3%
All sources of info	103 23.1%	0 0	24 12.6%	24 12.6%	79 31.1%B C	32 16.5%	10 11.1%	61 37.9%EF	5 9.1%	6 12.5%	38 22.5%H	36 35.6%HI L	2 16.7%	8 22.5%	1 12.5%	8 38.1%	34 18.5%	70 26.3%
preferred source of info	41 9.1%	0 0	15 7.6%	15 7.6%	26 10.3%	19 10.0%	6 6.6%	15 9.6%	1 1.5%	2 4.2%	19 11.2%H	12 12.2%H	1 8.3%H	3 7.5%	* 4.2%	3 14.3%	16 8.8%	25 9.4%
Other students inside your institution (NET)	25 5.5%	0 0	6 3.0%	6 3.0%	19 7.4%	4 2.2%	3 3.0%	17 10.8%EF	4 7.6%	4 8.3%	6 3.4%	9 8.9%	1 5.6%	1 2.5%	0 0	0 0	8 4.6%	16 6.1%
All sources of info	25 5.5%	0 0	6 3.0%	6 3.0%	19 7.4%	4 2.2%	3 3.0%	17 10.8%EF	4 7.6%	4 8.3%	6 3.4%	9 8.9%	1 5.6%	1 2.5%	0 0	0 0	8 4.6%	16 6.1%
preferred source of info	3 0.7%	0 0	2 0.9%	2 0.9%	1 0.5%	* 0.1%	2 1.9%	1 0.6%	2 3.0%J	0 0	0 0	0 0	* 2.8%JK	1 2.5%	0 0	0 0	1 0.6%	2 0.7%
Another institution's librarian (NET)	4 0.9%	0 0	3 1.5%	3 1.5%	1 0.4%	1 0.5%	2 2.2%	1 0.7%	1 1.5%	0 0	0 0	2 2.2%	0 0	1 2.5%	0 0	0 0	2 1.2%	2 0.7%

Proportions/Means: Columns Tested (5% risk level) - A/B/D - C/D - E/F/G - H/I/J/K/L/M/N - P/Q
* small base; ** very small base (under 30) ineligible for sig testing

Table 384
Page 1623

Outsell/Digital Library Federation Study (2002)
Weighted Tables

TABLE 143, continued

S7sum_10. Manuscripts and other primary source documents SUMMARY TABLE

		RESPONDENT TYPE				INSTITUTION TYPE			DISCIPLINE									GENDER	
	TOTAL SAMPLE	FACULTY MEMBER	GRAD. STUDENT	FACULTY /GRAD	UNDER GRAD. STUDENT	PUBLIC	PRIVATE	LIBERAL ARTS	BIOLOGIAL SCIENCES	PHYSICAL SCIENCES /MATH	SOCIAL SCIENCES	ARTS AND HUMAN.	ENGI-NEERING	BUSINESS	LAW	UNDEC. MAJOR	MALE	FEMALE
		(A)	(B)	(C)	(D)	(E)	(F)	(G)	(H)	(I)	(J)	(K)	(L)	(M)	(N)		(P)	(Q)
Base - Use Manuscripts and other primary source documents for coursework	447	0**	192	192	255	194	91*	161	58*	48*	167*	101*	10*	37*	4**	21*	182	265
All sources of info	4 0.9%	0 0	3 1.5%	3 1.5%	1 0.4%	1 0.5%	2 2.2%	1 0.7%	1 1.5%	0 0	0 0	2 2.2%	0 0	1 2.5%	0 0	0 0	2 1.2%	2 0.7%
preferred source of info	1 0.2%	0 0	1 0.5%	1 0.5%	0 0	1 0.5%	0 0	0 0	1 1.5%	0 0	0 0	0 0	0 0	0 0	0 0	0 0	0 0	1 0.3%
Faculty members outside your institution (NET)	2 0.5%	0 0	1 0.5%	1 0.5%	1 0.4%	0 0	1 1.0%	1 0.7%	0 0	0 0	0 0	1 1.1%	0 0	1 2.5%	0 0	0 0	1 0.6%	1 0.4%
All sources of info	2 0.5%	0 0	1 0.5%	1 0.5%	1 0.4%	0 0	1 1.0%	1 0.7%	0 0	0 0	0 0	1 1.1%	0 0	1 2.5%	0 0	0 0	1 0.6%	1 0.4%
preferred source of info	0 0	0 0	0 0	0 0	0 0	0 0	0 0	0 0	0 0	0 0	0 0	0 0	0 0	0 0	0 0	0 0	0 0	0 0
Other students outside your institution (NET)	1 0.3%	0 0	0 0	0 0	1 0.4%	0 0	0 0	1 0.7%	0 0	0 0	0 0	1 1.1%	0 0	0 0	0 0	0 0	1 0.6%	0 0
All sources of info	1 0.3%	0 0	0 0	0 0	1 0.4%	0 0	0 0	1 0.7%	0 0	0 0	0 0	1 1.1%	0 0	0 0	0 0	0 0	1 0.6%	0 0
preferred source of info	0 0	0 0	0 0	0 0	0 0	0 0	0 0	0 0	0 0	0 0	0 0	0 0	0 0	0 0	0 0	0 0	0 0	0 0

Proportions/Means: Columns Tested (5% risk level) - A/B/D - C/D - E/F/G - H/I/J/K/L/M/N - P/Q
* small base; ** very small base (under 30) ineligible for sig testing

Table 384
Page 1624

Outsell/Digital Library Federation Study (2002)
Weighted Tables

TABLE 143, continued

S7sum_10. Manuscripts and other primary source documents SUMMARY TABLE

	TOTAL SAMPLE	RESPONDENT TYPE: FACULTY MEMBER	GRAD. STUDENT	FACULTY /GRAD	UNDER GRAD. STUDENT	INSTITUTION TYPE: PUBLIC	PRIVATE	LIBERAL ARTS	DISCIPLINE: BIOLOGIAL SCIENCES	PHYSICAL SCIENCES /MATH	SOCIAL SCIENCES	ARTS AND HUMAN.	ENGI-NEERING	BUSINESS	LAW	UNDEC. MAJOR	GENDER: MALE	FEMALE
		(A)	(B)	(C)	(D)	(E)	(F)	(G)	(H)	(I)	(J)	(K)	(L)	(M)	(N)		(P)	(Q)
Base - Use Manuscripts and other primary source documents for coursework	447	0**	192	192	255	194	91*	161	58*	48*	167*	101*	10*	37*	4**	21*	182	265
Professional meetings (NET)	1 0.3%	0 0	1 0.6%	1 0.6%	0 0	1 0.6%	0 0	0 0	0 0	0 0	0 0	1 1.1%	0 0	0 0	0 0	0 0	1 0.6%	0 0
All sources of info	1 0.3%	0 0	1 0.6%	1 0.6%	0 0	1 0.6%	0 0	0 0	0 0	0 0	0 0	1 1.1%	0 0	0 0	0 0	0 0	1 0.6%	0 0
preferred source of info	1 0.3%	0 0	1 0.6%	1 0.6%	0 0	1 0.6%	0 0	0 0	0 0	0 0	0 0	1 1.1%	0 0	0 0	0 0	0 0	1 0.6%	0 0
LIBRARY FACILITIES/ PRINT	136 30.5%	0 0	61 31.9%	61 31.9%	75 29.4%	51 26.3%	27 29.5%	58 36.1%	11 18.2%	15 31.3%	45 27.0%	43 42.2%HJ	4 38.9%H	11 30.0%	2 41.7%	6 28.6%	67 37.0%Q	69 26.0%
Campus library (NET)	119 26.7%	0 0	53 27.4%	53 27.4%	67 26.2%	46 23.6%	19 20.4%	55 34.1%F	9 15.2%	13 27.1%	39 23.6%	37 36.7%H	3 33.3%H	10 27.5%	2 37.5%	6 28.6%	57 31.5%	62 23.4%
All sources of info	119 26.7%	0 0	53 27.4%	53 27.4%	67 26.2%	46 23.6%	19 20.4%	55 34.1%F	9 15.2%	13 27.1%	39 23.6%	37 36.7%H	3 33.3%H	10 27.5%	2 37.5%	6 28.6%	57 31.5%	62 23.4%
preferred source of info	66 14.8%	0 0	36 18.8%	36 18.8%	30 11.9%	29 14.7%	15 16.0%	23 14.4%	5 9.1%	8 16.7%	26 15.7%	16 15.6%	1 13.9%	7 20.0%	1 29.2%	1 4.8%	36 19.5%Q	31 11.6%
Another library (NET)	10 2.2%	0 0	4 2.1%	4 2.1%	6 2.3%	0 0	4 4.5%E	6 3.7%E	0 0	1 2.1%	6 3.4%	3 3.3%	0 0	0 0	0 0	0 0	10 5.5%Q	0 0
All sources of info	10 2.2%	0 0	4 2.1%	4 2.1%	6 2.3%	0 0	4 4.5%E	6 3.7%E	0 0	1 2.1%	6 3.4%	3 3.3%	0 0	0 0	0 0	0 0	10 5.5%Q	0 0

Proportions/Means: Columns Tested (5% risk level) - A/B/D - C/D - E/F/G - H/I/J/K/L/M/N - P/Q
* small base; ** very small base (under 30) ineligible for sig testing

Table 384
Page 1625

Outsell/Digital Library Federation Study (2002)
Weighted Tables

TABLE 143, continued

S7sum_10. Manuscripts and other primary source documents SUMMARY TABLE

		RESPONDENT TYPE				INSTITUTION TYPE			DISCIPLINE									GENDER	
	TOTAL SAMPLE	FACULTY MEMBER	GRAD. STUDENT	FACULTY /GRAD	UNDER GRAD. STUDENT	PUBLIC	PRIVATE	LIBERAL ARTS	BIOLOGIAL SCIENCES	PHYSICAL SCIENCES /MATH	SOCIAL SCIENCES	ARTS AND HUMAN.	ENGI-NEERING	BUSINESS	LAW	UNDEC. MAJOR	MALE	FEMALE
		(A)	(B)	(C)	(D)	(E)	(F)	(G)	(H)	(I)	(J)	(K)	(L)	(M)	(N)		(P)	(Q)
Base - Use Manuscripts and other primary source documents for coursework	447	0**	192	192	255	194	91*	161	58*	48*	167*	101*	10*	37*	4**	21*	182	265
preferred source of info	1 0.3%	0 0	1 0.6%	1 0.6%	0 0	0 0	1 1.2%	0 0	0 0	0 0	0 0	1 1.1%	0 0	0 0	0 0	0 0	1 0.6%	0 0
Physical bookstore (NET)	5 1.2%	0 0	4 2.1%	4 2.1%	1 0.4%	1 0.6%	3 3.1%	1 0.7%	0 0	1 2.1%	2 1.1%	1 1.1%	* 2.8%H	1 2.5%	0 0	0 0	1 0.7%	4 1.5%
All sources of info	5 1.2%	0 0	4 2.1%	4 2.1%	1 0.4%	1 0.6%	3 3.1%	1 0.7%	0 0	1 2.1%	2 1.1%	1 1.1%	* 2.8%H	1 2.5%	0 0	0 0	1 0.7%	4 1.5%
preferred source of info	1 0.2%	0 0	1 0.5%	1 0.5%	0 0	1 0.5%	0 0	0 0	0 0	0 0	0 0	0 0	0 0	1 2.5%	0 0	0 0	0 0	1 0.4%
Your own personal physical library/ files/bookshelves (NET)	5 1.2%	0 0	2 1.1%	2 1.1%	3 1.2%	0 0	4 4.4%E	1 0.7%	0 0	0 0	4 2.2%	1 1.1%	* 2.8%H	0 0	0 0	0 0	2 1.2%	3 1.1%
All sources of info	5 1.2%	0 0	2 1.1%	2 1.1%	3 1.2%	0 0	4 4.4%E	1 0.7%	0 0	0 0	4 2.2%	1 1.1%	* 2.8%H	0 0	0 0	0 0	2 1.2%	3 1.1%
preferred source of info	* 0.1%	0 0	* 0.2%	* 0.2%	0 0	0 0	* 0.3%	0 0	0 0	0 0	0 0	0 0	* 2.8%HJK	0 0	0 0	0 0	* 0.2%	0 0
References cited in books or journal articles (NET)	4 1.0%	0 0	3 1.8%	3 1.8%	1 0.4%	1 0.6%	2 2.5%	1 0.6%	1 1.5%	1 2.1%	0 0	2 2.2%	* 2.8%J	0 0	0 0	0 0	4 1.9%	1 0.3%

Proportions/Means: Columns Tested (5% risk level) - A/B/D - C/D - E/F/G - H/I/J/K/L/M/N - P/Q
* small base; ** very small base (under 30) ineligible for sig testing

Table 384
Page 1626

Outsell/Digital Library Federation Study (2002)
Weighted Tables

TABLE 143, continued

S7sum_10. Manuscripts and other primary source documents SUMMARY TABLE

		RESPONDENT TYPE				INSTITUTION TYPE			DISCIPLINE									GENDER	
	TOTAL SAMPLE	FACULTY MEMBER	GRAD. STUDENT	FACULTY /GRAD	UNDER GRAD. STUDENT	PUBLIC	PRIVATE	LIBERAL ARTS	BIOLOGIAL SCIENCES	PHYSICAL SCIENCES /MATH	SOCIAL SCIENCES	ARTS AND HUMAN.	ENGI-NEERING	BUSINESS	LAW	UNDEC. MAJOR	MALE	FEMALE
		(A)	(B)	(C)	(D)	(E)	(F)	(G)	(H)	(I)	(J)	(K)	(L)	(M)	(N)		(P)	(Q)
Base - Use Manuscripts and other primary source documents for coursework	447	0**	192	192	255	194	91*	161	58*	48*	167*	101*	10*	37*	4**	21*	182	265
All sources of info	4 1.0%	0 0	3 1.8%	3 1.8%	1 0.4%	1 0.6%	2 2.5%	1 0.6%	1 1.5%	1 2.1%	0 0	2 2.2%	* 2.8%J	0 0	0 0	0 0	4 1.9%	1 0.3%
preferred source of info	1 0.3%	0 0	1 0.7%	1 0.7%	0 0	0 0	1 1.5%	0 0	0 0	0 0	0 0	1 1.1%	* 2.8%HJ	0 0	0 0	0 0	1 0.8%	0 0
Printed library catalogues and finding aids (NET)	3 0.7%	0 0	1 0.5%	1 0.5%	2 0.7%	1 0.5%	0 0	2 1.2%	1 1.5%	0 0	2 1.1%	0 0	0 0	0 0	* 4.2%	0 0	2 1.1%	1 0.3%
All sources of info	3 0.7%	0 0	1 0.5%	1 0.5%	2 0.7%	1 0.5%	0 0	2 1.2%	1 1.5%	0 0	2 1.1%	0 0	0 0	0 0	* 4.2%	0 0	2 1.1%	1 0.3%
preferred source of info	0 0	0 0	0 0	0 0	0 0	0 0	0 0	0 0	0 0	0 0	0 0	0 0	0 0	0 0	0 0	0 0	0 0	0 0
Printed abstracting and indexing services (NET)	3 0.6%	0 0	0 0	0 0	3 1.1%	2 1.0%	0 0	1 0.6%	0 0	1 2.1%	2 1.1%	0 0	0 0	0 0	0 0	0 0	2 1.0%	1 0.4%
All sources of info	3 0.6%	0 0	0 0	0 0	3 1.1%	2 1.0%	0 0	1 0.6%	0 0	1 2.1%	2 1.1%	0 0	0 0	0 0	0 0	0 0	2 1.0%	1 0.4%
preferred source of info	2 0.4%	0 0	0 0	0 0	2 0.7%	2 1.0%	0 0	0 0	0 0	0 0	2 1.1%	0 0	0 0	0 0	0 0	0 0	2 1.0%	0 0

Proportions/Means: Columns Tested (5% risk level) - A/B/D - C/D - E/F/G - H/I/J/K/L/M/N - P/Q
* small base; ** very small base (under 30) ineligible for sig testing

Table 384
Page 1627

TABLE 143, continued

S7sum_10. Manuscripts and other primary source documents SUMMARY TABLE

		RESPONDENT TYPE				INSTITUTION TYPE			DISCIPLINE									GENDER	
	TOTAL SAMPLE	FACULTY MEMBER	GRAD. STUDENT	FACULTY /GRAD	UNDER GRAD. STUDENT	PUBLIC	PRIVATE	LIBERAL ARTS	BIOLOGIAL SCIENCES	PHYSICAL SCIENCES /MATH	SOCIAL SCIENCES	ARTS AND HUMAN.	ENGI- NEERING	BUSINESS	LAW	UNDEC. MAJOR	MALE	FEMALE
		(A)	(B)	(C)	(D)	(E)	(F)	(G)	(H)	(I)	(J)	(K)	(L)	(M)	(N)		(P)	(Q)
Base - Use Manuscripts and other primary source documents for coursework	447	0**	192	192	255	194	91*	161	58*	48*	167*	101*	10*	37*	4**	21*	182	265
Personal subscriptions to newspapers, magazines and journals (NET)	3 0.6%	0 0	* 0.2%	* 0.2%	2 0.9%	0 0	1 1.5%	1 0.7%	0 0	0 0	0 0	2 2.2%	* 2.8%HJ	0 0	0 0	0 0	1 0.8%	1 0.4%
All sources of info	3 0.6%	0 0	* 0.2%	* 0.2%	2 0.9%	0 0	1 1.5%	1 0.7%	0 0	0 0	0 0	2 2.2%	* 2.8%HJ	0 0	0 0	0 0	1 0.8%	1 0.4%
preferred source of info	0 0	0 0	0 0	0 0	0 0	0 0	0 0	0 0	0 0	0 0	0 0	0 0	0 0	0 0	0 0	0 0	0 0	0 0
Other (NET)	17 3.8%	0 0	8 4.3%	8 4.3%	9 3.5%	10 5.1%	5 5.3%	2 1.4%	1 1.5%	0 0	8 4.5%	4 4.4%	1 11.1%HI	2 5.0%	* 4.2%	1 4.8%	7 4.1%	10 3.6%
All sources of info	16 3.6%	0 0	8 4.3%	8 4.3%	8 3.1%	9 4.6%	5 5.3%	2 1.4%	1 1.5%	0 0	8 4.5%	4 4.4%	1 11.1%HI	1 2.5%	* 4.2%	1 4.8%	6 3.6%	10 3.6%
preferred source of info	6 1.4%	0 0	2 1.2%	2 1.2%	4 1.5%	3 1.5%	3 3.5%G	0 0	0 0	0 0	4 2.2%	0 0	* 2.8%HK	1 2.5%	* 4.2%	1 4.8%	1 0.8%	5 1.8%
Online (unspecified)	3 0.6%	0 0	1 0.6%	1 0.6%	1 0.6%	2 1.2%	* 0.3%	0 0	0 0	0 0	0 0	2 2.2%	* 2.8%HJ	0 0	0 0	0 0	1 0.8%	1 0.4%
All sources of info	3 0.6%	0 0	1 0.6%	1 0.6%	1 0.6%	2 1.2%	* 0.3%	0 0	0 0	0 0	0 0	2 2.2%	* 2.8%HJ	0 0	0 0	0 0	1 0.8%	1 0.4%

Proportions/Means: Columns Tested (5% risk level) - A/B/D - C/D - E/F/G - H/I/J/K/L/M/N - P/Q
* small base; ** very small base (under 30) ineligible for sig testing

Table 384
Page 1628

Outsell/Digital Library Federation Study (2002)
Weighted Tables

TABLE 143, continued

S7sum_10. Manuscripts and other primary source documents SUMMARY TABLE

	RESPONDENT TYPE				INSTITUTION TYPE			DISCIPLINE									GENDER	
	TOTAL SAMPLE	FACULTY MEMBER	GRAD. STUDENT	FACULTY /GRAD	UNDER GRAD. STUDENT	PUBLIC	PRIVATE	LIBERAL ARTS	BIOLOGIAL SCIENCES	PHYSICAL SCIENCES /MATH	SOCIAL SCIENCES	ARTS AND HUMAN.	ENGI- NEERING	BUSINESS	LAW	UNDEC. MAJOR	MALE	FEMALE
		(A)	(B)	(C)	(D)	(E)	(F)	(G)	(H)	(I)	(J)	(K)	(L)	(M)	(N)		(P)	(Q)
Base - Use Manuscripts and other primary source documents for coursework	447	0**	192	192	255	194	91*	161	58*	48*	167*	101*	10*	37*	4**	21*	182	265
preferred source of info	3 0.6%	0 0	1 0.6%	1 0.6%	1 0.6%	2 1.2%	* 0.3%	0 0	0 0	0 0	0 0	2 2.2%	* 2.8%HJ	0 0	0 0	0 0	1 0.8%	1 0.4%
E-journals	1 0.3%	0 0	0 0	0 0	1 0.4%	0 0	0 0	1 0.7%	0 0	0 0	0 0	1 1.1%	0 0	0 0	0 0	0 0	1 0.6%	0 0
All sources of info	1 0.3%	0 0	0 0	0 0	1 0.4%	0 0	0 0	1 0.7%	0 0	0 0	0 0	1 1.1%	0 0	0 0	0 0	0 0	1 0.6%	0 0
preferred source of info	0 0	0 0	0 0	0 0	0 0	0 0	0 0	0 0	0 0	0 0	0 0	0 0	0 0	0 0	0 0	0 0	0 0	0 0
DK/Refused	13 2.8%	0 0	6 2.9%	6 2.9%	7 2.8%	8 4.1%	3 3.1%	2 1.2%	2 3.0%	4 8.3%	4 2.2%	2 2.2%	0 0	1 2.5%	0 0	0 0	7 3.7%	6 2.2%

Proportions/Means: Columns Tested (5% risk level) - A/B/D - C/D - E/F/G - H/I/J/K/L/M/N - P/Q
* small base; ** very small base (under 30) ineligible for sig testing

TABLE 144

S7D/E_10. Manuscripts and other primary source documents SUMMARY TABLE

		RESPONDENT TYPE				INSTITUTION TYPE			DISCIPLINE								GENDER	
	TOTAL SAMPLE	FACULTY MEMBER	GRAD. STUDENT	FACULTY /GRAD	UNDER GRAD. STUDENT	PUBLIC	PRIVATE	LIBERAL ARTS	BIOLOGIAL SCIENCES	PHYSICAL SCIENCES /MATH	SOCIAL SCIENCES	ARTS AND HUMAN.	ENGI- NEERING	BUSINESS	LAW	UNDEC. MAJOR	MALE	FEMALE
		(A)	(B)	(C)	(D)	(E)	(F)	(G)	(H)	(I)	(J)	(K)	(L)	(M)	(N)		(P)	(Q)
Base - Use Manuscripts and other primary source documents for coursework	447	0**	192	192	255	194	91*	161	58*	48*	167*	101*	10*	37*	4**	21*	182	265
Borrow from or use in campus library (NET)	365 81.6%	0 0	153 79.7%	153 79.7%	212 83.1%	152 78.3%	72 78.7%	141 87.4%	43 74.2%	38 79.2%	141 84.3%L	90 88.9%HL M	7 69.4%	26 70.0%	3 70.8%	17 81.0%	154 84.5%	211 79.7%
All sources of info	365 81.6%	0 0	153 79.7%	153 79.7%	212 83.1%	152 78.3%	72 78.7%	141 87.4%	43 74.2%	38 79.2%	141 84.3%L	90 88.9%HL M	7 69.4%	26 70.0%	3 70.8%	17 81.0%	154 84.5%	211 79.7%
preferred source of info	298 66.7%	0 0	122 63.7%	122 63.7%	176 69.0%	126 64.7%	59 64.3%	113 70.4%	33 56.1%	31 64.6%	117 69.7%L	74 73.3%HL	5 47.2%	23 62.5%	2 45.8%	14 66.7%	124 68.3%	174 65.6%
Access online (NET)	147 32.9%	0 0	61 31.9%	61 31.9%	86 33.7%	62 32.0%	27 29.7%	58 35.8%	26 45.5%JK	18 37.5%	43 25.8%	24 23.3%	5 50.0%JK	17 45.0%JK	2 45.8%	12 57.1%	60 33.2%	87 32.7%
All sources of info	147 32.9%	0 0	61 31.9%	61 31.9%	86 33.7%	62 32.0%	27 29.7%	58 35.8%	26 45.5%JK	18 37.5%	43 25.8%	24 23.3%	5 50.0%JK	17 45.0%JK	2 45.8%	12 57.1%	60 33.2%	87 32.7%
preferred source of info	99 22.2%	0 0	53 27.9%D	53 27.9%D	46 17.9%	50 25.6%	24 25.7%	26 16.0%	23 39.4%JK	12 25.0%	28 16.9%	13 13.3%	4 36.1%JK	11 30.0%K	2 41.7%	6 28.6%	42 23.0%	57 21.6%
Borrow from or use in other libraries (NET)	30 6.8%	0 0	10 5.0%	10 5.0%	21 8.1%	5 2.5%	8 8.3%E	18 11.1%E	1 1.5%	2 4.2%	17 10.1%	9 8.9%	1 5.6%	1 2.5%	* 4.2%	0 0	11 6.0%	20 7.4%
All sources of info	30 6.8%	0 0	10 5.0%	10 5.0%	21 8.1%	5 2.5%	8 8.3%E	18 11.1%E	1 1.5%	2 4.2%	17 10.1%	9 8.9%	1 5.6%	1 2.5%	* 4.2%	0 0	11 6.0%	20 7.4%

Proportions/Means: Columns Tested (5% risk level) - A/B/D - C/D - E/F/G - H/I/J/K/L/M/N - P/Q
* small base; ** very small base (under 30) ineligible for sig testing

Table 387
Page 1636

Outsell/Digital Library Federation Study (2002)
Weighted Tables

TABLE 144, continued

S7D/E_10. Manuscripts and other primary source documents SUMMARY TABLE

		RESPONDENT TYPE				INSTITUTION TYPE			DISCIPLINE									GENDER	
	TOTAL SAMPLE	FACULTY MEMBER	GRAD. STUDENT	FACULTY /GRAD	UNDER GRAD. STUDENT	PUBLIC	PRIVATE	LIBERAL ARTS	BIOLOGIAL SCIENCES	PHYSICAL SCIENCES /MATH	SOCIAL SCIENCES	ARTS AND HUMAN.	ENGI- NEERING	BUSINESS	LAW	UNDEC. MAJOR	MALE	FEMALE
		(A)	(B)	(C)	(D)	(E)	(F)	(G)	(H)	(I)	(J)	(K)	(L)	(M)	(N)		(P)	(Q)
Base - Use Manuscripts and other primary source documents for coursework	447	0**	192	192	255	194	91*	161	58*	48*	167*	101*	10*	37*	4**	21*	182	265
preferred source of info	8 1.8%	0 0	4 2.1%	4 2.1%	4 1.6%	1 0.6%	4 4.2%	3 1.9%	1 1.5%	1 2.1%	4 2.2%	2 2.2%	0 0	0 0	* 4.2%	0 0	1 0.7%	7 2.6%
Faculty (NET)	22 5.0%	0 0	5 2.5%	5 2.5%	18 6.9%	2 1.3%	3 2.9%	17 10.7%EF	3 4.5%	1 2.1%	9 5.6%	6 5.6%	1 13.9%IM	1 2.5%	* 8.3%	1 4.8%	10 5.5%	12 4.6%
All sources of info	22 5.0%	0 0	5 2.5%	5 2.5%	18 6.9%	2 1.3%	3 2.9%	17 10.7%EF	3 4.5%	1 2.1%	9 5.6%	6 5.6%	1 13.9%IM	1 2.5%	* 8.3%	1 4.8%	10 5.5%	12 4.6%
preferred source of info	14 3.2%	0 0	3 1.8%	3 1.8%	11 4.3%	2 1.0%	2 1.7%	11 6.8%E	2 3.0%	1 2.1%	6 3.4%	3 3.3%	* 2.8%	1 2.5%	* 8.3%	1 4.8%	5 2.9%	9 3.4%
Interlibrary loan (NET)	16 3.5%	0 0	4 2.3%	4 2.3%	11 4.4%	2 1.0%	3 3.1%	11 6.8%E	0 0	1 2.1%	4 2.2%	9 8.9%HJ	1 8.3%HM	0 0	0 0	1 4.8%	9 4.8%	7 2.6%
All sources of info	16 3.5%	0 0	4 2.3%	4 2.3%	11 4.4%	2 1.0%	3 3.1%	11 6.8%E	0 0	1 2.1%	4 2.2%	9 8.9%HJ	1 8.3%HM	0 0	0 0	1 4.8%	9 4.8%	7 2.6%
preferred source of info	1 0.3%	0 0	0 0	0 0	1 0.6%	0 0	0 0	1 0.9%	0 0	0 0	0 0	1 1.1%	* 2.8%HJ	0 0	0 0	0 0	0 0	1 0.5%
Purchase from physical book store (NET)	13 3.0%	0 0	3 1.5%	3 1.5%	10 4.1%	4 2.1%	2 2.1%	7 4.6%	0 0	1 2.1%	6 3.4%	4 4.4%	* 2.8%H	2 5.0%	0 0	0 0	4 2.2%	9 3.5%

Proportions/Means: Columns Tested (5% risk level) - A/B/D - C/D - E/F/G - H/I/J/K/L/M/N - P/Q
* small base; ** very small base (under 30) ineligible for sig testing

Table 387
Page 1637

TABLE 144, continued

S7D/E_10. Manuscripts and other primary source documents SUMMARY TABLE

	TOTAL SAMPLE	RESPONDENT TYPE: FACULTY MEMBER	GRAD. STUDENT	FACULTY /GRAD	UNDER GRAD. STUDENT	INSTITUTION TYPE: PUBLIC	PRIVATE	LIBERAL ARTS	DISCIPLINE: BIOLOGIAL SCIENCES	PHYSICAL SCIENCES /MATH	SOCIAL SCIENCES	ARTS AND HUMAN.	ENGI-NEERING	BUSINESS	LAW	UNDEC. MAJOR	GENDER: MALE	FEMALE
		(A)	(B)	(C)	(D)	(E)	(F)	(G)	(H)	(I)	(J)	(K)	(L)	(M)	(N)		(P)	(Q)
Base - Use Manuscripts and other primary source documents for coursework	447	0**	192	192	255	194	91*	161	58*	48*	167*	101*	10*	37*	4**	21*	182	265
All sources of info	13 3.0%	0 0	3 1.5%	3 1.5%	10 4.1%	4 2.1%	2 2.1%	7 4.6%	0 0	1 2.1%	6 3.4%	4 4.4%	* 2.8%H	2 5.0%	0 0	0 0	4 2.2%	9 3.5%
preferred source of info	7 1.6%	0 0	1 0.5%	1 0.5%	6 2.5%	2 1.1%	2 2.1%	3 2.0%	0 0	1 2.1%	2 1.1%	2 2.2%	* 2.8%H	2 5.0%	0 0	0 0	* 0.2%	7 2.6%
Ask library to purchase source (NET)	3 0.7%	0 0	2 1.0%	2 1.0%	1 0.4%	2 1.0%	0 0	1 0.7%	0 0	0 0	2 1.1%	1 1.1%	0 0	0 0	0 0	0 0	1 0.6%	2 0.7%
All sources of info	3 0.7%	0 0	2 1.0%	2 1.0%	1 0.4%	2 1.0%	0 0	1 0.7%	0 0	0 0	2 1.1%	1 1.1%	0 0	0 0	0 0	0 0	1 0.6%	2 0.7%
preferred source of info	0 0	0 0	0 0	0 0	0 0	0 0	0 0	0 0	0 0	0 0	0 0	0 0	0 0	0 0	0 0	0 0	0 0	0 0
Purchase from online bookstore (NET)	3 0.7%	0 0	1 0.6%	1 0.6%	2 0.7%	0 0	1 1.2%	2 1.2%	0 0	0 0	2 1.1%	1 1.1%	0 0	0 0	0 0	0 0	3 1.6%	0 0
All sources of info	3 0.7%	0 0	1 0.6%	1 0.6%	2 0.7%	0 0	1 1.2%	2 1.2%	0 0	0 0	2 1.1%	1 1.1%	0 0	0 0	0 0	0 0	3 1.6%	0 0
preferred source of info	0 0	0 0	0 0	0 0	0 0	0 0	0 0	0 0	0 0	0 0	0 0	0 0	0 0	0 0	0 0	0 0	0 0	0 0

Proportions/Means: Columns Tested (5% risk level) - A/B/D - C/D - E/F/G - H/I/J/K/L/M/N - P/Q
* small base; ** very small base (under 30) ineligible for sig testing

Table 387
Page 1638

TABLE 144, continued

S7D/E_10. Manuscripts and other primary source documents SUMMARY TABLE

	TOTAL SAMPLE	RESPONDENT TYPE FACULTY MEMBER	GRAD. STUDENT	FACULTY /GRAD	UNDER GRAD. STUDENT	INSTITUTION TYPE PUBLIC	PRIVATE	LIBERAL ARTS	DISCIPLINE BIOLOGIAL SCIENCES	PHYSICAL SCIENCES /MATH	SOCIAL SCIENCES	ARTS AND HUMAN.	ENGI- NEERING	BUSINESS	LAW	UNDEC. MAJOR	GENDER MALE	FEMALE
		(A)	(B)	(C)	(D)	(E)	(F)	(G)	(H)	(I)	(J)	(K)	(L)	(M)	(N)		(P)	(Q)
Base - Use Manuscripts and other primary source documents for coursework	447	0**	192	192	255	194	91*	161	58*	48*	167*	101*	10*	37*	4**	21*	182	265
Personal Holdings (NET)	3 0.6%	0 0	* 0.2%	* 0.2%	2 0.9%	0 0	* 0.3%	2 1.4%	0 0	0 0	0 0	2 2.2%	* 2.8%HJ	0 0	0 0	0 0	1 0.8%	1 0.4%
All sources of info	3 0.6%	0 0	* 0.2%	* 0.2%	2 0.9%	0 0	* 0.3%	2 1.4%	0 0	0 0	0 0	2 2.2%	* 2.8%HJ	0 0	0 0	0 0	1 0.8%	1 0.4%
preferred source of info	3 0.6%	0 0	* 0.2%	* 0.2%	2 0.9%	0 0	* 0.3%	2 1.4%	0 0	0 0	0 0	2 2.2%	* 2.8%HJ	0 0	0 0	0 0	1 0.8%	1 0.4%
Home (NET)	1 0.3%	0 0	1 0.6%	1 0.6%	0 0	1 0.6%	0 0	0 0	0 0	0 0	0 0	1 1.1%	0 0	0 0	0 0	0 0	1 0.6%	0 0
All sources of info	1 0.3%	0 0	1 0.6%	1 0.6%	0 0	1 0.6%	0 0	0 0	0 0	0 0	0 0	1 1.1%	0 0	0 0	0 0	0 0	1 0.6%	0 0
preferred source of info	1 0.3%	0 0	1 0.6%	1 0.6%	0 0	1 0.6%	0 0	0 0	0 0	0 0	0 0	1 1.1%	0 0	0 0	0 0	0 0	1 0.6%	0 0
Order from on demand document delivery service (NET)	1 0.2%	0 0	0 0	0 0	1 0.4%	0 0	0 0	1 0.6%	0 0	0 0	0 0	0 0	0 0	0 0	0 0	1 4.8%	0 0	1 0.4%
All sources of info	1 0.2%	0 0	0 0	0 0	1 0.4%	0 0	0 0	1 0.6%	0 0	0 0	0 0	0 0	0 0	0 0	0 0	1 4.8%	0 0	1 0.4%
preferred source of info	0 0	0 0	0 0	0 0	0 0	0 0	0 0	0 0	0 0	0 0	0 0	0 0	0 0	0 0	0 0	0 0	0 0	0 0

Proportions/Means: Columns Tested (5% risk level) - A/B/D - C/D - E/F/G - H/I/J/K/L/M/N - P/Q
* small base; ** very small base (under 30) ineligible for sig testing

Table 387
Page 1639

Outsell/Digital Library Federation Study (2002)
Weighted Tables

TABLE 144, continued

S7D/E_10. Manuscripts and other primary source documents SUMMARY TABLE

		RESPONDENT TYPE				INSTITUTION TYPE			DISCIPLINE									GENDER	
	TOTAL SAMPLE	FACULTY MEMBER	GRAD. STUDENT	FACULTY /GRAD	UNDER GRAD. STUDENT	PUBLIC	PRIVATE	LIBERAL ARTS	BIOLOGIAL SCIENCES	PHYSICAL SCIENCES /MATH	SOCIAL SCIENCES	ARTS AND HUMAN.	ENGI-NEERING	BUSINESS	LAW	UNDEC. MAJOR	MALE	FEMALE
		(A)	(B)	(C)	(D)	(E)	(F)	(G)	(H)	(I)	(J)	(K)	(L)	(M)	(N)		(P)	(Q)
Base - Use Manuscripts and other primary source documents for coursework	447	0**	192	192	255	194	91*	161	58*	48*	167*	101*	10*	37*	4**	21*	182	265
Colleagues (NET)	* 0.1%	0 0	* 0.2%	* 0.2%	0 0	0 0	* 0.3%	0 0	0 0	0 0	0 0	0 0	* 2.8%HJK	0 0	0 0	0 0	* 0.2%	0 0
All sources of info	* 0.1%	0 0	* 0.2%	* 0.2%	0 0	0 0	* 0.3%	0 0	0 0	0 0	0 0	0 0	* 2.8%HJK	0 0	0 0	0 0	* 0.2%	0 0
preferred source of info	* 0.1%	0 0	* 0.2%	* 0.2%	0 0	0 0	* 0.3%	0 0	0 0	0 0	0 0	0 0	* 2.8%HJK	0 0	0 0	0 0	* 0.2%	0 0
Access book/journal/ journal article elsewhere online (NET)	0 0	0 0	0 0	0 0	0 0	0 0	0 0	0 0	0 0	0 0	0 0	0 0	0 0	0 0	0 0	0 0	0 0	0 0
All sources of info	0 0	0 0	0 0	0 0	0 0	0 0	0 0	0 0	0 0	0 0	0 0	0 0	0 0	0 0	0 0	0 0	0 0	0 0
preferred source of info	0 0	0 0	0 0	0 0	0 0	0 0	0 0	0 0	0 0	0 0	0 0	0 0	0 0	0 0	0 0	0 0	0 0	0 0
In class (NET)	0 0	0 0	0 0	0 0	0 0	0 0	0 0	0 0	0 0	0 0	0 0	0 0	0 0	0 0	0 0	0 0	0 0	0 0
All sources of info	0 0	0 0	0 0	0 0	0 0	0 0	0 0	0 0	0 0	0 0	0 0	0 0	0 0	0 0	0 0	0 0	0 0	0 0

Proportions/Means: Columns Tested (5% risk level) - A/B/D - C/D - E/F/G - H/I/J/K/L/M/N - P/Q
* small base; ** very small base (under 30) ineligible for sig testing

Table 387
Page 1640

Outsell/Digital Library Federation Study (2002)
Weighted Tables

TABLE 144, continued

S7D/E_10. Manuscripts and other primary source documents SUMMARY TABLE

		RESPONDENT TYPE				INSTITUTION TYPE			DISCIPLINE								GENDER	
	TOTAL SAMPLE	FACULTY MEMBER	GRAD. STUDENT	FACULTY /GRAD	UNDER GRAD. STUDENT	PUBLIC	PRIVATE	LIBERAL ARTS	BIOLOGIAL SCIENCES	PHYSICAL SCIENCES /MATH	SOCIAL SCIENCES	ARTS AND HUMAN.	ENGI-NEERING	BUSINESS	LAW	UNDEC. MAJOR	MALE	FEMALE
		(A)	(B)	(C)	(D)	(E)	(F)	(G)	(H)	(I)	(J)	(K)	(L)	(M)	(N)		(P)	(Q)
Base - Use Manuscripts and other primary source documents for coursework	447	0**	192	192	255	194	91*	161	58*	48*	167*	101*	10*	37*	4**	21*	182	265
preferred source of info	0 0	0 0	0 0	0 0	0 0	0 0	0 0	0 0	0 0	0 0	0 0	0 0	0 0	0 0	0 0	0 0	0 0	0 0
Dorm room (NET)	0 0	0 0	0 0	0 0	0 0	0 0	0 0	0 0	0 0	0 0	0 0	0 0	0 0	0 0	0 0	0 0	0 0	0 0
All sources of info	0 0	0 0	0 0	0 0	0 0	0 0	0 0	0 0	0 0	0 0	0 0	0 0	0 0	0 0	0 0	0 0	0 0	0 0
preferred source of info	0 0	0 0	0 0	0 0	0 0	0 0	0 0	0 0	0 0	0 0	0 0	0 0	0 0	0 0	0 0	0 0	0 0	0 0
Access from course website (NET)	0 0	0 0	0 0	0 0	0 0	0 0	0 0	0 0	0 0	0 0	0 0	0 0	0 0	0 0	0 0	0 0	0 0	0 0
All sources of info	0 0	0 0	0 0	0 0	0 0	0 0	0 0	0 0	0 0	0 0	0 0	0 0	0 0	0 0	0 0	0 0	0 0	0 0
preferred source of info	0 0	0 0	0 0	0 0	0 0	0 0	0 0	0 0	0 0	0 0	0 0	0 0	0 0	0 0	0 0	0 0	0 0	0 0
Other (NET)	12 2.7%	0 0	5 2.8%	5 2.8%	7 2.7%	10 5.0%G	2 2.6%	0 0	0 0	0 0	9 5.6%	2 2.2%	* 2.8%H	0 0	* 4.2%	0 0	2 0.9%	11 4.0%
All sources of info	12 2.7%	0 0	5 2.8%	5 2.8%	7 2.7%	10 5.0%G	2 2.6%	0 0	0 0	0 0	9 5.6%	2 2.2%	* 2.8%H	0 0	* 4.2%	0 0	2 0.9%	11 4.0%

Proportions/Means: Columns Tested (5% risk level) - A/B/D - C/D - E/F/G - H/I/J/K/L/M/N - P/Q
* small base; ** very small base (under 30) ineligible for sig testing

Table 387
Page 1641

Outsell/Digital Library Federation Study (2002)
Weighted Tables

TABLE 144, continued

S7D/E_10. Manuscripts and other primary source documents SUMMARY TABLE

		RESPONDENT TYPE				INSTITUTION TYPE			DISCIPLINE									GENDER	
	TOTAL SAMPLE	FACULTY MEMBER	GRAD. STUDENT	FACULTY /GRAD	UNDER GRAD. STUDENT	PUBLIC	PRIVATE	LIBERAL ARTS	BIOLOGIAL SCIENCES	PHYSICAL SCIENCES /MATH	SOCIAL SCIENCES	ARTS AND HUMAN.	ENGI- NEERING	BUSINESS	LAW	UNDEC. MAJOR	MALE	FEMALE
		(A)	(B)	(C)	(D)	(E)	(F)	(G)	(H)	(I)	(J)	(K)	(L)	(M)	(N)		(P)	(Q)
Base - Use Manuscripts and other primary source documents for coursework	447	0**	192	192	255	194	91*	161	58*	48*	167*	101*	10*	37*	4**	21*	182	265
preferred source of info	8 1.7%	0 0	2 1.1%	2 1.1%	6 2.2%	8 3.9%G	* 0.3%	0 0	0 0	0 0	8 4.5%	0 0	* 2.8%HK	0 0	0 0	0 0	* 0.2%	8 2.8%
DK/Refused	5 1.1%	0 0	3 1.5%	3 1.5%	2 0.7%	4 1.9%	1 1.1%	0 0	0 0	1 2.1%	4 2.2%	0 0	0 0	0 0	0 0	0 0	5 2.6%Q	0 0

Proportions/Means: Columns Tested (5% risk level) - A/B/D - C/D - E/F/G - H/I/J/K/L/M/N - P/Q
* small base; ** very small base (under 30) ineligible for sig testing

TABLE 145

S7sum_11. Proprietary software or application SUMMARY TABLE

		RESPONDENT TYPE				INSTITUTION TYPE			DISCIPLINE								GENDER	
	TOTAL SAMPLE	FACULTY MEMBER	GRAD. STUDENT	FACULTY /GRAD	UNDER GRAD. STUDENT	PUBLIC	PRIVATE	LIBERAL ARTS	BIOLOGIAL SCIENCES	PHYSICAL SCIENCES /MATH	SOCIAL SCIENCES	ARTS AND HUMAN.	ENGI-NEERING	BUSINESS	LAW	UNDEC. MAJOR	MALE	FEMALE
		(A)	(B)	(C)	(D)	(E)	(F)	(G)	(H)	(I)	(J)	(K)	(L)	(M)	(N)		(P)	(Q)
Base - Use Proprietary software or application for coursework	314	0**	140	140	174	144	76*	94*	43*	47*	86*	53*	24*	45*	3**	13*	178	136
ONLINE	182 57.8%	0 0	74 52.6%	74 52.6%	108 61.9%	79 54.7%	45 58.5%	58 62.0%	19 44.9%	27 57.4%	51 58.7%	35 66.0%H	14 58.3%	26 58.3%	3 83.3%	7 53.8%	103 57.8%	79 57.8%
Search engine (NET)	78 24.7%	0 0	18 13.0%	18 13.0%	59 34.1%B C	29 19.8%	17 21.6%	32 34.6%E	6 14.3%	10 21.3%	19 21.7%	17 31.9%H	6 22.6%	14 31.2%	* 11.1%	6 46.2%	44 24.4%	34 25.0%
All sources of info	78 24.7%	0 0	18 13.0%	18 13.0%	59 34.1%B C	29 19.8%	17 21.6%	32 34.6%E	6 14.3%	10 21.3%	19 21.7%	17 31.9%H	6 22.6%	14 31.2%	* 11.1%	6 46.2%	44 24.4%	34 25.0%
preferred source of info	49 15.7%	0 0	9 6.7%	9 6.7%	40 22.9%B C	24 16.9%	8 10.9%	17 17.7%	4 10.2%	6 12.8%	13 15.2%	10 19.1%	4 15.5%	7 14.6%	* 11.1%	5 38.5%	27 15.1%	22 16.4%
Your own institution's web site (NET)	34 10.8%	0 0	22 15.4%D	22 15.4%D	12 7.1%	19 12.9%	8 9.9%	8 8.4%	5 12.2%	6 12.8%	8 8.7%	4 8.5%	2 8.3%	7 14.6%	* 5.6%	2 15.4%	15 8.1%	19 14.3%
All sources of info	34 10.8%	0 0	22 15.4%D	22 15.4%D	12 7.1%	19 12.9%	8 9.9%	8 8.4%	5 12.2%	6 12.8%	8 8.7%	4 8.5%	2 8.3%	7 14.6%	* 5.6%	2 15.4%	15 8.1%	19 14.3%
preferred source of info	24 7.7%	0 0	15 10.7%	15 10.7%	9 5.2%	17 11.6%F	2 2.1%	6 6.3%	3 6.1%	5 10.6%	8 8.7%	3 6.4%	2 7.1%	4 8.3%	* 5.6%	0 0	11 6.3%	13 9.4%
Internet searches (NET)	26 8.3%	0 0	15 10.6%	15 10.6%	11 6.5%	13 8.8%	9 11.7%	5 4.9%	4 10.2%	4 8.5%	4 4.3%	8 14.9%	2 9.5%	4 8.3%	* 5.6%	0 0	18 10.0%	8 6.1%

Proportions/Means: Columns Tested (5% risk level) - A/B/D - C/D - E/F/G - H/I/J/K/L/M/N - P/Q
* small base; ** very small base (under 30) ineligible for sig testing

Table 391
Page 1654

Outsell/Digital Library Federation Study (2002)
Weighted Tables

TABLE 145, continued

S7sum_11. Proprietary software or application SUMMARY TABLE

	TOTAL SAMPLE	RESPONDENT TYPE: FACULTY MEMBER	GRAD. STUDENT	FACULTY /GRAD	UNDER GRAD. STUDENT	INSTITUTION TYPE: PUBLIC	PRIVATE	LIBERAL ARTS	DISCIPLINE: BIOLOGIAL SCIENCES	PHYSICAL SCIENCES /MATH	SOCIAL SCIENCES	ARTS AND HUMAN.	ENGI-NEERING	BUSINESS	LAW	UNDEC. MAJOR	GENDER: MALE	FEMALE
		(A)	(B)	(C)	(D)	(E)	(F)	(G)	(H)	(I)	(J)	(K)	(L)	(M)	(N)		(P)	(Q)
Base - Use Proprietary software or application for coursework	314	0**	140	140	174	144	76*	94*	43*	47*	86*	53*	24*	45*	3**	13*	178	136
All sources of info	26 8.3%	0 0	15 10.6%	15 10.6%	11 6.5%	13 8.8%	9 11.7%	5 4.9%	4 10.2%	4 8.5%	4 4.3%	8 14.9%	2 9.5%	4 8.3%	* 5.6%	0 0	18 10.0%	8 6.1%
preferred source of info	14 4.5%	0 0	8 5.4%	8 5.4%	7 3.8%	8 5.4%	5 6.8%	1 1.2%	1 2.0%	2 4.3%	4 4.3%	4 8.5%	1 4.8%	2 4.2%	0 0	0 0	9 5.1%	5 3.7%
Online databases (NET)	24 7.7%	0 0	8 5.9%	8 5.9%	16 9.1%	7 5.1%	7 9.4%	10 10.2%	2 4.1%	2 4.3%	13 15.2%L	3 6.4%	1 2.4%	2 4.2%	1 44.4%	0 0	14 8.1%	10 7.1%
All sources of info	24 7.7%	0 0	8 5.9%	8 5.9%	16 9.1%	7 5.1%	7 9.4%	10 10.2%	2 4.1%	2 4.3%	13 15.2%L	3 6.4%	1 2.4%	2 4.2%	1 44.4%	0 0	14 8.1%	10 7.1%
preferred source of info	16 5.1%	0 0	7 5.1%	7 5.1%	9 5.2%	5 3.2%	5 6.3%	7 7.3%	0 0	2 4.3%	9 10.9%H	1 2.1%	1 2.4%	2 4.2%	1 38.9%	0 0	10 5.8%	6 4.3%
Web directory/ subject related web site (NET)	21 6.6%	0 0	5 3.6%	5 3.6%	16 9.0%	6 4.2%	7 8.6%	8 8.7%	4 10.2%	4 8.5%	4 4.3%	2 4.3%	3 13.1%	3 6.2%	* 11.1%	0 0	11 6.4%	9 6.9%
All sources of info	21 6.6%	0 0	5 3.6%	5 3.6%	16 9.0%	6 4.2%	7 8.6%	8 8.7%	4 10.2%	4 8.5%	4 4.3%	2 4.3%	3 13.1%	3 6.2%	* 11.1%	0 0	11 6.4%	9 6.9%
preferred source of info	9 2.8%	0 0	2 1.5%	2 1.5%	7 3.8%	2 1.2%	4 5.3%	3 3.1%	3 6.1%	1 2.1%	2 2.2%	1 2.1%	1 4.8%	1 2.1%	0 0	0 0	5 2.9%	4 2.7%
Online library catalogues and finding aids (NET)	20 6.5%	0 0	6 4.2%	6 4.2%	15 8.3%	7 4.9%	4 4.6%	10 10.5%	1 2.0%	1 2.1%	6 6.5%	7 12.8%	2 8.3%	3 6.2%	* 11.1%	1 7.7%	12 6.7%	8 6.2%

Proportions/Means: Columns Tested (5% risk level) - A/B/D - C/D - E/F/G - H/I/J/K/L/M/N - P/Q
* small base; ** very small base (under 30) ineligible for sig testing

Table 391
Page 1655

Outsell/Digital Library Federation Study (2002)
Weighted Tables

TABLE 145, continued

S7sum_11. Proprietary software or application SUMMARY TABLE

	TOTAL SAMPLE	RESPONDENT TYPE: FACULTY MEMBER	GRAD. STUDENT	FACULTY /GRAD	UNDER GRAD. STUDENT	INSTITUTION TYPE: PUBLIC	PRIVATE	LIBERAL ARTS	DISCIPLINE: BIOLOGIAL SCIENCES	PHYSICAL SCIENCES /MATH	SOCIAL SCIENCES	ARTS AND HUMAN.	ENGI-NEERING	BUSINESS	LAW	UNDEC. MAJOR	GENDER: MALE	FEMALE
		(A)	(B)	(C)	(D)	(E)	(F)	(G)	(H)	(I)	(J)	(K)	(L)	(M)	(N)		(P)	(Q)
Base - Use Proprietary software or application for coursework	314	0**	140	140	174	144	76*	94*	43*	47*	86*	53*	24*	45*	3**	13*	178	136
All sources of info	20 6.5%	0 0	6 4.2%	6 4.2%	15 8.3%	7 4.9%	4 4.6%	10 10.5%	1 2.0%	1 2.1%	6 6.5%	7 12.8%	2 8.3%	3 6.2%	* 11.1%	1 7.7%	12 6.7%	8 6.2%
preferred source of info	14 4.3%	0 0	5 3.9%	5 3.9%	8 4.7%	7 4.9%	3 4.0%	4 3.8%	1 2.0%	1 2.1%	2 2.2%	4 8.5%	1 6.0%	3 6.2%	* 5.6%	1 7.7%	7 4.2%	6 4.5%
Department web page (NET)	12 3.8%	0 0	7 5.2%	7 5.2%	5 2.8%	5 3.5%	4 5.4%	3 3.1%	1 2.0%	3 6.4%	6 6.5%	0 0	1 2.4%	1 2.1%	0 0	1 7.7%	12 6.7%Q	0 0
All sources of info	12 3.8%	0 0	7 5.2%	7 5.2%	5 2.8%	5 3.5%	4 5.4%	3 3.1%	1 2.0%	3 6.4%	6 6.5%	0 0	1 2.4%	1 2.1%	0 0	1 7.7%	12 6.7%Q	0 0
preferred source of info	8 2.5%	0 0	7 4.9%D	7 4.9%D	1 0.5%	4 2.8%	4 5.0%G	0 0	1 2.0%	2 4.3%	4 4.3%	0 0	* 1.2%	1 2.1%	0 0	0 0	8 4.4%Q	0 0
Online reference service (NET)	8 2.5%	0 0	3 1.8%	3 1.8%	5 3.0%	5 3.1%	1 1.4%	2 2.3%	2 4.1%	1 2.1%	2 2.2%	1 2.1%	1 3.6%	1 2.1%	* 5.6%	0 0	6 3.2%	2 1.5%
All sources of info	8 2.5%	0 0	3 1.8%	3 1.8%	5 3.0%	5 3.1%	1 1.4%	2 2.3%	2 4.1%	1 2.1%	2 2.2%	1 2.1%	1 3.6%	1 2.1%	* 5.6%	0 0	6 3.2%	2 1.5%
preferred source of info	3 1.0%	0 0	* 0.2%	* 0.2%	3 1.7%	2 1.5%	0 0	1 1.1%	0 0	1 2.1%	2 2.2%	0 0	* 1.2%	0 0	0 0	0 0	1 0.7%	2 1.4%
Your own personal electronic library/files (NET)	2 0.7%	0 0	1 0.9%	1 0.9%	1 0.6%	* 0.2%	1 1.2%	1 1.1%	0 0	1 2.1%	0 0	0 0	* 1.2%	1 2.1%	0 0	0 0	2 1.2%	0 0

Proportions/Means: Columns Tested (5% risk level) - A/B/D - C/D - E/F/G - H/I/J/K/L/M/N - P/Q
* small base; ** very small base (under 30) ineligible for sig testing

Table 391
Page 1656

Outsell/Digital Library Federation Study (2002)
Weighted Tables

TABLE 145, continued

S7sum_11. Proprietary software or application SUMMARY TABLE

		RESPONDENT TYPE				INSTITUTION TYPE			DISCIPLINE									GENDER	
	TOTAL SAMPLE	FACULTY MEMBER	GRAD. STUDENT	FACULTY /GRAD	UNDER GRAD. STUDENT	PUBLIC	PRIVATE	LIBERAL ARTS	BIOLOGIAL SCIENCES	PHYSICAL SCIENCES /MATH	SOCIAL SCIENCES	ARTS AND HUMAN.	ENGI- NEERING	BUSINESS	LAW	UNDEC. MAJOR	MALE	FEMALE
		(A)	(B)	(C)	(D)	(E)	(F)	(G)	(H)	(I)	(J)	(K)	(L)	(M)	(N)		(P)	(Q)
Base - Use Proprietary software or application for coursework	314	0**	140	140	174	144	76*	94*	43*	47*	86*	53*	24*	45*	3**	13*	178	136
All sources of info	2 0.7%	0 0	1 0.9%	1 0.9%	1 0.6%	* 0.2%	1 1.2%	1 1.1%	0 0	1 2.1%	0 0	0 0	* 1.2%	1 2.1%	0 0	0 0	2 1.2%	0 0
preferred source of info	2 0.7%	0 0	1 0.9%	1 0.9%	1 0.6%	* 0.2%	1 1.2%	1 1.1%	0 0	1 2.1%	0 0	0 0	* 1.2%	1 2.1%	0 0	0 0	2 1.2%	0 0
Online abstracting and indexing services (NET)	2 0.6%	0 0	2 1.3%	2 1.3%	0 0	2 1.3%	0 0	0 0	0 0	0 0	2 2.2%	0 0	0 0	0 0	0 0	0 0	0 0	2 1.4%
All sources of info	2 0.6%	0 0	2 1.3%	2 1.3%	0 0	2 1.3%	0 0	0 0	0 0	0 0	2 2.2%	0 0	0 0	0 0	0 0	0 0	0 0	2 1.4%
preferred source of info	2 0.6%	0 0	2 1.3%	2 1.3%	0 0	2 1.3%	0 0	0 0	0 0	0 0	2 2.2%	0 0	0 0	0 0	0 0	0 0	0 0	2 1.4%
Online bookstore (NET)	* 0.1%	0 0	* 0.2%	* 0.2%	0 0	* 0.2%	0 0	0 0	0 0	0 0	0 0	0 0	* 1.2%	0 0	0 0	0 0	* 0.2%	0 0
All sources of info	* 0.1%	0 0	* 0.2%	* 0.2%	0 0	* 0.2%	0 0	0 0	0 0	0 0	0 0	0 0	* 1.2%	0 0	0 0	0 0	* 0.2%	0 0
preferred source of info	* 0.1%	0 0	* 0.2%	* 0.2%	0 0	* 0.2%	0 0	0 0	0 0	0 0	0 0	0 0	* 1.2%	0 0	0 0	0 0	* 0.2%	0 0
E-mail listservs (NET)	0 0	0 0	0 0	0 0	0 0	0 0	0 0	0 0	0 0	0 0	0 0	0 0	0 0	0 0	0 0	0 0	0 0	0 0

Proportions/Means: Columns Tested (5% risk level) - A/B/D - C/D - E/F/G - H/I/J/K/L/M/N - P/Q
* small base; ** very small base (under 30) ineligible for sig testing

Table 391
Page 1657

Outsell/Digital Library Federation Study (2002)
Weighted Tables

TABLE 145, continued

S7sum_11. Proprietary software or application SUMMARY TABLE

		RESPONDENT TYPE				INSTITUTION TYPE			DISCIPLINE									GENDER	
	TOTAL SAMPLE	FACULTY MEMBER	GRAD. STUDENT	FACULTY /GRAD	UNDER GRAD. STUDENT	PUBLIC	PRIVATE	LIBERAL ARTS	BIOLOGICAL SCIENCES	PHYSICAL SCIENCES /MATH	SOCIAL SCIENCES	ARTS AND HUMAN.	ENGI- NEERING	BUSINESS	LAW	UNDEC. MAJOR	MALE	FEMALE
		(A)	(B)	(C)	(D)	(E)	(F)	(G)	(H)	(I)	(J)	(K)	(L)	(M)	(N)		(P)	(Q)
Base - Use Proprietary software or application for coursework	314	0**	140	140	174	144	76*	94*	43*	47*	86*	53*	24*	45*	3**	13*	178	136
All sources of info	0 0	0 0	0 0	0 0	0 0	0 0	0 0	0 0	0 0	0 0	0 0	0 0	0 0	0 0	0 0	0 0	0 0	0 0
preferred source of info	0 0	0 0	0 0	0 0	0 0	0 0	0 0	0 0	0 0	0 0	0 0	0 0	0 0	0 0	0 0	0 0	0 0	0 0
PERSONAL ASSISTANCE	163 52.0%	0 0	76 54.5%	76 54.5%	87 50.0%	66 46.0%	44 58.0%	53 56.3%	29 67.3%J	24 51.1%	34 39.1%	31 59.6%	13 53.6%	25 56.2%	1 33.3%	6 46.2%	84 47.4%	79 58.0%
Faculty members inside your institution (NET)	99 31.5%	0 0	51 36.5%	51 36.5%	48 27.5%	39 26.7%	27 35.9%	33 35.4%	19 44.9%J	17 36.2%	21 23.9%	16 29.8%	10 41.7%J	14 31.2%	* 11.1%	2 15.4%	57 31.9%	42 31.0%
All sources of info	99 31.5%	0 0	51 36.5%	51 36.5%	48 27.5%	39 26.7%	27 35.9%	33 35.4%	19 44.9%J	17 36.2%	21 23.9%	16 29.8%	10 41.7%J	14 31.2%	* 11.1%	2 15.4%	57 31.9%	42 31.0%
preferred source of info	73 23.1%	0 0	40 28.4%	40 28.4%	33 18.8%	28 19.2%	20 26.0%	25 26.6%	12 28.6%	13 27.7%	17 19.6%	9 17.0%	7 28.6%	12 27.1%	* 11.1%	2 15.4%	44 24.8%	28 20.9%
A librarian in your institution (NET)	67 21.2%	0 0	17 12.3%	17 12.3%	50 28.4%B C	23 16.3%	13 17.5%	30 31.9%EF	7 16.3%	7 14.9%	15 17.4%	19 36.2%HIJ L	2 7.1%	11 25.0%L	1 22.2%	5 38.5%	29 16.0%	38 28.1%P
All sources of info	67 21.2%	0 0	17 12.3%	17 12.3%	50 28.4%B C	23 16.3%	13 17.5%	30 31.9%EF	7 16.3%	7 14.9%	15 17.4%	19 36.2%HIJ L	2 7.1%	11 25.0%L	1 22.2%	5 38.5%	29 16.0%	38 28.1%P

Proportions/Means: Columns Tested (5% risk level) - A/B/D - C/D - E/F/G - H/I/J/K/L/M/N - P/Q
* small base; ** very small base (under 30) ineligible for sig testing

TABLE 145, continued

S7sum_11. Proprietary software or application SUMMARY TABLE

	TOTAL SAMPLE	RESPONDENT TYPE: FACULTY MEMBER (A)	GRAD. STUDENT (B)	FACULTY /GRAD (C)	UNDER GRAD. STUDENT (D)	INSTITUTION TYPE: PUBLIC (E)	PRIVATE (F)	LIBERAL ARTS (G)	DISCIPLINE: BIOLOGIAL SCIENCES (H)	PHYSICAL SCIENCES /MATH (I)	SOCIAL SCIENCES (J)	ARTS AND HUMAN. (K)	ENGI-NEERING (L)	BUSINESS (M)	LAW (N)	UNDEC. MAJOR	GENDER: MALE (P)	FEMALE (Q)
Base - Use Proprietary software or application for coursework	314	0**	140	140	174	144	76*	94*	43*	47*	86*	53*	24*	45*	3**	13*	178	136
preferred source of info	32 10.1%	0 0	10 7.2%	10 7.2%	22 12.4%	11 7.7%	8 10.2%	13 13.7%	4 8.2%	3 6.4%	8 8.7%	8 14.9%L	* 1.2%	7 16.7%L	* 5.6%	2 15.4%	12 6.9%	19 14.3%
Other students inside your institution (NET)	39 12.3%	0 0	22 16.0%	22 16.0%	16 9.4%	17 12.0%	13 16.9%	9 9.3%	11 24.5%J	8 17.0%	6 6.5%	6 10.6%	4 17.9%J	5 10.4%	0 0	0 0	18 10.1%	21 15.3%
All sources of info	39 12.3%	0 0	22 16.0%	22 16.0%	16 9.4%	17 12.0%	13 16.9%	9 9.3%	11 24.5%J	8 17.0%	6 6.5%	6 10.6%	4 17.9%J	5 10.4%	0 0	0 0	18 10.1%	21 15.3%
preferred source of info	16 5.2%	0 0	11 7.8%	11 7.8%	5 3.1%	9 6.2%	5 7.2%	2 2.0%	5 12.2%J	5 10.6%J	0 0	3 6.4%J	2 7.1%J	1 2.1%	0 0	0 0	6 3.5%	10 7.4%
Another institution's librarian (NET)	3 0.9%	0 0	1 0.6%	1 0.6%	2 1.1%	2 1.3%	1 1.2%	0 0	1 2.0%	0 0	2 2.2%	0 0	0 0	0 0	0 0	0 0	0 0	3 2.0%
All sources of info	3 0.9%	0 0	1 0.6%	1 0.6%	2 1.1%	2 1.3%	1 1.2%	0 0	1 2.0%	0 0	2 2.2%	0 0	0 0	0 0	0 0	0 0	0 0	3 2.0%
preferred source of info	3 0.9%	0 0	1 0.6%	1 0.6%	2 1.1%	2 1.3%	1 1.2%	0 0	1 2.0%	0 0	2 2.2%	0 0	0 0	0 0	0 0	0 0	0 0	3 2.0%
Faculty members outside your institution (NET)	1 0.4%	0 0	0 0	0 0	1 0.6%	0 0	0 0	1 1.2%	0 0	0 0	0 0	1 2.1%	0 0	0 0	0 0	0 0	0 0	1 0.8%

Proportions/Means: Columns Tested (5% risk level) - A/B/D - C/D - E/F/G - H/I/J/K/L/M/N - P/Q
* small base; ** very small base (under 30) ineligible for sig testing

Table 391
Page 1659

Outsell/Digital Library Federation Study (2002)
Weighted Tables

TABLE 145, continued

S7sum_11. Proprietary software or application SUMMARY TABLE

		RESPONDENT TYPE				INSTITUTION TYPE			DISCIPLINE									GENDER	
	TOTAL SAMPLE	FACULTY MEMBER	GRAD. STUDENT	FACULTY /GRAD	UNDER GRAD. STUDENT	PUBLIC	PRIVATE	LIBERAL ARTS	BIOLOGIAL SCIENCES	PHYSICAL SCIENCES /MATH	SOCIAL SCIENCES	ARTS AND HUMAN.	ENGI- NEERING	BUSINESS	LAW	UNDEC. MAJOR	MALE	FEMALE
		(A)	(B)	(C)	(D)	(E)	(F)	(G)	(H)	(I)	(J)	(K)	(L)	(M)	(N)		(P)	(Q)
Base - Use Proprietary software or application for coursework	314	0**	140	140	174	144	76*	94*	43*	47*	86*	53*	24*	45*	3**	13*	178	136
All sources of info	1 0.4%	0 0	0 0	0 0	1 0.6%	0 0	0 0	1 1.2%	0 0	0 0	0 0	1 2.1%	0 0	0 0	0 0	0 0	0 0	1 0.8%
preferred source of info	0 0	0 0	0 0	0 0	0 0	0 0	0 0	0 0	0 0	0 0	0 0	0 0	0 0	0 0	0 0	0 0	0 0	0 0
Other students outside your institution (NET)	1 0.2%	0 0	1 0.4%	1 0.4%	0 0	* 0.2%	* 0.4%	0 0	0 0	0 0	0 0	0 0	1 2.4%	0 0	0 0	0 0	* 0.2%	* 0.2%
All sources of info	1 0.2%	0 0	1 0.4%	1 0.4%	0 0	* 0.2%	* 0.4%	0 0	0 0	0 0	0 0	0 0	1 2.4%	0 0	0 0	0 0	* 0.2%	* 0.2%
preferred source of info	* 0.1%	0 0	* 0.2%	* 0.2%	0 0	0 0	* 0.4%	0 0	0 0	0 0	0 0	0 0	* 1.2%	0 0	0 0	0 0	0 0	* 0.2%
Professional meetings (NET)	* 0.1%	0 0	* 0.3%	* 0.3%	0 0	0 0	* 0.6%	0 0	0 0	0 0	0 0	0 0	* 1.2%	0 0	* 5.6%	0 0	* 0.3%	0 0
All sources of info	* 0.1%	0 0	* 0.3%	* 0.3%	0 0	0 0	* 0.6%	0 0	0 0	0 0	0 0	0 0	* 1.2%	0 0	* 5.6%	0 0	* 0.3%	0 0
preferred source of info	0 0	0 0	0 0	0 0	0 0	0 0	0 0	0 0	0 0	0 0	0 0	0 0	0 0	0 0	0 0	0 0	0 0	0 0
LIBRARY FACILITIES/ PRINT	59 18.9%	0 0	25 17.9%	25 17.9%	34 19.7%	29 20.4%	12 16.0%	18 19.0%	4 10.2%	6 12.8%	19 21.7%	15 27.7%H	6 22.6%	7 14.6%	1 22.2%	3 23.1%	31 17.4%	28 20.9%

Proportions/Means: Columns Tested (5% risk level) - A/B/D - C/D - E/F/G - H/I/J/K/L/M/N - P/Q
* small base; ** very small base (under 30) ineligible for sig testing

Table 391
Page 1660

Outsell/Digital Library Federation Study (2002)
Weighted Tables

TABLE 145, continued

S7sum_11. Proprietary software or application SUMMARY TABLE

		RESPONDENT TYPE				INSTITUTION TYPE			DISCIPLINE									GENDER	
	TOTAL SAMPLE	FACULTY MEMBER	GRAD. STUDENT	FACULTY /GRAD	UNDER GRAD. STUDENT	PUBLIC	PRIVATE	LIBERAL ARTS	BIOLOGIAL SCIENCES	PHYSICAL SCIENCES /MATH	SOCIAL SCIENCES	ARTS AND HUMAN.	ENGI-NEERING	BUSINESS	LAW	UNDEC. MAJOR	MALE	FEMALE
		(A)	(B)	(C)	(D)	(E)	(F)	(G)	(H)	(I)	(J)	(K)	(L)	(M)	(N)		(P)	(Q)
Base - Use Proprietary software or application for coursework	314	0**	140	140	174	144	76*	94*	43*	47*	86*	53*	24*	45*	3**	13*	178	136
Campus library (NET)	50 15.8%	0 0	19 13.8%	19 13.8%	30 17.4%	22 15.5%	11 13.8%	17 18.0%	4 8.2%	5 10.6%	15 17.4%	13 25.5%H	5 19.0%	6 12.5%	1 16.7%	2 15.4%	24 13.5%	26 18.9%
All sources of info	50 15.8%	0 0	19 13.8%	19 13.8%	30 17.4%	22 15.5%	11 13.8%	17 18.0%	4 8.2%	5 10.6%	15 17.4%	13 25.5%H	5 19.0%	6 12.5%	1 16.7%	2 15.4%	24 13.5%	26 18.9%
preferred source of info	19 6.1%	0 0	5 3.5%	5 3.5%	14 8.1%	8 5.6%	3 3.8%	8 8.7%	2 4.1%	1 2.1%	8 8.7%	4 8.5%	1 4.8%	2 4.2%	* 11.1%	1 7.7%	11 6.2%	8 6.0%
Physical bookstore (NET)	5 1.6%	0 0	4 2.8%	4 2.8%	1 0.6%	3 1.9%	1 1.6%	1 1.2%	2 4.1%	1 2.1%	0 0	1 2.1%	* 1.2%	1 2.1%	0 0	0 0	3 1.7%	2 1.5%
All sources of info	5 1.6%	0 0	4 2.8%	4 2.8%	1 0.6%	3 1.9%	1 1.6%	1 1.2%	2 4.1%	1 2.1%	0 0	1 2.1%	* 1.2%	1 2.1%	0 0	0 0	3 1.7%	2 1.5%
preferred source of info	2 0.6%	0 0	2 1.4%	2 1.4%	0 0	1 0.7%	1 1.2%	0 0	0 0	1 2.1%	0 0	0 0	0 0	1 2.1%	0 0	0 0	2 1.1%	0 0
Your own personal physical library/ files/bookshelves (NET)	4 1.4%	0 0	1 0.4%	1 0.4%	4 2.2%	4 2.6%	1 0.8%	0 0	0 0	0 0	4 4.3%	0 0	1 2.4%	0 0	0 0	0 0	1 0.3%	4 2.8%
All sources of info	4 1.4%	0 0	1 0.4%	1 0.4%	4 2.2%	4 2.6%	1 0.8%	0 0	0 0	0 0	4 4.3%	0 0	1 2.4%	0 0	0 0	0 0	1 0.3%	4 2.8%
preferred source of info	* 0.1%	0 0	* 0.2%	* 0.2%	0 0	0 0	* 0.4%	0 0	0 0	0 0	0 0	0 0	* 1.2%	0 0	0 0	0 0	* 0.2%	0 0

Proportions/Means: Columns Tested (5% risk level) - A/B/D - C/D - E/F/G - H/I/J/K/L/M/N - P/Q
* small base; ** very small base (under 30) ineligible for sig testing

Table 391
Page 1661

Outsell/Digital Library Federation Study (2002)
Weighted Tables

TABLE 145, continued

S7sum_11. Proprietary software or application SUMMARY TABLE

		RESPONDENT TYPE				INSTITUTION TYPE			DISCIPLINE									GENDER	
	TOTAL SAMPLE	FACULTY MEMBER	GRAD. STUDENT	FACULTY /GRAD	UNDER GRAD. STUDENT	PUBLIC	PRIVATE	LIBERAL ARTS	BIOLOGIAL SCIENCES	PHYSICAL SCIENCES /MATH	SOCIAL SCIENCES	ARTS AND HUMAN.	ENGI-NEERING	BUSINESS	LAW	UNDEC. MAJOR	MALE	FEMALE
		(A)	(B)	(C)	(D)	(E)	(F)	(G)	(H)	(I)	(J)	(K)	(L)	(M)	(N)		(P)	(Q)
Base - Use Proprietary software or application for coursework	314	0**	140	140	174	144	76*	94*	43*	47*	86*	53*	24*	45*	3**	13*	178	136
References cited in books or journal articles (NET)	4 1.3%	0 0	2 1.3%	2 1.3%	2 1.3%	3 2.1%	0 0	1 1.2%	0 0	0 0	2 2.2%	2 4.3%	0 0	0 0	0 0	0 0	3 1.7%	1 0.8%
All sources of info	4 1.3%	0 0	2 1.3%	2 1.3%	2 1.3%	3 2.1%	0 0	1 1.2%	0 0	0 0	2 2.2%	2 4.3%	0 0	0 0	0 0	0 0	3 1.7%	1 0.8%
preferred source of info	3 1.0%	0 0	2 1.3%	2 1.3%	1 0.6%	3 2.1%	0 0	0 0	0 0	0 0	2 2.2%	1 2.1%	0 0	0 0	0 0	0 0	3 1.7%	0 0
Printed library catalogues and finding aids (NET)	2 0.8%	0 0	* 0.2%	* 0.2%	2 1.2%	1 0.8%	* 0.4%	1 1.1%	0 0	0 0	0 0	1 2.1%	* 1.2%	0 0	0 0	1 7.7%	2 1.4%	0 0
All sources of info	2 0.8%	0 0	* 0.2%	* 0.2%	2 1.2%	1 0.8%	* 0.4%	1 1.1%	0 0	0 0	0 0	1 2.1%	* 1.2%	0 0	0 0	1 7.7%	2 1.4%	0 0
preferred source of info	1 0.3%	0 0	0 0	0 0	1 0.6%	0 0	0 0	1 1.1%	0 0	0 0	0 0	0 0	0 0	0 0	0 0	1 7.7%	1 0.6%	0 0
Another library (NET)	2 0.5%	0 0	* 0.3%	* 0.3%	1 0.6%	* 0.2%	* 0.2%	1 1.2%	0 0	0 0	0 0	1 2.1%	* 1.2%	0 0	* 5.6%	0 0	* 0.3%	1 0.8%
All sources of info	2 0.5%	0 0	* 0.3%	* 0.3%	1 0.6%	* 0.2%	* 0.2%	1 1.2%	0 0	0 0	0 0	1 2.1%	* 1.2%	0 0	* 5.6%	0 0	* 0.3%	1 0.8%

Proportions/Means: Columns Tested (5% risk level) - A/B/D - C/D - E/F/G - H/I/J/K/L/M/N - P/Q
* small base; ** very small base (under 30) ineligible for sig testing

Table 391
Page 1662

Outsell/Digital Library Federation Study (2002)
Weighted Tables

TABLE 145, continued

S7sum_11. Proprietary software or application SUMMARY TABLE

		RESPONDENT TYPE				INSTITUTION TYPE			DISCIPLINE								GENDER	
	TOTAL SAMPLE	FACULTY MEMBER	GRAD. STUDENT	FACULTY /GRAD	UNDER GRAD. STUDENT	PUBLIC	PRIVATE	LIBERAL ARTS	BIOLOGIAL SCIENCES	PHYSICAL SCIENCES /MATH	SOCIAL SCIENCES	ARTS AND HUMAN.	ENGI- NEERING	BUSINESS	LAW	UNDEC. MAJOR	MALE	FEMALE
		(A)	(B)	(C)	(D)	(E)	(F)	(G)	(H)	(I)	(J)	(K)	(L)	(M)	(N)		(P)	(Q)
Base - Use Proprietary software or application for coursework	314	0**	140	140	174	144	76*	94*	43*	47*	86*	53*	24*	45*	3**	13*	178	136
preferred source of info	0 0	0 0	0 0	0 0	0 0	0 0	0 0	0 0	0 0	0 0	0 0	0 0	0 0	0 0	0 0	0 0	0 0	0 0
Personal subscriptions to newspapers, magazines and journals (NET)	1 0.5%	0 0	1 1.0%	1 1.0%	0 0	1 0.8%	* 0.4%	0 0	1 2.0%	0 0	0 0	0 0	1 2.4%	0 0	0 0	0 0	1 0.8%	0 0
All sources of info	1 0.5%	0 0	1 1.0%	1 1.0%	0 0	1 0.8%	* 0.4%	0 0	1 2.0%	0 0	0 0	0 0	1 2.4%	0 0	0 0	0 0	1 0.8%	0 0
preferred source of info	0 0	0 0	0 0	0 0	0 0	0 0	0 0	0 0	0 0	0 0	0 0	0 0	0 0	0 0	0 0	0 0	0 0	0 0
Printed abstracting and indexing services (NET)	0 0	0 0	0 0	0 0	0 0	0 0	0 0	0 0	0 0	0 0	0 0	0 0	0 0	0 0	0 0	0 0	0 0	0 0
All sources of info	0 0	0 0	0 0	0 0	0 0	0 0	0 0	0 0	0 0	0 0	0 0	0 0	0 0	0 0	0 0	0 0	0 0	0 0
preferred source of info	0 0	0 0	0 0	0 0	0 0	0 0	0 0	0 0	0 0	0 0	0 0	0 0	0 0	0 0	0 0	0 0	0 0	0 0

Proportions/Means: Columns Tested (5% risk level) - A/B/D - C/D - E/F/G - H/I/J/K/L/M/N - P/Q
* small base; ** very small base (under 30) ineligible for sig testing

Table 391
Page 1663

Outsell/Digital Library Federation Study (2002)
Weighted Tables

TABLE 145, continued

S7sum_11. Proprietary software or application SUMMARY TABLE

		RESPONDENT TYPE				INSTITUTION TYPE			DISCIPLINE									GENDER	
	TOTAL SAMPLE	FACULTY MEMBER	GRAD. STUDENT	FACULTY /GRAD	UNDER GRAD. STUDENT	PUBLIC	PRIVATE	LIBERAL ARTS	BIOLOGIAL SCIENCES	PHYSICAL SCIENCES /MATH	SOCIAL SCIENCES	ARTS AND HUMAN.	ENGI-NEERING	BUSINESS	LAW	UNDEC. MAJOR	MALE	FEMALE
		(A)	(B)	(C)	(D)	(E)	(F)	(G)	(H)	(I)	(J)	(K)	(L)	(M)	(N)		(P)	(Q)
Base - Use Proprietary software or application for coursework	314	0**	140	140	174	144	76*	94*	43*	47*	86*	53*	24*	45*	3**	13*	178	136
Other (NET)	19	0	9	9	9	10	5	3	3	2	6	2	3	1	*	2	13	5
	6.0%	0	6.7%	6.7%	5.4%	7.1%	6.7%	3.6%	6.1%	4.3%	6.5%	4.3%	13.1%M	2.1%	5.6%	15.4%	7.5%	4.0%
All sources of info	19	0	9	9	9	10	5	3	3	2	6	2	3	1	*	2	13	5
	6.0%	0	6.7%	6.7%	5.4%	7.1%	6.7%	3.6%	6.1%	4.3%	6.5%	4.3%	13.1%M	2.1%	5.6%	15.4%	7.5%	4.0%
preferred source of info	7	0	4	4	3	5	1	0	1	2	2	0	2	0	*	0	6	1
	2.1%	0	2.8%	2.8%	1.6%	3.7%	1.7%	0	2.0%	4.3%	2.2%	0	7.1%KM	0	5.6%	0	3.4%	0.4%
E-journals	2	0	0	0	2	0	0	2	0	0	2	0	0	0	0	0	2	0
	0.6%	0	0	0	1.1%	0	0	2.0%	0	0	2.2%	0	0	0	0	0	1.1%	0
All sources of info	2	0	0	0	2	0	0	2	0	0	2	0	0	0	0	0	2	0
	0.6%	0	0	0	1.1%	0	0	2.0%	0	0	2.2%	0	0	0	0	0	1.1%	0
preferred source of info	0	0	0	0	0	0	0	0	0	0	0	0	0	0	0	0	0	0
	0	0	0	0	0	0	0	0	0	0	0	0	0	0	0	0	0	0
Online (unspecified)	2	0	*	*	1	*	*	1	0	0	0	1	*	0	*	0	1	*
	0.5%	0	0.3%	0.3%	0.6%	0.2%	0.2%	1.2%	0	0	0	2.1%	1.2%	0	5.6%	0	0.8%	0.1%
All sources of info	2	0	*	*	1	*	*	1	0	0	0	1	*	0	*	0	1	*
	0.5%	0	0.3%	0.3%	0.6%	0.2%	0.2%	1.2%	0	0	0	2.1%	1.2%	0	5.6%	0	0.8%	0.1%
preferred source of info	2	0	*	*	1	*	*	1	0	0	0	1	*	0	*	0	1	*
	0.5%	0	0.3%	0.3%	0.6%	0.2%	0.2%	1.2%	0	0	0	2.1%	1.2%	0	5.6%	0	0.8%	0.1%

Proportions/Means: Columns Tested (5% risk level) - A/B/D - C/D - E/F/G - H/I/J/K/L/M/N - P/Q
* small base; ** very small base (under 30) ineligible for sig testing

Table 391
Page 1664

Outsell/Digital Library Federation Study (2002)
Weighted Tables

TABLE 145, continued

S7sum_11. Proprietary software or application SUMMARY TABLE

		RESPONDENT TYPE				INSTITUTION TYPE			DISCIPLINE								GENDER	
	TOTAL SAMPLE	FACULTY MEMBER	GRAD. STUDENT	FACULTY /GRAD	UNDER GRAD. STUDENT	PUBLIC	PRIVATE	LIBERAL ARTS	BIOLOGIAL SCIENCES	PHYSICAL SCIENCES /MATH	SOCIAL SCIENCES	ARTS AND HUMAN.	ENGI-NEERING	BUSINESS	LAW	UNDEC. MAJOR	MALE	FEMALE
		(A)	(B)	(C)	(D)	(E)	(F)	(G)	(H)	(I)	(J)	(K)	(L)	(M)	(N)		(P)	(Q)
Base - Use Proprietary software or application for coursework	314	0**	140	140	174	144	76*	94*	43*	47*	86*	53*	24*	45*	3**	13*	178	136
DK/Refused	21	0	7	7	14	9	5	7	5	3	8	1	1	2	0	1	10	11
	6.6%	0	4.8%	4.8%	8.0%	6.0%	6.5%	7.4%	12.2%	6.4%	8.7%	2.1%	3.6%	4.2%	0	7.7%	5.6%	7.8%

Proportions/Means: Columns Tested (5% risk level) - A/B/D - C/D - E/F/G - H/I/J/K/L/M/N - P/Q
* small base; ** very small base (under 30) ineligible for sig testing

Table 391
Page 1665

TABLE 146

S7D/E_11. Proprietary software or application SUMMARY TABLE

		RESPONDENT TYPE				INSTITUTION TYPE			DISCIPLINE									GENDER	
	TOTAL SAMPLE	FACULTY MEMBER	GRAD. STUDENT	FACULTY /GRAD	UNDER GRAD. STUDENT	PUBLIC	PRIVATE	LIBERAL ARTS	BIOLOGIAL SCIENCES	PHYSICAL SCIENCES /MATH	SOCIAL SCIENCES	ARTS AND HUMAN.	ENGI- NEERING	BUSINESS	LAW	UNDEC. MAJOR	MALE	FEMALE
		(A)	(B)	(C)	(D)	(E)	(F)	(G)	(H)	(I)	(J)	(K)	(L)	(M)	(N)		(P)	(Q)
Base - Use Proprietary software or application for coursework	314	0**	140	140	174	144	76*	94*	43*	47*	86*	53*	24*	45*	3**	13*	178	136
Access online (NET)	168 53.4%	0 0	70 50.0%	70 50.0%	98 56.0%	76 53.0%	39 51.6%	52 55.4%	16 36.7%	32 68.1%HLM	53 60.9%H	26 48.9%	11 46.4%	20 45.8%	2 55.6%	8 61.5%	102 57.1%	66 48.5%
All sources of info	168 53.4%	0 0	70 50.0%	70 50.0%	98 56.0%	76 53.0%	39 51.6%	52 55.4%	16 36.7%	32 68.1%HLM	53 60.9%H	26 48.9%	11 46.4%	20 45.8%	2 55.6%	8 61.5%	102 57.1%	66 48.5%
preferred source of info	146 46.4%	0 0	63 45.0%	63 45.0%	83 47.5%	63 43.8%	37 48.7%	45 48.4%	16 36.7%	28 59.6%HL	41 47.8%	24 44.7%	9 35.7%	19 41.7%	2 55.6%	8 61.5%	93 52.2%Q	53 38.7%
Borrow from or use in campus library (NET)	122 38.7%	0 0	41 29.6%	41 29.6%	80 46.1%B C	51 35.1%	27 35.8%	44 46.6%	16 36.7%	16 34.0%	34 39.1%	24 44.7%	8 32.1%	19 41.7%	1 33.3%	5 38.5%	58 32.7%	63 46.6%P
All sources of info	122 38.7%	0 0	41 29.6%	41 29.6%	80 46.1%B C	51 35.1%	27 35.8%	44 46.6%	16 36.7%	16 34.0%	34 39.1%	24 44.7%	8 32.1%	19 41.7%	1 33.3%	5 38.5%	58 32.7%	63 46.6%P
preferred source of info	83 26.5%	0 0	29 20.8%	29 20.8%	54 31.1%	37 25.9%	17 21.9%	29 31.2%	11 26.5%	8 17.0%	23 26.1%	21 40.4%IL	5 21.4%	11 25.0%	1 22.2%	3 23.1%	32 17.7%	52 38.0%P
Purchase from physical book store (NET)	30 9.6%	0 0	20 14.0%D	20 14.0%D	11 6.1%	14 10.0%	11 14.8%G	5 4.9%	4 10.2%	2 4.3%	8 8.7%	2 4.3%	4 16.7%IK	8 18.7%IK	1 22.2%	1 7.7%	25 14.0%Q	5 3.9%
All sources of info	30 9.6%	0 0	20 14.0%D	20 14.0%D	11 6.1%	14 10.0%	11 14.8%G	5 4.9%	4 10.2%	2 4.3%	8 8.7%	2 4.3%	4 16.7%IK	8 18.7%IK	1 22.2%	1 7.7%	25 14.0%Q	5 3.9%

Proportions/Means: Columns Tested (5% risk level) - A/B/D - C/D - E/F/G - H/I/J/K/L/M/N - P/Q
* small base; ** very small base (under 30) ineligible for sig testing

Table 394
Page 1672

Outsell/Digital Library Federation Study (2002)
Weighted Tables

TABLE 146, continued

S7D/E_11. Proprietary software or application SUMMARY TABLE

		RESPONDENT TYPE				INSTITUTION TYPE			DISCIPLINE									GENDER	
	TOTAL SAMPLE	FACULTY MEMBER	GRAD. STUDENT	FACULTY /GRAD	UNDER GRAD. STUDENT	PUBLIC	PRIVATE	LIBERAL ARTS	BIOLOGIAL SCIENCES	PHYSICAL SCIENCES /MATH	SOCIAL SCIENCES	ARTS AND HUMAN.	ENGI-NEERING	BUSINESS	LAW	UNDEC. MAJOR	MALE	FEMALE
		(A)	(B)	(C)	(D)	(E)	(F)	(G)	(H)	(I)	(J)	(K)	(L)	(M)	(N)		(P)	(Q)
Base - Use Proprietary software or application for coursework	314	0**	140	140	174	144	76*	94*	43*	47*	86*	53*	24*	45*	3**	13*	178	136
preferred source of info	20 6.4%	0 0	12 8.8%	12 8.8%	8 4.5%	9 6.5%	8 10.5%	3 2.8%	2 4.1%	1 2.1%	6 6.5%	2 4.3%	3 14.3%HIK	6 12.5%	* 11.1%	0 0	18 9.8%Q	3 1.8%
Faculty (NET)	24 7.6%	0 0	14 10.1%	14 10.1%	10 5.6%	9 6.1%	7 9.8%	8 8.1%	4 10.2%K	4 8.5%K	9 10.9%K	0 0	1 6.0%K	4 8.3%K	0 0	1 7.7%	15 8.2%	9 6.8%
All sources of info	24 7.6%	0 0	14 10.1%	14 10.1%	10 5.6%	9 6.1%	7 9.8%	8 8.1%	4 10.2%K	4 8.5%K	9 10.9%K	0 0	1 6.0%K	4 8.3%K	0 0	1 7.7%	15 8.2%	9 6.8%
preferred source of info	19 5.9%	0 0	10 7.2%	10 7.2%	9 4.9%	9 5.9%	3 4.4%	7 7.1%	4 10.2%K	2 4.3%	8 8.7%	0 0	1 3.6%	3 6.2%	0 0	1 7.7%	11 6.3%	7 5.4%
Purchase from online bookstore (NET)	7 2.2%	0 0	4 3.2%	4 3.2%	2 1.3%	3 1.9%	3 3.8%	1 1.2%	1 2.0%	0 0	2 2.2%	2 4.3%	1 3.6%	1 2.1%	0 0	0 0	5 2.7%	2 1.5%
All sources of info	7 2.2%	0 0	4 3.2%	4 3.2%	2 1.3%	3 1.9%	3 3.8%	1 1.2%	1 2.0%	0 0	2 2.2%	2 4.3%	1 3.6%	1 2.1%	0 0	0 0	5 2.7%	2 1.5%
preferred source of info	* 0.1%	0 0	* 0.2%	* 0.2%	0 0	0 0	* 0.4%	0 0	0 0	0 0	0 0	0 0	* 1.2%	0 0	0 0	0 0	* 0.2%	0 0
Colleagues (NET)	6 1.9%	0 0	2 1.6%	2 1.6%	4 2.2%	2 1.6%	0 0	4 4.0%	1 2.0%	0 0	4 4.3%	1 2.1%	* 1.2%	0 0	0 0	0 0	3 1.7%	3 2.2%
All sources of info	6 1.9%	0 0	2 1.6%	2 1.6%	4 2.2%	2 1.6%	0 0	4 4.0%	1 2.0%	0 0	4 4.3%	1 2.1%	* 1.2%	0 0	0 0	0 0	3 1.7%	3 2.2%

Proportions/Means: Columns Tested (5% risk level) - A/B/D - C/D - E/F/G - H/I/J/K/L/M/N - P/Q
* small base; ** very small base (under 30) ineligible for sig testing

Table 394
Page 1673

TABLE 146, continued

S7D/E_11. Proprietary software or application SUMMARY TABLE

		RESPONDENT TYPE				INSTITUTION TYPE			DISCIPLINE									GENDER	
	TOTAL SAMPLE	FACULTY MEMBER	GRAD. STUDENT	FACULTY /GRAD	UNDER GRAD. STUDENT	PUBLIC	PRIVATE	LIBERAL ARTS	BIOLOGIAL SCIENCES	PHYSICAL SCIENCES /MATH	SOCIAL SCIENCES	ARTS AND HUMAN.	ENGI-NEERING	BUSINESS	LAW	UNDEC. MAJOR	MALE	FEMALE
		(A)	(B)	(C)	(D)	(E)	(F)	(G)	(H)	(I)	(J)	(K)	(L)	(M)	(N)		(P)	(Q)
Base - Use Proprietary software or application for coursework	314	0**	140	140	174	144	76*	94*	43*	47*	86*	53*	24*	45*	3**	13*	178	136
preferred source of info	5 1.6%	0 0	1 0.8%	1 0.8%	4 2.2%	1 0.8%	0 0	4 4.0%	1 2.0%	0 0	4 4.3%	0 0	* 1.2%	0 0	0 0	0 0	3 1.7%	2 1.4%
Borrow from or use in other libraries (NET)	6 1.9%	0 0	2 1.5%	2 1.5%	4 2.1%	4 2.8%	0 0	2 1.9%	1 2.0%	0 0	4 4.3%	0 0	* 1.2%	1 2.1%	0 0	0 0	3 1.7%	3 2.1%
All sources of info	6 1.9%	0 0	2 1.5%	2 1.5%	4 2.1%	4 2.8%	0 0	2 1.9%	1 2.0%	0 0	4 4.3%	0 0	* 1.2%	1 2.1%	0 0	0 0	3 1.7%	3 2.1%
preferred source of info	2 0.7%	0 0	* 0.2%	* 0.2%	2 1.1%	2 1.5%	0 0	0 0	0 0	0 0	2 2.2%	0 0	* 1.2%	0 0	0 0	0 0	* 0.2%	2 1.4%
Interlibrary loan (NET)	4 1.4%	0 0	0 0	0 0	4 2.5%	1 0.8%	0 0	3 3.4%	1 2.0%	0 0	0 0	2 4.3%	* 1.2%	1 2.1%	0 0	0 0	1 0.8%	3 2.2%
All sources of info	4 1.4%	0 0	0 0	0 0	4 2.5%	1 0.8%	0 0	3 3.4%	1 2.0%	0 0	0 0	2 4.3%	* 1.2%	1 2.1%	0 0	0 0	1 0.8%	3 2.2%
preferred source of info	0 0	0 0	0 0	0 0	0 0	0 0	0 0	0 0	0 0	0 0	0 0	0 0	0 0	0 0	0 0	0 0	0 0	0 0
Home (NET)	3 1.0%	0 0	2 1.3%	2 1.3%	1 0.6%	3 2.1%	0 0	0 0	0 0	0 0	2 2.2%	1 2.1%	0 0	0 0	0 0	0 0	0 0	3 2.2%
All sources of info	3 1.0%	0 0	2 1.3%	2 1.3%	1 0.6%	3 2.1%	0 0	0 0	0 0	0 0	2 2.2%	1 2.1%	0 0	0 0	0 0	0 0	0 0	3 2.2%

Proportions/Means: Columns Tested (5% risk level) - A/B/D - C/D - E/F/G - H/I/J/K/L/M/N - P/Q
* small base; ** very small base (under 30) ineligible for sig testing

Table 394
Page 1674

Outsell/Digital Library Federation Study (2002)
Weighted Tables

TABLE 146, continued

S7D/E_11. Proprietary software or application SUMMARY TABLE

		RESPONDENT TYPE				INSTITUTION TYPE			DISCIPLINE									GENDER	
	TOTAL SAMPLE	FACULTY MEMBER	GRAD. STUDENT	FACULTY /GRAD	UNDER GRAD. STUDENT	PUBLIC	PRIVATE	LIBERAL ARTS	BIOLOGIAL SCIENCES	PHYSICAL SCIENCES /MATH	SOCIAL SCIENCES	ARTS AND HUMAN.	ENGI-NEERING	BUSINESS	LAW	UNDEC. MAJOR	MALE	FEMALE
		(A)	(B)	(C)	(D)	(E)	(F)	(G)	(H)	(I)	(J)	(K)	(L)	(M)	(N)		(P)	(Q)
Base - Use Proprietary software or application for coursework	314	0**	140	140	174	144	76*	94*	43*	47*	86*	53*	24*	45*	3**	13*	178	136
preferred source of info	3 1.0%	0 0	2 1.3%	2 1.3%	1 0.6%	3 2.1%	0 0	0 0	0 0	0 0	2 2.2%	1 2.1%	0 0	0 0	0 0	0 0	0 0	3 2.2%
Personal Holdings (NET)	2 0.7%	0 0	2 1.3%	2 1.3%	* 0.2%	1 0.9%	1 1.2%	0 0	1 2.0%	1 2.1%	0 0	0 0	* 1.2%	0 0	0 0	0 0	1 0.6%	1 0.9%
All sources of info	2 0.7%	0 0	2 1.3%	2 1.3%	* 0.2%	1 0.9%	1 1.2%	0 0	1 2.0%	1 2.1%	0 0	0 0	* 1.2%	0 0	0 0	0 0	1 0.6%	1 0.9%
preferred source of info	2 0.7%	0 0	2 1.3%	2 1.3%	* 0.2%	1 0.9%	1 1.2%	0 0	1 2.0%	1 2.1%	0 0	0 0	* 1.2%	0 0	0 0	0 0	1 0.6%	1 0.9%
Ask library to purchase source (NET)	1 0.4%	0 0	* 0.3%	* 0.3%	1 0.5%	1 0.6%	* 0.6%	0 0	1 2.0%	0 0	0 0	0 0	* 1.2%	0 0	* 5.6%	0 0	1 0.7%	* 0.1%
All sources of info	1 0.4%	0 0	* 0.3%	* 0.3%	1 0.5%	1 0.6%	* 0.6%	0 0	1 2.0%	0 0	0 0	0 0	* 1.2%	0 0	* 5.6%	0 0	1 0.7%	* 0.1%
preferred source of info	1 0.4%	0 0	* 0.2%	* 0.2%	1 0.5%	1 0.6%	* 0.4%	0 0	1 2.0%	0 0	0 0	0 0	* 1.2%	0 0	0 0	0 0	1 0.7%	0 0
Dorm room (NET)	1 0.4%	0 0	0 0	0 0	1 0.6%	0 0	0 0	1 1.2%	0 0	0 0	0 0	1 2.1%	0 0	0 0	0 0	0 0	1 0.6%	0 0
All sources of info	1 0.4%	0 0	0 0	0 0	1 0.6%	0 0	0 0	1 1.2%	0 0	0 0	0 0	1 2.1%	0 0	0 0	0 0	0 0	1 0.6%	0 0

Proportions/Means: Columns Tested (5% risk level) - A/B/D - C/D - E/F/G - H/I/J/K/L/M/N - P/Q
* small base; ** very small base (under 30) ineligible for sig testing

Table 394
Page 1675

Outsell/Digital Library Federation Study (2002)
Weighted Tables

TABLE 146, continued

S7D/E_11. Proprietary software or application SUMMARY TABLE

		RESPONDENT TYPE				INSTITUTION TYPE			DISCIPLINE									GENDER	
	TOTAL SAMPLE	FACULTY MEMBER	GRAD. STUDENT	FACULTY /GRAD	UNDER GRAD. STUDENT	PUBLIC	PRIVATE	LIBERAL ARTS	BIOLOGIAL SCIENCES	PHYSICAL SCIENCES /MATH	SOCIAL SCIENCES	ARTS AND HUMAN.	ENGI-NEERING	BUSINESS	LAW	UNDEC. MAJOR	MALE	FEMALE
		(A)	(B)	(C)	(D)	(E)	(F)	(G)	(H)	(I)	(J)	(K)	(L)	(M)	(N)		(P)	(Q)
Base - Use Proprietary software or application for coursework	314	0**	140	140	174	144	76*	94*	43*	47*	86*	53*	24*	45*	3**	13*	178	136
preferred source of info	0	0	0	0	0	0	0	0	0	0	0	0	0	0	0	0	0	0
	0	0	0	0	0	0	0	0	0	0	0	0	0	0	0	0	0	0
In class (NET)	1	0	0	0	1	*	*	0	0	0	0	0	1	0	0	0	*	*
	0.2%	0	0	0	0.3%	0.2%	0.4%	0	0	0	0	0	2.4%	0	0	0	0.2%	0.2%
All sources of info	1	0	0	0	1	*	*	0	0	0	0	0	1	0	0	0	*	*
	0.2%	0	0	0	0.3%	0.2%	0.4%	0	0	0	0	0	2.4%	0	0	0	0.2%	0.2%
preferred source of info	1	0	0	0	1	*	*	0	0	0	0	0	1	0	0	0	*	*
	0.2%	0	0	0	0.3%	0.2%	0.4%	0	0	0	0	0	2.4%	0	0	0	0.2%	0.2%
Order from on demand document delivery service (NET)	*	0	*	*	0	*	0	0	0	0	0	0	*	0	0	0	*	0
	0.1%	0	0.2%	0.2%	0	0.2%	0	0	0	0	0	0	1.2%	0	0	0	0.2%	0
All sources of info	*	0	*	*	0	*	0	0	0	0	0	0	*	0	0	0	*	0
	0.1%	0	0.2%	0.2%	0	0.2%	0	0	0	0	0	0	1.2%	0	0	0	0.2%	0
preferred source of info	0	0	0	0	0	0	0	0	0	0	0	0	0	0	0	0	0	0
	0	0	0	0	0	0	0	0	0	0	0	0	0	0	0	0	0	0
Access book/journal/ journal article elsewhere online (NET)	0	0	0	0	0	0	0	0	0	0	0	0	0	0	0	0	0	0
	0	0	0	0	0	0	0	0	0	0	0	0	0	0	0	0	0	0

Proportions/Means: Columns Tested (5% risk level) - A/B/D - C/D - E/F/G - H/I/J/K/L/M/N - P/Q
* small base; ** very small base (under 30) ineligible for sig testing

Table 394
Page 1676

Outsell/Digital Library Federation Study (2002)
Weighted Tables

TABLE 146, continued

S7D/E_11. Proprietary software or application SUMMARY TABLE

	TOTAL SAMPLE	RESPONDENT TYPE: FACULTY MEMBER	RESPONDENT TYPE: GRAD. STUDENT	RESPONDENT TYPE: FACULTY /GRAD	RESPONDENT TYPE: UNDER GRAD. STUDENT	INSTITUTION TYPE: PUBLIC	INSTITUTION TYPE: PRIVATE	INSTITUTION TYPE: LIBERAL ARTS	DISCIPLINE: BIOLOGIAL SCIENCES	DISCIPLINE: PHYSICAL SCIENCES /MATH	DISCIPLINE: SOCIAL SCIENCES	DISCIPLINE: ARTS AND HUMAN.	DISCIPLINE: ENGI-NEERING	DISCIPLINE: BUSINESS	DISCIPLINE: LAW	DISCIPLINE: UNDEC. MAJOR	GENDER: MALE	GENDER: FEMALE
		(A)	(B)	(C)	(D)	(E)	(F)	(G)	(H)	(I)	(J)	(K)	(L)	(M)	(N)		(P)	(Q)
Base - Use Proprietary software or application for coursework	314	0**	140	140	174	144	76*	94*	43*	47*	86*	53*	24*	45*	3**	13*	178	136
All sources of info	0 0	0 0	0 0	0 0	0 0	0 0	0 0	0 0	0 0	0 0	0 0	0 0	0 0	0 0	0 0	0 0	0 0	0 0
preferred source of info	0 0	0 0	0 0	0 0	0 0	0 0	0 0	0 0	0 0	0 0	0 0	0 0	0 0	0 0	0 0	0 0	0 0	0 0
Access from course website (NET)	0 0	0 0	0 0	0 0	0 0	0 0	0 0	0 0	0 0	0 0	0 0	0 0	0 0	0 0	0 0	0 0	0 0	0 0
All sources of info	0 0	0 0	0 0	0 0	0 0	0 0	0 0	0 0	0 0	0 0	0 0	0 0	0 0	0 0	0 0	0 0	0 0	0 0
preferred source of info	0 0	0 0	0 0	0 0	0 0	0 0	0 0	0 0	0 0	0 0	0 0	0 0	0 0	0 0	0 0	0 0	0 0	0 0
Other (NET)	29 9.3%	0 0	21 14.9%D	21 14.9%D	8 4.7%	13 9.3%	10 13.7%	5 5.6%	10 22.4%JK	6 12.8%J	0 0	3 6.4%J	4 16.7%J	5 10.4%J	* 11.1%	1 7.7%	15 8.7%	14 10.0%
All sources of info	28 9.0%	0 0	21 14.9%D	21 14.9%D	7 4.2%	13 9.3%	10 13.7%	4 4.6%	9 20.4%JK	6 12.8%J	0 0	3 6.4%J	4 16.7%J	5 10.4%J	* 11.1%	1 7.7%	15 8.7%	13 9.4%
preferred source of info	21 6.8%	0 0	17 12.1%D	17 12.1%D	4 2.5%	10 6.9%	8 10.7%	3 3.4%	5 12.2%J	5 10.6%J	0 0	2 4.3%	4 15.5%JK	5 10.4%J	* 11.1%	0 0	12 6.6%	9 7.0%
DK/Refused	11 3.5%	0 0	3 2.1%	3 2.1%	8 4.7%	7 4.8%	1 1.5%	3 3.1%	2 4.1%	2 4.3%	2 2.2%	2 4.3%	* 1.2%	2 4.2%	0 0	1 7.7%	7 3.9%	4 2.9%

Proportions/Means: Columns Tested (5% risk level) - A/B/D - C/D - E/F/G - H/I/J/K/L/M/N - P/Q
* small base; ** very small base (under 30) ineligible for sig testing

Table 394
Page 1677

Outsell/Digital Library Federation Study (2002)
Weighted Tables

TABLE 147

S7sum_12. Data SUMMARY TABLE

	TOTAL SAMPLE	RESPONDENT TYPE: FACULTY MEMBER	RESPONDENT TYPE: GRAD. STUDENT	RESPONDENT TYPE: FACULTY /GRAD	RESPONDENT TYPE: UNDER GRAD. STUDENT	INSTITUTION TYPE: PUBLIC	INSTITUTION TYPE: PRIVATE	INSTITUTION TYPE: LIBERAL ARTS	DISCIPLINE: BIOLOGIAL SCIENCES	DISCIPLINE: PHYSICAL SCIENCES /MATH	DISCIPLINE: SOCIAL SCIENCES	DISCIPLINE: ARTS AND HUMAN.	DISCIPLINE: ENGI-NEERING	DISCIPLINE: BUSINESS	DISCIPLINE: LAW	DISCIPLINE: UNDEC. MAJOR	GENDER: MALE	GENDER: FEMALE
		(A)	(B)	(C)	(D)	(E)	(F)	(G)	(H)	(I)	(J)	(K)	(L)	(M)	(N)		(P)	(Q)
Base - Use Data for coursework	572	0**	231	231	341	265	114	193	83*	85*	182*	91*	22*	75*	6*	28*	275	297
ONLINE	442 77.3%	0 0	176 75.9%	176 75.9%	267 78.3%	196 73.8%	87 76.4%	159 82.8%E	60 72.3%	69 81.2%	135 74.2%	73 80.2%	15 69.3%	60 80.2%	5 80.0%	25 89.3%	212 77.3%	230 77.4%
Search engine (NET)	174 30.4%	0 0	50 21.7%	50 21.7%	123 36.2%B C	56 21.1%	32 28.2%	85 44.4%EF	18 22.3%	35 41.2%HJL N	41 22.7%	30 33.3%	6 25.3%	28 37.0%HJ	1 20.0%	14 50.0%	87 31.8%	86 29.1%
All sources of info	174 30.4%	0 0	50 21.7%	50 21.7%	123 36.2%B C	56 21.1%	32 28.2%	85 44.4%EF	18 22.3%	35 41.2%HJL N	41 22.7%	30 33.3%	6 25.3%	28 37.0%HJ	1 20.0%	14 50.0%	87 31.8%	86 29.1%
preferred source of info	93 16.2%	0 0	20 8.4%	20 8.4%	73 21.5%B C	33 12.4%	16 14.4%	44 22.6%E	9 10.6%	14 16.5%	23 12.4%	13 14.8%	4 17.3%	21 28.4%HJ K	1 14.3%	8 28.6%	40 14.7%	52 17.6%
Online databases (NET)	105 18.4%	0 0	57 24.7%D	57 24.7%D	48 14.1%	46 17.2%	31 27.3%EG	28 14.7%	12 14.9%	10 11.8%	39 21.6%	17 18.5%	2 10.7%	18 23.5%I	3 42.9%HI JKLM	4 14.3%	58 21.3%	47 15.7%
All sources of info	105 18.4%	0 0	57 24.7%D	57 24.7%D	48 14.1%	46 17.2%	31 27.3%EG	28 14.7%	12 14.9%	10 11.8%	39 21.6%	17 18.5%	2 10.7%	18 23.5%I	3 42.9%HI JKLM	4 14.3%	58 21.3%	47 15.7%
preferred source of info	67 11.7%	0 0	39 17.1%D	39 17.1%D	27 8.1%	36 13.6%	17 14.9%G	14 7.3%	9 10.6%	9 10.6%	26 14.4%	6 6.2%	1 6.7%	12 16.0%K	2 28.6%HIJ KL	2 7.1%	40 14.7%	26 8.9%
Your own institution's web site (NET)	89 15.5%	0 0	31 13.5%	31 13.5%	58 16.9%	34 13.0%	19 16.5%	35 18.4%	14 17.0%	16 18.8%	21 11.3%	18 19.8%	3 16.0%	10 13.6%	* 5.7%	6 21.4%	36 13.1%	53 17.7%

Proportions/Means: Columns Tested (5% risk level) - A/B/D - C/D - E/F/G - H/I/J/K/L/M/N - P/Q
* small base; ** very small base (under 30) ineligible for sig testing

Table 398
Page 1689

Outsell/Digital Library Federation Study (2002)
Weighted Tables

TABLE 147, continued

S7sum_12. Data SUMMARY TABLE

	TOTAL SAMPLE	RESPONDENT TYPE: FACULTY MEMBER	RESPONDENT TYPE: GRAD. STUDENT	RESPONDENT TYPE: FACULTY /GRAD	RESPONDENT TYPE: UNDER GRAD. STUDENT	INSTITUTION TYPE: PUBLIC	INSTITUTION TYPE: PRIVATE	INSTITUTION TYPE: LIBERAL ARTS	DISCIPLINE: BIOLOGIAL SCIENCES	DISCIPLINE: PHYSICAL SCIENCES /MATH	DISCIPLINE: SOCIAL SCIENCES	DISCIPLINE: ARTS AND HUMAN.	DISCIPLINE: ENGI-NEERING	DISCIPLINE: BUSINESS	DISCIPLINE: LAW	DISCIPLINE: UNDEC. MAJOR	GENDER: MALE	GENDER: FEMALE
		(A)	(B)	(C)	(D)	(E)	(F)	(G)	(H)	(I)	(J)	(K)	(L)	(M)	(N)		(P)	(Q)
Base - Use Data for coursework	572	0**	231	231	341	265	114	193	83*	85*	182*	91*	22*	75*	6*	28*	275	297
All sources of info	89 15.5%	0 0	31 13.5%	31 13.5%	58 16.9%	34 13.0%	19 16.5%	35 18.4%	14 17.0%	16 18.8%	21 11.3%	18 19.8%	3 16.0%	10 13.6%	* 5.7%	6 21.4%	36 13.1%	53 17.7%
preferred source of info	54 9.4%	0 0	15 6.4%	15 6.4%	39 11.4%	23 8.8%	8 6.6%	23 11.8%	11 12.8%N	7 8.2%	19 10.3%	9 9.9%	2 8.0%	5 6.2%	0 0	2 7.1%	21 7.8%	32 10.9%
Internet searches (NET)	88 15.4%	0 0	36 15.5%	36 15.5%	52 15.4%	47 17.6%	19 16.4%	23 11.8%	11 13.8%	11 12.9%	28 15.5%	13 14.8%	4 20.0%	11 14.8%	1 8.6%	8 28.6%	38 13.7%	50 17.0%
All sources of info	88 15.4%	0 0	36 15.5%	36 15.5%	52 15.4%	47 17.6%	19 16.4%	23 11.8%	11 13.8%	11 12.9%	28 15.5%	13 14.8%	4 20.0%	11 14.8%	1 8.6%	8 28.6%	38 13.7%	50 17.0%
preferred source of info	48 8.4%	0 0	20 8.8%	20 8.8%	27 8.1%	30 11.2%G	13 11.7%G	5 2.5%	8 9.6%I	2 2.4%	21 11.3%I	4 4.9%	2 8.0%	7 8.6%	1 8.6%	4 14.3%	15 5.4%	33 11.1%P
Online library catalogues and finding aids (NET)	57 9.9%	0 0	21 9.0%	21 9.0%	36 10.6%	20 7.5%	13 11.5%	24 12.3%	11 12.8%N	7 8.2%	13 7.2%	11 12.3%	1 6.7%	8 11.1%	0 0	5 17.9%	23 8.3%	34 11.4%
All sources of info	57 9.9%	0 0	21 9.0%	21 9.0%	36 10.6%	20 7.5%	13 11.5%	24 12.3%	11 12.8%N	7 8.2%	13 7.2%	11 12.3%	1 6.7%	8 11.1%	0 0	5 17.9%	23 8.3%	34 11.4%
preferred source of info	30 5.2%	0 0	13 5.4%	13 5.4%	18 5.1%	15 5.6%	5 4.5%	10 5.2%	8 9.6%J	5 5.9%	4 2.1%	9 9.9%J	1 2.7%	3 3.7%	0 0	1 3.6%	13 4.6%	17 5.9%
Web directory/ subject related web site (NET)	51 8.8%	0 0	28 12.2%D	28 12.2%D	22 6.6%	20 7.6%	11 10.1%	19 9.8%	6 7.4%	7 8.2%	17 9.3%	8 8.6%	1 6.7%	8 11.1%	1 14.3%	2 7.1%	28 10.1%	23 7.7%

Proportions/Means: Columns Tested (5% risk level) - A/B/D - C/D - E/F/G - H/I/J/K/L/M/N - P/Q
* small base; ** very small base (under 30) ineligible for sig testing

Table 398
Page 1690

Outsell/Digital Library Federation Study (2002)
Weighted Tables

TABLE 147, continued

S7sum_12. Data SUMMARY TABLE

	TOTAL SAMPLE	RESPONDENT TYPE: FACULTY MEMBER	GRAD. STUDENT	FACULTY /GRAD	UNDER GRAD. STUDENT	INSTITUTION TYPE: PUBLIC	PRIVATE	LIBERAL ARTS	DISCIPLINE: BIOLOGIAL SCIENCES	PHYSICAL SCIENCES /MATH	SOCIAL SCIENCES	ARTS AND HUMAN.	ENGI-NEERING	BUSINESS	LAW	UNDEC. MAJOR	GENDER: MALE	FEMALE
		(A)	(B)	(C)	(D)	(E)	(F)	(G)	(H)	(I)	(J)	(K)	(L)	(M)	(N)		(P)	(Q)
Base - Use Data for coursework	572	0**	231	231	341	265	114	193	83*	85*	182*	91*	22*	75*	6*	28*	275	297
All sources of info	51 8.8%	0 0	28 12.2%D	28 12.2%D	22 6.6%	20 7.6%	11 10.1%	19 9.8%	6 7.4%	7 8.2%	17 9.3%	8 8.6%	1 6.7%	8 11.1%	1 14.3%	2 7.1%	28 10.1%	23 7.7%
preferred source of info	24 4.2%	0 0	13 5.7%	13 5.7%	11 3.3%	12 4.6%	2 2.0%	10 5.0%	4 4.3%	1 1.2%	11 6.2%	2 2.5%	1 4.0%	3 3.7%	1 8.6%I	2 7.1%	16 5.9%	8 2.7%
Online reference service (NET)	18 3.2%	0 0	10 4.1%	10 4.1%	9 2.6%	6 2.4%	5 4.5%	7 3.6%	1 1.1%	0 0	8 4.1%	4 4.9%I	* 1.3%	3 3.7%	* 5.7%HI	2 7.1%	11 4.1%	7 2.4%
All sources of info	18 3.2%	0 0	10 4.1%	10 4.1%	9 2.6%	6 2.4%	5 4.5%	7 3.6%	1 1.1%	0 0	8 4.1%	4 4.9%I	* 1.3%	3 3.7%	* 5.7%HI	2 7.1%	11 4.1%	7 2.4%
preferred source of info	4 0.8%	0 0	1 0.6%	1 0.6%	3 0.9%	* 0.1%	1 0.9%	3 1.6%	1 1.1%	0 0	2 1.0%	1 1.2%	* 1.3%	0 0	* 2.9%IM	0 0	2 0.9%	2 0.6%
Department web page (NET)	16 2.8%	0 0	11 4.7%D	11 4.7%D	5 1.5%	8 2.9%	4 3.9%	4 2.0%	2 2.1%	7 8.2%JK	0 0	1 1.2%	1 6.7%JK	4 4.9%J	0 0	1 3.6%	11 4.2%	5 1.6%
All sources of info	16 2.8%	0 0	11 4.7%D	11 4.7%D	5 1.5%	8 2.9%	4 3.9%	4 2.0%	2 2.1%	7 8.2%JK	0 0	1 1.2%	1 6.7%JK	4 4.9%J	0 0	1 3.6%	11 4.2%	5 1.6%
preferred source of info	14 2.4%	0 0	10 4.2%D	10 4.2%D	4 1.2%	7 2.8%	3 3.0%	3 1.5%	2 2.1%	6 7.1%J	0 0	1 1.2%	1 5.3%J	4 4.9%J	0 0	0 0	9 3.3%	5 1.6%
Online abstracting and indexing services (NET)	16 2.8%	0 0	8 3.3%	8 3.3%	8 2.4%	8 3.2%	2 1.8%	5 2.7%	1 1.1%	1 1.2%	8 4.1%	3 3.7%	0 0	2 2.5%	* 2.9%	1 3.6%	8 3.0%	8 2.5%
All sources of info	16 2.8%	0 0	8 3.3%	8 3.3%	8 2.4%	8 3.2%	2 1.8%	5 2.7%	1 1.1%	1 1.2%	8 4.1%	3 3.7%	0 0	2 2.5%	* 2.9%	1 3.6%	8 3.0%	8 2.5%

Proportions/Means: Columns Tested (5% risk level) - A/B/D - C/D - E/F/G - H/I/J/K/L/M/N - P/Q
* small base; ** very small base (under 30) ineligible for sig testing

Table 398
Page 1691

Outsell/Digital Library Federation Study (2002)
Weighted Tables

TABLE 147, continued

S7sum_12. Data SUMMARY TABLE

	TOTAL SAMPLE	RESPONDENT TYPE: FACULTY MEMBER	GRAD. STUDENT	FACULTY /GRAD	UNDER GRAD. STUDENT	INSTITUTION TYPE: PUBLIC	PRIVATE	LIBERAL ARTS	DISCIPLINE: BIOLOGIAL SCIENCES	PHYSICAL SCIENCES /MATH	SOCIAL SCIENCES	ARTS AND HUMAN.	ENGI- NEERING	BUSINESS	LAW	UNDEC. MAJOR	GENDER: MALE	FEMALE
		(A)	(B)	(C)	(D)	(E)	(F)	(G)	(H)	(I)	(J)	(K)	(L)	(M)	(N)		(P)	(Q)
Base - Use Data for coursework	572	0**	231	231	341	265	114	193	83*	85*	182*	91*	22*	75*	6*	28*	275	297
preferred source of info	7 1.3%	0 0	4 1.7%	4 1.7%	3 1.0%	4 1.4%	* 0.1%	3 1.7%	0 0	0 0	4 2.1%	2 2.5%	0 0	0 0	* 2.9%HIM	1 3.6%	2 0.9%	5 1.6%
Your own personal electronic library/files (NET)	4 0.7%	0 0	3 1.3%	3 1.3%	1 0.3%	* 0.1%	3 2.5%E	1 0.5%	0 0	1 1.2%	2 1.0%	0 0	* 1.3%	1 1.2%	0 0	0 0	2 0.8%	2 0.6%
All sources of info	4 0.7%	0 0	3 1.3%	3 1.3%	1 0.3%	* 0.1%	3 2.5%E	1 0.5%	0 0	1 1.2%	2 1.0%	0 0	* 1.3%	1 1.2%	0 0	0 0	2 0.8%	2 0.6%
preferred source of info	* 0.1%	0 0	* 0.1%	* 0.1%	0 0	* 0.1%	0 0	0 0	0 0	0 0	0 0	0 0	* 1.3%J	0 0	0 0	0 0	* 0.1%	0 0
E-mail listservs (NET)	1 0.2%	0 0	0 0	0 0	1 0.3%	0 0	0 0	1 0.5%	0 0	0 0	0 0	0 0	0 0	1 1.2%	0 0	0 0	1 0.3%	0 0
All sources of info	1 0.2%	0 0	0 0	0 0	1 0.3%	0 0	0 0	1 0.5%	0 0	0 0	0 0	0 0	0 0	1 1.2%	0 0	0 0	1 0.3%	0 0
preferred source of info	0 0	0 0	0 0	0 0	0 0	0 0	0 0	0 0	0 0	0 0	0 0	0 0	0 0	0 0	0 0	0 0	0 0	0 0
Online bookstore (NET)	0 0	0 0	0 0	0 0	0 0	0 0	0 0	0 0	0 0	0 0	0 0	0 0	0 0	0 0	0 0	0 0	0 0	0 0
All sources of info	0 0	0 0	0 0	0 0	0 0	0 0	0 0	0 0	0 0	0 0	0 0	0 0	0 0	0 0	0 0	0 0	0 0	0 0

Proportions/Means: Columns Tested (5% risk level) - A/B/D - C/D - E/F/G - H/I/J/K/L/M/N - P/Q
* small base; ** very small base (under 30) ineligible for sig testing

TABLE 147, continued

S7sum_12. Data SUMMARY TABLE

	TOTAL SAMPLE	RESPONDENT TYPE: FACULTY MEMBER (A)	GRAD. STUDENT (B)	FACULTY /GRAD (C)	UNDER GRAD. STUDENT (D)	INSTITUTION TYPE: PUBLIC (E)	PRIVATE (F)	LIBERAL ARTS (G)
Base - Use Data for coursework	572	0**	231	231	341	265	114	193
preferred source of info	0 0	0 0	0 0	0 0	0 0	0 0	0 0	0 0
PERSONAL ASSISTANCE	217 38.0%	0 0	92 39.7%	92 39.7%	125 36.8%	98 36.8%	48 42.0%	72 37.2%
Faculty members inside your institution (NET)	130 22.7%	0 0	68 29.3%D	68 29.3%D	62 18.3%	54 20.4%	35 30.7%E	41 21.2%
All sources of info	130 22.7%	0 0	68 29.3%D	68 29.3%D	62 18.3%	54 20.4%	35 30.7%E	41 21.2%
preferred source of info	59 10.3%	0 0	32 14.0%D	32 14.0%D	27 7.8%	21 8.0%	18 15.5%E	20 10.6%
A librarian in your institution (NET)	109 19.0%	0 0	27 11.7%	27 11.7%	81 23.9%B C	50 18.9%	12 10.6%	46 24.1%F
All sources of info	109 19.0%	0 0	27 11.7%	27 11.7%	81 23.9%B C	50 18.9%	12 10.6%	46 24.1%F
preferred source of info	51 9.0%	0 0	12 5.2%	12 5.2%	39 11.5%BC	23 8.5%	6 5.0%	23 12.0%

	DISCIPLINE: BIOLOGIAL SCIENCES (H)	PHYSICAL SCIENCES /MATH (I)	SOCIAL SCIENCES (J)	ARTS AND HUMAN. (K)	ENGI-NEERING (L)	BUSINESS (M)	LAW (N)	UNDEC. MAJOR	GENDER: MALE (P)	FEMALE (Q)
Base - Use Data for coursework	83*	85*	182*	91*	22*	75*	6*	28*	275	297
preferred source of info	0 0	0 0	0 0	0 0	0 0	0 0	0 0	0 0	0 0	0 0
PERSONAL ASSISTANCE	28 34.0%	36 42.4%M	73 40.2%	35 38.3%	10 44.0%M	20 25.9%	2 31.4%	14 50.0%	103 37.5%	114 38.4%
Faculty members inside your institution (NET)	20 24.5%	23 27.1%N	41 22.7%	18 19.8%	8 36.0%JKM N	12 16.0%	1 8.6%	7 25.0%	64 23.3%	66 22.2%
All sources of info	20 24.5%	23 27.1%N	41 22.7%	18 19.8%	8 36.0%JKM N	12 16.0%	1 8.6%	7 25.0%	64 23.3%	66 22.2%
preferred source of info	12 14.9%	8 9.4%	17 9.3%	9 9.9%	5 22.7%IJKM N	5 6.2%	* 5.7%	3 10.7%	30 11.1%	29 9.7%
A librarian in your institution (NET)	9 10.6%	14 16.5%	41 22.7%H	19 21.0%	3 16.0%	10 13.6%	2 28.6%HM	10 35.7%	47 17.0%	62 20.9%
All sources of info	9 10.6%	14 16.5%	41 22.7%H	19 21.0%	3 16.0%	10 13.6%	2 28.6%HM	10 35.7%	47 17.0%	62 20.9%
preferred source of info	4 5.3%	3 3.5%	24 13.4%I	11 12.3%I	1 5.3%	4 4.9%	1 8.6%	3 10.7%	22 7.9%	30 10.0%

Proportions/Means: Columns Tested (5% risk level) - A/B/D - C/D - E/F/G - H/I/J/K/L/M/N - P/Q
* small base; ** very small base (under 30) ineligible for sig testing

Table 398
Page 1693

Outsell/Digital Library Federation Study (2002)
Weighted Tables

TABLE 147, continued

S7sum_12. Data SUMMARY TABLE

	TOTAL SAMPLE	RESPONDENT TYPE: FACULTY MEMBER	GRAD. STUDENT	FACULTY /GRAD	UNDER GRAD. STUDENT	INSTITUTION TYPE: PUBLIC	PRIVATE	LIBERAL ARTS	DISCIPLINE: BIOLOGIAL SCIENCES	PHYSICAL SCIENCES /MATH	SOCIAL SCIENCES	ARTS AND HUMAN.	ENGI-NEERING	BUSINESS	LAW	UNDEC. MAJOR	GENDER: MALE	FEMALE
		(A)	(B)	(C)	(D)	(E)	(F)	(G)	(H)	(I)	(J)	(K)	(L)	(M)	(N)		(P)	(Q)
Base - Use Data for coursework	572	0**	231	231	341	265	114	193	83*	85*	182*	91*	22*	75*	6*	28*	275	297
Other students inside your institution (NET)	57 9.9%	0 0	32 13.9%D	32 13.9%D	24 7.2%	27 10.0%	16 13.8%	14 7.4%	6 7.4%	16 18.8%HJLM N	15 8.2%	10 11.1%	1 6.7%	5 6.2%	* 2.9%	3 10.7%	31 11.2%	26 8.7%
All sources of info	57 9.9%	0 0	32 13.9%D	32 13.9%D	24 7.2%	27 10.0%	16 13.8%	14 7.4%	6 7.4%	16 18.8%HJLM N	15 8.2%	10 11.1%	1 6.7%	5 6.2%	* 2.9%	3 10.7%	31 11.2%	26 8.7%
preferred source of info	12 2.2%	0 0	7 2.9%	7 2.9%	6 1.7%	8 2.8%	1 0.9%	4 2.0%	3 3.2%	7 8.2%JKLM	2 1.0%	0 0	0 0	1 1.2%	0 0	0 0	11 3.8%Q	2 0.6%
Faculty members outside your institution (NET)	3 0.6%	0 0	1 0.5%	1 0.5%	2 0.6%	0 0	1 1.0%	2 1.1%	0 0	1 1.2%	0 0	2 2.5%	0 0	0 0	0 0	0 0	1 0.4%	2 0.8%
All sources of info	3 0.6%	0 0	1 0.5%	1 0.5%	2 0.6%	0 0	1 1.0%	2 1.1%	0 0	1 1.2%	0 0	2 2.5%	0 0	0 0	0 0	0 0	1 0.4%	2 0.8%
preferred source of info	0 0	0 0	0 0	0 0	0 0	0 0	0 0	0 0	0 0	0 0	0 0	0 0	0 0	0 0	0 0	0 0	0 0	0 0
Other students outside your institution (NET)	2 0.4%	0 0	1 0.5%	1 0.5%	1 0.3%	0 0	1 1.0%	1 0.5%	0 0	0 0	0 0	1 1.2%	0 0	1 1.2%	0 0	0 0	1 0.3%	1 0.4%
All sources of info	2 0.4%	0 0	1 0.5%	1 0.5%	1 0.3%	0 0	1 1.0%	1 0.5%	0 0	0 0	0 0	1 1.2%	0 0	1 1.2%	0 0	0 0	1 0.3%	1 0.4%
preferred source of info	0 0	0 0	0 0	0 0	0 0	0 0	0 0	0 0	0 0	0 0	0 0	0 0	0 0	0 0	0 0	0 0	0 0	0 0

Proportions/Means: Columns Tested (5% risk level) - A/B/D - C/D - E/F/G - H/I/J/K/L/M/N - P/Q
* small base; ** very small base (under 30) ineligible for sig testing

Table 398
Page 1694

Outsell/Digital Library Federation Study (2002)
Weighted Tables

TABLE 147, continued

S7sum_12. Data SUMMARY TABLE

	TOTAL SAMPLE	RESPONDENT TYPE: FACULTY MEMBER	GRAD. STUDENT	FACULTY /GRAD	UNDER GRAD. STUDENT	INSTITUTION TYPE: PUBLIC	PRIVATE	LIBERAL ARTS	DISCIPLINE: BIOLOGIAL SCIENCES	PHYSICAL SCIENCES /MATH	SOCIAL SCIENCES	ARTS AND HUMAN.	ENGI-NEERING	BUSINESS	LAW	UNDEC. MAJOR	GENDER: MALE	FEMALE
		(A)	(B)	(C)	(D)	(E)	(F)	(G)	(H)	(I)	(J)	(K)	(L)	(M)	(N)		(P)	(Q)
Base - Use Data for coursework	572	0**	231	231	341	265	114	193	83*	85*	182*	91*	22*	75*	6*	28*	275	297
Another institution's librarian (NET)	1 0.2%	0 0	0 0	0 0	1 0.3%	1 0.4%	0 0	0 0	0 0	0 0	0 0	1 1.2%	0 0	0 0	0 0	0 0	0 0	1 0.4%
All sources of info	1 0.2%	0 0	0 0	0 0	1 0.3%	1 0.4%	0 0	0 0	0 0	0 0	0 0	1 1.2%	0 0	0 0	0 0	0 0	0 0	1 0.4%
preferred source of info	0 0	0 0	0 0	0 0	0 0	0 0	0 0	0 0	0 0	0 0	0 0	0 0	0 0	0 0	0 0	0 0	0 0	0 0
Professional meetings (NET)	* 0.1%	0 0	0 0	0 0	* 0.1%	* 0.1%	0 0	0 0	0 0	0 0	0 0	0 0	* 1.3%J	0 0	0 0	0 0	* 0.1%	0 0
All sources of info	* 0.1%	0 0	0 0	0 0	* 0.1%	* 0.1%	0 0	0 0	0 0	0 0	0 0	0 0	* 1.3%J	0 0	0 0	0 0	* 0.1%	0 0
preferred source of info	0 0	0 0	0 0	0 0	0 0	0 0	0 0	0 0	0 0	0 0	0 0	0 0	0 0	0 0	0 0	0 0	0 0	0 0
LIBRARY FACILITIES/ PRINT	169 29.5%	0 0	71 30.7%	71 30.7%	98 28.7%	59 22.4%	46 40.5%E	63 32.8%E	20 24.5%	35 41.2%HJM	43 23.7%	34 37.0%	6 26.7%	20 25.9%	2 40.0%	9 32.1%	95 34.4%Q	74 25.0%
Campus library (NET)	140 24.5%	0 0	59 25.6%	59 25.6%	81 23.8%	46 17.5%	38 33.6%E	56 28.9%E	18 22.3%	31 36.5%HJM	32 17.5%	26 28.4%	6 25.3%	17 22.2%	2 31.4%	9 32.1%	82 30.0%Q	58 19.5%
All sources of info	140 24.5%	0 0	59 25.6%	59 25.6%	81 23.8%	46 17.5%	38 33.6%E	56 28.9%E	18 22.3%	31 36.5%HJM	32 17.5%	26 28.4%	6 25.3%	17 22.2%	2 31.4%	9 32.1%	82 30.0%Q	58 19.5%

Proportions/Means: Columns Tested (5% risk level) - A/B/D - C/D - E/F/G - H/I/J/K/L/M/N - P/Q
* small base; ** very small base (under 30) ineligible for sig testing

Table 398
Page 1695

Outsell/Digital Library Federation Study (2002)
Weighted Tables

TABLE 147, continued

S7sum_12. Data SUMMARY TABLE

		RESPONDENT TYPE				INSTITUTION TYPE			DISCIPLINE								GENDER	
	TOTAL SAMPLE	FACULTY MEMBER	GRAD. STUDENT	FACULTY /GRAD	UNDER GRAD. STUDENT	PUBLIC	PRIVATE	LIBERAL ARTS	BIOLOGIAL SCIENCES	PHYSICAL SCIENCES /MATH	SOCIAL SCIENCES	ARTS AND HUMAN.	ENGI-NEERING	BUSINESS	LAW	UNDEC. MAJOR	MALE	FEMALE
		(A)	(B)	(C)	(D)	(E)	(F)	(G)	(H)	(I)	(J)	(K)	(L)	(M)	(N)		(P)	(Q)
Base - Use Data for coursework	572	0**	231	231	341	265	114	193	83*	85*	182*	91*	22*	75*	6*	28*	275	297
preferred source of info	69 12.1%	0 0	27 11.8%	27 11.8%	42 12.3%	25 9.6%	15 13.1%	29 15.0%	11 12.8%	16 18.8%M	17 9.3%	17 18.5%M	2 8.0%	5 6.2%	1 11.4%	2 7.1%	37 13.4%	33 11.0%
References cited in books or journal articles (NET)	15 2.7%	0 0	6 2.5%	6 2.5%	10 2.8%	7 2.7%	5 4.3%	3 1.7%	0 0	1 1.2%	8 4.1%	6 6.2%H	* 1.3%	1 1.2%	0 0	0 0	6 2.3%	9 3.0%
All sources of info	15 2.7%	0 0	6 2.5%	6 2.5%	10 2.8%	7 2.7%	5 4.3%	3 1.7%	0 0	1 1.2%	8 4.1%	6 6.2%H	* 1.3%	1 1.2%	0 0	0 0	6 2.3%	9 3.0%
preferred source of info	6 1.1%	0 0	5 2.1%	5 2.1%	1 0.4%	5 1.9%	1 0.9%	0 0	0 0	1 1.2%	4 2.1%	1 1.2%	* 1.3%	0 0	0 0	0 0	1 0.5%	5 1.6%
Physical bookstore (NET)	9 1.6%	0 0	3 1.4%	3 1.4%	6 1.8%	5 1.7%	2 1.6%	3 1.5%	0 0	3 3.5%	4 2.1%	0 0	* 1.3%	2 2.5%	* 5.7%HK	0 0	8 2.9%Q	1 0.5%
All sources of info	9 1.6%	0 0	3 1.4%	3 1.4%	6 1.8%	5 1.7%	2 1.6%	3 1.5%	0 0	3 3.5%	4 2.1%	0 0	* 1.3%	2 2.5%	* 5.7%HK	0 0	8 2.9%Q	1 0.5%
preferred source of info	2 0.4%	0 0	1 0.5%	1 0.5%	1 0.3%	* 0.1%	1 0.8%	1 0.5%	0 0	1 1.2%	0 0	0 0	0 0	1 1.2%	* 2.9%HJK	0 0	2 0.7%	* 0.1%
Another library (NET)	7 1.3%	0 0	2 0.8%	2 0.8%	6 1.6%	* 0.1%	2 1.7%	5 2.7%E	0 0	2 2.4%	4 2.1%	1 1.2%	1 2.7%HM	0 0	0 0	0 0	5 1.9%	2 0.7%
All sources of info	7 1.3%	0 0	2 0.8%	2 0.8%	6 1.6%	* 0.1%	2 1.7%	5 2.7%E	0 0	2 2.4%	4 2.1%	1 1.2%	1 2.7%HM	0 0	0 0	0 0	5 1.9%	2 0.7%

Proportions/Means: Columns Tested (5% risk level) - A/B/D - C/D - E/F/G - H/I/J/K/L/M/N - P/Q
* small base; ** very small base (under 30) ineligible for sig testing

Table 398
Page 1696

Outsell/Digital Library Federation Study (2002)
Weighted Tables

TABLE 147, continued

S7sum_12. Data SUMMARY TABLE

	TOTAL SAMPLE	RESPONDENT TYPE: FACULTY MEMBER	GRAD. STUDENT	FACULTY /GRAD	UNDER GRAD. STUDENT	INSTITUTION TYPE: PUBLIC	PRIVATE	LIBERAL ARTS	DISCIPLINE: BIOLOGIAL SCIENCES	PHYSICAL SCIENCES /MATH	SOCIAL SCIENCES	ARTS AND HUMAN.	ENGI-NEERING	BUSINESS	LAW	UNDEC. MAJOR	GENDER: MALE	FEMALE
		(A)	(B)	(C)	(D)	(E)	(F)	(G)	(H)	(I)	(J)	(K)	(L)	(M)	(N)		(P)	(Q)
Base - Use Data for coursework	572	0**	231	231	341	265	114	193	83*	85*	182*	91*	22*	75*	6*	28*	275	297
preferred source of info	0 0	0 0	0 0	0 0	0 0	0 0	0 0	0 0	0 0	0 0	0 0	0 0	0 0	0 0	0 0	0 0	0 0	0 0
Your own personal physical library/ files/bookshelves (NET)	7 1.3%	0 0	5 2.2%	5 2.2%	2 0.6%	2 0.7%	5 4.5%EG	* 0.2%	2 2.1%	1 1.2%	2 1.0%	1 1.2%	1 2.7%	1 1.2%	0 0	0 0	5 1.9%	2 0.7%
All sources of info	7 1.3%	0 0	5 2.2%	5 2.2%	2 0.6%	2 0.7%	5 4.5%EG	* 0.2%	2 2.1%	1 1.2%	2 1.0%	1 1.2%	1 2.7%	1 1.2%	0 0	0 0	5 1.9%	2 0.7%
preferred source of info	3 0.5%	0 0	3 1.2%	3 1.2%	* 0.1%	0 0	3 2.4%E	* 0.2%	1 1.1%	0 0	2 1.0%	0 0	* 1.3%	0 0	0 0	0 0	2 0.8%	1 0.3%
Printed abstracting and indexing services (NET)	6 1.1%	0 0	4 1.6%	4 1.6%	2 0.7%	2 0.7%	2 1.7%	2 1.2%	0 0	1 1.2%	2 1.0%	2 2.5%	0 0	1 1.2%	0 0	0 0	3 1.1%	3 1.0%
All sources of info	6 1.1%	0 0	4 1.6%	4 1.6%	2 0.7%	2 0.7%	2 1.7%	2 1.2%	0 0	1 1.2%	2 1.0%	2 2.5%	0 0	1 1.2%	0 0	0 0	3 1.1%	3 1.0%
preferred source of info	0 0	0 0	0 0	0 0	0 0	0 0	0 0	0 0	0 0	0 0	0 0	0 0	0 0	0 0	0 0	0 0	0 0	0 0
Printed library catalogues and finding aids (NET)	4 0.7%	0 0	* 0.1%	* 0.1%	4 1.1%	1 0.4%	* 0.1%	3 1.5%	2 2.1%	1 1.2%	0 0	1 1.2%	0 0	0 0	* 2.9%JM	0 0	1 0.4%	3 1.0%

Proportions/Means: Columns Tested (5% risk level) - A/B/D - C/D - E/F/G - H/I/J/K/L/M/N - P/Q
* small base; ** very small base (under 30) ineligible for sig testing

Table 398
Page 1697

Outsell/Digital Library Federation Study (2002)
Weighted Tables

TABLE 147, continued
S7sum_12. Data SUMMARY TABLE

		RESPONDENT TYPE				INSTITUTION TYPE			DISCIPLINE									GENDER	
	TOTAL SAMPLE	FACULTY MEMBER	GRAD. STUDENT	FACULTY /GRAD	UNDER GRAD. STUDENT	PUBLIC	PRIVATE	LIBERAL ARTS	BIOLOGIAL SCIENCES	PHYSICAL SCIENCES /MATH	SOCIAL SCIENCES	ARTS AND HUMAN.	ENGI-NEERING	BUSINESS	LAW	UNDEC. MAJOR	MALE	FEMALE
		(A)	(B)	(C)	(D)	(E)	(F)	(G)	(H)	(I)	(J)	(K)	(L)	(M)	(N)		(P)	(Q)
Base - Use Data for coursework	572	0**	231	231	341	265	114	193	83*	85*	182*	91*	22*	75*	6*	28*	275	297
All sources of info	4 0.7%	0 0	* 0.1%	* 0.1%	4 1.1%	1 0.4%	* 0.1%	3 1.5%	2 2.1%	1 1.2%	0 0	1 1.2%	0 0	0 0	* 2.9%JM	0 0	1 0.4%	3 1.0%
preferred source of info	2 0.4%	0 0	0 0	0 0	2 0.6%	1 0.4%	0 0	1 0.6%	0 0	1 1.2%	0 0	1 1.2%	0 0	0 0	0 0	0 0	0 0	2 0.7%
Personal subscriptions to newspapers, magazines and journals (NET)	3 0.5%	0 0	1 0.4%	1 0.4%	2 0.6%	2 0.7%	0 0	1 0.6%	0 0	0 0	0 0	1 1.2%	0 0	2 2.5%	0 0	0 0	2 0.7%	1 0.4%
All sources of info	3 0.5%	0 0	1 0.4%	1 0.4%	2 0.6%	2 0.7%	0 0	1 0.6%	0 0	0 0	0 0	1 1.2%	0 0	2 2.5%	0 0	0 0	2 0.7%	1 0.4%
preferred source of info	1 0.2%	0 0	0 0	0 0	1 0.3%	1 0.4%	0 0	0 0	0 0	0 0	0 0	0 0	0 0	1 1.2%	0 0	0 0	1 0.3%	0 0
Other (NET)	34 5.9%	0 0	9 4.0%	9 4.0%	24 7.1%	21 8.0%	6 4.8%	7 3.6%	4 4.3%	4 4.7%	17 9.3%	4 4.9%	1 4.0%	3 3.7%	0 0	1 3.6%	11 4.2%	22 7.5%
All sources of info	31 5.4%	0 0	9 4.0%	9 4.0%	21 6.3%	19 7.3%	5 4.0%	7 3.6%	4 4.3%	3 3.5%	15 8.2%	4 4.9%	1 4.0%	3 3.7%	0 0	1 3.6%	11 4.2%	19 6.5%
preferred source of info	10 1.7%	0 0	2 0.9%	2 0.9%	8 2.2%	7 2.5%G	3 2.7%G	0 0	0 0	2 2.4%	6 3.1%	1 1.2%	0 0	1 1.2%	0 0	0 0	2 0.7%	8 2.6%
Online (unspecified)	6 1.0%	0 0	1 0.6%	1 0.6%	4 1.3%	4 1.7%	* 0.3%	1 0.5%	0 0	1 1.2%	0 0	2 2.5%	1 2.7%HJ	2 2.5%	0 0	0 0	4 1.3%	2 0.7%

Proportions/Means: Columns Tested (5% risk level) - A/B/D - C/D - E/F/G - H/I/J/K/L/M/N - P/Q
* small base; ** very small base (under 30) ineligible for sig testing

Table 398
Page 1698

Outsell/Digital Library Federation Study (2002)
Weighted Tables

TABLE 147, continued

S7sum_12. Data SUMMARY TABLE

		RESPONDENT TYPE				INSTITUTION TYPE			DISCIPLINE									GENDER	
	TOTAL SAMPLE	FACULTY MEMBER	GRAD. STUDENT	FACULTY /GRAD	UNDER GRAD. STUDENT	PUBLIC	PRIVATE	LIBERAL ARTS	BIOLOGIAL SCIENCES	PHYSICAL SCIENCES /MATH	SOCIAL SCIENCES	ARTS AND HUMAN.	ENGI- NEERING	BUSINESS	LAW	UNDEC. MAJOR	MALE	FEMALE
		(A)	(B)	(C)	(D)	(E)	(F)	(G)	(H)	(I)	(J)	(K)	(L)	(M)	(N)		(P)	(Q)
Base - Use Data for coursework	572	0**	231	231	341	265	114	193	83*	85*	182*	91*	22*	75*	6*	28*	275	297
All sources of info	6 1.0%	0 0	1 0.6%	1 0.6%	4 1.3%	4 1.7%	* 0.3%	1 0.5%	0 0	1 1.2%	0 0	2 2.5%	1 2.7%HJ	2 2.5%	0 0	0 0	4 1.3%	2 0.7%
preferred source of info	4 0.8%	0 0	1 0.6%	1 0.6%	3 0.9%	4 1.5%	* 0.3%	0 0	0 0	0 0	0 0	2 2.5%	* 1.3%J	2 2.5%	0 0	0 0	2 0.9%	2 0.7%
E-journals	0 0	0 0	0 0	0 0	0 0	0 0	0 0	0 0	0 0	0 0	0 0	0 0	0 0	0 0	0 0	0 0	0 0	0 0
All sources of info	0 0	0 0	0 0	0 0	0 0	0 0	0 0	0 0	0 0	0 0	0 0	0 0	0 0	0 0	0 0	0 0	0 0	0 0
preferred source of info	0 0	0 0	0 0	0 0	0 0	0 0	0 0	0 0	0 0	0 0	0 0	0 0	0 0	0 0	0 0	0 0	0 0	0 0
DK/Refused	16 2.8%	0 0	7 3.2%	7 3.2%	9 2.6%	15 5.8%FG	* 0.3%	1 0.3%	1 1.1%	2 2.4%	8 4.1%	2 2.5%	1 6.7%H	2 2.5%	* 5.7%H	0 0	5 2.0%	11 3.7%

Proportions/Means: Columns Tested (5% risk level) - A/B/D - C/D - E/F/G - H/I/J/K/L/M/N - P/Q
* small base; ** very small base (under 30) ineligible for sig testing

Table 398
Page 1699

Outsell/Digital Library Federation Study (2002)
Weighted Tables

TABLE 148

S7D/E_12. Data SUMMARY TABLE

	TOTAL SAMPLE	RESPONDENT TYPE: FACULTY MEMBER	GRAD. STUDENT	FACULTY /GRAD	UNDER GRAD. STUDENT	INSTITUTION TYPE: PUBLIC	PRIVATE	LIBERAL ARTS	DISCIPLINE: BIOLOGIAL SCIENCES	PHYSICAL SCIENCES /MATH	SOCIAL SCIENCES	ARTS AND HUMAN.	ENGI-NEERING	BUSINESS	LAW	UNDEC. MAJOR	GENDER: MALE	FEMALE
		(A)	(B)	(C)	(D)	(E)	(F)	(G)	(H)	(I)	(J)	(K)	(L)	(M)	(N)		(P)	(Q)
Base - Use Data for coursework	572	0**	231	231	341	265	114	193	83*	85*	182*	91*	22*	75*	6*	28*	275	297
Borrow from or use in campus library (NET)	356 62.2%	0 0	125 53.9%	125 53.9%	231 67.8%B C	146 54.9%	64 56.6%	145 75.4%EF	50 60.6%	51 60.0%	120 66.0%M	63 69.1%LM N	11 52.0%	38 50.6%	3 48.6%	19 67.9%	157 57.0%	199 67.0%P
All sources of info	356 62.2%	0 0	125 53.9%	125 53.9%	231 67.8%B C	146 54.9%	64 56.6%	145 75.4%EF	50 60.6%	51 60.0%	120 66.0%M	63 69.1%LM N	11 52.0%	38 50.6%	3 48.6%	19 67.9%	157 57.0%	199 67.0%P
preferred source of info	251 43.9%	0 0	82 35.3%	82 35.3%	169 49.7%B C	102 38.3%	37 32.7%	112 58.1%EF	35 42.6%N	37 43.5%N	81 44.3%N	50 55.6%LM N	7 32.0%	26 34.6%	1 22.9%	13 46.4%	103 37.5%	148 49.7%P
Access online (NET)	330 57.8%	0 0	139 60.1%	139 60.1%	192 56.3%	146 54.9%	73 64.0%	112 58.1%	48 57.4%	53 62.4%	100 54.6%	45 49.4%	13 60.0%	50 66.7%K	4 71.4%K	18 64.3%	178 64.8%Q	152 51.3%
All sources of info	330 57.8%	0 0	139 60.1%	139 60.1%	192 56.3%	146 54.9%	73 64.0%	112 58.1%	48 57.4%	53 62.4%	100 54.6%	45 49.4%	13 60.0%	50 66.7%K	4 71.4%K	18 64.3%	178 64.8%Q	152 51.3%
preferred source of info	259 45.2%	0 0	115 49.7%	115 49.7%	144 42.2%	127 47.8%G	61 54.0%G	70 36.5%	37 44.7%	38 44.7%	81 44.3%	36 39.5%	10 48.0%	42 55.6%K	4 62.9%K	11 39.3%	137 49.7%	122 41.1%
Faculty (NET)	32 5.6%	0 0	21 9.1%D	21 9.1%D	11 3.3%	17 6.3%	7 6.5%	8 4.2%	6 7.4%	5 5.9%	9 5.2%	3 3.7%	2 10.7%K	5 6.2%	* 5.7%	1 3.6%	21 7.5%	12 3.9%
All sources of info	32 5.6%	0 0	21 9.1%D	21 9.1%D	11 3.3%	17 6.3%	7 6.5%	8 4.2%	6 7.4%	5 5.9%	9 5.2%	3 3.7%	2 10.7%K	5 6.2%	* 5.7%	1 3.6%	21 7.5%	12 3.9%
preferred source of info	23 4.0%	0 0	14 5.9%	14 5.9%	9 2.7%	13 4.8%	4 3.5%	6 3.2%	6 7.4%KM	3 3.5%	9 5.2%	1 1.2%	2 8.0%KM	0 0	* 5.7%M	1 3.6%	14 5.2%	8 2.8%

Proportions/Means: Columns Tested (5% risk level) - A/B/D - C/D - E/F/G - H/I/J/K/L/M/N - P/Q
* small base; ** very small base (under 30) ineligible for sig testing

Table 401
Page 1706

Outsell/Digital Library Federation Study (2002)
Weighted Tables

TABLE 148, continued

S7D/E_12. Data SUMMARY TABLE

	TOTAL SAMPLE	RESPONDENT TYPE: FACULTY MEMBER	GRAD. STUDENT	FACULTY /GRAD	UNDER GRAD. STUDENT	INSTITUTION TYPE: PUBLIC	PRIVATE	LIBERAL ARTS	DISCIPLINE: BIOLOGIAL SCIENCES	PHYSICAL SCIENCES /MATH	SOCIAL SCIENCES	ARTS AND HUMAN.	ENGI-NEERING	BUSINESS	LAW	UNDEC. MAJOR	GENDER: MALE	FEMALE
		(A)	(B)	(C)	(D)	(E)	(F)	(G)	(H)	(I)	(J)	(K)	(L)	(M)	(N)		(P)	(Q)
Base - Use Data for coursework	572	0**	231	231	341	265	114	193	83*	85*	182*	91*	22*	75*	6*	28*	275	297
Borrow from or use in other libraries (NET)	23 4.1%	0 0	7 3.0%	7 3.0%	17 4.8%	9 3.4%	3 2.7%	11 5.9%	5 6.4%M	4 4.7%	8 4.1%	4 4.9%	1 4.0%M	0 0	* 5.7%M	1 3.6%	12 4.4%	12 3.9%
All sources of info	23 4.1%	0 0	7 3.0%	7 3.0%	17 4.8%	9 3.4%	3 2.7%	11 5.9%	5 6.4%M	4 4.7%	8 4.1%	4 4.9%	1 4.0%M	0 0	* 5.7%M	1 3.6%	12 4.4%	12 3.9%
preferred source of info	10 1.7%	0 0	6 2.6%	6 2.6%	4 1.1%	5 1.8%	3 2.7%	2 1.0%	2 2.1%	1 1.2%	6 3.1%	0 0	* 1.3%	0 0	* 2.9%KM	1 3.6%	3 1.0%	7 2.4%
Interlibrary loan (NET)	18 3.1%	0 0	0 0	0 0	18 5.2%BC	2 0.8%	0 0	16 8.2%EF	2 2.1%	3 3.5%	6 3.1%	4 4.9%	0 0	0 0	0 0	3 10.7%	7 2.5%	11 3.7%
All sources of info	18 3.1%	0 0	0 0	0 0	18 5.2%BC	2 0.8%	0 0	16 8.2%EF	2 2.1%	3 3.5%	6 3.1%	4 4.9%	0 0	0 0	0 0	3 10.7%	7 2.5%	11 3.7%
preferred source of info	3 0.5%	0 0	0 0	0 0	3 0.9%	2 0.8%	0 0	1 0.5%	1 1.1%	1 1.2%	0 0	1 1.2%	0 0	0 0	0 0	0 0	1 0.4%	2 0.7%
Purchase from physical book store (NET)	10 1.8%	0 0	1 0.5%	1 0.5%	9 2.7%	5 2.1%	1 0.8%	4 2.1%	0 0	0 0	6 3.1%	1 1.2%	1 2.7%HI	2 2.5%	* 2.9%HI	1 3.6%	6 2.1%	5 1.6%
All sources of info	10 1.8%	0 0	1 0.5%	1 0.5%	9 2.7%	5 2.1%	1 0.8%	4 2.1%	0 0	0 0	6 3.1%	1 1.2%	1 2.7%HI	2 2.5%	* 2.9%HI	1 3.6%	6 2.1%	5 1.6%
preferred source of info	4 0.6%	0 0	1 0.5%	1 0.5%	2 0.7%	3 1.0%	1 0.8%	0 0	0 0	0 0	2 1.0%	0 0	1 2.7%HIK	1 1.2%	* 2.9%HIK	0 0	3 1.0%	1 0.3%

Proportions/Means: Columns Tested (5% risk level) - A/B/D - C/D - E/F/G - H/I/J/K/L/M/N - P/Q
* small base; ** very small base (under 30) ineligible for sig testing

Table 401
Page 1707

Outsell/Digital Library Federation Study (2002)
Weighted Tables

TABLE 148, continued

S7D/E_12. Data SUMMARY TABLE

		RESPONDENT TYPE				INSTITUTION TYPE			DISCIPLINE									GENDER	
	TOTAL SAMPLE	FACULTY MEMBER	GRAD. STUDENT	FACULTY /GRAD	UNDER GRAD. STUDENT	PUBLIC	PRIVATE	LIBERAL ARTS	BIOLOGIAL SCIENCES	PHYSICAL SCIENCES /MATH	SOCIAL SCIENCES	ARTS AND HUMAN.	ENGI-NEERING	BUSINESS	LAW	UNDEC. MAJOR	MALE	FEMALE
		(A)	(B)	(C)	(D)	(E)	(F)	(G)	(H)	(I)	(J)	(K)	(L)	(M)	(N)		(P)	(Q)
Base - Use Data for coursework	572	0**	231	231	341	265	114	193	83*	85*	182*	91*	22*	75*	6*	28*	275	297
Purchase from online bookstore (NET)	3 0.5%	0 0	2 0.9%	2 0.9%	1 0.3%	2 0.8%	1 0.8%	0 0	0 0	0 0	0 0	1 1.2%	0 0	2 2.5%	0 0	0 0	1 0.3%	2 0.7%
All sources of info	3 0.5%	0 0	2 0.9%	2 0.9%	1 0.3%	2 0.8%	1 0.8%	0 0	0 0	0 0	0 0	1 1.2%	0 0	2 2.5%	0 0	0 0	1 0.3%	2 0.7%
preferred source of info	1 0.2%	0 0	1 0.4%	1 0.4%	0 0	0 0	1 0.8%	0 0	0 0	0 0	0 0	0 0	0 0	1 1.2%	0 0	0 0	1 0.3%	0 0
Personal Holdings (NET)	3 0.5%	0 0	2 1.0%	2 1.0%	1 0.2%	1 0.5%	1 1.2%	* 0.2%	0 0	0 0	0 0	1 1.2%	1 4.0%HIJ	1 1.2%	0 0	0 0	2 0.7%	1 0.4%
All sources of info	3 0.5%	0 0	2 1.0%	2 1.0%	1 0.2%	1 0.5%	1 1.2%	* 0.2%	0 0	0 0	0 0	1 1.2%	1 4.0%HIJ	1 1.2%	0 0	0 0	2 0.7%	1 0.4%
preferred source of info	2 0.3%	0 0	1 0.5%	1 0.5%	1 0.2%	1 0.5%	* 0.3%	* 0.2%	0 0	0 0	0 0	0 0	1 4.0%HIJK	1 1.2%	0 0	0 0	2 0.7%	0 0
Home (NET)	2 0.4%	0 0	2 0.9%	2 0.9%	0 0	0 0	2 1.8%E	0 0	0 0	0 0	2 1.0%	0 0	0 0	0 0	* 2.9%HIKM	0 0	0 0	2 0.7%
All sources of info	2 0.4%	0 0	2 0.9%	2 0.9%	0 0	0 0	2 1.8%E	0 0	0 0	0 0	2 1.0%	0 0	0 0	0 0	* 2.9%HIKM	0 0	0 0	2 0.7%
preferred source of info	0 0	0 0	0 0	0 0	0 0	0 0	0 0	0 0	0 0	0 0	0 0	0 0	0 0	0 0	0 0	0 0	0 0	0 0
Access from course website (NET)	2 0.3%	0 0	1 0.4%	1 0.4%	1 0.3%	2 0.8%	0 0	0 0	0 0	1 1.2%	0 0	0 0	0 0	0 0	0 0	1 3.6%	2 0.7%	0 0

Proportions/Means: Columns Tested (5% risk level) - A/B/D - C/D - E/F/G - H/I/J/K/L/M/N - P/Q
* small base; ** very small base (under 30) ineligible for sig testing

Table 401
Page 1708

Outsell/Digital Library Federation Study (2002)
Weighted Tables

TABLE 148, continued

S7D/E_12. Data SUMMARY TABLE

		RESPONDENT TYPE				INSTITUTION TYPE			DISCIPLINE								GENDER	
	TOTAL SAMPLE	FACULTY MEMBER	GRAD. STUDENT	FACULTY /GRAD	UNDER GRAD. STUDENT	PUBLIC	PRIVATE	LIBERAL ARTS	BIOLOGIAL SCIENCES	PHYSICAL SCIENCES /MATH	SOCIAL SCIENCES	ARTS AND HUMAN.	ENGI- NEERING	BUSINESS	LAW	UNDEC. MAJOR	MALE	FEMALE
		(A)	(B)	(C)	(D)	(E)	(F)	(G)	(H)	(I)	(J)	(K)	(L)	(M)	(N)		(P)	(Q)
Base - Use Data for coursework	572	0**	231	231	341	265	114	193	83*	85*	182*	91*	22*	75*	6*	28*	275	297
All sources of info	2 0.3%	0 0	1 0.4%	1 0.4%	1 0.3%	2 0.8%	0 0	0 0	0 0	1 1.2%	0 0	0 0	0 0	0 0	0 0	1 3.6%	2 0.7%	0 0
preferred source of info	2 0.3%	0 0	1 0.4%	1 0.4%	1 0.3%	2 0.8%	0 0	0 0	0 0	1 1.2%	0 0	0 0	0 0	0 0	0 0	1 3.6%	2 0.7%	0 0
Order from on demand document delivery service (NET)	1 0.2%	0 0	* 0.1%	* 0.1%	1 0.3%	0 0	* 0.1%	1 0.5%	0 0	1 1.2%	0 0	0 0	0 0	0 0	* 2.9%HJKM	0 0	* 0.1%	1 0.3%
All sources of info	1 0.2%	0 0	* 0.1%	* 0.1%	1 0.3%	0 0	* 0.1%	1 0.5%	0 0	1 1.2%	0 0	0 0	0 0	0 0	* 2.9%HJKM	0 0	* 0.1%	1 0.3%
preferred source of info	0 0	0 0	0 0	0 0	0 0	0 0	0 0	0 0	0 0	0 0	0 0	0 0	0 0	0 0	0 0	0 0	0 0	0 0
Dorm room (NET)	1 0.2%	0 0	0 0	0 0	1 0.3%	0 0	0 0	1 0.5%	0 0	0 0	0 0	0 0	0 0	0 0	0 0	1 3.6%	1 0.4%	0 0
All sources of info	1 0.2%	0 0	0 0	0 0	1 0.3%	0 0	0 0	1 0.5%	0 0	0 0	0 0	0 0	0 0	0 0	0 0	1 3.6%	1 0.4%	0 0
preferred source of info	0 0	0 0	0 0	0 0	0 0	0 0	0 0	0 0	0 0	0 0	0 0	0 0	0 0	0 0	0 0	0 0	0 0	0 0
Colleagues (NET)	1 0.2%	0 0	1 0.4%	1 0.4%	0 0	0 0	1 0.8%	0 0	1 1.1%	0 0	0 0	0 0	0 0	0 0	0 0	0 0	0 0	1 0.3%
All sources of info	1 0.2%	0 0	1 0.4%	1 0.4%	0 0	0 0	1 0.8%	0 0	1 1.1%	0 0	0 0	0 0	0 0	0 0	0 0	0 0	0 0	1 0.3%

Proportions/Means: Columns Tested (5% risk level) - A/B/D - C/D - E/F/G - H/I/J/K/L/M/N - P/Q
* small base; ** very small base (under 30) ineligible for sig testing

Table 401
Page 1709

Outsell/Digital Library Federation Study (2002)
Weighted Tables

TABLE 148, continued

S7D/E_12. Data SUMMARY TABLE

		RESPONDENT TYPE				INSTITUTION TYPE			DISCIPLINE								GENDER	
	TOTAL SAMPLE	FACULTY MEMBER	GRAD. STUDENT	FACULTY /GRAD	UNDER GRAD. STUDENT	PUBLIC	PRIVATE	LIBERAL ARTS	BIOLOGIAL SCIENCES	PHYSICAL SCIENCES /MATH	SOCIAL SCIENCES	ARTS AND HUMAN.	ENGI-NEERING	BUSINESS	LAW	UNDEC. MAJOR	MALE	FEMALE
		(A)	(B)	(C)	(D)	(E)	(F)	(G)	(H)	(I)	(J)	(K)	(L)	(M)	(N)		(P)	(Q)
Base - Use Data for coursework	572	0**	231	231	341	265	114	193	83*	85*	182*	91*	22*	75*	6*	28*	275	297
preferred source of info	0 0	0 0	0 0	0 0	0 0	0 0	0 0	0 0	0 0	0 0	0 0	0 0	0 0	0 0	0 0	0 0	0 0	0 0
In class (NET)	0 0	0 0	0 0	0 0	0 0	0 0	0 0	0 0	0 0	0 0	0 0	0 0	0 0	0 0	0 0	0 0	0 0	0 0
All sources of info	0 0	0 0	0 0	0 0	0 0	0 0	0 0	0 0	0 0	0 0	0 0	0 0	0 0	0 0	0 0	0 0	0 0	0 0
preferred source of info	0 0	0 0	0 0	0 0	0 0	0 0	0 0	0 0	0 0	0 0	0 0	0 0	0 0	0 0	0 0	0 0	0 0	0 0
Ask library to purchase source (NET)	0 0	0 0	0 0	0 0	0 0	0 0	0 0	0 0	0 0	0 0	0 0	0 0	0 0	0 0	0 0	0 0	0 0	0 0
All sources of info	0 0	0 0	0 0	0 0	0 0	0 0	0 0	0 0	0 0	0 0	0 0	0 0	0 0	0 0	0 0	0 0	0 0	0 0
preferred source of info	0 0	0 0	0 0	0 0	0 0	0 0	0 0	0 0	0 0	0 0	0 0	0 0	0 0	0 0	0 0	0 0	0 0	0 0
Access book/journal/ journal article elsewhere online (NET)	0 0	0 0	0 0	0 0	0 0	0 0	0 0	0 0	0 0	0 0	0 0	0 0	0 0	0 0	0 0	0 0	0 0	0 0
All sources of info	0 0	0 0	0 0	0 0	0 .0	0 0	0 0	0 0	0 0	0 0	0 0	0 0	0 0	0 0	0 0	0 0	0 0	0 0

Proportions/Means: Columns Tested (5% risk level) - A/B/D - C/D - E/F/G - H/I/J/K/L/M/N - P/Q
* small base; ** very small base (under 30) ineligible for sig testing

Table 401
Page 1710

Outsell/Digital Library Federation Study (2002)
Weighted Tables

TABLE 148, continued

S7D/E_12. Data SUMMARY TABLE

		RESPONDENT TYPE				INSTITUTION TYPE			DISCIPLINE									GENDER	
	TOTAL SAMPLE	FACULTY MEMBER	GRAD. STUDENT	FACULTY /GRAD	UNDER GRAD. STUDENT	PUBLIC	PRIVATE	LIBERAL ARTS	BIOLOGIAL SCIENCES	PHYSICAL SCIENCES /MATH	SOCIAL SCIENCES	ARTS AND HUMAN.	ENGI- NEERING	BUSINESS	LAW	UNDEC. MAJOR	MALE	FEMALE
		(A)	(B)	(C)	(D)	(E)	(F)	(G)	(H)	(I)	(J)	(K)	(L)	(M)	(N)		(P)	(Q)
Base - Use Data for coursework	572	0**	231	231	341	265	114	193	83*	85*	182*	91*	22*	75*	6*	28*	275	297
preferred source of info	0 0	0 0	0 0	0 0	0 0	0 0	0 0	0 0	0 0	0 0	0 0	0 0	0 0	0 0	0 0	0 0	0 0	0 0
Other (NET)	27 4.7%	0 0	18 7.9%D	18 7.9%D	8 2.5%	17 6.3%G	7 6.0%	3 1.7%	4 4.3%	4 4.7%	9 5.2%	4 4.9%	1 2.7%	5 6.2%	* 2.9%	0 0	17 6.2%	10 3.3%
All sources of info	26 4.5%	0 0	17 7.5%D	17 7.5%D	8 2.5%	17 6.3%G	6 5.0%	3 1.7%	4 4.3%	4 4.7%	9 5.2%	3 3.7%	1 2.7%	5 6.2%	* 2.9%	0 0	17 6.2%	9 2.9%
preferred source of info	13 2.3%	0 0	9 3.8%	9 3.8%	4 1.3%	9 3.4%G	4 3.5%G	0 0	1 1.1%	3 3.5%	4 2.1%	2 2.5%	* 1.3%	3 3.7%	0 0	0 0	6 2.3%	7 2.3%
DK/Refused	5 1.0%	0 0	2 1.0%	2 1.0%	3 0.9%	2 0.9%	2 1.8%	1 0.5%	1 1.1%	1 1.2%	0 0	0 0	1 2.7%JK	2 2.5%	* 2.9%JK	1 3.6%	3 1.1%	3 0.8%

Proportions/Means: Columns Tested (5% risk level) - A/B/D - C/D - E/F/G - H/I/J/K/L/M/N - P/Q
* small base; ** very small base (under 30) ineligible for sig testing

Table 401
Page 1711

TABLE 149

S7sum_13. Photographs, prints and other visual resources SUMMARY TABLE

		RESPONDENT TYPE				INSTITUTION TYPE			DISCIPLINE									GENDER	
	TOTAL SAMPLE	FACULTY MEMBER	GRAD. STUDENT	FACULTY /GRAD	UNDER GRAD. STUDENT	PUBLIC	PRIVATE	LIBERAL ARTS	BIOLOGIAL SCIENCES	PHYSICAL SCIENCES /MATH	SOCIAL SCIENCES	ARTS AND HUMAN.	ENGI- NEERING	BUSINESS	LAW	UNDEC. MAJOR	MALE	FEMALE
		(A)	(B)	(C)	(D)	(E)	(F)	(G)	(H)	(I)	(J)	(K)	(L)	(M)	(N)		(P)	(Q)
Base - Use Photographs, prints and other visual resources for coursework	424	0**	143	143	281	183	87*	154	67*	50*	117*	111*	16*	46*	1**	17*	208	216
ONLINE	306 72.2%	0 0	96 67.0%	96 67.0%	210 74.9%	125 68.5%	61 70.3%	120 77.8%	44 65.8%	39 78.0%	81 69.4%	78 70.7%	12 72.7%	36 79.6%	1 100.0%	15 88.2%	160 76.9%	147 67.8%
Search engine (NET)	154 36.4%	0 0	34 24.0%	34 24.0%	120 42.7%B C	44 24.2%	27 30.6%	83 54.1%EF	16 23.7%	21 42.0%H	38 32.3%	41 37.4%	6 40.0%H	21 46.9%H	1 50.0%	10 58.8%	91 43.5%Q	64 29.5%
All sources of info	154 36.4%	0 0	34 24.0%	34 24.0%	120 42.7%B C	44 24.2%	27 30.6%	83 54.1%EF	16 23.7%	21 42.0%H	38 32.3%	41 37.4%	6 40.0%H	21 46.9%H	1 50.0%	10 58.8%	91 43.5%Q	64 29.5%
preferred source of info	99 23.4%	0 0	22 15.2%	22 15.2%	77 27.6%B C	32 17.6%	19 21.4%	49 31.5%E	12 18.4%	15 30.0%J	17 14.5%	25 22.2%	4 27.3%	19 40.8%HJ K	1 37.5%	7 41.2%	60 28.8%Q	39 18.3%
Internet searches (NET)	78 18.4%	0 0	33 22.7%	33 22.7%	45 16.2%	48 26.5%FG	12 14.2%	17 11.1%	12 18.4%	6 12.0%	23 19.4%	21 19.2%	3 20.0%	10 22.4%	* 25.0%	2 11.8%	37 17.9%	41 18.8%
All sources of info	78 18.4%	0 0	33 22.7%	33 22.7%	45 16.2%	48 26.5%FG	12 14.2%	17 11.1%	12 18.4%	6 12.0%	23 19.4%	21 19.2%	3 20.0%	10 22.4%	* 25.0%	2 11.8%	37 17.9%	41 18.8%
preferred source of info	51 12.0%	0 0	20 14.0%	20 14.0%	31 11.0%	35 19.3%FG	6 6.6%	10 6.5%	8 11.8%	5 10.0%	15 12.9%	11 10.1%	2 14.5%	8 18.4%	* 12.5%	1 5.9%	26 12.3%	25 11.8%
Online databases (NET)	48 11.3%	0 0	23 16.1%D	23 16.1%D	25 8.8%	13 7.3%	14 16.0%E	21 13.3%	5 7.9%	9 18.0%L	15 12.9%L	12 11.1%L	0 0	3 6.1%	* 25.0%	3 17.6%	24 11.8%	23 10.8%

Proportions/Means: Columns Tested (5% risk level) - A/B/D - C/D - E/F/G - H/I/J/K/L/M/N - P/Q
* small base; ** very small base (under 30) ineligible for sig testing

Table 405
Page 1723

TABLE 149, continued

S7sum_13. Photographs, prints and other visual resources SUMMARY TABLE

	TOTAL SAMPLE	RESPONDENT TYPE: FACULTY MEMBER	GRAD. STUDENT	FACULTY /GRAD	UNDER GRAD. STUDENT	INSTITUTION TYPE: PUBLIC	PRIVATE	LIBERAL ARTS	DISCIPLINE: BIOLOGIAL SCIENCES	PHYSICAL SCIENCES /MATH	SOCIAL SCIENCES	ARTS AND HUMAN.	ENGI-NEERING	BUSINESS	LAW	UNDEC. MAJOR	GENDER: MALE	FEMALE
		(A)	(B)	(C)	(D)	(E)	(F)	(G)	(H)	(I)	(J)	(K)	(L)	(M)	(N)		(P)	(Q)
Base - Use Photographs, prints and other visual resources for coursework	424	0**	143	143	281	183	87*	154	67*	50*	117*	111*	16*	46*	1**	17*	208	216
All sources of info	48 11.3%	0 0	23 16.1%D	23 16.1%D	25 8.8%	13 7.3%	14 16.0%E	21 13.3%	5 7.9%	9 18.0%L	15 12.9%L	12 11.1%L	0 0	3 6.1%	* 25.0%	3 17.6%	24 11.8%	23 10.8%
preferred source of info	22 5.1%	0 0	14 9.7%D	14 9.7%D	8 2.8%	9 4.9%	7 7.9%	6 3.8%	4 6.6%	4 8.0%	6 4.8%	4 4.0%	0 0	1 2.0%	* 25.0%	2 11.8%	11 5.5%	10 4.8%
Your own institution's web site (NET)	33 7.8%	0 0	12 8.6%	12 8.6%	21 7.4%	14 7.4%	11 12.4%	9 5.8%	9 13.2%	3 6.0%	8 6.5%	9 8.1%	1 7.3%	3 6.1%	0 0	1 5.9%	17 8.1%	16 7.6%
All sources of info	33 7.8%	0 0	12 8.6%	12 8.6%	21 7.4%	14 7.4%	11 12.4%	9 5.8%	9 13.2%	3 6.0%	8 6.5%	9 8.1%	1 7.3%	3 6.1%	0 0	1 5.9%	17 8.1%	16 7.6%
preferred source of info	17 4.1%	0 0	6 4.3%	6 4.3%	11 4.0%	6 3.2%	6 6.7%	6 3.8%	3 3.9%	2 4.0%	6 4.8%	4 4.0%	1 5.5%	2 4.1%	0 0	0 0	11 5.1%	7 3.2%
Online library catalogues and finding aids (NET)	32 7.5%	0 0	9 6.1%	9 6.1%	23 8.2%	10 5.5%	5 5.7%	17 10.7%	5 7.9%	4 8.0%	11 9.7%	7 6.1%	1 3.6%	3 6.1%	0 0	1 5.9%	13 6.4%	18 8.5%
All sources of info	32 7.5%	0 0	9 6.1%	9 6.1%	23 8.2%	10 5.5%	5 5.7%	17 10.7%	5 7.9%	4 8.0%	11 9.7%	7 6.1%	1 3.6%	3 6.1%	0 0	1 5.9%	13 6.4%	18 8.5%
preferred source of info	25 5.9%	0 0	5 3.5%	5 3.5%	20 7.1%	8 4.4%	2 2.5%	15 9.5%	4 6.6%	4 8.0%	8 6.5%	6 5.1%	1 3.6%	2 4.1%	0 0	1 5.9%	12 6.0%	13 5.8%

Proportions/Means: Columns Tested (5% risk level) - A/B/D - C/D - E/F/G - H/I/J/K/L/M/N - P/Q
* small base; ** very small base (under 30) ineligible for sig testing

Table 405
Page 1724

Outsell/Digital Library Federation Study (2002)
Weighted Tables

TABLE 149, continued

S7sum_13. Photographs, prints and other visual resources SUMMARY TABLE

		RESPONDENT TYPE				INSTITUTION TYPE			DISCIPLINE								GENDER	
	TOTAL SAMPLE	FACULTY MEMBER	GRAD. STUDENT	FACULTY /GRAD	UNDER GRAD. STUDENT	PUBLIC	PRIVATE	LIBERAL ARTS	BIOLOGIAL SCIENCES	PHYSICAL SCIENCES /MATH	SOCIAL SCIENCES	ARTS AND HUMAN.	ENGI-NEERING	BUSINESS	LAW	UNDEC. MAJOR	MALE	FEMALE
		(A)	(B)	(C)	(D)	(E)	(F)	(G)	(H)	(I)	(J)	(K)	(L)	(M)	(N)		(P)	(Q)
Base - Use Photographs, prints and other visual resources for coursework	424	0**	143	143	281	183	87*	154	67*	50*	117*	111*	16*	46*	1**	17*	208	216
Web directory/ subject related web site (NET)	28 6.6%	0 0	11 7.7%	11 7.7%	17 6.1%	7 3.8%	10 11.8%E	11 7.1%	7 10.5%	1 2.0%	6 4.8%	8 7.1%	1 3.6%	3 6.1%	* 12.5%	3 17.6%	16 7.7%	12 5.5%
All sources of info	28 6.6%	0 0	11 7.7%	11 7.7%	17 6.1%	7 3.8%	10 11.8%E	11 7.1%	7 10.5%	1 2.0%	6 4.8%	8 7.1%	1 3.6%	3 6.1%	* 12.5%	3 17.6%	16 7.7%	12 5.5%
preferred source of info	15 3.5%	0 0	6 4.1%	6 4.1%	9 3.1%	5 2.7%	6 6.8%	4 2.5%	4 6.6%	0 0	4 3.2%	3 3.0%	* 1.8%	1 2.0%	0 0	2 11.8%	7 3.4%	8 3.5%
Department web page (NET)	14 3.2%	0 0	1 0.8%	1 0.8%	12 4.4%	9 4.8%	1 1.0%	4 2.6%	3 3.9%	3 6.0%	2 1.6%	2 2.0%	1 5.5%	2 4.1%	* 12.5%	1 5.9%	8 3.8%	6 2.6%
All sources of info	14 3.2%	0 0	1 0.8%	1 0.8%	12 4.4%	9 4.8%	1 1.0%	4 2.6%	3 3.9%	3 6.0%	2 1.6%	2 2.0%	1 5.5%	2 4.1%	* 12.5%	1 5.9%	8 3.8%	6 2.6%
preferred source of info	7 1.7%	0 0	1 0.8%	1 0.8%	6 2.2%	6 3.0%	1 1.0%	1 0.6%	1 1.3%	1 2.0%	2 1.6%	1 1.0%	1 3.6%	1 2.0%	0 0	1 5.9%	4 1.7%	4 1.8%
Online reference service (NET)	10 2.4%	0 0	8 5.8%D	8 5.8%D	2 0.7%	7 3.6%G	4 4.3%G	0 0	3 3.9%	0 0	4 3.2%	3 3.0%	1 3.6%I	0 0	0 0	0 0	4 1.8%	7 3.1%
All sources of info	10 2.4%	0 0	8 5.8%D	8 5.8%D	2 0.7%	7 3.6%G	4 4.3%G	0 0	3 3.9%	0 0	4 3.2%	3 3.0%	1 3.6%I	0 0	0 0	0 0	4 1.8%	7 3.1%

Proportions/Means: Columns Tested (5% risk level) - A/B/D - C/D - E/F/G - H/I/J/K/L/M/N - P/Q
* small base; ** very small base (under 30) ineligible for sig testing

Table 405
Page 1725

Outsell/Digital Library Federation Study (2002)
Weighted Tables

TABLE 149, continued

S7sum_13. Photographs, prints and other visual resources SUMMARY TABLE

		RESPONDENT TYPE				INSTITUTION TYPE			DISCIPLINE									GENDER	
	TOTAL SAMPLE	FACULTY MEMBER	GRAD. STUDENT	FACULTY /GRAD	UNDER GRAD. STUDENT	PUBLIC	PRIVATE	LIBERAL ARTS	BIOLOGIAL SCIENCES	PHYSICAL SCIENCES /MATH	SOCIAL SCIENCES	ARTS AND HUMAN.	ENGI- NEERING	BUSINESS	LAW	UNDEC. MAJOR	MALE	FEMALE
		(A)	(B)	(C)	(D)	(E)	(F)	(G)	(H)	(I)	(J)	(K)	(L)	(M)	(N)		(P)	(Q)
Base - Use Photographs, prints and other visual resources for coursework	424	0**	143	143	281	183	87*	154	67*	50*	117*	111*	16*	46*	1**	17*	208	216
preferred source of info	2 0.5%	0 0	2 1.5%	2 1.5%	0 0	2 1.2%	0 0	0 0	0 0	0 0	2 1.6%	0 0	* 1.8%K	0 0	0 0	0 0	* 0.1%	2 0.9%
Online abstracting and indexing services (NET)	4 1.0%	0 0	3 1.8%	3 1.8%	2 0.7%	1 0.6%	1 1.6%	2 1.2%	0 0	0 0	2 1.6%	2 2.0%	* 1.8%	0 0	0 0	0 0	3 1.2%	2 0.9%
All sources of info	4 1.0%	0 0	3 1.8%	3 1.8%	2 0.7%	1 0.6%	1 1.6%	2 1.2%	0 0	0 0	2 1.6%	2 2.0%	* 1.8%	0 0	0 0	0 0	3 1.2%	2 0.9%
preferred source of info	0 0	0 0	0 0	0 0	0 0	0 0	0 0	0 0	0 0	0 0	0 0	0 0	0 0	0 0	0 0	0 0	0 0	0 0
Your own personal electronic library/files (NET)	2 0.5%	0 0	1 0.8%	1 0.8%	1 0.3%	0 0	1 1.3%	1 0.6%	1 1.3%	0 0	0 0	1 1.0%	0 0	0 0	0 0	0 0	0 0	2 0.9%
All sources of info	2 0.5%	0 0	1 0.8%	1 0.8%	1 0.3%	0 0	1 1.3%	1 0.6%	1 1.3%	0 0	0 0	1 1.0%	0 0	0 0	0 0	0 0	0 0	2 0.9%
preferred source of info	0 0	0 0	0 0	0 0	0 0	0 0	0 0	0 0	0 0	0 0	0 0	0 0	0 0	0 0	0 0	0 0	0 0	0 0
E-mail listservs (NET)	0 0	0 0	0 0	0 0	0 0	0 0	0 0	0 0	0 0	0 0	0 0	0 0	0 0	0 0	0 0	0 0	0 0	0 0

Proportions/Means: Columns Tested (5% risk level) - A/B/D - C/D - E/F/G - H/I/J/K/L/M/N - P/Q
* small base; ** very small base (under 30) ineligible for sig testing

Table 405
Page 1726

TABLE 149, continued

S7sum_13. Photographs, prints and other visual resources SUMMARY TABLE

		RESPONDENT TYPE				INSTITUTION TYPE			DISCIPLINE									GENDER	
	TOTAL SAMPLE	FACULTY MEMBER	GRAD. STUDENT	FACULTY /GRAD	UNDER GRAD. STUDENT	PUBLIC	PRIVATE	LIBERAL ARTS	BIOLOGIAL SCIENCES	PHYSICAL SCIENCES /MATH	SOCIAL SCIENCES	ARTS AND HUMAN.	ENGI-NEERING	BUSINESS	LAW	UNDEC. MAJOR	MALE	FEMALE
		(A)	(B)	(C)	(D)	(E)	(F)	(G)	(H)	(I)	(J)	(K)	(L)	(M)	(N)		(P)	(Q)
Base - Use Photographs, prints and other visual resources for coursework	424	0**	143	143	281	183	87*	154	67*	50*	117*	111*	16*	46*	1**	17*	208	216
All sources of info	0 0	0 0	0 0	0 0	0 0	0 0	0 0	0 0	0 0	0 0	0 0	0 0	0 0	0 0	0 0	0 0	0 0	0 0
preferred source of info	0 0	0 0	0 0	0 0	0 0	0 0	0 0	0 0	0 0	0 0	0 0	0 0	0 0	0 0	0 0	0 0	0 0	0 0
Online bookstore (NET)	0 0	0 0	0 0	0 0	0 0	0 0	0 0	0 0	0 0	0 0	0 0	0 0	0 0	0 0	0 0	0 0	0 0	0 0
All sources of info	0 0	0 0	0 0	0 0	0 0	0 0	0 0	0 0	0 0	0 0	0 0	0 0	0 0	0 0	0 0	0 0	0 0	0 0
preferred source of info	0 0	0 0	0 0	0 0	0 0	0 0	0 0	0 0	0 0	0 0	0 0	0 0	0 0	0 0	0 0	0 0	0 0	0 0
LIBRARY FACILITIES/ PRINT	151 35.5%	0 0	54 37.4%	54 37.4%	97 34.5%	53 29.1%	29 32.9%	69 44.5%E	27 40.8%LM	18 36.0%	39 33.9%	45 40.4%LM	3 18.2%	8 18.4%	1 50.0%	9 52.9%	64 30.7%	87 40.1%
Campus library (NET)	134 31.7%	0 0	48 33.2%	48 33.2%	87 30.9%	46 25.2%	26 29.5%	63 40.6%E	20 30.3%L	16 32.0%L	38 32.3%L	41 37.4%LM	2 12.7%	7 16.3%	1 50.0%	9 52.9%	55 26.4%	80 36.8%P
All sources of info	134 31.7%	0 0	48 33.2%	48 33.2%	87 30.9%	46 25.2%	26 29.5%	63 40.6%E	20 30.3%L	16 32.0%L	38 32.3%L	41 37.4%LM	2 12.7%	7 16.3%	1 50.0%	9 52.9%	55 26.4%	80 36.8%P
preferred source of info	77 18.1%	0 0	32 22.2%	32 22.2%	45 16.0%	29 15.7%	13 14.9%	35 22.6%	12 18.4%	8 16.0%	26 22.6%M	25 22.2%M	1 9.1%	3 6.1%	* 12.5%	1 5.9%	31 14.7%	46 21.3%

Proportions/Means: Columns Tested (5% risk level) - A/B/D - C/D - E/F/G - H/I/J/K/L/M/N - P/Q
* small base; ** very small base (under 30) ineligible for sig testing

Table 405
Page 1727

Outsell/Digital Library Federation Study (2002)
Weighted Tables

TABLE 149, continued

S7sum_13. Photographs, prints and other visual resources SUMMARY TABLE

		RESPONDENT TYPE				INSTITUTION TYPE			DISCIPLINE								GENDER	
	TOTAL SAMPLE	FACULTY MEMBER	GRAD. STUDENT	FACULTY /GRAD	UNDER GRAD. STUDENT	PUBLIC	PRIVATE	LIBERAL ARTS	BIOLOGIAL SCIENCES	PHYSICAL SCIENCES /MATH	SOCIAL SCIENCES	ARTS AND HUMAN.	ENGI-NEERING	BUSINESS	LAW	UNDEC. MAJOR	MALE	FEMALE
		(A)	(B)	(C)	(D)	(E)	(F)	(G)	(H)	(I)	(J)	(K)	(L)	(M)	(N)		(P)	(Q)
Base - Use Photographs, prints and other visual resources for coursework	424	0**	143	143	281	183	87*	154	67*	50*	117*	111*	16*	46*	1**	17*	208	216
Another library (NET)	9 2.1%	0 0	2 1.6%	2 1.6%	7 2.4%	2 1.1%	1 1.3%	6 3.8%	1 1.3%	1 2.0%	4 3.2%	2 2.0%	* 1.8%	1 2.0%	0 0	0 0	7 3.4%	2 0.9%
All sources of info	9 2.1%	0 0	2 1.6%	2 1.6%	7 2.4%	2 1.1%	1 1.3%	6 3.8%	1 1.3%	1 2.0%	4 3.2%	2 2.0%	* 1.8%	1 2.0%	0 0	0 0	7 3.4%	2 0.9%
preferred source of info	1 0.3%	0 0	0 0	0 0	1 0.4%	0 0	0 0	1 0.7%	0 0	0 0	0 0	1 1.0%	0 0	0 0	0 0	0 0	0 0	1 0.5%
Physical bookstore (NET)	9 2.0%	0 0	3 2.4%	3 2.4%	5 1.9%	2 1.2%	2 2.8%	4 2.6%	3 3.9%	2 4.0%	2 1.6%	1 1.0%	1 5.5%KM	0 0	* 12.5%	0 0	6 2.8%	3 1.3%
All sources of info	9 2.0%	0 0	3 2.4%	3 2.4%	5 1.9%	2 1.2%	2 2.8%	4 2.6%	3 3.9%	2 4.0%	2 1.6%	1 1.0%	1 5.5%KM	0 0	* 12.5%	0 0	6 2.8%	3 1.3%
preferred source of info	1 0.2%	0 0	0 0	0 0	1 0.3%	0 0	1 1.0%	0 0	1 1.3%	0 0	0 0	0 0	0 0	0 0	0 0	0 0	0 0	1 0.4%
Your own personal physical library/ files/bookshelves (NET)	7 1.6%	0 0	4 2.6%	4 2.6%	3 1.1%	2 1.3%	2 2.0%	3 1.9%	3 3.9%	0 0	2 1.6%	1 1.0%	* 1.8%	0 0	0 0	1 5.9%	1 0.6%	6 2.7%
All sources of info	7 1.6%	0 0	4 2.6%	4 2.6%	3 1.1%	2 1.3%	2 2.0%	3 1.9%	3 3.9%	0 0	2 1.6%	1 1.0%	* 1.8%	0 0	0 0	1 5.9%	1 0.6%	6 2.7%

Proportions/Means: Columns Tested (5% risk level) - A/B/D - C/D - E/F/G - H/I/J/K/L/M/N - P/Q
* small base; ** very small base (under 30) ineligible for sig testing

Table 405
Page 1728

TABLE 149, continued

S7sum_13. Photographs, prints and other visual resources SUMMARY TABLE

	TOTAL SAMPLE	RESPONDENT TYPE: FACULTY MEMBER	GRAD. STUDENT	FACULTY /GRAD	UNDER GRAD. STUDENT	INSTITUTION TYPE: PUBLIC	PRIVATE	LIBERAL ARTS	DISCIPLINE: BIOLOGIAL SCIENCES	PHYSICAL SCIENCES /MATH	SOCIAL SCIENCES	ARTS AND HUMAN.	ENGI-NEERING	BUSINESS	LAW	UNDEC. MAJOR	GENDER: MALE	FEMALE
		(A)	(B)	(C)	(D)	(E)	(F)	(G)	(H)	(I)	(J)	(K)	(L)	(M)	(N)		(P)	(Q)
Base - Use Photographs, prints and other visual resources for coursework	424	0**	143	143	281	183	87*	154	67*	50*	117*	111*	16*	46*	1**	17*	208	216
preferred source of info	4	0	2	2	2	*	2	2	2	0	2	0	*	0	0	0	*	4
	0.9%	0	1.2%	1.2%	0.8%	0.2%	2.0%	1.2%	2.6%	0	1.6%	0	1.8%K	0	0	0	0.1%	1.7%
References cited in books or journal articles (NET)	5	0	1	1	4	3	0	2	2	1	0	2	0	0	0	0	3	2
	1.2%	0	0.8%	0.8%	1.4%	1.6%	0	1.4%	2.6%	2.0%	0	2.0%	0	0	0	0	1.6%	0.8%
All sources of info	5	0	1	1	4	3	0	2	2	1	0	2	0	0	0	0	3	2
	1.2%	0	0.8%	0.8%	1.4%	1.6%	0	1.4%	2.6%	2.0%	0	2.0%	0	0	0	0	1.6%	0.8%
preferred source of info	2	0	0	0	2	1	0	1	1	1	0	0	0	0	0	0	1	1
	0.4%	0	0	0	0.7%	0.5%	0	0.6%	1.3%	2.0%	0	0	0	0	0	0	0.5%	0.4%
Printed library catalogues and finding aids (NET)	4	0	0	0	4	1	0	3	1	1	2	0	0	0	0	0	1	3
	0.9%	0	0	0	1.3%	0.5%	0	1.9%	1.3%	2.0%	1.6%	0	0	0	0	0	0.5%	1.3%
All sources of info	4	0	0	0	4	1	0	3	1	1	2	0	0	0	0	0	1	3
	0.9%	0	0	0	1.3%	0.5%	0	1.9%	1.3%	2.0%	1.6%	0	0	0	0	0	0.5%	1.3%
preferred source of info	0	0	0	0	0	0	0	0	0	0	0	0	0	0	0	0	0	0
	0	0	0	0	0	0	0	0	0	0	0	0	0	0	0	0	0	0

Proportions/Means: Columns Tested (5% risk level) - A/B/D - C/D - E/F/G - H/I/J/K/L/M/N - P/Q
* small base; ** very small base (under 30) ineligible for sig testing

Table 405
Page 1729

Outsell/Digital Library Federation Study (2002)
Weighted Tables

TABLE 149, continued

S7sum_13. Photographs, prints and other visual resources SUMMARY TABLE

		RESPONDENT TYPE				INSTITUTION TYPE			DISCIPLINE								GENDER	
	TOTAL SAMPLE	FACULTY MEMBER	GRAD. STUDENT	FACULTY /GRAD	UNDER GRAD. STUDENT	PUBLIC	PRIVATE	LIBERAL ARTS	BIOLOGIAL SCIENCES	PHYSICAL SCIENCES /MATH	SOCIAL SCIENCES	ARTS AND HUMAN.	ENGI- NEERING	BUSINESS	LAW	UNDEC. MAJOR	MALE	FEMALE
		(A)	(B)	(C)	(D)	(E)	(F)	(G)	(H)	(I)	(J)	(K)	(L)	(M)	(N)		(P)	(Q)
Base - Use Photographs, prints and other visual resources for coursework	424	0**	143	143	281	183	87*	154	67*	50*	117*	111*	16*	46*	1**	17*	208	216
Printed abstracting and indexing services (NET)	3 0.7%	0 0	0 0	0 0	3 1.1%	0 0	1 1.0%	2 1.4%	1 1.3%	0 0	0 0	1 1.0%	0 0	0 0	0 0	1 5.9%	2 1.0%	1 0.4%
All sources of info	3 0.7%	0 0	0 0	0 0	3 1.1%	0 0	1 1.0%	2 1.4%	1 1.3%	0 0	0 0	1 1.0%	0 0	0 0	0 0	1 5.9%	2 1.0%	1 0.4%
preferred source of info	0 0	0 0	0 0	0 0	0 0	0 0	0 0	0 0	0 0	0 0	0 0	0 0	0 0	0 0	0 0	0 0	0 0	0 0
Personal subscriptions to newspapers, magazines and journals (NET)	3 0.7%	0 0	0 0	0 0	3 1.0%	0 0	1 1.0%	2 1.3%	2 2.6%	0 0	0 0	1 1.0%	0 0	0 0	0 0	0 0	1 0.4%	2 0.9%
All sources of info	3 0.7%	0 0	0 0	0 0	3 1.0%	0 0	1 1.0%	2 1.3%	2 2.6%	0 0	0 0	1 1.0%	0 0	0 0	0 0	0 0	1 0.4%	2 0.9%
preferred source of info	0 0	0 0	0 0	0 0	0 0	0 0	0 0	0 0	0 0	0 0	0 0	0 0	0 0	0 0	0 0	0 0	0 0	0 0
PERSONAL ASSISTANCE	147 34.8%	0 0	46 32.1%	46 32.1%	101 36.1%	58 31.8%	33 37.6%	57 36.6%	18 27.6%	16 32.0%	51 43.5%	36 32.3%	6 34.5%	13 28.6%	1 62.5%	7 41.2%	68 32.7%	79 36.7%

Proportions/Means: Columns Tested (5% risk level) - A/B/D - C/D - E/F/G - H/I/J/K/L/M/N - P/Q
* small base; ** very small base (under 30) ineligible for sig testing

Table 405
Page 1730

TABLE 149, continued

S7sum_13. Photographs, prints and other visual resources SUMMARY TABLE

	TOTAL SAMPLE	RESPONDENT TYPE: FACULTY MEMBER (A)	GRAD. STUDENT (B)	FACULTY /GRAD (C)	UNDER GRAD. STUDENT (D)	INSTITUTION TYPE: PUBLIC (E)	PRIVATE (F)	LIBERAL ARTS (G)	DISCIPLINE: BIOLOGIAL SCIENCES (H)	PHYSICAL SCIENCES /MATH (I)	SOCIAL SCIENCES (J)	ARTS AND HUMAN. (K)	ENGI-NEERING (L)	BUSINESS (M)	LAW (N)	UNDEC. MAJOR	GENDER: MALE (P)	FEMALE (Q)
Base - Use Photographs, prints and other visual resources for coursework	424	0**	143	143	281	183	87*	154	67*	50*	117*	111*	16*	46*	1**	17*	208	216
Faculty members inside your institution (NET)	89 20.9%	0 0	36 25.3%	36 25.3%	53 18.7%	33 18.0%	22 25.0%	34 22.1%	14 21.1%	11 22.0%	32 27.4%M	20 18.2%	3 21.8%	5 10.2%	1 37.5%	3 17.6%	39 18.8%	50 23.0%
All sources of info	89 20.9%	0 0	36 25.3%	36 25.3%	53 18.7%	33 18.0%	22 25.0%	34 22.1%	14 21.1%	11 22.0%	32 27.4%M	20 18.2%	3 21.8%	5 10.2%	1 37.5%	3 17.6%	39 18.8%	50 23.0%
preferred source of info	37 8.7%	0 0	17 12.0%	17 12.0%	20 7.1%	15 8.4%	12 13.3%	10 6.5%	7 10.5%	5 10.0%	9 8.1%	10 9.1%	2 10.9%	3 6.1%	0 0	1 5.9%	18 8.9%	19 8.6%
A librarian in your institution (NET)	77 18.1%	0 0	10 6.8%	10 6.8%	67 23.9%B C	23 12.7%	13 14.9%	41 26.4%E	6 9.2%	9 18.0%	24 21.0%	24 21.2%H	2 10.9%	7 14.3%	1 37.5%	5 29.4%	36 17.1%	41 19.1%
All sources of info	77 18.1%	0 0	10 6.8%	10 6.8%	67 23.9%B C	23 12.7%	13 14.9%	41 26.4%E	6 9.2%	9 18.0%	24 21.0%	24 21.2%H	2 10.9%	7 14.3%	1 37.5%	5 29.4%	36 17.1%	41 19.1%
preferred source of info	38 9.0%	0 0	6 4.3%	6 4.3%	32 11.4%B C	20 11.2%	8 9.6%	9 6.0%	3 3.9%	4 8.0%	15 12.9%	12 11.1%	* 1.8%	3 6.1%	0 0	1 5.9%	16 7.8%	22 10.1%
Other students inside your institution (NET)	31 7.2%	0 0	17 11.7%D	17 11.7%D	14 4.9%	15 8.2%	6 6.6%	10 6.3%	6 9.2%	3 6.0%	11 9.7%	4 4.0%	2 10.9%	4 8.2%	* 12.5%	0 0	15 7.3%	15 7.1%

Proportions/Means: Columns Tested (5% risk level) - A/B/D - C/D - E/F/G - H/I/J/K/L/M/N - P/Q
* small base; ** very small base (under 30) ineligible for sig testing

Table 405
Page 1731

TABLE 149, continued

S7sum_13. Photographs, prints and other visual resources SUMMARY TABLE

	TOTAL SAMPLE	RESPONDENT TYPE: FACULTY MEMBER	GRAD. STUDENT	FACULTY /GRAD	UNDER GRAD. STUDENT	INSTITUTION TYPE: PUBLIC	PRIVATE	LIBERAL ARTS	DISCIPLINE: BIOLOGIAL SCIENCES	PHYSICAL SCIENCES /MATH	SOCIAL SCIENCES	ARTS AND HUMAN.	ENGI-NEERING	BUSINESS	LAW	UNDEC. MAJOR	GENDER: MALE	FEMALE
		(A)	(B)	(C)	(D)	(E)	(F)	(G)	(H)	(I)	(J)	(K)	(L)	(M)	(N)		(P)	(Q)
Base - Use Photographs, prints and other visual resources for coursework	424	0**	143	143	281	183	87*	154	67*	50*	117*	111*	16*	46*	1**	17*	208	216
All sources of info	31 7.2%	0 0	17 11.7%D	17 11.7%D	14 4.9%	15 8.2%	6 6.6%	10 6.3%	6 9.2%	3 6.0%	11 9.7%	4 4.0%	2 10.9%	4 8.2%	* 12.5%	0 0	15 7.3%	15 7.1%
preferred source of info	7 1.5%	0 0	3 1.8%	3 1.8%	4 1.4%	3 1.6%	1 0.7%	3 1.9%	1 1.3%	0 0	2 1.6%	2 2.0%	1 3.6%I	1 2.0%	0 0	0 0	2 0.8%	5 2.2%
Faculty members outside your institution (NET)	3 0.8%	0 0	1 0.8%	1 0.8%	2 0.8%	* 0.2%	1 1.3%	2 1.2%	0 0	0 0	2 1.6%	1 1.0%	* 1.8%	0 0	0 0	0 0	* 0.1%	3 1.4%
All sources of info	3 0.8%	0 0	1 0.8%	1 0.8%	2 0.8%	* 0.2%	1 1.3%	2 1.2%	0 0	0 0	2 1.6%	1 1.0%	* 1.8%	0 0	0 0	0 0	* 0.1%	3 1.4%
preferred source of info	0 0	0 0	0 0	0 0	0 0	0 0	0 0	0 0	0 0	0 0	0 0	0 0	0 0	0 0	0 0	0 0	0 0	0 0
Other students outside your institution (NET)	2 0.5%	0 0	1 1.0%	1 1.0%	1 0.3%	* 0.2%	2 2.3%	0 0	1 1.3%	0 0	0 0	1 1.0%	* 1.8%J	0 0	0 0	0 0	* 0.1%	2 0.9%
All sources of info	2 0.5%	0 0	1 1.0%	1 1.0%	1 0.3%	* 0.2%	2 2.3%	0 0	1 1.3%	0 0	0 0	1 1.0%	* 1.8%J	0 0	0 0	0 0	* 0.1%	2 0.9%
preferred source of info	0 0	0 0	0 0	0 0	0 0	0 0	0 0	0 0	0 0	0 0	0 0	0 0	0 0	0 0	0 0	0 0	0 0	0 0

Proportions/Means: Columns Tested (5% risk level) - A/B/D - C/D - E/F/G - H/I/J/K/L/M/N - P/Q
* small base; ** very small base (under 30) ineligible for sig testing

Table 405
Page 1732

Outsell/Digital Library Federation Study (2002)
Weighted Tables

TABLE 149, continued

S7sum_13. Photographs, prints and other visual resources SUMMARY TABLE

		RESPONDENT TYPE				INSTITUTION TYPE			DISCIPLINE									GENDER	
	TOTAL SAMPLE	FACULTY MEMBER	GRAD. STUDENT	FACULTY /GRAD	UNDER GRAD. STUDENT	PUBLIC	PRIVATE	LIBERAL ARTS	BIOLOGIAL SCIENCES	PHYSICAL SCIENCES /MATH	SOCIAL SCIENCES	ARTS AND HUMAN.	ENGI-NEERING	BUSINESS	LAW	UNDEC. MAJOR	MALE	FEMALE
		(A)	(B)	(C)	(D)	(E)	(F)	(G)	(H)	(I)	(J)	(K)	(L)	(M)	(N)		(P)	(Q)
Base - Use Photographs, prints and other visual resources for coursework	424	0**	143	143	281	183	87*	154	67*	50*	117*	111*	16*	46*	1**	17*	208	216
Another institution's librarian (NET)	1 0.3%	0 0	0 0	0 0	1 0.4%	0 0	0 0	1 0.7%	0 0	0 0	0 0	1 1.0%	0 0	0 0	0 0	0 0	0 0	1 0.5%
All sources of info	1 0.3%	0 0	0 0	0 0	1 0.4%	0 0	0 0	1 0.7%	0 0	0 0	0 0	1 1.0%	0 0	0 0	0 0	0 0	0 0	1 0.5%
preferred source of info	0 0	0 0	0 0	0 0	0 0	0 0	0 0	0 0	0 0	0 0	0 0	0 0	0 0	0 0	0 0	0 0	0 0	0 0
Professional meetings (NET)	0 0	0 0	0 0	0 0	0 0	0 0	0 0	0 0	0 0	0 0	0 0	0 0	0 0	0 0	0 0	0 0	0 0	0 0
All sources of info	0 0	0 0	0 0	0 0	0 0	0 0	0 0	0 0	0 0	0 0	0 0	0 0	0 0	0 0	0 0	0 0	0 0	0 0
preferred source of info	0 0	0 0	0 0	0 0	0 0	0 0	0 0	0 0	0 0	0 0	0 0	0 0	0 0	0 0	0 0	0 0	0 0	0 0
Other (NET)	26 6.2%	0 0	12 8.1%	12 8.1%	15 5.2%	17 9.6%G	3 4.0%	5 3.4%	4 5.3%	2 4.0%	8 6.5%	10 9.1%	1 5.5%	2 4.1%	* 25.0%	0 0	8 4.0%	18 8.3%
All sources of info	24 5.6%	0 0	11 8.0%	11 8.0%	12 4.4%	15 8.3%	3 3.8%	5 3.4%	4 5.3%	2 4.0%	8 6.5%	8 7.1%	1 5.5%	2 4.1%	* 12.5%	0 0	7 3.5%	17 7.7%
preferred source of info	10 2.3%	0 0	4 3.0%	4 3.0%	5 1.9%	8 4.4%	* 0.5%	1 0.7%	1 1.3%	0 0	4 3.2%	4 4.0%	* 1.8%	0 0	* 12.5%	0 0	3 1.6%	6 2.9%

Proportions/Means: Columns Tested (5% risk level) - A/B/D - C/D - E/F/G - H/I/J/K/L/M/N - P/Q
* small base; ** very small base (under 30) ineligible for sig testing

Table 405
Page 1733

Outsell/Digital Library Federation Study (2002)
Weighted Tables

TABLE 149, continued

S7sum_13. Photographs, prints and other visual resources SUMMARY TABLE

	TOTAL SAMPLE	RESPONDENT TYPE: FACULTY MEMBER	RESPONDENT TYPE: GRAD. STUDENT	RESPONDENT TYPE: FACULTY /GRAD	RESPONDENT TYPE: UNDER GRAD. STUDENT	INSTITUTION TYPE: PUBLIC	INSTITUTION TYPE: PRIVATE	INSTITUTION TYPE: LIBERAL ARTS	DISCIPLINE: BIOLOGIAL SCIENCES	DISCIPLINE: PHYSICAL SCIENCES /MATH	DISCIPLINE: SOCIAL SCIENCES	DISCIPLINE: ARTS AND HUMAN.	DISCIPLINE: ENGI-NEERING	DISCIPLINE: BUSINESS	DISCIPLINE: LAW	DISCIPLINE: UNDEC. MAJOR	GENDER: MALE	GENDER: FEMALE
		(A)	(B)	(C)	(D)	(E)	(F)	(G)	(H)	(I)	(J)	(K)	(L)	(M)	(N)		(P)	(Q)
Base - Use Photographs, prints and other visual resources for coursework	424	0**	143	143	281	183	87*	154	67*	50*	117*	111*	16*	46*	1**	17*	208	216
Online (unspecified)	7 1.5%	0 0	* 0.1%	* 0.1%	6 2.3%	3 1.8%	1 1.5%	2 1.2%	2 2.6%	0 0	4 3.2%	0 0	1 5.5%IKM	0 0	* 12.5%	0 0	4 1.7%	3 1.4%
All sources of info	7 1.5%	0 0	* 0.1%	* 0.1%	6 2.3%	3 1.8%	1 1.5%	2 1.2%	2 2.6%	0 0	4 3.2%	0 0	1 5.5%IKM	0 0	* 12.5%	0 0	4 1.7%	3 1.4%
preferred source of info	3 0.6%	0 0	0 0	0 0	3 0.9%	1 0.8%	1 1.3%	0 0	2 2.6%	0 0	0 0	0 0	1 5.5%IJKM	0 0	0 0	0 0	2 0.8%	1 0.4%
E-journals	1 0.2%	0 0	0 0	0 0	1 0.4%	0 0	0 0	1 0.6%	0 0	1 2.0%	0 0	0 0	0 0	0 0	0 0	0 0	1 0.5%	0 0
All sources of info	1 0.2%	0 0	0 0	0 0	1 0.4%	0 0	0 0	1 0.6%	0 0	1 2.0%	0 0	0 0	0 0	0 0	0 0	0 0	1 0.5%	0 0
preferred source of info	1 0.2%	0 0	0 0	0 0	1 0.4%	0 0	0 0	1 0.6%	0 0	1 2.0%	0 0	0 0	0 0	0 0	0 0	0 0	1 0.5%	0 0
DK/Refused	9 2.0%	0 0	3 2.3%	3 2.3%	5 1.9%	5 2.5%	3 3.4%	1 0.8%	1 1.3%	0 0	2 1.6%	2 2.0%	1 5.5%I	3 6.1%	0 0	0 0	4 1.9%	5 2.2%

Proportions/Means: Columns Tested (5% risk level) - A/B/D - C/D - E/F/G - H/I/J/K/L/M/N - P/Q
* small base; ** very small base (under 30) ineligible for sig testing

Table 405
Page 1734

Outsell/Digital Library Federation Study (2002)
Weighted Tables

TABLE 150

S7D/E_13. Photographs, prints and other visual resources SUMMARY TABLE

	TOTAL SAMPLE	RESPONDENT TYPE: FACULTY MEMBER	GRAD. STUDENT	FACULTY /GRAD	UNDER GRAD. STUDENT	INSTITUTION TYPE: PUBLIC	PRIVATE	LIBERAL ARTS	DISCIPLINE: BIOLOGICAL SCIENCES	PHYSICAL SCIENCES /MATH	SOCIAL SCIENCES	ARTS AND HUMAN.	ENGI-NEERING	BUSINESS	LAW	UNDEC. MAJOR	GENDER: MALE	FEMALE
		(A)	(B)	(C)	(D)	(E)	(F)	(G)	(H)	(I)	(J)	(K)	(L)	(M)	(N)		(P)	(Q)
Base - Use Photographs, prints and other visual resources for coursework	424	0**	143	143	281	183	87*	154	67*	50*	117*	111*	16*	46*	1**	17*	208	216
Borrow from or use in campus library (NET)	271 64.0%	0 0	87 60.9%	87 60.9%	184 65.5%	103 56.4%	49 56.4%	119 77.2%EF	39 57.9%L	31 62.0%LM	75 64.5%LM	90 80.8%HI JLM	6 40.0%	19 40.8%	1 62.5%	11 64.7%	122 58.8%	149 68.9%P
All sources of info	271 64.0%	0 0	87 60.9%	87 60.9%	184 65.5%	103 56.4%	49 56.4%	119 77.2%EF	39 57.9%L	31 62.0%LM	75 64.5%LM	90 80.8%HI JLM	6 40.0%	19 40.8%	1 62.5%	11 64.7%	122 58.8%	149 68.9%P
preferred source of info	200 47.1%	0 0	57 39.8%	57 39.8%	143 50.8%	74 40.5%	36 41.1%	90 58.1%EF	27 40.8%M	22 44.0%M	58 50.0%LM	74 66.7%HI JLM	4 27.3%	7 16.3%	* 25.0%	6 35.3%	85 40.9%	115 53.0%P
Access online (NET)	224 52.8%	0 0	78 54.2%	78 54.2%	146 52.1%	100 54.7%	45 51.6%	79 51.3%	38 56.6%K	32 64.0%K	60 51.6%K	36 32.3%	11 67.3%K	35 77.6%HJ K	1 75.0%	11 64.7%	125 59.9%Q	99 46.0%
All sources of info	224 52.8%	0 0	78 54.2%	78 54.2%	146 52.1%	100 54.7%	45 51.6%	79 51.3%	38 56.6%K	32 64.0%K	60 51.6%K	36 32.3%	11 67.3%K	35 77.6%HJ K	1 75.0%	11 64.7%	125 59.9%Q	99 46.0%
preferred source of info	185 43.7%	0 0	71 49.2%	71 49.2%	115 40.8%	85 46.7%	43 48.8%	57 37.1%	31 46.1%K	25 50.0%K	49 41.9%K	27 24.2%	9 58.2%K	33 73.5%HI JK	1 62.5%	10 58.8%	111 53.5%Q	74 34.1%
Faculty (NET)	19 4.5%	0 0	6 4.2%	6 4.2%	13 4.7%	9 5.0%	3 3.2%	7 4.6%	4 5.3%	1 2.0%	6 4.8%	6 5.1%	* 1.8%	2 4.1%	* 12.5%	1 5.9%	5 2.6%	14 6.3%

Proportions/Means: Columns Tested (5% risk level) - A/B/D - C/D - E/F/G - H/I/J/K/L/M/N - P/Q
* small base; ** very small base (under 30) ineligible for sig testing

Table 408
Page 1741

Outsell/Digital Library Federation Study (2002)
Weighted Tables

TABLE 150, continued

S7D/E_13. Photographs, prints and other visual resources SUMMARY TABLE

		RESPONDENT TYPE				INSTITUTION TYPE			DISCIPLINE								GENDER	
	TOTAL SAMPLE	FACULTY MEMBER	GRAD. STUDENT	FACULTY /GRAD	UNDER GRAD. STUDENT	PUBLIC	PRIVATE	LIBERAL ARTS	BIOLOGIAL SCIENCES	PHYSICAL SCIENCES /MATH	SOCIAL SCIENCES	ARTS AND HUMAN.	ENGI-NEERING	BUSINESS	LAW	UNDEC. MAJOR	MALE	FEMALE
		(A)	(B)	(C)	(D)	(E)	(F)	(G)	(H)	(I)	(J)	(K)	(L)	(M)	(N)		(P)	(Q)
Base - Use Photographs, prints and other visual resources for coursework	424	0**	143	143	281	183	87*	154	67*	50*	117*	111*	16*	46*	1**	17*	208	216
All sources of info	19 4.5%	0 0	6 4.2%	6 4.2%	13 4.7%	9 5.0%	3 3.2%	7 4.6%	4 5.3%	1 2.0%	6 4.8%	6 5.1%	* 1.8%	2 4.1%	* 12.5%	1 5.9%	5 2.6%	14 6.3%
preferred source of info	13 3.1%	0 0	5 3.4%	5 3.4%	8 2.9%	7 3.8%	3 3.2%	3 2.1%	3 3.9%	1 2.0%	4 3.2%	2 2.0%	* 1.8%	2 4.1%	* 12.5%	1 5.9%	2 1.2%	11 4.9%P
Borrow from or use in other libraries (NET)	16 3.8%	0 0	5 3.5%	5 3.5%	11 4.0%	7 3.9%	3 3.3%	6 4.0%	3 3.9%	1 2.0%	6 4.8%	7 6.1%	* 1.8%	0 0	0 0	0 0	5 2.5%	11 5.1%
All sources of info	16 3.8%	0 0	5 3.5%	5 3.5%	11 4.0%	7 3.9%	3 3.3%	6 4.0%	3 3.9%	1 2.0%	6 4.8%	7 6.1%	* 1.8%	0 0	0 0	0 0	5 2.5%	11 5.1%
preferred source of info	6 1.5%	0 0	1 0.8%	1 0.8%	5 1.9%	3 1.8%	2 2.3%	1 0.7%	1 1.3%	0 0	2 1.6%	3 3.0%	* 1.8%	0 0	0 0	0 0	* 0.1%	6 2.8%P
Interlibrary loan (NET)	8 1.9%	0 0	3 2.0%	3 2.0%	5 1.8%	3 1.8%	1 1.0%	4 2.4%	2 2.6%	0 0	4 3.2%	1 1.0%	* 1.8%	1 2.0%	0 0	0 0	2 1.1%	6 2.6%
All sources of info	8 1.9%	0 0	3 2.0%	3 2.0%	5 1.8%	3 1.8%	1 1.0%	4 2.4%	2 2.6%	0 0	4 3.2%	1 1.0%	* 1.8%	1 2.0%	0 0	0 0	2 1.1%	6 2.6%
preferred source of info	3 0.7%	0 0	2 1.4%	2 1.4%	1 0.3%	3 1.6%	0 0	0 0	1 1.3%	0 0	0 0	1 1.0%	0 0	1 2.0%	0 0	0 0	2 1.0%	1 0.4%

Proportions/Means: Columns Tested (5% risk level) - A/B/D - C/D - E/F/G - H/I/J/K/L/M/N - P/Q
* small base; ** very small base (under 30) ineligible for sig testing

Table 408
Page 1742

TABLE 150, continued

S7D/E_13. Photographs, prints and other visual resources SUMMARY TABLE

	TOTAL SAMPLE	RESPONDENT TYPE: FACULTY MEMBER	GRAD. STUDENT	FACULTY /GRAD	UNDER GRAD. STUDENT	INSTITUTION TYPE: PUBLIC	PRIVATE	LIBERAL ARTS	DISCIPLINE: BIOLOGICAL SCIENCES	PHYSICAL SCIENCES /MATH	SOCIAL SCIENCES	ARTS AND HUMAN.	ENGI-NEERING	BUSINESS	LAW	UNDEC. MAJOR	GENDER: MALE	FEMALE
		(A)	(B)	(C)	(D)	(E)	(F)	(G)	(H)	(I)	(J)	(K)	(L)	(M)	(N)		(P)	(Q)
Base - Use Photographs, prints and other visual resources for coursework	424	0**	143	143	281	183	87*	154	67*	50*	117*	111*	16*	46*	1**	17*	208	216
Purchase from physical book store (NET)	8 1.8%	0 0	1 1.0%	1 1.0%	6 2.2%	3 1.6%	1 1.7%	3 2.1%	2 2.6%	1 2.0%	0 0	3 3.0%	1 9.1%JM	0 0	0 0	0 0	6 2.7%	2 0.9%
All sources of info	8 1.8%	0 0	1 1.0%	1 1.0%	6 2.2%	3 1.6%	1 1.7%	3 2.1%	2 2.6%	1 2.0%	0 0	3 3.0%	1 9.1%JM	0 0	0 0	0 0	6 2.7%	2 0.9%
preferred source of info	4 1.0%	0 0	1 0.6%	1 0.6%	3 1.2%	2 1.3%	1 1.0%	1 0.6%	2 2.6%	1 2.0%	0 0	1 1.0%	* 1.8%J	0 0	0 0	0 0	3 1.6%	1 0.4%
Colleagues (NET)	6 1.3%	0 0	4 2.6%	4 2.6%	2 0.7%	6 3.1%G	0 0	0 0	1 1.3%	1 2.0%	4 3.2%	0 0	0 0	0 0	0 0	0 0	1 0.5%	5 2.1%
All sources of info	6 1.3%	0 0	4 2.6%	4 2.6%	2 0.7%	6 3.1%G	0 0	0 0	1 1.3%	1 2.0%	4 3.2%	0 0	0 0	0 0	0 0	0 0	1 0.5%	5 2.1%
preferred source of info	2 0.4%	0 0	2 1.3%	2 1.3%	0 0	2 1.0%	0 0	0 0	0 0	0 0	2 1.6%	0 0	0 0	0 0	0 0	0 0	0 0	2 0.9%
Personal Holdings (NET)	3 0.7%	0 0	3 2.2%D	3 2.2%D	0 0	2 1.1%	1 1.3%	0 0	1 1.3%	0 0	0 0	2 2.0%	0 0	0 0	0 0	0 0	2 1.0%	1 0.5%
All sources of info	3 0.7%	0 0	3 2.2%D	3 2.2%D	0 0	2 1.1%	1 1.3%	0 0	1 1.3%	0 0	0 0	2 2.0%	0 0	0 0	0 0	0 0	2 1.0%	1 0.5%
preferred source of info	1 0.3%	0 0	1 0.8%	1 0.8%	0 0	0 0	1 1.3%	0 0	0 0	0 0	0 0	1 1.0%	0 0	0 0	0 0	0 0	1 0.5%	0 0

Proportions/Means: Columns Tested (5% risk level) - A/B/D - C/D - E/F/G - H/I/J/K/L/M/N - P/Q
* small base; ** very small base (under 30) ineligible for sig testing

Table 408
Page 1743

Outsell/Digital Library Federation Study (2002)
Weighted Tables

TABLE 150, continued

S7D/E_13. Photographs, prints and other visual resources SUMMARY TABLE

		RESPONDENT TYPE				INSTITUTION TYPE			DISCIPLINE									GENDER	
	TOTAL SAMPLE	FACULTY MEMBER	GRAD. STUDENT	FACULTY /GRAD	UNDER GRAD. STUDENT	PUBLIC	PRIVATE	LIBERAL ARTS	BIOLOGIAL SCIENCES	PHYSICAL SCIENCES /MATH	SOCIAL SCIENCES	ARTS AND HUMAN.	ENGI- NEERING	BUSINESS	LAW	UNDEC. MAJOR	MALE	FEMALE
		(A)	(B)	(C)	(D)	(E)	(F)	(G)	(H)	(I)	(J)	(K)	(L)	(M)	(N)		(P)	(Q)
Base - Use Photographs, prints and other visual resources for coursework	424	0**	143	143	281	183	87*	154	67*	50*	117*	111*	16*	46*	1**	17*	208	216
In class (NET)	1 0.3%	0 0	1 0.8%	1 0.8%	* 0.1%	* 0.2%	1 1.3%	0 0	1 1.3%	0 0	0 0	0 0	1 3.6%IJK	0 0	0 0	0 0	* 0.1%	1 0.5%
All sources of info	1 0.3%	0 0	1 0.8%	1 0.8%	* 0.1%	* 0.2%	1 1.3%	0 0	1 1.3%	0 0	0 0	0 0	1 3.6%IJK	0 0	0 0	0 0	* 0.1%	1 0.5%
preferred source of info	1 0.3%	0 0	1 0.8%	1 0.8%	0 0	* 0.2%	1 1.0%	0 0	1 1.3%	0 0	0 0	0 0	* 1.8%JK	0 0	0 0	0 0	* 0.1%	1 0.4%
Ask library to purchase source (NET)	1 0.3%	0 0	0 0	0 0	1 0.4%	1 0.6%	0 0	0 0	0 0	0 0	0 0	1 1.0%	0 0	0 0	0 0	0 0	1 0.5%	0 0
All sources of info	1 0.3%	0 0	0 0	0 0	1 0.4%	1 0.6%	0 0	0 0	0 0	0 0	0 0	1 1.0%	0 0	0 0	0 0	0 0	1 0.5%	0 0
preferred source of info	0 0	0 0	0 0	0 0	0 0	0 0	0 0	0 0	0 0	0 0	0 0	0 0	0 0	0 0	0 0	0 0	0 0	0 0
Home (NET)	1 0.2%	0 0	0 0	0 0	1 0.3%	1 0.5%	0 0	0 0	0 0	0 0	0 0	0 0	0 0	1 2.0%	0 0	0 0	0 0	1 0.4%
All sources of info	1 0.2%	0 0	0 0	0 0	1 0.3%	1 0.5%	0 0	0 0	0 0	0 0	0 0	0 0	0 0	1 2.0%	0 0	0 0	0 0	1 0.4%
preferred source of info	0 0	0 0	0 0	0 0	0 0	0 0	0 0	0 0	0 0	0 0	0 0	0 0	0 0	0 0	0 0	0 0	0 0	0 0

Proportions/Means: Columns Tested (5% risk level) - A/B/D - C/D - E/F/G - H/I/J/K/L/M/N - P/Q
* small base; ** very small base (under 30) ineligible for sig testing

Table 408
Page 1744

Outsell/Digital Library Federation Study (2002)
Weighted Tables

TABLE 150, continued

S7D/E_13. Photographs, prints and other visual resources SUMMARY TABLE

		RESPONDENT TYPE				INSTITUTION TYPE			DISCIPLINE								GENDER	
	TOTAL SAMPLE	FACULTY MEMBER	GRAD. STUDENT	FACULTY /GRAD	UNDER GRAD. STUDENT	PUBLIC	PRIVATE	LIBERAL ARTS	BIOLOGIAL SCIENCES	PHYSICAL SCIENCES /MATH	SOCIAL SCIENCES	ARTS AND HUMAN.	ENGI-NEERING	BUSINESS	LAW	UNDEC. MAJOR	MALE	FEMALE
		(A)	(B)	(C)	(D)	(E)	(F)	(G)	(H)	(I)	(J)	(K)	(L)	(M)	(N)		(P)	(Q)
Base - Use Photographs, prints and other visual resources for coursework	424	0**	143	143	281	183	87*	154	67*	50*	117*	111*	16*	46*	1**	17*	208	216
Purchase from online bookstore (NET)	* 0.1%	0 0	* 0.2%	* 0.2%	0 0	* 0.2%	0 0	0 0	0 0	0 0	0 0	0 0	* 1.8%JK	0 0	0 0	0 0	* 0.1%	0 0
All sources of info	* 0.1%	0 0	* 0.2%	* 0.2%	0 0	* 0.2%	0 0	0 0	0 0	0 0	0 0	0 0	* 1.8%JK	0 0	0 0	0 0	* 0.1%	0 0
preferred source of info	* 0.1%	0 0	* 0.2%	* 0.2%	0 0	* 0.2%	0 0	0 0	0 0	0 0	0 0	0 0	* 1.8%JK	0 0	0 0	0 0	* 0.1%	0 0
Order from on demand document delivery service (NET)	0 0	0 0	0 0	0 0	0 0	0 0	0 0	0 0	0 0	0 0	0 0	0 0	0 0	0 0	0 0	0 0	0 0	0 0
All sources of info	0 0	0 0	0 0	0 0	0 0	0 0	0 0	0 0	0 0	0 0	0 0	0 0	0 0	0 0	0 0	0 0	0 0	0 0
preferred source of info	0 0	0 0	0 0	0 0	0 0	0 0	0 0	0 0	0 0	0 0	0 0	0 0	0 0	0 0	0 0	0 0	0 0	0 0
Access from course website (NET)	0 0	0 0	0 0	0 0	0 0	0 0	0 0	0 0	0 0	0 0	0 0	0 0	0 0	0 0	0 0	0 0	0 0	0 0
All sources of info	0 0	0 0	0 0	0 0	0 0	0 0	0 0	0 0	0 0	0 0	0 0	0 0	0 0	0 0	0 0	0 0	0 0	0 0
preferred source of info	0 0	0 0	0 0	0 0	0 0	0 0	0 0	0 0	0 0	0 0	0 0	0 0	0 0	0 0	0 0	0 0	0 0	0 0

Proportions/Means: Columns Tested (5% risk level) - A/B/D - C/D - E/F/G - H/I/J/K/L/M/N - P/Q
* small base; ** very small base (under 30) ineligible for sig testing

Table 408
Page 1745

Outsell/Digital Library Federation Study (2002)
Weighted Tables

TABLE 150, continued

S7D/E_13. Photographs, prints and other visual resources SUMMARY TABLE

		RESPONDENT TYPE				INSTITUTION TYPE			DISCIPLINE									GENDER	
	TOTAL SAMPLE	FACULTY MEMBER	GRAD. STUDENT	FACULTY /GRAD	UNDER GRAD. STUDENT	PUBLIC	PRIVATE	LIBERAL ARTS	BIOLOGIAL SCIENCES	PHYSICAL SCIENCES /MATH	SOCIAL SCIENCES	ARTS AND HUMAN.	ENGI- NEERING	BUSINESS	LAW	UNDEC. MAJOR	MALE	FEMALE
		(A)	(B)	(C)	(D)	(E)	(F)	(G)	(H)	(I)	(J)	(K)	(L)	(M)	(N)		(P)	(Q)
Base - Use Photographs, prints and other visual resources for coursework	424	0**	143	143	281	183	87*	154	67*	50*	117*	111*	16*	46*	1**	17*	208	216
Dorm room (NET)	0	0	0	0	0	0	0	0	0	0	0	0	0	0	0	0	0	0
	0	0	0	0	0	0	0	0	0	0	0	0	0	0	0	0	0	0
All sources of info	0	0	0	0	0	0	0	0	0	0	0	0	0	0	0	0	0	0
	0	0	0	0	0	0	0	0	0	0	0	0	0	0	0	0	0	0
preferred source of info	0	0	0	0	0	0	0	0	0	0	0	0	0	0	0	0	0	0
	0	0	0	0	0	0	0	0	0	0	0	0	0	0	0	0	0	0
Access book/journal/ journal article elsewhere online (NET)	0	0	0	0	0	0	0	0	0	0	0	0	0	0	0	0	0	0
	0	0	0	0	0	0	0	0	0	0	0	0	0	0	0	0	0	0
All sources of info	0	0	0	0	0	0	0	0	0	0	0	0	0	0	0	0	0	0
	0	0	0	0	0	0	0	0	0	0	0	0	0	0	0	0	0	0
preferred source of info	0	0	0	0	0	0	0	0	0	0	0	0	0	0	0	0	0	0
	0	0	0	0	0	0	0	0	0	0	0	0	0	0	0	0	0	0
Other (NET)	17	0	6	6	11	11	5	2	2	0	8	6	1	1	0	0	3	14
	4.0%	0	4.5%	4.5%	3.7%	5.8%G	5.2%	1.2%	2.6%	0	6.5%	5.1%	7.3%I	2.0%	0	0	1.6%	6.3%P
All sources of info	15	0	6	6	9	9	5	2	2	0	6	6	1	1	0	0	3	12
	3.6%	0	4.5%	4.5%	3.1%	4.8%	5.2%	1.2%	2.6%	0	4.8%	5.1%	7.3%I	2.0%	0	0	1.6%	5.4%

Proportions/Means: Columns Tested (5% risk level) - A/B/D - C/D - E/F/G - H/I/J/K/L/M/N - P/Q
* small base; ** very small base (under 30) ineligible for sig testing

Table 408
Page 1746

Outsell/Digital Library Federation Study (2002)
Weighted Tables

TABLE 150, continued

S7D/E_13. Photographs, prints and other visual resources SUMMARY TABLE

		RESPONDENT TYPE				INSTITUTION TYPE			DISCIPLINE								GENDER	
	TOTAL SAMPLE	FACULTY MEMBER	GRAD. STUDENT	FACULTY /GRAD	UNDER GRAD. STUDENT	PUBLIC	PRIVATE	LIBERAL ARTS	BIOLOGIAL SCIENCES	PHYSICAL SCIENCES /MATH	SOCIAL SCIENCES	ARTS AND HUMAN.	ENGI- NEERING	BUSINESS	LAW	UNDEC. MAJOR	MALE	FEMALE
		(A)	(B)	(C)	(D)	(E)	(F)	(G)	(H)	(I)	(J)	(K)	(L)	(M)	(N)		(P)	(Q)
Base - Use Photographs, prints and other visual resources for coursework	424	0**	143	143	281	183	87*	154	67*	50*	117*	111*	16*	46*	1**	17*	208	216
preferred source of info	7 1.5%	0 0	2 1.6%	2 1.6%	4 1.5%	5 3.0%	1 1.3%	0 0	2 2.6%	0 0	2 1.6%	1 1.0%	1 5.5%IK	1 2.0%	0 0	0 0	1 0.4%	6 2.6%
DK/Refused	2 0.5%	0 0	0 0	0 0	2 0.7%	0 0	0 0	2 1.3%	0 0	1 2.0%	0 0	0 0	0 0	1 2.0%	0 0	0 0	1 0.4%	1 0.5%

Proportions/Means: Columns Tested (5% risk level) - A/B/D - C/D - E/F/G - H/I/J/K/L/M/N - P/Q
* small base; ** very small base (under 30) ineligible for sig testing

TABLE 151

S7sum_14. Technical Reports SUMMARY TABLE

	TOTAL SAMPLE	RESPONDENT TYPE: FACULTY MEMBER	GRAD. STUDENT	FACULTY /GRAD	UNDER GRAD. STUDENT	INSTITUTION TYPE: PUBLIC	PRIVATE	LIBERAL ARTS	DISCIPLINE: BIOLOGIAL SCIENCES	PHYSICAL SCIENCES /MATH	SOCIAL SCIENCES	ARTS AND HUMAN.	ENGI-NEERING	BUSINESS	LAW	UNDEC. MAJOR	GENDER: MALE	FEMALE
		(A)	(B)	(C)	(D)	(E)	(F)	(G)	(H)	(I)	(J)	(K)	(L)	(M)	(N)		(P)	(Q)
Base - Use Technical Reports for coursework	235	0**	130	130	104*	115*	63*	57*	33*	41*	70*	21**	19*	44*	2**	6*	144	91*
ONLINE	184 78.5%	0 0	99 75.9%	99 75.9%	85 81.7%	83 72.6%	53 84.5%	48 83.8%	24 73.0%	34 82.9%	60 86.5%	12 57.9%	14 73.8%	33 74.5%	2 90.0%	6 100.0%	111 77.6%	73 80.0%
Search engine (NET)	56 23.8%	0 0	24 18.4%	24 18.4%	32 30.4%B C	20 17.1%	15 23.3%	22 37.8%E	6 18.9%	11 26.8%	11 16.2%	2 10.5%	4 21.5%	18 40.4%HJ L	* 20.0%	3 50.0%	36 24.8%	20 22.1%
All sources of info	56 23.8%	0 0	24 18.4%	24 18.4%	32 30.4%B C	20 17.1%	15 23.3%	22 37.8%E	6 18.9%	11 26.8%	11 16.2%	2 10.5%	4 21.5%	18 40.4%HJ L	* 20.0%	3 50.0%	36 24.8%	20 22.1%
preferred source of info	33 14.1%	0 0	15 11.6%	15 11.6%	18 17.2%	13 11.4%	9 14.0%	11 19.6%	4 13.5%	6 14.6%	6 8.1%	2 10.5%	1 7.7%	12 27.7%JL	* 10.0%	1 16.7%	23 15.9%	10 11.1%
Online databases (NET)	47 19.9%	0 0	25 19.4%	25 19.4%	21 20.6%	16 13.9%	22 35.1%EG	9 15.3%	6 18.9%	8 19.5%	19 27.0%L	2 10.5%	2 9.2%	9 21.3%	1 30.0%	0 0	25 17.7%	21 23.4%
All sources of info	47 19.9%	0 0	25 19.4%	25 19.4%	21 20.6%	16 13.9%	22 35.1%EG	9 15.3%	6 18.9%	8 19.5%	19 27.0%L	2 10.5%	2 9.2%	9 21.3%	1 30.0%	0 0	25 17.7%	21 23.4%
preferred source of info	37 15.6%	0 0	19 14.8%	19 14.8%	17 16.7%	15 13.1%	17 27.2%EG	5 8.1%	6 18.9%	4 9.8%	17 24.3%	2 10.5%	1 7.7%	6 12.8%	* 20.0%	0 0	20 14.1%	17 18.1%
Online library catalogues and finding aids (NET)	31 13.4%	0 0	19 14.8%	19 14.8%	12 11.6%	17 15.2%	8 13.3%	6 9.8%	4 10.8%	5 12.2%	11 16.2%	4 21.1%	2 12.3%	5 10.6%	* 10.0%	0 0	12 8.5%	19 21.1%P

Proportions/Means: Columns Tested (5% risk level) - A/B/D - C/D - E/F/G - H/I/J/K/L/M/N - P/Q
* small base; ** very small base (under 30) ineligible for sig testing

Table 412
Page 1759

Outsell/Digital Library Federation Study (2002)
Weighted Tables

TABLE 151, continued

S7sum_14. Technical Reports SUMMARY TABLE

		RESPONDENT TYPE				INSTITUTION TYPE			DISCIPLINE									GENDER	
	TOTAL SAMPLE	FACULTY MEMBER	GRAD. STUDENT	FACULTY /GRAD	UNDER GRAD. STUDENT	PUBLIC	PRIVATE	LIBERAL ARTS	BIOLOGIAL SCIENCES	PHYSICAL SCIENCES /MATH	SOCIAL SCIENCES	ARTS AND HUMAN.	ENGI-NEERING	BUSINESS	LAW	UNDEC. MAJOR	MALE	FEMALE
		(A)	(B)	(C)	(D)	(E)	(F)	(G)	(H)	(I)	(J)	(K)	(L)	(M)	(N)		(P)	(Q)
Base - Use Technical Reports for coursework	235	0**	130	130	104*	115*	63*	57*	33*	41*	70*	21**	19*	44*	2**	6*	144	91*
All sources of info	31 13.4%	0 0	19 14.8%	19 14.8%	12 11.6%	17 15.2%	8 13.3%	6 9.8%	4 10.8%	5 12.2%	11 16.2%	4 21.1%	2 12.3%	5 10.6%	* 10.0%	0 0	12 8.5%	19 21.1%P
preferred source of info	28 11.8%	0 0	18 14.1%	18 14.1%	9 8.9%	17 14.7%	7 11.4%	4 6.6%	4 10.8%	5 12.2%	9 13.5%	4 21.1%	1 7.7%	4 8.5%	* 10.0%	0 0	12 8.1%	16 17.7%P
Your own institution's web site (NET)	25 10.8%	0 0	13 10.3%	13 10.3%	12 11.4%	12 10.7%	5 7.8%	8 14.3%	4 10.8%	4 9.8%	9 13.5%	1 5.3%	3 18.5%M	2 4.3%	0 0	2 33.3%	14 10.1%	11 12.0%
All sources of info	25 10.8%	0 0	13 10.3%	13 10.3%	12 11.4%	12 10.7%	5 7.8%	8 14.3%	4 10.8%	4 9.8%	9 13.5%	1 5.3%	3 18.5%M	2 4.3%	0 0	2 33.3%	14 10.1%	11 12.0%
preferred source of info	21 8.9%	0 0	12 8.9%	12 8.9%	9 8.8%	10 8.6%	3 4.8%	8 13.8%	3 8.1%M	3 7.3%	9 13.5%M	1 5.3%	3 13.8%M	0 0	0 0	2 33.3%	12 8.1%	9 10.0%
Internet searches (NET)	24 10.0%	0 0	13 9.7%	13 9.7%	11 10.4%	10 9.1%	7 11.6%	6 10.1%	4 10.8%	3 7.3%	8 10.8%	1 5.3%	3 16.9%	5 10.6%	1 30.0%	0 0	16 11.2%	7 8.1%
All sources of info	24 10.0%	0 0	13 9.7%	13 9.7%	11 10.4%	10 9.1%	7 11.6%	6 10.1%	4 10.8%	3 7.3%	8 10.8%	1 5.3%	3 16.9%	5 10.6%	1 30.0%	0 0	16 11.2%	7 8.1%
preferred source of info	14 6.2%	0 0	9 7.2%	9 7.2%	5 4.9%	8 6.9%	6 9.0%	1 1.6%	2 5.4%	1 2.4%	6 8.1%	0 0	2 10.8%	4 8.5%	* 20.0%	0 0	9 6.5%	5 5.7%
Web directory/ subject related web site (NET)	13 5.4%	0 0	5 3.8%	5 3.8%	8 7.3%	5 4.2%	3 4.2%	5 9.0%	1 2.7%	4 9.8%J	0 0	0 0	2 9.2%J	5 10.6%J	* 20.0%	1 16.7%	9 5.9%	4 4.5%

Proportions/Means: Columns Tested (5% risk level) - A/B/D - C/D - E/F/G - H/I/J/K/L/M/N - P/Q
* small base; ** very small base (under 30) ineligible for sig testing

Table 412
Page 1760

Outsell/Digital Library Federation Study (2002)
Weighted Tables

TABLE 151, continued

S7sum_14. Technical Reports SUMMARY TABLE

	TOTAL SAMPLE	RESPONDENT TYPE: FACULTY MEMBER	RESPONDENT TYPE: GRAD. STUDENT	RESPONDENT TYPE: FACULTY /GRAD	RESPONDENT TYPE: UNDER GRAD. STUDENT	INSTITUTION TYPE: PUBLIC	INSTITUTION TYPE: PRIVATE	INSTITUTION TYPE: LIBERAL ARTS	DISCIPLINE: BIOLOGIAL SCIENCES	DISCIPLINE: PHYSICAL SCIENCES /MATH	DISCIPLINE: SOCIAL SCIENCES	DISCIPLINE: ARTS AND HUMAN.	DISCIPLINE: ENGI-NEERING	DISCIPLINE: BUSINESS	DISCIPLINE: LAW	DISCIPLINE: UNDEC. MAJOR	GENDER: MALE	GENDER: FEMALE
		(A)	(B)	(C)	(D)	(E)	(F)	(G)	(H)	(I)	(J)	(K)	(L)	(M)	(N)		(P)	(Q)
Base - Use Technical Reports for coursework	235	0**	130	130	104*	115*	63*	57*	33*	41*	70*	21**	19*	44*	2**	6*	144	91*
All sources of info	13	0	5	5	8	5	3	5	1	4	0	0	2	5	*	1	9	4
	5.4%	0	3.8%	3.8%	7.3%	4.2%	4.2%	9.0%	2.7%	9.8%J	0	0	9.2%J	10.6%J	20.0%	16.7%	5.9%	4.5%
preferred source of info	9	0	2	2	6	4	*	4	1	4	0	0	1	3	0	0	7	2
	3.6%	0	1.9%	1.9%	5.8%	3.6%	0.5%	7.3%	2.7%	9.8%J	0	0	4.6%J	6.4%	0	0	4.9%	1.7%
Online reference service (NET)	7	0	5	5	2	6	1	0	0	0	4	0	1	2	*	0	7	0
	2.8%	0	3.7%	3.7%	1.7%	5.0%	1.5%	0	0	0	5.4%	0	4.6%	4.3%	10.0%	0	4.6%	0
All sources of info	7	0	5	5	2	6	1	0	0	0	4	0	1	2	*	0	7	0
	2.8%	0	3.7%	3.7%	1.7%	5.0%	1.5%	0	0	0	5.4%	0	4.6%	4.3%	10.0%	0	4.6%	0
preferred source of info	2	0	2	2	*	2	0	0	0	0	2	0	*	0	*	0	2	0
	1.0%	0	1.6%	1.6%	0.3%	2.0%	0	0	0	0	2.7%	0	1.5%	0	10.0%	0	1.6%	0
Online abstracting and indexing services (NET)	4	0	2	2	2	2	2	*	1	2	0	0	*	1	0	0	4	0
	1.7%	0	1.5%	1.5%	2.0%	1.6%	3.2%	0.5%	2.7%	4.9%	0	0	1.5%	2.1%	0	0	2.9%	0
All sources of info	4	0	2	2	2	2	2	*	1	2	0	0	*	1	0	0	4	0
	1.7%	0	1.5%	1.5%	2.0%	1.6%	3.2%	0.5%	2.7%	4.9%	0	0	1.5%	2.1%	0	0	2.9%	0
preferred source of info	2	0	1	1	1	1	1	0	1	1	0	0	0	0	0	0	2	0
	0.8%	0	0.8%	0.8%	0.8%	0.8%	1.6%	0	2.7%	2.4%	0	0	0	0	0	0	1.3%	0
Department web page (NET)	2	0	1	1	1	0	1	1	1	0	0	0	*	0	0	1	1	1
	0.9%	0	0.7%	0.7%	1.2%	0	1.9%	1.8%	2.7%	0	0	0	1.5%	0	0	16.7%	0.8%	1.1%

Proportions/Means: Columns Tested (5% risk level) - A/B/D - C/D - E/F/G - H/I/J/K/L/M/N - P/Q
* small base; ** very small base (under 30) ineligible for sig testing

Table 412
Page 1761

Outsell/Digital Library Federation Study (2002)
Weighted Tables

TABLE 151, continued

S7sum_14. Technical Reports SUMMARY TABLE

		RESPONDENT TYPE				INSTITUTION TYPE			DISCIPLINE									GENDER	
	TOTAL SAMPLE	FACULTY MEMBER	GRAD. STUDENT	FACULTY /GRAD	UNDER GRAD. STUDENT	PUBLIC	PRIVATE	LIBERAL ARTS	BIOLOGIAL SCIENCES	PHYSICAL SCIENCES /MATH	SOCIAL SCIENCES	ARTS AND HUMAN.	ENGI- NEERING	BUSINESS	LAW	UNDEC. MAJOR	MALE	FEMALE
		(A)	(B)	(C)	(D)	(E)	(F)	(G)	(H)	(I)	(J)	(K)	(L)	(M)	(N)		(P)	(Q)
Base - Use Technical Reports for coursework	235	0**	130	130	104*	115*	63*	57*	33*	41*	70*	21**	19*	44*	2**	6*	144	91*
All sources of info	2	0	1	1	1	0	1	1	1	0	0	0	*	0	0	1	1	1
	0.9%	0	0.7%	0.7%	1.2%	0	1.9%	1.8%	2.7%	0	0	0	1.5%	0	0	16.7%	0.8%	1.1%
preferred source of info	2	0	1	1	1	0	1	1	1	0	0	0	*	0	0	1	1	1
	0.9%	0	0.7%	0.7%	1.2%	0	1.9%	1.8%	2.7%	0	0	0	1.5%	0	0	16.7%	0.8%	1.1%
Your own personal electronic library/files (NET)	2	0	2	2	0	2	0	0	0	1	0	1	0	0	0	0	1	1
	0.9%	0	1.6%	1.6%	0	1.8%	0	0	0	2.4%	0	5.3%	0	0	0	0	0.7%	1.2%
All sources of info	2	0	2	2	0	2	0	0	0	1	0	1	0	0	0	0	1	1
	0.9%	0	1.6%	1.6%	0	1.8%	0	0	0	2.4%	0	5.3%	0	0	0	0	0.7%	1.2%
preferred source of info	2	0	2	2	0	2	0	0	0	1	0	1	0	0	0	0	1	1
	0.9%	0	1.6%	1.6%	0	1.8%	0	0	0	2.4%	0	5.3%	0	0	0	0	0.7%	1.2%
E-mail listservs (NET)	0	0	0	0	0	0	0	0	0	0	0	0	0	0	0	0	0	0
	0	0	0	0	0	0	0	0	0	0	0	0	0	0	0	0	0	0
All sources of info	0	0	0	0	0	0	0	0	0	0	0	0	0	0	0	0	0	0
	0	0	0	0	0	0	0	0	0	0	0	0	0	0	0	0	0	0
preferred source of info	0	0	0	0	0	0	0	0	0	0	0	0	0	0	0	0	0	0
	0	0	0	0	0	0	0	0	0	0	0	0	0	0	0	0	0	0
Online bookstore (NET)	0	0	0	0	0	0	0	0	0	0	0	0	0	0	0	0	0	0
	0	0	0	0	0	0	0	0	0	0	0	0	0	0	0	0	0	0

Proportions/Means: Columns Tested (5% risk level) - A/B/D - C/D - E/F/G - H/I/J/K/L/M/N - P/Q
* small base; ** very small base (under 30) ineligible for sig testing

Table 412
Page 1762

Outsell/Digital Library Federation Study (2002)
Weighted Tables

TABLE 151, continued

S7sum_14. Technical Reports SUMMARY TABLE

		RESPONDENT TYPE				INSTITUTION TYPE			DISCIPLINE									GENDER	
	TOTAL SAMPLE	FACULTY MEMBER	GRAD. STUDENT	FACULTY /GRAD	UNDER GRAD. STUDENT	PUBLIC	PRIVATE	LIBERAL ARTS	BIOLOGIAL SCIENCES	PHYSICAL SCIENCES /MATH	SOCIAL SCIENCES	ARTS AND HUMAN.	ENGI-NEERING	BUSINESS	LAW	UNDEC. MAJOR	MALE	FEMALE
		(A)	(B)	(C)	(D)	(E)	(F)	(G)	(H)	(I)	(J)	(K)	(L)	(M)	(N)		(P)	(Q)
Base - Use Technical Reports for coursework	235	0**	130	130	104*	115*	63*	57*	33*	41*	70*	21**	19*	44*	2**	6*	144	91*
All sources of info	0 0	0 0	0 0	0 0	0 0	0 0	0 0	0 0	0 0	0 0	0 0	0 0	0 0	0 0	0 0	0 0	0 0	0 0
preferred source of info	0 0	0 0	0 0	0 0	0 0	0 0	0 0	0 0	0 0	0 0	0 0	0 0	0 0	0 0	0 0	0 0	0 0	0 0
PERSONAL ASSISTANCE	82 34.9%	0 0	39 29.5%	39 29.5%	43 41.7%	36 31.4%	17 27.2%	29 50.6%EF	10 29.7%	15 36.6%	26 37.8%	9 42.1%	6 29.2%	13 29.8%	1 30.0%	3 50.0%	52 36.1%	30 33.1%
Faculty members inside your institution (NET)	51 21.8%	0 0	24 18.7%	24 18.7%	27 25.6%	21 18.6%	10 15.4%	20 35.1%EF	8 24.3%	13 31.7%	11 16.2%	6 26.3%	3 18.5%	7 17.0%	* 20.0%	2 33.3%	36 25.4%	15 16.0%
All sources of info	51 21.8%	0 0	24 18.7%	24 18.7%	27 25.6%	21 18.6%	10 15.4%	20 35.1%EF	8 24.3%	13 31.7%	11 16.2%	6 26.3%	3 18.5%	7 17.0%	* 20.0%	2 33.3%	36 25.4%	15 16.0%
preferred source of info	28 12.0%	0 0	15 11.6%	15 11.6%	13 12.5%	12 10.3%	7 11.2%	9 16.2%	5 16.2%	7 17.1%	4 5.4%	3 15.8%	3 15.4%	5 10.6%	* 10.0%	1 16.7%	22 15.4%	6 6.5%
A librarian in your institution (NET)	39 16.5%	0 0	12 9.3%	12 9.3%	26 25.4%B C	12 10.9%	7 11.7%	19 33.1%EF	2 5.4%	4 9.8%	17 24.3%H	6 26.3%	1 7.7%	6 12.8%	* 20.0%	3 50.0%	23 15.9%	16 17.4%
All sources of info	39 16.5%	0 0	12 9.3%	12 9.3%	26 25.4%B C	12 10.9%	7 11.7%	19 33.1%EF	2 5.4%	4 9.8%	17 24.3%H	6 26.3%	1 7.7%	6 12.8%	* 20.0%	3 50.0%	23 15.9%	16 17.4%

Proportions/Means: Columns Tested (5% risk level) - A/B/D - C/D - E/F/G - H/I/J/K/L/M/N - P/Q
* small base; ** very small base (under 30) ineligible for sig testing

Table 412
Page 1763

Outsell/Digital Library Federation Study (2002)
Weighted Tables

TABLE 151, continued

S7sum_14. Technical Reports SUMMARY TABLE

	TOTAL SAMPLE	RESPONDENT TYPE: FACULTY MEMBER	GRAD. STUDENT	FACULTY /GRAD	UNDER GRAD. STUDENT	INSTITUTION TYPE: PUBLIC	PRIVATE	LIBERAL ARTS	DISCIPLINE: BIOLOGIAL SCIENCES	PHYSICAL SCIENCES /MATH	SOCIAL SCIENCES	ARTS AND HUMAN.	ENGI-NEERING	BUSINESS	LAW	UNDEC. MAJOR	GENDER: MALE	FEMALE
		(A)	(B)	(C)	(D)	(E)	(F)	(G)	(H)	(I)	(J)	(K)	(L)	(M)	(N)		(P)	(Q)
Base - Use Technical Reports for coursework	235	0**	130	130	104*	115*	63*	57*	33*	41*	70*	21**	19*	44*	2**	6*	144	91*
preferred source of info	15 6.3%	0 0	5 3.8%	5 3.8%	10 9.3%	6 4.9%	2 3.5%	7 12.1%	1 2.7%	1 2.4%	8 10.8%	2 10.5%	* 1.5%	3 6.4%	0 0	0 0	5 3.5%	10 10.7%P
Other students inside your institution (NET)	13 5.4%	0 0	8 6.2%	8 6.2%	4 4.3%	4 3.5%	4 7.1%	4 7.3%	2 5.4%	2 4.9%	2 2.7%	2 10.5%	2 9.2%	3 6.4%	* 10.0%	0 0	6 3.9%	7 7.7%
All sources of info	13 5.4%	0 0	8 6.2%	8 6.2%	4 4.3%	4 3.5%	4 7.1%	4 7.3%	2 5.4%	2 4.9%	2 2.7%	2 10.5%	2 9.2%	3 6.4%	* 10.0%	0 0	6 3.9%	7 7.7%
preferred source of info	1 0.2%	0 0	* 0.2%	* 0.2%	* 0.3%	* 0.3%	* 0.5%	0 0	0 0	0 0	0 0	0 0	1 3.1%	0 0	0 0	0 0	1 0.4%	0 0
Faculty members outside your institution (NET)	2 0.9%	0 0	0 0	0 0	2 2.0%	0 0	0 0	2 3.7%	0 0	1 2.4%	0 0	1 5.3%	0 0	0 0	0 0	0 0	1 0.7%	1 1.2%
All sources of info	2 0.9%	0 0	0 0	0 0	2 2.0%	0 0	0 0	2 3.7%	0 0	1 2.4%	0 0	1 5.3%	0 0	0 0	0 0	0 0	1 0.7%	1 1.2%
preferred source of info	0 0	0 0	0 0	0 0	0 0	0 0	0 0	0 0	0 0	0 0	0 0	0 0	0 0	0 0	0 0	0 0	0 0	0 0
Another institution's librarian (NET)	0 0	0 0	0 0	0 0	0 0	0 0	0 0	0 0	0 0	0 0	0 0	0 0	0 0	0 0	0 0	0 0	0 0	0 0
All sources of info	0 0	0 0	0 0	0 0	0 0	0 0	0 0	0 0	0 0	0 0	0 0	0 0	0 0	0 0	0 0	0 0	0 0	0 0

Proportions/Means: Columns Tested (5% risk level) - A/B/D - C/D - E/F/G - H/I/J/K/L/M/N - P/Q
* small base; ** very small base (under 30) ineligible for sig testing

Table 412
Page 1764

Outsell/Digital Library Federation Study (2002)
Weighted Tables

TABLE 151, continued

S7sum_14. Technical Reports SUMMARY TABLE

	RESPONDENT TYPE				INSTITUTION TYPE			DISCIPLINE								GENDER	
	TOTAL SAMPLE	FACULTY MEMBER	GRAD. STUDENT	FACULTY /GRAD	UNDER GRAD. STUDENT	PUBLIC	PRIVATE	LIBERAL ARTS	BIOLOGIAL SCIENCES	PHYSICAL SCIENCES /MATH	SOCIAL SCIENCES	ARTS AND HUMAN.	ENGI-NEERING	BUSINESS	LAW	UNDEC. MAJOR	MALE	FEMALE
		(A)	(B)	(C)	(D)	(E)	(F)	(G)	(H)	(I)	(J)	(K)	(L)	(M)	(N)		(P)	(Q)
Base - Use Technical Reports for coursework	235	0**	130	130	104*	115*	63*	57*	33*	41*	70*	21**	19*	44*	2**	6*	144	91*
preferred source of info	0 0	0 0	0 0	0 0	0 0	0 0	0 0	0 0	0 0	0 0	0 0	0 0	0 0	0 0	0 0	0 0	0 0	0 0
Other students outside your institution (NET)	0 0	0 0	0 0	0 0	0 0	0 0	0 0	0 0	0 0	0 0	0 0	0 0	0 0	0 0	0 0	0 0	0 0	0 0
All sources of info	0 0	0 0	0 0	0 0	0 0	0 0	0 0	0 0	0 0	0 0	0 0	0 0	0 0	0 0	0 0	0 0	0 0	0 0
preferred source of info	0 0	0 0	0 0	0 0	0 0	0 0	0 0	0 0	0 0	0 0	0 0	0 0	0 0	0 0	0 0	0 0	0 0	0 0
Professional meetings (NET)	0 0	0 0	0 0	0 0	0 0	0 0	0 0	0 0	0 0	0 0	0 0	0 0	0 0	0 0	0 0	0 0	0 0	0 0
All sources of info	0 0	0 0	0 0	0 0	0 0	0 0	0 0	0 0	0 0	0 0	0 0	0 0	0 0	0 0	0 0	0 0	0 0	0 0
preferred source of info	0 0	0 0	0 0	0 0	0 0	0 0	0 0	0 0	0 0	0 0	0 0	0 0	0 0	0 0	0 0	0 0	0 0	0 0
LIBRARY FACILITIES/ PRINT	62 26.3%	0 0	36 27.4%	36 27.4%	26 24.8%	31 26.6%	17 27.8%	14 23.9%	5 16.2%	15 36.6%H	19 27.0%	2 10.5%	6 29.2%	12 27.7%	1 40.0%	2 33.3%	41 28.4%	21 22.8%
Campus library (NET)	49 20.9%	0 0	26 20.0%	26 20.0%	23 22.0%	24 20.5%	13 20.5%	13 22.2%	4 13.5%	13 31.7%	13 18.9%	1 5.3%	5 24.6%	10 23.4%	1 30.0%	2 33.3%	34 23.8%	15 16.4%

Proportions/Means: Columns Tested (5% risk level) - A/B/D - C/D - E/F/G - H/I/J/K/L/M/N - P/Q
* small base; ** very small base (under 30) ineligible for sig testing

Table 412
Page 1765

Outsell/Digital Library Federation Study (2002)
Weighted Tables

TABLE 151, continued

S7sum_14. Technical Reports SUMMARY TABLE

		RESPONDENT TYPE				INSTITUTION TYPE			DISCIPLINE								GENDER	
	TOTAL SAMPLE	FACULTY MEMBER	GRAD. STUDENT	FACULTY /GRAD	UNDER GRAD. STUDENT	PUBLIC	PRIVATE	LIBERAL ARTS	BIOLOGIAL SCIENCES	PHYSICAL SCIENCES /MATH	SOCIAL SCIENCES	ARTS AND HUMAN.	ENGI- NEERING	BUSINESS	LAW	UNDEC. MAJOR	MALE	FEMALE
		(A)	(B)	(C)	(D)	(E)	(F)	(G)	(H)	(I)	(J)	(K)	(L)	(M)	(N)		(P)	(Q)
Base - Use Technical Reports for coursework	235	0**	130	130	104*	115*	63*	57*	33*	41*	70*	21**	19*	44*	2**	6*	144	91*
All sources of info	49 20.9%	0 0	26 20.0%	26 20.0%	23 22.0%	24 20.5%	13 20.5%	13 22.2%	4 13.5%	13 31.7%	13 18.9%	1 5.3%	5 24.6%	10 23.4%	1 30.0%	2 33.3%	34 23.8%	15 16.4%
preferred source of info	19 8.2%	0 0	12 9.1%	12 9.1%	7 7.2%	10 9.0%	5 7.6%	4 7.4%	4 10.8%	5 12.2%	2 2.7%	1 5.3%	3 15.4%J	4 8.5%	* 10.0%	1 16.7%	13 9.2%	6 6.7%
References cited in books or journal articles (NET)	6 2.6%	0 0	4 3.2%	4 3.2%	2 1.8%	3 2.6%	3 4.9%	0 0	0 0	0 0	4 5.4%	1 5.3%	* 1.5%	1 2.1%	0 0	0 0	2 1.6%	4 4.1%
All sources of info	6 2.6%	0 0	4 3.2%	4 3.2%	2 1.8%	3 2.6%	3 4.9%	0 0	0 0	0 0	4 5.4%	1 5.3%	* 1.5%	1 2.1%	0 0	0 0	2 1.6%	4 4.1%
preferred source of info	4 1.7%	0 0	4 3.0%	4 3.0%	0 0	3 2.6%	1 1.5%	0 0	0 0	0 0	2 2.7%	1 5.3%	0 0	1 2.1%	0 0	0 0	2 1.4%	2 2.1%
Another library (NET)	5 2.0%	0 0	4 2.9%	4 2.9%	1 1.0%	4 3.3%	0 0	1 1.8%	0 0	2 4.9%	2 2.7%	0 0	0 0	1 2.1%	0 0	0 0	4 2.7%	1 1.0%
All sources of info	5 2.0%	0 0	4 2.9%	4 2.9%	1 1.0%	4 3.3%	0 0	1 1.8%	0 0	2 4.9%	2 2.7%	0 0	0 0	1 2.1%	0 0	0 0	4 2.7%	1 1.0%
preferred source of info	1 0.4%	0 0	1 0.7%	1 0.7%	0 0	1 0.8%	0 0	0 0	0 0	0 0	0 0	0 0	0 0	1 2.1%	0 0	0 0	0 0	1 1.0%

Proportions/Means: Columns Tested (5% risk level) - A/B/D - C/D - E/F/G - H/I/J/K/L/M/N - P/Q
* small base; ** very small base (under 30) ineligible for sig testing

Table 412
Page 1766

Outsell/Digital Library Federation Study (2002)
Weighted Tables

TABLE 151, continued

S7sum_14. Technical Reports SUMMARY TABLE

		RESPONDENT TYPE				INSTITUTION TYPE			DISCIPLINE								GENDER	
	TOTAL SAMPLE	FACULTY MEMBER	GRAD. STUDENT	FACULTY /GRAD	UNDER GRAD. STUDENT	PUBLIC	PRIVATE	LIBERAL ARTS	BIOLOGIAL SCIENCES	PHYSICAL SCIENCES /MATH	SOCIAL SCIENCES	ARTS AND HUMAN.	ENGI- NEERING	BUSINESS	LAW	UNDEC. MAJOR	MALE	FEMALE
		(A)	(B)	(C)	(D)	(E)	(F)	(G)	(H)	(I)	(J)	(K)	(L)	(M)	(N)		(P)	(Q)
Base - Use Technical Reports for coursework	235	0**	130	130	104*	115*	63*	57*	33*	41*	70*	21**	19*	44*	2**	6*	144	91*
Your own personal physical library/ files/bookshelves (NET)	2 1.0%	0 0	1 1.0%	1 1.0%	1 0.9%	1 1.0%	1 1.9%	0 0	1 2.7%	0 0	0 0	0 0	* 1.5%	1 2.1%	* 10.0%	0 0	* 0.1%	2 2.3%
All sources of info	2 1.0%	0 0	1 1.0%	1 1.0%	1 0.9%	1 1.0%	1 1.9%	0 0	1 2.7%	0 0	0 0	0 0	* 1.5%	1 2.1%	* 10.0%	0 0	* 0.1%	2 2.3%
preferred source of info	* 0.1%	0 0	* 0.2%	* 0.2%	0 0	0 0	* 0.5%	0 0	0 0	0 0	0 0	0 0	* 1.5%	0 0	0 0	0 0	0 0	* 0.3%
Printed library catalogues and finding aids (NET)	2 0.8%	0 0	2 1.4%	2 1.4%	0 0	1 0.8%	1 1.4%	0 0	1 2.7%	0 0	0 0	0 0	0 0	1 2.1%	0 0	0 0	0 0	2 2.0%
All sources of info	2 0.8%	0 0	2 1.4%	2 1.4%	0 0	1 0.8%	1 1.4%	0 0	1 2.7%	0 0	0 0	0 0	0 0	1 2.1%	0 0	0 0	0 0	2 2.0%
preferred source of info	0 0	0 0	0 0	0 0	0 0	0 0	0 0	0 0	0 0	0 0	0 0	0 0	0 0	0 0	0 0	0 0	0 0	0 0
Printed abstracting and indexing services (NET)	1 0.5%	0 0	* 0.2%	* 0.2%	1 1.0%	0 0	* 0.5%	1 1.8%	0 0	1 2.4%	0 0	0 0	* 1.5%	0 0	0 0	0 0	1 0.9%	0 0
All sources of info	1 0.5%	0 0	* 0.2%	* 0.2%	1 1.0%	0 0	* 0.5%	1 1.8%	0 0	1 2.4%	0 0	0 0	* 1.5%	0 0	0 0	0 0	1 0.9%	0 0

Proportions/Means: Columns Tested (5% risk level) - A/B/D - C/D - E/F/G - H/I/J/K/L/M/N - P/Q
* small base; ** very small base (under 30) ineligible for sig testing

Table 412
Page 1767

Outsell/Digital Library Federation Study (2002)
Weighted Tables

TABLE 151, continued

S7sum_14. Technical Reports SUMMARY TABLE

		RESPONDENT TYPE				INSTITUTION TYPE			DISCIPLINE									GENDER	
	TOTAL SAMPLE	FACULTY MEMBER	GRAD. STUDENT	FACULTY /GRAD	UNDER GRAD. STUDENT	PUBLIC	PRIVATE	LIBERAL ARTS	BIOLOGIAL SCIENCES	PHYSICAL SCIENCES /MATH	SOCIAL SCIENCES	ARTS AND HUMAN.	ENGI-NEERING	BUSINESS	LAW	UNDEC. MAJOR	MALE	FEMALE
		(A)	(B)	(C)	(D)	(E)	(F)	(G)	(H)	(I)	(J)	(K)	(L)	(M)	(N)		(P)	(Q)
Base - Use Technical Reports for coursework	235	0**	130	130	104*	115*	63*	57*	33*	41*	70*	21**	19*	44*	2**	6*	144	91*
preferred source of info	0 0	0 0	0 0	0 0	0 0	0 0	0 0	0 0	0 0	0 0	0 0	0 0	0 0	0 0	0 0	0 0	0 0	0 0
Personal subscriptions to newspapers, magazines and journals (NET)	0 0	0 0	0 0	0 0	0 0	0 0	0 0	0 0	0 0	0 0	0 0	0 0	0 0	0 0	0 0	0 0	0 0	0 0
All sources of info	0 0	0 0	0 0	0 0	0 0	0 0	0 0	0 0	0 0	0 0	0 0	0 0	0 0	0 0	0 0	0 0	0 0	0 0
preferred source of info	0 0	0 0	0 0	0 0	0 0	0 0	0 0	0 0	0 0	0 0	0 0	0 0	0 0	0 0	0 0	0 0	0 0	0 0
Physical bookstore (NET)	0 0	0 0	0 0	0 0	0 0	0 0	0 0	0 0	0 0	0 0	0 0	0 0	0 0	0 0	0 0	0 0	0 0	0 0
All sources of info	0 0	0 0	0 0	0 0	0 0	0 0	0 0	0 0	0 0	0 0	0 0	0 0	0 0	0 0	0 0	0 0	0 0	0 0
preferred source of info	0 0	0 0	0 0	0 0	0 0	0 0	0 0	0 0	0 0	0 0	0 0	0 0	0 0	0 0	0 0	0 0	0 0	0 0
Other (NET)	11 4.7%	0 0	6 4.6%	6 4.6%	5 4.7%	6 5.4%	1 2.1%	3 6.0%	2 5.4%	1 2.4%	0 0	4 21.1%	1 7.7%J	1 2.1%	* 20.0%	1 16.7%	7 4.7%	4 4.6%

Proportions/Means: Columns Tested (5% risk level) - A/B/D - C/D - E/F/G - H/I/J/K/L/M/N - P/Q
* small base; ** very small base (under 30) ineligible for sig testing

Table 412
Page 1768

Outsell/Digital Library Federation Study (2002)
Weighted Tables

TABLE 151, continued

S7sum_14. Technical Reports SUMMARY TABLE

		RESPONDENT TYPE				INSTITUTION TYPE			DISCIPLINE									GENDER	
	TOTAL SAMPLE	FACULTY MEMBER	GRAD. STUDENT	FACULTY /GRAD	UNDER GRAD. STUDENT	PUBLIC	PRIVATE	LIBERAL ARTS	BIOLOGIAL SCIENCES	PHYSICAL SCIENCES /MATH	SOCIAL SCIENCES	ARTS AND HUMAN.	ENGI-NEERING	BUSINESS	LAW	UNDEC. MAJOR	MALE	FEMALE
		(A)	(B)	(C)	(D)	(E)	(F)	(G)	(H)	(I)	(J)	(K)	(L)	(M)	(N)		(P)	(Q)
Base - Use Technical Reports for coursework	235	0**	130	130	104*	115*	63*	57*	33*	41*	70*	21**	19*	44*	2**	6*	144	91*
All sources of info	11 4.7%	0 0	6 4.6%	6 4.6%	5 4.7%	6 5.4%	1 2.1%	3 6.0%	2 5.4%	1 2.4%	0 0	4 21.1%	1 7.7%J	1 2.1%	* 20.0%	1 16.7%	7 4.7%	4 4.6%
preferred source of info	3 1.2%	0 0	2 1.8%	2 1.8%	* 0.4%	2 1.5%	1 1.4%	* 0.3%	1 2.7%	0 0	0 0	1 5.3%	1 3.1%	0 0	* 10.0%	0 0	2 1.3%	1 1.0%
Online (unspecified)	6 2.6%	0 0	5 4.0%	5 4.0%	1 0.9%	5 4.6%	1 1.5%	0 0	0 0	0 0	4 5.4%	0 0	1 3.1%	2 4.3%	0 0	0 0	4 2.8%	2 2.4%
All sources of info	6 2.6%	0 0	5 4.0%	5 4.0%	1 0.9%	5 4.6%	1 1.5%	0 0	0 0	0 0	4 5.4%	0 0	1 3.1%	2 4.3%	0 0	0 0	4 2.8%	2 2.4%
preferred source of info	6 2.5%	0 0	5 3.8%	5 3.8%	1 0.9%	5 4.3%	1 1.5%	0 0	0 0	0 0	4 5.4%	0 0	* 1.5%	2 4.3%	0 0	0 0	4 2.8%	2 2.1%
E-journals	0 0	0 0	0 0	0 0	0 0	0 0	0 0	0 0	0 0	0 0	0 0	0 0	0 0	0 0	0 0	0 0	0 0	0 0
All sources of info	0 0	0 0	0 0	0 0	0 0	0 0	0 0	0 0	0 0	0 0	0 0	0 0	0 0	0 0	0 0	0 0	0 0	0 0
preferred source of info	0 0	0 0	0 0	0 0	0 0	0 0	0 0	0 0	0 0	0 0	0 0	0 0	0 0	0 0	0 0	0 0	0 0	0 0
DK/Refused	9 4.0%	0 0	4 3.3%	4 3.3%	5 4.7%	5 4.3%	1 2.1%	3 5.3%	2 5.4%	3 7.3%	2 2.7%	1 5.3%	1 3.1%	1 2.1%	0 0	0 0	6 3.9%	4 4.1%

Proportions/Means: Columns Tested (5% risk level) - A/B/D - C/D - E/F/G - H/I/J/K/L/M/N - P/Q
* small base; ** very small base (under 30) ineligible for sig testing

Table 412
Page 1769

TABLE 152

S7D/E_14. Technical Reports SUMMARY TABLE

		RESPONDENT TYPE				INSTITUTION TYPE			DISCIPLINE									GENDER	
	TOTAL SAMPLE	FACULTY MEMBER	GRAD. STUDENT	FACULTY /GRAD	UNDER GRAD. STUDENT	PUBLIC	PRIVATE	LIBERAL ARTS	BIOLOGIAL SCIENCES	PHYSICAL SCIENCES /MATH	SOCIAL SCIENCES	ARTS AND HUMAN.	ENGI-NEERING	BUSINESS	LAW	UNDEC. MAJOR	MALE	FEMALE
		(A)	(B)	(C)	(D)	(E)	(F)	(G)	(H)	(I)	(J)	(K)	(L)	(M)	(N)		(P)	(Q)
Base - Use Technical Reports for coursework	235	0**	130	130	104*	115*	63*	57*	33*	41*	70*	21**	19*	44*	2**	6*	144	91*
Borrow from or use in campus library (NET)	137 58.3%	0 0	75 57.4%	75 57.4%	62 59.4%	63 55.0%	38 61.2%	35 61.7%	18 54.1%	24 58.5%	45 64.9%	12 57.9%	13 69.2%M	21 48.9%	* 20.0%	3 50.0%	90 62.9%	47 51.1%
All sources of info	137 58.3%	0 0	75 57.4%	75 57.4%	62 59.4%	63 55.0%	38 61.2%	35 61.7%	18 54.1%	24 58.5%	45 64.9%	12 57.9%	13 69.2%M	21 48.9%	* 20.0%	3 50.0%	90 62.9%	47 51.1%
preferred source of info	95 40.4%	0 0	48 37.0%	48 37.0%	46 44.5%	48 42.1%	20 32.0%	26 46.0%	13 40.5%	16 39.0%	32 45.9%	8 36.8%	8 41.5%	15 34.0%	0 0	3 50.0%	62 43.0%	33 36.2%
Access online (NET)	133 56.9%	0 0	77 59.3%	77 59.3%	56 53.8%	60 52.3%	42 66.5%	32 55.6%	16 48.6%	28 68.3%L	36 51.4%	10 47.4%	9 46.2%	30 68.1%L	1 80.0%	4 66.7%	74 51.8%	59 64.8%
All sources of info	133 56.9%	0 0	77 59.3%	77 59.3%	56 53.8%	60 52.3%	42 66.5%	32 55.6%	16 48.6%	28 68.3%L	36 51.4%	10 47.4%	9 46.2%	30 68.1%L	1 80.0%	4 66.7%	74 51.8%	59 64.8%
preferred source of info	115 48.9%	0 0	70 53.9%	70 53.9%	45 42.7%	54 47.0%	38 60.0%	23 40.7%	15 45.9%	22 53.7%	30 43.2%	8 36.8%	8 41.5%	28 63.8%L	1 70.0%	3 50.0%	64 44.5%	51 55.9%
Faculty (NET)	16 6.6%	0 0	5 3.9%	5 3.9%	10 10.0%	3 2.4%	3 4.2%	10 17.7%EF	2 5.4%	1 2.4%	6 8.1%	3 15.8%	2 9.2%	2 4.3%	* 10.0%	0 0	10 6.8%	6 6.4%
All sources of info	16 6.6%	0 0	5 3.9%	5 3.9%	10 10.0%	3 2.4%	3 4.2%	10 17.7%EF	2 5.4%	1 2.4%	6 8.1%	3 15.8%	2 9.2%	2 4.3%	* 10.0%	0 0	10 6.8%	6 6.4%
preferred source of info	11 4.8%	0 0	4 2.8%	4 2.8%	8 7.3%	3 2.4%	1 1.8%	7 12.8%EF	2 5.4%	1 2.4%	4 5.4%	3 15.8%	1 6.2%M	0 0	* 10.0%	0 0	8 5.7%	3 3.3%

Proportions/Means: Columns Tested (5% risk level) - A/B/D - C/D - E/F/G - H/I/J/K/L/M/N - P/Q
* small base; ** very small base (under 30) ineligible for sig testing

Table 415
Page 1776

TABLE 152, continued

S7D/E_14. Technical Reports SUMMARY TABLE

	TOTAL SAMPLE	RESPONDENT TYPE: FACULTY MEMBER	GRAD. STUDENT	FACULTY /GRAD	UNDER GRAD. STUDENT	INSTITUTION TYPE: PUBLIC	PRIVATE	LIBERAL ARTS	DISCIPLINE: BIOLOGIAL SCIENCES	PHYSICAL SCIENCES /MATH	SOCIAL SCIENCES	ARTS AND HUMAN.	ENGI-NEERING	BUSINESS	LAW	UNDEC. MAJOR	GENDER: MALE	FEMALE
		(A)	(B)	(C)	(D)	(E)	(F)	(G)	(H)	(I)	(J)	(K)	(L)	(M)	(N)		(P)	(Q)
Base - Use Technical Reports for coursework	235	0**	130	130	104*	115*	63*	57*	33*	41*	70*	21**	19*	44*	2**	6*	144	91*
Interlibrary loan (NET)	5 2.2%	0 0	2 1.7%	2 1.7%	3 2.9%	4 3.6%	0 0	1 2.0%	2 5.4%	0 0	2 2.7%	1 5.3%	* 1.5%	0 0	* 10.0%	0 0	2 1.5%	3 3.3%
All sources of info	5 2.2%	0 0	2 1.7%	2 1.7%	3 2.9%	4 3.6%	0 0	1 2.0%	2 5.4%	0 0	2 2.7%	1 5.3%	* 1.5%	0 0	* 10.0%	0 0	2 1.5%	3 3.3%
preferred source of info	2 0.9%	0 0	* 0.2%	* 0.2%	2 1.8%	2 1.9%	0 0	0 0	0 0	0 0	2 2.7%	0 0	* 1.5%	0 0	0 0	0 0	* 0.2%	2 2.1%
Borrow from or use in other libraries (NET)	5 2.0%	0 0	3 2.5%	3 2.5%	1 1.4%	4 3.3%	0 0	1 1.8%	0 0	1 2.4%	2 2.7%	1 5.3%	1 3.1%	0 0	* 10.0%	0 0	5 3.2%	* 0.2%
All sources of info	5 2.0%	0 0	3 2.5%	3 2.5%	1 1.4%	4 3.3%	0 0	1 1.8%	0 0	1 2.4%	2 2.7%	1 5.3%	1 3.1%	0 0	* 10.0%	0 0	5 3.2%	* 0.2%
preferred source of info	* 0.2%	0 0	0 0	0 0	* 0.4%	* 0.4%	0 0	0 0	0 0	0 0	0 0	0 0	* 1.5%	0 0	* 10.0%	0 0	* 0.2%	* 0.2%
Purchase from physical book store (NET)	3 1.3%	0 0	2 1.4%	2 1.4%	1 1.1%	0 0	2 3.0%	1 2.0%	0 0	0 0	2 2.7%	1 5.3%	0 0	0 0	0 0	0 0	2 1.3%	1 1.2%
All sources of info	3 1.3%	0 0	2 1.4%	2 1.4%	1 1.1%	0 0	2 3.0%	1 2.0%	0 0	0 0	2 2.7%	1 5.3%	0 0	0 0	0 0	0 0	2 1.3%	1 1.2%
preferred source of info	0 0	0 0	0 0	0 0	0 0	0 0	0 0	0 0	0 0	0 0	0 0	0 0	0 0	0 0	0 0	0 0	0 0	0 0

Proportions/Means: Columns Tested (5% risk level) - A/B/D - C/D - E/F/G - H/I/J/K/L/M/N - P/Q
* small base; ** very small base (under 30) ineligible for sig testing

Table 415
Page 1777

Outsell/Digital Library Federation Study (2002)
Weighted Tables

TABLE 152, continued

S7D/E_14. Technical Reports SUMMARY TABLE

		RESPONDENT TYPE				INSTITUTION TYPE			DISCIPLINE									GENDER	
	TOTAL SAMPLE	FACULTY MEMBER	GRAD. STUDENT	FACULTY /GRAD	UNDER GRAD. STUDENT	PUBLIC	PRIVATE	LIBERAL ARTS	BIOLOGIAL SCIENCES	PHYSICAL SCIENCES /MATH	SOCIAL SCIENCES	ARTS AND HUMAN.	ENGI-NEERING	BUSINESS	LAW	UNDEC. MAJOR	MALE	FEMALE
		(A)	(B)	(C)	(D)	(E)	(F)	(G)	(H)	(I)	(J)	(K)	(L)	(M)	(N)		(P)	(Q)
Base - Use Technical Reports for coursework	235	0**	130	130	104*	115*	63*	57*	33*	41*	70*	21**	19*	44*	2**	6*	144	91*
Home (NET)	2 0.8%	0 0	1 0.7%	1 0.7%	1 0.9%	1 0.8%	1 1.4%	0 0	1 2.7%	0 0	0 0	0 0	0 0	1 2.1%	0 0	0 0	1 0.6%	1 1.0%
All sources of info	2 0.8%	0 0	1 0.7%	1 0.7%	1 0.9%	1 0.8%	1 1.4%	0 0	1 2.7%	0 0	0 0	0 0	0 0	1 2.1%	0 0	0 0	1 0.6%	1 1.0%
preferred source of info	1 0.4%	0 0	0 0	0 0	1 0.9%	1 0.8%	0 0	0 0	0 0	0 0	0 0	0 0	0 0	1 2.1%	0 0	0 0	1 0.6%	0 0
Ask library to purchase source (NET)	1 0.5%	0 0	1 0.9%	1 0.9%	0 0	1 1.0%	0 0	0 0	1 2.7%	0 0	0 0	0 0	* 1.5%	0 0	0 0	0 0	1 0.8%	0 0
All sources of info	1 0.5%	0 0	1 0.9%	1 0.9%	0 0	1 1.0%	0 0	0 0	1 2.7%	0 0	0 0	0 0	* 1.5%	0 0	0 0	0 0	1 0.8%	0 0
preferred source of info	* 0.1%	0 0	* 0.2%	* 0.2%	0 0	* 0.3%	0 0	0 0	0 0	0 0	0 0	0 0	* 1.5%	0 0	0 0	0 0	* 0.2%	0 0
Colleagues (NET)	1 0.5%	0 0	1 0.9%	1 0.9%	0 0	0 0	1 1.9%	0 0	1 2.7%	0 0	0 0	0 0	* 1.5%	0 0	0 0	0 0	1 0.8%	0 0
All sources of info	1 0.5%	0 0	1 0.9%	1 0.9%	0 0	0 0	1 1.9%	0 0	1 2.7%	0 0	0 0	0 0	* 1.5%	0 0	0 0	0 0	1 0.8%	0 0
preferred source of info	1 0.5%	0 0	1 0.9%	1 0.9%	0 0	0 0	1 1.9%	0 0	1 2.7%	0 0	0 0	0 0	* 1.5%	0 0	0 0	0 0	1 0.8%	0 0

Proportions/Means: Columns Tested (5% risk level) - A/B/D - C/D - E/F/G - H/I/J/K/L/M/N - P/Q
* small base; ** very small base (under 30) ineligible for sig testing

Table 415
Page 1778

Outsell/Digital Library Federation Study (2002)
Weighted Tables

TABLE 152, continued

S7D/E_14. Technical Reports SUMMARY TABLE

		RESPONDENT TYPE				INSTITUTION TYPE			DISCIPLINE									GENDER	
	TOTAL SAMPLE	FACULTY MEMBER	GRAD. STUDENT	FACULTY /GRAD	UNDER GRAD. STUDENT	PUBLIC	PRIVATE	LIBERAL ARTS	BIOLOGIAL SCIENCES	PHYSICAL SCIENCES /MATH	SOCIAL SCIENCES	ARTS AND HUMAN.	ENGI- NEERING	BUSINESS	LAW	UNDEC. MAJOR	MALE	FEMALE
		(A)	(B)	(C)	(D)	(E)	(F)	(G)	(H)	(I)	(J)	(K)	(L)	(M)	(N)		(P)	(Q)
Base - Use Technical Reports for coursework	235	0**	130	130	104*	115*	63*	57*	33*	41*	70*	21**	19*	44*	2**	6*	144	91*
Purchase from online bookstore (NET)	1 0.4%	0 0	1 0.7%	1 0.7%	0 0	0 0	1 1.4%	0 0	1 2.7%	0 0	0 0	0 0	0 0	0 0	0 0	0 0	1 0.6%	0 0
All sources of info	1 0.4%	0 0	1 0.7%	1 0.7%	0 0	0 0	1 1.4%	0 0	1 2.7%	0 0	0 0	0 0	0 0	0 0	0 0	0 0	1 0.6%	0 0
preferred source of info	1 0.4%	0 0	1 0.7%	1 0.7%	0 0	0 0	1 1.4%	0 0	1 2.7%	0 0	0 0	0 0	0 0	0 0	0 0	0 0	1 0.6%	0 0
Order from on demand document delivery service (NET)	1 0.4%	0 0	1 0.7%	1 0.7%	0 0	1 0.8%	0 0	0 0	1 2.7%	0 0	0 0	0 0	0 0	0 0	0 0	0 0	0 0	1 1.0%
All sources of info	1 0.4%	0 0	1 0.7%	1 0.7%	0 0	1 0.8%	0 0	0 0	1 2.7%	0 0	0 0	0 0	0 0	0 0	0 0	0 0	0 0	1 1.0%
preferred source of info	0 0	0 0	0 0	0 0	0 0	0 0	0 0	0 0	0 0	0 0	0 0	0 0	0 0	0 0	0 0	0 0	0 0	0 0
Access from course website (NET)	0 0	0 0	0 0	0 0	0 0	0 0	0 0	0 0	0 0	0 0	0 0	0 0	0 0	0 0	0 0	0 0	0 0	0 0
All sources of info	0 0	0 0	0 0	0 0	0 0	0 0	0 0	0 0	0 0	0 0	0 0	0 0	0 0	0 0	0 0	0 0	0 0	0 0
preferred source of info	0 0	0 0	0 0	0 0	0 0	0 0	0 0	0 0	0 0	0 0	0 0	0 0	0 0	0 0	0 0	0 0	0 0	0 0

Proportions/Means: Columns Tested (5% risk level) - A/B/D - C/D - E/F/G - H/I/J/K/L/M/N - P/Q
* small base; ** very small base (under 30) ineligible for sig testing

Table 415
Page 1779

Outsell/Digital Library Federation Study (2002)
Weighted Tables

TABLE 152, continued

S7D/E_14. Technical Reports SUMMARY TABLE

		RESPONDENT TYPE				INSTITUTION TYPE			DISCIPLINE									GENDER	
	TOTAL SAMPLE	FACULTY MEMBER	GRAD. STUDENT	FACULTY /GRAD	UNDER GRAD. STUDENT	PUBLIC	PRIVATE	LIBERAL ARTS	BIOLOGIAL SCIENCES	PHYSICAL SCIENCES /MATH	SOCIAL SCIENCES	ARTS AND HUMAN.	ENGI-NEERING	BUSINESS	LAW	UNDEC. MAJOR	MALE	FEMALE
		(A)	(B)	(C)	(D)	(E)	(F)	(G)	(H)	(I)	(J)	(K)	(L)	(M)	(N)		(P)	(Q)
Base - Use Technical Reports for coursework	235	0**	130	130	104*	115*	63*	57*	33*	41*	70*	21**	19*	44*	2**	6*	144	91*
Access book/journal/ journal article elsewhere online (NET)	0 0	0 0	0 0	0 0	0 0	0 0	0 0	0 0	0 0	0 0	0 0	0 0	0 0	0 0	0 0	0 0	0 0	0 0
All sources of info	0 0	0 0	0 0	0 0	0 0	0 0	0 0	0 0	0 0	0 0	0 0	0 0	0 0	0 0	0 0	0 0	0 0	0 0
preferred source of info	0 0	0 0	0 0	0 0	0 0	0 0	0 0	0 0	0 0	0 0	0 0	0 0	0 0	0 0	0 0	0 0	0 0	0 0
In class (NET)	0 0	0 0	0 0	0 0	0 0	0 0	0 0	0 0	0 0	0 0	0 0	0 0	0 0	0 0	0 0	0 0	0 0	0 0
All sources of info	0 0	0 0	0 0	0 0	0 0	0 0	0 0	0 0	0 0	0 0	0 0	0 0	0 0	0 0	0 0	0 0	0 0	0 0
preferred source of info	0 0	0 0	0 0	0 0	0 0	0 0	0 0	0 0	0 0	0 0	0 0	0 0	0 0	0 0	0 0	0 0	0 0	0 0
Dorm room (NET)	0 0	0 0	0 0	0 0	0 0	0 0	0 0	0 0	0 0	0 0	0 0	0 0	0 0	0 0	0 0	0 0	0 0	0 0
All sources of info	0 0	0 0	0 0	0 0	0 0	0 0	0 0	0 0	0 0	0 0	0 0	0 0	0 0	0 0	0 0	0 0	0 0	0 0
preferred source of info	0 0	0 0	0 0	0 0	0 .0	0 0	0 0	0 0	0 0	0 0	0 0	0 0	0 0	0 0	0 0	0 0	0 0	0 0

Proportions/Means: Columns Tested (5% risk level) - A/B/D - C/D - E/F/G - H/I/J/K/L/M/N - P/Q
* small base; ** very small base (under 30) ineligible for sig testing

Table 415
Page 1780

TABLE 152, continued

S7D/E_14. Technical Reports SUMMARY TABLE

		RESPONDENT TYPE				INSTITUTION TYPE			DISCIPLINE									GENDER	
	TOTAL SAMPLE	FACULTY MEMBER	GRAD. STUDENT	FACULTY /GRAD	UNDER GRAD. STUDENT	PUBLIC	PRIVATE	LIBERAL ARTS	BIOLOGIAL SCIENCES	PHYSICAL SCIENCES /MATH	SOCIAL SCIENCES	ARTS AND HUMAN.	ENGI-NEERING	BUSINESS	LAW	UNDEC. MAJOR	MALE	FEMALE
		(A)	(B)	(C)	(D)	(E)	(F)	(G)	(H)	(I)	(J)	(K)	(L)	(M)	(N)		(P)	(Q)
Base - Use Technical Reports for coursework	235	0**	130	130	104*	115*	63*	57*	33*	41*	70*	21**	19*	44*	2**	6*	144	91*
Personal Holdings (NET)	0 0	0 0	0 0	0 0	0 0	0 0	0 0	0 0	0 0	0 0	0 0	0 0	0 0	0 0	0 0	0 0	0 0	0 0
All sources of info	0 0	0 0	0 0	0 0	0 0	0 0	0 0	0 0	0 0	0 0	0 0	0 0	0 0	0 0	0 0	0 0	0 0	0 0
preferred source of info	0 0	0 0	0 0	0 0	0 0	0 0	0 0	0 0	0 0	0 0	0 0	0 0	0 0	0 0	0 0	0 0	0 0	0 0
Other (NET)	12 5.2%	0 0	6 4.5%	6 4.5%	6 6.1%	6 4.9%	2 2.8%	5 8.6%	3 8.1%	1 2.4%	4 5.4%	3 15.8%	1 3.1%	1 2.1%	0 0	0 0	9 6.5%	3 3.2%
All sources of info	12 5.2%	0 0	6 4.5%	6 4.5%	6 6.1%	6 4.9%	2 2.8%	5 8.6%	3 8.1%	1 2.4%	4 5.4%	3 15.8%	1 3.1%	1 2.1%	0 0	0 0	9 6.5%	3 3.2%
preferred source of info	3 1.5%	0 0	2 1.8%	2 1.8%	1 1.1%	3 2.2%	1 1.4%	0 0	1 2.7%	0 0	0 0	2 10.5%	* 1.5%	0 0	0 0	0 0	3 1.8%	1 1.0%
DK/Refused	5 2.0%	0 0	3 2.6%	3 2.6%	1 1.2%	3 2.9%	1 1.6%	* 0.5%	0 0	2 4.9%	2 2.7%	0 0	1 3.1%	0 0	* 10.0%	0 0	3 2.3%	1 1.4%

Proportions/Means: Columns Tested (5% risk level) - A/B/D - C/D - E/F/G - H/I/J/K/L/M/N - P/Q
* small base; ** very small base (under 30) ineligible for sig testing

Table 415
Page 1781

Outsell/Digital Library Federation Study (2002)
Weighted Tables

TABLE 153

S7sum_15. Pre-prints SUMMARY TABLE

		RESPONDENT TYPE				INSTITUTION TYPE			DISCIPLINE								GENDER	
	TOTAL SAMPLE	FACULTY MEMBER	GRAD. STUDENT	FACULTY /GRAD	UNDER GRAD. STUDENT	PUBLIC	PRIVATE	LIBERAL ARTS	BIOLOGIAL SCIENCES	PHYSICAL SCIENCES /MATH	SOCIAL SCIENCES	ARTS AND HUMAN.	ENGI-NEERING	BUSINESS	LAW	UNDEC. MAJOR	MALE	FEMALE
		(A)	(B)	(C)	(D)	(E)	(F)	(G)	(H)	(I)	(J)	(K)	(L)	(M)	(N)		(P)	(Q)
Base - Use Pre-prints for coursework	120*	0**	68*	68*	52*	61*	29**	30**	17**	19**	45**	10**	6**	18**	1**	4*	69*	51*
ONLINE	75 62.5%	0 0	41 60.0%	41 60.0%	34 66.0%	34 54.7%	19 64.2%	23 77.1%	13 78.9%	14 73.7%	23 50.0%	7 66.7%	3 45.5%	11 63.2%	1 50.0%	4 100.0%	40 57.3%	36 69.6%
Search engine (NET)	30 24.9%	0 0	12 18.0%	12 18.0%	18 34.0%	9 15.0%	4 13.9%	17 55.9%	4 21.1%	3 15.8%	11 25.0%	3 33.3%	1 18.2%	7 36.8%	0 0	1 25.0%	19 28.3%	10 20.3%
All sources of info	30 24.9%	0 0	12 18.0%	12 18.0%	18 34.0%	9 15.0%	4 13.9%	17 55.9%	4 21.1%	3 15.8%	11 25.0%	3 33.3%	1 18.2%	7 36.8%	0 0	1 25.0%	19 28.3%	10 20.3%
preferred source of info	17 14.3%	0 0	7 9.6%	7 9.6%	11 20.5%	6 10.2%	* 1.0%	11 35.5%	4 21.1%	0 0	8 16.7%	1 11.1%	1 18.2%	3 15.8%	0 0	1 25.0%	10 14.5%	7 13.9%
Internet searches (NET)	15 12.3%	0 0	5 7.2%	5 7.2%	10 19.0%	9 14.0%	3 10.7%	3 10.1%	4 21.1%	2 10.5%	6 12.5%	1 11.1%	1 9.1%	2 10.5%	0 0	0 0	8 11.8%	7 12.9%
All sources of info	15 12.3%	0 0	5 7.2%	5 7.2%	10 19.0%	9 14.0%	3 10.7%	3 10.1%	4 21.1%	2 10.5%	6 12.5%	1 11.1%	1 9.1%	2 10.5%	0 0	0 0	8 11.8%	7 12.9%
preferred source of info	7 5.6%	0 0	4 5.3%	4 5.3%	3 5.9%	5 7.9%	2 6.3%	0 0	4 21.1%	1 5.3%	0 0	0 0	* 4.5%	2 10.5%	0 0	0 0	3 4.5%	4 7.0%
Your own institution's web site (NET)	14 12.0%	0 0	7 10.2%	7 10.2%	7 14.3%	4 6.9%	5 17.5%	5 17.2%	0 0	4 21.1%	4 8.3%	2 22.2%	1 9.1%	3 15.8%	0 0	1 25.0%	8 12.1%	6 11.9%
All sources of info	14 12.0%	0 0	7 10.2%	7 10.2%	7 14.3%	4 6.9%	5 17.5%	5 17.2%	0 0	4 21.1%	4 8.3%	2 22.2%	1 9.1%	3 15.8%	0 0	1 25.0%	8 12.1%	6 11.9%

Proportions/Means: Columns Tested (5% risk level) - A/B/D - C/D - E/F/G - H/I/J/K/L/M/N - P/Q
* small base; ** very small base (under 30) ineligible for sig testing

Table 419
Page 1793

Outsell/Digital Library Federation Study (2002)
Weighted Tables

TABLE 153, continued

S7sum_15. Pre-prints SUMMARY TABLE

		RESPONDENT TYPE				INSTITUTION TYPE			DISCIPLINE								GENDER	
	TOTAL SAMPLE	FACULTY MEMBER	GRAD. STUDENT	FACULTY /GRAD	UNDER GRAD. STUDENT	PUBLIC	PRIVATE	LIBERAL ARTS	BIOLOGIAL SCIENCES	PHYSICAL SCIENCES /MATH	SOCIAL SCIENCES	ARTS AND HUMAN.	ENGI-NEERING	BUSINESS	LAW	UNDEC. MAJOR	MALE	FEMALE
		(A)	(B)	(C)	(D)	(E)	(F)	(G)	(H)	(I)	(J)	(K)	(L)	(M)	(N)		(P)	(Q)
Base - Use Pre-prints for coursework	120*	0**	68*	68*	52*	61*	29**	30**	17**	19**	45**	10**	6**	18**	1**	4*	69*	51*
preferred source of info	10	0	4	4	6	3	3	4	0	4	2	1	1	2	0	1	6	5
	8.7%	0	6.1%	6.1%	12.2%	5.4%	11.0%	13.4%	0	21.1%	4.2%	11.1%	9.1%	10.5%	0	25.0%	8.0%	9.7%
Online databases (NET)	14	0	12	12	2	8	5	1	2	5	4	0	0	2	*	1	6	8
	11.3%	0	17.0%	17.0%	3.7%	12.4%	17.0%	3.4%	10.5%	26.3%	8.3%	0	0	10.5%	16.7%	25.0%	8.5%	15.1%
All sources of info	14	0	12	12	2	8	5	1	2	5	4	0	0	2	*	1	6	8
	11.3%	0	17.0%	17.0%	3.7%	12.4%	17.0%	3.4%	10.5%	26.3%	8.3%	0	0	10.5%	16.7%	25.0%	8.5%	15.1%
preferred source of info	10	0	10	10	0	6	4	0	2	5	2	0	0	1	0	0	4	6
	8.0%	0	14.0%D	14.0%D	0	9.4%	13.2%	0	10.5%	26.3%	4.2%	0	0	5.3%	0	0	5.7%	11.1%
Web directory/ subject related web site (NET)	7	0	5	5	2	2	3	2	3	1	0	1	0	2	0	0	3	4
	5.5%	0	6.7%	6.7%	4.0%	2.9%	9.5%	6.9%	15.8%	5.3%	0	11.1%	0	10.5%	0	0	4.1%	7.5%
All sources of info	7	0	5	5	2	2	3	2	3	1	0	1	0	2	0	0	3	4
	5.5%	0	6.7%	6.7%	4.0%	2.9%	9.5%	6.9%	15.8%	5.3%	0	11.1%	0	10.5%	0	0	4.1%	7.5%
preferred source of info	4	0	2	2	2	0	2	2	2	0	0	1	0	1	0	0	2	2
	3.2%	0	2.6%	2.6%	4.0%	0	6.1%	6.9%	10.5%	0	0	11.1%	0	5.3%	0	0	2.6%	3.9%
Online reference service (NET)	4	0	3	3	1	1	3	0	0	2	0	2	0	0	*	0	1	3
	3.7%	0	4.8%	4.8%	2.2%	1.6%	11.8%	0	0	10.5%	0	22.2%	0	0	16.7%	0	1.7%	6.4%
All sources of info	4	0	3	3	1	1	3	0	0	2	0	2	0	0	*	0	1	3
	3.7%	0	4.8%	4.8%	2.2%	1.6%	11.8%	0	0	10.5%	0	22.2%	0	0	16.7%	0	1.7%	6.4%

Proportions/Means: Columns Tested (5% risk level) - A/B/D - C/D - E/F/G - H/I/J/K/L/M/N - P/Q
* small base; ** very small base (under 30) ineligible for sig testing

Table 419
Page 1794

Outsell/Digital Library Federation Study (2002)
Weighted Tables

TABLE 153, continued

S7sum_15. Pre-prints SUMMARY TABLE

		RESPONDENT TYPE				INSTITUTION TYPE			DISCIPLINE								GENDER	
	TOTAL SAMPLE	FACULTY MEMBER	GRAD. STUDENT	FACULTY /GRAD	UNDER GRAD. STUDENT	PUBLIC	PRIVATE	LIBERAL ARTS	BIOLOGIAL SCIENCES	PHYSICAL SCIENCES /MATH	SOCIAL SCIENCES	ARTS AND HUMAN.	ENGI-NEERING	BUSINESS	LAW	UNDEC. MAJOR	MALE	FEMALE
		(A)	(B)	(C)	(D)	(E)	(F)	(G)	(H)	(I)	(J)	(K)	(L)	(M)	(N)		(P)	(Q)
Base - Use Pre-prints for coursework	120*	0**	68*	68*	52*	61*	29**	30**	17**	19**	45**	10**	6**	18**	1**	4*	69*	51*
preferred source of info	1 0.9%	0 0	1 1.6%	1 1.6%	0 0	0 0	1 3.9%	0 0	0 0	0 0	0 0	1 11.1%	0 0	0 0	0 0	0 0	0 0	1 2.2%
Online library catalogues and finding aids (NET)	4 3.7%	0 0	3 4.5%	3 4.5%	1 2.5%	2 3.1%	1 4.2%	1 4.3%	1 5.3%	0 0	2 4.2%	0 0	* 4.5%	0 0	* 33.3%	1 25.0%	3 4.9%	1 2.0%
All sources of info	4 3.7%	0 0	3 4.5%	3 4.5%	1 2.5%	2 3.1%	1 4.2%	1 4.3%	1 5.3%	0 0	2 4.2%	0 0	* 4.5%	0 0	* 33.3%	1 25.0%	3 4.9%	1 2.0%
preferred source of info	4 3.5%	0 0	3 4.3%	3 4.3%	1 2.5%	2 3.1%	1 3.6%	1 4.3%	1 5.3%	0 0	2 4.2%	0 0	* 4.5%	0 0	* 16.7%	1 25.0%	3 4.7%	1 2.0%
Online abstracting and indexing services (NET)	2 1.8%	0 0	2 3.2%	2 3.2%	0 0	1 1.4%	1 4.5%	0 0	1 5.3%	1 5.3%	0 0	0 0	* 4.5%	0 0	0 0	0 0	1 1.9%	1 1.7%
All sources of info	2 1.8%	0 0	2 3.2%	2 3.2%	0 0	1 1.4%	1 4.5%	0 0	1 5.3%	1 5.3%	0 0	0 0	* 4.5%	0 0	0 0	0 0	1 1.9%	1 1.7%
preferred source of info	1 1.0%	0 0	1 1.7%	1 1.7%	0 0	1 1.4%	* 1.0%	0 0	1 5.3%	0 0	0 0	0 0	* 4.5%	0 0	0 0	0 0	* 0.4%	1 1.7%
Department web page (NET)	1 1.1%	0 0	1 1.9%	1 1.9%	0 0	1 1.6%	* 1.0%	0 0	0 0	1 5.3%	0 0	0 0	* 4.5%	0 0	0 0	0 0	1 1.9%	0 0
All sources of info	1 1.1%	0 0	1 1.9%	1 1.9%	0 0	1 1.6%	* 1.0%	0 0	0 0	1 5.3%	0 0	0 0	* 4.5%	0 0	0 0	0 0	1 1.9%	0 0

Proportions/Means: Columns Tested (5% risk level) - A/B/D - C/D - E/F/G - H/I/J/K/L/M/N - P/Q
* small base; ** very small base (under 30) ineligible for sig testing

Table 419
Page 1795

Outsell/Digital Library Federation Study (2002)
Weighted Tables

TABLE 153, continued

S7sum_15. Pre-prints SUMMARY TABLE

		RESPONDENT TYPE				INSTITUTION TYPE			DISCIPLINE								GENDER	
	TOTAL SAMPLE	FACULTY MEMBER	GRAD. STUDENT	FACULTY /GRAD	UNDER GRAD. STUDENT	PUBLIC	PRIVATE	LIBERAL ARTS	BIOLOGIAL SCIENCES	PHYSICAL SCIENCES /MATH	SOCIAL SCIENCES	ARTS AND HUMAN.	ENGI-NEERING	BUSINESS	LAW	UNDEC. MAJOR	MALE	FEMALE
		(A)	(B)	(C)	(D)	(E)	(F)	(G)	(H)	(I)	(J)	(K)	(L)	(M)	(N)		(P)	(Q)
Base - Use Pre-prints for coursework	120*	0**	68*	68*	52*	61*	29**	30**	17**	19**	45**	10**	6**	18**	1**	4*	69*	51*
preferred source of info	1 0.8%	0 0	1 1.5%	1 1.5%	0 0	1 1.6%	0 0	0 0	0 0	1 5.3%	0 0	0 0	0 0	0 0	0 0	0 0	1 1.4%	0 0
Online bookstore (NET)	* 0.2%	0 0	* 0.4%	* 0.4%	0 0	* 0.5%	0 0	0 0	0 0	0 0	0 0	0 0	* 4.5%	0 0	0 0	0 0	0 0	* 0.6%
All sources of info	* 0.2%	0 0	* 0.4%	* 0.4%	0 0	* 0.5%	0 0	0 0	0 0	0 0	0 0	0 0	* 4.5%	0 0	0 0	0 0	0 0	* 0.6%
preferred source of info	* 0.2%	0 0	* 0.4%	* 0.4%	0 0	* 0.5%	0 0	0 0	0 0	0 0	0 0	0 0	* 4.5%	0 0	0 0	0 0	0 0	* 0.6%
E-mail listservs (NET)	0 0	0 0	0 0	0 0	0 0	0 0	0 0	0 0	0 0	0 0	0 0	0 0	0 0	0 0	0 0	0 0	0 0	0 0
All sources of info	0 0	0 0	0 0	0 0	0 0	0 0	0 0	0 0	0 0	0 0	0 0	0 0	0 0	0 0	0 0	0 0	0 0	0 0
preferred source of info	0 0	0 0	0 0	0 0	0 0	0 0	0 0	0 0	0 0	0 0	0 0	0 0	0 0	0 0	0 0	0 0	0 0	0 0
Your own personal electronic library/files (NET)	0 0	0 0	0 0	0 0	0 0	0 0	0 0	0 0	0 0	0 0	0 0	0 0	0 0	0 0	0 0	0 0	0 0	0 0
All sources of info	0 0	0 0	0 0	0 0	0 0	0 0	0 0	0 0	0 0	0 0	0 0	0 0	0 0	0 0	0 0	0 0	0 0	0 0

Proportions/Means: Columns Tested (5% risk level) - A/B/D - C/D - E/F/G - H/I/J/K/L/M/N - P/Q
* small base; ** very small base (under 30) ineligible for sig testing

Table 419
Page 1796

Outsell/Digital Library Federation Study (2002)
Weighted Tables

TABLE 153, continued

S7sum_15. Pre-prints SUMMARY TABLE

		RESPONDENT TYPE				INSTITUTION TYPE			DISCIPLINE									GENDER	
	TOTAL SAMPLE	FACULTY MEMBER	GRAD. STUDENT	FACULTY /GRAD	UNDER GRAD. STUDENT	PUBLIC	PRIVATE	LIBERAL ARTS	BIOLOGIAL SCIENCES	PHYSICAL SCIENCES /MATH	SOCIAL SCIENCES	ARTS AND HUMAN.	ENGI-NEERING	BUSINESS	LAW	UNDEC. MAJOR	MALE	FEMALE
		(A)	(B)	(C)	(D)	(E)	(F)	(G)	(H)	(I)	(J)	(K)	(L)	(M)	(N)		(P)	(Q)
Base - Use Pre-prints for coursework	120*	0**	68*	68*	52*	61*	29**	30**	17**	19**	45**	10**	6**	18**	1**	4*	69*	51*
preferred source of info	0 0	0 0	0 0	0 0	0 0	0 0	0 0	0 0	0 0	0 0	0 0	0 0	0 0	0 0	0 0	0 0	0 0	0 0
PERSONAL ASSISTANCE	52 43.7%	0 0	26 38.1%	26 38.1%	26 51.1%	25 40.3%	11 38.5%	17 55.8%	4 26.3%	10 52.6%	21 45.8%	4 44.4%	3 45.5%	7 42.1%	1 50.0%	2 50.0%	31 44.7%	22 42.2%
Faculty members inside your institution (NET)	34 28.0%	0 0	19 27.7%	19 27.7%	15 28.3%	18 28.8%	9 31.0%	7 23.5%	4 26.3%	6 31.6%	11 25.0%	4 44.4%	3 40.9%	5 26.3%	* 16.7%	0 0	15 21.9%	18 36.3%
All sources of info	34 28.0%	0 0	19 27.7%	19 27.7%	15 28.3%	18 28.8%	9 31.0%	7 23.5%	4 26.3%	6 31.6%	11 25.0%	4 44.4%	3 40.9%	5 26.3%	* 16.7%	0 0	15 21.9%	18 36.3%
preferred source of info	21 17.2%	0 0	15 21.7%	15 21.7%	6 11.3%	13 21.0%	6 20.2%	2 6.5%	4 21.1%	4 21.1%	6 12.5%	2 22.2%	2 36.4%	3 15.8%	* 16.7%	0 0	11 16.4%	9 18.4%
A librarian in your institution (NET)	24 20.2%	0 0	5 7.4%	5 7.4%	19 37.1%B C	11 17.2%	* 0.6%	14 45.5%	0 0	2 10.5%	15 33.3%	1 11.1%	0 0	4 21.1%	* 33.3%	2 50.0%	13 19.5%	11 21.1%
All sources of info	24 20.2%	0 0	5 7.4%	5 7.4%	19 37.1%B C	11 17.2%	* 0.6%	14 45.5%	0 0	2 10.5%	15 33.3%	1 11.1%	0 0	4 21.1%	* 33.3%	2 50.0%	13 19.5%	11 21.1%
preferred source of info	13 11.2%	0 0	5 7.2%	5 7.2%	9 16.5%	7 11.1%	0 0	7 22.4%	0 0	1 5.3%	9 20.8%	0 0	0 0	2 10.5%	* 16.7%	1 25.0%	12 16.7%	2 3.7%

Proportions/Means: Columns Tested (5% risk level) - A/B/D - C/D - E/F/G - H/I/J/K/L/M/N - P/Q
* small base; ** very small base (under 30) ineligible for sig testing

Table 419
Page 1797

TABLE 153, continued

S7sum_15. Pre-prints SUMMARY TABLE

	TOTAL SAMPLE	RESPONDENT TYPE FACULTY MEMBER	 GRAD. STUDENT	 FACULTY /GRAD	 UNDER GRAD. STUDENT	INSTITUTION TYPE PUBLIC	 PRIVATE	 LIBERAL ARTS	DISCIPLINE BIOLOGIAL SCIENCES	 PHYSICAL SCIENCES /MATH	 SOCIAL SCIENCES	 ARTS AND HUMAN.	 ENGI-NEERING	 BUSINESS	 LAW	 UNDEC. MAJOR	GENDER MALE	 FEMALE
		(A)	(B)	(C)	(D)	(E)	(F)	(G)	(H)	(I)	(J)	(K)	(L)	(M)	(N)		(P)	(Q)
Base - Use Pre-prints for coursework	120*	0**	68*	68*	52*	61*	29**	30**	17**	19**	45**	10**	6**	18**	1**	4*	69*	51*
Other students inside your institution (NET)	8 6.9%	0 0	4 6.2%	4 6.2%	4 7.9%	2 3.5%	4 14.6%	2 6.3%	0 0	3 15.8%	4 8.3%	0 0	1 9.1%	1 5.3%	0 0	0 0	4 6.1%	4 7.9%
All sources of info	8 6.9%	0 0	4 6.2%	4 6.2%	4 7.9%	2 3.5%	4 14.6%	2 6.3%	0 0	3 15.8%	4 8.3%	0 0	1 9.1%	1 5.3%	0 0	0 0	4 6.1%	4 7.9%
preferred source of info	3 2.1%	0 0	2 3.2%	2 3.2%	* 0.6%	* 0.5%	2 7.7%	0 0	0 0	1 5.3%	0 0	0 0	1 9.1%	1 5.3%	0 0	0 0	2 3.2%	* 0.6%
Faculty members outside your institution (NET)	0 0	0 0	0 0	0 0	0 0	0 0	0 0	0 0	0 0	0 0	0 0	0 0	0 0	0 0	0 0	0 0	0 0	0 0
All sources of info	0 0	0 0	0 0	0 0	0 0	0 0	0 0	0 0	0 0	0 0	0 0	0 0	0 0	0 0	0 0	0 0	0 0	0 0
preferred source of info	0 0	0 0	0 0	0 0	0 0	0 0	0 0	0 0	0 0	0 0	0 0	0 0	0 0	0 0	0 0	0 0	0 0	0 0
Another institution's librarian (NET)	0 0	0 0	0 0	0 0	0 0	0 0	0 0	0 0	0 0	0 0	0 0	0 0	0 0	0 0	0 0	0 0	0 0	0 0
All sources of info	0 0	0 0	0 0	0 0	0 0	0 0	0 0	0 0	0 0	0 0	0 0	0 0	0 0	0 0	0 0	0 0	0 0	0 0
preferred source of info	0 0	0 0	0 0	0 0	0 0	0 0	0 0	0 0	0 0	0 0	0 0	0 0	0 0	0 0	0 0	0 0	0 0	0 0

Proportions/Means: Columns Tested (5% risk level) - A/B/D - C/D - E/F/G - H/I/J/K/L/M/N - P/Q
* small base; ** very small base (under 30) ineligible for sig testing

Table 419
Page 1798

Outsell/Digital Library Federation Study (2002)
Weighted Tables

TABLE 153, continued

S7sum_15. Pre-prints SUMMARY TABLE

	TOTAL SAMPLE	RESPONDENT TYPE: FACULTY MEMBER	GRAD. STUDENT	FACULTY /GRAD	UNDER GRAD. STUDENT	INSTITUTION TYPE: PUBLIC	PRIVATE	LIBERAL ARTS	DISCIPLINE: BIOLOGIAL SCIENCES	PHYSICAL SCIENCES /MATH	SOCIAL SCIENCES	ARTS AND HUMAN.	ENGI-NEERING	BUSINESS	LAW	UNDEC. MAJOR	GENDER: MALE	FEMALE
		(A)	(B)	(C)	(D)	(E)	(F)	(G)	(H)	(I)	(J)	(K)	(L)	(M)	(N)		(P)	(Q)
Base - Use Pre-prints for coursework	120*	0**	68*	68*	52*	61*	29**	30**	17**	19**	45**	10**	6**	18**	1**	4*	69*	51*
Other students outside your institution (NET)	0 0	0 0	0 0	0 0	0 0	0 0	0 0	0 0	0 0	0 0	0 0	0 0	0 0	0 0	0 0	0 0	0 0	0 0
All sources of info	0 0	0 0	0 0	0 0	0 0	0 0	0 0	0 0	0 0	0 0	0 0	0 0	0 0	0 0	0 0	0 0	0 0	0 0
preferred source of info	0 0	0 0	0 0	0 0	0 0	0 0	0 0	0 0	0 0	0 0	0 0	0 0	0 0	0 0	0 0	0 0	0 0	0 0
Professional meetings (NET)	0 0	0 0	0 0	0 0	0 0	0 0	0 0	0 0	0 0	0 0	0 0	0 0	0 0	0 0	0 0	0 0	0 0	0 0
All sources of info	0 0	0 0	0 0	0 0	0 0	0 0	0 0	0 0	0 0	0 0	0 0	0 0	0 0	0 0	0 0	0 0	0 0	0 0
preferred source of info	0 0	0 0	0 0	0 0	0 0	0 0	0 0	0 0	0 0	0 0	0 0	0 0	0 0	0 0	0 0	0 0	0 0	0 0
LIBRARY FACILITIES/ PRINT	29 24.1%	0 0	16 23.3%	16 23.3%	13 25.0%	9 15.5%	6 22.4%	13 43.5%	2 10.5%	5 26.3%	11 25.0%	3 33.3%	1 18.2%	5 26.3%	1 66.7%	1 25.0%	16 22.7%	13 26.0%
Campus library (NET)	27 22.3%	0 0	14 20.2%	14 20.2%	13 25.0%	7 11.9%	6 22.4%	13 43.5%	2 10.5%	5 26.3%	9 20.8%	3 33.3%	1 13.6%	5 26.3%	1 66.7%	1 25.0%	14 19.9%	13 25.4%
All sources of info	27 22.3%	0 0	14 20.2%	14 20.2%	13 25.0%	7 11.9%	6 22.4%	13 43.5%	2 10.5%	5 26.3%	9 20.8%	3 33.3%	1 13.6%	5 26.3%	1 66.7%	1 25.0%	14 19.9%	13 25.4%

Proportions/Means: Columns Tested (5% risk level) - A/B/D - C/D - E/F/G - H/I/J/K/L/M/N - P/Q
* small base; ** very small base (under 30) ineligible for sig testing

Table 419
Page 1799

Outsell/Digital Library Federation Study (2002)
Weighted Tables

TABLE 153, continued

S7sum_15. Pre-prints SUMMARY TABLE

		RESPONDENT TYPE				INSTITUTION TYPE			DISCIPLINE									GENDER	
	TOTAL SAMPLE	FACULTY MEMBER	GRAD. STUDENT	FACULTY /GRAD	UNDER GRAD. STUDENT	PUBLIC	PRIVATE	LIBERAL ARTS	BIOLOGIAL SCIENCES	PHYSICAL SCIENCES /MATH	SOCIAL SCIENCES	ARTS AND HUMAN.	ENGI- NEERING	BUSINESS	LAW	UNDEC. MAJOR	MALE	FEMALE
		(A)	(B)	(C)	(D)	(E)	(F)	(G)	(H)	(I)	(J)	(K)	(L)	(M)	(N)		(P)	(Q)
Base - Use Pre-prints for coursework	120*	0**	68*	68*	52*	61*	29**	30**	17**	19**	45**	10**	6**	18**	1**	4*	69*	51*
preferred source of info	12 9.9%	0 0	9 12.7%	9 12.7%	3 6.3%	3 5.2%	5 19.0%	3 10.9%	0 0	2 10.5%	6 12.5%	2 22.2%	1 9.1%	1 5.3%	1 50.0%	0 0	8 11.0%	4 8.5%
Your own personal physical library/ files/bookshelves (NET)	2 1.6%	0 0	2 2.7%	2 2.7%	0 0	2 3.1%	0 0	0 0	0 0	0 0	2 4.2%	0 0	0 0	0 0	0 0	0 0	2 2.7%	0 0
All sources of info	2 1.6%	0 0	2 2.7%	2 2.7%	0 0	2 3.1%	0 0	0 0	0 0	0 0	2 4.2%	0 0	0 0	0 0	0 0	0 0	2 2.7%	0 0
preferred source of info	0 0	0 0	0 0	0 0	0 0	0 0	0 0	0 0	0 0	0 0	0 0	0 0	0 0	0 0	0 0	0 0	0 0	0 0
Another library (NET)	1 1.2%	0 0	* 0.4%	* 0.4%	1 2.2%	* 0.5%	0 0	1 3.8%	0 0	0 0	0 0	1 11.1%	* 4.5%	0 0	0 0	0 0	* 0.4%	1 2.2%
All sources of info	1 1.2%	0 0	* 0.4%	* 0.4%	1 2.2%	* 0.5%	0 0	1 3.8%	0 0	0 0	0 0	1 11.1%	* 4.5%	0 0	0 0	0 0	* 0.4%	1 2.2%
preferred source of info	0 0	0 0	0 0	0 0	0 0	0 0	0 0	0 0	0 0	0 0	0 0	0 0	0 0	0 0	0 0	0 0	0 0	0 0
Physical bookstore (NET)	* 0.2%	0 0	* 0.4%	* 0.4%	0 0	* 0.5%	0 0	0 0	0 0	0 0	0 0	0 0	* 4.5%	0 0	0 0	0 0	0 0	* 0.6%
All sources of info	* 0.2%	0 0	* 0.4%	* 0.4%	0 0	* 0.5%	0 0	0 0	0 0	0 0	0 0	0 0	* 4.5%	0 0	0 0	0 0	0 0	* 0.6%

Proportions/Means: Columns Tested (5% risk level) - A/B/D - C/D - E/F/G - H/I/J/K/L/M/N - P/Q
* small base; ** very small base (under 30) ineligible for sig testing

Table 419
Page 1800

Outsell/Digital Library Federation Study (2002)
Weighted Tables

TABLE 153, continued

S7sum_15. Pre-prints SUMMARY TABLE

		RESPONDENT TYPE				INSTITUTION TYPE			DISCIPLINE								GENDER	
	TOTAL SAMPLE	FACULTY MEMBER	GRAD. STUDENT	FACULTY /GRAD	UNDER GRAD. STUDENT	PUBLIC	PRIVATE	LIBERAL ARTS	BIOLOGIAL SCIENCES	PHYSICAL SCIENCES /MATH	SOCIAL SCIENCES	ARTS AND HUMAN.	ENGI-NEERING	BUSINESS	LAW	UNDEC. MAJOR	MALE	FEMALE
		(A)	(B)	(C)	(D)	(E)	(F)	(G)	(H)	(I)	(J)	(K)	(L)	(M)	(N)		(P)	(Q)
Base - Use Pre-prints for coursework	120*	0**	68*	68*	52*	61*	29**	30**	17**	19**	45**	10**	6**	18**	1**	4*	69*	51*
preferred source of info	0 0	0 0	0 0	0 0	0 0	0 0	0 0	0 0	0 0	0 0	0 0	0 0	0 0	0 0	0 0	0 0	0 0	0 0
References cited in books or journal articles (NET)	0 0	0 0	0 0	0 0	0 0	0 0	0 0	0 0	0 0	0 0	0 0	0 0	0 0	0 0	0 0	0 0	0 0	0 0
All sources of info	0 0	0 0	0 0	0 0	0 0	0 0	0 0	0 0	0 0	0 0	0 0	0 0	0 0	0 0	0 0	0 0	0 0	0 0
preferred source of info	0 0	0 0	0 0	0 0	0 0	0 0	0 0	0 0	0 0	0 0	0 0	0 0	0 0	0 0	0 0	0 0	0 0	0 0
Printed library catalogues and finding aids (NET)	0 0	0 0	0 0	0 0	0 0	0 0	0 0	0 0	0 0	0 0	0 0	0 0	0 0	0 0	0 0	0 0	0 0	0 0
All sources of info	0 0	0 0	0 0	0 0	0 0	0 0	0 0	0 0	0 0	0 0	0 0	0 0	0 0	0 0	0 0	0 0	0 0	0 0
preferred source of info	0 0	0 0	0 0	0 0	0 0	0 0	0 0	0 0	0 0	0 0	0 0	0 0	0 0	0 0	0 0	0 0	0 0	0 0
Personal subscriptions to newspapers, magazines and journals (NET)	0 0	0 0	0 0	0 0	0 0	0 0	0 0	0 0	0 0	0 0	0 0	0 0	0 0	0 0	0 0	0 0	0 0	0 0

Proportions/Means: Columns Tested (5% risk level) - A/B/D - C/D - E/F/G - H/I/J/K/L/M/N - P/Q
* small base; ** very small base (under 30) ineligible for sig testing

Table 419
Page 1801

Outsell/Digital Library Federation Study (2002)
Weighted Tables

TABLE 153, continued

S7sum_15. Pre-prints SUMMARY TABLE

	TOTAL SAMPLE	RESPONDENT TYPE: FACULTY MEMBER	GRAD. STUDENT	FACULTY /GRAD	UNDER GRAD. STUDENT	INSTITUTION TYPE: PUBLIC	PRIVATE	LIBERAL ARTS	DISCIPLINE: BIOLOGIAL SCIENCES	PHYSICAL SCIENCES /MATH	SOCIAL SCIENCES	ARTS AND HUMAN.	ENGI-NEERING	BUSINESS	LAW	UNDEC. MAJOR	GENDER: MALE	FEMALE
		(A)	(B)	(C)	(D)	(E)	(F)	(G)	(H)	(I)	(J)	(K)	(L)	(M)	(N)		(P)	(Q)
Base - Use Pre-prints for coursework	120*	0**	68*	68*	52*	61*	29**	30**	17**	19**	45**	10**	6**	18**	1**	4*	69*	51*
All sources of info	0 0	0 0	0 0	0 0	0 0	0 0	0 0	0 0	0 0	0 0	0 0	0 0	0 0	0 0	0 0	0 0	0 0	0 0
preferred source of info	0 0	0 0	0 0	0 0	0 0	0 0	0 0	0 0	0 0	0 0	0 0	0 0	0 0	0 0	0 0	0 0	0 0	0 0
Printed abstracting and indexing services (NET)	0 0	0 0	0 0	0 0	0 0	0 0	0 0	0 0	0 0	0 0	0 0	0 0	0 0	0 0	0 0	0 0	0 0	0 0
All sources of info	0 0	0 0	0 0	0 0	0 0	0 0	0 0	0 0	0 0	0 0	0 0	0 0	0 0	0 0	0 0	0 0	0 0	0 0
preferred source of info	0 0	0 0	0 0	0 0	0 0	0 0	0 0	0 0	0 0	0 0	0 0	0 0	0 0	0 0	0 0	0 0	0 0	0 0
Other (NET)	11 8.9%	0 0	7 9.8%	7 9.8%	4 7.6%	7 10.6%	2 7.7%	2 6.3%	1 5.3%	0 0	6 12.5%	2 22.2%	0 0	2 10.5%	0 0	0 0	5 6.8%	6 11.6%
All sources of info	9 7.3%	0 0	5 7.1%	5 7.1%	4 7.6%	5 7.6%	2 7.7%	2 6.3%	0 0	0 0	6 12.5%	2 22.2%	0 0	1 5.3%	0 0	0 0	4 5.5%	5 9.9%
preferred source of info	8 6.4%	0 0	6 8.1%	6 8.1%	2 4.0%	7 10.6%	1 3.9%	0 0	1 5.3%	0 0	4 8.3%	1 11.1%	0 0	2 10.5%	0 0	0 0	3 4.1%	5 9.4%
Online (unspecified)	4 3.1%	0 0	0 0	0 0	4 7.3%BC	4 6.1%	0 0	0 0	0 0	0 0	4 8.3%	0 0	0 0	0 0	0 0	0 0	2 2.7%	2 3.7%

Proportions/Means: Columns Tested (5% risk level) - A/B/D - C/D - E/F/G - H/I/J/K/L/M/N - P/Q
* small base; ** very small base (under 30) ineligible for sig testing

Table 419
Page 1802

Outsell/Digital Library Federation Study (2002)
Weighted Tables

TABLE 153, continued

S7sum_15. Pre-prints SUMMARY TABLE

		RESPONDENT TYPE				INSTITUTION TYPE			DISCIPLINE									GENDER	
	TOTAL SAMPLE	FACULTY MEMBER	GRAD. STUDENT	FACULTY /GRAD	UNDER GRAD. STUDENT	PUBLIC	PRIVATE	LIBERAL ARTS	BIOLOGIAL SCIENCES	PHYSICAL SCIENCES /MATH	SOCIAL SCIENCES	ARTS AND HUMAN.	ENGI-NEERING	BUSINESS	LAW	UNDEC. MAJOR	MALE	FEMALE
		(A)	(B)	(C)	(D)	(E)	(F)	(G)	(H)	(I)	(J)	(K)	(L)	(M)	(N)		(P)	(Q)
Base - Use Pre-prints for coursework	120*	0**	68*	68*	52*	61*	29**	30**	17**	19**	45**	10**	6**	18**	1**	4*	69*	51*
All sources of info	4 3.1%	0 0	0 0	0 0	4 7.3%BC	4 6.1%	0 0	0 0	0 0	0 0	4 8.3%	0 0	0 0	0 0	0 0	0 0	2 2.7%	2 3.7%
preferred source of info	4 3.1%	0 0	0 0	0 0	4 7.3%BC	4 6.1%	0 0	0 0	0 0	0 0	4 8.3%	0 0	0 0	0 0	0 0	0 0	2 2.7%	2 3.7%
E-journals	0 0	0 0	0 0	0 0	0 0	0 0	0 0	0 0	0 0	0 0	0 0	0 0	0 0	0 0	0 0	0 0	0 0	0 0
All sources of info	0 0	0 0	0 0	0 0	0 0	0 0	0 0	0 0	0 0	0 0	0 0	0 0	0 0	0 0	0 0	0 0	0 0	0 0
preferred source of info	0 0	0 0	0 0	0 0	0 0	0 0	0 0	0 0	0 0	0 0	0 0	0 0	0 0	0 0	0 0	0 0	0 0	0 0
DK/Refused	5 3.9%	0 0	0 0	0 0	5 9.1%BC	4 6.1%	1 3.2%	0 0	0 0	0 0	4 8.3%	0 0	0 0	1 5.3%	0 0	0 0	3 4.1%	2 3.7%

Proportions/Means: Columns Tested (5% risk level) - A/B/D - C/D - E/F/G - H/I/J/K/L/M/N - P/Q
* small base; ** very small base (under 30) ineligible for sig testing

Table 419
Page 1803

Outsell/Digital Library Federation Study (2002)
Weighted Tables

TABLE 154

S7D/E_15. Pre-prints SUMMARY TABLE

		RESPONDENT TYPE				INSTITUTION TYPE			DISCIPLINE								GENDER	
	TOTAL SAMPLE	FACULTY MEMBER	GRAD. STUDENT	FACULTY /GRAD	UNDER GRAD. STUDENT	PUBLIC	PRIVATE	LIBERAL ARTS	BIOLOGIAL SCIENCES	PHYSICAL SCIENCES /MATH	SOCIAL SCIENCES	ARTS AND HUMAN.	ENGI- NEERING	BUSINESS	LAW	UNDEC. MAJOR	MALE	FEMALE
		(A)	(B)	(C)	(D)	(E)	(F)	(G)	(H)	(I)	(J)	(K)	(L)	(M)	(N)		(P)	(Q)
Base - Use Pre-prints for coursework	120*	0**	68*	68*	52*	61*	29**	30**	17**	19**	45**	10**	6**	18**	1**	4*	69*	51*
Borrow from or use in campus library (NET)	67 56.0%	0 0	30 44.0%	30 44.0%	37 71.9%B C	27 44.3%	16 56.6%	24 79.4%	4 21.1%	13 68.4%	28 62.5%	3 33.3%	4 63.6%	11 63.2%	1 83.3%	3 75.0%	41 59.3%	26 51.5%
All sources of info	67 56.0%	0 0	30 44.0%	30 44.0%	37 71.9%B C	27 44.3%	16 56.6%	24 79.4%	4 21.1%	13 68.4%	28 62.5%	3 33.3%	4 63.6%	11 63.2%	1 83.3%	3 75.0%	41 59.3%	26 51.5%
preferred source of info	51 42.2%	0 0	23 34.3%	23 34.3%	27 52.7%	21 34.7%	13 46.7%	16 53.4%	3 15.8%	10 52.6%	21 45.8%	2 22.2%	3 45.5%	9 52.6%	1 83.3%	2 50.0%	33 47.4%	18 35.1%
Access online (NET)	53 44.3%	0 0	30 43.2%	30 43.2%	24 45.7%	31 49.8%	11 37.3%	12 39.7%	11 63.2%	8 42.1%	17 37.5%	6 55.6%	3 50.0%	7 36.8%	* 33.3%	2 50.0%	24 35.3%	29 56.4%P
All sources of info	53 44.3%	0 0	30 43.2%	30 43.2%	24 45.7%	31 49.8%	11 37.3%	12 39.7%	11 63.2%	8 42.1%	17 37.5%	6 55.6%	3 50.0%	7 36.8%	* 33.3%	2 50.0%	24 35.3%	29 56.4%P
preferred source of info	44 37.0%	0 0	27 39.8%	27 39.8%	17 33.2%	25 41.4%	10 34.7%	9 30.0%	10 57.9%	6 31.6%	15 33.3%	4 44.4%	2 36.4%	5 26.3%	* 16.7%	2 50.0%	21 30.0%	24 46.3%
Faculty (NET)	17 14.3%	0 0	13 19.2%	13 19.2%	4 7.9%	8 12.9%	6 22.1%	3 9.7%	4 26.3%	3 15.8%	6 12.5%	1 11.1%	1 18.2%	2 10.5%	0 0	0 0	12 17.0%	5 10.7%
All sources of info	17 14.3%	0 0	13 19.2%	13 19.2%	4 7.9%	8 12.9%	6 22.1%	3 9.7%	4 26.3%	3 15.8%	6 12.5%	1 11.1%	1 18.2%	2 10.5%	0 0	0 0	12 17.0%	5 10.7%
preferred source of info	15 12.8%	0 0	12 17.7%	12 17.7%	3 6.2%	7 11.4%	5 18.6%	3 9.7%	4 21.1%	2 10.5%	6 12.5%	1 11.1%	1 18.2%	2 10.5%	0 0	0 0	11 15.5%	5 9.0%

Proportions/Means: Columns Tested (5% risk level) - A/B/D - C/D - E/F/G - H/I/J/K/L/M/N - P/Q
* small base; ** very small base (under 30) ineligible for sig testing

Table 422
Page 1810

Outsell/Digital Library Federation Study (2002)
Weighted Tables

TABLE 154, continued

S7D/E_15. Pre-prints SUMMARY TABLE

		RESPONDENT TYPE				INSTITUTION TYPE			DISCIPLINE									GENDER	
	TOTAL SAMPLE	FACULTY MEMBER	GRAD. STUDENT	FACULTY /GRAD	UNDER GRAD. STUDENT	PUBLIC	PRIVATE	LIBERAL ARTS	BIOLOGIAL SCIENCES	PHYSICAL SCIENCES /MATH	SOCIAL SCIENCES	ARTS AND HUMAN.	ENGI-NEERING	BUSINESS	LAW	UNDEC. MAJOR	MALE	FEMALE
		(A)	(B)	(C)	(D)	(E)	(F)	(G)	(H)	(I)	(J)	(K)	(L)	(M)	(N)		(P)	(Q)
Base - Use Pre-prints for coursework	120*	0**	68*	68*	52*	61*	29**	30**	17**	19**	45**	10**	6**	18**	1**	4*	69*	51*
Purchase from physical book store (NET)	4 3.2%	0 0	1 1.3%	1 1.3%	3 5.8%	2 3.3%	0 0	2 6.3%	1 5.3%	0 0	2 4.2%	1 11.1%	0 0	0 0	0 0	0 0	4 5.6%	0 0
All sources of info	4 3.2%	0 0	1 1.3%	1 1.3%	3 5.8%	2 3.3%	0 0	2 6.3%	1 5.3%	0 0	2 4.2%	1 11.1%	0 0	0 0	0 0	0 0	4 5.6%	0 0
preferred source of info	1 0.9%	0 0	0 0	0 0	1 2.2%	1 1.8%	0 0	0 0	0 0	0 0	0 0	1 11.1%	0 0	0 0	0 0	0 0	1 1.6%	0 0
Borrow from or use in other libraries (NET)	3 2.6%	0 0	* 0.4%	* 0.4%	3 5.5%	2 3.5%	0 0	1 3.1%	0 0	0 0	2 4.2%	0 0	* 4.5%	1 5.3%	0 0	0 0	1 1.8%	2 3.7%
All sources of info	3 2.6%	0 0	* 0.4%	* 0.4%	3 5.5%	2 3.5%	0 0	1 3.1%	0 0	0 0	2 4.2%	0 0	* 4.5%	1 5.3%	0 0	0 0	1 1.8%	2 3.7%
preferred source of info	1 0.8%	0 0	0 0	0 0	1 1.8%	0 0	0 0	1 3.1%	0 0	0 0	0 0	0 0	0 0	1 5.3%	0 0	0 0	1 1.3%	0 0
In class (NET)	2 1.6%	0 0	2 2.7%	2 2.7%	0 0	2 3.1%	0 0	0 0	0 0	0 0	2 4.2%	0 0	0 0	0 0	0 0	0 0	2 2.7%	0 0
All sources of info	2 1.6%	0 0	2 2.7%	2 2.7%	0 0	2 3.1%	0 0	0 0	0 0	0 0	2 4.2%	0 0	0 0	0 0	0 0	0 0	2 2.7%	0 0
preferred source of info	2 1.6%	0 0	2 2.7%	2 2.7%	0 ·0	2 3.1%	0 0	0 0	0 0	0 0	2 4.2%	0 0	0 0	0 0	0 0	0 0	2 2.7%	0 0

Proportions/Means: Columns Tested (5% risk level) - A/B/D - C/D - E/F/G - H/I/J/K/L/M/N - P/Q
* small base; ** very small base (under 30) ineligible for sig testing

Table 422
Page 1811

Outsell/Digital Library Federation Study (2002)
Weighted Tables

TABLE 154, continued

S7D/E_15. Pre-prints SUMMARY TABLE

		RESPONDENT TYPE				INSTITUTION TYPE			DISCIPLINE								GENDER	
	TOTAL SAMPLE	FACULTY MEMBER	GRAD. STUDENT	FACULTY /GRAD	UNDER GRAD. STUDENT	PUBLIC	PRIVATE	LIBERAL ARTS	BIOLOGIAL SCIENCES	PHYSICAL SCIENCES /MATH	SOCIAL SCIENCES	ARTS AND HUMAN.	ENGI- NEERING	BUSINESS	LAW	UNDEC. MAJOR	MALE	FEMALE
		(A)	(B)	(C)	(D)	(E)	(F)	(G)	(H)	(I)	(J)	(K)	(L)	(M)	(N)		(P)	(Q)
Base - Use Pre-prints for coursework	120*	0**	68*	68*	52*	61*	29**	30**	17**	19**	45**	10**	6**	18**	1**	4*	69*	51*
Interlibrary loan (NET)	1	0	1	1	0	1	0	0	1	0	0	0	0	0	0	0	1	0
	0.7%	0	1.3%	1.3%	0	1.4%	0	0	5.3%	0	0	0	0	0	0	0	1.3%	0
All sources of info	1	0	1	1	0	1	0	0	1	0	0	0	0	0	0	0	1	0
	0.7%	0	1.3%	1.3%	0	1.4%	0	0	5.3%	0	0	0	0	0	0	0	1.3%	0
preferred source of info	0	0	0	0	0	0	0	0	0	0	0	0	0	0	0	0	0	0
	0	0	0	0	0	0	0	0	0	0	0	0	0	0	0	0	0	0
Purchase from online bookstore (NET)	1	0	1	1	0	1	0	0	1	0	0	0	0	0	0	0	1	0
	0.7%	0	1.3%	1.3%	0	1.4%	0	0	5.3%	0	0	0	0	0	0	0	1.3%	0
All sources of info	1	0	1	1	0	1	0	0	1	0	0	0	0	0	0	0	1	0
	0.7%	0	1.3%	1.3%	0	1.4%	0	0	5.3%	0	0	0	0	0	0	0	1.3%	0
preferred source of info	0	0	0	0	0	0	0	0	0	0	0	0	0	0	0	0	0	0
	0	0	0	0	0	0	0	0	0	0	0	0	0	0	0	0	0	0
Colleagues (NET)	1	0	1	1	0	0	1	0	1	0	0	0	0	0	0	0	1	0
	0.7%	0	1.3%	1.3%	0	0	3.0%	0	5.3%	0	0	0	0	0	0	0	1.3%	0
All sources of info	1	0	1	1	0	0	1	0	1	0	0	0	0	0	0	0	1	0
	0.7%	0	1.3%	1.3%	0	0	3.0%	0	5.3%	0	0	0	0	0	0	0	1.3%	0
preferred source of info	0	0	0	0	0	0	0	0	0	0	0	0	0	0	0	0	0	0
	0	0	0	0	0	0	0	0	0	0	0	0	0	0	0	0	0	0

Proportions/Means: Columns Tested (5% risk level) - A/B/D - C/D - E/F/G - H/I/J/K/L/M/N - P/Q
* small base; ** very small base (under 30) ineligible for sig testing

Table 422
Page 1812

TABLE 154, continued

S7D/E_15. Pre-prints SUMMARY TABLE

		RESPONDENT TYPE				INSTITUTION TYPE			DISCIPLINE								GENDER	
	TOTAL SAMPLE	FACULTY MEMBER	GRAD. STUDENT	FACULTY /GRAD	UNDER GRAD. STUDENT	PUBLIC	PRIVATE	LIBERAL ARTS	BIOLOGIAL SCIENCES	PHYSICAL SCIENCES /MATH	SOCIAL SCIENCES	ARTS AND HUMAN.	ENGI-NEERING	BUSINESS	LAW	UNDEC. MAJOR	MALE	FEMALE
		(A)	(B)	(C)	(D)	(E)	(F)	(G)	(H)	(I)	(J)	(K)	(L)	(M)	(N)		(P)	(Q)
Base - Use Pre-prints for coursework	120*	0**	68*	68*	52*	61*	29**	30**	17**	19**	45**	10**	6**	18**	1**	4*	69*	51*
Order from on demand document delivery service (NET)	1 0.7%	0 0	1 1.3%	1 1.3%	0 0	1 1.4%	0 0	0 0	1 5.3%	0 0	0 0	0 0	0 0	0 0	0 0	0 0	0 0	1 1.7%
All sources of info	1 0.7%	0 0	1 1.3%	1 1.3%	0 0	1 1.4%	0 0	0 0	1 5.3%	0 0	0 0	0 0	0 0	0 0	0 0	0 0	0 0	1 1.7%
preferred source of info	1 0.7%	0 0	1 1.3%	1 1.3%	0 0	1 1.4%	0 0	0 0	1 5.3%	0 0	0 0	0 0	0 0	0 0	0 0	0 0	0 0	1 1.7%
Home (NET)	0 0	0 0	0 0	0 0	0 0	0 0	0 0	0 0	0 0	0 0	0 0	0 0	0 0	0 0	0 0	0 0	0 0	0 0
All sources of info	0 0	0 0	0 0	0 0	0 0	0 0	0 0	0 0	0 0	0 0	0 0	0 0	0 0	0 0	0 0	0 0	0 0	0 0
preferred source of info	0 0	0 0	0 0	0 0	0 0	0 0	0 0	0 0	0 0	0 0	0 0	0 0	0 0	0 0	0 0	0 0	0 0	0 0
Access from course website (NET)	0 0	0 0	0 0	0 0	0 0	0 0	0 0	0 0	0 0	0 0	0 0	0 0	0 0	0 0	0 0	0 0	0 0	0 0
All sources of info	0 0	0 0	0 0	0 0	0 0	0 0	0 0	0 0	0 0	0 0	0 0	0 0	0 0	0 0	0 0	0 0	0 0	0 0
preferred source of info	0 0	0 0	0 0	0 0	0 0	0 0	0 0	0 0	0 0	0 0	0 0	0 0	0 0	0 0	0 0	0 0	0 0	0 0

Proportions/Means: Columns Tested (5% risk level) - A/B/D - C/D - E/F/G - H/I/J/K/L/M/N - P/Q
* small base; ** very small base (under 30) ineligible for sig testing

Table 422
Page 1813

Outsell/Digital Library Federation Study (2002)
Weighted Tables

TABLE 154, continued

S7D/E_15. Pre-prints SUMMARY TABLE

		RESPONDENT TYPE				INSTITUTION TYPE			DISCIPLINE									GENDER	
	TOTAL SAMPLE	FACULTY MEMBER	GRAD. STUDENT	FACULTY /GRAD	UNDER GRAD. STUDENT	PUBLIC	PRIVATE	LIBERAL ARTS	BIOLOGIAL SCIENCES	PHYSICAL SCIENCES /MATH	SOCIAL SCIENCES	ARTS AND HUMAN.	ENGI-NEERING	BUSINESS	LAW	UNDEC. MAJOR	MALE	FEMALE
		(A)	(B)	(C)	(D)	(E)	(F)	(G)	(H)	(I)	(J)	(K)	(L)	(M)	(N)		(P)	(Q)
Base - Use Pre-prints for coursework	120*	0**	68*	68*	52*	61*	29**	30**	17**	19**	45**	10**	6**	18**	1**	4*	69*	51*
Access book/journal/ journal article elsewhere online (NET)	0 0	0 0	0 0	0 0	0 0	0 0	0 0	0 0	0 0	0 0	0 0	0 0	0 0	0 0	0 0	0 0	0 0	0 0
All sources of info	0 0	0 0	0 0	0 0	0 0	0 0	0 0	0 0	0 0	0 0	0 0	0 0	0 0	0 0	0 0	0 0	0 0	0 0
preferred source of info	0 0	0 0	0 0	0 0	0 0	0 0	0 0	0 0	0 0	0 0	0 0	0 0	0 0	0 0	0 0	0 0	0 0	0 0
Ask library to purchase source (NET)	0 0	0 0	0 0	0 0	0 0	0 0	0 0	0 0	0 0	0 0	0 0	0 0	0 0	0 0	0 0	0 0	0 0	0 0
All sources of info	0 0	0 0	0 0	0 0	0 0	0 0	0 0	0 0	0 0	0 0	0 0	0 0	0 0	0 0	0 0	0 0	0 0	0 0
preferred source of info	0 0	0 0	0 0	0 0	0 0	0 0	0 0	0 0	0 0	0 0	0 0	0 0	0 0	0 0	0 0	0 0	0 0	0 0
Dorm room (NET)	0 0	0 0	0 0	0 0	0 0	0 0	0 0	0 0	0 0	0 0	0 0	0 0	0 0	0 0	0 0	0 0	0 0	0 0
All sources of info	0 0	0 0	0 0	0 0	0 0	0 0	0 0	0 0	0 0	0 0	0 0	0 0	0 0	0 0	0 0	0 0	0 0	0 0
preferred source of info	0 0	0 0	0 0	0 0	0 0	0 0	0 0	0 0	0 0	0 0	0 0	0 0	0 0	0 0	0 0	0 0	0 0	0 0

Proportions/Means: Columns Tested (5% risk level) - A/B/D - C/D - E/F/G - H/I/J/K/L/M/N - P/Q
* small base; ** very small base (under 30) ineligible for sig testing

Table 422
Page 1814

Outsell/Digital Library Federation Study (2002)
Weighted Tables

TABLE 154, continued

S7D/E_15. Pre-prints SUMMARY TABLE

		RESPONDENT TYPE				INSTITUTION TYPE			DISCIPLINE									GENDER	
	TOTAL SAMPLE	FACULTY MEMBER	GRAD. STUDENT	FACULTY /GRAD	UNDER GRAD. STUDENT	PUBLIC	PRIVATE	LIBERAL ARTS	BIOLOGIAL SCIENCES	PHYSICAL SCIENCES /MATH	SOCIAL SCIENCES	ARTS AND HUMAN.	ENGI-NEERING	BUSINESS	LAW	UNDEC. MAJOR	MALE	FEMALE
		(A)	(B)	(C)	(D)	(E)	(F)	(G)	(H)	(I)	(J)	(K)	(L)	(M)	(N)		(P)	(Q)
Base - Use Pre-prints for coursework	120*	0**	68*	68*	52*	61*	29**	30**	17**	19**	45**	10**	6**	18**	1**	4*	69*	51*
Personal Holdings (NET)	0 0	0 0	0 0	0 0	0 0	0 0	0 0	0 0	0 0	0 0	0 0	0 0	0 0	0 0	0 0	0 0	0 0	0 0
All sources of info	0 0	0 0	0 0	0 0	0 0	0 0	0 0	0 0	0 0	0 0	0 0	0 0	0 0	0 0	0 0	0 0	0 0	0 0
preferred source of info	0 0	0 0	0 0	0 0	0 0	0 0	0 0	0 0	0 0	0 0	0 0	0 0	0 0	0 0	0 0	0 0	0 0	0 0
Other (NET)	5 4.3%	0 0	4 5.9%	4 5.9%	1 2.2%	3 4.7%	1 4.0%	1 3.8%	1 5.3%	1 5.3%	2 4.2%	1 11.1%	* 4.5%	0 0	0 0	0 0	3 4.4%	2 4.2%
All sources of info	5 4.3%	0 0	4 5.9%	4 5.9%	1 2.2%	3 4.7%	1 4.0%	1 3.8%	1 5.3%	1 5.3%	2 4.2%	1 11.1%	* 4.5%	0 0	0 0	0 0	3 4.4%	2 4.2%
preferred source of info	2 1.8%	0 0	1 1.5%	1 1.5%	1 2.2%	1 1.6%	0 0	1 3.8%	0 0	1 5.3%	0 0	1 11.1%	0 0	0 0	0 0	0 0	0 0	2 4.2%
DK/Refused	3 2.3%	0 0	2 2.7%	2 2.7%	1 1.8%	3 4.6%	0 0	0 0	0 0	0 0	2 4.2%	0 0	0 0	1 5.3%	0 0	0 0	1 1.3%	2 3.7%

Proportions/Means: Columns Tested (5% risk level) - A/B/D - C/D - E/F/G - H/I/J/K/L/M/N - P/Q
* small base; ** very small base (under 30) ineligible for sig testing

Table 422
Page 1815

Outsell/Digital Library Federation Study (2002)
Weighted Tables

TABLE 155

S7sum_16. Dissertations SUMMARY TABLE

	RESPONDENT TYPE				INSTITUTION TYPE			DISCIPLINE									GENDER	
	TOTAL SAMPLE	FACULTY MEMBER	GRAD. STUDENT	FACULTY /GRAD	UNDER GRAD. STUDENT	PUBLIC	PRIVATE	LIBERAL ARTS	BIOLOGIAL SCIENCES	PHYSICAL SCIENCES /MATH	SOCIAL SCIENCES	ARTS AND HUMAN.	ENGI-NEERING	BUSINESS	LAW	UNDEC. MAJOR	MALE	FEMALE
		(A)	(B)	(C)	(D)	(E)	(F)	(G)	(H)	(I)	(J)	(K)	(L)	(M)	(N)		(P)	(Q)
Base - Use Dissertations for coursework	243	0**	130*	130*	113*	107*	66*	70*	26**	29**	94*	59*	11*	18**	1**	5*	114*	129*
ONLINE	171 70.3%	0 0	97 74.6%	97 74.6%	74 65.4%	74 69.5%	49 74.8%	47 67.3%	18 72.4%	15 51.7%	68 72.0%	40 67.9%	8 71.1%	16 89.5%	1 50.0%	5 100.0%	83 72.6%	88 68.3%
Online library catalogues and finding aids (NET)	48 19.7%	0 0	30 23.2%	30 23.2%	18 15.8%	22 20.5%	13 19.7%	13 18.5%	4 13.8%	2 6.9%	24 26.0%	13 22.6%	2 15.8%	3 15.8%	0 0	0 0	24 20.7%	24 18.9%
All sources of info	48 19.7%	0 0	30 23.2%	30 23.2%	18 15.8%	22 20.5%	13 19.7%	13 18.5%	4 13.8%	2 6.9%	24 26.0%	13 22.6%	2 15.8%	3 15.8%	0 0	0 0	24 20.7%	24 18.9%
preferred source of info	36 14.7%	0 0	24 18.7%	24 18.7%	12 10.2%	18 16.8%	11 16.9%	7 9.5%	4 13.8%	2 6.9%	19 20.0%	8 13.2%	2 15.8%	2 10.5%	0 0	0 0	17 14.6%	19 14.8%
Online databases (NET)	42 17.4%	0 0	27 21.1%	27 21.1%	15 13.3%	17 15.7%	17 25.1%	9 12.8%	2 6.9%	3 10.3%	21 22.0%	11 18.9%	1 7.9%	5 26.3%	* 12.5%	0 0	20 17.1%	23 17.7%
All sources of info	42 17.4%	0 0	27 21.1%	27 21.1%	15 13.3%	17 15.7%	17 25.1%	9 12.8%	2 6.9%	3 10.3%	21 22.0%	11 18.9%	1 7.9%	5 26.3%	* 12.5%	0 0	20 17.1%	23 17.7%
preferred source of info	35 14.4%	0 0	25 19.0%	25 19.0%	10 9.2%	13 12.0%	15 22.7%	7 10.2%	1 3.4%	2 6.9%	17 18.0%	10 17.0%	* 2.6%	5 26.3%	* 12.5%	0 0	17 15.0%	18 13.9%
Search engine (NET)	40 16.5%	0 0	15 11.4%	15 11.4%	25 22.3%B C	13 12.2%	9 13.3%	18 25.9%E	5 20.7%	5 17.2%	11 12.0%	9 15.1%	2 15.8%	6 31.6%	* 12.5%	2 40.0%	23 19.8%	17 13.6%
All sources of info	40 16.5%	0 0	15 11.4%	15 11.4%	25 22.3%B C	13 12.2%	9 13.3%	18 25.9%E	5 20.7%	5 17.2%	11 12.0%	9 15.1%	2 15.8%	6 31.6%	* 12.5%	2 40.0%	23 19.8%	17 13.6%

Proportions/Means: Columns Tested (5% risk level) - A/B/D - C/D - E/F/G - H/I/J/K/L/M/N - P/Q
* small base; ** very small base (under 30) ineligible for sig testing

Table 426
Page 1827

Outsell/Digital Library Federation Study (2002)
Weighted Tables

TABLE 155, continued

S7sum_16. Dissertations SUMMARY TABLE

		RESPONDENT TYPE				INSTITUTION TYPE			DISCIPLINE									GENDER	
	TOTAL SAMPLE	FACULTY MEMBER	GRAD. STUDENT	FACULTY /GRAD	UNDER GRAD. STUDENT	PUBLIC	PRIVATE	LIBERAL ARTS	BIOLOGIAL SCIENCES	PHYSICAL SCIENCES /MATH	SOCIAL SCIENCES	ARTS AND HUMAN.	ENGI- NEERING	BUSINESS	LAW	UNDEC. MAJOR	MALE	FEMALE
		(A)	(B)	(C)	(D)	(E)	(F)	(G)	(H)	(I)	(J)	(K)	(L)	(M)	(N)		(P)	(Q)
Base - Use Dissertations for coursework	243	0**	130*	130*	113*	107*	66*	70*	26**	29**	94*	59*	11*	18**	1**	5*	114*	129*
preferred source of info	22 9.1%	0 0	8 5.8%	8 5.8%	15 12.8%	7 6.5%	4 6.5%	11 15.3%	2 6.9%	2 6.9%	8 8.0%	4 7.5%	1 5.3%	4 21.1%	0 0	2 40.0%	12 10.4%	10 7.9%
Your own institution's web site (NET)	29 11.9%	0 0	15 11.9%	15 11.9%	14 12.0%	9 8.5%	10 15.7%	10 13.6%	5 20.7%	4 13.8%	2 2.0%	10 17.0%J	2 18.4%J	4 21.1%	0 0	2 40.0%	12 10.1%	17 13.6%
All sources of info	29 11.9%	0 0	15 11.9%	15 11.9%	14 12.0%	9 8.5%	10 15.7%	10 13.6%	5 20.7%	4 13.8%	2 2.0%	10 17.0%J	2 18.4%J	4 21.1%	0 0	2 40.0%	12 10.1%	17 13.6%
preferred source of info	16 6.5%	0 0	9 6.8%	9 6.8%	7 6.3%	6 5.6%	6 8.7%	4 5.8%	4 13.8%	1 3.4%	2 2.0%	4 7.5%	1 10.5%J	2 10.5%	0 0	2 40.0%	4 3.5%	12 9.3%
Internet searches (NET)	25 10.4%	0 0	16 12.0%	16 12.0%	10 8.6%	13 11.8%	9 13.4%	4 5.5%	4 17.2%	3 10.3%	9 10.0%	3 5.7%	1 13.2%	4 21.1%	0 0	0 0	18 16.2%Q	7 5.3%
All sources of info	25 10.4%	0 0	16 12.0%	16 12.0%	10 8.6%	13 11.8%	9 13.4%	4 5.5%	4 17.2%	3 10.3%	9 10.0%	3 5.7%	1 13.2%	4 21.1%	0 0	0 0	18 16.2%Q	7 5.3%
preferred source of info	14 5.8%	0 0	7 5.5%	7 5.5%	7 6.2%	6 5.9%	7 10.2%	1 1.6%	3 10.3%	2 6.9%	6 6.0%	1 1.9%	1 7.9%	2 10.5%	0 0	0 0	12 10.6%Q	2 1.6%
Web directory/ subject related web site (NET)	17 6.8%	0 0	10 7.5%	10 7.5%	7 6.2%	8 7.6%	2 2.3%	7 9.9%	1 3.4%	1 3.4%	8 8.0%	2 3.8%	1 7.9%	3 15.8%	* 25.0%	1 20.0%	8 6.8%	9 6.9%
All sources of info	17 6.8%	0 0	10 7.5%	10 7.5%	7 6.2%	8 7.6%	2 2.3%	7 9.9%	1 3.4%	1 3.4%	8 8.0%	2 3.8%	1 7.9%	3 15.8%	* 25.0%	1 20.0%	8 6.8%	9 6.9%

Proportions/Means: Columns Tested (5% risk level) - A/B/D - C/D - E/F/G - H/I/J/K/L/M/N - P/Q
* small base; ** very small base (under 30) ineligible for sig testing

Table 426
Page 1828

Outsell/Digital Library Federation Study (2002)
Weighted Tables

TABLE 155, continued

S7sum_16. Dissertations SUMMARY TABLE

	TOTAL SAMPLE	RESPONDENT TYPE: FACULTY MEMBER (A)	RESPONDENT TYPE: GRAD. STUDENT (B)	RESPONDENT TYPE: FACULTY /GRAD (C)	RESPONDENT TYPE: UNDER GRAD. STUDENT (D)	INSTITUTION TYPE: PUBLIC (E)	INSTITUTION TYPE: PRIVATE (F)	INSTITUTION TYPE: LIBERAL ARTS (G)	DISCIPLINE: BIOLOGIAL SCIENCES (H)	DISCIPLINE: PHYSICAL SCIENCES /MATH (I)	DISCIPLINE: SOCIAL SCIENCES (J)	DISCIPLINE: ARTS AND HUMAN. (K)	DISCIPLINE: ENGI-NEERING (L)	DISCIPLINE: BUSINESS (M)	DISCIPLINE: LAW (N)	DISCIPLINE: UNDEC. MAJOR	GENDER: MALE (P)	GENDER: FEMALE (Q)
Base - Use Dissertations for coursework	243	0**	130*	130*	113*	107*	66*	70*	26**	29**	94*	59*	11*	18**	1**	5*	114*	129*
preferred source of info	9 3.9%	0 0	5 3.5%	5 3.5%	5 4.4%	4 4.0%	* 0.4%	5 7.0%	0 0	0 0	6 6.0%	1 1.9%	1 5.3%	1 5.3%	* 12.5%	1 20.0%	1 0.7%	9 6.8%P
Online abstracting and indexing services (NET)	6 2.3%	0 0	4 2.8%	4 2.8%	2 1.8%	3 2.9%	1 2.1%	1 1.6%	1 3.4%	0 0	2 2.0%	2 3.8%	1 5.3%	0 0	0 0	0 0	3 2.3%	3 2.3%
All sources of info	6 2.3%	0 0	4 2.8%	4 2.8%	2 1.8%	3 2.9%	1 2.1%	1 1.6%	1 3.4%	0 0	2 2.0%	2 3.8%	1 5.3%	0 0	0 0	0 0	3 2.3%	3 2.3%
preferred source of info	2 0.9%	0 0	2 1.7%	2 1.7%	0 0	2 1.8%	* 0.4%	0 0	0 0	0 0	2 2.0%	0 0	* 2.6%	0 0	0 0	0 0	* 0.3%	2 1.5%
Online reference service (NET)	5 2.1%	0 0	* 0.1%	* 0.1%	5 4.4%BC	2 1.6%	* 0.3%	3 4.6%	0 0	1 3.4%	0 0	3 5.7%	1 5.3%J	0 0	* 12.5%	0 0	4 3.5%	1 0.9%
All sources of info	5 2.1%	0 0	* 0.1%	* 0.1%	5 4.4%BC	2 1.6%	* 0.3%	3 4.6%	0 0	1 3.4%	0 0	3 5.7%	1 5.3%J	0 0	* 12.5%	0 0	4 3.5%	1 0.9%
preferred source of info	3 1.1%	0 0	* 0.1%	* 0.1%	3 2.2%	1 1.3%	* 0.3%	1 1.6%	0 0	0 0	0 0	2 3.8%	* 2.6%J	0 0	* 12.5%	0 0	3 2.4%	0 0
Department web page (NET)	4 1.7%	0 0	2 1.8%	2 1.8%	2 1.7%	2 2.2%	2 2.9%	0 0	0 0	0 0	2 2.0%	1 1.9%	* 2.6%	1 5.3%	0 0	0 0	3 2.7%	1 0.9%
All sources of info	4 1.7%	0 0	2 1.8%	2 1.8%	2 1.7%	2 2.2%	2 2.9%	0 0	0 0	0 0	2 2.0%	1 1.9%	* 2.6%	1 5.3%	0 0	0 0	3 2.7%	1 0.9%

Proportions/Means: Columns Tested (5% risk level) - A/B/D - C/D - E/F/G - H/I/J/K/L/M/N - P/Q
* small base; ** very small base (under 30) ineligible for sig testing

Table 426
Page 1829

Outsell/Digital Library Federation Study (2002)
Weighted Tables

TABLE 155, continued

S7sum_16. Dissertations SUMMARY TABLE

		RESPONDENT TYPE				INSTITUTION TYPE			DISCIPLINE									GENDER	
	TOTAL SAMPLE	FACULTY MEMBER	GRAD. STUDENT	FACULTY /GRAD	UNDER GRAD. STUDENT	PUBLIC	PRIVATE	LIBERAL ARTS	BIOLOGIAL SCIENCES	PHYSICAL SCIENCES /MATH	SOCIAL SCIENCES	ARTS AND HUMAN.	ENGI-NEERING	BUSINESS	LAW	UNDEC. MAJOR	MALE	FEMALE
		(A)	(B)	(C)	(D)	(E)	(F)	(G)	(H)	(I)	(J)	(K)	(L)	(M)	(N)		(P)	(Q)
Base - Use Dissertations for coursework	243	0**	130*	130*	113*	107*	66*	70*	26**	29**	94*	59*	11*	18**	1**	5*	114*	129*
preferred source of info	2 0.8%	0 0	2 1.6%	2 1.6%	0 0	2 1.9%	0 0	0 0	0 0	0 0	0 0	1 1.9%	0 0	1 5.3%	0 0	0 0	1 0.8%	1 0.9%
Your own personal electronic library/files (NET)	2 0.9%	0 0	2 1.7%	2 1.7%	0 0	2 2.0%	0 0	0 0	0 0	0 0	2 2.0%	0 0	* 2.6%	0 0	0 0	0 0	* 0.3%	2 1.5%
All sources of info	2 0.9%	0 0	2 1.7%	2 1.7%	0 0	2 2.0%	0 0	0 0	0 0	0 0	2 2.0%	0 0	* 2.6%	0 0	0 0	0 0	* 0.3%	2 1.5%
preferred source of info	2 0.9%	0 0	2 1.7%	2 1.7%	0 0	2 2.0%	0 0	0 0	0 0	0 0	2 2.0%	0 0	* 2.6%	0 0	0 0	0 0	* 0.3%	2 1.5%
E-mail listservs (NET)	0 0	0 0	0 0	0 0	0 0	0 0	0 0	0 0	0 0	0 0	0 0	0 0	0 0	0 0	0 0	0 0	0 0	0 0
All sources of info	0 0	0 0	0 0	0 0	0 0	0 0	0 0	0 0	0 0	0 0	0 0	0 0	0 0	0 0	0 0	0 0	0 0	0 0
preferred source of info	0 0	0 0	0 0	0 0	0 0	0 0	0 0	0 0	0 0	0 0	0 0	0 0	0 0	0 0	0 0	0 0	0 0	0 0
Online bookstore (NET)	0 0	0 0	0 0	0 0	0 0	0 0	0 0	0 0	0 0	0 0	0 0	0 0	0 0	0 0	0 0	0 0	0 0	0 0
All sources of info	0 0	0 0	0 0	0 0	0 0	0 0	0 0	0 0	0 0	0 0	0 0	0 0	0 0	0 0	0 0	0 0	0 0	0 0

Proportions/Means: Columns Tested (5% risk level) - A/B/D - C/D - E/F/G - H/I/J/K/L/M/N - P/Q
* small base; ** very small base (under 30) ineligible for sig testing

Table 426
Page 1830

Outsell/Digital Library Federation Study (2002)
Weighted Tables

TABLE 155, continued

S7sum_16. Dissertations SUMMARY TABLE

	TOTAL SAMPLE	RESPONDENT TYPE: FACULTY MEMBER (A)	GRAD. STUDENT (B)	FACULTY /GRAD (C)	UNDER GRAD. STUDENT (D)	INSTITUTION TYPE: PUBLIC (E)	PRIVATE (F)	LIBERAL ARTS (G)	DISCIPLINE: BIOLOGICAL SCIENCES (H)	PHYSICAL SCIENCES /MATH (I)	SOCIAL SCIENCES (J)	ARTS AND HUMAN. (K)	ENGI-NEERING (L)	BUSINESS (M)	LAW (N)	UNDEC. MAJOR	GENDER: MALE (P)	FEMALE (Q)
Base - Use Dissertations for coursework	243	0**	130*	130*	113*	107*	66*	70*	26**	29**	94*	59*	11*	18**	1**	5*	114*	129*
preferred source of info	0 0	0 0	0 0	0 0	0 0	0 0	0 0	0 0	0 0	0 0	0 0	0 0	0 0	0 0	0 0	0 0	0 0	0 0
PERSONAL ASSISTANCE	90 37.1%	0 0	38 29.4%	38 29.4%	52 46.0%B C	38 36.0%	17 25.3%	35 49.8%F	11 41.4%	16 55.2%	34 36.0%	19 32.1%	5 44.7%	4 21.1%	1 75.0%	1 20.0%	36 31.2%	54 42.3%
Faculty members inside your institution (NET)	63 26.0%	0 0	29 22.7%	29 22.7%	34 29.7%	28 26.3%	13 19.9%	22 31.2%	11 41.4%	11 37.9%	24 26.0%	10 17.0%	4 34.2%K	3 15.8%	1 37.5%	0 0	28 24.3%	35 27.5%
All sources of info	63 26.0%	0 0	29 22.7%	29 22.7%	34 29.7%	28 26.3%	13 19.9%	22 31.2%	11 41.4%	11 37.9%	24 26.0%	10 17.0%	4 34.2%K	3 15.8%	1 37.5%	0 0	28 24.3%	35 27.5%
preferred source of info	35 14.6%	0 0	12 9.4%	12 9.4%	23 20.5%B C	13 11.9%	6 8.4%	17 24.4%F	7 27.6%	10 34.5%	9 10.0%	7 11.3%	2 15.8%	0 0	1 37.5%	0 0	15 12.7%	21 16.2%
A librarian in your institution (NET)	45 18.6%	0 0	17 12.8%	17 12.8%	29 25.2%B C	16 15.2%	8 11.5%	21 30.4%EF	3 10.3%	6 20.7%	15 16.0%	15 24.5%	2 15.8%	4 21.1%	1 37.5%	1 20.0%	16 14.4%	29 22.3%
All sources of info	45 18.6%	0 0	17 12.8%	17 12.8%	29 25.2%B C	16 15.2%	8 11.5%	21 30.4%EF	3 10.3%	6 20.7%	15 16.0%	15 24.5%	2 15.8%	4 21.1%	1 37.5%	1 20.0%	16 14.4%	29 22.3%
preferred source of info	19 8.0%	0 0	6 4.9%	6 4.9%	13 11.6%	7 6.8%	2 3.1%	10 14.3%F	0 0	1 3.4%	11 12.0%	6 9.4%	* 2.6%	1 5.3%	* 25.0%	0 0	5 4.6%	14 11.0%

Proportions/Means: Columns Tested (5% risk level) - A/B/D - C/D - E/F/G - H/I/J/K/L/M/N - P/Q
* small base; ** very small base (under 30) ineligible for sig testing

Table 426
Page 1831

Outsell/Digital Library Federation Study (2002)
Weighted Tables

TABLE 155, continued

S7sum_16. Dissertations SUMMARY TABLE

		RESPONDENT TYPE				INSTITUTION TYPE			DISCIPLINE									GENDER	
	TOTAL SAMPLE	FACULTY MEMBER	GRAD. STUDENT	FACULTY /GRAD	UNDER GRAD. STUDENT	PUBLIC	PRIVATE	LIBERAL ARTS	BIOLOGIAL SCIENCES	PHYSICAL SCIENCES /MATH	SOCIAL SCIENCES	ARTS AND HUMAN.	ENGI- NEERING	BUSINESS	LAW	UNDEC. MAJOR	MALE	FEMALE
		(A)	(B)	(C)	(D)	(E)	(F)	(G)	(H)	(I)	(J)	(K)	(L)	(M)	(N)		(P)	(Q)
Base - Use Dissertations for coursework	243	0**	130*	130*	113*	107*	66*	70*	26**	29**	94*	59*	11*	18**	1**	5*	114*	129*
Other students inside your institution (NET)	16 6.4%	0 0	8 5.9%	8 5.9%	8 7.0%	6 6.0%	4 6.3%	5 7.1%	2 6.9%	6 20.7%	4 4.0%	2 3.8%	1 7.9%	1 5.3%	0 0	0 0	6 5.6%	9 7.2%
All sources of info	16 6.4%	0 0	8 5.9%	8 5.9%	8 7.0%	6 6.0%	4 6.3%	5 7.1%	2 6.9%	6 20.7%	4 4.0%	2 3.8%	1 7.9%	1 5.3%	0 0	0 0	6 5.6%	9 7.2%
preferred source of info	1 0.2%	0 0	1 0.4%	1 0.4%	0 0	* 0.3%	* 0.4%	0 0	0 0	0 0	0 0	0 0	1 5.3%JK	0 0	0 0	0 0	* 0.3%	* 0.2%
Professional meetings (NET)	2 0.8%	0 0	0 0	0 0	2 1.7%	0 0	0 0	2 2.7%	0 0	0 0	2 2.0%	0 0	0 0	0 0	0 0	0 0	0 0	2 1.5%
All sources of info	2 0.8%	0 0	0 0	0 0	2 1.7%	0 0	0 0	2 2.7%	0 0	0 0	2 2.0%	0 0	0 0	0 0	0 0	0 0	0 0	2 1.5%
preferred source of info	0 0	0 0	0 0	0 0	0 0	0 0	0 0	0 0	0 0	0 0	0 0	0 0	0 0	0 0	0 0	0 0	0 0	0 0
Faculty members outside your institution (NET)	* 0.1%	0 0	* 0.2%	* 0.2%	0 0	0 0	* 0.4%	0 0	0 0	0 0	0 0	0 0	* 2.6%J	0 0	0 0	0 0	* 0.3%	0 0
All sources of info	* 0.1%	0 0	* 0.2%	* 0.2%	0 0	0 0	* 0.4%	0 0	0 0	0 0	0 0	0 0	* 2.6%J	0 0	0 0	0 0	* 0.3%	0 0
preferred source of info	0 0	0 0	0 0	0 0	0 0	0 0	0 0	0 0	0 0	0 0	0 0	0 0	0 0	0 0	0 0	0 0	0 0	0 0

Proportions/Means: Columns Tested (5% risk level) - A/B/D - C/D - E/F/G - H/I/J/K/L/M/N - P/Q
* small base; ** very small base (under 30) ineligible for sig testing

Table 426
Page 1832

Outsell/Digital Library Federation Study (2002)
Weighted Tables

TABLE 155, continued

S7sum_16. Dissertations SUMMARY TABLE

		RESPONDENT TYPE				INSTITUTION TYPE			DISCIPLINE								GENDER	
	TOTAL SAMPLE	FACULTY MEMBER	GRAD. STUDENT	FACULTY /GRAD	UNDER GRAD. STUDENT	PUBLIC	PRIVATE	LIBERAL ARTS	BIOLOGIAL SCIENCES	PHYSICAL SCIENCES /MATH	SOCIAL SCIENCES	ARTS AND HUMAN.	ENGI-NEERING	BUSINESS	LAW	UNDEC. MAJOR	MALE	FEMALE
		(A)	(B)	(C)	(D)	(E)	(F)	(G)	(H)	(I)	(J)	(K)	(L)	(M)	(N)		(P)	(Q)
Base - Use Dissertations for coursework	243	0**	130*	130*	113*	107*	66*	70*	26**	29**	94*	59*	11*	18**	1**	5*	114*	129*
Other students outside your institution (NET)	0	0	0	0	0	0	0	0	0	0	0	0	0	0	0	0	0	0
	0	0	0	0	0	0	0	0	0	0	0	0	0	0	0	0	0	0
All sources of info	0	0	0	0	0	0	0	0	0	0	0	0	0	0	0	0	0	0
	0	0	0	0	0	0	0	0	0	0	0	0	0	0	0	0	0	0
preferred source of info	0	0	0	0	0	0	0	0	0	0	0	0	0	0	0	0	0	0
	0	0	0	0	0	0	0	0	0	0	0	0	0	0	0	0	0	0
Another institution's librarian (NET)	0	0	0	0	0	0	0	0	0	0	0	0	0	0	0	0	0	0
	0	0	0	0	0	0	0	0	0	0	0	0	0	0	0	0	0	0
All sources of info	0	0	0	0	0	0	0	0	0	0	0	0	0	0	0	0	0	0
	0	0	0	0	0	0	0	0	0	0	0	0	0	0	0	0	0	0
preferred source of info	0	0	0	0	0	0	0	0	0	0	0	0	0	0	0	0	0	0
	0	0	0	0	0	0	0	0	0	0	0	0	0	0	0	0	0	0
LIBRARY FACILITIES/ PRINT	71	0	43	43	28	33	20	18	11	10	23	19	4	3	*	1	39	32
	29.3%	0	33.2%	33.2%	24.8%	30.6%	30.8%	26.0%	44.8%	34.5%	24.0%	32.1%	36.8%	15.8%	25.0%	20.0%	34.1%	25.1%
Campus library (NET)	67	0	40	40	27	31	18	17	11	9	23	18	3	3	*	1	38	29
	27.7%	0	30.9%	30.9%	24.1%	29.5%	28.0%	24.8%	41.4%	31.0%	24.0%	30.2%	28.9%	15.8%	25.0%	20.0%	33.3%	22.8%
All sources of info	67	0	40	40	27	31	18	17	11	9	23	18	3	3	*	1	38	29
	27.7%	0	30.9%	30.9%	24.1%	29.5%	28.0%	24.8%	41.4%	31.0%	24.0%	30.2%	28.9%	15.8%	25.0%	20.0%	33.3%	22.8%

Proportions/Means: Columns Tested (5% risk level) - A/B/D - C/D - E/F/G - H/I/J/K/L/M/N - P/Q
* small base; ** very small base (under 30) ineligible for sig testing

Table 426
Page 1833

Outsell/Digital Library Federation Study (2002)
Weighted Tables

TABLE 155, continued

S7sum_16. Dissertations SUMMARY TABLE

	RESPONDENT TYPE				INSTITUTION TYPE			DISCIPLINE									GENDER	
	TOTAL SAMPLE	FACULTY MEMBER	GRAD. STUDENT	FACULTY /GRAD	UNDER GRAD. STUDENT	PUBLIC	PRIVATE	LIBERAL ARTS	BIOLOGIAL SCIENCES	PHYSICAL SCIENCES /MATH	SOCIAL SCIENCES	ARTS AND HUMAN.	ENGI- NEERING	BUSINESS	LAW	UNDEC. MAJOR	MALE	FEMALE
		(A)	(B)	(C)	(D)	(E)	(F)	(G)	(H)	(I)	(J)	(K)	(L)	(M)	(N)		(P)	(Q)
Base - Use Dissertations for coursework	243	0**	130*	130*	113*	107*	66*	70*	26**	29**	94*	59*	11*	18**	1**	5*	114*	129*
preferred source of info	35 14.6%	0 0	22 17.1%	22 17.1%	13 11.7%	18 16.5%	12 17.6%	6 8.9%	6 24.1%	8 27.6%	8 8.0%	12 20.8%	1 13.2%	0 0	0 0	0 0	21 18.3%	15 11.3%
Printed abstracting and indexing services (NET)	2 0.9%	0 0	2 1.6%	2 1.6%	0 0	1 1.1%	1 1.5%	0 0	0 0	1 3.4%	0 0	1 1.9%	0 0	0 0	0 0	0 0	0 0	2 1.6%
All sources of info	2 0.9%	0 0	2 1.6%	2 1.6%	0 0	1 1.1%	1 1.5%	0 0	0 0	1 3.4%	0 0	1 1.9%	0 0	0 0	0 0	0 0	0 0	2 1.6%
preferred source of info	0 0	0 0	0 0	0 0	0 0	0 0	0 0	0 0	0 0	0 0	0 0	0 0	0 0	0 0	0 0	0 0	0 0	0 0
Another library (NET)	2 0.8%	0 0	1 0.7%	1 0.7%	1 1.0%	0 0	1 1.3%	1 1.6%	1 3.4%	0 0	0 0	1 1.9%	0 0	0 0	0 0	0 0	2 1.8%	0 0
All sources of info	2 0.8%	0 0	1 0.7%	1 0.7%	1 1.0%	0 0	1 1.3%	1 1.6%	1 3.4%	0 0	0 0	1 1.9%	0 0	0 0	0 0	0 0	2 1.8%	0 0
preferred source of info	0 0	0 0	0 0	0 0	0 0	0 0	0 0	0 0	0 0	0 0	0 0	0 0	0 0	0 0	0 0	0 0	0 0	0 0
References cited in books or journal articles (NET)	2 0.7%	0 0	1 0.4%	1 0.4%	1 0.9%	* 0.3%	* 0.4%	1 1.4%	0 0	1 3.4%	0 0	0 0	1 5.3%JK	0 0	0 0	0 0	2 1.4%	0 0

Proportions/Means: Columns Tested (5% risk level) - A/B/D - C/D - E/F/G - H/I/J/K/L/M/N - P/Q
* small base; ** very small base (under 30) ineligible for sig testing

Table 426
Page 1834

Outsell/Digital Library Federation Study (2002)
Weighted Tables

TABLE 155, continued

S7sum_16. Dissertations SUMMARY TABLE

		RESPONDENT TYPE				INSTITUTION TYPE			DISCIPLINE								GENDER	
	TOTAL SAMPLE	FACULTY MEMBER	GRAD. STUDENT	FACULTY /GRAD	UNDER GRAD. STUDENT	PUBLIC	PRIVATE	LIBERAL ARTS	BIOLOGIAL SCIENCES	PHYSICAL SCIENCES /MATH	SOCIAL SCIENCES	ARTS AND HUMAN.	ENGI- NEERING	BUSINESS	LAW	UNDEC. MAJOR	MALE	FEMALE
		(A)	(B)	(C)	(D)	(E)	(F)	(G)	(H)	(I)	(J)	(K)	(L)	(M)	(N)		(P)	(Q)
Base - Use Dissertations for coursework	243	0**	130*	130*	113*	107*	66*	70*	26**	29**	94*	59*	11*	18**	1**	5*	114*	129*
All sources of info	2 0.7%	0 0	1 0.4%	1 0.4%	1 0.9%	* 0.3%	* 0.4%	1 1.4%	0 0	1 3.4%	0 0	0 0	1 5.3%JK	0 0	0 0	0 0	2 1.4%	0 0
preferred source of info	0 0	0 0	0 0	0 0	0 0	0 0	0 0	0 0	0 0	0 0	0 0	0 0	0 0	0 0	0 0	0 0	0 0	0 0
Physical bookstore (NET)	2 0.6%	0 0	2 1.2%	2 1.2%	0 0	1 0.9%	1 0.9%	0 0	0 0	0 0	0 0	0 0	1 5.3%JK	1 5.3%	0 0	0 0	2 1.3%	0 0
All sources of info	2 0.6%	0 0	2 1.2%	2 1.2%	0 0	1 0.9%	1 0.9%	0 0	0 0	0 0	0 0	0 0	1 5.3%JK	1 5.3%	0 0	0 0	2 1.3%	0 0
preferred source of info	* 0.1%	0 0	* 0.2%	* 0.2%	0 0	0 0	* 0.4%	0 0	0 0	0 0	0 0	0 0	* 2.6%J	0 0	0 0	0 0	* 0.3%	0 0
Printed library catalogues and finding aids (NET)	1 0.6%	0 0	1 0.4%	1 0.4%	1 0.8%	* 0.3%	* 0.4%	1 1.2%	1 3.4%	0 0	0 0	0 0	1 5.3%JK	0 0	0 0	0 0	1 0.5%	1 0.7%
All sources of info	1 0.6%	0 0	1 0.4%	1 0.4%	1 0.8%	* 0.3%	* 0.4%	1 1.2%	1 3.4%	0 0	0 0	0 0	1 5.3%JK	0 0	0 0	0 0	1 0.5%	1 0.7%
preferred source of info	* 0.1%	0 0	* 0.2%	* 0.2%	0 0	* 0.3%	0 0	0 0	0 0	0 0	0 0	0 0	* 2.6%J	0 0	0 0	0 0	* 0.3%	0 0

Proportions/Means: Columns Tested (5% risk level) - A/B/D - C/D - E/F/G - H/I/J/K/L/M/N - P/Q
* small base; ** very small base (under 30) ineligible for sig testing

Table 426
Page 1835

Outsell/Digital Library Federation Study (2002)
Weighted Tables

TABLE 155, continued

S7sum_16. Dissertations SUMMARY TABLE

	TOTAL SAMPLE	RESPONDENT TYPE: FACULTY MEMBER	GRAD. STUDENT	FACULTY /GRAD	UNDER GRAD. STUDENT	INSTITUTION TYPE: PUBLIC	PRIVATE	LIBERAL ARTS	DISCIPLINE: BIOLOGIAL SCIENCES	PHYSICAL SCIENCES /MATH	SOCIAL SCIENCES	ARTS AND HUMAN.	ENGI-NEERING	BUSINESS	LAW	UNDEC. MAJOR	GENDER: MALE	FEMALE
		(A)	(B)	(C)	(D)	(E)	(F)	(G)	(H)	(I)	(J)	(K)	(L)	(M)	(N)		(P)	(Q)
Base - Use Dissertations for coursework	243	0**	130*	130*	113*	107*	66*	70*	26**	29**	94*	59*	11*	18**	1**	5*	114*	129*
Personal subscriptions to newspapers, magazines and journals (NET)	0 0	0 0	0 0	0 0	0 0	0 0	0 0	0 0	0 0	0 0	0 0	0 0	0 0	0 0	0 0	0 0	0 0	0 0
All sources of info	0 0	0 0	0 0	0 0	0 0	0 0	0 0	0 0	0 0	0 0	0 0	0 0	0 0	0 0	0 0	0 0	0 0	0 0
preferred source of info	0 0	0 0	0 0	0 0	0 0	0 0	0 0	0 0	0 0	0 0	0 0	0 0	0 0	0 0	0 0	0 0	0 0	0 0
Your own personal physical library/ files/bookshelves (NET)	0 0	0 0	0 0	0 0	0 0	0 0	0 0	0 0	0 0	0 0	0 0	0 0	0 0	0 0	0 0	0 0	0 0	0 0
All sources of info	0 0	0 0	0 0	0 0	0 0	0 0	0 0	0 0	0 0	0 0	0 0	0 0	0 0	0 0	0 0	0 0	0 0	0 0
preferred source of info	0 0	0 0	0 0	0 0	0 0	0 0	0 0	0 0	0 0	0 0	0 0	0 0	0 0	0 0	0 0	0 0	0 0	0 0
Other (NET)	8 3.3%	0 0	1 0.9%	1 0.9%	7 6.1%	3 2.8%	1 1.8%	4 5.6%	1 3.4%	0 0	4 4.0%	2 3.8%	* 2.6%	1 5.3%	0 0	0 0	5 4.5%	3 2.3%
All sources of info	7 3.0%	0 0	1 0.9%	1 0.9%	6 5.3%	3 2.8%	1 1.8%	3 4.3%	1 3.4%	0 0	4 4.0%	2 3.8%	* 2.6%	0 0	0 0	0 0	4 3.7%	3 2.3%

Proportions/Means: Columns Tested (5% risk level) - A/B/D - C/D - E/F/G - H/I/J/K/L/M/N - P/Q
* small base; ** very small base (under 30) ineligible for sig testing

Table 426
Page 1836

Outsell/Digital Library Federation Study (2002)
Weighted Tables

TABLE 155, continued

S7sum_16. Dissertations SUMMARY TABLE

	TOTAL SAMPLE	RESPONDENT TYPE: FACULTY MEMBER	RESPONDENT TYPE: GRAD. STUDENT	RESPONDENT TYPE: FACULTY /GRAD	RESPONDENT TYPE: UNDER GRAD. STUDENT	INSTITUTION TYPE: PUBLIC	INSTITUTION TYPE: PRIVATE	INSTITUTION TYPE: LIBERAL ARTS	DISCIPLINE: BIOLOGIAL SCIENCES	DISCIPLINE: PHYSICAL SCIENCES /MATH	DISCIPLINE: SOCIAL SCIENCES	DISCIPLINE: ARTS AND HUMAN.	DISCIPLINE: ENGI-NEERING	DISCIPLINE: BUSINESS	DISCIPLINE: LAW	DISCIPLINE: UNDEC. MAJOR	GENDER: MALE	GENDER: FEMALE
		(A)	(B)	(C)	(D)	(E)	(F)	(G)	(H)	(I)	(J)	(K)	(L)	(M)	(N)		(P)	(Q)
Base - Use Dissertations for coursework	243	0**	130*	130*	113*	107*	66*	70*	26**	29**	94*	59*	11*	18**	1**	5*	114*	129*
preferred source of info	3 1.2%	0 0	0 0	0 0	3 2.5%	2 1.8%	0 0	1 1.3%	0 0	0 0	2 2.0%	0 0	0 0	1 5.3%	0 0	0 0	3 2.5%	0 0
Online (unspecified)	3 1.2%	0 0	1 0.7%	1 0.7%	2 1.7%	1 0.8%	2 2.9%	0 0	1 3.4%	1 3.4%	0 0	0 0	0 0	1 5.3%	0 0	0 0	1 0.8%	2 1.5%
All sources of info	3 1.2%	0 0	1 0.7%	1 0.7%	2 1.7%	1 0.8%	2 2.9%	0 0	1 3.4%	1 3.4%	0 0	0 0	0 0	1 5.3%	0 0	0 0	1 0.8%	2 1.5%
preferred source of info	0 0	0 0	0 0	0 0	0 0	0 0	0 0	0 0	0 0	0 0	0 0	0 0	0 0	0 0	0 0	0 0	0 0	0 0
E-journals	0 0	0 0	0 0	0 0	0 0	0 0	0 0	0 0	0 0	0 0	0 0	0 0	0 0	0 0	0 0	0 0	0 0	0 0
All sources of info	0 0	0 0	0 0	0 0	0 0	0 0	0 0	0 0	0 0	0 0	0 0	0 0	0 0	0 0	0 0	0 0	0 0	0 0
preferred source of info	0 0	0 0	0 0	0 0	0 0	0 0	0 0	0 0	0 0	0 0	0 0	0 0	0 0	0 0	0 0	0 0	0 0	0 0
DK/Refused	10 4.2%	0 0	5 4.1%	5 4.1%	5 4.2%	6 5.3%	3 3.8%	2 2.7%	0 0	1 3.4%	6 6.0%	2 3.8%	* 2.6%	1 5.3%	0 0	0 0	4 3.6%	6 4.7%

Proportions/Means: Columns Tested (5% risk level) - A/B/D - C/D - E/F/G - H/I/J/K/L/M/N - P/Q
* small base; ** very small base (under 30) ineligible for sig testing

Table 426
Page 1837

Outsell/Digital Library Federation Study (2002)
Weighted Tables

TABLE 156

S7D/E_16. Dissertations SUMMARY TABLE

		RESPONDENT TYPE				INSTITUTION TYPE			DISCIPLINE								GENDER	
	TOTAL SAMPLE	FACULTY MEMBER	GRAD. STUDENT	FACULTY /GRAD	UNDER GRAD. STUDENT	PUBLIC	PRIVATE	LIBERAL ARTS	BIOLOGIAL SCIENCES	PHYSICAL SCIENCES /MATH	SOCIAL SCIENCES	ARTS AND HUMAN.	ENGI- NEERING	BUSINESS	LAW	UNDEC. MAJOR	MALE	FEMALE
		(A)	(B)	(C)	(D)	(E)	(F)	(G)	(H)	(I)	(J)	(K)	(L)	(M)	(N)		(P)	(Q)
Base - Use Dissertations for coursework	243	0**	130*	130*	113*	107*	66*	70*	26**	29**	94*	59*	11*	18**	1**	5*	114*	129*
Borrow from or use in campus library (NET)	176 72.5%	0 0	87 67.4%	87 67.4%	89 78.4%	76 71.6%	45 67.6%	55 78.5%	18 69.0%	20 69.0%	70 74.0%	46 77.4%	8 71.1%	12 68.4%	1 87.5%	2 40.0%	86 75.2%	90 70.1%
All sources of info	176 72.5%	0 0	87 67.4%	87 67.4%	89 78.4%	76 71.6%	45 67.6%	55 78.5%	18 69.0%	20 69.0%	70 74.0%	46 77.4%	8 71.1%	12 68.4%	1 87.5%	2 40.0%	86 75.2%	90 70.1%
preferred source of info	135 55.5%	0 0	72 55.3%	72 55.3%	63 55.6%	55 51.1%	39 59.9%	41 57.9%	11 44.8%	15 51.7%	53 56.0%	40 67.9%	6 57.9%	7 42.1%	1 37.5%	1 20.0%	67 58.9%	67 52.4%
Access online (NET)	111 45.7%	0 0	53 41.1%	53 41.1%	58 51.0%	46 43.4%	26 39.3%	39 55.4%	12 48.3%	13 44.8%	47 50.0%K	18 30.2%	5 44.7%	10 57.9%	1 50.0%	5 100.0%	48 41.9%	63 49.1%
All sources of info	111 45.7%	0 0	53 41.1%	53 41.1%	58 51.0%	46 43.4%	26 39.3%	39 55.4%	12 48.3%	13 44.8%	47 50.0%K	18 30.2%	5 44.7%	10 57.9%	1 50.0%	5 100.0%	48 41.9%	63 49.1%
preferred source of info	86 35.4%	0 0	47 36.3%	47 36.3%	39 34.4%	42 39.6%	22 33.4%	22 30.9%	10 37.9%	12 41.4%	34 36.0%	15 24.5%	3 26.3%	8 47.4%	1 50.0%	4 80.0%	38 32.9%	48 37.6%
Interlibrary loan (NET)	19 7.6%	0 0	11 8.7%	11 8.7%	7 6.4%	8 7.4%	4 6.4%	6 9.1%	3 10.3%	1 3.4%	4 4.0%	9 15.1%J	* 2.6%	2 10.5%	0 0	0 0	9 8.3%	9 7.0%
All sources of info	19 7.6%	0 0	11 8.7%	11 8.7%	7 6.4%	8 7.4%	4 6.4%	6 9.1%	3 10.3%	1 3.4%	4 4.0%	9 15.1%J	* 2.6%	2 10.5%	0 0	0 0	9 8.3%	9 7.0%
preferred source of info	3 1.3%	0 0	2 1.5%	2 1.5%	1 1.0%	1 0.8%	1 1.7%	1 1.6%	1 3.4%	0 0	0 0	2 3.8%	0 0	0 0	0 0	0 0	1 1.0%	2 1.6%

Proportions/Means: Columns Tested (5% risk level) - A/B/D - C/D - E/F/G - H/I/J/K/L/M/N - P/Q
* small base; ** very small base (under 30) ineligible for sig testing

Table 429
Page 1844

Outsell/Digital Library Federation Study (2002)
Weighted Tables

TABLE 156, continued

S7D/E_16. Dissertations SUMMARY TABLE

		RESPONDENT TYPE				INSTITUTION TYPE			DISCIPLINE									GENDER	
	TOTAL SAMPLE	FACULTY MEMBER	GRAD. STUDENT	FACULTY /GRAD	UNDER GRAD. STUDENT	PUBLIC	PRIVATE	LIBERAL ARTS	BIOLOGIAL SCIENCES	PHYSICAL SCIENCES /MATH	SOCIAL SCIENCES	ARTS AND HUMAN.	ENGI-NEERING	BUSINESS	LAW	UNDEC. MAJOR	MALE	FEMALE
		(A)	(B)	(C)	(D)	(E)	(F)	(G)	(H)	(I)	(J)	(K)	(L)	(M)	(N)		(P)	(Q)
Base - Use Dissertations for coursework	243	0**	130*	130*	113*	107*	66*	70*	26**	29**	94*	59*	11*	18**	1**	5*	114*	129*
Borrow from or use in other libraries (NET)	12 4.9%	0 0	7 5.4%	7 5.4%	5 4.3%	4 3.5%	5 7.9%	3 4.3%	1 3.4%	1 3.4%	8 8.0%	2 3.8%	* 2.6%	0 0	0 0	0 0	5 4.5%	7 5.3%
All sources of info	12 4.9%	0 0	7 5.4%	7 5.4%	5 4.3%	4 3.5%	5 7.9%	3 4.3%	1 3.4%	1 3.4%	8 8.0%	2 3.8%	* 2.6%	0 0	0 0	0 0	5 4.5%	7 5.3%
preferred source of info	2 0.9%	0 0	2 1.7%	2 1.7%	0 0	2 1.8%	* 0.4%	0 0	0 0	0 0	2 2.0%	0 0	* 2.6%	0 0	0 0	0 0	* 0.3%	2 1.5%
Faculty (NET)	10 4.3%	0 0	3 2.7%	3 2.7%	7 6.1%	3 2.8%	1 1.1%	7 9.4%	4 13.8%	0 0	4 4.0%	1 1.9%	1 7.9%	1 5.3%	* 12.5%	0 0	5 4.7%	5 3.9%
All sources of info	10 4.3%	0 0	3 2.7%	3 2.7%	7 6.1%	3 2.8%	1 1.1%	7 9.4%	4 13.8%	0 0	4 4.0%	1 1.9%	1 7.9%	1 5.3%	* 12.5%	0 0	5 4.7%	5 3.9%
preferred source of info	9 3.5%	0 0	3 2.0%	3 2.0%	6 5.3%	2 2.0%	1 1.1%	6 8.2%	2 6.9%	0 0	4 4.0%	1 1.9%	1 7.9%	1 5.3%	* 12.5%	0 0	4 3.1%	5 3.9%
Ask library to purchase source (NET)	4 1.5%	0 0	4 2.9%	4 2.9%	0 0	4 3.5%	0 0	0 0	0 0	0 0	4 4.0%	0 0	0 0	0 0	0 0	0 0	2 1.6%	2 1.5%
All sources of info	4 1.5%	0 0	4 2.9%	4 2.9%	0 0	4 3.5%	0 0	0 0	0 0	0 0	4 4.0%	0 0	0 0	0 0	0 0	0 0	2 1.6%	2 1.5%
preferred source of info	0 0	0 0	0 0	0 0	0 0	0 0	0 0	0 0	0 0	0 0	0 0	0 0	0 0	0 0	0 0	0 0	0 0	0 0

Proportions/Means: Columns Tested (5% risk level) - A/B/D - C/D - E/F/G - H/I/J/K/L/M/N - P/Q
* small base; ** very small base (under 30) ineligible for sig testing

Table 429
Page 1845

Outsell/Digital Library Federation Study (2002)
Weighted Tables

TABLE 156, continued

S7D/E_16. Dissertations SUMMARY TABLE

		RESPONDENT TYPE				INSTITUTION TYPE			DISCIPLINE									GENDER	
	TOTAL SAMPLE	FACULTY MEMBER	GRAD. STUDENT	FACULTY /GRAD	UNDER GRAD. STUDENT	PUBLIC	PRIVATE	LIBERAL ARTS	BIOLOGIAL SCIENCES	PHYSICAL SCIENCES /MATH	SOCIAL SCIENCES	ARTS AND HUMAN.	ENGI-NEERING	BUSINESS	LAW	UNDEC. MAJOR	MALE	FEMALE
		(A)	(B)	(C)	(D)	(E)	(F)	(G)	(H)	(I)	(J)	(K)	(L)	(M)	(N)		(P)	(Q)
Base - Use Dissertations for coursework	243	0**	130*	130*	113*	107*	66*	70*	26**	29**	94*	59*	11*	18**	1**	5*	114*	129*
Purchase from online bookstore (NET)	2 0.8%	0 0	0 0	0 0	2 1.7%	2 1.8%	0 0	0 0	0 0	0 0	2 2.0%	0 0	0 0	0 0	0 0	0 0	0 0	2 1.5%
All sources of info	2 0.8%	0 0	0 0	0 0	2 1.7%	2 1.8%	0 0	0 0	0 0	0 0	2 2.0%	0 0	0 0	0 0	0 0	0 0	0 0	2 1.5%
preferred source of info	2 0.8%	0 0	0 0	0 0	2 1.7%	2 1.8%	0 0	0 0	0 0	0 0	2 2.0%	0 0	0 0	0 0	0 0	0 0	0 0	2 1.5%
Purchase from physical book store (NET)	* 0.1%	0 0	0 0	0 0	* 0.3%	* 0.3%	0 0	0 0	0 0	0 0	0 0	0 0	* 2.6%J	0 0	0 0	0 0	* 0.3%	0 0
All sources of info	* 0.1%	0 0	0 0	0 0	* 0.3%	* 0.3%	0 0	0 0	0 0	0 0	0 0	0 0	* 2.6%J	0 0	0 0	0 0	* 0.3%	0 0
preferred source of info	* 0.1%	0 0	0 0	0 0	* 0.3%	* 0.3%	0 0	0 0	0 0	0 0	0 0	0 0	* 2.6%J	0 0	0 0	0 0	* 0.3%	0 0
Order from on demand document delivery service (NET)	* 0.1%	0 0	0 0	0 0	* 0.3%	* 0.3%	0 0	0 0	0 0	0 0	0 0	0 0	* 2.6%J	0 0	0 0	0 0	0 0	* 0.2%
All sources of info	* 0.1%	0 0	0 0	0 0	* 0.3%	* 0.3%	0 0	0 0	0 0	0 0	0 0	0 0	* 2.6%J	0 0	0 0	0 0	0 0	* 0.2%
preferred source of info	0 0	0 0	0 0	0 0	0 0	0 0	0 0	0 0	0 0	0 0	0 0	0 0	0 0	0 0	0 0	0 0	0 0	0 0

Proportions/Means: Columns Tested (5% risk level) - A/B/D - C/D - E/F/G - H/I/J/K/L/M/N - P/Q
* small base; ** very small base (under 30) ineligible for sig testing

Table 429
Page 1846

Outsell/Digital Library Federation Study (2002)
Weighted Tables

TABLE 156, continued

S7D/E_16. Dissertations SUMMARY TABLE

	TOTAL SAMPLE	RESPONDENT TYPE: FACULTY MEMBER (A)	GRAD. STUDENT (B)	FACULTY /GRAD (C)	UNDER GRAD. STUDENT (D)	INSTITUTION TYPE: PUBLIC (E)	PRIVATE (F)	LIBERAL ARTS (G)	DISCIPLINE: BIOLOGIAL SCIENCES (H)	PHYSICAL SCIENCES /MATH (I)	SOCIAL SCIENCES (J)	ARTS AND HUMAN. (K)	ENGI-NEERING (L)	BUSINESS (M)	LAW (N)	UNDEC. MAJOR	GENDER: MALE (P)	FEMALE (Q)
Base - Use Dissertations for coursework	243	0**	130*	130*	113*	107*	66*	70*	26**	29**	94*	59*	11*	18**	1**	5*	114*	129*
Access from course website (NET)	0 0	0 0	0 0	0 0	0 0	0 0	0 0	0 0	0 0	0 0	0 0	0 0	0 0	0 0	0 0	0 0	0 0	0 0
All sources of info	0 0	0 0	0 0	0 0	0 0	0 0	0 0	0 0	0 0	0 0	0 0	0 0	0 0	0 0	0 0	0 0	0 0	0 0
preferred source of info	0 0	0 0	0 0	0 0	0 0	0 0	0 0	0 0	0 0	0 0	0 0	0 0	0 0	0 0	0 0	0 0	0 0	0 0
Home (NET)	0 0	0 0	0 0	0 0	0 0	0 0	0 0	0 0	0 0	0 0	0 0	0 0	0 0	0 0	0 0	0 0	0 0	0 0
All sources of info	0 0	0 0	0 0	0 0	0 0	0 0	0 0	0 0	0 0	0 0	0 0	0 0	0 0	0 0	0 0	0 0	0 0	0 0
preferred source of info	0 0	0 0	0 0	0 0	0 0	0 0	0 0	0 0	0 0	0 0	0 0	0 0	0 0	0 0	0 0	0 0	0 0	0 0
Access book/journal/ journal article elsewhere online (NET)	0 0	0 0	0 0	0 0	0 0	0 0	0 0	0 0	0 0	0 0	0 0	0 0	0 0	0 0	0 0	0 0	0 0	0 0
All sources of info	0 0	0 0	0 0	0 0	0 0	0 0	0 0	0 0	0 0	0 0	0 0	0 0	0 0	0 0	0 0	0 0	0 0	0 0
preferred source of info	0 0	0 0	0 0	0 0	0 0	0 0	0 0	0 0	0 0	0 0	0 0	0 0	0 0	0 0	0 0	0 0	0 0	0 0

Proportions/Means: Columns Tested (5% risk level) - A/B/D - C/D - E/F/G - H/I/J/K/L/M/N - P/Q
* small base; ** very small base (under 30) ineligible for sig testing

Table 429
Page 1847

Outsell/Digital Library Federation Study (2002)
Weighted Tables

TABLE 156, continued

S7D/E_16. Dissertations SUMMARY TABLE

		RESPONDENT TYPE				INSTITUTION TYPE			DISCIPLINE								GENDER	
	TOTAL SAMPLE	FACULTY MEMBER	GRAD. STUDENT	FACULTY /GRAD	UNDER GRAD. STUDENT	PUBLIC	PRIVATE	LIBERAL ARTS	BIOLOGIAL SCIENCES	PHYSICAL SCIENCES /MATH	SOCIAL SCIENCES	ARTS AND HUMAN.	ENGI-NEERING	BUSINESS	LAW	UNDEC. MAJOR	MALE	FEMALE
		(A)	(B)	(C)	(D)	(E)	(F)	(G)	(H)	(I)	(J)	(K)	(L)	(M)	(N)		(P)	(Q)
Base - Use Dissertations for coursework	243	0**	130*	130*	113*	107*	66*	70*	26**	29**	94*	59*	11*	18**	1**	5*	114*	129*
Colleagues (NET)	0 0	0 0	0 0	0 0	0 0	0 0	0 0	0 0	0 0	0 0	0 0	0 0	0 0	0 0	0 0	0 0	0 0	0 0
All sources of info	0 0	0 0	0 0	0 0	0 0	0 0	0 0	0 0	0 0	0 0	0 0	0 0	0 0	0 0	0 0	0 0	0 0	0 0
preferred source of info	0 0	0 0	0 0	0 0	0 0	0 0	0 0	0 0	0 0	0 0	0 0	0 0	0 0	0 0	0 0	0 0	0 0	0 0
In class (NET)	0 0	0 0	0 0	0 0	0 0	0 0	0 0	0 0	0 0	0 0	0 0	0 0	0 0	0 0	0 0	0 0	0 0	0 0
All sources of info	0 0	0 0	0 0	0 0	0 0	0 0	0 0	0 0	0 0	0 0	0 0	0 0	0 0	0 0	0 0	0 0	0 0	0 0
preferred source of info	0 0	0 0	0 0	0 0	0 0	0 0	0 0	0 0	0 0	0 0	0 0	0 0	0 0	0 0	0 0	0 0	0 0	0 0
Dorm room (NET)	0 0	0 0	0 0	0 0	0 0	0 0	0 0	0 0	0 0	0 0	0 0	0 0	0 0	0 0	0 0	0 0	0 0	0 0
All sources of info	0 0	0 0	0 0	0 0	0 0	0 0	0 0	0 0	0 0	0 0	0 0	0 0	0 0	0 0	0 0	0 0	0 0	0 0
preferred source of info	0 0	0 0	0 0	0 0	0 0	0 0	0 0	0 0	0 0	0 0	0 0	0 0	0 0	0 0	0 0	0 0	0 0	0 0
Personal Holdings (NET)	0 0	0 0	0 0	0 0	0 0	0 0	0 0	0 0	0 0	0 0	0 0	0 0	0 0	0 0	0 0	0 0	0 0	0 0

Proportions/Means: Columns Tested (5% risk level) - A/B/D - C/D - E/F/G - H/I/J/K/L/M/N - P/Q
* small base; ** very small base (under 30) ineligible for sig testing

Table 429
Page 1848

Outsell/Digital Library Federation Study (2002)
Weighted Tables

TABLE 156, continued

S7D/E_16. Dissertations SUMMARY TABLE

		RESPONDENT TYPE				INSTITUTION TYPE			DISCIPLINE								GENDER	
	TOTAL SAMPLE	FACULTY MEMBER	GRAD. STUDENT	FACULTY /GRAD	UNDER GRAD. STUDENT	PUBLIC	PRIVATE	LIBERAL ARTS	BIOLOGIAL SCIENCES	PHYSICAL SCIENCES /MATH	SOCIAL SCIENCES	ARTS AND HUMAN.	ENGI- NEERING	BUSINESS	LAW	UNDEC. MAJOR	MALE	FEMALE
		(A)	(B)	(C)	(D)	(E)	(F)	(G)	(H)	(I)	(J)	(K)	(L)	(M)	(N)		(P)	(Q)
Base - Use Dissertations for coursework	243	0**	130*	130*	113*	107*	66*	70*	26**	29**	94*	59*	11*	18**	1**	5*	114*	129*
All sources of info	0 0	0 0	0 0	0 0	0 0	0 0	0 0	0 0	0 0	0 0	0 0	0 0	0 0	0 0	0 0	0 0	0 0	0 0
preferred source of info	0 0	0 0	0 0	0 0	0 0	0 0	0 0	0 0	0 0	0 0	0 0	0 0	0 0	0 0	0 0	0 0	0 0	0 0
Other (NET)	7 2.8%	0 0	5 3.7%	5 3.7%	2 1.9%	4 3.5%	1 1.6%	2 3.0%	2 6.9%	1 3.4%	2 2.0%	1 1.9%	0 0	1 5.3%	* 12.5%	0 0	3 2.8%	4 2.8%
All sources of info	7 2.8%	0 0	5 3.7%	5 3.7%	2 1.9%	4 3.5%	1 1.6%	2 3.0%	2 6.9%	1 3.4%	2 2.0%	1 1.9%	0 0	1 5.3%	* 12.5%	0 0	3 2.8%	4 2.8%
preferred source of info	2 0.7%	0 0	2 1.4%	2 1.4%	0 0	1 0.9%	1 1.3%	0 0	1 3.4%	0 0	0 0	0 0	0 0	1 5.3%	0 0	0 0	1 0.8%	1 0.7%
DK/Refused	4 1.8%	0 0	2 1.8%	2 1.8%	2 1.8%	2 1.8%	1 2.1%	1 1.4%	1 3.4%	2 6.9%	0 0	1 1.9%	* 2.6%J	0 0	0 0	0 0	3 2.8%	1 0.9%

Proportions/Means: Columns Tested (5% risk level) - A/B/D - C/D - E/F/G - H/I/J/K/L/M/N - P/Q
* small base; ** very small base (under 30) ineligible for sig testing

Table 429
Page 1849

Outsell/Digital Library Federation Study (2002)
Weighted Tables

TABLE 157

S7sum_17. News SUMMARY TABLE

		RESPONDENT TYPE				INSTITUTION TYPE			DISCIPLINE									GENDER	
	TOTAL SAMPLE	FACULTY MEMBER	GRAD. STUDENT	FACULTY /GRAD	UNDER GRAD. STUDENT	PUBLIC	PRIVATE	LIBERAL ARTS	BIOLOGIAL SCIENCES	PHYSICAL SCIENCES /MATH	SOCIAL SCIENCES	ARTS AND HUMAN.	ENGI-NEERING	BUSINESS	LAW	UNDEC. MAJOR	MALE	FEMALE
		(A)	(B)	(C)	(D)	(E)	(F)	(G)	(H)	(I)	(J)	(K)	(L)	(M)	(N)		(P)	(Q)
Base - Use News for coursework	445	0**	148	148	296	183	94*	168	44*	35*	162*	84*	12*	71*	6*	31*	206	239
ONLINE	387 86.9%	0 0	126 85.2%	126 85.2%	260 87.7%	152 83.0%	86 91.5%	149 88.5%	38 86.0%	31 88.6%	145 89.5%	72 85.3%	10 83.7%	61 86.8%	5 88.9%	24 77.4%	176 85.6%	210 88.0%
Search engine (NET)	138 30.9%	0 0	33 22.0%	33 22.0%	105 35.4%B C	47 25.9%	23 24.9%	67 39.8%EF	11 26.0%	14 40.0%N	43 26.7%	27 32.0%	5 39.5%N	25 35.5%	1 16.7%	11 35.5%	67 32.3%	71 29.7%
All sources of info	138 30.9%	0 0	33 22.0%	33 22.0%	105 35.4%B C	47 25.9%	23 24.9%	67 39.8%EF	11 26.0%	14 40.0%N	43 26.7%	27 32.0%	5 39.5%N	25 35.5%	1 16.7%	11 35.5%	67 32.3%	71 29.7%
preferred source of info	90 20.1%	0 0	18 11.9%	18 11.9%	72 24.3%B C	35 18.9%	14 15.2%	41 24.3%	6 14.0%	11 31.4%N	28 17.4%	15 17.3%	3 27.9%N	18 25.0%	1 8.3%	8 25.8%	42 20.6%	47 19.7%
Web directory/ subject related web site (NET)	107 24.0%	0 0	41 27.3%	41 27.3%	66 22.4%	36 19.4%	28 29.7%	44 26.0%	11 26.0%	7 20.0%	34 20.9%	22 26.7%L	1 9.3%	20 28.9%L	2 27.8%L	9 29.0%	61 29.5%Q	46 19.3%
All sources of info	107 24.0%	0 0	41 27.3%	41 27.3%	66 22.4%	36 19.4%	28 29.7%	44 26.0%	11 26.0%	7 20.0%	34 20.9%	22 26.7%L	1 9.3%	20 28.9%L	2 27.8%L	9 29.0%	61 29.5%Q	46 19.3%
preferred source of info	75 16.8%	0 0	28 18.7%	28 18.7%	47 15.9%	29 16.0%	17 18.5%	28 16.9%	9 20.0%	4 11.4%	28 17.4%	12 14.7%	1 7.0%	17 23.7%L	1 16.7%	3 9.7%	46 22.2%Q	29 12.2%
Internet searches (NET)	86 19.4%	0 0	29 19.4%	29 19.4%	57 19.3%	42 22.8%G	22 23.5%	22 13.3%	8 18.0%	4 11.4%	38 23.3%	17 20.0%	3 25.6%	10 14.5%	1 22.2%	5 16.1%	34 16.5%	52 21.8%

Proportions/Means: Columns Tested (5% risk level) - A/B/D - C/D - E/F/G - H/I/J/K/L/M/N - P/Q
* small base; ** very small base (under 30) ineligible for sig testing

Table 433
Page 1861

Outsell/Digital Library Federation Study (2002)
Weighted Tables

TABLE 157, continued

S7sum_17. News SUMMARY TABLE

		RESPONDENT TYPE				INSTITUTION TYPE			DISCIPLINE									GENDER	
	TOTAL SAMPLE	FACULTY MEMBER	GRAD. STUDENT	FACULTY /GRAD	UNDER GRAD. STUDENT	PUBLIC	PRIVATE	LIBERAL ARTS	BIOLOGIAL SCIENCES	PHYSICAL SCIENCES /MATH	SOCIAL SCIENCES	ARTS AND HUMAN.	ENGI-NEERING	BUSINESS	LAW	UNDEC. MAJOR	MALE	FEMALE
		(A)	(B)	(C)	(D)	(E)	(F)	(G)	(H)	(I)	(J)	(K)	(L)	(M)	(N)		(P)	(Q)
Base - Use News for coursework	445	0**	148	148	296	183	94*	168	44*	35*	162*	84*	12*	71*	6*	31*	206	239
All sources of info	86 19.4%	0 0	29 19.4%	29 19.4%	57 19.3%	42 22.8%G	22 23.5%	22 13.3%	8 18.0%	4 11.4%	38 23.3%	17 20.0%	3 25.6%	10 14.5%	1 22.2%	5 16.1%	34 16.5%	52 21.8%
preferred source of info	61 13.7%	0 0	22 14.6%	22 14.6%	39 13.2%	32 17.7%G	14 15.2%	14 8.5%	7 16.0%	4 11.4%	30 18.6%	8 9.3%	3 20.9%	7 10.5%	1 13.9%	1 3.2%	29 14.1%	32 13.4%
Online databases (NET)	45 10.2%	0 0	22 14.9%D	22 14.9%D	23 7.9%	12 6.7%	18 18.8%EG	16 9.3%	4 10.0%	6 17.1%	17 10.5%	7 8.0%	* 2.3%	8 11.8%	2 27.8%HJK LM	1 3.2%	17 8.0%	29 12.1%
All sources of info	45 10.2%	0 0	22 14.9%D	22 14.9%D	23 7.9%	12 6.7%	18 18.8%EG	16 9.3%	4 10.0%	6 17.1%	17 10.5%	7 8.0%	* 2.3%	8 11.8%	2 27.8%HJK LM	1 3.2%	17 8.0%	29 12.1%
preferred source of info	41 9.1%	0 0	21 14.3%D	21 14.3%D	19 6.5%	11 6.1%	16 16.9%E	13 8.0%	4 8.0%	5 14.3%	17 10.5%	7 8.0%	* 2.3%	6 7.9%	2 25.0%HJK LM	1 3.2%	14 6.6%	27 11.3%
Online library catalogues and finding aids (NET)	35 7.9%	0 0	9 6.0%	9 6.0%	26 8.8%	13 7.3%	10 10.9%	11 6.8%	7 16.0%M	2 5.7%	11 7.0%	11 13.3%M	* 2.3%	1 1.3%	* 5.6%	2 6.5%	13 6.5%	22 9.1%
All sources of info	35 7.9%	0 0	9 6.0%	9 6.0%	26 8.8%	13 7.3%	10 10.9%	11 6.8%	7 16.0%M	2 5.7%	11 7.0%	11 13.3%M	* 2.3%	1 1.3%	* 5.6%	2 6.5%	13 6.5%	22 9.1%
preferred source of info	24 5.3%	0 0	5 3.2%	5 3.2%	19 6.4%	9 4.7%	7 7.3%	8 5.0%	5 12.0%M	1 2.9%	9 5.8%	6 6.7%M	* 2.3%M	0 0	* 2.8%M	2 6.5%	10 5.0%	13 5.6%

Proportions/Means: Columns Tested (5% risk level) - A/B/D - C/D - E/F/G - H/I/J/K/L/M/N - P/Q
* small base; ** very small base (under 30) ineligible for sig testing

Table 433
Page 1862

Outsell/Digital Library Federation Study (2002)
Weighted Tables

TABLE 157, continued

S7sum_17. News SUMMARY TABLE

	TOTAL SAMPLE	RESPONDENT TYPE: FACULTY MEMBER	GRAD. STUDENT	FACULTY /GRAD	UNDER GRAD. STUDENT	INSTITUTION TYPE: PUBLIC	PRIVATE	LIBERAL ARTS	DISCIPLINE: BIOLOGIAL SCIENCES	PHYSICAL SCIENCES /MATH	SOCIAL SCIENCES	ARTS AND HUMAN.	ENGI-NEERING	BUSINESS	LAW	UNDEC. MAJOR	GENDER: MALE	FEMALE
		(A)	(B)	(C)	(D)	(E)	(F)	(G)	(H)	(I)	(J)	(K)	(L)	(M)	(N)		(P)	(Q)
Base - Use News for coursework	445	0**	148	148	296	183	94*	168	44*	35*	162*	84*	12*	71*	6*	31*	206	239
Online reference service (NET)	34 7.5%	0 0	8 5.7%	8 5.7%	25 8.5%	10 5.6%	7 7.0%	17 10.0%	2 4.0%	4 11.4%	11 7.0%	2 2.7%	1 4.7%	9 13.2%K	1 22.2%HJK L	3 9.7%	16 7.7%	18 7.4%
All sources of info	34 7.5%	0 0	8 5.7%	8 5.7%	25 8.5%	10 5.6%	7 7.0%	17 10.0%	2 4.0%	4 11.4%	11 7.0%	2 2.7%	1 4.7%	9 13.2%K	1 22.2%HJK L	3 9.7%	16 7.7%	18 7.4%
preferred source of info	17 3.9%	0 0	3 1.9%	3 1.9%	14 4.9%	7 3.9%	2 2.4%	8 4.7%	2 4.0%	2 5.7%	4 2.3%	1 1.3%	1 4.7%	7 9.2%JK	1 8.3%K	1 3.2%	7 3.5%	10 4.2%
Your own institution's web site (NET)	32 7.2%	0 0	15 10.2%	15 10.2%	17 5.7%	14 7.5%	10 10.1%	9 5.1%	3 6.0%	1 2.9%	17 10.5%M	7 8.0%	2 14.0%IMN	1 1.3%	0 0	2 6.5%	9 4.6%	23 9.4%
All sources of info	32 7.2%	0 0	15 10.2%	15 10.2%	17 5.7%	14 7.5%	10 10.1%	9 5.1%	3 6.0%	1 2.9%	17 10.5%M	7 8.0%	2 14.0%IMN	1 1.3%	0 0	2 6.5%	9 4.6%	23 9.4%
preferred source of info	20 4.5%	0 0	10 6.6%	10 6.6%	10 3.4%	11 5.8%	2 2.6%	7 4.0%	2 4.0%	1 2.9%	9 5.8%	3 4.0%	1 11.6%M	1 1.3%	0 0	2 6.5%	5 2.6%	15 6.1%
Department web page (NET)	10 2.2%	0 0	3 1.8%	3 1.8%	7 2.4%	6 3.1%	1 1.0%	3 1.8%	1 2.0%	0 0	2 1.2%	2 2.7%	0 0	4 5.3%	0 0	1 3.2%	6 2.9%	4 1.6%
All sources of info	10 2.2%	0 0	3 1.8%	3 1.8%	7 2.4%	6 3.1%	1 1.0%	3 1.8%	1 2.0%	0 0	2 1.2%	2 2.7%	0 0	4 5.3%	0 0	1 3.2%	6 2.9%	4 1.6%
preferred source of info	7 1.5%	0 0	2 1.3%	2 1.3%	5 1:7%	3 1.5%	1 1.0%	3 1.8%	0 0	0 0	2 1.2%	1 1.3%	0 0	3 3.9%	0 0	1 3.2%	3 1.5%	4 1.6%

Proportions/Means: Columns Tested (5% risk level) - A/B/D - C/D - E/F/G - H/I/J/K/L/M/N - P/Q
* small base; ** very small base (under 30) ineligible for sig testing

Table 433
Page 1863

Outsell/Digital Library Federation Study (2002)
Weighted Tables

TABLE 157, continued

S7sum_17. News SUMMARY TABLE

		RESPONDENT TYPE				INSTITUTION TYPE			DISCIPLINE									GENDER	
	TOTAL SAMPLE	FACULTY MEMBER	GRAD. STUDENT	FACULTY /GRAD	UNDER GRAD. STUDENT	PUBLIC	PRIVATE	LIBERAL ARTS	BIOLOGIAL SCIENCES	PHYSICAL SCIENCES /MATH	SOCIAL SCIENCES	ARTS AND HUMAN.	ENGI-NEERING	BUSINESS	LAW	UNDEC. MAJOR	MALE	FEMALE
		(A)	(B)	(C)	(D)	(E)	(F)	(G)	(H)	(I)	(J)	(K)	(L)	(M)	(N)		(P)	(Q)
Base - Use News for coursework	445	0**	148	148	296	183	94*	168	44*	35*	162*	84*	12*	71*	6*	31*	206	239
Online abstracting and indexing services (NET)	2 0.5%	0 0	* 0.2%	* 0.2%	2 0.7%	0 0	* 0.3%	2 1.2%	0 0	0 0	0 0	1 1.3%	* 2.3%J	1 1.3%	0 0	0 0	2 1.1%	0 0
All sources of info	2 0.5%	0 0	* 0.2%	* 0.2%	2 0.7%	0 0	* 0.3%	2 1.2%	0 0	0 0	0 0	1 1.3%	* 2.3%J	1 1.3%	0 0	0 0	2 1.1%	0 0
preferred source of info	0 0	0 0	0 0	0 0	0 0	0 0	0 0	0 0	0 0	0 0	0 0	0 0	0 0	0 0	0 0	0 0	0 0	0 0
Your own personal electronic library/files (NET)	2 0.4%	0 0	2 1.3%	2 1.3%	0 0	2 1.1%	0 0	0 0	1 2.0%	0 0	0 0	1 1.3%	0 0	0 0	0 0	0 0	1 0.5%	1 0.4%
All sources of info	2 0.4%	0 0	2 1.3%	2 1.3%	0 0	2 1.1%	0 0	0 0	1 2.0%	0 0	0 0	1 1.3%	0 0	0 0	0 0	0 0	1 0.5%	1 0.4%
preferred source of info	1 0.2%	0 0	1 0.6%	1 0.6%	0 0	1 0.5%	0 0	0 0	1 2.0%	0 0	0 0	0 0	0 0	0 0	0 0	0 0	0 0	1 0.4%
Online bookstore (NET)	2 0.4%	0 0	2 1.3%	2 1.3%	0 0	2 1.0%	0 0	0 0	0 0	0 0	2 1.2%	0 0	0 0	0 0	0 0	0 0	0 0	2 0.8%
All sources of info	2 0.4%	0 0	2 1.3%	2 1.3%	0 0	2 1.0%	0 0	0 0	0 0	0 0	2 1.2%	0 0	0 0	0 0	0 0	0 0	0 0	2 0.8%
preferred source of info	2 0.4%	0 0	2 1.3%	2 1.3%	0 0	2 1.0%	0 0	0 0	0 0	0 0	2 1.2%	0 0	0 0	0 0	0 0	0 0	0 0	2 0.8%

Proportions/Means: Columns Tested (5% risk level) - A/B/D - C/D - E/F/G - H/I/J/K/L/M/N - P/Q
* small base; ** very small base (under 30) ineligible for sig testing

Table 433
Page 1864

Outsell/Digital Library Federation Study (2002)
Weighted Tables

TABLE 157, continued

S7sum_17. News SUMMARY TABLE

		RESPONDENT TYPE				INSTITUTION TYPE			DISCIPLINE								GENDER	
	TOTAL SAMPLE	FACULTY MEMBER	GRAD. STUDENT	FACULTY /GRAD	UNDER GRAD. STUDENT	PUBLIC	PRIVATE	LIBERAL ARTS	BIOLOGIAL SCIENCES	PHYSICAL SCIENCES /MATH	SOCIAL SCIENCES	ARTS AND HUMAN.	ENGI- NEERING	BUSINESS	LAW	UNDEC. MAJOR	MALE	FEMALE
		(A)	(B)	(C)	(D)	(E)	(F)	(G)	(H)	(I)	(J)	(K)	(L)	(M)	(N)		(P)	(Q)
Base - Use News for coursework	445	0**	148	148	296	183	94*	168	44*	35*	162*	84*	12*	71*	6*	31*	206	239
E-mail listservs (NET)	0 0	0 0	0 0	0 0	0 0	0 0	0 0	0 0	0 0	0 0	0 0	0 0	0 0	0 0	0 0	0 0	0 0	0 0
All sources of info	0 0	0 0	0 0	0 0	0 0	0 0	0 0	0 0	0 0	0 0	0 0	0 0	0 0	0 0	0 0	0 0	0 0	0 0
preferred source of info	0 0	0 0	0 0	0 0	0 0	0 0	0 0	0 0	0 0	0 0	0 0	0 0	0 0	0 0	0 0	0 0	0 0	0 0
LIBRARY FACILITIES/ PRINT	114 25.5%	0 0	42 28.2%	42 28.2%	72 24.2%	30 16.5%	29 31.3%E	54 32.1%E	8 18.0%	12 34.3%	32 19.8%	29 34.7%HJ	3 23.3%	20 28.9%	2 36.1%HJ	7 22.6%	52 25.4%	61 25.6%
Campus library (NET)	85 19.2%	0 0	26 17.2%	26 17.2%	60 20.2%	18 10.0%	21 22.4%E	46 27.4%E	4 10.0%	10 28.6%H	28 17.4%	24 28.0%HM	3 20.9%	9 13.2%	1 22.2%	6 19.4%	35 17.2%	50 20.9%
All sources of info	85 19.2%	0 0	26 17.2%	26 17.2%	60 20.2%	18 10.0%	21 22.4%E	46 27.4%E	4 10.0%	10 28.6%H	28 17.4%	24 28.0%HM	3 20.9%	9 13.2%	1 22.2%	6 19.4%	35 17.2%	50 20.9%
preferred source of info	44 9.9%	0 0	14 9.4%	14 9.4%	30 10.2%	10 5.5%	12 12.7%	22 13.2%E	4 8.0%	5 14.3%M	15 9.3%	16 18.7%MN	1 7.0%	2 2.6%	* 2.8%	2 6.5%	17 8.3%	27 11.3%
Personal subscriptions to newspapers, magazines and journals (NET)	25 5.6%	0 0	15 10.1%D	15 10.1%D	10 3.4%	7 3.7%	9 9.8%	9 5.4%	2 4.0%	3 8.6%	4 2.3%	4 5.3%	* 2.3%	9 13.2%J	1 8.3%	2 6.5%	13 6.3%	12 5.0%
All sources of info	25 5.6%	0 0	15 10.1%D	15 10.1%D	10 3.4%	7 3.7%	9 9.8%	9 5.4%	2 4.0%	3 8.6%	4 2.3%	4 5.3%	* 2.3%	9 13.2%J	1 8.3%	2 6.5%	13 6.3%	12 5.0%

Proportions/Means: Columns Tested (5% risk level) - A/B/D - C/D - E/F/G - H/I/J/K/L/M/N - P/Q
* small base; ** very small base (under 30) ineligible for sig testing

Table 433
Page 1865

Outsell/Digital Library Federation Study (2002)
Weighted Tables

TABLE 157, continued

S7sum_17. News SUMMARY TABLE

	TOTAL SAMPLE	RESPONDENT TYPE: FACULTY MEMBER (A)	GRAD. STUDENT (B)	FACULTY /GRAD (C)	UNDER GRAD. STUDENT (D)	INSTITUTION TYPE: PUBLIC (E)	PRIVATE (F)	LIBERAL ARTS (G)
Base - Use News for coursework	445	0**	148	148	296	183	94*	168
preferred source of info	7	0	4	4	2	1	3	2
	1.5%	0	3.0%	3.0%	0.7%	0.6%	3.6%	1.3%
Physical bookstore (NET)	7	0	3	3	3	2	3	1
	1.5%	0	2.2%	2.2%	1.1%	1.2%	3.4%	0.7%
All sources of info	7	0	3	3	3	2	3	1
	1.5%	0	2.2%	2.2%	1.1%	1.2%	3.4%	0.7%
preferred source of info	2	0	*	*	2	2	*	0
	0.5%	0	0.2%	0.2%	0.7%	1.2%	0.2%	0
Your own personal physical library/ files/bookshelves (NET)	6	0	4	4	2	2	3	1
	1.3%	0	2.6%	2.6%	0.7%	1.1%	3.0%	0.6%
All sources of info	6	0	4	4	2	2	3	1
	1.3%	0	2.6%	2.6%	0.7%	1.1%	3.0%	0.6%
preferred source of info	2	0	1	1	1	2	0	0
	0.5%	0	0.8%	0.8%	0.3%	1.1%	0	0
References cited in books or journal articles (NET)	3	0	1	1	2	1	0	2
	0.6%	0	0.7%	0.7%	0.6%	0.6%	0	1.1%

	DISCIPLINE: BIOLOGIAL SCIENCES (H)	PHYSICAL SCIENCES /MATH (I)	SOCIAL SCIENCES (J)	ARTS AND HUMAN. (K)	ENGI-NEERING (L)	BUSINESS (M)	LAW (N)	UNDEC. MAJOR	GENDER: MALE (P)	FEMALE (Q)
Base - Use News for coursework	44*	35*	162*	84*	12*	71*	6*	31*	206	239
preferred source of info	1	1	0	1	*	3	1	0	4	2
	2.0%	2.9%J	0	1.3%	2.3%J	3.9%J	8.3%JK	0	2.1%	1.0%
Physical bookstore (NET)	0	0	2	2	0	1	1	1	2	4
	0	0	1.2%	2.7%	0	1.3%	8.3%HIJ LM	3.2%	1.0%	1.9%
All sources of info	0	0	2	2	0	1	1	1	2	4
	0	0	1.2%	2.7%	0	1.3%	8.3%HIJ LM	3.2%	1.0%	1.9%
preferred source of info	0	0	0	1	0	1	*	0	1	1
	0	0	0	1.3%	0	1.3%	5.6%HIJ	0	0.5%	0.5%
Your own personal physical library/ files/bookshelves (NET)	0	1	2	1	0	2	0	0	4	2
	0	2.9%	1.2%	1.3%	0	2.6%	0	0	1.8%	0.9%
All sources of info	0	1	2	1	0	2	0	0	4	2
	0	2.9%	1.2%	1.3%	0	2.6%	0	0	1.8%	0.9%
preferred source of info	0	0	0	1	0	1	0	0	1	1
	0	0	0	1.3%	0	1.3%	0	0	0.5%	0.5%
References cited in books or journal articles (NET)	2	0	0	0	0	1	*	0	2	1
	4.0%J	0	0	0	0	1.3%	2.8%JK	0	1.0%	0.4%

Proportions/Means: Columns Tested (5% risk level) - A/B/D - C/D - E/F/G - H/I/J/K/L/M/N - P/Q
* small base; ** very small base (under 30) ineligible for sig testing

Table 433
Page 1866

Outsell/Digital Library Federation Study (2002)
Weighted Tables

TABLE 157, continued

S7sum_17. News SUMMARY TABLE

		RESPONDENT TYPE				INSTITUTION TYPE			DISCIPLINE								GENDER	
	TOTAL SAMPLE	FACULTY MEMBER	GRAD. STUDENT	FACULTY /GRAD	UNDER GRAD. STUDENT	PUBLIC	PRIVATE	LIBERAL ARTS	BIOLOGIAL SCIENCES	PHYSICAL SCIENCES /MATH	SOCIAL SCIENCES	ARTS AND HUMAN.	ENGI-NEERING	BUSINESS	LAW	UNDEC. MAJOR	MALE	FEMALE
		(A)	(B)	(C)	(D)	(E)	(F)	(G)	(H)	(I)	(J)	(K)	(L)	(M)	(N)		(P)	(Q)
Base - Use News for coursework	445	0**	148	148	296	183	94*	168	44*	35*	162*	84*	12*	71*	6*	31*	206	239
All sources of info	3 0.6%	0 0	1 0.7%	1 0.7%	2 0.6%	1 0.6%	0 0	2 1.1%	2 4.0%J	0 0	0 0	0 0	0 0	1 1.3%	* 2.8%JK	0 0	2 1.0%	1 0.4%
preferred source of info	0 0	0 0	0 0	0 0	0 0	0 0	0 0	0 0	0 0	0 0	0 0	0 0	0 0	0 0	0 0	0 0	0 0	0 0
Another library (NET)	2 0.5%	0 0	0 0	0 0	2 0.7%	0 0	0 0	2 1.3%	0 0	0 0	0 0	1 1.3%	0 0	0 0	0 0	1 3.2%	2 1.0%	0 0
All sources of info	2 0.5%	0 0	0 0	0 0	2 0.7%	0 0	0 0	2 1.3%	0 0	0 0	0 0	1 1.3%	0 0	0 0	0 0	1 3.2%	2 1.0%	0 0
preferred source of info	0 0	0 0	0 0	0 0	0 0	0 0	0 0	0 0	0 0	0 0	0 0	0 0	0 0	0 0	0 0	0 0	0 0	0 0
Printed library catalogues and finding aids (NET)	0 0	0 0	0 0	0 0	0 0	0 0	0 0	0 0	0 0	0 0	0 0	0 0	0 0	0 0	0 0	0 0	0 0	0 0
All sources of info	0 0	0 0	0 0	0 0	0 0	0 0	0 0	0 0	0 0	0 0	0 0	0 0	0 0	0 0	0 0	0 0	0 0	0 0
preferred source of info	0 0	0 0	0 0	0 0	0 0	0 0	0 0	0 0	0 0	0 0	0 0	0 0	0 0	0 0	0 0	0 0	0 0	0 0
Printed abstracting and indexing services (NET)	0 0	0 0	0 0	0 0	0 0	0 0	0 0	0 0	0 0	0 0	0 0	0 0	0 0	0 0	0 0	0 0	0 0	0 0

Proportions/Means: Columns Tested (5% risk level) - A/B/D - C/D - E/F/G - H/I/J/K/L/M/N - P/Q
* small base; ** very small base (under 30) ineligible for sig testing

Table 433
Page 1867

Outsell/Digital Library Federation Study (2002)
Weighted Tables

TABLE 157, continued

S7sum_17. News SUMMARY TABLE

		RESPONDENT TYPE				INSTITUTION TYPE			DISCIPLINE									GENDER	
	TOTAL SAMPLE	FACULTY MEMBER	GRAD. STUDENT	FACULTY /GRAD	UNDER GRAD. STUDENT	PUBLIC	PRIVATE	LIBERAL ARTS	BIOLOGIAL SCIENCES	PHYSICAL SCIENCES /MATH	SOCIAL SCIENCES	ARTS AND HUMAN.	ENGI- NEERING	BUSINESS	LAW	UNDEC. MAJOR	MALE	FEMALE
		(A)	(B)	(C)	(D)	(E)	(F)	(G)	(H)	(I)	(J)	(K)	(L)	(M)	(N)		(P)	(Q)
Base - Use News for coursework	445	0**	148	148	296	183	94*	168	44*	35*	162*	84*	12*	71*	6*	31*	206	239
All sources of info	0 0	0 0	0 0	0 0	0 0	0 0	0 0	0 0	0 0	0 0	0 0	0 0	0 0	0 0	0 0	0 0	0 0	0 0
preferred source of info	0 0	0 0	0 0	0 0	0 0	0 0	0 0	0 0	0 0	0 0	0 0	0 0	0 0	0 0	0 0	0 0	0 0	0 0
PERSONAL ASSISTANCE	73 16.4%	0 0	19 13.1%	19 13.1%	54 18.1%	28 15.4%	10 10.3%	35 20.9%F	3 6.0%	7 20.0%N	26 16.3%N	15 17.3%N	3 25.6%HMN	8 11.8%	0 0	11 35.5%	32 15.5%	41 17.2%
Faculty members inside your institution (NET)	48 10.7%	0 0	18 12.1%	18 12.1%	30 10.0%	18 9.7%	9 9.9%	20 12.2%	0 0	7 20.0%HMN	17 10.5%H	11 13.3%HM N	3 20.9%HMN	3 3.9%	0 0	7 22.6%	23 11.2%	25 10.3%
All sources of info	48 10.7%	0 0	18 12.1%	18 12.1%	30 10.0%	18 9.7%	9 9.9%	20 12.2%	0 0	7 20.0%HMN	17 10.5%H	11 13.3%HM N	3 20.9%HMN	3 3.9%	0 0	7 22.6%	23 11.2%	25 10.3%
preferred source of info	21 4.7%	0 0	9 6.4%	9 6.4%	11 3.9%	13 6.9%F	1 0.6%	8 4.6%	0 0	0 0	9 5.8%	4 5.3%	1 9.3%HI	2 2.6%	0 0	4 12.9%	11 5.4%	10 4.1%
A librarian in your institution (NET)	38 8.6%	0 0	6 3.7%	6 3.7%	33 11.1%BC	13 6.8%	3 2.7%	23 13.9%F	3 6.0%	3 8.6%	15 9.3%	4 5.3%	1 4.7%	6 7.9%	0 0	7 22.6%	17 8.2%	21 9.0%
All sources of info	38 8.6%	0 0	6 3.7%	6 3.7%	33 11.1%BC	13 6.8%	3 2.7%	23 13.9%F	3 6.0%	3 8.6%	15 9.3%	4 5.3%	1 4.7%	6 7.9%	0 0	7 22.6%	17 8.2%	21 9.0%
preferred source of info	10 2.2%	0 0	1 0.8%	1 0.8%	9 2.9%	5 2.6%	1 1.2%	4 2.2%	1 2.0%	0 0	2 1.2%	1 1.3%	0 0	3 3.9%	0 0	3 9.7%	6 2.8%	4 1.6%

Proportions/Means: Columns Tested (5% risk level) - A/B/D - C/D - E/F/G - H/I/J/K/L/M/N - P/Q
* small base; ** very small base (under 30) ineligible for sig testing

Table 433
Page 1868

Outsell/Digital Library Federation Study (2002)
Weighted Tables

TABLE 157, continued

S7sum_17. News SUMMARY TABLE

	TOTAL SAMPLE	RESPONDENT TYPE: FACULTY MEMBER	GRAD. STUDENT	FACULTY /GRAD	UNDER GRAD. STUDENT	INSTITUTION TYPE: PUBLIC	PRIVATE	LIBERAL ARTS	DISCIPLINE: BIOLOGIAL SCIENCES	PHYSICAL SCIENCES /MATH	SOCIAL SCIENCES	ARTS AND HUMAN.	ENGI- NEERING	BUSINESS	LAW	UNDEC. MAJOR	GENDER: MALE	FEMALE
		(A)	(B)	(C)	(D)	(E)	(F)	(G)	(H)	(I)	(J)	(K)	(L)	(M)	(N)		(P)	(Q)
Base - Use News for coursework	445	0**	148	148	296	183	94*	168	44*	35*	162*	84*	12*	71*	6*	31*	206	239
Other students inside your institution (NET)	19 4.3%	0 0	8 5.1%	8 5.1%	11 3.9%	6 3.1%	5 5.1%	9 5.1%	0 0	2 5.7%	9 5.8%	2 2.7%	1 4.7%H	3 3.9%	0 0	2 6.5%	7 3.5%	12 4.9%
All sources of info	19 4.3%	0 0	8 5.1%	8 5.1%	11 3.9%	6 3.1%	5 5.1%	9 5.1%	0 0	2 5.7%	9 5.8%	2 2.7%	1 4.7%H	3 3.9%	0 0	2 6.5%	7 3.5%	12 4.9%
preferred source of info	1 0.2%	0 0	0 0	0 0	1 0.3%	1 0.5%	0 0	0 0	0 0	0 0	0 0	0 0	0 0	1 1.3%	0 0	0 0	0 0	1 0.4%
Other students outside your institution (NET)	4 0.9%	0 0	2 1.5%	2 1.5%	2 0.6%	0 0	2 2.4%	2 1.1%	0 0	0 0	2 1.2%	2 2.7%	0 0	0 0	0 0	0 0	0 0	4 1.7%
All sources of info	4 0.9%	0 0	2 1.5%	2 1.5%	2 0.6%	0 0	2 2.4%	2 1.1%	0 0	0 0	2 1.2%	2 2.7%	0 0	0 0	0 0	0 0	0 0	4 1.7%
preferred source of info	0 0	0 0	0 0	0 0	0 0	0 0	0 0	0 0	0 0	0 0	0 0	0 0	0 0	0 0	0 0	0 0	0 0	0 0
Another institution's librarian (NET)	4 0.9%	0 0	0 0	0 0	4 1.3%	0 0	0 0	4 2.4%	0 0	1 2.9%	2 1.2%	1 1.3%	0 0	0 0	0 0	0 0	0 0	4 1.7%
All sources of info	4 0.9%	0 0	0 0	0 0	4 1.3%	0 0	0 0	4 2.4%	0 0	1 2.9%	2 1.2%	1 1.3%	0 0	0 0	0 0	0 0	0 0	4 1.7%
preferred source of info	1 0.3%	0 0	0 0	0 0	1 0.4%	0 0	0 0	1 0.7%	0 0	0 0	0 0	1 1.3%	0 0	0 0	0 0	0 0	0 0	1 0.5%

Proportions/Means: Columns Tested (5% risk level) - A/B/D - C/D - E/F/G - H/I/J/K/L/M/N - P/Q
* small base; ** very small base (under 30) ineligible for sig testing

Table 433
Page 1869

Outsell/Digital Library Federation Study (2002)
Weighted Tables

TABLE 157, continued

S7sum_17. News SUMMARY TABLE

		RESPONDENT TYPE				INSTITUTION TYPE			DISCIPLINE									GENDER	
	TOTAL SAMPLE	FACULTY MEMBER	GRAD. STUDENT	FACULTY /GRAD	UNDER GRAD. STUDENT	PUBLIC	PRIVATE	LIBERAL ARTS	BIOLOGIAL SCIENCES	PHYSICAL SCIENCES /MATH	SOCIAL SCIENCES	ARTS AND HUMAN.	ENGI-NEERING	BUSINESS	LAW	UNDEC. MAJOR	MALE	FEMALE
		(A)	(B)	(C)	(D)	(E)	(F)	(G)	(H)	(I)	(J)	(K)	(L)	(M)	(N)		(P)	(Q)
Base - Use News for coursework	445	0**	148	148	296	183	94*	168	44*	35*	162*	84*	12*	71*	6*	31*	206	239
Faculty members outside your institution (NET)	1 0.3%	0 0	1 0.8%	1 0.8%	0 0	0 0	1 1.2%	0 0	0 0	0 0	0 0	1 1.3%	0 0	0 0	0 0	0 0	0 0	1 0.5%
All sources of info	1 0.3%	0 0	1 0.8%	1 0.8%	0 0	0 0	1 1.2%	0 0	0 0	0 0	0 0	1 1.3%	0 0	0 0	0 0	0 0	0 0	1 0.5%
preferred source of info	0 0	0 0	0 0	0 0	0 0	0 0	0 0	0 0	0 0	0 0	0 0	0 0	0 0	0 0	0 0	0 0	0 0	0 0
Professional meetings (NET)	0 0	0 0	0 0	0 0	0 0	0 0	0 0	0 0	0 0	0 0	0 0	0 0	0 0	0 0	0 0	0 0	0 0	0 0
All sources of info	0 0	0 0	0 0	0 0	0 0	0 0	0 0	0 0	0 0	0 0	0 0	0 0	0 0	0 0	0 0	0 0	0 0	0 0
preferred source of info	0 0	0 0	0 0	0 0	0 0	0 0	0 0	0 0	0 0	0 0	0 0	0 0	0 0	0 0	0 0	0 0	0 0	0 0
Other (NET)	37 8.3%	0 0	21 14.3%D	21 14.3%D	15 5.2%	17 9.4%	10 10.9%	9 5.6%	3 6.0%	3 8.6%	15 9.3%	9 10.7%	1 7.0%	4 5.3%	1 8.3%	2 6.5%	21 10.1%	16 6.6%
All sources of info	36 8.2%	0 0	21 14.1%D	21 14.1%D	15 5.2%	17 9.4%	10 10.6%	9 5.6%	3 6.0%	3 8.6%	15 9.3%	9 10.7%	1 4.7%	4 5.3%	1 8.3%	2 6.5%	21 10.0%	16 6.6%
preferred source of info	9 2.0%	0 0	4 2.6%	4 2.6%	5 1.7%	2 1.2%	2 1.8%	5 3.1%	1 2.0%	1 2.9%	2 1.2%	3 4.0%	1 4.7%M	0 0	* 5.6%M	1 3.2%	4 1.8%	5 2.2%
Online (unspecified)	4 0.8%	0 0	2 1.3%	2 1.3%	2 0.6%	4 2.1%	0 0	0 0	1 2.0%	0 0	2 1.2%	0 0	0 0	0 0	0 0	1 3.2%	2 0.9%	2 0.8%

Proportions/Means: Columns Tested (5% risk level) - A/B/D - C/D - E/F/G - H/I/J/K/L/M/N - P/Q
* small base; ** very small base (under 30) ineligible for sig testing

Table 433
Page 1870

Outsell/Digital Library Federation Study (2002)
Weighted Tables

TABLE 157, continued

S7sum_17. News SUMMARY TABLE

		RESPONDENT TYPE				INSTITUTION TYPE			DISCIPLINE									GENDER	
	TOTAL SAMPLE	FACULTY MEMBER	GRAD. STUDENT	FACULTY /GRAD	UNDER GRAD. STUDENT	PUBLIC	PRIVATE	LIBERAL ARTS	BIOLOGIAL SCIENCES	PHYSICAL SCIENCES /MATH	SOCIAL SCIENCES	ARTS AND HUMAN.	ENGI-NEERING	BUSINESS	LAW	UNDEC. MAJOR	MALE	FEMALE
		(A)	(B)	(C)	(D)	(E)	(F)	(G)	(H)	(I)	(J)	(K)	(L)	(M)	(N)		(P)	(Q)
Base - Use News for coursework	445	0**	148	148	296	183	94*	168	44*	35*	162*	84*	12*	71*	6*	31*	206	239
All sources of info	4 0.8%	0 0	2 1.3%	2 1.3%	2 0.6%	4 2.1%	0 0	0 0	1 2.0%	0 0	2 1.2%	0 0	0 0	0 0	0 0	1 3.2%	2 0.9%	2 0.8%
preferred source of info	3 0.6%	0 0	2 1.3%	2 1.3%	1 0.3%	3 1.5%	0 0	0 0	1 2.0%	0 0	2 1.2%	0 0	0 0	0 0	0 0	0 0	1 0.4%	2 0.8%
E-journals	1 0.3%	0 0	0 0	0 0	1 0.4%	0 0	0 0	1 0.7%	0 0	0 0	0 0	1 1.3%	0 0	0 0	0 0	0 0	1 0.5%	0 0
All sources of info	1 0.3%	0 0	0 0	0 0	1 0.4%	0 0	0 0	1 0.7%	0 0	0 0	0 0	1 1.3%	0 0	0 0	0 0	0 0	1 0.5%	0 0
preferred source of info	0 0	0 0	0 0	0 0	0 0	0 0	0 0	0 0	0 0	0 0	0 0	0 0	0 0	0 0	0 0	0 0	0 0	0 0
DK/Refused	11 2.5%	0 0	2 1.3%	2 1.3%	9 3.0%	4 2.2%	1 0.9%	6 3.6%	2 4.0%	2 5.7%	2 1.2%	2 2.7%	0 0	1 1.3%	* 2.8%	2 6.5%	6 3.0%	5 2.0%

Proportions/Means: Columns Tested (5% risk level) - A/B/D - C/D - E/F/G - H/I/J/K/L/M/N - P/Q
* small base; ** very small base (under 30) ineligible for sig testing

TABLE 158

S7D/E_17. News SUMMARY TABLE

		RESPONDENT TYPE				INSTITUTION TYPE			DISCIPLINE									GENDER	
	TOTAL SAMPLE	FACULTY MEMBER	GRAD. STUDENT	FACULTY /GRAD	UNDER GRAD. STUDENT	PUBLIC	PRIVATE	LIBERAL ARTS	BIOLOGIAL SCIENCES	PHYSICAL SCIENCES /MATH	SOCIAL SCIENCES	ARTS AND HUMAN.	ENGI-NEERING	BUSINESS	LAW	UNDEC. MAJOR	MALE	FEMALE
		(A)	(B)	(C)	(D)	(E)	(F)	(G)	(H)	(I)	(J)	(K)	(L)	(M)	(N)		(P)	(Q)
Base - Use News for coursework	445	0**	148	148	296	183	94*	168	44*	35*	162*	84*	12*	71*	6*	31*	206	239
Access online (NET)	314 70.5%	0 0	108 72.5%	108 72.5%	206 69.5%	128 69.7%	69 73.3%	117 69.8%	30 68.0%	27 77.1%	117 72.1%	49 58.7%	8 65.1%	58 81.6%KL	5 83.3%K	20 64.5%	151 73.1%	163 68.2%
All sources of info	314 70.5%	0 0	108 72.5%	108 72.5%	206 69.5%	128 69.7%	69 73.3%	117 69.8%	30 68.0%	27 77.1%	117 72.1%	49 58.7%	8 65.1%	58 81.6%KL	5 83.3%K	20 64.5%	151 73.1%	163 68.2%
preferred source of info	265 59.5%	0 0	93 62.3%	93 62.3%	172 58.0%	112 61.0%	56 59.6%	97 57.7%	28 64.0%K	26 74.3%K	94 58.1%K	34 40.0%	7 58.1%	53 75.0%JK	5 75.0%K	18 58.1%	125 60.5%	140 58.6%
Borrow from or use in campus library (NET)	207 46.6%	0 0	55 36.8%	55 36.8%	153 51.6%B C	70 38.3%	43 46.3%	94 55.9%E	17 38.0%	11 31.4%	83 51.2%MN	49 58.7%HI MN	6 48.8%N	22 31.6%	1 22.2%	18 58.1%	88 42.9%	119 49.9%
All sources of info	207 46.6%	0 0	55 36.8%	55 36.8%	153 51.6%B C	70 38.3%	43 46.3%	94 55.9%E	17 38.0%	11 31.4%	83 51.2%MN	49 58.7%HI MN	6 48.8%N	22 31.6%	1 22.2%	18 58.1%	88 42.9%	119 49.9%
preferred source of info	135 30.4%	0 0	40 26.9%	40 26.9%	95 32.1%	47 25.6%	30 32.4%	58 34.4%	11 24.0%	6 17.1%	51 31.4%MN	39 46.7%HI JMN	4 30.2%	12 17.1%	1 11.1%	12 38.7%	58 28.1%	77 32.3%
Faculty (NET)	11 2.5%	0 0	2 1.6%	2 1.6%	9 3.0%	4 2.3%	2 2.3%	5 2.9%	1 2.0%	1 2.9%	6 3.5%	2 2.7%	1 4.7%M	0 0	0 0	1 3.2%	3 1.5%	8 3.4%
All sources of info	11 2.5%	0 0	2 1.6%	2 1.6%	9 3.0%	4 2.3%	2 2.3%	5 2.9%	1 2.0%	1 2.9%	6 3.5%	2 2.7%	1 4.7%M	0 0	0 0	1 3.2%	3 1.5%	8 3.4%
preferred source of info	8 1.8%	0 0	1 0.8%	1 0.8%	7 2:4%	4 2.3%	1 0.9%	3 1.8%	1 2.0%	0 0	4 2.3%	2 2.7%	* 2.3%M	0 0	0 0	1 3.2%	3 1.4%	5 2.2%

Proportions/Means: Columns Tested (5% risk level) - A/B/D - C/D - E/F/G - H/I/J/K/L/M/N - P/Q
* small base; ** very small base (under 30) ineligible for sig testing

Table 436
Page 1878

Outsell/Digital Library Federation Study (2002)
Weighted Tables

TABLE 158, continued

S7D/E_17. News SUMMARY TABLE

		RESPONDENT TYPE				INSTITUTION TYPE			DISCIPLINE								GENDER	
	TOTAL SAMPLE	FACULTY MEMBER	GRAD. STUDENT	FACULTY /GRAD	UNDER GRAD. STUDENT	PUBLIC	PRIVATE	LIBERAL ARTS	BIOLOGIAL SCIENCES	PHYSICAL SCIENCES /MATH	SOCIAL SCIENCES	ARTS AND HUMAN.	ENGI- NEERING	BUSINESS	LAW	UNDEC. MAJOR	MALE	FEMALE
		(A)	(B)	(C)	(D)	(E)	(F)	(G)	(H)	(I)	(J)	(K)	(L)	(M)	(N)		(P)	(Q)
Base - Use News for coursework	445	0**	148	148	296	183	94*	168	44*	35*	162*	84*	12*	71*	6*	31*	206	239
Borrow from or use in other libraries (NET)	10 2.3%	0 0	4 2.8%	4 2.8%	6 2.1%	5 2.8%	1 1.2%	4 2.3%	3 6.0%	1 2.9%	2 1.2%	3 4.0%	* 2.3%	1 1.3%	* 2.8%	0 0	6 3.0%	4 1.7%
All sources of info	10 2.3%	0 0	4 2.8%	4 2.8%	6 2.1%	5 2.8%	1 1.2%	4 2.3%	3 6.0%	1 2.9%	2 1.2%	3 4.0%	* 2.3%	1 1.3%	* 2.8%	0 0	6 3.0%	4 1.7%
preferred source of info	1 0.2%	0 0	1 0.6%	1 0.6%	0 0	1 0.5%	0 0	0 0	1 2.0%	0 0	0 0	0 0	0 0	0 0	0 0	0 0	1 0.4%	0 0
Purchase from physical book store (NET)	10 2.3%	0 0	1 0.3%	1 0.3%	10 3.2%	2 1.1%	2 2.5%	6 3.4%	3 6.0%	1 2.9%	2 1.2%	1 1.3%	0 0	1 1.3%	1 8.3%JKL M	2 6.5%	7 3.4%	3 1.3%
All sources of info	10 2.3%	0 0	1 0.3%	1 0.3%	10 3.2%	2 1.1%	2 2.5%	6 3.4%	3 6.0%	1 2.9%	2 1.2%	1 1.3%	0 0	1 1.3%	1 8.3%JKL M	2 6.5%	7 3.4%	3 1.3%
preferred source of info	* *	0 0	* 0.1%	* 0.1%	0 0	0 0	* 0.2%	0 0	0 0	0 0	0 0	0 0	0 0	0 0	* 2.8%HJKM	0 0	* 0.1%	0 0
Interlibrary loan (NET)	6 1.3%	0 0	2 1.3%	2 1.3%	4 1.3%	3 1.5%	1 1.2%	2 1.1%	1 2.0%	0 0	4 2.3%	1 1.3%	0 0	0 0	0 0	0 0	3 1.3%	3 1.3%
All sources of info	6 1.3%	0 0	2 1.3%	2 1.3%	4 1.3%	3 1.5%	1 1.2%	2 1.1%	1 2.0%	0 0	4 2.3%	1 1.3%	0 0	0 0	0 0	0 0	3 1.3%	3 1.3%
preferred source of info	2 0.4%	0 0	0 0	0 0	2 0.6%	2 1.0%	0 0	0 0	0 0	0 0	2 1.2%	0 0	0 0	0 0	0 0	0 0	2 0.9%	0 0

Proportions/Means: Columns Tested (5% risk level) - A/B/D - C/D - E/F/G - H/I/J/K/L/M/N - P/Q
* small base; ** very small base (under 30) ineligible for sig testing

Table 436
Page 1879

Outsell/Digital Library Federation Study (2002)
Weighted Tables

TABLE 158, continued

S7D/E_17. News SUMMARY TABLE

		RESPONDENT TYPE				INSTITUTION TYPE			DISCIPLINE									GENDER	
	TOTAL SAMPLE	FACULTY MEMBER	GRAD. STUDENT	FACULTY /GRAD	UNDER GRAD. STUDENT	PUBLIC	PRIVATE	LIBERAL ARTS	BIOLOGIAL SCIENCES	PHYSICAL SCIENCES /MATH	SOCIAL SCIENCES	ARTS AND HUMAN.	ENGI-NEERING	BUSINESS	LAW	UNDEC. MAJOR	MALE	FEMALE
		(A)	(B)	(C)	(D)	(E)	(F)	(G)	(H)	(I)	(J)	(K)	(L)	(M)	(N)		(P)	(Q)
Base - Use News for coursework	445	0**	148	148	296	183	94*	168	44*	35*	162*	84*	12*	71*	6*	31*	206	239
Dorm room (NET)	5 1.1%	0 0	0 0	0 0	5 1.7%	0 0	0 0	5 2.9%E	0 0	1 2.9%	2 1.2%	1 1.3%	0 0	1 1.3%	0 0	0 0	5 2.4%Q	0 0
All sources of info	5 1.1%	0 0	0 0	0 0	5 1.7%	0 0	0 0	5 2.9%E	0 0	1 2.9%	2 1.2%	1 1.3%	0 0	1 1.3%	0 0	0 0	5 2.4%Q	0 0
preferred source of info	5 1.1%	0 0	0 0	0 0	5 1.7%	0 0	0 0	5 2.9%E	0 0	1 2.9%	2 1.2%	1 1.3%	0 0	1 1.3%	0 0	0 0	5 2.4%Q	0 0
In class (NET)	3 0.6%	0 0	1 0.6%	1 0.6%	2 0.6%	3 1.5%	0 0	0 0	0 0	0 0	2 1.2%	0 0	0 0	1 1.3%	0 0	0 0	2 0.9%	1 0.4%
All sources of info	3 0.6%	0 0	1 0.6%	1 0.6%	2 0.6%	3 1.5%	0 0	0 0	0 0	0 0	2 1.2%	0 0	0 0	1 1.3%	0 0	0 0	2 0.9%	1 0.4%
preferred source of info	3 0.6%	0 0	1 0.6%	1 0.6%	2 0.6%	3 1.5%	0 0	0 0	0 0	0 0	2 1.2%	0 0	0 0	1 1.3%	0 0	0 0	2 0.9%	1 0.4%
Home (NET)	2 0.5%	0 0	* 0.2%	* 0.2%	2 0.6%	2 1.0%	* 0.3%	0 0	0 0	0 0	2 1.2%	0 0	* 2.3%KM	0 0	0 0	0 0	2 1.1%	0 0
All sources of info	2 0.5%	0 0	* 0.2%	* 0.2%	2 0.6%	2 1.0%	* 0.3%	0 0	0 0	0 0	2 1.2%	0 0	* 2.3%KM	0 0	0 0	0 0	2 1.1%	0 0
preferred source of info	2 0.4%	0 0	0 0	0 0	2 0.6%	2 1.0%	0 0	0 0	0 0	0 0	2 1.2%	0 0	0 0	0 0	0 0	0 0	2 0.9%	0 0
Personal Holdings (NET)	1 0.3%	0 0	1 0.9%	1 0.9%	0 .0	0 0	1 1.5%	0 0	0 0	0 0	0 0	1 1.3%	* 2.3%JM	0 0	0 0	0 0	0 0	1 0.6%

Proportions/Means: Columns Tested (5% risk level) - A/B/D - C/D - E/F/G - H/I/J/K/L/M/N - P/Q
* small base; ** very small base (under 30) ineligible for sig testing

Table 436
Page 1880

Outsell/Digital Library Federation Study (2002)
Weighted Tables

TABLE 158, continued

S7D/E_17. News SUMMARY TABLE

		RESPONDENT TYPE				INSTITUTION TYPE			DISCIPLINE									GENDER	
	TOTAL SAMPLE	FACULTY MEMBER	GRAD. STUDENT	FACULTY /GRAD	UNDER GRAD. STUDENT	PUBLIC	PRIVATE	LIBERAL ARTS	BIOLOGIAL SCIENCES	PHYSICAL SCIENCES /MATH	SOCIAL SCIENCES	ARTS AND HUMAN.	ENGI-NEERING	BUSINESS	LAW	UNDEC. MAJOR	MALE	FEMALE
		(A)	(B)	(C)	(D)	(E)	(F)	(G)	(H)	(I)	(J)	(K)	(L)	(M)	(N)		(P)	(Q)
Base - Use News for coursework	445	0**	148	148	296	183	94*	168	44*	35*	162*	84*	12*	71*	6*	31*	206	239
All sources of info	1 0.3%	0 0	1 0.9%	1 0.9%	0 0	0 0	1 1.5%	0 0	0 0	0 0	0 0	1 1.3%	* 2.3%JM	0 0	0 0	0 0	0 0	1 0.6%
preferred source of info	* 0.1%	0 0	* 0.2%	* 0.2%	0 0	0 0	* 0.3%	0 0	0 0	0 0	0 0	0 0	* 2.3%JKM	0 0	0 0	0 0	0 0	* 0.1%
Purchase from online bookstore (NET)	1 0.3%	0 0	0 0	0 0	1 0.4%	* 0.2%	0 0	1 0.6%	0 0	0 0	0 0	0 0	* 2.3%JKM	0 0	0 0	1 3.2%	1 0.5%	* 0.1%
All sources of info	1 0.3%	0 0	0 0	0 0	1 0.4%	* 0.2%	0 0	1 0.6%	0 0	0 0	0 0	0 0	* 2.3%JKM	0 0	0 0	1 3.2%	1 0.5%	* 0.1%
preferred source of info	* 0.1%	0 0	0 0	0 0	* 0.1%	* 0.2%	0 0	0 0	0 0	0 0	0 0	0 0	* 2.3%JKM	0 0	0 0	0 0	0 0	* 0.1%
Access from course website (NET)	1 0.2%	0 0	1 0.6%	1 0.6%	0 0	1 0.5%	0 0	0 0	0 0	0 0	0 0	0 0	0 0	1 1.3%	0 0	0 0	1 0.5%	0 0
All sources of info	1 0.2%	0 0	1 0.6%	1 0.6%	0 0	1 0.5%	0 0	0 0	0 0	0 0	0 0	0 0	0 0	1 1.3%	0 0	0 0	1 0.5%	0 0
preferred source of info	1 0.2%	0 0	1 0.6%	1 0.6%	0 0	1 0.5%	0 0	0 0	0 0	0 0	0 0	0 0	0 0	1 1.3%	0 0	0 0	1 0.5%	0 0
Colleagues (NET)	0 0	0 0	0 0	0 0	0 0	0 0	0 0	0 0	0 0	0 0	0 0	0 0	0 0	0 0	0 0	0 0	0 0	0 0
All sources of info	0 0	0 0	0 0	0 0	0 0	0 0	0 0	0 0	0 0	0 0	0 0	0 0	0 0	0 0	0 0	0 0	0 0	0 0

Proportions/Means: Columns Tested (5% risk level) - A/B/D - C/D - E/F/G - H/I/J/K/L/M/N - P/Q
* small base; ** very small base (under 30) ineligible for sig testing

Table 436
Page 1881

Outsell/Digital Library Federation Study (2002)
Weighted Tables

TABLE 158, continued

S7D/E_17. News SUMMARY TABLE

		RESPONDENT TYPE				INSTITUTION TYPE			DISCIPLINE								GENDER	
	TOTAL SAMPLE	FACULTY MEMBER	GRAD. STUDENT	FACULTY /GRAD	UNDER GRAD. STUDENT	PUBLIC	PRIVATE	LIBERAL ARTS	BIOLOGIAL SCIENCES	PHYSICAL SCIENCES /MATH	SOCIAL SCIENCES	ARTS AND HUMAN.	ENGI-NEERING	BUSINESS	LAW	UNDEC. MAJOR	MALE	FEMALE
		(A)	(B)	(C)	(D)	(E)	(F)	(G)	(H)	(I)	(J)	(K)	(L)	(M)	(N)		(P)	(Q)
Base - Use News for coursework	445	0**	148	148	296	183	94*	168	44*	35*	162*	84*	12*	71*	6*	31*	206	239
preferred source of info	0 0	0 0	0 0	0 0	0 0	0 0	0 0	0 0	0 0	0 0	0 0	0 0	0 0	0 0	0 0	0 0	0 0	0 0
Order from on demand document delivery service (NET)	0 0	0 0	0 0	0 0	0 0	0 0	0 0	0 0	0 0	0 0	0 0	0 0	0 0	0 0	0 0	0 0	0 0	0 0
All sources of info	0 0	0 0	0 0	0 0	0 0	0 0	0 0	0 0	0 0	0 0	0 0	0 0	0 0	0 0	0 0	0 0	0 0	0 0
preferred source of info	0 0	0 0	0 0	0 0	0 0	0 0	0 0	0 0	0 0	0 0	0 0	0 0	0 0	0 0	0 0	0 0	0 0	0 0
Ask library to purchase source (NET)	0 0	0 0	0 0	0 0	0 0	0 0	0 0	0 0	0 0	0 0	0 0	0 0	0 0	0 0	0 0	0 0	0 0	0 0
All sources of info	0 0	0 0	0 0	0 0	0 0	0 0	0 0	0 0	0 0	0 0	0 0	0 0	0 0	0 0	0 0	0 0	0 0	0 0
preferred source of info	0 0	0 0	0 0	0 0	0 0	0 0	0 0	0 0	0 0	0 0	0 0	0 0	0 0	0 0	0 0	0 0	0 0	0 0
Access book/journal/ journal article elsewhere online (NET)	0 0	0 0	0 0	0 0	0 0	0 0	0 0	0 0	0 0	0 0	0 0	0 0	0 0	0 0	0 0	0 0	0 0	0 0
All sources of info	0 0	0 0	0 0	0 0	0 0	0 0	0 0	0 0	0 0	0 0	0 0	0 0	0 0	0 0	0 0	0 0	0 0	0 0

Proportions/Means: Columns Tested (5% risk level) - A/B/D - C/D - E/F/G - H/I/J/K/L/M/N - P/Q
* small base; ** very small base (under 30) ineligible for sig testing

Table 436
Page 1882

Outsell/Digital Library Federation Study (2002)
Weighted Tables

TABLE 158, continued

S7D/E_17. News SUMMARY TABLE

		RESPONDENT TYPE				INSTITUTION TYPE			DISCIPLINE									GENDER	
	TOTAL SAMPLE	FACULTY MEMBER	GRAD. STUDENT	FACULTY /GRAD	UNDER GRAD. STUDENT	PUBLIC	PRIVATE	LIBERAL ARTS	BIOLOGIAL SCIENCES	PHYSICAL SCIENCES /MATH	SOCIAL SCIENCES	ARTS AND HUMAN.	ENGI-NEERING	BUSINESS	LAW	UNDEC. MAJOR	MALE	FEMALE
		(A)	(B)	(C)	(D)	(E)	(F)	(G)	(H)	(I)	(J)	(K)	(L)	(M)	(N)		(P)	(Q)
Base - Use News for coursework	445	0**	148	148	296	183	94*	168	44*	35*	162*	84*	12*	71*	6*	31*	206	239
preferred source of info	0 0	0 0	0 0	0 0	0 0	0 0	0 0	0 0	0 0	0 0	0 0	0 0	0 0	0 0	0 0	0 0	0 0	0 0
Other (NET)	32 7.3%	0 0	14 9.7%	14 9.7%	18 6.1%	14 7.5%	10 10.3%	9 5.4%	7 16.0%J	1 2.9%	6 3.5%	7 8.0%	1 7.0%	8 11.8%J	1 13.9%IJ	2 6.5%	15 7.4%	17 7.2%
All sources of info	31 7.0%	0 0	14 9.6%	14 9.6%	17 5.7%	12 6.8%	10 10.3%	9 5.4%	7 16.0%J	1 2.9%	6 3.5%	6 6.7%	1 7.0%	8 11.8%J	1 11.1%J	2 6.5%	15 7.4%	16 6.7%
preferred source of info	14 3.1%	0 0	6 4.3%	6 4.3%	8 2.5%	4 2.4%	5 5.4%	4 2.6%	3 6.0%	0 0	4 2.3%	6 6.7%	* 2.3%	1 1.3%	1 11.1%IJM	0 0	4 1.8%	10 4.3%
DK/Refused	6 1.4%	0 0	2 1.5%	2 1.5%	4 1.3%	5 2.8%	0 0	1 0.6%	1 2.0%	2 5.7%J	0 0	1 1.3%	* 2.3%J	2 2.6%	0 0	0 0	4 2.1%	2 0.8%

Proportions/Means: Columns Tested (5% risk level) - A/B/D - C/D - E/F/G - H/I/J/K/L/M/N - P/Q
* small base; ** very small base (under 30) ineligible for sig testing

Appendix 1: Institutions in Study Sample

Public Research Universities

Arizona State University Main
Auburn University
Ball State University
Bowling Green State University
City University of New York Graduate Center
Clemson University
Cleveland State University
College of William and Mary
Colorado School of Mines
Colorado State University
Florida Atlantic University
Florida International University
Florida State University
George Mason University
Georgia Institute of Technology
Georgia State University
Idaho State University
Illinois State University
Indiana State University
Indiana University at Bloomington
Indiana University of Pennsylvania
Indiana University-Purdue University Indianapolis
Iowa State University
Kansas State University
Kent State University Main Campus
Louisiana State University and Agricultural and Mechanical College
Louisiana Tech University
Miami University
Michigan State University
Michigan Technological University
Middle Tennessee State University
Mississippi State University
Montana State University - Bozeman
New Jersey Institute of Technology
New Mexico State University Main Campus
North Carolina State University
North Dakota State University Main Campus
Northern Arizona University
Northern Illinois University
Ohio State University Main Campus, The
Ohio University Main Campus
Oklahoma State University Main Campus
Old Dominion University
Oregon State University
Pennsylvania State University, University Park
Portland State University
Purdue University Main Campus
Rutgers, The State University of New Jersey, New Brunswick Campus
Rutgers, The State University of New Jersey, Newark Campus
San Diego State University
Southern Illinois University at Carbondale
State University of New York at Albany
State University of New York at Binghamton
State University of New York at Buffalo
State University of New York at Stony Brook
State University of New York College of Environmental Science & Forestry
Temple University
Tennessee State University
Texas A&M University
Texas A&M University - Commerce
Texas Southern University
Texas Tech University
Texas Woman's University
University of Akron, Main Campus, The
University of Alabama at Birmingham
University of Alabama in Huntsville
University of Alabama, The
University of Alaska Fairbanks
University of Arizona
University of Arkansas Main Campus
University of California-Berkeley
University of California-Davis
University of California-Irvine
University of California-Los Angeles
University of California-Riverside
University of California-San Diego
University of California-San Francisco
University of California-Santa Barbara
University of California-Santa Cruz
University of Central Florida
University of Cincinnati Main Campus
University of Colorado at Boulder
University of Colorado at Denver
University of Connecticut
University of Delaware
University of Florida
University of Georgia
University of Hawaii at Manoa
University of Houston
University of Idaho
University of Illinois at Chicago
University of Illinois at Urbana-Champaign
University of Iowa
University of Kansas Main Campus
University of Kentucky
University of Louisiana at Lafayette
University of Louisville
University of Maine
University of Maryland Baltimore County
University of Maryland College Park
University of Massachusetts
University of Massachusetts Lowell
University of Memphis, The
University of Michigan-Ann Arbor
University of Minnesota-Twin Cities
University of Mississippi
University of Missouri - Columbia
University of Missouri - Kansas City
University of Missouri - Rolla
University of Missouri - Saint Louis
University of Montana, The
University of Nebraska - Lincoln
University of Nevada, Reno
University of New Hampshire
University of New Mexico Main Campus
University of New Orleans
University of North Carolina at Chapel Hill
University of North Carolina at Greensboro
University of North Dakota Main Campus
University of North Texas
University of Northern Colorado
University of Oklahoma Norman Campus
University of Oregon
University of Pittsburgh, Pittsburgh Campus
University of Puerto Rico-Rio Piedras Campus
University of Rhode Island
University of South Carolina - Columbia
University of South Dakota
University of South Florida
University of Southern Mississippi
University of Tennessee, Knoxville
University of Texas at Arlington
University of Texas at Austin
University of Texas at Dallas
University of Toledo
University of Utah
University of Vermont
University of Virginia
University of Washington
University of Wisconsin-Madison
University of Wisconsin-Milwaukee
University of Wyoming
Utah State University
Virginia Commonwealth University
Virginia Polytechnic Institute and State University
Washington State University
Wayne State University
West Virginia University
Western Michigan University
Wichita State University
Wright State University Main Campus

Private Research Institutions

Adelphi University
American University
Andrews University
Baylor University
Biola University
Boston College
Boston University
Brandeis University
Brigham Young University
Brown University
California Institute of Technology
Carnegie Mellon University
Case Western Reserve University
Catholic University of America, The
Claremont Graduate University
Clark Atlanta University
Clark University
Clarkson University
Columbia University in the City of New York
Cornell University
Dartmouth College
DePaul University
Drexel University
Duke University
Duquesne University
Emory University
Florida Institute of Technology
Fordham University
George Washington University
Georgetown University
Harvard University
Hofstra University
Howard University
Illinois Institute of Technology
Johns Hopkins University
Lehigh University
Loma Linda University
Loyola University of Chicago
Marquette University
Massachusetts Institute of Technology
MCP Hahnemann University
New School University
New York University
Northeastern University
Northwestern University
Nova Southeastern University
Pace University New York Campus
Pepperdine University
Polytechnic University
Princeton University
Rensselaer Polytechnic Institute
Rice University
Rockefeller University
Saint John's University
Saint Louis University
Seton Hall University
Southern Methodist University
Stanford University
Stevens Institute of Technology
Syracuse University
Teachers College, Columbia University
Texas Christian University
Tufts University
Tulane University
Union Institute
United States International University
University of Chicago
University of Denver
University of Detroit Mercy
University of La Verne
University of Miami
University of Notre Dame
University of Pennsylvania
University of Rochester
University of San Diego
University of San Francisco
University of Southern California
University of the Pacific
University of Tulsa
Vanderbilt University
Wake Forest University
Washington University
Worcester Polytechnic Institute
Yale University
Yeshiva University

Liberal Arts Colleges

Agnes Scott College
Albion College
Albright College
Allegheny College
Alma College
Amherst College
Antioch College
Augustana College
Austin College
Bard College
Barnard College
Bates College
Beloit College
Bennington College
Bethany College
Birmingham-Southern College
Bowdoin College
Bryn Mawr College
Bucknell University
Carleton College
Central College
Centre College
Chatham College
Christendom College
Claremont McKenna College
Coe College
Colby College
Colgate University
College of Saint Benedict
College of the Atlantic
College of the Holy Cross
College of Wooster, The
Colorado College
Concordia College-Moorhead
Connecticut College
Cornell College
Davidson College
Denison University
DePauw University
Dickinson College
Drew University
Earlham College
Eckerd College
Erskine College
Franklin & Marshall College
Franklin College of Indiana
Furman University
Georgetown College
Gettysburg College
Gordon College
Goshen College
Goucher College
Grinnell College
Guilford College
Gustavus Adolphus College
Hamilton College
Hamline University
Hampden-Sydney College
Hampshire College
Hanover College
Hartwick College
Hastings College
Haverford College
Hendrix College
Hiram College
Hobart and William Smith Colleges
Hollins University
Hope College
Houghton College
Huntingdon College
Illinois College
Illinois Wesleyan University
Judson College
Juniata College
Kalamazoo College
Kenyon College
Knox College
Lafayette College
Lake Forest College
Lawrence University
Lewis and Clark College
Luther College
Macalester College
Manhattanville College

Marlboro College
Middlebury College
Mills College
Millsaps College
Monmouth College
Moravian College
Morehouse College
Mount Holyoke College
Muhlenberg College
Nebraska Wesleyan University
Oberlin College
Occidental College
Oglethorpe University
Ohio Wesleyan University
Pitzer College
Pomona College
Presbyterian College
Randolph-Macon College
Randolph-Macon Woman's College
Reed College
Rhodes College
Ripon College
Saint John's University
Saint Olaf College
Salem College
Sarah Lawrence College
Scripps College
Siena College
Simon's Rock College of Bard
Skidmore College
Smith College
Southwestern University
Spelman College
St. Andrews Presbyterian College
St. John's College
St. Lawrence University
Swarthmore College
Sweet Briar College
Thomas Aquinas College
Transylvania University
Trinity College
Union College
University of Dallas
University of Judaism
University of Puget Sound
University of the South
Ursinus College
Vassar College
Virginia Wesleyan College
Wabash College
Wartburg College
Washington and Jefferson College
Washington and Lee University
Washington College
Wellesley College
Wells College
Wesleyan College
Wesleyan University
Western Maryland College
Westminster College
Westmont College
Wheaton College
Whitman College
Whittier College
Willamette University
William Jewell College
Williams College
Wittenberg University
Wofford College